P9-BYO-540

NEWS ANALYSIS BOXES

FURTHER EXPLORATION BOXES

EIGHTH EDITION

PRINCIPLES OF ECONOMICS

EIGHTH EDITION

PRINCIPLES OF ECONOMICS

Karl E. Case
Wellesley College

Ray C. Fair
Yale University

PEARSON

Prentice Hall

Upper Saddle River, NJ 07458

Library of Congress Cataloging-in-Publication Data
Case, Karl E.
    Principles of economics/Karl E. Case, Ray C. Fair.—8th ed.
        p. cm.
    Includes index.
    ISBN 0-13-228914-8
    1. Economics.   I. Fair, Ray C.   II. Title.
    HB171.5.C3123 2006
    330—dc22   2006043413

Acquisitions Editor: Jon Axelrod
AVP/Executive Editor: David Alexander
VP/Editorial Director: Jeff Shelstad
Manager, Product Development: Pamela Hersperger
Editorial Assistant: Michael Dittamo
Development Editor: Sylvia Mallory
Media Project Manager: Peter Snell
AVP/Executive Marketing Manager: Sharon Koch
Associate Director, Production Editorial: Judy Leale
Senior Managing Editor: Cynthia Regan
Production Editor: Carol Samet
Permissions Coordinator: Charles Morris
Associate Director, Manufacturing: Vinnie Scelta
Production Manager: Arnold Vila
Design/Composition Manager: Christy Mahon
Composition Liaison: Nancy Thompson
Art Director: Kevin Kall
Interior Design: Sue Behnke
Cover Design: Kevin Kall
Illustration (Interior): Kenneth Batelman
Director, Image Resource Center: Melinda Reo
Manager, Rights and Permissions: Zina Arabia
Manager, Visual Research: Beth Brenzel
Image Permission Coordinator: Angelique Sharps
Photo Researcher: Sheila Norman
Composition: GGS Book Services
Full-Service Project Management: GGS Book Services
Printer/Binder: Quebecor
Typeface: 10.5/12 Minion

Credits and acknowledgments borrowed from other sources and reproduced, with permission, in this textbook appear on page P-1.

Pearson Prentice Hall™ is a trademark of Pearson Education, Inc.
Pearson® is a registered trademark of Pearson plc
Prentice Hall® is a registered trademark of Pearson Education, Inc.

Pearson Education LTD.
Pearson Education Singapore, Pte. Ltd
Pearson Education, Canada, Ltd
Pearson Education–Japan

Pearson Education Australia PTY, Limited
Pearson Education North Asia Ltd
Pearson Educación de Mexico, S.A. de C.V.
Pearson Education Malaysia, Pte. Ltd.

10 9 8 7 6 5 4 3
ISBN: 0-13-228914-8

To
Professor Richard A. Musgrave
and
Professor Robert M. Solow

About the Authors

Karl E. Case is the Katharine Coman and A. Barton Hepburn Professor of Economics at Wellesley College, where he has taught for 30 years, and is a Visiting Scholar at the Federal Reserve Bank of Boston.

Before coming to Wellesley, he served as Head Tutor (director of undergraduate studies) at Harvard, where he won the Allyn Young Teaching Prize. He is Associate Editor of the *Journal of Economic Perspectives* and has been a member of the AEA's Committee on Economic Education and was Associate Editor of the *Journal of Economic Education*, responsible for the section on innovations in teaching. He teaches at least one section of the principles course every year.

Professor Case received his B.A. from Miami University in 1968, spent three years on active duty in the Army, including a year in Vietnam, and received his Ph.D. in Economics from Harvard University in 1976.

Professor Case's research has been in the areas of real estate, housing, and public finance. He is author or co-author of five books, including *Principles of Economics, Economics and Tax Policy,* and *Property Taxation: The Need for Reform,* and has published numerous articles in professional journals.

He is also a founding partner in the real estate research firm of Fiserv Case Shiller Weiss, Inc., and serves as a member of the Boards of Directors of the Mortgage Guaranty Insurance Corporation (MGIC), The American Real Estate and Urban Economics Association, and Century Bank.

Ray C. Fair is Professor of Economics at Yale University. He is a member of the Cowles Foundation at Yale and a Fellow of the Econometric Society. He received a B.A. in economics from Fresno State College in 1964 and a Ph.D. in economics from M.I.T. in 1968. He taught at Princeton University from 1968 to 1974 and has been at Yale since 1974.

Professor Fair's research has primarily been in the areas of macroeconomics and econometrics, with particular emphasis on macroeconometric model building. He has also done work in the areas of finance, voting behavior, and aging in sports. His publications include *Specification, Estimation, and Analysis of Macroeconometric Models* (Harvard Press, 1984), *Testing Macroeconometric Models* (Harvard Press, 1994), and *Estimating How the Macroeconomy Works* (Harvard Press, 2004).

Professor Fair has taught introductory and intermediate economics at Yale. He has also taught graduate courses in macroeconomic theory and macroeconometrics.

Professor Fair's United States and multicountry models are available for use on the Internet free of charge. The address is **http://fairmodel.econ.yale.edu**. Many teachers have found that having students work with the United States model on the Internet is a useful complement to even an introductory macroeconomics course.

Brief Contents

Contents

Global Coverage

Because the study of economics crosses national boundaries, this book includes four chapters devoted to international issues: Chapter 33 (International Trade, Comparative Advantage, and Protectionism), Chapter 34 (Open-Economy Macroeconomics: The Balance of Payments and Exchange Rates), Chapter 35 (Globalization), and Chapter 36 (Economic Growth in Developing and Transitional Economies). We also include international examples and discussions in other chapters. The following is a summary of these examples and discussions.

PREFACE

Our goal in the eighth edition, as it was in the first edition, is to instill in students a fascination with both the functioning of the economy and the power and breadth of economics. The first line of every edition of our book has been "The study of economics should begin with a sense of wonder." We hope that readers will come away from our book with a basic understanding of how market economies function, an appreciation for the things that they do well, and a sense of the things that they do poorly. We hope too that they will learn that the proper role of government in a market economy is the subject of a great debate around the world. That debate serves as the organizing principle behind the structure of the material in this book.

For an economics text to be effective, it must address the economic issues of the time. Since the publication of our seventh edition, the economic landscape has changed substantially. In 2003, the U.S. economy had lost nearly 3 million jobs in the aftermath of 9/11 and a recession in 2001. The collapse of technology stocks contributed to a 45 percent decline in the Standard and Poor's index of stock prices, which wiped out trillions of dollars of wealth in a short period of time. The U.S.-led invasion of Afghanistan and subsequently of Iraq coupled with a rise in international terrorism led to a feeling of great uncertainty about the future of the economy.

Since the summer of 2003, some things have improved, some have gotten worse, and the big economic issues have changed. By the beginning of 2006, over 5 million jobs had been created in the United States, and the unemployment rate had fallen to 4.8 percent from 6.3 percent in 2003. In August 2005, Hurricane Katrina slammed into New Orleans and other parts of the Gulf Coast, killing nearly 1,500 people and destroying countless homes and businesses. Damages totaled over $75 billion, and the economy in the region was devastated. Loss of refinery capacity from the hurricane and tensions in the Middle East pushed the price of oil to over $70 a barrel.

As we go to press, a number of international economic issues dominate the headlines. First, the United States is running huge trade deficits with the rest of the world. Most notably the United States buys nearly $20 billion worth of goods and services from China every month, while China buys only about $4 billion worth of goods and services from the United States. At the same time, the U.S. government is spending hundreds of billions more than it is collecting in taxes, with the resulting budget deficit financed in large part by foreign countries.

Another concern is the housing market. Home prices have been rising in the United States in virtually every region for well over a decade. Home equity is a major part of the wealth of U.S. households. The United States has also been producing new houses at a record clip for five consecutive years. The real estate sector as a whole, including real estate agents, mortgage bankers, home remodeling and repair contractors, designers, and builders, accounts for a very substantial fraction of the jobs in the U.S. economy. Many foresee a "bursting bubble" that could send financial shock waves throughout the whole economic system.

NEW TO THIS EDITION

A concerted effort was made in this edition to focus on assessment. To that end, every chapter now contains at least one "News Analysis" box with related questions in the end-of-chapter material. This increases the number of homework problems from which you can choose from for each semester.

A new chapter: The material in Chapter 5 on elasticity has been extended into a full chapter.

All the current-events material used to illustrate economic points has been updated.

New concepts have been added to the material. For example, an important new concept is economic "outsourcing" where workers in countries like India connected by high-speed cable to U.S. producers do substantial work for other companies in other countries.

International material has been added and extended to continue the progress of the book from a basically domestic economics text to a truly international one. In the last edition, a new chapter on globalization was added.

New data for all economic time series have been extended to the latest possible date.

The report of the President's Tax Reform Commission in 2005 is discussed and highlighted.

THE FOUNDATION

Despite a new chapter and other revisions, the themes of *Principles of Economics*, Eighth Edition, are the same themes of the first seven editions. The purpose of this book is to introduce the discipline of economics and to provide a basic understanding of how economies function. This requires a blend of economic theory, institutional material, and real-world applications. We have maintained a balance between these ingredients in every chapter in this book. The hallmark features of our book are its

1. Three-tiered explanations of key concepts (*Stories-Graphs-Equations*)

2. Intuitive and accessible structure

3. International coverage

THREE-TIERED EXPLANATIONS: STORIES-GRAPHS-EQUATIONS

Professors who teach principles of economics are faced with a classroom of students with different abilities, backgrounds, and learning styles. For some, analytical material is difficult no matter how it is presented; for others, graphs and equations seem to come naturally. The problem facing instructors and textbook authors is how to convey the core principles of the discipline to as many students as possible without selling the better students short. Our approach to this problem is to present most core concepts in three ways:

First, we present each concept in the context of a simple intuitive *story* or example in words often followed by a table.

Second, we use a *graph* in most cases to illustrate the story or example.

A story helps capture student interest.

A graph illustrates the relationship between the variables in the story.

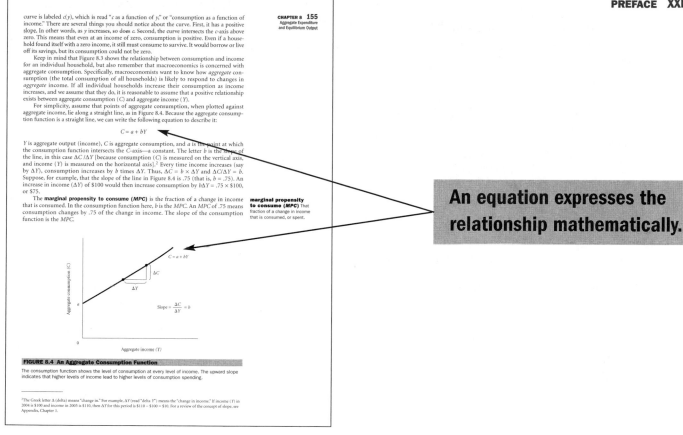

curve is labeled *c*(*y*), which is read "*c* as a function of *y*," or "consumption as a function of income." There are several things you should notice about the curve. First, it has a positive slope. In other words, as *y* increases, so does *c*. Second, the curve intersects the *c*-axis above zero. This means that even at an income of zero, consumption is positive. Even if a household found itself with a zero income, it still must consume to survive. It would borrow or live off its savings, but its consumption could not be zero.

Keep in mind that Figure 8.3 shows the relationship between consumption and income for an individual household, but also remember that macroeconomics is concerned with aggregate consumption. Specifically, macroeconomists want to know how *aggregate* consumption (the total consumption of all households) is likely to respond to changes in *aggregate* income. If all individual households increase their consumption as income increases, and we assume that they do, it is reasonable to assume that a positive relationship exists between aggregate consumption (*C*) and aggregate income (*Y*).

For simplicity, assume that points of aggregate consumption, when plotted against aggregate income, lie along a straight line, as in Figure 8.4. Because the aggregate consumption function is a straight line, we can write the following equation to describe it:

$$C = a + bY$$

Y is aggregate output (income), *C* is aggregate consumption, and *a* is the point at which the consumption function intersects the *C*-axis—a constant. The letter *b* is the slope of the line, in this case $\Delta C / \Delta Y$ [because consumption (*C*) is measured on the vertical axis, and income (*Y*) is measured on the horizontal axis].[2] Every time income increases (say by ΔY), consumption increases by *b* times ΔY. Thus, $\Delta C = b \times \Delta Y$ and $\Delta C / \Delta Y = b$. Suppose, for example, that the slope of the line in Figure 8.4 is .75 (that is, *b* = .75). An increase in income (ΔY) of $100 would then increase consumption by $b\Delta Y$ = .75 × $100, or $75.

The **marginal propensity to consume (MPC)** is the fraction of a change in income that is consumed. In the consumption function here, *b* is the MPC. An MPC of .75 means consumption changes by .75 of the change in income. The slope of the consumption function is the *MPC*.

marginal propensity to consume (MPC) That fraction of a change in income that is consumed, or spent.

FIGURE 8.4 An Aggregate Consumption Function

The consumption function shows the level of consumption at every level of income. The upward slope indicates that higher levels of income lead to higher levels of consumption spending.

[2]The Greek letter Δ (delta) means "change in." For example, ΔY (read "delta *Y*") means the "change in income." If income (*Y*) in 2004 is $100 and income in 2005 is $110, then ΔY for this period is $110 − $100 = $10. For a review of the concept of slope, see Appendix, Chapter 1.

An equation expresses the relationship mathematically.

And finally, in many cases where appropriate, we use an ***equation*** to present the concept with a mathematical formula.

MICROECONOMIC STRUCTURE

The organization of the microeconomic chapters continues to reflect our belief that the best way to understand how market economies operate—and the best way to understand basic economic theory—is to work through the perfectly competitive model first, including discussions of output markets (goods and services) and input markets (land, labor, and capital), and the connections between them, before turning to noncompetitive market structures, such as monopoly and oligopoly. When students understand how a simple, perfectly competitive system works, they can start thinking about how the pieces of the economy "fit together." We think this is a better approach to teaching economics than some of the more traditional approaches, which encourage students to think of economics as a series of disconnected alternative market models.

Learning perfect competition first also enables students to see the power of the market system. It is impossible to discuss the efficiency of markets as well as the problems that arise from markets until students have seen how a simple, perfectly competitive market system produces and distributes goods and services. This is our purpose in Chapters 6 through 11.

Chapter 12, "General Equilibrium and the Efficiency of Perfect Competition," is a pivotal chapter that links simple, perfectly competitive markets with a discussion of market imperfections and the role of government. Chapters 13 through 17 cover three noncompetitive market structures (monopoly, monopolistic competition, oligopoly), externalities, public goods, imperfect information, and income distribution as well as taxation and government finance. The accompanying visual gives you an overview of our structure.

Perfectly Competitive Markets

CHAPTER 6

Household Behavior

• Demand in output markets
• Supply in input markets

CHAPTER 9

Equilibrium in Competitive Output Markets

• Short run
• Long run

CHAPTERS 7–8

Firm Behavior

• Choice of technology
• Supply in output markets
• Demand in input markets

CHAPTERS 10–11

Competitive Input Markets

• Labor/land
• Capital

CHAPTER 12

The Competitive Market System

• General equilibrium and efficiency

Market Imperfections and the Role of Government

CHAPTERS 13–17

Market Imperfections and the Role of Government

• Imperfect market structures
  - Monopoly
  - Monopolistic competition
  - Oligopoly
• Externalities, public goods, imperfect information, social choice
• Income distribution and poverty
• Public finance: the economics of taxation

FIGURE 6.2 Understanding the Microeconomy and the Role of Government

To understand how the economy works, it helps to build from the ground up. We start in Chapters 6–8 with an overview of **household** and **firm** decision making in simple perfectly competitive markets. In Chapters 9–11 we see how firms and households interact in **output markets** (product markets) and **input markets** (labor/land and capital) to determine prices, wages, and profits. Once we have a picture of how a simple perfectly competitive economy works, we begin to relax assumptions. Chapter 12 is a pivotal chapter that links perfectly competitive markets with a discussion of market imperfections and the role of government. In Chapters 13–17 we cover the three noncompetitive market structures (monopoly, monopolistic competition, oligopoly), externalities, public goods, imperfect information, and income distribution as well as taxation and government finance.

MACROECONOMIC STRUCTURE

We remain committed to the view that it is a mistake simply to throw aggregate demand and aggregate supply curves at students in the first few chapters of a principles book. To understand the AS and AD curves, students need to know about the functioning of both the goods market and the money market. The logic behind the simple demand curve is wrong when applied to the relationship between aggregate demand and the price level. Similarly, the logic behind the simple supply curve is wrong when applied to the relationship between aggregate supply and the price level.

Part of teaching economics is teaching economic reasoning. Our discipline is built around deductive logic. Once we teach students a pattern of logic, we want and expect them to apply it to new circumstances. When they apply the logic of a simple demand curve or simply supply curve to the aggregate demand or aggregate supply curve, the logic does not fit. We believe the best way to teach the reasoning embodied in the aggregate demand and aggregate supply curves without creating serious confusion is to build up to them carefully.

In Chapters 21 and Chapter 22, we examine the market for goods and services. In Chapters 23 and 24 we examine the money market. We bring the two markets together in Chapter 25, which explains the links between the aggregate output (Y) and the interest rate (r). In Chapter 26, we explain how the aggregate demand curve can be derived from Chapter 25, and introduce the aggregate supply curve. This allows the price level (P) to be explained. We then explain in Chapter 27 how the labor market fits into this macroeconomic picture. The accompanying visual gives you an overview of our structure.

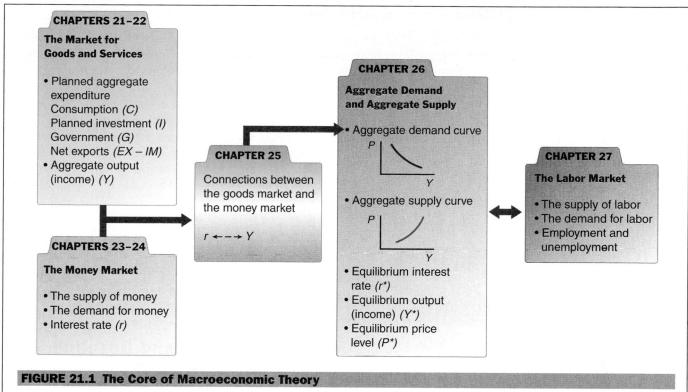

FIGURE 21.1 The Core of Macroeconomic Theory

We build up the macroeconomy slowly. In Chapters 21 and 22 we examine the market for goods and services, and in Chapters 23 and 24 we examine the money market. Then in Chapter 25 we bring the two markets together, in so doing explaining the links between aggregate output (Y) and the interest rate (r). In Chapter 26 we explain how the aggregate demand curve can be derived from Chapters 21 through 25, and we introduce the aggregate supply curve. This sets the stage for an explanation of the price level (P). We then explain in Chapter 27 how the labor market fits into the macroeconomic picture.

One of the big issues in the organization of the macroeconomic material is whether long-run growth issues should be taught before short-run chapters on the determination of national income and counter-cyclical policy. In the last three editions we moved a significant discussion of growth up to Chapter 20 and highlighted it. However, while we wrote the major chapters on long-run growth (Chapter 31) so that it can be taught either before or after the short-run chapters, we remain convinced that it is easier to understand the growth issue once a student has come to grips with the logic and controversies of short-run cycles, inflation, and unemployment.

INTERNATIONAL COVERAGE

We expanded international coverage in the seventh edition by including a new chapter on globalization (Chapter 35). This chapter covers the increasing economic interdependence among countries and their citizens. We focus on the causes and consequences of increased international trade of goods and services, increased cross-border movements of labor, and expanded international financial flows.

Since the publication of the seventh edition, there has been a dramatic acceleration in the "outsourcing" of jobs to lower wage labor markets outside the United States. What started with customer service representatives in Bangalore, India, has become a much bigger concern. Doctors who are paid a third of what a comparably educated doctor here would be paid are reading CAT scans, and foreign lawyers are doing back-office legal work in Malaysia. The whole topic of outsourcing is added in several places throughout the book including the globalization chapter.

As in previous editions, we continue to integrate international examples and applications in many chapters. International examples are listed in a table following the book's detailed table of contents. We continue to believe that a complete treatment of open-market macroeconomics should not be taught until students have mastered the logic of a simple closed macroeconomy. For this reason, we have chosen to place the "open-economy macroeconomics" chapter in the final part of the book, entitled "The World Economy." This part also includes the trade chapter, the globalization chapter, and the economic development chapter.

TOOLS FOR LEARNING

As authors and teachers, we understand the challenges of the principles of economics course. Our pedagogical features are designed to illustrate and reinforce key economic concepts through real-world examples and applications.

NEWS ANALYSIS

The "News Analysis" feature presents a news article that supports the key concept of the chapter and illustrates how economics is a part of students' daily lives. We have included news articles from various sources, including the *New York Times*, the *Economist*, the *Wall Street Journal*, and the *Washington Times*. Select articles include graphs or photos. The end-of-chapter problem sets include a question specific to each "News Analysis" article. Students can visit **www.myeconlab .com** for additional and updated news articles and exercises.

| crude oil prices, oil supply, oil demand | search |

○ Further Exploration   ● News Analysis

Economics and Global Affairs in 2005

Opportunity Costs and Internships

Mad Cow Disease Cuts Demand for Cattle in 2005

Hurricane Katrina and Gasoline Prices in 2005

Elasticity of Supply and House Prices

Hurricane Katrina and Gasoline Prices in 2005

AT THE END OF AUGUST 2005, THE coastlines of Louisiana and Mississippi suffered a direct hit from one of the most powerful storms ever to occur in the United States: Hurricane Katrina. The center of the storm passed very near to New Orleans, where broken levees led to unprecedented flooding, enormous loss of life, massive destruction of property, homelessness, and suffering. The storm knocked out a significant portion of the country's refinery capacity and had an immediate effect on the supply of gasoline at the pump. The following article from *CNN/Money* describes a pure shift of the gasoline supply curve to the left.

EXPERTS: $4 A GALLON GAS COMING SOON

Pricing analysts say consumers can expect even higher prices at the pump.
August 31, 2005: 4:11 PM EDT
By Grace Wong, CNN/Money staff writer

NEW YORK (CNN/Money)—Consumers can expect retail gas prices to rise to $4 a gallon soon, but whether they stay there depends on the long-term damage to oil facilities from Hurricane Katrina, oil and gas analysts said Wednesday.

"There's no question gas will hit $4 a gallon," Ben Brockwell, director of pricing at the Oil Price Information Service, said. "The question is how high will it go and how long will it last?"

Brockwell said with gasoline prices now exceeding $3 a gallon before even reaching the wholesale level, it "doesn't take a genius" to expect retail prices to hit $4 a gallon soon.

"Consumer haven't seen the worst of it yet," Brockwell said.

KATRINA PRESSURES GAS SUPPLIES
Katrina forced operators to close more than a tenth of the country's refining capacity and a quarter of its oil production, which sent gasoline prices surging.

Two major pipelines that supply gasoline to key terminals and distribution centers within the eastern U.S. were shut down due to power outages caused by the storm.

Colonial Pipeline said it hopes to be back in partial operation soon, while the date of Plantation Pipeline's restart is not clear. Each day the pipelines are closed, supplies get backlogged and distribution centers must rely on reserves.

"With this kind of hiccup in refinery capacity, in stretched markets like California, you could see over $4 a gallon in gas," Evan Smith, an analyst at U.S. Global Investors, told CNN/Money.

FURTHER EXPLORATION

Integrated in strategic places throughout the text, the "Further Exploration" feature provides students with applications as well as practical and historical information that supports the content of the chapter. The "Further Exploration" in Chapter 1, for example, highlights the various branches of economic study including economic law, international economics, and labor economics. In Chapter 29, the "Further Exploration" shows students how to read a bond table and the stock pages.

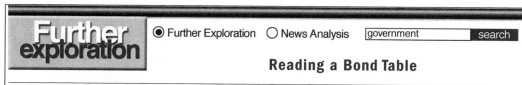

Reading a Bond Table

Figure 1 shows a small section of the corporate bond price quotations in the *Wall Street Journal* for July 24, 2003. What do all these signs and symbols mean?

The first column, under "Company," gives the name of the corporation that issued the bond and certain information about the terms under which the bond was originally issued. Let's take the last bond listed in the figure as an example. This bond was issued by the Comcast Cable Communications Holding Company. The "8.375" means the bond pays a coupon of $8.375 per $100 of face value of the bond. The bond matures in 2013. The column titled "Last Yield" shows the annual rate of return on the bond if the bond were purchased at the current price. If the current price were $100, then the annual rate of return would be 8.375 percent. The bond yields only 5.485 percent, however, so the current price of the bond must be higher than its face value of $100. (Remember: A decrease in the interest rate raises the price of a bond.)

The column "Vol" tells how many thousands of dollars in bonds were traded during the day. Here we see $89.953 million (at face value) of the Comcast bond were traded on July 24, 2003.

"Last Price" is the closing price of the bond. This is how much you would have to pay for the bond per $100 of face value. The Comcast bond's closing price was $121.38, which means a $100 bond was worth $121.38 at the end of the trading day.

"Est spread" and "UST" tell us something about the risk associated with the bond. "Est spread" is the difference in yield (stated in "basis points," with 100 basis points being the same as one percentage point) between the last yield on the Comcast bond and the current yield on a 10-year U.S. Treasury bond. Since the current yield on the Comcast bond is 5.485 and the spread is 131 (or 1.31 percent), the 10-year Treasury is paying 4.175 percent. Since the U.S. Treasury is backed by the "full faith and credit of the United States Government," Treasury bonds are the benchmark for a risk-free investment. The Comcast bond pays a higher effective yield because there is a small risk that Comcast will not be able to pay when the bond comes due.

Source: Wall Street Journal, July 25, 2003. WALL STREET JOURNAL. EASTERN EDITION [ONLY STAFF-PRODUCED MATERIALS MAY BE USED] by WALL STREET JOURNAL. Copyright 2003 by DOW JONES & CO INC. Reproduced with permission of DOW JONES & CO INC in the format Textbook via Copyright Clearance Center.

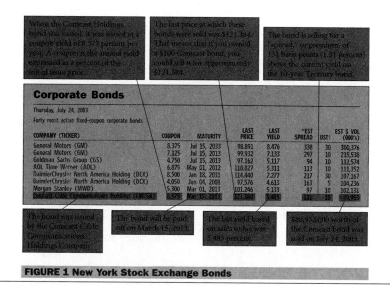

FIGURE 1 New York Stock Exchange Bonds

GRAPHS

Reading and interpreting graphs is a key part of understanding economic concepts. The Chapter 1 Appendix, "How to Read and Understand Graphs," shows readers how to interpret the 200+ graphs featured in this book. We use red curves to illustrate the behavior of firms and blue curves to show the behavior of households. We use a different shade of red and blue to signify a shift in a curve.

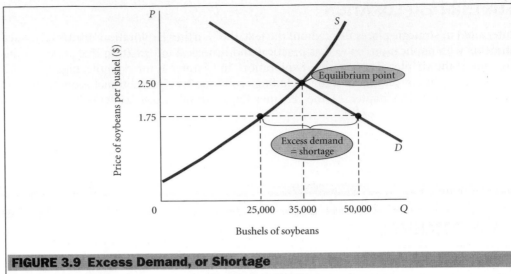

FIGURE 3.9 Excess Demand, or Shortage

At a price of $1.75 per bushel, quantity demanded exceeds quantity supplied. When excess *demand* arises, there is a tendency for price to rise. When quantity demanded equals quantity supplied, excess demand is eliminated and the market is in equilibrium. Here, the equilibrium price is $2.50, and the equilibrium quantity is 35,000 bushels.

HIGHLIGHTS OF MAJOR CONCEPTS

We have set major economic concepts off from the text in highlighted boxes. These highlights flow logically from the preceding text and into the text that follows. Students tell us that they find these very useful as a way of reviewing the key points in each chapter to prepare for exams.

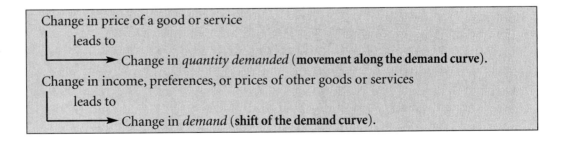

RUNNING GLOSSARY

Definitions of key terms appear in the margin so that they are easy to spot.

PROBLEM SETS AND SOLUTIONS

Each chapter and appendix ends with a problem set that asks students to think about what they've learned in the chapter. These problems are not simple memorization questions. Rather, they ask students to perform graphical analysis or to apply economics to a real-world situation or policy decision. More challenging problems are indicated by an asterisk. Additional questions, specific to the "News Analysis" articles, have been added. The worked-out solutions to all even-numbered problems are available in the back of the text so that students can check their understanding and progress. The solutions to all the problems are available in the Instructor's Manual.

INTEGRATED LEARNING PACKAGE

Case and Fair's text boasts an emphasis on quality assessment, and to that end, **MyEconLab**, the new standard in personalized online learning, is available as an integrated package with the eighth edition.

MyEconLab

MyEconLab provides problem-solving solutions for students and solves problems for you. It is a textbook-specific, online suite of tools designed with two purposes:

1. **Help students be more accountable for their own learning** To really understand economics, *to get ahead of the curve*, students need tools that fit their individual learning styles. MyEconLab puts those tools at their fingertips:
   - **Practice Tests** Practice tests for each section of the textbook enable students to test their understanding and identify the areas in which they need to do further work. Many practice-test questions ask students to work with graphs: interpreting them, manipulating them, and even drawing them. Instructors can customize the practice tests or let students use the supplied pre-built tests.
   - **Personalized Study Plan** Based on a student's performance on a practice test, a personal study plan is generated that shows where further study is needed. This study plan consists of a series of additional exercises, including many graphing questions.
   - **Additional Practice Exercises** Generated by the student's own performance on a practice test, additional practice exercises keyed to the textbook provide extensive practice and link students to the e-Text with animated graphs and to other tutorial instruction resources.
   - **Tutorial Instruction** Launched from the additional practice exercises, tutorial instruction is provided in the form of solutions to problems, step-by-step explanations, and other media-based explanations.
   - **Graphing Tools** Integrated into the practice tests and additional practice exercises, the graphing tool lets students manipulate and even draw graphs so that they get a better feel for how the concepts, numbers, and graphs are connected. Questions that use the graphing tool (like all other questions) can be submitted and graded.
   - **e-Text (optional) and e-Study Guide** The entire textbook and Study Guide are available in electronic format.
   - **Tutor Center** On-call for your students in the evenings—the Tutor Center offers live, qualified tutors who provide free and helpful support for your students.

2. **Help instructors save time** MyEconLab helps instructors track student performance and assess their progress by offering:
   - **Graded Homework** Instructors can create and assign tests, quizzes, or graded homework assignments.
   - **Graded Graphing Problems** MyEconLab can even grade assignments that require students to *draw* a graph.
   - **Gradebook** MyEconLab saves time by automatically grading all questions and tracking results in an online grade book.
   - **Supplementary Questions** The complete *Test Banks* are also preloaded into MyEconLab, giving instructors ample material from which they can create assignments.
   - **Weekly News Updates** Weekly news feeds with links to related Web sites, accompanied by homework and discussion questions, are provided and archived for use in class or as homework.
   - **Teaching Resources** Once registered for MyEconLab, instructors have access to downloadable supplements such as Instructor's Manuals, PowerPoint® lecture notes, and *Test Banks*.

For more information about MyEconLab, or to request an Instructor Access Code, visit **www.myeconlab.com**, or ask your local Prentice Hall representative.

ONLINE COURSE OFFERINGS

Blackboard and WebCT Course Content Prentice Hall offers fully customizable course content for the Blackboard and WebCT course management systems that include a link to the MyEconLab software hosting all of the course materials for Case and Fair's eighth edition.

The Companion Website (www.prenhall.com/casefair) This site connects students to Internet exercises and activities, practice quizzes that include many graphs from the text, and PowerPoint presentations. Each chapter contains multiple-choice, true-false, and essay quizzes. These quizzes immediately grade each answer submitted, provide feedback for correct and incorrect answers, and let students e-mail results to their professors.

STUDY GUIDES

Two comprehensive study guides, one for microeconomics and one for macroeconomics, provides students with additional applications and exercises.

Each chapter contains the following elements:

- **Point-by-Point Chapter Objectives** A list of learning goals for the chapter. Each objective is followed up with a summary of the material, learning tips for each concept, and practice questions with solutions.
- **Practice Tests** Consists of approximately 20 multiple-choice questions and answers.
- **Application Questions** A series of questions that require students to use graphic or numerical analysis to solve economic problems.
- **Solutions** Worked-out solutions to all questions in the *Study Guide*.
- **Comprehensive Part Exams** Exams to test the students' overall comprehension, consisting of multiple-choice and application questions. Solutions to all questions are also provided.

VANGONOTES

Study on the go with VangoNotes—chapter reviews from your text in downloadable mp3 format. Now wherever you are—whatever you're doing—you can study by listening to the following for each chapter of your textbook:

- **Big Ideas** Your "need to know" for each chapter
- **Practice Test** A gut check for the Big Ideas—tells you if you need to keep studying
- **Key Terms** Audio "flashcards" to help you review key concepts and terms
- **Rapid Review** A quick drill session—use it right before your test

VangoNotes are **flexible**. Download all the material from **www.vangonotes.com** directly to your mp3 player or only the chapters you need. They're also **efficient**. Use them in your car, at the gym, walking to class, wherever you want to go. So get yours today. And get studying.

SAFARIX WEBBOOK

SafariX Textbooks Online is an exciting new choice for students looking to save money. As an alternative to purchasing the print textbook, students can subscribe to the same content online and save up to 50% off the suggested list price of the print text. With a SafariX WebBook, students can search the text, make notes online, print out reading assignments that incorporate lecture notes, and bookmark important passages for later review. For more information, or to subscribe to the SafariX WebBook, visit **www.safarix.com**.

STUDENT SUBSCRIPTIONS

Staying on top of current economic issues is critical to understanding and applying micro-economic theory, in and out of class. Keep your students engaged by packaging, at a discount, a semester long subscription to the *Wall Street Journal*, the *Financial Times*, or the Economist.com with each student text. Contact your local Prentice Hall representative for package ISBNs.

Wall Street Journal **Global Events. Financial Markets. Your Personal Finances.** What's the one source that can tell you how all the pieces fit together? The *Wall Street Journal*, the world's most trusted source of vital business news and analysis.

In addition to daily home delivery of the *Wall Street Journal*, students receive all of the benefits of the *Wall Street Journal* Online, including:

- All the news from the *Wall Street Journal*—plus 24-hour-a-day updates
- The ability to search for past *Wall Street Journal* articles
- Detailed company research providing background, historical, and financial information
- News articles and press releases on nearly 30,000 companies
- Powerful personalization features, including online portfolios
- In-depth coverage of technology, and much more

As an adopting professor, you'll receive a free one-year subscription to both the print and online editions of the *Wall Street Journal.**

Financial Times Covering far more than just finance, the *Financial Times* is universally acknowledged as the world's leading business newspaper of global affairs. It is the only worldwide daily newspaper concentrating on international business, and its team of 600 journalists presents economic and business news from a truly global perspective.

In addition to daily home delivery of the *Financial Times*, students receive all of the benefits of FT.com (Level 1) including access to:

- **Exclusive FT news and commentary**
- **Industry-specific insight and analysis**
- **Surveys/in-depth reports**—industries, countries, and business trends
- **Power Search** tool searching through the last five-years of articles in the FT archive
- **View print edition**—exclusive previews from the *Financial Times* newspaper
- **PDA access**—download FT content to your PDA
- **News by e-mail**—news summaries and alerts direct to your inbox

As an adopting professor, you will qualify for a complimentary one-year personal subscription to the *Financial Times.**

Economist.com Economist.com is the premier online source for the analysis of world business and current affairs, providing authoritative insight and opinion on international news, world politics, business, finance, science and technology, as well as overviews of cultural trends and regular industry, business, and country surveys.

Economist.com publishes all articles from the *Economist* print edition plus:

- The **Advanced Search** feature retrieves over 30,000 *Economist* articles and surveys published since May 1997 from the Economist.com archives, making our library your personal intelligence source.
- The **Global Agenda** offers analysis of the international issues and events that matter most, when they matter most: a rolling selection of six to eight editorial briefings on the most important issues and events in global current affairs and business.
- **Country Briefings** offer continuously updated reports, forecasts, economic statistics, news, and analysis on 60 countries around the world.
- **Markets & Data** features global market data and charting, economic indicators from the *Economist*, stock quotes, foreign exchange graphs for 164 countries, a currency converter, and our annual favorite: The Big Mac Index.

As an adopting professor, you will qualify for a complimentary six-month personal subscription to the *Economist.com*.*

TECHNOLOGY SUPPLEMENTS FOR THE INSTRUCTOR

The following technology supplements are designed to make teaching and testing flexible and easy.

INSTRUCTOR'S RESOURCE CENTER

The Instructor's Resource Center contains all faculty and student resources that support this text. Instructors have the ability to download the Instructor's Manuals, TestGen-EQ, and PowerPoint presentations.

TESTGEN-EQ

Microeconomics and *Macroeconomics* Test Item Files 1 and 2 appear in print and as computer files that may be used with this TestGen-EQ test-generating software. This test-generating program permits instructors to edit, add, or delete questions from the test banks; edit or create; analyze test results; and organize a database of tests and student results. This software allows for flexibility and ease of use. It provides many options for organizing and displaying tests, along with a search and sort feature. *Principles of Economics*, Eighth Edition, is supported by a comprehensive set of six test-item files. The test-item files are described in detail under the "Print Supplements" section of this preface.

POWERPOINT LECTURE PRESENTATIONS

The PowerPoint presentations offer summaries and reinforcement of key text material. Many graphs "build" over a sequencing of slides so that students may see the step-by-step process of economic analysis.

Instructors can use these to create full-color, professional-looking presentations and customized handouts for students.

The PowerPoint presentations are available for download on the Instructor's Resource Center and are also available for use in conjunction with classroom response systems.

CLASSROOM RESPONSE SYSTEMS

- Enhance interactivity
- Capture attention
- Get instant feedback
- Assess comprehension

Pearson Education is pleased to offer you and your school the benefits of our partnerships with a number of leading providers of classroom response systems.

Whether you are considering a system for the first time or are interested in expanding a program department-wide, we can help you select the best system for your needs to accompany *Principles of Economics*, Eighth Edition.

DIGITAL IMAGE LIBRARY

All graphs and tables from the text are available electronically.

---

*Package adoptions of over 10 copies qualify for complimentary professor subscriptions.

Principles of Economics, Eighth Edition, has a comprehensive print supplement package for both student and instructor.

INSTRUCTOR'S MANUAL

Two instructor's manuals, one for *Principles of Microeconomics* and one for *Principles of Macroeconomics*, are designed to provide the utmost teaching support for instructors. It includes the following:

- Detailed *Chapter Outlines* include key terminology, teaching notes, and lecture suggestions.
- *Topics for Class Discussion* provide topics and real-world situations that help make economic concepts resonate with students.
- *Teaching Tips* provide tips for alternative ways to cover the material or brief reminders on additional help to provide students. These tips can include suggestions for exercises or experiments to complete in class.
- *Extended Applications* include exercises, activities, and experiments to help make economics relevant to students.
- *Solutions* to all problems in the book.

SIX TEST BANKS

In our effort to focus on assessment with the eighth edition of *Principles of Economics*, we tailored the test item files so that they are useful to the instructors who use them. To help instructors select questions more quickly and efficiently, we have used the skill descriptors of *fact, definition, conceptual,* and *analytical*. A question labeled *fact* tests a student's knowledge of factual information presented in the text. A *definition* question asks the student to define an economic term or concept. *Conceptual* questions test a student's understanding of a concept. *Analytical* questions require the student to apply an analytical procedure to answer the question.

To aid instructors in building tests, each question is also keyed by degree of difficulty as *easy, moderate,* or *difficult. Easy* questions involve straightforward recall of information in the text. *Moderate* questions require some analysis on the student's part. *Difficult* questions usually entail more complex analysis.

The test banks include questions with tables that students must analyze to solve for numerical answers. They also contain questions based on the graphs that appear in the book. The questions ask students to interpret the information presented in the graph. There are also many questions in the test banks that require students to sketch out a graph on their own and interpret curve movements.

THREE TEST BANKS FOR MICROECONOMICS

Microeconomics Test Bank 1   Test Item File 1 includes over 2,200 questions. All questions are machine-gradable and are either multiple-choice or true-false. This test bank is for use with the eighth edition of *Principles of Economics* in the first year of publication. This test bank is available in a computerized format using TestGen-EQ test-generating software.

Microeconomics Test Bank 2   This additional test bank contains another 2,200, machine-gradable questions based on the TIF1 but regenerated to provide instructors with fresh questions when using the book in the second year. This test bank is available in a computerized format using TestGen-EQ test-generating software.

Microeconomics Test Bank 3   This third test bank includes 1,000 conceptual problems, essay questions, and short-answer questions. Application-type problems ask students to draw graphs and analyze tables. The Word files are available on the Instructor's Resource Center.

THREE TEST BANKS FOR MACROECONOMICS

Macroeconomics Test Bank 1   Test Item File 1 includes over 2,500 questions. All questions are machine-gradable and are either multiple-choice or true-false. This test bank is for use with the eighth edition of *Principles of Economics* in the first year of publication. This test bank is available in a computerized format using TestGen-EQ test-generating software.

Macroeconomics Test Bank 2   This additional test bank contains another 2,500, machine-gradable questions based on the TIF1 but regenerated to provide instructors with fresh questions when using the book in the second year. This test bank is available in a computerized format using TestGen-EQ test-generating software.

Macroeconomics Test Bank 3   This third test bank includes over 1,000 conceptual problems, essay questions, and short-answer questions. Application-type problems ask students to draw graphs and analyze tables. The Word files are available on the Instructor's Resource Center.

ACKNOWLEDGMENTS

We are grateful to the many people who helped us prepare the eighth edition. We thank Jon Axelrod, editor for economics, and Pam Hersperger, product development manager at Prentice Hall, for their help and enthusiasm. We are also grateful to Sylvia Mallory, developmental editor, for overseeing the entire project. The quality of the book owes much to her guidance. The technology supplements that accompany this book are the result of the dedication of Peter Snell, media project manager. Sharon Koch, executive marketing manager, and David Theisen, national sales director for key markets, carefully crafted the marketing message. Carol Samet, production editor, and Cynthia Regan, our production managing editor, ensured that the production process of the book went smoothly. In addition, we also want to thank Heidi Allgair of GGS Book Services who kept us on schedule, and Sheila Norman, who researched the many photographs that appear in the book. We want to give special thanks to Samantha Ernst for her research assistance and proofreading of the manuscript.

We also owe a debt of gratitude to those who reviewed and accuracy checked the eighth edition. They all provided us with valuable insight as we prepared this edition and its supplement package.

ACCURACY REVIEWERS AND SUPPLEMENT AUTHORS

A dedicated team of economics professors accuracy checked the text and prepared a complete supplements package for the eighth edition:

Thomas Beveridge, North Carolina State University

Charles Callahan, III, State University of New York at Brockport

Richard Gosselin, Houston Community College

Anthony K. Lima, California State University at Hayward

Marvin Margolis, Millersville University of Pennsylvania

Jim Moreno, Blinn College

Fernando Quijano, Dickinson State University

Yvonn Quijano, Dickinson State University

James Swofford, University of South Alabama

REVIEWERS OF THE CURRENT EDITION

The guidance and recommendations of the following professors helped us develop the revision plans for our new edition and shape the content of the new chapters:

Douglas K. Adie, Ohio University

Moshen Bahmani, University of Wisconsin-Milwaukee

A. Paul Ballantyne, University of Colorado at Colorado Springs

Frank Bonello, University of Notre Dame

David Brownstone, University of California-Irvine

Yvonne Durham, Western Washington University

Mathew Forstater, University of Missouri-Kansas City

Donna Ginther, University of Kansas

Thomas A. Gresik, University of Notre Dame

Arthur Kartman, San Diego State University

Brett Katzman, Kennesaw State University

Fred Keast, Portland State University

Stephanie Kelton, University of Missouri-Kansas City

Hwagyun Kim, State University of New York at Buffalo

Heather Kohls, Marquette University

Charles R. Link, University of Delaware

Ming Chien Lo, St. Cloud State University

Meghan Millea, Mississippi State University

Art Meyer, Lincoln Land Community College

Carrie Meyer, George Mason University

Terry D. Monson, Michigan Tech University

Myra Moore, University of Georgia

W. Douglas Morgan, University of California, Santa Barbara

Mike Pogodzinski, San Jose State University

Abe Qastin, Lakeland College

Paul Rappoport, Temple University

Stephen L Shapiro, University of North Florida

Chris Stufflebean, Southwestern Oklahoma State University

Samia Tavares, Rochester Institute of Technology

Henry Terrell, University of Maryland, College Park

Robert Tokle, Idaho State University

REVIEWERS OF PREVIOUS EDITIONS

The following individuals were of immense help in reviewing all or part of previous editions of this book and the teaching/learning package in various stages of development:

Lew Abernathy, University of North Texas

Jack Adams, University of Maryland

Douglas Agbetsiafa, Indiana University at South Bend

Sheri Aggarwal, University of Virginia

Sam Alapati, Rutgers University

John W. Allen, Texas A&M University

Polly Allen, University of Connecticut

Stuart Allen, University of North Carolina at Greensboro

Alex Anas, University at Buffalo, The State University of New York

Jim Angresano, Hampton-Sydney College

Kenneth S. Arakelian, University of Rhode Island

Harvey Arnold, Indian River Community College

Nick Apergis, Fordham University

Richard Ashley, Virginia Technical University

Kidane Asmeron, Pennsylvania State University

James Aylesworth, Lakeland Community College

Richard J. Ballman, Jr., Augustana College

Mohammad Bajwa, Northampton Community College

King Banaian, St. Cloud State University

Kari Battaglia, University of North Texas

Leon Battista, Bronx Community College

Willie J. Belton, Jr., Georgia Institute of Technology

Daniel K. Benjamin, Clemson University

Charles A. Bennett, Gannon University

Daniel Berkowitz, University of Pittsburgh

Bruce Bolnick, Northeastern University

Jeffrey Bookwalter, University of Montana

Maristella Botticini, Boston University

G. E. Breger, University of South Carolina

Dennis Brennan, William Rainey Harper Junior College

Anne E. Bresnock, California State Polytechnic University, Pomona, and the University of California, Los Angeles

Charles Callahan, III, State University of New York at Brockport

Lindsay Caulkins, John Carroll University

Atreya Chakraborty, Boston College

Winston W. Chang, University at Buffalo, The State University of New York

Janie Chermak, University of New Mexico

Harold Christensen, Centenary College

Daniel Christiansen, Albion College

Susan Christoffersen, Philadelphia University

Samuel Kim-Liang Chuah, Walla Walla College

David Colander, Middlebury College

Daniel Condon, University of Illinois at Chicago; Moraine Valley Community College

David Cowen, University of Texas at Austin

Peggy Crane, Southwestern College

Minh Quang Dao, Eastern Illinois University

Vernon J. Dixon, Haverford College

Michael Donihue, Colby College

Joanne M. Doyle, James Madison University

Robert Driskill, The Ohio State University

James Dulgeroff, San Bernardino Valley College

Debra Sabatini Dwyer, State University of New York at Stony Brook
Gary Dymski, University of Southern California
David Eaton, Murray State University
Jay Egger, Towson State University
Ronald D. Elkins, Central Washington University
Noel J. J. Farley, Bryn Mawr College
Mosin Farminesh, Temple University
Dan Feaster, Miami University of Ohio
Susan Feiner, Virginia Commonwealth University
Getachew Felleke, Albright College
Lois Fenske, South Puget Sound Community College
William Field, DePauw University
Mary Flannery, Santa Clara University
Richard Fowles, University of Utah
Bill Foeller, State University of New York at Fredonia
Roger Nils Folsom, San Jose State University
Sean Fraley, College of Mount Saint Joseph
Roger Frantz, San Diego State University
Alejandro Gallegos, Winona State University
N. Galloro, Chabot College
Martin A. Garrett, Jr., College of William and Mary
Tom Gausman, Northern Illinois University, DeKalb
Shirley J. Gedeon, University of Vermont
Lisa Giddings, University of Wisconsin at La Crosse
Gary Gigliotti, Rutgers University
Lynn Gillette, Texas A&M University
James N. Giordano, Villanova University
Sarah L. Glavin, Boston College
Roy Gobin, Loyola University of Chicago
Bill Goffe, University of Mississippi
Devra Golbe, Hunter College
Roger Goldberg, Ohio Northern University
Richard Gosselin, Houston Community College
John W. Graham, Rutgers University
Douglas Greenley, Morehead State University
Lisa M. Grobar, California State University at Long Beach
Wayne A. Grove, Syracuse University
Benjamin Gutierrez, Indiana University at Bloomington
A. R. Gutowsky, California State University at Sacramento
David R. Hakes, University of Missouri at St. Louis
Stephen Happel, Arizona State University
Mitchell Harwitz, University at Buffalo, The State University of New York

David Hoaas, Centenary College
Harry Holzer, Michigan State University
Bobbie Horn, University of Tulsa
John Horowitz, Ball State University
Janet Hunt, University of Georgia
E. Bruce Hutchinson, University of Tennessee at Chattanooga
Fred Inaba, Washington State University
Richard Inman, Boston College
Russell A. Janis, University of Massachusetts Amherst
Eric Jensen, The College of William & Mary
Shirley Johnson, Vassar College
Farhoud Kafi, Babson College
R. Kallen, Roosevelt University
Arthur E. Kartman, San Diego State University
Hirshel Kasper, Oberlin College
Bruce Kaufman, Georgia State University
Dominique Khactu, The University of North Dakota
Phillip King, San Francisco State University
Barbara Kneeshaw, Wayne County Community College
Inderjit Kohli, Santa Clara University
Barry Kotlove, Elmira College
David Kraybill, University of Georgia at Athens
Rosung Kwak, University of Texas at Austin
Steven Kyle, Cornell University
Anil K. Lal, Pittsburg State University
Melissa Lam, Wellesley College
Micheal Lawlor, Wake Forest University
Jim Lee, Fort Hays State University
Judy Lee, Leeward Community College
Sang H. Lee, Southeastern Louisiana University
Don Leet, California State University at Fresno
Robert J. Lemke, Lake Forest College
Gary Lemon, DePauw University
Alan Leonard, Northern Illinois University
Mary Lesser, Iona College
George Lieu, Tuskegee University
Stephen E. Lile, Western Kentucky University
Jane Lillydahl, University of Colorado at Boulder
Anthony K. Lima, California State University at Hayward
Al Link, University of North Carolina at Greensboro
Robert Litro, U.S. Air Force Academy
Burl F. Long, University of Florida
Gerald Lynch, Purdue University
Karla Lynch, University of North Texas
Marvin S. Margolis, Millersville University of Pennsylvania

Michael Magura, University of Toledo

Don Maxwell, Central State University

Nan Maxwell, California State University at Hayward

Cynthia S. McCarty, Jacksonville State University

J. Harold McClure, Jr., Villanova University

Rick McIntyre, University of Rhode Island

James J. McLain, University of New Orleans

K. Mehtaboin, College of St. Rose

Jenny Minier, University of Miami

Shahruz Mohtadi, Suffolk University

Barbara A. Moore, University of Central Florida

Joe L. Moore, Arkansas Technical University

Robert Moore, Occidental College

Doug Morgan, University of California, Santa Barbara

Norma C. Morgan, Curry College

John Murphy, North Shore Community College, Massachusetts

Veena Nayak, University at Buffalo, The State University of New York

Ron Necoechea, Robert Wesleyan College

Randy Nelson, Colby College

David Nickerson, University of British Columbia

Rachel Nugent, Pacific Lutheran University

Akorlie A. Nyatepe-Coo, University of Wisconsin at LaCrosse

Norman P. Obst, Michigan State University

William C. O'Connor, Western Montana College

Martha L. Olney, University of California, Berkeley

Kent Olson, Oklahoma State University

Theresa Osborne, Hunter College

Jaime Ortiz, Florida Atlantic University

Donald J. Oswald, California State University at Bakersfield

Niki Papadopoulou, University of Cyprus

Walter Park, American University

Carl Parker, Fort Hays State University

Spirog Patton, Neumann College

Mary Ann Pevas, Winona State University

Tony Pizelo, Spokane Community College

Elizabeth Porter, University of North Florida

Kevin Quinn, St. Norbert College

Michael Rendich, Westchester Community College

Lynn Rittenoure, University of Tulsa

Michael Rolleigh, University of Minnesota

S. Scanlon Romer, Delta College

David C. Rose, University of Missouri at St. Louis

Greg Rose, Sacramento City College

Richard Rosenberg, Pennsylvania State University

Robert Rosenman, Washington State University

Paul Rothstein, Washington University

Jeff Rubin, Rutgers University

Mark Rush, University of Florida at Gainesville

Dereka Rushbrook, Ripon College

Jerard Russo, University of Hawaii

David L. Schaffer, Haverford College

Ramon Schreffler, Houston Community College System (retired)

Jerry Schwartz, Broward Community College

Gary Sellers, University of Akron

Jean Shackleford, Bucknell University

Linda Shaffer, California State University, Fresno

Geoff Shepherd, University of Massachusetts Amherst

Bih-Hay Sheu, University of Texas at Austin

Alden Shiers, California Polytechnic State University

Scott Simkins, North Carolina Agricultural and Technical State University

Sue Skeath, Wellesley College

Paula Smith, Central State University, Oklahoma

David Sobiechowski, Wayne State University

John Solow, University of Iowa at Iowa City

David J. St. Clair, California State University at Hayward

Rebecca Stein, University of Pennsylvania

Susan Stojanovic, Washington University, St. Louis

Ernst W. Stromsdorfer, Washington State University

Rodney B. Swanson, University of California, Los Angeles

James Swofford, University of Alabama

Michael Taussig, Rutgers University

Timothy Taylor, Stanford University

Sister Beth Anne Tercek, SND, Notre Dame College of Ohio

Karen M. Travis, Pacific Lutheran University

Jack Trierweler, Northern State University

Brian M. Trinque, University of Texas at Austin

Ann Velenchik, Wellesley College

Lawrence Waldman, University of New Mexico

Chris Waller, Indiana University at Bloomington

Walter Wessels, North Carolina State University

Joan Whalen-Ayyappan, DeVry Institute of Technology

Robert Whaples, Wake Forest University

Leonard A. White, University of Arkansas

Paula Worthington, Northwestern University

Ben Young, University of Missouri-Kansas City
Darrel Young, University of Texas
Michael Youngblood, Rock Valley College
Abera Zeyege, Ball State University

James Ziliak, Indiana University at Bloomington
Jason Zimmerman, South Dakota State University

We welcome comments about the eighth edition. Please write to us care of Economics Editor, Prentice Hall Higher Education Division, One Lake Street, Upper Saddle River, NJ 07458.

Karl E. Case

Ray C. Fair

Save a Tree!
Many of the components of the teaching and learning package are available online. Online supplements conserve paper and allow you to select and print only the material you plan to use. For more information, please contact your Prentice Hall sales representative.

FLEXIBILITY CHART

Micro

Core Chapters

1. The Scope and Method of Economics.
2. The Economic Problem: Scarcity and Choice.
3. Demand, Supply, and Market Equilibrium.
4. Demand and Supply Applications.
5. Elasticity.
6. Household Behavior and Consumer Choice.
7. The Production Process: The Behavior of Profit-Maximizing Firms.
8. Short-Run Costs and Output Decisions.
9. Long-Run Costs and Output Decisions.
10. Input Demand: The Labor and Land Markets.
11. Input Demand: The Capital Market and the Investment Decision.
12. General Equilibrium and the Efficiency of Perfect Competition.
13. Monopoly and Antitrust Policy.
14. Monopolistic Competition and Oligopoly.
15. Externalities, Public Goods, Imperfect Information, and Social Choice.

Short Core Chapters

1. The Scope and Method of Economics.
2. The Economic Problem: Scarcity and Choice.
3. Demand, Supply, and Market Equilibrium.
4. Demand and Supply Applications.
5. Elasticity.
6. Household Behavior and Consumer Choice.
7. The Production Process: The Behavior of Profit-Maximizing Firms.
8. Short-Run Costs and Output Decisions.
9. Long-Run Costs and Output Decisions.
13. Monopoly and Antitrust Policy.
14. Monopolistic Competition and Oligopoly.
15. Externalities, Public Goods, Imperfect Information, and Social Choice.

Optional Chapters

16. Income Distribution and Poverty.
17. Public Finance: The Economics of Taxation.
18. International Trade, Comparative Advantage, and Protectionism.
19. Globalization.
20. Economic Growth in Developing and Transitional Economies.

Macro

Core Chapters

18. Introduction to Macroeconomics.
19. Measuring National Output and National Income.
20. Long-Run and Short-Run Concerns: Growth, Productivity, Unemployment, and Inflation.
21. Aggregate Expenditure and Equilibrium Output.

Short Core Chapters

18. Introduction to Macroeconomics.
19. Measuring National Output and National Income.
20. Long-Run and Short-Run Concerns: Growth, Productivity, Unemployment, and Inflation.
21. Aggregate Expenditure and Equilibrium Output.

Optional Chapters

29. The Stock Market and the Economy.
30. Household and Firm Behavior in the Macroeconomy: A Further Look.
35. Globalization.
36. Economic Growth in Developing and Transitional Economies.

(continued)

Macro

Core Chapters

22. The Government and Fiscal Policy.
23. The Money Supply and the Federal Reserve System.
24. Money Demand, the Equilibrium Interest Rate, |and Monetary Policy.
25. Money, the Interest Rate, and Output: Analysis and Policy.
26. Aggregate Demand, Aggregate Supply, and Inflation.
27. The Labor Market, Unemployment, and Inflation.
31. Long-Run Growth.
32. Debates in Macroeconomics: Monetarism, New Classical Theory, and Supply Side-Economics.
34. Open-Economy Macroeconomics: The Balance of Payments and Exchange Rates.

Short Core Chapters

22. The Government and Fiscal Policy.
23. The Money Supply and the Federal Reserve System.
24. Money Demand, the Equilibrium Interest Rate, and Monetary Policy.
25. Money, the Interest Rate, and Output: Analysis and Policy.
26. Aggregate Demand, Aggregate Supply, and Inflation.
31. Long-Run Growth.

Optional Chapters

Combined = 2 semester Core, short core and optional

one semester – core

Micro

1. The Scope and Method of Economics.
2. The Economic Problem: Scarcity and Choice
3. Demand, Supply, and Market Equilibrium.
4. Demand and Supply Applications
5. Elasticity
6. Household Behavior and Consumer Choice
7. The Production Process: The Behavior of Profit-Maximizing Firms.
8. Short-Run Costs and Output Decisions.
9. Long-Run Costs and Output Decisions.
10. Input Demand: The Labor and Land Markets.
13. Monopoly and Antitrust Policy.

Macro

18. Introduction to Macroeconomics.
19. Measuring National Output and National Income.
20. Long-Run and Short-Run Concerns: Growth, Productivity, Unemployment, and Inflation.
21. Aggregate Expenditure and Equilibrium Output.
22. The Government and Fiscal Policy.
23. The Money Supply and the Federal Reserve System.
24. Money Demand, the Equilibrium Interest Rate, and Monetary Policy.
25. Money, the Interest Rate, and Output: Analysis and Policy.
26. Aggregate Demand, Aggregate Supply, and Inflation.

EIGHTH EDITION

PRINCIPLES OF ECONOMICS

The Scope and Method of Economics

1

The study of economics should begin with a sense of wonder. Pause for a moment and consider a typical day in your life. For breakfast you might have bread made in a local bakery with flour produced in Minnesota from wheat grown in Kansas and bacon from pigs raised in Ohio packaged in plastic made in New Jersey. You spill coffee from Colombia on your shirt made in Texas from textiles shipped from South Carolina.

After class you drive with a friend in a Japanese car on an interstate highway that is part of a system that took 20 years and billions of dollars to build. You stop for gasoline refined in Louisiana from Saudi Arabian crude oil brought to the United States on a supertanker that took 3 years to build at a shipyard in Maine.

Later you log onto the Web with a laptop computer assembled in Indonesia from parts made in China and send e-mail to your brother in Mexico City, and you call a buddy on a cell phone made by a company in Finland. It is picked up by a microwave dish hiding in a church steeple rented from the church by a cellular company that was just bought by a European conglomerate.

You use or consume tens of thousands of things, both tangible and intangible, every day: buildings, rock music, compact discs (CDs), telephone services, staples, paper, toothpaste, tweezers, soap, digital watches, fire protection, banks, electricity, eggs, insurance, football fields, computers, buses, rugs, subways, health services, sidewalks, and so forth. Somebody made all these things. Somebody organized men and women and materials to produce them and distribute them. Thousands of decisions went into their completion. Somehow they got to you.

In the United States over 140 million people—almost half the total population—work at hundreds of thousands of different jobs producing over $12 trillion worth of goods and services every year. Some cannot find work; some choose not to work. Some are rich; others are poor.

The United States imports over $240 billion worth of automobiles and parts and about $180 billion worth of petroleum and petroleum products each year; it exports around $62 billion worth of agricultural products, including food. High-rise office buildings go up in central cities. Condominiums and homes are built in the suburbs. In other places homes are abandoned and boarded up.

Some countries are wealthy. Others are impoverished. Some are growing. Some are not. Some businesses are doing well. Others are going bankrupt.

At any moment in time every society faces constraints imposed by nature and by previous generations. Some societies are handsomely endowed by nature with fertile land, water, sunshine, and natural resources. Others have deserts and few mineral resources. Some societies receive much from previous generations—art, music, technical knowledge, beautiful buildings, and productive factories. Others are left with overgrazed, eroded land, cities leveled by war, or polluted natural environments. *All* societies face limits.

economics The study of how individuals and societies choose to use the scarce resources that nature and previous generations have provided.

Economics is the study of how individuals and societies choose to use the scarce resources that nature and previous generations have provided. The key word in this definition is *choose*. Economics is a behavioral, or social, science. In large measure it is the study of how people make choices. The choices that people make, when added up, translate into societal choices.

The purpose of this chapter and the next is to elaborate on this definition and to introduce the subject matter of economics. What is produced? How is it produced? Who gets it? Why? Is the result good or bad? Can it be improved?

WHY STUDY ECONOMICS?

There are four main reasons to study economics: to learn a way of thinking, to understand society, to understand global affairs, and to be an informed voter.

TO LEARN A WAY OF THINKING

Probably the most important reason for studying economics is to learn a way of thinking. A good way to approach economics is to understand three of its most fundamental concepts: *opportunity cost, marginalism,* and *efficient markets*. It is a good bet that after studying economics, you will use these concepts every day in making decisions.

Opportunity Cost What happens in an economy is the outcome of thousands of individual decisions. Households must decide how to divide their incomes among all the goods and services available in the marketplace. People must decide whether to work or not to work, whether to go to school, and how much to save. Businesses must decide what to produce, how much to produce, how much to charge, and where to locate. It is not surprising that economic analysis focuses on the process of decision making.

Nearly all decisions involve trade-offs. A key concept that recurs in analyzing the decision-making process is the notion of *opportunity cost*. The full "cost" of making a specific choice includes what we give up by not making the alternative choice. The best alternative that we forgo, or give up, when we make a choice or a decision is called the **opportunity cost** of that decision.

opportunity cost The best alternative that we forgo, or give up, when we make a choice or a decision.

This concept applies to individuals, businesses, and entire societies. The opportunity cost of going to a movie is the value of the other things you could have done with the same money and time. If you decide to take time off from work, the opportunity cost of your leisure is the pay that you would have earned had you worked. Part of the cost of a college education is the income you could have earned by working full-time instead of going to school. If a firm purchases a new piece of equipment for $3,000, it does so because it expects that equipment to generate more profit. There is an opportunity cost, however, because that $3,000 could have been deposited in an interest-earning account. To a society, the opportunity cost of using resources to launch astronauts on a space shuttle is the value of the private/civilian or other government goods that could have been produced with the same resources.

scarce Limited.

Opportunity costs arise because resources are scarce. **Scarce** simply means "limited." Consider one of our most important resources—time. There are only 24 hours in a day, and we must live our lives under this constraint. A farmer in rural Brazil must decide whether it is better to continue to farm or to go to the city and look for a job. A hockey player at the University of Vermont must decide whether she will play on the varsity team or spend more time improving her academic work.

Marginalism and Sunk Costs   A second key concept used in analyzing choices is the notion of **marginalism**. In weighing the costs and benefits of a decision, it is important to weigh only the costs and benefits that arise from the decision. Suppose, for example, that you live in New Orleans and that you are weighing the costs and benefits of visiting your mother in Iowa. If business required that you travel to Kansas City, the cost of visiting Mom would be only the additional, or *marginal*, time and money cost of getting to Iowa from Kansas City.

Consider the cost of producing this book. Assume that 10,000 copies are produced. The total cost of producing the copies includes the cost of the authors' time in writing the book, the cost of editing, the cost of making the plates for printing, and the cost of the paper and ink. If the total cost were $600,000, then the average cost of one copy would be $60, which is simply $600,000 divided by 10,000.

Although average cost is an important concept, a book publisher must know more than simply the average cost of a book. For example, suppose a second printing is being debated. That is, should another 10,000 copies be produced? In deciding whether to proceed, the costs of writing, editing, making plates, and so forth are irrelevant, because they have already been incurred—they are *sunk costs*. **Sunk costs** are costs that cannot be avoided, regardless of what is done in the future, because they have already been incurred. All that matters is the costs associated with the additional, or marginal, books to be printed. Technically, *marginal cost* is the cost of producing one more unit of output.

There are numerous examples in which the concept of marginal cost is useful. For an airplane that is about to take off with empty seats, the marginal cost of an extra passenger is essentially zero; the total cost of the trip is roughly unchanged by the addition of an extra passenger. Thus, setting aside a few seats to be sold at big discounts through priceline.com or other Web sites can be profitable even if the fare for those seats is far below the average cost per seat of making the trip. As long as the airline succeeds in filling seats that would otherwise have been empty, doing so is profitable.

Efficient Markets—No Free Lunch   Suppose you are ready to check out of a busy grocery store on the day before a storm, and seven checkout registers are open with several people in each line. Which line should you choose? It is usually the case that the waiting time is approximately the same no matter which register you choose (assuming you have more than 12 items). If one line is much shorter than the others, people will quickly move into it until the lines are equalized again.

As you will see later, the term *profit* in economics has a very precise meaning. Economists, however, often loosely refer to "good deals" or risk-free ventures as *profit opportunities*. Using the term loosely, a profit opportunity exists at the checkout lines if one line is shorter than the others. In general, such profit opportunities are rare. At any time there are many people searching for them, and as a consequence, few exist. Markets like this, where any profit opportunities are eliminated almost instantaneously, are said to be **efficient markets**. (We discuss *markets*, the institutions through which buyers and sellers interact and engage in exchange, in detail in Chapter 2.)

The common way of expressing the efficient markets concept is "there's no such thing as a free lunch." How should you react when a stockbroker calls up with a hot tip on the stock market? With skepticism. There are thousands of individuals each day looking for hot tips in the market. If a particular tip about a stock is valid, there will be an immediate rush to buy the stock, which will quickly drive its price up. This view that very few profit opportunities exist can, of course, be carried too far. There is a story about two people walking along, one an economist and one not. The noneconomist sees a $20 bill on the sidewalk and says, "There's a $20 bill on the sidewalk." The economist replies, "That is not possible. If there were, somebody would already have picked it up."

There are clearly times when profit opportunities exist. Someone has to be first to get the news, and some people have quicker insights than others. Nevertheless, news travels fast, and there are thousands of people with quick insights. The general view that large profit opportunities are rare is close to the mark.

> **marginalism** The process of analyzing the additional or incremental costs or benefits arising from a choice or decision.

> **sunk costs** Costs that cannot be avoided, regardless of what is done in the future, because they have already been incurred.

> **efficient market** A market in which profit opportunities are eliminated almost instantaneously.

The study of economics teaches us a way of thinking and helps us make decisions.

TO UNDERSTAND SOCIETY

Another reason for studying economics is to understand society better. Past and present economic decisions have an enormous influence on the character of life in a society. The current state of the physical environment, the level of material well-being, and the nature and number of jobs are all products of the economic system.

To get a sense of the ways in which economic decisions have shaped our environment, imagine looking out of a top-floor window of an office tower in any large city. The workday is about to begin. All around you are other tall glass and steel buildings full of workers. In the distance you see the smoke of factories. Looking down, you see thousands of commuters pouring off trains and buses, and cars backed up on freeway exit ramps. You see trucks carrying goods from one place to another. You also see the face of urban poverty: Just beyond the freeway is a large public housing project and, beyond that, burned-out and boarded-up buildings.

What you see before you is the product of millions of economic decisions made over hundreds of years. People at some point decided to spend time and money building those buildings and factories. Somebody cleared the land, laid the tracks, built the roads, and produced the cars and buses.

Economic decisions not only have shaped the physical environment but also have determined the character of society. At no time has the impact of economic change on a society been more evident than in England during the late eighteenth and early nineteenth centuries, a period that we now call the **Industrial Revolution**. Increases in the productivity of agriculture, new manufacturing technologies, and development of more efficient forms of transportation led to a massive movement of the British population from the countryside to the city. At the beginning of the eighteenth century, approximately 2 out of 3 people in Great Britain worked in agriculture. By 1812, only 1 in 3 remained in agriculture; by 1900, the figure was fewer than 1 in 10. People jammed into overcrowded cities and worked long hours in factories. England had changed completely in two centuries—a period that in the run of history was nothing more than the blink of an eye.

It is not surprising that the discipline of economics began to take shape during this period. Social critics and philosophers looked around them and knew that their philosophies must expand to accommodate the changes. Adam Smith's *Wealth of Nations* appeared in 1776. It was followed by the writings of David Ricardo, Karl Marx, Thomas Malthus, and others. Each tried to make sense out of what was happening. Who was building the factories? Why? What determined the level of wages paid to workers or the price of food? What would happen in the future, and what should happen? The people who asked these questions were the first economists.

Similar changes continue to affect the character of life in more recent times. In fact, many argue that the late 1990s marked the beginning of a new Industrial Revolution. As we turned the corner into the new millennium, the "e" revolution was clearly having an impact on virtually every aspect of our lives: the way we buy and sell products, the way we get news, the way we plan vacations, the way we communicate with each other, the way we teach and take classes, and on and on. These changes have had and will clearly continue to have profound impacts on societies across the globe, from Beijing to Calcutta to New York.

These changes have been driven by economics. Although the government was involved in the early years of the World Wide Web, private firms that exist to make a profit (such as Yahoo!, Microsoft, Google, Monster.com, Amazon.com, and E-Trade) created almost all the new innovations and products. How does one make sense of all this? What will the effects be on the number of jobs, the character of those jobs, the family incomes, the structure of our cities, and the political process, both in the United States and in other countries?

Even more recently, during the last days of August 2005, Hurricane Katrina slammed into the coasts of Louisiana and Mississippi, causing widespread devastation, killing thousands, and leaving hundreds of thousands homeless. The economic impact of this catastrophic storm will be huge and will not be known for years. Yet thinking about the various markets involved helps frame the problem.

First of all the labor market was massively affected. By some estimates over 400,000 jobs were lost as the storm hit. Hotels, restaurants, small businesses, oil refineries, and on and on were destroyed. All the people who worked in those establishments instantaneously lost their jobs and their incomes. While the cleanup and rebuilding process will take time to organize, it will eventually create a great deal of employment.

Industrial Revolution The period in England during the late eighteenth and early nineteenth centuries in which new manufacturing technologies and improved transportation gave rise to the modern factory system and a massive movement of the population from the countryside to the cities.

Economics and Global Affairs in 2005

IT IS IMPOSSIBLE TO UNDERSTAND the workings of an economy without first understanding the ways in which economies are connected across borders. The United States was importing goods and services at a rate of nearly $2 trillion per year in 2005 and was exporting at a rate of nearly $1.5 trillion per year.

While debates about free trade in goods and services have been going on for hundreds of years, public attention has recently turned to the labor market. Increasingly, the market for labor has become "globalized," touching off a debate among both economic theorists and policy makers.[1] Some argue that we are "exporting" good jobs and creating unemployment in the United States. Others contend that lower production costs make products less expensive and that buyers who pay less will spend more on other goods and services produced by workers in the United States. They argue that it is possible to have a fully employed economy and still use foreign labor in production.

The following article appeared in the *New York Times*.

SAN FRANCISCO, June 20—Philip Chigos and Mary Domenico are busy building a children's pajama business. They are refining patterns, picking fabrics and turning the basement of their two-bedroom apartment into an office.

Then there is the critical step of finding the right seamstresses in China.

Instead of looking for garment workers in this city, they plan to have their wares manufactured by low-cost workers overseas. In doing so, they've become micro-outsourcers, adopting a tactic of major American corporations, which are increasingly sending production work abroad.

A growing number of mom-and-pop operations, outsourcing experts say, are braving a host of potential complications and turning to places like Sri Lanka, China, Mexico, and Eastern Europe to make clothes, jewelry, trinkets, and even software programs.

"We'd love it to say 'made in the U.S.' and use American textiles and production," Mr. Chigos said of his product. But, he said, the cost of that would be 4 to 10 times what was planned. "We didn't want to sell our pajamas for $120."

The ability of Mr. Chigos, 26, and Ms. Domenico, 25, to reach across borders has as much to do with technology as it does with the globalization of the labor market.

Computers, the Internet, and modern telecommunications already make it possible for start-ups to market their goods to customers anywhere in the country. That infrastructure also enables even the smallest entrepreneurs to find workers tens of thousands of miles away in countries they will never visit and in factories they will never inspect.

---

[1]See for example Jagdish Bhagwati, "Why Your Job Is Not Moving to Bangalore," *New York Times*, January 22, 2004, and Paul A. Samuelson, "Where Ricardo and Mill Rebut and Confirm Arguments of Mainstream Economists Supporting Globalization," *Journal of Economic Perspectives*, Volume 18, No. 3, Summer 2004.

The storm created a major disruption in world oil markets. Loss of refinery capacity sent gasoline prices up immediately, nearly 40 percent to over $4 per gallon in some locations. The price per gallon of crude oil rose to over $70 per barrel. Local governments found their tax bases destroyed, with no resources to pay teachers and local officials. Hundreds of hospitals were destroyed and colleges and universities were forced to close their doors, causing tens of thousands of students to change their plans.

While the horror of the storm hit all kinds of people, the worst hit were the very poor, who could not get out of the way because they didn't have cars or other means of escape. The storm raised fundamental issues of fairness, which we will be discussing for years to come.

We will learn a great deal of economics from the way the system responds to this horrible tragedy.

> The study of economics is an essential part of the study of society.

TO UNDERSTAND GLOBAL AFFAIRS

A third reason for studying economics is to understand global affairs. News headlines are filled with economic stories. International events often have enormous economic consequences. The destruction of the World Trade Center towers in New York City and the subsequent war on terror in Afghanistan and elsewhere led to a huge decline in both tourism and business travel. Several major airlines, including U.S. Airways and Swissair, went bankrupt. Hotel operators worldwide suffered huge losses. The war in Iraq and a strike in Venezuela in 2003 sent oil markets gyrating dramatically, initially increasing the cost of energy across the globe. The dramatic decline in the value of stocks traded in U.S. stock markets during the first three years of this century reduced household wealth in the United States by over $6 trillion, drove down the value of the U.S. dollar on foreign exchange markets, and had a huge effect on world trading patterns. The rapid spread of HIV and AIDS across Africa will have terrible economic consequences for the continent and ultimately for the world.

Some claim that economic considerations dominate international relations. Certainly politicians place the economic well-being of their citizens near the top of their priority lists. It would be surprising if that were not so. Thus, the economic consequences of things like environmental policy, free trade, and immigration play a huge role in international negotiations and policies.

Great Britain and the other countries of the European Union have struggled with the agreement among most members to adopt a common currency, the euro. In 2005, France and the Netherlands rejected a proposed European constitution that would have gone a long way toward a completely open economy in Europe. The nations of the former Soviet Union are wrestling with a growing phenomenon that clouds their efforts to "privatize" formerly state-owned industries: organized crime.

Another important issue in today's world is the widening gap between rich and poor nations. In 2005, world population was over 6.5 billion. Of that number, over 5 billion lived in less-developed countries and 1.5 billion lived in more-developed countries. The 75 percent of the world's population that lives in the less-developed countries receives less than 20 percent of the world's income. In dozens of countries, per capita income is only a few hundred dollars a year.

After the events of September 11, 2001, more of society's resources were spent on guarding against terrorism.

> An understanding of economics is essential to an understanding of global affairs.

TO BE AN INFORMED VOTER

A knowledge of economics is essential to be an informed voter. During the last 35 years, the U.S. economy has been on a roller coaster. In 1973–1974, the Organization of Petroleum Exporting Countries (OPEC) succeeded in raising the price of crude oil by 400 percent. Simultaneously, a sequence of events in the world food market drove food prices up by 25 percent. By mid-1974, prices in the United States were rising across the board at a very rapid rate. Partially as a result of government policy to fight runaway inflation, the economy went into a recession in 1975. (An *inflation* is an increase in the overall price level in the economy; a *recession* is a period of decreasing output and rising unemployment.) The recession succeeded in slowing price increases, but in the process millions found themselves unemployed.

From 1979 through 1983, it happened all over again. Prices rose rapidly, the government reacted with more policies designed to stop prices from rising, and the United States ended up with an even worse recession in 1982. By the end of that year, 10.8 percent of the work force was unemployed. Then, in mid-1990—after almost 8 years of strong economic performance—the U.S. economy went into another recession. During the third and fourth quarters of 1990 and the first quarter of 1991, *gross domestic product (GDP,* a measure of the total output of the U.S. economy) fell, and unemployment again increased sharply. The election of Bill Clinton late in 1992 was no doubt in part influenced by the so-called "jobless recovery."

From the second quarter of 1991 through the early part of the new millennium, the U.S. economy experienced the longest expansion in its history. More than 24 million new jobs were created, pushing unemployment below 4 percent by the year 2000. The stock market boomed to historic levels, and the biggest worry facing the American economy was that things were too good!

The presidential election of 2000 was close, to say the least, with the outcome not known until early December. In mid-December President-Elect George W. Bush and his economic advisers began to worry about the possibility of a recession occurring in 2001. The stock market was below its highs for the year; corporate profits were not coming in as well as expected; and there were some signs that demand for goods was slowing.

Indeed, following the election the economy slipped into recession, and economic conditions were made worse by the September 11, 2001, attacks on the World Trade Center and on the Pentagon. The stock market, which suffered losses as early as 2000, fell for 3 consecutive years, reducing the wealth of U.S. households by trillions of dollars. Total employment dropped by nearly 2.7 million. But by 2002 the economy began to grow again, slowly, and by 2005 nearly 3.5 million jobs had been created.

The war in Iraq and the threat of international terrorism following the 9/11 attacks increased military expenditures in the United States substantially. At the same time, tax cuts proposed by President Bush and passed by the Congress led to large deficits in the federal budget. All of these developments drew attention to the potential problems of two large government programs: Medicare and Social Security. These complex programs, which provide benefits to the elderly and the disabled, are estimated to require spending of nearly $1 trillion in 2006. Reform of Social Security became a major priority of the Bush administration in 2004.

As we approach the election of 2008, the important issues will be determined to a large extent by the performance of the economy during the years prior to the election. Will the economy continue to grow, or will it slip into recession? Will unemployment rise or fall? Will inflation reemerge after years of moderate price growth?

When we participate in the political process, we are voting on issues that require a basic understanding of economics.

THE SCOPE OF ECONOMICS

Most students taking economics for the first time are surprised by the breadth of what they study. Some think that economics will teach them about the stock market or what to do with their money. Others think that economics deals exclusively with problems like inflation and unemployment. In fact, it deals with all these subjects, but they are pieces of a much larger puzzle.

Economics has deep roots in, and close ties to, social philosophy. An issue of great importance to philosophers, for example, is distributional justice. Why are some people rich and others poor, and, whatever the answer, is this fair? A number of nineteenth-century social philosophers wrestled with these questions, and out of their musings economics as a separate discipline was born.

The easiest way to get a feel for the breadth and depth of what you will be studying is to explore briefly the way economics is organized. First of all, there are two major divisions of economics: microeconomics and macroeconomics.

MICROECONOMICS AND MACROECONOMICS

microeconomics The branch of economics that examines the functioning of individual industries and the behavior of individual decision-making units—that is, business firms and households.

Microeconomics deals with the functioning of individual industries and the behavior of individual economic decision-making units: business firms and households. Firms' choices about what to produce and how much to charge, and households' choices about what and how much to buy, help to explain why the economy produces the things it does.

Another big question addressed by microeconomics is who gets the things that are produced. Wealthy households get more than poor households, and the forces that determine this distribution of output are the province of microeconomics. Why does poverty exist? Who is poor? Why do some jobs pay more than others?

Think again about all the things you consume in a day, and then think back to that view over a big city. Somebody decided to build those factories. Somebody decided to construct the roads, build the housing, produce the cars, and smoke the bacon. Why? What is going on in all those buildings? It is easy to see that understanding individual microdecisions is very important to any understanding of society.

macroeconomics The branch of economics that examines the economic behavior of aggregates—income, employment, output, and so on—on a national scale.

Macroeconomics looks at the economy as a whole. Instead of trying to understand what determines the output of a single firm or industry or the consumption patterns of a single household or group of households, macroeconomics examines the factors that determine national output, or national product. Microeconomics is concerned with *household* income; macroeconomics deals with *national* income.

Whereas microeconomics focuses on individual product prices and relative prices, macroeconomics looks at the overall price level and how quickly (or slowly) it is rising (or falling). Microeconomics questions how many people will be hired (or fired) this year in a particular industry or in a certain geographic area, and focuses on the factors that determine how much labor a firm or an industry will hire. Macroeconomics deals with *aggregate* employment and unemployment: how many jobs exist in the economy as a whole, and how many people who are willing to work are not able to find work.

To summarize:

> Microeconomics looks at the individual unit—the household, the firm, the industry. It sees and examines the "trees." Macroeconomics looks at the whole, the aggregate. It sees and analyzes the "forest."

Table 1.1 summarizes these divisions of economics and some of the subjects with which they are concerned.

THE DIVERSE FIELDS OF ECONOMICS

Individual economists focus their research and study in many diverse areas. Many of these specialized fields are reflected in the advanced courses offered at most colleges and universities. Some are concerned with economic history or the history of economic thought.

TABLE 1.1 Examples of Microeconomic and Macroeconomic Concerns

DIVISION OF ECONOMICS	PRODUCTION	PRICES	INCOME	EMPLOYMENT
Microeconomics	*Production/output in individual industries and businesses*	*Prices of individual goods and services*	*Distribution of income and wealth*	*Employment by individual businesses and industries*
	How much steel	Price of medical care	Wages in the auto industry	Jobs in the steel industry
	How much office space	Price of gasoline	Minimum wage	Number of employees in a firm
	How many cars	Food prices	Executive salaries	Number of accountants
		Apartment rents	Poverty	
Macroeconomics	*National production/output*	*Aggregate price level*	*National income*	*Employment and unemployment in the economy*
	Total industrial output	Consumer prices	Total wages and salaries	Total number of jobs
	Gross domestic product	Producer prices	Total corporate profits	Unemployment rate
	Growth of output	Rate of inflation		

The Fields of Economics

A good way to convey the diversity of economics is to describe some of its major fields of study and the issues that economists address.

■ *Comparative economic systems* examines the ways alternative economic systems function. What are the advantages and disadvantages of different systems? What is the best way to convert the planned economies of the former Soviet Union to market systems?

■ *Econometrics* applies statistical techniques and data to economic problems in an effort to test hypotheses and theories. Most schools require economics majors to take at least one course in statistics or econometrics.

■ *Economic development* focuses on the problems of low income countries. What can be done to promote development in these nations? Important concerns of development economists include population growth and control, provision for basic needs, and strategies for international trade.

■ *Economic history* traces the development of the modern economy. What economic and political events and scientific advances caused the Industrial Revolution? What explains the tremendous growth and progress of post–World War II Japan? What caused the Great Depression of the 1930s?

■ *Economics of race and gender* examines the role of race and gender in economic theory, in economic life, and in policymaking. How has discrimination by race or gender affected the well-being of households and the distribution of income and wealth?

■ *Environmental economics* studies the potential failure of the market system to account fully for the impacts of production and consumption on the environment and on natural resource depletion. Have alternative public policies and new economic institutions been effective in correcting these potential failures?

■ *Finance* examines the ways in which households and firms actually pay for, or finance, their purchases. It involves the study of capital markets (including the stock and bond mar-

An important issue in economic development is education.

kets), futures and options, capital budgeting, and asset valuation.

■ *The history of economic thought,* which is grounded in philosophy, studies the development of economic ideas and theories over time, from Adam Smith in the eighteenth century to the works of economists such as Thomas Malthus, Karl Marx, and John Maynard Keynes. Because economic theory is constantly developing and changing, studying the history of ideas helps give meaning to modern theory and puts it in perspective.

■ *Industrial organization* looks carefully at the structure and performance of industries and firms within an economy. How do businesses compete? Who gains and who loses?

■ *International economics* studies trade flows among countries and international financial institutions. What are the advantages and disadvantages for a country that allows its citizens to buy and sell freely in world markets? Why is the dollar strong or weak?

■ *Labor economics* deals with the factors that determine wage rates, employment, and unemployment. How do people decide

whether to work, how much to work, and at what kind of job? How have the roles of unions and management changed in recent years?

■ *Law and economics* analyzes the economic function of legal rules and institutions. How does the law change the behavior of individuals and businesses? Do different liability rules make accidents and injuries more or less likely? What are the economic costs of crime?

■ *Public economics* examines the role of government in the economy. What are the economic functions of government, and what should they be? How should the government finance the services that it provides? What kinds of government programs should confront the problems of poverty, unemployment, and pollution? What problems does government involvement create?

■ *Urban and regional economics* studies the spatial arrangement of economic activity. Why do we have cities? Why are manufacturing firms locating farther and farther from the center of urban areas?

Others focus on international economics or growth in less-developed countries. Still others study the economics of cities (urban economics) or the relationship between economics and law. (See the Further Exploration box titled "The Fields of Economics" for more details.)

Economists also differ in the emphasis they place on theory. Some economists specialize in developing new theories, whereas others spend their time testing the theories of others.

Some economists hope to expand the frontiers of knowledge, whereas others are more interested in applying what is already known to the formulation of public policies.

As you begin your study of economics, look through your school's course catalog and talk to the faculty about their interests. You will discover that economics encompasses a broad range of inquiry and is linked to many other disciplines.

THE METHOD OF ECONOMICS

positive economics An approach to economics that seeks to understand behavior and the operation of systems without making judgments. It describes what exists and how it works.

normative economics An approach to economics that analyzes outcomes of economic behavior, evaluates them as good or bad, and may prescribe courses of action. Also called *policy economics*.

Economics asks and attempts to answer two kinds of questions, positive and normative. **Positive economics** attempts to understand behavior and the operation of economic systems *without making judgments* about whether the outcomes are good or bad. It strives to describe what exists and how it works. What determines the wage rate for unskilled workers? What would happen if we abolished the corporate income tax? The answers to such questions are the subject of positive economics.

In contrast, **normative economics** looks at the outcomes of economic behavior and asks whether they are good or bad and whether they can be made better. Normative economics involves judgments and prescriptions for courses of action. Should the government subsidize or regulate the cost of higher education? Should medical benefits to the elderly under Medicare be available only to those with incomes below some threshold? Should the United States allow importers to sell foreign-produced goods that compete with U.S.-produced products? Should we reduce or eliminate inheritance taxes? Normative economics is often called *policy economics*.

Of course, most normative questions involve positive questions. To know whether the government *should* take a particular action, we must know first if it *can* and second what the consequences are likely to be. (For example, if we lower import fees, will there be more competition and lower prices?)

Some claim that positive, value-free economic analysis is impossible. They argue that analysts come to problems with biases that cannot help but influence their work. Furthermore, even in choosing what questions to ask or what problems to analyze, economists are influenced by political, ideological, and moral views.

Although this argument has some merit, it is nevertheless important to distinguish between analyses that attempt to be positive and those that are intentionally and explicitly normative. Economists who ask explicitly normative questions should be forced to specify their grounds for judging one outcome superior to another.

descriptive economics The compilation of data that describe phenomena and facts.

Descriptive Economics and Economic Theory   Positive economics is often divided into descriptive economics and economic theory. **Descriptive economics** is simply the compilation of data that describe phenomena and facts. Examples of such data appear in the *Statistical Abstract of the United States*, a large volume of data published by the Department of Commerce every year that describes many features of the U.S. economy. Massive volumes of data can now also be found on the World Wide Web. As an example look at **www.bls.gov** (Bureau of Labor Statistics).

Where do all these data come from? The Census Bureau collects an enormous amount of raw data every year, as do the Bureau of Labor Statistics, the Bureau of Economic Analysis, and nongovernment agencies such as the University of Michigan Survey Research Center. One important study now published annually is the *Survey of Consumer Expenditure*, which asks individual households to keep careful records of all their expenditures over a long period of time. Another is the *National Longitudinal Survey of Labor Force Behavior*, conducted over many years by the Center for Human Resource Development at The Ohio State University.

economic theory A statement or set of related statements about cause and effect, action and reaction.

Economic theory attempts to generalize about data and interpret them. An **economic theory** is a statement or set of related statements about cause and effect, action and reaction. One of the first theories you will encounter in this text is the *law of demand*, which was most clearly stated by Alfred Marshall in 1890: When the price of a product rises, people tend to buy less of it; when the price of a product falls, they tend to buy more.

Theories do not always arise out of formal numerical data. All of us have been collecting observations of people's behavior and their responses to economic stimuli for most of our lives. We may have observed our parents' reaction to a sudden increase—or decrease—in income or to the loss of a job or the acquisition of a new one. We all have seen people standing in line waiting for a bargain. Of course, our own actions and reactions are another important source of data.

THEORIES AND MODELS

In many disciplines, including physics, chemistry, meteorology, political science, and economics, theorists build formal models of behavior. A **model** is a formal statement of a theory. It is usually a mathematical statement of a presumed relationship between two or more variables.

A **variable** is a measure that can change from time to time or from observation to observation. Income is a variable—it has different values for different people, and different values for the same person at different times. The rental price of a movie on a DVD is a variable; it has different values at different stores and at different times. There are countless other examples.

Because all models simplify reality by stripping part of it away, they are abstractions. Critics of economics often point to abstraction as a weakness. Most economists, however, see abstraction as a real strength.

The easiest way to see how abstraction can be helpful is to think of a map. A map is a representation of reality that is simplified and abstract. A city or state appears on a piece of paper as a series of lines and colors. The amount of reality that the mapmaker can strip away before the map loses something essential depends on what the map will be used for. If I want to drive from St. Louis to Phoenix, I need to know only the major interstate highways and roads. I lose absolutely nothing and gain clarity by cutting out the local streets and roads. However, if I need to get around in Phoenix, I may need to see every street and alley.

Most maps are two-dimensional representations of a three-dimensional world; they show where roads and highways go but do not show hills and valleys along the way. Trail maps for hikers, however, have "contour lines" that represent changes in elevation. When you are in a car, changes in elevation matter very little; they would make a map needlessly complex and much more difficult to read. However, if you are on foot carrying a 50-pound pack, a knowledge of elevation is crucial.

Like maps, economic models are abstractions that strip away detail to expose only those aspects of behavior that are important to the question being asked. The principle that irrelevant detail should be cut away is called the principle of **Ockham's razor** after the fourteenth-century philosopher William of Ockham.

Be careful—although abstraction is a powerful tool for exposing and analyzing specific aspects of behavior, it is possible to oversimplify. Economic models often strip away a good deal of social and political reality to get at underlying concepts. When an economic theory is used to help formulate actual government or institutional policy, political and social reality must often be reintroduced if the policy is to have a chance of working.

The key here is that the appropriate amount of simplification and abstraction depends on the use to which the model will be put. To return to the map example: You do not want to walk around San Francisco with a map made for drivers—there are too many very steep hills.

All Else Equal: *Ceteris Paribus* It is almost always true that whatever you want to explain with a model depends on more than one factor. Suppose, for example, that you want to explain the total number of miles driven by automobile owners in the United States. The number of miles driven will change from year to year or month to month; it is a variable. The issue, if we want to understand and explain changes that occur, is what factors cause those changes.

Obviously, many things might affect total miles driven. First, more or fewer people may be driving. This number, in turn, can be affected by changes in the driving age, by population growth, or by changes in state laws. Other factors might include the price of gasoline, the household's income, the number and age of children in the household, the distance from home to work, the location of shopping facilities, and the availability and quality of public

model A formal statement of a theory, usually a mathematical statement of a presumed relationship between two or more variables.

variable A measure that can change from time to time or from observation to observation.

Maps are useful abstract representations of reality.

Ockham's razor The principle that irrelevant detail should be cut away.

transport. When any of these variables change, the members of the household may drive more or less. If changes in any of these variables affect large numbers of households across the country, the total number of miles driven will change.

Very often we need to isolate or separate these effects. For example, suppose we want to know the impact on driving of a higher tax on gasoline. This change would raise the price of gasoline at the pump, but would not (at least in the short run) affect income, workplace location, number of children, and so forth.

ceteris paribus, or all else equal A device used to analyze the relationship between two variables while the values of other variables are held unchanged.

To isolate the impact of one single factor, we use the device of **ceteris paribus**, or **all else equal**. We ask: What is the impact of a change in gasoline price on driving behavior, *ceteris paribus*, or assuming that nothing else changes? If gasoline prices rise by 10 percent, how much less driving will there be, assuming no simultaneous change in anything else—that is, assuming that income, number of children, population, laws, and so on all remain constant?

> Using the device of *ceteris paribus* is one part of the process of abstraction. In formulating economic theory, the concept helps us simplify reality to focus on the relationships that interest us.

Expressing Models in Words, Graphs, and Equations Consider the following statements: "Lower airline ticket prices cause people to fly more frequently." "Higher interest rates slow the rate of home sales." "When firms produce more output, employment increases." "Higher gasoline prices cause people to drive less and to buy more fuel-efficient cars."

Each of these statements expresses a relationship between two variables that can be quantified. In each case there is a stimulus and a response, a cause and an effect. Quantitative relationships can be expressed in a variety of ways. Sometimes words are sufficient to express the essence of a theory, but often it is necessary to be more specific about the nature of a relationship or about the size of a response. The most common method of expressing the quantitative relationship between two variables is *graphing* that relationship on a two-dimensional plane. In fact, we will use graphic analysis extensively in Chapter 2 and beyond. Because it is essential that you be familiar with the basics of graphing, the Appendix to this chapter presents a careful review of graphing techniques.

Quantitative relationships between variables can also be presented through *equations*. For example, suppose we discovered that over time, U.S. households collectively spend, or consume, 90 percent of their income and save 10 percent of their income. We could then write:

$$C = .90\,Y \quad \text{and} \quad S = .10Y$$

where C is consumption spending, Y is income, and S is saving. Writing explicit algebraic expressions like these helps us understand the nature of the underlying process of decision making. Understanding this process is what economics is all about.

Cautions and Pitfalls In formulating theories and models, it is especially important to avoid two pitfalls: the *post hoc* fallacy and the fallacy of composition.

The Post Hoc Fallacy Theories often make statements, or sets of statements, about cause and effect. It can be quite tempting to look at two events that happen in sequence and assume that the first caused the second to happen. This is not always the case. This common error is called the **post hoc, ergo propter hoc** (or "after this, therefore because of this") fallacy.

post hoc, ergo propter hoc Literally, "after this (in time), therefore because of this." A common error made in thinking about causation: If Event A happens before Event B, it is not necessarily true that A caused B.

There are thousands of examples. The Colorado Rockies have won seven games in a row. Last night, I went to the game and they lost. I must have "jinxed" them. They lost *because I went to the game.*

Stock market analysts indulge in what is perhaps the most striking example of the *post hoc* fallacy in action. Every day the stock market goes up or down, and every day some analyst on some national news program singles out one or two of the day's events as *the* cause of some change in the market: "Today the Dow Jones industrial average rose five points on heavy trading; analysts say that the increase was due to progress in talks between Israel and Syria." Research has shown that daily changes in stock market averages are very largely random. Although major news events clearly have a direct influence on certain stock prices, most daily changes cannot be directly linked to specific news stories.

Whatever happens to the price of oil daily, it is used to explain the stock market. When Hurricane Katrina hit New Orleans and the Gulf Coast, there was an immediate run up in the price of oil to over $70 a barrel. With each day that passed following the devastating storm, there was a new report about destroyed refineries, drilling platforms, and slowing demand, and every day the behavior of the stock market was blamed on oil. In fact, there are literally thousands of ways that individual firms can be hurt or helped by rising or falling of oil prices. Oil companies themselves clearly benefit. In addition, the impact of the storm on insurance companies, tourism, and agriculture, to name just a few industries, is likely to be huge. The point is to beware of simple explanations for complex economic events.

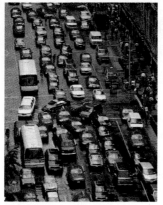

Cars probably don't *cause* crime.

Very closely related to the *post hoc* fallacy is the often erroneous link between correlation and causation. Two variables are said to be *correlated* if one variable changes when the other variable changes. However, correlation does not imply causation. Cities that have high crime rates also have lots of automobiles, so there is a very high degree of correlation between number of cars and crime rates. Can we argue, then, that cars *cause* crime? No. The reason for the correlation may have nothing to do with cause and effect. Big cities have lots of people, lots of people have lots of cars, and therefore big cities have lots of cars. Big cities also have high crime rates for many reasons—crowding, poverty, anonymity, unequal distribution of wealth, and readily available drugs, to mention only a few. However, the presence of cars is probably not one of them.

This caution must also be viewed in reverse. Sometimes events that seem entirely unconnected actually *are* connected. In 1978, Governor Michael Dukakis of Massachusetts ran for reelection. Still quite popular, Dukakis was nevertheless defeated in the Democratic primary that year by a razor-thin margin. The weekend before, the Boston Red Sox, in the thick of the division championship race, had been badly beaten by the New York Yankees in four straight games. Some very respectable political analysts believe that hundreds of thousands of Boston sports fans vented their anger on the incumbent governor the following Tuesday.

The Fallacy of Composition   To conclude that what is true for a part is necessarily true for the whole is to fall into the **fallacy of composition**. Suppose that a large group of cattle ranchers graze their cattle on the same range. To an individual rancher, more cattle and more grazing mean a higher income. However, because its capacity is limited, the land can support only so many cattle. If every cattle rancher increased the number of cattle sent out to graze, the land would become overgrazed and barren, and everyone's income would fall. In short, theories that seem to work well when applied to individuals or households often break down when they are applied to the whole.

fallacy of composition
The erroneous belief that what is true for a part is necessarily true for the whole.

Testing Theories and Models: Empirical Economics

In science, a theory is rejected when it fails to explain what is observed or when another theory better explains what is observed. Prior to the sixteenth century almost everyone believed that Earth was the center of the universe and that the sun and stars rotated around it. The astronomer Ptolemy (A.D. 127 to 151) built a model that explained and predicted the movements of the heavenly bodies in a geocentric (Earth-centered) universe. Early in the sixteenth century, however, the Polish astronomer Nicholas Copernicus found himself dissatisfied with the Ptolemaic model and proposed an alternative theory or model, placing the sun at the center of the known universe and relegating Earth to the status of one planet among many. The battle between the competing models was waged, at least in part, with data based on observations—actual measurements of planetary movements. The new model ultimately predicted much better than the old, and in time it came to be accepted.

In the seventeenth century, building on the works of Copernicus and others, Sir Isaac Newton constructed yet another body of theory that seemed to predict planetary motion with still more accuracy. Newtonian physics became the accepted body of theory, relied on for almost 300 years. Then in the early twentieth century Albert Einstein's theory of relativity replaced Newtonian physics for particular types of problems because it was able to explain some things that earlier theories could not.

Economic theories are also confronted with new and often conflicting data from time to time. The collection and use of data to test economic theories is called **empirical economics**.

Numerous large data sets are available to facilitate economic research. For example, economists studying the labor market can now test behavioral theories against the actual working experiences of thousands of randomly selected people who have been surveyed continuously since the 1960s by economists at The Ohio State University. Macroeconomists continuously monitoring and studying the behavior of the national economy pass thousands of items of data, collected by both government agencies and private companies, back and forth over the Internet.

Scientific research often seeks to isolate and measure the responsiveness of one variable to a change in another variable, *ceteris paribus*. Physical scientists such as physicists and geologists can often impose the condition of *ceteris paribus* by conducting controlled experiments. They can, for example, measure the effect of one chemical on another while literally holding all else constant in an environment that they control completely. Social scientists, who study people, rarely have this luxury.

Although controlled experiments are difficult in economics and other social sciences, they are not impossible. During recent presidential and congressional elections, many candidates pointed to dramatic declines in crime rates in most American cities. Of course, incumbent candidates took credit, claiming that the decline was due to their policies. In fact, careful analysis shows that the decline in crime was largely due to two factors essentially beyond the control of political leaders: fewer people in the age groups that tend to commit crimes and a very strong economy with low unemployment. How do researchers know this? They look at data over time on crimes committed by people of various ages; they look at crime rates across states with different economic conditions; and they look at the pattern of crime rates nationally over time under different economic conditions. Even though economists cannot generally do controlled experiments, fluctuations in economic conditions and factors like birthrate patterns in a way set up natural experiments.

ECONOMIC POLICY

Economic theory helps us understand how the world works, but the formulation of *economic policy* requires a second step. We must have objectives. What do we want to change? Why? What is good and what is bad about the way the system is operating? Can we make it better?

Such questions force us to be specific about the grounds for judging one outcome superior to another. What does it mean to be better? Four criteria are frequently applied in making these judgments:

> Criteria for judging economic outcomes:
> **1.** Efficiency
> **2.** Equity
> **3.** Growth
> **4.** Stability

Efficiency   In physics, "efficiency" refers to the ratio of useful energy delivered by a system to the energy supplied to it. An efficient automobile engine, for example, is one that uses up a small amount of fuel per mile for a given level of power.

In economics, **efficiency** means *allocative efficiency*. An efficient economy is one that produces what people want at the least possible cost. If the system allocates resources to the production of things that nobody wants, it is inefficient. If all members of a particular society were vegetarian and somehow half of all that society's resources were used to produce meat, the result would be inefficient. It is inefficient when steel beams lie in the rain and rust because somebody fouled up a shipping schedule. If a firm could produce its product using 25 percent less labor and energy without sacrificing quality, it too is inefficient.

The clearest example of an efficient change is a voluntary exchange. If you and I each want something that the other has and we agree to exchange, we are both better off, and no one loses. When a company reorganizes its production or adopts a new technology that enables it to produce more of its product with fewer resources, without sacrificing quality, it has made an efficient change. At least potentially, the resources saved could be used to produce more of something.

Inefficiencies can arise in numerous ways. Sometimes they are caused by government regulations or tax laws that distort otherwise sound economic decisions. Suppose that land in Ohio is best suited for corn production and that land in Kansas is best suited for wheat production. A law that requires Kansas to produce only corn and Ohio to produce only wheat would be inefficient. If firms that cause environmental damage are not held accountable for their actions, the incentive to minimize those damages is lost, and the result is inefficient.

Equity   While efficiency has a fairly precise definition that can be applied with some degree of rigor, **equity** (fairness) lies in the eye of the beholder. To many, fairness implies a more equal distribution of income and wealth. Fairness may imply alleviating poverty, but the extent to which the poor should receive cash benefits from the government is the subject of enormous disagreement. For thousands of years philosophers have wrestled with the principles of justice that should guide social decisions. They will probably wrestle with such questions for thousands of years to come.

equity Fairness.

Despite the impossibility of defining equity or fairness universally, public policy makers judge the fairness of economic outcomes all the time. Rent control laws were passed because some legislators thought that landlords treated low-income tenants unfairly. Certainly most social welfare programs are created in the name of equity.

Growth   As the result of technological change, the building of machinery, and the acquisition of knowledge, societies learn to produce new things and to produce old things better. In the early days of the U.S. economy, it took nearly half the population to produce the required food supply. Today less than 2.5 percent of the country's population works in agriculture.

When we devise new and better ways of producing the things we use now, and when we develop new products and services, the total amount of production in the economy increases. **Economic growth** is an increase in the total output of an economy. If output grows faster than the population, output per capita rises and standards of living increase. Presumably, when an economy grows it produces more of what people want. Rural and agrarian societies become modern industrial societies as a result of economic growth and rising per capita output.

economic growth An increase in the total output of an economy.

Some policies discourage economic growth and others encourage it. Tax laws, for example, can be designed to encourage the development and application of new production techniques. Research and development in some societies are subsidized by the government. Building roads, highways, bridges, and transport systems in developing countries may speed up the process of economic growth. If businesses and wealthy people invest their wealth outside their country rather than in its own industries, growth in their home country may be slowed.

Stability   Economic **stability** refers to the condition in which national output is growing steadily, with low inflation and full employment of resources. During the 1950s and 1960s, the U.S. economy experienced a long period of relatively steady growth, stable prices, and low unemployment. Between 1951 and 1969, consumer prices never rose more than 5 percent in a single year, and in only 2 years did the number of unemployed exceed 6 percent of the labor force. From the end of the Gulf War in 1991 to the beginning of 2001, the U.S. economy enjoyed price stability and strong economic growth with rising employment. It was the longest expansion in American history.

stability A condition in which national output is growing steadily, with low inflation and full employment of resources.

The decades of the 1970s and 1980s, however, were not as stable. The United States experienced two periods of rapid price inflation (over 10 percent) and two periods of severe unemployment. In 1982, for example, 12 million people (10.8 percent of the workforce) were looking for work. The beginning of the 1990s was another period of instability, with a recession occurring in 1990–1991. Around the world, economic fluctuations have been severe in recent years. During the late 1990s, many economies in Asia fell into recessions with falling incomes and rising unemployment. The transition economies of Eastern Europe and the former Soviet Union have experienced periods of decline as well as periods of rapidly rising prices since the fall of the Berlin Wall in 1989.

The causes of instability and the ways in which governments have attempted to stabilize the economy are the subject matter of macroeconomics.

AN INVITATION

This chapter has prepared you for your study of economics. The first part of the chapter invited you into an exciting discipline that deals with important issues and questions. You cannot begin to understand how a society functions without knowing something about its economic history and its economic system.

The second part of the chapter introduced the method of reasoning that economics requires and some of the tools that economics uses. We believe that learning to think in this very powerful way will help you better understand the world.

As you proceed, it is important that you keep track of what you have learned in earlier chapters. This book has a plan; it proceeds step by step, each section building on the last. It would be a good idea to read each chapter's table of contents and scan each chapter before you read it to be sure you understand where it fits in the big picture.

SUMMARY

1. *Economics* is the study of how individuals and societies choose to use the scarce resources that nature and previous generations have provided.

WHY STUDY ECONOMICS?

2. There are many reasons to study economics, including (a) to learn a way of thinking, (b) to understand society, (c) to understand global affairs, and (d) to be an informed voter.

3. The best alternative that we forgo when we make a choice or a decision is the *opportunity cost* of that decision.

THE SCOPE OF ECONOMICS

4. *Microeconomics* deals with the functioning of individual markets and industries and with the behavior of individual decision-making units: business firms and households.

5. *Macroeconomics* looks at the economy as a whole. It deals with the economic behavior of aggregates—national output, national income, the overall price level, and the general rate of inflation.

6. Economics is a broad and diverse discipline with many special fields of inquiry. These include economic history, international economics, and urban economics.

THE METHOD OF ECONOMICS

7. Economics asks and attempts to answer two kinds of questions: positive and normative. *Positive economics* attempts to understand behavior and the operation of economies without making judgments about whether the outcomes are good or bad. *Normative economics* looks at the results of economic behavior and asks whether they are good or bad and whether they can be improved.

8. Positive economics is often divided into two parts. *Descriptive economics* involves the compilation of data that accurately describe economic facts and events. *Economic theory* attempts to generalize and explain what is observed. It involves statements of cause and effect—of action and reaction.

9. An economic *model* is a formal statement of an economic theory. Models simplify and abstract from reality.

10. It is often useful to isolate the effects of one variable on another while holding "all else constant." This is the device of *ceteris paribus.*

11. Models and theories can be expressed in many ways. The most common ways are in words, in graphs, and in equations.

12. Because one event happens before another, the second event does not necessarily happen as a result of the first. To assume that "after" implies "because" is to commit the fallacy of *post hoc, ergo propter hoc.* The erroneous belief that what is true for a part is necessarily true for the whole is the *fallacy of composition.*

13. *Empirical economics* involves the collection and use of data to test economic theories. In principle, the best model is the one that yields the most accurate predictions.

14. To make policy, one must be careful to specify criteria for making judgments. Four specific criteria are used most often in economics: *efficiency, equity, growth,* and *stability.*

REVIEW TERMS AND CONCEPTS

ceteris paribus, 12
descriptive economics, 10
economic growth, 15
economic theory, 10
economics, 2
efficiency, 14
efficient market, 3
empirical economics, 14

equity, 15
fallacy of composition, 13
Industrial Revolution, 4
macroeconomics, 8
marginalism, 3
microeconomics, 8
model, 11
normative economics, 10

Ockham's razor, 11
opportunity cost, 2
positive economics, 10
post hoc, ergo propter hoc, 12
scarce, 2
stability, 15
sunk costs, 3
variable, 11

PROBLEM SET

1. One of the scarce resources that constrain our behavior is time. Each of us has only 24 hours in a day. How do you go about allocating your time in a given day among competing alternatives? How do you go about weighing the alternatives? Once you choose a most important use of time, why do you not spend all your time on it? Use the notion of opportunity cost in your answer.

2. In early 2005, the economy of the United States was sending mixed signals to consumers and investors. Following the recession of 2001, the economy began to grow, and it grew strongly in 2004. One of the indicators of a growing economy is increasing employment. Go to **www.bls.gov** and click on the "employment situation" for the most recent quarter. How many new jobs were created in the United States in the most recent quarter? In the last year? Does the economy seem to be growing or shrinking?

3. Which of the following statements are examples of positive economic analysis? Which are examples of normative analysis?
   a. The inheritance tax should be repealed because it is unfair.
   b. In 2005, France and the Netherlands rejected the new European constitution. As a result, the European economy is likely to be less efficient and will grow more slowly in the years ahead.
   c. Allowing Chile to join NAFTA would cause wine prices in the United States to drop.
   d. The first priorities of the new regime in the Democratic Republic of Congo (DRC, formerly Zaire) should be to rebuild schools and highways and to provide basic health care.

4. Selwyn signed up with an Internet provider for a fixed fee of $19.95 per month. For this fee he gets unlimited access to the World Wide Web. During the average month in 2006 he was logged onto the Web for 17 hours. What is the average cost of an hour of Web time to Selwyn? What is the marginal cost of an additional hour?

5. A question facing many U.S. states is whether to allow casino gambling. States with casino gambling have seen a substantial increase in tax revenue flowing to state government. This revenue can be used to finance schools, repair roads, maintain social programs, or reduce other taxes.
   a. Recall that efficiency means producing what people want at least cost. Can you make an efficiency argument in favor of allowing casinos to operate?
   b. What nonmonetary costs might be associated with gambling? Would these costs have an impact on the efficiency argument you presented in part a?
   c. Using the concept of equity, argue for or against the legalization of casino gambling.

6. For each of the following situations, identify the full cost (opportunity costs) involved:
   a. A worker earning an hourly wage of $8.50 decides to cut back to half-time to attend Houston Community College.
   b. Sue decides to drive to Los Angeles from San Francisco to visit her son, who attends UCLA.
   c. Tom decides to go to a wild fraternity party and stays out all night before his physics exam.
   d. Annie spends $200 on a new dress.
   e. The Confab Company spends $1 million to build a new branch plant that will probably be in operation for at least 10 years.
   f. Alex's father owns a small grocery store in town. Alex works 40 hours a week in the store but receives no compensation.

7. As you saw in the box on page 5, the press has focused a great deal of attention on the problem of outsourcing in recent years. Go to Google or to one of the Web sites of the major news magazines like *Newsweek* or *Businessweek* and search for the term *outsourcing*. Make a list of the countries that you see mentioned. Can you generalize about this list? Are there common characteristics? You might go to **www.worldbank.org** and click on "research and statistics" and then look at the data for each. What is GDP per capita? How fast are these countries growing? How high is unemployment? Can you draw any conclusions about these data? Discuss both the costs and potential benefits to the United States of outsourcing.

APPENDIX

HOW TO READ AND UNDERSTAND GRAPHS

Economics is the most quantitative of the social sciences. If you flip through the pages of this or any other economics text, you will see countless tables and graphs. These serve a number of purposes. First, they illustrate important economic relationships. Second, they make difficult problems easier to understand and analyze. Finally, they can show patterns and regularities that may not be discernible in simple lists of numbers.

A **graph** is a two-dimensional representation of a set of numbers, or data. There are many ways that numbers can be illustrated by a graph.

TIME SERIES GRAPHS

It is often useful to see how a single measure or variable changes over time. One way to present this information is to plot the values of the variable on a graph, with each value corresponding to a different time period. A graph of this kind is called a **time series graph**. On a time series graph, time is measured along the horizontal scale and the variable being graphed is measured along the vertical scale. Figure 1A.1 is a time series graph that presents the total disposable personal income in the U.S. economy for each year between 1975 and 2005.[1] This graph is based on the data found in Table 1A.1. By displaying these data graphically, we can see that (1) total disposable personal income has increased steadily since 1975, and (2) during certain periods, income has increased at a faster rate than during other periods.

[1]The measure of income presented in Table 1A.1 and in Figure 1A.1 is disposable personal income in billions of dollars. It is the total personal income received by all households in the United States minus the taxes that they pay.

GRAPHING TWO VARIABLES ON A CARTESIAN COORDINATE SYSTEM

More important than simple graphs of one variable are graphs that contain information on two variables at the same time. The most common method of graphing two variables is the **Cartesian coordinate system**. This system is constructed by simply drawing two perpendicular lines: a horizontal line, or **X-axis**, and a vertical line, or **Y-axis**. The axes contain measurement scales that intersect at 0 (zero). This point is called the **origin**. On the vertical scale, positive numbers lie above the horizontal axis (that is, above the origin) and negative numbers lie below it. On the horizontal scale, positive numbers lie to the right of the vertical axis (to the

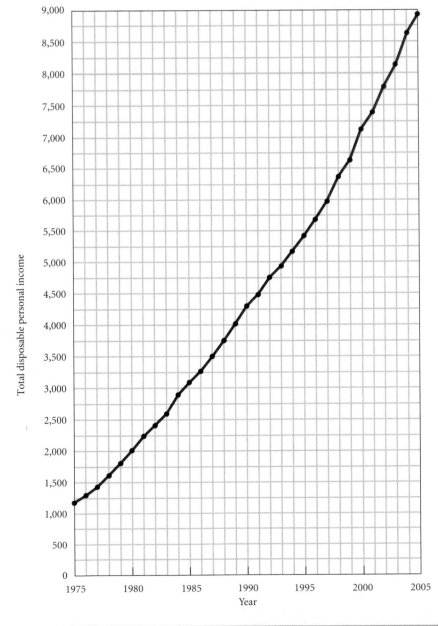

FIGURE 1A.1 Total Disposable Personal Income in the United States: 1975–2005 (in billions of dollars)

Source: See Table 1A.1.

TABLE 1A.1	Total Disposable Personal Income in the United States, 1975–2005 (in billions of dollars)		
YEAR	TOTAL DISPOSABLE PERSONAL INCOME	YEAR	TOTAL DISPOSABLE PERSONAL INCOME
1975	1,181.4	1991	4,474.8
1976	1,299.9	1992	4,754.6
1977	1,436.0	1993	4,935.3
1978	1,614.8	1994	5,165.4
1979	1,808.2	1995	5,422.6
1980	2,019.8	1996	5,677.7
1981	2,247.9	1997	5,968.2
1982	2,406.8	1998	6,355.6
1983	2,586.0	1999	6,627.4
1984	2,887.6	2000	7,120.2
1985	3,086.5	2001	7,393.2
1986	3,262.5	2002	7,827.7
1987	3,459.5	2003	8,159.9
1988	3,752.4	2004	8,646.9
1989	4,016.3	2005	8,945.6
1990	4,293.6		

Source: U.S. Department of Commerce, Bureau of Economic Analysis.

right of the origin) and negative numbers lie to the left of it. The point at which the graph intersects the Y-axis is called the **Y-intercept**. The point at which the graph intersects the X-axis is called the **X-intercept**.

When two variables are plotted on a single graph, each point represents a pair of numbers. The first number is measured on the X-axis and the second number is measured on the Y-axis. For example, the following points (X, Y) are plotted on the set of axes drawn in Figure 1A.2: (4, 2), (2, −1), (−3, 4),

$(-3, -2)$. Most, but not all, of the graphs in this book are plots of two variables where both values are positive numbers [such as (4, 2) in Fig. 1A.2]. On these graphs, only the upper right quadrant of the coordinate system (i.e., the quadrant in which all X and Y values are positive) will be drawn.

PLOTTING INCOME AND CONSUMPTION DATA FOR HOUSEHOLDS

Table 1A.2 presents some data collected by the Bureau of Labor Statistics (BLS). In a recent survey, 5,000 households were asked to keep careful track of all their expenditures. Table 1A.2 shows average income and average spending for those households, ranked by income. For example, the average income for the top fifth (20 percent) of the households was $127,146. The average spending for the top 20 percent was $81,731.

Figure 1A.3 presents the numbers from Table 1A.2 graphically using the Cartesian coordinate system. Along the horizontal scale, the X-axis, we measure average income. Along the vertical scale, the Y-axis, we measure average consumption spending. Each of the five pairs of numbers from the table is represented by a point on the graph. Because all numbers are positive numbers, we need to show only the upper right quadrant of the coordinate system.

To help you read this graph, we have drawn a dotted line connecting all the points where consumption and income would be equal. *This 45° line does not represent any data.* Instead, it represents the line along which all variables on the X-axis correspond exactly to the variables on the Y-axis, for example, [10,000, 10,000], [20,000, 20,000], [37,000, 37,000], and so forth. The heavy blue line traces the data; the dotted line is only to help you read the graph.

There are several things to look for when reading a graph. The first thing you should notice is whether the line slopes upward or downward as you move from left to right. The blue line in Figure 1A.3 slopes upward, indicating that there seems to be a **positive relationship** between income and spending: The higher a household's income, the more a household tends to consume. If we had graphed the percentage of each group receiving welfare payments along the Y-axis, the line would presumably slope downward, indicating that welfare payments are lower at higher income levels. The income level/welfare payment relationship is thus a **negative relationship**.

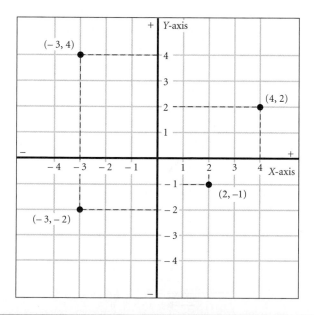

FIGURE 1A.2 A Cartesian Coordinate System

A Cartesian coordinate system is constructed by drawing two perpendicular lines: a vertical axis (the Y-axis) and a horizontal axis (the X-axis). Each axis is a measuring scale.

TABLE 1A.2	Consumption Expenditures and Income, 2003	
	AVERAGE INCOME BEFORE TAXES	AVERAGE CONSUMPTION EXPENDITURES
Bottom fifth	$ 8,201	$18,492
2nd fifth	21,478	26,729
3rd fifth	37,542	36,213
4th fifth	61,132	50,468
Top fifth	127,146	81,731

Source: Consumer Expenditures in 2003, U.S. Bureau of Labor Statistics; Report 986, June 2005.

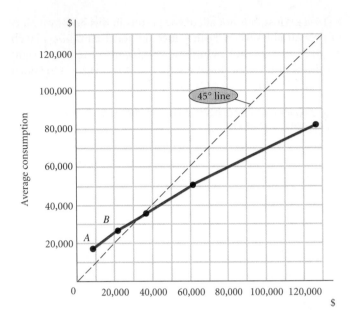

FIGURE 1A.3 Household Consumption and Income

A graph is a simple two-dimensional geometric representation of data. This graph displays the data from Table 1A.2. Along the horizontal scale (*X*-axis), we measure household income. Along the vertical scale (*Y*-axis), we measure household consumption. *Note:* At point *A*, consumption equals $18,492 and income equals $8,201. At point *B*, consumption equals $26,729 and income equals $21,478.

Source: See Table 1A.2.

SLOPE

The **slope** of a line or curve is a measure that indicates whether the relationship between the variables is positive or negative and how much of a response there is in *Y* (the variable on the vertical axis) when *X* (the variable on the horizon-

tal axis) changes. The slope of a line between two points is the change in the quantity measured on the *Y*-axis divided by the change in the quantity measured on the *X*-axis. We will normally use Δ (the Greek letter *delta*) to refer to a change in a variable. In Figure 1A.4, the slope of the line between points *A* and *B* is Δ*Y* divided by Δ*X*. Sometimes it is easy to remember slope as "the rise over the run," indicating the vertical change over the horizontal change.

> To be precise, Δ*X* between two points on a graph is simply X_2 minus X_1, where X_2 is the *X* value for the second point and X_1 is the *X* value for the first point. Similarly, Δ*Y* is defined as Y_2 minus Y_1, where Y_2 is the *Y* value for the second point and Y_1 is the *Y* value for the first point. Slope is equal to
>
> $$\frac{\Delta Y}{\Delta X} = \frac{Y_2 - Y_1}{X_2 - X_1}$$

As we move from *A* to *B* in Figure 1A.4(a), both *X* and *Y* increase; the slope is thus a positive number. However, as we move from *A* to *B* in Figure 1A.4(b), *X* increases [$(X_2 - X_1)$ is a positive number], but *Y* decreases [$(Y_2 - Y_1)$ is a negative number]. The slope in Figure 1A.4(b) is thus a negative number, because a negative number divided by a positive number gives a negative quotient.

To calculate the numerical value of the slope between points *A* and *B* in Figure 1A.3, we need to calculate Δ*Y* and Δ*X*. Because consumption is measured on the *Y*-axis, Δ*Y* is 8,237 [$(Y_2 - Y_1) = (26,729 - 18,492)$]. Because income is measured along the *X*-axis, Δ*X* is 13,277 [$(X_2 - X_1) = (21,478 - 8,201)$]. The slope between *A* and *B* is Δ*Y*/Δ*X* = 8,237/13,277 = + .620.

Another interesting thing to note about the data graphed in Figure 1A.3 is that all the points lie roughly along a straight line. (If you look very closely, however, you can see that the

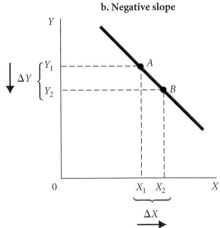

FIGURE 1A.4 A Curve with (a) Positive Slope and (b) Negative Slope

A *positive* slope indicates that increases in *X* are associated with increases in *Y* and that decreases in *X* are associated with decreases in *Y*. A *negative* slope indicates the opposite—when *X* increases, *Y* decreases and when *X* decreases, *Y* increases.

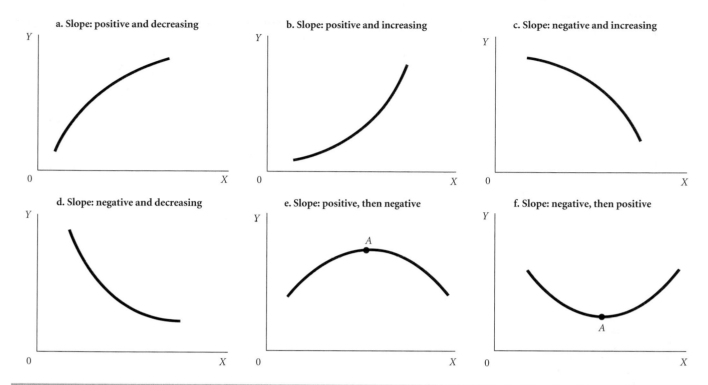

FIGURE 1A.5 Changing Slopes Along Curves

slope declines as one moves from left to right; the line becomes slightly less steep.) A straight line has a constant slope. That is, if you pick any two points along it and calculate the slope, you will always get the same number. A horizontal line has a zero slope (ΔY is zero); a vertical line has an "infinite" slope, because ΔY is too big to be measured.

Unlike the slope of a straight line, the slope of a *curve* is continually changing. Consider, for example, the curves in Figure 1A.5. Figure 1A.5(a) shows a curve with a positive slope that decreases as you move from left to right. The easiest way to think about the concept of increasing or decreasing slope is to imagine what it is like walking up a hill from left to right. If the hill is steep, as it is in the first part of Figure 1A.5(a), you are moving a lot in the Y direction for each step you take in the X direction. If the hill is less steep, as it is further along in Figure 1A.5(a), you are moving less in the Y direction for every step you take in the X direction. Thus, when the hill is steep, slope ($\Delta Y/\Delta X$) is a larger number than it is when the hill is flatter. The curve in Figure 1A.5(b) has a positive slope, but its slope *increases* as you move from left to right.

The same analogy holds for curves that have a negative slope. Figure 1A.5(c) shows a curve with a negative slope that increases (in absolute value) as you move from left to right. This time think about skiing down a hill. At first, the descent in Figure 1A.5(c) is gradual (low slope), but as you proceed down the hill (to the right), you descend more quickly (high slope). Figure 1A.5(d) shows a curve with a negative slope that *decreases* in absolute value as you move from left to right.

In Figure 1A.5(e), the slope goes from positive to negative as X increases. In Figure 1A.5(f), the slope goes from negative to positive. At point A in both, the slope is zero. [Remember, slope is defined as $\Delta Y/\Delta X$. At point A, Y is not changing ($\Delta Y = 0$). Therefore, slope at point A is zero.]

SOME PRECAUTIONS

When you read a graph, it is important to think carefully about what the points in the space defined by the axes represent. Table 1A.3 and Figure 1A.6 present a graph of consumption and income that is very different from the one in

TABLE 1A.3 Aggregate National Income and Consumption for the United States, 1930–2004 (in billions of dollars)		
	AGGREGATE NATIONAL INCOME	**AGGREGATE CONSUMPTION**
1930	75.6	70.2
1940	81.1	71.2
1950	241.0	192.7
1960	427.5	332.3
1970	837.5	648.9
1980	2,243.0	1,762.9
1990	4,642.1	3,831.5
2000	7,984.4	6,683.7
2004	10,339.6	8,229.9

Source: U.S. Department of Commerce, Bureau of Economic Analysis. News release, June 29, 2005.

FIGURE 1A.6 National Income and Consumption

It is important to think carefully about what is represented by points in the space defined by the axes of a graph. In this graph, we have graphed income with consumption, as in Figure 1A.3, but here each observation point is national income and aggregate consumption in *different years*, measured in billions of dollars.

Source: See Table 1A.3.

Table 1A.2 and Figure 1A.3. First, each point in Figure 1A.6 represents a different year; in Figure 1A.3, each point represented a different group of households at the *same* point in time (2003). Second, the points in Figure 1A.6 represent *aggregate* consumption and income for the whole nation measured in *billions* of dollars; in Figure 1A.3, the points represented average *household* income and consumption measured in dollars.

It is interesting to compare these two graphs. All points on the aggregate consumption curve in Figure 1A.6 lie below the 45° line, which means that aggregate consumption is always less than aggregate income. However, the graph of average household income and consumption in Figure 1A.3 crosses the 45° line, implying that for some households consumption is larger than income.

SUMMARY

1. A *graph* is a two-dimensional representation of a set of numbers, or data. A *time series graph* illustrates how a single variable changes over time.

2. The most common method of graphing two variables on one graph is the *Cartesian coordinate system*, which includes an *X* (horizontal)-*axis* and a *Y* (vertical)-*axis*. The points at which the two axes intersect is called the *origin*. The point at which a graph intersects the *Y*-axis is called the *Y-intercept*. The point at which a graph intersects the *X*-axis is called the *X-intercept*.

3. The *slope* of a line or curve indicates whether the relationship between the two variables graphed on a Cartesian coordinate system is positive or negative and how much of a response there is in *Y* (the variable on the vertical axis) when *X* (the variable on the horizontal axis) changes. The slope of a line between two points is the change in the quantity measured on the *Y*-axis divided by the change in the quantity measured on the *X*-axis.

REVIEW TERMS AND CONCEPTS

Cartesian coordinate system A common method of graphing two variables that makes use of two perpendicular lines against which the variables are plotted. 18

graph A two-dimensional representation of a set of numbers, or data. 17

negative relationship A relationship between two variables, *X* and *Y*, in which a decrease in *X* is associated with an increase in *Y*, and an increase in *X* is associated with a decrease in *Y*. 19

origin On a Cartesian coordinate system, the point at which the horizontal and vertical axes intersect. 18

positive relationship A relationship between two variables, *X* and *Y*, in which a decrease in *X* is associated with a decrease in *Y*, and an increase in *X* is associated with an increase in *Y*. 19

slope A measurement that indicates whether the relationship between variables is positive or negative and how much of a response there is in *Y* (the variable on the vertical axis) when *X* (the variable on the horizontal axis) changes. 20

time series graph   A graph illustrating how a variable changes over time.   17

X-axis   On a Cartesian coordinate system, the horizontal line against which a variable is plotted.   18

X-intercept   The point at which a graph intersects the X-axis.   19

Y-axis   On a Cartesian coordinate system, the vertical line against which a variable is plotted.   18

Y-intercept   The point at which a graph intersects the Y-axis.   19

PROBLEM SET

1. Graph each of the following sets of numbers. Draw a line through the points and calculate the slope of each line.

1		2		3		4		5		6	
X	Y	X	Y	X	Y	X	Y	X	Y	X	Y
1	5	1	25	0	0	0	40	0	0	0.1	100
2	10	2	20	10	10	10	30	10	10	0.2	75
3	15	3	15	20	20	20	20	20	20	0.3	50
4	20	4	10	30	30	30	10	30	10	0.4	25
5	25	5	5	40	40	40	0	40	0	0.5	0

2. For each of the graphs in Figure 1 below, say whether the curve has a positive or negative slope. Give an intuitive explanation for what is happening with the slope of each curve.

3. For each of the following equations, graph the line and calculate its slope.
   a. $P = 10 - 2q_D$ (Put q_D on the X-axis)
   b. $P = 100 - 4q_D$ (Put q_D on the X-axis)
   c. $P = 50 + 6q_S$ (Put q_S on the X-axis)
   d. $I = 10,000 - 500r$ (Put I on the X-axis)

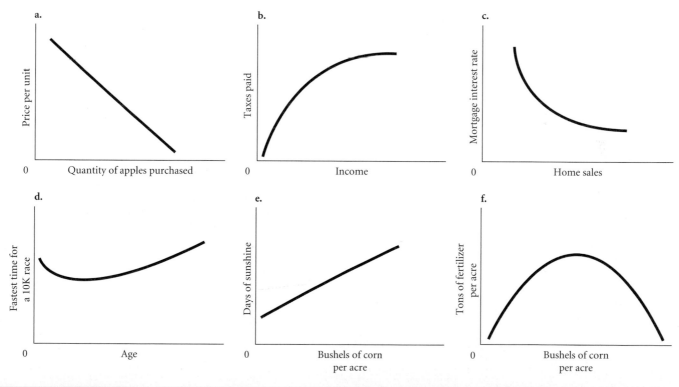

FIGURE 1

The Economic Problem: Scarcity and Choice

2

Chapter 1 began with a very broad definition of economics. Every society, no matter how small or how large, no matter how simple or how complex, has a system or process that works to transform the resources that nature and previous generations provide into useful form. Economics is the study of that process and its outcomes.

Figure 2.1 illustrates three basic questions that must be answered to understand the functioning of the economic system:

- What gets produced?
- How is it produced?
- Who gets what is produced?

This chapter explores these questions in detail. In a sense, this entire chapter *is* the definition of economics. It lays out the central problems addressed by the discipline and presents a framework that will guide you through the rest of the book. The starting point is the presumption that *human wants are unlimited, but resources are not.* Limited or scarce resources force individuals and societies to choose among competing uses of resources—alternative combinations of produced goods and services—and among alternative final distributions of what is produced among households.

These questions are *positive* or *descriptive*. That is, they ask "How does the system function?" without passing judgment about whether the result is good or bad. They must be answered first before we ask more normative questions like

- Is the outcome good or bad?
- Can it be improved?

The term *resources* is very broad. The sketch on the left side of Figure 2.1 shows several categories of resources. Some resources are the products of nature: land, wildlife, a fertile soil, minerals, timber, energy, and even the rain and the wind. In addition, the resources available to an economy include things, like buildings and equipment, that have been produced in the past but are now being used to produce other things. And, of course, perhaps the most important resource of a society is its human workforce with people's talents, skills, and knowledge.

Things that are themselves produced and that are then used in the production of other goods and services are called capital resources, or simply **capital**. Buildings, equipment, desks, chairs, software, roads, bridges, and highways are a part of the nation's stock of capital.

capital Things that are themselves produced and that are then used in the production of other goods and services.

25

The three basic questions:

1. What gets produced?

2. How is it produced?

3. Who gets what is produced?

Mix of output

Resources

Allocation of resources

Producers

Distribution of output

Households

FIGURE 2.1 The Three Basic Questions

Every society has some system or process that transforms that society's scarce resources into useful goods and services. In doing so it must decide what gets produced, how it is produced, and to whom it is distributed. The primary resources that must be allocated are land, labor, and capital.

factors of production (or factors) The inputs into the process of production. Another word for resources.

production The process that transforms scarce resources into useful goods and services.

inputs or resources Anything provided by nature or previous generations that can be used directly or indirectly to satisfy human wants.

outputs Usable products.

The basic resources available to a society are often referred to as **factors of production**, or simply **factors**. The three key factors of production are land, labor, and capital. The process that transforms scarce resources into useful goods and services is called **production**. In many societies most of the production of goods and services is done by private firms. Private airlines in the United States use land (runways), labor (pilots and mechanics), as well as capital (airplanes) to produce transportation services. But in all societies some production is done by the public sector, or government. Examples of government-produced or -provided goods and services include national defense, public education, police protection, fire protection, and so forth.

Resources or factors of production are the **inputs** into the process of production; goods and services of value to households are the **outputs** of the process of production.

SCARCITY, CHOICE, AND OPPORTUNITY COST

In the second half of this chapter, we discuss the global economic landscape. Before you can understand the different types of economic systems, it is important to master the basic economic concepts of scarcity, choice, and opportunity cost.

SCARCITY AND CHOICE IN A ONE-PERSON ECONOMY

The simplest economy is one in which a single person lives alone on an island. Consider Bill, the survivor of a plane crash, who finds himself cast ashore in such a place. Here, individual and society are one; there is no distinction between social and private. *Nonetheless, nearly all the same basic decisions that characterize complex economies must also be made in a simple economy.* That is, although Bill will get whatever he produces, he still must decide how to allocate the island's resources, what to produce, and how and when to produce it.

First, Bill must decide *what* he wants to produce. Notice that the word *needs* does not appear here. Needs are absolute requirements, but beyond just enough water, basic nutrition, and shelter to survive, they are very difficult to define. What is an "absolute necessity" for one person may not be for another. In any case, Bill must put his wants in some order of priority and make some choices.

Next he must look at the *possibilities*. What can he do to satisfy his wants, given the limits of the island? In every society, no matter how simple or complex, people are constrained in what they can do. In this society of one, Bill is constrained by time, his physical condition, his knowledge, his skills, and the resources and climate of the island.

Given that resources are limited, Bill must decide *how* to best use them to satisfy his hierarchy of wants. Food would probably come close to the top of his list. Should he

Opportunity Costs and Internships

SUMMERS PRESENT COLLEGE students with often difficult choices. While most must work at least part-time to help pay for their education, some find internships, and others devote a substantial part of their time to lying on the beach, playing a sport, or sleeping.

Opportunity costs are everywhere in decisions about how to use time during the summer. Many internships are unpaid. When a student accepts an unpaid internship, she gives up what she could have earned in a paying job. When a student decides to take a job working in a grocery store, he may give up the potential benefits of an interesting internship that could pay off in the long run.

Sleeping and lying on the beach are great, but the opportunity costs of not working are high.

The following excerpt from the *New York Times* highlights some of the trade-offs facing students today.

Summer, for many, is about looking before you leap. Internships have become as coveted and prestigious as colleges—yet another "must have" on the polished résumé. But while most of the talk is about how these internships help start you off into becoming all you want to be, the quieter reality is how they can help you decide all you don't want to be.

Careers are a lot like flypaper. Once you're trapped, work can be sticky. Internships provide a chance to buzz around without getting stuck.

If not for an internship Julia Cwiebel might still be working in a research lab. That's where she spent 12 weeks last summer deciding whether she wanted to do scientific research the rest of her life. "It was a very neat project," says Ms. Cwiebel, who was a pre-med student at the University of Cincinnati at the time. Her internship assignment was to research the plight of the American chestnut tree, which is nearing extinction.

But though the work was worthy, Ms. Cwiebel said she found it boring.

While internships provide an ideal way to try the working world on for size, they come with a price tag. Most internships are volunteer work, which means the only people who can apply are those who can afford not to be paid. Ms. Cwiebel received a $4,000 stipend from her university. The money came from the University of Cincinnati's version of a program known as WISE—Women in Science and Engineering—one of a growing number of efforts around the country to recognize the importance of giving students the chance to make mistakes and learn from them before the mistakes start to "count."

Yancie Davis is also a senior, and he also changed his career plans

Students face opportunity costs in the summer.

after the institute subsidized his internship. A summer at a mechanical engineering firm in San Francisco taught him that scouring blueprints for possible fracture points in ventilation systems just wasn't as creative as he wanted to be. "I like to design things and create things," he says. "I wouldn't have known this wasn't what I wanted to do unless I tried it."

spend his time simply gathering fruits and berries? Should he hunt for game? Should he clear a field and plant seeds? The answers to these questions depend on the character of the island, its climate, its flora and fauna (*are* there any fruits and berries?), the extent of his skills and knowledge (does he know anything about farming?), and his preferences (he may be a vegetarian).

Opportunity Cost   The concepts of *constrained choice* and *scarcity* are central to the discipline of economics. They can be applied when discussing the behavior of individuals like Bill and when analyzing the behavior of large groups of people in complex societies.

Given the scarcity of time and resources, Bill has less time to gather fruits and berries if he chooses to hunt—he trades more meat for less fruit. There is a trade-off between food and shelter, too. If Bill likes to be comfortable, he may work on building a nice place to live, but that may require giving up the food he might have produced. As we noted in Chapter 1, the best alternative that we forgo when we make a choice is the **opportunity cost** of that choice.

opportunity cost The best alternative that we give up, or forgo, when we make a choice or decision.

27

Bill may occasionally decide to rest, to lie on the beach, and to enjoy the sun. In one sense, that benefit is free—he does not have to pay for the privilege. In reality, however, it does have an opportunity cost. The true cost of that leisure is the value of the other things Bill could have produced, but did not, during the time he spent on the beach.

In February 2003 the space shuttle *Columbia* broke up over Texas and seven astronauts lost their lives. That disaster set off a national debate over the "costs" of the U.S. space program. Many argued that the potential benefits of manned space exploration were not worth the costs, including human lives. More specifically, they argued that the resources consumed by the program could be used for other purposes. What are the opportunity costs of continuing the manned space program? Among other things, taxes might be lower. That would mean more income for people to spend on other goods and services. Those same resources could also be used by the government to expand medical research, to improve education, to repair roads and bridges, to aid the elderly by paying for prescription drugs, or to support the arts. The manned space program resumed in July 2005 with the launch of the shuttle *Discovery*.

In making everyday decisions, it is often helpful to think about opportunity costs. Should I go to the dorm party or not? First, it costs $4 to attend. When I pay money for anything, I give up the other things that I could have bought with that money. Second, it costs 2 or 3 hours. Time is a valuable commodity for a college student. I have exams next week and I need to study. I could go to a movie instead of the party. I could go to another party. I could sleep. Just as Bill must weigh the value of sunning on the beach against more food or better housing, so I must weigh the value of the fun I may have at the party against everything else I might otherwise do with the time and money.

SCARCITY AND CHOICE IN AN ECONOMY OF TWO OR MORE

Now suppose that another survivor of the crash, Colleen, appears on the island. Now that Bill is not alone, things are more complex, and some new decisions must be made. Bill's and Colleen's preferences about what things to produce are likely to be different. They will probably not have the same knowledge or skills. Perhaps Colleen is very good at tracking animals, and Bill has a knack for building things. How should they split the work that needs to be done? Once things are produced, the two castaways must decide how to divide them. How should their products be distributed?

The mechanism for answering these fundamental questions is clear when Bill is alone on the island. The "central plan" is his; he simply decides what he wants and what to do about it. The minute someone else appears, however, a number of decision-making arrangements immediately become possible. One or the other may take charge, in which case that person will decide for both of them. The two may agree to cooperate, with each having an equal say, and come up with a joint plan, or they may agree to split the planning, as well as the production duties. Finally, they may go off to live alone at opposite ends of the island. Even if they live apart, however, they may take advantage of each other's presence by specializing and trading.

Modern industrial societies must answer exactly the same questions that Colleen and Bill must answer, but the mechanics of larger economies are naturally more complex. Instead of two people living together, the United States has over 290 million. Still, decisions must be made about what to produce, how to produce it, and who gets it.

Education takes time. Time spent in the classroom has an opportunity cost.

Specialization, Exchange, and Comparative Advantage

The idea that members of society benefit by specializing in what they do best has a long history and is one of the most important and powerful ideas in all of economics. David Ricardo, a major nineteenth-century British economist, formalized the point precisely. According to Ricardo's **theory of comparative advantage**, specialization and free trade will benefit all trading parties, even when some are "absolutely" more efficient producers than others. Ricardo's basic point applies just as much to Colleen and Bill as it does to different nations.

To keep things simple, suppose that Colleen and Bill have only two tasks to accomplish each week: gathering food to eat and cutting logs to burn. If Colleen could cut more logs than Bill in 1 day, and Bill could gather more nuts and berries than Colleen could, specialization would clearly lead to more total production. Both would benefit if Colleen only cuts logs and Bill only gathers nuts and berries, as long as they can trade. Suppose that Bill is slow and somewhat clumsy in his nut gathering and that Colleen is better at both cutting logs *and*

theory of comparative advantage Ricardo's theory that specialization and free trade will benefit all trading parties, even those that may be absolutely more efficient producers.

gathering food. Ricardo points out that it still pays for them to specialize and exchange. (Refer to Figure 2.2 in the following discussion.)

Suppose Colleen can cut 10 logs per day and Bill can cut only 4. Also suppose Colleen can gather 10 bushels of food per day and Bill can gather only 8. A producer has an **absolute advantage** over another in the production of a good or service if it can produce the good or service using fewer resources, including its time. Since Colleen can cut more logs per day than Bill, we say she has an absolute advantage in the production of logs. Similarly, Colleen has an absolute advantage over Bill in the production of food.

Thinking just about productivity and the output of food and logs, you might conclude that it would pay Colleen to move to the other side of the island and be by herself. Since she is more productive in cutting logs and gathering food, won't she be better off on her own? How could she benefit by hanging out with Bill and sharing what they produce?

To answer this question we must think in terms of opportunity cost. A producer has a **comparative advantage** over another in the production of a good or service if it can produce the good or service at a lower opportunity cost. First, think about Bill. He can produce 8 bushels of food per day or he can cut 4 logs. To get 8 additional bushels of food, he must give up cutting 4 logs. Thus, *for Bill the opportunity cost of 8 bushels of food is 4 logs.* Think next

absolute advantage A producer has an absolute advantage over another in the production of a good or service if it can produce that product using fewer resources.

comparative advantage A producer has a comparative advantage over another in the production of a good or service if it can produce that product at a lower *opportunity* cost.

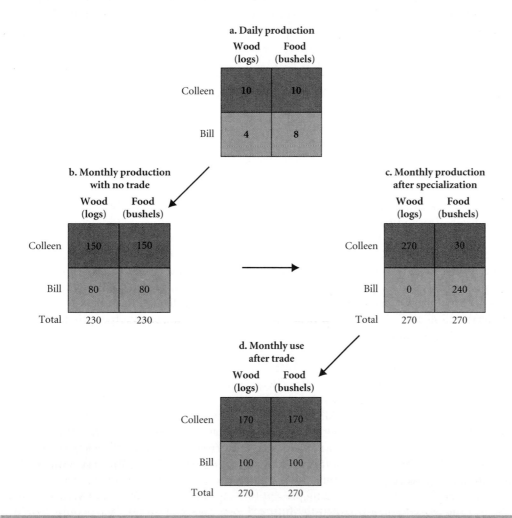

FIGURE 2.2 Comparative Advantage and the Gains from Trade

In this figure, (a) shows the number of logs and bushels of food that Colleen and Bill can produce for every day spent at the task; (b) shows how much output they could produce in a month assuming they wanted an equal number of logs and bushels. Colleen would split her time 50/50, devoting 15 days to each task and achieving total output of 150 logs and 150 bushels of food. Bill would spend 20 days on cutting wood and 10 days on gathering food. As shown in (c) and (d), by specializing and trading, both Colleen and Bill will be better off. Going from (c) to (d), Colleen trades 100 logs to Bill in exchange for 140 bushels of food.

about Colleen. She can produce 10 bushels of food per day or she can cut 10 logs. She thus gives up 1 log for each additional bushel, and so *for Colleen the opportunity cost of 8 bushels of food is 8 logs.* Bill has a comparative advantage over Colleen in the production of food because he gives up only 4 logs for an additional 8 bushels whereas Colleen gives up 8 logs.

Think now about what Colleen must give up in terms of food to get 10 logs. To produce 10 logs she must work a whole day. If she spends a day cutting 10 logs she gives up a day of gathering 10 bushels of food. Thus *for Colleen the opportunity cost of 10 logs is 10 bushels of food.* What must Bill give up to get 10 logs? To produce 4 logs he must work a day. For each day he cuts logs he gives up 8 bushels of food. He thus gives up 2 bushels of food for each log, and so *for Bill the opportunity cost of 10 logs is 20 bushels of food.* Colleen has a comparative advantage over Bill in the production of logs since she gives up only 10 bushels of food for an additional 10 logs whereas Bill gives up 20 bushels.

Ricardo then argues that two parties can benefit from specialization and trade even if one party has an absolute advantage in the production of both goods. Suppose Colleen and Bill both want equal numbers of logs and bushels of food. If Colleen goes off on her own, in a 30-day month she can produce 150 logs and 150 bushels, devoting 15 days to each task. For Bill to produce equal numbers of logs and bushels on his own requires that he spend 10 days on food and 20 days on logs. This yields 80 bushels of food (10 days × 8 bushels per day) and 80 logs (20 days × 4 logs per day). Between the two, they produce 230 logs and 230 bushels of food.

Let's see if specialization and trade can work. If Bill spends all his time on food, he produces 240 bushels in a month (30 days × 8 bushels per day). If Colleen spends 3 days on food and 27 days on logs, she produces 30 bushels of food (3 days × 10 bushels per day) and 270 logs (27 days × 10 logs per day). Between the two, they produce 270 logs and 270 bushels of food, which is more than the 230 logs and 230 bushels they produced when not specializing. Thus, by specializing in the production of the good in which they enjoyed a comparative advantage, there is more of both goods.

Even if Colleen were to live at another place on the island, she could specialize, producing 30 bushels of food and 270 logs, and then trade 100 of her logs to Bill for 140 bushels of food. This would leave her with 170 logs and 170 bushels of food, which is more than the 150 of each she could produce on her own. Bill would specialize completely in food, producing 240 bushels. Trading 140 bushels of food to Colleen for 100 logs leaves him with 100 of each, which is more than the 80 of each he could produce on his own.

The degree of specialization in modern industrial societies is breathtaking. Let your mind wander over the range of products and services available or under development today. As knowledge expands, specialization becomes a necessity. This is true not only for scientists and doctors but also in every career from tree surgeons to divorce lawyers to Web masters. Understanding specialization and trade will help you to explain much of what goes on in today's global economy.

Weighing Present and Expected Future Costs and Benefits

Very often we find ourselves weighing benefits available today against benefits available tomorrow. Here too the notion of opportunity cost is helpful.

While alone on the island, Bill had to choose between cultivating a field and just gathering wild nuts and berries. Gathering nuts and berries provides food now; gathering seeds and clearing a field for planting will yield food tomorrow, if all goes well. Using today's time to farm may well be worth the effort if doing so will yield more food than Bill would otherwise have in the future. By planting, Bill is trading present value for future values.

The simplest example of trading present for future benefits is the act of saving. When I put income aside today for use in the future, I give up some things that I could have had today in exchange for something tomorrow. Because nothing is certain, some judgment about future events and expected values must be made. What will my income be in 10 years? How long am I likely to live?

We trade off present and future benefits in small ways all the time. If you decide to study instead of going to the dorm party, you are trading present fun for the expected future benefits of higher grades. If you decide to go outside on a very cold day and run 5 miles, you are trading discomfort in the present for being in better shape later.

Capital Goods and Consumer Goods A society trades present for expected future benefits when it devotes a portion of its resources to research and development or to investment in capital. As we said earlier in this chapter, *capital* in its broadest definition is anything that has already been produced that will be used to produce other valuable goods or services over time.

Building capital means trading present benefits for future ones. Bill and Colleen might trade gathering berries or lying in the sun for cutting logs to build a nicer house in the future. In a modern society, resources used to produce capital goods could have been used to produce **consumer goods**—that is, goods for present consumption. Heavy industrial machinery does not directly satisfy the wants of anyone, but producing it requires resources that could instead have gone into producing things that do satisfy wants directly—for example, food, clothing, toys, or golf clubs.

consumer goods Goods produced for present consumption.

Capital is everywhere. A road is capital. Once it is built, we can drive on it or transport goods and services over it for many years to come. A house is also capital. Before a new manufacturing firm can start up, it must put some capital in place. The buildings, equipment, and inventories that it uses comprise its capital. As it contributes to the production process, this capital yields valuable services through time.

In Chapter 1, we talked about the enormous amount of capital—buildings, factories, housing, cars, trucks, telephone lines, and so forth—that you might see from a window high in a skyscraper. Much of it was put in place by previous generations, yet it continues to provide valuable services today; it is part of this generation's endowment of resources. To build every building, every road, every factory, every house, and every car or truck, society must forgo using resources to produce consumer goods today. To get an education, I pay tuition and put off joining the workforce for a while.

Capital does not need to be tangible. When you spend time and resources developing skills or getting an education, you are investing in human capital—your own human capital. This capital will continue to exist and yield benefits to you for years to come. A computer program produced by a software company may come on a compact disc (CD) that costs 75¢ to make, but its true intangible value comes from the ideas embodied in the program itself, which will drive computers to do valuable, time-saving tasks over time. It too is capital.

The process of using resources to produce new capital is called **investment**. (In everyday language, the term *investment* often refers to the act of buying a share of stock or a bond, as in "I invested in some Treasury bonds." In economics, however, investment *always* refers to the creation of capital: the purchase or putting in place of buildings, equipment, roads, houses, and the like.) A wise investment in capital is one that yields future benefits that are more valuable than the present cost. When you spend money for a house, for example, presumably you value its future benefits. That is, you expect to gain more from living in it than you would from the things you could buy today with the same money.

investment The process of using resources to produce new capital.

> Because resources are scarce, the opportunity cost of every investment in capital is forgone present consumption.

THE PRODUCTION POSSIBILITY FRONTIER

A simple graphic device called the **production possibility frontier (ppf)** illustrates the principles of constrained choice, opportunity cost, and scarcity. The ppf is a graph that shows all the combinations of goods and services that can be produced if all society's resources are used efficiently. Figure 2.3 shows a ppf for a hypothetical economy.

production possibility frontier (ppf) A graph that shows all the combinations of goods and services that can be produced if all of society's resources are used efficiently.

On the *Y*-axis, we measure the quantity of capital goods produced and on the *X*-axis, the quantity of consumer goods. All points below and to the left of the curve (the shaded area) represent combinations of capital and consumer goods that are possible for the society given the resources available and existing technology. Points above and to the right of the curve, such as point *G*, represent combinations that cannot be reached. If an economy were to end up at point *A* on the graph, it would be producing no consumer goods at all; all resources would be used for the production of capital. If an economy were to end up at point *B*, it would be devoting all its resources to the production of consumer goods and none of its resources to the formation of capital.

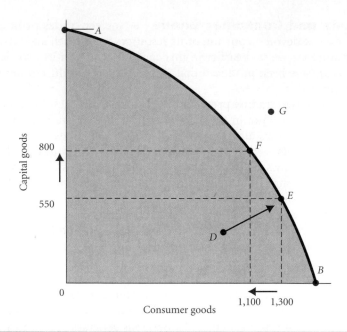

FIGURE 2.3 Production Possibility Frontier

The ppf illustrates a number of economic concepts. One of the most important is *opportunity cost*. The opportunity cost of producing more capital goods is fewer consumer goods. Moving from *E* to *F*, the number of capital goods increases from 550 to 800, but the number of consumer goods decreases from 1,300 to 1,100.

While all economies produce some of each kind of good, different economies emphasize different things. About 17.1 percent of gross output in the United States in 2005 was new capital. In Japan, capital historically accounted for a much higher percent of gross output, while in the Congo the figure was 7 percent. Japan is closer to point *A* on its ppf, the Congo is closer to *B*, and the United States is somewhere in between.

Points that are actually on the ppf are points of both full resource employment and production efficiency. (Recall from Chapter 1 that an efficient economy is one that produces the things that people want at least cost. *Production efficiency* is a state in which a given mix of outputs is produced at least cost.) Resources are not going unused, and there is no waste. Points that lie within the shaded area, but that are not on the frontier, represent either unemployment of resources or production inefficiency. An economy producing at point *D* in Figure 2.3 can produce more capital goods and more consumer goods, for example, by moving to point *E*. This is possible because resources are not fully employed at point *D* or are not being used efficiently.

Unemployment During the Great Depression of the 1930s, the U.S. economy experienced prolonged unemployment. Millions of workers found themselves without jobs. In 1933, 25 percent of the civilian labor force was unemployed. This figure stayed above 14 percent until 1940, when increased defense spending by the United States created millions of jobs. In June 1975, the unemployment rate went over 9 percent for the first time since the 1930s. In December 1982, when the unemployment rate hit 10.8 percent, nearly 12 million were looking for work. In 2005, the figure was over 8 million.

In addition to the hardship that falls on the unemployed themselves, unemployment of labor means unemployment of capital. During economic downturns or recessions, industrial plants run at less than their total capacity. When there is unemployment of labor and capital, we are not producing all that we can.

Periods of unemployment correspond to points inside the ppf, points like *D* in Figure 2.3. Moving onto the frontier from a point like *D* means achieving full employment of resources.

Inefficiency Although an economy may be operating with full employment of its land, labor, and capital resources, it may still be operating inside its ppf (at a point like *D* in Figure 2.3). It could be using those resources *inefficiently*.

Waste and mismanagement are the results of a firm's operating below its potential. If I am the owner of a bakery and I forget to order flour, my workers and ovens stand idle while I figure out what to do.

Sometimes, inefficiency results from mismanagement of the economy instead of mismanagement of individual private firms. Suppose, for example, that the land and climate in Ohio are best suited for corn production, and the land and climate in Kansas are best suited for wheat production. If Congress passes a law forcing Ohio farmers to plant 50 percent of their acreage in wheat and Kansas farmers to plant 50 percent in corn, neither corn nor wheat production will be up to potential. The economy will be at a point like *A* in Figure 2.4— inside the ppf. Allowing each state to specialize in producing the crop that it produces best increases the production of both crops and moves the economy to a point like *B* in Figure 2.4.

The Efficient Mix of Output   To be efficient, an economy must produce what people want. This means that, in addition to operating *on* the ppf, the economy must be operating at the *right point* on the ppf. Suppose that an economy devotes 100 percent of its resources to beef production and that the beef industry runs efficiently, using the most modern techniques. Also suppose that everyone in the society is a vegetarian. The result is a total waste of resources (assuming that the society cannot trade its beef for vegetables produced in another country).

Both points *B* and *C* in Figure 2.4 are points of production efficiency and full employment. Whether *B* is more or less efficient than *C*, however, depends on the preferences of members of society and is not shown in the ppf graph.

Negative Slope and Opportunity Cost   As we have seen, points that lie on the ppf represent points of full resource employment and production efficiency. Society can choose only one point on the curve. Because a society's choices are constrained by available resources and existing technology, when those resources are fully and efficiently employed, it can produce more capital goods only by reducing production of consumer goods. The opportunity cost of the additional capital is the forgone production of consumer goods.

The fact that scarcity exists is illustrated by the negative slope of the ppf. (If you need a review of slope, see the Appendix to Chapter 1.) In moving from point *E* to point *F* in Figure 2.3, capital production *increases* by 800 − 550 = 250 units (a positive change), but that increase in capital can be achieved only by shifting resources out of the production of consumer goods. Thus, in moving from point *E* to point *F* in Figure 2.3, consumer goods production *decreases* by 1,300 − 1,100 = 200 units of the consumer goods (a negative change).

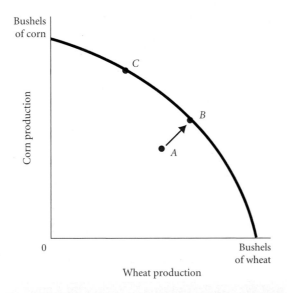

FIGURE 2.4 Inefficiency from Misallocation of Land in Farming

Society can end up inside its ppf at a point like *A* by using its resources inefficiently. If, for example, Ohio's climate and soil were best suited for corn production and those of Kansas were best suited for wheat production, a law forcing Kansas farmers to produce corn and Ohio farmers to produce wheat would result in less of both. In such a case, society might be at point *A* instead of point *B*.

TABLE 2.1 Production Possibility Schedule for Total Corn and Wheat Production in Ohio and Kansas

POINT ON PPF	TOTAL CORN PRODUCTION (MILLIONS OF BUSHELS PER YEAR)	TOTAL WHEAT PRODUCTION (MILLIONS OF BUSHELS PER YEAR)
A	700	100
B	650	200
C	510	380
D	400	500
E	300	550

The slope of the curve, the ratio of the change in capital goods to the change in consumer goods, is negative.

The value of the slope of a society's ppf is called the **marginal rate of transformation (MRT)**. In Figure 2.3, the MRT between points *E* and *F* is simply the ratio of the change in capital goods (a positive number) to the change in consumer goods (a negative number).

marginal rate of transformation (MRT)
The slope of the production possibility frontier (ppf).

The Law of Increasing Opportunity Cost   The negative slope of the ppf indicates the trade-off that a society faces between two goods. We can learn something further about the shape of the frontier and the terms of this trade-off. Let us look at the trade-off between corn and wheat production in Ohio and Kansas. In a recent year, Ohio and Kansas together produced 510 million bushels of corn and 380 million bushels of wheat. Table 2.1 presents these two numbers, plus some hypothetical combinations of corn and wheat production that might exist for Ohio and Kansas together. Figure 2.5 graphs the data from Table 2.1.

Suppose that society's demand for corn dramatically increases. If this happens, farmers would probably shift some of their acreage from wheat production to corn production. Such a shift is represented by a move from point *C* (where corn = 510 and wheat = 380) up and to the left along the ppf toward points *A* and *B* in Figure 2.5. As this happens, it becomes more and more difficult to produce additional corn. The best land for corn production was presumably already in corn, and the best land for wheat production was already in wheat. As we try to produce more and more corn, the land is less and less well suited to that crop. As we take more and

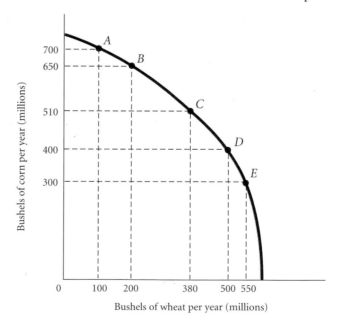

FIGURE 2.5 Corn and Wheat Production in Ohio and Kansas

The ppf illustrates that the opportunity cost of corn production increases as we shift resources from wheat production to corn production. Moving from points *E* to *D*, we get an additional 100 million bushels of corn at a cost of 50 million bushels of wheat. Moving from points *B* to *A*, we get only 50 million bushels of corn at a cost of 100 million bushels of wheat. The *cost per bushel* of corn—measured in lost wheat—has increased.

more land out of wheat production, we will be taking increasingly better wheat-producing land. All this is to say that the opportunity cost of more corn, measured in terms of wheat, increases.

Moving from points *E* to *D*, Table 2.1 shows that we can get 100 million bushels of corn (400 − 300) by sacrificing only 50 million bushels of wheat (550 − 500)—that is, we get 2 bushels of corn for every bushel of wheat. However, when we are already stretching the ability of the land to produce corn, it becomes more difficult to produce more, and the opportunity cost increases. Moving from points *B* to *A*, we can get only 50 million bushels of corn (700 − 650) by sacrificing 100 million bushels of wheat (200 − 100). For every bushel of wheat, we now get only half a bushel of corn. However, if the demand for *wheat* were to increase substantially and we were to move down and to the right along the ppf, it would become increasingly difficult to produce wheat, and the opportunity cost of wheat, in terms of corn, would increase. This is the *law of increasing opportunity cost.*

It is important to remember that the ppf represents choices available within the constraints imposed by the current state of agricultural technology. In the long run, technology may improve, and when that happens, we have *growth*.

Economic Growth   **Economic growth** is characterized by an increase in the total output of an economy. It occurs when a society acquires new resources or learns to produce more with existing resources. New resources may mean a larger labor force or an increased capital stock. The production and use of new machinery and equipment (capital) increase workers' productivity. (Give a man a shovel, and he can dig a bigger hole; give him a steam shovel, and wow!) Improved productivity also comes from technological change and *innovation*, the discovery and application of new, more efficient production techniques.

In the past few decades, the productivity of U.S. agriculture has increased dramatically. Based on data compiled by the Department of Agriculture, Table 2.2 shows that yield per acre in corn production has increased fivefold since the late 1930s, while the labor required to produce it has dropped significantly. Productivity in wheat production has also increased, at only a slightly less remarkable rate: Output per acre has more than tripled, while labor requirements are down nearly 90 percent. These increases are the result of more efficient farming techniques, more and better capital (tractors, combines, and other equipment), and advances in scientific knowledge and technological change (hybrid seeds, fertilizers, and so on). As you can see in Figure 2.6, increases such as these shift the ppf up and to the right.

Sources of Growth and the Dilemma of the Poor Countries   Economic growth arises from many sources, the two most important of which, over the years, have been the accumulation of capital and technological advances. For poor countries, capital is essential; they must build the communication networks and transportation systems necessary to develop industries that function efficiently. They also need capital goods to develop their agricultural sectors.

economic growth An increase in the total output of an economy. It occurs when a society acquires new resources or when it learns to produce more using existing resources.

TABLE 2.2 Increasing Productivity in Corn and Wheat Production in the United States, 1935–2006

	CORN		WHEAT	
	Yield Per Acre (Bushels)	Labor Hours Per 100 Bushels	Yield Per Acre (Bushels)	Labor Hours Per 100 Bushels
1935–1939	26.1	108	13.2	67
1945–1949	36.1	53	16.9	34
1955–1959	48.7	20	22.3	17
1965–1969	78.5	7	27.5	11
1975–1979	95.3	4	31.3	9
1981–1985	107.2	3	36.9	7
1985–1990	112.8	NA[a]	38.0	NA[a]
1990–1995	120.6	NA[a]	38.1	NA[a]
1998	134.4	NA[a]	43.2	NA[a]
2001	138.2	NA[a]	43.5	NA[a]
2006	145.6	NA[a]	42.3	NA[a]

[a]Data not available.
Sources: U.S. Department of Agriculture, Economic Research Service, Agricultural Statistics, Crop Summary. **www.ers.usda.gov**, February 2005.

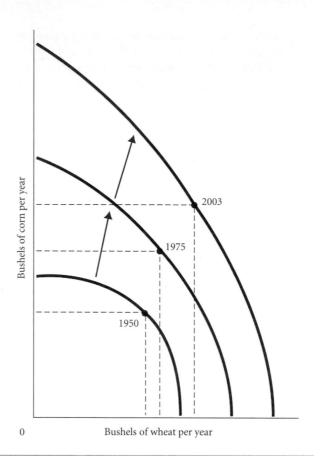

FIGURE 2.6 Economic Growth Shifts the ppf Up and to the Right

Productivity increases have enhanced the ability of the United States to produce both corn and wheat. As Table 2.2 shows, productivity increases were more dramatic for corn than for wheat. The shifts in the ppf were thus not parallel.

Note: The ppf also shifts if the amount of land or labor in corn and wheat production changes. Although we empha-size productivity increases here, the actual shifts between years were in part due to land and labor changes.

Recall that capital goods are produced only at a sacrifice of consumer goods. The same can be said for technological advances. Technological advances come from research and development that use resources; thus they too must be paid for. The resources used to pro-duce capital goods—to build a road, a tractor, or a manufacturing plant—*and* to develop new technologies could have been used to produce consumer goods.

When a large part of a country's population is very poor, taking resources out of the production of consumer goods (such as food and clothing) is very difficult. In addition, in some countries people wealthy enough to invest in domestic industries choose instead to invest abroad because of political turmoil at home. As a result, it often falls to the govern-ments of poor countries to generate revenues for capital production and research out of tax collections.

All these factors have contributed to the growing gap between some poor and rich nations. Figure 2.7 shows the result, using ppf's. On the left, the rich country devotes a larger portion of its production to capital, while the poor country produces mostly consumer goods. On the right, you see the result: The ppf of the rich country shifts up and out farther and faster.

COMPARATIVE ADVANTAGE AND THE GAINS FROM TRADE

Production possibility frontiers can also be used to show the benefits from specialization and trade. Recall the story earlier in the chapter of Colleen and Bill on a desert island. In that example we assumed that Colleen could cut 10 logs per day or she could gather 10 bushels of food per day. To construct her production possibility frontier (see Figure 2.8(a)), we start with the end points. If she were to devote an entire month (30 days) to log production, she

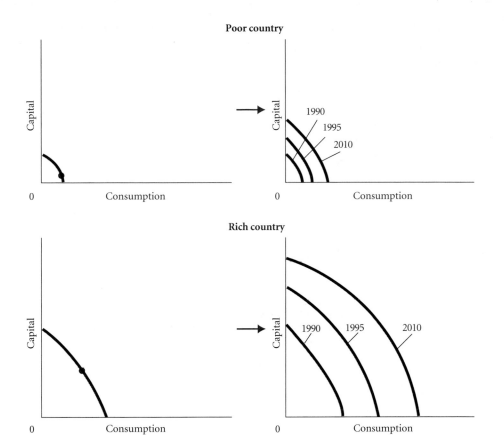

FIGURE 2.7 Capital Goods and Growth in Poor and Rich Countries

Rich countries find it easier to devote resources to the production of capital than poor countries do, but the more resources that flow into capital production, the faster the rate of economic growth. Thus the gap between poor and rich countries has grown over time.

could cut 300 logs—10 logs per day × 30 days. Similarly, if she were to devote an entire month to food gathering, she could produce 300 bushels. If she chose to split her time evenly (15 days to logs and 15 days to food), she would have 150 bushels and 150 logs. Her production possibilities are illustrated by the straight line between *A* and *B*. The ppf illustrates the trade-off that she faces between logs and food: By reducing her time spent in food gathering, she is able to devote more time to logs, and for every 10 bushels of food that she gives up she gets 10 logs.

In Figure 2.8(b), we construct Bill's ppf. Recall that Bill can produce 8 bushels of food per day, but he can cut only 4 logs. Again, starting with the end points, if Bill devoted all his time to food production, he could produce 240 bushels—8 bushels of food per day × 30 days. Similarly, if he were to devote the entire 30 days to log cutting, he could cut 120 logs—4 logs per day × 30 days. By splitting his time, with 20 days spent on log cutting and 10 days spent gathering food, Bill could produce 80 logs and 80 bushels of food. His production possibilities are illustrated by the straight line between *D* and *E*. By shifting his resources and time from logs to food, he gets 2 bushels for every log.

Figures 2.8(a) and 2.8(b) illustrate the maximum amounts of food and logs that Bill and Colleen can produce acting independently with no specialization or trade, which is 230 logs and 230 bushels. Let's now have each specialize in producing the good in which he or she has a comparative advantage. Back in Figure 2.2 we showed that if Bill devotes all his time to food production, producing 240 bushels (30 days × 8 bushels per day), and Colleen devotes the vast majority of her time to cutting logs (27 days) and just a few days to gathering food (3 days), their combined total would be 270 logs and 270 bushels of food. Colleen would produce 270 logs and 30 bushels of food to go with Bill's 240 bushels of food.

Finally, we arrange a trade, and the result is shown in Figures 2.9(a) and 2.9(b). Bill trades 140 bushels of food to Colleen for 100 logs, and he ends up with 100 logs and 100 bushels of food, 20 more of each than he would have had before the specialization and trade.

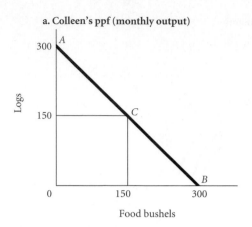

a. Colleen's ppf (monthly output)

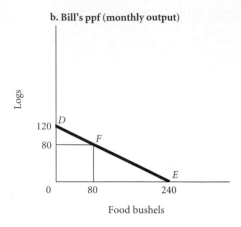

b. Bill's ppf (monthly output)

FIGURE 2.8 Production Possibility Frontiers with No Trade

The figure in (a) shows all of the combinations of logs and bushels of food that Colleen can produce by herself. If she spends all 30 days each month on logs, she produces 300 logs and no food (point *A*). If she spends all 30 days on food, she produces 300 bushels of food and no logs (point *B*). If she spends 15 days on logs and 15 days on food, she produces 150 of each (point *C*).

The figure in (b) shows all the combinations of logs and bushels of food that Bill can produce by himself. If he spends all 30 days each month on logs, he produces 120 logs and no food (point *D*). If he spends all 30 days on food, he produces 240 bushels of food and no logs (point *E*). If he spends 20 days on logs and 10 days on food, he produces 80 of each (point *F*).

Colleen ends up with 170 logs and 170 bushels, again 20 more of each than she would have had before the specialization and trade. Both are better off. Both move out beyond their individual production possibilities.

Although it exists only as an abstraction, the ppf illustrates a number of very important concepts that we shall use throughout the rest of this book: scarcity, unemployment, inefficiency, opportunity cost, the law of increasing opportunity cost, economic growth, and the gains from trade.

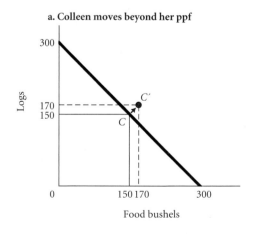

a. Colleen moves beyond her ppf

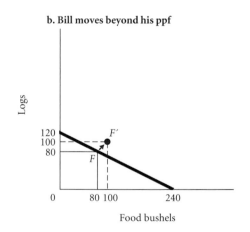

b. Bill moves beyond his ppf

FIGURE 2.9 Colleen and Bill Gain from Trade

By specializing and engaging in trade, Colleen and Bill can move beyond their own production possibilities. If Bill spends all his time producing food, he produces 240 bushels of food and no logs. If he can trade 140 of his bushels to Colleen for 100 logs, he ends up with 100 logs and 100 bushels of food. The figure in (b) shows that he can move from point *F* on his ppf to point *F'*.

If Colleen spends 27 days cutting logs and 3 days producing food, she produces 270 logs and 30 bushels of food. If she can trade 100 of her logs to Bill for 140 bushels of food, she ends up with 170 logs and 170 bushels of food. The figure in (a) shows that she can move from point *C* on her ppf to point *C'*.

THE ECONOMIC PROBLEM

Recall the three basic questions facing all economic systems: (1) What gets produced? (2) How is it produced? and (3) Who gets it?

When Bill was alone on the island, the mechanism for answering these questions was simple: He thought about his own wants and preferences, looked at the constraints imposed by the resources of the island and his own skills and time, and made his decisions. As he set about his work, he allocated available resources quite simply, more or less by dividing up his available time. Distribution of the output was irrelevant. Because Bill was the society, he got it all.

Introducing even one more person into the economy—in this case, Colleen—changed all that. With Colleen on the island, resource allocation involves deciding not only how each person spends time but also who does what; and now there are two sets of wants and preferences. If Bill and Colleen go off on their own and form two completely separate self-sufficient economies, there will be lost potential. Two people can do many more things together than one person can do alone. They may use their comparative advantages in different skills to specialize. Cooperation and coordination may give rise to gains that would otherwise not be possible.

When a society consists of millions of people, the problem of coordination and cooperation becomes enormous, but so does the potential for gain. In large, complex economies, specialization can go wild, with people working in jobs as different in their detail as an impressionist painting is from a blank page. The range of products available in a modern industrial society is beyond anything that could have been imagined a hundred years ago, and so is the range of jobs.

The amount of coordination and cooperation in a modern industrial society is almost impossible to imagine. Yet something seems to drive economic systems, if sometimes clumsily and inefficiently, toward producing the things that people want. Given scarce resources, how exactly do large, complex societies go about answering the three basic economic questions? This is the economic problem, and this is what this text is about.

ECONOMIC SYSTEMS

Now that you understand the economic problem, we can explore how different economic systems go about answering the three basic questions.

It is probably fair to argue that the ideological struggle over economic systems—the debate between the competing systems of the Soviet Union and the United States and the emerging power of Communist China—was the world's biggest problem for half a century. The continuing threat of nuclear war was held in the balance.

In recent years, however, the world has changed dramatically. China has become a magnet for private capital and entrepreneurship and has one of the most rapidly growing economies in the world. For the last decade, China has been growing at double-digit rates. Between 2001 and 2004, China's national output went up almost 50 percent. In the single month of June 2005, the Chinese sold $21 billion worth of goods and services to the United States, while we sold only $3.4 billion to them. On the other hand, the Russian Federation has been growing, but not very rapidly, since the fall of the Soviet Union in 1989. The danger to the world now lies in international terrorism and a more complex set of ideological struggles with wars in Iraq and Afghanistan.

COMMAND ECONOMIES

In a pure **command economy**, the basic economic questions are answered by a central government. Through a combination of government ownership of state enterprises and central planning, the government, either directly or indirectly, sets output targets, incomes, and prices.

While the extremes of central planning have been rejected, so too has the idea that "markets solve all problems." The real debate is not about whether we have government at all, it is about the extent and the character of a limited government role in the economy. One of the major themes of this book is that government involvement, in theory, may improve the effi-

command economy An economy in which a central government either directly or indirectly sets output targets, incomes, and prices.

ciency and fairness of the allocation of a nation's resources. At the same time, a poorly functioning government can destroy incentives, lead to corruption, and result in the waste of a society's resources.

LAISSEZ-FAIRE ECONOMIES: THE FREE MARKET

laissez-faire economy
Literally from the French: "allow [them] to do." An economy in which individual people and firms pursue their own self-interests without any central direction or regulation.

market The institution through which buyers and sellers interact and engage in exchange.

At the opposite end of the spectrum from the command economy is the **laissez-faire economy**. The term *laissez faire*, which, translated literally from French, means "allow [them] to do," implies a complete lack of government involvement in the economy. In this type of economy, individuals and firms pursue their own self-interest without any central direction or regulation; the sum total of millions of individual decisions ultimately determines all basic economic outcomes. The central institution through which a laissez-faire system answers the basic questions is the **market**, a term that is used in economics to mean an institution through which buyers and sellers interact and engage in exchange.

The interactions between buyers and sellers in any market range from simple to complex. Early explorers of the North American Midwest who wished to exchange with Native Americans did so simply by bringing their goods to a central place and trading them. Today, the World Wide Web is revolutionizing exchange. A jewelry maker in upstate Maine can exhibit wares through digital photographs on the Web. Buyers can enter orders or make bids and pay by credit card. Companies like eBay facilitate the worldwide interaction of tens of thousands of buyers and sellers sitting at their computers.

In short:

> Some markets are simple and others are complex, but they all involve buyers and sellers engaging in exchange. The behavior of buyers and sellers in a laissez-faire economy determines what gets produced, how it is produced, and who gets it.

The following chapters explore market systems in great depth. A quick preview is worthwhile here, however.

consumer sovereignty
The idea that consumers ultimately dictate what will be produced (or not produced) by choosing what to purchase (and what not to purchase).

Consumer Sovereignty In a free, unregulated market, goods and services are produced and sold only if the supplier can make a profit. In simple terms, making a *profit* means selling goods or services for more than it costs to produce them. You cannot make a profit unless someone wants the product that you are selling. This logic leads to the notion of **consumer sovereignty**: The mix of output found in any free market system is dictated ultimately by the tastes and preferences of consumers, who "vote" by buying or not buying. Businesses rise and fall in response to consumer demands. No central directive or plan is necessary.

free enterprise The freedom of individuals to start and operate private businesses in search of profits.

Individual Production Decisions: Free Enterprise Under a free market system, individual producers must also figure how to organize and coordinate the actual production of their products or services. The owner of a small shoe repair shop must alone buy the needed equipment and tools, hang signs, and set prices. In a big corporation, so many people are involved in planning the production process that in many ways corporate planning resembles the planning in a command economy. In a free market economy, producers may be small or large. One person who hand paints eggshells may start to sell them as a business; a person good at computers may start a business designing Web sites. On a larger scale, a group of furniture designers may put together a large portfolio of sketches, raise several million dollars, and start a bigger business. At the extreme are huge corporations like Microsoft, Mitsubishi, and Intel, each of which sells tens of billions of dollars' worth of products every year. Whether the firms are large or small, however, production decisions in a market economy are made by separate private organizations acting in what they perceive to be their own interests.

Often the market system is called a free enterprise system. **Free enterprise** means the freedom of individuals to start private businesses in search of profits. Because new businesses require capital investment before they can begin operation, starting a new business involves risk. A well-run business that produces a product for which demand exists will succeed; a poorly run business or one that produces a product for which little demand exists now or in the future is likely to fail. It is through free enterprise that new products and new production techniques find their way into use.

Proponents of free market systems argue that free enterprise leads to more efficient production and better response to diverse and changing consumer preferences. If a producer produces inefficiently, competitors will come along, fight for the business, and eventually take it away. Thus, in a free market economy, competition forces producers to use efficient techniques of production. It is competition, then, that ultimately dictates how outputs are produced.

Distribution of Output   In a free market system, the distribution of output—who gets what—is also determined in a decentralized way. The amount that any one household gets depends on its income and wealth. *Income* is the amount that a household earns each year. It comes in a number of forms: wages, salaries, interest, and the like. *Wealth* is the amount that households have accumulated out of past income through saving or inheritance.

To the extent that income comes from working for a wage, it is at least in part determined by individual choice. You will work for the wages available in the market only if these wages (and the things they can buy) are sufficient to compensate you for what you give up by working. Your leisure certainly has a value also. You may discover that you can increase your income by getting more education or training. You *cannot* increase your income, however, if you acquire a skill that no one wants and can pay for.

Price Theory   The basic coordinating mechanism in a free market system is price. A price is the amount that a product sells for per unit, and it reflects what society is willing to pay. Prices of inputs—labor, land, and capital—determine how much it costs to produce a product. Prices of various kinds of labor, or *wage rates*, determine the rewards for working in different jobs and professions. Many of the independent decisions made in a market economy involve the weighing of prices and costs, so it is not surprising that much of economic theory focuses on the factors that influence and determine prices. This is why microeconomic theory is often simply called *price theory*.

In sum:

New businesses arise each day and some go out of business in response to profit opportunities and losses.

> In a free market system, the basic economic questions are answered without the help of a central government plan or directives. This is what the "free" in free market means—the system is left to operate on its own, with no outside interference. Individuals pursuing their own self-interest will go into business and produce the products and services that people want. Others will decide whether to acquire skills; whether to work; and whether to buy, sell, invest, or save the income that they earn. The basic coordinating mechanism is price.

MIXED SYSTEMS, MARKETS, AND GOVERNMENTS

The differences between command economies and laissez-faire economies in their pure forms are enormous. In fact, these pure forms do not exist in the world; all real systems are in some sense "mixed." That is, individual enterprise exists and independent choice is exercised even in economies in which the government plays the major role.

Conversely, no market economies exist without government involvement and government regulation. The United States has basically a free market economy, but government purchases accounted for about 18 percent of its total production in 2005. Governments in the United States (local, state, and federal) directly employ about 16 percent of all workers, counting the military. They also redistribute income by means of taxation and social welfare expenditures, and they regulate many economic activities.

One of the major themes in this book, and indeed in economics, is the tension between the advantages of free, unregulated markets and the desire for government involvement. Advocates of free markets argue that such markets work best when left to themselves. They produce only what people want; without buyers, sellers go out of business. Competition forces firms to adopt efficient production techniques. Wage differentials lead people to acquire needed skills. Competition also leads to innovation in both production techniques and products. The result is quality and variety, but market systems have problems too.

Even staunch defenders of the free enterprise system recognize that market systems are not perfect. First, they do not always produce what people want at lowest cost—there are inefficiencies. Second, rewards (income) may be unfairly distributed, and some groups may be left out. Third, periods of unemployment and inflation recur with some regularity.

Many people point to these problems as reasons for government involvement. Indeed, for some problems government involvement may be the only solution. However, government decisions are made by people who presumably, like the rest of us, act in their own self-interest. While governments may indeed be called on to improve the functioning of the economy, there is no guarantee that they will do so. Just as markets may fail to produce an allocation of resources that is perfectly efficient and fair, governments may fail to improve matters. We return to this debate many times throughout this text.

LOOKING AHEAD

This chapter has described the economic problem in broad terms. We have outlined the questions that all economic systems must answer. We also discussed very broadly the two kinds of economic systems. In the next chapter we analyze the way market systems work.

SUMMARY

1. Every society has some system or process for transforming into useful form what nature and previous generations have provided. Economics is the study of that process and its outcomes.

2. *Producers* are those who take resources and transform them into usable products, or *outputs*. Private firms, households, and governments all produce something.

SCARCITY, CHOICE, AND OPPORTUNITY COST

3. All societies must answer *three basic questions*: What gets produced? How is it produced? Who gets what is produced? These three questions make up the *economic problem*.

4. One person alone on an island must make the same basic decisions that complex societies make. When a society consists of more than one person, questions of distribution, cooperation, and specialization arise.

5. Because resources are scarce relative to human wants in all societies, using resources to produce one good or service implies *not* using them to produce something else. This concept of *opportunity cost* is central to an understanding of economics.

6. Using resources to produce *capital* that will in turn produce benefits in the future implies *not* using those resources to produce consumer goods in the present.

7. Even if one individual or nation is absolutely more efficient at producing goods than another, all parties will gain if they specialize in producing goods in which they have a *comparative advantage*.

8. A *production possibility frontier* (ppf) is a graph that shows all the combinations of goods and services that can be produced if all society's resources are used efficiently. The ppf illustrates a number of important economic concepts: scarcity, unemployment, inefficiency, increasing opportunity cost, and economic growth.

9. *Economic growth* occurs when society produces more, either by acquiring more resources or by learning to produce more with existing resources. Improved productivity may come from additional capital or from the discovery and application of new, more efficient techniques of production.

10. The ppf can be used to illustrate the gains from trade and the theory of comparative advantage. Trade and specialization enable people and countries to move out beyond their own productive possibilities.

ECONOMIC SYSTEMS

11. In some modern societies, government plays a big role in answering the three basic questions. In pure *command economies*, a central authority directly or indirectly sets output targets, incomes, and prices.

12. A *laissez-faire economy* is one in which individuals independently pursue their own self-interest, without any central direction or regulation, and ultimately determine all basic economic outcomes.

13. A *market* is an institution through which buyers and sellers interact and engage in exchange. Some markets involve simple face-to-face exchange; others involve a complex series of transactions, often over great distance or electronically.

14. There are no purely planned economies and no pure laissez-faire economies; all economies are mixed. Individual enterprise, independent choice, and relatively free markets exist in centrally planned economies; and there is significant government involvement in market economies such as that of the United States.

15. One of the great debates in economics revolves around the tension between the advantages of free, unregulated markets and the desire for government involvement in the economy. Free markets produce what people want, and competition forces firms to adopt efficient production techniques. The need for government intervention arises because free markets are characterized by inefficiencies and an unequal distribution of income and experience regular periods of inflation and unemployment.

REVIEW TERMS AND CONCEPTS

absolute advantage, 29
capital, 25
command economy, 39
comparative advantage, 29
consumer goods, 31
consumer sovereignty, 40
economic growth, 35

factors of production (or factors), 26
free enterprise, 40
inputs or resources, 26
investment, 31
laissez-faire economy, 40
marginal rate of transformation (MRT), 34

market, 40
opportunity cost, 27
outputs, 26
production, 26
production possibility frontier (ppf), 31
theory of comparative advantage, 28

PROBLEM SET

1. For each of the following, describe some of the potential opportunity costs:
   a. Studying for your economics test
   b. Spending 2 hours playing computer games
   c. Buying a new car instead of keeping the old one
   d. A local community voting to raise property taxes to increase school expenditures and to reduce class size
   e. A number of countries working together to build a space station
   f. Going to graduate school

2. "As long as all resources are fully employed, and every firm in the economy is producing its output using the best available technology, the result will be efficient." Do you agree or disagree with the statement? Explain your answer.

3. You are an intern to the editor of a small-town newspaper in Mallsburg, Pennsylvania. Your boss, the editor, asks you to write the first draft of an editorial for this week's paper. Your assignment is to describe both the costs and the benefits of a new bridge across the railroad tracks in the center of town. Currently, most people who live in this town must drive 2 miles through thickly congested traffic to the existing bridge to get to the main shopping and employment center. The bridge will cost the citizens of Mallsburg $25 million, which will be paid for with a tax on their incomes over the next 20 years. What are the opportunity costs of building this bridge? What are the benefits that citizens will likely receive if the bridge is built? What other factors might you consider in writing this editorial?

4. Kristen and Anna live in the beach town of Santa Monica. They own a small business in which they make wristbands and potholders and sell them to people on the beach. Kristen can make 15 wristbands per hour but only 3 potholders. Anna is a bit slower and can make only 12 wristbands or 2 potholders in an hour.

	OUTPUT PER HOUR	
	Kristen	**Anna**
Wristbands	15	12
Potholders	3	2

   a. For Kristen and for Anna what is the opportunity cost of a potholder? Who has a comparative advantage in the production of potholders? Explain.
   b. Who has a comparative advantage in the production of wristbands? Explain.
   c. Assume that Kristen works 20 hours per week in the business. If Kristen were in business on her own, graph the possible

combinations of potholders and wristbands that she could produce in a week. Do the same for Anna.

   d. If Kristen devoted half of her time (10 out of 20 hours) to wristbands and half of her time to potholders, how many of each would she produce in a week? If Anna did the same, how many of each would she produce? How many wristbands and potholders would be produced in total?

   e. Suppose that Anna spent all 20 hours of her time on wristbands and Kristen spent 17 hours on potholders and 3 hours on wristbands. How many of each would be produced?

   f. Suppose that Kristen and Anna can sell all their wristbands for $1 each and all their potholders for $5.50 each. If each of them worked 20 hours per week, how should they split their time between wristbands and potholders? What is their maximum joint revenue?

5. Briefly describe the trade-offs involved in each of the following decisions. Specifically, list some of the opportunity costs associated with the decision, paying particular attention to the trade-offs between present and future consumption.

   a. After a stressful senior year in high school, Sherice decides to take the summer off instead of working before going to college.

   b. Frank is overweight and decides to work out every day and to go on a diet.

   c. Mei is very diligent about taking her car in for routine maintenance, even though it takes 2 hours of her time and costs $100 four times each year.

   d. Jim is in a big hurry. He runs a red light on the way to work.

*6. The countries of Figistan and Blah are small island countries in the South Pacific. Both produce fruit and timber. Each island has a labor force of 1,200. The table below gives production per month for each worker in each country:

	BASKETS OF FRUIT	BOARD FEET OF TIMBER
Figistan workers	10	5
Blah workers	30	10

Productivity of one worker for one month

   a. Which country has an absolute advantage in the production of fruit? Which country has an absolute advantage in the production of timber?

   b. Which country has a comparative advantage in the production of fruit? Of timber?

   c. Sketch the production possibility frontiers for both countries.

   d. Assuming no trading between the two, if both countries desired to have equal numbers of feet of timber and baskets of fruit, how would they allocate workers to the two sectors?

   e. Show that specialization and trade can move both countries beyond their production possibility frontiers.

7. Suppose that a simple society has an economy with only one resource, labor. Labor can be used to produce only two commodities—X, a necessity good (food), and Y, a luxury good (music and merriment). Suppose that the labor force consists of 100 workers. One laborer can produce either 5 units of necessity per month (by hunting and gathering) or 10 units of luxury per month (by writing songs, playing the guitar, dancing, and so on).

   a. On a graph, draw the economy's production possibility frontier (ppf). Where does the ppf intersect the Y-axis? Where does it intersect the X-axis? What meaning do those points have?

   b. Suppose the economy produced at a point *inside* the ppf. Give at least two reasons why this could occur. What could be done to move the economy to a point *on* the ppf?

   c. Suppose you succeeded in lifting your economy to a point on its ppf. What point would you choose? How might your small society decide the point at which it wanted to be?

   d. Once you have chosen a point on the ppf, you still need to decide how your society's product will be divided. If you were a dictator, how would you decide? What would happen if you left product distribution to the free market?

*8. Match each diagram in Figure 1 on the next page with its description below. Assume that the economy is producing or attempting to produce at point A, and most members of society like meat and not fish. Some descriptions apply to more than one diagram, and some diagrams have more than one description.

   a. Inefficient production of meat and fish

   b. Productive efficiency

   c. An inefficient mix of output

   d. Technological advances in the production of meat and fish

   e. The law of increasing opportunity cost

   f. An impossible combination of meat and fish

9. A nation with fixed quantities of resources is able to produce any of the following combinations of bread and ovens:

LOAVES OF BREAD (MILLIONS)	OVENS (THOUSANDS)
75	0
60	12
45	22
30	30
15	36
0	40

These figures assume that a certain number of previously produced ovens are available in the current period for baking bread.

   a. Using the data in the table, graph the ppf (with ovens on the vertical axis).

   b. Does the principle of "increasing opportunity cost" hold in this nation? Explain briefly. (*Hint:* What happens to the opportunity cost of bread—measured in number of ovens—as bread production increases?)

   c. If this country chooses to produce both ovens and bread, what will happen to the ppf over time? Why?

   Now suppose that a new technology is discovered that allows twice as many loaves of bread to be baked in each existing oven.

   d. Illustrate (on your original graph) the effect of this new technology on the production possibility curve.

   e. Suppose that before the new technology is introduced, the nation produces 22 ovens. After the new technology is introduced, the nation produces 30 ovens. What is the

---

*Note: Problems marked with an asterisk are more challenging.

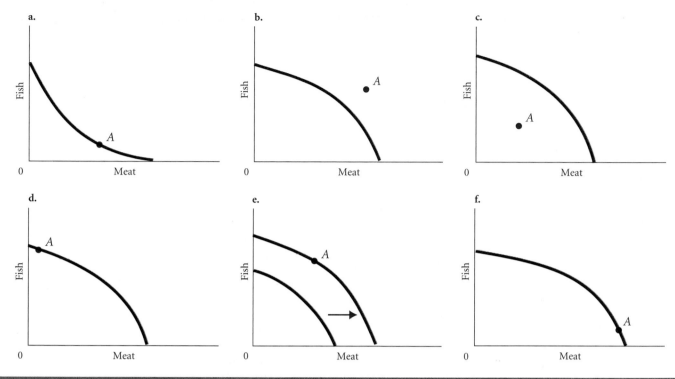

FIGURE 1

effect of the new technology on the production of bread? (Give the number of loaves before and after the change.)

10. Most college students work for pay at least part-time. The box on page 27 describes the decision to work or to hold a summer internship faced by a full-time student. Part-time students in most cases juggle school and work routinely, and all

students have faced the trade-offs that are associated with the allocation of time. Do you work during the school year? During the summer? What were the specific opportunity costs that you faced in deciding whether to work or not to work? How did you go about evaluating the alternative costs and benefits of working and not working?

Demand, Supply, and Market Equilibrium

3

Chapters 1 and 2 introduced the discipline, methodology, and subject matter of economics. We now begin the task of analyzing how a market economy actually works. This chapter and the next present an overview of the way individual markets work. They introduce some of the concepts needed to understand both microeconomics and macroeconomics.

As we proceed to define terms and make assumptions, it is important to keep in mind what we are doing. In Chapter 1 we explained what economic theory attempts to do. Theories are abstract representations of reality, like a map that represents a city. We believe that the models presented here will help you understand the workings of the economy just as a map helps you find your way around a city. Just as a map presents one view of the world, so too does any given theory of the economy. Alternatives exist to the theory that we present. We believe, however, that the basic model presented here, while sometimes abstract, is useful in gaining an understanding of how the economy works.

In the simple island society discussed in Chapter 2, Bill and Colleen solved the economic problem directly. They allocated their time and used the island's resources to satisfy their wants. Bill might be a farmer, Colleen a hunter and carpenter. He might be a civil engineer, she a doctor. Exchange occurred, but complex markets were not necessary.

In societies of many people, however, production must satisfy wide-ranging tastes and preferences. Producers therefore specialize. Farmers produce more food than they can eat so that they can sell it to buy manufactured goods. Physicians are paid for specialized services, as are attorneys, construction workers, and editors. When there is specialization, there must be exchange, and *markets* are the institutions through which exchange takes place.

This chapter begins to explore the basic forces at work in market systems. The purpose of our discussion is to explain how the individual decisions of households and firms together, without any central planning or direction, answer the three basic questions: What gets produced, how is it produced, and who gets what is produced? We begin with some definitions.

FIRMS AND HOUSEHOLDS: THE BASIC DECISION-MAKING UNITS

Throughout this book, we discuss and analyze the behavior of two fundamental decision-making units: *firms*—the primary producing units in an economy—and *households*—the consuming units in an economy. Both are made up of people performing different functions and playing different roles. In essence, what we are developing is a theory of human behavior.

firm An organization that transforms resources (inputs) into products (outputs). Firms are the primary producing units in a market economy.

A **firm** exists when a person or a group of people decides to produce a product or products by transforming *inputs*—that is, resources in the broadest sense—into *outputs*, the products that are sold in the market. Some firms produce goods; others produce services. Some are large, many are small, and some are in between. All firms exist to transform resources into things that people want. The Colorado Symphony Orchestra takes labor, land, a building, musically talented people, instruments, and other inputs and combines them to produce concerts. The production process can be extremely complicated. For example, the first flautist in the orchestra uses training, talent, previous performance experience, score, instrument, conductor's interpretation, and personal feelings about the music to produce just one contribution to an overall performance.

Most firms exist to make a profit for their owners, but some do not. Columbia University, for example, fits the description of a firm: It takes inputs in the form of labor, land, skills, books, and buildings and produces a service that we call education. Although it sells that service for a price, it does not exist to make a profit, but instead to provide education of the highest quality possible.

Still, most firms exist to make a profit. They engage in production because they can sell their product for more than it costs to produce it. The analysis of firm behavior that follows rests on the assumption that *firms make decisions in order to maximize profits*.

entrepreneur A person who organizes, manages, and assumes the risks of a firm, taking a new idea or a new product and turning it into a successful business.

An **entrepreneur** is one who organizes, manages, and assumes the risks of a firm. When a new firm is created, someone must organize the new firm, arrange financing, hire employees, and take risks. That person is an entrepreneur. Sometimes existing companies introduce new products, and sometimes new firms develop or improve on an old idea, but at the root of it all is entrepreneurship, which some see as the core of the free enterprise system.

At the heart of the debate about the potential of free enterprise in formerly socialist Eastern Europe is the question of entrepreneurship. Does an entrepreneurial spirit exist in that part of the world? If not, can it be developed? Without it, the free enterprise system breaks down.

households The consuming units in an economy.

The consuming units in an economy are **households**. A household may consist of any number of people: a single person living alone, a married couple with four children, or 15 unrelated people sharing a house. Household decisions are presumably based on individual tastes and preferences. The household buys what it wants and can afford. In a large, heterogeneous, and open society such as the United States, wildly different tastes find expression in the marketplace. A six-block walk in any direction on any street in Manhattan or a drive from the Chicago Loop south into rural Illinois should be enough to convince someone that it is difficult to generalize about what people like and do not like.

Even though households have wide-ranging preferences, they also have some things in common. All—even the very rich—have ultimately limited incomes, and all must pay in some way for the things they consume. Although households may have some control over their incomes—they can work more hours or fewer hours—they are also constrained by the availability of jobs, current wages, their own abilities, and their accumulated and inherited wealth (or lack thereof).

INPUT MARKETS AND OUTPUT MARKETS: THE CIRCULAR FLOW

product or output markets The markets in which goods and services are exchanged.

Households and firms interact in two basic kinds of markets: product (or output) markets and input (or factor) markets. Goods and services that are intended for use by households are exchanged in **product** or **output markets**. In output markets, firms *supply* and households *demand*.

To produce goods and services, firms must buy resources in **input** or **factor markets**. Firms buy inputs from households, which supply these inputs. When a firm decides how much to produce (supply) in output markets, it must simultaneously decide how much of each input it needs to produce the desired level of output. To produce automobiles, Ford Motor Company must use many inputs, including tires, steel, complicated machinery, and many different kinds of labor.

Figure 3.1 shows the *circular flow* of economic activity through a simple market economy. Note that the flow reflects the direction in which goods and services flow through input and output markets. For example, goods and services flow from firms to households through output markets. Labor services flow from households to firms through input markets. Payment (most often in money form) for goods and services flows in the opposite direction.

In input markets, households *supply* resources. Most households earn their incomes by working—they supply their labor in the **labor market** to firms that demand labor and pay workers for their time and skills. Households may also loan their accumulated or inherited savings to firms for interest, or exchange those savings for claims to future profits, as when a household buys shares of stock in a corporation. In the **capital market**, households supply the funds that firms use to buy capital goods. Households may also supply land or other real property in exchange for rent in the **land market**.

Inputs into the production process are also called **factors of production**. Land, labor, and capital are the three key factors of production. Throughout this text, we use the terms *input* and *factor of production* interchangeably. Thus, input markets and factor markets mean the same thing.

input or factor markets
The markets in which the resources used to produce products are exchanged.

labor market The input/factor market in which households supply work for wages to firms that demand labor.
capital market The input/factor market in which households supply their savings, for interest or for claims to future profits, to firms that demand funds to buy capital goods.

land market The input/factor market in which households supply land or other real property in exchange for rent.

factors of production The inputs into the production process. Land, labor, and capital are the three key factors of production.

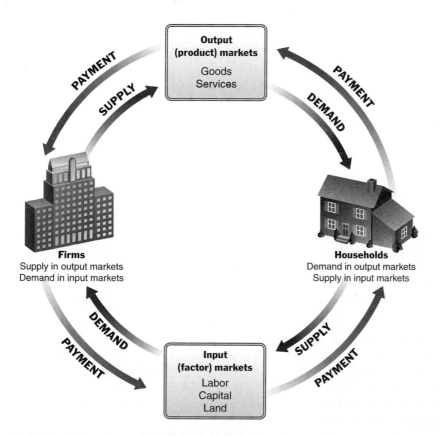

FIGURE 3.1 The Circular Flow of Economic Activity

Diagrams like this one show the circular flow of economic activity, hence the name *circular flow diagram*. Here, goods and services flow clockwise: Labor services supplied by households flow to firms, and goods and services produced by firms flow to households. Payment (usually money) flows in the opposite (counterclockwise) direction: Payment for goods and services flows from households to firms, and payment for labor services flows from firms to households.

Note: Color Guide—In Figure 3.1 households are depicted in blue and firms are depicted in *red*. From now on all diagrams relating to the behavior of households will be blue or shades of blue, and all diagrams relating to the behavior of firms will be in red or shades of red.

Early economics texts included entrepreneurship as a type of input, just like land, labor, and capital. Treating entrepreneurship as a separate factor of production has fallen out of favor, however, partially because it is unmeasurable. Most economists today implicitly assume that it is in plentiful supply. That is, if profit opportunities exist, it is likely that entrepreneurs will crop up to take advantage of them. This assumption has turned out to be a good predictor of actual economic behavior and performance.

The supply of inputs and their prices ultimately determine household income. The amount of income a household earns thus depends on the decisions it makes concerning what types of inputs it chooses to supply. Whether to stay in school, how much and what kind of training to get, whether to start a business, how many hours to work, whether to work at all, and how to invest savings are all household decisions that affect income.

As you can see:

> Input and output markets are connected through the behavior of both firms and households. Firms determine the quantities and character of outputs produced and the types of quantities of inputs demanded. Households determine the types and quantities of products demanded and the quantities and types of inputs supplied.[1]

The following analysis of demand and supply will lead up to a theory of how market prices are determined. Prices are determined by the interaction between demanders and suppliers. To understand this interaction, we first need to know how product prices influence the behavior of demanders and suppliers *separately*. We therefore discuss output markets by focusing first on demanders, then on suppliers, and finally on their interaction.

DEMAND IN PRODUCT/OUTPUT MARKETS

In real life, households make many decisions at the same time. To see how the forces of demand and supply work, however, let us focus first on the amount of a *single* product that an *individual* household decides to consume within some given period of time, such as a month or a year.

> A household's decision about what quantity of a particular output, or product, to demand depends on a number of factors including:
>
> - The *price of the product* in question
> - The *income available* to the household
> - The household's *amount of accumulated wealth*
> - The *prices of other products* available to the household
> - The household's *tastes and preferences*
> - The household's *expectations* about future income, wealth, and prices

quantity demanded The amount (number of units) of a product that a household would buy in a given period if it could buy all it wanted at the current market price.

Quantity demanded is the amount (number of units) of a product that a household would buy in a given period *if it could buy all it wanted at the current market price*. Of course, the amount of a product that households finally purchase depends on the amount of product actually available in the market. The phrase *if it could buy all it wanted* is critical to the definition of quantity demanded because it allows for the possibility that quantity supplied and quantity demanded are unequal.

---

[1] Our description of markets begins with the behavior of firms and households. Modern orthodox economic theory essentially combines two distinct but closely related theories of behavior. The "theory of household behavior," or "consumer behavior," has its roots in the works of nineteenth-century utilitarians such as Jeremy Bentham, William Jevons, Carl Menger, Leon Walras, Vilfredo Parcto, and F.Y. Edgeworth. The "theory of the firm" developed out of the earlier classical political economy of Adam Smith, David Ricardo, and Thomas Malthus. In 1890, Alfred Marshall published the first of many editions of his *Principles of Economics*. That volume pulled together the main themes of both the classical economists and the utilitarians into what is now called "neoclassical economics." While there have been many changes over the years, the basic structure of the model that we build can be found in Marshall's work.

The most important relationship in individual markets is that between market price and quantity demanded. For this reason, we need to begin our discussion by analyzing the likely response of households to changes in price using the device of *ceteris paribus*, or "all else equal." That is, we will attempt to derive a relationship between the quantity demanded of a good per time period and the price of that good, holding income, wealth, other prices, tastes, and expectations constant.

It is very important to distinguish between price changes, which affect the quantity of a good demanded, and changes in other factors (such as income), which change the entire relationship between price and quantity. For example, if a family begins earning a higher income, it might buy more of a good at every possible price. To be sure that we distinguish between changes in price and other changes that affect demand, we will throughout the rest of the text be very precise about terminology. Specifically:

> Changes in the price of a product affect the *quantity demanded* per period. Changes in any other factor, such as income or preferences, affect *demand*. Thus, we say that an increase in the price of Coca-Cola is likely to cause a decrease in the *quantity of Coca-Cola demanded*. However, we say that an increase in income is likely to cause an increase in the *demand* for most goods.

PRICE AND QUANTITY DEMANDED: THE LAW OF DEMAND

A **demand schedule** shows the quantities of a product that a household would be willing to buy at different prices. Table 3.1 presents a hypothetical demand schedule for Anna, a student who goes off to college to study economics while her boyfriend goes to art school. If telephone calls were free (a price of zero), Anna would call her boyfriend every day, or 30 times a month. At a price of $.50 per call, she makes 25 calls a month. When the price hits $3.50, she cuts back to seven calls a month. This same information presented graphically is called a **demand curve**. Anna's demand curve is presented in Figure 3.2.

You will note in Figure 3.2 that *quantity* (*q*) is measured along the horizontal axis, and *price* (*P*) is measured along the vertical axis. This is the convention we follow throughout this book.

Demand Curves Slope Downward   The data in Table 3.1 show that at lower prices, Anna calls her boyfriend more frequently; at higher prices, she calls less frequently. There is thus a *negative, or inverse, relationship between quantity demanded and price*. When price rises, quantity demanded falls, and when price falls, quantity demanded rises. Thus demand curves always slope downward. This negative relationship between price and quantity demanded is often referred to as the **law of demand**, a term first used by economist Alfred Marshall in his 1890 textbook.

Some people are put off by the abstraction of demand curves. Of course, we do not actually draw our own demand curves for products. When we want to make a purchase, we usually face only a single price, and how much we would buy at other prices is irrelevant. However, demand

demand schedule A table showing how much of a given product a household would be willing to buy at different prices.

demand curve A graph illustrating how much of a given product a household would be willing to buy at different prices.

law of demand The negative relationship between price and quantity demanded: As price rises, quantity demanded decreases. As price falls, quantity demanded increases.

TABLE 3.1 Anna's Demand Schedule for Telephone Calls

PRICE (PER CALL)	QUANTITY DEMANDED (CALLS PER MONTH)
$ 0	30
.50	25
3.50	7
7.00	3
10.00	1
15.00	0

FIGURE 3.2 Anna's Demand Curve

The relationship between price *(P)* and quantity demanded *(q)* presented graphically is called a demand curve. Demand curves have a negative slope, indicating that lower prices cause quantity demanded to increase. Note that Anna's demand curve is blue; demand in product markets is determined by house-hold choice.

curves help analysts understand the kind of behavior that households are *likely* to exhibit if they are actually faced with a higher or lower price. We know, for example, that if the price of a good rises enough, the quantity demanded must ultimately drop to zero. The demand curve is thus a tool that helps us explain economic behavior and predict reactions to possible price changes.

Marshall's definition of a social "law" captures the idea:

> The term "law" means nothing more than a general proposition or statement of tendencies, more or less certain, more or less definite . . . a *social law* is a statement of social tendencies; that is, that a certain course of action may be expected from the members of a social group under certain conditions.[2]

It seems reasonable to expect that consumers will demand more of a product at a lower price and less of it at a higher price. Households must divide their incomes over a wide range of goods and services. If I spend $4.50 for a pound of prime beef, I am sacrificing the other things that I might have bought with that $4.50. If the price of prime beef were to jump to $7 per pound, while chicken breasts remained at $1.99 (remember *ceteris paribus*—we are holding all else constant), I would have to give up more chicken and/or other items to buy that pound of beef. So I would probably eat more chicken and less beef. Anna calls her boyfriend three times when phone calls cost $7 each. A fourth call would mean sacrificing $7 worth of other purchases. At a price of $3.50, however, the opportunity cost of each call is lower, and she calls more frequently.

Another explanation for the fact that demand curves slope downward rests on the notion of *utility*. Economists use the concept of *utility* to mean happiness or satisfaction. Presumably, we consume goods and services because they give us utility. As we consume more of a product within a given period of time, it is likely that each additional unit consumed will yield successively less satisfaction. The utility I gain from a second ice cream cone is likely to be less than the utility I gained from the first; the third is worth even less; and so forth. This *law of diminishing marginal utility* is an important concept in economics. If each successive unit of a good is worth less to me, I am not going to be willing to pay as much for it. It is thus reasonable to expect a downward slope in the demand curve for that good.

---

[2]Alfred Marshall, *Principles of Economics*, 8th ed. (New York: Macmillan, 1948), p. 33. (The first edition was published in 1890.)

The idea of diminishing marginal utility also helps to explain Anna's behavior. The demand curve is a way of representing what she is willing to pay per phone call. At a price of $7, she calls her boyfriend three times per month. A fourth call, however, is worth less than the third—that is, the fourth call is worth less than $7 to her—so she stops at three. If the price were only $3.50, however, she would keep right on calling. Even at $3.50, she would stop at seven calls per month. This behavior reveals that the eighth call has less value to Anna than the seventh.

Thinking about the ways that people are affected by price changes also helps us see what is behind the law of demand. Consider this example: Luis lives and works in Mexico City. His elderly mother lives in Santiago, Chile. Last year, the airlines servicing South America got into a price war, and the price of flying between Mexico City and Santiago dropped from 20,000 pesos to 10,000 pesos. How might Luis's behavior change?

First, he is better off. Last year he flew home to Chile three times at a total cost of 60,000 pesos. This year he can fly to Chile the same number of times, buy exactly the same combination of other goods and services that he bought last year, and have 30,000 pesos left over. Because he is better off—his income can buy more—he may fly home more frequently. Second, the opportunity cost of flying home has changed. Before the price war, Luis had to sacrifice 20,000 pesos worth of other goods and services each time he flew to Chile. After the price war he must sacrifice only 10,000 pesos worth of other goods and services for each trip. The trade-off has changed. Both of these effects are likely to lead to a higher quantity demanded in response to the lower price.

In sum:

> It is reasonable to expect quantity demanded to fall when price rises, *ceteris paribus*, and to expect quantity demanded to rise when price falls, *ceteris paribus*. Demand curves have a negative slope.

Other Properties of Demand Curves

Two additional things are notable about Anna's demand curve. First, it intersects the *Y*-, or price, axis. This means that there is a price above which no calls will be made. In this case, Anna simply stops calling when the price reaches $15 per call.

> As long as households have limited incomes and wealth, all demand curves will intersect the price axis. For any commodity, there is always a price above which a household will not, or cannot, pay. Even if the good or service is very important, all households are ultimately constrained, or limited, by income and wealth.

Second, Anna's demand curve intersects the *X*-, or quantity, axis. Even at a zero price, there is a limit to the number of phone calls Anna will make. If telephone calls were free, she would call 30 times a month, but not more.

> That demand curves intersect the quantity axis is a matter of common sense. Demand in a given period of time is limited, if only by time, even at a zero price.

To summarize what we know about the shape of demand curves:

1. They have a negative slope. An increase in price is likely to lead to a decrease in quantity demanded, and a decrease in price is likely to lead to an increase in quantity demanded.
2. They intersect the quantity (*X*-) axis, a result of time limitations and diminishing marginal utility.
3. They intersect the price (*Y*-) axis, a result of limited incomes and wealth.

That is all we can say; it is not possible to generalize further. The actual shape of an individual household demand curve—whether it is steep or flat, whether it is bowed in or bowed out—depends on the unique tastes and preferences of the household and other factors. Some households may be very sensitive to price changes; other households may respond little to a change in price. In some cases, plentiful substitutes are available; in other cases, they are not. Thus, to fully understand the shape and position of demand curves, we must turn to the other determinants of household demand.

OTHER DETERMINANTS OF HOUSEHOLD DEMAND

Of the many factors likely to influence a household's demand for a specific product, we have considered only the price of the product itself. Other determining factors include household income and wealth, the prices of other goods and services, tastes and preferences, and expectations.

Income and Wealth Before we proceed, we need to define two terms that are often confused, *income* and *wealth*. A household's **income** is the sum of all the wages, salaries, profits, interest payments, rents, and other forms of earnings received by the household *in a given period of time*. Income is thus a *flow* measure: We must specify a time period for it—income *per month* or *per year*. You can spend or consume more or less than your income in any given period. If you consume less than your income, you save. To consume more than your income in a period, you must either borrow or draw on savings accumulated from previous periods.

Wealth is the total value of what a household owns less what it owes. Another word for wealth is **net worth**—the amount a household would have left if it sold off all its possessions and paid off all its debts. Wealth is a *stock* measure: It is measured at a given point in time. If, in a given period, you spend less than your income, you save; the amount that you save is added to your wealth. Saving is the flow that affects the stock of wealth. When you spend more than your income, you *dissave*—you reduce your wealth.

Households with higher incomes and higher accumulated savings or inherited wealth can afford to buy more things. In general, we would expect higher demand at higher levels of income/wealth and lower demand at lower levels of income/wealth. Goods for which demand goes up when income is higher and for which demand goes down when income is lower are called **normal goods**. Movie tickets, restaurant meals, telephone calls, and shirts are all normal goods.

However, generalization in economics can be hazardous. Sometimes demand for a good falls when household income rises. Consider, for example, the various qualities of meat available. When a household's income rises, it is likely to buy higher-quality meats—its demand for filet mignon is likely to rise—but its demand for lower-quality meats—chuck steak, for example—is likely to fall. Transportation is another example. At higher incomes, people can afford to fly. People who can afford to fly are less likely to take the bus long distances. Thus, higher income may *reduce* the number of times someone takes a bus. Goods for which demand tends to fall when income rises are called **inferior goods**.

Prices of Other Goods and Services No consumer decides in isolation on the amount of any one commodity to buy. Instead, each decision is part of a larger set of decisions that are made simultaneously. Households must apportion their incomes over many different goods and services. As a result, the price of any one good can and does affect the demand for other goods.

This is most obviously the case when goods are substitutes for one another. To return to our lonesome first-year student: If the price of a telephone call rises to $10, Anna will call her boyfriend only once a month (see Table 3.1). Of course, she can get in touch with him in other ways. Presumably she substitutes some other, less costly, form of communication, such as writing more letters or sending more e-mails.

When an *increase* in the price of one good causes demand for another good to *increase* (a positive relationship), we say that the goods are **substitutes**. A *fall* in the price of a good causes a *decline* in demand for its substitutes. Substitutes are goods that can serve as replacements for one another.

To be substitutes, two products do not need to be identical. Identical products are called **perfect substitutes**. Japanese cars are not identical to American cars. Nonetheless, all have four wheels, are capable of carrying people, and run on gasoline. Thus, significant changes in the price of one country's cars can be expected to influence demand for the other country's

income The sum of all a household's wages, salaries, profits, interest payments, rents, and other forms of earnings in a given period of time. It is a flow measure.

wealth or **net worth** The total value of what a household owns minus what it owes. It is a stock measure.

normal goods Goods for which demand goes up when income is higher and for which demand goes down when income is lower.

inferior goods Goods for which demand tends to fall when income rises.

substitutes Goods that can serve as replacements for one another; when the price of one increases, demand for the other goes up.

perfect substitutes Identical products.

cars. Restaurant meals are substitutes for meals eaten at home, and flying from New York to Washington is a substitute for taking the train.

Often, two products "go together"—that is, they complement each other. Our lonesome letter writer, for example, will find her demand for stamps and stationery rising as she writes more letters, and her demand for Internet access rising as she sends more e-mails. Bacon and eggs are **complementary goods**, as are cars and gasoline, and cameras and film. When two goods are complements, a *decrease* in the price of one results in *increase* in demand for the other, and vice versa.

Because any one good may have many potential substitutes and complements at the same time, a single price change may affect a household's demands for many goods simultaneously; the demand for some of these products may rise while the demand for others may fall. For example, consider the compact disc read-only memory (CD-ROM). Massive amounts of data can be stored digitally on CDs that can be read by personal computers with a CD-ROM drive. When these drives first came on the market they were quite expensive, selling for several hundred dollars each. Now they are much less expensive, and most new computers have them built in. As a result, the demand for CD-ROM discs (complementary goods) has soared. As more and more students adopted the CD technology and the price of CDs and CD hardware fell, fewer bought printed reference books such as encyclopedias and dictionaries (substitute goods).

complements, complementary goods
Goods that "go together"; a decrease in the price of one results in an increase in demand for the other, and vice versa.

Running shoes are substitutes, but not perfect substitutes.

Tastes and Preferences Income, wealth, and prices of goods available are the three factors that determine the combinations of things that a household is *able* to buy. You know that you cannot afford to rent an apartment at $1,200 per month if your monthly income is only $400, but within these constraints, you are more or less free to choose what to buy. Your final choice depends on your individual tastes and preferences.

Changes in preferences can and do manifest themselves in market behavior. Thirty years ago the major big-city marathons drew only a few hundred runners. Now tens of thousands enter and run. The demand for running shoes, running suits, stopwatches, and other running items has greatly increased. For many years people drank soda for refreshment. Today convenience stores are filled with a dizzying array of iced teas, fruit juices, natural beverages, and mineral waters.

Within the constraints of prices and incomes, preference shapes the demand curve, but it is difficult to generalize about tastes and preferences. First, they are volatile: Five years ago, more people smoked cigarettes and fewer people had computers. Second, they are idiosyncratic: Some people like to talk on the telephone, whereas others prefer the written word; some people prefer dogs, whereas others are crazy about cats; some people like chicken wings, whereas others prefer legs. The diversity of individual demands is almost infinite.

Expectations What you decide to buy today certainly depends on today's prices and your current income and wealth. You also have expectations about what your position will be in the future. You may have expectations about future changes in prices, too, and these may affect your decisions today.

There are many examples of the ways expectations affect demand. When people buy a house or a car, they often must borrow part of the purchase price and repay it over a number of years. In deciding what kind of house or car to buy, they presumably must think about their income today, as well as what their income is likely to be in the future.

As another example, consider a student in the final year of medical school living on a scholarship of $12,000. Compare that student with another person earning $6 an hour at a full-time job, with no expectation of a significant change in income in the future. The two have virtually identical incomes because there are about 2,000 working hours in a year (40 hours per week × 50 work weeks per year). But even if they have the same tastes, the medical student is likely to demand different things, simply because of the expectation of a major increase in income later on.

Increasingly, economic theory has come to recognize the importance of expectations. We will devote a good deal of time to discussing how expectations affect more than just demand. For the time being, however, it is important to understand that demand depends on more than just *current* incomes, prices, and tastes.

SHIFT OF DEMAND VERSUS MOVEMENT ALONG A DEMAND CURVE

Recall that a demand curve shows the relationship between quantity demanded and the price of a good. Such demand curves are derived while holding income, tastes, and other prices constant. If this condition of *ceteris paribus* were relaxed, we would have to derive an entirely new relationship between price and quantity.

Let us return once again to Anna (see Table 3.1 and Figure 3.2). Suppose that when we derived the demand schedule in Table 3.1, Anna had a part-time job that paid $300 per month. Now suppose that her parents inherit some money and begin sending her an additional $300 per month. Assuming that she keeps her job, Anna's income is now $600 per month.

With her higher income, Anna would probably call her boyfriend more frequently, regardless of the price of a call. Table 3.2 and Figure 3.3 present Anna's original income schedule (D_0) and increased income demand schedule (D_1). At $.50 per call, the frequency of her calls (the quantity she demands) increases from 25 to 33 calls per month; at $3.50 per call, frequency increases from 7 to 18 calls per month; at $10 per call, frequency increases from 1 to 7 calls per month. (Note in Figure 3.3 that even if calls are free, Anna's income matters; at zero price, her demand increases. With a higher income, she may visit her boyfriend more, for example, and more visits might mean more phone calls to organize and plan.)

The fact that demand *increased* when income increased implies that telephone calls are *normal goods* to Anna.

The conditions that were in place at the time we drew the original demand curve have now changed. In other words, a factor that affects Anna's demand for telephone calls (in this case, her income) has changed, and there is now a new relationship between price and quantity demanded. Such a change is referred to as a **shift of the demand curve**.

It is very important to distinguish between a change in quantity demanded—that is, some movement *along* a demand curve—and a shift of demand. Demand schedules and demand curves show the relationship between the price of a good or service and the quantity demanded per period, *ceteris paribus*. If price changes, quantity demanded will change—this is a **movement along the demand curve**. When any of the *other* factors that influence demand change, however, a new relationship between price and quantity demanded is established—this is a *shift of the demand curve*. The result, then, is a *new* demand curve. Changes in income, preferences, or prices of other goods cause the demand curve to shift:

shift of a demand curve The change that takes place in a demand curve corresponding to a new relationship between quantity demanded of a good and price of that good. The shift is brought about by a change in the original conditions.

movement along a demand curve The change in quantity demanded brought about by a change in price.

> Change in price of a good or service
> leads to
> → Change in *quantity demanded* (**movement along the demand curve**).
> Change in income, preferences, or prices of other goods or services
> leads to
> → Change in *demand* (**shift of the demand curve**).

TABLE 3.2 Shift of Anna's Demand Schedule Due to Increase in Income

Price (Per Call)	SCHEDULE D_0 Quantity Demanded (Calls Per Month at an Income of $300 Per Month)	SCHEDULE D_1 Quantity Demanded (Calls Per Month at an Income of $600 Per Month)
$ 0	30	35
.50	25	33
3.50	7	18
7.00	3	12
10.00	1	7
15.00	0	2
20.00	0	0

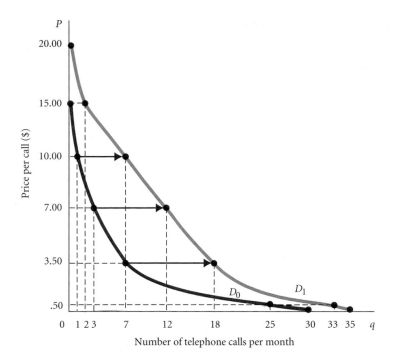

FIGURE 3.3 Shift of a Demand Curve Following a Rise in Income

When the price of a good changes, we move *along* the demand curve for that good. When any other factor that influences demand changes (income, tastes, and so on), the relationship between price and quantity is different; there is a *shift* of the demand curve, in this case from D_0 to D_1. Telephone calls are normal goods.

Figure 3.4 illustrates the differences between movement along a demand curve and shifting demand curves. In Figure 3.4(a), an increase in household income causes demand for hamburger (an inferior good) to decline, or shift to the left from D_0 to D_1. (Because quantity is measured on the horizontal axis, a decrease means a *shift to the left*.) In contrast, demand for steak (a normal good) increases, or *shifts to the right*, when income rises.

In Figure 3.4(b), an increase in the price of hamburger from $1.49 to $3.09 a pound causes a household to buy less hamburger each month. In other words, the higher price causes the *quantity demanded* to decline from 10 pounds to 5 pounds per month. This change represents a movement *along* the demand curve for hamburger. In place of hamburger, the household buys more chicken. The household's demand for chicken (a substitute for hamburger) rises—the demand curve shifts to the right. At the same time, the demand for catsup (a good that complements hamburger) declines—its demand curve shifts to the left.

FROM HOUSEHOLD DEMAND TO MARKET DEMAND

Market demand is simply the sum of all the quantities of a good or service demanded per period by all the households buying in the market for that good or service. Figure 3.5 shows the derivation of a market demand curve from three individual demand curves. (Although this market demand curve is derived from the behavior of only three people, most markets have thousands or even millions of demanders.) As the table in Figure 3.5 shows, when the price of a pound of coffee is $3.50, both A and C would purchase 4 pounds per month, while B would buy none. At that price, presumably, B drinks tea. Market demand at $3.50 would thus be a total of 4 + 4 or 8 pounds. At a price of $1.50 per pound, however, A would purchase 8 pounds per month; B, 3 pounds; and C, 9 pounds. Thus, at $1.50 per pound, market demand would be 8 + 3 + 9, or 20 pounds of coffee per month.

The total quantity demanded in the marketplace at a given price is simply the sum of all the quantities demanded by all the individual households shopping in the market *at that price*. A market demand curve shows the total amount of a product that would be sold at each price if households could buy all they wanted at that price. As Figure 3.5 shows, the market demand curve is the sum of all the individual demand curves—that is, the sum of all

market demand The sum of all the quantities of a good or service demanded per period by all the households buying in the market for that good or service.

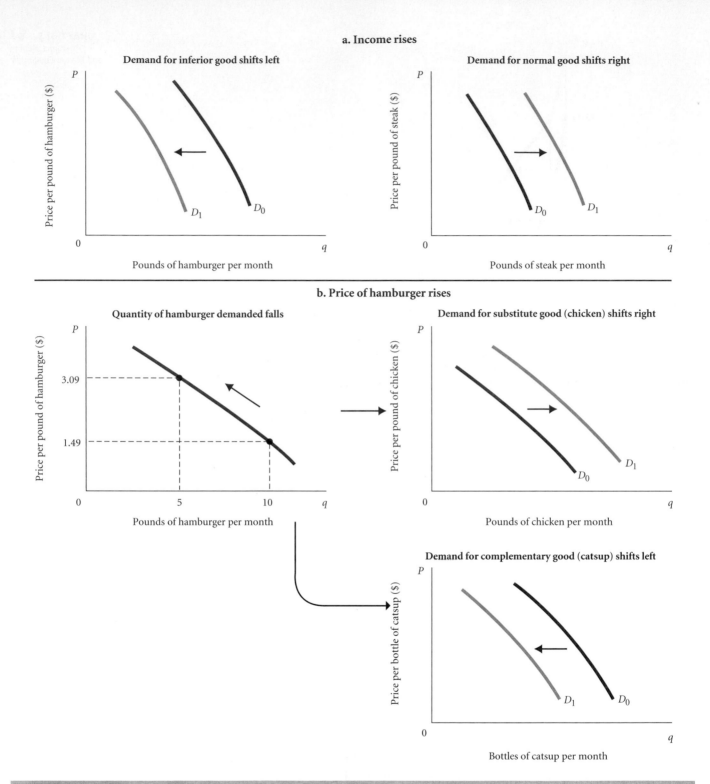

FIGURE 3.4 Shifts versus Movement along a Demand Curve

a. When income increases, the demand for inferior goods *shifts to the left* and the demand for normal goods *shifts to the right*. **b.** If the price of hamburger rises, the quantity of hamburger demanded declines—this is a movement along the demand curve. The same price rise for hamburger would shift the demand for chicken (a substitute for hamburger) to the right and the demand for catsup (a complement to hamburger) to the left.

the individual quantities demanded at each price. The market demand curve thus takes its shape and position from the shapes, positions, and number of individual demand curves. If more people decide to shop in a market, more demand curves must be added, and the market demand curve will shift to the right. Market demand curves may also shift as a result of preference changes, income changes, or changes in the number of demanders.

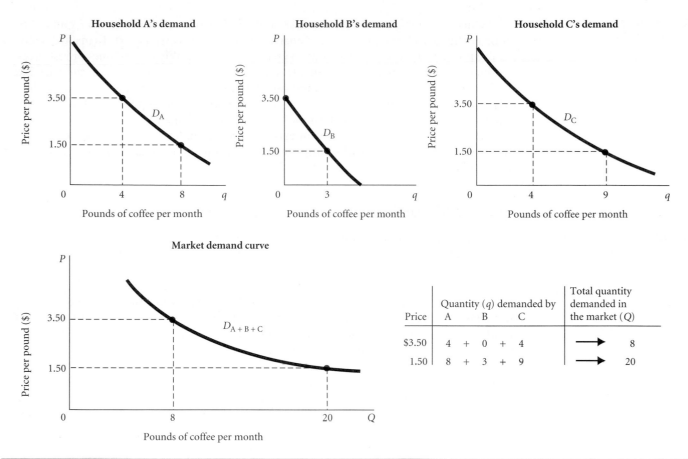

FIGURE 3.5 Deriving Market Demand from Individual Demand Curves

Total demand in the marketplace is simply the sum of the demands of all the households shopping in a particular market. It is the sum of all the individual demand curves—that is, the sum of all the individual quantities demanded at each price.

As a general rule throughout this book, capital letters refer to the entire market and lower-case letters refer to individual households or firms. Thus, in Figure 3.5, Q refers to total quantity demanded in the market, while q refers to the quantity demanded by individual households.

SUPPLY IN PRODUCT/OUTPUT MARKETS

In addition to dealing with household demands for outputs, economic theory deals with the behavior of business firms, which supply in output markets and demand in input markets (see again Figure 3.1). Firms engage in production, and we assume that they do so for profit. Successful firms make profits because they are able to sell their products for more than it costs to produce them.

Supply decisions can thus be expected to depend on profit potential. Because **profit** is the simple difference between revenues and costs, supply is likely to react to changes in revenues and changes in production costs. The amount of revenue earned by a firm depends on the price of its product in the market and on how much it sells. Costs of production depend on many factors, the most important of which are (1) the kinds of inputs needed to produce the product, (2) the amount of each input required, and (3) the prices of inputs.

The supply decision is just one of several decisions that firms make to maximize profit. There are usually a number of ways to produce any given product. A golf course can be built by hundreds of workers with shovels and grass seed or by a few workers with heavy earth-moving equipment and sod blankets. Hamburgers can be fried individually by a short-order cook or grilled by the hundreds on a mechanized moving grill. Firms must choose the production technique most appropriate to their products and projected levels of production. The best method of production is the one that minimizes cost, thus maximizing profit.

profit The difference between revenues and costs.

Which production technique is best, in turn, depends on the prices of inputs. Where labor is cheap and machinery is expensive and difficult to transport, firms are likely to choose production techniques that use a great deal of labor. Where machines or resources to produce machines are readily available and labor is scarce or expensive, they are likely to choose more capital-intensive methods. Obviously, the technique ultimately chosen determines input requirements. Thus, by choosing an output supply target and the most appropriate technology, firms determine which inputs to demand.

With the caution that no decision exists in a vacuum, let us begin our examination of firm behavior by focusing on the output supply decision and the relationship between quantity supplied and output price, *ceteris paribus*.

PRICE AND QUANTITY SUPPLIED: THE LAW OF SUPPLY

quantity supplied The amount of a particular product that a firm would be willing and able to offer for sale at a particular price during a given time period.

supply schedule A table showing how much of a product firms will sell at different prices.

Quantity supplied is the amount of a particular product that a firm would be willing and able to offer for sale at a particular price during a given time period. A **supply schedule** shows how much of a product a firm will sell at alternative prices. Table 3.3 itemizes the quantities of soybeans that an individual farmer such as Clarence Brown might sell at various prices. If the market paid $1.50 or less a bushel for soybeans, Brown would not supply any soybeans. For one thing, it costs more than $1.50 to produce a bushel of soybeans; for another, Brown can use his land more profitably to produce something else. At $1.75 per bushel, however, at least some soybean production takes place on Brown's farm, and a price increase from $1.75 to $2.25 per bushel causes the quantity supplied by Brown to increase from 10,000 to 20,000 bushels per year. The higher price may justify shifting land from wheat to soybean production or putting previously fallow land into soybeans, or it may lead to more intensive farming of land already in soybeans, using expensive fertilizer or equipment that was not cost-justified at the lower price.

Generalizing from Farmer Brown's experience, we can reasonably expect an increase in market price, *ceteris paribus*, to lead to an increase in quantity supplied. In other words, there is a positive relationship between the quantity of a good supplied and price. This statement sums up the **law of supply**: An increase in market price will lead to an increase in quantity supplied, and a decrease in market price will lead to a decrease in quantity supplied.

law of supply The positive relationship between price and quantity of a good supplied: An increase in market price will lead to an increase in quantity supplied, and a decrease in market price will lead to a decrease in quantity supplied.

supply curve A graph illustrating how much of a product a firm will sell at different prices.

The information in a supply schedule may be presented graphically in a **supply curve**. Supply curves slope upward. The upward, or positive, slope of Brown's curve in Figure 3.6 reflects this positive relationship between price and quantity supplied.

Note in Brown's supply schedule, however, that when price rises from $4 to $5, quantity supplied no longer increases. Often an individual firm's ability to respond to an increase in price is constrained by its existing scale of operations, or capacity, in the short run. For example, Brown's ability to produce more soybeans depends on the size of his farm, the fertility of his soil, and the types of equipment he has. The fact that output stays constant at 45,000 bushels per year suggests that he is running up against the limits imposed by the size of his farm, the quality of his soil, and his existing technology.

In the longer run, however, Brown may acquire more land, or technology may change, allowing for more soybean production. The terms *short run* and *long run* have very precise meanings in economics; we will discuss them in detail later. Here it is important only to understand that time plays a critical role in supply decisions. When prices change, firms'

TABLE 3.3 Clarence Brown's Supply Schedule for Soybeans

PRICE (PER BUSHEL)	QUANTITY SUPPLIED (BUSHELS PER YEAR)
$1.50	0
1.75	10,000
2.25	20,000
3.00	30,000
4.00	45,000
5.00	45,000

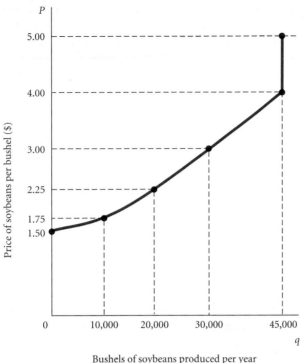

FIGURE 3.6 Clarence Brown's Individual Supply Curve

A producer will supply more when the price of output is higher. The slope of a supply curve is positive.
Note that the supply curve is red: Supply is determined by choices made by firms.

immediate response may be different from what they are able to do after a month or a year.
Short-run and long-run supply curves are often different.

OTHER DETERMINANTS OF SUPPLY

Of the factors we have listed that are likely to affect the quantity of output supplied by a
given firm, we have thus far discussed only the price of output. Other factors that affect supply include the cost of producing the product and the prices of related products.

The Cost of Production   Regardless of the price that a firm can command for its product, revenue must exceed the cost of producing the output for the firm to make a profit. Thus,
the supply decision is likely to change in response to changes in the cost of production. Cost
of production depends on a number of factors, including the available technologies and the
prices and quantities of the inputs needed by the firm (labor, land, capital, energy, and so on).

Technological change can have an enormous impact on the cost of production over
time. Consider agriculture. The introduction of fertilizers, the development of complex farm
machinery, and the use of bioengineering to increase the yield of individual crops have all
powerfully affected the cost of producing agricultural products. Farm productivity in the
United States has been increasing dramatically for decades. Yield per acre of corn production
has increased fivefold since the late 1930s, and the amount of labor required to produce 100
bushels of corn has fallen from 108 hours in the late 1930s, to 20 hours in the late 1950s, to
less than 3 hours today. (See Table 2.2.)

When a technological advance lowers the cost of production, output is likely to increase.
When yield per acre increases, individual farmers can and do produce more. The output of
the Ford Motor Company increased substantially after the introduction of assembly-line
techniques. The production of electronic calculators, and later personal computers, boomed
with the development of inexpensive techniques to produce microprocessors.

Cost of production is also affected directly by the price of the factors of production. In
the summer of 2005, the world price of oil rose to more than $60 per barrel from below $20

in 2002. As a result, cab drivers faced higher gasoline prices, airlines faced higher fuel costs, and manufacturing firms faced higher heating bills. The result: Cab drivers probably spent less time driving around looking for customers, airlines cut a few low-profit routes, and some manufacturing plants stopped running extra shifts. The moral of this story: Increases in input prices raise costs of production and are likely to reduce supply.

The Prices of Related Products Firms often react to changes in the prices of related products. For example, if land can be used for either corn or soybean production, an increase in soybean prices may cause individual farmers to shift acreage out of corn production and into soybeans. Thus, an increase in soybean prices actually affects the amount of corn supplied.

Similarly, if beef prices rise, producers may respond by raising more cattle. However, leather comes from cowhide. Thus, an increase in beef prices may actually increase the supply of leather.

To summarize:

> Assuming that its objective is to maximize profits, a firm's decision about what quantity of output, or product, to supply depends on
>
> 1. The price of the good or service
> 2. The cost of producing the product, which in turn depends on
>   - The price of required inputs (labor, capital, and land)
>   - The technologies that can be used to produce the product
> 3. The prices of related products

A factory supplies goods to the market.

movement along a supply curve The change in quantity supplied brought about by a change in price.

shift of a supply curve The change that takes place in a supply curve corresponding to a new relationship between quantity supplied of a good and the price of that good. The shift is brought about by a change in the original conditions.

SHIFT OF SUPPLY VERSUS MOVEMENT ALONG A SUPPLY CURVE

A supply curve shows the relationship between the quantity of a good or service supplied by a firm and the price that good or service brings in the market. Higher prices are likely to lead to an increase in quantity supplied, *ceteris paribus*. Remember: The supply curve is derived holding everything constant except price. When the price of a product changes *ceteris paribus*, a change in the quantity supplied follows—that is, a **movement along the supply curve** takes place. As you have seen, supply decisions are also influenced by factors other than price. New relationships between price and quantity supplied come about when factors other than price change, and the result is a **shift of the supply curve**. When factors other than price cause supply curves to shift, we say that there has been a *change in supply*.

Recall that the cost of production depends on the price of inputs and the technologies of production available. Now suppose that a major breakthrough in the production of soybeans has occurred: Genetic engineering has produced a superstrain of disease- and pest-resistant seed. Such a technological change would enable individual farmers to supply more soybeans at *any* market price. Table 3.4 and Figure 3.7 describe this change. At $3 a bushel, farmers would have produced 30,000 bushels from the old seed (schedule S_0 in Table 3.4); with the lower cost of production and higher yield resulting from the new seed, they produce 40,000 bushels (schedule S_1 in Table 3.4). At $1.75 per bushel, they would have produced 10,000 bushels from the old seed; but with the lower costs and higher yields, output rises to 23,000 bushels.

TABLE 3.4 Shift of Supply Schedule for Soybeans Following Development of a New Disease-Resistant Seed Strain

Price (Per Bushel)	SCHEDULE S_0 Quantity Supplied (Bushels Per Year Using Old Seed)	SCHEDULE S_1 Quantity Supplied (Bushels Per Year Using New Seed)
$1.50	0	5,000
1.75	10,000	23,000
2.25	20,000	33,000
3.00	30,000	40,000
4.00	45,000	54,000
5.00	45,000	54,000

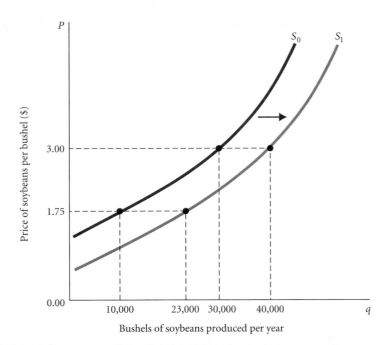

FIGURE 3.7 Shift of Supply Curve for Soybeans Following Development of a New Seed Strain

When the price of a product changes, we move *along* the supply curve for that product; the quantity supplied rises or falls. When any other factor affecting supply changes, the supply curve *shifts*.

Increases in input prices may also cause supply curves to shift. If Farmer Brown faces higher fuel costs, for example, his supply curve will shift to the left—that is, he will produce less at any given market price. If Brown's soybean supply curve shifted far enough to the left, it would intersect the price axis at a higher point, meaning that it would take a higher market price to induce Brown to produce any soybeans at all.

As with demand, it is very important to distinguish between *movements along* supply curves (changes in quantity supplied) and *shifts in* supply curves (changes in supply):

Change in price of a good or service

    leads to

        Change in *quantity supplied* (**movement along a supply curve**).

Change in costs, input prices, technology, or prices of related goods and services

    leads to

        Change in *supply* (**shift of a supply curve**).

FROM INDIVIDUAL SUPPLY TO MARKET SUPPLY

Market supply is determined in the same fashion as market demand. It is simply the sum of all that is supplied each period by all producers of a single product. Figure 3.8 derives a market supply curve from the supply curves of three individual firms. (In a market with more firms, total market supply would be the sum of the amounts produced by each of the firms in that market.) As the table in Figure 3.8 shows, at a price of $3 farm A supplies 30,000 bushels of soybeans, farm B supplies 10,000 bushels, and farm C supplies 25,000 bushels. At this price, the total amount supplied in the market is 30,000 + 10,000 + 25,000, or 65,000 bushels. At a price of $1.75, however, the total amount supplied is only 25,000 bushels (10,000 + 5,000 + 10,000). The market supply curve is thus the simple addition of the individual supply curves of all the firms in a particular market—that is, the sum of all the individual quantities supplied at each price.

The position and shape of the market supply curve depend on the positions and shapes of the individual firms' supply curves from which it is derived. They also depend on the number of firms that produce in that market. If firms that produce for a particular market are earning

market supply The sum of all that is supplied each period by all producers of a single product.

Firm A's supply

Firm B's supply

Firm C's supply

Market supply curve

Price	Quantity (q) supplied by			Total quantity supplied in the market (Q)
	A	B	C	
$3.00	30,000 +	10,000 +	25,000	→ 65,000
1.75	10,000 +	5,000 +	10,000	→ 25,000

FIGURE 3.8 Deriving Market Supply from Individual Firm Supply Curves

Total supply in the marketplace is the sum of all the amounts supplied by all the firms selling in the market. It is the sum of all the individual quantities supplied at each price.

high profits, other firms may be tempted to go into that line of business. When the technology to produce computers for home use became available, literally hundreds of new firms got into the act. The popularity and profitability of professional football has three times led to the formation of new leagues. When new firms enter an industry, the supply curve shifts to the right. When firms go out of business, or "exit" the market, the supply curve shifts to the left.

MARKET EQUILIBRIUM

So far, we have identified a number of factors that influence the amount that households demand and the amount that firms supply in product (output) markets. The discussion has emphasized the role of market price as a determinant both of quantity demanded and quantity supplied. We are now ready to see how supply and demand in the market interact to determine the final market price.

We have been very careful in our discussions thus far to separate household decisions about how much to demand from firm decisions about how much to supply. The operation of the market, however, clearly depends on the interaction between suppliers and demanders. At any moment, one of three conditions prevails in every market: (1) The quantity demanded exceeds the quantity supplied at the current price, a situation called *excess demand*; (2) the quantity supplied exceeds the quantity demanded at the current price, a situation called *excess supply*; or (3) the quantity supplied equals the quantity demanded at the current price, a situation called **equilibrium**. At equilibrium, no tendency for price to change exists.

EXCESS DEMAND

Excess demand, or a **shortage**, exists when quantity demanded is greater than quantity supplied at the current price. Figure 3.9, which plots both a supply curve and a demand curve on the same graph, illustrates such a situation. As you can see, market demand at $1.75 per bushel (50,000 bushels) exceeds the amount that farmers are currently supplying (25,000 bushels).

When excess demand occurs in an unregulated market, there is a tendency for price to rise as demanders compete against each other for the limited supply. The adjustment mechanisms may differ, but the outcome is always the same. For example, consider the mechanism of an auction. In an auction, items are sold directly to the highest bidder. When the auctioneer starts the bidding at a low price, many people bid for the item. At first there is a shortage: Quantity demanded exceeds quantity supplied. As would-be buyers offer higher and higher prices, bidders drop out, until the one who offers the most ends up with the item being auctioned. Price rises until quantity demanded and quantity supplied are equal.

At a price of $1.75 (see Figure 3.9 again), farmers produce soybeans at a rate of 25,000 bushels per year, but at that price the demand is for 50,000 bushels. Most farm products are sold to local dealers who in turn sell large quantities in major market centers, where bidding would push prices up if quantity demanded exceeded quantity supplied. As price rises above $1.75, two things happen: (1) The quantity demanded falls as buyers drop out of the market and perhaps choose a substitute, and (2) the quantity supplied increases as farmers find themselves receiving a higher price for their product and shift additional acres into soybean production.[3]

This process continues until the shortage is eliminated. In Figure 3.9, this occurs at $2.50, where quantity demanded has fallen from 50,000 to 35,000 bushels per year and quantity supplied has increased from 25,000 to 35,000 bushels per year. When quantity demanded and

equilibrium The condition that exists when quantity supplied and quantity demanded are equal. At equilibrium, there is no tendency for price to change.

excess demand or shortage The condition that exists when quantity demanded exceeds quantity supplied at the current price.

Bidding at an auction starts with excess demand and ends up with quantity demanded and quantity supplied equal.

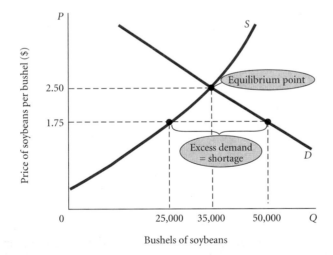

FIGURE 3.9 Excess Demand, or Shortage

At a price of $1.75 per bushel, quantity demanded exceeds quantity supplied. When excess *demand* arises, there is a tendency for price to rise. When quantity demanded equals quantity supplied, excess demand is eliminated and the market is in equilibrium. Here, the equilibrium price is $2.50, and the equilibrium quantity is 35,000 bushels.

[3]Once farmers have produced in any given season, they cannot change their minds and produce more, of course. When we derived Clarence Brown's supply schedule in Table 3.3, we imagined him reacting to prices that existed at the time he decided how much land to plant in soybeans. In Figure 3.9, the upward slope shows that higher prices justify shifting land from other crops. Final price may not be determined until final production figures are in. For our purposes here, however, we have ignored this timing problem. The best way to think about it is that demand and supply are *flows*, or *rates*, of production—that is, we are talking about the number of bushels produced *per production period*. Adjustments in the rate of production may take place over a number of production periods.

quantity supplied are equal and there is no further bidding, the process has achieved an equilibrium, a situation in which *there is no natural tendency for further adjustment.* Graphically, the point of equilibrium is the point at which the supply curve and the demand curve intersect.

Increasingly, items are auctioned over the Internet. Companies like eBay connect buyers and sellers of everything from automobiles to wine and from computers to airline tickets. Auctions are occurring simultaneously with participants located across the globe. The principles through which prices are determined in these auctions are the same: When excess demand exists, prices rise.

While the principles are the same, the process through which excess demand leads to higher prices is different in different markets. Consider the market for houses in the hypothetical town of Boomville with a population of 25,000 people, most of whom live in single-family homes. Normally, about 75 homes are sold in the Boomville market each year. However, last year a major business opened a plant in town, creating 1,500 new jobs that pay good wages. This attracted new residents to the area, and real estate agents now have more buyers than there are properties for sale. Quantity demanded now exceeds quantity supplied. In other words, there is a shortage.

Auctions are not unheard of in the housing market, but they are rare. This market usually works more subtly, but the outcome is the same. Properties are sold very quickly and housing prices begin to rise. Boomville sellers soon learn that there are more buyers than usual, and they begin to hold out for higher offers. As prices for Boomville houses rise, quantity demanded eventually drops off and quantity supplied increases. Quantity supplied increases in at least two ways: (1) Encouraged by the high prices, builders begin constructing new houses, and (2) some people, attracted by the higher prices their homes will fetch, put their houses on the market. Discouraged by higher prices, however, some potential buyers (demanders) may begin to look for housing in neighboring towns and settle on commuting. Eventually, equilibrium will be reestablished, with the quantity of houses demanded just equal to the quantity of houses supplied.

Although the mechanics of price adjustment in the housing market differ from the mechanics of an auction, the outcome is exactly the same:

> When quantity demanded exceeds quantity supplied, price tends to rise. When the price in a market rises, quantity demanded falls and quantity supplied rises until an equilibrium is reached at which quantity demanded and quantity supplied are equal.

This process is called *price rationing.* When a shortage exists, some people will be satisfied and some will not. When the market operates without interference, price increases will distribute what is available to those who are willing and able to pay the most. As long as there is a way for buyers and sellers to interact, those who are willing to pay more will make that fact known somehow. (We discuss the nature of the price system as a rationing device in detail in Chapter 4.)

EXCESS SUPPLY

excess supply or **surplus** The condition that exists when quantity supplied exceeds quantity demanded at the current price.

Excess supply, or a **surplus**, exists when the quantity supplied exceeds the quantity demanded at the current price. As with a shortage, the mechanics of price adjustment in the face of a surplus can differ from market to market. For example, if automobile dealers find themselves with unsold cars in the fall when the new models are coming in, you can expect to see price cuts. Sometimes dealers offer discounts to encourage buyers; sometimes buyers themselves simply offer less than the price initially asked. In any event, products do no one any good sitting in dealers' lots or on warehouse shelves. The auction metaphor introduced earlier can also be applied here: If the initial asking price is too high, no one bids, and the auctioneer tries a lower price. It is almost always true, and 2005 was no exception, that certain items do not sell as well as anticipated during the Christmas holidays. After Christmas, most stores have big sales during which they lower the prices of overstocked items. Quantities supplied exceeded quantities demanded at the current prices, so stores cut prices.

Across the state from Boomville is Bustville, where last year a drug manufacturer shut down its operations and 1,500 people found themselves out of work. With no other prospects for work, many residents decided to pack up and move. They put their houses up for sale, but there were few buyers. The result was an excess supply, or surplus, of houses: The quantity of houses supplied exceeded the quantity demanded at the current prices.

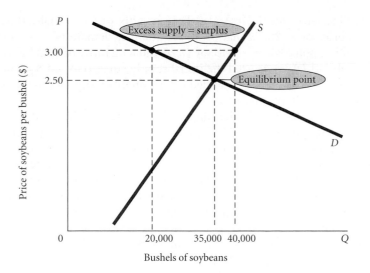

FIGURE 3.10 Excess Supply, or Surplus

At a price of $3, quantity supplied exceeds quantity demanded by 20,000 bushels. This excess supply
will cause price to fall.

As houses sit unsold on the market for months, sellers start to cut their asking prices.
Potential buyers begin offering considerably less than sellers are asking. As prices fall, two
things are likely to happen. First, the low housing prices may attract new buyers. People
who might have bought in a neighboring town see that there are housing bargains to be
had in Bustville, and quantity demanded rises in response to price decline. Second, some
of those who put their houses on the market may be discouraged by the lower prices and
decide to stay in Bustville. Developers are certainly not likely to be building new housing
in town. Lower prices thus lead to a decline in quantity supplied as potential sellers pull
their houses from the market. This was exactly the situation in New England and
California in the early 1990s.

Figure 3.10 illustrates another excess supply/surplus situation. At a price of $3 per
bushel, suppose farmers are supplying soybeans at a rate of 40,000 bushels per year, but buyers are demanding only 20,000. With 20,000 (40,000 minus 20,000) bushels of soybeans
going unsold, the market price falls. As price falls from $3 to $2.50, quantity supplied
decreases from 40,000 bushels per year to 35,000. The lower price causes quantity demanded
to rise from 20,000 to 35,000. At $2.50, quantity demanded and quantity supplied are equal.
For the data shown here, $2.50 and 35,000 bushels are the equilibrium price and quantity.

Although oil prices rose to record levels in 2005, back in 2001, crude oil production worldwide exceeded the quantity demanded, and prices fell significantly as competing producer countries tried to maintain their share of world markets. Although the mechanism by which price is
adjusted is different for automobiles, housing, soybeans, and crude oil, the outcome is the same:

> When quantity supplied exceeds quantity demanded at the current price, the price
> tends to fall. When price falls, quantity supplied is likely to decrease and quantity
> demanded is likely to increase until an equilibrium price is reached where quantity
> supplied and quantity demanded are equal.

CHANGES IN EQUILIBRIUM

When supply and demand curves shift, the equilibrium price and quantity change. The following example will help to illustrate this point.

South America is a major producer of coffee beans. A cold snap there can reduce the coffee harvest enough to affect the world price of coffee beans. In the mid-1990s, a major freeze
hit Brazil and Colombia and drove up the price of coffee on world markets to a record $2.40
per pound. Severe hurricanes in the Caribbean caused a similar shift of supply in 2005.

Figure 3.11 illustrates how the freeze pushed up coffee prices. Initially, the market was in equilibrium at a price of $1.20. At that price, the quantity demanded was equal to quantity supplied (13.2 billion pounds). At a price of $1.20 and a quantity of 13.2 billion pounds, the demand curve (labeled D) intersected the initial supply curve (labeled S_0). (Remember that equilibrium exists when quantity demanded equals quantity supplied—the point at which the supply and demand curves intersect.)

The freeze caused a decrease in the supply of coffee beans. That is, it caused the supply curve to shift to the left. In Figure 3.11, the new supply curve (the supply curve that shows the relationship between price and quantity supplied after the freeze) is labeled S_1.

At the initial equilibrium price, $1.20, there is now a shortage of coffee. If the price were to remain at $1.20, quantity demanded would not change; it would remain at 13.2 billion pounds. However, at that price, quantity supplied would drop to 6.6 billion pounds. At a price of $1.20, quantity demanded is greater than quantity supplied.

When excess demand exists in a market, price can be expected to rise, and rise it did. As the figure shows, price rose to a new equilibrium at $2.40. At $2.40, quantity demanded is again equal to quantity supplied, this time at 9.9 billion pounds—the point at which the new supply curve (S_1) intersects the demand curve.

Notice that as the price of coffee rose from $1.20 to $2.40, two things happened. First, the quantity demanded declined (a movement along the demand curve) as people shifted to substitutes such as tea and hot cocoa. Second, the quantity supplied began to rise, but within the limits imposed by the damage from the freeze. (It might also be that some countries or areas with high costs of production, previously unprofitable, came into production and shipped to the world market at the higher price.) That is, the quantity supplied increased in response to the higher price *along* the new supply curve, which lies to the left of the old supply curve. The final result was a higher price ($2.40), a smaller quantity finally exchanged in the market (9.9 billion pounds), and coffee bought only by those willing to pay $2.40 per pound.

Since many market prices are driven by the interaction of millions of buyers and sellers, it is often hard to predict how they will change. A series of events in the mid-1990s led to the leftward shift in supply, thus driving up the price of coffee, but the opposite occurred between 1995 and 2003, when the world supply of coffee beans shifted sharply rightward. Brazil's crop was up 39 percent in 2003 alone. Brazil and the other large pro-

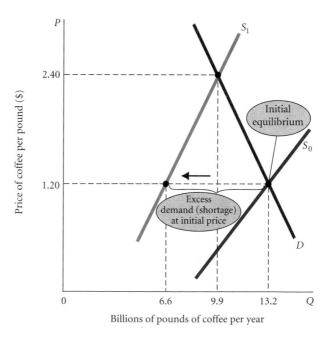

FIGURE 3.11 The Coffee Market: A Shift of Supply and Subsequent Price Adjustment

Before the freeze, the coffee market was in equilibrium at a price of $1.20. At that price, quantity demanded equaled quantity supplied. The freeze shifted the supply curve to the left (from S_0 to S_1), increasing equilibrium price to $2.40.

ducing nations of Mexico, Vietnam, Indonesia, and Colombia combined to produce the largest crop ever in 2003. The result was that coffee prices fell to 40 cents per pound, the lowest price since July 1969. Very low coffee prices hurt the producing countries that rely heavily on coffee revenues. Finally, prices rose back near $1 per pound with a decline in Brazil's crop in 2005.

Figure 3.12 summarizes the possible supply and demand shifts that have been discussed and the resulting changes in equilibrium price and quantity. Be sure to go through each graph carefully and ensure that you understand each.

FIGURE 3.12 Examples of Supply and Demand Shifts for Product X

DEMAND AND SUPPLY IN PRODUCT MARKETS: A REVIEW

As you continue your study of economics, you will discover that it is a discipline full of controversy and debate. There is, however, little disagreement about the basic way that the forces of supply and demand operate in free markets. If you hear that a freeze in Florida has destroyed a good portion of the citrus crop, you can bet that the price of oranges will rise.[4] If you read that the weather in the Midwest has been good and a record corn crop is expected, you can bet that corn prices will fall. When fishermen in Massachusetts go on strike and stop bringing in the daily catch, you can bet that the price of fish will go up. For additional examples of how the forces of supply and demand work, see the News Analysis feature titled "Mad Cow Disease Cuts Demand for Cattle in 2005."

Here are some important points to remember about the mechanics of supply and demand in product markets:

1. A demand curve shows how much of a product a household would buy if it could buy all it wanted at the given price. A supply curve shows how much of a product a firm would supply if it could sell all it wanted at the given price.

2. Quantity demanded and quantity supplied are always per time period—that is, per day, per month, or per year.

3. The demand for a good is determined by price, household income and wealth, prices of other goods and services, tastes and preferences, and expectations.

4. The supply of a good is determined by price, costs of production, and prices of related products. Costs of production are determined by available technologies of production and input prices.

5. Be careful to distinguish between movements along supply and demand curves and shifts of these curves. When the price of a good changes, the quantity of that good demanded or supplied changes—that is, a movement occurs along the curve. When any other factor changes, the curve shifts, or changes position.

6. Market equilibrium exists only when quantity supplied equals quantity demanded at the current price.

LOOKING AHEAD: MARKETS AND THE ALLOCATION OF RESOURCES

You can already begin to see how markets answer the basic economic questions of what is produced, how it is produced, and who gets what is produced. A firm will produce what is profitable to produce. If it can sell a product at a price that is sufficient to leave a profit after production costs are paid, the firm will in all likelihood produce that product. Resources will flow in the direction of profit opportunities.

■ Demand curves reflect what people are willing and able to pay for products; they are influenced by incomes, wealth, preferences, prices of other goods, and expectations. Because product prices are determined by the interaction of supply and demand, prices reflect what people are willing to pay. If people's preferences or incomes change, resources will be allocated differently. Consider, for example, an increase in demand—a shift in the market demand curve. Beginning at an equilibrium, households simply begin buying more. At the equilibrium price, quantity demanded becomes greater than quantity supplied. When there is excess demand, prices will rise, and higher prices mean higher profits for firms in the industry. Higher profits, in turn, provide existing firms

---

[4]In economics you have to think twice, however, even about a "safe" bet. If you bet that the price of frozen orange juice will rise after a freeze, you will lose your money. It turns out that much of the crop that is damaged by a freeze can be used, but for only one thing—to make frozen orange juice. Thus, a freeze actually *increases* the supply of frozen juice on the national market. Following two recent hard freezes in Florida, the price of oranges shot up, but the price of orange juice fell sharply.

News ANALYSIS

beef production, beef consumption, supply and demand   search

○ Further Exploration   ● News Analysis

Mad Cow Disease Cuts Demand for Cattle in 2005

IN JUNE 2005, A CASE OF MAD COW disease caused demand for cattle to shift to the left, and price dropped.

New York Times, July 3, 2005
ST. LOUIS, July 2 (AP)—There will be no ribs or steaks on the grill this Fourth of July weekend at the Brown house. Worried by the latest confirmed case of mad cow disease, the family plans to eat chicken.

Just days before one of the biggest grilling weekends of the year, federal authorities said mad cow disease had been found in a beef cow from a Texas ranch, the first documented case of the illness in a livestock animal born and raised in the United States. The only other known case in the United States surfaced in 2003 in Washington State, in a dairy cow that had been imported from Canada.

Mad cow disease, formally known as bovine spongiform encephalopathy, causes holes to develop in the brain. It is thought to be spread through previously accepted feeding practices, including using certain animal by-products in feed.

In people, a rare and deadly form of the illness, called variant Creutzfeldt-Jakob disease, has been linked to eating tissue from infected cows. Mad cow disease was blamed for the deaths of 150 people in Britain in the 1980s and 1990s, but no human cases originating in the United States have been documented.

New York Times, June 28, 2005
TULIA, Texas (AP)—Rancher Kevin Crooks lost about $1 million in the year following the country's first case of mad cow 18 months ago. He really doesn't want that to happen again.

If he'd had cattle big enough to sell at the Tulia Livestock Auction on Monday, he wouldn't have brought any. "I took my lumps last time," Crooks said. "It took all my profit. I basically did everything that year for free."

The auction was the first opportunity to see how live cattle sales in Texas were affected by last week's announcement of a second case of mad cow in the country, apparently the first in a U.S.-born animal. The Holstein in the country's first case in December 2003 was from a Canadian herd.

Others at the weekly sale barn brought far fewer animals to try to cut their losses. Tim Wilhelm, who owns about 5,000 head and ranches near Tulia, said he planned to bring 1,300 head of cattle Monday. But concern about possible plummeting prices dropped that number to 575 animals.

At the June 20 sale, steers sold for $113 per hundredweight. Monday's price slipped about $4 to about $109 per hundredweight.

1. At price P_0, before the discovery of mad cow disease, quantity demanded and quantity supplied are equal at q_0.

2. When the disease is discovered, demand declines (a shift of demand) from D_0 to D_1.

3. At the original price, quantity demanded drops to q_1. Now quantity demanded (q_1) is less than quantity supplied (q_0).

4. The excess supply on the market causes price to fall to P_1.

5. As price falls, the quantity supplied drops, moving us along the supply curve to q_2, and the quantity demanded rises back to q_2. At the lower price, P_1, the quantity demanded again equals the quantity supplied and equilibrium is restored.

Sources: The Associated Press, The New York Times, *"Despite Fears of Mad Cow, Grillers Get Set for Holiday," July 3, 2005. The Associated Press,* The New York Times, *"Some Ranchers Shy During Cattle Auction," June 28, 2005. Reprinted by permission.*

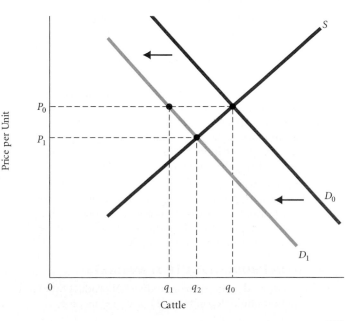

with an incentive to expand and new firms with an incentive to enter the industry. Thus, the decisions of independent private firms responding to prices and profit opportunities determine *what* will be produced. No central direction is necessary.

Adam Smith saw this self-regulating feature of markets more than 200 years ago:

> Every individual . . . by pursuing his own interest . . . promotes that of society. He is led . . . by an invisible hand to promote an end which was no part of his intention.[5]

The term Smith coined, the *invisible hand*, has passed into common parlance and is still used by economists to refer to the self-regulation of markets.

- Firms in business to make a profit have a good reason to choose the best available technology—lower costs mean higher profits. Thus, individual firms determine *how* to produce their products, again with no central direction.

- So far, we have barely touched on the question of distribution—*who* gets what is produced? You can see part of the answer in the simple supply and demand diagrams. When a good is in short supply, price rises. As it does, those who are willing and able to continue buying do so; others stop buying.

The next chapter begins with a more detailed discussion of these topics. How, exactly, is the final allocation of resources (the mix of output and the distribution of output) determined in a market system?

---

[5]Adam Smith, *The Wealth of Nations,* Modern Library Edition (New York: Random House, 1937), p. 456 (1st ed., 1776).

SUMMARY

1. In societies with many people, production must satisfy wide-ranging tastes and preferences, and producers must therefore specialize.

FIRMS AND HOUSEHOLDS: THE BASIC DECISION-MAKING UNITS

2. A *firm* exists when a person or a group of people decides to produce a product or products by transforming resources, or *inputs*, into *outputs*—the products that are sold in the market. Firms are the primary producing units in a market economy. We assume firms make decisions to try to maximize profits.

3. *Households* are the primary consuming units in an economy. All households' incomes are subject to constraints.

INPUT MARKETS AND OUTPUT MARKETS: THE CIRCULAR FLOW

4. Households and firms interact in two basic kinds of markets: *product* or *output markets* and *input* or *factor markets.* Goods and services intended for use by households are exchanged in output markets. In output markets, competing firms supply and competing households demand. In input markets, competing firms demand and competing households supply.

5. Ultimately, firms choose the quantities and character of outputs produced, the types and quantities of inputs demanded, and the technologies used in production. Households choose the types and quantities of products demanded and the types and quantities of inputs supplied.

DEMAND IN PRODUCT/OUTPUT MARKETS

6. The quantity demanded of an individual product by an individual household depends on (1) price, (2) income,

(3) wealth, (4) prices of other products, (5) tastes and preferences, and (6) expectations about the future.

7. Quantity demanded is the amount of a product that an individual household would buy in a given period if it could buy all it wanted at the current price.

8. A *demand schedule* shows the quantities of a product that a household would buy at different prices. The same information can be presented graphically in a *demand curve.*

9. The *law of demand* states that there is a negative relationship between price and quantity demanded: As price rises, quantity demanded decreases, and vice versa. Demand curves slope downward.

10. All demand curves eventually intersect the price axis because there is always a price above which a household cannot, or will not, pay. All demand curves also eventually intersect the quantity axis because demand for most goods is limited, if only by time, even at a zero price.

11. When an increase in income causes demand for a good to rise, that good is a *normal good.* When an increase in income causes demand for a good to fall, that good is an *inferior good.*

12. If a rise in the price of good X causes demand for good Y to increase, the goods are *substitutes.* If a rise in the price of X causes demand for Y to fall, the goods are *complements.*

13. Market demand is simply the sum of all the quantities of a good or service demanded per period by all the households buying in the market for that good or service. It is the sum of all the individual quantities demanded at each price.

SUPPLY IN PRODUCT/OUTPUT MARKETS

14. Quantity supplied by a firm depends on (1) the price of the good or service; (2) the cost of producing the product, which includes the prices of required inputs and the technologies that can be used to produce the product; and (3) the prices of related products.

15. Market supply is the sum of all that is supplied in each period by all producers of a single product. It is the sum of all the individual quantities supplied at each price.

16. It is very important to distinguish between *movements* along demand and supply curves and *shifts* of demand and supply curves. The demand curve shows the relationship between price and quantity demanded. The supply curve shows the relationship between price and quantity supplied. A change in price is a movement along the curve. Changes in tastes, income, wealth, expectations, or prices of other goods and services cause demand curves to shift; changes in costs, input prices, technology, or prices of related goods and services cause supply curves to shift.

MARKET EQUILIBRIUM

17. When quantity demanded exceeds quantity supplied at the current price, *excess demand* (or a *shortage*) exists and the price tends to rise. When prices in a market rise, quantity demanded falls and quantity supplied rises until an equilibrium is reached at which quantity supplied and quantity demanded are equal. At *equilibrium*, there is no further tendency for price to change.

18. When quantity supplied exceeds quantity demanded at the current price, *excess supply* (or a *surplus*) exists and the price tends to fall. When price falls, quantity supplied decreases and quantity demanded increases until an equilibrium price is reached where quantity supplied and quantity demanded are equal.

REVIEW TERMS AND CONCEPTS

capital market, 49

complements, complementary goods, 55

demand curve, 51

demand schedule, 51

entrepreneur, 48

equilibrium, 65

excess demand or shortage, 65

excess supply or surplus, 66

factors of production, 49

firm, 48

households, 48

income, 54

inferior goods, 54

input or factor markets, 49

labor market, 49

land market, 49

law of demand, 51

law of supply, 60

market demand, 57

market supply, 63

movement along a demand curve, 56

movement along a supply curve, 62

normal goods, 54

perfect substitutes, 54

product or output markets, 48

profit, 59

quantity demanded, 50

quantity supplied, 60

shift of a demand curve, 56

shift of a supply curve, 62

substitutes, 54

supply curve, 60

supply schedule, 60

wealth or net worth, 54

PROBLEM SET

1. Illustrate the following with supply and demand curves:
   a. With increased access to wireless technology and lighter weight, the demand for laptop computers has increased substantially. Laptops have also become easier and cheaper to produce as new technology has come online. Despite the shift of demand, prices have fallen.
   b. Cranberry production in Massachusetts totaled 1.8 million barrels in 2004, a 28 percent increase from the previous year's production. This year's crop yield averaged 127.9 barrels per acre, an increase of over 30 barrels per acre from the 2003 crop. But demand increased by even more than supply, actually pushing 2004 prices above 2003 prices.
   c. During the high-tech boom in the late 1990s, San Jose office space was in very high demand and rents were very high. With the national recession that began in March 2001, however, the market for office space in San Jose (Silicon Valley) was hit very hard, with rents per square foot falling. In 2005, the employment numbers from San Jose were rising slowly and rents began to rise again. Assume for simplicity that no new office space was built during the period.
   d. Before economic reforms were implemented in the countries of Eastern Europe, regulation held the price of bread substantially below equilibrium. When reforms were implemented, prices were deregulated and the price of bread rose dramatically. As a result, the quantity of bread demanded fell and the quantity of bread supplied rose sharply.
   e. The steel industry has been lobbying for high taxes on imported steel. Russia, Brazil, and Japan have been producing and selling steel on world markets at $22 per metric ton, well below what equilibrium would be in the United States with no imports. If no imported steel were permitted into the country, the equilibrium price would be $35 per metric ton. Show supply and demand curves for the United States assuming no imports; then show what the graph would look like if U.S. buyers could purchase all the steel that they wanted from world markets at $22; show the quantity of imported steel. In

2002, President George W. Bush imposed a 30 percent tariff on imported steel.

2. On Tuesday, June 28, 2005, the New York Mets and the New York Yankees played baseball at Yankee Stadium. Both teams were in pursuit of league championships. Tickets to the game were sold out, and many more fans would have attended if more tickets had been available. On that same night, two bottom-ranked teams, the Toronto Blue Jays and the Tampa Bay Devil Rays, played one another and sold tickets to only 8,545 people in Tampa.

   The Devil Rays stadium, Tropicana Field, holds 43,772. Yankee Stadium holds 57,478. Assume for simplicity that tickets to all regular-season games are priced at $35.

   a. Draw supply and demand curves for the tickets to each of the two games. (*Hint:* Supply is fixed. It does not change with price.) Draw one graph for each game.

   b. Is there a pricing policy that would have filled the ballpark for the Tampa game? If the Devil Rays adopted such a strategy, would it bring in more or less revenue?

   c. The price system was not allowed to work to ration the New York tickets when they were initially sold to the public. How do you know? How do you suppose the tickets were rationed?

3. During 2005, Orlando, Florida, was growing rapidly, with new jobs luring young people into the area. Despite increases in population and income growth that expanded demand for housing, the price of existing houses barely increased. Why? Illustrate your answer with supply and demand curves.

4. Do you agree or disagree with each of the following statements? Briefly explain your answers and illustrate with supply and demand curves.

   a. The price of a good rises, causing the demand for another good to fall. The two goods are therefore substitutes.

   b. A shift in supply causes the price of a good to fall. The shift must have been an increase in supply.

   c. During 2005, incomes rose sharply for most Americans. This change would likely lead to an increase in the prices of both normal and inferior goods.

   d. Two normal goods cannot be substitutes for each other.

   e. If demand increases and supply increases at the same time, price will clearly rise.

   f. The price of good A falls. This causes an increase in the price of good B. Goods A and B are therefore complements.

5. The U.S. government administers two programs that affect the market for cigarettes. Media campaigns and labeling requirements are aimed at making the public aware of the health dangers of cigarettes. At the same time, the Department of Agriculture maintains price supports for tobacco. Under this program, the supported price is above the market equilibrium price, and the government limits the amount of land that can be devoted to tobacco production. Are these two programs at odds with the goal of reducing cigarette consumption? As a part of your answer, illustrate graphically the effects of both policies on the market for cigarettes.

6. Housing prices in Boston and Los Angeles have been on a roller coaster ride. Illustrate each of the following situations with supply and demand curves:

   a. In both cities an increase in income combined with expectations of a strong market shifted demand and caused prices to rise rapidly during the mid- to late 1980s.

   b. By 1990, the construction industry boomed as more and more developers started new residential projects. Those new projects expanded the supply of housing just as demand was shifting as a result of falling incomes and expectations during the 1990–1991 recession.

   c. In 2005, housing in higher-income towns in some parts of the Midwest was experiencing price increases at the same time as housing in lower-income towns was experiencing price decreases. In part this effect was due to "trade-up" buyers selling houses in lower-income areas and buying houses in higher-income areas.

7. The following two sets of statements contain common errors. Identify and explain each.

   a. Demand increases, causing prices to rise. Higher prices cause demand to fall. Therefore, prices fall back to their original levels.

   b. The supply of meat in Russia increases, causing meat prices to fall. Lower prices always mean that Russian households spend more on meat.

8. For each of the following, draw a diagram that illustrates the likely effect on the market for eggs. Indicate in each case the impact on equilibrium price and equilibrium quantity.

   a. A surgeon general warns that high-cholesterol foods cause heart attacks.

   b. The price of bacon, a complementary product, decreases.

   c. An increase in the price of chicken feed occurs.

   d. Caesar salads become trendy at dinner parties. (The dressing is made with raw eggs.)

   e. A technological innovation reduces egg breakage during packing.

*9. Suppose the demand and supply curves for eggs in the United States are given by the following equations:

$$Q_d = 100 - 20P$$
$$Q_s = 10 + 40P$$

where Q_d = millions of dozens of eggs Americans would like to buy each year; Q_s = millions of dozens of eggs U.S. farms would like to sell each year; P = price per dozen eggs.

   a. Fill in the following table:

PRICE (PER DOZEN)	QUANTITY DEMANDED (Q_d)	QUANTITY SUPPLIED (Q_s)
$.50	_____	_____
$1.00	_____	_____
$1.50	_____	_____
$2.00	_____	_____
$2.50	_____	_____

   b. Use the information in the table to find the equilibrium price and equilibrium quantity.

   c. Graph the demand and supply curves, and identify the equilibrium price and quantity.

*10. Housing policy analysts debate the best way to increase the number of housing units available to low-income households. One strategy—the demand-side strategy—is to provide people with housing "vouchers," paid for by the government, that can be used to rent housing supplied by the private market. Another—a supply-side strategy—is to have the government subsidize housing suppliers or to build public housing.

   a. Illustrate supply- and demand-side strategies using supply and demand curves. Which results in higher rents?

---

*Note: Problems marked with an asterisk are more challenging.

b. Critics of housing vouchers (the demand-side strategy) argue that because the supply of housing to low-income households is limited and will not respond at all to higher rents, demand vouchers will serve only to drive up rents and make landlords better off. Illustrate their point with supply and demand curves.

*11. Suppose the market demand for pizza is given by $Q_d = 300 - 20P$ and the market supply for pizza is given by $Q_s = 20P - 100$, where P = price (per pizza).

    a. Graph the supply and demand schedules for pizza using $5 through $15 as the value of P.

    b. In equilibrium, how many pizzas would be sold and at what price?

    c. What would happen if suppliers set the price of pizza at $15? Explain the market adjustment process.

    d. Suppose the price of hamburgers, a substitute for pizza, doubles. This leads to a doubling of the demand for pizza (at each price consumers demand twice as much pizza as before). Write the equation for the new market demand for pizza.

    e. Find the new equilibrium price and quantity of pizza.

12. Review the impact of mad cow disease on beef and cattle prices in 2004 and 2005 in the box on page 71. The following table presents data on beef imports and exports for the years 1999 through 2004. You can see a large decline in exports in 2004. What was not discussed was the fact that imports also rose quite significantly between 1999 and 2004. Assuming that imports affect the supply of beef, how would this change the diagram in the box? Would it be a shift of supply to the left or to the right? Considering both the drop in export demand and the increase in imports, would prices decline more or less than the diagram would indicate? Despite these trends, the price of beef cattle actually rose significantly in 2004 and 2005. Can you offer an explanation?

Beef and Veal Exports Versus Imports (Carcass Weight Equivalent)

Year	EXPORTS (Mil lb.)	IMPORTS (Mil lb.)
1999	2,328	2,874
2000	2,516	3,032
2001	2,271	3,161
2002	2,447	3,218
2003	2,523	3,006
2004	462	3,679

Sources: USDA and Cattle-Fax.

Demand and Supply Applications

Every society has a system of institutions that determines what is produced, how it is produced, and who gets what is produced. In some societies, these decisions are made centrally, through planning agencies or by government directive. However, in every society many decisions are made in a *decentralized* way, through the operation of markets.

Markets exist in all societies, and Chapter 3 provided a bare-bones description of how markets operate. In this chapter, we continue our examination of demand, supply, and the price system.

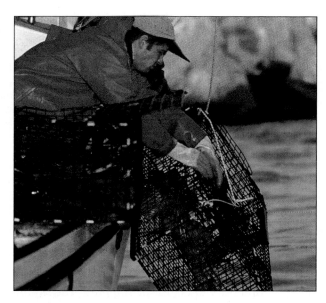

THE PRICE SYSTEM: RATIONING AND ALLOCATING RESOURCES

The market system, also called the *price system*, performs two important and closely related functions. First, it provides an automatic mechanism for distributing scarce goods and services. That is, it serves as a **price rationing** device for allocating goods and services to consumers when the quantity demanded exceeds the quantity supplied. Second, the price system ultimately determines both the allocation of resources among producers and the final mix of outputs.

price rationing The process by which the market system allocates goods and services to consumers when quantity demanded exceeds quantity supplied.

PRICE RATIONING

Consider first the simple process by which the price system eliminates a shortage. Figure 4.1 shows hypothetical supply and demand curves for lobsters caught off the coast of New England.

Lobsters are considered a delicacy. Maine produces most of the lobster catch in the United States, and anyone who drives up the Maine coast cannot avoid the hundreds of restaurants selling lobster rolls, steamed lobster, and baked stuffed lobster.

As Figure 4.1 shows, the equilibrium price of live New England lobsters was $5.25 per pound in the summer of 2005. At this price, lobster boats brought in lobsters at a rate of 81 million pounds per year—an amount that was just enough to satisfy demand.

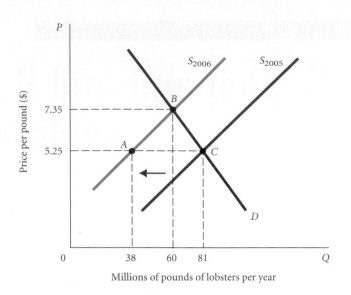

FIGURE 4.1 **The Market for Lobsters**

Suppose in 2006 that 15,000 square miles of lobstering waters off the coast of Maine are closed. The supply curve shifts to the left. Before the waters are closed, the lobster market is in equilibrium at the price of $5.25 and a quantity of 81 million pounds. The decreased supply of lobster leads to higher prices, and a new equilibrium is reached at $7.35 and 60 million pounds (point B).

Market equilibrium existed at $5.25 per pound, because at that price quantity demanded was equal to quantity supplied. (Remember that equilibrium occurs at the point where the supply and demand curves intersect. In Figure 4.1, this occurs at point C.)

Now suppose in 2006 that the waters off a section of the Maine coast become contaminated with a poisonous parasite. As a result, the Department of Agriculture is forced to close 15,000 square miles of the most productive lobstering areas. Even though many of the lobster boats shift their trapping activities to other waters, there is a sharp reduction in the quantity of lobster available for trapping. The supply curve shifts to the left, from S_{2005} to S_{2006}. This shift in the supply curve creates a situation of excess demand at $5.25. At that price, the quantity demanded is 81 million pounds and the quantity supplied is 38 million pounds. Quantity demanded exceeds quantity supplied by 43 million pounds.

The reduced supply causes the price of lobster to rise sharply. As the price rises, the available supply is "rationed." Those who are willing and able to pay the most get it.

You can see the market's price rationing function clearly in Figure 4.1. As the price rises from $5.25, the quantity demanded declines along the demand curve, moving from point C (81 million pounds) toward point B (60 million pounds). The higher prices mean that restaurants must charge much more for lobster rolls and stuffed lobsters. As a result, many people simply stop buying lobster or order it less frequently when they dine out. Some restaurants drop it from the menu entirely, and some shoppers at the fish counter turn to lobster substitutes such as swordfish and salmon.

As the price rises, lobster trappers (suppliers) also change their behavior. They stay out longer and put out more traps than they did when the price was $5.25 per pound. Quantity supplied increases from 38 million pounds to 60 million pounds. This increase in price brings about a movement along the 2006 supply curve from point A to point B.

When supply is fixed or something for sale is unique, its price is *demand deter-mined*. Price is what the highest bidder is willing to pay. In 2004, the highest bidder was willing to pay $104.1 million for Picasso's *Boy with a Pipe*.

Finally, a new equilibrium is established at a price of $7.35 per pound and a total output of 60 million pounds. The market has determined who gets the lobsters: *The lower total supply is rationed to those who are willing and able to pay the higher price.*

This idea of "willingness to pay" is central to the distribution of available supply, and willingness depends on both desire (preferences) and income/wealth. Willingness to pay does not necessarily mean that only the very rich will continue to buy lobsters when the price increases. Lower-income people may continue to buy some lobster, but they will have to be willing to sacrifice more of other goods to do so.

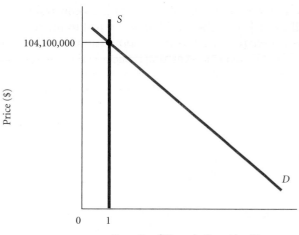

FIGURE 4.2 Market for a Rare Painting

There is some price that will clear any market, even if supply is strictly limited. In an auction for a unique painting, the price (bid) will rise to eliminate excess demand until there is only one bidder willing to purchase the single available painting.

In sum:

> The adjustment of price is the rationing mechanism in free markets. Price rationing means that whenever there is a need to ration a good—that is, when a shortage exists—in a free market, the price of the good will rise until quantity supplied equals quantity demanded—that is, until the market clears.

There is some price that will clear any market you can think of. Consider the market for a famous painting such as Picasso's *Boy with a Pipe*, illustrated in Figure 4.2. At a low price, there would be an enormous excess demand for such an important painting. The price would be bid up until there was only one remaining demander. Presumably, that price would be very high. In fact, Picasso's *Boy with a Pipe* sold for a record $104.1 million in 2004. If the product is in strictly scarce supply, as a single painting is, its price is said to be *demand determined*. That is, its price is determined solely and exclusively by the amount that the highest bidder or highest bidders are willing to pay.

One might interpret the statement that "there is some price that will clear any market" to mean "everything has its price," but that is not exactly what it means. Suppose you own a small silver bracelet that has been in your family for generations. It is quite possible that you would not sell it for *any* amount of money. Does this mean that the market is not working, or that quantity supplied and quantity demanded are not equal? Not at all. It means simply that *you* are the highest bidder. By turning down all bids, you must be willing to forgo what anybody offers for it.

CONSTRAINTS ON THE MARKET AND ALTERNATIVE RATIONING MECHANISMS

On occasion, both governments and private firms decide to use some mechanism other than the market system to ration an item for which there is excess demand at the current price. Policies designed to stop price rationing are commonly justified in a number of ways.

The rationale most often used is fairness. It is not "fair" to let landlords charge high rents, not fair for oil companies to run up the price of gasoline, not fair for insurance companies to charge enormous premiums, and so on. After all, the argument goes, we have no choice but to pay—housing and insurance are necessary, and one needs gasoline to get to work. Although it is not precisely true that price rationing allocates goods and services solely on the basis of income and wealth, income and wealth do constrain our wants. Why should all the gasoline or all the tickets to the World Series go just to the rich?

Various schemes to keep price from rising to equilibrium are based on several perceptions of injustice, among them (1) that price-gouging is bad, (2) that income is unfairly distributed, and (3) that some items are necessities, and everyone should be able to buy them at a "reasonable" price. Regardless of the rationale, the following examples will make two things clear:

> **1.** Attempts to bypass price rationing in the market and to use alternative rationing devices are much more difficult and costly than they would seem at first glance.
>
> **2.** Very often, such attempts distribute costs and benefits among households in unintended ways.

price ceiling A maximum price that sellers may charge for a good, usually set by government.

Oil, Gasoline, and OPEC
In 1973 and 1974, the Organization of Petroleum Exporting Countries (OPEC) imposed an embargo on shipments of crude oil to the United States. What followed was a drastic reduction in the quantity of gasoline available at local gas pumps.

Had the market system been allowed to operate, refined gasoline prices would have increased dramatically until quantity supplied was equal to quantity demanded. However, the government decided that rationing gasoline to only those who were willing and able to pay the most was unfair, and Congress imposed a **price ceiling**, or maximum price, of $0.57 per gallon of leaded regular gasoline. That price ceiling was intended to keep gasoline "affordable," but it also perpetuated the shortage. At the restricted price, quantity demanded remained greater than quantity supplied, and the available gasoline had to be divided up somehow among all potential demanders.

You can see the effects of the price ceiling by looking carefully at Figure 4.3. If the price had been set by the interaction of supply and demand, it would have increased to approximately $1.50 per gallon. Instead, Congress made it illegal to sell gasoline for more than $0.57

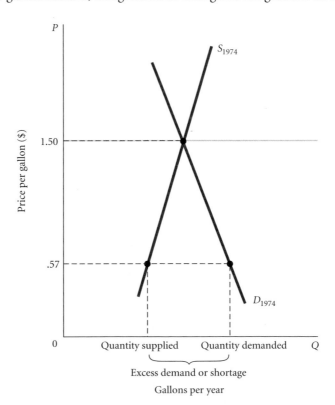

FIGURE 4.3 Excess Demand (Shortage) Created by a Price Ceiling

In 1974, a ceiling price $0.57 cents per gallon of leaded regular gasoline was imposed. If the price had instead been set by the interaction of supply and demand, it would have increased to approximately $1.50 per gallon. At $0.57 per gallon, the quantity demanded exceeded the quantity supplied. Because the price system was not allowed to function, an alternative rationing system had to be found to distribute the available supply of gasoline.

per gallon. At that price, quantity demanded exceeded quantity supplied and a shortage existed. Because the price system was not allowed to function, an alternative rationing system had to be found to distribute the available supply of gasoline.

Several devices were tried. The most common of all nonprice rationing systems is **queuing**, a term that simply means waiting in line. During 1974, very long lines formed daily at gas stations, starting as early as 5 A.M. Under this system, gasoline went to those who were willing to pay the most, but the sacrifice was measured in hours and aggravation instead of dollars.[1]

A second nonprice rationing device used during the gasoline crisis was that of **favored customers**. Many gas station owners decided not to sell gasoline to the general public at all but to reserve their scarce supplies for friends and favored customers. Not surprisingly, many customers tried to become "favored" by offering side payments to gas station owners. Owners also charged high prices for service. By doing so, they increased the real price of gasoline but hid it in service overcharges to get around the ceiling.

Yet another method of dividing up available supply is the use of **ration coupons**. It was suggested in both 1974 and 1979 that families be given ration tickets, or coupons, that would entitle them to purchase a certain number of gallons of gasoline each month. That way, everyone would get the same amount, regardless of income. Such a system had been employed in the United States during the 1940s, when wartime price ceilings on meat, sugar, butter, tires, nylon stockings, and many other items were imposed.

When ration coupons are used with no prohibition against trading them, however, the result is almost identical to a system of price rationing. Those who are willing and able to pay the most simply buy up the coupons and use them to purchase gasoline, chocolate, fresh eggs, or anything else that is sold at a restricted price.[2] This means that the price of the restricted good will effectively rise to the market-clearing price. For instance, suppose that you decide not to sell your ration coupon. You are then forgoing what you would have received by selling the coupon. Thus the "real" price of the good you purchase will be higher (if only in opportunity cost) than the restricted price.

Even when trading coupons is declared illegal, it is virtually impossible to stop black markets from developing. In a **black market**, illegal trading takes place at market-determined prices.

queuing Waiting in line as a means of distributing goods and services: a nonprice rationing mechanism.

favored customers Those who receive special treatment from dealers during situations of excess demand.

ration coupons Tickets or coupons that entitle individuals to purchase a certain amount of a given product per month.

black market A market in which illegal trading takes place at market-determined prices.

NCAA March Madness: College Basketball's National Championship

On Sunday, March 16, 2003, The National Collegiate Athletic Association (NCAA) announced the 65 teams that would compete in the NCAA Division I Men's Basketball Championship. "NCAA March Madness" had begun. The 65 teams were whittled down over the next three weeks to a final four. The semifinals were held on Saturday, April 5, and the championship game took place at the Louisiana Superdome in New Orleans on Monday, April 7, between Syracuse and Kansas.

The NCAA controlled the distribution of 54,000 Final Four tickets. The face value of each ticket was between a minimum of $100 for upper-level, distant-view seats and a maximum of $160 for lower-level seats. Clearly, the potential demand for these tickets was enormous, and the NCAA made a decision to price them below equilibrium. How do we know that they were priced below equilibrium? Many ticket agencies had tickets for sale, and a check of prices being paid over the Web in mid-March 2003 showed that upper-level tickets were being sold for over $1,750, while lower-level tickets between the baskets in the first 20 rows were going for an astonishing $10,000!

There are many ways to deal with the excess demand to premiere sporting events such as the NCAA finals, but it is hard to keep tickets from those who are willing to pay high prices. Syracuse played Kansas in the NCAA championship game in 2003.

---

[1]You can also show formally that the result is inefficient—that there is a resulting net loss of total value to society. First, there is the cost of waiting in line. Time has a value. With price rationing, no one has to wait in line and the value of that time is saved. Second, there may be additional lost value if the gasoline ends up in the hands of someone who places a lower value on it than someone else who gets no gas. Suppose, for example, that the market price of gasoline if unconstrained would rise to $2, but that the government has it fixed at $1. There will be long lines to get gas. Imagine that to motorist A, 10 gallons of gas is worth $35 but that she fails to get it because her time is too valuable to wait in line. To motorist B, 10 gallons is worth only $15, but his time is worth much less, so he gets the gas. In the end, A could pay B for the gas and both could be better off. If A pays B $30 for the gas, A is $5 better off and B is $15 better off. In addition, A does not have to wait in line. Thus, the allocation that results from nonprice rationing involves a net loss of value. Such losses are called *deadweight losses*.

[2]Of course, if you are assigned a number of tickets and you sell them, you are better off than you would be with price rationing. Ration coupons thus serve as a way of redistributing income.

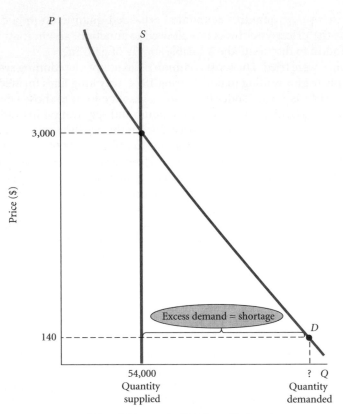

A pair of tickets to the semifinals and final of the NCAA men's basketball tournament in 2003 was originally priced at an average of about $140. The Superdome in New Orleans holds 54,000. Thus, the supply is vertical at 54,000. At $140, the quantity demanded far exceeded the quantity supplied. The diagram shows an equilibrium at $3,000.

Let us say that the average price at which the original tickets were sold was $140 and that the equilibrium price that would equate the quantity supplied and the quantity demanded was $3,000. Figure 4.4 shows the story graphically. Supply is fixed at 54,000. The quantity demanded at the original sales price is not known, but it is probably a very large number.

One obvious question is, if the market were not used to ration or distribute the originally available tickets on the basis of ability and willingness to pay, how were they distributed? Several methods were used. First, 4,500 tickets were saved for each of the Final Four institutions. Presumably, these went to school officials, players and their families, big donors, and season ticket holders. Each school, no doubt, had a different priority list. Next, 15,000 tickets were sold to the general public through a drawing all the way back in July 2002. Anyone could send in a check for the face amount of the tickets, the lucky winners were drawn at random, and the money was returned to those who were not drawn.

The remaining 21,000 tickets went to a variety of groups. The largest allotment went to corporate sponsors and the media. In a way, these groups "pay" for their tickets. CBS, for example, paid millions of dollars for the rights to televise the tournament. That payment was distributed among the teams by a formula. Corporate sponsors paid CBS and the NCAA millions for the rights to advertise. In return, each group received a set number of tickets to distribute as it saw fit.

What happened next was that a market arose. As long as people who are willing to pay very high prices (those who are represented by the upper left portion of the demand curve in Figure 4.4) can communicate with those who somehow were able to get tickets at face value, there will be trades! The Internet provides a convenient way for potential buyers to communicate with potential sellers. A simple search turns up dozens of organized ticket sellers.

Let us suppose that I was selected in the drawing in July and bought a pair of $100 tickets. How much must I *really* pay to go to the game? The answer is "what I can sell

Hurricane Katrina and Gasoline Prices in 2005

AT THE END OF AUGUST 2005, THE coastlines of Louisiana and Mississippi suffered a direct hit from one of the most powerful storms ever to occur in the United States: Hurricane Katrina. The center of the storm passed very near to New Orleans, where broken levees led to unprecedented flooding, enormous loss of life, massive destruction of property, homelessness, and suffering. The storm knocked out a significant portion of the country's refinery capacity and had an immediate effect on the supply of gasoline at the pump. The following article from *CNN/ Money* describes a pure shift of the gasoline supply curve to the left.

EXPERTS: $4 A GALLON GAS COMING SOON

Pricing analysts say consumers can expect even higher prices at the pump.
August 31, 2005: 4:11 PM EDT
By Grace Wong, CNN/Money staff writer

NEW YORK (CNN/Money)—Consumers can expect retail gas prices to rise to $4 a gallon soon, but whether they stay there depends on the long-term damage to oil facilities from Hurricane Katrina, oil and gas analysts said Wednesday.

"There's no question gas will hit $4 a gallon," Ben Brockwell, director of pricing at the Oil Price Information Service, said. "The question is how high will it go and how long will it last?"

Brockwell said with gasoline prices now exceeding $3 a gallon before even reaching the wholesale level, it "doesn't take a genius" to expect retail prices to hit $4 a gallon soon.

"Consumer haven't seen the worst of it yet," Brockwell said.

KATRINA PRESSURES GAS SUPPLIES

Katrina forced operators to close more than a tenth of the country's refining capacity and a quarter of its oil production, which sent gasoline prices surging.

Two major pipelines that supply gasoline to key terminals and distribution centers within the eastern U.S. were shut down due to power outages caused by the storm.

Colonial Pipeline said it hopes to be back in partial operation soon, while the date of Plantation Pipeline's restart is not clear. Each day the pipelines are closed, supplies get backlogged and distribution centers must rely on reserves.

"With this kind of hiccup in refinery capacity, in stretched markets like California, you could see over $4 a gallon in gas," Evan Smith, an analyst at U.S. Global Investors, told CNN/Money.

those tickets for." If I can sell the tickets for $4,000 a pair, I must turn down the $4,000 market price in order to go to the game. There is an opportunity cost. I must reveal that it is worth at least $4,000 because I forgo $4,000 if a friend and I go to the game.

What, then, can we conclude about alternatives to the price rationing system?

> No matter how good the intentions of private organizations and governments, it is very difficult to prevent the price system from operating and to stop willingness to pay from asserting itself. Every time an alternative is tried, the price system seems to sneak in the back door. With favored customers and black markets, the final distribution may be even more unfair than that which would result from simple price rationing.

PRICES AND THE ALLOCATION OF RESOURCES

Thinking of the market system as a mechanism for allocating scarce goods and services among competing demanders is very revealing, but the market determines much more than just the distribution of final outputs. It also determines what gets produced and how resources are allocated among competing uses.

Consider a change in consumer preferences that leads to an increase in demand for a specific good or service. During the 1980s, for example, people began going to restaurants much more frequently than before. Researchers think that this trend, which continues today, is partially the result of social changes (such as dramatic rise in the number of two-earner families) and partially the result of rising incomes. The market responded to this change in demand by shifting resources, both capital and labor, into more and better restaurants.

With the increase in demand for restaurant meals, the price of eating out rose, and the restaurant business became more profitable. The higher profits attracted new businesses and provided old restaurants with an incentive to expand. As new capital, seeking profits, flowed into the restaurant business, so did labor. New restaurants need chefs. Chefs need training, and the higher wages that came with increased demand provided an incentive for them to get it. In response to the increase in demand for training, new cooking schools opened and existing schools began to offer courses in the culinary arts.

This story could run on and on, but the point is clear:

> Price changes resulting from shifts of demand in output markets cause profits to rise or fall. Profits attract capital; losses lead to disinvestment. Higher wages attract labor and encourage workers to acquire skills. At the core of the system, supply, demand, and prices in input and output markets determine the allocation of resources and the ultimate combinations of things produced.

PRICE FLOORS

price floor A minimum price below which exchange is not permitted.

minimum wage A price floor set under the price of labor.

As we have seen, price ceilings, often imposed because price rationing is sometimes viewed as unfair, result in alternative rationing mechanisms that are inefficient and may be equally unfair. Some of the same arguments can be made for price floors. A **price floor** is a minimum price below which exchange is not permitted. If a price floor is set above the equilibrium price, the result will be excess supply; quantity supplied will be greater than quantity demanded.

The most common example of a price floor is the **minimum wage**, which is a floor set under the price of labor. Employers (who demand labor) are not permitted under federal law to pay a wage less than $5.15 per hour to workers (who supply labor). Critics argue that since the minimum wage is above equilibrium, the result will be wasteful unemployment. At the wage of $5.15, the quantity of labor demanded is less than the quantity of labor supplied.

Whenever a price floor is set above equilibrium, an excess supply will be on the market. A lower price would increase the quantity demanded, since buyers would pay a lower price, and quantity supplied would fall, as resources are transferred to more productive uses. We will return to this topic in more detail in Chapter 16.

SUPPLY AND DEMAND ANALYSIS: AN OIL IMPORT FEE

The basic logic of supply and demand is a powerful tool of analysis. As an extended example of the power of this logic, we will consider a recent proposal to impose a tax on imported oil. The idea of raising the federal gasoline tax is hotly debated, with many arguing strongly for such a tax. Many economists, however, believe that a fee on imported crude oil, which is used to produce gasoline, would have better effects on the economy than would a gasoline tax.

Consider the facts. Between 1985 and 1989, the United States increased its dependence on oil imports dramatically. In 1989, total U.S. demand for crude oil was 13.6 million barrels per day. Of that amount, only 7.7 million barrels per day (57 percent) were supplied by U.S. producers, with the remaining 5.9 million barrels per day (43 percent) imported. The price of oil on world markets that year averaged about $18. This heavy dependence on foreign oil left the United States vulnerable to the price shock that followed the Iraqi invasion of Kuwait in August 1990. In the months following the invasion, the price of crude oil on world markets shot up to $40 per barrel.

Even before the invasion, many economists and some politicians had recommended a stiff oil import fee (or tax) that would, it was argued, reduce the U.S. dependence on foreign oil by (1) reducing overall consumption and (2) providing an incentive for increased domestic production. An added bonus would be improved air quality from the reduction in driving.

Supply and demand analysis makes the arguments of the import fee proponents easier to understand. Figure 4.5(a) shows the U.S. market for oil. The world price of oil is assumed to be $18, and the United States is assumed to be able to buy *all the oil that it wants* at this price. This means that domestic producers cannot get away with charging any more than $18 per barrel. The curve labeled *Supply*$_{US}$ shows the amount that domestic suppliers will produce at each price level. At a price of $18, domestic production is 7.7 million barrels. Stated somewhat differently, U.S. producers will produce at point *A* on the supply curve. The total quantity of oil demanded in the United States in 1989 was 13.6 million barrels per day. At a price of $18, the quantity demanded in the United States is point *B* on the demand curve.

The difference between the total quantity demanded (13.6 million barrels per day) and domestic production (7.7 million barrels per day) is total imports (5.9 million barrels per day).

Now suppose that the government levies a tax of $33\frac{1}{3}$ percent on imported oil. Because the import price is $18, a tax of $6 (or .3333 × $18) per barrel means that importers of oil in the United States will pay a total of $24 per barrel ($18 + $6). This new, higher price means that U.S. producers can also charge up to $24 for a barrel of crude. Note, however, that the tax is paid only on imported oil. Thus the entire $24 paid for domestic crude goes to domestic producers.

Figure 4.5(b) shows the result of the tax. First, because of higher price the quantity demanded drops to 12.2 million barrels per day. This is a movement *along* the demand curve from point *B* to point *D*. At the same time, the quantity supplied by domestic producers increased to 9.0 million barrels per day. This is a movement *along* the supply curve from point *A* to point *C*. With an increase in domestic quantity supplied and a decrease in domestic quantity demanded, imports decrease to 3.2 million barrels per day (12.2 − 9.0).[3]

---

[3]These figures were not chosen randomly. It is interesting to note that in 1985 the world price of crude oil averaged about $24 a barrel. Domestic production was 9.0 million barrels per day, and domestic consumption was 12.2 million barrels per day, with imports of only 3.2 million. The drop in the world price between 1985 and 1989 increased imports to 5.9 million, an 84 percent increase. By 2003, domestic production had fallen to 5.9 million barrels per day, and imports were up to 8.6 million barrels per day.

a. U.S. market, 1989

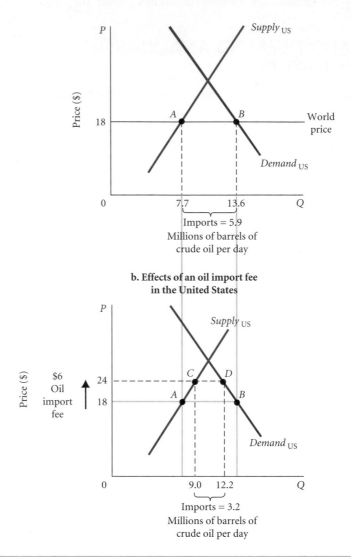

b. Effects of an oil import fee
in the United States

FIGURE 4.5 The U.S. Market for Crude Oil, 1989

At a world price of $18, domestic production is 7.7 million barrels per day and the total quantity of oil demanded in the United States is 13.6 million barrels per day. The difference is total imports (5.9 million barrels per day).

If the government levies a 33 percent tax on imports, the price of a barrel of oil rises to $24. The quantity demanded falls to 12.2 million barrels per day. At the same time, the quantity supplied by domestic producers increases to 9.0 million barrels per day, and the quantity imported falls to 3.2 million barrels per day.

The tax also generates revenues for the federal government. The total tax revenue collected is equal to the tax per barrel ($6) times the number of imported barrels. When the quantity imported is 3.2 million barrels per day, total revenue is $6 × 3.2 million, or $19.2 million *per day* (about $7 billion per year).

What does all of this mean? In the final analysis, an oil import fee would (1) increase domestic production and (2) reduce overall consumption. This would in turn help with the problem of air pollution and simultaneously reduce U.S. dependence on foreign oil.

SUPPLY AND DEMAND AND MARKET EFFICIENCY

Clearly, supply and demand curves help explain the way that markets and market prices work to allocate scarce resources. Recall that when we try to understand "how the system works," we are doing "positive economics."

Supply and demand curves can also be used to illustrate the idea of market efficiency, an important aspect of "normative economics." To understand the ideas you first must understand the concepts of consumer and producer surplus.

CONSUMER SURPLUS

The argument, made several times already, that the market forces us to reveal a great deal about our personal preferences is an extremely important one, and it bears repeating at least once more here. If you are free to choose within the constraints imposed by prices and your income, and you decide to buy (say) a hamburger for $2.50, you have "revealed" that a hamburger is worth at least $2.50 to you.

A simple market demand curve such as the one in Figure 4.6(a) illustrates this point quite clearly. At the current market price of $2.50, consumers will purchase 7 million hamburgers per month. There is only one price in the market, and the demand curve tells us how many hamburgers households would buy if they could purchase all they wanted at the posted price of $2.50. Anyone who values a hamburger at $2.50 or more will buy it. Anyone who does not value it that highly will not.

Some people, however, value hamburgers at more than $2.50. As Figure 4.6(a) shows, even if the price were $5.00, consumers would still buy 1 million hamburgers. If these people were able to buy the good at a price of $2.50, they would earn a **consumer surplus**. Consumer surplus is the difference between the maximum amount a person is willing to pay for a good and its current market price. The consumer surplus earned by the people willing to pay $5.00 for a hamburger is approximately equal to the shaded area between point A and the price, $2.50.

consumer surplus The difference between the maximum amount a person is willing to pay for a good and its current market price.

The second million hamburgers in Figure 4.6(a) are valued at more than the market price as well, although the consumer surplus gained is slightly less. Point B on the market demand curve shows the maximum amount that consumers would be willing to pay for the second million hamburgers. The consumer surplus earned by these people is equal to the shaded area between B and the price, $2.50. Similarly, for the third million hamburgers, maximum willingness to pay is given by point C; consumer surplus is a bit lower than it is at points A and B, but it is still significant.

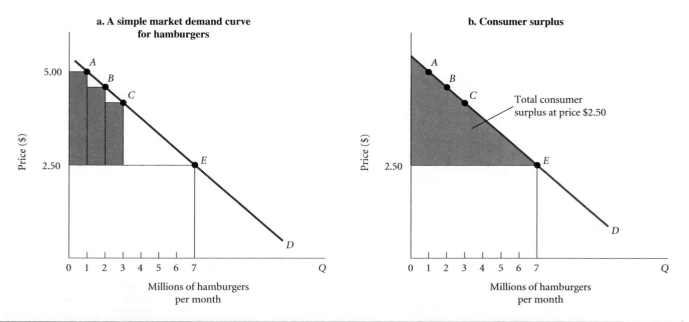

FIGURE 4.6 Market Demand and Consumer Surplus

As illustrated in Figure 4.6(a), some consumers (see point A) are willing to pay as much as $5.00 each for hamburgers. Since the market price is just $2.50, they receive a consumer surplus of $2.50 for each hamburger that they consume. Others (see point B) are willing to pay something less than $5.00 and receive a slightly smaller surplus. Since the market price of hamburgers is just $2.50, the area of the shaded triangle in Figure 4.6(b) is equal to total consumer surplus.

The total value of the consumer surplus suggested by the data in Figure 4.6(a) is roughly equal to the area of the shaded triangle in Figure 4.6(b). To understand why this is so, think about offering hamburgers to consumers at successively lower prices. If the good were actually sold for $2.50, those near point A on the demand curve would get a large surplus; those at point B would get a smaller surplus. Those at point E would get no surplus.

PRODUCER SURPLUS

Similarly, the supply curve in a market shows the amount that firms willingly produce and supply to the market at various prices. Presumably it is because the price is sufficient to cover the costs or the opportunity costs of production and give producers enough profit to keep them in business. When speaking of cost of production, we include everything that a producer must give up in order to produce a good.

A simple market supply curve like the one in Figure 4.7(a) illustrates this point quite clearly. At the current market price of $2.50, producers will produce and sell 7 million hamburgers. There is only one price in the market, and the supply curve tells us the quantity supplied at each price.

Notice, however, that if the price were just $0.75 (75 cents), although production would be much lower—most producers would be out of business at that price—a few producers would actually be supplying burgers. In fact, producers would supply about 1 million burgers to the market. These firms must have lower costs: They are either more efficient, or they have access to raw beef at a lower price, or perhaps they can hire low-wage labor.

producer surplus The difference between the current market price and the full cost of production for the firm.

If these efficient, low-cost producers are able to charge $2.50 for each hamburger, they are earning what is called a **producer surplus**. Producer surplus is the difference between the current market price and the full cost of production for the firm. The first 1 million hamburgers would generate a producer surplus of $2.50 minus $0.75 or $1.75 per hamburger: a total of $1.75 million. The second million hamburgers would also generate a producer surplus because the price of $2.50 exceeds the producers' total cost of producing these hamburgers, which is above $0.75 but much less than $2.50.

The total value of the producer surplus received by producers of hamburgers at a price of $2.50 per burger is roughly equal to the shaded triangle in Figure 4.7(b). Those producers just able to make a profit producing burgers will be near point E on the supply curve and will earn very little in the way of surplus.

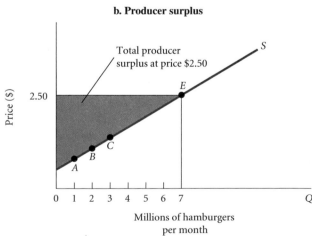

FIGURE 4.7 Market Supply and Producer Surplus

As illustrated in Figure 4.7(a), some producers are willing to produce hamburgers for a price of $0.75 each. Since they are paid $2.50, they earn a producer surplus equal to $1.75. Other producers are willing to supply hamburgers at a price of $1.00; they receive a producer surplus equal to $1.50. Since the market price of hamburgers is $2.50, the area of the shaded triangle in Figure 4.7(b) is equal to total producer surplus.

COMPETITIVE MARKETS MAXIMIZE THE SUM OF PRODUCER AND CONSUMER SURPLUS

In the preceding example, the quantity of hamburgers supplied and the quantity of hamburgers demanded are equal. Figure 4.8 shows the total net benefits to consumers and producers resulting from the production of 7 million hamburgers. Consumers receive benefits, in excess of the price they pay, equal to the blue shaded area between the demand curve and the price line at $2.50; the area is equal to the amount of consumer surplus being earned. Producers receive compensation, in excess of costs, equal to the red shaded area between the supply curve and the price line at $2.50; the area is equal to the amount of producer surplus being earned.

Now consider the result to consumers and producers if production were to be reduced to 4 million burgers. Look carefully at Figure 4.9(a). At 4 million burgers, consumers are willing to pay $3.75 for hamburgers and there are firms whose cost makes it worthwhile to supply at a price as low as $1.50, yet something is stopping production at 4 million. The result is a loss of both consumer and producer surplus. You can see in Figure 4.9(a) that if production were expanded from 4 million to 7 million, the market would yield more consumer surplus and more producer surplus. The total loss of producer and consumer surplus from *underproduction* or, as we will see shortly, also from overproduction, is referred to as a **deadweight loss**. In Figure 4.9(a) the deadweight loss is equal to the area of triangle *ABC* shaded in yellow.

Figure 4.9(b) illustrates how a deadweight loss of both producer and consumer surplus can result from *overproduction* as well. For every hamburger produced above 7 million, consumers are willing to pay less than the cost of production. The cost of the resources needed to produce hamburgers above 7 million exceeds the benefits to consumers, resulting in a net loss of producer and consumer surplus equal to the yellow shaded area *ABC*.

deadweight loss The net loss of producer and consumer surplus from underproduction or overproduction.

POTENTIAL CAUSES OF DEADWEIGHT LOSS FROM UNDER- AND OVERPRODUCTION

Most of the next few chapters will discuss perfectly competitive markets in which prices are determined by the free interaction of supply and demand. As you will see, when supply and demand interact freely, competitive markets produce what people want at least

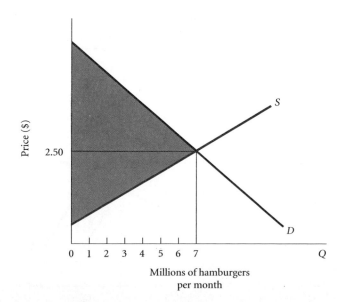

FIGURE 4.8 Total Producer and Consumer Surplus

Total producer and consumer surplus is greatest where supply and demand curves intersect at equilibrium.

The Drug Wars: A Matter of Supply and Demand

For years a debate has raged between those who favor strategies for reducing the supply of illegal drugs and those who favor strategies designed to reduce the demand for illegal drugs. The president's budget for 2006 contained $12.4 billion dollars for the "war on drugs," and its focus was on supply. Of the total, roughly 67 percent was spent on the supply side: actions to destroy drugs where they are grown; stopping drugs from entering the United States; and efforts to stop domestic distribution. The remaining 33 percent was spent on reducing demand, specifically for things like treatment and prevention.

Clearly, if the supply-side efforts are successful, they will drive up the price of drugs on the street. Higher prices mean that fewer people are willing to buy drugs and the quantity demanded drops.

Critics of the supply-side approach argue that programs designed to reduce supply in the past have failed. The reason, they claim, is that the high price of drugs makes it very profitable to produce. Thus, as production from one country is reduced, supply will come from other sources.

You can see the essence of the debate in Figure 1. Supply shifts to the left, and the equilibrium price rises. As the price rises, quantity demanded declines along the demand curve as fewer people are willing to buy drugs, and quantity supplied increases along the supply curve as the higher price spurs new production elsewhere.

What are the alternatives? Some argue that we should shift the focus to reducing the demand for illegal drugs. If we succeed, the resulting lower price

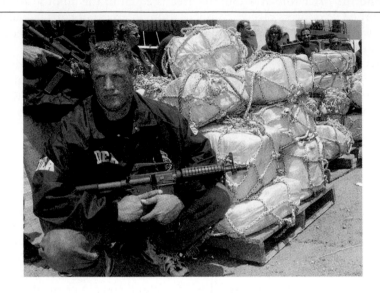

would take the profit out of production and reduce the quantity supplied. You can see this point in Figure 2. Demand shifts to the left, and the equilibrium price falls. As the price falls, the quantity supplied falls, a movement along the supply curve.

A second, perhaps more radical, set of critics argues that legalization is the best solution. Legalization would reduce the cost of production substantially. No longer would it take enormous expenses to smuggle drugs across the border, and sellers would no longer face the risk of prosecution. Legalization would shift the supply curve to the right, substantially reducing the price of drugs on

the street. Proponents of legalization argue that it is the very high price of drugs that forces many into criminal activity to support their habits. Opponents of legalization point to the fact that the lower price would lead to a higher quantity demanded and, thus, to more addiction.

Of course, the arguments on all sides of this issue are very complex, but the laws of supply and demand put them in a framework that helps clarify the debate.

Source: "The President's National Drug Control Policy," White House, February 2005.

FIGURE 1

FIGURE 2

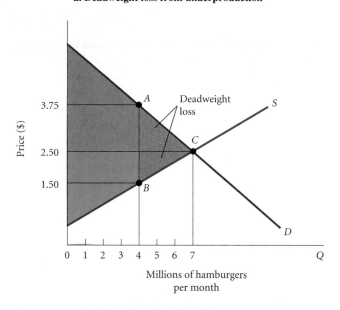

a. Deadweight loss from underproduction

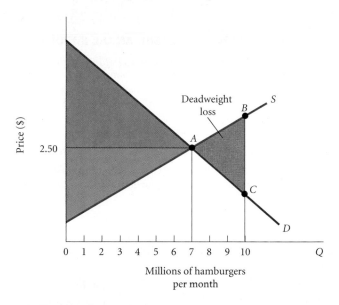

b. Deadweight loss from overproduction

FIGURE 4.9 Deadweight Loss

Figure 4.9(a) shows the consequences of producing 4 million hamburgers per month instead of 7 million hamburgers per month. Total producer and consumer surplus is reduced by the area of triangle *ABC* shaded in yellow. This is called the deadweight loss from underproduction. Figure 4.9(b) shows the consequences of producing 10 million hamburgers per month instead of 7 million hamburgers per month. As production increases from 7 to 10 million hamburgers, the full cost of production rises above consumers' willingness to pay, resulting in a deadweight loss equal to the area of triangle *ABC*.

cost, that is, they are efficient. Beginning in Chapter 12, however, we will begin to relax assumptions, and we will discover a number of naturally occurring sources of market failure. Monopoly power gives firms the incentive to underproduce and overprice, taxes and subsidies may distort consumer choices, external costs such as pollution and congestion may lead to over- or underproduction of some goods, and artificial price floors and price ceilings may have the same effects.

LOOKING AHEAD

We have now examined the basic forces of supply and demand and discussed the market/price system. These fundamental concepts will serve as building blocks for what comes next. Whether you are studying microeconomics or macroeconomics, you will be studying the functions of markets and the behavior of market participants in more detail in the following chapters.

Because the concepts presented in the first four chapters are so important to your understanding of what is to come, this might be a good point for you to review Part I.

SUMMARY

THE PRICE SYSTEM: RATIONING AND ALLOCATING RESOURCES

1. In a market economy, the market system (or price system) serves two functions. It determines the allocation of resources among producers and the final mix of outputs. It also distributes goods and services on the basis of willingness and ability to pay. In this sense, it serves as a *price rationing* device.

2. Governments, as well as private firms, sometimes decide not to use the market system to ration an item for which

there is excess demand. Examples of nonprice rationing systems include *queuing, favored customers,* and *ration coupons.* The most common rationale for such policies is "fairness."

3. Attempts to bypass the market and use alternative nonprice rationing devices are much more difficult and costly than it would seem at first glance. Schemes that open up opportunities for favored customers, black markets, and side payments often end up less "fair" than the free market.

SUPPLY AND DEMAND ANALYSIS: AN OIL IMPORT FEE

4. The basic logic of supply and demand is a powerful tool for analysis. For example, supply and demand analysis shows that an oil import tax will reduce quantity of oil demanded, increase domestic production, and generate revenues for the government.

SUPPLY AND DEMAND AND MARKET EFFICIENCY

5. Supply and demand curves can also be used to illustrate the idea of market efficiency, an important aspect of "normative economics."

6. *Consumer surplus* is the difference between the maximum amount a person is willing to pay for a good and the current market price.

7. *Producer surplus* is the difference between the current market price and the full cost of production for the firm.

8. At free market equilibrium with competitive markets, the sum of consumer surplus and producer surplus is maximized.

9. The net loss of producer and consumer surplus from underproduction or overproduction is referred to as a *deadweight loss*.

REVIEW TERMS AND CONCEPTS

black market, 81	minimum wage, 84	price rationing, 77
consumer surplus, 87	price ceiling, 80	queuing, 80
deadweight loss, 89	price floor, 84	ration coupons, 81
favored customers, 81	producer surplus, 88	

PROBLEM SET

1. Illustrate the following with supply and demand curves:
   a. In May 2005, a 1963 painting by Andy Warhol called *Liz* was sold in New York for $12.6 million.
   b. In 2005, hogs in the United States were selling for $67 each, down from $75 a year before. This was primarily due to the fact that supply had increased during the period to 1.8 million hogs per week.
   c. Early in 2007, a survey of greenhouses indicated that the demand for houseplants was rising sharply. At the same time, large numbers of low-cost producers started growing plants for sale. The overall result was a drop in the average price of houseplants and an increase in the number of plants sold.

2. Every demand curve must eventually hit the quantity axis because with limited incomes there is always a price so high that there is no demand for the good. Do you agree or disagree?

3. When excess demand exists for tickets to a major sporting event or a concert, profit opportunities exist for scalpers. Explain briefly, using supply and demand curves to illustrate. Some argue that scalpers work to the advantage of everyone and are "efficient." Do you agree or disagree? Explain briefly.

4. In an effort to "support" the price of some agricultural goods, the Department of Agriculture pays farmers a subsidy in cash for every acre that they leave *unplanted*. The Agriculture Department argues that the subsidy increases the "cost" of planting and that it will reduce supply and increase the price of competitively produced agricultural goods. Critics argue that because the subsidy is a payment to farmers, it will reduce costs and lead to lower prices. Which argument is correct? Explain.

5. "The rent for apartments in New York City has been rising sharply. Demand for apartments in New York City has been rising sharply as well. This is hard to explain because the law of demand says that higher prices should lead to lower demand." Do you agree or disagree? Explain your answer.

6. Illustrate the following with supply and/or demand curves:
   a. The federal government "supports" the price of wheat by paying farmers not to plant wheat on some of their land.
   b. An increase in the price of chicken has an impact on the price of hamburger.
   c. Incomes rise, shifting the demand for gasoline. Crude oil prices rise, shifting the supply of gasoline. At the new equilibrium, the quantity of gasoline sold is less than it was before. (Crude oil is used to produce gasoline.)

7. Illustrate the following with supply and/or demand curves:
   a. A situation of excess labor supply (unemployment) caused by a "minimum wage" law
   b. The effect of a sharp increase in heating oil prices on the demand for insulation material

8. Suppose that the world price of oil is $30 per barrel, and suppose that the United States can buy all the oil it wants at this price. Suppose also that the demand and supply schedules for oil in the United States are as follows:

PRICE ($ PER BARREL)	U.S. QUANTITY DEMANDED	U.S. QUANTITY SUPPLIED
28	16	4
30	15	6
32	14	8
34	13	10
36	12	12

   a. On graph paper, draw the supply and demand curves for the United States.
   b. With free trade in oil, what price will Americans pay for their oil? What quantity will Americans buy? How much of this will be supplied by American producers? How much will be imported? Illustrate total imports on your graph of the U.S. oil market.

c. Suppose the United States imposes a tax of $4 per barrel on imported oil. What quantity would Americans buy? How much of this would be supplied by American producers? How much would be imported? How much tax would the government collect?

d. Briefly summarize the impact of an oil import tax by explaining who is helped and who is hurt among the following groups: domestic oil consumers, domestic oil producers, foreign oil producers, and the U.S. government.

9. Use the data in the preceding problem to answer the following questions. Now suppose that the United States allows no oil imports.

a. What are the equilibrium price and quantity for oil in the United States?

b. If the United States imposed a price ceiling of $34 per barrel on the oil market and prohibited imports, would there be an excess supply or an excess demand for oil? How much?

c. Under the price ceiling, quantity supplied and quantity demanded differ. Which of the two will determine how much oil is purchased? Briefly explain why.

10. Use the diagram below to calculate total consumer surplus at a price of $8 and production of 6 million meals per day. For the same equilibrium, calculate total producer surplus. If price remained at $8 but production were cut to 3 million meals per day, calculate producer surplus and consumer surplus. Calculate the deadweight loss from underproduction.

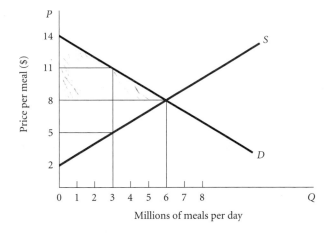

11. The box on page 90 describes the war on drugs and the potential impacts on the supply of and demand for cocaine. Suppose that the United States government simultaneously legalized drugs and launched a highly successful antidrug advertising campaign. Draw a supply and demand diagram to illustrate the effects of such changes on the price of cocaine. Proponents of legalization argue that it would reduce the crime rate. What links are there likely to be between the price of drugs and the crime rate? Opponents of legalization argue that the resulting expansion of supply and decline in price would cause the quantity demanded to increase as more people become addicted. Show on a supply and demand diagram what would happen if supply shifted to the right, but the advertising campaign failed to shift demand.

12. The box on page 83 presents an article from *CNN/Money* written in September of 2005. It predicts that in a relatively short period of time, unleaded regular gasoline at the pump would be selling for over $4. Do some research on the price of gasoline. Have those dire predictions materialized? What is the price of unleaded regular today in your city or town? If it is below $4 per gallon, what are the reasons why? Similarly, if it is higher than $4, what has happened to drive up the price? Illustrate with supply and demand curves.

Elasticity

5

In economics, simple logic often tells us how a change in one variable, like the price of a good or the interest rate, is likely to affect behavior. It is a safe bet, for example, that if gasoline prices rise, people will drive less. Also, when a store runs a big sale and cuts prices, its number of sales goes up.

The last two chapters have shown that principles of supply and demand enable us to predict changes in household and firm behavior in both national and international markets. We can say, for example, that a surge in housing construction in the United States in 2000–2005 shifted the demand for lumber and pushed up lumber and timber prices in world markets. We can also say the resulting higher price of timber caused an increase in logging.

But what we really need to know is, how big are these reactions? How much will a store sell if it runs a sale? A big increase in the number of sales will increase revenues, but a small increase may actually reduce revenues since prices are lower. How much less will people drive if gas prices surge? How many trees are being cut in response to the housing boom?

Consider the oil-producing countries, which have had some success keeping oil prices high by controlling supply. To some extent, reducing supply and driving up prices has increased the total oil revenues to the producing countries. As a result we might expect this strategy to work for everyone. If the organization of banana-exporting countries (OBEC) had done the same thing, however, the strategy would not have worked.

Why? Suppose OBEC decides to cut production by 30 percent to drive up the world price of bananas. At first, when the quantity of bananas supplied declines, the quantity demanded is greater than the quantity supplied, and the world price rises. The issue for OBEC, however, is *how much* the world price will rise. That is, how much will people be willing to pay to continue consuming bananas? Unless the percentage *increase* in price is greater than the percentage *decrease* in output, the OBEC countries will lose revenues.

A little research shows us that the prospects are not good for OBEC. There are many reasonable substitutes for bananas. As the price of bananas rises, people simply eat fewer bananas as they switch to eating more pineapples or oranges. Many people are simply not willing to pay a higher price for bananas. The quantity of bananas demanded declines 30 percent—to the new quantity supplied—after only a modest price rise, and OBEC fails in its mission; its revenues decrease instead of increase.

The quantity of oil demanded is not nearly as responsive as bananas to a change in price because no substitutes for oil are readily available. When the price of crude oil went up in the early 1970s, 130 million motor vehicles, getting an average of 12 miles per gallon and consuming over 100 billion gallons of gasoline each year, were on the road in the United States. Millions of homes were heated with oil, and industry ran on equipment that used petroleum products. When the oil-producing countries (OPEC) cut production, the price of oil rose sharply. Quantity demanded fell somewhat, but price increased over 400 percent. What makes the cases of OPEC and OBEC different is the *magnitude* of the response in the quantity demanded to a change of price.

The importance of actual measurement cannot be overstated. Without the ability to measure and predict how much people are likely to respond to economic changes, all the economic theory in the world would be of little help to policy makers. In fact, most of the research being done in economics today involves the collection and analysis of quantitative data that measure behavior. This is a dramatic change in the discipline of economics that has taken place only in the last 30 years.

elasticity A general concept used to quantify the response in one variable when another variable changes.

Economists commonly measure responsiveness using the concept of **elasticity**. Elasticity is a general concept that can be used to quantify the response in one variable when another variable changes. If some variable *A* changes in response to changes in another variable *B*, the elasticity of *A* with respect to *B* is equal to the percentage change in *A* divided by the percentage change in *B*:

$$\text{elasticity of } A \text{ with respect to } B = \frac{\%\Delta A}{\%\Delta B}$$

We may speak of the elasticity of demand or supply with respect to price, of the elasticity of investment with respect to the interest rate, or of the elasticity of tax payments with respect to income. We begin with a discussion of price elasticity of demand.

PRICE ELASTICITY OF DEMAND

You have already seen the law of demand at work. Recall that, *ceteris paribus*, when prices rise, quantity demanded can be expected to decline. When prices fall, quantity demanded can be expected to rise. The normal negative relationship between price and quantity demanded is reflected in the downward slope of demand curves.

SLOPE AND ELASTICITY

The slope of a demand curve may in a rough way reveal the responsiveness of the quantity demanded to price changes, but slope can be quite misleading. In fact, it is not a good formal measure of responsiveness.

Consider the two identical demand curves in Figure 5.1. The only difference between the two is that quantity demanded is measured in pounds in the graph on the left and in ounces in the graph on the right. When we calculate the numerical value of each slope, however, we get very different answers. The curve on the left has a slope of −1/5, and the curve on the right has a slope of −1/80, yet the two curves represent the *exact same behavior*. If we had changed dollars to cents on the *Y*-axis, the two slopes would be −20 and −1.25, respectively. (Review the Appendix to Chapter 1 if you do not understand how these numbers are calculated.)

The problem is that the numerical value of slope depends on the units used to measure the variables on the axes. To correct this problem, we must convert the changes in price and quantity to *percentages*. The price increase in Figure 5.1 leads to a decline of 5 pounds, or 80 ounces, in the quantity of steak demanded—a decline of 50 percent from the initial 10 pounds, or 160 ounces, whether we measure the steak in pounds or ounces.

price elasticity of demand The ratio of the percentage of change in quantity demanded to the percentage of change in price; measures the responsiveness of quantity demanded to changes in price.

We define **price elasticity of demand** simply as the ratio of the percentage of change in quantity demanded to the percentage change in price.

$$\text{price elasticity of demand} = \frac{\%\text{ change in quantity demanded}}{\%\text{ change in price}}$$

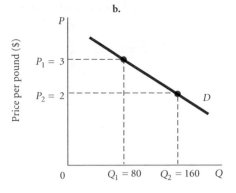

$$\text{Slope: } \frac{\Delta Y}{\Delta X} = \frac{P_2 - P_1}{Q_2 - Q_1}$$

$$= \frac{2 - 3}{10 - 5} = -\frac{1}{5}$$

$$\text{Slope: } \frac{\Delta Y}{\Delta X} = \frac{P_2 - P_1}{Q_2 - Q_1}$$

$$= \frac{2 - 3}{160 - 80} = -\frac{1}{80}$$

FIGURE 5.1 Slope Is Not a Useful Measure of Responsiveness

Changing the unit of measure from pounds to ounces changes the numerical value of the demand slope dramatically, but the behavior of buyers in the two diagrams is identical.

Percentage changes should always carry the sign (plus or minus) of the change. Positive changes, or increases, take a (+). Negative changes, or decreases, take a (−). The law of demand implies that price elasticity of demand is nearly always a negative number: Price increases (+) will lead to decreases in quantity demanded (−), and vice versa. Thus, the numerator and denominator should have opposite signs, resulting in a negative ratio.

TYPES OF ELASTICITY

Table 5.1 gives the hypothetical responses of demanders to a 10 percent price increase in four markets. Insulin is absolutely necessary to an insulin-dependent diabetic, and the quantity demanded is unlikely to respond to an increase in price. When the quantity demanded does not respond at all to a price change, the percentage of change in quantity demanded is zero, and the elasticity is zero. In this case, we say that the demand for the product is **perfectly inelastic**. Figure 5.2(a) illustrates the perfectly inelastic demand for insulin. Because quantity demanded does not change *at all* when price changes, the demand curve is simply a vertical line.

Unlike insulin, basic telephone service is generally considered a necessity, but not an absolute necessity. If a 10 percent increase in telephone rates results in a 1 percent decline in the quantity of service demanded, demand elasticity is $(-1 \div 10) = -.1$.

When the percentage change in quantity demanded is smaller in absolute size than the percentage change in price, as is the case with telephone service, then elasticity is less than 1 in absolute size.[1] When a product has an elasticity between zero and −1, we say that demand

perfectly inelastic demand Demand in which quantity demanded does not respond at all to a change in price.

TABLE 5.1 Hypothetical Demand Elasticities for Four Products

PRODUCT	% CHANGE IN PRICE (% ΔP)	% CHANGE IN QUANTITY DEMANDED (% ΔQ_D)	ELASTICITY (% Δ Q_D ÷ %ΔP)	
Insulin	+10%	0%	.0	➤ Perfectly inelastic
Basic telephone service	+10%	−1%	−.1	➤ Inelastic
Beef	+10%	−10%	−1.0	➤ Unitarily elastic
Bananas	+10%	−30%	−3.0	➤ Elastic

[1]The term *absolute size* or *absolute value* means ignoring the sign. The absolute value of −4 is 4; the absolute value of −3.8 is greater than the absolute value of 2.

a. Perfectly inelastic demand   b. Perfectly elastic demand

FIGURE 5.2 Perfectly Inelastic and Perfectly Elastic Demand Curves

Figure 5.2(a) shows a perfectly inelastic demand curve for insulin. Price elasticity of demand is zero. Quantity demanded is fixed; it does not change at all when price changes. Figure 5.2(b) shows a perfectly elastic demand curve facing a wheat farmer. A tiny price increase drives the quantity demanded to zero. In essence, perfectly elastic demand implies that individual producers can sell all they want at the going market price but cannot charge a higher price.

inelastic demand Demand that responds somewhat, but not a great deal, to changes in price. Inelastic demand always has a numerical value between zero and −1.

is **inelastic**. The demand for basic telephone service is inelastic at −.1. Stated simply, inelastic demand means that there is some responsiveness of demand, but not a great deal, to a change in price.

> A warning: You must be very careful about signs. Because it is generally understood that demand elasticities are negative (demand curves have a negative slope), they are often reported and discussed without the negative sign. For example, a technical paper might report that the demand for housing "appears to be inelastic with respect to price, or less than 1 (.6)." What the writer means is that the estimated elasticity is −.6, which is between zero and −1. Its absolute value is less than 1.

Returning to Table 5.1, we see that a 10 percent increase in beef prices drives down the quantity of beef demanded by 10 percent. Demand elasticity is thus $(-10 \div 10) = -1$. When the percentage change in quantity of product demanded is the same as the percentage change in price in absolute value, we say that the demand for that product has **unitary elasticity**. The elasticity is minus one (−1). As Table 5.1 shows, the demand for beef has unitary elasticity.

unitary elasticity A demand relationship in which the percentage change in quantity of a product demanded is the same as the percentage change in price in absolute value (a demand elasticity of −1).

When the percentage change in quantity demanded is larger than the percentage change in price in absolute size, we say that demand is **elastic**. The demand for bananas, for example, is likely to be quite elastic because there are many substitutes for bananas—other fruits, for instance. If a 10 percent increase in the price of bananas leads to a 30 percent decrease in the quantity of bananas demanded, the price elasticity of demand for bananas is $(-30 \div 10) = -3$. When the absolute value of elasticity exceeds 1, demand is elastic.

elastic demand A demand relationship in which the percentage change in quantity demanded is larger than the percentage change in price in absolute value (a demand elasticity with an absolute value greater than 1).

Finally, if a small increase in the price of a product causes the quantity demanded to drop immediately to zero, demand for that product is said to be **perfectly elastic**. Suppose, for example, that you produce a product that can be sold only at a predetermined, fixed price. If you charged even one penny more, no one would buy your product because people would simply buy from another producer who had not raised the price. This is very close to reality for farmers, who cannot charge more than the current market price for their crops.

perfectly elastic demand Demand in which quantity drops to zero at the slightest increase in price.

A perfectly elastic demand curve is illustrated in Figure 5.2(b). Because the quantity demanded drops to zero above a certain price, the demand curve for such a good is a horizontal line. A good way to remember the difference between the two "perfect" elasticities is:

Perfectly **E**lastic
and Perfectly **I**nelastic

Elasticity of Supply and House Prices

ONE OF THE HOTTEST TOPICS IN THE news in 2005 was the potential bursting of the "Housing Bubble." House prices in a number of specific markets, particularly in the Northeast and in California, increased by much more than incomes had risen over the 1995–2005 period. This huge run-up in prices is described in the following press release from the Office of Federal Housing Enterprise Oversight issued on September 1, 2005.

Housing price increases are good for those who own. But house price increases make it harder for those who do not own to make the leap to ownership. In addition, when house prices rise, owners tend to take out "home equity" loans to finance spending on other things. The housing and home building sector employs many people, from construction workers to real estate agents to mortgage bankers. If the housing bubble were to burst and prices were to fall sharply, the impact on the economy could be severe.

A bubble occurs when the price of an asset rises beyond what the fundamentals of supply and demand can support. The United States had a stock market bubble in the late 1990s built on overblown expectations about stock values during the dot-com revolution. The bursting of the dot-com bubble in 2000 wiped out trillions of dollars in household saving.

What causes a bubble to occur? In housing, one ingredient must be a relatively **inelastic supply of housing** or land to build on. In places where land is plentiful and inexpensive, housing gets built quickly whenever demand increases, and prices do not rise very much. In Midwestern cities surrounded by developable farm land, housing can be built quickly when demand increases. But in places where land for building is in short supply or where zoning rules make it difficult to get building permits, supply does not respond quickly and shifts of demand can push up prices quickly.

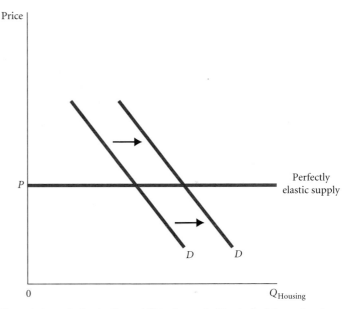

If supply is perfectly elastic, a shift in demand will not result in a price rise.

Largest U.S. House Price Increases in More Than 25 Years

WASHINGTON, D.C.—Average U.S. home prices increased **13.43 percent** from the second quarter of 2004 through the second quarter of 2005. Appreciation for the most recent quarter was **3.20 percent**, or an annualized rate of 12.8 percent. The new data represent the largest four-quarter increase since the second quarter of 1979. The figures were released today by OFHEO Acting Director Stephen A. Blumenthal, as part of the House Price Index (HPI), a quarterly report analyzing housing price appreciation trends.

"There is no evidence here of prices topping out," said OFHEO Chief Economist Patrick Lawler. "On the contrary, house price inflation continues to accelerate, as some areas that have experienced relatively slow appreciation are picking up steam."

House prices grew considerably faster over the past year than did prices of non-housing goods and services reflected in the Consumer Price Index. House prices rose 13.4 percent, while prices of other goods and services rose only 3.1 percent.

The Pacific Census Division continues to exhibit the fastest appreciation while the slowest growing area continues to be the West South Central division, which includes Texas, Oklahoma, Arkansas, and Louisiana. Arizona and Nevada continue to exhibit striking appreciation rates.

"The continued price increases are a result of many factors including low mortgage interest rates and the apparent impact of speculative investing," said Lawler. "The robust appreciation rates are striking both in terms of their magnitude and in their geographic scope. However, they are likely unsustainable given the underlying inflation rate, income growth and other factors," Lawler said.

CALCULATING ELASTICITIES

Elasticities must be calculated cautiously. Return for a moment to the demand curves in Figure 5.1. The fact that these two identical demand curves have dramatically different slopes should be enough to convince you that slope is a poor measure of responsiveness.

The concept of elasticity circumvents the measurement problem posed by the graphs in Figure 5.1 by converting the changes in price and quantity into percentage changes. Recall that elasticity of demand is the *percentage* change in quantity demanded divided by the *percentage* change in price.

CALCULATING PERCENTAGE CHANGES

Because we need to know percentage changes to calculate elasticity, let us begin our example by calculating the percentage change in quantity demanded. Figure 5.1(a) shows that the quantity of steak demanded increases from 5 pounds (Q_1) to 10 pounds (Q_2) when price drops from \$3 to \$2 per pound. Thus, the change in quantity demanded is equal to $Q_2 - Q_1$, or 5 pounds.

To convert this change into a percentage change, we must decide on a *base* against which to calculate the percentage. It is often convenient to use the initial value of quantity demanded (Q_1) as the base.

To calculate percentage change in quantity demanded using the initial value as the base, the following formula is used:

$$\% \text{ change in quantity demanded} = \frac{\text{change in quantity demanded}}{Q_1} \times 100\%$$

$$= \frac{Q_2 - Q_1}{Q_1} \times 100\%$$

In Figure 5.1, $Q_2 = 10$ and $Q_1 = 5$. Thus,

$$\% \text{ change in quantity demanded} = \frac{10 - 5}{5} \times 100\% = \frac{5}{5} \times 100\% = 100\%$$

Expressing this equation verbally, we can say that an increase in quantity demanded from 5 pounds to 10 pounds is a 100 percent increase from 5 pounds. Note that you arrive at exactly the same result if you use the diagram in Figure 5.1(b), in which quantity demanded is measured in ounces. An increase from Q_1 (80 ounces) to Q_2 (160 ounces) is a 100 percent increase.

We can calculate the percentage change in price in a similar way. Once again, let us use the initial value of P—that is, P_1—as the base for calculating the percentage. By using P_1 as the base, the formula for calculating the percentage of change in P is simply:

$$\% \text{ change in price} = \frac{\text{change in price}}{P_1} \times 100\%$$

$$= \frac{P_2 - P_1}{P_1} \times 100\%$$

In Figure 5.1(a), P_2 equals 2, and P_1 equals 3. Thus, the change in P, or ΔP, is a negative number: $P_2 - P_1 = 2 - 3 = -1$. This is true because the change is a decrease in price. Plugging the values of P_1 and P_2 into the preceding equation, we get:

$$\% \text{ change in price} = \frac{2 - 3}{3} \times 100\% = \frac{-1}{3} \times 100\% = -33.3\%$$

In other words, decreasing the price from \$3 to \$2 is a 33.3 percent decline.

Once the changes in quantity demanded and price have been converted into percentages, calculating elasticity is a matter of simple division. Recall the formal definition of elasticity:

$$\text{price elasticity of demand} = \frac{\%\ \text{change in quantity demanded}}{\%\ \text{change in price}}$$

If demand is elastic, the ratio of percentage change in quantity demanded to percentage change in price will have an absolute value greater than 1. If demand is inelastic, the ratio will have an absolute value between 0 and 1. If the two percentages are exactly equal, so that a given percentage change in price causes an equal percentage change in quantity demanded, elasticity is equal to −1; this is unitary elasticity.

Substituting the preceding percentages, we see that a 33.3 percent decrease in price leads to a 100 percent increase in quantity demanded; thus,

$$\text{price elasticity of demand} = \frac{+100\%}{-33.3\%} = -3.0$$

According to these calculations, the demand for steak is elastic.

THE MIDPOINT FORMULA

Although simple, the use of the initial values of P and Q as the bases for calculating percentage changes can be misleading. Let us return to the example of demand for steak in Figure 5.1(a), where we have a change in quantity demanded of 5 pounds. Using the initial value Q_1 as the base, we calculated that this change represents a 100 percent increase over the base. Now suppose that the price of steak rises back to $3, causing the quantity demanded to drop back to 5 pounds. How much of a percentage decrease in quantity demanded is this? We now have $Q_1 = 10$ and $Q_2 = 5$. With the same formula we used earlier, we get

$$\%\ \text{change in quantity demanded} = \frac{\text{change in quantity demanded}}{Q_1} \times 100\%$$

$$= \frac{Q_2 - Q_1}{Q_1} \times 100\%$$

$$= \frac{5 - 10}{10} \times 100\% = -50\%$$

Thus, an increase from 5 pounds to 10 pounds is a 100 percent increase (because the initial value used for the base is 5), but a decrease from 10 pounds to 5 pounds is only a 50 percent decrease (because the initial value used for the base is 10). This does not make much sense because in both cases we are calculating elasticity on the same interval on the demand curve. Changing the "direction" of the calculation should not change the elasticity.

To describe percentage changes more accurately, a simple convention has been adopted. Instead of using the initial values of Q and P as the bases for calculating percentages, we use the *midpoints* of these variables as the bases. That is, we use the value halfway between P_1 and P_2 for the base in calculating the percentage change in price, and the value halfway between Q_1 and Q_2 as the base for calculating percentage change in quantity demanded.

Thus, the **midpoint formula** for calculating the percentage change in quantity demanded becomes

midpoint formula A more precise way of calculating percentages using the value halfway between P_1 and P_2 for the base in calculating the percentage change in price, and the value halfway between Q_1 and Q_2 as the base for calculating the percentage change in quantity demanded.

$$\%\ \text{change in quantity demanded} = \frac{\text{change in quantity demanded}}{(Q_1 + Q_2)\,/\,2} \times 100\%$$

$$= \frac{Q_2 - Q_1}{(Q_1 + Q_2)\,/\,2} \times 100\%$$

Substituting the numbers from the original Figure 5.1(a), we get

$$\% \text{ change in quantity demanded} = \frac{10 - 5}{(5 + 10)\,/\,2} \times 100\% = \frac{5}{7.5} \times 100\% = 66.7\%$$

Using the point halfway between P_1 and P_2 as the base for calculating the percentage change in price, we get

$$\% \text{ change in price} = \frac{\text{change in price}}{(P_1 + P_2)\,/\,2} \times 100\%$$

$$= \frac{P_2 - P_1}{(P_1 + P_2)\,/\,2} \times 100\%$$

Substituting the numbers from the original Figure 5.1(a) yields

$$\% \text{ change in price} = \frac{2 - 3}{(3 + 2)\,/\,2} \times 100\% = \frac{-1}{2.5} \times 100\% = -40.0\%$$

We can thus say that a change from a quantity of 5 to a quantity of 10 is a +66.7 percent change using the midpoint formula, and a change in price from $3 to $2 is a −40 percent change using the midpoint formula.

Using these percentages to calculate elasticity yields

$$\text{price elasticity of demand} = \frac{\% \text{ change in quantity demanded}}{\% \text{ change in price}} = \frac{66.7\%}{-40.0\%} = -1.67$$

Using the midpoint formula in this case gives a lower demand elasticity, but the demand remains elastic because the percentage change in quantity demanded is still greater than the percentage change in price in absolute size.

The calculations based on the midpoint approach are summarized in Table 5.2.

ELASTICITY CHANGES ALONG A STRAIGHT-LINE DEMAND CURVE

An interesting and important point is that elasticity changes from point to point along a demand curve even if the slope of that demand curve does not change—that is, even along a straight-line demand curve. Indeed, the differences in elasticity along a demand curve can be quite large.

Consider the demand schedule shown in Table 5.3 and the demand curve in Figure 5.3. Herb works about 22 days per month in a downtown San Francisco office tower. On the top floor of the building is a nice dining room. If lunch in the dining room costs $10, Herb

---

TABLE 5.2 Calculating Price Elasticity with the Midpoint Formula

First, Calculate Percentage Change in Quantity Demanded (%ΔQ_D):

$$\% \text{ change in quantity demanded} = \frac{\text{change in quantity demanded}}{(Q_1 + Q_2)\,/\,2} \times 100\% = \frac{Q_2 - Q_1}{(Q_1 + Q_2)\,/\,2} \times 100\%$$

By substituting the numbers from Figure 5.1(a):

$$\% \text{ change in quantity demanded} = \frac{10 - 5}{(5 + 10)\,/\,2} \times 100\% = \frac{5}{7.5} \times 100\% = 66.7\%$$

Next, Calculate Percentage Change in Price (%ΔP):

$$\% \text{ change in price} = \frac{\text{change in price}}{(P_1 + P_2)\,/\,2} \times 100\% = \frac{P_2 - P_1}{(P_1 + P_2)\,/\,2} \times 100\%$$

By substituting the numbers from Figure 5.1(a):

$$\% \text{ change in price} = \frac{2 - 3}{(3 + 2)\,/\,2} \times 100\% = \frac{-1}{2.5} \times 100\% = -40.0\%$$

PRICE ELASTICITY COMPARES THE PERCENTAGE CHANGE IN QUANTITY DEMANDED AND THE PERCENTAGE CHANGE IN PRICE:

$$\frac{\%\Delta Q_D}{\%\Delta P} = \frac{66.7\%}{-40.0\%}$$

$$= -1.67$$

= PRICE ELASTICITY OF DEMAND

DEMAND IS ELASTIC

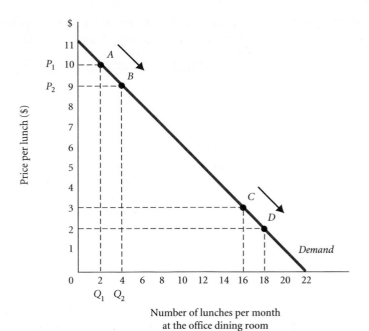

TABLE 5.3 Demand Schedule for Office Dining Room Lunches

PRICE (PER LUNCH)	QUANTITY DEMANDED (LUNCHES PER MONTH)
$11	0
10	2
9	4
8	6
7	8
6	10
5	12
4	14
3	16
2	18
1	20
0	22

FIGURE 5.3 Demand Curve for Lunch at the Office Dining Room

Between points *A* and *B*, demand is quite elastic at −6.4. Between points *C* and *D*, demand is quite inelastic at −.294.

would eat there only twice a month. If the price of lunch falls to $9, he would eat there 4 times a month. (Herb would bring his lunch to work on other days.) If lunch were only a dollar, he would eat there 20 times a month.

Let us calculate price elasticity of demand between points *A* and *B* on the demand curve in Figure 5.3. Moving from *A* to *B*, the price of a lunch drops from $10 to $9 (a decrease of $1) and the number of dining room lunches that Herb eats per month increases from two to four (an increase of two). We will use the midpoint approach.

First, we calculate the percentage change in quantity demanded:

$$\% \text{ change in quantity demanded} = \frac{Q_2 - Q_1}{(Q_1 + Q_2) / 2} \times 100\%$$

Substituting the numbers from Figure 5.3, we get

$$\% \text{ change in quantity demanded} = \frac{4 - 2}{(2 + 4) / 2} \times 100\% = \frac{2}{3} \times 100\% = 66.7\%$$

Next, we calculate the percentage change in price:

$$\% \text{ change in price} = \frac{P_2 - P_1}{(P_1 + P_2) / 2} \times 100\%$$

By substituting the numbers from Figure 5.3:

$$\% \text{ change in price} = \frac{9 - 10}{(10 + 9) / 2} \times 100\% = \frac{-1}{9.5} \times 100\% = -10.5\%$$

Finally, we calculate elasticity by dividing:

$$\text{elasticity of demand} = \frac{\% \text{ change in quantity demanded}}{\% \text{ change in price}}$$

$$= \frac{66.7\%}{-10.5\%} = -6.4$$

The percentage change in quantity demanded is 6.4 times larger than the percentage change in price. In other words, Herb's demand between points *A* and *B* is quite responsive; his demand between points *A* and *B* is elastic.

Now consider a different movement along the *same* demand curve in Figure 5.3. Moving from point *C* to point *D*, the graph indicates that at a price of $3, Herb eats in the office dining room 16 times per month. If the price drops to $2, he eats there 18 times per month. These changes expressed in numerical terms are exactly the same as the price and quantity changes between points *A* and *B* in the figure—price falls $1, and quantity demanded increases by two meals. Expressed in *percentage* terms, however, these changes are very different.

By using the midpoints as the base, the $1 price decline is only a 10.5 percent reduction when price is around $9.50, between points *A* and *B*. The same $1 price decline is a 40 percent reduction when price is around $2.50, between points *C* and *D*. The two-meal increase in quantity demanded is a 66.7 percent increase when Herb averages only 3 meals per month, but it is only an 11.76 percent increase when he averages 17 meals per month. The elasticity of demand between points *C* and *D* is thus 11.76 percent divided by −40 percent, or −.294. (Work these numbers out for yourself by using the midpoint formula.)

The percentage changes between *A* and *B* are very different from those between *C* and *D*, and so are the elasticities. Herb's demand is quite elastic (−6.4) between points *A* and *B*; a 10.5 percent reduction in price caused a 66.7 percent increase in quantity demanded. However, his demand is inelastic (−.294) between points *C* and *D*; a 40 percent decrease in price caused only an 11.76 percent increase in quantity demanded.

ELASTICITY AND TOTAL REVENUE

We have seen that oil-producing countries often can increase their revenues by restricting supply and pushing up the market price of crude oil. We also argued that a similar strategy by banana-producing countries would probably fail. Why? The quantity of oil demanded is not as responsive to a change in price as is the quantity of bananas demanded. In other words, the demand for oil is more inelastic than is the demand for bananas.

We can now use the more formal definition of elasticity to make more precise our argument of why oil producers would succeed and banana producers would fail. In any market, $P \times Q$ is total revenue (*TR*) received by producers:

$$TR = P \times Q$$

total revenue = price × quantity

The oil producers' total revenue is the price per barrel of oil (*P*) times the number of barrels its participant countries sell (*Q*). To banana producers, total revenue is the price per bunch times the number of bunches sold.

When price increases in a market, quantity demanded declines. As we have seen, when price (*P*) declines, quantity demanded (Q_D) increases. The two factors, *P* and Q_D, move in opposite directions:

effects of price changes on quantity demanded:
$$P \uparrow \rightarrow Q_D \downarrow$$
and
$$P \downarrow \rightarrow Q_D \uparrow$$

Because total revenue is the product of *P* and *Q*, whether *TR* rises or falls in response to a price increase depends on which is bigger, the percentage increase in price or the percentage decrease in quantity demanded. If the percentage decrease in quantity demanded is smaller than the percentage increase in price, total revenue will rise. This occurs when demand is *inelastic*. In this case, the percentage price rise simply outweighs the percentage quantity decline, and $P \times Q = (TR)$ rises:

effect of price increase on a product with inelastic demand:
$$\uparrow P \times Q_D \downarrow = TR \uparrow$$

If, however, the percentage decline in quantity demanded following a price increase is larger than the percentage increase in price, total revenue will fall. This occurs when demand is *elastic*. The percentage price increase is outweighed by the percentage quantity decline:

$$\text{effect of price increase on a product with elastic demand:} \quad \uparrow P \times Q_D \downarrow = TR \downarrow$$

The opposite is true for a price cut. When demand is elastic, a cut in price increases total revenues:

$$\text{effect of price cut on a product with elastic demand:} \quad \downarrow P \times Q_D \uparrow = TR \uparrow$$

When demand is inelastic, a cut in price reduces total revenues:

$$\text{effect of price cut on a product with inelastic demand:} \quad \downarrow P \times Q_D \uparrow = TR \downarrow$$

Review the logic of these equations to make sure you understand the reasoning thoroughly.

With this knowledge, we can now easily see why the oil cartel was so effective. The demand for oil is inelastic. Restricting the quantity of oil available led to a huge increase in the price of oil—the percentage of increase was larger in absolute value than the percentage decrease in the quantity of oil demanded. Hence, oil producers' total revenues went up. In contrast, a banana cartel would not be effective because the demand for bananas is elastic. A small increase in the price of bananas results in a large decrease in the quantity of bananas demanded and thus causes total revenues to fall. For details on the elasticity experiences of some other businesses, see the Further Exploration feature titled "London Newspapers and New York Restaurants Learn about Elasticity" on page 106.

THE DETERMINANTS OF DEMAND ELASTICITY

Elasticity of demand is a way of measuring the responsiveness of consumers' demand to changes in price. As a measure of behavior, it can be applied to individual households or to market demand as a whole. I love peaches and I would hate to give them up. My demand for peaches is therefore inelastic. However, not everyone is crazy about peaches, and, in fact, the market demand for peaches is relatively elastic. Because no two people have exactly the same preferences, reactions to price changes will be different for different people, and this makes generalizations risky. Nonetheless, a few principles do seem to hold.

AVAILABILITY OF SUBSTITUTES

Perhaps the most obvious factor affecting demand elasticity is the availability of substitutes. Consider a number of farm stands lined up along a country road. If every stand sells fresh corn of roughly the same quality, Mom's Green Thumb will find it very difficult to charge a price much higher than the competition charges, because a nearly perfect substitute is available just down the road. The demand for Mom's corn is thus likely to be very elastic: An increase in price will lead to a rapid decline in the quantity demanded of Mom's corn.

In Table 5.1, we considered two products that have no readily available substitutes, local telephone service and insulin for diabetics. There are many others. Demand for these products is likely to be quite inelastic.

THE IMPORTANCE OF BEING UNIMPORTANT

When an item represents a relatively small part of our total budget, we tend to pay little attention to its price. For example, if I pick up a pack of mints once in a while, I might not notice an increase in price from 25 cents to 35 cents. Yet this is a 40 percent increase in price

London Newspapers and New York Restaurants Learn about Elasticity

Businesses must carefully consider the demand elasticity for their products when adjusting prices. Consider these two examples:

1. **The London *Independent*** Recently, the *Independent*, a daily newspaper printed in London, announced a price cut to 30 pence from 50 pence. As a result, daily circulation increased from 240,000 copies to 280,000 copies. At first glance, the price cut might seem successful, but look closely at the result.

   A price cut from 50 pence to 30 pence is a 40 percent reduction (50 percent using the midpoint formula). The increase in circulation each day is only 16.6 percent (15.4 percent using the midpoint formula). Thus, demand is *inelastic*:

   $$\text{elasticity} = \frac{+15.4\%}{-50.0\%} = -.31$$

   When demand is inelastic, a cut in price leads to a reduction in daily revenues.

   Before: 50 pence × 240,000 copies = 12,000,000 pence in revenue

   After: 30 pence × 280,000 copies = 8,400,000 pence in revenue

2. **Restaurants in New York City** In the early 1990s, New York City was experiencing economic hard times. Unemployment was up, incomes were down, and there was great uncertainty about the future. Like other businesses, restaurants were suffering. Fewer people were dining out, and those who were avoided the most expensive restaurants.

The 1992 Democratic National Convention in July brought thousands of visiting delegates and journalists to the city, but many feared the out-of-town visitors would suffer "sticker shock" and avoid the city's most expensive restaurants. (Prices in New York are much higher than in most other parts of the country.) Thus, a plan was hatched. A group of 100 restaurants got together and offered lunch for $19.92, and a number of them

added special dinner menus with meals priced at $24.92. These prices may sound high to you, but they were a substantial reduction for most of the participating restaurants.

The result: Revenues were up during the convention, but what happened after the delegates left? Many restaurants decided to keep their prices down and got a real surprise: Local demand was elastic. Lower prices brought in more total revenue.

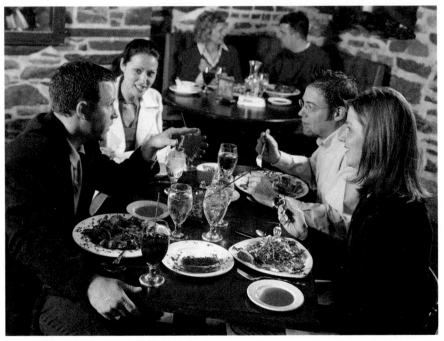

All businesses, including expensive restaurants, must face the fact that the quantity demanded for their product depends on price.

(33.3 percent using the midpoint formula). In cases such as these, we are not likely to respond very much to changes in price, and demand is likely to be inelastic.

THE TIME DIMENSION

When the oil-producing nations first cut output and succeeded in pushing up the price of crude oil, few substitutes were immediately available. Demand was relatively inelastic, and prices rose substantially. During the last 30 years, however, there has been some adjustment to higher oil prices. Automobiles manufactured today get on average more miles per gallon, and some drivers have cut down on their driving. Millions have insulated their homes, most have turned down their thermostats, and some have explored alternative energy sources.

Oil prices again rose dramatically during the weeks following Hurricane Katrina in 2005. Once again the response of demand to the resulting higher gasoline prices took place slowly over time. This time, many former SUV drivers switched to hybrids.

All of this illustrates a very important point:

> The elasticity of demand in the short run may be very different from the elasticity of demand in the long run. In the longer run, demand is likely to become more elastic, or responsive, simply because households make adjustments over time and producers develop substitute goods.

OTHER IMPORTANT ELASTICITIES

So far we have been discussing price elasticity of demand, which measures the responsiveness of quantity demanded to changes in price. However, as we noted earlier, elasticity is a perfectly general concept. If B causes a change in A and we can measure the change in both, we can calculate the elasticity of A with respect to B. Let us look briefly at three other important types of elasticity.

INCOME ELASTICITY OF DEMAND

Income elasticity of demand, which measures the responsiveness of demand to changes in income, is defined as

$$\text{income elasticity of demand} = \frac{\%\ \text{change in quantity demanded}}{\%\ \text{change in income}}$$

income elasticity of demand Measures the responsiveness of demand to changes in income.

Measuring income elasticity is important for many reasons. Government policy makers spend a great deal of time and money weighing the relative merits of different policies. During the 1970s, for example, the Department of Housing and Urban Development (HUD) conducted a huge experiment in four cities to estimate the income elasticity of housing demand. In this "housing allowance demand experiment," low-income families received housing vouchers over an extended period of time, and researchers watched their housing consumption for several years. Most estimates, including the ones from the HUD study, put the income elasticity of housing demand between .5 and .8. That is, a 10 percent increase in income can be expected to raise the quantity of housing demanded by a household by 5 percent to 8 percent.

CROSS-PRICE ELASTICITY OF DEMAND

Cross-price elasticity of demand, which measures the response of quantity of one good demanded to a change in the price of another good, is defined as

$$\text{cross-price elasticity of demand} = \frac{\%\ \text{change in quantity of } Y \text{ demanded}}{\%\ \text{change in price of } X}$$

cross-price elasticity of demand A measure of the response of the quantity of one good demanded to a change in the price of another good.

Like income elasticity, cross-price elasticity can be either positive or negative. A *positive* cross-price elasticity indicates that an increase in the price of X causes the demand for Y to rise. This implies that the goods are substitutes. If cross-price elasticity turns out to be *negative*, an increase in the price of X causes a decrease in the demand for Y. This implies that the goods are complements.

ELASTICITY OF SUPPLY

Elasticity of supply, which measures the response of quantity of a good supplied to a change in price of that good, is defined as

$$\text{elasticity of supply} = \frac{\%\ \text{change in quantity supplied}}{\%\ \text{change in price}}$$

elasticity of supply A measure of the response of quantity of a good supplied to a change in price of that good. Likely to be positive in output markets.

elasticity of labor supply A measure of the response of labor supplied to a change in the price of labor.

In output markets, the elasticity of supply is likely to be a positive number—that is, a higher price leads to an increase in the quantity supplied, *ceteris paribus*. (Recall our discussion of upward-sloping supply curves in the preceding two chapters.)

In input markets, however, some interesting problems arise. Perhaps the most studied elasticity of all is the **elasticity of labor supply**, which measures the response of labor supplied to a change in the price of labor. Economists have examined household labor supply responses to such government programs as welfare, Social Security, the income tax system, need-based student aid, and unemployment insurance, among others.

In simple terms, the elasticity of labor supply is defined as

$$\text{elasticity of labor supply} = \frac{\text{\% change in quantity of labor supplied}}{\text{\% change in the wage rate}}$$

It seems reasonable at first glance to assume that an increase in wages increases the quantity of labor supplied. That would imply an upward-sloping supply curve and a positive labor supply elasticity, but this is not necessarily so. An increase in wages makes workers better off: They can work the same amount and have higher incomes. One of the things that they might like to "buy" with that higher income is more leisure time. "Buying" leisure simply means working fewer hours, and the "price" of leisure is the lost wages. Thus it is quite possible that an increase in wages to some groups and above some level will lead to a reduction in the quantity of labor supplied.

LOOKING AHEAD

The purpose of this chapter was to convince you that measurement is important. If all we can say is that a change in one economic factor causes another to change, we cannot say whether the change is important or not, or whether a particular policy is likely to work or not work. The most commonly used tool of measurement is elasticity, and the term will recur as we explore economics in more depth.

We now return to the study of basic economics by looking in detail at household behavior. Recall that households *demand* goods and services in product markets but *supply* labor and savings in input or factor markets.

SUMMARY

ELASTICITY

1. *Elasticity* is a general measure of responsiveness that can be used to quantify many different relationships. If one variable A changes in response to changes in another variable B, the elasticity of A with respect to B is equal to the percentage change in A divided by the percentage change in B.

2. The slope of a demand curve is an inadequate measure of responsiveness, because its value depends on the units of measurement used. For this reason, elasticities are calculated using percentages.

3. *Price elasticity of demand* is the ratio of the percentage change in quantity demanded of a good to the percentage change in price of that good.

4. *Perfectly inelastic* demand is demand whose quantity demanded does not respond at all to changes in price; its numerical value is zero.

5. *Inelastic* demand is demand whose quantity demanded responds somewhat, but not a great deal, to changes in price; its numerical value is between zero and −1.

6. *Elastic* demand is demand in which the percentage change in quantity demanded is larger in absolute value than the percentage change in price. Its numerical value is less than −1.

7. *Unitary elasticity* of demand describes a relationship in which the percentage change in the quantity of a product demanded is the same as the percentage change in price; unitary elasticity has a numerical value of −1.

8. *Perfectly elastic* demand describes a relationship in which a small increase in the price of a product causes the quantity demanded for that product to drop to zero.

9. If demand is elastic, a price increase will reduce the quantity demanded by a larger percentage than the percentage increase in price, and total revenue ($P \times Q$) will fall. If demand is inelastic, a price increase will increase total revenue.

10. If demand is elastic, a price cut will cause quantity demanded to increase by a greater percentage than the percentage decrease in price, and total revenue will rise. If demand is inelastic, a price cut will cause quantity demanded to increase by a smaller percentage than the percentage decrease in price, and total revenue will fall.

11. The elasticity of demand depends on (1) the availability of substitutes, (2) the importance of the item in individual budgets, and (3) the time frame in question.

12. There are several important elasticities. *Income elasticity of demand* measures the responsiveness of the quantity demanded with respect to changes in income. *Cross-price elasticity of demand* measures the response of the quantity of one good demanded to a change in the price of another good. *Elasticity of supply* measures the response of the quantity of a good supplied to a change in the price of that good. The *elasticity of labor supply* measures the response of the quantity of labor supplied to a change in the price of labor.

REVIEW TERMS AND CONCEPTS

cross-price elasticity of demand, 107
elastic demand, 98
elasticity, 96
elasticity of labor supply, 108

elasticity of supply, 107
income elasticity of demand, 107
inelastic demand, 98
midpoint formula, 101

perfectly elastic demand, 98
perfectly inelastic demand, 97
price elasticity of demand, 96
unitary elasticity, 98

PROBLEM SET

1. Fill in the missing amounts in the following table:

	% CHANGE IN PRICE	% CHANGE IN QUANTITY	ELASTICITY
Demand for Ben & Jerry's Ice Cream	+10%	−12%	a.
Demand for beer at San Francisco 49ers football games	−20%	b.	−.5
Demand for Broadway theater tickets in New York	c.	−15%	−1.0
Supply of chickens	+10%	d.	+1.2
Supply of beef cattle	−15%	−10%	e.

2. Use the table in the preceding problem to defend your answers to the following questions:
   a. Would you recommend that Ben & Jerry's move forward with a plan to raise prices if the company's only goal is to increase revenues?
   b. Would you recommend that beer stands cut prices to increase revenues at 49ers games next year?

3. Using the midpoint formula, calculate elasticity for each of the following changes in demand by a household.

Demand for:	P_1	P_2	Q_1	Q_2
a. Long-distance telephone service	$0.25 per min.	$0.15 per min.	300 min. per month	400 min. per month
b. Orange juice	1.49 per qt	1.89 per qt	14 qt per month	12 qt per month
c. Big Macs	2.89	1.00	3 per week	6 per week
d. Cooked shrimp	9.00 per lb	12.00 per lb	2 lb per month	1.5 lb per month

4. A sporting goods store has estimated the demand curve for a popular brand of running shoes as a function of price. Use the following diagram to answer the questions below it.

Shoe sales per week

a. Calculate demand elasticity using the midpoint formula between points *A* and *B*, between points *C* and *D*, and between points *E* and *F*.
b. If the store currently charges a price of $50, then increases this price to $60, what happens to total revenue from shoe sales (calculate $P \times Q$ before and after the price change)? Repeat the exercise for initial prices being decreased to $40 and $20, respectively.
c. Explain why the answers to a. can be used to predict the answers to b.

5. For each of the following, say whether you agree or disagree and explain your answer.
   a. If the elasticity of demand for cocaine is −.2, and the Drug Enforcement Administration succeeds in reducing supply substantially, causing the street price of the drug to rise by 50%, buyers will spend less on cocaine.
   b. Every year, Christmas tree vendors bring tens of thousands of trees from the forests of New England to New York City and Boston. During the last two years the market has been very competitive, and as a result price has fallen by 10%. If the price elasticity of demand was −1.3, vendors would lose revenues altogether as a result of the price decline.

c. If the demand for a good has unitary elasticity, or elasticity is −1, it is always true that an increase in its price will lead to more revenues for sellers taken as a whole.

*6. For the following, say whether you agree or disagree and explain your answer.

a. The demand curve pictured next is elastic.

b. If supply were to increase somewhat in the following diagram, prices would fall and firms would earn less revenue.

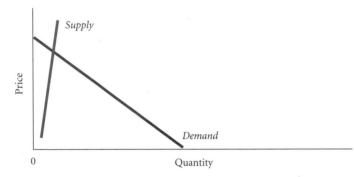

7. Taxicab fares in most cities are regulated. Several years ago, taxicab drivers in Boston obtained permission to raise their fares 10 percent, and they anticipated that revenues would increase by about 10 percent as a result. They were disappointed, however. When the commissioner granted the 10 percent increase, revenues increased by only about 5 percent. What can you infer about the elasticity of demand for taxicab rides? What were taxicab drivers assuming about the elasticity of demand?

*8. Studies have fixed the short-run price elasticity of demand for gasoline at the pump at −.20. Suppose that international hostilities lead to a sudden cutoff of crude oil supplies. As a result, U.S. supplies of refined gasoline drop 10 percent.

a. If gasoline was selling for $1.40 per gallon before the cutoff, how much of a price increase would you expect to see in the coming months?

b. Suppose that the government imposes a price ceiling on gas at $1.40 per gallon. How would the relationship between consumers and gas station owners change?

9. The box on page 99 describes the ingredients in a "housing bubble." One key is that the supply of housing must be relatively inelastic when prices are rising. That is, if the quantity supplied increases rapidly whenever house prices rise, price increases will remain small. Many have suggested government policies to increase the elasticity of supply. What specific policies might hold prices down when demand increases? Explain.

---

*Note: Problems marked with an asterisk are more challenging.

APPENDIX

POINT ELASTICITY (OPTIONAL)

Two different elasticities were calculated along the demand curve in Figure 5.3. Between points A and B we discovered that Herb's demand for lunches in the fancy dining room was very elastic: A price decline of only 10.5 percent resulted in his eating 66.7 percent more lunches in the dining room (elasticity = −6.4). Between points C and D, however, on the same demand curve, we discovered that his demand for meals was very inelastic: A price decline of 40 percent resulted in only a modest increase in lunches consumed of 11.8 percent (elasticity = −.295).

Now consider the straight-line demand curve in Figure 5A.1. We can write an expression for elasticity at point C as follows:

$$\text{elasticity} = \frac{\%\Delta Q}{\%\Delta P} = \frac{\dfrac{\Delta Q}{Q} \cdot 100}{\dfrac{\Delta P}{P} \cdot 100} = \frac{\dfrac{\Delta Q}{Q_1}}{\dfrac{\Delta P}{P_1}} = \boxed{\frac{\Delta P}{P} \cdot \frac{P_1}{Q_1}}$$

$\Delta Q / \Delta P$ is the *reciprocal* of the slope of the curve. Slope in the diagram is constant along the curve, and it is negative. To calculate the reciprocal of the slope to plug into the electricity

equation above, we take Q_1B, or M_1, and divide by *minus* the length of line segment CQ_1. Thus,

$$\frac{\Delta Q}{\Delta P} = \frac{M_1}{CQ_1}$$

Since the length of CQ_1 is equal to P_1, we can write:

$$\frac{\Delta Q}{\Delta P} = \frac{M_1}{P_1}$$

By substituting we get:

$$\text{elasticity} = \frac{M_1}{P_1} \cdot \frac{P_1}{Q_1} = \frac{M_1}{P_1} \cdot \frac{P_1}{M_2} = \boxed{\frac{M_1}{M_2}}$$

(The second equal sign uses the fact that Q_1 equals M_2 in Figure 5A.1.)

Elasticity at point C is simply the ratio of line segment M_1 to line segment M_2. It is easy to see that if we had chosen a point to the left of Q_1, M_1 would have been larger and M_2 would have been smaller, indicating a higher elasticity. If we had chosen a point to the right of Q_1, M_1 would have been

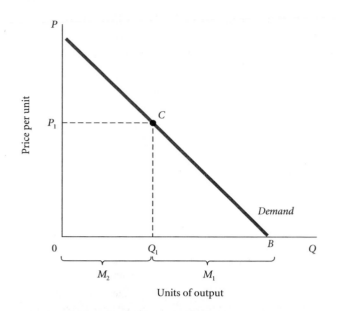

FIGURE 5A.1 Elasticity at a Point Along a Demand Curve

point *A*. At points to the left, such as Q_1, segment Q_1C (M_1) is larger than segment $0Q_1$ (M_2). This means that the absolute size of the ratio is *greater than 1*, and demand is elastic at point *B*.

Compare the results here with the results using the midpoint formula for elasticity for Herb.

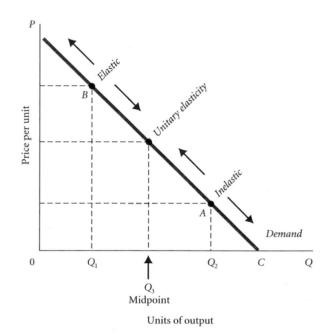

FIGURE 5A.2 Point Elasticity Changes Along a Demand Curve

smaller and M_2 would have been larger, indicating a lower elasticity.

In Figure 5A.2, you can see that elasticity is unitary (equal to -1) at the midpoint of the demand curve, Q_3. At points to the right, such as Q_2, segment Q_2C (M_1 from Figure 5A.1) is smaller than segment $0Q_2$ (M_2 from Figure 5A.1). This means that the absolute size of the ratio is *less than 1*, and demand is *inelastic* at

Household Behavior and Consumer Choice

6

Now that we have discussed the basic forces of supply and demand, we can explore the underlying behavior of the two fundamental decision-making units in the economy, households and firms.

Figure 6.1 presents a diagram of a simple competitive economy. The figure is an expanded version of the circular flow diagram first presented in Figure 3.1. It is designed to guide you through Part II (Chapters 6 through 12) of this book. You will see the "big picture" much more clearly if you follow this diagram closely as you work your way through this part of the book. (For your convenience, the diagram will be repeated several times in the next few chapters.)

Recall that households and firms interact in two kinds of markets: output (product) markets, shown at the top of Figure 6.1, and input (factor) markets, shown at the bottom. Households *demand* outputs and *supply* inputs. In contrast, firms *supply* outputs and *demand* inputs. This chapter explores the behavior of households, focusing first on household demand for outputs and then on household supply in labor and capital markets.

The remaining chapters in Part II focus on firms and the interaction between firms and households. Chapters 7 through 9 analyze the behavior of firms in output markets in both the short run and the long run. Chapter 10 focuses on the behavior of firms in input markets in general, especially the labor and land markets. Chapter 11 discusses the capital market in more detail. Chapter 12 puts all the pieces together and analyzes the functioning of a complete market system. Following Chapter 12, Part III of the book relaxes many assumptions and analyzes market imperfections, as well as the potential for and pitfalls of government involvement in the economy. The plan for Chapters 6 through 17 is outlined in Figure 6.2.

Recall that throughout this book, all diagrams that describe the behavior of households are drawn or highlighted in *blue*. All diagrams that describe the behavior of firms are drawn or highlighted in *red*. Look carefully at the supply and demand diagrams in Figure 6.1, and notice that in both the labor and capital markets, the supply curves are blue. The reason is that labor and capital are supplied by households. The demand curves for labor and capital are red because firms demand these inputs for production.

In Figure 6.1 much of the detail of the real world is stripped away just as it is on a highway map. A map is a highly simplified version of reality, but it is a very useful tool

FIGURE 6.1 Firm and Household Decisions

Households demand in output markets and supply labor and capital in input markets. To simplify our analysis, we have not included the government and international sectors in this circular flow diagram. These topics will be discussed in detail later.

when you need to know where you are. This diagram is intended to serve as a map to help you understand basic market forces before we add more complicated market structures and government.

Assumptions Before we proceed with our discussion of household choice, we need to make a few basic assumptions. The key assumption that we make in Chapters 6 through 12 is that all markets are *perfectly competitive.*

perfect competition An industry structure in which there are many firms, each small relative to the industry and producing virtually identical products, and in which no firm is large enough to have any control over prices.

Perfect competition is a very precisely defined form of industry structure. (The word *perfect* here does not refer to virtue. It simply means "total," or "complete.") In a perfectly competitive industry, no single firm has any control over prices. That is, no single firm is large enough to affect the market price of its product or the prices of the inputs that it buys. This follows from two characteristics of competitive industries. First, a competitive industry is composed of many firms, each small relative to the size of the industry. Second, every firm in a perfectly competitive industry produces exactly the same

Perfectly Competitive Markets

Market Imperfections and the Role of Government

CHAPTER 6

Household Behavior

- Demand in output markets
- Supply in input markets

CHAPTER 9

Equilibrium in Competitive Output Markets

- Short run
- Long run

CHAPTERS 7–8

Firm Behavior

- Choice of technology
- Supply in output markets
- Demand in input markets

CHAPTERS 10–11

Competitive Input Markets

- Labor/land
- Capital

CHAPTER 12

The Competitive Market System

- General equilibrium and efficiency

CHAPTERS 13–17

Market Imperfections and the Role of Government

- Imperfect market structures
  - Monopoly
  - Monopolistic competition
  - Oligopoly
- Externalities, public goods, imperfect information, social choice
- Income distribution and poverty
- Public finance: the economics of taxation

FIGURE 6.2 Understanding the Microeconomy and the Role of Government

To understand how the economy works, it helps to build from the ground up. We start in Chapters 6–8 with an overview of **household** and **firm** decision making in simple perfectly competitive markets. In Chapters 9–11 we see how firms and households interact in **output markets** (product markets) and **input markets** (labor/land and capital) to determine prices, wages, and profits. Once we have a picture of how a simple perfectly competitive economy works, we begin to relax assumptions. Chapter 12 is a pivotal chapter that links perfectly competitive markets with a discussion of market imperfections and the role of government. In Chapters 13–17 we cover the three noncompetitive market structures (monopoly, monopolistic competition, oligopoly), externalities, public goods, imperfect information, and income distribution as well as taxation and government finance.

product; the output of one firm cannot be distinguished from the output of the others. Products in a perfectly competitive industry are said to be **homogeneous**.

These characteristics limit the decisions open to competitive firms and simplify the analysis of competitive behavior. Because all firms in a perfectly competitive industry produce virtually identical products, and because each firm is small relative to the market, perfectly competitive firms have no control over the prices at which they sell their output. By taking prices as a given, each firm can decide only how much output to produce and how to produce it.

Consider agriculture, the classic example of a perfectly competitive industry. A wheat farmer in South Dakota has absolutely no control over the price of wheat. Prices are determined not by the individual farmers, but instead by the interaction of many suppliers and many demanders. The only decisions left to the wheat farmer are how much wheat to plant and when and how to produce the crop.

We can assume that each household is small relative to the size of the market. Households face a set of product prices that they individually cannot control. Prices, again, are set by the interaction of many suppliers and many demanders.

We also assume that households and firms possess all the information they need to make market choices. Specifically, we assume that households possess knowledge of the qualities and prices of everything available in the market. Firms know all that there is to know about wage rates, capital costs, and output prices. This assumption is often called the assumption of **perfect knowledge**.

homogeneous products Undifferentiated outputs; products that are identical to, or indistinguishable from, one another.

perfect knowledge The assumption that households possess a knowledge of the qualities and prices of everything available in the market and that firms have all available information concerning wage rates, capital costs, and output prices.

By the end of Chapter 10 we will have a complete picture of an economy, but it will be based on this set of fairly restrictive assumptions. At first, this may seem unrealistic to you. Keep the following in mind, however:

> Much of the economic analysis in the chapters that follow applies to all forms of market structure. Indeed, much of the power of economic reasoning is that it is quite general. As we continue in microeconomics, in Chapter 13 we will define and explore several different kinds of market organization and structure, including monopoly, oligopoly, and monopolistic competition. Because monopolists, oligopolists, monopolistic competitors, and perfect competitors share the objective of maximizing profits, it should not be surprising that their behavior is in many ways similar. We focus here on perfect competition because many of these basic principles are easier to learn in the simplest of cases first.

HOUSEHOLD CHOICE IN OUTPUT MARKETS

Every household must make three basic decisions:

> **1.** How much of each product, or output, to demand
> **2.** How much labor to supply
> **3.** How much to spend today and how much to save for the future

In the pages that follow, we examine each of these decisions.

As we begin our look at demand in output markets, you must keep in mind that the choices underlying the demand curve are only part of the larger household choice problem. Closely related decisions about how much to work and how much to save are equally important and must be made simultaneously with output-demand decisions.

THE DETERMINANTS OF HOUSEHOLD DEMAND

As we saw in Chapter 3:

> Several factors influence the quantity of a given good or service demanded by a single household:
>
> - The price of the product
> - The income available to the household
> - The household's amount of accumulated wealth
> - The prices of other products available to the household
> - The household's tastes and preferences
> - The household's expectations about future income, wealth, and prices

Recall that demand schedules and demand curves express the relationship between quantity demanded and price, *ceteris paribus*. A change in price leads to a movement along a demand curve. Changes in income, in other prices, or in preferences shift demand curves to the left or right. We refer to these shifts as "changes in demand." However, the interrelationship among these variables is more complex than the simple exposition in Chapter 3 might lead you to believe.

THE BUDGET CONSTRAINT

Before we examine the household choice process, we need to discuss exactly what choices are open or not open to households. If you look carefully at the list of items that influence household demand, you will see that the first four actually define the set of options available:

Information on household income and wealth, together with information on product prices, makes it possible to distinguish those combinations of goods and services that are affordable from those that are not.[1]

Income, wealth, and prices thus define what we call household **budget constraint**. The budget constraint facing any household results primarily from limits imposed externally by one or more markets. In competitive markets, for example, households cannot control prices; they must buy goods and services at market-determined prices. A household has some control over its income: Its members can choose to work or not, and they can sometimes decide how many hours to work and how many jobs to hold. However, constraints exist in the labor market, too. The amount that household members are paid is limited by current market wage rates. Whether they can get a job is determined by the availability of jobs.

Although income does in fact depend, at least in part, on the choices that households make, we will treat it as a given for now. Later on in this chapter we will relax this assumption and explore labor supply choices in more detail.

The income, wealth, and price constraints that surround choice are best illustrated with an example. Consider Barbara, a recent graduate of a midwestern university, who takes a job as an account manager at a public relations firm. Let us assume that she receives a salary of $1,000 per month (after taxes) and that she has no wealth and no credit. Barbara's monthly expenditures are limited to her flow of income. Table 6.1 summarizes some of the choices open to her.

A careful search of the housing market reveals four vacant apartments. The least expensive is a one-room studio with a small kitchenette that rents for $400 per month, including utilities (option A). If she lived there, Barbara could afford to spend $250 per month on food and still have $350 left over for other things.

About four blocks away is a one-bedroom apartment with wall-to-wall carpeting and a larger kitchen. It has much more space, but the rent is $600, including utilities. If Barbara took this apartment, she might cut her food expenditures by $50 per month and have only $200 per month left for everything else.

In the same building as the one-bedroom apartment is an identical unit on the top floor of the building with a balcony facing west toward the sunset. The balcony and view add $100 to the monthly rent. To live there, Barbara would be left with only $300 to split between food and other expenses.

Just because she was curious, Barbara took a look at a townhouse in the suburbs that was renting for $1,000 per month. Obviously, unless she could get along without eating or doing anything else that costs money, she could not afford it. The combination of the townhouse and any amount of food is outside her budget constraint.

Notice that we have used the information that we have on income and prices to identify different combinations of housing, food, and other items that are available to a single-person household with an income of $1,000 per month. We have said nothing about the process of choosing. Instead, we have carved out what is called a **choice set** or **opportunity set**, the set of options that is defined and limited by Barbara's budget constraint.

budget constraint The limits imposed on household choices by income, wealth, and product prices.

choice set or **opportunity set** The set of options that is defined and limited by a budget constraint.

TABLE 6.1 Possible Budget Choices of a Person Earning $1,000 Per Month After Taxes

OPTION	MONTHLY RENT	FOOD	OTHER EXPENSES	TOTAL	AVAILABLE?
A	$ 400	$250	$350	$1,000	Yes
B	600	200	200	1,000	Yes
C	700	150	150	1,000	Yes
D	1,000	100	100	1,200	No

[1]Remember that we drew the distinction between income and wealth in Chapter 3. *Income* is the sum of household earnings within a given period; it is a flow variable. In contrast, *wealth* is a stock variable; it is what a household owns minus what it owes at a given point in time.

Preferences play a key role in determining demand. Some people like the blues or jazz, some like classical, while others love country music.

Preferences, Tastes, Trade-Offs, and Opportunity Cost So far, we have identified only the combinations of goods and services that are available to Barbara and those that are not. Within the constraints imposed by limited incomes and fixed prices, however, households are free to choose what they will buy and what they will not buy. Their ultimate choices are governed by their individual preferences and tastes.

It will help you to think of the household choice process as a process of allocating income over a large number of available goods and services. Final demand of a household for any single product is just one of many outcomes that result from the decision-making process. Think, for example, of a demand curve that shows a household's reaction to a drop in the price of air travel. During certain periods when people travel less frequently, special fares flood the market and many people decide to take trips that they otherwise would not have taken. However, if I live in Florida and decide to spend $400 to visit my mother in Nashville, I cannot spend that $400 on new clothes, dinners at a restaurant, or a new set of tires.

A change in the price of a single good changes the constraints within which households choose, and this may change the entire allocation of income. Demand for some goods and services may rise while demand for others falls. A complicated set of trade-offs lies behind the shape and position of a household demand curve for a single good. Whenever a household makes a choice, it is really weighing the good or service it chooses against all the other things that the same money could buy. For more information on the ways choice sets have changed over the years, see the Further Exploration feature titled: "Opportunity Costs—Then and Now."

Consider again our young account manager and her options as listed in Table 6.1. If she hates to cook, likes to eat at restaurants, and goes out three nights a week, she will probably trade off some housing for dinners out and money to spend on clothes and other things. She will probably rent the studio for $400. She may, however, love to spend long evenings at home reading, listening to classical music, and sipping tea while watching the sunset. In that case, she will probably trade off some restaurant meals, evenings out, and travel expenses for the added comfort of the larger apartment with the balcony and the view.

> As long as a household faces a limited budget—and all households ultimately do—the real cost of any good or service is the value of the other goods and services that could have been purchased with the same amount of money. The real cost of a good or service is its opportunity cost, and opportunity cost is determined by relative prices.

The Budget Constraint More Formally Ann and Tom are struggling graduate students in economics at the University of Virginia. Their tuition is completely paid by graduate fellowships. They live as resident advisers in a first-year dormitory, in return for which they receive an apartment and meals. Their fellowships also give them $200 each month to cover all their other expenses. To simplify things, let us assume that Ann and Tom spend their money on only two things: meals at the local Thai restaurant and nights at the local jazz club, The Hungry Ear. Thai meals go for a fixed price of $20 per couple. Two tickets to the jazz club, including espresso, are $10.

As Figure 6.3 shows, we can graphically depict the choices that are available to our dynamic duo. The axes measure the *quantities* of the two goods that Ann and Tom buy. The horizontal axis measures the number of Thai meals consumed per month, and the vertical axis measures the number of trips to The Hungry Ear. (Note that price is not on the vertical axis here.) Every point in the space between the axes represents some combination of Thai meals and nights at the jazz club. The question is: Which of these points can Ann and Tom purchase with a fixed budget of $200 per month? That is, which points are in the opportunity set and which are not?

One possibility is that the kids in the dorm are driving Ann and Tom crazy. The two grad students want to avoid the dining hall at all costs. Thus they might decide to spend all their money on Thai food and none of it on jazz. This decision would be represented by a point *on* the horizontal axis because all the points on that axis are points at which Ann and Tom make no jazz club visits. How many meals can Ann and Tom afford? The answer is simple: If income is $200 and the price of Thai meals is $20, they can afford $200 ÷ $20 = 10 meals. This point is labeled *A* on the budget constraint in Figure 6.3.

Another possibility is that general exams are coming up and Ann and Tom decide to chill out at The Hungry Ear to relieve stress. Suppose that they choose to spend all their

⦿ Further Exploration   ○ News Analysis | opportunity costs | search |

Opportunity Costs—Then and Now

The real cost of buying a $19 compact disc (CD) is the total of all the other things you could have bought with that $19. In other words, the real cost of a good or service is its *opportunity cost*.

A good's opportunity cost is determined by the price of that good *relative to* the prices of other goods and services. If a sandwich at your favorite eatery costs $4, and sandwiches are your second choice after CDs, the real cost of a CD is nearly 5 sandwiches. As relative prices have changed over the years, so have the trade-offs among goods and services:

	PRICE IN 1970	PRICE IN 2005	CHANGE (%)
Prices in general [a]	1.00	5.04	404
Long-playing album/CD	4.00	18.98	375
Standard 20-in. color TV	325	150	−116
Big Mac at McDonald's	.55	2.49	353
Basic Ford automobile (Taurus)[b]	2,850	20,127	606
Tuition[c] at University of Michigan			
Resident	1,073	15,232	1,320
Nonresident	2,935	33,058	1,026
Standard refrigerator	220	550	150
Ticket to a Broadway show	9	120	1,233
Half-gallon of milk	.57	2.09	266
One pound of sirloin steak	1.35	6.19	359

Note: Incomes have gone up too—by one measure (after-tax personal income per capita) income went from $3,545 in 1970 to $30,250 in February 2005, an increase of 753 percent.

[a]As measured by the consumer price index.

[b]1970 Fairlane/2005 Taurus

[c]Including room and board.

money on jazz and none of it on Thai food. This decision would be represented by a point *on* the vertical axis because all the points on this axis are points at which Ann and Tom eat no Thai meals. How many jazz club visits can they afford? Again, the answer is simple: With an income of $200 and with the price of jazz/espresso at $10, they can go to The Hungry Ear $200 ÷ $10 = 20 times. This is the point labeled *B* in Figure 6.3. The line connecting points *A* and *B* is Ann and Tom's budget constraint.

What about all the points between *A* and *B* on the budget constraint? Starting from point *B*, suppose Ann and Tom give up trips to the jazz club to buy more Thai meals. Each additional Thai meal "costs" two trips to The Hungry Ear. The opportunity cost of a Thai meal is two jazz club trips.

Point *C* on the budget constraint represents a compromise. Here Ann and Tom go to the club 10 times and eat at the Thai restaurant 5 times. To verify that point *C* is on the budget constraint, price it out: 10 jazz club trips cost a total of $10 × 10 = $100, and 5 Thai meals cost a total of $20 × 5 = $100. The total is thus $100 + $100 = $200.

The budget constraint divides all the points between the axes into two groups: those that can be purchased for $200 or less (the opportunity set) and those that are unavailable. Point *D* on the diagram costs less than $200; point *E* costs more than $200. (Verify that this is true.) The opportunity set is the shaded area in Figure 6.3.

Clearly, both prices and incomes affect the size of a household's opportunity set. If a price or a set of prices falls, but income stays the same, the opportunity set gets bigger and the household is better off. If we define **real income** as the set of opportunities to purchase real goods and services, then "real income" has gone up in this case even if the household's money income has not. You can see this clearly in Figure 6.4, where the opportunity set expands as the result of a price decrease. On the other hand, if money income increases and prices go up even more, we would say that the household's "real income" has fallen.

The concept of real income is very important in macroeconomics, which is concerned with measuring real output and the price level.

real income Set of opportunities to purchase real goods and services available to a household as determined by prices and money income.

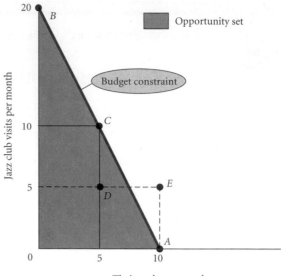

FIGURE 6.3 Budget Constraint and Opportunity Set for Ann and Tom

A budget constraint separates those combinations of goods and services that are available, given limited income, from those that are not. The available combinations make up the opportunity set.

THE EQUATION OF THE BUDGET CONSTRAINT

Yet another way to look at the budget constraint is to write down the consumer's problem as an equation. In the example above, the constraint is that total expenditure on Thai meals plus total expenditure on jazz club visits must be less than or equal to Ann and Tom's income. Total expenditure on Thai meals is equal to the *price* of Thai meals times the number, or *quantity*, of meals consumed. Total expenditure on jazz club visits is equal to the *price* of a visit times the number, or *quantity*, of visits. That is,

$$\$20 \times \text{Thai meals} + \$10 \times \text{jazz visits} \leq \$200$$

If we let X represent the number of Thai meals and we let Y represent the number of jazz club visits and we assume that Ann and Tom spend their entire income on either X or Y, this can be written

$$20X + 10Y = \$200$$

This is the equation of the budget constraint—the line connecting points A and B in Figure 6.3. Notice that if Ann and Tom spend nothing at the jazz club, then $Y = 0$. If you plug

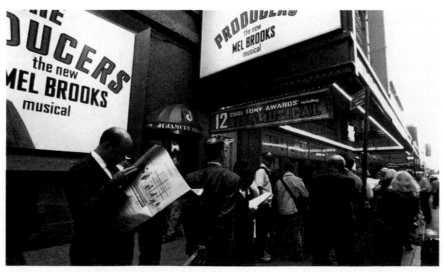

There is an opportunity cost to standing in line.

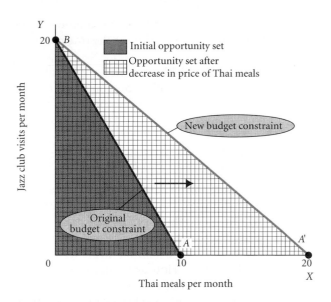

Y
20 B
Initial opportunity set
Opportunity set after
decrease in price of Thai meals

Jazz club visits per month

New budget constraint

Original
budget constraint

A

A'

0   10   20
                        X
Thai meals per month

FIGURE 6.4 The Effect of a Decrease in Price on Ann and Tom's Budget Constraint

When the price of a good decreases, the budget constraint swivels to the right, increasing the opportunities available and expanding choice.

$Y = 0$ into the equation of the budget constraint, then $20X = 200$ and $X = 10$. Since X is the number of Thai meals, they eat Thai food 10 times. Similarly, if $X = 0$, you can solve for Y, which equals 20. If they eat no Thai food, they can go to the jazz club 20 times.

In general, the budget constraint can be written:

$$P_X X + P_Y Y = I,$$

where P_X = the price of X, X = the quantity of X consumed, P_Y = the price of Y, Y = the quantity of Y consumed, and I = household income.[2]

Budget Constraints Change When Prices Rise or Fall   Now suppose that the Thai restaurant is offering two-for-one certificates good during the month of November. In effect, this means that the price of Thai meals drops to $10 for Ann and Tom. How would the budget constraint in Figure 6.3 change?

First, point B would not change. If Ann and Tom spend all their money on jazz, the price of Thai meals is irrelevant. Ann and Tom can still afford only 20 trips to the jazz club. What has changed is point A, which moves to point A' in Figure 6.4. At the new lower price of $10, if Ann and Tom spent all their money on Thai meals, they could buy twice as many, $200 ÷ $10 = 20. The budget constraint *swivels*, as shown in Figure 6.4.

The new, flatter budget constraint reflects the new trade-off between Thai meals and Hungry Ear visits. Now, after the price of Thai meals drops to $10, the opportunity cost of a Thai meal is only one jazz club visit. The opportunity set has expanded because at the lower price more combinations of Thai meals and jazz are available.

Figure 6.4 thus illustrates a very important point. When the price of a single good changes, more than just the quantity demanded of that good may be affected. The household now faces an entirely different choice problem—the opportunity set has expanded. At the same income of $200, the new lower price means that Ann and Tom might choose more Thai meals, more jazz club visits, or more of both. They are clearly better off.

> The budget constraint is defined by income, wealth, and prices. Within those limits, households are free to choose, and the household's ultimate choice depends on its own likes and dislikes.

---

[2]You can calculate the slope of the budget constraint as $-P_X/P_Y$, the ratio of the price of X to the price of Y. This gives the trade-off facing consumers. In the example, $-P_X/P_Y = -2$, meaning to get another Thai meal Ann and Tom must give up 2 trips to the jazz club.

Notice that when the price of meals falls to $10, the equation of the budget constraint changes to $10X + 10Y = 200$, which is the equation of the line connecting points A' and B in Figure 6.4.

The range of goods and services available in a modern society is as vast as consumer tastes are variable, and this makes any generalization about the household choice process risky. Nonetheless, the theory of household behavior that follows is an attempt to derive some logical propositions about the way households make choices.

THE BASIS OF CHOICE: UTILITY

Somehow, from the millions of things that are available, each of us manages to sort out a set of goods and services to buy. When we make our choices, we make specific judgments about the relative worth of things that are very different.

During the nineteenth century, the weighing of values was formalized into a concept called utility. Whether one item is preferable to another depends on how much **utility**, or satisfaction, it yields relative to its alternatives. How do we decide on the relative worth of a new puppy or a stereo? A trip to the mountains or a weekend in New York City? Working or not working? As we make our choices, we are effectively weighing the utilities we would receive from all the possible available goods.

Certain problems are implicit in the concept of utility. First, it is impossible to measure utility. Second, it is impossible to compare the utilities of different people—that is, one cannot say whether person A or person B has a higher level of utility. Despite these problems, however, the idea of utility helps us understand the process of choice better.

DIMINISHING MARGINAL UTILITY

In making their choices, most people spread their incomes over many different kinds of goods. One reason people prefer variety is that consuming more and more of any one good reduces the marginal, or extra, satisfaction they get from further consumption of the same good. Formally, **marginal utility (MU)** is the additional satisfaction gained by the consumption or use of *one* more unit of something.

It is important to distinguish marginal utility from total utility. **Total utility** is the total amount of satisfaction obtained from consumption of a good or service. Marginal utility comes only from the *last unit* consumed; total utility comes from *all* units consumed.

Suppose that you live next to a store that sells homemade ice cream that you are crazy about. Even though you get a great deal of pleasure from eating ice cream, you do not spend your entire income on it. The first cone of the day tastes heavenly. The second is merely delicious. The third is still very good, but it is clear that the glow is fading. Why? The answer is because the more of any one good we consume in a given period, the less satisfaction, or utility, we get from each additional, or marginal, unit. In 1890, Alfred Marshall called this "familiar and fundamental tendency of human nature" the **law of diminishing marginal utility**.

Consider this simple example. Frank loves country music, and a country band is playing seven nights a week at a club near his house. Table 6.2 shows how the utility he derives from

utility The satisfaction, or reward, a product yields relative to its alternatives. The basis of choice.

marginal utility (MU) The additional satisfaction gained by the consumption or use of *one more* unit of something.

total utility The total amount of satisfaction obtained from consumption of a good or service.

law of diminishing marginal utility The more of any one good consumed in a given period, the less satisfaction (utility) generated by consuming each additional (marginal) unit of the same good.

TABLE 6.2 Total Utility and Marginal Utility of Trips to the Club Per Week		
TRIPS TO CLUB	TOTAL UTILITY	MARGINAL UTILITY
1	12	12
2	22	10
3	28	6
4	32	4
5	34	2
6	34	0

the band might change as he goes to the club more and more frequently. The first visit generates 12 "utils," or units of utility. If Frank goes back another night he enjoys it, but not quite as much as the first night. The second night by itself yields 10 additional utils. *Marginal utility* is 10, while the *total utility* derived from two nights at the club is 22. Three nights per week at the club provide 28 total utils; the marginal utility of the third night is 6, because total utility rose from 22 to 28. Figure 6.5 graphs total and marginal utility using the data in Table 6.2. Total utility increases up through Frank's fifth trip to the club, but levels off on the sixth night. Marginal utility, which has declined from the beginning, is now at zero.

ALLOCATING INCOME TO MAXIMIZE UTILITY

How many times in one week would Frank go to the club to hear his favorite band? The answer depends on three things: Frank's income, the price of admission to the club, and the alternatives available. If the price of admission were zero and no alternatives existed, he would probably go to the club five nights a week. (Remember, the sixth does not increase his utility, so why should he bother to go?) However, Frank is also a basketball fan. His city has many good high school and college teams, and he can go to games six nights a week if he wants to.

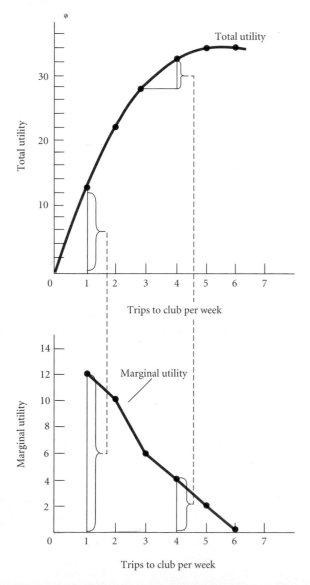

FIGURE 6.5 Graphs of Frank's Total and Marginal Utility

Marginal utility is the additional utility gained by consuming one additional unit of a commodity—in this case, trips to the club. When marginal utility is zero, total utility stops rising.

Let us say for now that admission to both the country music club and the basketball games is free—that is, there is no price/income constraint. There is a time constraint, however, because there are only seven nights in a week. Table 6.3 lists Frank's total and marginal utilities from attending basketball games and going to country music clubs. From column 3 of the table we can conclude that on the first night Frank will go to a basketball game. The game is worth far more to him (21 utils) than a trip to the club (12 utils).

On the second night, Frank's decision is not so easy. Because he has been to one basketball game this week, the second is worth less (12 utils, as compared to 21 for the first basketball game). In fact, it is worth exactly the same as a first trip to the club, so he is indifferent to whether he goes to the game or the club. So he splits the next two nights: One night he sees ballgame number two (12 utils); the other he spends at the club (12 utils). At this point, Frank has been to two ballgames and spent one night at the club. Where will Frank go on evening four? He will go to the club again, because the marginal utility from a second trip to the club (10 utils) is greater than the marginal utility from attending a third basketball game (9 utils).

Frank is splitting his time between the two activities to maximize total utility. At each successive step, he chooses the activity that yields the most marginal utility. Continuing with this logic, you can see that spending three nights at the club and four nights watching basketball produces total utility of 76 utils each week (28 plus 48). No other combination of games and club trips can produce as much utility.

So far, the only cost of a night of listening to country music is a forgone basketball game, and the only cost of a basketball game is a forgone night of country music. Now let us suppose that it costs $3 to get into the club and $6 to go to a basketball game. Suppose further that after paying rent and taking care of other expenses Frank has only $21 left over to spend on entertainment. Typically, consumers allocate limited incomes, or budgets, over a large set of goods and services. Here we have a limited income ($21) being allocated between only two goods, but the principle is the same. Income ($21) and prices ($3 and $6) define Frank's budget constraint. Within that constraint, Frank chooses to maximize utility.

Because the two activities now cost different amounts, we need to find the *marginal utility per dollar* spent on each activity. If Frank is to spend his money on the combination of activities lying within his budget constraint that gives him the most total utility, each night he must choose the activity that gives him the *most utility per dollar spent*. As you can see from column 5 in Table 6.3, Frank gets 4 utils per dollar on the first night he goes to the club (12 utils ÷ $3 = 4 utils per dollar). On night two he goes to a game and gets 3.5 utils per dollar (21 utils ÷ $6 = 3.5 utils per dollar). On night three it is back to the club. Then what happens? When all is said and done—work this out for yourself—

TABLE 6.3 Allocation of Fixed Expenditure per Week Between Two Alternatives

(1) TRIPS TO CLUB PER WEEK	(2) TOTAL UTILITY	(3) MARGINAL UTILITY (*MU*)	(4) PRICE (*P*)	(5) MARGINAL UTILITY PER DOLLAR (*MU/P*)
1	12	12	$3.00	4.0
2	22	10	3.00	3.3
3	28	6	3.00	2.0
4	32	4	3.00	1.3
5	34	2	3.00	.7
6	34	0	3.00	0

(1) BASKETBALL GAMES PER WEEK	(2) TOTAL UTILITY	(3) MARGINAL UTILITY (*MU*)	(4) PRICE (*P*)	(5) MARGINAL UTILITY PER DOLLAR (*MU/P*)
1	21	21	$6.00	3.5
2	33	12	6.00	2.0
3	42	9	6.00	1.5
4	48	6	6.00	1.0
5	51	3	6.00	.5
6	51	0	6.00	0

Frank ends up going to two games and spending three nights at the club. No other combination of activities that $21 will buy yields more utility.

THE UTILITY-MAXIMIZING RULE

◀ Optional Material

In general, utility-maximizing consumers spread out their expenditures until the following condition holds:

$$\text{utility-maximizing rule:} \quad \frac{MU_X}{P_X} = \frac{MU_Y}{P_Y} \text{ for all goods}$$

where MU_X is the marginal utility derived from the last unit of X consumed, MU_Y is the marginal utility derived from the last unit of Y consumed, P_X is the price per unit of X, and P_Y is the price per unit of Y.

To see why this **utility-maximizing rule** is true, think for a moment about what would happen if it were *not* true. For example, suppose MU_X/P_X were greater than MU_Y/P_Y; that is, suppose that a consumer purchased a bundle of goods so that the marginal utility from the last dollar spent on X were greater than the marginal utility from the last dollar spent on Y. This would mean that the consumer could increase his utility by spending a dollar less on Y and a dollar more on X. As the consumer shifts to buying more X and less Y, he runs into diminishing marginal utility. Buying more units of X *decreases* the marginal utility derived from consuming additional units of X. As a result, the marginal utility of another dollar spent on X falls. Now *less* is being spent on Y, and that means its marginal utility *increases*. This process continues until $MU_X/P_X = MU_Y/P_Y$. When this condition holds, there is no way for the consumer to increase his utility by changing the bundle of goods purchased.

You can see how the utility-maximizing rule works in Frank's choice between country music and basketball. At each stage, Frank chooses the activity that gives him the most utility per dollar. If he goes to a game, the utility he will derive from the next game—marginal utility—falls. If he goes to the club, the utility he will derive from his next visit falls, and so forth. ◀

utility-maximizing rule
Equating the ratio of the marginal utility of a good to its price for all goods.

DIMINISHING MARGINAL UTILITY AND DOWNWARD-SLOPING DEMAND

The concept of diminishing marginal utility offers us one reason why people spread their incomes over a variety of goods and services instead of spending them all on one or two items. It also leads us to conclude that demand curves slope downward.

To see why this is so, let us return to our friends Ann and Tom, the struggling graduate students. Recall that they chose between meals at a Thai restaurant and trips to a jazz club. Now think about their demand curve for Thai meals, shown in Figure 6.6. When the price of a meal is $40, they decide not to buy any Thai meals. What they are really deciding is that the utility gained from even that first scrumptious meal each month is not worth the utility that would come from the other things that $40 can buy.

Now consider a price of $25. At this price, Ann and Tom buy five Thai meals. The first, second, third, fourth, and fifth meals each generate enough utility to justify the price. Tom and Ann "reveal" this by buying five meals. After the fifth meal, the utility gained from the next meal is not worth $25.

Ultimately, every demand curve hits the quantity (horizontal) axis as a result of diminishing marginal utility—in other words, demand curves slope downward. How many times will Ann and Tom go to the Thai restaurant if meals are free? Twenty-five times is the answer, and after 25 times a month, they are so sick of Thai food that they will not eat any more even if it is free. That is, marginal utility—the utility gained from the last meal—has dropped to zero. If you think this is unrealistic, ask yourself how much water you drank today.

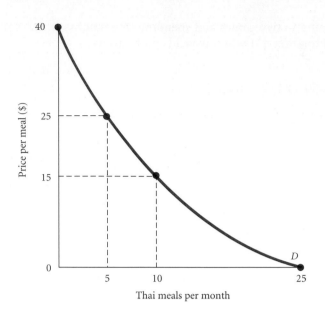

FIGURE 6.6 Diminishing Marginal Utility and Downward-Sloping Demand

At a price of $40, the utility gained from even the first Thai meal is not worth the price. However, a lower price of $25 lures Ann and Tom into the Thai restaurant 5 times a month. (The utility from the sixth meal is not worth $25.) If the price is $15, Ann and Tom will eat Thai meals 10 times a month—until the marginal utility of a Thai meal drops below the utility they could gain from spending $15 on other goods. At 25 meals a month, they cannot tolerate the thought of another Thai meal even if it is free.

INCOME AND SUBSTITUTION EFFECTS

Although the idea of utility is, we believe, a helpful way of thinking about the choice process, there is an explanation for downward-sloping demand curves that does not rely on the concept of utility or the assumption of diminishing marginal utility. This explanation centers on income and substitution effects.

Keeping in mind that consumers face constrained choices, consider the probable response of a household to a decline in the price of some heavily used product, *ceteris paribus*. How might a household currently consuming many goods be likely to respond to a fall in the price of one of those goods if its income, its preferences, and all other prices remained unchanged? The household would face a new budget constraint, and its final choice of all goods and services might change. A decline in the price of gasoline, for example, may affect not only how much gasoline you purchase but also what kind of car you buy, when and how much you travel, where you go, and (not so directly) how many movies you see this month and how many projects around the house you get done.

THE INCOME EFFECT

Price changes affect households in two ways. First, if we assume that households confine their choices to products that improve their well-being, then a decline in the price of any product, *ceteris paribus*, makes the household unequivocally better off. In other words, if a household continues to buy the exact same amount of every good and service after the price decrease, it will have income left over. That extra income may be spent on the product whose price has declined, hereafter called good *X*, or on other products. The change in consumption of *X* due to this improvement in well-being is called the *income effect of a price change*.

Suppose that I live in Florida and that four times a year I fly to Nashville to visit my mother. Suppose further that last year a round-trip ticket to Nashville cost $400. Thus, I spend a total of $1,600 per year on trips to visit Mom. This year, however, increased competition among the airlines has led one airline to offer round-trip tickets to Nashville for $200. Assuming that the price remains at $200 all year, I can now fly home exactly the same number of times, and I will have spent $800 less for airline tickets than I did last year. Now that I am better off, I have additional opportunities. I could fly home a fifth time this year, leaving

JetBlue has led to increased competition among airlines.

Marginal Utility and the Capacity to Consume

ONE OF THE THINGS THAT YOU SHOULD take away from this chapter is that it is very difficult to generalize about consumer behavior. The world that we live in is very diverse, and we are each unique. Our preferences, our likes and dislikes, and the things that we are or are not willing to pay for are determined by our cultures, our experiences, our families, our religions, and so forth.

Yet we argue that demand curves slope downward. At higher prices, *ceteris paribus*, the quantity demanded falls. One of the earliest explanations for this "law of demand" was that people's behavior reflected "diminishing marginal utility." As we consume more of a given product, the utility that we gain from an added unit of that product in a given time period declines eventually to zero! The fourteenth dish of fresh apple pie in a day does not bring with it the same satisfaction or joy as the first few, and at some point I can't eat any more. Ultimately, even if price falls to zero (the good is made available free), we don't consume an infinite amount of it. Marginal utility falls to zero, and the demand curve hits the *X*-axis.

Why? The answer is simple. Since we defined the quantity demanded as the quantity of a product consumed per *time period*, there is a limit to how much you can consume in a given length of time. If you absolutely loved and craved Ben and Jerry's ice cream, how much could you physically eat in a day?

The following news article shows that for at least one product, the hot dog, we have evidence of just what that limit is.

2005 Nathan's Famous Fourth of July International Hot Dog-Eating Contest

Date: 07/04/2005
Location: Coney Island, NY
Winner: Takeru Kobayashi, 49 Nathan's Famous Hot Dogs and Buns in 12 Minutes
Total Prizes: Mustard Yellow International Belt

Recap
On July 4, 2005, the eyes of the world were focused on Coney Island, NY, for the 90th install-

ment of the Nathan's Famous Fourth of July International Hot Dog-Eating Contest. Five-time world champion Takeru Kobayashi of Japan successfully defended his title at Nathan's Famous in Coney Island by consuming 49 Nathan's Famous hot dogs and buns in 12 minutes.

At 8:01 a.m. Thursday, Megumi Suzuki and her six friends were the first to nudge the barricades set up at the corner of Surf and Stillwell to keep the crowd from getting too close to the competitors at Coney Island.

"We call him 'Prince,'" said Suzuki, of the man they came to see. They know he already has a girlfriend, but they giggle at the mention of his name just like the girls who scream and dream for Yankees shortstop Derek Jeter.

"I myself compared him to Tiger Woods last year," said Rich Shea, president of the International Federation of Competitive Eating (IFOCE), which sanctions 100 events each year. "I've often heard people say he's the Michael Jordan of eating.

Source: Courtesy of International Federation of Competitive Eating (IFOCE).

$600 ($800 − $200) to spend on other things, or I could fly home the same number of times (four) and spend all the extra $800 on other things.

When the price of something we buy falls, we are *better off*. When the price of something we buy rises, we are *worse off*.

Look back at Figure 6.4. When the price of Thai meals fell, the opportunity set facing Tom and Ann expanded—they were able to afford more Thai meals, more jazz club trips, or more of both. They were unequivocally better off because of the price decline. In a sense, their "real" income was higher.

Now recall from Chapter 3 the definition of a *normal good*. When income rises, demand for normal goods increases. Most goods are normal goods. Because of the price decline, Tom and Ann can afford to buy more. If Thai food is a normal good, a decline in the price of Thai food should lead to an increase in the quantity demanded of Thai food.

THE SUBSTITUTION EFFECT

The fact that a price decline leaves households better off is only part of the story. When the price of a product falls, that product also becomes *relatively* cheaper. That is, it becomes more attractive relative to potential substitutes. A fall in the price of product *X* might cause a household to shift its purchasing pattern away from substitutes toward *X*. This shift is called the *substitution effect of a price change.*

Earlier, we made the point that the "real" cost or price of a good is what one must sacrifice to consume it. This opportunity cost is determined by relative prices. To see why this is so, consider again the choice that I face when a round-trip ticket to Nashville costs $400. Each trip that I take requires a sacrifice of $400 worth of other goods and services. When the price drops to $200, the opportunity cost of a ticket has dropped by $200. In other words, after the price decline, I have to sacrifice only $200 (instead of $400) worth of other goods and services to visit Mom.

To clarify the distinction between the income and substitution effects in your mind, imagine how I would be affected if two things happened to me at the same time. First, the price of round-trip air travel between Florida and Nashville drops from $400 to $200. Second, my income is reduced by $800. I am now faced with new relative prices, but—assuming I flew home four times last year—I am no better off now than I was before the price of a ticket declined. The decrease in the price of air travel has exactly offset my decrease in income.

I am still likely to take more trips home. Why? The opportunity cost of a trip home is now lower, *ceteris paribus*—that is, assuming no change in the prices of other goods and services. A trip to Nashville now requires a sacrifice of only $200 worth of other goods and services, not the $400 worth that it did before. Thus, I will substitute away from other goods toward trips to see my mother.

Everything works in the opposite direction when a price rises, *ceteris paribus*. A price increase makes households worse off. If income and other prices do not change, spending the same amount of money buys less, and households will be forced to buy less. This is the income effect. In addition, when the price of a product rises, that item becomes more expensive relative to potential substitutes, and the household is likely to substitute other goods for it. This is the substitution effect.

What do the income and substitution effects tell us about the demand curve?

> Both the income and the substitution effects imply a negative relationship between price and quantity demanded—in other words, downward-sloping demand. When the price of something falls, *ceteris paribus*, we are better off, and we are likely to buy more of that good and other goods (income effect). Because lower price also means "less expensive relative to substitutes," we are likely to buy more of the good (substitution effect). When the price of something rises, we are worse off, and we will buy less of it (income effect). Higher price also means "more expensive relative to substitutes," and we are likely to buy less of it and more of other goods (substitution effect).[3]

Figure 6.7 summarizes the income and substitution effects of a price change.

CONSUMER SURPLUS

As we have seen, the market forces households to reveal their preferences. If you decide to buy a DVD player for $175, you reveal that the DVD player is worth at least as much as the other things that $175 could buy. The true cost of an item is the value of the other things that you give up when you buy it. The true cost is the opportunity cost.

---

[3]For some goods, the income and substitution effects work in opposite directions. When our income rises, we may buy less of some goods. In Chapter 3, we called such goods *inferior goods.*

When the price of an inferior good rises, it is, like any other good, more expensive relative to substitutes, and we are likely to replace it with lower-priced substitutes. However, when we are worse off, we increase our demand for inferior goods. Thus, the income effect could lead us to buy more of the good, partially offsetting the substitution effect.

Even if a good is "very inferior," demand curves will slope downward as long as the substitution effect is larger than the income effect. It is possible, at least in theory, for the income effect to be larger. In such a case, a price increase would actually lead to an increase in quantity demanded. This possibility was pointed out by Alfred Marshall in *Principles of Economics.* Marshall attributes the notion of an upward-sloping demand curve to Sir Robert Giffen, and for this reason the notion is often referred to as *Giffen's paradox.* Fortunately or unfortunately, no one has ever demonstrated that a Giffen good has ever existed.

Price of a
good or service:

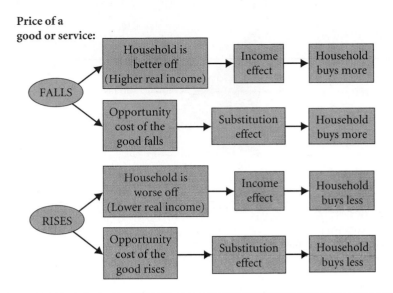

FIGURE 6.7 Income and Substitution Effects of a Price Change

For normal goods, the income and substitution effects work in the same direction. Higher prices lead to a lower quantity demanded, and lower prices lead to a higher quantity demanded.

In Chapter 4 we introduced the notion of **consumer surplus**. In competitive markets, each good sells for a single market price, and consumers can buy all they want and can afford of each good at its market price. For many, the amount that they are willing to pay for a good is greater than what they must pay for it. To the extent that a household's willingness to pay for a good exceeds the good's market price, the household earns a surplus, called consumer surplus. As we showed, the total consumer surplus enjoyed by households in a given market is equal to the area under the demand curve and above the equilibrium price (see Chapter 4).

The idea of consumer surplus helps to explain an old paradox that dates back to Plato. Adam Smith wrote about it in 1776:

> The things which have the greatest value in use have frequently little or no value in exchange; and on the contrary, those which have the greatest value in exchange have frequently little or no value in use. Nothing is more useful than water: but it will purchase scarce any thing; scarce anything can be had in exchange for it. A diamond, on the contrary, has scarce any value in use; but a very great quantity of other goods may frequently be had in exchange for it.[4]

Although diamonds have arguably more than "scarce any value in use" today (for example, they are used to cut glass), Smith's **diamond/water paradox** is still instructive, at least where water is concerned.

The low price of water owes much to the fact that it is in plentiful supply. Even at a price of zero we do not consume an infinite amount of water. We consume up to the point where *marginal* utility drops to zero. The *marginal* value of water is zero. Each of us enjoys an enormous consumer surplus when we consume nearly free water. At a price of zero, consumer surplus is the entire area under the demand curve, as you can see from Figure 6.8. We tend to take water for granted, but imagine what would happen to its price if there were simply not enough for everyone. It would command a high price indeed.

Consumer surplus measurement is a key element in **cost-benefit analysis**, the formal technique by which the benefits of a public project are weighed against its costs. To decide whether to build a new electrical power plant, we need to know the value, to consumers, of the electricity that it will produce. Just as the value of water to consumers is not just its price times the quantity that people consume, the value of electricity generated is not just the price

consumer surplus The difference between the maximum amount a person is willing to pay for a good and its current market price.

diamond/water paradox A paradox stating that (1) the things with the greatest value in use frequently have little or no value in exchange, and (2) the things with the greatest value in exchange frequently have little or no value in use.

cost-benefit analysis The formal technique by which the benefits of a public project are weighed against its costs.

---

[4]Adam Smith, *The Wealth of Nations*, Modern Library Edition (New York: Random House, 1937), p. 28 (1st ed. 1776). The cheapness of water is referred to by Plato in *Euthydem.*, 304B.

FIGURE 6.8 The Diamond/Water Paradox

At a price of zero you might argue that water has no value. But in fact, the value of water is great. Because it is plentiful in most places, consumers enjoy a huge consumer surplus equal to the shaded area in the diagram. Household willingness to pay far exceeds the zero price.

of electricity times the quantity the new plant will produce. The total value that should be weighed against the costs of the plant includes the consumer surplus that electricity users will enjoy if the plant is built.

HOUSEHOLD CHOICE IN INPUT MARKETS

So far, we have focused on the decision-making process that lies behind output demand curves. Households with limited incomes allocate those incomes across various combinations of goods and services that are available and affordable. In looking at the factors affecting choices in the output market, we assumed that income was fixed, or given. We noted at the outset, however, that income is in fact partially determined by choices that households make in input markets (look back at Figure 6.1). We now turn to a brief discussion of the two decisions households make in input markets: the labor supply decision and the saving decision.

THE LABOR SUPPLY DECISION

Most income in the United States is wage and salary income paid in compensation for labor. Household members supply labor in exchange for wages or salaries. As in output markets, households face constrained choices in input markets. They must decide

1. Whether to work
2. How much to work
3. What kind of a job to work at

In essence, household members must decide how much labor to supply. The choices they make are affected by

1. Availability of jobs
2. Market wage rates
3. Skills they possess

As with decisions in output markets, the labor supply decision involves a set of trade-offs. There are basically two alternatives to working for a wage: (1) not working, and (2) unpaid work. If I do not work, I sacrifice income for the benefits of staying at home and reading, watching TV, swimming, or sleeping. Another option is to work, but not for a money wage. In this case, I sacrifice money income for the benefits of growing my own food, bringing up my children, or taking care of my house.

As with the trade-offs in output markets, my final choice depends on how I value the alternatives available. If I work, I earn a wage that I can use to buy things. Thus, the trade-off is between the value of the goods and services I can buy with the wages I earn versus the value of things I can produce at home—home-grown food, manageable children, clean clothes, and so on—or the value I place on leisure. This choice is illustrated in Figure 6.9. In general, then:

> The wage rate can be thought of as the price—or the opportunity cost—of the benefits of either unpaid work or leisure.

THE PRICE OF LEISURE

In our analysis in the early part of this chapter, households had to allocate a limited budget across a set of goods and services. Now they must choose among goods, services, and *leisure*.

When we add leisure to the picture, we do so with one important distinction. Trading off one good for another involves buying less of one and more of another, so households simply reallocate *money* from one good to the other. "Buying" more leisure, however, means reallocating time between work and nonwork activities. For each hour of leisure that I decide to consume, I give up one hour's wages. Thus the wage rate is the *price of leisure*.

Conditions in the labor market determine the budget constraints and final opportunity sets that face households. The availability of jobs and these job wage rates determine the final combinations of goods and services that a household can afford. The final choice within these constraints depends on the unique tastes and preferences of each household. Different people place more or less value on leisure—but everyone needs to put food on the table.

INCOME AND SUBSTITUTION EFFECTS OF A WAGE CHANGE

A **labor supply curve** shows the quantity of labor supplied at different wage rates. The shape of the labor supply curve depends on how households react to changes in the wage rate.

Consider an increase in wages. First, an increase in wages makes households better off. If they work the same number of hours—that is, if they supply the same amount of labor—

labor supply curve A diagram that shows the quantity of labor supplied at different wage rates. Its shape depends on how households react to changes in the wage rate.

FIGURE 6.9 The Trade-Off Facing Households

The decision to enter the workforce involves a trade-off between wages (and the goods and services that wages will buy) on the one hand, and leisure and the value of nonmarket production on the other.

they will earn higher incomes and be able to buy more goods and services. They can also buy more leisure. If leisure is a normal good—that is, a good for which demand increases as income increases—an increase in income will lead to a higher demand for leisure and a lower labor supply. This is the *income effect of a wage increase*.

However, there is also a potential *substitution effect of a wage increase*. A higher wage rate means that leisure is more expensive. If you think of the wage rate as the price of leisure, each individual hour of leisure consumed at a higher wage costs more in forgone wages. As a result, we would expect households to substitute other goods for leisure. This means working more, or a lower quantity demanded of leisure and a higher quantity supplied of labor.

Note that in the labor market the income and substitution effects work in *opposite* directions when leisure is a normal good. The income effect of a wage increase implies buying more leisure and working less; the substitution effect implies buying less leisure and working more. Whether households will supply more labor overall or less labor overall when wages rise depends on the relative strength of both the income and the substitution effects.

If the substitution effect is greater than the income effect, the wage increase will increase labor supply. This suggests that the labor supply curve slopes upward, or has a positive slope, like the one in Figure 6.10(a). If the income effect outweighs the substitution effect, however, a higher wage will lead to added consumption of leisure, and labor supply will decrease. This implies that the labor supply curve "bends back," as the one in Figure 6.10(b) does.

During the early years of the Industrial Revolution in late eighteenth-century Great Britain, the textile industry operated under what was called the "putting-out" system. Spinning and weaving were done in small cottages to supplement the family farm income—hence the term "cottage industry." During that period, wages and household incomes rose considerably. Some economic historians claim that this higher income actually led many households to take more leisure and work fewer hours; the empirical evidence suggests a backward-bending labor supply curve.

Just as income and substitution effects helped us understand household choices in output markets, they now help us understand household choices in input markets. The point here is simple:

> When leisure is added to the choice set, the line between input and output market decisions becomes blurred. In fact, households decide simultaneously how much of each good to consume and how much leisure to consume.

FIGURE 6.10 Two Labor Supply Curves

When the substitution effect outweighs the income effect, the labor supply curve slopes upward (a). When the income effect outweighs the substitution effect, the result is a "backward-bending" labor supply curve: The labor supply curve slopes downward (b).

SAVING AND BORROWING: PRESENT VERSUS FUTURE CONSUMPTION

We began this chapter by examining the way households allocate a fixed income over a large number of goods and services. We then pointed out that, at least in part, choices made by households determine income levels. Within the constraints imposed by the market, households decide whether to work and how much to work.

So far, however, we have talked about only the current period—the allocation of current income among alternative uses and the work/leisure choice *today*. Households can also (1) use present income to finance future spending—they can *save*—or (2) use future income to finance present spending—they can *borrow*.

When a household decides to save, it is using current income to finance future consumption. That future consumption may come in 3 years, when you use your savings to buy a car; in 10 years, when you sell stock to put a deposit on a house; or in 45 years, when you retire and begin to receive money from your pension plan. Most people cannot finance large purchases— a house or condominium, for example—out of current income and savings. They almost always borrow money and sign a mortgage. When a household borrows, it is, in essence, financing a current purchase with future income. It pays back the loan out of future income.

Even in simple economies such as the two-person, desert-island economy of Colleen and Bill (see Chapter 2), people must make decisions about *present versus future consumption*. Colleen and Bill could (1) produce goods for today's consumption by hunting and gathering, (2) consume leisure by sleeping on the beach, or (3) work on projects to enhance future consumption opportunities. Building a house or a boat over a 5-year period is trading present consumption for future consumption.

When a household saves, it usually puts the money into something that will generate income. There is no sense in putting money under your mattress when you can make it work in so many ways: savings accounts, money market funds, stocks, corporate bonds, and so forth—many of which are virtually risk free. When you put your money in any of these places, you are actually lending it out, and the borrower pays you a fee for its use. This fee usually takes the form of *interest*.

Just as changes in wage rates affect household behavior in the labor market, so do changes in interest rates affect household behavior in capital markets. Higher interest rates mean that borrowing is more expensive—required monthly payments on a newly purchased house or car will be higher. Higher interest rates also mean that saving will earn a higher return: $1,000 invested in a 5 percent savings account or bond yields $50 per year. If rates rise to 10 percent, the annual interest rises to $100.

What impact do interest rates have on saving behavior? As with the effect of wage changes on labor supply, the effect of changes in interest rates on saving can best be understood in terms of income and substitution effects. Suppose, for example, that I have been saving for a number of years for retirement. Will an increase in interest rates lead to an increase or a decrease in my saving? The answer is not obvious. First, because each dollar saved will earn a higher rate of return, the "price" of spending today in terms of forgone future spending is higher. That is, each dollar that I spend today (instead of saving) costs me more in terms of future consumption because my saving will now earn a higher return. On this score I will be led to save *more*, and this is the substitution effect at work.

However, higher interest rates mean more than that. Higher interest rates mean that it will take less saving today to reach a specific target amount of savings tomorrow. I will not need to save as much for retirement or future consumption as I did before. One hundred dollars put into a savings account with 5 percent compound interest will double in 14 years. If interest were paid at a rate of 10 percent, I would have my $200 in just 7 years. Consequently, I may be led to save less, and this is the income effect at work. Higher interest rates mean savers are better off, and so higher interest rates may lead to less saving. The final impact of a change in interest rates on saving depends on the relative size of the income and substitution effects.

> Most empirical evidence indicates that saving tends to increase as the interest rate rises. In other words, the substitution effect is larger than the income effect.

financial capital market
The complex set of institutions
in which suppliers of capital
(households that save) and the
demand for capital (business
firms wanting to invest) interact.

Saving and investment decisions involve a huge and complex set of institutions, the **financial capital market**, in which the suppliers of capital (households that save) and the demand for capital (business firms that want to invest) interact. The amount of capital investment in an economy is constrained in the long run by that economy's saving rate. You can think of household *saving* as the economy's supply of capital. When a firm borrows to finance a capital acquisition, it is almost as if households have supplied the capital for the fee we call interest. We treat capital markets in detail in Chapter 11.[5]

A REVIEW: HOUSEHOLDS IN OUTPUT AND INPUT MARKETS

In probing the behavior of households in both input and output markets and examining the nature of constrained choice, we went behind the household demand curve, using the simplifying assumption that income was fixed and given. Income, wealth, and prices set the limits, or *constraints*, within which households make their choices in output markets. Within those limits, households make their choices on the basis of personal tastes and preferences.

The notion of *utility* helps to explain the process of choice. The law of *diminishing marginal utility* partly explains why people seem to spread their incomes over many different goods and services and why demand curves have a negative slope. Another important explanation behind the negative relationship between price and quantity demanded lies in *income effects* and *substitution effects*.

As we turned to input markets, we relaxed the assumption that income was fixed and given. In the labor market, households are forced to weigh the value of leisure against the value of goods and services that can be bought with wage income. Once again, we found household preferences for goods and leisure operating within a set of constraints imposed by the market. Households also face the problem of allocating income and consumption over more than one period of time. They can finance spending in the future with today's income by saving and earning interest, or they can spend tomorrow's income today by borrowing.

We now have a rough sketch of the factors that determine output demand and input supply. (You can review these in Figure 6.1.) In the next three chapters, we turn to firm behavior and explore in detail the factors that affect output supply and input demand.

---

[5]Here we are looking at a country as if it were isolated from the rest of the world. Very often, however, capital investment is financed by funds loaned or provided by foreign citizens or governments. For example, in recent years a substantial amount of foreign savings has found its way into the United States to buy stocks, bonds, and other financial instruments. In part, these flows finance capital investment. Also, the United States and other countries that contribute funds to the World Bank and the International Monetary Fund have provided billions in outright grants and loans to help developing countries produce capital. For more information on these institutions, see the last chapter of this text.

SUMMARY

1. In perfectly competitive markets, prices are determined by the forces of supply and demand, and no single household or firm has any control over them. The assumption of a perfectly competitive market underlies all our discussions through Chapter 12. Much of what we say in these chapters, however, can be generalized to the other forms of market structure. We also assume that households possess *perfect knowledge* of the qualities and prices of everything available in the market.

HOUSEHOLD CHOICE IN OUTPUT MARKETS

2. Every household must make three basic decisions: (1) how much of each product, or output, to demand; (2) how much labor to supply; and (3) how much to spend today and how much to save for the future.

3. Income, wealth, and prices define household *budget constraint*. The budget constraint separates those combinations

of goods and services that are available from those that are not. All the points below and to the left of a graph of a household budget constraint make up the *choice set*, or *opportunity set*.

4. It is best to think of the household choice problem as one of allocating income over a large number of goods and services. A change in the price of one good may change the entire allocation. Demand for some goods may rise while demand for others may fall.

5. As long as a household faces a limited income, the real cost of any single good or service is the value of the next preferred *other* goods and services that could have been purchased with the same amount of money.

6. Within the constraints of prices, income, and wealth, household decisions ultimately depend on preferences—likes, dislikes, and tastes.

THE BASIS OF CHOICE: UTILITY

7. Whether one item is preferable to another depends on how much *utility*, or satisfaction, it yields relative to its alternatives.

8. The *law of diminishing marginal utility* says that the more of any good we consume in a given period of time, the less satisfaction, or utility, we get out of each additional (or marginal) unit of that good.

9. Households allocate income among goods and services to maximize utility. This implies choosing activities that yield the highest marginal utility per dollar. In a two-good world, households will choose so as to equate the marginal utility per dollar spent on *X* with the marginal utility per dollar spent on *Y*. This is the *utility-maximizing rule*.

INCOME AND SUBSTITUTION EFFECTS

10. The fact that demand curves have a negative slope can be explained in two ways: (1) Marginal utility for all goods diminishes, and (2) for most normal goods both the *income and the substitution effects* of a price decline lead to more consumption of the good.

CONSUMER SURPLUS

11. When any good is sold at a fixed price, households must "reveal" whether that good is worth the price being asked. For many people who buy in a given market, the product is worth more than its current price. Those people receive a *consumer surplus*.

HOUSEHOLD CHOICE IN INPUT MARKETS

12. In the labor market, a trade-off exists between the value of the goods and services that can be bought in the market or produced at home and the value that one places on leisure. The opportunity cost of paid work is leisure and unpaid work. The wage rate is the price, or opportunity cost, of the benefits of unpaid work or of leisure.

13. The income and substitution effects of a change in the wage rate work in opposite directions. Higher wages mean that (1) leisure is more expensive (likely response: people work *more*—substitution effect), and (2) more income is earned in a given number of hours, so some time may be spent on leisure (likely response: people work *less*—income effect).

14. In addition to deciding how to allocate its present income among goods and services, a household may also decide to save or borrow. When a household decides to save part of its current income, it is using current income to finance future spending. When a household borrows, it finances current purchases with future income.

15. An increase in interest rates has a positive effect on saving if the substitution effect dominates the income effect, and a negative effect if the income effect dominates the substitution effect. Most empirical evidence shows that the substitution effect dominates here.

REVIEW TERMS AND CONCEPTS

budget constraint, 117

choice set or opportunity set, 117

consumer surplus, 129

cost-benefit analysis, 129

diamond/water paradox, 129

financial capital market, 134

homogeneous products, 115

labor supply curve, 131

law of diminishing marginal utility, 122

marginal utility (*MU*) 122

perfect competition, 114

perfect knowledge, 115

real income, 119

total utility, 122

utility, 122

utility-maximizing rule, 125

PROBLEM SET

1. For each of the following events, consider how you might react. What things might you consume more or less of? Would you work more or less? Would you increase or decrease your saving? Are your responses consistent with the discussion of household behavior in this chapter?
   a. You have a very close friend who lives in another city, a 3-hour bus ride away. The price of a round-trip ticket rises from $20 to $45.
   b. Tuition at your college is cut 25 percent.
   c. You receive an award that pays you $300 per month for the next 5 years.
   d. Interest rates rise dramatically, and savings accounts are now paying 10% interest annually.
   e. The price of food doubles. (If you are on a meal plan, assume that your board charges double.)
   f. A new business opens up nearby offering part-time jobs at $20 per hour.

2. The following table gives a hypothetical total utility schedule for the Cookie Monster (CM):

NUMBER OF COOKIES	TOTAL UTILITY
0	0
1	100
2	200
3	275
4	325
5	350
6	360
7	360

Calculate the CM's marginal utility schedule. Draw a graph of total and marginal utility. If cookies cost the CM 5 cents each and CM had a good income, what is the maximum number of cookies he would most likely eat?

3. Kamika lives in Chicago but goes to school in Tucson, Arizona. For the last 2 years, she has made four trips home each year. During 2006, the price of a round-trip ticket from Chicago to Tucson increased from $350 to $600. As a result, Kamika decided not to buy a new outfit that year and decided not to drive to Phoenix with friends for an expensive rock concert.
   a. Explain how Kamika's demand for clothing and concert tickets can be affected by an increase in air travel prices.
   b. By using this example, explain why both income and substitution effects might be expected to reduce the number of trips home that Kamika takes.

4. Sketch the following budget constraints:

	P_X	P_Y	INCOME
a.	$20	$50	$1,000
b.	40	50	1,000
c.	20	100	1,000
d.	20	50	2,000
e.	0.25	0.25	7.00
f.	0.25	0.50	7.00
g.	0.50	0.25	7.00

5. On January 1, Professor Smith made a resolution to lose some weight and save some money. He decided that he would strictly budget $100 for lunches each month. For lunch he has only two choices: the faculty club, where the price of a lunch is $5, and Alice's Restaurant, where the price of a lunch is $10. Every day that he does not eat lunch, he runs 5 miles.
   a. Assuming that Professor Smith spends the $100 each month at either Alice's or the club, sketch his budget constraint. Show actual numbers on the axes.
   b. Last month Professor Smith chose to eat at the club 10 times and at Alice's 5 times. Does this choice fit within his budget constraint?
   c. Last month, Alice ran a half-price lunch special all month. All lunches were reduced to $5. Show the effect on Professor Smith's budget constraint.

6. During 2005 and 2006, the Congress debated the advisability of several tax cut proposals that had been put forward by President Bush. By reducing tax rates across the board, take-home pay for all taxpaying workers would increase. The purpose, in part, was to encourage work and increase the supply of labor. Households would respond the way the president hoped, but only if income effects were stronger than substitution effects. Do you agree or disagree? Explain your answer.

7. Assume that Mei has $100 per month to divide between dinners at a Chinese restaurant and nights at Zanzibar, a local pub. Assume that going to Zanzibar costs $20 and eating at the Chinese restaurant costs $10. Suppose that Mei spends two nights at Zanzibar and eats six times at the Chinese restaurant.
   a. Draw Mei's budget constraint and show that she can afford six dinners and two nights at Zanzibar.
   b. Assume that Mei comes into some money and can now spend $200 per month. Draw her new budget constraint.

c. As a result of the increase in income, Mei decides to spend eight nights at Zanzibar and eat at the Chinese restaurant four times. What kind of a good is Chinese food? What kind of a good is a night at Zanzibar?
   d. What part of the increase in Zanzibar trips is due to the income effect, and which part is due to the substitution effect? Explain your answer.

8. Say whether you agree or disagree with each of the following statements, and explain your reason:
   a. If the income effect of a wage change dominates the substitution effect for a given household, and the household works longer hours following a wage change, wages must have risen.
   b. In product markets when a price falls, the substitution effect leads to more consumption, but for normal goods, the income effect leads to less consumption.

9. Suppose that the price of X is $5 and the price of Y is $10 and a hypothetical household has $500 to spend per month on goods X and Y.
   a. Sketch the household budget constraint.
   b. Assume that the household splits its income equally between X and Y. Show where the household ends up on the budget constraint.
   c. Suppose that the household income doubles to $1,000. Sketch the new budget constraint facing the household.
   d. Suppose after the change the household spends $200 on Y and $800 on X. Does this imply that X is a normal or an inferior good? What about Y?

10. For this problem, assume that Joe has $80 to spend on books and movies each month, and that both goods must be purchased whole (no fractional units). Movies cost $8 each, and books cost $20 each. Joe's preferences for movies and books are summarized by the following information:

	MOVIES				BOOKS		
No. per Month	TU	MU	MU/$	No. per Month	TU	MU	MU/$
1	50	—	—	1	22	—	—
2	80	—	—	2	42	—	—
3	100	—	—	3	52	—	—
4	110	—	—	4	57	—	—
5	116	—	—	5	60	—	—
6	121	—	—	6	62	—	—
7	123	—	—	7	63	—	—

a. Fill in the figures for marginal utility and marginal utility per dollar for both movies and books.
   b. Are these preferences consistent with the "law of diminishing marginal utility"? Explain briefly.
   c. Given the budget of $80, what quantity of books and what quantity of movies will maximize Joe's level of satisfaction? Explain briefly.
   d. Draw the budget constraint (with books on the horizontal axis) and identify the optimal combination of books and movies as point A.
   e. Now suppose the price of books falls to $10. Which of the columns in the table must be recalculated? Do the required recalculations.
   f. After the price change, how many movies and how many books will Joe purchase?

g. Draw in the new budget constraint and identify the new optimal combination of books and movies as point *B*.

h. If you calculated correctly, you have found that a decrease in the price of books has caused this person to buy more movies as well as more books. How can this be?

11. The News Analysis box on page 127 argues that the limited capacity of households to consume a good in a given time period causes individual demand curves to "hit the *X*-axis." What about the *Y*-axis, or the "price axis"? Do individual demand curves hit the price axis? Why or why not?

APPENDIX

INDIFFERENCE CURVES

Early in this chapter, we saw how a consumer choosing between two goods is constrained by the prices of those goods and by his or her income. This appendix returns to that example and analyzes the process of choice more formally. (Before we proceed, carefully review the text under the heading "The Budget Constraint More Formally.")

ASSUMPTIONS

We base the following analysis on four assumptions:

1. We assume that this analysis is restricted to goods that yield positive marginal utility, or, more simply, that "more is better." One way to justify this assumption is to say that if more of something actually makes you worse off, you can simply throw it away at no cost. This is the assumption of free disposal.

2. The **marginal rate of substitution** is defined as MU_X/MU_Y, or the ratio at which a household is willing to substitute *X* for *Y*. When MU_X/MU_Y is equal to 4, for example, I would be willing to trade four units of *Y* for one additional unit of *X*.

    We assume a diminishing marginal rate of substitution. That is, as more of *X* and less of *Y* are consumed, MU_X/MU_Y declines. As you consume more of *X* and less of *Y*, *X* becomes less valuable in terms of units of *Y*, or *Y* becomes more valuable in terms of *X*. This is almost, but not precisely, equivalent to assuming diminishing marginal utility.

3. We assume that consumers have the ability to choose among the combinations of goods and services available. Confronted with the choice between two alternative combinations of goods and services, *A* and *B*, a consumer will respond in one of three ways: (1) She prefers *A* over *B*, (2) she prefers *B* over *A*, or (3) she is indifferent between *A* and *B*—that is, she likes *A* and *B* equally.

4. We assume that consumer choices are consistent with a simple assumption of rationality. If a consumer shows that she prefers *A* to *B* and subsequently shows that she prefers *B* to a third alternative, *C*, she should prefer *A* to *C* if confronted with a choice between the two.

DERIVING INDIFFERENCE CURVES

If we accept these four assumptions, we can construct a "map" of a consumer's preferences. These preference maps are made up of indifference curves. An **indifference curve** is a set of points, each point representing a combination of goods *X* and *Y*, all of which yield the same total utility.

Figure 6A.1 shows how we might go about deriving an indifference curve for a hypothetical consumer. Each point in the diagram represents some amount of *X* and some amount of *Y*. Point *A* in the diagram, for example, represents X_A units of *X* and Y_A units of *Y*. Now suppose that we take some amount of *Y* away from our hypothetical consumer, moving the individual to *A'*. At *A'* the consumer has the same amount of *X*—that is, X_A units—but less *Y*, and now has only Y_C units of *Y*. Because "more is better," our consumer is unequivocally worse off at *A'* than at *A*.

To compensate for the loss of *Y*, we now begin giving our consumer some more *X*. If we give the individual just a little, our consumer will still be worse off than at *A*. If we give this individual lots of *X*, our consumer will be better off. There must be some quantity of *X* that will just compensate for the loss of *Y*. By giving the consumer that amount, we

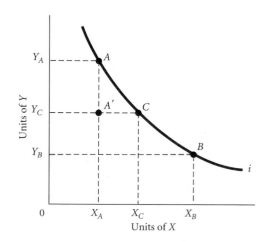

FIGURE 6A.1 An Indifference Curve

An indifference curve is a set of points, each representing a combination of some amount of good *X* and some amount of good *Y*, that all yield the same amount of total utility. The consumer depicted here is indifferent between bundles *A* and *B*, *B* and *C*, and *A* and *C*.

will have put together a bundle, Y_C and X_C, that yields the same total utility as bundle A. This is bundle C in Figure 6A.1. If confronted with a choice between bundles A and C, our consumer will say, "Either one; I do not care." In other words, the consumer is *indifferent* between A and C. When confronted with a choice between bundles C and B (which represents X_B and Y_B units of X and Y), this person is also indifferent. The points along the curve labeled i in Figure 6A.1 represent all the combinations of X and Y that yield the same total utility to our consumer. That curve is thus an indifference curve.

Each consumer has a whole set of indifference curves. Return for a moment to Figure 6A.1. Starting at point A again, imagine that we give the consumer a tiny bit more X *and* a tiny bit more Y. Because more is better, we know that the new bundle will yield a higher level of total utility, and the consumer will be better off. Now, just as we constructed the first indifference curve, we can construct a second one. What we get is an indifference curve that is *higher* and to the *right* of the first curve. Because utility along an indifference curve is constant at all points, every point along the new curve represents a higher level of total utility than every point along the first.

Figure 6A.2 shows a set of four indifference curves. The curve labeled i_4 represents the combinations of X and Y that yield the highest level of total utility among the four. Many other indifference curves exist between those shown on the diagram; in fact, their number is infinite. Notice that as you move up and to the right, utility increases.

The shapes of the indifference curves depend on the preferences of the consumer, and the whole set of indifference curves is called a **preference map**. Each consumer has a unique preference map.

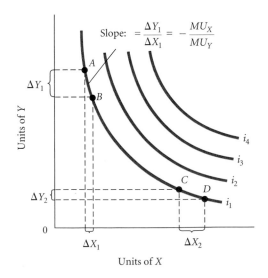

FIGURE 6A.2 A Preference Map: A Family of Indifference Curves

Each consumer has a unique family of indifference curves called a preference map. Higher indifference curves represent higher levels of total utility.

PROPERTIES OF INDIFFERENCE CURVES

The indifference curves shown in Figure 6A.2 are drawn bowing in toward the origin, or zero point, on the axes. In other words, the absolute value of the slope of the indifference curves decreases, or the curves get flatter, as we move to the right. Thus, we say that indifference curves are convex toward the origin. This shape follows directly from the assumption of diminishing marginal rate of substitution and makes sense if you remember the law of diminishing marginal utility.

To understand the convex shape, compare the segment of curve i_1 between A and B with the segment of the same curve between C and D. Moving from A to B, the consumer is willing to give up a substantial amount of Y to get a small amount of X. (Remember that total utility is constant along an indifference curve; the consumer is therefore indifferent between A and B.) Moving from C and D, however, the consumer is willing to give up only a small amount of Y to get more X.

This changing trade-off makes complete sense when you remember the law of diminishing marginal utility. Notice that between A and B, a lot of Y is consumed, and the marginal utility derived from a unit of Y is likely to be small. At the same time, though, only a little of X is being consumed, so the marginal utility derived from consuming a unit of X is likely to be high.

Suppose, for example, that X is pizza and Y is soda. Near A and B, a thirsty, hungry football player who has 10 sodas in front of him but only one slice of pizza will trade several sodas for another slice. Down around C and D, however, he has 20 slices of pizza and only a single soda. Now he will trade several slices of pizza to get an additional soda.

We can show how the trade-off changes more formally by deriving an expression for the slope of an indifference curve. Let us look at the arc (that is, the section of the curve) between A and B. We know that in moving from A to B, total utility remains constant. That means that the utility lost as a result of consuming less Y must be matched by the utility gained from consuming more X. We can approximate the loss of utility by multiplying the marginal utility of Y (MU_Y) by the number of units by which consumption of Y is curtailed (ΔY). Similarly, we can approximate the utility gained from consuming more X by multiplying the marginal utility of X (MU_X) by the number of additional units of X consumed (ΔX). Remember: Because the consumer is indifferent between points A and B, total utility is the same at both points. Thus, these two must be equal in magnitude—that is, the gain in utility from consuming more X must equal the loss in utility from consuming less Y. Because ΔY is a negative number (because consumption of Y decreases from A to B), it follows that

$$MU_X \cdot \Delta X = -(MU_Y \cdot \Delta Y)$$

If we divide both sides by MU_Y and by ΔX, we obtain

$$\frac{\Delta Y}{\Delta X} = -\left(\frac{MU_X}{MU_Y}\right)$$

Recall that the slope of any line is calculated by dividing the change in Y—that is, ΔY—by the change in X—that is, ΔX. This leads us to conclude:

> The slope of an indifference curve is the ratio of the marginal utility of X to the marginal utility of Y, and it is negative.

Now let us return to our pizza (X) and soda (Y) example. As we move down from the $A{:}B$ area to the $C{:}D$ area, our football player is consuming less soda and more pizza. The marginal utility of pizza (MU_X) is falling and the marginal utility of soda (MU_Y) is rising. That means that MU_X/MU_Y (**the marginal rate of substitution**) is falling, and the absolute value of the slope of the indifference curve is declining. Indeed, it does get flatter.

CONSUMER CHOICE

As you recall, demand depends on income, the prices of goods and services, and preferences or tastes. We are now ready to see how preferences as embodied in indifference curves interact with budget constraints to determine how the final quantities of X and Y will be chosen.

In Figure 6A.3 a set of indifference curves is superimposed on a consumer's budget constraint. Recall that the budget constraint separates those combinations of X and Y that are available from those that are not. The constraint simply shows those combinations that can be purchased with an income of I at prices P_X and P_Y. The budget constraint crosses the X-axis at I/P_X, or the number of units of X that can be purchased with I if nothing is spent on Y. Similarly, the budget constraint crosses the Y-axis at I/P_Y, or the number of units of Y that can be purchased with an income of I if nothing is spent on X. The shaded area is the consumer's opportunity set. The slope of a budget constraint is $-P_X/P_Y$.

Consumers will choose from among available combinations of X and Y the one that maximizes utility. In graphic terms, a consumer will move along the budget constraint until he or she is on the highest possible indifference curve. Utility rises by moving from points such as A or C (which lie on i_1) toward B (which lies on i_2). Any movement away from point B moves the consumer to a lower indifference curve—a lower level of utility. In this case, utility is maximized when our consumer buys X^* units of X and Y^* units of Y. At point B, the budget constraint is just tangent to—that is, just touches—indifference curve i_2.

> As long as indifference curves are convex to the origin, utility maximization will take place at the point at which the indifference curve is just tangent to the budget constraint.

The tangency condition has important implications. Where two curves are tangent, they have the same slope, which implies that the slope of the indifference curve is exactly equal

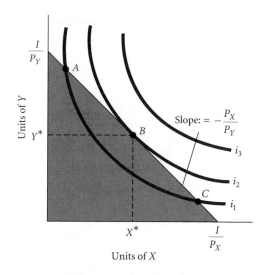

FIGURE 6A.3 Consumer Utility-Maximizing Equilibrium

Consumers will choose the combination of X and Y that maximizes total utility. Graphically, the consumer will move along the budget constraint until the highest possible indifference curve is reached. At that point, the budget constraint and the indifference curve are tangent. This point of tangency occurs at X^* and Y^* (point B).

to the slope of the budget constraint at the point of tangency:

$$-\frac{MU_X}{MU_Y} = -\frac{P_X}{P_Y}$$

slope of indifference curve = slope of budget constraint

By multiplying both sides of this equation by MU_Y and dividing both sides by P_X, we can rewrite this utility-maximizing rule as

$$\frac{MU_X}{P_X} = \frac{MU_Y}{P_Y}$$

This is the same rule derived in our earlier discussion without using indifference curves. We can describe this rule intuitively by saying that consumers maximize their total utility by equating the marginal utility per dollar spent on X with the marginal utility per dollar spent on Y. If this rule did not hold, utility could be increased by shifting money from one good to the other.

DERIVING A DEMAND CURVE FROM INDIFFERENCE CURVES AND BUDGET CONSTRAINTS

We now turn to the task of deriving a simple demand curve from indifference curves and budget constraints. A demand curve shows the quantity of a single good, X in this case, that a consumer will demand at various prices. To derive the demand curve, we need to confront our consumer with several alternative prices for X while keeping other prices, income, and preferences constant.

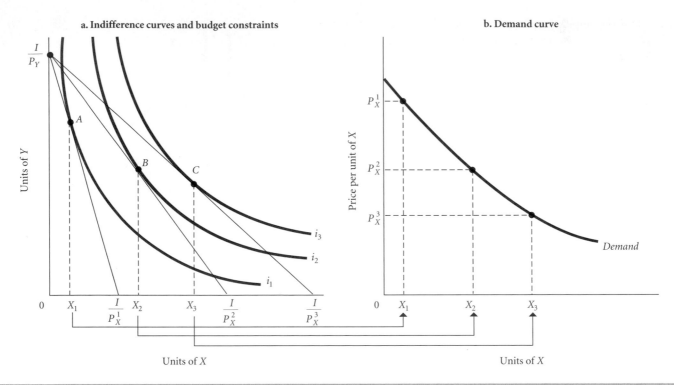

FIGURE 6A.4 Deriving a Demand Curve from Indifference Curves and Budget Constraint

Indifference curves are labeled i_1, i_2, and i_3; budget constraints are shown by the three diagonal lines from I/P_Y, to I/P_X^1, I/P_X^2, and I/P_X^3. Lowering the price of X from P_X^1 to P_X^2 and then to P_X^3 swivels the budget constraint to the right. At each price there is a different utility-maximizing combination of X and Y. Utility is maximized at point A on i_1, point B on i_2, and point C on i_3. Plotting the three prices against the quantities of X chosen results in a standard downward-sloping demand curve.

Figure 6.A4 shows the derivation. We begin with price P_X^1. At that price, the utility-maximizing point is A, where the consumer demands X_1 units of X. Therefore, in the right-hand diagram, we plot P_X^1 against X_1. This is the first point on our demand curve.

Now we 7 the price of X to P_X^2. Lowering the price expands the opportunity set, and the budget constraint swivels to the right. Because the price of X has fallen, if our consumer spends all of the income on X, the individual can buy more of it. Our

consumer is also better off, because of being able to move to a higher indifference curve. The new utility-maximizing point is B, where the consumer demands X2 units of X. Because the consumer demands X2 units of X at a price of P_X^2, we plot P_X^2 against X2 in the right-hand diagram. A second price cut to P_X^3 moves our consumer to point C, with a demand of X_3 units of X, and so on. Thus, we see how the demand curve can be derived from a consumer's preference map and budget constraint.

SUMMARY

1. An *indifference curve* is a set of points, each point representing a combination of goods X and Y, all of which yield the same total utility. A particular consumer's set of indifference curves is called a *preference map*.

2. The slope of an indifference curve is the ratio of the marginal utility of X to the marginal utility of Y, and it is negative.

3. As long as indifference curves are convex to the origin, utility maximization will take place at that point at which the indifference curve is just tangent to—that is, just touches—the budget constraint. The utility-maximizing rule can also be written as $MU_X/P_X = MU_Y/P_Y$.

REVIEW TERMS AND CONCEPTS

Indifference curve A set of points, each point representing a combination of goods X and Y, all of which yield the same total utility. 137

Marginal rate of substitution MU_X/MU_Y; the ratio at which a household is willing to substitute good Y for good X. 137

Preference map A consumer's set of indifference curves. 138

PROBLEM SET

1. Which of the four assumptions that were made at the beginning of the Appendix are violated by the indifference curves in Figure 1? Explain.

2. Assume that a household receives a weekly income of $100. If Figure 2 represents the choices of that household as the price of X changes, plot three points on the household demand curve.

*3. If Ann's marginal rate of substitution of X for Y is 5—that is, $MU_X/MU_Y = 5$—the price of X is $9.00, and the price of Y is $2.00, she is spending too much of her income on Y. Do you agree or disagree? Explain your answer using a graph.

*4. Assume that Jim is a rational consumer who consumes only two goods, apples (A) and nuts (N). Assume that his marginal rate of substitution of apples for nuts is given by the following formula:

$$MRS = MU_N/MU_A = A/N$$

That is, Jim's MRS is simply equal to the ratio of the number of apples consumed to the number of nuts consumed.

a. Assume that Jim's income is $100, the price of nuts is $5, and the price of apples is $10. What quantities of apples and nuts will he consume?

b. Find two additional points on his demand curve for nuts ($P_N = $10 and $P_N = $2).

c. Sketch one of the equilibrium points on an indifference curve graph.

*Note: Problems marked with an asterisk are more challenging.

FIGURE 1

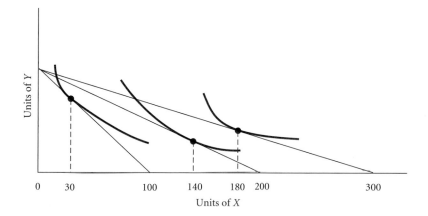

FIGURE 2

The Production Process:
The Behavior of
Profit-Maximizing Firms

7

In Chapter 6, we took a brief look at the household decisions that lie behind supply and demand curves. We spent some time discussing household choices: how much to work and how to choose among the wide range of goods and services available within the constraints of prices and income. We also identified some of the influences on household demand in output markets, as well as some of the influences on household supply behavior in input markets.

We now turn to the other side of the system and examine the behavior of firms. Business firms purchase inputs to produce and sell outputs that range from computers to string quartet performances. In other words, they *demand* factors of production in input markets and *supply* goods and services in output markets. Figure 7.1 repeats the now familiar circular flow diagram you first encountered in Chapter 6. In this chapter we look inside the firm at the production process that transforms inputs into outputs.

Although Chapters 7 through 12 describe the behavior of perfectly competitive firms, much of what we say in these chapters also applies to firms that are not perfectly competitive. For example, when we turn to monopoly in Chapter 13, we will be describing firms that are similar to competitive firms in many ways. All firms, whether competitive or not, demand inputs, engage in production, and produce outputs. All firms have an incentive to maximize profits and thus to minimize costs.

Central to our analysis is **production**, the process by which inputs are combined, transformed, and turned into outputs. Firms vary in size and internal organization, but they all take inputs and transform them into things for which there is some demand. For example, an independent accountant combines labor, paper, telephone and e-mail service, time, learning, and a Web site to provide help to confused taxpayers. An automobile plant uses steel, labor, plastic, electricity, machines, and countless other inputs to produce cars. Before we begin our discussion of the production process, however, we need to clarify some of the assumptions on which our analysis is based.

production The process by which inputs are combined, transformed, and turned into outputs.

Production Is Not Limited to Firms   Although our discussions in the next several chapters focus on profit-making business firms, it is important to understand that production and productive activity are not confined to private business firms. Households also

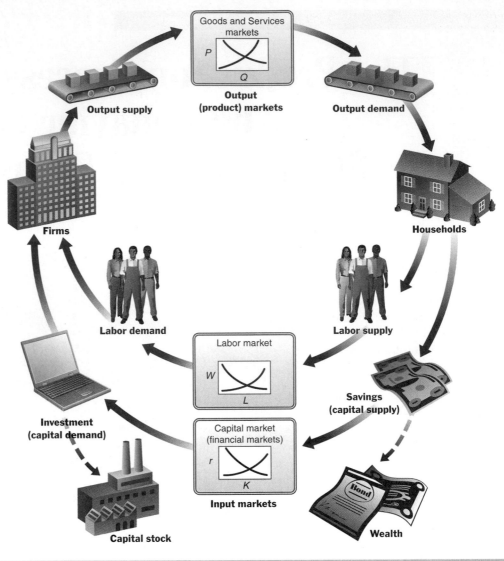

FIGURE 7.1 Firm and Household Decisions

engage in transforming factors of production (labor, capital, energy, natural resources, and so on) into useful things. When I work in my garden, I am combining land, labor, fertilizer, seeds, and tools (capital) into the vegetables I eat and the flowers I enjoy. The government also combines land, labor, and capital to produce public services for which demand exists: national defense, homeland security, police and fire protection, and education, to name a few.

Private business firms are set apart from other producers, such as households and government, by their purpose. A **firm** exists when a person or a group of people decides to produce a good or service to meet a perceived demand. Firms engage in production—that is, they transform inputs into outputs—because they can sell their products for more than it costs to produce them.

Even among firms that exist to make a profit, however, there are many important differences. A firm's behavior is likely to depend on its internal organization and on its relationship to the firms with which it competes. How many competitors are there? How large are they? How do they compete? Although many different kinds of market organization can be observed in the economy, it makes sense to begin the analysis with the simplest: perfect competition.

Perfect Competition   **Perfect competition** exists in an industry that contains many relatively small firms producing identical products. In a perfectly competitive industry, no single firm has any control over prices. In other words, an individual firm cannot affect the market price of its product or the prices of the inputs that it buys. This important characteristic follows from two assumptions. First, a competitive industry is composed of many firms, each small relative to the size of the industry. Second, every firm in a perfectly competitive

---

firm An organization that comes into being when a person or a group of people decides to produce a good or service to meet a perceived demand. Most firms exist to make a profit.

perfect competition An industry structure in which there are many firms, each small relative to the industry, producing virtually identical products and in which no firm is large enough to have any control over prices. In perfectly competitive industries, new competitors can freely enter and exit the market.

industry produces **homogeneous products**, which means that one firm's output cannot be distinguished from the output of the others.

These assumptions limit the decisions open to competitive firms and simplify the analysis of competitive behavior. Firms in perfectly competitive industries do not differentiate their products and do not make decisions about price. Instead, each firm takes prices as given—that is, as determined in the market by the laws of supply and demand—and decides only how much to produce and how to produce it.

The idea that competitive firms are "price-takers" is central to our discussion. Of course, we do not mean that firms cannot affix price tags to their merchandise; all firms have this ability. We simply mean that, given the availability of perfect substitutes, any product priced over the market price will not be sold.

These assumptions also imply that the demand for the product of a competitive firm is perfectly elastic (see Chapter 5). For example, consider the Ohio corn farmer whose situation is shown in Figure 7.2. The left side of the diagram represents the current conditions in the market. Corn is currently selling for $2.45 per bushel.[1] The right side of the diagram shows the demand for corn as the farmer sees it. If she were to raise her price, she would sell no corn at all; because there are perfect substitutes available, the quantity demanded of her corn would drop to zero. To lower her price would be silly because she can sell all she wants at the current price. (Remember, each farmer's production is very small relative to the entire corn market.)

In perfect competition we also assume easy entry—that firms can easily enter and exit the industry. If firms in an industry are earning high profits, new firms are likely to spring up. There are no barriers that prevent a new firm from competing. Fast-food restaurants are quick to spring up when a new shopping center opens, and new gas stations appear when a housing development or a new highway is built. When it became clear a few years ago that many people would be buying products online, thousands of e-commerce start-ups flooded the Web with new online "shops."

We also assume *easy exit*. When a firm finds itself suffering losses or earning low profits, one option is to go out of business, or exit the industry. Everyone knows a favorite restaurant that went out of business. Changes in cost of production, falling prices from international or regional competition, and changing technology may all turn business profits into losses and failure.

The best examples of perfect competition are probably found in agriculture. In that industry, products are absolutely homogeneous—it is impossible to distinguish one farmer's wheat from another's—and prices are set by the forces of supply and demand in a huge national market.

homogeneous products Undifferentiated products; products that are identical to, or indistinguishable from, one another.

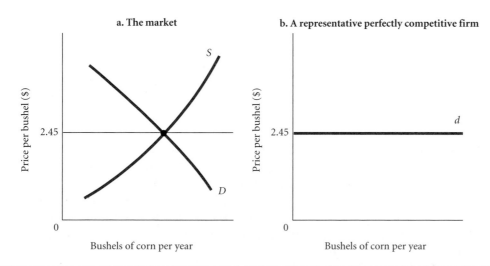

a. The market

b. A representative perfectly competitive firm

FIGURE 7.2 Demand Facing a Single Firm in a Perfectly Competitive Market

If a representative firm in a perfectly competitive market raises the price of its output above $2.45, the quantity demanded of *that firm's* output will drop to zero. Each firm faces a perfectly elastic demand curve, *d*.

---

[1]Capital letters refer to the entire market and lowercase letters refer to representative firms. For example, in Figure 7.2, the market demand curve is labeled *D* and the demand curve facing the firm is labeled *d*.

145

THE BEHAVIOR OF PROFIT-MAXIMIZING FIRMS

All firms must make several basic decisions to achieve what we assume to be their primary objective—maximum profits.

> The three decisions that all firms must make include:
>
> **1.** How much output to supply (quantity of product)
> **2.** How to produce that output (which production technique/technology to use)
> **3.** How much of each input to demand

The first and last choices are linked by the second choice. Once a firm has decided how much to produce, the choice of a production method determines the firm's input requirements. If a sweater company decides to produce 5,000 sweaters this month, it knows how many production workers it will need, how much electricity it will use, how much raw yarn to purchase, and how many sewing machines to run.

Similarly, given a technique of production, any set of input quantities determines the amount of output that can be produced. Certainly the number of machines and workers employed in a sweater mill determines how many sweaters can be produced.

Changing the *technology* of production will change the relationship between input and output quantities. An apple orchard that uses expensive equipment to raise pickers up into the trees will harvest more fruit with fewer workers in a given period of time than an orchard in which pickers use simple ladders. It is also possible that two different technologies can produce the same quantity of output. For example, a fully computerized textile mill with only a few workers running the machines may produce the same number of sweaters as a mill with no sophisticated machines but many workers. A profit-maximizing firm chooses the technology that minimizes its costs for a given level of output.

Remember as we proceed that we are discussing and analyzing the behavior of *perfectly competitive* firms. Thus, we will say nothing about price-setting behavior, product quality, and other characteristics of the product—choices that lead to product differentiation. In perfect competition, both input and output prices are beyond a firm's control—they are determined in the market and are not the decisions of any individual firm. Remember that all firms in a given industry produce the same exact product. When we analyze the behavior of firms in other kinds of markets (in Chapters 13 and 14), the three basic decisions will be expanded to include the setting of prices and the determination of product quality.

PROFITS AND ECONOMIC COSTS

profit (economic profit)
The difference between total revenue and total cost.

We assume that firms are in business to make a profit and that a firm's behavior is guided by the goal of maximizing profits. What is profit? **Profit** is the difference between total revenue and total cost:

$$\text{profit} = \text{total revenue} - \text{total cost}$$

total revenue The amount received from the sale of the product ($q \times P$).

total cost (total economic cost) The total of (1) out-of-pocket costs, (2) normal rate of return on capital, and (3) opportunity cost of each factor of production.

Total revenue is the amount received from the sale of the product; it is equal to the number of units sold (q) times the price received per unit (P). **Total cost** is less straightforward to define. We define total cost here to include (1) out-of-pocket costs and (2) full opportunity cost of all inputs or factors of production. *Out-of-pocket costs* are sometimes referred to as *explicit costs* or *accounting costs*. These refer to costs as an accountant would calculate them. *Economic costs* include the full opportunity cost of every input. These opportunity costs are often referred to as *implicit costs*.

1. How much output to supply	2. Which production technology to use	3. How much of each input to demand

FIGURE 7.3 The Three Decisions That All Firms Must Make

The term *profit* will from here on refer to *economic profit*. So whenever we say profit = total revenue − total cost, what we really mean is

economic profit = total revenue − total economic cost

The reason we take opportunity costs into account is that we are interested in analyzing the behavior of firms from the standpoint of a potential investor or a potential new competitor. If I am thinking about buying a firm, or shares in a firm, or entering an industry as a new firm, I need to consider the *full* costs of production. For example, if a family business employs three family members but pays them no wage, there is still a cost: the opportunity cost of their labor. In evaluating the business from the outside, these costs must be added.

The most important opportunity cost that is included in economic cost is the opportunity cost of capital. The way we treat the opportunity cost of capital is to add a *normal rate of return* to capital as part of economic cost.

Unless otherwise stated, we will use this definition of profit, not the accounting definition, in what follows.

Normal Rate of Return   When someone decides to start a firm, that person must commit resources. To operate a manufacturing firm, you need a plant and some equipment. To start a restaurant, you need to buy grills, ovens, tables, chairs, and so forth. In other words, you must invest in capital. To start an e-business, you need a host site, some computer equipment, some software, and a Web-site design. Such investment requires resources that stay tied up in the firm as long as it operates. Even firms that have been around a long time must continue to invest. Plant and equipment wear out and must be replaced. Firms that decide to expand must put new capital in place. This is as true of proprietorships, where the resources come directly from the proprietor, as it is of corporations, where the resources needed to make investments come from shareholders.

Whenever resources are used to invest in a business, there is an opportunity cost. Instead of opening a candy store, I could put my funds into an alternative use such as a certificate of deposit or a government bond, both of which earn interest. Instead of using its retained earnings to build a new plant, a firm could simply earn interest on those funds or pay them out to shareholders.

Rate of return is the annual flow of net income generated by an investment expressed as a percentage of the total investment. For example, if someone makes a $100,000 investment in capital to start a small restaurant and the restaurant produces a flow of profit of $15,000 every year, we say the project has a "rate of return" of 15 percent. Sometimes we refer to the rate of return as the *yield* of the investment.

A **normal rate of return** is the rate that is just sufficient to keep owners and investors satisfied. If the rate of return were to fall below normal, it would be difficult or impossible for managers to raise resources needed to purchase new capital. Owners of the firm would be receiving a rate of return that was lower than they could receive elsewhere in the economy, and they would have no incentive to invest in the firm.

If the firm has fairly steady revenues and the future looks secure, the normal rate of return should be very close to the interest rate on risk-free government bonds. I certainly will not keep investors interested in my firm if I do not pay them a rate of return at least as high as they can get from a risk-free government or corporate bond. If my firm is rock solid and the economy is steady, I may not have to pay a much higher rate. However, if my firm is in a very speculative industry and the future of the economy is shaky, I may have to pay substantially more to keep my shareholders happy. In exchange for taking such a risk, they will expect a higher return.

A normal rate of return is considered a part of the total cost of a business. Adding a normal rate of return to total cost has an important implication: When a firm earns exactly a normal rate of return, it is earning a zero profit as we have defined profit. If the level of profit is positive, the firm is earning an above-normal rate of return on capital.

A simple example will illustrate the concepts of a normal rate of return being part of total cost. Suppose that Sue and Ann decide to start a small business selling turquoise belts in the Denver airport. To get into the business they need to invest in a fancy pushcart. The price of the pushcart is $20,000 with all the displays and attachments included. Suppose that Sue and Ann estimate that they will sell 3,000 belts each year for $10 each. Further, assume that each belt costs $5 from the supplier. Finally, the cart must be staffed by one clerk, who works for an annual wage of $14,000. Is this business going to make a profit?

normal rate of return
A rate of return on capital that is just sufficient to keep owners and investors satisfied. For relatively risk-free firms, it should be nearly the same as the interest rate on risk-free government bonds.

An Idea, a Firm, and Profits in 2005

THIS CHAPTER FOCUSES ON THE behavior of profit-seeking firms. Firms produce goods and services that people want and are willing to pay for. They supply products to output markets and demand labor and capital in input markets. Successful firms earn profits. They take in more from sales of their product than it costs to produce it. When *economic profits*, that is, profits above a normal return to investment, are likely, you would expect to see new firms or products arise or to see existing, profitable industries expand.

This is the description of a new profit-seeking firm.

Small Business; Student's Start-Up Draws Attention and $13 Million

By ELLEN ROSEN (NYT)
Published: May 26, 2005

It is not easy capturing the attention of Jim Breyer, one of Silicon Valley's leading venture capitalists. But Mark Zuckerberg, a 21-year-old Harvard student, managed to do it with a Web site that has attracted 2.8 million registered users on more than 800 campuses since it began in February 2004.

Mr. Breyer was so taken with Mr. Zuckerberg's company, thefacebook. com, which creates online interactive college-student networks, that his firm, Accel Partners, plans to announce a $13 million investment in the start-up today.

Mr. Zuckerberg and his two roommates, Dustin Moskovitz and Chris Hughes, started the venture in February 2004 as an online directory of all Harvard's students, a big step up from the photo books of incoming freshmen the school produced annually.

The premise—and the process— were both simple: students wanting to join needed a current ".edu" e-mail address to register without fees. They could then supply a digital photo and create a profile of themselves.

The partners declined to disclose revenue, which comes solely from advertising, though they say the company is profitable. With the infusion of outside cash, they are also able to pay themselves salaries and rent an office in Palo Alto.

The site is becoming ubiquitous at the 840 colleges where it is available.

Laura Hofmann, who just finished her sophomore year at Loyola College in Baltimore, said that when thefacebook. com was introduced at her school in the fall, "everyone was addicted; at first, I was on five times a day."

While the breakout success of thefacebook.com is unusual, those in Silicon Valley say there is plenty of room for other Internet companies. According to Allen Wiener, an analyst at the research firm Gartner Inc., a successful company needs to have a "clearly articulated product and service," that will "save time or money, offer something someone can't find somewhere else."

To answer this question, we must determine total revenue and total cost. First, annual revenue is simply $30,000 (3,000 belts × $10). Total cost includes the cost of the belts— $15,000 (3,000 belts × $5)—plus the labor cost of $14,000, for a total of $29,000. Thus, on the basis of the annual revenue and cost flows, the firm *seems* to be making a profit of $1,000 ($30,000 − $29,000).

What about the $20,000 initial investment in the pushcart? This investment is *not* a direct part of the cost of Sue and Ann's firm. If we assume that the cart maintains its value over time, *the only thing that Sue and Ann are giving up is the interest that they might have earned had they not tied up their funds in the pushcart.* That is, the only real cost is the opportunity cost of the investment, which is the forgone interest on the $20,000.

TABLE 7.1 Calculating Total Revenue, Total Cost, and Profit

INITIAL INVESTMENT: MARKET INTEREST RATE AVAILABLE:	$20,000 0.10 OR 10%
Total revenue (3,000 belts × $10 each)	$30,000
Costs	
Belts from Supplier	$15,000
Labor cost	14,000
Normal return/Opportunity Cost of Capital ($20,000 × 0.10)	2,000
Total Cost	**$31,000**
Profit = total revenue − total cost	**−$ 1,000**[a]

[a]There is a loss of $1,000.

Now suppose that Sue and Ann want a minimum return equal to 10 percent—which is, say, the rate of interest that they could have gotten by purchasing corporate bonds. This implies a normal return of 10 percent, or $2,000 annually (=$20,000 × 0.10) on the $20,000 investment. As we determined earlier, Sue and Ann will earn only $1,000 annually. This is only a 5 percent return on their investment. Thus, they are really earning a below-normal return. Recall that the opportunity cost of capital must be added to total cost in calculating profit. Thus, the total cost in this case is $31,000 ($29,000 + $2,000 in forgone interest on the investment). The level of profit is negative: $30,000 minus $31,000 equals −$1,000. These calculations are summarized in Table 7.1. Because the level of profit is negative, Sue and Ann are actually suffering a *loss* on their belt business.

When a firm earns a *positive* level of profit, it is earning more than is sufficient to retain the interest of investors. In fact, positive profits are likely to attract new firms into an industry and cause existing firms to expand.

When a firm suffers a *negative* level of profit—that is, when it incurs a loss—it is earning at a rate below that required to keep investors happy. Such a loss may or may not be a loss as an accountant would measure it. Even if I earn a rate of return of 10 percent on my assets, I am earning a below-normal rate of return, or a loss, if a normal return for my industry is 15 percent. Losses may cause some firms to exit the industry; others will contract in size. Certainly new investment will not flow into such an industry.

SHORT-RUN VERSUS LONG-RUN DECISIONS

The decisions made by a firm—how much to produce, how to produce it, and what inputs to demand—all take time into account. If a firm decides that it wants to double or triple its output, it may need time to arrange financing, hire architects and contractors, and build a new plant. Planning for a major expansion can take years. In the meantime, the firm must decide how much to produce within the constraint of its existing plant. If a firm decides to get out of a particular business, it may take time to arrange an orderly exit. There may be contract obligations to fulfill, equipment to sell, and so forth. Once again, the firm must decide what to do in the meantime.

A firm's immediate response to a change in the economic environment may differ from its response over time. Consider, for example, a small restaurant with 20 tables that becomes very popular. The immediate problem is getting the most profit within the constraint of the existing restaurant. The owner might consider adding a few tables or speeding up service to squeeze in a few more customers. Some popular restaurants do not take reservations, forcing people to wait at the bar. This practice increases drink revenues and keeps tables full at all times. At the same time, the owner may be thinking of expanding the current facility, moving to a larger facility, or opening a second restaurant. In the future, the owner might buy the store next door and double the capacity. Such decisions might require negotiating a lease, buying new equipment, and hiring more staff. It takes time to make and implement these decisions.

short run The period of time for which two conditions hold: The firm is operating under a fixed scale (fixed factor) of production, and firms can neither enter nor exit an industry.

Because the character of immediate response differs from long-run adjustment, it is useful to define two time periods: the short run and the long run. Two assumptions define the **short run** (1) a fixed scale (or a fixed factor of production) and (2) no entry into or exit from the industry. First, the short run is defined as that period during which existing firms have some *fixed factor of production*—that is, during which time some factor locks them into their current scale of operations. Second, new firms cannot enter, and existing firms cannot exit, an industry in the short run. Firms may curtail operations, but they are still locked into some costs, even though they may be in the process of going out of business.

Just which factor or factors of production are fixed in the short run differs from industry to industry. For a manufacturing firm, the size of the physical plant is often the greatest limitation. A factory is built with a given production rate in mind. Although that rate can be increased, output cannot increase beyond a certain limit in the short run. For a private physician, the limit may be the capacity to see patients; the day has only so many hours. In the long run, the doctor may invite others to join the practice and expand, but for now, in the short run, this sole physician *is* the firm, with a capacity that is the firm's only capacity. For a farmer, the fixed factor may be land. The capacity of a small farm is limited by the number of acres being cultivated.

long run That period of time for which there are no fixed factors of production: Firms can increase or decrease the scale of operation, and new firms can enter and existing firms can exit the industry.

In the **long run**, there are no fixed factors of production. Firms can plan for any output level they find desirable. They can double or triple output, for example. In addition, new firms can start up operations (enter the industry), and existing firms can go out of business (exit the industry).

No hard-and-fast rule specifies how long the short run is. The point is simply that firms make two basic kinds of decisions: those that govern the day-to-day operations of the firm and those that involve longer-term strategic planning. Sometimes major decisions can be implemented in weeks. Often, however, the process takes years.

THE BASES OF DECISIONS: MARKET PRICE OF OUTPUTS, AVAILABLE TECHNOLOGY, AND INPUT PRICES

As we said earlier, a firm's three fundamental decisions are made with the objective of maximizing profits. Because profits equal total revenues minus total costs, each firm needs to know how much it costs to produce its product and how much its product can be sold for.

To know how much it costs to produce a good or service, I need to know something about the production techniques that are available and about the prices of the inputs required. To estimate how much it will cost me to operate a gas station, for instance, I need to know what equipment I need, how many workers, what kind of a building, and so forth. I also need to know the going wage rates for mechanics and unskilled laborers, the cost of gas pumps, interest rates, the rents per square foot of land on high-traffic corners, and the wholesale price of gasoline. Of course, I also need to know how much I can sell gasoline and repair services for.

In the language of economics, I need to know three things:

The bases of decision making:

1. The market price of output

2. The techniques of production that are available

3. The prices of inputs

Output price determines potential revenues. The techniques available tell me how much of each input I need, and input prices tell me how much they will cost. Together, the available production techniques and the prices of inputs determine costs.

optimal method of production The production method that minimizes cost.

The rest of this chapter and the whole next chapter focus on costs of production. We begin at the heart of the firm, with the production process itself. Faced with a set of input prices, firms must decide on the best, or optimal, method of production (Figure 7.4). The **optimal method of production** is the one that minimizes cost. With cost determined and the market price of output known, a firm will make a final judgment about the quantity of product to produce and the quantity of each input to demand.

FIGURE 7.4 Determining the Optimal Method of Production

THE PRODUCTION PROCESS

Production is the process through which inputs are combined and transformed into outputs. **Production technology** relates inputs to outputs. Specific quantities of inputs are needed to produce any given service or good. A loaf of bread requires certain amounts of water, flour, and yeast, some kneading and patting, as well as an oven and gas or electricity. A trip from downtown New York to Newark, New Jersey, can be produced with a taxicab, 45 minutes of a driver's labor, some gasoline, and so forth.

Most outputs can be produced by a number of different techniques. You can tear down an old building and clear a lot to create a park in several ways, for example. Five hundred men and women could descend on it with sledgehammers and carry the pieces away by hand; this would be a **labor-intensive technology**. The same park could be produced by two people with a wrecking crane, a steam shovel, a backhoe, and a dump truck; this would be a **capital-intensive technology**. Similarly, different inputs can be combined to transport people from Oakland to San Francisco. The Bay Area Rapid Transit carries thousands of people simultaneously under San Francisco Bay and uses a massive amount of capital relative to labor. Cab rides to San Francisco require much more labor relative to capital; a driver is needed for every few passengers.

In choosing the most appropriate technology, firms choose the one that minimizes the cost of production. For a firm in an economy with a plentiful supply of inexpensive labor but not much capital, the optimal method of production will involve labor-intensive techniques. For example, assembly of items like running shoes is done most efficiently by hand. That is why Nike produces virtually all its shoes in developing countries where labor costs are very low. In contrast, firms in an economy with high wages and high labor costs have an incentive to substitute away from labor and to use more capital-intensive, or labor-saving, techniques. Suburban office parks use more land and have more open space in part because land in the suburbs is more plentiful and less expensive than land in the middle of a big city.

PRODUCTION FUNCTIONS: TOTAL PRODUCT, MARGINAL PRODUCT, AND AVERAGE PRODUCT

The relationship between inputs and outputs—that is, the production technology—expressed numerically or mathematically is called a **production function** (or **total product function**). A production function shows units of total product as a function of units of inputs.

Imagine, for example, a small sandwich shop. All the sandwiches made in the shop are grilled, and the shop owns only one grill, which can accommodate only two people comfortably. As columns 1 and 2 of the production function in Table 7.2 show, one person working alone can produce only 10 sandwiches per hour, in addition to answering the phone, waiting

production technology
The quantitative relationship between inputs and outputs.

labor-intensive technology Technology that relies heavily on human labor instead of capital.

capital-intensive technology Technology that relies heavily on capital instead of human labor.

production function or **total product function**
A numerical or mathematical expression of a relationship between inputs and outputs. It shows units of total product as a function of units of inputs.

TABLE 7.2 Production Function

(1) LABOR UNITS (EMPLOYEES)	(2) TOTAL PRODUCT (SANDWICHES PER HOUR)	(3) MARGINAL PRODUCT OF LABOR	(4) AVERAGE PRODUCT OF LABOR (TOTAL PRODUCT ÷ LABOR UNITS)
0	0	–	–
1	10	10	10.0
2	25	15	12.5
3	35	10	11.7
4	40	5	10.0
5	42	2	8.4
6	42	0	7.0

on customers, keeping the tables clean, and so on. The second worker can stay at the grill full-time and not worry about anything except making sandwiches. Because the two workers together can produce 25 sandwiches, the second worker can produce 25 − 10 = 15 sandwiches per hour. A third person trying to use the grill produces crowding, but, with careful use of space, more sandwiches can be produced. The third worker adds 10 sandwiches per hour. Note that the added output from hiring a third worker is less because of the capital constraint, *not* because the third worker is somehow less efficient or hardworking. We assume that all workers are equally capable.

The fourth and fifth workers can work at the grill only while the first three are putting the pickles, onions, and wrapping on the sandwiches they have made. Then the first three must wait to get back to the grill. Worker four adds 5 sandwiches per hour to the total, and worker five adds just 2. Adding a sixth worker adds no output at all: The current maximum capacity of the shop is 42 sandwiches per hour.

Figure 7.5(a) graphs the total product data from Table 7.2.

marginal product The additional output that can be produced by adding one more unit of a specific input, *ceteris paribus*.

Marginal Product and the Law of Diminishing Returns   **Marginal product** is the additional output that can be produced by hiring one more unit of a specific input, holding all other inputs constant. As column 3 of Table 7.2 shows, the marginal product of the first unit of labor in the sandwich shop is 10 sandwiches; the marginal product of the second is 15; the third, 10; and so forth. The marginal product of the sixth worker is zero. Figure 7.5(b) graphs the marginal product of labor curve from the data in Table 7.2.

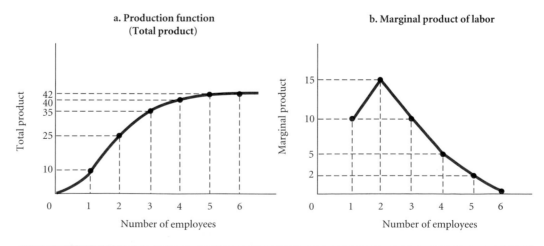

**a. Production function
(Total product)**

b. Marginal product of labor

FIGURE 7.5 Production Function for Sandwiches

A *production function* is a numerical representation of the relationship between inputs and outputs. In Figure 7.5(a), total product (sandwiches) is graphed as a function of labor inputs. The *marginal product* of labor is the additional output that one additional unit of labor produces. Figure 7.5(b) shows that the marginal product of the second unit of labor at the sandwich shop is 15 units of output; the marginal product of the fourth unit of labor is 5 units of output.

The **law of diminishing returns** states that *after a certain point, when additional units of a variable input are added to fixed inputs* (in this case, the building and grill), *the marginal product of the variable input* (in this case, labor) *declines*. The British economist David Ricardo first formulated the law of diminishing returns on the basis of his observations of agriculture in nineteenth-century England. Within a given area of land, he noted, successive "doses" of labor and capital yielded smaller and smaller increases in crop output. The law of diminishing returns is true in agriculture because only so much more can be produced by farming the same land more intensely. In manufacturing, diminishing returns set in when a firm begins to strain the capacity of its existing plant.

law of diminishing returns When additional units of a variable input are added to fixed inputs after a certain point, the marginal product of the variable input declines.

At our sandwich shop, diminishing returns set in when the third worker is added. The marginal product of the second worker is actually higher than the first [see Figure 7.5(b)]. The first worker takes care of the phone and the tables, thus freeing the second worker to concentrate exclusively on sandwich making. From that point on, the grill gets crowded.

Diminishing returns characterize many productive activities. Consider, for example, an independent accountant who works primarily for private citizens preparing their tax returns. As more and more clients are added, the accountant must work later and later into the evening. An hour spent working at 1 A.M. after a long day is likely to be less productive than an hour spent working at 10 A.M. Here the fixed factor of production is the accountant, whose mind and body capacity ultimately limit production, much as the walls of a plant limit production in a factory.

Diminishing returns, or *diminishing marginal product*, begin to show up when more and more units of a variable input are added to a fixed input, such as the scale of the plant. Recall that we defined the short run as that period in which some fixed factor of production constrains the firm. It then follows that

Diminishing returns always apply in the short run, and in the short run every firm will face diminishing returns. This means that every firm finds it progressively more difficult to increase its output as it approaches capacity production.

Marginal Product Versus Average Product
Average product is the average amount produced by each unit of a variable factor of production. At our sandwich shop with one grill, that variable factor is labor. In Table 7.2, you saw that the first two workers together produce 25 sandwiches per hour. Their average product is therefore 12.5 (25 ÷ 2). The third worker adds only 10 sandwiches per hour to the total. These 10 sandwiches are the *marginal product* of labor. The *average product* of the first three units of labor, however, is 11.7 (the average of 10, 15, and 10). Stated in equation form, the average product of labor is the *total* product divided by total units of labor:

average product The average amount produced by each unit of a variable factor of production.

$$\text{average product of labor} = \frac{\text{total product}}{\text{total units of labor}}$$

Average product "follows" marginal product, but it does not change as quickly. If marginal product is above average product, the average rises; if marginal product is below average product, the average falls. Suppose, for example, that you have had six exams and that your average is 86. If you score 75 on the next exam, your average score will fall, but not all the way to 75. In fact, it will fall only to 84.4. If you score a 95 instead, your average will rise to 87.3. As columns 3 and 4 of Table 7.2 show, marginal product at the sandwich shop declines continuously after the third worker is hired. Average product also decreases, but more slowly.

Figure 7.6 shows a typical production function and the marginal and average product curves derived from it. The marginal product curve is a graph of the slope of the total product curve—that is, of the production function. Average product and marginal product start out equal, as they do in Table 7.2. As marginal product climbs, the graph of average product follows it, but more slowly, up to L_1 (point A).

Notice that marginal product starts out increasing. (It did so in the sandwich shop as well.) Most production processes are designed to be run well by more than one worker. Take an assembly line, for example. To work efficiently, an assembly line needs a worker at every

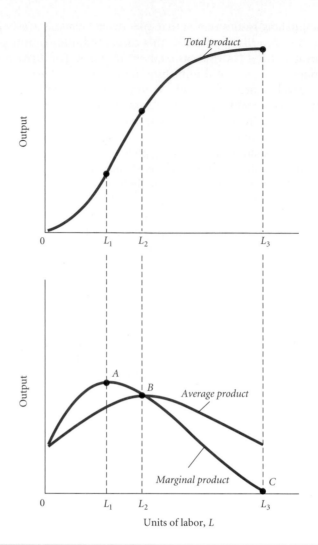

FIGURE 7.6 Total Average and Marginal Product

Marginal and average product curves can be derived from total product curves. Average product is at its maximum at the point of intersection with marginal product.

station; it's a cooperative process. The marginal product of the first workers is low or zero. As workers are added, the process starts to run and marginal product rises.

At point A (L_1 units of labor), marginal product begins to fall. Because every plant has a finite capacity, efforts to increase production will always run into the limits of that capacity. At point B (L_2 units of labor), marginal product has fallen to equal the average product, which has been increasing. Between point B and point C (between L_2 and L_3 units of labor), marginal product falls below average product, and average product begins to follow it *down*. Average product is at its maximum at point B, where it is equal to marginal product.

At L_3 more labor yields no more output, and marginal product is zero—the assembly line has no more positions, the grill is jammed, and the accountant is too tired to see another client. (If you have trouble understanding the relationships among the three curves in Figure 7.6, review the calculations in Table 7.2, and review the Appendix on graphing in Chapter 1.)

PRODUCTION FUNCTIONS WITH TWO VARIABLE FACTORS OF PRODUCTION

So far we have considered production functions with only one variable factor of production. However, inputs work together in production. In general, additional capital increases the productivity of labor. Because capital—buildings, machines, and so on—is of no use without people to operate it, we say that capital and labor are *complementary inputs*.

A simple example will clarify this point. Consider again the sandwich shop. If the demand for sandwiches began to exceed the capacity of the shop to produce them, the shop's owner might decide to expand capacity. This would mean purchasing more capital in the form of a new grill.

A second grill would essentially double the shop's productive capacity. The new higher capacity would mean that the sandwich shop would not run into diminishing returns as quickly. With only one grill, the third and fourth workers are less productive because the single grill gets crowded. With two grills, however, the third and fourth workers could produce 15 sandwiches per hour using the second grill. In essence, the added capital raises the *productivity* of labor—that is, the amount of output produced per worker per hour.

Just as the new grill enhances the productivity of workers in the sandwich shop, new businesses and the capital that they put in place raise the productivity of workers in countries like Malaysia, India, and Kenya.

This simple relationship lies at the heart of worries about productivity at the national and international levels. Building new, modern plants and equipment enhances a nation's productivity. Since the 1950s, for example, Japan has accumulated capital (that is, built plant and equipment) faster than any other country in the world. The result is a very high average quantity of output per worker in Japan.

A labor intensive plant.

CHOICE OF TECHNOLOGY

As our sandwich shop example shows, inputs (factors of production) are complementary. Capital enhances the productivity of labor. Workers in the sandwich shop are more productive when they are not crowded on a single grill. Similarly, labor enhances the productivity of capital. When more workers are hired at a plant that is operating at 50 percent of capacity, previously idle machines suddenly become productive.

However, inputs can also be substituted for one another. If labor becomes expensive, firms can adopt labor-saving technologies; that is, they can substitute capital for labor. Assembly lines can be automated by replacing human beings with machines, and capital can be substituted for land when land is scarce. If capital becomes relatively expensive, firms can substitute labor for capital. In short, most goods and services can be produced in a number of ways, using alternative technologies. One of the key decisions that all firms must make is which technology to use.

Consider the choices available to the diaper manufacturer in Table 7.3. Five different techniques of producing 100 diapers are available. Technology *A* is the most labor intensive, requiring 10 hours of labor and two units of capital to produce 100 diapers. (You can think of units of capital as machine hours.) Technology *E* is the most capital intensive, requiring only 2 hours of labor but 10 hours of machine time.

To choose a production technique, the firm must look to input markets to find out the current market prices of labor and capital. What is the wage rate (P_L), and what is the cost per hour of capital (P_K)?

Suppose that labor and capital are both available at a price of $1 per unit. Column 4 of Table 7.4 presents the calculations required to determine which technology is the best. The winner is technology *C*. Assuming that the firm's objective is to maximize profits, it will choose the least-cost technology. Using technology *C*, the firm can produce 100 diapers for $8. All four of the other technologies produce 100 diapers at a higher cost.

TABLE 7.3 Inputs Required to Produce 100 Diapers Using Alternative Technologies

TECHNOLOGY	UNITS OF CAPITAL (*K*)	UNITS OF LABOR (*L*)
A	2	10
B	3	6
C	4	4
D	6	3
E	10	2

News
ANALYSIS

Increasing Substitution of Capital for Labor Raises Labor Productivity

MODERN TECHNOLOGY HAS DRAMATI-cally changed the process of production in many industries and in everyday life. Automobiles are increasingly assembled by industrial robots; computer systems are doing everything from accounting to making decisions about whether a loan should be made to a bank customer; and the chores of everyday life, such as washing dishes and buying a gift from Amazon.com, are done at high speeds with the aid of machines and computers.

The main benefit is that modern technology requires less labor—less human time—to produce the same output, thus raising the productivity of labor. Higher productivity in household production frees up time for leisure activities.

Agricultural production has been evolving for thousands of years. The latest technology has had a huge impact on the production of milk.

More modern technologies substitute capital (machines) for labor.

The Flexible Farmer Lets the Robot Do the Milking

—New York Times

NAVAN, Ontario—For most of the last 20 years, the milking at the Cloverdale Farm was an unwelcome ritual for both the cows and the people. Every morning the owner, Wayne Edwards, and an assistant would wake up at 5:30 and spend the next two hours milking. Then every afternoon at 4 the process began again, this time lasting about three hours with cleanup.

"You had to be there, there was no way around it," Mr. Edwards said. The cows were not happy with the rigid schedule either, he said.

Today, if he wants, Mr. Edwards can sleep in or attend his children's afternoon sports events at a nearby arena. And his cows can get milked pretty much whenever they fancy, day or night.

Cloverdale, in this hamlet on the rural fringes of Ottawa, is among the North American dairy farms that are letting robots do the milking. Cows are admitted to the milking area by com-puter, and a robotic arm does the job of washing the teats and placing the milking cups, using a laser to guide it. No person needs to be present. Rising labor costs, problems with conventional milking methods and a desire for more flexibility have persuaded dozens of farmers in Canada and a handful in the United States to follow the lead of thousands of European dairy farmers in turning the crucial part of their operation to machines.

Now suppose that the wage rate (P_L) were to rise sharply, from $1 to $5. You might guess that this increase would lead the firm to substitute labor-saving capital for workers, and you would be right. As column 5 of Table 7.4 shows, the increase in the wage rate means that technology E is now the cost-minimizing choice for the firm. Using 10 units of capital and only 2 units of labor, the firm can produce 100 diapers for $20. All other technologies are now more costly.

Two things determine the cost of production: (1) technologies that are available and (2) input prices. Profit-maximizing firms will choose the technology that minimizes the cost of production given current market input prices.

TABLE 7.4 Cost-Minimizing Choice Among Alternative Technologies (100 Diapers)

(1) TECHNOLOGY	(2) UNITS OF CAPITAL (K)	(3) UNITS OF LABOR (L)	(4) COST = $(L \times P_L) + (K \times P_K)$ $P_L = \$1$ $P_K = \$1$	(5) COST = $(L \times P_L) + (K \times P_K)$ $P_L = \$5$ $P_K = \$1$
A	2	10	$12	$52
B	3	6	9	33
C	4	4	[8]	24
D	6	3	9	21
E	10	2	12	[20]

LOOKING AHEAD: COST AND SUPPLY

So far, we have looked only at a *single* level of output. That is, we have determined how much it will cost to produce 100 diapers using the best available technology when $P_K = \$1$ and $P_L = \$1$ or 5. The best technique for producing 1,000 diapers or 10,000 diapers may be entirely different. The next chapter explores the relationship between cost and the level of output in some detail. One of our main objectives in that chapter will be to determine the amount that a competitive firm will choose to *supply* during a given time period.

SUMMARY

1. Firms vary in size and internal organization, but they all take inputs and transform them into outputs through a process called *production*.

2. In perfect competition, no single firm has any control over prices. This follows from two assumptions: (1) Perfectly competitive industries are composed of many firms, each small relative to the size of the industry; and (2) each firm in a perfectly competitive industry produces *homogeneous products*.

3. The demand curve facing a competitive firm is perfectly elastic. If a single firm raises its price above the market price, it will sell nothing. Because it can sell all it produces at the market price, a firm has no incentive to reduce price.

THE BEHAVIOR OF PROFIT-MAXIMIZING FIRMS

4. Profit-maximizing firms in all industries must make three choices: (1) how much output to supply, (2) how to produce that output, and (3) how much of each input to demand.

5. Profit equals total revenue minus total cost. Total cost (economic cost) includes (1) out-of-pocket costs and (2) the opportunity cost of each factor of production, including a normal rate of return on capital.

6. A *normal rate of return* to capital is included in total cost because tying up resources in a firm's capital stock has an opportunity cost. If you start a business or buy a share of stock in a corporation, you do so because you expect to make a normal rate of return. Investors will not invest their money in a business unless they expect to make a normal rate of return.

7. A positive *profit* level occurs when a firm is earning an above-normal rate of return on capital.

8. Two assumptions define the *short run*: (1) a fixed scale or fixed factor of production and (2) no entry to or exit from the industry. In the *long run*, firms can choose any scale of operations they want, and new firms can enter and leave the industry.

9. To make decisions, firms need to know three things: (1) the market price of their output, (2) the production techniques that are available, and (3) the prices of inputs.

THE PRODUCTION PROCESS

10. The relationship between inputs and outputs (the *production technology*) expressed numerically or mathematically is called a *production function* or *total product function*.

11. The *marginal product* of a variable input is the additional output that an added unit of that input will produce if all other inputs are held constant. According to the *law of diminishing returns*, when additional units of a variable input are added to fixed inputs after a certain point, the marginal product of the variable input will decline.

12. *Average product* is the average amount of product produced by each unit of a variable factor of production. If marginal product is above average product, the average product rises; if marginal product is below average product, the average product falls.

13. Capital and labor are at the same time complementary and substitutable inputs. Capital enhances the productivity of labor, but it can also be substituted for labor.

CHOICE OF TECHNOLOGY

14. Once of the key decisions that all firms must make is which technology to use. Profit-maximizing firms will choose that combination of inputs that minimizes costs and therefore maximizes profits.

REVIEW TERMS AND CONCEPTS

average product, 153

capital-intensive technology, 151

firm, 144

homogeneous products, 145

labor-intensive technology, 151

law of diminishing returns, 153

long run, 150

marginal product, 152

normal rate of return, 147

optimal method of production, 150

perfect competition, 144

production, 143

production function or total product function, 151

production technology, 151

profit (economic profit), 146

short run, 150

total cost (total economic cost), 146

total revenue, 146

1. Profit = total revenue – total cost

2. $\dfrac{\text{Average product}}{\text{of labor}} = \dfrac{\text{total product}}{\text{total units of labor}}$

PROBLEM SET

1. Consider a firm that uses capital and labor as inputs and sells 5,000 units of output per year at the going market price of $10. Also assume that total labor costs to the firm are $45,000 annually. Assume further that the total capital stock of the firm is currently worth $100,000, that the return available to investors with comparable risks is 10 percent annually, and that there was no depreciation. Is this a profitable firm? Explain your answer.

2. Two former Northwestern University students worked in an investment bank at a salary of $60,000 each for 2 years after they graduated. Together they saved $50,000. After 2 years, they decided to quit their jobs and start a business designing Web sites. They used the $50,000 to buy computer equipment, desks, and chairs. For the next 2 years they took in $40,000 in revenue each year, paid themselves $10,000 annually each, and rented an office for $18,000 per year. Prior to the investment, their $50,000 was in bonds earning interest at a rate of 10 percent. Are they now earning economic profits? Explain your answer.

3. Suppose that in 2006 you became president of a small nonprofit theater company. Your playhouse has 120 seats and a small stage. The actors have national reputations, and demand for tickets is enormous relative to the number of seats available; every performance is sold out months in advance. You are elected because you have demonstrated an ability to raise funds successfully. Describe some of the decisions that you must make in the short run. What might you consider to be your "fixed factor"? What alternative decisions might you be able to make in the long run? Explain.

4. The following table gives total output or total product as a function of labor units used:

LABOR	TOTAL OUTPUT
0	0
1	5
2	9
3	12
4	14
5	15

   a. Define diminishing returns.
   b. Does the table indicate a situation of diminishing returns? Explain your answer.

5. Suppose that wimps can be produced using two different production techniques, A and B. The following table provides the total input requirements for each of five different total output levels:

	Q = 1		Q = 2		Q = 3		Q = 4		Q = 5	
TECH.	K	L	K	L	K	L	K	L	K	L
A	2	5	1	10	5	14	6	18	8	20
B	5	2	8	3	11	4	14	5	16	6

   a. Assuming that the price of labor (P_L) is $1 and the price of capital (P_K) is $2, calculate the total cost of production for each of the five levels of output using the optimal (least-cost) technology at each level.
   b. How many labor hours (units of labor) would be employed at each level of output? How many machine hours (units of capital)?
   c. Graph total cost of production as a function of output. (Put cost on the Y-axis and output, q, on the X-axis.) Again, assume that the optimal technology is used.
   d. Repeat a. through c. under the assumption that the price of labor (P_L) rises from $1 to $3 while the price of capital (P_K) remains at $2.

6. A female student who lives on the fourth floor of Bates Hall is assigned to a new room on the seventh floor during her junior year. She has 11 heavy boxes of books and "stuff" to move. Discuss the alternative combinations of capital and labor that might be used to make the move. How would your answer differ if the move were to a new dorm 3 miles across campus, and to a new college 400 miles away?

7. The following is a production function:

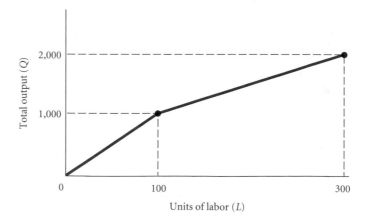

a. Draw a graph of marginal product as a function of output. (*Hint:* Marginal product is the additional number of units of output per unit of labor at each level of output.)

b. Does this graph exhibit diminishing returns?

8. During the early phases of industrialization, the number of persons engaged in agriculture usually drops sharply, even as agricultural output is growing. Given what you know about production technology and production functions, can you explain this seeming inconsistency?

9. The number of repairs produced by a computer repair shop depends on the number of workers as follows:

NUMBER OF WORKERS (PER WEEK)	NUMBER OF REPAIRS
0	0
1	8
2	20
3	35
4	45
5	52
6	57
7	60

Assume that all inputs (office space, telephone, utilities) other than labor are fixed in the short run.

a. Add two additional columns to the table, and enter the marginal product and average product for each number of workers.

b. Over what range of labor input are there increasing returns to labor? Diminishing returns to labor? Negative returns to labor?

c. Over what range of labor input is marginal product greater than average product? What is happening to average product as employment increases over this range?

d. Over what range of labor input is marginal product smaller than average product? What is happening to average product as employment increases over this range?

10. Since the end of World War II, manufacturing firms in the United States and in Europe have been moving farther and farther outside of central cities. At the same time, firms in finance, insurance, and other parts of the service sector have been locating near the downtown areas in tall buildings. One major reason seems to be that manufacturing firms find it difficult to substitute capital for land, while service-sector firms that use office space do not.

a. What kinds of buildings represent substitution of capital for land?

b. Why do you think that manufacturing firms might find it difficult to substitute capital for land?

c. Why is it relatively easier for a law firm or an insurance company to substitute capital for land?

d. Why is the demand for land likely to be very high near the center of a city?

*e. One of the reasons for substituting capital for land near the center of a city is that land is more expensive near the center. What is true about the relative supply of land near the center of a city? (*Hint:* What is the formula for the area of a circle?)

11. Ted Baxter runs a small, very stable newspaper company in southern Oregon. The paper has been in business for 25 years. The total value of the firm's capital stock is $1 million, which Ted owns outright. This year the firm earned a total of $250,000 after out-of-pocket expenses. Without taking the opportunity cost of capital into account, this means that Ted is earning a 25 percent return on his capital. Suppose that risk-free bonds are currently paying a rate of 10 percent to those who buy them.

a. What is meant by the "opportunity cost of capital"?

b. Explain why opportunity costs are "real" costs even though they do not necessarily involve out-of-pocket expenses.

c. What is the opportunity cost of Ted's capital?

d. How much excess profit is Ted earning?

12. A firm can use three different production technologies, with capital and labor requirements at each level of output as follows:

Daily Output	TECHNOLOGY 1		TECHNOLOGY 2		TECHNOLOGY 3	
	K	L	K	L	K	L
100	3	7	4	5	5	4
150	3	10	4	7	5	5
200	4	11	5	8	6	6
250	5	13	6	10	7	8

a. Suppose the firm is operating in a high-wage country, where capital cost is $100 per unit per day and labor cost is $80 per worker per day. For each level of output, which technology is the cheapest?

b. Now suppose the firm is operating in a low-wage country, where capital cost is $100 per unit per day but labor cost is only $40 per unit per day. For each level of output, which technology is the cheapest?

c. Suppose the firm moves from a high-wage to a low-wage country but that its level of output remains constant at 200 units per day. How will its total employment change?

---

*Note: Problems marked with an asterisk are more challenging.

APPENDIX

ISOQUANTS AND ISOCOSTS

This chapter has shown that the cost structure facing a firm depends on two key pieces of information: (1) input (factor) prices and (2) technology. This appendix presents a more formal analysis of technology and factor prices and their relationship to cost.

NEW LOOK AT TECHNOLOGY: ISOQUANTS

Table 7A.1 is expanded from Table 7.3 to show the various combinations of capital (K) and labor (L) that can be used to produce three different levels of output (q). For example, 100 units of X can be produced with 2 units of capital and 10 units of labor, or with 3 units of K and 6 units of L, or with 4 units of K and 4 units of L, and so forth. Similarly, 150 units of X can be

TABLE 7A.1	Alternative Combinations of Capital (K) and Labor (L) Required to Produce 50, 100, and 150 Units of Output					
	$Q_X = 50$		$Q_X = 100$		$Q_X = 150$	
	K	L	K	L	K	L
A	1	8	2	10	3	10
B	2	5	3	6	4	7
C	3	3	4	4	5	5
D	5	2	6	3	7	4
E	8	1	10	2	10	3

produced with 3 units of K and 10 units of L, or with 4 units of K and 7 units of L, and so forth.

A graph that shows all the combinations of capital and labor that can be used to produce a given amount of output is called an **isoquant**. Figure 7A.1 graphs three isoquants, one each for $q_X = 50$, $q_X = 100$, and $q_X = 150$, based on the data in Table 7A.1. Notice that all the points on the graph have been connected, indicating that there are an infinite number of combinations of labor and capital that can produce each level of output. For example, 100 units of output can also be produced with 3.50 units of labor and 4.75 units of capital. (Verify that this point is on the isoquant labeled $q_X = 100$.)

Figure 7A.1 shows only three isoquants, but there are many more not shown. For example, there are separate isoquants for $q_X = 101$, $q_X = 102$, and so on. If we assume that producing fractions of a unit of output is possible, there must be an isoquant for $q_X = 134.57$, for $q_X = 124.82$, and so on. One could imagine an infinite number of isoquants in Figure 7A.1. The higher the level of output, the farther up and to the right the isoquant will lie.

Figure 7A.2 derives the slope of an isoquant. Because points F and G are both on the $q_X = 100$ isoquant, the two

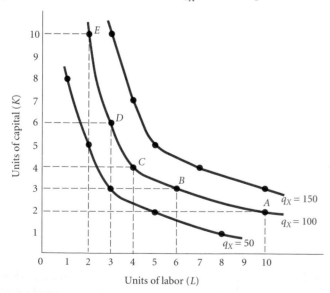

FIGURE 7A.1 Isoquants Showing All Combinations of Capital and Labor That Can Be Used to Produce 50, 100, and 150 Units of Output

FIGURE 7A.2 The Slope of an Isoquant Is Equal to the Ratio of MP_L to MP_K

points represent two different combinations of K and L that can be used to produce 100 units of output. In moving from point F to point G along the curve, less capital is employed but more labor is used. An approximation of the amount of output lost by using less capital is ΔK times the marginal product of capital (MP_K). The *marginal product of capital* is the number of units of output produced by a single marginal unit of capital. Thus, $\Delta K \cdot MP_K$ is the total output lost by using less capital.

For output to remain constant (as it must, because F and G are on the same isoquant), the loss of output from using less capital must be exactly matched by the added output produced by using more labor. This amount can be approximated by ΔL times the marginal product of labor (MP_L). Because the two must be equal, it follows that

$$\Delta K \cdot MP_K = -\Delta L \cdot MP_L{}^1$$

If we then divide both sides of this equation by ΔL and then by MP_K, we arrive at the following expression for the slope of the isoquant:

$$\text{slope of isoquant: } \frac{\Delta K}{\Delta L} = -\frac{MP_L}{MP_K}$$

The ratio of MP_L to MP_K is called the **marginal rate of technical substitution**. It is the rate at which a firm can substitute capital for labor and hold output constant.

FACTOR PRICES AND INPUT COMBINATIONS: ISOCOSTS

A graph that shows all the combinations of capital and labor that are available for a given total cost is called an **isocost line**. (Recall that total cost includes opportunity costs and normal

---

[1]We need to add the negative sign to ΔL because in moving from point F to point G, ΔK is a negative number and ΔL is a positive number. The minus sign is needed to balance the equation.

rate of return.) Just as there are an infinite number of isoquants (one for every possible level of output), there are an infinite number of isocost lines, one for every possible level of total cost.

Figure 7A.3 shows three simple isocost lines assuming that the price of labor (P_L) is \$1 per unit and the price of capital (P_K) is \$1 per unit. The lowest isocost line shows all the combinations of K and L that can be purchased for \$5. For example, \$5 will buy 5 units of labor and no capital (point A), or 3 units of labor and 2 units of capital (point B), or no units of labor and 5 units of capital (point C). All these points lie along a straight line. The equation of that straight line is

$$(P_K \cdot K) + (P_L \cdot L) = TC$$

Substituting our data for the lowest isocost line into this general equation, we get

$$(\$1 \cdot K) + (\$1 \cdot L) = \$5, \quad \text{or } K + L = 5$$

Remember that the X- and Y-scales are units of labor and units of capital, not dollars.

On the same graph are two additional isocosts showing the various combinations of K and L available for a total cost of \$6 and \$7. These are only three of an infinite number of isocosts. At any total cost, there is an isocost that shows all the combinations of K and L available for that amount.

Figure 7A.4 shows another isocost line. This isocost assumes a different set of factor prices, $P_L = \$5$ and $P_K = \$1$. The diagram shows all the combinations of K and L that can be bought for \$25. One way to draw the line is to determine the endpoints. For example, if the entire \$25 were spent on labor,

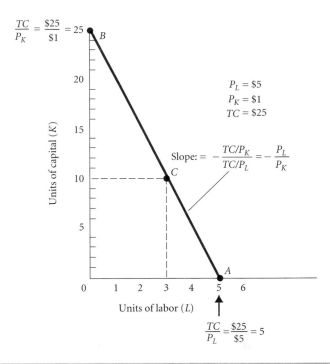

FIGURE 7A.4 Isocost Line Showing All Combinations of Capital and Labor Available for \$25

One way to draw an isocost line is to determine the endpoints of that line and draw a line connecting them.

how much labor could be purchased? The answer is, of course, 5 units (\$25 divided by \$5 per unit). Thus, point A, which represents 5 units of labor and no capital, is on the isocost line. Similarly, if all of the \$25 were spent on capital, how much capital could be purchased? The answer is 25 units (\$25 divided by \$1 per unit). Thus, point B, which represents 25 units of capital and no labor, is also on the isocost line. Another point on this particular isocost is 3 units of labor and 10 units of capital, point C.

The slope of an isocost line can be calculated easily if you first find the endpoints of the line. In Figure 7A.4, we can calculate the slope of the isocost line by taking $\Delta K / \Delta L$ between points B and A. Thus

$$\text{slope of isocost line: } \frac{\Delta K}{\Delta L} = -\frac{TC / P_K}{TC / P_L} = -\frac{P_L}{P_K}$$

Plugging in the endpoints from our example, we get

$$\text{slope of line } AB = -\frac{\$5}{\$1} = -5$$

FINDING THE LEAST-COST TECHNOLOGY WITH ISOQUANTS AND ISOCOSTS

Figure 7A.5 superimposes the isoquant for $q_X = 50$ on the isocost lines in Figure 7A.3, which assume that $P_K = \$1$ and $P_L = \$1$. The question now becomes one of choosing among the combinations of K and L that can be used to produce 50 units of output. Recall that each point on the isoquant (labeled $q_X = 50$ in Figure 7A.5)

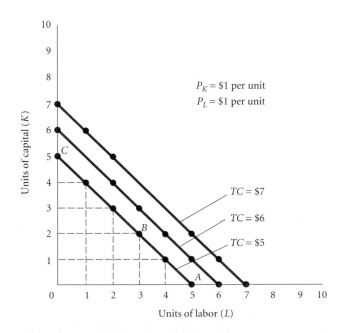

FIGURE 7A.3 Isocost Lines Showing the Combinations of Capital and Labor Available for \$5, \$6, and \$7

An isocost line shows all the combinations of capital and labor that are available for a given total cost.

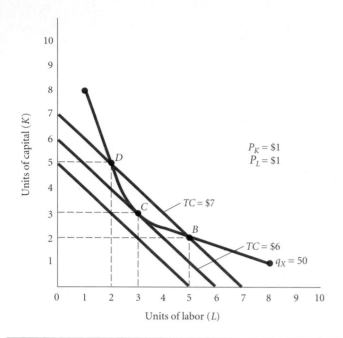

FIGURE 7A.5 Finding the Least-Cost Combination of Capital and Labor to Produce 50 Units of Output

Profit-maximizing firms will minimize costs by producing their chosen level of output with the technology represented by the point at which the isoquant is tangent to an isocost line. Here, the cost-minimizing technology—3 units of capital and 3 units of labor—is represented by point C.

FIGURE 7A.6 Minimizing Cost of Production for $q_X = 50$, $q_X = 100$, and $q_X = 150$

Plotting a series of cost-minimizing combinations of inputs—shown in this graph as points A, B, and C—on a separate graph results in a *cost curve* like the one shown in Figure 7A.7.

represents a different technology—a different combination of K and L.

We assume that our firm is a perfectly competitive, profit maximizing firm that will choose the combination that minimizes cost. Because every point on the isoquant lies on some particular isocost line, we can determine the total cost for each combination along the isoquant. For example, point D (5 units of capital and 2 units of labor) lies along the isocost for a total cost of $7. Notice that 5 units of capital and 2 units of labor cost a total of $7. (Remember, $P_K = \$1$ and $P_L = \$1$.) The same amount of output (50 units) can be produced at lower cost. Specifically, by using 3 units of labor and 3 units of capital (point C), total cost is reduced to $6. *No other combination of* K *and* L *along isoquant* $q_X = 50$ *is on a lower isocost line.* In seeking to maximize profits, then

> The firm will choose the combination of inputs that is least costly. The least costly way to produce any given level of output is indicated by the point of tangency between an isocost line and the isoquant corresponding to that level of output.[2]

In Figure 7A.5, the least-cost technology of producing 50 units of output is represented by point C, the point at which the $q_X = 50$ isoquant is just tangent to—that is, just touches—the isocost line.

Figure 7A.6 adds the other two isoquants from Figure 7A.1 to Figure 7A.5. Assuming that $P_K = \$1$ and $P_L = \$1$, the firm will move along each of the three isoquants until it finds the least-cost combination of K and L that can be used to produce that particular level of output. The result is plotted in Figure 7A.7. The minimum cost of producing 50 units of X is $6; the minimum cost of producing 100 units of X is $8; and the minimum cost of producing 150 units of X is $10.

THE COST-MINIMIZING EQUILIBRIUM CONDITION

At the point where a line is just tangent to a curve, the two have the same slope. (We have already derived expressions for the slope of an isocost and the slope of an isoquant.) At each point of tangency (such as at points A, B, and C in Figure 7A.6), the following must be true:

$$\text{slope of isoquant} = -\frac{MP_L}{MP_K} = \text{slope of isocost} = -\frac{P_L}{P_K}$$

Thus,

$$\frac{MP_L}{MP_K} = \frac{P_L}{P_K}$$

---

[2]This assumes that the isoquants are continuous and convex (bowed) toward the origin.

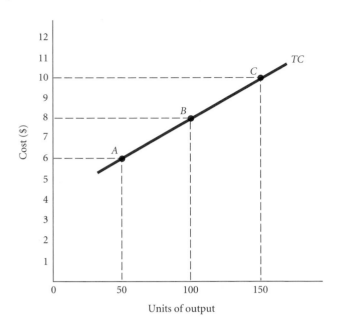

FIGURE 7A.7 A Cost Curve Shows the *Minimum* Cost of Producing Each Level of Output

Dividing both sides by P_L and multiplying both sides by MP_K, we get

$$\frac{MP_L}{P_L} = \frac{MP_K}{P_K}$$

This is the firm's cost-minimizing equilibrium condition.

This expression makes sense if you think about what it says. The left side of the equation is the marginal product of labor divided by the price of a unit of labor. Thus, it is the product derived from the last dollar spent on labor. The right-hand side of the equation is the product derived from the last dollar spent on capital. If the product derived from the last dollar spent on labor were not equal to the product derived from the last dollar spent on capital, the firm could decrease costs by using more labor and less capital or by using more capital and less labor.

Look back to Chapter 6 and see if you can find a similar expression and some similar logic in our discussion of household behavior. In fact, there is great symmetry between the theory of the firm and the theory of household behavior.

SUMMARY

1. An *isoquant* is a graph that shows all the combinations of capital and labor that can be used to produce a given amount of output. The slope of an isoquant is equal to $-MP_L/MP_K$. The ratio of MP_L to MP_K is the *marginal rate of technical substitution.* It is the rate at which a firm can substitute capital for labor and hold output constant.

2. An *isocost line* is a graph that shows all the combinations of capital and labor that are available for a given total cost. The slope of an isocost line is equal to $-P_L/P_K$.

3. The least-cost method of producing a given amount of output is found graphically at the point at which an isocost line is just tangent to—that is, just touches—the isoquant corresponding to that level of production. The firm's cost-minimizing equilibrium condition is $MP_L/P_L = MP_K/P_K$.

REVIEW TERMS AND CONCEPTS

isocost line A graph that shows all the combinations of capital and labor available for a given total cost.   160

isoquant A graph that shows all the combinations of capital and labor that can be used to produce a given amount of output.   160

marginal rate of technical substitution The rate at which a firm can substitute capital for labor and hold output constant.   160

1. Slope of isoquant:

$$\frac{\Delta K}{\Delta L} = -\frac{MP_L}{MP_K}$$

2. Slope of isocost line:

$$\frac{\Delta K}{\Delta L} = -\frac{TC\,/\,P_K}{TC\,/\,P_L} = -\frac{P_L}{P_K}$$

PROBLEM SET

1. Assume that $MP_L = 5$ and $MP_K = 10$. Assume also that $P_L = \$2$ and $P_K = \$5$. This implies that the firm should substitute labor for capital. Explain why.

2. In the isoquant/isocost diagram (Figure 1) suppose that the firm is producing 1,000 units of output at point A using 100 units of labor and 200 units of capital. As an outside consultant,

what actions would you suggest to management to improve profits? What would you recommend if the firm were operating at point *B*, using 100 units of capital and 200 units of labor?

3. Using the information from the isoquant/isocost diagram (Figure 2) and assuming that $P_L = P_K = \$2$, complete Table 1.

TABLE 1

OUTPUT UNITS	TOTAL COST OF OUTPUT	UNITS OF LABOR DEMANDED	UNITS OF CAPITAL DEMANDED
100			
200			
300			

FIGURE 1

FIGURE 2

Short-Run Costs and Output Decisions

This chapter continues our examination of the decisions that firms make in their quest for profits. You have seen that firms in perfectly competitive industries make three specific decisions (Figure 8.1). These decisions are:

1. How much output to supply
2. How to produce that output—that is, which production technique/technology to use
3. What quantity of each input to demand

Remember, though, that *all* types of firms make these decisions, not just those in perfectly competitive industries. We continue to use perfectly competitive firms as a teaching device, but much of the material in this chapter applies to firms in noncompetitive industries as well.

We have assumed so far that firms are in business to earn profits and that they make choices to maximize those profits. (Remember that *profit* refers to economic profit, the difference between revenues and costs—full economic costs.) Because firms in perfectly competitive markets are price-takers in both input and output markets, many decisions depend on prices over which firms have no control. Like households, firms also face market constraints.

In the last chapter, we focused on the production process. This chapter focuses on the *costs* of production. To calculate costs, a firm must know two things: what quantity and combination of inputs it needs to produce its product and how much those inputs cost. (Do not forget that economic costs include a normal return to capital—the opportunity cost of capital.)

Take a moment and look back at the circular flow diagram, Figure 7.1. There you can see exactly where we are in our study of the competitive market system. The goal of this chapter is to look behind the supply curve in output markets. It is important to understand, however, that producing output implies demanding inputs at the same time. You can also see in Figure 7.1 two of the information sources that firms use in their output supply and input demand decisions: Firms look to *output markets* for the price of output and to *input markets* for the prices of capital and labor.

COSTS IN THE SHORT RUN

Our emphasis in this chapter is on costs *in the short run only*. Recall that the short run is that period during which two conditions hold: (1) Existing firms face limits imposed by some fixed factor of production, and (2) new firms cannot enter, and existing firms cannot exit, an industry.

DECISIONS	are based on	INFORMATION
1. The quantity of output to *supply*		1. The price of output
2. How to produce that output (which technique to use)		2. Techniques of production available*
3. The quantity of each input to *demand*		3. The price of inputs*
		*Determines production costs

FIGURE 8.1 Decisions Facing Firms

fixed cost Any cost that does not depend on the firm's level of output. These costs are incurred even if the firm is producing nothing. There are no fixed costs in the long run.

variable cost A cost that depends on the level of production chosen.

total cost (TC) Fixed costs plus variable costs.

In the short run, all firms (competitive and noncompetitive) have costs that they must bear regardless of their output. In fact, some costs must be paid even if the firm stops producing—that is, even if output is zero. These kinds of costs are called **fixed costs**, and firms can do nothing in the short run to avoid them or to change them. In the long run, a firm has no fixed costs, because it can expand, contract, or exit the industry.

Firms do have certain costs in the short run that depend on the level of output they have chosen. These kinds of costs are called **variable costs**. Fixed costs and variable costs together make up **total costs**:

$$TC = TFC + TVC$$

where *TC* denotes total costs, *TFC* denotes total fixed costs, and *TVC* denotes total variable costs. We will return to this equation after discussing fixed costs and variable costs in detail.

FIXED COSTS

In discussing fixed costs, we must distinguish between total fixed costs and average fixed costs.

Total Fixed Cost (TFC)   Total fixed cost is sometimes called *overhead*. If you operate a factory, you must heat the building to keep the pipes from freezing in the winter. Even if no production is taking place, you may have to keep the roof from leaking, pay a guard to protect the building from vandals, and make payments on a long-term lease. There may also be insurance premiums, taxes, and city fees to pay, as well as contract obligations to workers.

Fixed costs represent a larger portion of total costs for some firms than for others. Electric companies, for instance, maintain generating plants, thousands of miles of distribution wires, poles, transformers, and so forth. Usually, such plants are financed by issuing bonds to the public—that is, by borrowing. The interest that must be paid on these bonds represents a substantial part of the utilities' operating cost and is a fixed cost in the short run, no matter how much (if any) electricity they are producing.

For the purposes of our discussion in this chapter, we will assume that firms use only two inputs: labor and capital. Although this may seem unrealistic, virtually everything that we will say about firms using these two factors can easily be generalized to firms that use many factors of production. Recall that capital yields services over time in the production of other goods and services. It is the plant and equipment of a manufacturing firm; the computers, desks, chairs, doors, and walls of a law office; it is the software of a Web-based firm, and the boat that Bill and Colleen built on their desert island. It is sometimes assumed that capital is a fixed input in the short run and that labor is the only variable input. To be a bit more realistic, however, we will assume that capital has both a fixed *and* a variable component. After all, some capital can be purchased in the short run.

Consider a small consulting firm that employs several economists, research assistants, and secretaries. It rents space in an office building and has a 5-year lease. The rent on the office space can be thought of as a fixed cost in the short run. The monthly electric and heating bills are also essentially fixed (although the amounts may vary slightly from month to month). So are the salaries of the basic administrative staff. Payments on some capital equipment—a large copying machine and the main word processing system, for instance—can also be thought of as fixed.

TABLE 8.1 Short-Run Fixed Cost (Total and Average) of a Hypothetical Firm

(1) Q	(2) TFC	(3) AFC (TFC/Q)
0	$1,000	$ —
1	1,000	1,000
2	1,000	500
3	1,000	333
4	1,000	250
5	1,000	200

The same firm also has costs that vary with output. When there is a lot of work, the firm hires more employees at both the professional and research assistant levels. The capital used by the consulting firm may also vary, even in the short run. Payments on the computer system do not change, but the firm may rent additional computer time when necessary. It can buy additional personal computers, network terminals, or databases quickly, if needed. It must pay for the copy machine, but the machine costs more when it is running than when it is not.

Total fixed costs (*TFC*) are those costs that do not change with output, even if output is zero. Column 2 of Table 8.1 presents data on the fixed costs of a hypothetical firm. Fixed costs are $1,000 at all levels of output (q). Figure 8.2(a) shows total fixed costs as a function of output. Because *TFC* does not change with output, the graph is simply a straight horizontal line at $1,000. The important thing to remember here is that

> Firms have no control over fixed costs in the short run. For this reason, fixed costs are sometimes called **sunk costs**.

total fixed costs (*TFC*) or overhead The total of all costs that do not change with output, even if output is zero.

sunk costs Another name for fixed costs in the short run because firms have no choice but to pay them.

Average Fixed Cost (*AFC*) **Average fixed cost (*AFC*)** is total fixed cost (*TFC*) divided by the number of units of output (q):

$$AFC = \frac{TFC}{q}$$

average fixed cost (*AFC*) Total fixed cost divided by the number of units of output; a per-unit measure of fixed costs.

a. Total fixed cost

b. Average fixed cost

FIGURE 8.2 Short-Run Fixed Cost (Total and Average) of a Hypothetical Firm

Average fixed cost is simply total fixed cost divided by the quantity of output. As output increases, average fixed cost declines because we are dividing a fixed number ($1,000) by a larger and larger quantity.

spreading overhead The
process of dividing total fixed
costs by more units of output.
Average fixed cost declines as
quantity rises.

For example, if the firm in Figure 8.2 produced 3 units of output, average fixed costs would be $333 ($1,000 divided by 3). If the same firm produced 5 units of output, average fixed cost would be $200 ($1,000 divided by 5). *Average fixed cost falls as output rises*, because the same total is being spread over, or divided by, a larger number of units (see column 3 of Table 8.1). This phenomenon is sometimes called **spreading overhead**.

Graphs of average fixed cost, like that in Figure 8.2(b) (which presents the average fixed cost data from Table 8.1), are downward-sloping curves. Notice that *AFC* approaches zero as the quantity of output increases. If output were 100,000 units, average fixed cost would equal only 1 cent per unit in our example ($1,000 ÷ 100,000 = $0.01). *AFC* never actually reaches zero.

VARIABLE COSTS

total variable cost (*TVC*)
The total of all costs that vary
with output in the short run.

Total Variable Cost (*TVC*)   **Total variable cost (*TVC*)** is the sum of those costs that vary with the level of output in the short run. To produce more output, a firm uses more inputs. The cost of additional output depends directly on what additional inputs are required and how much they cost.

As you saw in Chapter 7, input requirements are determined by technology. Firms generally have a number of production techniques available to them, and the option they choose is assumed to be the one that produces the desired level of output at the least cost. To find out which technology involves the least cost, a firm must compare the total variable costs of producing that level of output using different production techniques.

This is as true of small businesses as it is of large manufacturing firms. Suppose, for example, that you are a small farmer. A certain amount of work has to be done to plant and harvest your 120 acres. You might hire four farmhands and divide up the tasks, or you might buy several pieces of complex farm machinery (capital) and do the work single-handedly. Your final choice depends on a number of things. What machinery is available? What does it do? Will it work on small fields such as yours? How much will it cost to buy each piece of equipment? What wage will you have to pay farmhands? How many will you need to get the job done? If machinery is expensive and labor is cheap, you will probably choose the labor-intensive technology. If farm labor is expensive and the local farm equipment dealer is going out of business, you might get a good deal on some machinery and choose the capital-intensive method.

Having compared the costs of alternative production techniques, the firm may be influenced in its choice by the current scale of its operation. Remember, in the short run a firm is locked into a *fixed* scale of operations. A firm currently producing on a small scale may find that a labor-intensive technique is the least costly, whether or not labor is comparatively expensive. The same firm producing on a larger scale might find a capital-intensive technique less costly.

**total variable cost
curve** A graph that shows the
relationship between total
variable cost and the level of a
firm's output.

The **total variable cost curve** is a graph that shows the relationship between total variable cost and the level of a firm's output (q). At any given level of output, total variable cost depends on (1) the techniques of production that are available and (2) the prices of the inputs required by each technology. To examine this relationship in more detail, let us look at some hypothetical production figures.

Table 8.2 presents an analysis that might lie behind three points on a typical firm's total variable cost curve. In this case, there are two production techniques available, *A* and *B*, one

TABLE 8.2 Derivation of Total Variable Cost Schedule from Technology and Factor Prices

| PRODUCE | USING TECHNIQUE | UNITS OF INPUT REQUIRED (PRODUCTION FUNCTION) | | TOTAL VARIABLE COST ASSUMING $P_K = \$2$, $P_L = \$1$ $TVC = (K \times P_K) + (L \times P_L)$ |
		K	L	
1 Unit of output	A	4	4	$(4 \times \$2) + (4 \times \$1) = \$12$
	B	2	6	$(2 \times \$2) + (6 \times \$1) = \boxed{\$10}$
2 Units of output	A	7	6	$(7 \times \$2) + (6 \times \$1) = \$20$
	B	4	10	$(4 \times \$2) + (10 \times \$1) = \boxed{\$18}$
3 Units of output	A	9	6	$(9 \times \$2) + (6 \times \$1) = \boxed{\$24}$
	B	6	14	$(6 \times \$2) + (14 \times \$1) = \$26$

somewhat more capital intensive than the other. We will assume that the price of labor is $1 per unit and the price of capital is $2 per unit. For the purposes of this example, we focus on *variable capital*—that is, on capital that can be changed in the short run. In practice, some capital (such as buildings and large, specialized machines) is fixed in the short run. In our example, we will use K to denote variable capital. Remember, however, that the firm has other capital, capital that is fixed in the short run.

Analysis reveals that to produce one unit of output, the labor-intensive technique is least costly. Technique A requires four units of both capital and labor, which would cost a total of $12. Technique B requires six units of labor but only two units of capital for a total cost of only $10. To maximize profits, the firm would use technique B to produce one unit. The total variable cost of producing one unit of output would thus be $10.

The relatively labor-intensive technique B is also the best method of production for two units of output. By using B, the firm can produce two units for $18. If the firm decides to produce three units of output, however, technique A is cheaper. By using the least-cost technology (A), the total variable cost of production is $24. The firm will use nine units of capital at $2 each and six units of labor at $1 each.

Figure 8.3 graphs the relationship between variable costs and output based on the data in Table 8.2, assuming the firm chooses, for each output, the least-cost technology.

> The total variable cost curve embodies information about both factor, or input, prices and technology. It shows the cost of production using the best available technique at each output level given current factor prices.

Marginal Cost (MC)

Marginal Cost (MC)   The most important of all cost concepts is that of **marginal cost (MC)**, the increase in total cost that results from the production of one more unit of output. Let us say, for example, that a firm is producing 1,000 units of output per period and decides to raise its rate of output to 1,001. Producing the extra unit raises costs, and the increase—that is, the cost of producing the 1,001st unit—is the marginal cost. Focusing on the "margin" is one way of looking at variable costs: Marginal costs reflect changes in variable costs because they vary when output changes. Fixed costs do not change when output changes.

Table 8.3 shows how marginal cost is derived from total variable cost by simple subtraction. The total variable cost of producing the first unit of output is $10. Raising production from one unit to two units increases total variable cost from $10 to $18; the difference is the marginal cost of the second unit, or $8. Raising output from two to three units increases total variable cost from $18 to $24. The marginal cost of the third unit, therefore, is $6.

marginal cost (MC) The increase in total cost that results from producing one more unit of output. Marginal costs reflect changes in variable costs.

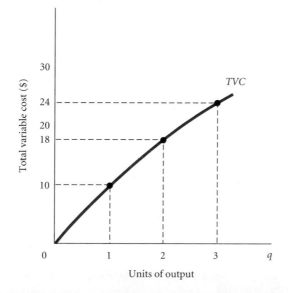

FIGURE 8.3 Total Variable Cost Curve

In Table 8.2 total variable cost is derived from production requirements and input prices. A total variable cost curve expresses the relationship between *TVC* and total output.

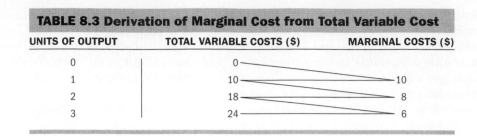

TABLE 8.3 Derivation of Marginal Cost from Total Variable Cost

UNITS OF OUTPUT	TOTAL VARIABLE COSTS ($)	MARGINAL COSTS ($)
0	0	
1	10	10
2	18	8
3	24	6

It is important to think for a moment about the nature of marginal cost. Specifically, marginal cost is the cost of the added inputs, or resources, needed to produce one additional unit of output. Look back at Table 8.2, and think about the additional capital and labor needed to go from 1 unit to 2 units. Producing 1 unit of output with technique *B* requires 2 units of capital and 6 units of labor; producing 2 units of output using the same technique requires 4 units of capital and 10 units of labor. Thus, the second unit requires 2 *additional* units of capital and 4 *additional* units of labor. What, then, is the added, or marginal, cost of the second unit? Two units of capital cost $2 each ($4 total) and 4 units of labor cost $1 each (another $4), for a total marginal cost of $8, which is exactly the number we derived in Table 8.3.

> Although the easiest way to derive marginal cost is to look at total variable cost and subtract, do not lose sight of the fact that when a firm increases its output level, it hires or demands more inputs. *Marginal cost* measures the *additional* cost of inputs required to produce each successive unit of output.

The Shape of the Marginal Cost Curve in the Short Run The assumption of a fixed factor of production in the short run means that a firm is stuck at its current scale of operation (in our example, the size of the plant). As a firm tries to increase its output, it will eventually find itself trapped by that scale. Thus, our definition of the short run also implies that *marginal cost eventually rises with output*. The firm can hire more labor and use more materials—that is, it can add variable inputs—but diminishing returns eventually set in.

Recall the sandwich shop, with one grill and too many workers trying to prepare sandwiches on it, from Chapter 7. With a fixed grill capacity, more laborers could make more sandwiches, but the marginal product of each successive cook declined as more people tried to use the grill. If each additional unit of labor adds less and less to total output, *it follows that it requires more labor to produce each additional unit of output*. Thus, each additional unit of output costs more to produce. In other words, *diminishing returns, or decreasing marginal product, imply increasing marginal cost* (Figure 8.4).

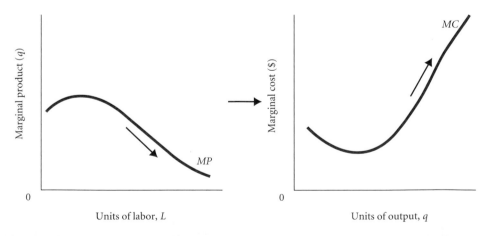

FIGURE 8.4 Declining Marginal Product Implies That Marginal Cost Will Eventually Rise with Output

In the short run, every firm is constrained by some fixed factor of production. A fixed factor implies diminishing returns (declining marginal product) and a limited capacity to produce. As that limit is approached, marginal costs rise.

Recall too the accountant who helps people file their tax returns. He has an office in his home and works alone. His fixed factor of production is that there are only 24 hours in a day and he has only so much stamina. In the long run, he may decide to hire and train an associate, but in the meantime (the short run) he has to decide how much to produce, and that decision is constrained by his current scale of operations. The biggest component of the accountant's cost is time. When he works, he gives up leisure and other things that he could do with his time. With more and more clients, he works later and later into the night. As he does so, he becomes less and less productive, and his hours become more and more valuable for sleep and relaxation. In other words, the marginal cost of doing each successive tax return rises.

To reiterate:

When an independent accountant works until late at night, he faces diminishing returns. The marginal cost of his time increases.

> In the short run, every firm is constrained by some fixed input that (1) leads to diminishing returns to variable inputs and (2) limits its capacity to produce. As a firm approaches that capacity, it becomes increasingly costly to produce successively higher levels of output. Marginal costs ultimately increase with output in the short run.

Graphing Total Variable Costs and Marginal Costs   Figure 8.5 shows the total variable cost curve and the marginal cost curve of a typical firm. Notice first that the shape of the marginal cost curve is consistent with short-run diminishing returns. At first MC declines, but eventually the fixed factor of production begins to constrain the firm, and marginal cost rises. Up to 100 units of output, producing each successive unit of output costs

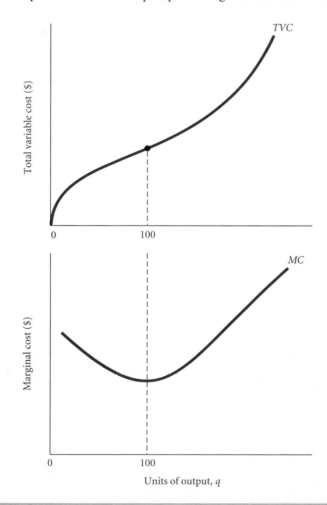

FIGURE 8.5 Total Variable Cost and Marginal Cost for a Typical Firm

Total variable costs always increase with output. Marginal cost is the cost of producing each additional unit. Thus, the marginal cost curve shows how total variable cost changes with single-unit increases in total output.

slightly less than producing the one before. Beyond 100 units, however, the cost of each successive unit is greater than the one before. (Remember the sandwich shop.)

More output costs more than less output. Total variable costs (*TVC*), therefore, *always increase* when output increases. Even though the cost of each additional unit changes, *total variable cost rises when output rises*. Thus the *total* variable cost curve always has a positive slope.

You might think of the total variable cost curve as a staircase. Each step takes you out along the quantity axis by a single unit, and the height of each step is the increase in total variable cost. As you climb the stairs, you are always going up, but the steps have different heights. At first, the stairway is steep, but as you climb, the steps get smaller (marginal cost declines). The 100th stair is the smallest. As you continue to walk out beyond 100 units, the steps begin to get larger; the staircase gets steeper (marginal cost increases).

Remember that the slope of a line is equal to the change in the units measured on the *Y*-axis divided by the change in the units measured on the *X*-axis. The slope of a total variable cost curve is thus the change in total variable cost divided by the change in output ($\Delta TVC/\Delta q$). Because marginal cost is by definition the change in total variable cost resulting from an increase in output of one unit ($\Delta q = 1$), *marginal cost actually is the slope of the total variable cost curve*:

$$\text{slope of } TVC = \frac{\Delta TVC}{\Delta q} = \frac{\Delta TVC}{1} = \Delta TVC = MC$$

Notice that up to 100 units, marginal cost decreases and the variable cost curve becomes flatter. The slope of the total variable cost curve is declining—that is, total variable cost increases, but at a *decreasing rate*. Beyond 100 units of output, marginal cost increases and the total variable cost curve gets steeper—total variable costs continue to increase, but at an *increasing rate*.

A more complete picture of the costs of a hypothetical firm appears in Table 8.4. Column 2 shows total variable costs—derived from information on input prices and technology. Column 3 derives marginal cost by simple subtraction. For example, raising output from three units to four units increases variable costs from $24 to $32, making the marginal cost of the fourth unit $8 ($32 − $24). The marginal cost of the fifth unit is $10, the difference between $32 (*TVC*) for four units and $42 (*TVC*) for five units.

average variable cost (AVC) Total variable cost divided by the number of units of output.

Average Variable Cost (AVC)   Average variable cost (AVC) is total variable cost divided by the number of units of output (*q*):

$$AVC = \frac{TVC}{q}$$

In Table 8.4, we calculate *AVC* in column 4 by dividing the numbers in column 2 (*TVC*) by the numbers in column 1 (*q*). For example, if the total variable cost of producing five units of output is $42, then the average variable cost is $42 ÷ 5, or $8.40.

TABLE 8.4 Short-Run Costs of a Hypothetical Firm

(1) q	(2) TVC	(3) MC (Δ TVC)	(4) AVC (TVC/q)	(5) TFC	(6) TC (TVC + TFC)	(7) AFC (TFC/q)	(8) ATC (TC/q OR AFC + AVC)
0	$ 0	$ −	$ −	$1,000	$1,000	$ −	$ −
1	10	10	10	1,000	1,010	1,000	1,010
2	18	8	9	1,000	1,018	500	509
3	24	6	8	1,000	1,024	333	341
4	32	8	8	1,000	1,032	250	258
5	42	10	8.4	1,000	1,042	200	208.4
−	−	−	−	−	−	−	−
−	−	−	−	−	−	−	−
−	−	−	−	−	−	−	−
500	8,000	20	16	1,000	9,000	2	18

Marginal cost is the cost of *one additional unit*. Average variable cost is the total variable cost divided by the total number of units produced.

Graphing Average Variable Costs and Marginal Costs   The relationship between average variable cost and marginal cost can be illustrated graphically. When marginal cost is *below* average variable cost, average variable cost declines toward it. When marginal cost is *above* average variable cost, average variable cost increases toward it.

Figure 8.6 duplicates the lower diagram for a typical firm in Figure 8.5 but adds average variable cost. As the graph shows, average variable cost *follows* marginal cost, but lags behind. As we move from left to right, we are looking at higher and higher levels of output per period. As we increase production, marginal cost—which at low levels of production is above $3.50 per unit—falls as coordination and cooperation begin to play a role. At 100 units of output, marginal cost has fallen to $2.50. Notice that average variable cost falls as well, but not as rapidly as marginal cost.

After 100 units of output, we begin to see diminishing returns. Marginal cost begins to increase as higher and higher levels of output are produced. However, notice that average cost is still falling until 200 units because marginal cost remains below it. At 100 units of output, marginal cost is $2.50 per unit but the *average* variable cost of production is $3.50. Thus, even though marginal cost is rising after 100 units, it is still pulling the average of $3.50 downward.

At 200 units, however, marginal cost has risen to $3.00 and average cost has fallen to $3.00; marginal and average costs are equal. At this point marginal cost continues to rise with higher output. From 200 units upward, *MC* is *above AVC*, and thus exerts an upward pull on the average variable cost curve. At levels of output below 200 units, marginal cost is below average variable cost, and average variable cost decreases as output increases. At levels of output above 200 units, *MC* is above *AVC*, and *AVC* increases as output increases. If you follow this logic you will see that

Marginal cost intersects average variable cost at the lowest, or minimum, point of *AVC*.

An example using test scores should help you to understand the relationship between *MC* and *AVC*. Consider the following sequence of test scores: 95, 85, 92, 88. The average of these four is 90. Suppose you get an 80 on your fifth test. This score will drag down your average to 88. Now suppose that you get an 85 on your sixth test. This score is higher than 80, but it's still *below* your 88 average. As a result, your average continues to fall (from 88 to 87.5), even though your marginal test score rose. If instead of an 85 you get an 89—just one point over your average—you have turned your average around; it is now rising.

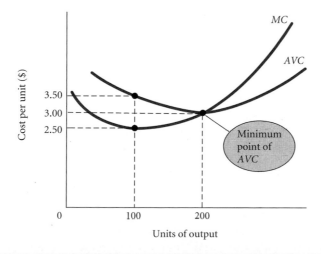

FIGURE 8.6 More Short-Run Costs

When marginal cost is *below* average cost, average cost is declining. When marginal cost is *above* average cost, average cost is increasing. Rising marginal cost intersects average variable cost at the minimum point of *AVC*.

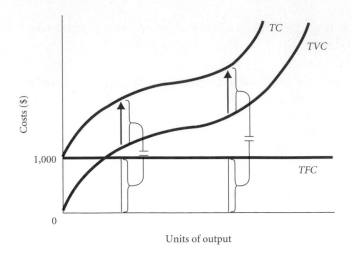

FIGURE 8.7 Total Cost = Total Fixed Cost + Total Variable Cost

Adding *TFC* to *TVC* means adding the same amount of total fixed cost to every level of total variable cost. Thus, the total cost curve has the same shape as the total variable cost curve; it is simply higher by an amount equal to *TFC*.

TOTAL COSTS

We are now ready to complete the cost picture by adding total fixed costs to total variable costs. Recall that

$$TC = TFC + TVC$$

Total cost is graphed in Figure 8.7, where the same vertical distance (equal to *TFC*, which is constant) is simply added to *TVC* at every level of output. In Table 8.4, column 6 adds the total fixed cost of $1,000 to total variable cost to arrive at total cost.

average total cost (ATC)
Total cost divided by the number of units of output.

Average Total Cost (ATC) Average total cost **(ATC)** is total cost divided by the number of units of output (q):

$$ATC = \frac{TC}{q}$$

Column 8 in Table 8.4 shows the result of dividing the costs in column 6 by the quantities in column 1. For example, at five units of output, *total* cost is $1,042; *average* total cost is $1,042 ÷ 5, or $208.40. The average total cost of producing 500 units of output is only $18—that is, $9,000 ÷ 500.

Another, more revealing, way of deriving average total cost is to add average fixed cost and average variable cost together:

$$ATC = AFC + AVC$$

For example, column 8 in Table 8.4 is the sum of column 4 (*AVC*) and column 7 (*AFC*).

Figure 8.8 derives average total cost graphically for a typical firm. The bottom part of the figure graphs average fixed cost. At 100 units of output, average fixed cost is *TFC/q* = $1,000 ÷ 100 = $10. At 400 units of output, *AFC* = $1,000 ÷ 400 = $2.50. The top part of Figure 8.8 shows the declining *AFC* added to *AVC* at each level of output. Because *AFC* gets smaller and smaller, *ATC* gets closer and closer to *AVC* as output increases, but the two lines never meet.

The Relationship Between Average Total Cost and Marginal Cost

The relationship between average *total* cost and marginal cost is exactly the same as the relationship between average *variable* cost and marginal cost. The average total cost curve

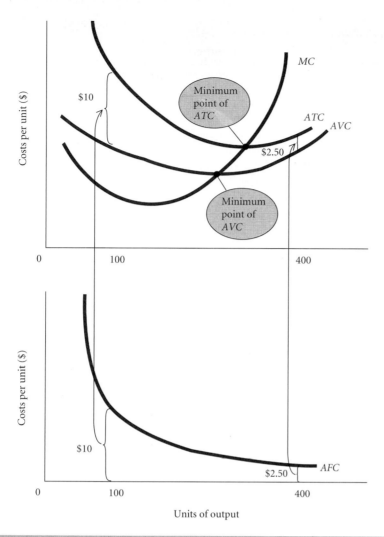

FIGURE 8.8 Average Total Cost = Average Variable Cost + Average Fixed Cost

To get average total cost, we add average fixed and average variable costs at all levels of output. Because average fixed cost falls with output, an ever-declining amount is added to *AVC*. Thus, *AVC* and *ATC* get closer together as output increases, but the two lines never meet.

follows the marginal cost curve but lags behind because it is an average over all units of output. The average total cost curve lags behind the marginal cost curve even more than the average variable cost curve does, because the cost of each added unit of production is now averaged not only with the variable cost of all previous units produced but also with fixed costs.

Fixed costs equal $1,000 and are incurred even when the output level is zero. Thus, the first unit of output in the example in Table 8.4 costs $10 in variable cost to produce. The second unit costs only $8 in variable cost to produce. The total cost of two units is $1,018; average total cost of the two is ($1,010 + $8)/2, or $509. The marginal cost of the third unit is only $6. The total cost of three units is thus $1,024, or $1,018 + $6, and the average total cost of three units is ($1,010 + $8 + $6)/3, or $341.

As you saw with the test scores example, marginal cost is what drives changes in average total cost:

> If marginal cost is *below* average total cost, average total cost will *decline* toward marginal cost. If marginal cost is *above* average total cost, average total cost will *increase*. As a result, marginal cost intersects average *total* cost at *ATC*'s minimum point, for the same reason that it intersects the average *variable* cost curve at its minimum point.

TABLE 8.5 A Summary of Cost Concepts

TERM	DEFINITION	EQUATION
Accounting costs	Out-of-pocket costs or costs as an accountant would define them. Sometimes referred to as *explicit costs*.	—
Economic costs	Costs that include the full opportunity costs of all inputs. These include what are often called *implicit costs*.	—
Total fixed costs	Costs that do not depend on the quantity of output produced. These must be paid even if output is zero.	TFC
Total variable costs	Costs that vary with the level of output.	TVC
Total cost	The total economic cost of all the inputs used by a firm in production.	$TC = TFC + TVC$
Average fixed costs	Fixed costs per unit of output.	$AFC = TFC/q$
Average variable costs	Variable costs per unit of output.	$AVC = TVC/q$
Average total costs	Total costs per unit of output.	$ATC = TC/q \quad ATC = AFC + AVC$
Marginal costs	The increase in total cost that results from producing one additional unit of output.	$MC = \Delta TC/\Delta q$

SHORT-RUN COSTS: A REVIEW

Let us now pause to review what we have learned about the behavior of firms. We know that firms make three basic choices: how much product or output to produce or supply, how to produce that output, and how much of each input to demand to produce what they intend to supply. We assume that these choices are made to maximize profits. Profits are equal to the difference between a firm's revenue from the sale of its product and the costs of producing that product: profit = total revenue − total cost.

So far, we have looked only at costs, but costs are just one part of the profit equation. To complete the picture, we must turn to the output market and see how these costs compare with the price that a product commands in the market. Before we do so, however, it is important to consolidate what we have said about costs.

Before a firm does anything else, it needs to know the different methods that it can use to produce its product. The technologies available determine the combinations of inputs that are needed to produce each level of output. Firms choose the technique that produces the desired level of output at least cost. The cost curves that result from the analysis of all this information show the cost of producing each level of output using the best available technology.

Remember that so far we have talked only about short-run costs. The curves we have drawn are therefore *short-run cost curves*. The shape of these curves is determined in large measure by the assumptions that we make about the short run, especially the assumption that some fixed factor of production leads to diminishing returns. Given this assumption, marginal costs eventually rise, and average cost curves are likely to be U-shaped. Table 8.5 summarizes the cost concepts that we have discussed.

After gaining a complete knowledge of how to produce a product and how much it will cost to produce it at each level of output, the firm turns to the market to find out what it can sell its product for. It is to the output market that we now turn our attention.

OUTPUT DECISIONS: REVENUES, COSTS, AND PROFIT MAXIMIZATION

To calculate potential profits, firms must combine their cost analyses with information on potential revenues from sales. After all, if a firm cannot sell its product for more than the cost of production, it will not be in business long. In contrast, if the market gives the firm a price that is significantly greater than the cost it incurs to produce a unit of its product, the firm may have an incentive to expand output. Large profits might also attract new competitors to the market.

Let us now examine in detail how a firm goes about determining how much output to produce. For the sake of simplicity, we will continue to examine the decisions of a perfectly

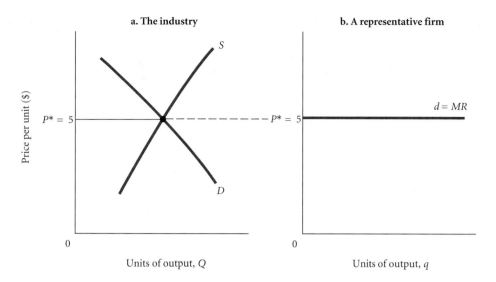

FIGURE 8.9 Demand Facing a Typical Firm in a Perfectly Competitive Market

Because perfectly competitive firms are very small relative to the market, they have no control over price. A firm can sell all it wants at the market price but would sell nothing if it charged a higher price. Thus, the demand curve facing a perfectly competitive firm is simply a horizontal line at the market equilibrium price, P^*.

competitive firm. A perfectly competitive industry has many firms that are small relative to the size of the market, and the output of one firm is identical to the output of its competitors. In such an environment, product price is determined by the interaction of many suppliers and many demanders.

Figure 8.9 shows a typical firm in a perfectly competitive industry. Price is determined in the market at $P^* = \$5$. The individual firm can charge any price that it wants for its product, but if it charges above \$5, the quantity demanded falls to zero, and the firm will not sell anything. The firm could also sell its product for less than \$5, but there is no reason to do so.

> In the short run, a competitive firm faces a demand curve that is simply a horizontal line at the market equilibrium price. In other words, competitive firms face perfectly elastic demand in the short run.

In Figure 8.9, the market equilibrium price is $P^* = \$5$ and the firm's perfectly elastic demand curve is labeled d.

TOTAL REVENUE (*TR*) AND MARGINAL REVENUE (*MR*)

Profit is the difference between total revenue and total cost. **Total revenue** is the total amount that a firm takes in from the sale of its product. A perfectly competitive firm sells each unit of product for the same price, regardless of the output level it has chosen. Therefore, total revenue is simply the price per unit times the quantity of output that the firm decides to produce:

total revenue (*TR*) The total amount that a firm takes in from the sale of its product: the price per unit times the quantity of output the firm decides to produce ($P \times q$).

$$\text{total revenue} = \text{price} \times \text{quantity}$$
$$TR = P \times q$$

Marginal revenue (*MR*) is the added revenue that a firm takes in when it increases output by one additional unit. If a firm producing 10,521 units of output per month increases that output to 10,522 units per month, it will take in an additional amount of revenue each month. The revenue associated with the 10,522nd unit is simply the amount that the firm sells that one unit for. Thus, for a competitive firm, marginal revenue is simply equal to the

marginal revenue (*MR*) The additional revenue that a firm takes in when it increases output by one additional unit. In perfect competition, $P = MR$.

current market price of each additional unit sold. In Figure 8.9, for example, the market price is $5. Thus, if the representative firm raises its output from 10,521 units to 10,522 units, its revenue will increase by $5.

A firm's *marginal revenue curve* shows how much revenue the firm will gain by raising output by one unit at every level of output. The *marginal revenue curve and the demand curve facing a competitive firm are identical*. The horizontal line in Figure 8.9(b) can be thought of as both the demand curve facing the firm and its marginal revenue curve:

$$P^* = d = MR$$

COMPARING COSTS AND REVENUES TO MAXIMIZE PROFIT

The discussion in the next few paragraphs conveys one of the most important concepts in all of microeconomics. As we pursue our analysis, remember that we are working under two assumptions: (1) that the industry we are examining is perfectly competitive and (2) that firms choose the level of output that yields the maximum total profit.

The Profit-Maximizing Level of Output   Look carefully at the diagrams in Figure 8.10. Once again we have the whole market, or industry, on the left and a single, typical small firm on the right. And again the current market price is P^*.

First, the firm observes market price [see Figure 8.10(a)] and knows that it can sell all that it wants to for $P^* = \$5$ per unit. Next, it must decide how much to produce. It might seem reasonable to pick the output level where marginal cost is at its minimum point—in this case, at an output of 100 units. Here the difference between marginal revenue, $5, and marginal cost, $2.50, is the greatest.

Remember that a firm wants to maximize the difference between *total* revenue and *total* cost, not the difference between *marginal* revenue and *marginal* cost. The fact that marginal revenue is greater than marginal cost actually indicates that profit is *not* being maximized. Think about the 101st unit. Adding that single unit to production each period adds $5 to revenues but adds only about $2.50 to cost. Profits each period would be higher by about $2.50. Thus, the optimal (profit-maximizing) level of output is clearly higher than 100 units.

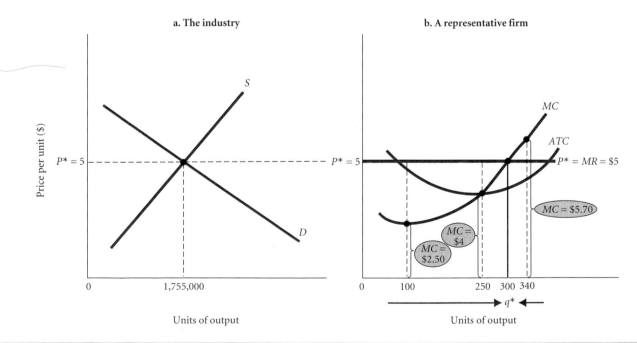

a. The industry   b. A representative firm

FIGURE 8.10 The Profit-Maximizing Level of Output for a Perfectly Competitive Firm

If price is above marginal cost, as it is at 100 and 250 units of output, profits can be increased by raising output; each additional unit increases revenues by more than it costs to produce the additional output. Beyond $q^* = 300$, however, added output will reduce profits. At 340 units of output, an additional unit of output costs more to produce than it will bring in revenue when sold on the market. Profit-maximizing output is thus q^*, the point at which $P^* = MC$.

Now look at an output level of 250 units. Here, once again, raising output increases profit. The revenue gained from producing the 251st unit (marginal revenue) is still $5, and the cost of the 251st unit (marginal cost) is only about $4.

> As long as marginal revenue is greater than marginal cost, even though the difference between the two is getting smaller, added output means added profit. Whenever marginal revenue exceeds marginal cost, the revenue gained by increasing output by one unit per period exceeds the cost incurred by doing so.

This logic leads us to 300 units of output. At 300 units, marginal cost has risen to $5. At 300 units of output, $P^* = MR = MC = \$5$.

Notice that if the firm were to produce *more* than 300 units, marginal cost rises above marginal revenue. At 340 units of output, for example, the cost of the 341st unit is about $5.70 while that added unit of output still brings in only $5 in revenue, thus reducing profit. It simply does not pay to increase output above the point where marginal cost rises above marginal revenue because such increases will *reduce* profit.

> The profit-maximizing perfectly competitive firm will produce up to the point where the price of its output is just equal to short-run marginal cost—the level of output at which $P^* = MC$.

Thus, in Figure 8.10, the profit-maximizing level of output, q^*, is 300 units.

Keep in mind, though, that all types of firms (not just those in perfectly competitive industries) are profit maximizers. Thus,

> The profit-maximizing output level for *all* firms is the output level where $MR = MC$.

In perfect competition, however, $MR = P$, as shown earlier. Hence, for perfectly competitive firms we can rewrite our profit-maximizing condition as $P = MC$.

Important note: The key idea here is that firms will produce as long as marginal revenue exceeds marginal cost. If marginal cost rises smoothly, as it does in Figure 8.10, then the profit-maximizing condition is that MR (or P) *exactly equals MC.* If marginal cost moves up in increments—as it does in the following numerical example—marginal revenue or price may never exactly equal marginal cost. The key idea still holds.

A Numerical Example Table 8.6 presents some data for another hypothetical firm. Let us assume that the market has set a $15 unit price for the firm's product. Total revenue in column 6 is the simple product of $P \times q$ (the numbers in column 1 times $15). The table derives total, marginal, and average costs exactly as Table 8.4 did. Here, however, we have included revenues, and we can calculate the profit, which is shown in column 8.

Column 8 shows that a profit-maximizing firm would choose to produce four units of output. At this level, profits are $20. At all other output levels, they are lower. Now let us see if "marginal" reasoning leads us to the same conclusion.

TABLE 8.6 Profit Analysis for a Simple Firm

(1)	(2)	(3)	(4)	(5)	(6) TR	(7) TC	(8) PROFIT
q	TFC	TVC	MC	P = MR	($P \times q$)	(TFC + TVC)	(TR − TC)
0	$10	$ 0	$−	$15	$ 0	$10	$−10
1	10	10	10	15	15	20	−5
2	10	15	5	15	30	25	5
3	10	20	5	15	45	30	15
4	10	30	10	15	60	40	20
5	10	50	20	15	75	60	15
6	10	80	30	15	90	90	0

Case Study in Marginal Analysis:
An Ice Cream Parlor

The following is a description of the decisions made in 2000 by the owner of a small ice cream parlor in Ohio. After being in business for 1 year, this entrepreneur had to ask herself, should I stay in business?

The cost figures on which she based her decisions are presented next. These numbers are real, but they do not include one important item: the managerial labor provided by the owner. In her calculations, the entrepreneur did not include a wage for herself, but we will assume an opportunity cost of $30,000 per year ($2,500 per month).

FIXED COSTS

The fixed components of the store's monthly costs include the following:

Rent (1,150 square feet)	$2,012.50
Electricity	325.00
Interest on loan	737.50
Maintenance	295.00
Telephone	65.00
Total	$3,435.00

Not all the items on this list are strictly fixed, however. Electricity costs, for example, would be slightly higher if the store produced more ice cream and stayed open longer, but the added cost would be minimal.

VARIABLE COSTS

The ice cream store's variable costs include two components: (1) behind-the-counter labor costs, and (2) cost of making ice cream. The store employs high school students at a wage of $5.15 per hour. Including the employer's share of the *Social Security tax*, the gross cost of each hour of labor is $5.54 per hour. There are two employees working in the store at all times. The full cost of producing ice cream is $3.27 per gallon. Each gallon contains approximately 12 servings. Customers can add toppings free of charge, and the average cost of the toppings taken by a customer is about $.05:

Gross labor costs	$5.54/hour
Costs of producing one gallon of ice cream (12 servings per gallon)	$3.27
Average cost of added toppings per serving	$.05

REVENUES

The store sells ice cream cones, sundaes, and floats. The average price of a purchase at the store is $1.45. The store is open 8 hours per day,

Marginal analysis is as important to the owner of a small ice cream store as it is to the managers of million-dollar operations.

26 days a month, and serves an average of 240 customers per day:

Average purchase	$1.45
Days open per month	26
Average number of customers per day . .	240

From the preceding information, it is possible to calculate the store's average monthly profit. Total revenue is equal to 240 customers × $1.45 per customer × 26 open days in an average month: $TR = $9,048 per month.

PROFITS

The store sells 240 servings per day. Because there are 12 servings of ice cream per gallon, the store uses exactly 20 gallons per day (240 servings divided by 12). Total costs are $3.27 × 20, or $65.40, per day for ice cream and $12 per day for toppings (240 × $.05). The cost of variable labor is $5.54 × 8 hours × 2 workers, or $88.64 per day. Total variable costs are therefore $166.04 ($65.40 + $12.00 + $88.64) per day. The store is open 26 days a month, so the total variable cost per month is $4,317.04.

Adding fixed costs of $3,435 to variable costs of $4,317.04, we get a total cost of operation of $7,752.04 per month. Thus, the firm is averaging a profit of $1,295.96 per month ($9,048 − $7,752.04). *This is not an "economic profit" because we have not accounted for the opportunity cost of the owner's time and efforts.* In fact, when we factor in an implicit wage of $2,500 per month for the owner, we see that the store is suffering *losses* of $1,204.04 per month ($1,295.96 − $2,500).

Total revenue (*TR*)	$9,048.00
Total fixed cost (*TFC*)	3,435.00
+ Total variable cost (*TVC*)	4,317.04
Total costs (*TC*)	7,752.04
Total profit (*TR − TC*)	1,295.96
Adjustment for implicit wage	2,500.00
Economic profit	−1,204.04

Should the entrepreneur stay in business? If she wants to make $2,500 per month and she thinks that nothing about her business will change, she must shut down in the long run. However, two things keep her going: (1) a decision to stay open longer and (2) hope for more customers in the future.

OPENING LONGER HOURS: MARGINAL COSTS AND MARGINAL REVENUES

The store's normal hours of operation are noon until 8 P.M. On an experimental basis, the owner extends its hours until 11 P.M. for 1 month. The following table shows the average number of additional customers for each of the added hours:

HOURS (P.M.)	Customers
8-9	41
9-10	20
10-11	8

Assuming that the late customers spend an average of $1.45, we can calculate the marginal revenue and the marginal cost of staying open longer. The marginal cost of one serving of ice cream is $3.27 divided by 12 = $0.27 + .05 (for topping) = $0.32. (See table that follows.)

Marginal analysis tells us that the store should stay open for 2 additional hours. Each day that the store stays open from 8 to 9 P.M. it will make an added profit of $59.45 − $24.20, or $35.25. Staying open from 9 to 10 P.M. adds $29.00 − $17.48, or $11.52, to profit. Staying open the third hour, however, *decreases* profits because the marginal revenue generated by staying open from 10 to 11 P.M. is less than the marginal cost. The entrepreneur decides to stay open for 2 additional hours per day. This adds $46.77 ($35.25 + 11.52) to profits each day, a total of $1,216.02 per month.

By adding the 2 hours, the store turns an economic loss of $1,204.04 per month into a small ($11.98) profit after accounting for the owner's implicit wage of $2,500 per month.

The owner decided to stay in business. She now serves over 350 customers per day, and the price of a dish of ice cream has risen to $2.50 while costs have not changed very much. In 2001, she cleared a profit of nearly $10,000 per month.

HOUR (P.M.)	MARGINAL REVENUE (MR)	MARGINAL COST (MC)		ADDED PROFIT PER HOUR (MR − MC)
8–9	$1.45 × 41 = $59.45	Ice cream: $0.32 × 41 = $13.12		$35.25
		Labor: 2 × $5.54 = 11.08		
		Total $24.20		
9–10	1.45 × 20 = $29.00	Ice cream: $0.32 × 20 = $ 6.40		$11.52
		Labor: 2 × $5.54 = 11.08		
		Total $17.48		
10–11	1.45 × 8 = $11.60	Ice cream: $0.32 × 8 = $ 2.56		−$2.04
		Labor: 2 × $5.54 = 11.08		
		Total $13.64		

First, should the firm produce at all? If it produces nothing, it suffers losses equal to $10. If it increases output to one unit, marginal revenue is $15 (remember that it sells each unit for $15), and marginal cost is $10. Thus, it gains $5, reducing its loss from $10 each period to $5.

Should the firm increase output to two units? The marginal revenue from the second unit is again $15, but the marginal cost is only $5. Thus, by producing the second unit, the firm gains $10 ($15 − $5) and turns a $5 loss into a $5 profit. The third unit adds $10 to profits. Again, marginal revenue is $15 and marginal cost is $5, an increase in profit of $10, for a total profit of $15.

The fourth unit offers still more profit. Price is still above marginal cost, which means that producing that fourth unit will increase profits. Price, or marginal revenue, is $15, and marginal cost is just $10. Thus, the fourth unit adds $5 to profit. At unit number five, however, diminishing returns push marginal cost up above price. The marginal revenue from producing the fifth unit is $15, while marginal cost is now $20. As a result, profit per period drops by $5, to $15 per period. Clearly, the firm will not produce the fifth unit.

The profit-maximizing level of output is thus four units. The firm produces as long as price (marginal revenue) is greater than marginal cost. For an in-depth example of profit maximization, see the Further Exploration box titled "Case Study in Marginal Analysis: An Ice Cream Parlor."

THE SHORT-RUN SUPPLY CURVE

Consider how the typical firm shown in Figure 8.10 would behave in response to an increase in price. In Figure 8.11(a), assume that something causes demand to increase (shift to the right), driving price from $5 to $6 and finally to $7. When price is $5, a profit-maximizing firm will choose output level 300 in Figure 8.11(b). To produce any less, or to raise output above that level, would lead to a lower level of profit. At $6, the same firm would increase output to 350, but it would stop there. Similarly, at $7, the firm would raise output to 400 units of output.

The *MC* curve in Figure 8.11(b) relates price and quantity supplied. At any market price, the marginal cost curve shows the output level that maximizes profit. A curve that shows how much output a profit-maximizing firm will produce at every price also fits the definition of a supply curve. (Review Chapter 3 if this point is not clear to you.) It, therefore, follows that

The marginal cost curve of a competitive firm is the firm's short-run supply curve.

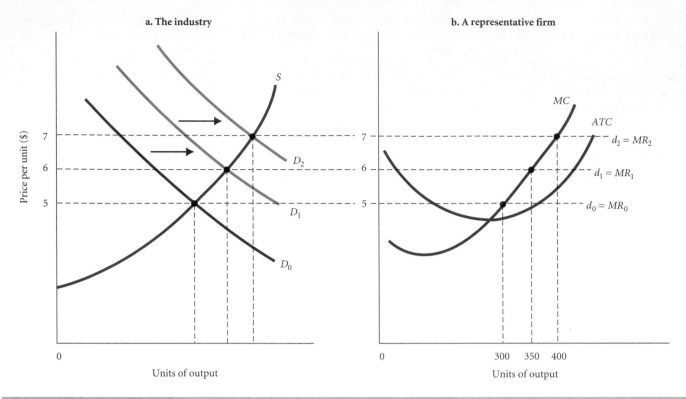

a. The industry

b. A representative firm

FIGURE 8.11 Marginal Cost Is the Supply Curve of a Perfectly Competitive Firm

At any market price,[a] the marginal cost curve shows the output level that maximizes profit. Thus, the marginal cost curve of a perfectly competitive profit-maximizing firm is the firm's short-run supply curve.

[a]This is true except when price is so low that it pays a firm to shut down—a point that will be discussed in Chapter 9.

As you will see, one very important exception exists to this general rule: There is some price level below which the firm will shut down its operations and simply bear losses equal to fixed costs even if price is above marginal cost. This important point is discussed in Chapter 9.

LOOKING AHEAD

At the beginning of this chapter we set out to combine information on technology, factor prices, and output prices to understand the supply curve of a competitive firm. We have now accomplished that goal.

Because marginal cost is such an important concept in microeconomics, you should carefully review any sections of this chapter that were unclear to you. Above all, keep in mind that the *marginal cost curve* carries information about both *input prices* and *technology*. The firm looks to output markets for information on potential revenues, and the current market price defines the firm's marginal revenue curve. The point where price (which is equal to marginal revenue in perfect competition) is just equal to marginal cost is the perfectly competitive firm's profit-maximizing level of output. Thus, with one important exception, the marginal cost curve *is* the perfectly competitive firm's supply curve in the short run.

In the next chapter, we turn to the long run. What happens when firms are free to choose their scale of operations without being limited by a fixed factor of production? Without diminishing returns that set in as a result of a fixed scale of production, what determines the shape of cost curves? What happens when new firms can enter industries in which profits are being earned? How do industries adjust when losses are being incurred? How does the structure of an industry evolve over time?

SUMMARY

1. Profit-maximizing firms make decisions to maximize profit (total revenue minus total cost).

2. To calculate production costs, firms must know two things: (1) the quantity and combination of inputs they need to produce their product, and (2) the cost of those inputs.

COSTS IN THE SHORT RUN

3. *Fixed costs* are costs that do not change with a firm's output. In the short run, firms cannot avoid them or change them, even if production is zero.

4. *Variable costs* are those costs that depend on the level of output chosen. Fixed costs plus variable costs equal *total costs* ($TC = TFC + TVC$).

5. *Average fixed cost* (*AFC*) is total fixed cost divided by the quantity of output. As output rises, average fixed cost declines steadily because the same total is being spread over a larger and larger quantity of output. This phenomenon is called *spreading overhead*.

6. Numerous combinations of inputs can be used to produce a given level of output. *Total variable cost* (*TVC*) is the sum of all costs that vary with output in the short run.

7. *Marginal cost* (*MC*) is the increase in total cost that results from the production of one more unit of output. If a firm is producing 1,000 units, the additional cost of increasing output to 1,001 units is marginal cost. Marginal cost measures the cost of the additional inputs required to produce each successive unit of output. Because fixed costs do not change when output changes, marginal costs reflect changes in variable costs.

8. In the short run, a firm is limited by a fixed factor of production, or a fixed scale of plant. As a firm increases output, it will eventually find itself trapped by that scale. Because of the fixed scale, marginal cost eventually rises with output.

9. Marginal cost is the slope of the total variable cost curve. The total variable cost curve always has a positive slope, because total costs always rise with output. However, increasing marginal cost means that total costs ultimately rise at an increasing rate.

10. *Average variable cost* (*AVC*) is equal to total variable cost divided by the quantity of output.

11. When marginal cost is above average variable cost, average variable cost is *increasing*. When marginal cost is below average variable cost, average variable cost is *declining*. Marginal cost intersects average variable cost at *AVC*'s minimum point.

12. *Average total cost* (*ATC*) is equal to total cost divided by the quantity of output. It is also equal to the sum of average fixed cost and average variable cost.

13. If marginal cost is below average total cost, average total cost will decline toward marginal cost. If marginal cost is above average total cost, average total cost will increase. Marginal cost intersects average total cost at *ATC*'s minimum point.

OUTPUT DECISIONS: REVENUES, COSTS, AND PROFIT MAXIMIZATION

14. A perfectly competitive firm faces a demand curve that is a horizontal line (in other words, perfectly elastic demand).

15. *Total revenue* (*TR*) is simply price times the quantity of output that a firm decides to produce and sell. *Marginal revenue* (*MR*) is the additional revenue that a firm takes in when it increases output by one unit.

16. For a perfectly competitive firm, marginal revenue is equal to the current market price of its product.

17. A profit-maximizing firm in a perfectly competitive industry will produce up to the point at which the price of its output is just equal to short-run marginal cost: $P = MC$. The more general profit-maximizing formula is $MR = MC$ ($P = MR$ in perfect competition). The marginal cost curve of a perfectly competitive firm is the firm's short-run supply curve, with one exception (discussed in Chapter 9).

REVIEW TERMS AND CONCEPTS

average fixed cost (*AFC*), 167

average total cost (*ATC*), 174

average variable cost (*AVC*), 172

fixed cost, 166

marginal cost (*MC*), 169

marginal revenue (*MR*), 177

spreading overhead, 168

sunk costs, 167

total cost (*TC*), 166

total fixed costs (*TFC*), or overhead, 167

total revenue (*TR*), 177

total variable cost (*TVC*), 168

total variable cost curve, 168

variable cost, 166

1. $TC = TFC + TVC$

2. $AFC = TFC/q$

3. Slope of $TVC = MC$

4. $AVC = TVC/q$

5. $ATC = TC/q = AFC + AVC$

6. $TR = P \times q$

7. Profit-maximizing level of output for all firms: $MR = MC$

8. Profit-maximizing level of output for perfectly competitive firms: $P = MC$

PROBLEM SET

1. Consider the following costs of owning and operating a car. A $15,000 Ford Taurus financed over 5 years at 10 percent interest means a monthly payment of $318.71. Insurance costs $100 a month regardless of how much you drive. The car gets 20 miles per gallon and uses unleaded regular that costs $1.50 per gallon. Finally suppose that wear and tear on the car costs about 15 cents a mile. Which costs are fixed and which are variable? What is the marginal cost of a mile driven? In deciding whether to drive from New York to Pittsburgh (about 1,000 miles round-trip) to visit a friend, which costs would you consider? Why?

2. July 18, 2005 LONDON (Reuters)—The sixth volume of the Harry Potter saga sold more than 8.9 million copies in the first 24 hours it went on sale in the United States and Britain to become the fastest-selling book in history, publishers said. In book publishing fixed costs are very high and marginal costs are very low and fairly constant. Suppose that the fixed cost of producing the new Harry Potter volume is $30 million. What is the *average fixed cost* if the publisher produces 5 million copies? 10 million copies? 20 million copies?

    Now suppose that the marginal cost of a Harry Potter book is $1.50 per book and is the same for each book up to 40 million copies. Assume this includes all variable costs. Explain why in this case marginal cost is a horizontal line, as is average variable cost. What is the *average total cost* of the book if the publisher produces 5 million copies? 10 million copies? 20 million copies?

    Sketch the average fixed cost curve and the average total cost curve facing the publisher.

3. Do you agree or disagree with this statement? Firms minimize costs; thus, a firm earning short-run economic profits will choose to produce at the minimum point on its average total cost function.

4. The following table gives capital and labor requirements for 10 different levels of production:

q	K	L
0	0	0
1	2	5
2	4	9
3	6	12
4	8	15
5	10	19
6	12	24
7	14	30
8	16	37
9	18	45
10	20	54

    a. Assuming that the price of labor (P_L) is $5 per unit and the price of capital (P_K) is $10 per unit, compute and graph the total variable cost curve, the marginal cost curve, and the average variable cost curve for the firm.
    b. Do the curves have the shapes that you might expect? Explain.
    c. Using the numbers here, explain the relationship between marginal cost and average variable cost.
    d. Using the numbers here, explain the meaning of "marginal cost" in terms of additional inputs needed to produce a marginal unit of output.

    e. If the output price was $57, how many units of output would the firm produce? Explain.

5. Do you agree or disagree with each of the following statements? Explain your reasons.
    a. For a competitive firm facing a market price above average total cost, the existence of economic profits means the firm should increase output in the short run even if price is below marginal cost.
    b. If marginal cost is rising with increasing output, average cost must also be rising.
    c. Fixed cost is constant at every level of output except zero. When a firm produces no output, fixed costs are zero in the short run.

6. A firm's cost curves are given by the following table:

Q	TC	TFC	TVC	AVC	ATC	MC
0	$100	$100	—	—	—	—
1	130	100	—	—	—	—
2	150	100	—	—	—	—
3	160	100	—	—	—	—
4	172	100	—	—	—	—
5	185	100	—	—	—	—
6	210	100	—	—	—	—
7	240	100	—	—	—	—
8	280	100	—	—	—	—
9	330	100	—	—	—	—
10	390	100	—	—	—	—

    a. Complete the table.
    b. Graph *AVC, ATC,* and *MC* on the same graph. What is the relationship between the *MC* curve and the *ATC,* and between *MC* and *AVC*?
    c. Suppose that market price is $30. How much will the firm produce in the short run? How much are total profits?
    d. Suppose that market price is $50. How much will the firm produce in the short run? What are total profits?
    e. Suppose that market price is $10. How much would the firm produce in the short run? What are total profits?

7. A 2006 Georgia Tech graduate inherited her mother's printing company. The capital stock of the firm consists of three machines of various vintages, all in excellent condition. All machines can be running at the same time:

	COST OF PRINTING AND BINDING PER BOOK	MAXIMUM TOTAL CAPACITY (BOOKS) PER MONTH
Machine 1	$1.00	100
Machine 2	2.00	200
Machine 3	3.00	500

    a. Assume that "cost of printing and binding per book" includes *all* labor and materials, including the owner's own wages. Assume further that Mom signed a long-term contract (50 years) with a service company to keep the machines in good repair for a fixed fee of $100 per month.
    (1) Derive the firm's marginal cost curve.
    (2) Derive the firm's total cost curve.
    b. At a price of $2.50, how many books would the company produce? What would total revenues, total costs, and total profits be?

8. The following is a total cost curve. Sketch the corresponding marginal cost curve. If the price of output is $3 and there are no fixed costs, what is the profit-maximizing level of output?

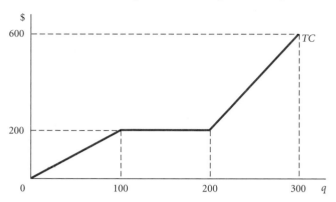

9. The following curve is a production function for a firm that uses just one variable factor of production, labor. It shows total output, or product, for every level of inputs:
   a. Derive and graph the marginal product curve.
   b. Suppose that the wage rate is $4. Derive and graph the firm's marginal cost curve.
   c. If output sells for $6, what is the profit-maximizing level of output? How much labor will the firm hire?

10. Elena and Emmanuel live on the Black Sea in Bulgaria and own a small fishing boat. A crew of four is required to take the boat out fishing. The current wage paid to the four crew members is a total of 5,000 levs per day (a lev is the Bulgarian unit of currency). Assume that the cost of operating and maintaining the boat is 1,000 levs per day when fishing, and zero otherwise. The following schedule gives the appropriate catch for each period during the year:

PERIOD	CATCH PER DAY (KILOGRAMS)
Prime fishing: 180 days	100
Month 7: 30 days	80
Month 8: 30 days	60
Rest of the year	40

The price of fish in Bulgaria is no longer regulated by the government and is now determined in competitive markets. Suppose that the price has been stable all year at 80 levs per kilogram.
   a. What is the marginal product of a day's worth of fishing during prime fishing season? During month 7? During month 8?
   b. What is the marginal cost of a kilogram of fish during prime fishing season? During month 7, during month 8, and during the rest of the year?
   c. If you were Elena and Emmanuel, how many months per year would you hire the crew and go out fishing? Explain your answer using marginal logic.

11. For each of the following businesses, what is the likely fixed factor of production that defines the short run?
   a. Potato farm of 160 acres
   b. Chinese restaurant
   c. Dentist in private practice
   d. Car dealership
   e. Bank

Long-Run Costs and Output Decisions

9

The last two chapters discussed the behavior of profit-maximizing competitive firms in the short run. Recall that all firms must make three fundamental decisions: (1) how much output to produce or supply, (2) how to produce that output, and (3) how much of each input to demand.

Firms use information on input prices, output prices, and technology to make the decisions that will lead to the most profit. Because profits equal revenues minus costs, firms must know how much their products will sell for and how much production will cost, using the most efficient technology.

In Chapter 8, we saw how cost curves can be derived from production functions and input prices. Once a firm has a clear picture of its short-run costs, the price at which it sells its output determines the quantity of output that will maximize profit. Specifically, a profit-maximizing perfectly competitive firm will supply output up to the point that price (marginal revenue) equals marginal cost. The marginal cost curve of such a firm is thus the same as its supply curve.

In this chapter, we turn from the short run to the long run. The condition in which firms find themselves in the short run (Are they making profits? Are they incurring losses?) determines what is likely to happen in the long run. Remember that output (supply) decisions in the long run are less constrained than in the short run, for two reasons. First, in the long run, the firm has no fixed factor of production that confines its production to a given scale. Second, firms are free to enter industries to seek profits and to leave industries to avoid losses.

The long run has important implications for the shape of cost curves. As we saw in the short run, a fixed factor of production eventually causes marginal cost to increase along with output. This is not the case in the long run, however. With no fixed scale, the shapes of cost curves become more complex and less easy to generalize about. The shapes of long-run cost curves have important implications for the way an industry's structure is likely to evolve over time.

We begin our discussion of the long run by looking at firms in three short-run circumstances: (1) firms earning economic profits, (2) firms suffering economic losses but continuing to operate to reduce or minimize those losses, and (3) firms that decide to shut down and bear losses just equal to fixed costs. We then examine how these firms will alter their decisions in response to these short-run conditions.

Although we continue to focus on perfectly competitive firms, it should be stressed that *all* firms are subject to the spectrum of short-run profit or loss situations, regardless of *market structure*. Assuming perfect competition allows us to simplify our analysis and provides us with a strong background for understanding the discussions of imperfectly competitive behavior in later chapters.

SHORT-RUN CONDITIONS AND LONG-RUN DIRECTIONS

Before beginning our examination of firm behavior, let us review the concept of profit. Recall that a normal rate of return is included in the definition of total cost (see Chapter 7). A *normal rate of return* is a rate that is just sufficient to keep current investors interested in the industry. Because we define *profit* as total revenue minus total cost and because total cost includes a normal rate of return, our concept of profit takes into account the opportunity cost of capital. If a firm is earning an above-normal rate of return, it has a positive profit level, but otherwise not. When there are positive profits in an industry, new investors are likely to be attracted to the industry.

When we say that a firm is suffering a *loss*, we mean that it is earning a rate of return that is below normal. Such a firm may be suffering a loss as an accountant would measure it, or it may simply be earning at a very low—that is, below normal—rate. Investors are not going to be attracted to an industry in which there are losses. A firm that is **breaking even**, or earning a zero level of profit, is one that is earning exactly a normal rate of return. New investors are not attracted, but current ones are not running away, either.

With these distinctions in mind, then, we can say that for any firm one of three conditions holds at any given moment: (1) The firm is making positive profits, (2) the firm is suffering losses, or (3) the firm is just breaking even. Profitable firms will want to maximize their profits in the short run, while firms suffering losses will want to minimize those losses in the short run.

breaking even The situation in which a firm is earning exactly a normal rate of return.

MAXIMIZING PROFITS

The best way to understand the behavior of a firm that is currently earning profits is by way of example.

Example: The Blue Velvet Car Wash   When a firm earns revenues in excess of costs (including a normal rate of return), it is earning positive profits. Let us take as an example the Blue Velvet Car Wash. Suppose that investors have put up $500,000 to construct a building and purchase all the equipment required to wash cars. Let us also suppose that investors expect to earn a minimum return of 10 percent on their investment. If the money to set up the business had been borrowed from the bank instead, the car wash owners would have paid a 10 percent interest rate. In either case, total cost must include $50,000 per year (10 percent of $500,000).

The car wash is open 50 weeks per year and is capable of washing up to 800 cars per week. Whether it is open and operating or not, the car wash has fixed costs. Those costs include $1,000 per week to investors—that is, the $50,000 per year normal return to investors—and $1,000 per week in other fixed costs—a basic maintenance contract on the equipment, insurance, and so forth.

When the car wash is operating, there are also variable costs. Workers must be paid, and materials such as soap and wax must be purchased. The wage bill is $1,000 per week. Materials, electricity, and so forth run $600 at full capacity. If the car wash is not in operation, there are no variable costs. Table 9.1 summarizes the costs of the Blue Velvet Car Wash.

This car wash business is quite competitive. There are many car washes of equal quality in the area, and they offer their service at $5. If Blue Velvet wants customers, it cannot charge a price above $5. (Recall the perfectly elastic demand curve facing perfectly competitive firms; review Chapter 8 if necessary.) If we assume that Blue Velvet washes 800 cars each week, it takes in revenues of $4,000 from operating (800 cars × $5). Is this total revenue enough to make a positive profit?

The answer is yes. Revenues of $4,000 are sufficient to cover both fixed costs of $2,000 and variable costs of $1,600, leaving a positive profit of $400 per week.

TABLE 9.1 Blue Velvet Car Wash Weekly Costs

TOTAL FIXED COSTS (*TFC*)		TOTAL VARIABLE COSTS (*TVC*) (800 WASHES)		TOTAL COSTS (*TC = TFC + TVC*)	$3,600
1. Normal return		1. Labor	$1,000	Total revenue (*TR*)	
to investors	$1,000	2. Materials	600	at *P* = $5 (800 × $5)	**$4,000**
2. Other fixed costs			**$1,600**	Profit (*TR − TC*)	**$ 400**
(maintenance contract,					
insurance, etc.)	1,000				
	$2,000				

Graphic Presentation   Figure 9.1 graphs the performance of a firm that is earning positive profits in the short run. Figure 9.1(a) illustrates the industry, or the market, and Figure 9.1(b) illustrates a representative firm. At present, the market is clearing at a price of $5. Thus, we assume that the individual firm can sell all it wants at a price of $P^* = \$5$, but that it is constrained by its capacity. Its marginal cost curve rises in the short run because of a fixed factor. You already know that a perfectly competitive profit-maximizing firm produces up to the point where price equals marginal cost. As long as price (marginal revenue) exceeds marginal cost, firms can push up profits by increasing short-run output. The firm in the diagram, then, will supply $q^* = 300$ units of output (point *A*, where $P = MC$).

Both revenues and costs are shown graphically. *Total revenue* (*TR*) is simply the product of price and quantity: $P^* \times q^* = \$5 \times 300 = \$1,500$. On the diagram, total revenue is equal to the area of the rectangle P^*Aq^*0. (The area of a rectangle is equal to its length times its width.) At output q^*, average total cost is $4.20 (point *B*). Numerically, it is equal to the length of line segment q^*B. Because average total cost is derived by dividing total cost by q, we can get back to total cost by *multiplying* average total cost by q. That is,

$$ATC = \frac{TC}{q}$$

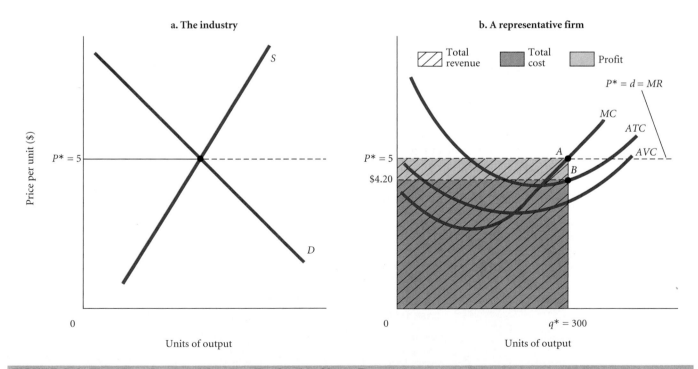

a. The industry
b. A representative firm

FIGURE 9.1 Firm Earning Positive Profits in the Short Run

A profit-maximizing perfectly competitive firm will produce up to the point where $P^* = MC$. Profits are the difference between total revenue and total costs. At $q^* = 300$, total revenue is $5 × 300 = $1,500; total cost is $4.20 × 300 = $1,260; and total profit = $1,500 − $1,260 = $240.

and

$$TC = ATC \times q$$

Total cost (*TC*), then, is $4.20 \times 300 = \$1,260$, the area shaded blue in the diagram. *Profit* is simply the difference between total revenue (*TR*) and total cost (*TC*), or $240. This is the area that is shaded gray in the diagram. This firm is earning positive profits.

A firm that is earning positive profits in the short run and expects to continue doing so has an incentive to expand its scale of operation in the long run. Those profits also give new firms an incentive to enter and compete in the market.

MINIMIZING LOSSES

A firm that is not earning positive profits or breaking even is suffering a loss. Firms suffering losses fall into two categories: (1) those that find it advantageous to shut down operations immediately and bear losses equal to fixed costs, and (2) those that continue to operate in the short run to minimize their losses. The most important thing to remember here is that firms cannot exit the industry in the short run. The firm can shut down, but it cannot get rid of its fixed costs by going out of business. Fixed costs must be paid in the short run no matter what the firm does.

Whether a firm suffering losses decides to produce or not to produce in the short run depends on the advantages and disadvantages of continuing production. If a firm shuts down, it earns no revenues and has no variable costs to bear. If it continues to produce, it both earns revenues and incurs variable costs. Because a firm must bear fixed costs *whether or not* it shuts down, its decision depends *solely on whether revenues from operating are sufficient to cover variable costs.* **Operating profit (or loss)** (sometimes called **net operating revenue**) is defined as total revenue (*TR*) minus total variable cost (*TVC*). In general,

operating profit (or loss) or net operating revenue Total revenue minus total variable cost (*TR* − *TVC*).

- If revenues exceed variable costs, operating profit is positive and can be used to offset fixed costs and reduce losses, and it will pay the firm to keep operating.
- If revenues are smaller than variable costs, the firm suffers operating losses that push total losses above fixed costs. In this case, the firm can minimize its losses by shutting down.

Producing at a Loss to Offset Fixed Costs: The Blue Velvet Revisited

Suppose that competitive pressure pushes the price per wash down to $3. Total revenues for Blue Velvet would fall to $2,400 per week (800 cars × $3). If variable costs remained at $1,600, total costs would be $3,600 ($1,600 + $2,000 fixed costs), a figure higher than total revenues. The firm would then be suffering losses of $3,600 − $2,400 = $1,200. In the long run, Blue Velvet may want to go out of business, but in the short run it is stuck, and it must decide what to do.

The car wash has two options: operate or shut down. If it shuts down, it has no variable costs, but it also earns no revenues, and its losses will be equal to its fixed costs of $2,000 (Table 9.2, Case 1). If it decides to stay open (Table 9.2, Case 2), it will make operating profits. Revenues will be $2,400, more than sufficient to cover variable costs of $1,600. By operat-

TABLE 9.2 A Firm Will Operate If Total Revenue Covers Total Variable Cost

CASE 1: SHUT DOWN		CASE 2: OPERATE AT PRICE = $3	
Total revenue (*q* = 0)	$ 0	Total revenue ($3 × 800)	$2,400
Fixed costs	$2,000	Fixed costs	$2,000
Variable costs	+ 0	Variable costs	+ 1,600
Total costs	$2,000	Total costs	$3,600
Profit/loss (*TR* − *TC*)	−$2,000	Operating profit/loss (*TR* − *TVC*)	$ 800
		Total profit/loss (*TR* − *TC*)	−$1,200

ing, the firm gains $800 per week operating profits that it can use to offset its fixed costs. By operating, the firm reduces its losses from $2,000 to $1,200.

Graphic Presentation   Figure 9.2 graphs a firm suffering losses. The market price, set by the forces of supply and demand, is $P^* = \$3.50$. If the firm decides to operate, it will do best by producing up to the point where price (marginal revenue) is equal to marginal cost—in this case, at an output of $q^* = 225$ units.

Once again, total revenue (TR) is simply the product of price and quantity ($P^* \times q^*$) = $\$3.50 \times 225 = \$787.50$, or the area of rectangle $P^*\, Aq^*0$. Average total cost at $q^* = 225$ is $\$4.10$, and it is equal to the length of q^*B. Total cost is the product of average total cost and q^* ($ATC \times q^*$), or $\$4.10 \times 225 = \$922.50$. Because total cost is greater than total revenue, the firm is suffering losses of $\$135$, shown on the graph by the pink-shaded rectangle.

Operating profit—the difference between total revenue and total *variable* cost—can also be identified. On the graph, total revenue (as we said) is $\$787.50$. *Average* variable cost at q^* is the length of q^*E. Total variable cost is the product of average variable cost and q^* and is therefore equal to $\$3.10 \times 225 = \$697.50$. Profit on operation is thus $\$787.50 - \$697.50 = \$90$, the area of the gray-shaded rectangle.

Remember that average total cost is equal to average fixed cost plus average variable cost. This means that at every level of output, average fixed cost is the difference between average total and average variable cost:

$$ATC = AFC + AVC$$
$$\text{or}$$
$$AFC = ATC - AVC = \$4.10 - \$3.10 = \$1.00$$

In Figure 9.2, therefore, average fixed cost is equal to the length of BE (the difference between ATC and AVC at q^*, or $\$1.00$). Because total fixed cost is simply average fixed cost of $\$1.00$ times $q^* = \$225$, total fixed cost is equal to $\$225$, the entire pink- and gray-shaded rectangle. Thus, if the firm had shut down, its losses would be equal to $\$225$. By operating, the firm earns an operating profit equal to the gray-shaded area ($\$90$) covering some fixed costs and reducing losses to the red-shaded area ($\$135$).

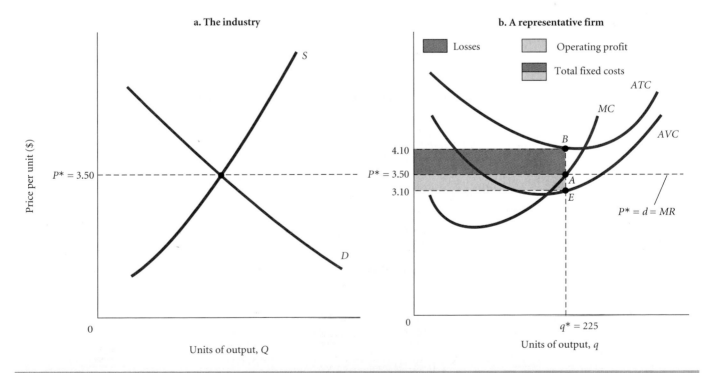

FIGURE 9.2 Firm Suffering Losses but Showing an Operating Profit in the Short Run

When price is sufficient to cover average variable costs, firms suffering short-run losses will continue operating instead of shutting down. Total revenues ($P^* \times q^*$) cover variable costs, leaving an operating profit of $90 to cover part of fixed costs and reduce losses to $135.

If we think only in averages, it seems logical that a firm in this position will continue to operate:

> As long as price (which is equal to average revenue per unit) is sufficient to cover average variable costs, the firm stands to gain by operating instead of shutting down.

Shutting Down to Minimize Loss   When revenues are insufficient to cover even variable costs, firms suffering losses find it advantageous to shut down, even in the short run.

Suppose, for example, that competition and the availability of sophisticated new machinery pushed the price of a car wash all the way down to $1.50. Washing 800 cars per week would then yield revenues of only $1,200 (Table 9.3). With variable costs at $1,600, operating would mean losing an additional $400 *over and above* fixed costs of $2,000. This means that total losses would amount to $2,400. A profit-maximizing/loss-minimizing car wash would reduce its losses from $2,400 to $2,000 by shutting down, even in the short run.

> Any time that price (average revenue) is below the minimum point on the average variable cost curve, total revenue will be less than total variable cost, and operating profit will be negative—that is, there will be a loss on operation. In other words, when price is below all points on the average variable cost curve, the firm will suffer operating losses at any possible output level the firm could choose. When this is the case, the firm will stop producing and bear losses equal to fixed costs. This is why the bottom of the average variable cost curve is called the **shut-down point**. At all prices above it, the marginal cost curve shows the profit-maximizing level of output. At all prices below it, optimal short-run output is zero.

shut-down point The lowest point on the average variable cost curve. When price falls below the minimum point on *AVC*, total revenue is insufficient to cover variable costs and the firm will shut down and bear losses equal to fixed costs.

We can now refine our earlier statement that a perfectly competitive firm's marginal cost curve is actually its short-run supply curve. Recall that a profit-maximizing perfectly competitive firm will produce up to the point at which $P = MC$. As we have just seen, though, a firm will shut down when P is less than the minimum point on the *AVC* curve. Also recall that the marginal cost curve intersects the *AVC* curve at *AVC*'s lowest point. It therefore follows that

> The short-run supply curve of a competitive firm is that portion of its marginal cost curve that lies above its average variable cost curve (Figure 9.3).

THE SHORT-RUN INDUSTRY SUPPLY CURVE

Supply in a competitive industry is simply the sum of the quantity supplied by the individual firms in the industry at each price level. The **short-run industry supply curve** is the sum of the individual firm supply curves—that is, the marginal cost curves (above *AVC*) of all the firms in the industry. Because quantities are being added—that is, because we are finding the total quantity supplied in the industry at each price level—the curves are added horizontally.

short-run industry supply curve The sum of the marginal cost curves (above *AVC*) of all the firms in an industry.

TABLE 9.3 A Firm Will Shut Down If Total Revenue Is Less Than Total Variable Cost

CASE 1: SHUT DOWN		CASE 2: OPERATE AT PRICE = $1.50	
Total revenue (q = 0)	$ 0	Total revenue ($1.50 × 800)	$1,200
Fixed costs	$2,000	Fixed costs	$2,000
Variable costs	+ 0	Variable costs	+ 1,600
Total costs	$2,000	Total costs	$3,600
Profit/loss (TR − TC):	−$2,000		
		Operating profit/loss (TR − TVC)	−$ 400
		Total profit/loss (TR − TC)	−$2,400

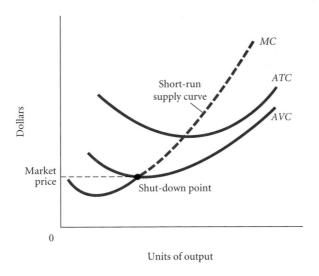

FIGURE 9.3 Short-Run Supply Curve of a Perfectly Competitive Firm

At prices below average variable cost, it pays a firm to shut down rather than continue operating. Thus, the short-run supply curve of a competitive firm is the part of its marginal cost curve that lies *above* its average variable cost curve.

Figure 9.4 shows the supply curve for an industry with just three firms.[1] At a price of $6, firm 1 produces 100 units, the output where $P = MC$. Firm 2 produces 200 units, and firm 3 produces 150 units. The total amount supplied on the market at a price of $6 is thus 450 (100 + 200 + 150). At a price of $5, firm 1 produces 90 units, firm 2 produces 180 units, and firm 3 produces 120 units. At a price of $5, the industry thus supplies 390 units (90 + 180 + 120).

Two things can cause the industry supply curve to shift. In the short run, the industry supply curve shifts if something—a decrease in the price of some input, for instance—shifts the marginal cost curves of all the individual firms simultaneously. For example, when the cost of producing components of home computers decreased, the marginal cost curves of all computer manufacturers shifted downward. Such a shift amounted to the same thing as an outward shift in their supply curves. Each firm was willing to supply more computers at each price level because computers were now cheaper to produce.

In the long run, an increase or decrease in the number of firms—and, therefore, in the number of individual firm supply curves—shifts the total industry supply curve. If new

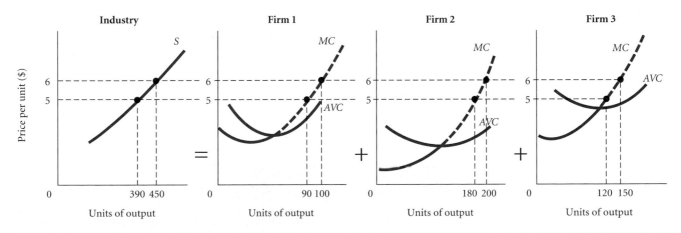

FIGURE 9.4 The Industry Supply Curve in the Short Run Is the Horizontal Sum of the Marginal Cost Curves (above AVC) of All the Firms in an Industry

If there are only three firms in the industry, the industry supply curve is simply the sum of all the products supplied by the three firms at each price. For example, at $6, firm 1 supplies 100 units, firm 2 supplies 200 units, and firm 3 supplies 150 units, for a total industry supply of 450.

---

[1]Perfectly competitive industries are assumed to have many firms. Many is, of course, more than three. We use three firms here simply for the purposes of illustration.

TABLE 9.4 Profits, Losses, and Perfectly Competitive Firm Decisions in the Long and Short Run

	SHORT-RUN CONDITION	SHORT-RUN DECISION	LONG-RUN DECISION
Profits	$TR > TC$	$P = MC$: operate	Expand: new firms enter
Losses	1. With operating profit ($TR \geq TVC$)	$P = MC$: operate (losses < fixed costs)	Contract: firms exit
	2. With operating losses ($TR < TVC$)	Shut down: losses = fixed costs	Contract: firms exit

firms enter the industry, the industry supply curve moves to the right; if firms exit the industry, the industry supply curve moves to the left.

We return to shifts in industry supply curves and discuss them further when we take up long-run adjustments later in this chapter.

LONG-RUN DIRECTIONS: A REVIEW

Table 9.4 summarizes the different circumstances that perfectly competitive firms may face as they plan for the long run. Profit-making firms will produce up to the point where price and marginal cost are equal in the short run. If there are positive profits, in the long run there is an incentive for firms to expand their scales of plant and for new firms to enter the industry.

Firms suffering losses will produce if, and only if, revenues are sufficient to cover variable costs. Such firms, like profitable firms, will also produce up to the point where $P = MC$. If firms suffering losses cannot cover variable costs by operating, they will shut down and bear losses equal to fixed costs. Whether or not a firm that is suffering losses decides to shut down in the short run, it has an incentive to contract in the long run. The simple fact is that when firms are suffering losses, they will generally exit the industry in the long run.

In the short run, a firm's decision about how much to produce depends on the market price of its product and the shapes of its cost curves. Remember that the short-run cost curves show costs that are determined by the *current* scale of plant. In the long run, however, firms have to choose among many *potential* scales of plant.

The long-run decisions of individual firms depend on what their costs are likely to be at different scales of operation. Just as firms have to analyze different technologies to arrive at a cost structure in the short run, they must also compare their costs at different scales of plant to arrive at long-run costs. Perhaps a larger scale of operations will reduce production costs and provide an even greater incentive for a profit-making firm to expand, or perhaps large firms will run into problems that constrain growth. The analysis of long-run possibilities is even more complex than the short-run analysis, because more things are variable—scale of plant is not fixed, for example, and there are no fixed costs because firms can exit their industry in the long run. In theory, firms may choose *any* scale of operation, and so they must analyze many possible options.

Now let us turn to an analysis of cost curves in the long run.

LONG-RUN COSTS: ECONOMIES AND DISECONOMIES OF SCALE

The shapes of short-run cost curves follow directly from the assumption of a fixed factor of production. As output increases beyond a certain point, the fixed factor (which we usually think of as fixed scale of plant) causes diminishing returns to other factors and thus increasing marginal costs. In the long run, however, there is no fixed factor of production. Firms can choose any scale of production. They can double or triple output or go out of business completely.

increasing returns to scale, or economies of scale An increase in a firm's scale of production leads to lower costs per unit produced.

The shape of a firm's *long-run* average cost curve depends on how costs vary with scale of operations. For some firms, increased scale, or size, reduces costs. For others, increased scale leads to inefficiency and waste. When an increase in a firm's scale of production leads to lower average costs, we say that there are **increasing returns to scale**, or **economies of scale**. When average costs do not change with the scale of production, we say that there are **constant returns to scale**. Finally, when an increase in a firm's scale of production leads to higher average costs, we say that there are **decreasing returns to scale**, or **diseconomies of scale**. Because these economies of scale all are found within the individual firm, they are considered *internal* economies of scale. In the Appendix to this chapter, we talk about *external* economies of scale, which describe economies or diseconomies of scale on an industry-wide basis.

INCREASING RETURNS TO SCALE

Technically, the phrase *increasing returns to scale* refers to the relationship between inputs and outputs. When we say that a production function exhibits increasing returns, we mean that a given percentage of increase in inputs leads to a *larger* percentage of increase in the production of output. For example, if a firm doubled or tripled inputs, it would more than double or triple output.

When firms can count on fixed input prices—that is, when the prices of inputs do not change with output levels—increasing returns to scale also means that as output rises, average cost of production falls. The term *economies of scale* refers directly to this reduction in cost per unit of output that follows from larger-scale production.

The Sources of Economies of Scale
Most of the economies of scale that immediately come to mind are technological in nature. Automobile production, for example, would be much more costly per unit if a firm were to produce 100 cars per year by hand. Early in this century, Henry Ford introduced standardized production techniques that increased output volume, reduced costs per car, and made the automobile available to almost everyone.

Some economies of scale result not from technology but from sheer size. Very large companies, for instance, can buy inputs in volume at discounted prices. Large firms may also produce some of their own inputs at considerable savings, and they can certainly save in transport costs when they ship items in bulk.

Economies of scale can be seen all around us. A bus that carries 100 people between Vancouver and Seattle uses less labor, capital, and gasoline than 100 people driving 100 different automobiles. The cost per passenger (average cost) is lower on the bus. Roommates who share an apartment are taking advantage of economies of scale. Costs per person for heat, electricity, and space are lower when an apartment is shared than if each person rented a separate apartment.

Example: Economies of Scale in Egg Production
Nowhere are economies of scale more visible than in agriculture. Consider the following example. A few years ago a major agribusiness moved into a small Ohio town and set up a huge egg-producing operation. The new firm, Chicken Little Egg Farms Inc., is completely mechanized. Complex machines feed the chickens and collect and box the eggs. Large refrigerated trucks transport the eggs all over the state daily. In the same town, some small farmers still own fewer than 200 chickens. These farmers collect the eggs, feed the chickens, clean the coops by hand, and deliver the eggs to county markets.

Table 9.5 presents some hypothetical cost data for Homer Jones's small operation and for Chicken Little Inc. Jones has his operation working well. He has several hundred chickens and spends about 15 hours per week feeding, collecting, delivering, and so forth. In the rest of his time he raises soybeans. We can value Jones's time at $8 per hour, because that is the wage he could earn working at a local manufacturing plant. When we add up all Jones's costs, including a rough estimate of the land and capital costs attributable to egg production, we arrive at $177 per week. Total production on the Jones farm runs about 200 dozen, or 2,400, eggs per week, which means that Jones's average cost comes out to $0.074 per egg.

The costs of Chicken Little Inc. are much higher in total; weekly costs run over $30,000. A much higher percentage of costs are capital costs—the firm uses lots of sophisticated machinery that cost millions to put in place. Total output is 1.6 million eggs per week, and the product is shipped all over the Midwest. The comparatively huge scale of plant has driven average production costs all the way down to $0.019 per egg.

Although these numbers are hypothetical, you can see why small farmers in the United States are finding it difficult to compete with large-scale agribusiness concerns that can real-

TABLE 9.5 Weekly Costs Showing Economies of Scale in Egg Production

JONES FARM	TOTAL WEEKLY COSTS
15 hours of labor (implicit value $8 per hour)	$120
Feed, other variable costs	25
Transport costs	15
Land and capital costs attributable to egg production	17
	$177
Total output	2,400 eggs
Average cost	$0.074 per egg
CHICKEN LITTLE EGG FARMS INC.	**TOTAL WEEKLY COSTS**
Labor	$ 5,128
Feed, other variable costs	4,115
Transport costs	2,431
Land and capital costs	19,230
	$30,904
Total output	1,600,000 eggs
Average cost	$0.019 per egg

ize significant economies of scale. For more on this topic, see the Further Exploration box titled "Why Small Farmers Have Trouble Competing: Economies of Scale in Agriculture and Hog Raising" on the next page.

long-run average cost curve (LRAC) A graph that shows the different scales on which a firm can choose to operate in the long run.

Graphic Presentation   A firm's **long-run average cost curve (LRAC)** shows the different scales on which it can choose to operate in the long run. In other words, a firm's *LRAC* curve traces out the position of all its possible short-run curves, each corresponding to a different scale. At any time, the existing scale of plant determines the position and shape of the firm's short-run cost curves, but the firm must consider in its long-run strategic planning whether to build a plant of a *different* scale. The long-run average cost curve simply shows the positions of the different sets of short-run curves among which the firm must choose. The long-run average cost curve is the "envelope" of a series of short-run curves; it "wraps around" the set of all possible short-run curves like an envelope. (The Further Exploration feature on page 203 titled "The Long-Run Average Cost Curve: Flat or U-Shaped?" describes the debate on how the *LRAC* is constructed.)

Figure 9.5 shows short-run and long-run average cost curves for a firm that realizes economies of scale up to about 100,000 units of production and roughly constant returns to

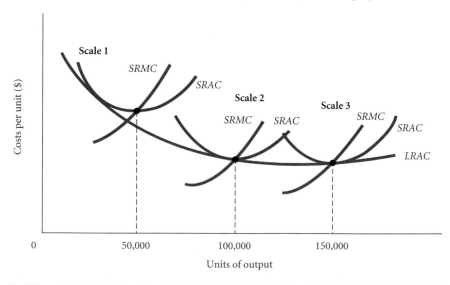

FIGURE 9.5 A Firm Exhibiting Economies of Scale

The long-run average cost curve of a firm shows the different scales on which the firm can choose to operate in the long run. Each scale of operation defines a different short run. Here we see a firm exhibiting economies of scale; moving from scale 1 to scale 3 reduces average cost.

Why Small Farmers Have Trouble Competing: Economies of Scale in Agriculture

Economies of scale, or increasing returns to scale, exist when larger firms have lower average costs than smaller firms. If economies of scale exist in agriculture, one would expect the average size of farms to increase over time as smaller operations find themselves unable to compete. Indeed, over the past 65 years the number of farms in the United States has dropped by more than two-thirds and average farm size has increased nearly threefold:

YEAR	NUMBER OF FARMS (THOUSANDS)	AVERAGE SIZE (ACRES)
1940	6,350	167
1950	5,648	213
1960	3,963	297
1970	2,949	374
1980	2,439	426
1990	2,146	460
2000	2,166	436
2004	2,113	443

As a result of economies of scale in agriculture, family-owned farms are increasingly being replaced by large-scale agribusinesses.

Numerous studies have found evidence of scale economies in farming. In a recent article in the *Journal of Economic History*, Nancy Virts found that large-scale tenant plantations in the post–Civil War South had cost advantages over smaller plantations. In another article in the *American Journal of Agricultural Economics*, Stephen Cooke found that between 1974 and 1983 very large corn producers (500–1,000 acres) were 4 to 8 percent more cost-efficient than large producers (300–460 acres) and 8 to 15 percent more cost-efficient than medium-sized producers (175–290 acres).[a]

In an article examining the potential of smaller farms to compete with larger farms, Catherine Paul argues that "family farms are both scale and technically inefficient." These characteristics have led to a decline in both profitability and competitiveness among small family farms.

Source: Catherine Morrison Paul, "Scale Economics and Efficiency in U.S. Agriculture: Are Traditional Farms History?" with Richard Nehring, David Banker, and Agapi Somwaru, Journal of Productivity Analysis 22 (2004), 185–205.

[a]Nancy Virts, "The Efficiency of Southern Tenant Plantations, 1900-1945," *Journal of Economic History* 51(2), June 1991, 385-95; Stephen Cooke, "Cost Efficiency in U.S. Corn Production," *American Journal of Agricultural Economics* 71(4), November 1989, 1003–10.

scale after that. The diagram shows three potential scales of operation, each with its own set of short-run cost curves. Each point on the *LRAC* curve represents the minimum cost at which the associated output level can be produced.

Once the firm chooses a scale on which to produce, it becomes locked into one set of cost curves in the short run. If the firm were to settle on scale 1, it would not realize the major cost advantages of producing on a larger scale. By roughly doubling its scale of operations from 50,000 to 100,000 units (scale 2), the firm reduces average costs per unit significantly.

Figure 9.5 shows that at every moment firms face two different cost constraints. In the long run, firms can change their scale of operation, and costs may be different as a result. However, at any *given* moment, a particular scale of operation exists, constraining the firm's capacity to produce in the short run. That is why we see both short- and long-run curves in the same diagram.

CONSTANT RETURNS TO SCALE

Technically, the term *constant returns* means that the quantitative relationship between input and output stays constant, or the same, when output is increased. If a firm doubles inputs, it doubles output; if it triples inputs, it triples output; and so forth. Furthermore, if input economies of scale, long run costs, returns to scales   search

○ Further Exploration   ● News Analysis

Economies of Scale in Banking, 2005

FOR THE PAST TWO DECADES, THE banking industry in the United States has been consolidating. Smaller banks have been gobbled up by larger banks, and larger banks have been merging, in part to take advantage of *economies of scale*. Clearly, banking is a very competitive industry. Even in small to moderate-size towns, major intersections can have several branches. A merger between two banks with branches next door to each other allows the newly created larger bank to eliminate a branch and to reduce its average costs without losing much business. Larger banks can also take advantage of computer operating systems that may be less costly. Between 1985 and 2004, the number of commercial banks in the United States fell from 14,417 to 7,630, while average size increased dramatically.[1]

At the same time, smaller banks can and do sometimes thrive, as the following article from the *New York Times* indicates. The question is, can they survive in the long run if the bigger banks continue to consolidate and reduce average costs in the process?

Economies of scale make it difficult for small banks to survive.

Small Banking in a Big Bank World

By Eve Tahmincioglu (NYT)
Published: June 30, 2005

Bank of America, after absorbing FleetBoston last year in a $50 billion deal, now has 5,800 branches in 30 states. J. P. Morgan Chase, having bought Bank One for $60 billion in stock in another 2004 mega-merger, now counts 2,500 branches. Royal Bank of Scotland, the parent of Citizens Bank, increased its presence in the United States to 1,500 branches after its acquisition of Charter One, also last year.

Then there is the Western National Bank in Phoenix. It has a single location, at the intersection of 24th Street and Camelback Road, on the ground floor of an office tower in a business district known as the Camelback Corridor. And it does not even have a drive-through window, because the entrepreneur who opened it in February [William D. Hinz] could not find a piece of real estate that would accommodate one.

"We found that especially with small-business lending and banking, being able to know your customer is critical," he said. "Being part of the community in which they work is critical. The big bank networks aren't really built to take care of smaller loans."

So far, his business strategy is paying off. In just four months, Western National has accumulated more than 400 accounts and about $32 million in assets, more than twice his goal. And while he had estimated it would take 18 months to become profitable, he now predicts it will take less than a year.

Mr. Hinz belongs to a hearty band of entrepreneurs, many of them former managers of small banks that were gobbled up by the big boys, who smelled opportunity in customers' longing to be pampered. While competing against the likes of Bank of America can be daunting, they say, the Internet has given them tools that were not available before.

[1]www.fdic.gov

prices are fixed, constant returns imply that average cost of production does not change with scale. In other words, constant returns to scale mean that the firm's long-run average cost curve remains flat.

The firm in Figure 9.5 exhibits roughly constant returns to scale between scale 2 and scale 3. The average cost of production is about the same in each. If the firm exhibited constant returns at levels above 150,000 units of output, the *LRAC* would continue as a flat, straight line.

Economists have studied cost data extensively over the years to estimate the extent to which economies of scale exist. Evidence suggests that in most industries firms do not have to be gigantic to realize cost savings from scale economies. For example, automobile production is accomplished in thousands of separate assembly operations, each with its own economies of scale. Perhaps the best example of efficient production on a small scale is the manufacturing sector in Taiwan. Taiwan has enjoyed very rapid growth based on manufacturing firms that employ fewer than 100 workers.

One simple argument supports the empirical result that most industries seem to exhibit constant returns to scale (a flat *LRAC*) after some level of output. Competition always pushes firms to adopt the least-cost technology and scale. If cost advantages result with larger-scale operations, the firms that shift to that scale will drive the smaller, less efficient firms out of business. A firm that wants to grow when it has reached its "optimal" size can do so by building another identical plant. It thus seems logical to conclude that most firms face constant returns to scale *as long as* they can replicate their existing plants. Thus, when you look at developed industries, from breweries to banks and from software to home building, you can expect to see firms of different sizes operating with similar costs. These firms produce using roughly the same scale of plant, but larger firms simply have more plants. (See box on page 198 for a discussion of banking.)

DECREASING RETURNS TO SCALE

When average cost increases with scale of production, a firm faces *decreasing returns to scale*, or *diseconomies of scale*. The most often cited example of a diseconomy of scale is bureaucratic inefficiency. As size increases beyond a certain point, operations tend to become more difficult to manage. You can easily imagine what happens when a firm grows top-heavy with managers who have accumulated seniority and high salaries. The coordination function is more complex for larger firms than for smaller ones, and the chances that it will break down are greater.

A large firm is also more likely than a small firm to find itself facing problems with organized labor. Unions can demand higher wages and more benefits, go on strike, force firms to incur legal expenses, and take other actions that increase production costs. (This does not mean that unions are "bad" but instead that their activities often increase costs.)

Figure 9.6 describes a firm that exhibits both economies of scale and diseconomies of scale. Average costs decrease with scale of plant up to q^* and increase with scale after that. This long-run average cost curve looks very much like the short-run average cost curves we have examined in the last two chapters, but do not confuse the two:

> All short-run average cost curves are U-shaped, because we assume a fixed scale of plant that constrains production and drives marginal cost upward as a result of diminishing returns. In the long run, we make no such assumption; instead, we assume that scale of plant can be changed.

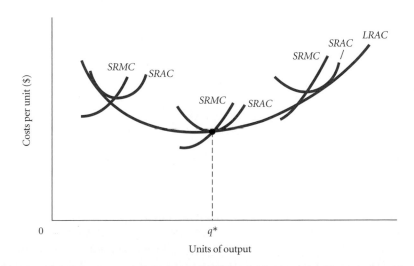

FIGURE 9.6 A Firm Exhibiting Economies and Diseconomies of Scale

Economies of scale push this firm's average costs down to q^*. Beyond q^*, the firm experiences diseconomies of scale; q^* is the level of production at lowest average cost, using optimal scale.

optimal scale of plant

The scale of plant that minimizes
average cost.

Thus, the same firm can face diminishing returns—a short-run concept—and still have a long-run cost curve that exhibits economies of scale.

The shape of a firm's long-run average cost curve depends on how costs react to changes in scale. Some firms do see economies of scale, and their long-run average cost curves slope downward. Most firms seem to have flat long-run average cost curves. Still others encounter diseconomies, and their long-run average cost curves slope upward.

It is important to note that economic efficiency requires taking advantage of economies of scale (if they exist) and avoiding diseconomies of scale. The **optimal scale of plant** is the one that minimizes average cost. In fact, as we will see next, competition forces firms to use the optimal scale.

LONG-RUN ADJUSTMENTS TO SHORT-RUN CONDITIONS

We began this chapter by discussing the different short-run positions in which firms may find themselves. Firms can be operating at a profit or suffering economic losses; they can be shut down or producing. The industry is not in long-run equilibrium if firms have an incentive to enter or exit in the long run. Thus, when firms are earning economic profits (profits above normal, or positive) or are suffering economic losses (profits below normal, or negative), the industry is not at an equilibrium, and firms will change their behavior. What they are likely to do depends in part on costs in the long run. This is why we have spent a good deal of time discussing economies and diseconomies of scale.

We can now put these two ideas together and discuss the actual long-run adjustments that are likely to take place in response to short-run profits and losses.

SHORT-RUN PROFITS: EXPANSION TO EQUILIBRIUM

We begin our analysis of long-run adjustments with a perfectly competitive industry in which firms are earning positive profits. We assume that all firms in the industry are producing with the same technology of production, and that each firm has a long-run average cost curve that is U-shaped. A U-shaped long-run average cost curve implies that there are some economies of scale to be realized in the industry, and that all firms ultimately begin to run into diseconomies at some scale of operation.

Figure 9.7 shows a representative perfectly competitive firm initially producing at scale 1. Market price is $P_0 = \$12$, and individual firms are enjoying economic profits. Total

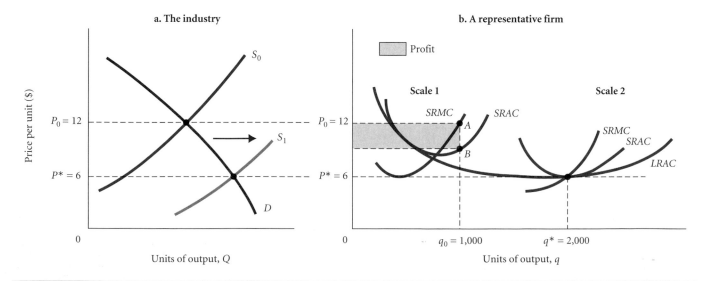

a. The industry   **b. A representative firm**

FIGURE 9.7 Firms Expand in the Long Run When Increasing Returns to Scale Are Available

When economies of scale can be realized, firms have an incentive to expand. Thus firms will be pushed by competition to produce at their optimal scales. Price will be driven to the minimum point on the *LRAC* curve.

revenue at our representative firm, which is producing 1,000 units of output per period, exceeds total cost. Our firm's profit per period is equal to the gray-shaded rectangle. (Make sure you understand why the gray rectangle represents profits. Remember that perfectly competitive firms maximize profit by producing at $P = MC$ —in Figure 9.7, at point A.)

At this point, our representative firm has not realized all the economies of scale available to it. By expanding to scale 2, it will reduce average costs significantly, and it will increase profits unless price drops. As long as firms are enjoying profits and economies of scale exist, firms will expand. Thus, we assume that the firm in Figure 9.7 shifts to scale 2.

At the same time, the existence of positive profits will attract new entrants to the industry. Both the entrance of new firms and the expansion of existing firms have the same effect on the short-run industry supply curve [Figure 9.7(a)]. Both cause the short-run supply curve to shift to the right, from S_0 to S_1. Because the short-run industry supply curve is the sum of all the marginal cost curves (above the minimum point of AVC) of all the firms in the industry, it will shift to the right, for two reasons. First, because all firms in the industry are expanding to a larger scale, their individual short-run marginal cost curves shift to the right. Second, with new firms entering the industry, there are more firms and thus more marginal cost curves to add up.

As capital flows into the industry, the supply curve in Figure 9.7(a) shifts to the right and price falls. The question is: Where will the process stop? In general:

Firms will continue to expand as long as there are economies of scale to be realized, and new firms will continue to enter as long as positive profits are being earned.

In Figure 9.7(a), final equilibrium is achieved only when price falls to $P^* = \$6$ and firms have exhausted all the economies of scale available in the industry. At $P^* = \$6$, no economic profits are being earned and none can be earned by changing the level of output.

Look carefully at the final equilibrium in Figure 9.7. Each firm will choose the scale of plant that produces its product at minimum long-run average cost. Competition drives firms to adopt not just the most efficient technology in the *short* run but also the most efficient scale of operation in the *long* run.

In the long run, equilibrium price (P^*) is equal to long-run average cost, short-run marginal cost, and short-run average cost. Profits are driven to zero:

$$P^* = SRMC = SRAC = LRAC$$

where $SRMC$ denotes short-run marginal cost, $SRAC$ denotes short-run average cost, and $LRAC$ denotes long-run average cost. No other price is an equilibrium price. Any price above P^* means that there are profits to be made in the industry, and new firms will continue to enter. Any price below P^* means that firms are suffering losses, and firms will exit the industry. Only at P^* will economic profits be just equal to zero, and only at P^* will the industry be in equilibrium.

SHORT-RUN LOSSES: CONTRACTION TO EQUILIBRIUM

Firms that suffer short-run losses have an incentive to leave the industry in the long run but cannot do so in the short run. As we have seen, some firms incurring losses will choose to shut down and bear losses equal to fixed costs. Others will continue to produce in the short run in an effort to minimize their losses.

Figure 9.8 depicts a firm that will continue to produce $q_0 = 1,000$ units of output in the short run, despite its losses. (We are assuming here that the firm is earning losses that are smaller than the firm's fixed costs.) With losses, the long-run picture will change. Firms have an incentive to get out of the industry. As they exit, the industry's short-run supply curve shifts to the left. As it shifts, the equilibrium price rises, from $8 to $9.

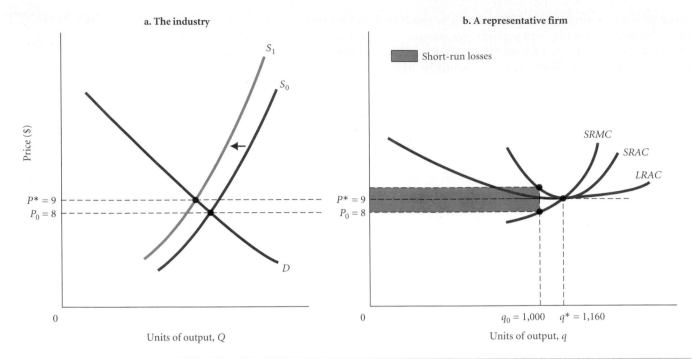

a. The industry

b. A representative firm

Short-run losses

$$P^* = SRMC = SRAC = LRAC$$

(axis labels from figure)
Price ($)
S_1
S_0
$P^* = 9$
$P_0 = 8$
D
Units of output, Q
$SRMC$
$SRAC$
$LRAC$
$P^* = 9$
$P_0 = 8$
$q_0 = 1,000$ $q^* = 1,160$
Units of output, q

FIGURE 9.8 Long-Run Contraction and Exit in an Industry Suffering Short-Run Losses

When firms in an industry suffer losses, there is an incentive for them to exit. As firms exit, the supply curve shifts from S_0 to S_1, driving price up to P^*. As price rises, losses are gradually eliminated and the industry returns to equilibrium.

Once again the question is: How long will this adjustment process continue? In general:

As long as losses are being sustained in an industry, firms will shut down and leave the industry, thus reducing supply—shifting the supply curve to the left. As this happens, price rises. This gradual price rise reduces losses for firms remaining in the industry until those losses are ultimately eliminated.

In Figure 9.8, equilibrium occurs when price rises to $P^* = \$9$. At that point, remaining firms will maximize profits by producing $q^* = 1,160$ units of output. Price is just sufficient to cover average costs, and economic profits and losses are zero.

Whether we begin with an industry in which firms are earning profits or suffering losses, the final long-run competitive equilibrium condition is the same:

$$P^* = SRMC = SRAC = LRAC$$

and profits are zero. At this point, individual firms are operating at the most efficient scale of plant—that is, at the minimum point on their *LRAC* curve.

THE LONG-RUN ADJUSTMENT MECHANISM: INVESTMENT FLOWS TOWARD PROFIT OPPORTUNITIES

The central idea in our discussion of entry, exit, expansion, and contraction is this:

In efficient markets, investment capital flows toward profit opportunities. The actual process is complex and varies from industry to industry.

We talked about efficient markets in Chapter 1. In efficient markets, profit opportunities are quickly eliminated as they develop. To illustrate this point, we described driving up to a toll booth and suggested that shorter-than-average lines are quickly eliminated as cars shift

When firms in an industry are making positive profits, capital is likely to flow into that industry. Entrepreneurs start new firms, and firms producing entirely different products may join the competition. The success of Ben and Jerry's has inspired a slew of imitators to compete in the ice cream industry.

202

The Long-Run Average Cost Curve: Flat or U-Shaped?

The long-run average cost curve has been a source of controversy in economies for many years. A long-run average cost curve was first drawn as the "envelope" of a series of short-run curves in a classic article written by Jacob Viner in 1931.[a] In preparing that article, Viner gave his draftsman the task of drawing the long-run curve through the minimum points of all the short-run average cost curves.

In a supplementary note written in 1950, Viner commented:

> . . . the error in Chart IV is left uncorrected so that future teachers and students may share the pleasure of many of their predecessors of pointing out that if I had known what an envelope was, I would not have given my excellent draftsman the technically impossible and economically inappropriate task of drawing an *AC* curve which would pass through the lowest cost points of all the *AC* curves yet not rise above any *AC* curve at any point . . . .[b]

While this story is an interesting part of the lore of economics, a more recent debate concentrates on the economic content of this controversy. In 1986, Professor Herbert Simon of Carnegie-Mellon University stated bluntly:

> I think the textbooks are a scandal . . . the most widely used textbooks use the old long-run and short-run cost curves to illustrate the theory of the firm. . . . [the U-shaped long-run cost curve] postulated that in the long run the size of the firm would increase to a scale associated with the minimum cost on the long-run curve. It was supposed to predict something about the size distribution of firms in the industry. It doesn't do that and there are other problems. Most serious is the fact that most empirical studies show the firm's cost curves not to be U-shaped, but in fact to slope down to the right and then level off, without a clearly defined minimum point.[c]

Professor Simon makes an important point. Suppose that we were to redraw Figure 9.7(b) with

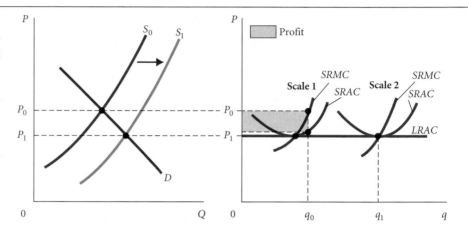

FIGURE 1 Long-Run Expansion in an Industry with Constant Returns to Scale

a flat long-run average cost curve. Figure 1 shows a firm earning short-run profits using scale 1, but there are no economies of scale to be realized.

Despite the lack of economies of scale, expansion of such an industry would likely take place in much the same way as we have described. First, existing firms have an incentive to expand because they are making profits. At current prices, a firm that doubles its scale would earn twice the profits even if cost did not fall with expansion. Of course, as long as profits persist, new firms have an incentive to enter the industry. Both events will shift the short-run industry supply curve to the right, from S_0 to S_1 and price will fall, from P_0 to P_1. Expansion and entry will stop only when price has fallen to *LRAC*. Only then will profits be eliminated. At equilibrium:

$$P = SRMC = SRAC = LRAC$$

This model does not predict the final firm size or the structure of the industry. When the long-run *AC* curve is U-shaped, firms stop expanding at the minimum point on *LRAC* because further expan-

sion means higher costs. Thus, optimal firm size is determined technologically. If the *LRAC* curve is flat, however, small firms and large firms have identical average costs.

If this is true, and it seems to be in many industries, the structure of the industry in the long run will depend on whether existing firms expand faster than new firms enter. If new firms enter quickly in response to profit opportunities, the industry will end up with large numbers of small firms, but if existing firms expand more rapidly than new firms enter, the industry may end up with only a few very large firms. There is thus an element of randomness in the way industries expand. In fact, most industries contain some large firms and some small firms, which is exactly what Simon's flat *LRAC* model predicts.

Sources: [a]Jacob Viner, "Cost Curves and Supply Curves," Zeitschrift fur Nationalokonomie, Vol. 3 (1–1931), 23–46; [b]George J. Stigler and Kenneth E. Boulding, eds., AEA Readings in Price Theory, Vol. 6 (Chicago: Richard D. Irwin, 1952), p. 227; [c]Interview with Herbert A. Simon, "The Failure of Armchair Economics," Challenge, November–December, 1986, 23–24.

into them. So, too, are profits in competitive industries eliminated as new competing firms move into open slots, or perceived opportunities, in the industry.

In practice, the entry and exit of firms in response to profit opportunities usually involve the financial capital market. In capital markets, people are constantly looking for profits. When firms in an industry do well, capital is likely to flow into that industry in a variety of forms. Entrepreneurs start new firms, and firms producing entirely different products may join the competition to break into new markets. It happens all around us. The tremendous success of premium ice cream makers Ben and Jerry's and Häagen-Dazs spawned dozens of competitors. In one Massachusetts town of 35,000, a small ice cream store opened to rave reviews, long lines, and high prices and positive profits. Within a year there were four new ice cream/frozen yogurt stores, no lines, and lower prices. Magic? No: just the natural functioning of competition.

long-run competitive equilibrium When $P = SRMC = SRAC = LRAC$ and profits are zero.

Many believe that part of the explosion of technology-based dot-com companies is due to the very low barriers to entry. All it takes to start a company is an idea, a terminal, and Web access. The number of new firms entering the industry is so large that statistical agencies cannot even keep pace.

When there is promise of positive profits, investments are made and output expands. When firms end up suffering losses, firms contract, and some go out of business. It can take quite a while, however, for an industry to achieve **long-run competitive equilibrium**, the point at which $P = SRMC = SRAC = LRAC$ and profits are zero. In fact, because costs and tastes are in a constant state of flux, very few industries ever really get there. The economy is always changing. There are always some firms making profits and some firms suffering losses.

This, then, is a story about tendencies:

> Investment—in the form of new firms and expanding old firms—will over time tend to favor those industries in which profits are being made, and over time industries in which firms are suffering losses will gradually contract from disinvestment.

OUTPUT MARKETS: A FINAL WORD

In the last four chapters, we have been building a model of a simple market system under the assumption of perfect competition. Let us provide just one more example to review the actual response of a competitive system to a change in consumer preferences.

Over the past two decades, Americans have developed a taste for wine in general and for California wines in particular. We know that household demand is constrained by income, wealth, and prices, and that income is (at least in part) determined by the choices that households make. Within these constraints, households increasingly choose—or demand—wine. The demand curve for wine has shifted to the right, causing excess demand followed by an increase in price.

With higher prices, wine producers find themselves earning positive profits. *This increase in price and consequent rise in profits is the basic signal that leads to a reallocation of society's resources.* In the short run, wine producers are constrained by their current scales of operation. California has only a limited number of vineyards and only a limited amount of vat capacity, for example.

In the long run, however, we would expect to see resources flow in to compete for these profits, and this is exactly what happens. New firms enter the wine-producing business. New vines are planted and new vats and production equipment are purchased and put in place. Vineyard owners move into new states—Rhode Island, Texas, and Maryland—and established growers increase production. Overall, more wine is produced to meet the new consumer demand. At the same time, competition is forcing firms to operate using the most efficient technology available.

What starts as a shift in preferences thus ends up as a shift in resources. Land is reallocated and labor moves into wine production. All this is accomplished without any central planning or direction.

You have now seen what lies behind the demand curves and supply curves in competitive output markets. The next two chapters take up competitive *input* markets and complete the picture.

SUMMARY

1. For any firm, one of three conditions holds at any given moment: (1) The firm is earning positive profits, (2) the firm is suffering losses, or (3) the firm is just breaking even—that is, earning a normal rate of return and thus zero profits.

SHORT-RUN CONDITIONS AND LONG-RUN DIRECTIONS

2. A firm that is earning positive profits in the short run and expects to continue doing so has an incentive to expand in the long run. Profits also provide an incentive for new firms to enter the industry.

3. In the short run, firms suffering losses are stuck in the industry. They can shut down operations ($q = 0$), but they must still bear fixed costs. In the long run, firms suffering losses can exit the industry.

4. A firm's decision about whether to shut down in the short run depends solely on whether its revenues from operating are sufficient to cover its variable costs. If revenues exceed variable costs, the *operating profits* can be used to pay some fixed costs and thus reduce losses.

5. Any time that price is below the minimum point on the average variable cost curve, total revenue will be less than

total variable cost, operating profit will be negative, and the firm will shut down. The minimum point on the average variable cost curve (which is also the point where marginal cost and average variable cost intersect) is called the *shut-down point*. At all prices above the shut-down point, the *MC* curve shows the profit-maximizing level of output. At all prices below it, optimal short-run output is zero.

6. The *short-run supply curve* of a firm in a perfectly competitive industry is the portion of its marginal cost curve that lies above its average variable cost curve.

7. Two things can cause the industry supply curve to shift: (1) in the short run, anything that causes marginal costs to change across the industry, such as an increase in the price of a particular input; and (2) in the long run, entry or exit of firms.

LONG-RUN COSTS: ECONOMIES AND DISECONOMIES OF SCALE

8. When an increase in a firm's scale of production leads to lower average costs, the firm exhibits *increasing returns to scale*, or *economies of scale*. When average costs do not

change with the scale of production, the firm exhibits *constant returns to scale*. When an increase in a firm's scale of production leads to higher average costs, the firm exhibits *decreasing returns to scale*, or *diseconomies of scale*.

9. A firm's *long-run average cost curve* (*LRAC*) shows the costs associated with different scales on which it can choose to operate in the long run.

LONG-RUN ADJUSTMENTS TO SHORT-RUN CONDITIONS

10. When short-run profits exist in an industry, firms will enter and existing firms will expand. These events shift the industry supply curve to the right. When this happens, price falls and ultimately profits are eliminated.

11. When short-run losses are suffered in an industry, some firms exit and some firms reduce scale. These events shift the industry supply curve to the left, raising price and eliminating losses.

12. *Long-run competitive equilibrium* is reached when $P = SRMC = SRAC = LRAC$ and profits are zero.

13. In efficient markets investment capital flows toward profit opportunities.

REVIEW TERMS AND CONCEPTS

breaking even, 188

constant returns to scale, 195

decreasing returns to scale, or diseconomies of scale, 195

increasing returns to scale, or economies of scale, 194

long-run average cost curve (*LRAC*), 196

long-run competitive equilibrium, 204

operating profit (or loss) or net operating revenue, 190

optimal scale of plant, 200

short-run industry supply curve, 192

shut-down point, 192

long-run competitive equilibrium, $P = SRMC = SRAC = LRAC$

PROBLEM SET

1. For each of the following say whether you agree or disagree and explain your answer:
   a. Firms that exhibit constant returns to scale have U-shaped long-run average cost curves.
   b. A firm suffering losses in the short run will continue to operate as long as total revenue will at least cover fixed cost.

2. Ajax is a competitive firm operating under the following conditions: Price of output is $5, the profit-maximizing level of output is 20,000 units of output, and the total cost (full economic cost) of producing 20,000 units is $120,000. The firm's *only* fixed factor of production is a $300,000 stock of capital (a building). If the interest rate available on comparable risks is 10 percent, should this firm shut down immediately in the short run?

3. Explain why it is possible that a firm with a production function that exhibits increasing returns to scale can run into diminishing returns at the same time.

4. Which of the following industries do you think are likely to exhibit large economies of scale? Explain why in each case.
   a. Home building
   b. Electric power generation
   c. Vegetable farming

   d. Software development
   e. Aircraft manufacturing

5. For cases *A* through *F* below, would you (1) operate or shut down in the short run, and (2) expand your plant or exit the industry in the long run?

	A	B	C	D	E	F
Total revenue	1,500	2,000	2,000	5,000	5,000	5,000
Total cost	1,500	1,500	2,500	6,000	7,000	4,000
Total fixed cost	500	500	200	1,500	1,500	1,500

6. Do you agree or disagree with the following statements? Explain why in a sentence or two.
   a. A firm will never sell its product for less than it costs to produce it.
   b. If the short-run marginal cost curve is U-shaped, the long-run average cost curve is likely to be U-shaped as well.

7. The Smythe chicken farm outside of Little Rock, Arkansas, produces 25,000 chickens per month. Total cost of production at the Smythe Farm is $28,000. Down the road are two other farms. The Faubus Farm produces 55,000 chickens a month

and total cost is $50,050. Mega Farm produces 100,000 chickens per month at a total cost of $91,000. These data suggest that there are significant economies of scale in chicken production. Do you agree or disagree with this statement? Explain your answer.

8. Indicate whether you agree or disagree with each of the following statements. Briefly explain your answers.
   a. Firms that exhibit constant returns to scale have U-shaped long-run average cost curves.
   b. The supply curve of a competitive firm in the short run is its marginal cost curve above average total cost.
   c. A firm suffering losses in the short run will continue to operate as long as total revenue will at least cover fixed cost.

9. You are given the following cost data:

q	TFC	TVC
0	12	0
1	12	5
2	12	9
3	12	14
4	12	20
5	12	28
6	12	38

If the price of output is $7, how many units of output will this firm produce? What is the total revenue? What is the total cost? Will the firm operate or shut down in the short run, and in the long run? Briefly explain your answers.

10. In the box on page 198, data were presented showing a substantial decline in the number of banks in the United States between 1985 and 2004. Go to the Web site of the Federal Deposit Insurance Corporation (**www.fdic.gov**) and click on "Industry Analysis." Explore the data presented there to determine if the trend toward mergers and larger banks has continued since 2004. If you have a bank account, is it at a large national bank with many branches or is it at a small bank? As a customer of a bank, what advantages or disadvantages do you find associated with its size? Do you think that economies of scale exist in banking?

11. The following problem traces the relationship between firm decisions, market supply, and market equilibrium in a perfectly competitive market.
   a. Complete the following table for a single firm in the short run:

OUTPUT	TFC	TVC	TC	AVC	ATC	MC
0	$300	$ 0	—	—	—	—
1	—	100	—	—	—	—
2	—	150	—	—	—	—
3	—	210	—	—	—	—
4	—	290	—	—	—	—
5	—	400	—	—	—	—
6	—	540	—	—	—	—
7	—	720	—	—	—	—
8	—	950	—	—	—	—
9	—	1,240	—	—	—	—
10	—	1,600	—	—	—	—

   b. Using the information in the table, fill in the following supply schedule for this individual firm under perfect competition, and indicate profit (positive or negative) at each output level. (*Hint:* At each hypothetical price, what is the MR of produc-

ing one more unit of output? Combine this with the MC of another unit to figure out the quantity supplied.)

PRICE	QUANTITY SUPPLIED	PROFIT
$50	$\frac{2}{3}$	—
70	—	—
100	—	—
130	—	—
170	—	—
220	—	—
280	—	—
350	—	—

   c. Now suppose there are 100 firms in this industry, all with identical cost schedules. Fill in the market quantity supplied at each price in this market:

PRICE	MARKET QUANTITY SUPPLIED	MARKET QUANTITY DEMANDED
$50	—	1,000
70	—	900
100	—	800
130	—	700
170	—	600
220	—	500
280	—	400
350	—	300

   d. Fill in the blanks: From the market supply and demand schedules in c., the equilibrium market price for this good is _____ and the equilibrium market quantity is _____. Each firm will produce a quantity of _____ and earn a _____ (profit/loss) equal to _____.
   e. In d., your answers characterize the short-run equilibrium in this market. Do they characterize the long-run equilibrium as well? If yes, explain why. If no, explain why not (that is, what would happen in the long run to change the equilibrium, and why?).

*12. Assume that you are hired as an analyst at a major New York consulting firm. Your first assignment is to do an industry analysis of the tribble industry. After extensive research and two all-nighters, you have obtained the following information.
   ■ *Long-run costs*:
     Capital costs: $5 per unit of output
     Labor costs: $2 per unit of output
   ■ No economies or diseconomies of scale
   ■ Industry currently earning a normal return to capital (profit of zero)
   ■ Industry perfectly competitive, with each of 100 firms producing the same amount of output
   ■ *Total industry output*: 1.2 million tribbles
   Demand for tribbles is expected to grow rapidly over the next few years to a level twice as high as it is now, but (due to short-run diminishing returns) each of the 100 existing firms is likely to be producing only 50 percent more.
   a. Sketch the long-run cost curve of a representative firm.
   b. Show the current conditions by drawing two diagrams, one showing the industry and one showing a representative firm.
   c. Sketch the increase in demand and show how the industry is likely to respond in the short run and in the long run.

_____
*Note: Problems marked with an asterisk are more challenging.

APPENDIX

EXTERNAL ECONOMIES AND DISECONOMIES AND THE LONG-RUN INDUSTRY SUPPLY CURVE

Sometimes average costs increase or decrease with the size of the industry, in addition to responding to changes in the size of the firm itself. When long-run average costs decrease as a result of industry growth, we say that there are **external economies**. When average costs increase as a result of industry growth, we say that there are **external diseconomies**. (Remember the distinction between internal and external economies: *Internal* economies of scale are found within firms, whereas *external* economies occur on an industry-wide basis.)

The expansion of the home building sector of the economy between 2000 and 2005 illustrates how external diseconomies of scale arise and how they imply a rising long-run average cost curve.

Beginning in year 2000, the overall economy suffered a slowdown as the dot-com exuberance turned to a bursting stock market bubble, and the events of 9/11/2001 raised the specter of international terrorism.

One sector, however, came alive between the years 2000 and 2005: housing. Very low interest rates lowered the monthly cost of home ownership, immigration increased the number of households, millions of baby boomers traded up and bought second homes, and investors who had been burned by the stock market bust turned to housing as a "real" asset.

All of this increased the demand for single-family homes and condominiums around the country. Table 9A.1 shows what happened to house prices, output, and the costs of inputs during the first 5 years of the decade.

First, house prices began to rise faster than other prices while the cost of construction materials stayed flat. Profitability in the home building sector took off. Next, as existing builders expanded their operations, new firms started

up. The number of new housing units "started" stood at just over 1.5 million annually in 2000 and then rose to over 2 million by 2005. All of this put pressure on the prices of construction materials like lumber and wall board. The table shows that construction materials costs rose more than 8 percent in 2004. These input prices increased the costs of home building. The expanding *industry* caused external diseconomies of scale.

THE LONG-RUN INDUSTRY SUPPLY CURVE

Recall that long-run competitive equilibrium is achieved when entering firms responding to profits or exiting firms fleeing from losses drive price to a level that just covers long-run average costs. Profits are zero, and $P = LRAC = SRAC = SRMC$. At this point, individual firms are operating at the most efficient scale of plant—that is, at the minimum point on their $LRAC$ curve.

As we saw in the text, long-run equilibrium is not easily achieved. Even if a firm or an industry does achieve long-run equilibrium, it will not remain at that point indefinitely. Economies are dynamic. As population and the stock of capital grow, and as preferences and technology change, some sectors will expand and some will contract. How do industries adjust to long-term changes? The answer depends on both internal and external factors.

The extent of *internal* economies (or diseconomies) determines the shape of a firm's long-run average cost curve ($LRAC$). If a firm changes its scale and either expands or contracts, its average costs will increase, decrease, or stay the same *along* the $LRAC$ curve. Recall that the $LRAC$ curve shows the relationship between a firm's output (q) and average total cost (ATC). A firm enjoying internal economies will see costs decreasing as it expands its scale; a firm facing internal diseconomies will see costs increasing as it expands its scale.

TABLE 9A.1 Construction of New Housing and Construction Materials Costs, 2000–2005

YEAR	HOUSE PRICES % OVER THE PREVIOUS YEAR	HOUSING STARTS (thousands)	HOUSING STARTS % CHANGE OVER THE PREVIOUS YEAR	CONSTRUCTION MATERIALS PRICES % CHANGE OVER THE PREVIOUS YEAR	CONSUMER PRICES % CHANGE OVER THE PREVIOUS YEAR
2000	–	1,573	–	–	–
2001	7.5	1,661	56%	0%	2.8%
2002	7.5	1,710	2.9%	1.5%	1.5%
2003	7.9	1,853	8.4%	1.6%	2.3%
2004	12.0	1,949	5.2%	8.3%	2.7%
2005	13.0	2,053	5.3%	5.4%	2.5%

Source: Economy.com and the Office of Federal Housing Enterprise Oversight (OFHEO).

However, external economies and diseconomies have nothing to do with the size of *individual* firms in a competitive market. Because individual firms in perfectly competitive industries are very small relative to the market, other firms are affected only minimally when an individual firm changes its output or scale of operation. *External* economies and diseconomies arise from industry expansions; that is, they arise when many firms increase their output simultaneously or when new firms enter an industry. If industry expansion causes costs to increase (external diseconomies), the *LRAC* curves facing individual firms shift upward; costs increase regardless of the level of output finally chosen by the firm. Similarly, if industry expansion causes costs to decrease (external economies), the *LRAC* curves facing individual firms shift downward; costs decrease at all potential levels of output.

An example of an expanding industry facing external economies is illustrated in Figure 9A.1. Initially, the industry and the representative firm are in long-run competitive equilibrium at the price P_0 determined by the intersection of the initial demand curve D_0 and the initial supply curve S_0. P_0 is the long-run equilibrium price; it intersects the initial long-run average cost curve ($LRAC_0$) at its minimum point. At this point, economic profits are zero.

Let us assume that as time passes, demand increases—that is, the demand curve shifts to the right from D_0 to D_1. This increase in demand will push price all the way to P_1. Without drawing the short-run cost curves, we know that economic profits now exist and that firms are likely to enter the industry to

compete for them. In the absence of external economies or diseconomies, firms would enter the industry, shifting the supply curve to the right and driving price back to the bottom of the long-run average cost curve, where profits are zero. Nevertheless, the industry in Figure 9A.1 enjoys external economies. As firms enter and the industry expands, costs decrease; and as the supply curve shifts to the right from S_0 toward S_1, the long-run average cost curve shifts downward to $LRAC_2$. Thus, to reach the new long-run equilibrium level of price and output, the supply curve must shift all the way to S_1. Only when the supply curve reaches S_1 is price driven down to the new equilibrium price of P_2, the minimum point on the *new* long-run average cost curve.

Presumably, further expansion would lead to even greater savings because the industry encounters external economies. The dashed line in Figure 9A.1(a) that traces out price and total output over time as the industry expands is called the **long-run industry supply curve (LRIS)**. When an industry enjoys external economies, its long-run supply curve slopes down. Such an industry is called a **decreasing-cost industry**.

Figure 9A.2 shows the long-run industry supply curve for an industry that faces external *diseconomies*. (These were suffered in the construction industry, you will recall, when increased house-building activity drove up lumber prices.) As demand expands from D_0 to D_1, price is driven up from P_0 to P_1. In response to the resulting higher profits, firms enter, shifting the short-run supply schedule to the right and driving price down. However, this time, as the industry expands, the long-run average cost curve shifts up to $LRAC_2$ as a result of

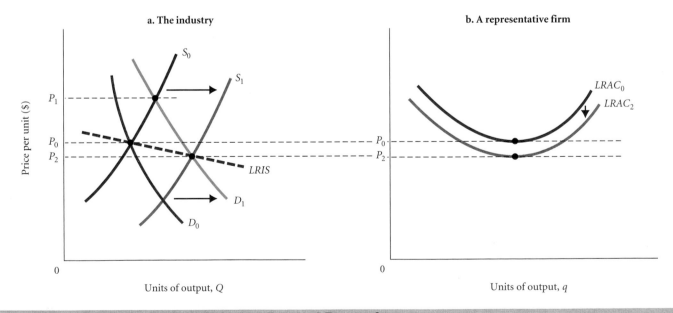

a. The industry   b. A representative firm

FIGURE 9A.1 A Decreasing-Cost Industry: External Economies

In a decreasing-cost industry, average cost declines as the industry expands. As demand expands from D_0 to D_1, price rises from P_0 to P_1. As new firms enter and existing firms expand, supply shifts from S_0 to S_1, driving price down. If costs decline as a result of the expansion to $LRAC_2$, the final price will be below P_0 at P_2. The long-run industry supply curve (*LRIS*) slopes downward in a decreasing-cost industry.

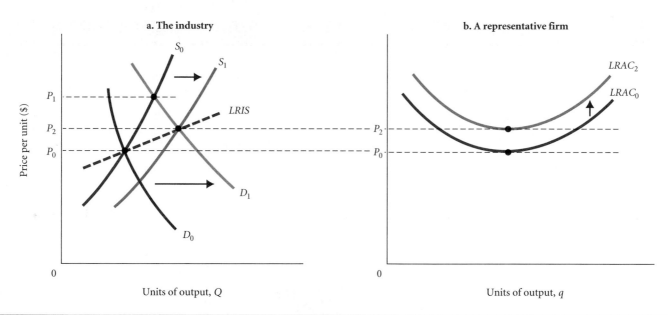

FIGURE 9A.2 An Increasing-Cost Industry: External Diseconomies

In an increasing-cost industry, average cost increases as the industry expands. As demand shifts from D_0 to D_1, price rises from P_0 to P_1. As new firms enter and existing firms expand output, supply shifts from S_0 to S_1, driving price down. If long-run average costs rise as a result to $LRAC_2$, the final price will be P_2. The long-run industry supply curve ($LRIS$) slopes up in an increasing-cost industry.

external diseconomies. Now, price has to fall back only to P_2 (the minimum point on $LRAC_2$), not all the way to P_0, to eliminate economic profits. This type of industry, whose long-run industry supply curve slopes up to the right, is called an **increasing-cost industry**.

It should not surprise you to know that industries in which there are no external economies or diseconomies of scale have flat, or horizontal, long-run industry supply curves. These industries are called **constant-cost industries**.

SUMMARY

EXTERNAL ECONOMIES AND DISECONOMIES

1. When long-run average costs decrease as a result of industry growth, we say that the industry exhibits *external economies*. When long-run average costs increase as a result of industry growth, we say that the industry exhibits *external diseconomies*.

THE LONG-RUN INDUSTRY SUPPLY CURVE

2. The *long-run industry supply curve* (*LRIS*) is a graph that traces out price and total output over time as an industry

expands. A *decreasing-cost industry* is one in which average costs fall as the industry expands. It exhibits external economies, and its long-run industry supply curve slopes downward. An *increasing-cost industry* is one in which average costs rise as the industry expands. It exhibits external diseconomies, and its long-run industry supply curve slopes upward. A *constant-cost industry* is one that shows no external economies or diseconomies as the industry grows. Its long-run industry supply curve is horizontal, or flat.

REVIEW TERMS AND CONCEPTS

constant-cost industry An industry that shows no economies or diseconomies of scale as the industry grows. Such industries have flat, or horizontal, long-run supply curves. 209

decreasing-cost industry An industry that realizes external economies—that is, average costs decrease as the industry grows. The

long-run supply curve for such an industry has a negative slope. 208

external economies and **diseconomies** When industry growth results in a decrease of long-run average costs, there are *external economies*; when industry growth results in an increase of long-run average costs, there are *external diseconomies*. 207

increasing-cost industry An industry that encounters external diseconomies—that is, average costs increase as the industry grows. The long-run supply curve for such an industry has a positive slope. 209

long-run industry supply curve (*LRIS*) A graph that traces out price and total output over time as an industry expands. 208

PROBLEM SET

1. In deriving the short-run industry supply curve (the sum of firms' marginal cost curves), we assumed that input prices are constant because competitive firms are price-takers. This same assumption holds in the derivation of the long-run industry supply curve. Do you agree or disagree? Explain.

2. Consider an industry that exhibits external diseconomies of scale. Suppose that over the next 10 years, demand for that industry's product increases rapidly. Describe in detail the adjustments likely to follow. Use diagrams in your answer.

3. A representative firm producing cloth is earning a normal profit at a price of $10 per yard. Draw a supply and demand diagram showing equilibrium at this price. Assuming that the industry is a constant-cost industry, use the diagram to show the long-term adjustment of the industry as demand grows over time. Explain the adjustment mechanism.

Input Demand: The Labor and Land Markets

10

As we have seen, all business firms must make three decisions: (1) how much to produce and supply in output markets; (2) how to produce that output— that is, which technology to use; and (3) how much of each input to demand. So far, our discussion of firm behavior has focused on the first two questions. In Chapters 7 through 9, we explained how profit-maximizing firms choose among alternative technologies and decide how much to supply in output markets.

We now turn to the behavior of firms in perfectly competitive *input* markets, going behind input demand curves in much the same way that we went behind output supply curves in the previous two chapters. When we look behind input demand curves, we discover the exact same set of decisions that we saw when we analyzed output supply curves. In a very real sense, we have already talked about everything covered in this chapter. It is the *perspective* that is new.

The three main inputs are labor, land, and capital. Transactions in the labor and land markets are fairly straightforward. Households supply their labor to firms that demand it in exchange for a salary or a wage. Landowners sell or rent land to others. Capital markets are a bit more complex but are conceptually very similar. Households supply the resources used for the production of capital by saving and giving up present consumption. Savings flow through financial markets to firms that use these savings to procure capital to be used in production. Households receive interest, dividends, or profits in exchange. This chapter discusses input markets in general; the next chapter focuses on the capital market in some detail. Figure 10.1 outlines the interactions of households and firms in the labor and capital markets.

INPUT MARKETS: BASIC CONCEPTS

Before we begin our discussion of input markets, it will be helpful to establish some basic concepts: derived demand, complementary and substitutable inputs, diminishing returns, and marginal revenue product.

DEMAND FOR INPUTS: A *DERIVED* DEMAND

A firm cannot make a profit unless there is a demand for its product. Households must be willing to pay for the firm's output. The quantity of output that a firm produces (in both the long run and the short run) thus depends on the value placed by the market on the firm's

Output supply

Goods and Services markets

P

Q

**Output
(product) markets**

Output demand

Firms

Households

Labor demand

Labor supply

Labor market

W

L

Savings
(capital supply)

Investment
(capital demand)

Capital market
(financial markets)

r

K

Input markets

Capital stock

Wealth

FIGURE 10.1 Firm and Household Decisions

Firms and households interact in both input and output markets. This chapter highlights firm choices in input markets.

derived demand The
demand for resources (inputs)
that is dependent on the demand
for the outputs those resources
can be used to produce.

productivity of an input
The amount of output produced
per unit of that input.

product. This means that demand for inputs depends on the demand for outputs. In other words, input demand is **derived** from output demand.

The value attached to a product and the inputs needed to produce that product define the input's productivity. Formally, the **productivity of an input** is the amount of output produced per unit of that input. When a large amount of output is produced per unit of an input, the input is said to exhibit *high productivity*. When only a small amount of output is produced per unit of the input, the input is said to exhibit *low productivity*.

Inputs are demanded by a firm if and only if households demand the good or service produced by that firm.

Prices in competitive input markets depend on firms' demand for inputs, households' supply of inputs, and interaction between the two. In the labor market, for example, households must decide whether to work and how much to work. In Chapter 6 we saw that the opportunity cost of working for a wage is either leisure or the value derived from unpaid labor—working in the garden, for instance, or raising children. In general, firms will demand workers as long as the value of what those workers produce exceeds what they must be paid. Households will supply labor as long as the wage they receive exceeds the value of leisure or the value that they derive from nonpaid work.

INPUTS: COMPLEMENTARY AND SUBSTITUTABLE

Inputs can be *complementary* or *substitutable*. Two inputs used together may enhance, or complement, each other. For example, a new machine is often useless without someone to run it. Machines can also be substituted for labor, or—less often perhaps—labor can be substituted for machines.

All this means that a firm's input demands are tightly linked to one another. An increase or decrease in wages naturally causes the demand for labor to change, but it may also have an effect on the demand for capital or land. If we are to understand the demand for inputs, therefore, we must understand the connections among labor, capital, and land.

DIMINISHING RETURNS

Recall that the short run is the period during which some fixed factor of production limits a firm's capacity to expand. Under these conditions, the firm that decides to increase output will eventually encounter diminishing returns. Stated more formally, a fixed scale of plant means that the marginal product of variable inputs eventually declines.

Recall also that **marginal product of labor (MP_L)** is the additional output produced if a firm hires one additional unit of labor. For example, if a firm pays for 400 hours of labor per week—10 workers working 40 hours each—and asks 1 worker to stay an extra hour, the product of the 401st hour is the marginal product of labor for that firm.

marginal product of labor (MP_L) The additional output produced by one additional unit of labor.

In Chapter 7, we talked at some length about declining marginal product at a sandwich shop. The first two columns of Table 10.1 reproduce some of the production data from that shop. You may remember that the shop has only one grill, at which only two or three people can work comfortably. In this example, the grill is the fixed factor of production in the short run. Labor is the variable factor. The first worker can produce 10 sandwiches per hour, and the second can produce 15 (see column 3 of Table 10.1). The second worker can produce more because the first is busy answering the phone and taking care of customers, as well as making sandwiches. After the second worker, however, marginal product declines. The third worker adds only 10 sandwiches per hour, because the grill gets crowded. The fourth worker can squeeze in quickly while the others are serving or wrapping, but adds only 5 additional sandwiches each hour, and so forth.

In this case, the grill's capacity ultimately limits output. To see how the firm might make a rational choice about how many workers to hire, we need to know more about the value of the firm's product and the cost of labor.

MARGINAL REVENUE PRODUCT

The **marginal revenue product (MRP)** of a variable input is the additional revenue a firm earns by employing one additional unit of that input, *ceteris paribus*. If labor is the variable factor, for example, hiring an additional unit will lead to added output (the *marginal product* of labor). The sale of that added output will yield revenue. *Marginal revenue product* is the revenue

marginal revenue product (MRP) The additional revenue a firm earns by employing one additional unit of input, *ceteris paribus*.

TABLE 10.1 Marginal Revenue Product per Hour of Labor in Sandwich Production (One Grill)				
(1) TOTAL LABOR UNITS (EMPLOYEES)	**(2)** TOTAL PRODUCT (SANDWICHES PER HOUR)	**(3)** MARGINAL PRODUCT OF LABOR (MP_L) (SANDWICHES PER HOUR)	**(4)** PRICE (P_X) (VALUE ADDED PER SANDWICH)[a]	**(5)** MARGINAL REVENUE PRODUCT ($MP_L \times P_X$) (PER HOUR)
0	0	—	—	—
1	10	10	$0.50	$5.00
2	25	15	0.50	7.50
3	35	10	0.50	5.00
4	40	5	0.50	2.50
5	42	2	0.50	1.00
6	42	0	0.50	0

[a]The "price" is essentially profit per sandwich; see discussion in text.

produced by selling the good or service that is produced by the marginal unit of labor. In a competitive firm, marginal revenue product is the value of a factor's marginal product.

By using labor as our variable factor, we can state this proposition more formally by saying that if MP_L is the marginal product of labor and P_X is the price of output, then the marginal revenue product of labor is:

$$MRP_L = MP_L \times P_X$$

When calculating marginal revenue product, we need to be precise about what is being produced. A sandwich shop, to be sure, sells sandwiches, but it does not produce the bread, meat, cheese, mustard, and mayonnaise that go into the sandwiches. What the shop is pro-

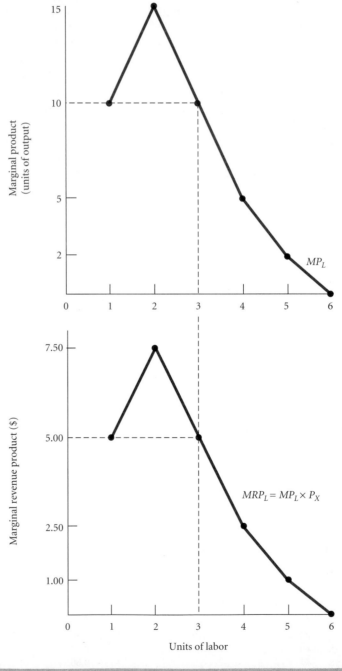

FIGURE 10.2 Deriving a Marginal Revenue Product Curve from Marginal Product

The marginal revenue product of labor is the price of output, P_X, times the marginal product of labor, MP_L.

ducing is "sandwich cooking and assembly services." The shop is "adding value" to the meat, bread, and other ingredients by preparing and putting them all together in ready-to-eat form. With this in mind, let us assume that each finished sandwich in our shop sells for $0.50 over and above the costs of its ingredients. Thus, the *price of the service* the shop is selling is $0.50 per sandwich, and the only variable cost of providing that service is that of the labor used to put the sandwiches together. Thus, if X is the product of our shop, $P_X = \$0.50$.

Table 10.1, column 5, calculates the marginal revenue product of each worker if the shop charges $0.50 per sandwich over and above the costs of its ingredients. The first worker produces 10 sandwiches per hour, which, at $0.50 each, generates revenues of $5 per hour. The addition of a second worker yields $7.50 an hour in revenues. After the second worker, diminishing returns drive MRP_L down. The marginal revenue product of the third worker is $5 per hour, of the fourth worker is only $2.50, and so forth.

Figure 10.2 graphs the data from Table 10.1. Notice that the marginal revenue product curve has the same downward slope as the marginal product curve, but that MRP is measured in dollars, not units of output. The MRP curve shows the dollar value of labor's marginal product.

LABOR MARKETS

Let us begin our discussion of input markets simply by discussing a firm that uses only one variable factor of production.

A FIRM USING ONLY ONE VARIABLE FACTOR OF PRODUCTION: LABOR

Demand for an input depends on that input's marginal revenue product and its unit cost, or price. The price of labor, for example, is the wage determined in the labor market. (At this point we are continuing to assume that the sandwich shop uses only one variable factor of production—labor. Remember that competitive firms are price-takers in both output and input markets. Such firms can hire all the labor they want to hire as long as they pay the market wage.) We can think of the hourly wage at the sandwich shop as the marginal cost of a unit of labor.

A profit-maximizing firm will add inputs—in the case of labor, it will hire workers—as long as the marginal revenue product of that input exceeds the market price of that input—in the case of labor, the wage.

Look again at the figures for the sandwich shop in Table 10.1, column 5. Now suppose that the going wage for sandwich makers is $4 per hour. A profit-maximizing firm would hire three workers. The first worker would yield $5 per hour in revenues and the second would yield $7.50, but they each would cost only $4 per hour. The third worker would bring in $5 per hour, but still cost only $4 in marginal wages. The marginal product of the fourth worker, however, would not bring in enough revenue ($2.50) to pay this worker's salary. Total profit is thus maximized by hiring three workers.

Figure 10.3 presents this same concept graphically. The labor market appears in Figure 10.3(a); Figure 10.3(b) shows a single firm that employs workers. This firm, incidentally, does not represent just the firms in a single industry. Because firms in many different industries demand labor, the representative firm in Figure 10.3(b) represents any firm in any industry that uses labor.

The firm faces a market wage rate of $10. We can think of this as the marginal cost of a unit of labor. (Note that we are now discussing the margin in units of *labor*; in previous chapters, we talked about marginal units of *output*.) Given a wage of $10, how much labor would the firm demand?

One might think that 100 units would be hired, the point at which the difference between marginal revenue product and wage rate is greatest. However, the firm is interested in maximizing *total* profit, not *marginal* profit. Hiring the 101st unit of labor generates $20 in revenue at a cost of only $10. Because MRP_L is greater than the cost of the input required

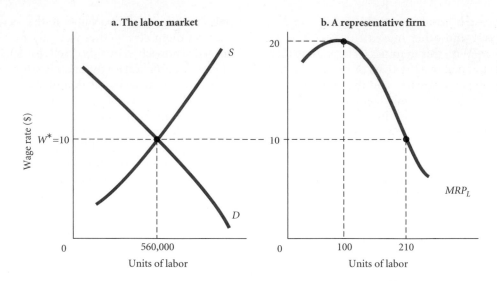

FIGURE 10.3 Marginal Revenue Product and Factor Demand for a Firm Using One Variable Input (Labor)

A competitive firm using only one variable factor of production will use that factor as long as its marginal revenue product exceeds its unit cost. A perfectly competitive firm will hire labor as long as MRP_L is greater than the going wage, W^*. The hypothetical firm will demand 210 units of labor.

to produce it, hiring one more unit of labor adds to profit. This will continue to be true as long as MRP_L remains above $10, which is all the way to 210 units. At that point, the wage rate is equal to the marginal revenue product of labor, or:

$$W^* = MRP_L = 10$$

The firm will not demand labor beyond 210 units, because the cost of hiring the 211th unit of labor would be greater than the value of what that unit produces. (Recall that the fourth sandwich maker can produce only an extra $2.50 an hour in sandwiches, while receiving a salary of $4 per hour.)

Thus the curve in Figure 10.3(b) tells us how much labor a firm that uses only one variable factor of production will hire at each potential market wage rate. If the market wage falls, the quantity of labor demanded will rise. If the market wage rises, the quantity of labor demanded will fall. This description should sound familiar to you—it is, in fact, the description of a demand curve. Therefore we can now say that

> When a firm uses only one variable factor of production, that factor's marginal revenue product curve is the firm's demand curve for that factor in the short run.

For another example of the relevance of marginal revenue product, see the News Analysis box, "Baseball Salaries and Marginal Revenue Product in 2005."

Comparing Marginal Revenue and Marginal Cost to Maximize Profits

In Chapter 8, we saw that a competitive firm's marginal cost curve is the same as its supply curve. That is, at any output price, the marginal cost curve determines how much output a profit-maximizing firm will produce. We came to this conclusion by comparing the marginal revenue that a firm would earn by producing one more unit of output with the marginal cost of producing that unit of output.

There is no difference between the reasoning in Chapter 8 and the reasoning in this chapter. The only difference is that what is being measured at the margin has changed. In Chapter 8, the firm was comparing the marginal revenues and costs of producing *another unit of output*. Here, the firm is comparing the marginal revenues and costs of employing *another unit of input*. To see this similarity, look at Figure 10.4. If the only variable factor of production is labor, the condition $W^* = MRP_L$ is the same condition as $P = MC$. The two statements say exactly the same thing.

Baseball Salaries and Marginal Revenue Product in 2005

THE HIGHEST-PAID PLAYER IN MAJOR league baseball in 2005 was Alex Rodriguez of the New York Yankees. He was paid $26.2 million. The question is, was he worth it? Did his performance bring enough revenue to the Yankees to essentially pay his salary? In economic terms, what was his marginal revenue product? Believe it or not, research suggests that many baseball players, even some with very high salaries, are paid less than their contribution to team revenues would suggest.

Alex Rodriguez signed a 10-year, $252 million contract with the Texas Rangers in 2000, making him the highest-salaried player in professional sports history. Rodriguez played his first major league baseball game at age 18 and became the starting shortstop for the Seattle Mariners at age 20. Nicknamed "A-Rod," he hit .358 with 36 homers in 1996, his first full season in the majors. His power, defensive skills, charisma, and fan-friendly Hispanic heritage made him an attractive free agent after the 2000 season, and Texas owner Tom Hicks signed Rodriguez to the unprecedented $252 million deal. Rodriguez played well for the Rangers (winning the American League MVP award in 2003), but the team finished last in its

Is Alex Rodriguez "worth" $26 million to the New York Yankees franchise?

division for three straight years, and some felt that Rodriguez's mammoth contract had hobbled the team. In 2004, Rodriguez was traded to the New York Yankees, where he moved to third base to play alongside Yankee shortstop Derek Jeter. In 2005, he was still the highest-paid player in the majors with an annual salary of $26.2 million.

In 2005, the New York Yankees had the highest payroll in baseball by a wide margin. The total salary of the 24 active-roster players was $205,938,439, an average of $8.6 million per player. Ten of the Yankees earned more than $10 million per year. The team with the lowest salary total in 2005 was the Kansas City Royals at $36.9 million, an average of a mere $1.5 million per player.

Sources:
http://who2.com/jeeves/alexrodriguez.html; May the Best Team Win: Baseball Economics and Public Policy *by Andrew Zimbalist, Brookings Institution, 2003; Andrea Marie Bell, "Are Professional Basketball Players Overpaid?" Thesis prepared for Honors in Economics, Wellesley College, 2003.*

In both cases, the firm is comparing the cost of production with potential revenues from the sale of product *at the margin.* In Chapter 8, the firm compared the price of output (*P*, which is equal to *MR* in perfect competition) directly with cost of production (*MC*), where cost was derived from information on factor prices and technology. (Review the derivation of cost curves in Chapter 8 if this is unclear.) Here, information on output price and technology is contained in the marginal revenue product curve, which is compared with information on input price to determine the optimal level of input to demand.

The assumption of one variable factor of production makes the trade-off facing firms easy to see. Figure 10.5 shows that in essence firms weigh the value of labor as reflected in the market wage against the value of the product of labor as reflected in the price of output.

Assuming that labor is the only variable input, if society values a good more than it costs firms to hire the workers to produce that good, the good will be produced. In general, the same logic also holds for more than one input. Firms weigh the value of outputs as reflected in output price against the value of inputs as reflected in marginal costs.

FIGURE 10.4 The Two Profit-Maximizing Conditions Are Simply Two Views of the Same Choice Process

Deriving Input Demands For the small sandwich shop, calculating the marginal product of a variable input (labor) and marginal revenue product was easy. Although it may be more complex, the decision process is essentially the same for both big corporations and small proprietorships.

When an airline hires more flight attendants, for example, it increases the quality of its service to attract more passengers and thus to sell more of its product. In deciding how many to hire, the airline must figure out how much new revenue the added flight attendants are likely to generate relative to their wages.

At the sandwich shop, diminishing returns set in at a certain point. The same holds true for an airplane. Once a sufficient number of attendants are on a plane, additional attendants add little to the quality of service, and beyond a certain level might even give rise to negative marginal product. The presence of too many attendants could bother the passengers and make it difficult to get to the restrooms.

In making your own decisions, you, too, compare marginal gains with input costs in the presence of diminishing returns. Suppose you grow vegetables in your yard. First, you save

FIGURE 10.5 The Trade-Off Facing Firms

Firms weigh the cost of labor as reflected in wage rates against the value of labor's marginal product. Assume that labor is the only variable factor of production. Then, if society values a good more than it costs firms to hire the workers to produce that good, the good will be produced.

money at the supermarket. Second, you can plant what you like, and the vegetables taste better fresh from the garden. Third, you simply like to work in the garden.

Like the sandwich shop and the airline, you also face diminishing returns. You have only 625 square feet of garden to work with, and with land as a fixed factor in the short run, your marginal product will certainly decline. You can work all day every day, but your limited space will produce only so many string beans. The first few hours you spend each week watering, fertilizing, and dealing with major weed and bug infestations probably have a high marginal product. However, after 5 or 6 hours, there is little else you can do to increase yield. Diminishing returns also apply to your sense of satisfaction. The farmers' markets are now full of cheap fresh produce that tastes nearly as good as yours. Once you have been out in the garden for a few hours, the hot sun and hard work start to lose their charm.

Although your gardening does not involve a salary (unlike the sandwich shop and the airline, which pay out wages), the labor you supply has a value that must be weighed. When the returns diminish beyond a certain point, you must weigh the value of additional gardening time against leisure and the other options available to you.

Less labor is likely to be employed as the cost of labor rises. If the competitive labor market pushed the daily wage to $6 per hour, the sandwich shop would hire only two workers instead of three (see Table 10.1). If you suddenly became very busy at school, your time would become more valuable, and you would probably devote fewer hours to gardening.

In the "new economy" there is a common example of what may seem to be an exception to the rule that workers will be hired only if the revenues they generate are equal to or greater than their wages. Many start-up companies pay salaries to workers before they begin to take in revenue. This has been particularly true for Internet start-ups in recent years. How does a company pay workers if it is not earning any revenues? The answer is that the entrepreneur, or the venture capital fund supporting the entrepreneur, is betting that the firm will earn substantial revenues in the future. Workers are hired because the entrepreneur expects that their current efforts will produce future revenues greater than their wage costs.

A FIRM EMPLOYING TWO VARIABLE FACTORS OF PRODUCTION IN THE SHORT AND LONG RUN

◀ Optional Material

When a firm employs more than one variable factor of production, the analysis of input demand becomes more complicated, but the principles stay the same. We shall now consider a firm that employs variable capital (K) and labor (L) inputs and thus faces factor prices P_K and P_L.[1] (Recall that *capital* refers to plant, equipment, and inventory used in production. We assume that some portion of the firm's capital stock is fixed in the short run, but that some of it is variable—for example, some machinery and equipment can be installed quickly.) Our analysis can be applied to any two factors of production and can easily be generalized to three or more. It can also be applied to the long run, when all factors of production are variable.

You have seen that inputs can be complementary or substitutable. Land, labor, and capital are used *together* to produce outputs. The worker who uses a shovel digs a bigger hole than one with no shovel. Add a steam shovel and that worker becomes even more productive. When an expanding firm adds to its stock of capital, it raises the productivity of its labor, and vice versa. Thus, each factor complements the other. At the same time, though, land, labor, and capital can also be *substituted* for one another. If labor becomes expensive, some labor-saving technology—robotics, for example—may take its place.

In firms employing just one variable factor of production, a change in the price of that factor affects only the demand for the factor itself. When more than one factor can vary, however, we must consider the impact of a change in one factor price on the demand for other factors as well.

Substitution and Output Effects of a Change in Factor Price Table 10.2 presents data on a hypothetical firm that employs variable capital and labor. Suppose that the firm faces a choice between two available technologies of production—technique *A*,

---

[1]The price of labor, P_L, is the same as the wage rate, W. We will often use the term P_L instead of W to stress the symmetry between labor and capital.

TABLE 10.2 Response of a Firm to an Increasing Wage Rate

TECHNOLOGY	INPUT REQUIREMENTS PER UNIT OF OUTPUT		UNIT COST IF $P_L = \$1$ $P_K = \$1$ $(P_L \times L) + (P_K \times K)$	UNIT COST IF $P_L = \$2$ $P_K = \$1$ $(P_L \times L) + (P_K \times K)$
	K	L		
A (capital intensive)	10	5	$15	$20
B (labor intensive)	3	10	$13	$23

which is capital-intensive, and technique B, which is labor-intensive. When the market price of labor is $1 per unit and the market price of capital is $1 per unit, the labor-intensive method of producing output is less costly. Each unit costs only $13 to produce using technique B, while the unit cost of production using technique A is $15. If the price of labor rises to $2, however, technique B is no longer less costly. Labor has become more expensive relative to capital. The unit cost rises to $23 for labor-intensive technique B, but to only $20 for capital-intensive technique A.

Table 10.3 shows the impact of such an increase in the price of labor on both capital and labor demand when a firm produces 100 units of output. When each input factor costs $1 per unit, the firm chooses technique B and demands 300 units of capital and 1,000 units of labor. Total variable cost is $1,300. An increase in the price of labor to $2 causes the firm to switch from technique B to technique A. In doing so, it *substitutes* capital for labor. The amount of labor demanded drops from 1,000 to 500 units. The amount of capital demanded increases from 300 to 1,000 units, while total variable cost increases to $2,000.

The tendency of firms to substitute away from a factor whose relative price has risen and toward a factor whose relative price has fallen is called the **factor substitution effect**. The factor substitution effect is part of the reason that *input demand curves slope downward*. When an input, or factor of production, becomes less expensive, firms tend to substitute it for other factors and thus buy *more* of it. When a particular input becomes more expensive, firms tend to substitute other factors and buy *less* of it.

The firm described in Tables 10.2 and 10.3 continued to produce 100 units of output after the wage rate doubled. An *increase* in the price of a production factor, however, also means an increase in the costs of production. Notice that total variable cost increased from $1,300 to $2,000. When a firm faces higher costs, it is likely to produce less in the short run. When a firm decides to decrease output, its demand for all factors declines—including, of course, the factor whose price increased in the first place. This is called the **output effect of a factor price increase**.

A *decrease* in the price of a factor of production, in contrast, means lower costs of production. If their output price remains unchanged, firms will increase output. This, in turn, means that demand for all factors of production will increase. This is the **output effect of a factor price decrease**.

The output effect helps explain why input demand curves slope downward. Output effects and factor substitution effects work in the same direction. Consider, for example, a

factor substitution effect The tendency of firms to substitute away from a factor whose price has risen and toward a factor whose price has fallen.

output effect of a factor price increase (decrease) When a firm decreases (increases) its output in response to a factor price increase (decrease), this decreases (increases) its demand for all factors.

TABLE 10.3 The Substitution Effect of an Increase in Wages on a Firm Producing 100 Units of Output

	To Produce 100 Units of Output		
	TOTAL CAPITAL DEMANDED	TOTAL LABOR DEMANDED	TOTAL VARIABLE COST
When $P_L = \$1, P_K = \$1$, firm uses technology B	300	1,000	$1,300
When $P_L = \$2, P_K = \$1$, firm uses technology A	1,000	500	$2,000

decline in the wage rate. Lower wages mean that a firm will substitute labor for capital and other inputs. Stated somewhat differently, the factor substitution effect leads to an increase in the quantity of labor demanded. Lower wages mean lower costs, and lower costs lead to more output. This increase in output means that the firm will hire more of all factors of production, including labor itself. This is the output effect of a factor price decrease. Notice that both effects lead to an increase in the quantity demanded for labor when the wage rate falls. ◄

MANY LABOR MARKETS

Although Figure 10.1 depicts "*the* labor market," many labor markets exist. There is a market for baseball players, for carpenters, for chemists, for college professors, and for unskilled workers. Still other markets exist for taxi drivers, assembly-line workers, secretaries, and corporate executives. Each market has a set of skills associated with it and a supply of people with the requisite skills.

> If labor markets are competitive, the wages in those markets are determined by the interaction of supply and demand. As we have seen, firms will hire workers only as long as the value of their product exceeds the relevant market wage. This is true in all competitive labor markets.

LAND MARKETS

Unlike labor and capital, land has a special feature that we have not yet considered: It is in strictly fixed (perfectly inelastic) supply in total. The only real questions about land thus center around how much it is worth and how it will be used.

Because land is fixed in supply, we say that its price is **demand determined**. In other words, the price of land is determined exclusively by what households and firms are willing to pay for it. The return to any factor of production in fixed supply is called a **pure rent**.

Thinking of the price of land as demand determined can be confusing because all land is not the same. Some land is clearly more valuable than other land. What lies behind these differences? As with any other factor of production, land will presumably be sold or rented to the user who is willing to pay the most for it. The value of land to a potential user may depend on the characteristics of the land itself or on its location. For example, more fertile land should produce more farm products per acre and thus command a higher price than less fertile land. A piece of property located at the intersection of two highways may be of great value as a site for a gas station because of the amount of traffic that passes the intersection daily.

A numerical example may help to clarify our discussion. Consider the potential uses of a corner lot in a suburb of Kansas City. Alan wants to build a clothing store on the lot. He anticipates that he can earn economic profits of $10,000 per year there because of the land's excellent location. Bella, another person interested in buying the corner lot, believes that she can earn $35,000 per year in economic profit if she builds a pharmacy there. Because of the higher profit that she expects to earn, Bella will be able to outbid Alan, and the landowner will sell (or rent) to the highest bidder.

Because location is often the key to profits, landowners are frequently able to "squeeze" their renters. One of the most popular locations in the Boston area, for example, is Harvard Square. There are dozens of restaurants in and around the square, and most of them are full most of the time. Despite this seeming success, most Harvard Square restaurant owners are not getting rich. Why? Because they must pay very high rents on the location of their restaurants. A substantial portion of each restaurant's revenues goes to rent the land that (by virtue of its scarcity) is the key to unlocking those same revenues.

Although Figure 10.6 shows that the supply of land is perfectly inelastic (a vertical line), the supply of land in a *given use* may not be perfectly inelastic or fixed. Think, for example, about farmland and land available for housing developments. As a city's population grows, housing developers find themselves willing to pay more and more for land. As land becomes more valuable for development, some farmers sell out, and the supply of land available for

demand determined price The price of a good that is in fixed supply; it is determined exclusively by what firms and households are willing to pay for the good.

pure rent The return to any factor of production that is in fixed supply.

FIGURE 10.6 The Rent on Land Is Demand Determined

Because land in general (and each parcel in particular) is in fixed supply, its price is demand determined. Graphically, a fixed supply is represented by a vertical, perfectly inelastic supply curve. Rent, R_0, depends exclusively on demand—what people are willing to pay.

development increases. This analysis would lead us to draw an upward-sloping supply curve (not a perfectly inelastic supply curve) for land in the land-for-development category.

Nonetheless, our major point—that land earns a pure rent—is still valid:

> The supply of land of a *given quality* at a *given location* is truly fixed in supply. Its value is determined exclusively by the amount that the highest bidder is willing to pay for it. Because land cannot be reproduced, supply is perfectly inelastic.

RENT AND THE VALUE OF OUTPUT PRODUCED ON LAND

Because the price of land is demand determined, rent depends on what the potential users of the land are willing to pay for it. As we have seen, land will end up being used by whoever is willing to pay the most for it. What determines this willingness to pay? Let us now connect our discussion of land markets with our earlier discussions of factor markets in general.

As our example of two potential users bidding for a plot of land shows, the bids depend on the land's potential for profit. Alan's plan would generate $10,000 a year; Bella's would generate $35,000 a year. Nevertheless, these profits do not just materialize. Instead, they come from producing and selling an output that is valuable to households. Land in a popular downtown location is expensive because of what can be produced on it. Note that land is needed as an input into the production of nearly all goods and services. A restaurant located next to a popular theater can charge a premium price because it has a relatively captive clientele. The restaurant must produce a quality product to stay in business, but the location alone provides a substantial profit opportunity.

It should come as no surprise that the demand for land follows the same rules as the demand for inputs in general. A profit-maximizing firm will employ an additional factor of production as long as its marginal revenue product exceeds its market price. For example, a profit-maximizing firm will hire labor as long as the revenue earned from selling labor's product is sufficient to cover the cost of hiring additional labor—which for perfectly competitive firms equals the wage rate. The same thing is true for land:

> A firm will pay for and use land as long as the revenue earned from selling the product produced on that land is sufficient to cover the price of the land. Stated in equation form, the firm will use land up to the point at which $MRP_A = P_A$, where A is land (acres).

The demand for land is a derived demand. Agricultural or even desert land will be developed when there is a demand for housing because land is a key input used in the production of housing.

Just as the demand curve for labor reflects the value of labor's product as determined in output markets, so the demand for land depends on the value of land's product in output markets. The profitability of the restaurant located next to the theater results from the fact that the meals produced there command a price in the marketplace.

The allocation of a given plot of land among competing uses thus depends on the trade-off between competing products that can be produced there. Agricultural land becomes developed when its value in producing housing or manufactured goods, or providing space for a minimall, exceeds its value in producing crops. A corner lot in Kansas City becomes the site of a pharmacy instead of a clothing store because the people in that neighborhood have a greater need for a pharmacy.

One final word about land: Because land cannot be moved physically, the value of any one parcel depends to a large extent on the uses to which adjoining parcels are put. A factory belching acrid smoke will probably reduce the value of adjoining land, while a new highway that increases accessibility may enhance it.

THE FIRM'S PROFIT-MAXIMIZATION CONDITION IN INPUT MARKETS

◀Optional Material

Thus far we have discussed the labor and land markets in some detail. Although we will put off a detailed discussion of capital until the next chapter, it is now possible to generalize about competitive demand for factors of production. Every firm has an incentive to use variable inputs as long as the revenue generated by those inputs covers the costs of those inputs at the margin. More formally, firms will employ each input up to the point that its price equals its marginal revenue product. This condition holds for all factors at all levels of output:

> Profit-maximizing condition for the perfectly competitive firm is
>
> $$P_L = MRP_L = (MP_L \times P_X)$$
> $$P_K = MRP_K = (MP_K \times P_X)$$
> $$P_A = MRP_A = (MP_A \times P_X)$$
>
> where L is labor, K is capital, A is land (acres), X is output, and P_X is the price of that output.

When all these conditions are met, the firm will be using the optimal, or least costly, combination of inputs. If all these conditions hold at the same time, it is possible to rewrite them in another way:

$$\frac{MP_L}{P_L} = \frac{MP_K}{P_K} = \frac{MP_A}{P_A} = \frac{1}{P_X}$$

Your intuition tells you much the same thing that these equations do: The marginal product of the last dollar spent on labor must be equal to the marginal product of the last dollar spent on capital, which must be equal to the marginal product of the last dollar spent on land, and so forth. If this were not the case, the firm could produce more with less and reduce cost. Suppose, for example, that $MP_L/P_L > MP_K/P_K$. In this situation, the firm can produce more output by shifting dollars out of capital and into labor. Hiring more labor drives down the marginal product of labor, and using less capital increases the marginal product of capital. This means that the ratios come back to equality as the firm shifts out of capital and into labor.

So far we have used very general terms to discuss the nature of input demand by firms in competitive markets, where input prices and output prices are taken as given. The most important point here is that demand for a factor depends on the value that the market places on its marginal product.[2] The rest of this chapter explores the forces that determine the shapes and positions of input demand curves. ◄

INPUT DEMAND CURVES

In Chapter 5, we considered the factors that influence the responsiveness, or elasticity, of output demand curves. We have not yet talked about *input* demand curves in any detail, however, and we now need to say more about what lies behind them.

SHIFTS IN FACTOR DEMAND CURVES

Factor (input) demand curves are derived from information on technology—that is, production functions—and output price (see Figure 10.4). A change in the demand for outputs, a change in the quantity of complementary or substitutable inputs, changes in the prices of other inputs, and technological change all can cause factor demand curves to shift. These shifts in demand are important because they directly affect the allocation of resources among alternative uses, as well as the level and distribution of income.

The Demand for Outputs A firm will demand an input as long as its marginal revenue product exceeds its market price. Marginal revenue product, which in perfect competition is equal to a factor's marginal product times the price of output, is the value of the factor's marginal product:

$$MRP_L = MP_L \times P_X$$

The amount that a firm is willing to pay for a factor of production depends directly on the value of the things that the firm produces. It follows that

> If product demand increases, product price will rise and marginal revenue product (factor demand) will increase—the *MRP* curve will shift to the right. If product demand declines, product price will fall and marginal revenue product (factor demand) will decrease—the *MRP* curve will shift to the left.

Go back and raise the price of sandwiches from $0.50 to $1 in the sandwich shop example examined in Table 10.1 to see that this is so.

To the extent that any input is used intensively in the production of some product, changes in the demand for that product cause factor demand curves to shift and the prices of those inputs to change. Land prices are a good example. Forty years ago, the area in Manhattan along the west side of Central Park from about 80th Street north was a run-down neighborhood full of abandoned houses. The value of land there was virtually zero. During the mid-1980s, increased demand for housing caused rents to hit record levels. Some single-room apartments, for example, rented for as much as $1,400 per month. With the higher price of output (rent), input prices increased substantially. Small buildings on 80th Street and Central Park West sold for well over a million dollars, and the value of the land figures very importantly in these building prices. In essence, a shift in demand for an output (housing in the area) pushed up the marginal revenue product of land from zero to very high levels.

---

[2]If you worked through the Appendix to Chapter 7, you saw this same condition derived graphically from an isocost/isoquant diagram. *Note:* $MP_L/P_L = MP_K/P_K \rightarrow MP_L/MP_K = P_L/P_K$.

The Quantity of Complementary and Substitutable Inputs   In our discussion thus far, we have kept coming back to the fact that factors of production complement one another. The productivity of, and thus the demand for, any one factor of production depends on the quality and quantity of the other factors with which it works.

The effect of capital accumulation on wages is one of the most important themes in all of economics. In general,

> The production and use of capital enhances the productivity of labor and normally increases the demand for labor and drives up wages.

Take as an example transportation. In a poor country like Bangladesh, one person with an ox cart can move a small load over bad roads very slowly. By contrast, the stock of capital used by workers in the transportation industry in the United States is enormous. A truck driver in the United States works with a substantial amount of capital. The typical 18-wheel tractor trailer, for example, is a piece of capital worth over $100,000. The roads themselves are capital that was put in place by the government. The amount of material that a single driver can now move between distant points in a short time is staggering relative to what it was just 35 years ago.

The Prices of Other Inputs   When a firm has a choice among alternative technologies, the choice it makes depends to some extent on relative input prices. You saw in Tables 10.2 and 10.3 that an increase in the price of labor substantially increased the demand for capital as the firm switched to a more capital-intensive production technique.

During the 1970s, the large increase in energy prices relative to prices of other factors of production had a number of effects on the demand for those other inputs. Insulation of new buildings, installation of more efficient heating plants, and similar efforts substantially raised the demand for capital as capital was substituted for energy in production. It has also been argued that the energy crisis led to an increase in demand for labor. If capital and energy are complementary inputs—that is, if technologies that are capital-intensive are also energy-intensive—the argument goes, the higher energy prices tended to push firms away from capital-intensive techniques and toward more labor-intensive techniques. A new highly automated technique, for example, might need fewer workers, but it would also require a vast amount of electricity to operate. High electricity prices could lead a firm to reject the new techniques and stick with an old, more labor-intensive, method of production.

Technological Change   Closely related to the impact of capital accumulation on factor demand is the potential impact of **technological change**—that is, the introduction of new methods of production or new products. New technologies usually introduce ways to produce outputs with fewer inputs by increasing the productivity of existing inputs or by raising marginal products. Because marginal revenue product reflects productivity, increases in productivity directly shift input demand curves. If the marginal product of labor rises, for example, the demand for labor shifts to the right (increases).

technological change The introduction of new methods of production or new products intended to increase the productivity of existing inputs or to raise marginal products.

> Technological change can and does have a powerful influence on factor demands. As new products and new techniques of production are born, so are demands for new inputs and new skills. As old products become obsolete, so, too, do the labor skills and other inputs needed to produce them.

RESOURCE ALLOCATION AND THE MIX OF OUTPUT IN COMPETITIVE MARKETS

We now have a complete, but simplified, picture of household and firm decision making. We have also examined some of the basic forces that determine the allocation of resources and the mix of output in perfectly competitive markets.

In this competitive environment, profit-maximizing firms make three fundamental decisions: (1) how much to produce and supply in output markets, (2) how to produce (which technology to use), and (3) how much of each input to demand. Chapters 7 to 9 looked at these three decisions from the perspective of the output market. We derived the supply curve of a competitive firm in the short run and discussed output market adjustment in the long run. Deriving cost curves, we learned, involves evaluating and choosing among alternative technologies. Finally, we saw how a firm's decision about how much product to supply in output markets implicitly determines input demands. Input demands, we argued, are also derived demands. That is, they are ultimately linked to the demand for output.

To show the connection between output and input markets, this chapter took these same three decisions and examined them from the perspective of input markets. Firms hire up to the point at which each input's marginal revenue product is equal to its price.

THE DISTRIBUTION OF INCOME

In the last few chapters, we have been focusing primarily on the firm. Throughout our study of microeconomics, we have also been building a theory that explains the distribution of income among households. We can now put the pieces of this puzzle together.

As we saw in this chapter, income is earned by households as payment for the factors of production that household members supply in input markets. Workers receive wages in exchange for their labor, owners of capital receive profits and interest in exchange for supplying capital (saving), and landowners receive rents in exchange for the use of their land. The incomes of workers depend on the wage rates determined in the market. The incomes of capital owners depend on the market price of capital (the amount households are paid for the use of their savings). The incomes of landowners depend on the rental values of their land.

marginal productivity theory of income distribution At equilibrium, all factors of production end up receiving rewards determined by their productivity as measured by marginal revenue product.

If markets are competitive, the equilibrium price of each input is equal to its marginal revenue product ($W = MRP_L$, and so forth). In other words, at equilibrium, each factor ends up receiving rewards determined by its productivity as measured by marginal revenue product. This is referred to as the **marginal productivity theory of income distribution**. We will turn to a more complete analysis of income distribution in Chapter 16.

LOOKING AHEAD

We have now completed our discussion of competitive labor and land markets. The next chapter takes up the complexity of what we have been loosely calling the "capital market." There we discuss the relationship between the market for physical capital and financial capital markets, and look at some of the ways that firms make investment decisions. Once we examine the nature of overall competitive equilibrium in Chapter 12, we can finally begin relaxing some of the assumptions that have restricted the scope of our inquiry—most importantly, the assumption of perfect competition in input and output markets.

SUMMARY

1. The exact same set of decisions that lies behind output supply curves also lies behind input demand curves. It is only the perspective that is different.

INPUT MARKETS: BASIC CONCEPTS

2. Demand for inputs depends on demand for the outputs that they produce; input demand is thus a *derived demand. Productivity* is a measure of the amount of output produced per unit of input.

3. In general, firms will demand workers as long as the value of what those workers produce exceeds what they must be paid. Households will supply labor as long as the wage exceeds the value of leisure or the value that they derive from nonpaid work.

4. Inputs are at the same time *complementary* and *substitutable.*

5. In the short run, some factor of production is fixed. This means that all firms encounter diminishing returns in the short run. Stated somewhat differently, diminishing returns means that all firms encounter declining marginal product in the short run.

6. The *marginal revenue product* (*MRP*) of a variable input is the additional revenue a firm earns by employing one additional unit of the input, *ceteris paribus. MRP* is equal to the input's marginal product times the price of output.

LABOR MARKETS

7. Demand for an input depends on that input's marginal revenue product. Profit-maximizing perfectly competitive firms will buy an input (e.g., hire labor) up to the point where the input's marginal revenue product equals its price.

For a firm employing only one variable factor of production, the *MRP* curve is the firm's demand curve for that factor in the short run.

8. For a perfectly competitive firm employing one variable factor of production, labor, the condition $W = MRP_L$ is exactly the same as the condition $P = MC$. Firms weigh the value of outputs as reflected in output price against the value of inputs as reflected in marginal costs.

9. When a firm employs two variable factors of production, a change in factor price has both a *factor substitution effect* and an *output effect*.

10. A wage increase may lead a firm to substitute capital for labor and thus cause the quantity demanded of labor to decline. This is the *factor substitution effect of the wage increase*.

11. A wage increase increases cost, and higher cost may lead to lower output and less demand for all inputs, including labor. This is the *output effect of the wage increase*. The effect is the opposite for a wage decrease.

LAND MARKETS

12. Because land is in strictly fixed supply, its price is *demand determined*—that is, its price is determined exclusively by what households and firms are willing to pay for it. The return to any factor of production in fixed supply is called a *pure rent*. A firm will pay for and use land as long as the revenue earned from selling the product produced on that land is sufficient to cover the price of the land. The firm will use land up to the point at which $MRP_A = P_A$, where A is land (acres).

THE FIRM'S PROFIT-MAXIMIZING CONDITION IN INPUT MARKETS

13. Every firm has an incentive to use variable inputs as long as the revenue generated by those inputs covers the costs of those inputs at the margin. Therefore, firms will employ each input up to the point that its price equals its marginal revenue product. This profit-maximizing condition holds for all factors at all levels of output.

INPUT DEMAND CURVES

14. A shift in a firm's demand curve for a factor of production can be influenced by the demand for the firm's product, the quantity of complementary and substitutable inputs, the prices of other inputs, and changes in technology.

RESOURCE ALLOCATION AND THE MIX OF OUTPUT IN COMPETITIVE MARKETS

15. Because the price of a factor at equilibrium in competitive markets is equal to its marginal revenue product, the distribution of income among households depends in part on the relative productivity of factors. This is the *marginal productivity theory of income distribution*.

REVIEW TERMS AND CONCEPTS

demand determined price, 221

derived demand, 212

factor substitution effect, 220

marginal product of labor (MP_L), 213

marginal productivity theory of income distribution, 226

marginal revenue product (*MRP*), 213

output effect of a factor price increase (decrease), 220

productivity of an input, 212

pure rent, 221

technological change, 225

Equations:

$MRP_L = MP_L \times P_X$

$W^* = MRP_L$

PROBLEM SET

1. In June of 2005, average weekly earnings in manufacturing were $539. A decade earlier they were $398. All else equal, such an increase in wages would be expected to reduce the demand for labor, and employment should fall. Instead, the quantity demanded for labor has increased dramatically with more than 16.5 million jobs being created between 1995 and 2005. How can you explain this seeming discrepancy?

2. Assume that a firm that manufactures widgets can produce them with one of three processes, used alone or in combination. The following table indicates the amounts of capital and labor required by each of the three processes to produce one widget.

	UNITS OF LABOR	UNITS OF CAPITAL
Process 1	4	1
Process 2	2	2
Process 3	1	3

a. Assuming that capital costs $3 per unit and labor costs $1 per unit, which process will be employed?

b. Plot the three points on the firm's *TVC* curve corresponding to $q = 10$, $q = 30$, and $q = 50$.

c. At each of the three output levels, how much K and L will be demanded?

d. Repeat parts a. through c., assuming the price of capital is $3 per unit and that the price of labor has risen to $4 per unit.

3. During the two decades leading up to the new millennium, wage inequality in the United States increased substantially. That is, high-income workers saw their salaries increase substantially, while wages of lower-income workers stagnated or even fell. Using the logic of marginal revenue product, give an explanation for this change in the distribution of income. In your explanation you may want to consider the rise of the high-technology, high-skill sector and the decline of industries requiring low-skill labor.

4. The following schedule shows the technology of production at the Delicious Apple Orchard for 2006:

WORKERS	TOTAL BUSHELS OF APPLES PER DAY
0	0
1	40
2	70
3	90
4	100
5	105
6	102

If apples sell for $2 per bushel and workers can be hired in a competitive labor market for $30 per day, how many workers should be hired? What if workers unionized and the wage rose to $50? (*Hint:* Create marginal product and marginal revenue product columns for the table.) Explain your answers clearly.

5. The following graph is the production function for a firm using only one variable factor of production, labor.
   a. Graph the marginal product of labor for the firm as a function of the number of labor units hired.
   b. Assuming that the price of output, P_X, is equal to $6, graph the firm's marginal revenue product schedule as a function of the number of labor units hired.
   c. If the current equilibrium wage rate is $4 per hour, how many hours of labor will you hire? How much output will you produce?

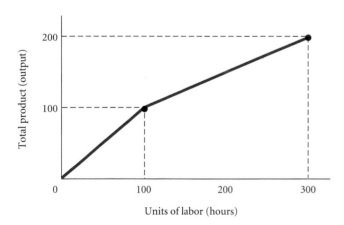

6. Describe how each of the following events would affect (1) demand for construction workers and (2) construction wages in Portland, Oregon. Illustrate with supply and demand curves.
   a. A sharp increase in interest rates on new-home mortgages reduces the demand for new houses substantially.
   b. The economy of the area booms. Office rents rise, creating demand for new office space.
   c. A change in the tax laws in 2005 made real estate developments more profitable. As a result, three major developers start planning to build major shopping centers.

7. The demand for land is a derived demand. Think of a popular location near your school. What determines the demand for land in that area? What outputs are sold by businesses located

there? Discuss the relationship between land prices and the prices of those products.

8. Many states provide firms with an "investment tax credit" that effectively reduces the price of capital. In theory, these credits are designed to stimulate new investment and thus create jobs. Critics have argued that if there are strong factor substitution effects, these subsidies could actually *reduce* employment in the state. Explain their arguments.

9. Doug's farm in Idaho has four major fields that he uses to grow potatoes. The productivity of each field follows:

	ANNUAL YIELD, HUNDREDS OF POUNDS
Field 1	10,000
Field 2	8,000
Field 3	5,000
Field 4	3,000

Assume that each field is the same size and that the variable costs of farming are $25,000 per year per field. The variable costs cover labor and machinery time, which is rented. Doug must decide each year how many fields to plant. In 2004, potato farmers received $6.35 per 100 pounds. How many fields did Doug plant? Explain. By 2006, the price of potatoes had fallen to $4.50 per 100 pounds. How will this price decrease change Doug's decision? How will it affect his demand for labor? How will it affect the value of Doug's land?

10. Assume that you are living in a house with two other people and that the house has a big lawn that has to be mowed. One of your roommates, who hates to work outdoors, suggests hiring a neighbor's daughter to mow the grass for $40 per week instead of sharing the work and doing it yourselves. How would you go about deciding who will mow the lawn? What factors would you raise in deciding? What are the trade-offs here?

11. Consider the following information for a T-shirt manufacturing firm that can sell as many T-shirts as it wants for $3 per shirt:

NUMBER OF WORKERS	NUMBER OF SHIRTS PRODUCED PER DAY	MP_L	TR	MRP_L
0	0	—	—	—
1	30	—	—	—
2	80	—	—	—
3	110	—	—	—
4	135	—	—	—
5	—	20	—	—
6	170	—	—	—
7	—	—	—	30
8	—	—	—	15

a. Fill in all the blanks in the table.
b. Verify that MRP_L for this firm can be calculated in two ways: (1) change in TR from adding another worker and (2) MP_L times the price of output.
c. If this firm must pay a wage rate of $40 per worker per day, how many workers should it hire? Briefly explain why.
d. Suppose the wage rate rises to $50 per worker. How many workers should be hired now? Why?
e. Suppose the firm adopts a new technology that doubles output at each level of employment and that the price of shirts remains at $3. What is the effect of this new technol-

ogy on MP_L, and on MRP_L? At a wage of $50, how many workers should the firm hire now?

*12. For a given firm, MRP_L = $50, and MRP_K = $100, while P_L = $10 and P_K = $20.

    a. Is the firm maximizing profits? Why or why not?

    b. Can you identify a specific action that would increase this firm's profits?

13. Review the box on page 217. Do a Web search and find out who was the highest-paid player in baseball in 2006. Do you think such salaries are justified? Why or why not?

---

*Note: Problems marked with an asterisk are more challenging.

Input Demand: The Capital Market and the Investment Decision

11

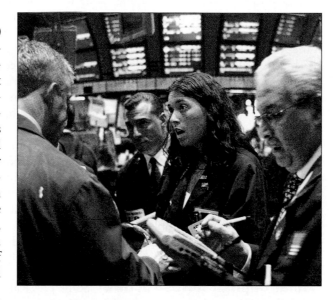

We saw in Chapter 10 that perfectly competitive firms hire factors of production (inputs) up to the point at which each factor's marginal revenue product is equal to that factor's price. The three main factors of production are land, labor, and capital. We also saw that factor prices are determined by the interaction of supply and demand in the factor markets. The wage rate is determined in the labor market, the price of land is determined in the land market, and the price of capital is determined in the capital market.

In Chapter 10, we explored the labor and land markets in some detail. In this chapter we consider the capital market more fully. Transactions between households and firms in the labor and land markets are direct. In the labor market, households offer their labor directly to firms in exchange for wages. In the land market, landowners rent or sell their land directly to firms in exchange for rent or an agreed-to price. In the capital market, though, households often *indirectly* supply the financial resources necessary for firms to purchase capital. When households save and add funds to their bank accounts, for example, firms can borrow these funds from the bank to finance their capital purchases.

Earlier, in Chapter 9, we discussed the incentives new firms have to enter industries in which profit opportunities exist and the incentives that existing firms have to leave industries in which they are suffering losses. We also described the conditions under which existing firms have an incentive either to expand or to reduce their scales of operation. That chapter was in a preliminary way describing the process of capital allocation. When new firms enter an industry or an existing firm expands, someone pays to put capital (plant, equipment, and inventory) in place. Because the future is uncertain, capital investment decisions always involve risk. In market capitalist systems, the decision to put capital to use in a particular enterprise is made by private citizens putting their savings at risk in search of private gain. This chapter describes the set of institutions through which such transactions take place.

CAPITAL, INVESTMENT, AND DEPRECIATION

Before we proceed with our analysis of the capital market, we need to review some basic economic principles and introduce some related concepts.

231

CAPITAL

One of the most important concepts in all of economics is the concept of **capital**.

> Capital goods are those goods produced by the economic system that are used as inputs to produce other goods and services in the future. Capital goods thus yield valuable productive services over time.

capital Those goods produced by the economic system that are used as inputs to produce other goods and services in the future.

Tangible Capital   When we think of capital, we generally think of the physical, material capital employed by business firms. The major categories of **physical**, or **tangible, capital** are (1) nonresidential structures (for example, office buildings, power plants, factories, shopping centers, warehouses, and docks); (2) durable equipment (machines, trucks, sandwich grills, automobiles, and so on); (3) residential structures; and (4) inventories of inputs and outputs that firms have in stock.

Most firms need tangible capital, along with labor and land, to produce their products. A restaurant's capital requirements include a kitchen, ovens and grills, tables and chairs, silverware, dishes, and light fixtures. These items must be purchased up front and maintained if the restaurant is to function properly. A manufacturing firm must have a plant, specialized machinery, trucks, and inventories of parts. A winery needs casks, vats, piping, temperature-control equipment, and cooking and bottling machinery.

physical, or tangible, capital Material things used as inputs in the production of future goods and services. The major categories of physical capital are nonresidential structures, durable equipment, residential structures, and inventories.

The capital stock of a retail pharmacy is made up mostly of inventories. Pharmacies do not produce the aspirin, vitamins, and toothbrushes that they sell. Instead, they buy those things from manufacturers and put them on display. The product actually produced and sold by a pharmacy is convenience. Like any other product, convenience is produced with labor and capital in the form of a store with lots of products, or inventory, displayed on the sales floor and kept in storerooms. The inventories of inputs and outputs that manufacturing firms maintain are also capital. To function smoothly and meet the demands of buyers, for example, the Ford Motor Company maintains inventories of both auto parts (tires, windshields, and so on) and completed cars.

An apartment building is also capital. Produced by the economic system, it yields valuable services over time, and it is used as an input to produce housing services, which are rented.

Social Capital: Infrastructure   Some physical or tangible capital is owned by the public instead of private firms. **Social capital**, sometimes called **infrastructure**, is capital that provides services to the public. Most social capital takes the form of public works like highways, roads, bridges, mass transit systems, and sewer and water systems. Police stations, fire stations, city halls, courthouses, and police cars all are forms of social capital that are used as inputs to produce the services that government provides.

social capital, or infrastructure Capital that provides services to the public. Most social capital takes the form of public works (roads and bridges) and public services (police and fire protection).

All firms use some forms of social capital in producing their outputs. Recent economic research has shown that a country's infrastructure plays a very important role in helping private firms produce their products efficiently. When public capital is not properly cared for—for example, when roads deteriorate or when airports are not modernized to accommodate increasing traffic—private firms that depend on efficient transportation networks suffer.

Intangible Capital   Not all capital is physical. Some things that are intangible (nonmaterial) satisfy every part of our definition of capital. When a business firm invests in advertising to establish a brand name, it is producing a form of **intangible capital** called goodwill. This goodwill yields valuable services to the firm over time.

intangible capital Nonmaterial things that contribute to the output of future goods and services.

When a firm establishes a training program for employees, it is investing in its workers' skills. One can think of such an investment as the production of an intangible form of capital called **human capital**. It is produced with labor (instructors) and capital (classrooms, computers, projectors, and books). Human capital in the form of new or augmented skills is an input—it will yield valuable productive services for the firm in the future.

human capital A form of intangible capital that includes the skills and other knowledge that workers have or acquire through education and training and that yields valuable services to a firm over time.

When research produces valuable results, such as a new production process that reduces costs or a new formula that creates a new product, the new technology itself can be considered capital. Furthermore, even ideas can be patented and the rights to them can be sold.

A large number of "new economy" start-up technology companies have responded to the growth of the Internet in recent years. These dot-com and e-commerce companies generally start with limited capital, and most of that capital is in the skills and knowledge of their employees: human capital.

The Time Dimension The most important dimension of capital is the fact that it exists through time. Labor services are used at the time they are provided. Households consume services and nondurable goods[1] almost immediately after purchase. However, capital exists now and into the future. Therefore:

> The value of capital is only as great as the value of the services it will render over time.[2]

Measuring Capital Labor is measured in hours, and land is measured in square feet or acres. Because capital comes in so many forms, it is virtually impossible to measure it directly in physical terms. The indirect measure generally used is *current market value*. The measure of a firm's **capital stock** is the current market value of its plant, equipment, inventories, and intangible assets. By using value as a measuring stick, business managers, accountants, and economists can, in a sense, add buildings, barges, and bulldozers into a measure of total capital.

Capital is measured as a *stock* value. That is, it is measured at a point in time. The capital stock of the XYZ Corporation on July 31, 2006, is $3,453,231. According to Department of Commerce estimates, the capital stock of the U.S. economy in 2003 was about $31.4 trillion. Of that amount, $13.1 trillion was residential structures, $6.5 trillion was owned by the government (for example, aircraft carriers), and $5.3 trillion was equipment and software.[3]

Although it is measured in terms of money, or value, it is very important to think of the actual capital stock itself:

> When we speak of capital, we refer not to money or to financial assets such as bonds and stocks, but instead to the firm's physical plant, equipment, inventory, and intangible assets.

capital stock For a single firm, the current market value of the firm's plant, equipment, inventories, and intangible assets.

INVESTMENT AND DEPRECIATION

Recall the difference between stock and flow measures discussed in earlier chapters. *Stock measures* are valued at a particular point in time, whereas *flow measures* are valued over a period of time. The easiest way to think of the difference between a stock and a flow is to think about a tub of water. The volume of water in the tub is measured at a point in time and is a stock. The amount of water that flows into the tub *per hour* and the amount of water that evaporates out of the tub *per day* are flow measures. Flow measures have meaning only when the time dimension is added. Water flowing into the tub at a rate of 5 gallons per hour is very different from water flowing at a rate of 5 gallons per year.

Capital stocks are affected over time by two flows: investment and depreciation. When a firm produces or puts in place new capital—a new piece of equipment, for example—it has invested. **Investment** is a flow that increases the stock of capital. Because it has a time dimension, we speak of investment per period (by the month, quarter, or year).

As you proceed, be careful to keep in mind that the term *investing* is *not* used in economics to describe the act of buying a share of stock or a bond. Although people commonly use the term this way ("I invested in some Union Carbide stock" or "he invested in Treasury bonds"), the term *investment* when used correctly refers *only to an increase in capital*.

Table 11.1 presents data on private investment in the United States economy in 2004. About half of the total was equipment and software. Almost all the rest was investment in structures, both residential (apartment buildings, condominiums, houses, and so on) and nonresidential (factories, shopping malls, and so on). Inventory investment was small.

investment New capital additions to a firm's capital stock. Although capital is measured at a given point in time (a stock), investment is measured over a period of time (a flow). The flow of investment increases the capital stock.

---

[1]Consumer goods are generally divided into two categories: durables and nondurables. Technically, *durable goods* are goods expected to last for more than 1 year. *Nondurable goods* are goods expected to last less than 1 year.
[2]Conceptually, consumer durable goods, such as automobiles, washing machines, and the like, are capital. They are produced, they yield services over time, and households use them as inputs to produce services such as transportation and clean laundry.
[3]U.S. Department of Commerce, Bureau of Economic Analysis, *Survey of Current Business*, September 2004.

TABLE 11.1 Private Investment in the U.S. Economy, 2004

GDP = 11,734.3
Gross private domestic investment = 1,928.1

	BILLIONS OF CURRENT DOLLARS	AS A PERCENTAGE OF TOTAL GROSS INVESTMENT	AS A PERCENTAGE OF GDP
Nonresidential structures	298.4	15.5	2.5
Equipment and software	900.4	46.7	7.7
Change in private inventories	55.4	2.9	0.5
Residential structures and equipment	673.8	34.9	5.7
Total gross private investment	1928.1	100.0	16.4
− depreciation	−1206.2	−62.6	−10.3
Net investment =			
gross investment − depreciation	721.9	37.4	6.1

Source: U.S. Department of Commerce, Bureau of Economic Analysis.

depreciation The decline in an asset's economic value over time.

Depreciation is the decline in an asset's (resource's) economic value over time. If you have ever owned a car, you are aware that its resale value falls with age. Suppose you bought a new 2006 Mercury Mariner hybrid SUV for $30,500 and you decide to sell it 2 years and 25,000 miles later. Checking the newspaper and talking to several dealers, you find out that, given its condition and the mileage, you can expect to get $22,000 for it. It has depreciated $8,500 ($30,500 − $22,000). Table 11.1 shows that in 2004 private depreciation in the U.S. economy was $1,206.2 billion.

A capital asset can depreciate because it wears out physically or because it becomes obsolete. Take, for example, a computer control system in a factory. If a new, technologically superior system does the same job for half the price, the old system may be replaced even if it still functions well. The Mercury Mariner depreciated because of wear and tear *and* because new models had become available.

THE CAPITAL MARKET

Where does capital come from? How and why is it produced? How much and what kinds of capital are produced? Who pays for it? These questions are answered in the complex set of institutions in which households supply their savings to firms that demand funds to buy capital goods. Collectively, these institutions are called the **capital market**.

capital market The market in which households supply their savings to firms that demand funds to buy capital goods.

Although governments and households make some capital investment decisions, most decisions to produce new capital goods—that is, to invest—are made by firms. However, a firm cannot invest unless it has the funds to do so. Although firms can invest in many ways, it is always the case that:

> The funds that firms use to buy capital goods come, directly or indirectly, from households. When a household decides not to consume a portion of its income, it saves. Investment by firms is the *demand for capital*. Saving by households is the *supply of capital*. Various financial institutions facilitate the transfer of households' savings to firms that use them for capital investment.

Let us use a simple example to see how the system works. Suppose that some firm wants to purchase a machine that costs $1,000 and that some household decides at the same time to save $1,000 from its income. Figure 11.1 shows one way that the household's decision to save might connect with the firm's decision to invest.

bond A contract between a borrower and a lender, in which the borrower agrees to pay the loan at some time in the future, along with interest payments along the way.

Either directly or through a financial intermediary (such as a bank), the household agrees to loan its savings to the firm. In exchange, the firm contracts to pay the household interest at some agreed-to rate each period. Interest is the fee paid by a borrower to a lender or by a bank to a depositor for the use of funds. The interest rate is that fee paid annually, expressed as a percentage of the loan or deposit. If the household lends directly to the firm, the firm gives the household a **bond**, which is nothing more than a contract promising to

Lends $1,000

Issues $1,000 bond

Firms

Investment decision

Buys
$1,000 machine

Capital market
(financial markets)

Saves $1,000

Issues $1,000 bond

Households

Saving decision

Bond

**Capital stock
increases $1,000**

**Net worth
increases $1,000**

FIGURE 11.1 $1,000 in Savings Becomes $1,000 of Investment

repay the loan at some specific time in the future. The bond also specifies the flow of interest to be paid in the meantime.

The new saving adds to the household's stock of wealth. The household's *net worth* has increased by the $1,000, which it holds in the form of a bond.[4] The bond represents the firm's promise to repay the $1,000 at some future date with interest. The firm uses the $1,000 to buy a new $1,000 machine, which it adds to its capital stock. In essence, the household has supplied the capital demanded by the firm. It is almost as if the household bought the machine and rented it to the firm for an annual fee. Presumably, this investment will generate added revenues that will facilitate the payment of interest to the household.

> In general, projects are undertaken as long as the revenues likely to be realized from the investment are sufficient to cover the interest payments to the household.

Sometimes the transfer of household savings through the capital market into investment occurs without a financial intermediary. An *entrepreneur* is one who organizes, manages, and assumes the risk of a new firm. When entrepreneurs start a new business by buying capital with their own savings, they are both demanding capital and supplying the resources (that is, their savings) needed to purchase that capital. No third party is involved in the transaction. Most investment, however, is accomplished with the help of financial intermediaries (third parties such as banks, insurance companies, and pension funds) that stand between the supplier (saver) and the demander (investing firm). The part of the capital market in which savers and investors interact through intermediaries is often called the **financial capital market**.

financial capital market
The part of the capital market in which savers and investors interact through intermediaries.

CAPITAL INCOME: INTEREST AND PROFITS

It should now be clear to you how capital markets fit into the circular flow: They facilitate the movement of household savings into the most productive investment projects. When households allow their savings to be used to purchase capital, they receive payments, and these payments (along with wages and salaries) are part of household incomes. Income that is earned on savings that have been put to use through financial capital markets is called

---

[4]Note that the *act of saving* increases the household's wealth, not the act of buying the bond. Buying the bond simply transforms one financial asset (money) into another (a bond). The household could simply have held on to the money.

capital income. Capital income is received by households in many forms, the two most important of which are *interest* and *profits*.

Interest   The most common form of capital income received by households is interest. In simplest terms, **interest** is the payment made for the use of money. Banks pay interest to depositors, whose deposits are loaned out to businesses or individuals who want to make investments.[5] Banks also *charge* interest to those who borrow money. Corporations pay interest to households that buy their bonds. The government borrows money by issuing bonds, and the buyers of those bonds receive interest payments.

The **interest rate** is almost always expressed as an annual rate. It is the annual interest payment expressed as a percentage of the loan or deposit. For example, a $1,000 bond (representing a $1,000 loan from a household to a firm) that carries a fixed 10 percent interest rate will pay the household $100 per year ($1,000 × .10) in interest. A savings account that carries a 5 percent annual interest rate will pay $50 annually on a balance of $1,000.

The interest rate is usually agreed to at the time a loan or deposit is made. Sometimes borrowers and lenders agree to periodically adjust the level of interest payments depending on market conditions. These types of loans are called *adjustable* or *floating-rate loans*. (*Fixed-rate loans* are loans in which the interest rate never varies.) In recent years there have even been adjustable rates of interest on savings accounts and certificates of deposit.

A loan's interest rate depends on a number of factors. A loan that involves more risk will generally pay a higher interest rate than a loan with less risk. Similarly, firms that are considered bad credit risks will pay higher interest rates than firms with good credit ratings. You have probably heard radio or TV advertisements by finance companies offering to loan money to borrowers "regardless of credit history." This means that they will loan to people or businesses that pose a relatively high risk of *defaulting*, or not paying off the loan. What they do not tell you is that the interest rate will be quite high.

It is generally agreed that the safest borrower is the U.S. government. With the "full faith and credit" of the U.S. government pledged to buyers of U.S. Treasury bonds and bills, most people believe that there is little risk that the government will not repay its loans. For this reason, the U.S. government can borrow money at a lower interest rate than any other borrower.

Profits   *Profits* is another word for the net income of a firm: revenue minus costs of production. Some firms are simply owned by individuals or partners, who sell their products for more than it costs to produce them. The profits of proprietors or partnerships generally go directly to the owner or owners who run the firm. Corporations are firms owned by shareholders who are normally not otherwise connected with the firms. Corporations are organized and chartered under state laws that grant limited liability status to their owners or shareholders. Essentially that means that shareholders cannot lose more than they have invested if the company incurs liabilities it cannot pay.

A *share of common stock* is a certificate that represents the ownership of a share of a business, almost always a corporation. For example, Lincoln Electric is a Cleveland-based company that makes welding and cutting equipment. The company has 41 million shares of common stock that are owned by tens of thousands of shareholders, some of whom are simply private individuals, some of whom are institutions like Carlton College, and some of whom may be employees of the firm. Shareholders are entitled to a share of the company's profit. When profits are paid directly to shareholders, the payment is called a *dividend*. Lincoln Electric made a profit in a recent year of $54 million, which was $1.31 per share, of which $0.43 was paid out to shareholders as dividends and the rest retained for investment.

Shares of common stock are traded openly on private stock exchanges or markets, the biggest of which is the New York Stock Exchange (NYSE). Most of the billions of shares traded every day are simply one shareholder selling shares to another and these trades have nothing to do with the company. When shares are first issued, the proceeds are used to buy capital or to "buy out" the entrepreneurs who started the firm.

---

[5]Although we are focusing on investment by businesses, households can and do make investments also. The most important form of household investment is the construction of a new house, usually financed by borrowing in the form of a mortgage. A household may also borrow to finance the purchase of an existing house, but when it does so, no new investment is taking place.

In discussing profit, it is important to distinguish between profit as defined by generally accepting *accounting* practices and *economic* profits as we defined them back in Chapter 7.

Recall that our definition of **profit** is total revenue minus total cost, where total cost includes the normal rate of return on capital. We defined profit in this way because true economic cost includes the opportunity cost of capital.

Suppose, for example, that I decide to open a candy store that requires an initial investment of $100,000. If I borrow the $100,000 from a bank, I am not making a profit until I cover the interest payments on my loan. Even if I use my own savings or raise the funds I need by selling shares in my business, I am not making a profit until I cover the opportunity cost of using those funds to start my business. Because I always have the option of lending my funds at the current market interest rate, I earn a profit only when my total revenue is large enough to cover my total cost, including the forgone interest revenue I could make from lending my funds at the current market interest rate.

As another example, suppose that the Kauai Lamp Company was started in 2006, and that 100 percent of the $1 million needed to start up the company (to buy the plant and equipment) was raised by selling shares of stock. Now suppose that the company earns $200,000 per year, all of which is paid out to shareholders. Because $200,000 is 20 percent of the company's total capital stock, the shareholders are earning a rate of return of 20 percent, but only part of the $200,000 is profit. If the market interest rate is 11 percent, then 11 percent of $1 million ($110,000) is part of the cost of capital. The shareholders are only earning a profit of $90,000 given our definition of profit.

profit The excess of revenues over cost in a given period.

A business that cannot cover the interest payments on its loans or a firm that does not generate a normal rate of return to its owners will likely exit the industry in the long run.

Functions of Interest and Profit   Capital income serves several functions. First, interest may function as an incentive to postpone gratification. When you save, you pass up the chance to buy things that you want right now. One view of interest holds that it is the reward for postponing consumption.

Second, profit serves as a reward for innovation and risk taking. Every year *Forbes* magazine publishes the names of the richest people in the United States, and virtually every major fortune listed there is traceable to the founding of some business enterprise that "made it big." In recent years, big winners have included retail stores (the Walton family of Wal-Mart), high-tech companies (Bill Gates of Microsoft and Michael Dell of Dell), and a real estate empire (the Pritzker family).

Many argue that rewards for innovation and risk taking are the essence of the U.S. free enterprise system. Innovation is at the core of economic growth and progress. More efficient production techniques mean that the resources saved can be used to produce new things. There is another side to this story, however: Critics of the free enterprise system claim that such large rewards are not justified and that accumulations of great wealth and power are not in society's best interests.

FINANCIAL MARKETS IN ACTION

When a firm issues a fixed-interest-rate bond, it borrows funds and pays interest at an agreed-to rate to the person or institution that buys the bond. Many other mechanisms, four of which are illustrated in Figure 11.2, also channel household savings into investment projects.

Case A: Business Loans   As I look around my hometown, I see several ice cream stores doing very well, but I think that I can make better ice cream than they do. To go into the business, I need capital: ice cream-making equipment, tables, chairs, freezers, signs, and a store. Because I put up my house as collateral, I am not a big risk, and the bank grants me a loan at a fairly reasonable interest rate. Banks have these funds to lend only because households deposit their savings there.

Case B: Venture Capital   A scientist at a leading university develops an inexpensive method of producing a very important family of virus-fighting drugs, using microorganisms created through gene splicing. The business could very well fail within 12 months, but if it succeeds, the potential for profit is huge.

Our scientist goes to a *venture capital fund* for financing. Such funds take household savings and put them into high-risk ventures in exchange for a share of the profits if the new businesses succeed. By investing in many different projects, the funds reduce the risk of going

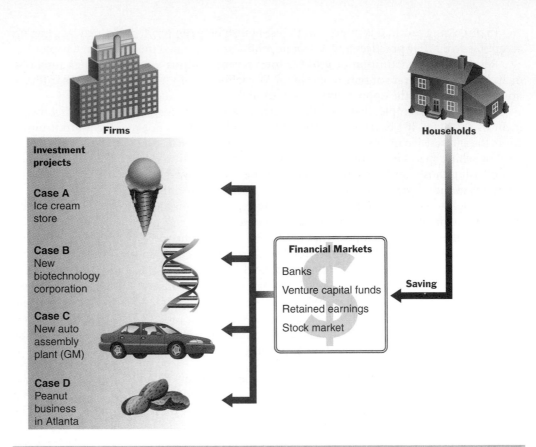

FIGURE 11.2 Financial Markets Link Household Saving and Investment by Firms

broke. Once again, household funds make it possible for firms to undertake investments. If a venture succeeds, those owning shares in the venture capital fund receive substantial profits.

Case C: Retained Earnings
General Motors Corporation (GM) decides that it wants to build a new assembly plant in Tennessee, and it discovers that it has enough funds to pay for the new facility. The new investment is thus paid for through internal funds, or *retained earnings*.

The result is exactly the same as if the firm had gone to households via some financial intermediary and borrowed the funds. If GM uses its profits to buy new capital, it does so only with the shareholders' implicit consent. When a firm takes its own profit and uses it to buy capital assets instead of paying it out to its shareholders, the total value of the firm goes up, as does the value of the shares held by stockholders. As in our other examples, GM capital stock increases, and so does the net worth of households.

When a household owns a share of stock that *appreciates*, or increases in value, the appreciation is part of the household's income. Unless the household sells the stock and consumes the gain, that gain is part of saving. In essence, when a firm retains earnings for investment purposes, it is actually saving on behalf of its shareholders.

Case D: The Stock Market
A former high-ranking government official decides to start a new peanut processing business in Atlanta, and he also decides to raise the funds needed by issuing shares of stock. Households buy the shares with income that they decide not to spend. In exchange, they are entitled to a share of the peanut firm's profits.

The shares of stock become part of households' net worth. The proceeds from stock sales are used to buy plant equipment and inventory. Savings flow into investment, and the firm's capital stock goes up by the same amount as household net worth.

CAPITAL ACCUMULATION AND ALLOCATION

You can see from the preceding examples that various, and sometimes complex, connections between households and firms facilitate the movement of savings into productive investment. The methods may differ, but the results are the same.

Putting Their Money Where the Future Is in 2005

THE FOLLOWING ARTICLE FROM THE *New York Times* describes the response of venture capital firms to the demand for alternative energy sources in 2005.

Green Tinge Is Attracting Seed Money to Ventures

By GARY RIVLIN (NYT)
June 22, 2005

Ira Ehrenpreis may be a kind of prophet advocating investments in alternative energy companies, but don't accuse him of being noble.

In recent months, Mr. Ehrenpreis, a venture capitalist at Technology Partners in Palo Alto, Calif., has been asked any number of times to speak to audiences about "clean tech," a term that encompasses such things as solar energy, water purification systems, and alternative automotive fuels.

He begins and ends every speech the same way: with a slide that stresses that to the extent his motivations are tinged green, it has to do with the color of money.

In Silicon Valley these days, more venture capitalists are following Mr. Ehrenpreis's lead. They are driven in

part by the high price of oil, which hovered around $59 a barrel on Tuesday, and the vast unmet demand for electricity in China and India.

"The reason we're allocating dollars to this sector is we think we can deliver attractive returns," said Mr. Ehrenpreis, who also serves as co-chairman of the advisory board of the Cleantech Venture Network. "It's not because we want to do great things for the environment or great things for the

world," though he adds that that is a "great byproduct."

That message is resonating with venture capitalists and individual investors in the Valley, where growing rich through doing good is considered the ideal.

Think again about Colleen and Bill, whom we discussed in Chapter 2. They found themselves alone on a deserted island. They had to make choices about how to allocate available resources, including their time. By spending long hours working on a house or a boat, Colleen and Bill are saving and investing. First, they are using resources that could be used to produce more immediate rewards—they could gather more food or simply lie in the sun and relax. Second, they are applying those resources to the production of capital and capital accumulation.

Industrialized or agrarian, small or large, simple or complex, all societies exist through time and must allocate resources over time. In simple societies, investment and saving decisions are made by the same people. However:

In modern industrial societies, investment decisions (capital production decisions) are made primarily by firms. Households decide how much to save, and in the long run savings limit or constrain the amount of investment that firms can undertake. The capital market exists to direct savings into profitable investment projects.

THE DEMAND FOR NEW CAPITAL AND THE INVESTMENT DECISION

We saw in Chapter 9 that firms have an incentive to expand in industries that earn positive profits—that is, a rate of return above normal—and in industries in which economies of scale lead to lower average costs at higher levels of output. We also saw that positive profits in an industry stimulate the entry of new firms. The expansion of existing firms and the creation of new firms both involve investment in new capital.

Even when there are no profits in an industry, firms must still do some investing. First, equipment wears out and must be replaced if the firm is to stay in business. Second, firms are constantly changing. A new technology may become available, sales patterns may shift, or the firm may expand or contract its product line.

With these points in mind, we now turn to a discussion of the investment decision process within the individual firm. In the end we will see (just as we did in Chapter 10) that a perfectly competitive firm invests in capital up to the point at which the marginal revenue product of capital is equal to the price of capital. (Because we based much of our discussion in Chapter 10 on the assumption of perfect competition, it makes sense to continue doing so here. Keep in mind, though, that much of what we say here also applies to firms that are not perfectly competitive.)

FORMING EXPECTATIONS

We have already said that the most important dimension of capital is time. Capital produces useful services over *some period of time.* In building an office tower, a developer makes an investment that will be around for decades. In deciding where to build a branch plant, a manufacturing firm commits a large amount of resources to purchase capital that will be in place for a long time.

It is important to remember, though, that capital goods do not begin to yield benefits until they are *used.* Often the decision to build a building or purchase a piece of equipment must be made years before the actual project is completed. Although the acquisition of a small business computer may take only days, the planning process for downtown development projects in big U.S. cities has been known to take decades.

The purchase of trucks by a firm is a form of investment.

The Expected Benefits of Investments Decision makers must have expectations about what is going to happen in the future. A new plant will be very valuable—that is, it will produce much profit—if the market for a firm's product grows and the price of that product remains high. The same plant will be worth little if the economy goes into a slump or consumers grow tired of the firm's product. An office tower may turn out to be an excellent investment, but not if many new office buildings go up at the same time, flooding the office space market, pushing up the vacancy rate, and driving down rents. It follows, then, that:

> The investment process requires that the potential investor evaluate the expected flow of future productive services that an investment project will yield.

Remember that households, business firms, and governments all undertake investments. A household must evaluate the future services that a new roof will yield. A firm must evaluate the flow of future revenues that a new plant will generate. Governments must estimate how much benefit society will derive from a new bridge or a war memorial.

An official of the General Electric Corporation (GE) once described the difficulty involved in making such predictions. GE subscribes to a number of different economic forecasting services. In the early 1980s, those services provided the firm with 10-year predictions of new housing construction that ranged from a low of 400,000 new units per year to a high of 4 million new units per year. Because GE sells millions of household appliances to contractors building new houses, condominiums, and apartments, the forecast was critical. If GE decided that the high number was more accurate, it would need to spend literally billions of dollars on new plant and equipment to prepare for the extra demand. If GE decided that the low number was more accurate, it would need to begin closing several of its larger plants and disinvesting. In fact, GE took the middle road. It assumed that housing production would be between 1.5 and 2 million units—which, in fact, it was.

GE is not an exception. All firms must rely on forecasts to make sensible investment and production decisions, but forecasting is an inexact science because so much depends on events that cannot be foreseen.

Many believe that the Internet and the rise of e-commerce have brought revolutionary change to the world economy and created "a new economy." There is a great deal of uncertainty about where the "information age" is headed, and this makes expectations all the more important and volatile. A great deal of capital was allocated to thousands and thousands of new technology companies in the 1990s. Many of those firms failed during the dot.com crash of 2000–2003. Only time will tell which will finally bear fruit for investors.

The Expected Costs of Investments The benefits of any investment project take the form of future profits. These profits must be forecast, but costs must also be evaluated. Like households, firms have access to financial markets, both as borrowers and as lenders. If a firm borrows, it must *pay* interest over time. If it lends, it will *earn* interest. If the firm borrows to finance a project, the interest on the loan is part of the cost of the project.

Even if a project is financed with the firm's own fund instead of by borrowing, an opportunity cost is involved. A thousand dollars put into a capital investment project will generate an expected flow of future profit; the same $1,000 put into the financial market (in essence, loaned to another firm) will yield a flow of interest payments. The project will not be undertaken unless it is expected to yield more than the market interest rate. The cost of an investment project may thus be direct or indirect because:

> The ability to lend at the market rate of interest means that there is an *opportunity cost* associated with every investment project. The evaluation process thus involves not only estimating future benefits but also comparing them with the possible alternative uses of the funds required to undertake the project. At a minimum, those funds could earn interest in financial markets.

COMPARING COSTS AND EXPECTED RETURN

Once expectations have been formed, firms must quantify them—that is, they must assign some dollars-and-cents value to them. One way to quantify expectations is to calculate an **expected rate of return** on the investment project. For example, if a new computer network that costs $400,000 is likely to save $100,000 per year in data processing costs forever after, the expected rate of return on that investment is 25 percent per year. Each year the firm will save $100,000 as a result of the $400,000 investment. The expected rate of return will be less than 25 percent if the computer network wears out or becomes obsolete after a while and the cost saving ceases. In short:

expected rate of return The annual rate of return that a firm expects to obtain through a capital investment.

> The expected rate of return on an investment project depends on the price of the investment, the expected length of time the project provides additional cost savings or revenue, and the expected amount of revenue attributable each year to the project.

Table 11.2 presents a menu of investment choices and expected rates of return that face a hypothetical firm. Because expected rates of return are based on forecasts of future profits attributable to the investments, any change in expectations would change all the numbers in column 2.

Figure 11.3 graphs the total amount of investment in millions of dollars that the firm would undertake at various interest rates. If the interest rate were 24 percent, the firm would fund only project A, the new computer network. It can borrow at 24 percent and invest in a computer that is expected to yield 25 percent. At 24 percent, the firm's total investment is $400,000. The first vertical red line in Figure 11.3 shows that at any interest rate above 20 percent and below 25 percent, only $400,000 worth of investment (that is, project A) will be undertaken.

If the interest rate were 18 percent, the firm would fund projects A and B, and its total investment would rise to $3 million ($400,000 + $2,600,000). If the firm could borrow at 18 percent, the flow of additional profits generated by the new computer and the new plant would more than cover the costs of borrowing, but none of the other projects would be justified. The rates of return on projects A and B (25 percent and 20 percent, respectively) both

TABLE 11.2 Potential Investment Projects and Expected Rates of Return for a Hypothetical Firm, Based on Forecasts of Future Profits Attributable to the Investment

PROJECT	(1) TOTAL INVESTMENT (DOLLARS)	(2) EXPECTED RATE OF RETURN (PERCENT)
A. New computer network	400,000	25
B. New branch plant	2,600,000	20
C. Sales office in another state	1,500,000	15
D. New automated billing system	100,000	12
E. Ten new delivery trucks	400,000	10
F. Advertising campaign	1,000,000	7
G. Employee cafeteria	100,000	5

exceed the 18 percent interest rate. Only if the interest rate fell below 5 percent would the firm fund all seven investment projects.

The investment schedule in Table 11.2 and its graphic depiction in Figure 11.3 describe the firm's demand for new capital, expressed as a function of the market interest rate. If we add the total investment undertaken by *all* firms at every interest rate, we arrive at the demand for new capital in the economy as a whole. In other words, the market demand curve for new capital is simply the sum of all the individual demand curves for new capital in the economy (Figure 11.4). In a sense, the investment demand schedule is a ranking of all the investment opportunities in the economy in order of expected yield.

Only those investment projects in the economy that are expected to yield a rate of return higher than the market interest rate will be funded. At lower market interest rates, more investment projects are undertaken.

The most important thing to remember about the investment demand curve is that its shape and position depend critically on the *expectations* of those making the investment

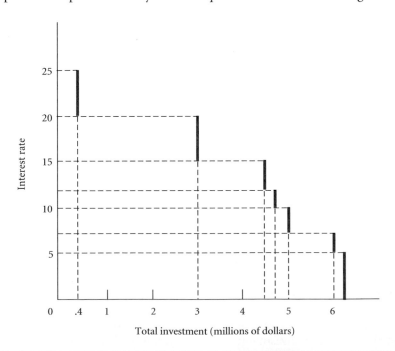

FIGURE 11.3 Total Investment as a Function of the Market Interest Rate

The demand for new capital depends on the interest rate. When the interest rate is low, firms are more likely to invest in new plant and equipment than when the interest rate is high. This is so because the interest rate determines the direct cost (interest on a loan) or the opportunity cost (alternative investment) of each project.

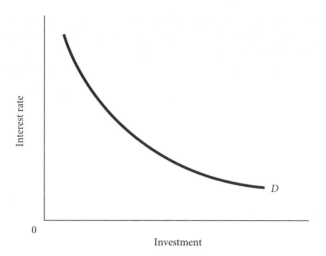

FIGURE 11.4 Investment Demand

Lower interest rates are likely to stimulate investment in the economy as a whole, whereas higher interest rates are likely to slow investment.

decisions. Because many influences affect these expectations, they are usually volatile and subject to frequent change. Thus, although lower interest rates tend to stimulate investment, and higher interest rates tend to slow it, many other hard-to-measure and hard-to-predict factors also affect the level of investment spending. These might include government policy changes, election results, global affairs, inflation, and changes in currency exchange rates.

The Expected Rate of Return and the Marginal Revenue Product of Capital

The concept of the expected rate of return on investment projects is analogous to the concept of the marginal revenue product of capital (MRP_K). Recall that we defined an input's marginal revenue product as the additional revenue a firm earns by employing one additional unit of that input, *ceteris paribus.* Also recall our earlier discussion of labor demand in a sandwich shop in Chapter 7. If an additional worker can produce 15 sandwiches in 1 hour (the marginal product of labor: $MP_L = 15$) and each sandwich brings in $0.50 (the price of the service produced by the sandwich shop: $P_X = \$0.50$), the marginal revenue product of labor is equal to $7.50 ($MRP_L = MP_L \times P_X = 15 \times \$0.50 = \$7.50$).

Now think carefully about the return to an additional unit of new capital (the marginal revenue product of capital). Suppose that the rate of return on an investment in a new machine is 15 percent. This means that the investment project yields the same return as a bond yielding 15 percent. If the current interest rate is less than 15 percent, the investment project will be undertaken because:

A perfectly competitive profit-maximizing firm will keep investing in new capital up to the point at which the expected rate of return is equal to the interest rate. This is analogous to saying that the firm will continue investing up to the point at which the marginal revenue product of capital is equal to the price of capital, or $MRP_K = P_K$, which is what we learned in Chapter 10.

A FINAL WORD ON CAPITAL

The concept of capital is one of the central ideas in economics. Capital is produced by the economic system itself. Capital generates services over time, and it is used as an input in the production of goods and services.

The enormous productivity of modern industrial societies is due in part to the tremendous amount of capital that they have accumulated over the years. It may surprise you to know that the average worker in the United States works with about $170,000 worth of capital. Recall that in the United States total investment (new capital) was 16.4 percent of GDP in 2004 (see Table 11.1). High rates of investment have had enormous impacts in countries such as China and Malaysia. According to recent World Bank figures, capital goods represent 40 percent of China's total output of goods and services, and in Malaysia the figure is 32 percent. In 2005, China had a growth rate of output of over 9 percent and Malaysia of over 7 percent.

The bulk of this chapter described the institutions and processes that determine the amount and types of capital produced in a market economy. Existing firms in search of increased profits, potential new entrants to the markets, and entrepreneurs with new ideas all are continuously evaluating potential investment projects. At the same time, households are saving. Each year households save some portion of their after-tax incomes. These new savings become part of their net worth, and they want to earn a return on them. Each year a good portion of the savings finds its way into the hands of firms that use it to buy new capital goods.

Between households and firms is the financial capital market. Millions of people participate in financial markets every day. There are literally thousands of financial managers, pension funds, mutual funds, brokerage houses, options traders, and banks whose sole purpose is to earn the highest possible rate of return on people's savings.

Brokers, bankers, and financial managers are continuously scanning the financial horizons for profitable investments. What businesses are doing well? What businesses are doing poorly? Should we lend to an expanding firm? All the analysis done by financial managers seeking to earn a high yield for clients, by managers of firms seeking to earn high profits for their stockholders, and by entrepreneurs seeking profits from innovation serves to channel capital into its most productive uses. Within firms, the evaluation of individual investment projects involves forecasting costs and benefits and valuing streams of potential income that will be earned only in future years.

We have now completed our discussion of competitive input and output markets. We have looked at household and firm choices in output markets, labor markets, land markets, and capital markets.

We now turn to a discussion of the allocative process that we have described. How do all the parts of the economy fit together? Is the result good or bad? Can we improve on it? All of this is the subject of Chapter 12.

SUMMARY

CAPITAL, INVESTMENT, AND DEPRECIATION

1. In market capitalist systems, the decision to put capital to use in a particular enterprise is made by private citizens putting their savings at risk in search of private gain. The set of institutions through which such transactions occur is called the *capital market*.

2. *Capital goods* are those goods produced by the economic system that are used as inputs to produce other goods and services in the future. Capital goods thus yield valuable productive services over time.

3. The major categories of *physical*, or *tangible*, *capital* are non-residential structures, durable equipment, residential structures, and inventories. *Social capital* (or *infrastructure*) is capital that provides services to the public. *Intangible (non-material) capital* includes *human capital* and goodwill.

4. The most important dimension of capital is that it exists through time. Therefore, its value is only as great as the value of the services it will render over time.

5. The most common measure of a firm's *capital stock* is the current market value of its plant, equipment, inventories, and intangible assets. However, in thinking about capital it is important to focus on the actual capital stock instead of its simple monetary value.

6. In economics, the term *investment* refers to the creation of new capital, not to the purchase of a share of stock or a bond. Investment is a flow that increases the capital stock.

7. *Depreciation* is the decline in an asset's economic value over time. A capital asset can depreciate because it wears out physically or because it becomes obsolete.

THE CAPITAL MARKET

8. Income that is earned on savings that have been put to use through *financial capital markets* is called *capital income*. The two most important forms of capital income are *interest* and *profits*. Interest is the fee paid by a borrower to a lender. Interest rewards households for postponing gratification, and profit rewards entrepreneurs for innovation and risk taking.

9. In modern industrial societies, investment decisions (capital production decisions) are made primarily by firms. Households decide how much to save, and in the long run, saving limits the amount of investment that firms can

undertake. The capital market exists to direct savings into profitable investment projects.

THE DEMAND FOR NEW CAPITAL AND THE INVESTMENT DECISION

10. Before investing, investors must evaluate the expected flow of future productive services that an investment project will yield.

11. The availability of interest to lenders means that there is an opportunity cost associated with every investment project. This cost must be weighed against the stream of earnings that a project is expected to yield.

12. A firm will decide whether to undertake an investment project by comparing costs with expected returns. The *expected rate of return* on an investment project depends on the price of the investment, the expected length of time the project provides additional cost savings or revenue, and the expected amount of revenue attributable each year to the project.

13. The investment demand curve shows the demand for capital in the economy as a function of the market interest rate. Only those investment projects that are expected to yield a rate of return higher than the market interest rate will be funded. Lower interest rates should stimulate investment.

14. A perfectly competitive profit-maximizing firm will keep investing in new capital up to the point at which the expected rate of return is equal to the interest rate. This is equivalent to saying that the firm will continue investing up to the point at which the marginal revenue product of capital is equal to the price of capital, or $MRP_K = P_K$.

REVIEW TERMS AND CONCEPTS

bond, 234

capital, 232

capital income, 236

capital market, 234

capital stock, 233

depreciation, 234

expected rate of return, 241

financial capital market, 235

human capital, 232

intangible capital, 232

interest, 236

interest rate, 236

investment, 233

physical, or tangible, capital, 232

social capital, or infrastructure, 232

PROBLEM SET

1. Which of the following are capital, and which are not? Explain your answers.
   a. A video poker game machine at a local bar that takes quarters
   b. A $10 bill
   c. A college education
   d. The Golden Gate Bridge
   e. The shirts on the rack in Sears
   f. A government bond
   g. The Empire State Building
   h. A savings account
   i. The Washington Monument
   j. A Honda plant in Marysville, Ohio

2. For each of the following say whether you agree or disagree and explain your answer:
   a. *Savings* and *investment* are just two words for the same thing.
   b. When I buy a share of Microsoft stock, I have invested; when I buy a government bond, I have not.
   c. Higher interest rates lead to more investment because those investments pay a higher return.

3. You and 99 other partners are offered the chance to buy a gas station. Each partner would put up $10,000. The revenues from the operation of the station have been steady at $420,000 per year for several years and are projected to remain steady into the future. The costs (not including opportunity costs) of operating the station (including maintenance and repair, depreciation, salaries, and so on) have also been steady at $360,000 per year.

Currently, 5-year Treasury bills are yielding 7.5 percent interest. Would you go in on the deal?

4. The board of directors of the Quando Company in Singapore was presented with the following list of investment projects for implementation in 2005:

PROJECT	TOTAL COST SINGAPORE DOLLARS	ESTIMATED RATE OF RETURN
Factory in Kuala Lumpur	17,356,400	13%
Factory in Bangkok	15,964,200	15
A new company aircraft	10,000,000	12
A factory outlet store	3,500,000	18
A new computer network	2,000,000	20
A cafeteria for workers	1,534,000	7

Sketch total investment as a function of the interest rate (with the interest rate on the *Y*-axis). Currently, the interest rate in Singapore is 8 percent. How much investment would you recommend to Quando's board?

5. The Federal Reserve Board of Governors has the power to raise or lower short-term interest rates. Between 2003 and 2005, the Fed aggressively increased the benchmark federal funds interest rate from 1 percent in June 2003 to 3.75 percent in October 2005. Assuming that other interest rates also increased, what effects do you think that move had on investment spending in the economy? Explain your answer. What do you think the Fed's objective was?

6. Give at least three examples of how savings can be channeled into productive investment. Why is investment so important for an economy? What do you sacrifice when you save today?

7. From a newspaper like the *Wall Street Journal*, from the business section of your local daily, or from the Internet, look up the prime interest rate, the corporate bond rate, and the interest rate on 10-year U.S. government bonds today. List some of the reasons these three rates are different.

8. Explain what we mean when we say that "households supply capital and firms demand capital."

9. Suppose that I decide to start a small business. To raise start-up funds, I sell 1,000 shares of stock for $100 each. For the next 5 years, I take in annual revenues of $50,000. My total annual costs of operating the business are $20,000. If all of my earnings

are paid out as dividends to shareholders, how much of my total annual earnings can be considered profit? Assume that the current interest rate is 10 percent.

10. Describe the capital stock of your college or university. How would you go about measuring its value? Has your school made any major investments in recent years? If so, describe them. What does your school hope to gain from these investments?

11. In August 1997, the Prudential Insurance Company of America put the Prudential Center, the largest commercial complex in Boston (including a 52-story office tower), up for sale. If you were a real estate investment company considering bidding on the complex, what would you want to know first? What specific factors would you need to form expectations about? What information would you need to help form those expectations?

APPENDIX

CALCULATING PRESENT VALUE

We have seen in this chapter that a firm's major goal in making investment decisions is to evaluate revenue streams that will not materialize until the future. One way for the firm to decide whether or not to undertake an investment project is to compare the expected rate of return from the investment with the current interest rate available (assuming comparable risk) in the financial market. We discussed this procedure in the text. The purpose of this appendix is to present a more complete method of evaluating future revenue streams through present-value analysis.

PRESENT VALUE

Consider the investment project described in Table 11A.1. We use the word *project* in this example to refer to actually buying a machine or a piece of capital for $1,200 and receiving the cash flow given in the right-hand column of the table. Would you do the project or not? At first glance, you might answer yes. After all, the total flow of cash that you will receive is $1,600, which is $400 greater than the amount that you have to pay. But be careful: The $1,600 comes to you over a 5-year period, and your $1,200 must be paid right now. You must consider the alternative uses and opportunity costs of the $1,200. At the same time, you must consider the risks that you are taking.

What are these other alternatives? At a bare minimum the same $1,200 could be put into a bank account, where it would earn interest. In addition, there are always other things that you could do with the same money. You could buy Treasury bonds from the federal government that guarantee you interest of 4 percent for 5 years. Or you could possibly find other projects with a similar degree of risk that might produce more than $1,600.

Recall that the *interest rate* is the amount of money that a borrower agrees to pay a lender, or a bank agrees to pay a depositor, each year expressed as a percentage of the deposit or the loan. For example, if I deposited $1,000 in an account paying 10 percent interest, I would receive $100 per year for the term of the deposit. Sometimes we use the term *rate of return* to refer to the amount of money that the lender receives from her investment each year expressed as a percent of the investment.

The idea is that in deciding to do any project, you must consider the opportunity costs: What are you giving up? If you did not do this project but rather put the money to use elsewhere, would you do better?

Almost all investments that you might consider involve risks: The project might not work out the way you anticipate, the economy may change, or market interest rates could go up or down. To assess the opportunity costs and to decide whether this project is worth it or not, you first have to think about those risks and decide on the rate of return that you require to compensate yourself for taking the risks involved.

If there were no risk, the opportunity cost of investing in a project would be simply the government-guaranteed or bank-guaranteed interest rate. But in considering a project that involves risk, you would clearly want more profit in return for bearing that risk. For example, you might invest in a sure deal if you received a 3 percent annual return comparable to what you might earn in a bank account or certificate of deposit, whereas you

TABLE 11A.1 Expected Profits from a $1,200 Investment Project

Year 1	$100
Year 2	100
Year 3	400
Year 4	500
Year 5	500
All later years	0
Total	1,600

might demand 15 percent or even 20 percent on a very risky investment.

Evaluating the opportunity costs of any investment project requires taking the following steps.

Step 1: The first step in evaluating the opportunity costs of an investment project is to look at the market. What are interest rates today? What rates of interest are people earning by putting their money in bank accounts? If there is risk that something could go wrong, what interest rate is the market paying to those who accept that risk?

> The *discount rate* used to evaluate an investment project is the interest rate that you could earn by investing a similar amount of money in an alternative investment *of comparable risk.*

Let's suppose that the investment project described in Table 11A.1 involved some risk. While you are quite certain that the expected flow of profits in years 1–5 ($100, $100, $400, and so on) is a very good estimate, the future is always uncertain. Let's further suppose that alternative investments of comparable risks are paying a 10 percent rate of interest (rate of return). So you will not do this project unless it earns at least 10 percent. We will thus use a 10 percent discount rate in evaluating the project.

Step 2: Now comes the trick. Is your investment worth it? By doing the project you must consider the opportunity cost of the money. To do this, imagine a bank that will pay 10 percent on deposits. The question that you must answer is, *How much would you have to put in a bank paying 10 percent interest on deposits in order to get the exact same flow of profits that you would get if you did the project?*

If it turns out that you can replicate the flow of profits for *less* money up front than the project costs— $1,200—you will *not* do the project. The project would be paying you less than a 10 percent rate of return. On the other hand, if it turns out that you would have to put *more* than $1,200 into the bank to replicate the flow of profits from the project, then the project would be earning more than 10 percent, and you would do it.

The amount of money that you would have to put in the imaginary bank to replicate the flow of profits from an investment project is called the **present discounted value (PDV)** or simply the **present value (PV)** of the expected flow of profits from the project. To determine that flow, we have to look at the flow *one year at a time.*

At the end of a year you will receive $100 if you do the project. To receive $100 a year from now from your hypothetical bank, how much would you have to deposit now? The answer is clearly less than $100

because you will earn interest. Let's call the interest rate r. In the example $r = .10$ (10 percent). To get back $100 next year, you need to deposit X, where X plus a year's interest on X is equal to $100. That is,

$$X + rX = \$100 \quad \text{or} \quad X(1 + r) = \$100$$

And if we solve for X, we get

$$X = \frac{\$100}{(1 + r)}$$

and that means if $r = .10$,

$$X = \frac{\$100}{1.1}$$

or

$$X = \$90.91$$

To convince yourself that this is right, think of putting $90.91 into your hypothetical bank and coming back in a year. You get back your $90.91 plus interest of 10 percent, which is $9.09. When you add the interest to the initial deposit you get $90.91 + 9.09 or exactly $100! *We say that the present value of $100 a year from now at a discount rate of 10 percent ($r = .10$) is $90.91.*

Notice that if you paid more than $90.91 for the $100 that you will receive from the project after a year, you would be receiving *less than a 10 percent return.* For example, suppose that you paid $95. If you put $95 in an account and came back after a year and found exactly $100, you would have received $5 in interest. Since $5 is just about .0526 (or 5.26 percent) of $95, the interest rate that the bank paid you is actually only 5.26 percent, not 10 percent.

Now what about the next year and the years after that? At the end of year 2 you get another $100. How much would you have to put in the bank today to be able to come back in *2* years and take away $100? Assume that you put amount X in the bank today. Then at the end of year 1 you have $X + rX$, which you keep in the account. At the end of year 2 you have $X + rX$ *plus* interest on $X + rX$, so that at the end of year 2 you have

$$(X + rX) + r(X + rX)$$

which can be written

$$X(1 + r) + rX(1 + r) \quad \text{or} \quad X(1 + r)(1 + r) \quad \text{or} \quad X(1 + r)^2$$

Therefore,

$$X = \frac{\$100}{(1 + r)^2}$$

is the amount you must deposit today to get back $100 in two years.

If $r = .10$, then

$$X = \frac{\$100}{(1.1)^2} \quad \text{or} \quad X = \$82.65$$

To convince yourself that this calculation is right, if you put $82.65 in your hypothetical bank today and came back to check the balance after a year, you would have $82.65 plus interest of 10 percent, or $8.26, which is $90.91. But this time you leave it in the bank and receive 10 percent on the entire balance during the second year, which is $9.09. Adding the additional 10 percent you get back to $100. Thus, if you deposit $82.65 in an account and come back in two years, you will have $100. The present value of $100 two years from now is $82.65.

Now on to year 3. This time you receive a check for $400 but you don't get it until three years have passed. Again, how much would you have to put in your hypothetical bank to end up with $400? Without doing all the math, you can show that X, the amount that you must deposit to get back $400 in three years, is

$$X = \frac{\$400}{(1 + r)^3}$$

and if $r = .10$,

$$X = \frac{\$400}{(1.1)^3} \quad \text{or} \quad X = \$300.53$$

In general, the present value (PV) or present discounted value of R dollars to be received in t years is

$$PV = \frac{R}{(1 + r)^t}$$

Step 3: Once you have looked at the project one year at a time, you must add up the total present value to see what the whole project is worth. In Table 11A.2, the right-hand column shows the present value of each year's return separately. If you add up the total, you have arrived at the amount that you would have to put into your hypothetical bank (that pays interest on deposits at 10 percent) today in order to receive the exact flow that is expected to come from the project. That total is $1,126.06.

So if you go to the bank today and put in $1,126.06, then come back in a year and withdraw $100, then come back after 2 years and withdraw another $100, then come back in three years and withdraw $400, and so forth, until 5 years have passed, when you show up to close the account at the end of the fifth year there will be exactly $500 left to withdraw. Lo and behold, you have figured out that you can receive the exact flow of profit that the project is expected to yield for $1,126.06. If you were looking for a 10 percent yield, you would *not* spend $1,200 for it. You would not do the project.

TABLE 11A.2 Calculation of Total Present Value of a Hypothetical Investment Project (Assuming r = 10 Percent)

END OF . . .	(r)	DIVIDED BY $(1 + r)^t$	=	PRESENT VALUE ($)
Year 1	100	(1.1)		90.91
Year 2	100	$(1.1)^2$		82.65
Year 3	400	$(1.1)^3$		300.53
Year 4	500	$(1.1)^4$		341.51
Year 5	500	$(1.1)^5$		310.46
Total present value				1,126,06

What you have done is to convert an expected *flow* of dollars from an investment project that comes to you over some extended period of time to a *single number*: the present value of the flow.

We can restate the point this way:

> If the present value of the income stream associated with an investment is less than the full cost of the investment project, the investment should not be undertaken.

This is illustrated in Figure 11A.1.

FIGURE 11A.1 Investment Project: Go or No? A Thinking Map

It is important to remember here that we are discussing the *demand for new capital*. Business firms must evaluate potential investments to decide whether they are worth undertaking. This involves predicting the flow of potential future profits arising from each project and comparing those future profits with the return available in the financial market at the current interest rate. The present-value method allows firms to calculate how much it would *cost today* to purchase a contract for the exact same flow of earnings in the financial market.

LOWER INTEREST RATES, HIGHER PRESENT VALUES

Now consider what would happen if you used a lower discount rate in calculating the present value of a flow of earnings. You might use a lower rate in the analysis because interest rates in general have gone down in financial markets, making the opportunity cost of investment lower in general. You might also find out that the project itself is less risky than you believed earlier. For whatever reason, let's say that you would now do the project if it produced a return of 5 percent.

In evaluating the present value, the firm now looks at each year's flow of profit and asked how much it would cost to earn that amount if it were able to earn exactly 5 percent on its money in a hypothetical bank. With a lower interest rate, the firm will have to *pay more* now to purchase the same number of future dollars. Take, for example, the present value of $100 in two years. We saw that if the firm puts aside $82.65 at 10 percent interest, it will have $100 in two years—at a 10 percent interest rate, the present discounted value, or current market price, of $100 in two years is $82.65. However, $82.65 put aside at a 5 percent interest rate would generate only $4.13 in interest in the first year and $4.34 in the second year, for a total balance of $91.11 after two years. To get $100 in two years, the firm needs to put aside more than $82.65 now. Solving for X as we did before:

$$X = \frac{\$100}{(1+r)^2} = \frac{\$100}{(1.05)^2} = \$90.70$$

TABLE 11A.3 Calculation of Total Present Value of a Hypothetical Investment Project (Assuming $r = 5$ Percent)

END OF . . .	$	DIVIDED BY $(1 + r)^t$	=	PRESENT VALUE ($)
Year 1	100	(1.05)		95.24
Year 2	100	$(1.05)^2$		90.70
Year 3	400	$(1.05)^3$		345.54
Year 4	500	$(1.05)^4$		411.35
Year 5	500	$(1.05)^5$		391.76
Total present value				1,334.59

When the interest rate falls from 10 percent to 5 percent, the present value of $100 in two years rises by $8.05 ($90.70 − $82.65).

Table 11A.3 recalculates the present value of the full stream at the lower interest rate; it shows that a decrease in the interest rate from 10 percent to 5 percent causes the total present value to rise to $1,334.59. Because the investment project costs less than this (only $1,200), it should be undertaken. It is now a better deal than can be obtained in the financial market. Under these conditions, a profit-maximizing firm will make the investment. As discussed in the chapter, a lower interest rate leads to more investment.

The basic rule is:

> If the present value of an expected stream of earnings from an investment exceeds the cost of the investment necessary to undertake it, then the investment should be undertaken. However, if the present value of an expected stream of earnings falls short of the cost of the investment, then the financial market can generate the same stream of income for a smaller initial investment, and the investment should not be undertaken.

SUMMARY

1. The present value (PV) of R dollars to be paid t years in the future is the amount you need to pay today, at current interest rates, to ensure that you end up with R dollars t years from now. It is the current market value of receiving R dollars in t years.

2. If the present value of the income stream associated with an investment is less than the full cost of the investment project, the investment project should not be undertaken. If the present value of an expected stream of income exceeds the cost of the investment necessary to undertake it, then the investment should be undertaken.

REVIEW TERMS AND CONCEPTS

present discounted value (PDV), or present value (PV) The present discounting value of R dollars to be paid t years in the future is the amount you need to pay today, at current interest rates, to ensure that you end up with R dollars t years from now. It is the current market value of receiving R dollars in t years.   247

$$PV = \frac{R}{(1 + r)^t}$$

PROBLEM SET

1. Suppose that you were offered $2,000 to be delivered in 1 year. Further suppose that you had the alternative of putting money into a safe certificate of deposit paying annual interest at 10 percent. Would you pay $1,900 in exchange for the $2,000 after 1 year? What is the *maximum* amount you would pay for the offer of $2,000? Suppose that the offer was $2,000, but delivery was to be in 2 years instead of 1. What is the maximum amount you would be willing to pay?

2. Your Uncle Joe has just died and left $10,000 payable to you when you turn 30 years old. You are now 20. Currently, the annual rate of interest one can obtain by buying 10-year bonds is 6.5 percent. Your brother offers you $6,000 cash right now to sign over your inheritance. Should you do it?

3. A special task force has determined that the present discounted value of the benefits from a bridge project comes to $23,786,000. The total construction cost of the bridge is $25,000,000. This implies that the bridge should be built. Do you agree with this conclusion? Explain your answer. What impact could a substantial decline in interest rates have on your answer?

4. Calculate the present value of the income streams A to E in Table 1 at an 8 percent interest rate and again at a 10 percent rate.

   Suppose that the investment behind the flow of income in E is a machine that cost $1,235 at the beginning of year 1. Would you buy the machine if the interest rate were 8 percent? If the interest rate were 10 percent?

5. Determine what someone should be willing to pay for each of the following bonds when the market interest rate for borrowing and lending is 5 percent.
   a. A bond that promises to pay $3,000 in a lump-sum payment after 1 year.
   b. A bond that promises to pay $3,000 in a lump-sum payment after 2 years.
   c. A bond that promises to pay $1,000 per year for 3 years.

6. What should someone be willing to pay for each of the bonds in question 5 if the interest rate is 10 percent?

7. Based on your answers to questions 5 and 6, state whether each of the following is true or false:
   a. *Ceteris paribus*, the price of a bond increases when the interest rate increases.
   b. *Ceteris paribus*, the price of a bond increases when any given amount of money is received sooner rather than later.

8. Assume that the present discounted value of an investment project (commercial development) at a discount rate of 7 percent is $234,756,000. Assume that the building just sold for $254,000,000. Will the buyer earn a rate of return of more than 7 percent, exactly 7 percent, or less than 7 percent? Briefly explain.

9. Assume that I promise to pay you $100 at the end of each of the next 3 years. Using the following formula,

   $$X = 100/(1 + r) + 100/(1 + r)^2 + 100/(1 + r)^3$$

   if $r = 0.075$, then $X = \$260.06$.

   Assuming that somebody of roughly comparable reliability offers to pay out 7.5 percent on anything you let him borrow from you, would you be willing to pay me $270 for my promise?

TABLE 1

END OF YEAR	A	B	C	D	E
1	$ 80	$ 80	$ 100	$ 100	$500
2	80	80	100	100	300
3	80	80	1,100	100	400
4	80	80	0	100	300
5	1,080	80	0	100	0
6	0	80	0	1,100	0
7	0	1,080	0	0	0

General Equilibrium and the Efficiency of Perfect Competition

12

In the last nine chapters we have built a model of a simple, perfectly competitive economy. Our discussion has revolved around the two fundamental decision-making units, *households* and *firms*, which interact in two basic market arenas, *input markets* and *output markets*. (Look again at the circular flow diagram, shown in Figure 12.1.) By limiting our discussion to perfectly competitive firms, we have been able to examine how the basic decision-making units interact in the two basic market arenas.

Households make constrained choices in both input and output markets. In Chapters 3 and 4, we discussed an individual household demand curve for a single good or service. Then in Chapter 6, we went behind the demand curve and saw how income, wealth, and prices define the budget constraints within which households exercise their tastes and preferences. We soon discovered, however, that we cannot look at household decisions in output markets without thinking about the decisions made simultaneously in input markets. Household income, for example, depends on choices made in input markets: whether to work, how much to work, what skills to acquire, and so forth. Input market choices are constrained by such factors as current wage rates, the availability of jobs, and interest rates.

Firms are the primary producing units in a market economy. Profit-maximizing firms, to which we have limited our discussion, earn their profits by selling products and services for more than it costs to produce them. With firms, as with households, output markets and input markets cannot be analyzed separately. All firms make three specific decisions simultaneously: (1) how much output to supply, (2) how to produce that output—that is, which technology to use, and (3) how much of each input to demand.

In Chapters 7 to 9, we explored these three decisions from the viewpoint of output markets. We saw that the portion of the marginal cost curve that lies above a firm's average variable cost curve is the supply curve of a perfectly competitive firm in the short run. Implicit in the marginal cost curve is a choice of technology and a set of input demands. In Chapters 10 and 11, we looked at the perfectly competitive firm's three basic decisions from the viewpoint of input markets.

Output and input markets are connected because firms and households make simultaneous choices in both arenas, but there are other connections among markets as well. Firms buy in both capital and labor markets, for example, and they can substitute capital for labor and vice versa. A change in the price of one factor can easily change the demand for other

FIGURE 12.1 Firm and Household Decisions

Firms and households interact in both input and output markets.

factors. Buying more *capital*, for instance, usually changes the marginal revenue product of *labor* and shifts the labor demand curve. Similarly, a change in the price of a single good or service usually affects household demand for other goods and services, as when a price decrease makes one good more attractive than other close substitutes. The same change also makes households better off when they find that the same amount of income will buy more. Such additional "real income" can be spent on any of the other goods and services that the household buys.

The point here is simple:

> Input and output markets cannot be considered separately or as if they operated independently. Although it is important to understand the decisions of individual firms and households and the functioning of individual markets, we now need to add it all up, to look at the operation of the system as a whole.

You have seen the concept of equilibrium applied both to markets and to individual decision-making units. In individual markets, supply and demand determine an equilibrium price. Perfectly competitive firms are in short-run equilibrium when price and marginal cost are equal ($P = MC$). In the long run, however, equilibrium in a competitive market is achieved only when economic profits are eliminated. Households are in equilibrium when they have equated the marginal utility per dollar spent on each good to the marginal utility per dollar spent on all other goods. This process of examining the equilibrium conditions in individual markets and for individual households and firms separately is called **partial equilibrium analysis**.

A **general equilibrium** exists when all markets in an economy are in simultaneous equilibrium. An event that disturbs the equilibrium in one market may disturb the equilibrium in many other markets as well. The ultimate impact of the event depends on the way *all* markets adjust to it. Thus, partial equilibrium analysis, which looks at adjustments in one isolated market, may be misleading.

Thinking in terms of a general equilibrium leads to some important questions. Is it possible for all households and firms and all markets to be in equilibrium simultaneously? Are the equilibrium conditions that we have discussed separately compatible with one another? Why is an event that disturbs an equilibrium in one market likely to disturb many others simultaneously?

In talking about general equilibrium, the first concept we explore in this chapter, we continue our exercise in *positive economics*— that is, we seek to understand how systems operate without making value judgments about outcomes. Later in the chapter, we turn from positive economics to *normative economics* as we begin to judge the economic system. Are its results good or bad? Can we make them better?

In judging the performance of any economic system, you will recall, it is essential first to establish specific criteria to judge by. In this chapter, we use two such criteria: *efficiency* and *equity* (fairness). First, we demonstrate the **efficiency** of the allocation of resources—that is, the system produces what people want and does so at the least possible cost—if all the assumptions that we have made thus far hold. When we begin to relax some of our assumptions, however, it will become apparent that free markets may *not* be efficient. Several sources of inefficiency naturally occur within an unregulated market system. In the final part of this chapter, we introduce the potential role of government in correcting market inefficiencies and achieving fairness.

partial equilibrium analysis The process of examining the equilibrium conditions in individual markets and for households and firms separately.

general equilibrium The condition that exists when all markets in an economy are in simultaneous equilibrium.

efficiency The condition in which the economy is producing what people want at least possible cost.

GENERAL EQUILIBRIUM ANALYSIS

Two examples will help us illustrate some of the insights that we can gain when we move from partial to general equilibrium analysis. In this section, we will consider the impact on the economy of (1) a major technological advance and (2) a shift in consumer preferences. As you read, remember that we are looking for the connections between markets, particularly between input and output markets.

AN EARLY TECHNOLOGICAL ADVANCE: THE ELECTRONIC CALCULATOR

Students working in quantitative fields of study in the late 1960s, and even as late as the early 1970s, recall classrooms filled with noisy mechanical calculators. At that time, a calculator weighed about 40 pounds and was only able to add, subtract, multiply, and divide. These machines had no memories, and they took 20 to 25 seconds to do one multiplication problem.

Major corporations had rooms full of accountants with such calculators on their desks, and the sound when 30 or 40 of them were running was deafening. During the 1950s and 1960s, most firms had these machines, but few people had a calculator in their homes because the cost of a single machine was several hundred dollars. Some high schools had calculators for accounting classes, but most schoolchildren in the United States had never seen one.

In the 1960s, Wang Laboratories developed an electronic calculator. Bigger than a modern personal computer, it had several keyboards attached to a single main processor. It could add, subtract, multiply, and divide, but it also had a memory. Its main virtues were speed and quiet. It did calculations instantaneously without any noise. The Wang machine sold for around $1,500.

stock market, capital market, investment   search

○ Further Exploration   ● News Analysis

The Dot-Com Bust and the Labor Market: 2003

ONE OF THE IMPORTANT POINTS OF THIS chapter is that input and output markets are closely connected to each other. Clearly, the demand for labor in a particular sector is a derived demand—derived from the demand for product. A sector will demand labor only if the product that it sells is in demand. As a result, when demand for a product declines, there are impacts on the job market. Nowhere is this more evident than in the market for high-technology equipment and software. This sector had an incredible boom during the late 1990s and a stunning decline from 2000 to 2003. The following article from the *New York Times* illustrates the impact on the job market. Labor resources are naturally attracted to expanding industries and away from contracting industries.

Computing's Lost Allure

—*New York Times*

On a sunny May afternoon, Brian Harvey's introductory computer science class at the University of California convened for the last time before the final exam. By the time Dr. Harvey was full tilt into his lecture, reviewing recursive functions and binary search trees, the cavernous hall was lightly peppered with about 100 students, backpacks at their sides, a few legs slung over the backs of empty seats.

Sparse attendance is, of course, an end-of-semester inevitability. Many students viewed the lecture by Webcast, if at all. But more significantly, just 350 students signed up for the course this spring, in striking contrast to enrollment in the fall of 2000, when the same lecture hall was engorged at the start of the semester with 700 students sitting and standing in every available pocket of space.

So full was the room the first few sessions that a fire marshal showed up

to size up the situation as a potential hazard. "Even the corridors were jammed," recalled Dr. Harvey, who has taught the introductory course for 16 years. The following semester was little different, with 600 students hoping to enroll in the class.

Today, empty classroom seats, like the vacant offices once occupied by high-flying start-ups, are among the unmistakable repercussions of the dot-com bust.

At the height of the Internet boom in the late 90's, computer science talent was in such demand that recruiters offered signing bonuses to students who agreed to drop out of school. Now, spooked by layoffs and disabused of visions of overnight riches, many undergraduates are turning away from computer science as if it were somehow cursed.

Berkeley's experience is mirrored elsewhere. At Carnegie-Mellon University, applications to the School of Computer Science for next fall are down 36 percent from their peak in 2001; applications to Virginia Tech's computer science department have declined 40 percent since 2001. At M.I.T., renowned for its computer science curriculum, 20 percent fewer freshmen declared electrical engineering and computer science as their central focus this spring than did in 2001 or 2002.

"People aren't seeing the glory in computer science that they used to," said Nirav Dave, 20, a senior and an electrical and computer engineering major at Carnegie-Mellon who has seen the ranks of his fellow majors decline. "It used to be that you would do this and you would be a millionaire."

Shaun McCormick, 19, who will be a sophomore next fall at the University of Texas at Austin, started out in computer science but switched at midyear to communications and plans to focus on advertising.

Not only was he daunted by the difficulty of the coursework, Mr. McCormick said, but his job prospects also worried him.

According to the Taulbee Survey, enrollment in computer science departments nearly doubled between 1995 and 2000. So great was the demand for programmers that many students enjoyed the luxury of not even having to prepare a résumé.

"It used to be that even before students had graduated they had three job offers and by the time they had to make a decision, they had 10," said Gabby Silberman, program director for the Centers for Advanced Studies at I.B.M.'s T.J. Watson Research Center, who spends much of his time recruiting.

Undergraduates who might otherwise have chosen computer science appear to be fanning out to related yet more applied fields like business information technology, biotechnology and bioinformatics, which involves managing and manipulating databases of genetic information.

At the University of Texas, pharmacy appears to be a popular alternative, a phenomenon that mystifies Dr. Moore. "All these kids need a lot of chemistry courses, so it's put a real load on the chemistry department," he said. Many others have shifted to biology.

Jennifer Li, a junior at Carnegie-Mellon who is majoring in computer science, said that more people in her field were choosing second majors to enhance their job prospects in other fields like graphic arts and bioinformatics. For her part, Ms. Li has chosen two minors: business administration and multimedia production.

The beginning of the 1970s saw the industry develop rapidly. First, calculators shrank in size. The Bomar Corporation made one of the earliest hand calculators, the Bomar Brain. These early versions could do nothing more than add, subtract, multiply, and divide; they had no memories; and they still sold for several hundred dollars. Then, in the early 1970s, a number of technological breakthroughs made it possible to mass-produce very small electronic circuits (silicon chips). These circuits in turn made calculators very inexpensive to produce, and this is the beginning of our general equilibrium story. Costs in the calculator industry shifted downward dramatically [Figure 12.2(b)]. As costs fell, profits increased. Attracted by economic profits, new firms rapidly entered the market. Instead of one or two firms producing state-of-the-art machines, dozens of firms began cranking them out by the thousands. As a result, the industry supply curve shifted out to the right, driving down prices toward the new lower costs [see Figure 12.2(a)].

As the price of electronic calculators fell, the market for the old mechanical calculators died a quiet death. With no more demand for their product, producers found themselves suffering losses and got out of the business. As the price of electronic calculators kept falling, thousands of people who had never had a calculator began to buy them. By 1973, calculators were available at discount appliance stores for $60 to $70, and by 1975, 18.1 million were produced annually and sold at an average price of $62. The average price fell to under $30 and sales hit 30.9 million by 1983. You can now buy a basic calculator for less than $5, or get one free with a magazine subscription. In 1987, 33.8 million calculators were produced. In 1990, the Commerce Department stopped counting.

The rapid decline in the cost of producing calculators led to a rapid expansion of supply and a decline in price [see Figure 12.2(a)]. The lower prices increased the quantity demanded to such an extent that most U.S. homes now have at least one calculator. Nowadays, most cell phones even have a calculator feature.

This is only a partial equilibrium story, however. The events we have described also had effects on many other markets. In other words, they disturbed the general equilibrium. When mechanical calculators became obsolete, many people who had over the years developed the skills required to produce and repair those complex machines found themselves unemployed. At the same time, demand boomed for workers in the production, distribution, and sales of the new electronic calculators. The new technology thus caused a reallocation of labor across the labor market.

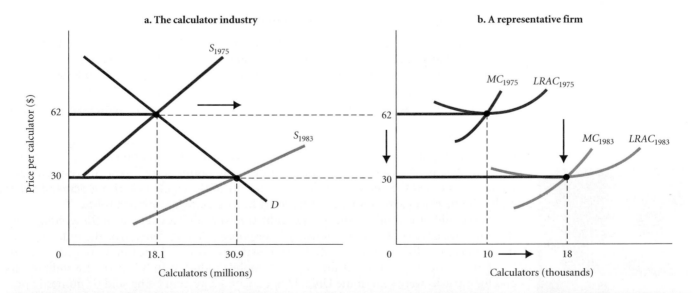

FIGURE 12.2 Cost Saving Technological Change in the Calculator Industry

In the 1970s and 1980s, major technological changes occurred in the calculator industry. In 1975, 18.1 million calculators were sold at an average price of $62. As technology made it possible to produce at lower costs, cost curves shifted downward. As new firms entered the industry and existing firms expanded, output rose and market price dropped. In 1983, 30.9 million calculators were produced and sold at an average price of under $30.

Capital was also reallocated. New firms invested in the plant and equipment needed to produce electronic calculators. Old capital owned by the firms that previously made mechanical calculators became obsolete and depreciated, and it ended up on the scrap heap. The mechanical calculators themselves, once an integral part of the capital stocks of accounting firms, banks, and so forth, were scrapped and replaced by the cheaper, more efficient calculators.

When a new billion-dollar industry suddenly appears, it earns billions of dollars in revenues that might have been spent on other things. Even though the effects of this success on any one other industry were probably small, general equilibrium analysis tells us that in the absence of the new industry and the demand for its product, households will demand other goods and services, and other industries will produce more. In this case, society has benefited a great deal. Everyone can now buy a very useful product at a low price. The new calculators have raised the productivity of certain kinds of labor and reduced costs in many industries.

Of course, the electronic calculator was just the beginning of a process of product evolution that has led to a complete change in the way we live. Thirty years ago Kenneth Olsen, the president of Digital Equipment Corporation, is widely quoted to have asked, "Why would anyone need their own computer?" Today, we do everything from watching movies, to paying bills, shopping, dating, and blogging on small but powerful laptops with huge hard drives. A hotel without Wi-Fi, wireless access, is considered a second-class hotel.

Apple sold a staggering 6 million iPods for over a billion dollars during the first 3 months of 2005. The immense popularity of the iPod has fueled the market for music downloads, which are fast becoming the technology of choice for storing and playing music for millions of people worldwide. The betting is that CDs and CD players are now obsolete and will fade out as the new technology pushes aside yet another frontier.

All of this change has happened through the market. Declining costs of production and fierce competition have continuously pushed prices down and provided us with a never-ending stream of new and more powerful consumer electronics.

> A significant—if not sweeping—technological change in a single industry affects many markets. Households face a different structure of prices and must adjust their consumption of many products. Labor reacts to new skill requirements and is reallocated across markets. Capital is also reallocated.

MARKET ADJUSTMENT TO CHANGES IN DEMAND

One thing we know about the U.S. economy and the world economy is that they are dynamic: Change occurs all the time. Markets experience shifts of demand, both up and down; costs and technology change; and prices and outputs change. To show how a change in one market affects other markets and the general equilibrium, we will describe a simple economy with two sectors, X and Y. The story will be of an increase in demand in one sector and a decline in demand in the other.

As you go through the following diagrams and discussion, you can think of any major sector that might be experiencing an increase in demand. For example, beginning around the year 2000 the housing market entered a dramatic boom period. Low interest rates and rising incomes led the demand for housing to shift to the right. This rising demand led to higher home prices and new entry by building firms seeking economic profits.

You could also think of the airline industry. New airlines such as JetBlue, Song, and AirTran have entered the airline industry in response to rising demand as the industry continues to recover from a dramatic decline following the World Trade Center tragedy of 2001.

Finally, you might think of the huge automobile industry. In July 2005, 1.8 million cars and light trucks were sold in the United States, with 82 percent being sold by domestic producers. Auto workers accounted for over 1 million workers out of just over 14 million workers in manufacturing in 2005. The auto sector moves cyclically, and periodically demand increases.

So imagine that sector X is one of these large sectors and that sector Y is the rest of the economy.

Recent entrants into the airline industry include JetBlue.

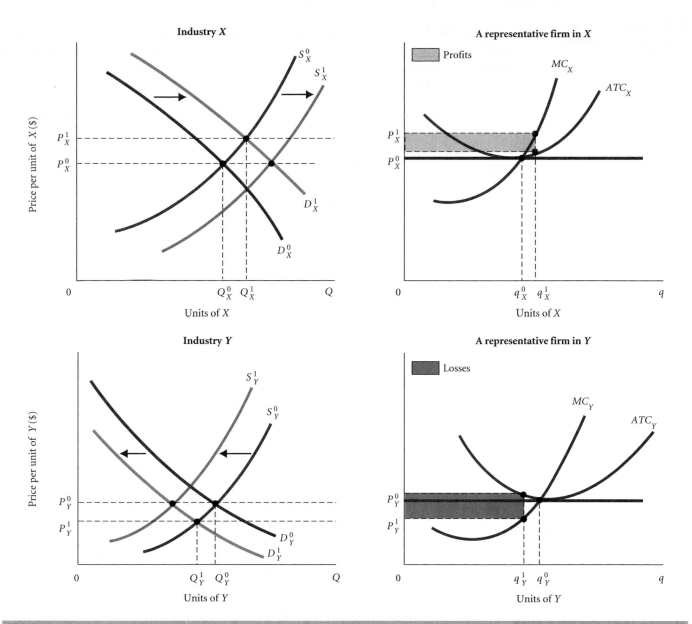

FIGURE 12.3 Adjustment in an Economy with Two Sectors

Initially, demand for X shifts from D_X^0 to D_X^1. This shift pushes the price of X up to P_X^1, creating profits. Demand for Y shifts down from D_Y^0 to D_Y^1, pushing the price of Y down to P_Y^1 and creating losses. Firms have an incentive to leave sector Y and an incentive to enter sector X. Exiting sector Y shifts supply in that industry to S_Y^1, raising price and eliminating losses. Entry shifts supply in X to S_X^1, thus reducing and eliminating profits.

Figure 12.3 shows the initial equilibrium in sectors X and Y. We assume that both sectors are initially in long-run competitive equilibrium. Total output in sector X is Q_X^0, the product is selling for a price of P_X^0, and each firm in the industry produces up to where P_X^0 is equal to marginal cost—q_X^0. At that point, price is just equal to average cost, and economic profits are zero. The same condition holds initially in sector Y. The market is in zero profit equilibrium at a price of P_Y^0.

Now assume that a change in consumer preferences (or in the age distribution of the population or in something else) shifts the demand for X out to the right from D_X^0 to D_X^1. That shift drives the price up to P_X^1. If households decide to buy more X, without an increase in income they must buy *less* of something else. Because everything else is represented by Y in this example, the demand for Y must decline, and the demand curve for Y shifts to the left, from D_Y^0 to D_Y^1.

With the shift in demand for X, price rises to P_X^1 and profit-maximizing firms immediately increase output to q_X^1 (the point where $P_X^1 = MC_X$). However, now there are positive profits in X. With the downward shift of demand in Y, price falls to P_Y^1. Firms in sector Y cut back to q_Y^1 (the point where $P_Y^1 = MC_Y$), and the lower price causes firms producing Y to suffer losses.

In the short run, adjustment is simple. Firms in both industries are constrained by their current scales of plant. Firms can neither enter nor exit their respective industries. Each firm in industry X raises output somewhat, from q_X^0 to q_X^1. Firms in industry Y cut back from q_Y^0 to q_Y^1.

In response to the existence of profit in sector X, the capital market begins to take notice. In Chapter 9 we saw that new firms are likely to enter an industry in which there are profits to be earned. Financial analysts see the profits as a signal of future healthy growth, and entrepreneurs may become interested in moving into the industry.

Adding all of this together, we would expect to see investment begin to favor sector X. This is indeed the case: Capital begins to flow into sector X. As new firms enter, the short-run supply curve in the industry shifts to the right and continues to do so until all profits are eliminated. In the top left diagram in Figure 12.3, the supply curve shifts out from S_X^0 to S_X^1, a shift that drives the price back down to P_X^0.

We would also expect to see a movement out of sector Y because of losses. Some firms will exit the industry. In the bottom left diagram in Figure 12.3, the supply curve shifts back from S_Y^0 to S_Y^1, a shift that drives the price back up to P_Y^0. At this point all losses are eliminated.

Note that a new general equilibrium is not reached until equilibrium is reestablished in all markets. If costs of production remain unchanged, as they do in Figure 12.3, this equilibrium occurs at the initial product prices, but with more resources and production in X and fewer in Y. In contrast, if an expansion in X drives up the prices of resources used specifically in X, the cost curves in X will shift upward and the final, postexpansion, zero-profit equilibrium will occur at a higher price. Such an industry is called an *increasing-cost industry*.

FORMAL PROOF OF A GENERAL COMPETITIVE EQUILIBRIUM

Economic theorists have struggled with the question of whether a set of prices that equates supply and demand in all markets simultaneously can actually exist when there are literally thousands and thousands of markets. If such a set of prices were not possible, the result could be continuous cycles of expansion, contraction, and instability.

The nineteenth-century French economist Leon Walras struggled with the problem, but he could never provide a formal proof. By using advanced mathematical tools, economists Kenneth Arrow and Gerard Debreu and mathematicians John von Neumann and Abraham Wald showed the existence of at least one set of prices that *will* clear all markets in a large system simultaneously.

ALLOCATIVE EFFICIENCY AND COMPETITIVE EQUILIBRIUM

Chapters 3 through 11 built a complete model of a simple, perfectly competitive economic system; however, recall that in Chapters 3 and 4 we made a number of important assumptions. We assumed that both output markets and input markets are perfectly competitive—that is, that no individual household or firm is large enough relative to the market to have any control over price. In other words, we assumed that firms and households are *price-takers*.

We also assumed that households have perfect information on product quality and on all prices available, and that firms have perfect knowledge of technologies and input prices. Finally, we said that decision makers in a competitive system always consider all the costs and benefits of their decisions—that there are no "external" costs.

If all these assumptions hold, the economy will produce an efficient allocation of resources. As we relax these assumptions one by one, however, you will discover that the allocation of resources is no longer efficient and that a number of sources of inefficiency occur naturally.

PARETO EFFICIENCY

In Chapter 1 we introduced several specific criteria used by economists to judge the performance of economic systems and to evaluate alternative economic policies. These criteria are (1) efficiency, (2) equity, (3) growth, and (4) stability. In Chapter 1 you also learned that an *efficient* economy is one that produces the things that people want at least cost. The idea behind the efficiency criterion is that the economic system exists to serve the wants and needs of the people. If resources can be somehow reallocated to make the people "better off," then they should be. We want to use the resources at our disposal to produce maximum well-being. The trick is defining "maximum well-being."

For many years, social philosophers wrestled with the problem of "aggregation," or "adding up." When we say "maximum well-being" we mean maximum *for society*. Societies are made up of many people, however, and the problem has always been how to maximize satisfaction, or well-being, for all members of society. What has emerged is the now widely accepted concept of *allocative efficiency*, first developed by the Italian economist Vilfredo Pareto in the nineteenth century. Pareto's very precise definition of efficiency is often referred to as **Pareto efficiency** or **Pareto optimality**.

Pareto efficiency or **Pareto optimality** A condition in which no change is possible that will make some members of society better off without making some other members of society worse off.

Specifically, a change is said to be efficient if it makes some members of society better off without making other members of society worse off. An efficient, or *Pareto optimal*, system is one in which no such changes are possible. An example of a change that makes some people better off and nobody worse off is a simple voluntary exchange. I have apples; you have nuts. I like nuts; you like apples. We trade. We both gain, and no one loses.

For such a definition to have any real meaning, we must answer two questions: (1) What do we mean by "better off"? and (2) How do we account for changes that make some people better off and others worse off?

The answer to the first question is simple. People themselves decide what "better off" and "worse off" mean. I am the only one who knows whether I am better off after a change. If you and I exchange one item for another because I like what you have and you like what I have, we both "reveal" that we are better off after the exchange because we agreed to it voluntarily. If everyone in the neighborhood wants a park and the residents all contribute to a fund to build one, they have consciously changed the allocation of resources, and they all are better off for it.

The answer to the second question is more complex. Nearly every change that one can imagine leaves some people better off and some people worse off. If some gain and some lose as the result of a change, and it can be demonstrated that the value of the gains exceeds the value of the losses, then the change is said to be *potentially efficient*. In practice, however, the distinction between a *potentially* and an *actually* efficient change is often ignored, and all such changes are simply called *efficient*.

Example: Budget Cuts in Massachusetts

Several years ago, in an effort to reduce state spending, the budget of the Massachusetts Registry of Motor Vehicles was cut substantially. Among other things, the state sharply reduced the number of clerks in each office. Almost immediately Massachusetts residents found themselves waiting in line for hours when they had to register their automobiles or get their driver's licenses.

Drivers and car owners began paying a price: standing in line, which uses time and energy that could otherwise be used more productively. However, before we can make sensible efficiency judgments, we must be able to measure, or at least approximate, the value of both the gains and the losses produced by the budget cut. To approximate the losses to car owners and drivers, we might ask how much people would be willing to pay to avoid standing in those long lines.

One office estimated that 500 people stood in line every day for about 1 hour each. If each person were willing to pay just $2 to avoid standing in line, the damage incurred would be $1,000 (500 × $2) per day. If the registry were open 250 days per year, the reduction in labor force at that office alone would create a cost to car owners, conservatively estimated, of $250,000 (250 × $1,000) per year.

Estimates also showed that taxpayers in Massachusetts saved about $80,000 per year by having fewer clerks at that office. If the clerks were reinstated, there would be some gains and some losses. Car owners and drivers would gain, and taxpayers would lose. However, because we can show that the value of the gains would substantially exceed the value of the losses, it can be argued that reinstating the clerks would be an efficient change. Note that the only *net* losers would be those taxpayers who do not own a car and do not hold driver's licenses.[1]

THE EFFICIENCY OF PERFECT COMPETITION

In Chapter 2 we discussed the "economic problem" of dividing up scarce resources among alternative uses. We also discussed the three basic questions that all societies must answer, and we set out to explain how these three questions are answered in a competitive economy.

The three basic questions included:

1. *What gets produced?* What determines the final mix of output?

2. *How is it produced?* How do capital, labor, and land get divided up among firms? In other words, what is the allocation of resources among producers?

3. *Who gets what is produced?* What determines which households get how much? What is the distribution of output among consuming households?

To determine whether it is efficient to hire additional clerks at the Registry of Motor Vehicles, the cost must be weighed against the value of people's time spent waiting in lines.

The following discussion of efficiency uses these three questions and their answers to prove informally that perfect competition is efficient. To demonstrate that the perfectly competitive system leads to an efficient, or Pareto optimal, allocation of resources, we need to show that no changes are possible that will make some people better off without making others worse off. Specifically, we will show that under perfect competition (1) resources are allocated among firms efficiently, (2) final products are distributed among households efficiently, and (3) the system produces the things that people want.

Efficient Allocation of Resources among Firms The simple definition of efficiency holds that firms must produce their products using the best available—that is, lowest-cost—technology. If more output could be produced with the same amount of inputs, it would be possible to make some people better off without making others worse off.

The perfectly competitive model we have been using rests on several assumptions that assure us that resources in such a system would indeed be efficiently allocated among firms. Most important of these is the assumption that individual firms maximize profits. To maximize profit, a firm must minimize the cost of producing its chosen level of output. With a full knowledge of existing technologies, firms will choose the technology that produces the output they want at least cost.

There is more to this story than meets the eye, however. Inputs must be allocated *across* firms in the best possible way. If we find that it is possible, for example, to take capital from firm A and swap it for labor from firm B and produce more product in both firms, then the original allocation was inefficient. Recall our example from Chapter 2. Farmers in Ohio and Kansas both produce wheat and corn. The climate and soil in most of Kansas are best suited to wheat production; the climate and soil in Ohio are best suited to corn production. Kansas should produce most of the wheat, and Ohio should produce most of the corn. A law that forces Kansas land into corn production and Ohio land into wheat production would result in less of both—an inefficient allocation of resources. However, if markets are free and open, Kansas farmers will naturally find a higher return by planting wheat, and Ohio farmers will find a higher return in corn. The free market, then, should lead to an efficient allocation of resources among firms.

The same argument can be made more general. Misallocation of resources among firms is unlikely as long as every single firm faces the same set of prices and trade-offs in input markets. Recall from Chapter 10 that perfectly competitive firms will hire additional factors of production as long as their marginal revenue product exceeds their market price. As long as all firms have access to the *same* factor markets and the *same* factor prices, the last unit of

---

[1]You might ask, are there not other gainers and losers? What about the clerks themselves? In analysis like this, it is usually assumed that the citizens who pay lower taxes now spend their added income on other things. The producers of those other things need to expand to meet the new demand, and they hire more labor. Thus, a contraction of 100 jobs in the public sector will open up 100 jobs in the private sector. If the economy is fully employed, the transfer of labor to the private sector is assumed to create no net gains or losses to the workers themselves.

a factor hired will produce the same value in each firm. Certainly firms will use different technologies and factor combinations, but at the margin, no single profit-maximizing firm can get more value out of a factor than that factor's current market price. For example, if workers can be hired in the labor market at a wage of $6.50, *all* firms will hire workers as long as the marginal revenue product (MRP_L) produced by the marginal worker (labor's MRP_L) remains above $6.50. *No* firms will hire labor beyond the point at which MRP_L falls below $6.50. Thus, at equilibrium, additional workers are not worth more than $6.50 to any firm, and switching labor from one firm to another will not produce output of any greater value to society. Each firm has hired the profit-maximizing amount of labor. In short:

> The assumptions that factor markets are competitive and open, that all firms pay the same prices for inputs, and that all firms maximize profits lead to the conclusion that the allocation of resources among firms is efficient.

Efficient Distribution of Outputs among Households Even if the system is producing the right things, and is doing so efficiently, these things still have to get to the right people. Just as open, competitive factor markets ensure that firms do not end up with the wrong inputs, open, competitive output markets ensure that households do not end up with the wrong goods and services.

Within the constraints imposed by income and wealth, households are free to choose among all the goods and services available in output markets. A household will buy a good as long as that good generates utility, or subjective value, greater than its market price. Utility value is revealed in market behavior. You do not go out and buy something unless you are willing to pay *at least* the market price.

Remember that the value you place on any one good depends on what you must give up to have that good. The trade-offs available to you depend on your budget constraint. The trade-offs that are desirable depend on your preferences. If you buy a $300 MP3 player, you may be giving up a trip home. If I buy it, I may be giving up four new tires for my car. We have both revealed that the MP3 player is worth at least as much to us as all the other things that $300 can buy. As long as we are free to choose among all the things that $300 can buy, we will not end up with the wrong things; it is not possible to find a trade that will make us both better off.

> We all know that people have different tastes and preferences, and that they will buy very different things in very different combinations. As long as everyone shops freely in the same markets, no redistribution of final outputs among people will make them better off. If you and I buy in the same markets and pay the same prices, and I buy what I want and you buy what you want, we cannot possibly end up with the wrong combination of things. Free and open markets are essential to this result.

Producing What People Want: The Efficient Mix of Output It does no good to produce things efficiently or to distribute them efficiently if the system produces the wrong things. Will competitive markets produce the things that people want?

If the system is producing the wrong mix of output, we should be able to show that producing more of one good and less of another will make people better off. To show that perfectly competitive markets are efficient, we must demonstrate that no such changes in the final mix of output are possible.

The condition that ensures that the right things are produced is $P = MC$. That is, in both the long run and the short run, a perfectly competitive firm will produce at the point where the price of its output is equal to the marginal cost of production. The logic is this: When a firm weighs price and marginal cost, it weighs the value of its product to society *at the margin* against the value of the things that could otherwise be produced with the same resources. Figure 12.4 summarizes this logic.

The argument is quite straightforward. *First, price reflects households' willingness to pay.* By purchasing a product, individual households reveal that it is worth at least as much as the other things that the same money could buy. Thus, current price reflects the value that households place on a good.

If $P_X > MC_X$, society gains value by producing *more* X.
If $P_X < MC_X$, society gains value by producing *less* X.

| The value placed on good X by society through the market, or the social value of a marginal unit of X. | $P_X = MC_X$ | Market-determined value of resources needed to produce a marginal unit of X. MC_X is equal to the opportunity cost of those resources: lost production of other goods or the value of the resources left unemployed (leisure, vacant land, etc.). |

FIGURE 12.4 The Key Efficiency Condition: Price Equals Marginal Cost

Second, marginal cost reflects the opportunity cost of the resources needed to produce a good. If a firm producing X hires a worker, it must pay the market wage. That wage must be sufficient to attract that worker out of leisure or away from firms producing other products. The same argument holds for capital and land.

Thus, if the price of a good ends up greater than marginal cost, producing more of it will generate benefits to households in excess of opportunity costs, and society gains. Similarly, if the price of a good ends up below marginal cost, resources are being used to produce something that households value less than opportunity costs. Producing less of it creates gains to society.[2]

> Society will produce the efficient mix of output if all firms equate price and marginal cost.

Figure 12.5 shows how a simple competitive market system leads individual households and firms to make efficient choices in input and output markets. For simplicity, the

FIGURE 12.5 Efficiency in Perfect Competition Follows from a Weighing of Values by Both Households and Firms

---

[2]It is important to understand that firms do not act *consciously* to balance social costs and benefits. In fact, the usual assumption is that firms are self-interested, private profit-maximizers. It just works out that in perfectly competitive markets, when firms are weighing private benefits against private costs, they are actually (perhaps without knowing it) weighing the benefits and costs to society as well.

figure assumes only one factor of production, labor. Households weigh the market wage against the value of leisure and time spent in unpaid household production. However, the wage is a measure of labor's potential product because firms weigh labor cost (wages) against the value of the product produced and hire up to the point at which $W = MRP_L$. Households use wages to buy market-produced goods. Thus, households implicitly weigh the value of market-produced goods against the value of leisure and household production.

When a firm's scale is balanced, it is earning maximum profit; when a household's scale is balanced, it is maximizing utility. Under these conditions, no changes can improve social welfare.

PERFECT COMPETITION VERSUS REAL MARKETS

So far, we have built a model of a perfectly competitive market system that produces an efficient allocation of resources, an efficient mix of output, and an efficient distribution of output. The perfectly competitive model is built on a set of assumptions, all of which must hold for our conclusions to be fully valid. We have assumed that all firms and households are price-takers in input and output markets, that firms and households have perfect information, and that all firms maximize profits.

These assumptions do not always hold in real-world markets. When this is the case, the conclusion breaks down that free, unregulated markets will produce an efficient outcome. The remainder of this chapter discusses some inefficiencies that occur naturally in markets and some of the strengths, as well as the weaknesses, of the market mechanism. We also discuss the usefulness of the competitive model for understanding the real economy.

THE SOURCES OF MARKET FAILURE

In suggesting some of the problems encountered in real markets and some of the possible solutions to these problems, the rest of this chapter previews the next part of this book, which focuses on the economics of market failure and the potential role of government in the economy.

Market failure occurs when resources are misallocated, or allocated inefficiently. The result is waste or lost value. In this section, we briefly describe four important sources of market failure: (1) *imperfect market structure*, or noncompetitive behavior, (2) the existence of *public goods*, (3) the presence of *external costs and benefits*, and (4) *imperfect information*. Each condition results from the failure of one of the assumptions basic to the perfectly competitive model, and each is discussed in more detail in later chapters. Each also points to a potential role for government in the economy. The desirability and extent of actual government involvement in the economy are hotly debated subjects.

market failure Occurs when resources are misallocated, or allocated inefficiently. The result is waste or lost value.

IMPERFECT MARKETS

Until now we have operated on the assumption that the number of buyers and sellers in each market is large. When each buyer and each seller is only one of a great many in the market, no individual buyer or seller can independently influence price. Thus, all economic decision makers are by virtue of their relatively small size forced to take input prices and output prices as given. When this assumption does not hold—that is, when single firms have some control over price and potential competition—the result is **imperfect competition** and an inefficient allocation of resources.

A Kansas wheat farmer is probably a "price-taker," but Microsoft and Daimler Chrysler Corporation most certainly are not. Many firms in many industries do have some control over price. The degree of control that is possible depends on the character of competition in the industry itself.

An industry that comprises just one firm producing a product for which there are no close substitutes is called a **monopoly**. Although a monopoly has no other firms to compete with, it is still constrained by market demand. To be successful, the firm still has to produce something that people want. Essentially, a monopoly must choose both price and quantity of

imperfect competition An industry in which single firms have some control over price and competition. Imperfectly competitive industries give rise to an inefficient allocation of resources.

monopoly An industry composed of only one firm that produces a product for which there are no close substitutes and in which significant barriers exist to prevent new firms from entering the industry.

output simultaneously because the amount that it will be able to sell depends on the price it sets. If the price is too high, it will sell nothing. Presumably, a monopolist sets price to maximize profit. That price is generally significantly above average costs, and such a firm usually earns economic profits.

In competition, economic profits will attract the entry of new firms into the industry. A rational monopolist who is not restrained by the government does everything possible to block any such entry to preserve economic profits in the long run. As a result, society loses the benefits of more products and lower prices. A number of barriers to entry can be raised. Sometimes a monopoly is actually licensed by government, and entry into its market is prohibited by law. Taiwan has only one beer company; many areas in the United States have only one local telephone company. Ownership of a natural resource can also be the source of monopoly power. If I buy up all the coal mines in the United States and I persuade Congress to restrict coal imports, no one can enter the coal industry and compete with me.

Between monopoly and perfect competition are a number of other imperfectly competitive market structures. *Oligopolistic industries* are made up of a small number of firms, each with a degree of price-setting power. *Monopolistically competitive industries* are made up of a large number of firms that acquire price-setting power by differentiating their products or by establishing a brand name. Only General Mills can produce Wheaties, for example, and only Bayer AG can produce Alka-Seltzer.

> In all imperfectly competitive industries, output is lower—the product is underproduced—and price is higher than it would be under perfect competition. The equilibrium condition $P = MC$ does not hold, and the system does not produce the most efficient product mix.

In Chapter 13 we will demonstrate that firms with market power underproduce and the result is a deadweight loss of producer and consumer surplus. (See the discussion of deadweight loss in Chapter 4.)

In the United States, many forms of noncompetitive behavior are illegal. A firm that attempts to monopolize an industry or that conspires with other firms to reduce competition risks serious penalties. The most famous recent antitrust case was brought by the Justice Department against Microsoft in the late 1990s. Microsoft was accused of attempting to monopolize the Internet browser market and other anticompetitive practices. In June 2000, the court agreed that Microsoft violated U.S. antitrust laws and ordered that Microsoft be broken up into two separate companies. Although the Microsoft break-up was stopped on appeal, Microsoft was convicted of violating the antitrust laws and is still involved in litigation. In 2005, Microsoft was struggling with numerous cases in the courts of the European Union. This sort of behavior, the Justice Department argued, prevents society from enjoying the benefits of free competition.

Recently, three industries once thought to be "natural monopolies" are shifting away from government regulation toward becoming fully competitive industries: local telephone service, electricity, and natural gas. (All this is discussed in much more detail in Chapters 13 and 14.)

PUBLIC GOODS

public goods, or social goods Goods or services that bestow collective benefits on members of society. Generally, no one can be excluded from enjoying their benefits. The classic example is national defense.

A second major source of inefficiency lies in the fact that private producers simply do not find it in their best interest to produce everything that members of society want. More specifically, there is a whole class of goods called **public goods**, or **social goods**, that will be underproduced or not produced at all in a completely unregulated market economy.[3]

Public goods are goods or services that bestow collective benefits on society; they are, in a sense, collectively consumed. The classic example is national defense, but there are countless others—police protection, homeland security, preservation of wilderness lands, and public health, to name a few. These things are "produced" using land, labor, and capital just like any other good. Some public goods, such as national defense, benefit the whole nation.

---

[3]Although they are normally referred to as public *goods*, many of the things we are talking about are *services*.

Others, such as clean air, may be limited to smaller areas—the air may be clean in a Kansas town but dirty in a southern California city.

Public goods are consumed by everyone, not just by those who pay for them. Once the good is produced, no one can be excluded from enjoying its benefits. Producers of **private goods**, such as hamburgers, can make a profit because they do not hand over the product to you until you pay for it. Chapters 3 through 11 centered on the production of private goods.

If the provision of public goods were left to private, profit-seeking producers with no power to force payment, a serious problem would arise. Suppose, for example, that I value some public good, X. If there were a functioning market for X, I would be willing to pay for it. Suppose that I am asked to contribute voluntarily to the production of X. Should I contribute? Perhaps I should on moral grounds, but not on the basis of pure self-interest.

At least two problems can get in the way. First, because I cannot be excluded from using X for not paying, I get the good whether I pay or not. Why should I pay if I do not have to? Second, because public goods that provide collective benefits to large numbers of people are expensive to produce, any one person's contribution is not likely to make much difference to the amount of the good ultimately produced. Would the national defense suffer, for example, if you did not pay your share of the bill? Probably not. Thus, nothing happens if you do not pay. The output of the good does not change much, and you get it whether you pay or not.

Private provision of public goods fails. A completely laissez-faire market system will not produce everything that all members of a society might want. Citizens must band together to ensure that desired public goods are produced, and this is generally accomplished through government spending financed by taxes.

Public goods are the subject of Chapter 15.

EXTERNALITIES

A third major source of inefficiency is the existence of external costs and benefits. An **externality** is a cost or benefit imposed or bestowed on an individual or group that is outside, or external to, the transaction—in other words, something that affects a third party. In a city, external costs are pervasive. The classic example is pollution, but there are thousands of others, such as noise, congestion, and painting your house a color that the neighbors think is ugly.

Not all externalities are negative, however. For example, housing investment may yield benefits for neighbors. A farm located near a city provides residents in the area with nice views, fresher air, and a less congested environment.

Externalities are a problem only if decision makers do not take them into account. The logic of efficiency presented earlier in this chapter required that firms weigh social benefits against social costs. If a firm in a competitive environment produces a good, it is because the value of that good to society exceeds the social cost of producing it—this is the logic of $P = MC$. If social costs or benefits are overlooked or left out of the calculations, inefficient decisions result.

The market itself has no automatic mechanism that provides decision makers an incentive to consider external effects. Through government, however, society has established over the years a number of different institutions for dealing with externalities. Tort law, for example, is a body of legal rules that deal with third-party effects. Under certain circumstances, those who impose costs are held strictly liable for them. In other circumstances, liability is assessed only if the cost results from "negligent" behavior. Tort law deals with small problems as well as larger ones. If your neighbors spray their lawn with a powerful chemical and kill your prize shrub, you can take them to court and force them to pay for it.

The effects of externalities can be enormous. For years, companies piled chemical wastes indiscriminately into dump sites near water supplies and residential areas. In some locations, those wastes seeped into the ground and contaminated the drinking water. In response to the evidence that smoking damages not only the smoker but also others, governments have increased prohibitions against smoking on airplanes and in public places. In 1997, attorneys general for a majority of states approved a tentative agreement with the tobacco industry to pay billions of dollars in damage claims to avoid pending lawsuits filed on behalf of citizens damaged

private goods Products produced by firms for sale to individual households.

A classic example of a *public good* is a park such as Central Park in Manhattan producing *collective* benefits for New Yorkers and tourists.

externality A cost or benefit resulting from some activity or transaction that is imposed or bestowed on parties outside the activity or transaction.

by smoking or breathing secondhand smoke. In July 2005, the Justice Department asked the Supreme Court for the legal authority to seek $280 billion in damages from the tobacco industry.

For years, economists have suggested that a carefully designed set of taxes and subsidies could help to "internalize" external effects. For example, if a paper mill that pollutes the air and waterways is taxed in proportion to the damage caused by that pollution, it would consider those costs in its production decisions.

Sometimes, interaction among and between parties can lead to the proper consideration of externality without government involvement. If someone plays a radio loudly on the fourth floor of your dormitory, that person imposes an externality on the other residents of the building. The residents, however, can get together and negotiate a set of mutually acceptable rules to govern radio playing.

> The market does not always force consideration of all the costs and benefits of decisions. Yet for an economy to achieve an efficient allocation of resources, all costs and benefits must be weighed.

We discuss externalities in detail in Chapter 15.

IMPERFECT INFORMATION

imperfect information
The absence of full knowledge concerning product characteristics, available prices, and so forth.

The fourth major source of inefficiency is **imperfect information** on the part of buyers and sellers:

> The conclusion that markets work efficiently rests heavily on the assumption that consumers and producers have full knowledge of product characteristics, available prices, and so forth. The absence of full information can lead to transactions that are ultimately disadvantageous.

Some products are so complex that consumers find it difficult to judge the potential benefits and costs of purchase. Buyers of life insurance have a very difficult time sorting out the terms of the more complex policies and determining the true "price" of the product. Consumers of almost any service that requires expertise, such as plumbing or medical care, have a hard time evaluating what is needed, much less how well it is done. It is difficult for a used-car buyer to find out the true "quality" of the cars in Big Jim's Car Emporium.

Some forms of misinformation can be corrected with simple rules such as truth-in-advertising regulations. In some cases, the government provides information to citizens; job banks and consumer information services exist for this purpose. In certain industries, such as medical care, there is no clear-cut solution to the problem of noninformation or misinformation. We discuss all these topics in detail in Chapter 15.

EVALUATING THE MARKET MECHANISM

Is the market system good or bad? Should the government be involved in the economy, or should it leave the allocation of resources to the free market? So far, our information is mixed and incomplete. To the extent that the perfectly competitive model reflects the way markets really operate, there seem to be some clear advantages to the market system. When we relax the assumptions and expand our discussion to include noncompetitive behavior, public goods, externalities, and the possibility of imperfect information, we see at least a potential role for government.

The market system does seem to provide most participants with the incentive to weigh costs and benefits and to operate efficiently. Firms can make profits only if a demand for their products exists. If there are no externalities, or if such costs or benefits are properly internalized, firms _will_ weigh social benefits and costs in their production decisions. Under these circumstances, the profit motive should provide competitive firms with an incentive to minimize cost and to produce their products using the most efficient technologies. Likewise, competitive input markets should provide households with the incentive to weigh the value of their time against the social value of what they can produce in the labor force.

However, markets are far from perfect. Freely functioning markets in the real world do not always produce an efficient allocation of resources, and this result provides a potential role for government in the economy. Many have called for government involvement in the economy to correct for market failure—that is, to help markets function more efficiently. As you will see, however, many feel that government involvement in the economy creates more inefficiency than it cures.

An example of inefficiency brought about by government regulation was discussed in Chapter 4. If market-determined prices bring supply and demand into equilibrium, the total value of consumer surplus plus producer surplus is maximized. Often the government imposes price ceilings and price floors in the name of fairness, or equity. An example of a price ceiling is rent control. By holding price below equilibrium, the quantity supplied is reduced and the quantity demanded is increased. The result is a deadweight loss. An example of a price floor is the minimum wage that holds the wage rate above equilibrium in the labor market. As we will see in Chapter 16, the minimum wage also produces a deadweight loss if it is higher than the equilibrium wage.

In addition, we have thus far discussed only the criterion of efficiency, and economic systems and economic policies must be judged by many other criteria, not the least of which is *equity*, or fairness. Indeed, some contend that the outcome of any free market is ultimately unfair, because some become rich while others remain very poor.

Part III, which follows, explores the issue of market imperfections and government involvement in the economy in greater depth.

SUMMARY

GENERAL EQUILIBRIUM ANALYSIS

1. Both firms and households make simultaneous choices in both input and output markets. For example, input prices determine output costs and affect firms' output supply decisions. Wages in the labor market affect labor supply decisions, income, and ultimately how much output households can and do purchase.

2. A *general equilibrium* exists when all markets in an economy are in simultaneous equilibrium. An event that disturbs the equilibrium in one market may disturb the equilibrium in many other markets as well. *Partial equilibrium* analysis can be misleading, because it looks only at adjustments in one isolated market.

ALLOCATIVE EFFICIENCY AND COMPETITIVE EQUILIBRIUM

3. An *efficient* economy is one that produces the goods and services that people want at least possible cost. A change is said to be efficient if it makes some members of society better off without making others worse off. An efficient, or *Pareto optimal*, system is one in which no such changes are possible.

4. If a change makes some people better off and some people worse off, but it can be shown that the value of the gains exceeds the value of the losses, the change is said to be *potentially efficient*, or simply *efficient*.

5. If all the assumptions of perfect competition hold, the result is an efficient, or Pareto optimal, allocation of resources. To prove this statement, it is necessary to show that resources are allocated efficiently among firms, that final products are distributed efficiently among households, and that the system produces what people want.

6. The assumptions that factor markets are competitive and open, that all firms pay the same prices for inputs, and that all firms maximize profits lead to the conclusion that the allocation of resources among firms is efficient.

7. People have different tastes and preferences, and they buy very different things in very different combinations. As long as everyone shops freely in the same markets, no redistribution of outputs among people will make them better off. This leads to the conclusion that final products are distributed efficiently among households.

8. Because perfectly competitive firms will produce as long as the price of their product is greater than the marginal cost of production, they will continue to produce as long as a gain for society is possible. The market thus guarantees that the right things are produced. In other words, the perfectly competitive system produces what people want.

THE SOURCES OF MARKET FAILURE

9. When the assumptions of perfect competition do not hold, the conclusion breaks down that free, unregulated markets will produce an efficient allocation of resources.

10. An imperfectly competitive industry is one in which single firms have some control over price and competition. Forms of *imperfect competition* include monopoly, monopolistic competition, and oligopoly. In all imperfectly competitive industries, output is lower and price is higher than they would be in perfect competition. Imperfect competition is a major source of market inefficiency.

11. *Public*, or *social*, *goods* bestow collective benefits on members of society. Because the benefits of social goods are collective, people cannot in most cases be excluded from enjoying them. Thus, private firms usually do not find it profitable to produce public goods. The need for public goods is thus another source of inefficiency.

12. An *externality* is a cost or benefit that is imposed or bestowed on an individual or group that is outside, or external to, the transaction. If such social costs or benefits are overlooked, the decisions of households or firms are likely to be wrong or inefficient.

13. Market efficiency depends on the assumption that buyers have perfect information on product quality and price and

that firms have perfect information on input quality and price. *Imperfect information* can lead to wrong choices and inefficiency.

EVALUATING THE MARKET MECHANISM

14. Sources of market failure—such as imperfect markets, public goods, externalities, and imperfect information—are considered by many to justify the existence of government and governmental policies that seek to redistribute costs and income on the basis of efficiency, equity, or both.

REVIEW TERMS AND CONCEPTS

efficiency, 253

externality, 265

general equilibrium, 253

imperfect competition, 263

imperfect information, 266

market failure, 263

monopoly, 263

Pareto efficiency, or Pareto optimality, 259

partial equilibrium analysis, 253

private goods, 265

public goods, or social goods, 264

Key efficiency condition in perfect competition: $P_X = MC_X$

PROBLEM SET

1. Recently, cellular telephones have become very popular. At the same time new technology has made them less expensive to produce. By assuming the technological advance caused cost curves to shift downward at the same time that demand was shifting to the right, draw a diagram or diagrams to show what will happen in the short and in the long run.

2. Numerous times in history, the courts have issued consent decrees requiring large companies to break up into smaller, competing companies for violating the antitrust laws. The two best-known examples are American Telephone and Telegraph (AT&T) in the 1980s and Microsoft 20 years later. (AT&T was broken up into the "Baby Bells," but the Microsoft breakup was successfully appealed and the breakup never occurred.)

   Many argue that breaking up a monopoly is a Pareto-efficient change. This interpretation cannot be so because breaking up a monopoly makes its owners (or shareholders) worse off. Do you agree or disagree? Explain your answer.

3. During the first three quarters of 2001, the U.S. economy was in recession. The nation's output of goods and services fell. The recession began with a sharp drop in demand for investment goods—particularly computer equipment and software. The dot-com bubble had burst. The result was a steep drop in employment in California's Silicon Valley and in other high-technology–producing areas of the United States. Describe the likely impacts of the decline in demand for investment goods on the labor market and on the capital markets. How might such a decline impact on other sectors of the economy such as the housing market or the office market in San Jose, California?

4. A medium-sized bakery has just opened in Slovakia. A loaf of bread is currently selling for 14 koruna (the Slovakian currency) over and above the cost of intermediate goods (flour, yeast, and so on). Assuming that labor is the only variable factor of production, the following table gives the production function for the bread:

WORKERS	LOAVES OF BREAD
0	0
1	15
2	30
3	42
4	52
5	60
6	66
7	70

a. Suppose that the current wage rate in Slovakia is 119 koruna per hour. How many workers will the bakery employ?

b. Suppose that the economy of Slovakia begins to grow, incomes rise, and the price of a loaf of bread is pushed up to 20 koruna. Assuming no increase in the price of labor, how many workers will the bakery hire?

c. An increase in the demand for labor pushes up wages to 125 koruna per hour. What impact will this increase in cost have on employment and output in the bakery at the 20-koruna price of bread?

d. If all firms behaved like our bakery, would the allocation of resources in Slovakia be efficient? Explain your answer.

5. Country A has soil that is suited to corn production and yields 135 bushels per acre. Country B has soil that is not suited for corn and yields only 45 bushels per acre. Country A has soil that is not suited for soybean production and yields 15 bushels per acre. Country B has soil that is suited for soybeans and yields 35 bushels per acre. In 2004, there was no trade between A and B because of high taxes, and both countries together produced huge quantities of corn and soybeans. In 2005, taxes were eliminated because of a new trade agreement. What is likely to happen? Can you justify the trade agreement on the basis of Pareto efficiency? Why or why not?

6. Do you agree or disagree with each of the following statements? Explain your answer.

a. "Housing is a public good and should be produced by the public sector because private markets will fail to produce it efficiently."

b. "Monopoly power is inefficient, because large firms will produce too much product, dumping it on the market at artificially low prices."

c. "Medical care is an example of a potentially inefficient market because consumers do not have perfect information about the product."

7. Which of the following are examples of Pareto-efficient changes? Explain your answers.

a. Cindy trades her laptop computer to Bob for his old car.

b. Competition is introduced into the electric industry and electricity rates drop. A study shows that benefits to consumers are larger than the lost monopoly profits.

c. A high tax on wool sweaters deters buyers. The tax is repealed.

d. A federal government agency is reformed and costs are cut 23 percent with no loss of service quality.

8. A major source of chicken feed in the United States is anchovies, small fish that can be scooped up out of the ocean at low cost. Every 7 years, the anchovies disappear to spawn, and producers must turn to grain, which is more expensive, to feed their chickens. What is likely to happen to the cost of chicken when the anchovies disappear? What are substitutes for chicken? How are the markets for these substitutes affected? Name some complements to chicken. How are the markets for these complements affected? How might the allocation of farmland be changed as a result of the disappearance of anchovies?

9. Suppose two passengers both end up with a reservation for the last seat on a train from San Francisco to Los Angeles. Two alternatives are proposed:

a. Toss a coin.

b. Sell the ticket to the highest bidder.

Compare the two from the standpoint of efficiency and equity.

10. Assume that there are two sectors in an economy: goods (*G*) and services (*S*). Both sectors are perfectly competitive, with large numbers of firms and constant returns to scale. As income rises, households spend a larger portion of their income on *S* and a smaller portion on *G*. Using supply and demand curves for both sectors and a diagram showing a representative firm in each sector, explain what would happen to output and prices in the short run and the long run in response to an increase in income. (Assume that the increase in income causes demand for *G* to shift left and demand for *S* to shift right.) In the long run, what would happen to employment in the goods sector, and in the service sector? (*Hint:* See Figure 12.3.)

11. Which of the following are actual Pareto-efficient changes? Explain briefly.

a. You buy three oranges for $1 from a street vendor.

b. You are near death from thirst in the desert and must pay a passing vagabond $10,000 for a glass of water.

c. A mugger steals your wallet.

d. You take a taxi ride in downtown Manhattan during rush hour.

12. Each instance that follows is an example of one of the four types of market failure discussed in this chapter. In each case identify the type of market failure and defend your choice briefly.

a. An auto repair shop convinces you that you need a $2,000 valve job, when all you really need is an oil change.

b. Everyone in a neighborhood would benefit if an empty lot were turned into a park, but no entrepreneur will come forward to finance the transformation.

c. Someone who lives in an apartment building buys a Gretchen Wilson album and then blasts it at full volume at 3 A.M.

d. The only two airlines flying direct between St. Louis and Atlanta make an agreement to raise their prices.

13. Two factories in the same town hire workers with exactly the same skills. Union agreements require factory A to pay its workers $10 per hour, while factory B must pay $6 per hour. Each factory hires the profit-maximizing number of workers. Is the allocation of labor between these two factories efficient? Explain why or why not.

Monopoly and Antitrust Policy

13

I n Chapters 6 through 12, we built a model of a perfectly competitive economy. To do so, we needed to make some assumptions. In Chapter 12 we began to see what happens when we relax them.

A number of assumptions, you will recall, underlie the logic of perfect competition. One is that a large number of firms and households interact in each output market. Another is that firms in a given market produce undifferentiated, or homogeneous, products. Together, these two conditions limit firms' choices. With many firms in each market, no single firm has any control over market prices. Single firms may decide how much to produce and how to produce, but the market determines output price. The assumption that new firms are free to enter industries and to compete for profits led us to conclude that opportunities for economic profit are eliminated in the long run as competition drives price to a level equal to the average cost of production.

In the next two chapters, we explore the implications of relaxing these assumptions. In this chapter, we focus on the case of a single firm in an industry—a monopoly.

IMPERFECT COMPETITION AND MARKET POWER: CORE CONCEPTS

A market, or industry, in which individual firms have some control over the price of their output is **imperfectly competitive**. All firms in an imperfectly competitive market have one thing in common: They exercise **market power**, the ability to raise price without losing all of the quantity demanded for their product. Imperfect competition and market power are major sources of inefficiency.

> Imperfect competition does not mean that *no* competition exists in the market. In some imperfectly competitive markets competition occurs in *more* arenas than in perfectly competitive markets. Firms can differentiate their products, advertise, improve quality, market aggressively, cut prices, and so forth.

For a firm to exercise control over the price of its product, it must be able to *limit competition* by blocking other firms from entering the market. If your firm produces T-shirts,

imperfectly competitive industry An industry in which single firms have some control over the price of their output.

market power An imperfectly competitive firm's ability to raise price without losing all of the quantity demanded for its product.

271

and if other firms can enter freely into the industry and produce exactly the same T-shirts that you produce, the result will be the outcome that you would expect in a perfectly competitive industry: The supply will increase, the price of T-shirts will be driven down to their average cost, and economic profits will be eliminated.

However, note that T-shirts having the official National Basketball Association team logo are more expensive than generic T-shirts. If your firm can prevent other firms from producing exactly the same product, or if it can prevent other firms from entering the market, then it has a chance of preserving its economic profits. Only the NBA's licensees are allowed to use the official logo.

DEFINING INDUSTRY BOUNDARIES

There are several different market structures. A *monopoly* is an industry with a single firm in which the entry of new firms is blocked. An *oligopoly* is an industry in which there is a small number of firms, each large enough to have an impact on the market price of its outputs. Firms that differentiate their products in industries with many producers and free entry are called *monopolistic competitors*, but where do we set the boundary of an industry? Although Procter & Gamble is the only firm that can produce Ivory, there are many other brands of soap. In general:

> The ease with which consumers can substitute for a product limits the extent to which a monopolist can exercise market power. The more broadly a market is defined, the more difficult it becomes to find substitutes.

Consider hamburger. A firm that produces brand X hamburger faces stiff competition from other hamburger sellers, even though it is the only producer of brand X. The brand X firm has little market power because near-perfect substitutes for its hamburger are available. If a firm were the *only* producer of hamburger (or, better yet, the only producer of beef), it would have more market power because fewer (or no) alternatives would be available. When fewer substitutes exist, a monopolist has more power to raise price because demand for its product is less elastic, as Figure 13.1 shows. A monopolist that produces all the food in an economy would exercise enormous market power because there are no substitutes at all for food as a category.

To be meaningful, therefore, our definition of a monopolistic industry must be more precise.

> We define **pure monopoly** as an industry (1) with a single firm that produces a product for which there are *no close substitutes* and (2) in which significant barriers to entry prevent other firms from entering the industry to compete for profits.

pure monopoly An industry with a single firm that produces a product for which there are no close substitutes and in which significant barriers to entry prevent other firms from entering the industry to compete for profits.

barrier to entry Something that prevents new firms from entering and competing in imperfectly competitive industries.

government franchise A monopoly by virtue of government directive.

BARRIERS TO ENTRY

Firms that already have market power can maintain that power either by preventing other firms from producing an exact duplicate of their product or by preventing firms from entering the industry. A number of **barriers to entry** can be erected.

Government Franchises   Many firms are monopolies by virtue of government directive. Although the industry was largely deregulated in 1996, local telephone-operating companies, for example, are still granted exclusive licenses by most states to provide "local exchange service." State governments also grant electric companies the sole right to supply power within given areas. The usual defense of this kind of monopoly power by **government franchise** is that it is more efficient for a single firm to produce the particular product (usually a service) than for many firms to produce the same product. If very large economies of scale are possible, it makes no sense to have many small firms producing the same thing at much higher costs. (We discuss these so-called *natural monopolies* later in this chapter.)

Public utility commissions in each state watch over electric companies and locally operating telephone companies. One of government's responsibilities is to regulate the prices charged by these utilities to ensure that they do not abuse their monopoly power.

FIGURE 13.1 The Boundary of a Market and Elasticity

We can define an industry as broadly or as narrowly as we like. The more broadly we define the industry, the fewer substitutes there are, and the less elastic the demand for that industry's product is likely to be. A monopoly is an industry with one firm that produces a product for which there are *no close substitutes*. The producer of brand X hamburger cannot properly be called a monopolist because this producer has no control over market price and there are many substitutes for brand X hamburger.

Fairness, or equity, is another frequently cited defense of government-regulated monopoly. Technological progress in the telecommunications industry has reduced the advantages that come from size, for example, but some states are clearly not ready to open local exchange service to competition. The reason is that most state governments want to ensure that everyone has access to a telephone at affordable rates. In most states, private households are provided with telephone service at a price below the cost of producing it; local telephone companies earn the bulk of their profits from business users, who are charged a price above cost. Deregulating local service, it is argued, would mean higher telephone bills for households, a change that many would consider unfair.

Large economies of scale and equity are not the only justifications that governments give for granting monopoly licenses, however. Sometimes government wants to maintain control of an industry, and a monopoly is easier to control than a competitive industry. Iowa, Maine, New Hampshire, and Ohio, for example, permit liquor to be sold only through state-controlled and -managed liquor stores. However, when large economies of scale do not exist in an industry, or when equity is not a concern, the arguments in favor of government-run monopolies are much weaker. One argument is that the state wants to prevent private parties from encouraging and profiting from "sin." Another is that government monopolies are a convenient source of revenues. How can anyone criticize the state-licensed, implicit taxation of drinking or gambling?

Patents Another legal barrier that prevents entry into an industry is a **patent**, which grants exclusive use of the patented product or process to the inventor. Patents are issued in the United States under the authority of Article I, Section 8, of the Constitution, which gives Congress the power to "promote the progress of science and the useful arts, by securing for limited times to authors and inventors the exclusive right to their respective writings and discoveries." Patent protection in the United States is currently granted for a period of 20 years.

Patents provide an incentive for invention and innovation. New products and new processes are developed through research undertaken by individual inventors and by firms. Research requires resources and time, which have opportunity costs. Without the protection

patent A barrier to entry that grants exclusive use of the patented product or process to the inventor.

that a patent provides, the results of research would become available to the general public very quickly. If research did not lead to expanded profits, very little research would be done. On the negative side, though, patents do serve as a barrier to competition, and they do slow down the benefits of research flowing through the market to consumers.

The expiration of patents after a given number of years represents an attempt to balance the benefits of firms and the benefits of households: On the one hand, it is important to stimulate invention and innovation; on the other hand, invention and innovation do society no good unless their benefits eventually flow to the public.[1]

In recent years, public attention has been focused on the high costs of health care. One factor contributing to these costs is the very high price of many prescription drugs. Equipped with newly developed tools of bioengineering, the pharmaceutical industry has been granted thousands of patents for new drugs. When a new drug for treating a disease is developed, the patent holder can charge a very high price for it. The drug companies argue that these rewards are justified by high research and development costs; others say these profits are the result of a monopoly protected by the patent system.

Economies of Scale and Other Cost Advantages   Some products can be produced efficiently only in big, expensive production facilities. For example, it is estimated that an oil refinery large enough to achieve maximum-scale economies in the production of gasoline would cost well over a billion dollars to build. A small entrepreneur is not going to jump into the refining business in search of economic profit. The need to raise an initial investment of over a billion dollars is compounded by the riskiness of the business. Hence, large capital requirements are often a barrier to entry.

Sometimes large economies of scale are not production related. Breakfast cereal can be produced efficiently on a very small scale, for example; large-scale production does not reduce costs. However, to compete, a new firm would need an advertising campaign costing millions of dollars. The large front-end investment requirement in the presence of risk is likely to deter would-be entrants to the cereal market.

The DeBeers Company of South Africa controls about 80 percent of the market for uncut diamonds.

Ownership of a Scarce Factor of Production   You cannot enter the diamond-producing business unless you own a diamond mine. There are not many diamond mines in the world, and most are already owned by a single firm, the DeBeers Company of South Africa. Once, the Aluminum Company of America (now Alcoa) owned or controlled virtually 100 percent of the bauxite deposits in the world and until the 1940s monopolized the production and distribution of aluminum. Obviously, if production requires a particular input, and one firm owns the entire supply of that input, that firm will control the industry. Ownership alone is a barrier to entry.

PRICE: THE FOURTH DECISION VARIABLE

To review: A firm has market power when it has some control over the price of its product—raising the price of its product without losing all of the quantity demanded. The exercise of market power requires that the firm be able to limit competition in some way. It does this either by erecting barriers to the entry of new firms or by preventing other firms from producing the same product.

Regardless of the source of market power, output price is not taken as given by the firm. Instead:

> Price is a decision variable for imperfectly competitive firms. Firms with market power must decide not only (1) how much to produce, (2) how to produce it, and (3) how much to demand in each input market (see Figure 7.3), but also (4) *what price to charge for their output.*

---

[1]Another alternative is *licensing*. With licensing, the new technology is used by all producers, and the inventor splits the benefits with consumers. Because forcing the non-patent-holding producers to use an inefficient technology results in waste, some analysts have proposed adding mandatory licensing to the current patent system.

profitability — search

○ Further Exploration ● News Analysis

The Drug Wars in 2005

DRUG COMPANIES SPEND BILLIONS OF dollars on research each year. When that research bears fruit and a drug has been found to be effective, the drug company secures a patent and becomes a monopolist. The patent enables the drug company to charge a price generally far above the marginal cost of production. Patented prescription drugs have become very expensive in recent years. Successful drugs are very profitable for their producers; that profitability is what finances the research that has produced spectacular results over the years.

This presents no problem for those who can afford to pay for drugs or for those who have health insurance with drug coverage. What about those who cannot afford to pay the prices charged by the drug companies? Clearly there is a trade-off. We need incentives and resources to fund research, but should a beneficial drug be denied to sick people because they have low incomes?

This debate has played itself out dramatically in the case of cancer treatments. The following article from the *New York Times* illustrates the dilemma.

Cancer Drugs Offer Hope, but at a Huge Expense
by ALEX BERENSON
—New York Times
July 12, 2005

Ten thousand dollars once seemed a lot to pay for a few months' supply of a drug.

No more. Avastin. Erbitux. Gleevec. Herceptin. Rituxan. Tarceva. These are among the first in a wave of new drugs giving hope to millions of cancer patients by treating the disease in new ways, like blocking the blood vessels that feed tumors.

But they are all highly expensive, up to $100,000 for a course of treatment that lasts a few months. That is hundreds of times the cost of older, more toxic cancer drugs, and several times the annual cost of AIDS drugs, whose prices caused widespread anger during the 1990's.

Health care economists say the rising costs of the new cancer treatments and other drugs will force difficult questions on doctors and policy makers. Should patients be guaranteed access to drugs no matter what their cost? And should physicians be encouraged to consider cost when they decide on treat-

ment—something most doctors in this country now say they do not do?

Drug companies say many factors drive the pricing of their drugs, including the high cost of research and development, complex and expensive manufacturing processes and the value the drugs provide for patients.

For now, most patients are able to obtain the new drugs, either through insurance coverage or assistance programs. Shawnette Treat, 37, was diagnosed with lung cancer early last year and was told her life expectancy was less than two years. She now takes Tarceva, which costs almost $90 a day, or $31,000 a year.

Ms. Treat, who lives with her husband and two children in Melbourne, Ark., has private insurance, which covers 80 percent of Tarceva's cost. But she stopped working in March after undergoing a double mastectomy when the cancer spread. She said she could not afford her insurer's $500 monthly co-payment for Tarceva.

"My husband's the only one working, and we have bills and stuff that we have to pay, and it takes all he makes for us to make it," Ms. Treat said. "Five hundred dollars is a lot to us a month."

This does not mean that "market power" allows a firm to charge any price it likes. The market demand curve constrains the behavior even of a pure monopolist. To sell its product successfully, a firm must produce something that people want and sell it at a price they are willing to pay.

PRICE AND OUTPUT DECISIONS IN PURE MONOPOLY MARKETS

To analyze monopoly behavior, we make two assumptions: (1) that entry to the market is blocked, and (2) that firms act to maximize profits.

Initially, we also assume that our pure monopolist buys in competitive input markets. Even though the firm is the only one producing for its product market, it is only one among many firms buying factors of production in input markets. The local telephone company must hire labor like any other firm. To attract workers it must pay the market wage; to buy fiber-optic cable, it must pay the going price. In these input markets the monopolistic firm is a price-taker.

On the cost side of the profit equation, a pure monopolist does not differ one bit from a perfect competitor. Both choose the technology that minimizes the cost of production. The cost curve of each represents the minimum cost of producing each level of output. The difference arises on the revenue, or demand, side of the equation, where we begin our analysis.

DEMAND IN MONOPOLY MARKETS

A perfectly competitive firm, you will recall, faces a fixed, market-determined price, and we assume it can sell all it wants to sell at that price; it is constrained only by its current capacity in the short run. The demand curve facing such a firm is thus a horizontal line (Figure 13.2). Raising the price of its product means losing all demand, because perfect substitutes are available. The perfectly competitive firm has no incentive to charge a lower price either.

Because a perfectly competitive firm can charge only one price, regardless of the output level chosen, its *marginal revenue*—the additional revenue that it earns by raising output by one unit—is simply the price of the output, or $P^* = \$5$ in Figure 13.2. Remember that marginal revenue is important because a profit-maximizing firm will increase output as long as marginal revenue exceeds marginal cost.

The most important distinction between perfect competition and monopoly is that:

> With one firm in a monopoly market, there is no distinction between the firm and the industry. In a monopoly, the firm *is* the industry. The market demand curve is the demand curve facing the firm, and the total quantity supplied in the market is what the firm decides to produce.

To proceed, we need a few more assumptions. First, we assume that a monopolistic firm cannot price discriminate. It sells its product to all demanders at the same price. (*Price discrimination* means selling to different consumers or groups of consumers at different prices.)

We also assume that the monopoly faces a known demand curve. That is, we assume that the firm has enough information to predict how households will react to different prices. (Many firms use statistical methods to estimate the elasticity of demand for their products. Other firms may use less formal methods, including trial and error, sometimes called "price searching." All firms with market power must have some sense of how consumers are likely

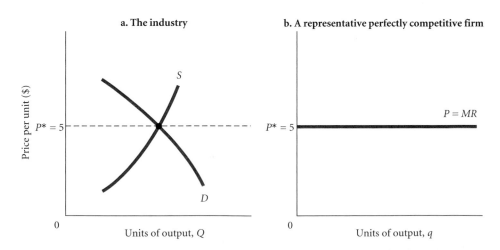

a. The industry   **b. A representative perfectly competitive firm**

FIGURE 13.2 The Demand Curve Facing a Perfectly Competitive Firm Is Perfectly Elastic; in a Monopoly, the Market Demand Curve Is the Demand Curve Facing the Firm

Perfectly competitive firms are price-takers; they are small relative to the size of the market and thus cannot influence market price. The implication is that the demand curve facing a perfectly competitive firm is perfectly elastic. If the firm raises its price, it sells nothing, and there is no reason for the firm to lower its price if it can sell all it wants at $P^* = \$5$. In a monopoly, the firm *is* the industry. Thus the market demand curve is the demand curve facing the monopoly, and the total quantity supplied in the market is what the monopoly decides to produce.

TABLE 13.1 Marginal Revenue Facing a Monopolist

(1) QUANTITY	(2) PRICE	(3) TOTAL REVENUE	(4) MARGINAL REVENUE
0	$11	0	–
1	10	$10	$10
2	9	18	8
3	8	24	6
4	7	28	4
5	6	30	2
6	5	30	0
7	4	28	–2
8	3	24	–4
9	2	18	–6
10	1	10	–8

to react to various prices.) By knowing the demand curve it faces, the firm must *simultaneously* choose both the quantity of output to supply and the price of that output. Once the firm chooses a price, the market determines how much will be sold. Stated somewhat differently, the monopoly chooses the point on the market demand curve where it wants to be.

Marginal Revenue and Market Demand   Just like a competitor, a profit-maximizing monopolist will continue to produce output as long as marginal revenue exceeds marginal cost. Because the market demand curve is the demand curve for a monopoly, a monopolistic firm faces a downward-sloping demand curve.

Consider the hypothetical demand schedule in Table 13.1. Column 3 lists the total revenue that the monopoly would take in at different levels of output. If it were to produce one unit, that unit would sell for $10, and total revenue would be $10. Two units would sell for $9 each, in which case total revenue would be $18. As column 4 shows, marginal revenue from the second unit would be $8 ($18 minus $10). Notice that the marginal revenue from increasing output from one unit to two units ($8) is *less* than the price of the second unit ($9).

Now consider what happens when the firm considers setting production at four units instead of three. The fourth unit would sell for $7, but because the firm cannot price discriminate, it must sell *all four* units for $7 each. Had the firm chosen to produce only three units, it could have sold those three units for $8 each. Thus, offsetting the revenue gain of $7 is a revenue loss of $3—that is, $1 for each of the three units that would have sold at the higher price. The marginal revenue of the fourth unit is $7 minus $3, or $4, which is considerably below the price of $7. (Remember, unlike a monopoly, a perfectly competitive firm does not have to charge a lower price to sell more; thus $P = MR$ in competition.)

> For a monopolist, an increase in output involves not just producing more and selling it, but also reducing the price of its output to sell it.

Marginal revenue can also be derived simply by looking at the change in total revenue as output changes by one unit. At three units of output, total revenue is $24; at four units of output, total revenue is $28. Marginal revenue is the difference, or $4.

Moving from six to seven units of output actually reduces total revenue for the firm. At seven units, marginal revenue is negative. Although it is true that the seventh unit will sell for a positive price ($4), the firm must sell all seven units for $4 each (for a total revenue of $28). If output had been restricted to six units, each would have sold for $5. Thus, offsetting the revenue gain of $4 is a revenue loss of $6—that is, $1 for each of the six units that the firm would have sold at the higher price. Increasing output from six to seven units actually decreases revenue by $2. Figure 13.3 graphs the marginal revenue schedule derived in Table 13.1. Notice that at every level of output except one unit, marginal revenue is *below* price. Marginal revenue turns from positive to negative after six units of output. When the demand curve is a straight line, the marginal revenue curve bisects the quantity axis between the origin and the point where the demand curve hits the quantity axis, as in Figure 13.4.

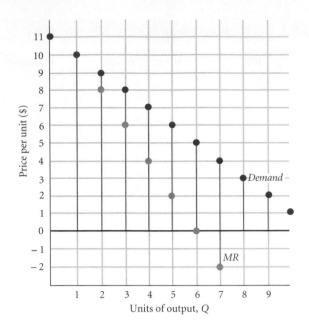

FIGURE 13.3 Marginal Revenue Curve Facing a Monopolist

At every level of output except one unit, a monopolist's marginal revenue (*MR*) is below price. This is so because (1) we assume that the monopolist must sell all its product at a single price (no price discrimination), and (2) to raise output and sell it, the firm must lower the price it charges. Selling the additional output will raise revenue, but this increase is offset somewhat by the lower price charged for all units sold. Therefore, the increase in revenue from increasing output by one (the marginal revenue) is less than the price.

Look carefully at Figure 13.4. What you can see in the diagram is that:

A monopoly's marginal revenue curve shows the change in total revenue that results as a firm moves along the segment of the demand curve that lies directly above it.

Consider starting at an output of zero units per period in the top panel of Figure 13.4. At zero units, of course, total revenue (shown in the bottom panel) is zero because nothing is sold. To begin selling, the firm must lower the product price. Marginal revenue is positive, and total revenue begins to increase. To sell increasing quantities of the good, the firm must lower its price more and more. As output increases between zero and Q^* and the firm moves down its demand curve from point *A* to point *B*, marginal revenue remains positive and total revenue continues to increase. The quantity of output (Q) is rising, which tends to push total revenue ($P \times Q$) *up*. At the same time, the price of output (P) is falling, which tends to push total revenue ($P \times Q$) *down*. Up to point *B*, the effect of increasing Q dominates the effect of falling P, and total revenue rises: Marginal revenue is positive (above the quantity axis).[2]

What happens as we move farther along the quantity axis above Q^*—that is, farther down the demand curve from point *B* toward point *C*? We are still lowering *P* to sell more output, but above (to the right of) Q^*, marginal revenue is negative and total revenue in the bottom panel starts to fall. Beyond Q^*, the effect of cutting price on total revenue is larger than the effect of increasing quantity. As a result, total revenue ($P \times Q$) falls. At point *C*, revenue once again is at zero, this time because price has dropped to zero.[3]

The Monopolist's Profit-Maximizing Price and Output   We have spent much time in defining and explaining marginal revenue because it is an important factor in the monopolist's choice of profit-maximizing price and output. Figure 13.5 superimposes a

---

[2]Recall from Chapter 4 that if the percentage change in Q is greater than the percentage in P as you move along a demand curve, the absolute value of elasticity of demand is greater than 1. Thus, as we move along the demand curve in Figure 13.4 between point A and point B, demand is *elastic*.

[3]Beyond Q^*, between points B and C on the demand curve in Figure 13.4, the decline in price must be bigger in percentage terms than the increase in quantity. Thus the absolute value of elasticity beyond point B is less than 1: Demand is inelastic. At point B, marginal revenue is zero; the decrease in P exactly offsets the increase in Q, and elasticity is unitary or equal to −1.

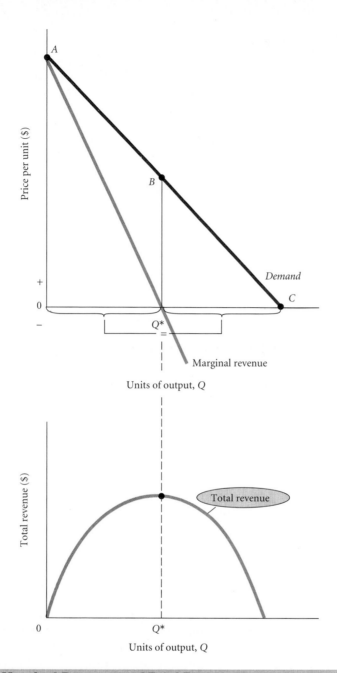

FIGURE 13.4 Marginal Revenue and Total Revenue

A monopoly's marginal revenue curve bisects the quantity axis between the origin and the point where the demand curve hits the quantity axis. A monopoly's *MR* curve shows the change in total revenue that results as a firm moves along the segment of the demand curve that lies exactly above it.

demand curve and the marginal revenue curve derived from it over a set of cost curves. In determining price and output, a monopolistic firm must go through the same basic decision process that a competitive firm goes through. Any profit-maximizing firm will raise its production as long as the added revenue from the increase outweighs the added cost. In more specific terms, we can say that:

All firms, including monopolies, raise output as long as marginal revenue is greater than marginal cost. Any positive difference between marginal revenue and marginal cost can be thought of as marginal profit.

The optimal price/output combination for the monopolist in Figure 13.5 is $P_m = \$4.00$ and $Q_m = 4,000$ units, the quantity at which the marginal revenue curve and the marginal cost curve intersect. At any output below 4,000, marginal revenue is greater than marginal

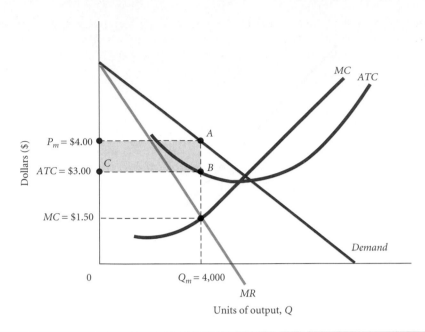

FIGURE 13.5 Price and Output Choice for a Profit-Maximizing Monopolist

A profit-maximizing monopolist will raise output as long as marginal revenue exceeds marginal cost. Maximum profit is at an output of 4,000 units per period and a price of $4. Above 4,000 units of output, marginal cost is greater than marginal revenue; increasing output beyond 4,000 units would reduce profit. At 4,000 units, $TR = P_m A Q_m 0$, $TC = CBQ_m 0$, and profit = $P_m ABC$.

cost. At any output above 4,000, increasing output would reduce profits, because marginal cost exceeds marginal revenue. This leads us to conclude that:

> The profit-maximizing level of output for a monopolist is the one at which marginal revenue equals marginal cost: $MR = MC$.

Because marginal revenue for a monopoly lies below the demand curve, the final price chosen by the monopolist will be above marginal cost ($P_m = \$4.00$ is greater than $MC = \$1.50$). At 4,000 units of output, price will be fixed at $4 (point A on the demand curve), and total revenue will be $P_m \times Q_m = \$4 \times 4,000 = \$16,000$ (area $P_m A Q_m 0$). Total cost is the product of average total cost and units of output, $\$3 \times 4,000 = \$12,000$ (area $CBQ_m 0$). Total profit is the difference between total revenue and total cost, $\$16,000 - \$12,000 = \$4,000$. In Figure 13.5, total profit is the area of the gray rectangle $P_m ABC$.

Among competitive firms, the presence of positive profits provides an incentive for new firms to enter the industry, thus shifting supply to the right, driving down price, and eliminating profits. Remember, however, that for monopolies we assume that barriers to entry have been erected and that profits are protected.

The Absence of a Supply Curve in Monopoly In perfect competition, the supply curve of a firm in the short run is the same as the portion of the firm's marginal cost curve that lies above the average variable cost curve. As the price of the good produced by the firm changes, the perfectly competitive firm simply moves up or down its marginal cost curve in choosing how much output to produce.

As you can see, however, Figure 13.5 contains nothing that we can point to and call a supply curve. The amount of output that a monopolist produces depends on its marginal cost curve *and* on the shape of the demand curve that it faces. In other words, the amount of output that a monopolist supplies is not independent of the shape of the demand curve.

> A monopoly firm has no supply curve that is independent of the demand curve for its product.

To see why, consider what a firm's supply curve means. A supply curve shows the quantity of output the firm is willing to supply at each price. If we ask a monopolist how much output she is willing to supply at a given price, the monopolist will say her supply behavior depends not just on marginal cost, but also on the marginal revenue associated with that price. To know what that marginal revenue would be, the monopolist must know what her demand curve looks like.

In sum: In perfect competition, we can draw a firm's supply curve without knowing anything more than the firm's marginal cost curve. The situation for a monopolist is more complicated:

> A monopolist sets both price and quantity, and the amount of output that it supplies depends on both its marginal cost curve and the demand curve that it faces.

Monopoly in the Long and Short Run In our analysis of perfectly competitive markets we distinguished between the long run and the short run. In the short run, all firms face some fixed factor of production, and no entry into or exit from the industry is possible. The assumption of a fixed factor of production is the primary reason that marginal cost increases with output in the short run. That is, the short-run marginal cost curve of a typical competitive firm slopes upward and to the right because of the limitations imposed by the fixed factor. In the long run, however, firms can enter and exit the industry. Long-run equilibrium is established when the entry and exit of firms drives profits in the industry to zero.

The distinction between the long and short runs is less important in monopoly markets. In the short run, monopolists are limited by a fixed factor of production, as competitive firms are. The cost curves in Figure 13.5 reflect the diminishing returns to the monopoly's fixed factor of production—for example, plant size.

What will happen to the monopoly in the long run? If the monopoly is earning positive profits (a rate of return above the normal rate of return to capital), nothing will happen. In competition, positive profits lead to expansion and entry, but in a monopoly, entry is blocked. In addition, because we assume that the monopoly is a profit-maximizing firm, it will operate at the most efficient scale of production, and it will neither expand nor contract in the long run. Thus, Figure 13.5 will not change in the long run.

It is possible for a monopoly to find itself suffering losses (a rate of return below the normal rate). A monopoly that finds itself unable to cover total costs is illustrated in Figure 13.6.

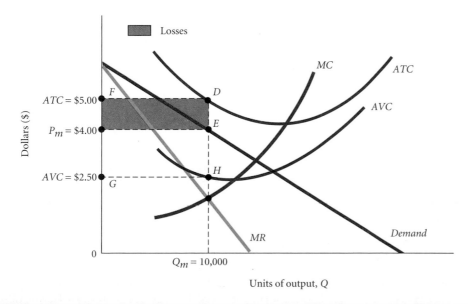

FIGURE 13.6 Price and Output Choice for a Monopolist Suffering Losses in the Short Run

It is possible for a profit-maximizing monopolist to suffer short-run losses. At 10,000 units of output (the point at which $MR = MC$), total revenue is sufficient to cover variable cost but not to cover total cost. Thus, the firm will operate in the short run but go out of business in the long run. At 10,000 units, $TR = P_m EQ_m 0$, $TC = FDQ_m 0$, and losses $= FDEP_m$.

The best that the firm can do is produce $Q_m = 10,000$ units of output (the point at which $MR = MC$) and charge $P_m = \$4$ for its output (point E on the demand curve). However, at 10,000 units of output per period, total revenue of \$40,000 ($P_m \times Q_m$, where $P_m = \$4$ and $Q_m = 10,000$), which is equal to the area $P_m E Q_m 0$, is not sufficient to cover total costs of \$50,000 ($ATC \times Q_m$, where $ATC = \$5$ and $Q_m = 10,000$), which is equal to the area $FDQ_m 0$. The firm thus suffers losses equal to \$10,000, the shaded area (rectangle $FDEP_m$). Notice, however, that total revenue is sufficient to cover the level of *variable* costs, which equals \$25,000 ($AVC \times Q_m$, where $AVC = \$2.50$ and $Q_m = 10,000$). Thus, operating in the short run generates a profit on operation (total revenue minus total variable costs is greater than zero) that can be used to cover some of the firm's short-run fixed costs. The basis of the monopolist's decision is thus exactly the same as that for a perfectly competitive firm:

> If a firm can reduce its losses by operating in the short run, it will do so.

Similarly, in the long run, a firm that cannot generate enough revenue to cover total costs will go out of business, whether it is perfectly competitive or a monopoly. Because the demand curve in Figure 13.6 lies completely below the average total cost curve, the monopoly will go out of business in the long run, and its product will not be produced because it is simply not worth the cost of production to buyers.

PERFECT COMPETITION AND MONOPOLY COMPARED

One way to understand monopoly is to compare equilibrium output and price in a perfectly competitive industry with the output and price that would be chosen if the same industry were organized as a monopoly. To make this comparison meaningful, let us exclude from consideration any technological advantage that a single large firm might enjoy.

We begin our comparison with a perfectly competitive industry made up of a large number of firms operating with a production technology that exhibits constant returns to scale in the long run. (Recall that *constant returns to scale* means that average cost is the same whether the firm operates one large plant or many small plants.) Figure 13.7 shows a perfectly competitive industry at long-run equilibrium, a condition in which price is equal to long-run average costs and in which there are no profits.

Now suppose that the industry were to fall under the control of a single private monopolist. The monopolist now owns one firm with many plants. However, technology has not

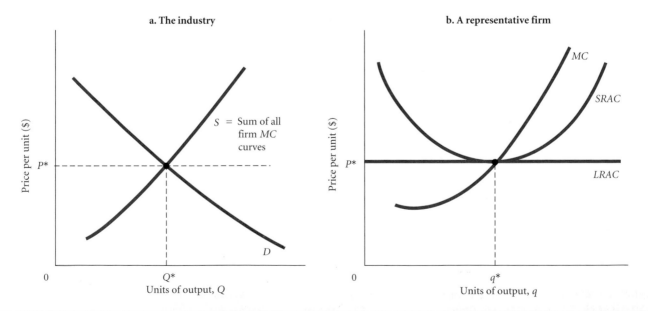

a. The industry   **b. A representative firm**

FIGURE 13.7 A Perfectly Competitive Industry in Long-Run Equilibrium

In a perfectly competitive industry in the long run, price will be equal to long-run average cost. The market supply curve is the sum of all the short-run marginal cost curves of the firms in the industry. Here we assume that firms are using a technology that exhibits constant returns to scale: *LRAC* is flat. Big firms enjoy no cost advantage.

changed; only the location of decision-making power has. To analyze the monopolist's decisions, we must derive the consolidated cost curves now facing the monopoly.

The marginal cost curve of the new monopoly will simply be the horizontal sum of the marginal cost curves of the smaller firms, which are now branches of the larger firm. That is, to get the large firm's *MC* curve, at each level of *MC* we add together the output quantities from each separate plant. To understand why, consider this simple example. Suppose that there is perfect competition and that the industry is made up of just two small firms, A and B, each with upward-sloping marginal cost curves. Suppose that for firm A, $MC = \$5$ at an output of 10,000 units and for firm B, $MC = \$5$ at an output of 20,000 units. If these firms were merged, what would the marginal cost of the 30,000th unit of output per period be? The answer is $5, because the new larger firm would produce 10,000 units in plant A and 20,000 in plant B. This means that the marginal cost curve of the new firm is *exactly the same curve* as the supply curve in the industry when it was competitively organized. [Recall from Chapter 9 that the industry supply curve in a perfectly competitive industry is the sum of the marginal cost curves (above average variable cost) of all the individual firms in that industry.][4]

Figure 13.8 illustrates the cost curves, marginal revenue curve, and demand curve of the consolidated monopoly industry. If the industry were competitively organized, total industry output would have been $Q_c = 4,000$ and price would have been $P_c = \$3$. These price and output decisions are determined by the intersection of the competitive supply curve, S_c, and the market demand curve.

No longer faced with a price that it cannot influence, however, the monopolist can choose any price/quantity combination along the demand curve. The output level that maximizes profits to the monopolist is $Q_m = 2,500$—the point at which marginal revenue intersects marginal cost. Output will be priced at $P_m = \$4$. To increase output beyond 2,500 units or to charge a price below $4 (which represents the amount consumers are willing to pay) would reduce profit. The result:

> Relative to a perfectly competitive industry, a monopolist restricts output, charges higher prices, and earns positive profits.

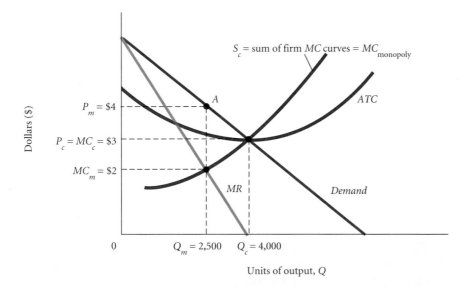

FIGURE 13.8 Comparison of Monopoly and Perfectly Competitive Outcomes for a Firm with Constant Returns to Scale

In the newly organized monopoly, the marginal cost curve is exactly the same as the supply curve that represented the behavior of all the independent firms when the industry was organized competitively. Quantity produced by the monopoly will be less than the perfectly competitive level of output, and the monopoly price will be higher than the price under perfect competition. Under monopoly, $P = P_m = \$4$ and $Q = Q_m = 2,500$. Under perfect competition, $P = P_c = \$3$ and $Q = Q_c = 4,000$.

---

[4]The same logic will show that the average cost curve of the consolidated firm is simply the sum of the average cost curves of the individual plants.

Also remember that all we did was to transfer decision-making power from the individual small firms to a consolidated owner. The new firm gains nothing at all technologically from being big.

COLLUSION AND MONOPOLY COMPARED

collusion The act of working with other producers in an effort to limit competition and increase joint profits.

Suppose now that the industry just discussed did not become a monopoly. Instead, suppose the individual firm owners simply decide to work together in an effort to limit competition and increase joint profits, a behavior called **collusion**. In this case, the outcome would be exactly the same as the outcome of a monopoly in the industry. Firms certainly have an incentive to collude. When they act independently, they compete away whatever profits they can find. However, as we saw in Figure 13.8, when price increases to $4 across the industry, the monopolistic firm earns positive profits.

Despite the fact that collusion is illegal, it has taken place in some industries. In one significant case in the 1960s, a number of executives of well-known electrical equipment manufacturers were successfully prosecuted for meeting secretly to fix prices and divide up markets. In January 1987, a judge moved to end a pricing agreement among milk producers in New York City that had existed since the 1930s. As a result, the wholesale price of milk dropped between $0.30 and $0.71 per gallon in 1 week. More recently, illegal price fixing was discovered among Italian bread bakeries in New York City. And in 2005 the courts were hearing dozens of price-fixing cases. Among others, actions were filed against concrete producers in Indiana and ob-gyn physicians in Cincinnati.

THE SOCIAL COSTS OF MONOPOLY

So far we have seen that a monopoly produces less output and charges a higher price than a competitively organized industry if no large economies of scale exist for the monopoly. You are probably thinking at this point that producing less and charging more to earn positive profits is not likely to be in the best interests of consumers, and you are right.

INEFFICIENCY AND CONSUMER LOSS

In Chapter 12, we argued that price must equal marginal cost ($P = MC$) for markets to produce what people want. This argument rests on two propositions: (1) that price provides a good approximation of the social value of a unit of output, and (2) that marginal cost, in the absence of externalities (costs or benefits to external parties not weighed by firms), provides a good approximation of the product's social opportunity cost. In a pure monopoly, price is above the product marginal cost. When this happens, the firm is underproducing from society's point of view; society would be better off if the firm produced more and charged a lower price. We can, therefore, conclude that:

> Monopoly leads to an inefficient mix of output.

A slightly simplified version of the monopoly diagram appears in Figure 13.9, which shows how we might make a rough estimate of the size of the loss to social welfare that arises from monopoly. (For clarity we will ignore the short-run cost curves and assume constant returns to scale in the long run.) Under competitive conditions, firms would produce output up to $Q_c = 4,000$ units, and price would ultimately settle at $P_c = \$2$, equal to long-run average cost. Any price above $2 will mean positive profits, which would be eliminated by the entry of new competing firms in the long run. (You should remember all this from Chapter 9.)

A monopoly firm in the same industry, however, would produce only $Q_m = 2,000$ units per period and charge a price of $P_m = \$4$, because $MR = MC$ at $Q_m = 2,000$ units. The monopoly would make a profit equal to total revenue minus total cost, or $P_m \times Q_m$ minus $ATC \times Q_m$. Profit to the monopoly is thus equal to the area $P_m ACP_c$, or $4,000. [($4 \times 2,000$) − ($2 \times 2,000$) = $8,000 − $4,000 = $4,000. Remember $P_c = ATC$ in this example.]

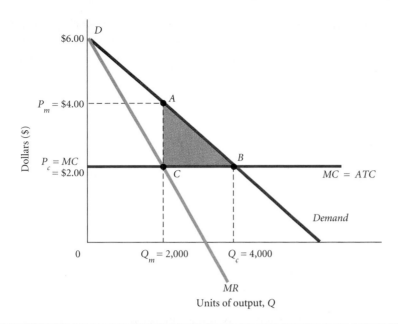

FIGURE 13.9 Welfare Loss from Monopoly

A demand curve shows the amounts that people are willing to pay at each potential level of output. Thus the demand curve can be used to approximate the benefits to the consumer of raising output above 2,000 units. *MC* reflects the marginal cost of the resources needed. The triangle *ABC* roughly measures the net social gain of moving from 2,000 units to 4,000 units (or the loss that results when monopoly decreases output from 4,000 units to 2,000 units).

Now consider the gains and losses associated with increasing price from $2 to $4 and cutting output from 4,000 units to 2,000 units. As you might guess, the winner will be the monopolist and the loser will be the consumer, but let us see how it works out.

At $P_c = \$2$, the price under perfect competition, there are no profits. Consumers are paying a price of $2, but the demand curve shows that many are willing to pay more than that. For example, a substantial number of people would pay $4 or more. Those people willing to pay more than $2 are receiving what we earlier called a *consumer surplus*. Consumer surplus is the difference between what households are willing to pay for a product and the current market price. The demand curve shows approximately how much households are willing to pay at each level of output, and thus the area of triangle DBP_c gives us a rough measure of the "consumer surplus" being enjoyed by households when the price is $2. Consumers willing to pay exactly $4 get a surplus equal to $2. Those who place the highest value on this good—that is, those who are willing to pay the most ($6)—get a surplus equal to DP_c, or $4.

Now the industry is reorganized as a monopoly that cuts output to 2,000 units and raises price to $4. The big winner is the monopolist, who ends up earning profits equal to $4,000. The big losers are the consumers. Their "surplus" now shrinks from the area of triangle DBP_c to the area of triangle DAP_m. Part of that loss (which is equal to DBP_c minus DAP_m, or the area P_mABP_c) is covered by the monopolist's gain of P_mACP_c, but not all of it. The loss to consumers exceeds the gain to the monopoly by the area of triangle ABC (P_mABP_c minus P_mACP_c), which roughly measures the net loss in social welfare associated with monopoly power in this industry. Because the area of a triangle is half its base times its height, the welfare loss is $1/2 \times 2,000 \times \$2 = \$2,000$. If we could push price back down to the competitive level and increase output to 4,000 units, consumers would gain more than the monopolist would lose, and the gain in social welfare would approximate the area of *ABC*, or $2,000.

In this example, the presence of a monopoly also causes an important change in the distribution of real income. In Figure 13.9, area P_mACP_c is profit of $4,000 flowing every period to the monopolist. If price were pushed down to $2 by competition or regulation, those profits would pass to consumers in the form of lower prices. Society may value this resource transfer on equity grounds in addition to efficiency grounds.

Of course, monopolies may have social costs that do not show up on these diagrams. Monopolies, which are protected from competition by barriers to entry, do not face the same pressures to cut costs and to innovate as competitive firms do. A competitive firm that does not use the most efficient technology will be driven out of business by firms that do. One of the significant arguments against tariffs and quotas to protect such industries as automobiles and steel from foreign competition is that protection removes the incentive to be efficient and competitive.

RENT-SEEKING BEHAVIOR

In recent years, economists have encountered another serious worry. Triangle *ABC* in Figure 13.9 represents a real net loss to society, but part of rectangle P_mACP_c (the $4,000 monopoly profit) may also end up lost. To understand why, we need to think about the incentives facing potential monopolists.

The area of rectangle P_mACP_c shows positive profits. If entry into the market were easy and competition were open, these profits would eventually be competed to zero. Owners of businesses earning profits have an incentive to prevent this development. In fact, the diagram shows exactly how much they would be willing to pay to prevent it. A rational owner of a monopoly firm would be willing to pay any amount less than the entire rectangle. Any portion of profits left over after expenses is better than zero, which would be the case if free competition eliminated all profits.

There are many things that potential monopolists can do to protect their profits. One obvious approach is to push the government to impose restrictions on competition. A classic example is the behavior of taxicab driver organizations in New York and other large cities. To operate a cab legally in New York City, you need a license. The city tightly controls the number of licenses available. If entry into the taxi business were open, competition would hold down cab fares to the cost of operating cabs. However, cab drivers have become a powerful lobbying force and have muscled the city into restricting the number of licenses issued. This restriction keeps fares high and preserves monopoly profits.

There are countless other examples. The steel industry and the automobile industry spend large sums lobbying Congress for tariff protection.[5] Some experts claim that both the establishment of the now-defunct Civil Aeronautics Board in 1937 to control competition in the airline industry and the extensive regulation of trucking by the FTC prior to deregulation in the 1970s came about partly through industry efforts to restrict competition and preserve profits.

This kind of behavior, in which households or firms take action to preserve positive profits, is called **rent-seeking behavior**. Recall from Chapter 10 that rent is the return to a factor of production in strictly limited supply. Rent-seeking behavior has two important implications.

First, this behavior consumes resources. Lobbying and building barriers to entry are not costless activities. Lobbyists' wages, expenses of the regulatory bureaucracy, and the like must be paid. Periodically faced with the prospect that the city of New York will issue new taxi licenses, cab owners and drivers have become so well organized that they can bring the city to a standstill with a strike or even a limited job action. Indeed, positive profits may be completely consumed through rent-seeking behavior that produces nothing of social value; all it does is help to preserve the current distribution of income.

Second, the frequency of rent-seeking behavior leads us to another view of government. So far we have considered only the role that government might play in helping to achieve an efficient allocation of resources in the face of market failure—in this case, failures that arise from imperfect market structure. Later in this chapter we survey the measures government might take to ensure that resources are efficiently allocated when monopoly power arises. However, the idea of rent-seeking behavior introduces the notion of **government failure**, in which the government becomes the tool of the rent seeker and the allocation of resources is made even less efficient than before.

This idea of government failure is at the center of **public choice theory**, which holds that governments are made up of people, just as business firms are. These people—politicians and

rent-seeking behavior Actions taken by households or firms to preserve positive profits.

government failure Occurs when the government becomes the tool of the rent seeker and the allocation of resources is made even less efficient by the intervention of government.

public choice theory An economic theory that the public officials who set economic policies and regulate the players act in their own self-interest, just as firms do.

---

[5]A tariff is a tax on imports designed to give a price advantage to domestic producers.

bureaucrats—can be expected to act in their own self-interest, just as owners of firms do. We turn to the economics of public choice in Chapter 15.

PRICE DISCRIMINATION

So far in our discussion of monopoly we have assumed that the firm faces a known downward-sloping demand curve and must choose a *single price* and a single quantity of output. Indeed, the reason that price and marginal revenue are different for a monopoly and the same for a perfectly competitive firm is that if a monopoly decides to sell more output, it must lower price in order to do so.

In the world, however, there are lots of examples of firms that charge different prices to different groups of buyers. Charging different prices to different buyers is called **price discrimination**. The motivation for price discrimination is fairly obvious: If a firm can identify those who are willing to pay a higher price for a good, it can earn more profit from them by charging a higher price. The idea is best illustrated using the extreme case where a firm knows what each buyer is willing to pay. A firm that charges the maximum amount that buyers are willing to pay for each unit is practicing **perfect price discrimination**.

Figure 13.10(a) is similar to Figure 13.9. For simplicity, assume a firm with a constant marginal cost equal to $2 per unit. A non-price-discriminating monopolist would have to set one and only one price. That firm would face the marginal revenue curve shown in the diagram and would produce as long as MR is above MC: Output would be Q_m and price would be set at $4 per unit. The firm would earn an economic profit of $2 per unit for every unit up to Q_m. Consumers would enjoy a consumer surplus equal to the shaded area. Consumer A, for example, is willing to pay $5.75 but has to pay only $4.

Now consider what would happen if the firm could charge each consumer the maximum amount that that consumer was willing to pay. In Figure 13.10(a), if the firm could charge consumer A a price of $5.75, the firm would earn $3.75 in profit on that unit and the consumer would get no consumer surplus. Going on to consumer B, if the firm could determine B's maximum willingness to pay and charge $5.50, profit would be $3.50 and consumer surplus for B would again be zero. This would continue all the way to point C on the demand curve, where total profit would be equal to the entire area under the demand curve and above the $MC = ATC$ line. See Figure 13.10(b).

Another way to look at the diagram in Figure 13.10(b) is to notice that the demand curve actually becomes the same as the marginal revenue curve. If a firm can charge the maximum that anyone is willing to pay *for each unit*, then that price *is* marginal revenue. There is no need to draw a separate MR curve as there was when the firm could charge only one price to all consumers. Once again, profit is the entire shaded area and consumer surplus is zero.

It is interesting to note that a perfectly price-discriminating monopolist will actually produce the *efficient* quantity of output—Q_c in Figure 13.10(b), which is the same as the amount that would be produced had the industry been perfectly competitive. The firm will continue to produce as long as benefits to consumers exceed marginal cost; it doesn't stop at Q_m in Figure 13.10(a). But when a monopolist can price discriminate, it reaps all the net benefits from higher production. There is no deadweight loss, but there is no consumer surplus either.

EXAMPLES OF PRICE DISCRIMINATION

Examples of price discrimination are all around us. It used to be that airlines routinely charged those who stayed over Saturday nights a much lower fare than those who did not. Business travelers generally travel during the week, and often are unwilling to stay over Saturdays and generally are willing to pay more for tickets.

Airlines, movie theaters, hotels, and many other industries routinely charge a lower price for children and the elderly. The reason is that children and the elderly generally have a lower willingness to pay. Telephone companies have so many ways of getting at different groups that it is difficult to know what they are really charging!

In each case, the objective of the firm is to segment the market into different identifiable groups, with each group having a different elasticity of demand. It can be shown, although

price discrimination
Charging different prices to different buyers.

perfect price discrimination Occurs when a firm charges the maximum amount that buyers are willing to pay for each unit.

FIGURE 13.10 Price Discrimination

In Figure 13.10(a), consumer A is willing to pay $5.75. If the price-discriminating firm can charge $5.75 to A, profit is $3.75. A monopolist who cannot price discriminate would maximize profit by charging $4. At a price of $4, the firm makes $2 in profit and consumer A enjoys a consumer surplus of $1.75. In Figure 13.10(b), for a perfectly price-discriminating monopolist the demand curve is the same as marginal revenue. The firm will produce as long as MR > MC, up to Q_c. At Q_c profit is the entire shaded area and consumer surplus is zero.

we will not present the analysis here, that the optimal strategy for a firm that can sell in more than one market is to charge higher prices in markets with low demand elasticities.

REMEDIES FOR MONOPOLY: ANTITRUST POLICY

Historically, governments in market economies have assumed two basic and seemingly contradictory roles with respect to imperfectly competitive industries: (1) They *promote* competition and restrict market power, primarily through antitrust laws, and (2) they *restrict* competition by regulating industries.

THE DEVELOPMENT OF ANTITRUST LAW: HISTORICAL BACKGROUND

The period immediately following the Civil War was one of rapid growth and change in the United States. As migrants headed to the open spaces, population swelled in the West as well as in the East. Railroads were built between all major cities, and in 1869 a golden spike driven at Promontory Point, Utah, completed the transcontinental railroad line linking the East with California. Between 1864 and 1874, what was already a substantial rail network doubled in size. At the same time, factories sprang up to accommodate new methods of production. Between 1870 and 1913, the economy grew faster than at any other time in U.S. history.

Before the Civil War, most firms had been small and their markets local. The high cost of horse-drawn and water transportation limited access to local markets, and production technologies were efficient only on a small scale. However, the railroads opened up the nation, and firms began to compete for national markets. Many of the new technologies exhibited economies of scale; real advantages to size in some industries soon became apparent.

Communications technology also changed. In 1877, an inventor offered to sell to Western Union, for $100,000, a patent on a new method of sending information over wires. Alexander Graham Bell's asking price was too high for Western Union, and it turned down the offer. Within 10 years, telephone lines operated by Bell companies crisscrossed the country, linking city after city.

As all these forces drew the United States together, the character of the economy changed. Small firms selling to local markets were replaced by large firms selling to regional and national markets. With size came power, and with power came hunger for more power. Competition was fierce and often brutal.

The successful exercise of power meant driving competition out of business and controlling markets, and for many firms these became explicit goals. Thousands of smaller firms were gobbled up by big ones. Cartels fixed prices and controlled output. Price cutting to drive competitors out of business was common. In this climate, the **trust** flourished. Under a trust arrangement, shareholders of independent firms agreed to give up their stock in exchange for trust certificates that entitled them to a share of the trust's common profits. A group of trustees then operated the trust as a monopoly, controlling output and setting price.

It was not long before people saw that something was wrong with the system that had emerged. Small independent farmers facing large powerful railroads and declining agricultural prices began to organize. Formed in 1867, the National Grange became a strong pressure group on behalf of farmers against the power of big business. At the same time, life for the laboring classes in the cities and in factory towns was grim, with child labor, long hours, meager wages, and crowded housing in slums.

"Big business" was held responsible, and its image was probably best captured in cartoons of grotesquely fat men with big cigars and diamond stickpins crushing workers and farmers underfoot. Perhaps the best known and most vilified of these "robber barons" was Jay Gould, who made a fortune manipulating railroad stocks and trying to monopolize the railroad business. In 1881, Gould controlled more miles of railroad track than any other individual or group. While recent research shows that Gould may not have been as evil as most history books portray him, there is no question that he wielded enormous power.

LANDMARK ANTITRUST LEGISLATION

Even though public sentiment increasingly favored reform, faith in the market and in private enterprise also remained strong. In response to public pressure, Congress began to formulate antitrust legislation. In 1887, it created the **Interstate Commerce Commission (ICC)** to oversee and correct abuses in the railroad industry; in 1890, it passed the **Sherman Act**, which declared monopoly and trade restraints illegal. To control monopoly power in general, the Sherman Act turned not to regulation and public enterprise, but instead to competition and the market.

trust An arrangement in which shareholders of independent firms agree to give up their stock in exchange for trust certificates that entitle them to a share of the trust's common profits. A group of trustees then operates the trust as a monopoly, controlling output and setting price.

Interstate Commerce Commission (ICC) A federal regulatory group created by Congress in 1887 to oversee and correct abuses in the railroad industry.

Sherman Act Passed by Congress in 1890, the act declared every contract or conspiracy to restrain trade among states or nations illegal and declared any attempt at monopoly, successful or not, a misdemeanor. Interpretation of which specific behaviors were legal fell to the courts.

The early days of antitrust enforcement, 1881.
Uncle Sam breaking the Gould-Vanderbilt
monopoly—notice the bags of money under
the desk.

Standard Oil controlled about
91 percent of the refining
industry in 1911.

The Sherman Act of 1890   The real substance of the Sherman Act is contained in
two short sections:

> *Section 1.* Every contract, combination in the form of trust or otherwise, or conspir-
> acy, in restraint of trade or commerce among the several States, or with foreign
> nations, is hereby declared to be illegal. . . .
>
> *Section 2.* Every person who shall monopolize, or attempt to monopolize, or com-
> bine or conspire with any other person or persons, to monopolize any part of the
> trade or commerce among the several States, or with foreign nations, shall be
> deemed guilty of a misdemeanor, and, on conviction thereof, shall be punished by
> fine not exceeding five thousand dollars, or by imprisonment not exceeding one
> year, or by both said punishments, in the discretion of the court.

The biggest problem with the Sherman Act lay in its interpretation. Its language seemed
to declare monopolistic structure, as well as certain kinds of monopolistic conduct, to be
illegal, but it was unclear what specific acts were to be considered "restraints of trade."
Competition itself can act as a restraint.

When a statute is unclear, it usually falls to the courts to provide clarification.
Unfortunately, the courts only added to the confusion in the early years of antitrust legislation and enforcement. In 1911, two major antitrust cases were brought before the
Supreme Court. The two companies involved, Standard Oil and American Tobacco,
seemed to epitomize the textbook definition of monopoly, and both appeared to exhibit
the structure and the conduct outlawed by the Sherman Act. Standard Oil controlled about
91 percent of the refining industry; and although the exact figure is still disputed, the
American Tobacco Trust probably controlled between 75 percent and 90 percent of the
market for all tobacco products except cigars. Both companies had used tough tactics to
swallow up competition or to drive it out of business. Not surprisingly, the Supreme Court
found both firms guilty of violating Sections 1 and 2 of the Sherman Act and ordered their
dissolution.[6]

The Court made clear, however, that the Sherman Act did not outlaw every action that
seemed to restrain trade, only those that were "unreasonable." In enunciating this **rule of
reason**, the Court seemed to say that structure alone was not a criterion for unreasonable-
ness. Thus it was possible for a near-monopoly not to violate the Sherman Act as long as it
had won its market using "reasonable" tactics.

Subsequent court cases confirmed that a firm could be convicted of violating the
Sherman Act only if it had exhibited *unreasonable conduct*. Between 1911 and 1920, cases
were brought against Eastman Kodak, International Harvester, United Shoe Machinery, and

rule of reason The criterion
introduced by the Supreme Court
in 1911 to determine whether a
particular action was illegal
("unreasonable") or legal
("reasonable") within the terms
of the Sherman Act.

---

[6]*United States v. Standard Oil Co. of New Jersey,* 221 U.S. 1 (1911); *United States v. American Tobacco Co.,* 221 U.S. 106 (1911).

United States Steel. The first three controlled overwhelming shares of their respective markets and the fourth controlled 60 percent of the country's capacity to produce steel. Nonetheless, all four cases were dismissed on the grounds that these companies had shown no evidence of "unreasonable conduct."

The enunciation of the rule of reason did little to clarify the language of the Sherman Act, and just what explicit acts the courts would deem "unreasonable" remained a mystery. The original supporters of the act were upset by the lack of enforcement; business simply wanted to know the rules of the game. In response, Congress went back to the drawing board in 1914 and passed the Clayton Act and the Federal Trade Commission Act.

The Clayton Act and the Federal Trade Commission, 1914   Designed both to strengthen the Sherman Act and to clarify the rule of reason, the **Clayton Act** of 1914 outlawed a number of specific practices. First, it made *tying contracts* illegal. Such contracts force a customer to buy one product to obtain another. Second, it limited mergers that would "substantially lessen competition or tend to create a monopoly." Third, it banned *price discrimination*—charging different customers different prices for reasons other than changes in cost or matching competitors' prices.

The **Federal Trade Commission (FTC)**, created by Congress in 1914, was established to investigate "the organization, business conduct, practices, and management" of companies that engage in interstate commerce. At the same time, the act establishing the commission added another vaguely worded prohibition to the books: "Unfair methods of competition in commerce are hereby declared unlawful." The determination of what constituted "unfair" behavior was left up to the commission. The FTC was also given the power to issue "cease-and-desist orders" where it found behavior in violation of the law.

Nonetheless, the legislation of 1914 retained the focus on *conduct*, and thus the rule of reason remained central to all antitrust action in the courts.

The Alcoa Case, 1945   The history of antitrust law has been an ongoing struggle between the rule of reason and various actions and outcomes that the courts have declared *per se* (intrinsic) violations of antitrust law. For example, a **per se rule** against price fixing evolved over a number of years until 1926, when the Supreme Court held unequivocally that price fixing violates Section 1 of the Sherman Act whether the resulting price is reasonable or not.

Prior to 1945, most antitrust law enforcement continued to focus on *conduct*. In most cases, the rule of reason determined whether the conduct was or was not illegal. Even though United States Steel grew large enough to dominate the market for iron and steel, for example, it did not coerce its remaining rivals or conspire to fix prices, and thus it did not engage in unreasonable conduct. As the Court said, "The law does not make *mere size* [italics added] an offense or the existence of unexerted power an offense." In short, the courts decreed it was not illegal to be a benevolent monopoly.

This was the basic position of the courts until 1945, when the rule of reason was challenged in a different way in the landmark Alcoa case.[7] The United States charged the Aluminum Company of America (Alcoa) with violating Section 2 of the Sherman Act by monopolizing the market for newly refined aluminum. At the time, Alcoa controlled 90 percent of the raw aluminum market.

The Court did not hold that any specific behavior, or conduct, by which Alcoa achieved its monopoly position was in itself illegal. It said, in fact, that Alcoa had used "normal, prudent, but not predatory business practices. . . . These included building capacity well ahead of demand." Instead, it was the *structure* of the market itself that led Judge Learned Hand to order the dissolution of Alcoa:

> No monopolist monopolizes unconscious of what he is doing. So here "Alcoa" meant to keep, and did keep, that complete and exclusive hold upon the ingot market with which it started. That was to "monopolize" that market, however innocently it otherwise proceeded.

Clayton Act Passed by Congress in 1914 to strengthen the Sherman Act and clarify the rule of reason, the act outlawed specific monopolistic behaviors such as tying contracts, price discrimination, and unlimited mergers.

Federal Trade Commission (FTC) A federal regulatory group created by Congress in 1914 to investigate the structure and behavior of firms engaging in interstate commerce, to determine what constitutes unlawful "unfair" behavior, and to issue cease-and-desist orders to those found in violation of antitrust law.

per se rule A rule enunciated by the courts declaring a particular action or outcome to be a *per se* (intrinsic) violation of antitrust law, whether the result is reasonable or not.

---

[7] *United States v. Aluminum Co. of America*, 148 F. 2nd 416 (1945).

292 **PART III**

Market Imperfections
and the Role of Government

One other case is worth a brief note here, because it extended the Sherman Act as it was interpreted in the Alcoa case to cover an oligopoly that was acting like a monopoly. In 1946, the United States brought suit against the three largest domestic cigarette producers. The Court found no specific evidence of collusion, but did rule that the firms had acted *as if* they were taking account of each other's behavior in setting prices. The case, in essence, extended the law to include tacit collusion as well as explicit conspiracy.

THE ENFORCEMENT OF ANTITRUST LAW

With this brief history of the antitrust laws, we turn to antitrust enforcement.

INITIATING ANTITRUST ACTIONS

Two different administrative bodies have the responsibility for initiating actions on behalf of the U.S. government against individuals or companies thought to be in violation of the antitrust laws. These agencies are the Antitrust Division of the Justice Department and the FTC. In addition, private citizens can initiate antitrust actions.

Government Actions: The Antitrust Division and the FTC The 1914 legislation that established the FTC, and the **Wheeler-Lea Act** that followed, gave the FTC broad powers to forbid "unfair and deceptive" conduct. The FTC is composed of five members appointed by the president and confirmed by the Senate for terms of 7 years. A large staff of lawyers and economists investigates and prosecutes offenders. The FTC can issue cease-and-desist orders to offenders, but such orders carry no criminal or civil penalties for past damages or monetary fines. In essence, the FTC exists to prevent *further* unlawful action, and in practice most FTC proceedings end in formal agreements instead of cease-and-desist orders.

The FTC has also established a set of trade regulation rules that make clear what practices it deems unfair and subject to action. One such rule, for example, states that a service station that fails to display octane ratings clearly on gas pumps is guilty of an "unfair or deceptive act or practice." These rules simplify the process of adjudication by making the standards of conduct clear.

Along with the **Antitrust Division of the Department of Justice**, the FTC initiates actions against those who violate antitrust law. The power to impose penalties and remedies formally rests with the courts, but the Antitrust Division decides which cases to prosecute. All cases involving criminal complaints against individuals or companies originate in the Antitrust Division, but it is fairly small. Its resources are limited, and the vigor with which it pursues antitrust violators changes with the views of the president and the attorney general.

Private Actions Antitrust cases may also be brought to the courts by private citizens. Since 1914, private persons have been empowered to bring suits as long as they can clearly demonstrate a significant injury or threat of injury. Much like the old rule of reason, however, the law is vague about what constitutes a "significant injury or threat." The original suit against AT&T that ended in the divestiture in 1982 was brought by a private company, MCI.

SANCTIONS AND REMEDIES

The courts are empowered to impose a number of remedies if they find that antitrust law has been violated. Certain civil and criminal penalties can be exacted for past wrongs, and other measures can prevent future wrongs. Specifically, the courts can "(1) forbid the continuation of illegal acts, (2) force the defendants to dispose of the fruits of their wrong, and (3) restore competitive conditions":

> In fashioning effective relief, the courts have considerable discretion in their choice of remedy. Antitrust decrees have, for example, ordered defendants to dispose of subsidiary companies; to create a company with appropriate assets and personnel to compete effectively with defendant; to make patents, trademarks and trade secrets

Wheeler-Lea Act (1938) Extended the language of the Federal Trade Commission Act to include "deceptive" as well as "unfair" methods of competition.

Antitrust Division (of the Department of Justice) One of two federal agencies empowered to act against violators of antitrust laws. It initiates action against those who violate antitrust laws and decides which cases to prosecute and against whom to bring criminal charges.

or know-how available to competitors at reasonable royalties or even without any royalties; to provide goods and services to all who wish to buy; to revise the terms on which defendant buys or sells; and to cancel, shorten or modify outstanding agreements with competitors, suppliers or customers.[8]

Consent Decrees

Between 75 percent and 80 percent of all government-initiated civil suits are settled with the signing of a consent decree. **Consent decrees** are formal agreements between the prosecuting government and the defendants that must be approved by the courts. Such decrees can be signed before, during, or after a trial. Because antitrust cases are long and expensive to litigate, both parties benefit if settlement comes early. A recent case involving allegations of price-fixing by Ivy League colleges was settled before trial when eight of the nine schools involved signed a consent decree.

consent decrees Formal agreements on remedies between all the parties to an antitrust case that must be approved by the courts. Consent decrees can be signed before, during, or after a trial.

Consent decrees have encompassed a variety of agreements. A company may agree to give up a patent that is serving as a barrier to effective competition, for example, or it may agree to be broken up into separate competing companies, as in the AT&T case.

The most celebrated recent consent decree involved Microsoft, which the Justice Department accused of using its dominance in operating-system software to gain market power in other areas. (Virtually all IBM and IBM-compatible personal computers use Microsoft DOS or Windows as their main operating system.) In July 1994, the Justice Department reached a tentative agreement with Microsoft and did not move to file a formal complaint. Under the consent decree, Microsoft agreed to give computer manufacturers more freedom to install software from other software companies. In 1997, Microsoft found itself charged with violating the terms of the consent decree and was back in court. In 2000, the company was found guilty of violating the antitrust laws and a judge ordered it split into two companies. But Microsoft appealed and the decision to split the company was replaced with a consent decree requiring Microsoft to behave more competitively, including a provision that computer makers would have the ability to sell competitors' software without fear of retaliation. In the fall of 2005, Microsoft finally put its antitrust troubles behind itself in the United States after agreeing to pay RealNetworks $761 million to settle one final lawsuit.

Criminal Actions

In 1955 and again in 1974, the sanctions for violating the Sherman Act were changed. The original act held that violations were misdemeanors, and made no distinction between individuals and corporations. Today the penalties are considerably more severe:

> Every person who shall make any contract or engage in any combination or conspiracy hereby declared to be illegal shall be deemed guilty of a *felony*, and on conviction thereof, shall be punished by a fine not exceeding *one million dollars* if a corporation, or, if any other person, *one hundred thousand dollars* or by imprisonment not exceeding three years, or by both said punishments, in the discretion of the court.[9]

The practice of the Antitrust Division has been to limit criminal proceedings to outrageous violations, where intent to violate is clear. In 1961, for example, seven prominent executives of major U.S. corporations that produced electrical equipment were found guilty of flagrantly violating well-established laws. They had secretly met and agreed to fix prices. All seven received 30-day jail sentences.

Treble Damages

Any person or private company that sustains injury or financial loss because of an antitrust violation can recover damages from the guilty party over and above any fines levied. The award made by the court must be three times the actual damages (*treble damages*):

> [A]ny person injured in his business or property by reason of anything forbidden in the antitrust laws. . . . shall recover threefold the damages by him sustained, and the cost of suit, including a reasonable attorney's fee.[10]

---

[8]Phillip Areeda, *Antitrust Analysis: Problems, Text and Cases*, 3rd ed. (Boston: Little, Brown, 1986), p. 61.
[9]26 Stat. 209 (1890), as amended 15 U.S.C.A. 1–7 (1980). Changes to the statute are italicized in the text.
[10]Phillip Areeda, *Antitrust Analysis: Problems, Text and Cases*, 3rd ed. (Boston: Little, Brown, 1986).

News ANALYSIS

anti-trust, price fixing, collusion	search

Price-Fixing Cases in 2005

TWO AMONG DOZENS OF PRESS releases from the Department of Justice in 2005 are excerpted below. Both of the cases described resulted in executives' serving time. One shows how narrowly a market may be defined: several counties in Indiana. The other illustrates that the antitrust laws reach across international borders. Both indicate that the Department of Justice takes price-fixing very seriously.

Indiana Ready Mixed Concrete Producer Indicted on Price-Fixing Charge
Thursday, May 19, 2005

WASHINGTON, D.C.—A federal grand jury in Indianapolis yesterday indicted a North Vernon, Indiana, producer and distributor of ready mixed concrete for fixing the price of ready mixed concrete sold in certain counties in Indiana, the Department of Justice announced.

According to the indictment filed in the U.S. District Court in Indianapolis, Lee's Ready Mix & Trucking Inc. was charged with participating in a conspiracy to fix the price at which ready mixed concrete was sold in the Indiana counties of Bartholomew, Jackson, and Jennings, beginning in or about February 2003 and continuing until approximately June 2004.

As stated in the indictment, Lee's Ready Mix and its co-conspirators agreed to specific price increases for ready mixed concrete as well as to the specific timing of those price increases. During the period covered by the conspiracy, Lee's Ready Mix sold at least $7 million worth of ready mixed concrete that was affected by the conspiracy to its customers using the agreed-upon prices.

"Today's indictment demonstrates the Antitrust Division's resolve to aggressively prosecute price-fixers," said Scott D. Hammond, the Antitrust Division's Deputy Assistant Attorney General for Criminal Enforcement.

This case is the second to arise out of the investigation of the ready mixed concrete industry. On May 13, 2005, Larry Lee, the former president of Lee's Ready Mix, agreed to plead guilty, to serve eight months in prison, and to pay a $70,000 criminal fine for his role in the conspiracy.

Former Bayer AG Executive Agrees to Plead Guilty in International Rubber Chemicals Price-Fixing Conspiracy

FORMER EXECUTIVE FACES JAIL TIME IN U.S.
Monday, May 16, 2005

WASHINGTON, D.C.—A former executive of Bayer AG, the German chemicals and pharmaceutical giant based in Leverkusen, Germany, has agreed to plead guilty, serve time in prison and pay a criminal fee for his role in an international conspiracy to fix prices in the rubber chemicals market, the Department of Justice announced today.

In a felony case filed in the U.S. District Court in San Francisco, Wolfgang Koch was charged with fixing the prices of certain rubber chemicals sold in the United States and elsewhere from January 1999 until December 2001. Koch, a German national, was product manager of rubber chemicals at Bayer during the time he participated in the conspiracy. Under the plea agreement, which must be approved by the court, Koch has agreed to serve a four-month prison term, pay a $50,000 fine, and assist the government in its ongoing rubber chemicals investigation.

Thus far, more than $100 million in criminal fines have resulted from the Antitrust Division's ongoing investigation into the rubber chemicals market.

Rubber chemicals are a group of additives used to improve the elasticity, strength, and durability of rubber products, such as tires, outdoor furniture, hoses, belts, and footwear. Approximately $1 billion of rubber chemicals are sold annually in the United States.

This provision, of course, provides a powerful incentive for private parties to invoke the antitrust laws.

A NATURAL MONOPOLY

In comparing monopoly and competition, we assumed there were constant returns to scale. When this is the case, there is no technological reason to have big firms instead of small firms. In some industries, however, there are technological economies of scale so large that it makes sense to have just one firm. Examples are rare, but public utilities—the electric company and the local telephone company, for example—are among them. A firm that realizes such large economies of scale is called a **natural monopoly**.

natural monopoly An industry that realizes such large economies of scale in producing its product that single-firm production of that good or service is most efficient.

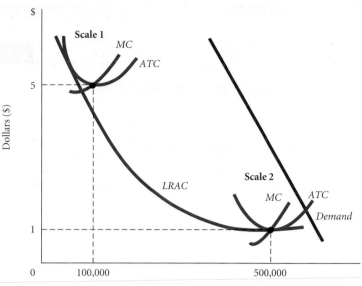

FIGURE 13.11 A Natural Monopoly

A natural monopoly is a firm in which the most efficient scale is very large. Here average total cost declines until a single firm is producing nearly the entire amount demanded in the market. With one firm producing 500,000 units, average total cost is $1 per unit. With five firms each producing 100,000 units, average total cost is $5 per unit.

Although Figure 13.11 presents an exaggerated picture, it does serve to illustrate our point. One large-scale plant (scale 2) can produce 500,000 units of output at an average unit cost of $1. If the industry were restructured into five firms, each producing on a smaller scale (scale 1), the industry could produce the same amount, but average unit cost would be five times as high ($5). Consumers thus see a considerable gain when economies of scale are realized. The critical point here is that:

Economies of scale must be realized at a scale that is close to total demand in the market.

Notice in Figure 13.11 that the long-run average cost curve continues to decline almost until it hits the market demand curve. If at a price of $1 market demand is 5 *million* units of output, there would be no reason to have only one firm in the industry. Ten firms could each produce 500,000 units, and each could reap the full benefits of the available economies of scale.

DO NATURAL MONOPOLIES STILL EXIST?

The classic examples of natural monopolies over the years have been public utilities: the telephone company, the electric company, and the gas company. The basic idea was that huge fixed costs to develop transmission lines and distribution pipes meant large economies of scale. It also made no sense to have five electric companies all running wires down every street.

Until very recently, state governments have allowed public utility companies to exist as monopolies subject to tight regulation of prices. Today everything is changing. The long-distance telephone service market has been fiercely competitive since AT&T was broken up by the courts in 1982. Even local telephone service is moving toward competition. See the News Analysis box, "From a Natural Monopoly to Near-Perfect Competition." Electricity and natural gas are not far behind. California was the first state to allow utility consumers to buy electricity from any supplier; the new regulations took effect in 1998. The trick is to force local utilities to allow low-cost suppliers to transmit power over their lines for a fee.

From a Natural Monopoly to Near-Perfect Competition

IN NO INDUSTRY HAS TECHNOLOGY changed the structure of the market more than it has in telecommunications. The following short piece from the *New York Times* describes one aspect of the current, highly competitive cell phone market in 2005.

Cell Phones? Over There, Right Next to the Nachos
By MATT RICHTEL and KEN BELSON
—*The New York Times*

Jeanne Yanaro long associated 7-Eleven with Big Gulps and last-minute groceries. But late last year she turned to her local convenience store for a more substantial purchase: a cellular phone.

"It would have been the last place I'd have thought to go for a phone," said Ms. Yanaro, a marketing manager who lives in Chelmsford, Mass.

When 7-Eleven started its own mobile phone service last year, stocking handsets on the shelves near the beef jerky and burritos, it became one of dozens of companies, many with no experience in the phone business, making a new sideline of selling mobile communications.

In years past, only corporations with billions of dollars could afford to buy radio spectrum and build complex networks to deliver phone services. Now, companies with an advertising budget and a market to pursue can start their own service by ordering phones from Nokia or Motorola and reselling network capacity leased at wholesale rates from carriers like Sprint or Cingular.

The growth of this business highlights how cell phones have become just another inexpensive commodity and also a means of consumer self-expression. The mobile phone has evolved into such an everyday staple that choosing a provider can be something like choosing a credit card.

Many of these providers—known as mobile virtual network operators—also offer a cheaper alternative to traditional calling plans by selling prepaid minutes at a flat rate, like 20 cents a minute. The minutes do not expire and customers pay for more time only if they use up their supply.

By contrast, national carriers generally sell plans that offer a set number of minutes for a monthly fee. While the per-minute costs might be lower, the monthly charge is recurring. And if users exceed the number of minutes on their plan, they are charged about 45 cents a minute.

The prepaid model is one way virtual operators have won over budget-conscious users, younger customers and people who use their phones infrequently.

Although the trend is clearly away from regulation and toward competition, regulatory commissions are still firmly in control of most state utility markets.

IMPERFECT MARKETS: A REVIEW AND A LOOK AHEAD

A firm has *market power* when it exercises some control over the price of its output or the prices of the inputs that it uses. The extreme case of a firm with market power is the pure monopolist. In a pure monopoly, a single firm produces a product for which there are no close substitutes in an industry in which all new competitors are barred from entry.

Our focus in this chapter on pure monopoly (which occurs rarely) has served a number of purposes. First, the monopoly model describes a number of industries quite well. Second, the monopoly case illustrates the observation that imperfect competition leads to an inefficient allocation of resources. Finally, the analysis of pure monopoly offers insights into the more commonly encountered market models of monopolistic competition and oligopoly, which we discussed briefly in this chapter and will discuss in detail in the next chapter.

SUMMARY

1. A number of assumptions underlie the logic of perfect competition. Among them: (1) A large number of firms and households are interacting in each market; (2) firms in a given market produce undifferentiated, or homogeneous, products; and (3) new firms are free to enter industries and to compete for profits. The first two imply that firms have no control over input prices or output prices; the third implies that opportunities for positive profit are eliminated in the long run.

IMPERFECT COMPETITION AND MARKET POWER: CORE CONCEPTS

2. A market in which individual firms have some control over price is imperfectly competitive. Such firms exercise *market power*. The three forms of *imperfect competition* are monopoly, oligopoly, and monopolistic competition.

3. A *pure monopoly* is an industry with a single firm that produces a product for which there are no close substitutes and in which there are significant *barriers to entry*.

4. There are many barriers to entry, including government franchises and licenses, patents, economies of scale, and ownership of scarce factors of production.

5. Market power means that firms must make four decisions instead of three: (1) how much to produce, (2) how to produce it, (3) how much to demand in each input market, and (4) *what price to charge for their output.*

6. Market power does not imply that a monopolist can charge any price it wants. Monopolies are constrained by market demand. They can sell only what people will buy and only at a price that people are willing to pay.

PRICE AND OUTPUT DECISIONS IN PURE MONOPOLY MARKETS

7. In perfect competition, many firms supply homogeneous products. With only one firm in a monopoly market, however, there is no distinction between the firm and the industry—the firm *is* the industry. The market demand curve is thus the firm's demand curve, and the total quantity supplied in the market is what the monopoly firm decides to produce.

8. For a monopolist, an increase in output involves not just producing more and selling it but also reducing the price of its output to sell it. Thus marginal revenue, to a monopolist, is not equal to product price, as it is in competition. Instead, marginal revenue is lower than price because to raise output one unit *and to be able to sell* that one unit, the firm must lower the price it charges to all buyers.

9. A profit-maximizing monopolist will produce up to the point at which marginal revenue is equal to marginal cost ($MR = MC$).

10. Monopolies have no identifiable supply curves. They simply choose a point on the market demand curve. That is, they choose a price and quantity to produce, which depend on both the marginal cost and the shape of the demand curve.

11. In the short run, monopolists are limited by a fixed factor of production, just as competitive firms are. Monopolies that do not generate enough revenue to cover costs will go out of business in the long run.

12. Compared with a competitively organized industry, a monopolist restricts output, charges higher prices, and earns positive profits. Because *MR* always lies below the demand curve for a monopoly, monopolists will always charge a price higher than *MC* (the price that would be set by perfect competition).

THE SOCIAL COSTS OF MONOPOLY

13. When firms price above marginal cost, the result is an inefficient mix of output. The decrease in consumer surplus is larger than the monopolist's profit, thus causing a net loss in social welfare.

14. Actions that firms take to preserve positive profits, such as lobbying for restrictions on competition, are called rent seeking. *Rent-seeking behavior* consumes resources and adds to social cost, thus reducing social welfare even further.

PRICE DISCRIMINATION

15. Charging different prices to different buyers is called *price discrimination*. The motivation for price discrimination is fairly obvious: If a firm can identify those who are willing to pay a higher price for a good, it can earn more profit from them by charging a higher price.

16. A firm that charges the maximum amount that buyers are willing to pay for each unit is practicing *perfect price discrimination*.

17. A perfectly price-discriminating monopolist will actually produce the *efficient* quantity of output.

18. Examples of price discrimination are all around us. Airlines routinely charge those who stay over Saturday nights a much lower fare than those who do not. Business travelers generally travel during the week, often are unwilling to stay over Saturdays, and generally are willing to pay more for tickets.

REMEDIES FOR MONOPOLY: ANTITRUST POLICY

19. Governments have assumed two roles with respect to imperfectly competitive industries: (1) They *promote* competition and restrict market power, primarily through antitrust laws and other congressional acts, and (2) they *restrict* competition by regulating industries.

20. Congress created the *Interstate Commerce Commission* in 1887 to regulate the railroads and in 1890 passed the *Sherman Act*, which declared monopoly and trade restraints illegal. In 1911, the Supreme Court enunciated the *rule of reason*, which implied that monopolistic structure alone was not a criterion for antitrust enforcement.

21. In 1914, Congress passed the *Clayton Act*, which was designed to strengthen the Sherman Act and to clarify exactly what specific forms of conduct were "unreasonable" restraints of trade. In the same year, the *Federal Trade Commission* was established and given broad power to investigate and regulate unfair methods of competition.

THE ENFORCEMENT OF ANTITRUST LAW

22. Responsibility for the enforcement of the antitrust laws rests primarily with the *Antitrust Division* of the Justice Department and the Federal Trade Commission. Antitrust complaints can also be brought to the courts by private citizens.

23. The courts are empowered to impose a number of remedies if they find that antitrust laws have been violated. These include civil and criminal penalties, *consent decrees* that specifically forbid future illegal acts, and treble damages.

A NATURAL MONOPOLY

24. When a firm exhibits economies of scale so large that average costs continuously decline with output, it may be efficient to have only one firm in an industry. Such an industry is called a *natural monopoly*.

REVIEW TERMS AND CONCEPTS

Antitrust Division (of the Department of Justice), 292

barrier to entry, 272

Clayton Act, 291

collusion, 284

consent decree, 293

Federal Trade Commission (FTC), 291

government failure, 286

government franchise, 272

imperfectly competitive industry, 271

Interstate Commerce Commission (ICC), 289

market power, 271

natural monopoly, 294

patent, 273

perfect price discrimination, 287

per se rule, 291

price discrimination, 287

public choice theory, 286

pure monopoly, 272

rent-seeking behavior, 286

rule of reason, 290

Sherman Act, 289

trust, 289

Wheeler-Lea Act, 292

PROBLEM SET

1. Do you agree or disagree with each of the following statements? Explain your reasoning.
   a. For a monopoly, price is equal to marginal revenue because a monopoly has the power to control price.
   b. Because a monopoly is the only firm in an industry, it can charge virtually any price for its product.
   c. It is always true that if demand elasticity is equal to −1, marginal revenue is equal to 0.

2. Explain why the marginal revenue curve facing a competitive firm differs from the marginal revenue curve facing a monopolist.

3. Assume that the potato chip industry in the Northwest in 2005 was competitively structured and in long-run competitive equilibrium; firms were earning a normal rate of return. In 2006, two smart lawyers quietly bought up all the firms and began operations as a monopoly called "Wonks." To operate efficiently, Wonks hired a management consulting firm, which estimated long-run costs and demand. These results are presented in the following figure:

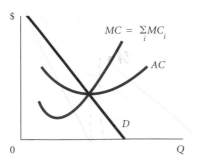

($\Sigma_i MC_i$ = the horizontal sum of the marginal cost curves of the individual branches/firms.)
   a. Indicate 2005 output and price on the diagram.
   b. By assuming that the monopolist is a profit-maximizer, indicate on the graph total revenue, total cost, and total profit after the consolidation.
   c. Compare the perfectly competitive outcome with the monopoly outcome.
   d. In 2007, an old buddy from law school files a complaint with the Antitrust Division of the Justice Department claiming that Wonks has monopolized the potato chip industry. Justice concurs and prepares a civil suit. Suppose you work in the White House and the president asks you to prepare a brief memo (two or three paragraphs) outlining the issues. In your response, be sure to include
   (1) The economic justification for action
   (2) A proposal to achieve an efficient market outcome

4. Willy's Widgets, a monopoly, faces the following demand schedule (sales in widgets per month):

Price	$20	$30	$40	$50	$60	$70	$80	$90	$100
Quantity demanded	40	35	30	25	20	15	10	5	0

Calculate marginal revenue over each interval in the schedule—for example, between $q = 40$ and $q = 35$. Recall that marginal revenue is the added revenue from an additional *unit* of production/sales and assume that *MR* is constant within each interval.

If marginal cost is constant at $20 and fixed cost is $100, what is the profit-maximizing level of output? (Choose one of the specific levels of output from the schedule.) What is the level of profit? Explain your answer using marginal cost and marginal revenue.

Repeat the exercise for $MC = \$40$.

5. The following diagram illustrates the demand curve facing a monopoly in an industry with no economies or diseconomies of scale and no fixed costs. In the short and long run $MC = ATC$. Copy the diagram and indicate:

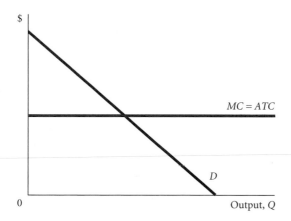

a. Optimal output
b. Optimal price
c. Total revenue
d. Total cost
e. Total monopoly profits
f. Total "excess burden" or "welfare costs" of the monopoly (briefly explain)

6. The following diagram shows the cost structure of a monopoly firm as well as market demand. Identify on the graph and calculate the following:
a. Profit-maximizing output level 10,000
b. Profit-maximizing price 4
c. Total revenue 40,000
d. Total cost 50,000
e. Total profit or loss -10,000

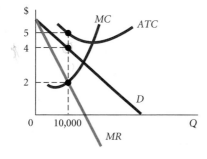

7. Consider the following monopoly that produces paperback books:

$$\text{fixed costs} = \$1,000$$
$$\text{marginal cost} = \$1 \text{ (and is constant)}$$

a. Draw the average total cost curve and the marginal cost curve on the same graph.
b. Assume that all households have the same demand schedule, given by the following relationship:

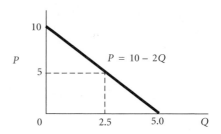

If there are 400 households in the economy, draw the market demand curve and the marginal revenue schedule facing the monopolist.
c. What is the monopolist's profit-maximizing output? What is the monopolist's price?
d. What is the "efficient price," assuming no externalities?
e. Suppose that the government "imposed" the efficient price by setting a ceiling on price at the efficient level. What is the long-run output of the monopoly?
f. Can you suggest an alternative approach for achieving an efficient outcome?

*8. In Taiwan, there is only one beer producer, a government-owned monopoly called Taiwan Beer. Suppose that the company were run in a way to maximize profit for the government. That is, assume it behaved like a private profit-maximizing monopolist. Assuming that demand and cost conditions are given on the following diagram, at what level would Taiwan Beer target output, and what price would it charge?

Now suppose that Taiwan Beer decided to begin competing in the highly competitive American market. Assume further that Taiwan maintains import barriers so that American producers cannot sell in Taiwan, but that they are not immediately reciprocated. Assuming that Taiwan Beer can sell all that it can produce in the American market at a price $P = P_{US}$ indicate:

a. Total output
b. Output sold in Taiwan
c. New price in Taiwan
d. Total sold in the United States
e. Total profits
f. Total profits on U.S. sales
g. Total profits on Taiwan sales

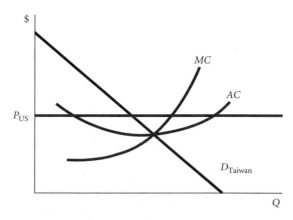

_____
*Note: Problems marked with an asterisk are more challenging.

9. The News Analysis Box on page 275 describes the trade-off facing health policy makers. The patent system provides drug makers monopoly power and the ability to charge very high prices to those who suffer from diseases that can be helped by a new drug. Nowhere was this dilemma more powerful than in the case of AIDS drugs in Africa. Since the mid-1990s the pharmaceutical companies have developed a set of drug compounds that effectively prolong the lives of AIDS victims, but they are so expensive that 90 percent of the millions of AIDS victims or their governments will not be able to pay. What solutions have been suggested to deal with the pandemic? Are any of them working?

Monopolistic Competition and Oligopoly

14

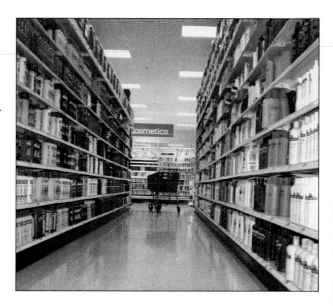

We have now examined two "pure" market structures. At one extreme is *perfect competition*, a market structure in which many firms, each small relative to the size of the market, produce undifferentiated products and have no market power at all. Each competitive firm takes price as given and faces a perfectly elastic demand for its product. At the other extreme is *pure monopoly*, a market structure in which only one firm is the industry. The monopoly holds the power to set price and is protected against competition by barriers to entry. Its market power would be complete if it did not face the discipline of the market demand curve. Even a monopoly, however, must produce a product that people want and are willing to pay for.

Most industries in the United States fall somewhere between these two extremes. In this chapter, we focus on two types of industries in which firms exercise some market power but at the same time face competition. One type, *monopolistic competition*, differs from perfect competition only in that firms can differentiate their products. Entry to a monopolistically competitive industry is easy, and each industry is made up of many firms.

The other type, *oligopoly*, is a broad category that covers many kinds of firm behavior and industry structure. An oligopoly is an industry comprising a small number of competitors; each firm in an oligopoly is large enough to have some control over market price, but beyond that the character of competition varies greatly from industry to industry. An oligopoly may have 2 firms or 20, and those firms may produce differentiated or undifferentiated products.

Thus far we have defined four types of market or industry structure. These are important because how firms within any industry behave depends upon how that industry is organized—whether there are many firms or few, whether they are large firms or small, whether the products of one firm are good substitutes for the products of others in the industry, and whether entry is easy or difficult. Figure 14.1 summarizes the four main types of market organization: perfect competition, monopoly, monopolistic competition, and oligopoly. Although not every industry fits neatly into one of these categories, the categories do provide a useful and convenient framework for thinking about industry structure and behavior.

	Number of firms	Products differentiated or homogeneous	Price a decision variable	Easy entry	Distinguished by	Examples
Perfect competition	Many	Homogeneous	No	Yes	No price competition	Wheat farmer Textile firm
Monopoly	One	A single, unique product	Yes	No	Still constrained by market demand	Public utility Patented drug
Monopolistic competition	Many	Differentiated	Yes, but limited	Yes	Price and quality competition	Restaurants Hand soap
Oligopoly	Few	Either	Yes	Limited	Strategic behavior	Automobiles Aluminum

FIGURE 14.1 Characteristics of Different Market Organizations

MONOPOLISTIC COMPETITION

monopolistic competition
A common form of industry (market) structure in the United States, characterized by a large number of firms, none of which can influence market price by virtue of size alone. Some degree of market power is achieved by firms producing differentiated products. New firms can enter and established firms can exit such an industry with ease.

A **monopolistically competitive industry** has the following characteristics:

1. A large number of firms
2. No barriers to entry
3. Product differentiation

While pure monopoly and perfect competition are rare, monopolistic competition is common in the United States, for example, in the restaurant business. In the San Francisco Yellow Pages, 26 pages are devoted to listing over 1,500 different restaurants in the area. Each produces a slightly different product and attempts to distinguish itself in consumers' minds. Entry to the market is certainly not blocked. At one location near Union Square, five different restaurants opened and went out of business in 5 years. Although many restaurants fail, small ones can compete and survive because there are no economies of scale in the restaurant business.

The feature that distinguishes monopolistic competition from monopoly and oligopoly is that firms that are monopolistic competitors cannot influence market price by virtue of their size. No one restaurant is big enough to affect the market price of a prime rib dinner, even though all restaurants can control their *own* prices. Instead, firms gain control over price in monopolistic competition by *differentiating* their products. You make it in the restaurant business by producing a product that people want that others are not producing or by establishing a reputation for good food and good service. By producing a unique product or establishing a particular reputation, a firm becomes, in a sense, a "monopolist"—that is, no one else can produce the exact same good.

The feature that distinguishes monopolistic competition from pure monopoly is that good substitutes are available in a monopolistically competitive industry. With 1,500 restaurants in the San Francisco area, there are dozens of good Italian, Chinese, and French restaurants. San Francisco's Chinatown, for example, has about 50 small Chinese restaurants, with over a dozen packed on a single street. The menus are nearly identical, and they all charge virtually the same prices. At the other end of the spectrum are restaurants, with established names and prices far above the cost of production, that are always booked. That is the goal of every restaurateur who ever put a stockpot on the range.

Table 14.1 presents some data on nine national manufacturing industries that have the characteristics of monopolistic competition. Each of these industries includes hundreds of individual firms, some larger than others, but all small relative to the industry. The top four firms in book printing, for example, account for 32 percent of total shipments. The top 20 firms account for 59 percent of the market, while the market's remaining 41 percent is split among almost 690 separate firms.

Monopolistic Competition
and Oligopoly

TABLE 14.1 Percentage of Value of Shipments Accounted for by the Largest Firms in Selected Industries, 1997

INDUSTRY DESIGNATION	FOUR LARGEST FIRMS	EIGHT LARGEST FIRMS	TWENTY LARGEST FIRMS	NUMBER OF FIRMS
Travel trailers and campers	26	35	50	761
Dolls	31	51	72	239
Wood office furniture	35	42	55	639
Book printing	32	45	59	690
Curtains and draperies	26.5	36.3	50.1	2,012
Fresh or frozen seafood	13.6	22.9	42.2	586
Women's dresses	14.2	23.7	39.4	747
Miscellaneous plastic products	5	8	14	7,522

Source: U.S. Department of Commerce, Bureau of Census, 1997 Census of Manufacturers, *Concentration Ratios in Manufacturing.* Subject Series Ec92m 315, June 2001.

Firms in a monopolistically competitive industry are small relative to the total market. New firms can enter the industry in pursuit of profit, and relatively good substitutes for the firms' products are available. Firms in monopolistically competitive industries try to achieve a degree of market power by differentiating their products—by producing something new, different, or better, or by creating a unique identity in the minds of consumers.

To discuss the behavior of such firms, we begin with a few words about advertising and product differentiation.

PRODUCT DIFFERENTIATION, ADVERTISING, AND SOCIAL WELFARE

Monopolistically competitive firms achieve whatever degree of market power they command through **product differentiation**. To be chosen over competitors, products must have distinct positive identities in consumers' minds. This differentiation is often accomplished through advertising.

In 2003, firms spent over $200 billion on advertising, as Table 14.2 shows. Advertising reaches us through every medium of communication. Table 14.3 shows national magazine

product differentiation
A strategy that firms use to achieve market power. Accomplished by producing products that have distinct positive identities in consumers' minds.

TABLE 14.2 Total Advertising Expenditures in 2003

	DOLLARS (BILLIONS)
Newspapers	45.4
Television	62.2
Direct mail	49.1
Yellow pages	13.9
Internet	5.6
Radio	19.5
Magazines	11.8

Source: Universal McCann, Reported in U.S. Bureau of the Census, *Statistical Abstract of the United States,* 2004–2005, Table 1274.

TABLE 14.3 Magazine Advertising Revenues by Category, 2003

	DOLLARS (MILLIONS)
Automotive	2,088
Technology	
Telecommunications	243
Computers and software	729
Home furnishings and supplies	1,554
Toiletries and cosmetics	1,699
Apparel and accessories	1,513
Financial, insurance, and real estate	896
Food and food products	1,391
Drugs and remedies	1,663
Retail stores	986
Beer, wine, and liquor	394
Sporting goods	253

Source: Publishers Information Bureau, *Statistical Abstract of the United States,* 2004–2005, Table 1275.

advertising expenditures by major industrial category. The automobile industry leads the pack with expenditures of nearly $2.1 billion in magazine advertising in 2003. In 2005, 30 seconds of prime commercial advertising time during Super Bowl XXXIX cost $2.4 million.

The effects of product differentiation in general, and advertising in particular, on the allocation of resources have been hotly debated for years. Advocates claim that these forces give the market system its vitality and power. Critics argue that they cause waste and inefficiency. Before we proceed to the models of monopolistic competition and oligopoly, let us look at this debate.

The Case for Product Differentiation and Advertising

The big advantage of product competition is that it provides us with the variety inherent in a steady stream of new products while ensuring the quality of those products. A modern economy can satisfy a tremendous variety of tastes and preferences. A walk through several neighborhoods of a big city, or an hour in a modern department store or mall, should convince you that human wants are infinite—well, nearly—in their variety.

Spirited competition with differentiated products is the only way to satisfy all of us. Think of the variety of music we listen to—bluegrass, heavy metal, country, folk, rap, classical, and grunge. Business firms engage in constant market research to satisfy these wants. What do consumers want? What colors? What cuts? What sizes? The only firms that succeed are the ones that answer these questions correctly and thereby satisfy an existing demand.

In recent years, quite a few of us have taken up the sport of running. The market has responded in a big way. Now there are numerous running magazines; hundreds of orthotic shoes designed specifically for runners with particular running styles; running suits of every color, cloth, and style; weights for the hands, ankles, and shoelaces; tiny radios to slip into your sweatbands; and so forth. Even physicians have differentiated their products: Sports medicine clinics have diets for runners, therapies for runners, and doctors specializing in shin splints or Morton's toe.

The products that satisfy a real demand survive. The market shows no mercy to products no one wants. They sit on store shelves, are sold at heavily discounted prices or not at all, and eventually disappear. Firms making products that do not sell go out of business, the victims of an economic Darwinism in which only the products that can thrive in a competitive environment survive.

The standard of living rises when the technology of production improves—that is, when we learn to produce more with fewer resources. The standard of living also rises when we have product *innovation*, when new and better products come on the market. Think of all the things today that did not exist 20 years ago: iPods, DVD players, many features of personal computers, and so on.

Variety is also important to us psychologically. The astonishing range of products available exists not just because your tastes differ from mine. Human beings get bored easily. We grow tired of things, and diminishing marginal utility sets in. I do not go only to French restaurants; it is nice to eat Greek or Chinese food once in a while too. To satisfy many people with different preferences that change over time, the market must be able to respond with new products.

Restaurants and rock bands are good examples of monopolistic competitors that face intense competition.

People who visit planned economies always comment on the lack of variety. Before the Berlin Wall came down in 1989 and East and West Germany were reunited in 1990, those who were allowed passed from colorful and exciting West Berlin into dull and gray East Berlin; variety seemed to vanish. As the Wall came down, thousands of Germans from the East descended on the department stores of the West. Visitors to China since the economic reforms of the mid-1980s claim that the biggest visible sign of change is the increase in the selection of products available to the population.

Proponents of product differentiation also argue that it leads to efficiency. If my product is of higher quality than my competition's, my product will sell more and my firm will do better. If I can produce something of high quality more cheaply—that is, more efficiently—than my competition can, I will force them to do likewise or go out of business. Creating a brand name through advertising also helps to ensure quality. Firms that have spent millions to establish a brand name or a reputation for quality have something of value to protect.

For product differentiation to be successful, consumers must know about product quality and availability. In perfect competition, where all products are alike, we assume that consumers have perfect information; without it, the market fails to produce an efficient allocation of resources. Complete information is even more important when we allow for product differentiation. Consumers get this information through advertising, at least in part. The basic function of advertising, according to its proponents, is to assist consumers in making informed, rational choices.

Supporters of product differentiation and advertising also claim that these techniques promote competition. New products can compete with old, established brands only if they can get their messages through to consumers. When consumers are informed about a wide variety of potential substitutes, they can more effectively resist the power of monopolies.

> The advocates of spirited competition believe that differentiated products and advertising give the market system its vitality and are the basis of its power. They are the only ways to begin to satisfy the enormous range of tastes and preferences in a modern economy. Product differentiation also helps to ensure high quality and efficient production, and advertising provides consumers with the valuable information on product availability, quality, and price that they need to make efficient choices in the marketplace.

The Case Against Product Differentiation and Advertising Product differentiation and advertising waste society's scarce resources, argue critics. They say enormous sums of money are spent to create minute, meaningless differences among products.

Drugs, both prescription and nonprescription, are an example. Companies spend millions of dollars to "hype" brand-name drugs that contain exactly the same compounds as those available under their generic names. The antibiotics erythromycin and erythrocin have the same ingredients, yet the latter is half as expensive. Aspirin is aspirin, yet we pay twice the price for an advertised brand because the manufacturer has convinced us that there is a tangible—or intangible—difference.

Do we really need 50 different kinds of soap, all of whose prices are inflated substantially by the cost of advertising? For a firm producing a differentiated product, advertising is part of the everyday cost of doing business; its price is built into the average cost curve and thus into the price of the product in the short run and the long run. Thus, consumers pay to finance advertising.

In a way, advertising and product differentiation turn the market system completely around. An economic system is supposed to meet the needs and satisfy the desires of members of society. Advertising is intended to change people's preferences and to create wants that otherwise would not have existed. From the advertiser's viewpoint, people exist to satisfy the needs of the economy.

Critics also argue that the information content of advertising is minimal at best and deliberately deceptive at worst. It is meant to change our minds, to persuade us, and to create brand "images." Try to determine how much real information there is in the next 10 advertisements you see on television. To the extent that no information is conveyed, critics argue, advertising creates no real value, and thus a substantial portion of the over $200 billion worth of resources that we devote to advertising is wasted.

Competitive advertising can also easily turn into unproductive warfare. Suppose there are five firms in an industry and one firm begins to advertise heavily. To survive, the others respond in kind. If one firm drops out of the race, it will certainly lose out. Advertising of this sort may not increase demand for the product or improve profitability for the industry. Instead, it is often a "zero sum game"—a game in which the sum of the gains equals the sum of the losses.

Advertising may reduce competition by creating a barrier to the entry of new firms into an industry. One famous case study taught at the Harvard Business School calculates the cost of entering the breakfast cereal market. To be successful, a potential entrant would have to start with millions of dollars in an extensive advertising campaign to establish a brand name recognized by consumers. Entry to the breakfast cereal game is not completely blocked, but such financial requirements make it much more difficult.

Finally, some argue that advertising by its very nature imposes a cost on society. We are continuously bombarded by bothersome jingles and obtrusive images. When driving home from school or work, we may pass 50 billboards and listen to 15 minutes of news and 20 minutes of advertising on the radio. When we get home, we throw away 10 pieces of unsolicited junk mail, glance at a magazine containing 50 pages of writing and 75 pages of advertisements, and perhaps watch a television show that is interrupted every 5 minutes for a "message."

> The bottom line, critics of product differentiation and advertising argue, is waste and inefficiency. Enormous sums are spent to create minute, meaningless, and possibly nonexistent differences among products. Advertising raises the cost of products and frequently contains very little information. Often, it is merely an annoyance. Product differentiation and advertising have turned the system upside down: People exist to satisfy the needs of the economy, not vice versa. Advertising can lead to unproductive warfare and may serve as a barrier to entry, thus reducing real competition.

No Right Answer   You will see over and over as you study economics that many questions have no right answers. There are strong arguments on both sides of the advertising debate, and even the empirical evidence yields to conflicting conclusions. Some studies show that advertising leads to concentration and positive profits; others, that advertising improves the functioning of the market.

PRICE AND OUTPUT DETERMINATION IN MONOPOLISTIC COMPETITION

Recall that monopolistically competitive industries are made up of a large number of firms, each small relative to the size of the total market. Thus, no one firm can affect market price by virtue of its size alone. Firms do differentiate their products, however. By doing so, they gain some control over price.

Product Differentiation and Demand Elasticity   Perfectly competitive firms face a perfectly elastic demand for their product: All firms in a perfectly competitive industry produce exactly the same product. If firm A tried to raise price, buyers would go elsewhere and firm A would sell nothing. When a firm can distinguish its product from all others in the

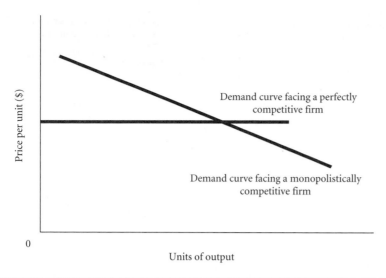

FIGURE 14.2 Product Differentiation Reduces the Elasticity of Demand Facing a Firm

The demand curve faced by a monopolistic competitor is likely to be less elastic than the demand curve faced by a perfectly competitive firm, but more elastic than the demand curve faced by a monopolist because close substitutes for the products of a monopolistic competitor are available.

minds of consumers, as we assume it can under monopolistic competition, it probably can raise price without losing all quantity demanded. Figure 14.2 shows how product differentiation might make demand somewhat less elastic for a hypothetical firm.

A monopoly is an industry with a single firm that produces a good for which there are no close substitutes. A monopolistically competitive firm is like a monopoly in that it is the only producer of its unique product. Only one firm can produce Cheerios or Wheat Thins or Johnson's Baby Shampoo or Oreo cookies. However, unlike the product in a monopoly market, the product of a monopolistically competitive firm has many close substitutes competing for the consumer's favor.

> Although the demand curve faced by a monopolistic competitor is likely to be less elastic than the demand curve faced by a perfectly competitive firm, it is likely to be more elastic than the demand curve faced by a monopoly.

Price/Output Determination in the Short Run   Under conditions of monopolistic competition, a profit-maximizing firm behaves much like a monopolist in the short run. First, marginal revenue is not equal to price, because the monopolistically competitive firm has some control over output price. Like a monopolistic firm, a monopolistically competitive firm must lower price to increase output and sell it. The monopolistic competitor's marginal revenue curve thus lies *below* its demand curve, intersecting the quantity axis midway between the origin and the point at which the demand curve intersects it. (If necessary, review Chapter 13 to get a grip on this idea.) The firm chooses that output–price combination that maximizes profit.

> To maximize profit, the monopolistically competitive firm will increase production until the marginal revenue from increasing output and selling it no longer exceeds the marginal cost of producing it. This occurs at the point at which marginal revenue equals marginal cost: $MR = MC$.

In Figure 14.3(a), the profit-maximizing output is $q_0 = 2,000$, where marginal revenue equals marginal cost. To sell 2,000 units, the firm must charge $6. Total revenue is $P_0 \times q_0 = \$12,000$, or the area of $P_0 A q_0 0$. Total cost is equal to average total cost times q_0, which is $10,000, or $CBq_0 0$. Total profit is the difference, $2,000 (the gray-shaded area $P_0 ABC$).

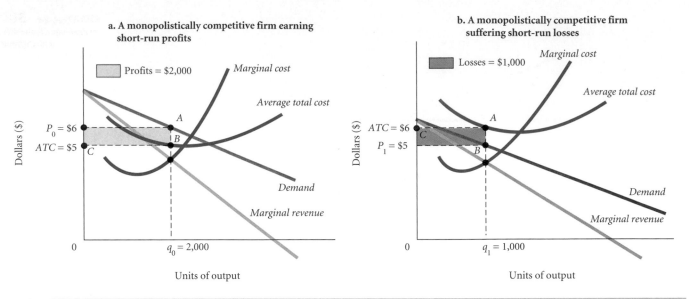

FIGURE 14.3 Monopolistic Competition in the Short Run

In the short run, a monopolistically competitive firm will produce up to the point $MR = MC$. At $q_0 = 2,000$ in panel a, the firm is earning short-run profits equal to $P_0ABC = \$2,000$. In panel b, another monopolistically competitive firm with a similar cost structure is shown facing a weaker demand and suffering short-run losses at $q_1 = 1,000$, equal to $CABP_1 = \$1,000$.

Nothing guarantees that a firm in a monopolistically competitive industry will earn positive profits in the short run. Figure 14.3(b) shows what happens when a firm with similar cost curves faces a weaker market demand. Even though the firm does have some control over price, market demand is insufficient to make the firm profitable.

As in perfect competition, such a firm minimizes its losses by producing up to the point where marginal revenue is equal to marginal cost. Of course, as in perfect competition, the price that the firm charges must be sufficient to cover variable costs. Otherwise, the firm will shut down and suffer losses equal to total fixed costs, instead of increasing losses by producing more. In other words, the firm must make a profit on operation. In Figure 14.3(b), the loss-minimizing level of output is $q_1 = 1,000$ at a price of \$5. Total revenue is $P_1 \times q_1 = \$5,000$, or P_1Bq_10. Total cost is $ATC \times q_1 = \$6,000$, or CAq_10. Because total cost is greater than revenue, the firm suffers a loss of \$1,000, equal to the pink-shaded area, $CABP_1$.

Price/Output Determination in the Long Run

In analyzing monopolistic competition, we assume entry and exit are easy in the long run. Firms can enter an industry when there are profits to be made, and firms suffering losses can go out of business. However, entry into an industry of this sort is somewhat different from entry into perfect competition, because products are differentiated in monopolistic competition. A firm that enters a monopolistically competitive industry is producing a close substitute for the good in question, *but not the same good.*

Let us begin with a firm earning positive profits in the short run. Those profits provide an incentive for new firms to enter the industry. The new firms compete by offering close substitutes, driving down the demand for the product of the firm that was earning profits. If several restaurants seem to be doing well in a particular location, others may start up and attract business from them.

New firms will continue to enter the market until profits are eliminated. As the new firms enter, the demand curve facing each old firm begins to shift to the left, pushing the marginal revenue curve along with it. (Review Chapter 13 if you are unsure why.) This shift continues until profits are eliminated, which occurs when the demand curve slips down to the average total cost curve. Graphically, this is the point at which the demand curve and the average total cost curve are tangent (the point at which they just touch and have the same slope). Figure 14.4 shows a monopolistically competitive industry in long-run equilibrium. At q^* and P^*, price and average total cost are equal, so there are no profits or losses.

FIGURE 14.4 Monopolistically Competitive Firm at Long-Run Equilibrium

As new firms enter a monopolistically competitive industry in search of profits, the demand curves of profit-making existing firms begin to shift to the left, pushing marginal revenue with them as consumers switch to the new close substitutes. This process continues until profits are eliminated, which occurs for a firm when its demand curve is just tangent to its average total cost curve.

Look carefully at this tangency, which in Figure 14.4 is at output level q^*. The tangency occurs at the profit-maximizing level of output. At this point, marginal cost is equal to marginal revenue. At any level of output other than q^*, ATC lies above the demand curve. This means that at any other level of output, ATC is greater than the price that the firm can charge. (Recall that the demand curve shows the price that can be charged at every level of output.) Hence, price equals average total cost at q^* and profits equal zero.

This equilibrium must occur at the point at which the demand curve is *just tangent* to the average total cost curve. If the demand curve cut across the average cost curve, intersecting it at two points, the demand curve would be *above* the average total cost curve at some levels of output. Producing at those levels of output would mean positive profits. Positive profits would attract entrants, shifting the market demand curve to the left and lowering profits. If the demand curve were always *below* the average total cost curve, all levels of output would produce losses for the firm. This would cause firms to exit the industry, shifting the market demand curve to the right and increasing profits (or reducing losses) for those firms still in the industry.

The firm's demand curve must end up tangent to its average total cost curve for profits to equal zero. This is the condition for long-run equilibrium in a monopolistically competitive industry.

Even if some monopolistically competitive firms start with losses, the long-run equilibrium will be zero profits for all firms remaining in the industry. (Look back at Figure 14.3(b), which shows a firm suffering losses.) Suppose many restaurants open in a small area, for example. In Columbus, Ohio, near the intersection of I-270 and Fishinger Road, there are a dozen or so "quick dinner" restaurants crowded into a small area. Given so many restaurants, it seems likely that there will be a "shake-out" sometime in the near future—that is, one or more of the restaurants suffering losses will decide to drop out.

When this happens, the firms remaining in the industry will get a larger share of the total business, and their demand curves will shift to the right. Firms will continue to drop out and thus the demand curves of the remaining firms will continue to shift until all losses are eliminated. Thus, we end up with the same long-run equilibrium as when we started out with firms earning positive profits. At equilibrium, demand is tangent to average total cost, and there are no profits or losses.

ECONOMIC EFFICIENCY AND RESOURCE ALLOCATION

We have already noted some of the similarities between monopolistic competition and perfect competition. Because entry is easy and economic profits are eliminated in the long run, we might conclude that the result of monopolistic competition is efficient. There are two problems, however.

First, once a firm achieves any degree of market power by differentiating its product (as is the case in monopolistic competition), its profit-maximizing strategy is to hold down production and charge a price above marginal cost, as you saw in Figures 14.3 and 14.4. Remember from Chapter 12 that price is the value that society places on a good, and marginal cost is the value that society places on the resources needed to produce that good. By holding production down and price above marginal cost, monopolistically competitive firms prevent the efficient use of resources. More product could be produced at a resource cost below the value that consumers place on the product.

Second, as Figure 14.4 shows, the final equilibrium in a monopolistically competitive firm is necessarily to the left of the low point on its average total cost curve. That means a typical firm in a monopolistically competitive industry will not realize all the economies of scale available. (In perfect competition, you will recall, firms are pushed to the bottom of their long-run average cost curves, and the result is an efficient allocation of resources.)

Suppose a number of firms enter an industry and build plants on the basis of initially profitable positions. As more and more firms compete for those profits, individual firms find themselves with smaller and smaller market shares, and they end up eventually with "excess capacity." The firm in Figure 14.4 is not fully using its existing capacity because competition drove its demand curve to the left. In monopolistic competition we end up with many firms, each producing a slightly different product at a scale that is less than optimal. Would it not be more efficient to have a smaller number of firms, each producing on a slightly larger scale?

The costs of less-than-optimal production, however, need to be balanced against the gains that can accrue from aggressive competition among products. If product differentiation leads to the introduction of new products, improvements in old products, and greater variety, then an important gain in economic welfare may counteract (and perhaps outweigh) the loss of efficiency from pricing above marginal cost or not fully realizing all economies of scale.

Most industries that comfortably fit the model of monopolistic competition are very competitive. Price competition coexists with product competition, and firms do not earn incredible profits and do not violate any of the antitrust laws that we discussed in the last chapter. Monopolistically competitive firms have not been a subject of great concern among economic policy makers. Their behavior appears to be sufficiently controlled by competitive forces, and no serious attempt has been made to regulate or control them.

OLIGOPOLY

oligopoly A form of industry (market) structure characterized by a few dominant firms. Products may be homogenous or differentiated. The behavior of any one firm in an oligopoly depends to a great extent on the behavior of others.

An **oligopoly** is an industry dominated by a few firms that, by virtue of their individual sizes, are large enough to influence the market price. Oligopolies exist in many forms. In some oligopoly markets, products are differentiated—the classic example is the automobile industry. In others, products are nearly homogeneous. In primary copper production, for example, only eight firms produce virtually all the basic metal. Some oligopolies have a very small number of firms, each large enough to influence price—only five firms are involved in cellulosic man-made fibers (a $1.8 billion industry), for example. Others have many firms, of which only a few control market price—four firms control 86 percent of the market for electrical lamps, but 76 firms compete in the industry.

An industry that has a relatively small number of firms that dominate the market is called a *concentrated industry*. Oligopolies are concentrated industries. Table 14.4 contains some data on 10 industries that are relatively concentrated. Although the largest firms account for most of the output in each of these industries, some seem to support a large number of smaller firms.

The complex interdependence that usually exists among firms in these industries makes oligopoly difficult to analyze. The behavior of any one firm depends on the reactions it expects of all the others in the industry. Because individual firms make so many decisions—

TABLE 14.4 Percentage of Value of Shipments Accounted for by the Largest Firms in High-Concentration Industries, 1997

INDUSTRY DESIGNATION	FOUR LARGEST FIRMS	EIGHT LARGEST FIRMS	NUMBER OF FIRMS
Cellulosic man-made fiber	100		4
Primary copper	95	99	9
Household laundry equipment	90	99	10
Cigarettes	99	100	8
Malt beverages (beer)	90	93	494
Electric lamp bulbs	89	94	54
Cereal breakfast foods	83	94	48
Motor vehicles	82	92	325
Small arms ammunition	89	94	107
Household refrigerators and freezers	82	97	21

Source: U.S. Department of Commerce, Bureau of the Census, 1997 Census of Manufacturers, *Concentration Ratios in Manufacturing*, Subject Series 2001.

how much output to produce, what price to charge, how much to advertise, whether and when to introduce new product lines, and so forth—industrial strategies are usually complex and difficult to generalize about.

OLIGOPOLY MODELS

Because many different types of oligopolies exist, a number of different oligopoly models have been developed. The following provides a sample of the alternative approaches to the behavior (or conduct) of oligopolistic firms. As you will see, all kinds of oligopoly have one thing in common:

> The behavior of any given oligopolistic firm depends on the behavior of the other firms in the industry comprising the oligopoly.

The Collusion Model   In Chapter 13, we examined what happens when a perfectly competitive industry falls under the control of a single profit-maximizing firm. In that analysis, we assumed neither technological nor cost advantages to having one firm instead of many. We saw that when many competing firms act independently, they produce more, charge a lower price, and earn less profit than they would have if they had acted as a single unit. If these firms get together and agree to cut production and increase price—that is, if firms can agree *not* to price compete—they will have a bigger total-profit pie to carve. When a group of profit-maximizing oligopolists colludes on price and output, the result is exactly the same as it would be if a monopolist controlled the entire industry.

> The colluding oligopoly will face market demand and produce only up to the point at which marginal revenue and marginal cost are equal ($MR = MC$), and price will be set above marginal cost.

Review "Collusion and Monopoly Compared" in Chapter 13 if you are not sure why.

A group of firms that gets together and makes price and output decisions jointly is called a **cartel**. Perhaps the most familiar example of a cartel today is the Organization of Petroleum Exporting Countries (OPEC). As early as 1970, the OPEC cartel began to cut petroleum production. Its decisions in this matter led to a 400 percent increase in the price of crude oil on world markets during 1973 and 1974. Although OPEC controls a smaller portion of world production today, OPEC production restrictions were an important factor during a substantial increase in world oil prices in more recent times.

Price-fixing is not controlled internationally, but it is illegal in the United States. Nonetheless, the incentive to fix prices can be irresistible, and industries are caught in the act

cartel A group of firms that gets together and makes joint price and output decisions to maximize joint profits.

from time to time. One famous case in the 1950s involved explicit agreements among a number of electrical equipment manufacturers. In that case, 12 people from five companies met secretly on a number of occasions and agreed to set prices and split up contracts and profits. The scheme involved rotating the winning bids among the firms. Ultimately, the scheme was exposed and the participants were tried, convicted, and sent to jail.

For a cartel to work, a number of conditions must be present. First, demand for the cartel's product must be inelastic. If many substitutes are readily available, the cartel's price increases may become self-defeating as buyers switch to substitutes. Second, the members of the cartel must play by the rules. If a cartel is holding up prices by restricting output, there is a big incentive for members to cheat by increasing output. Breaking ranks can mean very large profits.

Collusion occurs when price- and quantity-fixing agreements are explicit. **Tacit collusion** occurs when firms end up fixing price without a specific agreement, or when such agreements are implicit. A small number of firms with market power may fall into the practice of setting similar prices or following the lead of one firm without ever meeting or setting down formal agreements.

As we saw in some detail in Chapter 13, the exercise of monopoly power or attempts to exercise monopoly power are illegal. In addition, the Department of Justice and the Federal Trade Commission have the power granted by Congress jointly to regulate mergers that may result in reduced competition. We will return to the subject of merger regulation later in the chapter. (See box titled "Regulation of Mergers by the Department of Justice and the Federal Trade Commission," p. 313.)

The Cournot Model   Perhaps the oldest model of oligopoly behavior was put forward by French economist Augustin Cournot almost 150 years ago. The **Cournot model** is based on three assumptions: (1) There are just two firms in an industry—a *duopoly*; (2) each firm takes the output of the other as given; and (3) both firms maximize profits.

The story begins with a new firm producing nothing and the existing firm producing everything. The existing firm takes the market demand curve as its own, acting like a monopolist. When the new firm starts operating, it assumes that the existing firm will continue to produce the same level of output and charge the same price as before. The market demand of the new firm is market demand less the amount that the existing firm is currently selling. In essence, the new firm assumes that its demand curve is everything on the market demand curve below the price charged by the older firm.

When the new firm starts operation, the existing firm discovers that its demand has eroded because some output is now sold by the new firm. The old firm now assumes that the new firm's output will remain constant, subtracts the new firm's demand from market demand, and produces a new, lower level of output. However, that throws the ball back to the new firm, which now finds that the competition is producing *less*.

These adjustments get smaller and smaller, with the new firm raising output in small steps and the older firm lowering output in small steps until the two firms split the market and charge the same price. Like the collusion model:

> The Cournot model of oligopoly results in a quantity of output somewhere between output that would prevail if the market were perfectly competitive and output that would be set by a monopoly.

Although the Cournot model illustrates the interdependence of decisions in oligopoly, its assumptions about strategic reactions are quite naive. The two firms in the model react only after the fact and never anticipate the competition's moves.

The Kinked Demand Curve Model   Another common model of oligopolistic behavior assumes that firms believe that rivals will follow if they *cut* prices but not if they *raise* prices. This **kinked demand curve model** assumes that the elasticity of demand in response to an increase in price is different from the elasticity of demand in response to a price cut. The result is a "kink" in the demand for a single firm's product.

You can see some of these reactions in the demand curve in Figure 14.5. If the initial price of firm B's product is P^*, raising its price above P^* would cause firm B to face an elastic demand curve if its rivals did not also raise their prices (segment d_1 of the demand curve). That is, in response to the price increase, quantity demanded for firm B's product would fall

tacit collusion Collusion occurs when price- and quantity-fixing agreements among producers are explicit. *Tacit collusion* occurs when such agreements are implicit.

Cournot model A model of a two-firm industry (duopoly) in which a series of output-adjustment decisions leads to a final level of output between the output that would prevail if the market were organized competitively and the output that would be set by a monopoly.

kinked demand curve model A model of oligopoly in which the demand curve facing each individual firm has a "kink" in it. The kink results from the assumption that competitor firms will follow if a single firm cuts price but will not follow if a single firm raises price.

Regulation of Mergers by the Department of Justice and the Federal Trade Commission

The following is the introduction to the published *Guidelines* underlying the regulation of mergers jointly by the Department of Justice and the Federal Trade Commission as of 2005:

> Mergers are motivated by the prospect of financial gains. The possible sources of the financial gains from mergers are many, and the Guidelines do not attempt to identify all possible sources of gain in every merger. Instead, the Guidelines focus on the one potential source of gain that is of concern under the antitrust laws: market power.
>
> The unifying theme of the Guidelines is that mergers should not be permitted to create or enhance market power or to facilitate its exercise. Market power to a seller is the ability profitably to maintain prices above competitive levels for a significant period of time. In some circumstances, a sole seller (a "monopolist") of a product with no good substitutes can maintain a selling price that is above the level that would prevail if the market were competitive. Similarly, in some circumstances, where only a few firms account for most of the sales of a product, those firms can exercise market power, perhaps even approximating the performance of a monopolist, by either explicitly or implicitly coordinating their actions. Circumstances also may permit a single firm, not a monopolist, to exercise market power through unilateral or non-coordinated conduct—conduct the success of which does not rely on the concurrence of other firms in the market or on coordinated responses by those firms. In any case, the result of the exercise of market power is a transfer of wealth from buyers to sellers or a misallocation of resources.

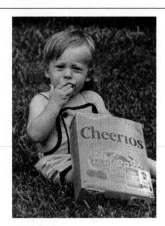

off quickly. The reaction to a price *decrease* would not be as great, however, because rivals would decrease price too. Firm B would lose some of its market share by increasing price, but it would not gain a larger share by decreasing price (segment d_2 of the demand curve).

Recall the very important point that a firm's marginal revenue curve reflects the changes in demand occurring along the demand curve *directly above it.* (Review the derivation of the marginal revenue curve in Chapter 13 if this is not fresh in your mind.) This being the case, MR_1

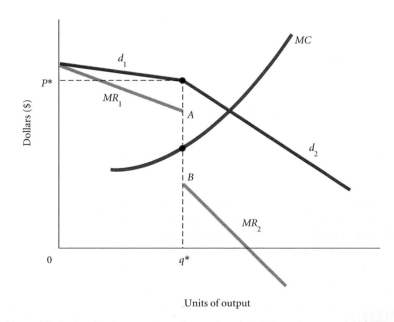

FIGURE 14.5 A Kinked Demand Curve Oligopoly Model

The kinked demand model assumes that competing firms follow price cuts but not price increases. Thus, if firm B increases its price, the competition will not, and quantity demanded of firm B's product will fall off quickly. If firm B cuts price, other firms will also cut price and the price cut will not gain as much quantity demanded for firm B as it would if other firms did not follow. At prices above P^*, demand is relatively elastic. Below P^*, demand is less elastic.

313

reflects the changes in P and q along demand curve segment d_1. MR_2 reflects changes in P and q along demand curve segment d_2. Because the demand curve changes slope at q^*, the marginal revenue curve is discontinuous, jumping from point A all the way down to point B.

As always, profit-maximizing firms will produce as long as marginal revenue is greater than marginal cost. If, as in Figure 14.5, the marginal cost curve passes through q^* at any point between A and B, the optimal price is P^* and the optimal output is q^*. To the left of q^*, marginal revenue is greater than marginal cost. To maximize profits the firm should increase output. To the right of q^*, marginal cost is greater than marginal revenue—the firm should decrease output.

Notice that this model predicts that price in oligopolistic industries is likely to be more stable than costs. In Figure 14.5, the marginal cost curve can shift up or down by a substantial amount before it becomes advantageous for the firm to change price at all. A number of attempts have been made to test whether oligopolistic prices are indeed more stable than costs. Although the results do not support the hypothesis of stable prices, the evidence is far from conclusive.

The kinked demand curve model has been criticized because (1) it fails to explain why price is at P^* to begin with, and (2) the assumption that competing firms will follow price cuts but not price increases is overly simple—real-world oligopolistic pricing strategies are much more complex.

The Price-Leadership Model   In another form of oligopoly, one firm dominates an industry and all the smaller firms follow the leader's pricing policy—hence its name **price leadership**. If the dominant firm knows that the smaller firms will follow its lead, it will derive its own demand curve simply by subtracting from total market demand the amount of demand that the smaller firms will satisfy at each potential price.

The price-leadership model assumes that (1) the industry is made up of one large firm and a number of smaller, competitive firms; (2) the dominant firm maximizes profit subject to the constraint of market demand *and* subject to the behavior of the smaller, competitive firms; and (3) the dominant firm allows the smaller firms to sell all they want at the price the leader has set. The difference between the quantity demanded in the market and the amount supplied by the smaller firms is the amount that the dominant firm will produce.

The result has the quantity demanded in the market split between the smaller firms and the dominant firm. This result is based entirely on the dominant firm's market power. The only constraint facing a monopoly firm, you will recall, is the behavior of demanders—that is, the market demand curve. In this case, however, the presence of smaller firms acts to constrain the dominant firm's power. If we were to assume that the smaller firms were out of the way, the dominant firm would face the market demand curve on its own. This means the dominant firm has a clear incentive to push the smaller firms out of the industry. One way is to lower the price until all of the smaller firms go out of business and then raise the price once the market has been monopolized. The practice by which a large, powerful firm drives smaller firms out of the market by temporarily selling at an artificially low price is called *predatory pricing*. Such behavior, common during the nineteenth century in the United States, became illegal with the passage of antimonopoly legislation around the turn of the century.

price leadership A form of oligopoly in which one dominant firm sets prices and all the smaller firms in the industry follow its pricing policy.

> As in the other oligopoly models, an oligopoly with a dominant price leader will produce a level of output between the output that would prevail under perfect competition and the output that a monopolist would choose in the same industry. It will also set a price between the monopoly price and the perfectly competitive price. Some competition is usually more efficient than none at all.

GAME THEORY

The firms in Cournot's model do not anticipate the moves of the competition. Yet in choosing strategies in an oligopolistic market, real-world firms can and do try to guess what the opposition will do in response.

In 1944, mathematician John von Neumann and economist Oskar Morgenstern published a path-breaking work in which they analyzed a set of problems, or *games*, in which two or more people or organizations pursue their own interests and in which no one of them can dictate the outcome. During the last few years, game theory has become an increasingly popular field of study and a fertile area for research. The notions of game theory have been applied to analyses of firm behavior, politics, international relations, nuclear war, military strategy, and foreign policy. In 1994, the Nobel Prize in Economic Science was awarded jointly to three early game theorists: John F. Nash of Princeton University, John C. Harsanyi of the University of California at Berkeley, and Reinhard Selten of the University of Bonn.

Game theory goes something like this: In all conflict situations, and thus all games, there are decision makers (or players), rules of the game, and payoffs (or prizes). Players choose strategies without knowing with certainty what strategy the opposition will use. At the same time, though, some information that indicates how their opposition may be "leaning" may be available to the players.

Figure 14.6 illustrates what is called a payoff matrix for a very simple game. Each of two firms, A and B, must decide whether to mount an expensive advertising campaign. If each firm decides not to advertise, each will earn a profit of $50,000. If one firm advertises and the other does not, the firm that does will increase its profit by 50 percent (to $75,000), while driving the competition into the loss column. If both firms decide to advertise, they will each earn profits of $10,000. They may generate a bit more demand by advertising, but not enough to offset the expense of the advertising itself.

If firms A and B could collude (and we assume that they cannot), their optimal strategy would be to agree not to advertise. That solution maximizes the joint profits to both firms. If both firms do not advertise, joint profits are $100,000. If both firms advertise, joint profits are only $20,000. If only one of the firms advertises, joint profits are $75,000 − $25,000 = $50,000.

The strategy that firm A will actually choose depends on the information available concerning B's likely strategy. In this case, it is possible to predict behavior. Consider A's choice of strategy. Regardless of what B does, it pays A to advertise. If B does not advertise, A makes $25,000 more by advertising than by not advertising. Thus, A will advertise. If B does advertise, A must advertise to avoid a loss. The same logic holds for B. Regardless of the strategy pursued by A, it pays B to advertise. A **dominant strategy** is one that is best no matter what the opposition does. In this game, both players have a dominant strategy, which is to advertise.

The result of the game in Figure 14.6 is an example of what is called a **prisoners' dilemma**. The term comes from a game in which two prisoners (call them Ginger and Rocky) are accused of robbing the local 7-11 together, but the evidence is shaky. If both confess, they each get 5 years in prison for armed robbery. If each one refuses to confess, they are convicted of a lesser charge, shoplifting, and get 1 year in prison each. The problem is that

game theory Analyzes oligopolistic behavior as a complex series of strategic moves and reactive countermoves among rival firms. In game theory, firms are assumed to anticipate rival reactions.

dominant strategy In game theory, a strategy that is best no matter what the opposition does.

prisoners' dilemma A game in which the players are prevented from cooperating and in which each has a dominant strategy that leaves them both worse off than if they could cooperate.

FIGURE 14.6 Payoff Matrix for Advertising Game

Both players have a dominant strategy. If B doesn't advertise, A will because $75,000 beats $50,000. If B does advertise, A will advertise because a profit of $10,000 beats a loss of $25,000. A will advertise *regardless* of what B does. Similarly, B will advertise regardless of what A does. If A does not advertise, B will because $75,000 beats $50,000. If A does advertise, B will too because a $10,000 profit beats a loss of $25,000.

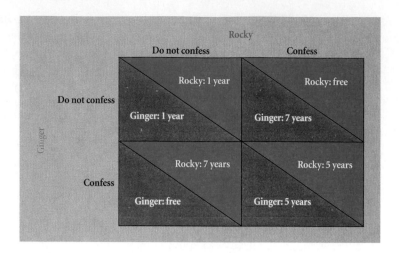

FIGURE 14.7 The Prisoners' Dilemma

Both players have a dominant strategy and will confess. If Rocky does *not* confess, Ginger will because going free beats a year in jail. Similarly, if Rocky *does* confess, Ginger will confess because 5 years in the slammer is better than 7. Rocky has the same set of choices. If Ginger does *not* confess, Rocky will because going free beats a year in jail. Similarly, if Ginger *does* confess, Rocky will confess because 5 years in the slammer is better than 7. Both will confess *regardless* of what the other does.

the district attorney has offered each of them a deal independently. If Ginger confesses and Rocky does not, Ginger goes free and Rocky gets 7 years. If Rocky confesses and Ginger does not, Rocky goes free and Ginger gets 7 years. The payoff matrix for the prisoners' dilemma is given in Figure 14.7.

By looking carefully at the payoffs, you may notice that both Ginger and Rocky have dominant strategies: to confess. That is, Ginger is better off confessing regardless of what Rocky does, and Rocky is better off confessing regardless of what Ginger does. The likely outcome is thus that both will confess, even though they would be better off if they both kept their mouths shut.

Is there any way out of this dilemma? There may be under circumstances in which the game is played over and over. Look back at Figure 14.6. The best outcome for each firm is not to advertise. Suppose firm A decided not to advertise for one period to see how firm B would respond. If firm B continued to advertise, A would have to resume advertising to survive. Suppose that B decided to simply match A's strategy. In this case, both firms might—with no explicit collusion—end up not advertising after A figures out what B is doing. We return to this below in the discussion of repeated games.

There are many games in which one player does not have a dominant strategy but in which the outcome is predictable. Consider the game in Figure 14.8(a) in which C does not have a dominant strategy. If D plays the left strategy, C will play the top strategy. If D plays the right strategy, C will play the bottom strategy. What strategy will D choose to play? If C knows the options, she will see that D has a dominant strategy and is likely to play it. D does better playing the right-hand strategy regardless of what C does; he can guarantee himself a $100 win by choosing right and is guaranteed to win nothing by playing left. Because D's behavior is predictable (he will play the right-hand strategy), C will play bottom. When all players are playing their best strategy *given* what their competitors are doing, the result is called a **Nash equilibrium**.

Nash equilibrium In game theory, the result of all players' playing their best strategy given what their competitors are doing.

Now suppose that the game in Figure 14.8(a) were changed. Suppose that all the payoffs are the same except that if D chooses left and C chooses bottom, C loses $10,000 [Figure 14.8(b)]. While D still has a dominant strategy (playing right), C now stands to lose a great deal by choosing bottom on the off-chance that D chooses left instead. When uncertainty and risk are introduced, the game changes. C is likely to play top and guarantee herself a $100 profit instead of playing bottom and risk losing $10,000 in the off-chance that D plays left. A **maximin strategy** is one chosen by a player to maximize the minimum gain that it can earn. In essence, one who plays a maximin strategy assumes that the opposition will play the strategy that does the most damage.

maximin strategy In game theory, a strategy chosen to maximize the minimum gain that can be earned.

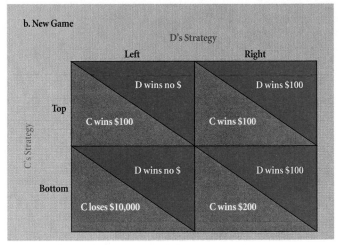

FIGURE 14.8 Payoff Matrixes for Left/Right–Top/Bottom Strategies

In the original game (a), C does not have a dominant strategy. If D plays left, C plays top; if D plays right, C plays bottom. D, on the other hand, *does* have a dominant strategy: D will play right regardless of what C does. If C believes that D is rational, she will predict that D will play right. If C concludes that D will play right, C will play bottom. The result is a Nash equilibrium because each player is doing the best that he or she can *given* what the other is doing.

In the new game (b), C had better be very sure that D will play right because if D plays left and C plays bottom, C is in big trouble, losing $10,000. C will probably play top to minimize the potential loss if the probability of D's choosing left is at all significant.

REPEATED GAMES

Clearly, games are not played once. Firms must decide on advertising budgets, investment strategies, and pricing policies continuously. While explicit collusion violates the antitrust statutes, strategic reaction does not. Yet strategic reaction in a repeated game may have the same effect as tacit collusion.

Consider the game in Figure 14.9. Suppose that British Airways and Lufthansa were competing for business on the New York to London route during the off-season. To lure travelers, they were offering discount fares. The question is, how much to discount? Both airlines were considering a deep discount of $400 round-trip or a moderate discount of $600. Since the average per trip cost to the airline is $200, each $600 ticket produces profit of $400, and each $400 ticket produces profit of $200.

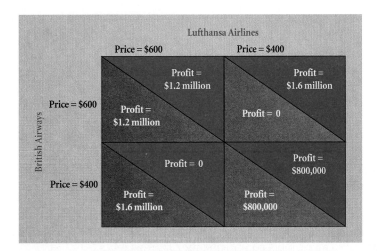

FIGURE 14.9 Payoff Matrix for Airline Game

In a single play, both British Airways (BA) and Lufthansa Airlines (LA) have dominant strategies. If LA prices at $600, BA will price at $400 because $1.6 million beats $1.2 million. If, on the other hand, LA prices at $400, BA will again choose to price at $400 because $800,000 beats zero. Similarly, LA will choose to price at $400 regardless of which strategy BA chooses.

Clearly, demand is sensitive to price. Assume that studies of demand elasticity have determined that if *both* airlines offer tickets for $600, they will attract 6,000 passengers per week (3,000 for each airline), and each airline will make a profit of $1.2 million per week ($400 dollar profit times 3,000 passengers). However, if both airlines offer the deep discount fares of $400 they will attract 2,000 additional customers per week for a total of 8,000 (4,000 for each airline). While they will have more passengers, each ticket brings in less profit and total profit falls to $800,000 per week ($200 profit times 4,000 passengers).

What if the two airlines offer different prices? To keep things simple, we will ignore brand loyalty and assume that whichever airline offers the deep discount gets all of the 8,000 passengers. If British Airways offers the $400 fare it will sell 8,000 tickets per week and make $200 profit each, for a total of $1.6 million. Since Lufthansa holds out for $600, it sells no tickets and makes no profit. Similarly, if Lufthansa were to offer tickets for $400, it would make $1.6 million per week while British Airways would make zero.

Looking carefully at the payoff matrix in Figure 14.9, do you conclude that either or both of the airlines have a dominant strategy? In fact, both do. If Lufthansa prices at $600, British Airways will price at the deep discount, $400, because $1.6 million per week is more than $1.2 million. On the other hand, if Lufthansa offers the deep discount, British Airways must as well. If it doesn't, it will earn nothing, and $800,000 beats nothing! Similarly, Lufthansa has a dominant strategy to offer the $400 fare because it makes more regardless of what British Airways does.

The result is that both airlines will offer the deep discount fare and each will make $800,000 per week. This is a classic prisoners' dilemma. If they were permitted to collude on price, they would both charge $600 per ticket and make $1.2 million per week instead—a 50 percent increase.

It was precisely this logic that led American Airlines President Robert Crandall to suggest to Howard Putnam of Braniff Airways in 1983, "I think this is dumb as hell . . . to sit here and pound the @#%* out of each other and neither one of us making a @#%* dime." . . . "I have a suggestion for you, raise your @#%* fares 20 percent. I'll raise mine the next morning."

Since competing firms are prohibited from even talking about prices, Crandall got into a lot of trouble with the Justice Department when Putnam turned over a tape of the call in which these comments were made. But could they have colluded without talking to each other? Suppose that prices are announced each week at a given time. It is like playing the game in Figure 14.9 a number of times in succession, a repeated game. After a few weeks of making $800,000, British Airways raises its price to $600. Lufthansa knows that if it simply sits on its $400 fare, it will double its profit from $800,000 to $1.6 million per week. But what is British Airways up to? It must know that its profit will drop to zero unless Lufthansa raises its fare too. The fare increase could clearly be just a signal that both firms would be better off at the higher price, and that if I lead and I can count on you to follow, we will both be better off. The strategy to respond in a way that lets your competitor know you will follow its lead is called a **tit-for-tat strategy**.

If Lufthansa figures out that British Airways will simply play the same strategy that Lufthansa is playing, both will end up charging $600 per ticket and earning $1.2 million, instead of charging $400 and earning only $800,000 per week even though there has been no explicit price-fixing.

A GAME WITH MANY PLAYERS: COLLECTIVE ACTION CAN BE BLOCKED BY A PRISONERS' DILEMMA

Some games have many players and can result in the same kinds of prisoners' dilemmas as we have just discussed. The following game illustrates how coordinated collective action in everybody's interest can be blocked under some circumstances.

Suppose that I am your professor in an economics class of 100 students. I ask you to bring $10 to class. In front of the room I place two boxes marked Box A and Box B. I tell you that you must put the sum of $10 in the two boxes split in any way you would like. You can put all $10 in Box A and nothing in Box B. You can put all $10 in Box B and nothing in Box A. On the other hand, you can put $2.50 in box A and $7.50 in Box B. Any combination totaling $10 is all right, and no one will ever know how you split up your money except me.

tit-for-tat strategy A company's strategy that lets a competitor know the company will follow the competitor's lead.

At the end of the class, every dollar put into Box A will be returned to the person who put it in. You get back exactly what you put in. But Box B is special. I will add 20 cents to Box B for every dollar put into it. That is, if there is $100 in the box, I will add $20. But here is the wrinkle: The money that ends up in Box B, *including* my 20 percent contribution, will be divided up equally among everyone in the class regardless of the amount that an individual student puts in.

You can think of Box A as representing a private market where we get what we pay for. We pay $10 and we get $10 in value back. Think of Box B as representing something we want to do collectively where the benefits go to all members of the class regardless of whether they have contributed. In Chapter 12 we discussed the concept of a *public good*. People cannot be excluded from enjoying the benefits of a public good once it is produced. Examples include clean air, a lower crime rate from law enforcement, and national defense. You can think of Box B as representing a public good.

Now, where do you put your money? If you were smart you would call a class meeting and get everyone to agree to put his or her entire $10 in Box B. Then everybody would walk out with $12. There would be $1,000 in the box, I would add $200, and the total of $1,200 would be split evenly among the 100 students.

But suppose you were not allowed to get together, in the same way that Ginger and Rocky were kept in separate cells in the jailhouse? Further suppose that everyone acts in his or her best interest. Everyone plays a strategy that maximizes the amount that he or she walks out with. If you think carefully, the dominant strategy for each individual class member is to put all $10 in Box A. *Regardless of what anyone else does*, I will get more if I put all my money in Box A than I will get from any other split of the $10. And if I put all my money into A, no one will walk out of the room with more money than I will!

How can this be? It's simple. Suppose that everyone else puts all $10 in B but I put all mine in A. Box B ends up with $990 plus a 20 percent bonus from me of $198, for a grand total of $1,188, just $12 short of the maximum possible of $1,200. What do I get? My share of Box B—which is $11.88, *plus* my $10 back, for a total of $21.88. Pretty slimy but clearly optimal for me. If I had put all my money in B, I would get only $12 back. You can do exactly the same analysis for cases in which the others split their income up in any way, and your optimal strategy is still to put your whole $10 in Box A.

Another way to think about it is, what part of what you ultimately get out is linked to or dependent upon what you put in? For every dollar you put in A, you get a dollar back. For every dollar *you yourself* put in B, you get back only one cent, one one-hundredth of a dollar, because your dollar gets split up among all 100 members of the class.

Thus, the game is a classic prisoners' dilemma, where collusion would result in an optimal outcome but where dominant strategies result in a suboptimal outcome.

How do we break this particular dilemma? We call a town meeting (class meeting) and pass a law that requires us to contribute to the production of public goods by paying taxes. Then, of course, we run the risk that government becomes a player! We will return to this theme in Chapters 15 and 17.

CONTESTABLE MARKETS

Before we discuss the performance of oligopolies, we should note one relatively new theory of behavior that has limited applications but some important implications for understanding imperfectly competitive market behavior.

A market is **perfectly contestable** if entry into it *and* exit from it are costless. That is, a market is perfectly contestable if a firm can move into it in search of profits but lose nothing if it fails. To be part of a perfectly contestable market, a firm must have capital that is both mobile and easily transferable from one market to another.

perfectly contestable market A market in which entry and exit are costless.

Take, for example, a small airline that can move its capital stock from one market to another with little cost. Cape Air flies between Boston, Martha's Vineyard, Nantucket, and Cape Cod during the summer months. During the winter, the same planes are used in Florida, where they fly up and down that state's west coast between Naples, Fort Meyers, Tampa, and other cities. A similar situation may occur when a new industrial complex is built at a fairly remote site and a number of trucking companies offer their services. Because the trucking companies' capital stock is mobile, they can move their trucks somewhere else at no great cost if business is not profitable.

Because entry is cheap, participants in a contestable market are continuously faced with competition or the threat of it. Even if only a few firms are competing, the openness of the market forces all of them to produce efficiently or be driven out of business. This threat of competition remains high because new firms face little risk in going after a new market. If things do not work out in a crowded market, they do not lose their investment. They can simply transfer their capital to a different place or different use.

In contestable markets, even large oligopolistic firms end up behaving like perfectly competitive firms. Prices are pushed to long-run average cost by competition, and positive profits do not persist.

Review Oligopoly is a market structure that is consistent with a variety of behaviors.

The only necessary condition of oligopoly is that firms are large enough to have some control over price. Oligopolies are concentrated industries. At one extreme is the cartel, in which a few firms get together and jointly maximize profits—in essence, acting as a monopolist. At the other extreme, the firms within the oligopoly vigorously compete for small, contestable markets by moving capital quickly in response to observed profits. In between are a number of alternative models, all of which stress the interdependence of oligopolistic firms.

OLIGOPOLY AND ECONOMIC PERFORMANCE

How well do oligopolies perform? Should they be regulated or changed? Are they efficient, or do they lead to an inefficient use of resources? On balance, are they good or bad?

With the exception of the contestable-markets model, all the models of oligopoly we have examined lead us to conclude that concentration in a market leads to pricing above marginal cost and output below the efficient level. When price is above marginal cost at equilibrium, consumers are paying more for the good than it costs to produce that good in terms of products forgone in other industries. To increase output would be to create value that exceeds the social cost of the good, but profit-maximizing oligopolists have an incentive not to increase output.

Entry barriers in many oligopolistic industries also prevent new capital and other resources from responding to profit signals. Under competitive conditions or in contestable markets, positive profits would attract new firms and thus increase production. This does not happen in most oligopolistic industries. The problem is most severe when entry barriers exist and firms explicitly or tacitly collude. The results of collusion are identical to the results of a monopoly. Firms jointly maximize profits by fixing prices at a high level and splitting up the profits.

Product differentiation under oligopoly presents us with the same dilemma that we encountered in monopolistic competition. On the one hand, vigorous product competition among oligopolistic competitors produces variety and leads to innovation in response to the wide variety of consumer tastes and preferences. It can thus be argued that vigorous product competition is efficient. On the other hand, product differentiation may lead to waste and inefficiency. Product differentiation accomplished through advertising may have nothing to do with product quality, and advertising itself may have little or no information content. If it serves as an entry barrier that blocks competition, product differentiation can cause the market allocation mechanism to fail.

Oligopolistic, or concentrated, industries are likely to be inefficient for several reasons. First, profit-maximizing oligopolists are likely to price above marginal cost. When price is above marginal cost, there is underproduction from society's point of view—in other words, society could get more for less, but it does not. Second, strategic behavior can lead to outcomes that are not in society's best interest. Specifically, strategically competitive firms can force themselves into deadlocks that waste resources. Finally, to the extent that oligopolies differentiate their products and advertise, there is the promise of new and exciting products. At the same time, however, there remains a real danger of waste and inefficiency.

INDUSTRIAL CONCENTRATION AND TECHNOLOGICAL CHANGE

One of the major sources of economic growth and progress throughout history has been technological advance. Innovation, both in methods of production and in the creation of new and better products, is one of the engines of economic progress. Much innovation starts with research and development efforts undertaken by firms in search of profit.

Several economists, notably Joseph Schumpeter and John Kenneth Galbraith, argued in works now considered classics that industrial concentration, where a relatively small number of firms control the marketplace, actually increases the rate of technological advance. As Schumpeter put it in 1942:

> As soon as we . . . inquire into the individual items in which progress was most conspicuous, the trail leads not to the doors of those firms that work under conditions of comparatively free competition but precisely to the doors of the large concerns . . . and a shocking suspicion dawns upon us that big business may have had more to do with creating that standard of life than keeping it down.[1]

This interpretation caused the economics profession to pause and take stock of its theories. The conventional wisdom had been that concentration and barriers to entry insulate firms from competition and lead to sluggish performance and slow growth.

The evidence concerning where innovation comes from is mixed. Certainly, most small businesses do not engage in research and development, and most large firms do. When R&D expenditures are considered as a percentage of sales, firms in industries with high concentration ratios spend more on research and development than firms in industries with low concentration ratios.

Oligopolistic companies such as AT&T have done a great deal of research. AT&T's Bell Laboratories (now a separate company called Lucent Technologies) has probably done more important research over the last several decades than any other organization in the country. It has been estimated that Bell Labs conducted 10 percent of *all* the basic industrial research in the United States during the 1970s. IBM, which despite its recent problems set the industry standard in personal computers, has certainly introduced as much new technology to the computer industry as any other firm.

However, the "high-tech revolution" grew out of many tiny start-up operations. Companies such as Sun Microsystems, Cisco Systems, and even Microsoft barely existed only a generation ago. The new biotechnology firms that are just beginning to work miracles with genetic engineering are still tiny operations that started with research done by individual scientists in university laboratories.

As with the debate about product differentiation and advertising, significant ambiguity on this subject remains. Indeed, there may be no right answer. Technological change seems to come in fits and starts, sometimes from small firms and sometimes from large ones.

THE ROLE OF GOVERNMENT

REGULATION OF MERGERS

The Clayton Act of 1914 (as mentioned in Chapter 13) had given government the authority to limit mergers that might "substantially lessen competition in an industry." The **Celler-Kefauver Act of 1950** enabled the Justice Department to monitor and enforce these provisions.

In 1968, the Justice Department issued its first guidelines designed to reduce uncertainty about the mergers it would find acceptable. The 1968 guidelines were strict. For example, if the largest four firms in an industry controlled 75 percent or more of a market, an acquiring firm with a 15 percent market share would be challenged if it wanted to acquire a firm that controlled as little as an additional 1 percent of the market.

In 1982, the Antitrust Division—in keeping with President Reagan's hands-off policy toward big business—issued a new set of far more lenient guidelines. Revised in 1984, they

Celler-Kefauver Act (1950) Extended the government's authority to ban vertical and conglomerate mergers.

---

[1] J. A. Schumpeter, *Capitalism, Socialism, and Democracy* (New York: Harper, 1942); and J. K. Galbraith, *American Capitalism* (Boston: Houghton Mifflin, 1952).

TABLE 14.5 Calculation of a Simple Herfindahl-Hirschman Index for Four Hypothetical Industries, Each with No More Than Four Firms

	PERCENTAGE SHARE OF:				HERFINDAHL-HIRSCHMAN INDEX
	Firm 1	Firm 2	Firm 3	Firm 4	
Industry A	50	50	–	–	$50^2 + 50^2 = 5{,}000$
Industry B	80	10	10	–	$80^2 + 10^2 + 10^2 = 6{,}600$
Industry C	25	25	25	25	$25^2 + 25^2 + 25^2 + 25^2 = 2{,}500$
Industry D	40	20	20	20	$40^2 + 20^2 + 20^2 + 20^2 = 2{,}800$

Herfindahl-Hirschman Index (HHI) A mathematical calculation that uses market share figures to determine whether or not a proposed merger will be challenged by the government.

FIGURE 14.10 Department of Justice Merger Guidelines (revised 1984)

Note: See Phillip Areeda, *Antitrust Analysis*, 3rd ed. 1986 Supplement (Boston: Little Brown, 1986), p. 185.

remain in place today. The standards are based on a measure of market structure called the **Herfindahl-Hirschman Index (HHI)**. The HHI is calculated by expressing the market share of each firm in the industry as a percentage, squaring these figures, and adding. For example, in an industry in which two firms each control 50 percent of the market, the index is

$$50^2 + 50^2 = 2{,}500 + 2{,}500 = 5{,}000$$

For an industry in which four firms each control 25 percent of the market, the index is:

$$25^2 + 25^2 + 25^2 + 25^2 = 625 + 625 + 625 + 625 = 2{,}500$$

Table 14.5 shows HHI calculations for several hypothetical industries. The Justice Department's courses of action, summarized in Figure 14.10, are as follows:

If the Herfindahl-Hirschman Index is less than 1,000, the industry is considered unconcentrated, and any proposed merger will go unchallenged by the Justice Department. If the index is between 1,000 and 1,800, the department will challenge any merger that would increase the index by over 100 points. Herfindahl indexes above 1,800 mean that the industry is considered concentrated already, and the Justice Department will challenge any merger that pushes the index up more than 50 points.

Some years ago, two breweries, Pabst and Heileman, proposed a merger. At the time, the Herfindahl index in the beer industry was about 1,772. Before the merger, each firm had about 7.5 percent of the market. Thus, after a merger, the new firm would have a combined share of 15 percent. The merger would thus raise the index by 112.5:

$$\underbrace{(15^2)}_{\text{Postmerger}} - \underbrace{(7.5^2 + 7.5^2)}_{\text{Premerger}} = 225 - 112.5 = 112.5$$

Because the merger increased the index by more than 100 points, it was challenged by the Justice Department.

In 1984, the same two companies reapplied to the Justice Department for permission to merge. This time Pabst agreed to sell four of its brands—accounting for over one-third of its total production—and one brewery to a third party. The sale was sufficient to bring the merger within the guidelines, and the Antitrust Division dropped its objections. However, the merger never took place. Heileman was bought by an Australian company and in 1991 went bankrupt.

In 1997, the Department of Justice and the FTC issued joint Horizontal Merger Guidelines updating and expanding the 1984 guidelines. The most interesting part of the new provisions is that the government will examine each potential merger to determine if it enhances the firms' power to engage in "coordinated interaction" with other firms in the industry. The guidelines define "coordinated interaction" as

actions by a group of firms that are profitable for each of them only as the result of the accommodating reactions of others. This behavior includes tacit or express collusion, and may or may not be lawful in and of itself.[2]

---

[2]U.S. Department of Justice, Federal Trade Commission, *Horizontal Merger Guidelines*, 2005.

Footwear Giant Adidas Buys Reebok in 2005

IN AUGUST 2005 THE GERMAN ATHLETIC footwear giant Adidas bought the American firm Reebok for nearly $4 billion in cash. The acquisition immediately set off a debate among antitrust regulators about whether the deal violated national or international regulations. Certainly, the combined firm will have substantial market power, but the industry is a highly competitive industry, with some very big players, including Nike.

The following pieces from the *New York Times* and CNN/*Money* describe the merger and the likelihood of regulatory approval.

FRANKFURT, Aug. 3—When Herbert Hainer sat down for a drink with Paul B. Fireman during the Athens Olympic Games last summer, the conversation drifted, as it often does with people in the athletic-shoe trade, to the vast American market, which is dominated by Nike.

"We talked about what's good, what's bad," said Mr. Hainer, the chief executive of Adidas-Salomon, of the chat with Mr. Fireman, the chairman of Reebok International. "There was a natural sympathy between us."

On Wednesday, that sympathy gave birth to a $3.8 billion deal, in which Adidas of Germany will acquire Reebok, creating a formidable competitor to Nike for the first time in more than a decade.

At heart, the merger is about the United States market, which accounts for more than half the sales of athletic footwear in the world. Adidas has pushed hard to increase its American market share, but it remains a distant No. 3 after Nike and Reebok.

Even after the merger, Nike, which has sales of $12.2 billion, will have the largest market share in the United States, at 36.3 percent. But Adidas's share will jump to 21.1 percent, from 8.9 percent. And in the global market

share, the gap between the two will narrow: 32.9 percent for Nike versus 26.3 percent for Adidas-Reebok, according to Mr. Horan.

Size will also give Adidas leverage in dealing with powerful retail chains like Foot Locker. "You're confronting the retail community with two huge companies, with 60 percent of the market," Mr. Horan said.

He said the merger would put pressure on the industry's smaller players, among them Puma and New Balance. Shares of Puma rose 3.86 percent here on Wednesday, as investors anticipated further deals.

In February, Reebok introduced the market slogan "I am what I am." The ads have featured hip-hop stars like Jay-Z and 50 Cent, the actress Lucy Liu, and Mr. Iverson.

BRUSSELS—Germany's Adidas-Salomon EUR3.1 billion bid for Massachusetts-based Reebok International Ltd will likely gain quick antitrust clearance in the U.S. and Europe, analysts say.

The combined firms will have a 30 percent share of the $33 billion global athletic footwear business, but will still trail Oregon-based Nike Inc.'s 37 percent stake, according to analysts' data.

Regulators allowed Nike to buy Converse Inc. in 2003. At the time, Nike controlled 39 percent of the U.S. athletic footwear market and Converse had a 3 percent stake. U.S. and European regulators generally use 50 percent market share as a threshold for identifying antitrust concerns.

"If Nike can add to its dominant market share by buying Converse, then Adidas and Reebok shouldn't be a problem," said John-Paul O'Meara, a retail analyst at Dresdner Kleinwort Wasserstein.

Sources: Mark Landler, "Two Brands Running as a Team to Overtake Nike," The New York Times, August 4, 2005. Adam Cohen, "Adidas-Reebok Likely to Clear Antitrust Hurdles—Analysts," CNN/Money, August 4, 2005. Reprinted by permission.

A PROPER ROLE?

Certainly there is much to guard against in the behavior of large, concentrated industries. Barriers to entry, large size, and product differentiation all lead to market power and to potential inefficiency. Barriers to entry and collusive behavior stop the market from working toward an efficient allocation of resources.

For several reasons, however, economists no longer attack industry concentration with the same fervor they once did. First, the theory of contestable markets shows that even firms in highly concentrated industries can be pushed to produce efficiently under certain market circumstances. Second, the benefits of product differentiation and product competition are real, at least in part. After all, a constant stream of new products and new variations of old products comes to the market almost daily. Third, the effects of concentration on the rate of research and development spending are, at worst, mixed. It is certainly true that large firms do a substantial amount of the total research in the United States. Finally, in some industries, substantial economies of scale simply preclude a completely competitive structure.

In addition to the debate over the desirability of industrial concentration, there is a never-ending debate concerning the role of government in regulating markets. One view is that high levels of concentration lead to inefficiency and that government should act to improve the allocation of resources—to help the market work more efficiently. This logic has been used to justify the laws and other regulations aimed at moderating noncompetitive behavior.

An opposing view holds that the clearest examples of effective barriers to entry are those actually created by government. This view holds that government regulation in past years has been ultimately anticompetitive and has made the allocation of resources less efficient than it would have been with no government involvement. Recall from Chapter 13 that those who earn positive profits have an incentive to spend resources to protect themselves and their profits from competitors. This *rent-seeking* behavior may include using the power of government.

Complicating the debate further is international competition. Increasingly, firms are faced with competition from foreign firms in domestic markets at the same time that they are competing with other multinational firms for a share of foreign markets. We live in a truly global economy today. Thus, firms that dominate a domestic market may be fierce competitors in the international arena. This has implications for the proper role of government. Some contend that instead of breaking up AT&T, the government should have allowed it to be a bigger, stronger international competitor. We will return to this debate in the next chapter.

SUMMARY

MONOPOLISTIC COMPETITION

1. A monopolistically competitive industry has the following structural characteristics: (1) a large number of firms, (2) no barriers to entry, and (3) *product differentiation*. Relatively good substitutes for a monopolistic competitor's products are available. Monopolistic competitors try to achieve a degree of market power by differentiating their products.

2. Advocates of free and open competition believe that differentiated products and advertising give the market system its vitality and are the basis of its power. Critics argue that product differentiation and advertising are wasteful and inefficient.

3. By differentiating their products, firms hope to be able to raise price without losing all demand. The demand curve facing a monopolistic competitor is less elastic than the demand curve faced by a perfectly competitive firm but more elastic than the demand curve faced by a monopoly.

4. To maximize profit in the short run, a monopolistically competitive firm will produce as long as the marginal revenue from increasing output and selling it exceeds the marginal cost of producing it. This occurs at the point at which $MR = MC$.

5. When firms enter a monopolistically competitive industry, they introduce close substitutes for the goods being produced. This attracts demand away from the firms already in the industry. Demand faced by each firm shifts left, and profits are ultimately eliminated in the long run. This long-run equilibrium occurs at the point where the demand curve is just tangent to the average total cost curve.

6. Monopolistically competitive firms end up pricing above marginal cost. This is inefficient, as is the fact that monopolistically competitive firms will not realize all economies of scale available.

OLIGOPOLY

7. An *oligopoly* is an industry dominated by a few firms that, by virtue of their individual sizes, are large enough to influence market price. The behavior of a single oligopolistic firm depends on the reactions it expects of all the other firms in the industry. Industrial strategies usually are very complicated and difficult to generalize about.

8. When firms collude, either explicitly or tacitly, they jointly maximize profits by charging an agreed-to price or by setting output limits and splitting profits. The result is exactly the same as it would be if one firm monopolized the industry: The firm will produce up to the point at which $MR = MC$, and price will be set above marginal cost.

9. The *Cournot model* of oligopoly is based on three assumptions: (1) that there are just two firms in an industry—a situation called *duopoly*; (2) that each firm takes the output of the other as a given; and (3) that both firms maximize prof-

its. The model holds that a series of output-adjustment decisions in the duopoly leads to a final level of output between that which would prevail under perfect competition and that which would be set by a monopoly.

10. A firm faces a kinked demand curve if competitors follow price cuts but fail to respond to price increases. The *kinked demand curve* model predicts that in oligopolistic industries price is likely to be more stable than costs.

11. The *price-leadership* model of oligopoly leads to a result similar but not identical to the collusion model. In this organization, the dominant firm in the industry sets a price and allows competing firms to supply all they want at that price. An oligopoly with a dominant price leader will produce a level of output between what would prevail under competition and what a monopolist would choose in the same industry. It will also set a price between the monopoly price and the competitive price.

12. *Game theory* analyzes the behavior of firms as if their behavior were a series of strategic moves and countermoves. It helps us understand the problem of oligopoly but leaves us with an incomplete and inconclusive set of propositions about the likely behavior of individual oligopolistic firms.

13. A market is *perfectly contestable* if entry into it and exit from it are costless—that is, if a firm can move into a market in search of profits but loses nothing if it fails. Firms in such industries must have mobile capital. In contestable markets, even large oligopolistic firms end up behaving like perfect competitors: Prices are pushed to long-run average cost by competition, and positive profits do not persist.

THE ROLE OF GOVERNMENT

14. The *Clayton Act* of 1914 (see Chapter 13) gave the government the authority to limit mergers that might "substantially lessen competition in an industry." The *Celler-Kefauver Act* of 1950 enabled the Justice Department to move against a proposed merger. Currently, the Justice Department uses the *Herfindahl-Hirschman Index* to determine whether or not it will challenge a proposed merger.

15. Some argue that the regulation of mergers is no longer a proper role for government.

REVIEW TERMS AND CONCEPTS

cartel, 311
Celler-Kefauver Act, 321
Cournot model, 312
dominant strategy, 315
game theory, 315
Herfindahl-Hirschman Index (HHI), 322

kinked demand curve model, 312
maximin strategy, 316
monopolistic competition, 302
Nash equilibrium, 316
oligopoly, 310
perfectly contestable market, 319

price leadership model, 314
prisoners' dilemma, 315
product differentiation, 303
tacit collusion, 312
tit-for-tat strategy, 318

PROBLEM SET

1. Which of the following industries would you classify as an oligopoly? Which would you classify as monopolistically competitive? Explain your answer. If you are not sure, what information do you need to know to decide?
   a. Athletic shoes
   b. Restaurants
   c. Watches
   d. Aircraft
   e. Ice cream

2. For each of the following, state whether you agree or disagree and explain your answer:
   a. Monopolistically competitive firms product their economic profits with barriers to entry.
   b. The soft-drink industry is made up of two very large firms and thousands of smaller firms. Because there are so many firms, it cannot be classified as an oligopoly.
   c. Monopolistically competitive firms are efficient because in the long run price falls to equal marginal cost.

3. Consider the local music scene in your area. Name some of the local live bands that play in clubs and music halls, both on and off campus. Look in your local paper for advertisements of upcoming shows or performances. How would you characterize the market for local musicians? Is there product differentiation? In what specific ways do firms (individual performers or bands) compete? To what degree are they able to exercise market power? Are there barriers to entry? How profitable do you think they are?

4. Write a brief essay explaining each statement:
   a. "A dominant firm price leader in an oligopolistic industry may actually function as a monopolistically competitive firm in the face of international competition in *world* markets."
   b. "The Beatles were once a monopolistically competitive firm that became a monopolist."

5. Which of the following markets are likely to be perfectly contestable? Explain your answers.
   a. Shipbuilding
   b. Trucking
   c. Housecleaning services
   d. Wine production

6. The matrix in Figure 1 shows payoffs based on the strategies chosen by two firms. If they collude and hold prices at $10, each will earn profits of $5 million. If A cheats on the agreement,

FIGURE 1

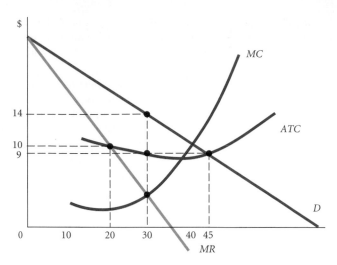

FIGURE 2

lowering its price, but B does not, A will get 75 percent of the business and earn profits of $8 million and B will lose $2 million. Similarly, if B cheats and A does not, B will earn $8 million and A will lose $2 million. If both cut prices, they will end up with $2 million each in profits.

Which strategy minimizes the maximum potential loss for A, and for B? If you were A, which strategy would you choose? Why? If A cheats, what will B do? If B cheats, what will A do? What is the most likely outcome of such a game? Explain.

7. Assume that you are in the business of building houses. You have analyzed the market carefully, and you know that at a price of $120,000 you will sell 800 houses per year. In addition, you know that at any price above $120,000 no one will buy your houses because the government provides equal-quality houses to anyone who wants one at $120,000. You also know that for every $20,000 you lower your price, you will be able to sell an additional 200 units. For example, at a price of $100,000 you can sell 1,000 houses, at a price of $8,000 you can sell 1,200 houses, and so forth.
   a. Sketch the demand curve facing your firm.
   b. Sketch the effective marginal revenue curve facing your firm.
   c. If the marginal cost of building a house is $100,000, how many will you build, and what price will you charge? What if $MC = \$85,000$?

8. Examine the short-run graph in Figure 2 for a monopolistically competitive firm.
   a. What is the profit-maximizing level of output?
   b. What price will be charged in the short run?
   c. How much are short-run total revenue, total cost, and total profit?
   d. Describe what will happen to this firm in the long run.

9. The payoff matrixes in Figure 3 show the payoffs for two games. The payoffs are given in parentheses. The figure on the left refers

to the payoff to A, the figure on the right to the payoff to B. Hence (2, 25) means a $2 payoff to A and a $25 payoff to B.
   a. Is there a dominant strategy in each game for each player?
   b. If game 1 were repeated a large number of times, and you were A and you could change your strategy, what might you do?
   c. Which strategy would you play in game 2? Why?

Game 1: Pricing

		Firm B	
		Price high	Price low
Firm A	Price high	(15, 15)	(2, 25)
	Price low	(25, 2)	(5, 5)

Game 2: Chicken

		Bob (B)	
		Swerve	Don't swerve
Ann (A)	Swerve	(5, 5)	(3, 10)
	Do not swerve	(10, 3)	(−10, −10)

FIGURE 3

Externalities, Public Goods, Imperfect Information, and Social Choice

15

In Chapters 6 through 12, we built a complete model of a perfectly competitive economy under a set of assumptions. By Chapter 12, we had demonstrated that the allocation of resources under perfect competition is efficient, and we began to relax some of the assumptions on which the perfectly competitive model is based. We introduced the idea of **market failure**, and in Chapters 13 and 14 we talked about three kinds of imperfect markets: monopoly, oligopoly, and monopolistic competition. We also discussed some of the ways government has responded to the inefficiencies of imperfect markets and to the development of market power.

market failure Occurs when resources are misallocated or allocated inefficiently.

As we continue our examination of market failure, we look first at *externalities* as a source of inefficiency. Often when we engage in transactions or make economic decisions, second or third parties suffer consequences that decision makers have no incentive to consider. For example, for many years manufacturing firms and power plants had no reason to worry about the impact of smoke from their operations on the quality of the air we breathe. Now we know that air pollution—an externality—harms people.

Next, we consider a second type of market failure that involves products that private firms find unprofitable to produce even if members of society want them. These products are called *public goods* or *social goods*. Public goods yield collective benefits, and in most societies, governments produce them or arrange to provide them. The process of choosing what social goods to produce is very different from the process of private choice.

A third source of market failure is *imperfect information*. In Chapters 6 through 12, we assumed that households and firms make choices in the presence of perfect information—that households know all that there is to know about product availability, quality, and price, and that firms know all there is to know about factor availability, quality, and price. When information is imperfect, a misallocation of resources may result.

Finally, while the existence of externalities, public goods, and imperfect information are examples of market failure, it is not necessarily true that government involvement will always improve matters. Just as markets can fail, so too can governments. When we look at the incentives facing government decision makers, we find several reasons behind government failure.

EXTERNALITIES AND ENVIRONMENTAL ECONOMICS

externality A cost or benefit resulting from some activity or transaction that is imposed or bestowed on parties outside the activity or transaction. Sometimes called *spillovers* or *neighborhood effects*.

An **externality** exists when the actions or decisions of one person or group impose a cost or bestow a benefit on second or third parties. Externalities are sometimes called *spillovers* or *neighborhood effects*. Inefficient decisions result when decision makers fail to consider social costs and benefits.

The presence of externalities is a significant phenomenon in modern life. Examples are everywhere: Air, water, land, sight, and sound pollution; traffic congestion; automobile accidents; abandoned housing; nuclear accidents; and secondhand cigarette smoke are only a few. The study of externalities is a major concern of *environmental economics*.

The opening of Eastern Europe in 1989 and 1990 revealed that environmental externalities are not limited to free market economies. Part of the logic of a planned economy is that when economic decisions are made socially (by the government, presumably acting on behalf of the people) instead of privately, planners can and will take all costs—private and social—into account. This has not been the case, however. When East and West Germany were reunited and the borders of Europe were opened, we saw the disastrous condition of the environment in virtually all Eastern Europe.

As societies become more urbanized, externalities become more important: When we live more closely together, our actions are more likely to affect others.

MARGINAL SOCIAL COST AND MARGINAL-COST PRICING

Profit-maximizing perfectly competitive firms will produce output up to the point at which price is equal to marginal cost ($P = MC$). Let us take a moment here to review why this is essential to the proposition that perfectly competitive markets produce what people want—an efficient mix of output.

When a firm weighs price and marginal cost and no externalities exist, it is weighing the full benefits to society of additional production against the full costs to society of that production. Those who benefit from the production of a product are the people or households who end up consuming it. The price of a product is a good measure of what an additional unit of that product is "worth," because those who value it more highly already buy it. People who value it less than the current price are not buying it. If marginal cost includes all costs—that is, all costs *to society*—of producing a marginal unit of a good, then additional production is efficient, provided that P is greater than MC. Up to the point where $P = MC$, each unit of production yields benefits in excess of cost.

Consider a firm in the business of producing laundry detergent. As long as the price per unit that consumers pay for that detergent exceeds the cost of the resources needed to produce one marginal unit of it, the firm will continue to produce. Producing up to the point where $P = MC$ is efficient, because for every unit of detergent produced, consumers derive benefits that exceed the cost of the resources needed to produce it. Producing at a point where $MC > P$ is inefficient, because marginal cost will rise above the unit price of the detergent. For every unit produced beyond the level at which $P = MC$, society uses up resources that cost more than the benefits that consumers place on detergent. Figure 15.1(a) shows a firm and an industry in which no externalities exist.

Suppose, however, that the production of the firm's product imposes external costs on society as well. If it does not factor those additional costs into its decisions, the firm is likely to overproduce. In Figure 15.1(b), a certain measure of external costs is added to the firm's marginal cost curve. We see these external costs in the diagram, but the firm is ignoring them. The curve labeled *MSC*, **marginal social cost**, is the sum of the marginal costs of producing the product plus the correctly measured damage costs imposed in the process of production.

marginal social cost (MSC) The total cost to society of producing an additional unit of a good or service. *MSC* is equal to the sum of the marginal costs of producing the product and the correctly measured damage costs involved in the process of production.

If the firm does not have to pay for these damage costs, it will produce exactly the same level of output (q^*) as before, and price (P^*) will continue to reflect only the costs that the firm actually pays to produce its product. The firms in this industry will continue to produce, and consumers will continue to consume their product, but the market price takes into account only part of the full cost of producing the good. At equilibrium (q^*), marginal social costs are considerably greater than *price*. (Recall that *price* is a measure of the full value to consumers of a unit of the product at the margin.)

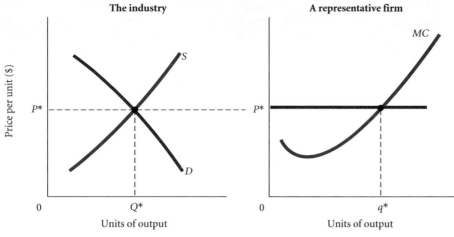

a. A profit-maximizing firm: No externalities

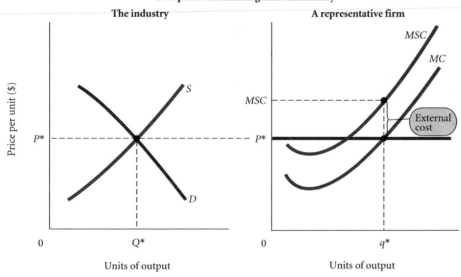

b. A profit-maximizing firm: Externality

FIGURE 15.1 Profit-Maximizing Perfectly Competitive Firms Will Produce up to the Point That Price Equals Marginal Cost (P = MC)

If we assume that the current price reflects what consumers are willing to pay for a product at the margin, firms that create external costs without weighing them in their decisions are likely to produce too much. At q*, marginal social cost exceeds the price paid by consumers.

Suppose our detergent plant freely dumps untreated toxic waste into a river. The waste imposes specific costs on people who live downstream: It kills the fish in the river, it makes the river ugly to look at and rotten to smell, and it destroys the river for recreational use. There may also be health hazards, depending on what chemicals the firm is dumping. Obviously, the plant's product provides certain benefits. Its soap is valuable to consumers, who are willing and able to pay for it. The firm employs people and capital, and its revenues are sufficient to cover all costs. The issue is how the *net benefits* produced by the plant compare with the damage that it does. You do not need an economic model to know that *someone* should consider the costs of those damages.

Acid Rain and the Clean Air Act Acid rain is an excellent example of an externality and of the issues and conflicts in dealing with externalities. Manufacturing firms and power plants in the Midwest burn coal with a high sulfur content. When the smoke from those plants mixes with moisture in the atmosphere, the result is a dilute acid that is windblown north to Canada and east to New York and New England, where it falls to the earth in the rain. The subject of a major conflict between the U.S. and Canadian governments and between industry and environmental groups, this acid rain is imposing enormous costs where it falls. Estimates of damage from fish kills, building deterioration, and deforestation range into the billions of dollars.

Decision makers at the manufacturing firms and public utilities using high-sulfur coal should weigh these costs, of course, but there is another side to this story. Burning cheap coal and not worrying about the acid rain that may be falling on someone else means jobs and cheap power for residents of the Midwest. Forcing coal-burning plants to pay for past damages from acid rain or even requiring them to begin weighing the costs that they are presently imposing will undoubtedly raise electricity prices and production costs in the Midwest. Some firms will be driven out of business and some jobs will be lost. However, if the electricity and other products produced in the Midwest are worth the full costs imposed by acid rain, plants would not shut down; consumers would pay higher prices. If those goods are not worth the full cost, they should not be produced, at least not in current quantities or by using current production methods.

The case of acid rain highlights the fact that efficiency analysis ignores the *distribution* of gains and losses. That is, to establish efficiency we need only to demonstrate that the total value of the gains exceeds the total value of the losses. If midwestern producers and consumers of their products were forced to pay an amount equal to the damages they cause, the gains from reduced damage in the East and in Canada would be at least as great as costs in the Midwest. The beneficiaries of forcing midwestern firms to consider these costs would be the households and firms in the East and in Canada. After many years of debate, Congress passed and President George H. W. Bush signed the Clean Air Act of 1990. Included in the law are strict emissions standards aimed, in part, at controlling the production and distribution of acid rain. An interesting provision of the Clean Air Act is its use of "tradable pollution rights," which we discuss later in this chapter.

Other Externalities   Other examples of external effects are all around us. When I drive my car into the center of the city at rush hour, I contribute to the congestion and impose costs (in the form of lost time and auto emissions) on others. One focus of a 1992 world environmental conference called the Earth Summit was the possibility of worldwide climate warming as a result of "greenhouse emissions" (like carbon dioxide) from industrial plants and automobiles. While potential costs are high, great uncertainty, both in the scientific evidence and in the magnitude of the potential costs, surrounds the issue. Many do believe that the effects are already being felt. A number of reputable scientific studies suggest that rising ocean temperatures have increased the frequency and intensity of hurricanes. The devastating 2005 hurricane season included Katrina, which hit New Orleans with unprecedented fury.

Secondhand cigarette smoke has become a matter of public concern. In December 1994, a judge in Florida ruled that nonsmokers could bring a class-action suit based on the health consequences of passive smoke. Smoking has been banned on domestic air carriers, and many states have passed laws severely restricting smoking in public places. In 1997, the big tobacco firms signed an agreement to pay over $350 billion to compensate those harmed by smoke and to reimburse states for smoking-related medical expenses paid under the Medicaid program.

Despite these problems, not all externalities are negative: An abandoned house in an urban neighborhood that is restored and occupied makes the neighborhood better and adds value to the neighbors' homes.

PRIVATE CHOICES AND EXTERNAL EFFECTS

To help us understand externalities, let us use a simple two-person example. Harry lives in a dormitory at a big public college in the Southwest, where he is a first-year student. When he graduated from high school, his family gave him an expensive stereo system. Unfortunately, the walls of Harry's dorm are made of quarter-inch sheetrock over 3-inch aluminum studs. You can hear people sleeping four rooms away. Harry likes bluegrass music of the "twangy" kind. Because of a hearing loss after an accident on the Fourth of July some years ago, he often does not notice the volume of his music.

Jake, who lives next door to Harry, is not much of a music lover, but when he does listen, it is to Brahms and occasionally Mozart. So Harry's music bothers Jake.

Let us assume there are no further external costs or benefits to anyone other than Harry and Jake. Figure 15.2 diagrams the decision process that the two dorm residents face. The

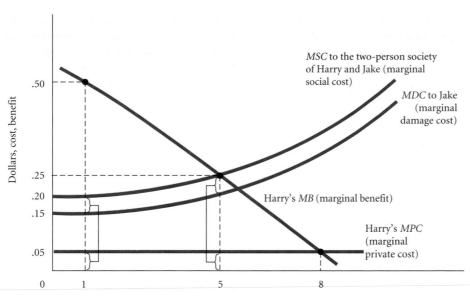

FIGURE 15.2 Externalities in a College Dormitory

The marginal benefits to Harry exceed the marginal costs he must bear to play his stereo system for a period of up to 8 hours. When the stereo is playing, a cost is being imposed on Jake. When we add the costs borne by Harry to the damage costs imposed on Jake, we get the full cost of the stereo to the two-person society made up of Harry and Jake. Playing the stereo more than 5 hours is inefficient because the benefits to Harry are less than the social cost for every hour above 5. If Harry considers only his private costs, he will play the stereo for too long a time from society's point of view.

downward-sloping curve labeled *MB* represents the value of the marginal benefits that Harry derives from listening to his music. Of course, Harry does not sit down to draw this curve, any more than anyone else (other than an economics student) sits down to draw actual demand curves. Curves like this are simply abstract representations of the way people behave. If you think about it, such a curve must exist. To ask how much an hour of listening to music is worth to you is to ask how much you would be willing to pay to have it. Start at $0.01 and raise the "price" slowly in your mind. Presumably, you must stop at some point; where you stop depends on your taste for music and your income.

You can think about the benefits Harry derives from listening to bluegrass as the maximum amount of money that he would be willing to pay to listen to his music for an hour. For the first hour, for instance, the figure for *MB* is $0.50. We assume diminishing marginal utility, of course. The more hours Harry listens, the lower the additional benefits from each successive hour. As the diagram shows, the *MB* curve falls below $0.05 per hour after 8 hours of listening.

We call the costs that Harry must pay for each additional hour of listening to music **marginal private costs**, labeled *MPC* in Figure 15.2. These include the cost of electricity and so forth. These costs are constant at $0.05 per hour.

Then there is Jake. Although Harry's music does not poison Jake, give him lung cancer, or even cause him to lose money, it damages him nonetheless: He gets a headache, loses sleep, and cannot concentrate on his work. Jake is harmed, and it is possible (at least conceptually) to measure that harm in terms of the maximum amount that he would be willing to pay to avoid it. The damage, or cost, imposed on Jake is represented in Figure 15.2 by the curve labeled *MDC*. Formally, **marginal damage cost (MDC)** is the additional harm done by increasing the level of an externality-producing activity by one unit. By assuming Jake would be willing to pay some amount of money to avoid the music, it is reasonable to assume the amount increases each successive hour. His headache gets worse with each additional hour he is forced to listen to bluegrass.

In the simple society of Jake and Harry, it is easy to add up social benefits and costs. At every level of output (stereo playing time), total social cost is the sum of the private costs borne by Harry and the damage costs borne by Jake. In Figure 15.2, *MPC* (constant at $0.05 per hour) is added to *MDC* to get *MSC*.

marginal private cost (MPC) The amount that a consumer pays to consume an additional unit of a particular good.

marginal damage cost (MDC) The additional harm done by increasing the level of an externality-producing activity by one unit. If producing product *X* pollutes the water in a river, *MDC* is the additional cost imposed by the added pollution that results from increasing output by one unit of *X* per period.

Consider now what would happen if Harry simply ignored Jake.[1] If Harry decides to play the stereo, Jake will be damaged. As long as Harry gains more in personal benefits from an additional hour of listening to music than he incurs in costs, the stereo system will stay on. He will play it for 8 hours (the point where Harry's $MB = MPC$). This result is inefficient; for every hour of play beyond 5, the marginal social cost borne by society—in this case, a society made up of Harry and Jake—exceeds the marginal benefits to Harry—that is, $MSC >$ Harry's MB. It is generally true that

> When economic decisions ignore external costs, whether those costs are borne by one person or by society, those decisions are likely to be inefficient.

We will return to Harry and Jake to see how they deal with their problem. First, we need to discuss the general problem of correcting for externalities.

INTERNALIZING EXTERNALITIES

A number of mechanisms are available to provide decision makers with incentives to weigh the external costs and benefits of their decisions, a process called *internalization*. In some cases, externalities are internalized through bargaining and negotiation without government involvement. In other cases, private bargains fail and the only alternative may be government action of some kind.

Five approaches have been taken to solving the problem of externalities: (1) government-imposed taxes and subsidies, (2) private bargaining and negotiation, (3) legal rules and procedures, (4) sale or auctioning of rights to impose externalities, and (5) direct government regulation. While each is best suited for a different set of circumstances, all five provide decision makers with an incentive to weigh the external effects of their decisions.

Taxes and Subsidies   Traditionally, economists have advocated marginal taxes and subsidies as a direct way of forcing firms to consider external costs or benefits. When a firm imposes an external social cost, the reasoning goes, a per-unit tax should be imposed equal to the damages of each successive unit of output produced by the firm—the tax should be *exactly equal* to marginal damage costs.[2]

Figure 15.3 repeats the diagram that appears as Figure 15.1(b), but this time the damage costs are paid by the firm in the form of a per-unit tax—that is, the tax = MDC. The firm now faces a marginal cost curve that is the same as the marginal social cost curve ($MC_1 = MSC$). Remember that the industry supply curve is the sum of the marginal cost curves of the individual firms. This means that as a result of the tax the industry supply curve shifts to the left, driving up price from P_0 to P_1. The efficient level of output is q_1, where $P = MC_1$. (Recall our general equilibrium analysis from Chapter 12.)

Because a profit-maximizing firm equates price with marginal cost, the new price to consumers covers both the resource costs of producing the product and the damage costs. The consumer decision process is once again efficient at the margin, because marginal social benefit as reflected in market price is equal to the full marginal cost of the product.

Measuring Damages   The biggest problem with this approach is that damages must be estimated in financial terms. For the detergent plant polluting the nearby river to be properly taxed, the government must evaluate the damages done to residents downstream in money terms. This is difficult but not impossible. When legal remedies are pursued, judges are forced to make such estimates as they decide on compensation to be paid. Surveys of "willingness to pay," studies of property values in affected versus nonaffected areas, and sometimes the market value of recreational activities can provide basic data.

---

[1] It may actually be easier for people to ignore the social costs imposed by their actions when those costs fall on large numbers of other people whom they do not have to look in the eye or whom they do not know personally. For the moment, however, we assume that Harry takes no account of Jake.

[2] As we discuss later in this chapter, damage costs are difficult to measure. It is often assumed that they are proportional to the volume of pollutants discharged into the air or water. Instead of taxes, governments often impose *effluent charges*, which make the cost to polluters proportional to the amount of pollution caused. We will use "tax" to refer to both taxes and effluent charges.

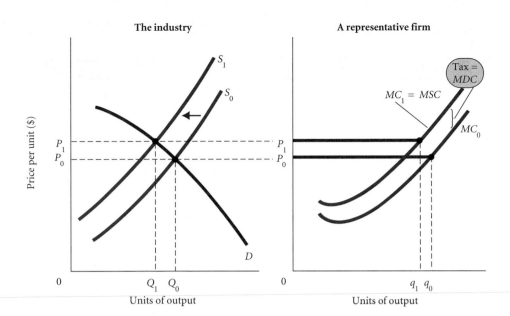

FIGURE 15.3 Tax Imposed on a Firm Equal to Marginal Damage Cost

If a per-unit tax exactly equal to marginal damage costs is imposed on a firm, the firm will weigh the tax, and thus the damage costs, in its decisions. At the new equilibrium price, P_1, consumers will be paying an amount sufficient to cover full resource costs as well as the cost of damage imposed. The efficient level of output for the firm is q_1.

The monetary value of damages to health and loss of life is, naturally, much more difficult to estimate, and any measurement of such losses is controversial. Even here, policy makers frequently make judgments that implicitly set values on life and health. Tens of thousands of deaths and millions of serious injuries result from traffic accidents in the United States every year, yet Americans are unwilling to give up driving or to reduce the speed limit to 40 miles per hour—the costs of either course of action would be too high. If most Americans are willing to increase the risk of death in exchange for shorter driving times, the value we place on life has its limits.

Be sure to realize that taxing externality-producing activities may not eliminate damages. Taxes on these activities are not designed to eliminate externalities; they are simply meant to force decision makers to consider the full costs of their decisions. Even if we assume that a tax correctly measures all the damage done, the decision maker may find it advantageous to continue causing the damage. The detergent manufacturer may find it most profitable to pay the tax and go on polluting the river. It can continue to pollute because the revenues from selling its product are sufficient to cover the cost of resources used *and to compensate the damaged parties fully*. In such a case, producing the product in spite of the pollution is "worth it" to society. It would be inefficient for the firm to stop polluting. Only if damage costs were very high would it make sense to stop. Thus, you can see the importance of proper measurement of damage costs.

Reducing Damages to an Efficient Level Taxes also provide firms with an incentive to use the most efficient technology for dealing with damage. If a tax reflects true damages, and if it is reduced when damages are reduced, firms may choose to avoid or reduce the tax by using a different technology that causes less damage. Suppose our soap manufacturer is taxed $10,000 per month for polluting the river. If the soap plant can ship its waste to a disposal site elsewhere at a cost of $7,000 per month and thereby avoid the tax, it will do so. If a plant belching sulfides into the air can install "smoke scrubbers" that eliminate emissions for an amount less than the tax imposed for polluting the air, it will do so.

The Incentive to Take Care and to Avoid Harm You should understand that all externalities involve at least two parties and that it is not always clear which party is "causing" the damage. Take our friends Harry and Jake. Harry enjoys music; Jake enjoys quiet. If Harry plays his music, he imposes a cost on Jake. If Jake can force Harry to stop listening to music, he imposes a cost on Harry.

Externalities Are All Around Us

EXTERNALITIES ARISE FROM MANY sources. The most common example is the automobile. Use of private automobiles generates a number of negative externalities including congestion and pollution. Another source of externality that arises from time to time is described in the following article published in the *New York Times*. The article proposes a way of internalizing these externalities that is likely to be controversial!

The Big City: Urban Menace Stalks Streets in Diapers
—*New York Times*

Any journalist who covers the Upper West Side quickly becomes combat-hardened, but even the veterans at *The West Side Spirit* have never seen anything like the current war. It was set off by their front-page headline: "Your Kids Are Driving Me Crazy!"

The battle cry came from Gail Bryce, a nonparent appalled at the children running amok in her Starbucks.

"We let baby carriages and strollers steamroll over us on crowded sidewalks and in stores, as if it's a papal edict that they have the right of way," she wrote in an article last month. "We let brats terrorize us in restaurants. We stand passively on public transportation, looking down at the tops of the heads of kids who are riding for free in the seats that should go to us fare-paying adults."

I can't help sympathizing with Ms. Bryce's band of activists. In a place as congested and cramped as Manhattan, other people's children are a special burden. Until my own perfect child arrived, I shared their belief that this island should operate like the one on "Survivor." When parenthood hits, a

voice should announce, "It's time for you to go."

If parents insist on staying, they have to make peace with the childless majority. Here, to start negotiations, are a couple of olive branches:

Demilitarized zones. Any peace process begins by separating the combatants. Already, there are informal child-free refuges: cafes with tables too closely packed for strollers, restaurants with menus too pricy for families. (But some New Yorkers refuse to take a hint. They need to see the equivalent of a no-smoking sign clearly posted at the door; a baby with a red slash across it.)

The brat tax. Children shorter than 44 inches are allowed to ride free on subways. If you think of a screaming child as an environmental disturbance, then giving a child a discount is like offering a subsidy to a polluter. A child should pay at least full fare, and the fairest policy would be to impose a surcharge, as *The Economist* magazine once explained in analyzing the "negative externalities" created by children in another cramped, congested environment.

The Economist proposed that airlines segregate families at the back of the plane and charge children more than adults. The surcharge could be used to subsidize a buffer zone; a row of seats in front of the children for adults willing to endure noise in return for a special discount.

It would be complicated to set up subsidized buffer zones and special children's fares in the subway, but a brave restau-

Do children produce external costs?

rateur could certainly try the experiment. Parents wouldn't like paying extra for kiddie meals, of course, but in one way they too would benefit—or at least the ones who now sit mortified when their kids turn into monsters.

With a brat tax, they could hold their heads high as their little darlings rampaged. If any nearby diners glared, if any adult-rights activists tried to complain, the parent could smile and calmly reply, "I paid for that tantrum."

Often, the best solution to an externality problem may not involve stopping the externality-generating activity. Suppose Jake and Harry's dormitory has a third resident, Pete. Pete hates silence and loves bluegrass music. The resident adviser on Harry's floor arranges for Pete and Jake to switch rooms. What was once an external cost has been transformed into an external benefit. Everyone is better off. Harry and Pete get to listen to music, and Jake gets his silence.

Sometimes the most efficient solution to an externality problem is for the damaged party to avoid the damage. However, if full compensation is paid by the damager, damaged parties may have no incentive to do so. Consider a laundry located next to the exhaust fans from the kitchen of a Chinese restaurant. Suppose damages run to $1,000 per month because the laundry must use special air filters in its dryers so that the clothes will not smell of Szechuan spices. The laundry looks around and finds a perfectly good alternative location away from the restaurant that rents for only $500 per month above its current rent. Without any compensation from the Chinese restaurant, the laundry will move and the total damage will be the $500 per month extra rent that it must pay. But if the restaurant compensates the laundry for damages of $1,000 a month, why should the laundry move? Under these conditions, a move is unlikely, even though it would be efficient.

Subsidizing External Benefits Sometimes activities or decisions generate external benefits instead of costs, as in the case of Harry and Pete. Real estate investment provides another example. Investors who revitalize a downtown area—an old theater district in a big city, for example—provide benefits to many people, both in the city and in surrounding areas.

Activities that provide such external social benefits may be subsidized at the margin to give decision makers an incentive to consider them. Just as ignoring social costs can lead to inefficient decisions, so too can ignoring social benefits. Government subsidies for housing and other development, either directly through specific expenditure programs or indirectly through tax exemptions, have been justified on such grounds.

Bargaining and Negotiation In a notable article written in 1960, economist Ronald Coase pointed out that the government does not need to be involved in every case of externality.[3] Coase argued that private bargains and negotiations are likely to lead to an efficient solution in many social damage cases, without any government involvement at all. This argument is referred to as the **Coase theorem**.

For Coase's solution to work, three conditions must be satisfied. First, the basic rights at issue must be clearly understood. Either Harry has the right to play his stereo system or Jake has the right to silence. These rights will probably be spelled out in dorm rules. Second, there must be no impediments to bargaining. Parties must be willing and able to discuss the issues openly and without cost. Third, only a few people can be involved. Serious problems can develop when one of the parties to a bargain is a large group of people, such as all the residents of a large town.

For the sake of our example, let us say that all three of these conditions hold for Harry and Jake and that no room swap with someone like Pete is possible. The dorm rules establish basic rights in this case by specifying that during certain hours of the day, Harry has the right to play his stereo as loudly as he pleases. Returning to Figure 15.2 and our earlier discussion, suppose that under the rules Harry is free to choose any number of music-playing hours between zero and 8.

Because Harry is under no legal constraint to pay any attention to Jake's wishes, you might be tempted to think that he will ignore Jake and play his stereo for 8 hours. (Recall that up to 8 hours, the marginal benefits to Harry exceed the marginal costs that he must pay.) However, Jake is willing to pay Harry to play his stereo fewer than 8 hours. For the first hour of play, the marginal damage to Jake is $0.15, so Jake would be willing to pay Harry $0.15 in the first hour to have Harry turn off his stereo. The opportunity cost to Harry of playing the first hour is thus $0.15 plus the (constant) marginal private cost of $0.05, or $0.20. Because the marginal gain to Harry in the first hour is $0.50, Harry would not accept the bribe. Likewise, for hours 2 through 5 the marginal benefit to Harry exceeds the bribe that Jake would be willing to pay plus the marginal private cost.

After 5 hours, however, Jake is willing to pay $0.20 per hour to have Harry turn off his stereo. This means that the opportunity cost to Harry is $0.25. After 5 hours the marginal benefit to Harry of another hour of listening to his stereo falls below $0.25. Harry will thus accept the bribe not to listen to his music in the sixth hour. Similarly, a bribe of $0.25 per hour is sufficient to have Harry not play the stereo in the seventh and eighth hours, and Jake would be willing to pay such a bribe. Five hours is the efficient amount of playing time. More hours or fewer hours reduce net total benefits to Harry and Jake.

Coase theorem Under certain conditions, when externalities are present, private parties can arrive at the efficient solution without government involvement.

---

[3]See Ronald Coase, "The Problem of Social Cost," *Journal of Law and Economics*, 1960.

Coase also pointed out that bargaining will bring the contending parties to the right solution regardless of where rights are initially assigned. For example, suppose that the dorm rules state that Jake has the right to silence. This being the case, Jake can go to the dorm administrators and have them enforce the rule. Now when Harry plays the stereo and Jake asks him to turn it off, Harry must comply.

Now the tables are turned. Accepting the dorm rules (as he must), Harry knocks on Jake's door. Jake's damages from the first hour are only $0.15. This means that if he were compensated by more than $0.15, he would allow the music to be played. Now the stage is set for bargaining. Harry gets $0.45 in net benefit from the first hour of playing the stereo ($0.50 minus private cost of $0.05). Thus, he is willing to pay up to $0.45 for the privilege. If there are no impediments to bargaining, money will change hands. Harry will pay Jake some amount between $0.15 and $0.45 and, just as before, the stereo will continue to play. Jake has, in effect, sold his right to have silence to Harry. As before, bargaining between the two parties will lead to 5 hours of stereo playing. At exactly 5 hours, Jake will stop taking compensation and tell Harry to turn the stereo off. (Look again at Figure 15.2 to see that this is true.)

In both cases the offer of compensation might be made in some form other than cash. Jake may offer Harry goodwill, a favor or two, or the use of his Harley-Davidson for an hour.

Coase's critics are quick to point out that the conditions required for bargaining to produce the efficient result are not always present. The biggest problem with Coase's system is also a common problem. Very often one party to a bargain is a large group of people, and our reasoning may be subject to a fallacy of composition.

Suppose a power company in Pittsburgh is polluting the air. The damaged parties are the 100,000 people who live near the plant. Let us assume the plant has the right to pollute. The Coase theorem predicts that the people who are damaged by the smoke will get together and offer a bribe (as Jake offered a bribe to Harry). If the bribe is sufficient to induce the power plant to stop polluting or reduce the pollutants with air scrubbers, then it will accept the bribe and cut down on the pollution. If it is not, the pollution will continue, but the firm will have weighed all the costs (just as Harry did when he continued to play the stereo) and the result will be efficient.

However, not everyone will contribute to the bribe fund. First, each contribution is so small relative to the whole that no single contribution makes much of a difference. Making a contribution may seem unimportant or unnecessary to some. Second, all people get to breathe the cleaner air, whether they contribute to the bribe or not. Many people will not participate simply because they are not compelled to, and the private bargain breaks down— the bribe that the group comes up with will be less than the full damages unless everyone participates. (We discuss these two problems—the *drop-in-the-bucket* and the *free-rider*— later in this chapter.) When the number of damaged parties is large, government taxes or regulation may be the only avenue to a remedy.

Legal Rules and Procedures   For bargaining to result in an efficient outcome, the initial assignment of rights must be clear to both parties. When rights are established by law, more often than not some mechanism to protect those rights is also built into the law. In some cases where a nuisance exists, for example, there may be injunctive remedies. In such cases, the victim can go to court and ask for an **injunction** that forbids the damage-producing behavior from continuing. If the dorm rules specifically give Jake the right to silence, Jake's getting the resident adviser to speak to Harry is something like getting an injunction.

Injunctive remedies are irrelevant when the damage has already been done. Consider accidents. If your leg has already been broken as the result of an automobile accident, enjoining the driver of the other car from drinking and driving will not work—it is too late. In these cases, rights must be protected by **liability rules**, rules that require A to compensate B for damages imposed. In theory, such rules are designed to do exactly the same thing that taxing a polluter is designed to do: provide decision makers with an incentive to weigh all the consequences, actual and potential, of their decisions. Just as taxes do not stop all pollution, liability rules do not stop all accidents.

However, the threat of liability actions does induce people to take more care than they might otherwise. Product liability is a good example. If a person is damaged in some way because a product is defective, the producing company is in most cases held liable for the

injunction A court order forbidding the continuation of behavior that leads to damages.

liability rules Laws that require A to compensate B for damages imposed.

damages, even if the company took reasonable care in producing the product. Producers have a powerful incentive to be careful. If consumers know they will be generously compensated for any damages, however, they may not have as powerful an incentive to be careful when using the product.

Selling or Auctioning Pollution Rights   We have already established that not all externality-generating activities should be banned. Around the world, the private automobile has become the clearest example of an externality-generating activity whose benefits (many believe) outweigh its costs.

Many externalities are imposed when we drive our cars. First, congestion is an externality. Even though the marginal "harm" imposed by any one driver is small, the sum total is a serious cost to all who spend hours in traffic jams. Second, most of the air pollution in the United States comes from automobiles. The problem is most evident in Los Angeles, where smog loaded with harmful emissions (mostly from cars) blankets the city virtually every day. Finally, driving increases the likelihood of accidents, raising insurance costs to all.

While we do not ignore these costs from the standpoint of public policy, we certainly have not banned driving. This is also true for many other forms of pollution. In many cases, we have consciously opted to allow ocean dumping, river pollution, and air pollution within limits.

The right to impose environmental externalities is beneficial to the parties causing the damage. In a sense, the right to dump in a river or pollute the air or the ocean is a resource. Thinking of the privilege to dump in this way suggests an alternative mechanism for controlling pollution: selling or auctioning the pollution rights to the highest bidder. The Clean Air Act of 1990 takes this approach by limiting the quantity of emissions from the nation's power plants. To minimize the initial cost of compliance and to distribute the burden fairly, each plant is issued tradable pollution rights. These rights can be sold at auction to those plants whose costs of compliance are highest.

Externalities are, of course, not limited by international boundaries. Global warming is one of the most controversial issues involving externalities. The European Union began an aggressive experimental program of emissions trading designed to reduce global warming in January 2005. See the Further Exploration box titled "Global Warming: A Global Externality?" on page 338.

Another example of selling externality rights comes from Singapore, where the right to buy a car is auctioned each year. Despite very high taxes and the need for permits to drive in downtown areas, the roads in Singapore have become congested. The government decided to limit the number of new cars on the road because the external costs associated with them (congestion and pollution) have become very high. With these limits imposed, the decision was made to distribute car-ownership rights to those who place the highest value on them. It seems likely that taxi drivers, trucking companies, bus lines, and traveling salespeople will buy the licenses; families who drive for convenience instead of taking public transportation will find them too expensive. Congestion and pollution are not the only externalities that Singapore takes seriously: In 2005 the fine for littering was as high as $1,000; for failing to flush a public toilet, over $100; and for eating on a subway, $300.

Singapore is known for its many laws designed to reduce negative externalities. Littering, chewing gum in public, eating on a subway car, failing to flush a toilet, and vandalizing public property are all considered serious offenses that are punishable by imprisonment, fines, and/or public chastisement.

Direct Regulation of Externalities   Taxes, subsidies, legal rules, and public auction are all methods of indirect regulation designed to induce firms and households to weigh the social costs of their actions against their benefits. The actual size of the external cost/benefit depends on the reaction of households and firms to the incentives provided by the taxes, subsidies, and rules.

For obvious reasons, many externalities are too important to be regulated indirectly. Dumping cancer-causing chemicals into the ground near a public water supply is simply illegal, and those who do it can be prosecuted and sent to jail.

Direct regulation of externalities takes place at the federal, state, and local level. The Environmental Protection Agency (EPA) is a federal agency established by an act of Congress in 1970. Since the 1960s, Congress has passed lots of legislation that sets specific standards for permissible discharges into the air and water. Every state has a division or department charged with regulating activities that are likely to harm the environment. Most airports in the United States have landing patterns and hours that are regulated by local governments to minimize noise.

Global Warming: A Global Externality?

One of the most hotly debated issues involving externalities is the potential cost of global warming. There is currently no incentive for steel producers pumping carbon dioxide into the atmosphere to consider the fact that they may be contributing to widespread damage to the climate in 40 years. While many observers point to the high level of uncertainty in measuring such costs, others stress potentially disastrous results if we do nothing.

In testimony before Congress in July 2005 the president of the National Academy of Sciences addressed the controversial issue of global warming. The following is from that testimony:

> The Earth is warming. Weather station records and ship-based observations indicate that global mean surface air temperature increased about 0.7°F since the early 1970s. Although the magnitude of warming varies locally, the warming trend is widespread and is consistent with an array of other evidence (e.g., melting glaciers and ice caps, sea level rise, extended growing seasons, and changing in the geographical distributions of plant and animal species). The ocean, which represents the largest reservoir of heat in the climate system, has warmed by about 0.12°F.
>
> Laboratory measurements . . . have shown that for hundreds of thousands of years, changes in temperatures have closely tracked atmospheric carbon dioxide concentrations. Burning

fossil fuel for energy, industrial processes, and transportation releases carbon dioxide to the atmosphere. Carbon dioxide in the atmosphere is now at its highest level in 400,000 years and continues to rise. Nearly all climate scientists today believe that much of Earth's current warming has been caused by increases in the amount of greenhouse gases in the atmosphere, mostly from the burning of fossil fuels.

It is important to recognize, however, that while future climate change and its impacts are inherently uncertain, they are far from unknown. The combined effects of ice melting and sea water expansion from ocean warming will likely cause the global average sea level to rise. In colder climates, such warming could bring longer growing seasons and less severe winters. Those in coastal communities, many in developing nations, will experience increased flooding due to sea-level rise and are likely to experience more severe storms and surges. In the Arctic regions, where temperatures have risen more than the global average, the landscape and ecosystems are being altered rapidly.

THE KYOTO PROTOCOL

The Kyoto Protocol is an international treaty on global warming negotiated by the United Nations in the 1990s. It came into force after being ratified by Russia in February 2005. A total of 141 countries have ratified the agreement, which commits them to reduce their emissions of carbon

dioxide and five other greenhouse gases or to engage in emissions trading. Although the United States has not ratified the treaty, the European Union began an aggressive experimental program of emissions trading in January 2005. The 25 participating countries each have a target for allowable emissions of carbon dioxide generated in four sectors: production of iron and steel, energy, pulp and paper, and other materials such as glass.

Once those targets have been established and each country has allocated the "rights to pollute," those rights can be sold. The existence of the market provides incentives for firms to distribute the costs of reducing emissions in the most efficient way. Once up and running, the program will likely lead to billions of dollars worth of trading, and it will be one of the largest social policy experiments in world history. Although many problems must be overcome to make this program successful, it is one of the only cases where global concerns about environmental externalities have led to collective action.

Sources: Ralph J. Cicerone, Ph.D., President, National Academy of Sciences, The National Academies, before the Subcommittee on Global Climate Change and Impacts Committee on Commerce, Science, and Transportation. U.S. Senate, July 20, 2005; Wallace Oates, "What Is the EU Emissions Trading System?" unpublished.

Many criminal penalties and sanctions for violating environmental regulations are like the taxes imposed on polluters. Not all violations and crimes are stopped, but violators and criminals face "costs." For the outcome to be efficient, the penalties they expect to pay should reflect the damage their actions impose on society.

PUBLIC (SOCIAL) GOODS

public goods (social or collective goods) Goods that are nonrival in consumption and/or their benefits are nonexcludable.

Another source of market failure lies in **public goods**, often called **social**, or **collective**, **goods**. Public goods are defined by two closely related characteristics: They are nonrival in consumption and/or their benefits are nonexcludable. As we will see, these goods represent a market failure because they have characteristics that make it difficult for the private sector to produce them profitably:

> In an unregulated market economy with no government to see that they are produced, public goods would at best be produced in insufficient quantity and at worst not produced at all.

nonrival in consumption A characteristic of public goods: One person's enjoyment of the benefits of a public good does not interfere with another's consumption of it.

THE CHARACTERISTICS OF PUBLIC GOODS

A good is **nonrival in consumption** when A's consumption of it does not interfere with B's consumption of it. This means that the benefits of the goods are collective—they accrue to everyone. National defense, for instance, benefits us all. The fact that I am protected in no way detracts from the fact that you are protected; every citizen is protected just as much as every other citizen. If the air is cleaned up, my breathing that air does not interfere with your breathing it, and (under ordinary circumstances) that air is not used up as more people breathe it. Private goods in contrast are *rival in consumption*. If I eat a hamburger, you cannot eat it too.

Goods can sometimes generate collective benefits and still be rival in consumption. This happens when crowding occurs. A park or a pool can accommodate many people at the same time, generating collective benefits for everyone. However, when too many people crowd in on a hot day, they begin to interfere with each other's enjoyment.

Most public goods are also **nonexcludable**. Once the good is produced, people cannot be excluded for any reason from enjoying its benefits. Once a national defense system is established, it protects everyone.

nonexcludable A characteristic of most public goods: Once a good is produced, no one can be excluded from enjoying its benefits.

Before we go on, it is very important to note that goods are either public or private by virtue of their characteristics (nonrival and nonexcludable) and *not* by virtue of whether or not they are produced by the public sector. If the government decided to make it a law that hamburgers were an entitlement, that is, all the people could have all the hamburgers they wanted at government expense, that decision would not make hamburgers into public goods. It is an example of the government's providing a private good free of charge to all. The government's decision not to exercise the power to exclude doesn't change the nature of a hamburger.

The real problem with public goods is that private producers may simply not have any incentive to produce them or to produce the right amount. For a private profit-making firm to produce a good and make a profit, it must be able to withhold that good from those who do not pay. McDonald's can make money selling chicken sandwiches only because you do not get the chicken sandwich unless you pay for it first. If payment were voluntary, McDonald's would not be in business for long.

Consider an entrepreneur who decides to offer better police protection to the city of Metropolis. Careful (and we assume correct) market research reveals that the citizens of Metropolis want high-quality protection and are willing to pay for it. Not everyone is willing to pay the same amount. Some can afford more, others less, and people have different preferences and different feelings about risk. Our entrepreneur hires a salesforce and begins to sell his service. Soon he encounters a problem. Because his is a private company, payment is voluntary. He cannot force anyone to pay. Payment for a hamburger is voluntary too, but a hamburger can be withheld for nonpayment. The good that our new firm is selling, however, is by nature a public good.

As a potential consumer of a public good, I face a dilemma. I want more police protection, and, let us say, I am even willing to pay $50 a month for it. But nothing is contingent on my payment. First, if the good is produced, the crime rate falls and all residents benefit. I get that benefit whether I pay for it or not. I get a free ride. That is why this dilemma is called the **free-rider problem**. Second, my payment is very small relative to the amount that must be collected to provide the service. Thus, the amount of police protection actually produced will not be significantly affected by how much I contribute or whether I contribute at all. This is the **drop-in-the-bucket problem**.

free-rider problem A problem intrinsic to public goods: Because people can enjoy the benefits of public goods whether they pay for them or not, they are usually unwilling to pay for them.

drop-in-the-bucket problem A problem intrinsic to public goods: The good or service is usually so costly that its provision generally does not depend on whether or not any single person pays.

> Consumers acting in their own self-interest have no incentive to contribute voluntarily to the production of public goods. Some will feel a moral responsibility or social pressure to contribute, and those people indeed may do so. Nevertheless, the economic incentive is missing, and most people do not find room in their budgets for many voluntary payments.

The public goods problem can also be thought of as a large-number, prisoners' dilemma game theory problem (for a full discussion see Chapter 14).

INCOME DISTRIBUTION AS A PUBLIC GOOD?

In the next chapter, we add the issues of justice and equity to the matters of economic efficiency that we are considering here. There we explain that the government may wish to change the distribution of income that results from the operation of the unregulated market on the grounds that the distribution is not fair. Before we do so, we need to note that some economists have argued for redistribution of income on grounds that it generates public benefits.

For example, let us say that many members of U.S. society want to eliminate hunger in the United States. Suppose you are willing to give $200 per year in exchange for the knowledge that people are not going to bed hungry. Many private charities in the United States use the money they raise to feed the poor. If you want to contribute, you can do so privately, through charity. So why do we need government involvement?

To answer this, we must consider the benefits of eliminating hunger. First, it generates collective psychological benefits; simply knowing that people are not starving helps us sleep better. Second, eliminating hunger may reduce disease, and this has lots of beneficial effects. People who are fit and strong are more likely to stay in school and to get and keep jobs. This reduces welfare claims and contributes positively to the economy. If people are less likely to get sick, insurance premiums for everyone will go down. Robberies may decline because fewer people are desperate for money. This means that all of us are less likely to be victims of crime, now and in the future.

These are goals that members of society may want to achieve. But just as there is no economic incentive to contribute voluntarily to national defense, so there is no economic incentive to contribute to private causes. If hunger is eliminated, you benefit whether you contributed or not—the free-rider problem. At the same time, poverty is a huge problem and your contribution cannot possibly have any influence on the amount of national hunger—the drop-in-the-bucket problem. The goals of income redistribution may be more like national defense than like a chicken sandwich from McDonald's.

> If we accept the idea that redistributing income generates a public good, private endeavors may fail to do what we want them to do, and government involvement may be called for.

PUBLIC PROVISION OF PUBLIC GOODS

All societies, past and present, have had to face the problem of providing public goods. When members of society get together to form a government, they do so to provide themselves with goods and services that will not be provided if they act separately. Like any other good or service, a body of laws (or system of justice) is produced with labor, capital, and other inputs. Law and the courts yield social benefits, and they must be set up and administered by some sort of collective, cooperative effort.

Notice that we are talking about public *provision*, not public *production*. Once the government decides what service it wants to provide, it often contracts with the private sector to produce the good. Much of the material for national defense is produced by private defense contractors. Highways, government offices, data processing services, and so forth are usually produced by private firms.

One of the immediate problems of public provision is that it frequently leads to public dissatisfaction. It is easy to be angry at government. Part, but certainly not all, of the reason for this dissatisfaction lies in the nature of the goods that government provides. Firms that produce or sell private goods post a price—we can choose to buy any quantity we want or we can walk away without any. It makes no sense to get mad at a shoe store, because no one can force you to shop there.

You cannot shop for collectively beneficial public goods. When it comes to national defense, the government must choose one and only one kind and quantity of (collective) output to produce. Because none of us can choose how much should be spent or on what, we are all dissatisfied. Even if the government does its job with reasonable efficiency, at any given time about half of us think that we have too much national defense and about half of us think that we have too little.

OPTIMAL PROVISION OF PUBLIC GOODS

In the early 1950s, economist Paul Samuelson demonstrated that there exists an *optimal*, or a *most efficient*, level of output for every public good.[4] The discussion of the Samuelson solution that follows leads us straight to the thorny problem of how societies, as opposed to individuals, make choices.

---

[4]Paul A. Samuelson, "Diagrammatic Exposition of a Theory of Public Expenditure," *Review of Economics and Statistics*, 37, 1955, 350–56.

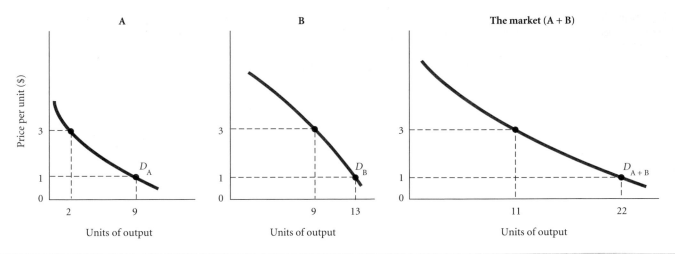

FIGURE 15.4 With Private Goods, Consumers Decide What Quantity to Buy; Market Demand Is the Sum of Those Quantities at Each Price

At a price of $3, A buys 2 units and B buys 9 for a total of 11. At a price of $1, A buys 9 units and B buys 13 for a total of 22. We all buy the quantity of each private good that we want. Market demand is the horizontal sum of all individual demand curves.

Samuelson's Theory   An efficient economy produces what people want. Private producers, whether perfect competitors or monopolists, are constrained by the market demand for their products. If they cannot sell their products for more than it costs to produce them, they are out of business. Because private goods permit exclusion, firms can withhold their products until households pay. Buying a product at a posted price reveals that it is "worth" at least that amount to you and to everyone who buys it.

Market demand for a private good is the sum of the quantities that each household decides to buy (as measured on the horizontal axis). The diagrams in Figure 15.4 review the derivation of a market demand curve. Assume society consists of two people, A and B. At a price of $1, A demands 9 units of the private good and B demands 13. Market demand at a price of $1 is 22 units. If price were to rise to $3, A's quantity demanded would drop to 2 units and B's would drop to 9 units; market demand at a price of $3 is 2 + 9 = 11 units. The point is that

> The price mechanism forces people to reveal what they want, and it forces firms to produce only what people are willing to pay for, but it works this way only because exclusion is possible.

People's preferences and demands for public goods are conceptually no different from their preferences and demands for private goods. You may want fire protection and be willing to pay for it in the same way you want to listen to a CD. To demonstrate that an efficient level of production exists, Samuelson assumes we know people's preferences. Figure 15.5 shows demand curves for buyers A and B. If the public good were available in the private market at a price of $6, A would buy X_1 units. Put another way, A is willing to pay $6 per unit to obtain X_1 units of the public good. B is willing to pay only $3 per unit to obtain X_1 units of the public good.

Remember, public goods are nonrival and/or nonexcludable—benefits accrue simultaneously to everyone. One, and only one, quantity can be produced, and that is the amount that everyone gets. If X_1 units are produced, A gets X_1 and B gets X_1. If X_2 units are produced, A gets X_2 and B gets X_2.

To arrive at market demand for public goods, we do not sum quantities. Instead, *we add the amounts that individual households are willing to pay for each potential level of output.* In Figure 15.5, A is willing to pay $6 per unit for X_1 units and B is willing to pay $3 per unit for X_1 units. Thus, if society consists only of A and B, society is willing to pay $9 per unit for X_1 units of public good X. For X_2 units of output, society is willing to pay a total of $4 per unit.

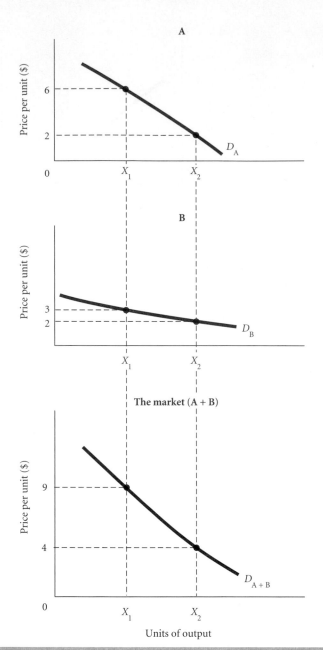

FIGURE 15.5 With Public Goods, There Is Only *One* Level of Output, and Consumers Are Willing to Pay Different Amounts for Each Level

A is willing to pay $6 per unit for X_1 units of the public good. B is willing to pay only $3 for X_1 units. Society—in this case A and B—is willing to pay a total of $9 for X_1 units of the good. Because only one level of output can be chosen for a public good, we must add A's contribution to B's to determine market demand. This means adding demand curves vertically.

For private goods, market demand is the horizontal sum of individual demand curves—we add the different *quantities* that households consume (as measured on the *horizontal* axis). For public goods, market demand is the vertical sum of individual demand curves—we add the different *amounts* that households are willing to pay to obtain each level of output (as measured on the *vertical* axis).

Samuelson argued that once we know how much society is willing to pay for a public good, we need only compare that amount to the cost of its production. Figure 15.6 reproduces A's and B's demand curves and the total demand curve for the public good. As long as society (in this case, A and B) is willing to pay more than the marginal cost of production, the good should be produced. If A is willing to pay $6 per unit of public good and B is willing to pay $3 per unit, society is willing to pay $9.

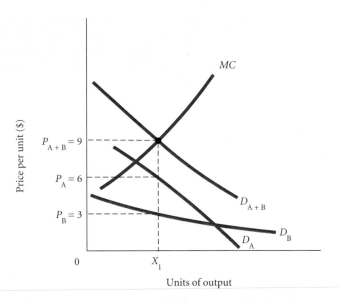

FIGURE 15.6 Optimal Production of a Public Good

Optimal production of a public good means producing as long as society's total willingness to pay per unit (D_{A+B}) is greater than the marginal cost of producing the good.

Given the *MC* curve as drawn in Figure 15.6, the efficient level of output is X_1 units. If at that level A is charged a fee of $6 per unit of X produced and B is charged a fee of $3 per unit of X, everyone should be happy. Resources are being drawn from the production of other goods and services only to the extent that people want the public good and are willing to pay for it. We have arrived at the **optimal level of provision for public goods**.

> At the optimal level, society's total willingness to pay per unit is equal to the marginal cost of producing the good.

The Problems of Optimal Provision   One major problem exists, however. To produce the optimal amount of each public good, the government must know something that it cannot possibly know—everyone's preferences. Because exclusion is impossible, nothing forces households to reveal their preferences. Furthermore, if we ask households directly about their willingness to pay, we run up against the same problem encountered by our protection-services salesman mentioned earlier. If my actual payment depends on my answer, I have an incentive to hide my true feelings. Knowing that I cannot be excluded from enjoying the benefits of the good and that my payment is not likely to have an appreciable influence on the level of output finally produced, what incentive do I have to tell the truth—or to contribute?

How does society decide which public goods to provide? We assume that members of society want certain public goods. Private producers in the market cannot make a profit by producing these goods, and the government cannot obtain enough information to measure society's demands accurately. No two societies have dealt with this dilemma in the same way. In some countries, dictators simply decide for the people. In others, representative political bodies speak for the people's preferences. In still others, people vote directly. None of these solutions works perfectly. We will return to the problem of social choice at the end of the chapter.

optimal level of provision for public goods The level at which resources are drawn from the production of other goods and services only to the extent that people want the public good and are willing to pay for it. At this level, society's willingness to pay per unit is equal to the marginal cost of producing the good.

LOCAL PROVISION OF PUBLIC GOODS: TIEBOUT HYPOTHESIS

In 1956, economist Charles Tiebout made this point: To the extent that local governments are responsible for providing public goods, an efficient market-choice mechanism may exist. Consider a set of towns that are identical except for police protection. Towns that choose to spend a lot of money on police are likely to have a lower crime rate. A lower crime rate will attract households who are risk averse and are willing to pay higher taxes for a lower risk of being a crime victim. Those who are willing to bear greater risk may choose to live in the low-

Tiebout hypothesis An efficient mix of public goods is produced when local land/housing prices and taxes come to reflect consumer preferences just as they do in the market for private goods.

tax/high-crime towns. Also, if some town is very efficient at crime prevention, it will attract residents—given that each town has limited space, property values will be bid up in this town. The higher home price in this town is the "price" of the lower crime rate.

According to the **Tiebout hypothesis**, an efficient mix of public goods is produced when local prices (in the form of taxes or higher housing costs) come to reflect consumer preferences just as they do in the market for private goods. What is different in the Tiebout world is that people exercise consumer sovereignty not by "buying" different combinations of goods in a market, but by "voting with their feet" (choosing among bundles of public goods and tax rates produced by different towns and participating in local government).

MIXED GOODS

Finally, we should mention the case of mixed goods. Most goods are easy to classify as either public or private. A hamburger is a pure private good. It is clearly possible to exclude people from consuming a burger, and if I eat it, you cannot. That is, a hamburger is both excludable and rival in consumption. On the other hand, clean air is a pure public good. Once air is produced, no one can be excluded from breathing it if he or she didn't pay, and my breathing it in no way interferes with your breathing it. That is, clean air is *not* excludable and is nonrival in consumption.

mixed goods Goods that are part public goods and part private goods. Education is a key example.

Many goods, however, are not easy to classify. Such goods have characteristics that are part public and part private, and we call them **mixed goods**. The classic example of a mixed good is elementary and secondary education.

First of all, note that education, at least a basic level of primary and secondary education, is a right or an entitlement in every state in the United States. Thus, we have decided that exclusion will not be exercised. But is education "excludable"? The answer is yes. It is possible to exclude a student from attending class at a private school if she or her parents don't pay tuition. Certainly, at both the college level and the high school level, private schools are numerous, and the prime benefits of an education belong to the individual student: a higher income in the future, perhaps access to a more desirable profession, or maybe something as simple as learning to appreciate literature, art, or music. Thus, education is essentially a private good.

But many argue that education does produce public benefits that are nonexcludable. The essential argument is that all members of society benefit when citizens are educated. The Nobel laureate Milton Friedman argued that "a stable democratic society is impossible without a minimum degree of literacy and knowledge on the part of most citizens." An educated society is likely to have a lower crime rate, higher productivity, and thus higher wages. Higher wages to others also benefit me because neighborhoods will be more attractive.

Another way of describing the same idea is that education is a private good that creates a positive externality. When mixed goods generate significant positive externalities, we often turn to government involvement to help provide the optimal level of production.

IMPERFECT INFORMATION

In Chapters 6 through 12, we assumed households and firms have complete information on products and inputs. To make informed choices among goods and services available in the market, households must have full information on product quality, availability, and price. To make sound judgments about what inputs to use, firms must have full information on input availability, quality, and price.

The absence of full information can cause households and firms to make mistakes. A voluntary exchange is almost always evidence that both parties benefit. Thus most voluntary exchanges are efficient. However, in the presence of imperfect information, not all exchanges are efficient. An obvious example is fraud. Frank sells a bottle of colored water to Ed claiming it will grow hair on Ed's bald head. Had Ed known what was really in the bottle, he would not have purchased it.

Firms as well as consumers can be the victims of incomplete or inaccurate information. Recall that a profit-maximizing competitive firm will hire workers as long as the marginal revenue product of labor (MRP_L) is greater than the wage rate. How can a firm judge the *productivity* of a potential hire? Also, suppose that a worker steals from the firm. The cost of employing that worker is greater than just the wage of that employee.

ADVERSE SELECTION: ASYMMETRIC INFORMATION

The problem of **adverse selection** can occur when a buyer or seller enters an exchange with another party who has more information. In such a case, there is said to be *asymmetric information*. Suppose there are only two types of workers: lazy workers and hard workers. Workers know which type they are, but employers cannot tell. If there is only one wage rate, lazy workers will be overpaid relative to their productivity and hard workers will be underpaid. Recall that workers weigh the value of leisure and nonmarket production against the wage in deciding whether to enter the labor force. Because hard workers will end up underpaid relative to their productivity, fewer hard workers than is optimal will be attracted into the labor force. Similarly, because lazy workers are overpaid relative to their productivity, more of them will be attracted into the labor force than is optimal. Hence, the market has selected among workers adversely.

The classic case of adverse selection is the used-car market. Suppose owners (potential sellers) of used cars have all the information about the real quality of their cars. Suppose further that half of all used cars are "lemons" (bad cars) and that half are "cherries" (good cars), and consumers (potential used-car buyers) are willing to pay $6,000 for a cherry but only $2,000 for a lemon.

If half the cars for sale were lemons and half were cherries, the market price of a car would be about $4,000, and consumers would have a 50–50 chance of getting a lemon. There is an adverse selection problem because of unequal information: Used-car *sellers* know whether they have a lemon or a cherry whereas used-car *buyers* do not. Lemon owners know they are making out like bandits by selling at $4,000, while cherry owners know they are not getting what their car is really worth. Thus, more lemon owners are attracted into selling their cars than are cherry owners.

Over time, buyers come to understand that the probability of getting a lemon is greater than the probability of getting a cherry, and the price of used cars drops. This makes matters worse because it provides even less incentive for cherry owners to sell their cars. This process will continue until only lemons are left in the market. Once again, the unequal information leads to an adverse selection.

Adverse selection is also a problem in insurance markets. Insurance companies insure people against risks such as health problems and accidents. Individuals know more about their own health than anyone else, even with required medical exams. If medical insurance rates are set at the same level for everyone, then medical insurance is a better deal for those who are unhealthy than for those who are healthy and likely never to have a claim. This means more unhealthy people will buy insurance, an outcome that forces insurance companies to raise premiums. As with used cars, fewer healthy people and more unhealthy people will end up with insurance.

adverse selection Can occur when a buyer or seller enters into an exchange with another party who has more information.

MORAL HAZARD

Another information problem that arises in insurance markets is *moral hazard*. Often, people enter into contracts in which the result of the contract, at least in part, depends on one of the parties' future behavior. A **moral hazard** problem arises when one party to a contract passes the cost of its behavior on to the other party to the contract. For example, accident insurance policies are contracts that agree to pay for repairs to your car if it is damaged in an accident. Whether you have an accident or not in part depends on whether you drive cautiously. Similarly, apartment leases may specify that the landlord will perform routine maintenance around the apartment. If you punch the wall every time you get angry, your landlord ultimately pays the repair bill.

Such contracts can lead to inefficient behavior. The problem is like the externality problem in which firms and households have no incentive to consider the full costs of their behavior. If my car is fully insured against theft, why should I lock it? If visits to the dentist are free under my dental insurance plan, why not get my teeth cleaned six times a year?

Like adverse selection, the moral hazard problem is an information problem. Contracting parties cannot always determine the future behavior of the person with whom they are contracting. If all future behavior could be predicted, contracts could be written to try to eliminate undesirable behavior. Sometimes this is possible. Life insurance companies do not pay off in the case of suicide. Fire insurance companies will not write a policy unless

moral hazard Arises when one party to a contract passes the cost of its behavior on to the other party to the contract.

you have smoke detectors. If you cause unreasonable damage to an apartment, your landlord can retain your security deposit.

> It is impossible to know everything about behavior and intentions. If a contract absolves one party of the consequences of its action, and people act in their own self-interest, the result is inefficient.

MARKET SOLUTIONS

Imperfect information violates one of the assumptions of perfect competition, but not all information problems are market failures. In fact, information is itself valuable, and there is an incentive for perfectly competitive producers to produce it. As with any other good, there is an efficient quantity of information production.

Often, information is produced by consumers and producers themselves. The information-gathering process is called *market search*. When we go shopping for a "good buy" or for the "right" sweater, we are collecting the information that we need to make an informed choice. Just as products are produced as long as the marginal benefit from additional output exceeds the marginal cost of production, consumers have an incentive to continue searching out information until the expected marginal benefit from an additional hour of search is equal to the cost of that additional hour. After I have looked in 11 different stores that sell sweaters, I know a great deal about the quality and prices available. Continuing to look takes up valuable time and effort that could be used doing other things. In shopping for a house or a car, I may spend much more time and effort searching out information than I might for a sweater, because the potential benefits (or losses) are much greater.

The rapid development of the Internet has had an enormous effect on the availability of information to consumers. The Web allows instantaneous comparative shopping for everything from automobiles to airplane tickets to mortgage rates. For some goods, the Internet has effectively "solved" the imperfect information problem, but the Internet itself is not always reliable. The information that consumers take off the Web is only as good as what is put in.

Firms also spend time and resources searching for information. Potential employers ask for letters of reference, résumés, and interviews before offering employment. Market research helps firms respond to consumer preferences. It should come as no surprise to you that the general rule is

> Like consumers, profit-maximizing firms will gather information as long as the marginal benefits from continued search are greater than the marginal costs.

Many firms produce information for consumers and businesses. *Consumer Reports* is a magazine that tests consumer products and sells the results in the form of a periodical. Credit bureaus keep track of people's credit histories and sell credit reports to firms that need them to evaluate potential credit customers. "Head-hunting" firms collect information and search out applicants for jobs.

Because the market handles many information problems efficiently, we do not need to assume perfect information in order to arrive at an efficient allocation of resources. However, some information problems are not handled well by the market.

GOVERNMENT SOLUTIONS

Information is essentially a public good. If a set of test results on the safety of various products is produced, my having access to that information in no way reduces the value of that information to others. In other words, information is nonrival in consumption. When information is very costly for individuals to collect and disperse, it may be cheaper for government to produce it once for everybody.

In many cases, the government has set up special administrative agencies to ensure that accurate information reaches the public. As we noted in Chapter 13, Congress established the Federal Trade Commission (FTC) in 1914 specifically to deal with unfair and deceptive trade practices. The FTC regulates advertising, sets standards for disclosure of contents, and so forth. The Consumer Product Safety Commission sets standards of safety for potentially unsafe products. The Food and Drug Administration regulates the content of foods and drugs permitted on the market. It is illegal to sell a drug that has not been demonstrated to be effective. Many state governments have passed "lemon laws" that grant car buyers certain rights in case they end up with a troublesome car.

SOCIAL CHOICE

One view of government, or the public sector, holds that it exists to provide things that "society wants." A society is a collection of individuals, and each has a unique set of preferences. Defining what society wants, therefore, becomes a problem of **social choice**—of somehow adding up, or aggregating, individual preferences.

It is also important to understand that government is made up of individuals—politicians and government workers—whose *own* objectives in part determine what government does. To understand government, we must understand the incentives facing politicians and public servants, as well as the difficulties of aggregating the preferences of the members of a society.

social choice The problem of deciding what society wants. The process of adding up individual preferences to make a choice for society as a whole.

THE VOTING PARADOX

Democratic societies use ballot procedures to determine aggregate preferences and to make the social decisions that follow from them. If all votes could be unanimous, efficient decisions would be guaranteed. Unfortunately, unanimity is virtually impossible to achieve when hundreds of millions of people, with their own different preferences, are involved.

The most common social decision-making mechanism is majority rule—but it is not perfect. In 1951, economist Kenneth Arrow proved the **impossibility theorem**[5]—that it is impossible to devise a voting scheme that respects individual preferences and gives consistent, nonarbitrary results.

One example of a seemingly irrational result emerging from majority-rule voting is the voting paradox. Suppose that, faced with a decision about the future of the institution, the president of a major university opts to let its three top administrators vote on the following options: Should the university (A) increase the number of students and hire more faculty, (B) maintain the current size of the faculty and student body, or (C) cut back on faculty and reduce the student body? Figure 15.7 represents the preferences of the three administrators diagrammatically.

The vice president for finance (VP1) wants growth, preferring A to B and B to C. The vice president for development (VP2), however, does not want to rock the boat, preferring the maintenance of the current size of the institution, option B, to either of the others. If the status quo is out of the question, VP2 would prefer option C. The dean believes in change, wanting to shake the place up and not caring whether that means an increase or a decrease. The dean prefers C to A and A to B.

impossibility theorem A proposition demonstrated by Kenneth Arrow showing that no system of aggregating individual preferences into social decisions will always yield consistent, nonarbitrary results.

FIGURE 15.7 Preferences of Three Top University Officials

VP1 prefers A to B and B to C. VP2 prefers B to C and C to A. The dean prefers C to A and A to B.

[5]Kenneth Arrow, *Social Choice and Individual Values* (New York: John Wiley, 1951).

TABLE 15.1 Results of Voting on University's Plans: The Voting Paradox

	VOTES OF:			
Vote	VP1	VP2	Dean	Result[a]
A versus B	A	B	A	A wins: A > B
B versus C	B	B	C	B wins: B > C
C versus A	A	C	C	C wins: C > A

[a]A > B is read "A is preferred to B."

Table 15.1 shows the results of the vote. When the three vote on A versus B, they vote in favor of A—to increase the size of the university instead of keeping it the same size. VP1 and the dean outvote VP2. Voting on B and C produces a victory for option B; two of the three would prefer to hold the line than to decrease the size of the institution. After two votes we have the result that A (an increase) is preferred to B (no change) and that B (no change) is preferred to C (a decrease).

The problem arises when we then have the three vote on A against C. Both VP2 and the dean vote for C, giving it the victory; C is actually preferred to A. Nevertheless, if A beats B, and B beats C, how can C beat A? The results are inconsistent.

The **voting paradox** illustrates several points. Most important is that when preferences for public goods differ across individuals, any system for adding up, or aggregating, those preferences can lead to inconsistencies. In addition, it illustrates just how much influence the person who sets the agenda has. If a vote had been taken on A and C first, the first two votes might never have occurred. This is why rules committees in both houses of Congress have enormous power; they establish the rules under which, as well as the order in which, legislation will be considered.

Another problem with majority-rule voting is that it leads to logrolling. **Logrolling** occurs when representatives trade votes—D helps get a majority in favor of E's program, and in exchange E helps D get a majority on D's program. It is not clear whether any bill could get through any legislature without logrolling. It is also not clear whether logrolling is, on balance, a good thing or a bad thing from the standpoint of efficiency. On the one hand, a program that benefits one region or group of people might generate enormous net social gains, but because the group of beneficiaries is fairly small, it will not command a majority of delegates. If another bill that is likely to generate large benefits to another area is also awaiting a vote, a trade of support between the two sponsors of the bills should result in the passage of two good pieces of efficient legislation. On the other hand, logrolling can also turn out unjustified, inefficient, "pork barrel" legislation.

A number of other problems also follow from voting as a mechanism for public choice. For one, voters do not have much of an incentive to become well informed. When you go out to buy a car or, on a smaller scale, a CD player, you are the one who suffers the full consequences of a bad choice. Similarly, you are the beneficiary of the gains from a good choice. This is not so in voting. Although many of us believe that we have a civic responsibility to vote, no one really believes that his or her vote will actually determine the outcome of an election. The time and effort it takes just to get to the polls are enough to deter many people. Becoming informed involves even more costs, and it is not surprising that many people do not do it.

Beyond the fact that a single vote is not likely to be decisive is the fact that the costs and benefits of wise and unwise social choices are widely shared. If the congressman that I elect makes a bad mistake and wastes a billion dollars, I bear only a small fraction of that cost. Even though the sums involved are large in aggregate, individual voters find little incentive to become informed.

Two additional problems with voting are that choices are almost always limited to *bundles* of publicly provided goods, and we vote infrequently. Many of us vote for Republicans or Democrats. We vote for president only every 4 years. We elect senators for 6-year terms. In private markets, we can look at each item separately and decide how much of each we want. We also can shop daily. In the public sector, though, we vote for a platform or

voting paradox A simple demonstration of how majority-rule voting can lead to seemingly contradictory and inconsistent results. A commonly cited illustration of the kind of inconsistency described in the impossibility theorem.

logrolling Occurs when congressional representatives trade votes, agreeing to help each other get certain pieces of legislation passed.

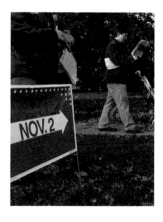

a party that takes a particular position on a whole range of issues. In the public sector it is very difficult, or impossible, for voters to unbundle issues.

CHAPTER 15 **349**
Externalities, Public Goods, Imperfect
Information, and Social Choice

There is, of course, a reason why bundling occurs in the sphere of public choice. It is difficult enough to convince people to go to the polls once a year. If we voted separately on every appropriation bill, we would spend our lives at the polls. This is one reason for representative democracy. We elect officials who we hope will become informed and represent our interests and preferences.

GOVERNMENT INEFFICIENCY: THEORY OF PUBLIC CHOICE

Recent work in economics has focused not just on the government as an extension of individual preferences but also on government officials as people with their own agendas and objectives. That is, government officials are assumed to maximize their own utility, not the social good. To understand the way government functions, we need to look less at the preferences of individual members of society and more at the incentive structures that exist around public officials.

The officials whom we seem to worry about are the people who run government agencies—the Social Security Administration, the Department of Housing and Urban Development, and state registries of motor vehicles, for example. What incentive do these people have to produce a good product and to be efficient? Might such incentives be lacking?

In the private sector, where firms compete for profits, only efficient firms producing goods that consumers will buy survive. If a firm is inefficient—if it is producing at a higher-than-necessary cost—the market will drive it out of business. This is not necessarily so in the public sector. If a government bureau is producing a necessary service, or one mandated by law, it does not need to worry about customers. No matter how bad the service is at the registry of motor vehicles, everyone with a car must buy its product.

The efficiency of a government agency's internal structure depends on the way incentives facing workers and agency heads are structured. If the budget allocation of an agency is based on the last period's spending alone, for example, agency heads have a clear incentive to spend more money, however inefficiently. This point is not lost on government officials, who have experimented with many ways of rewarding agency heads and employees for cost-saving suggestions.

However, critics say such efforts to reward productivity and punish inefficiency are rarely successful. It is difficult to punish, let alone dismiss, a government employee. Elected officials are subject to recall, but it usually takes gross negligence to rouse voters into instituting such a measure. Also, elected officials are rarely associated with problems of bureaucratic mismanagement, which they decry daily.

Critics of "the bureaucracy" argue that no set of internal incentives can ever match the discipline of the market, and they point to studies of private versus public garbage collection, airline operations, fire protection, mail service, and so forth, all of which suggest significantly lower costs in the private sector. One theme of the Reagan and first Bush administrations was "privatization." If the private sector can possibly provide a service, it is likely to do so more efficiently—so the public sector should allow the private sector to take over.

One concern regarding wholesale privatization is the potential effect it may have on distribution. Late in his administration, President Reagan suggested that the federal government sell its entire stock of public housing to the private sector. Would the private sector continue to provide housing to poor people? The worry is that it would not, because it may not be profitable to do so.

Like voters, public officials suffer from a lack of incentive to become fully informed and to make tough choices. Consider an elected official. If the real objective of an elected official is to get reelected, then the real incentive must be to provide visible goods for that official's constituency while hiding the costs or spreading them thin. Self-interest may easily lead to poor decisions and public irresponsibility.

Looking at the public sector from the standpoint of the behavior of public officials and the potential for inefficient choices and bureaucratic waste rather than in terms of its potential for improving the allocation of resources has become quite popular. This is the viewpoint of what is called the *public choice* field in economics that builds heavily on the work of Nobel laureate James Buchanan.

RENT-SEEKING REVISITED

Another problem with public choice is that special-interest groups can and do spend resources to influence the legislative process. As we said before, individual voters have little incentive to become well informed and to participate fully in the legislative process. Favor-seeking special-interest groups have a great deal of incentive to participate in political decision making. We saw in Chapter 13 that a monopolist would be willing to pay to prevent competition from eroding its economic profits. Many—if not all—industries lobby for favorable treatment, softer regulation, or antitrust exemption. This, as you recall, is *rent-seeking*.

Rent-seeking extends far beyond those industries that lobby for government help in preserving monopoly powers. Any group that benefits from a government policy has an incentive to use its resources to lobby for that policy. Farmers lobby for farm subsidies, oil producers lobby for oil import taxes, and the American Association of Retired Persons lobbies against cuts in Social Security.

In the absence of well-informed and active voters, special-interest groups assume an important and perhaps a critical role. But there is another side to this story. Some have argued that favorable legislation is, in effect, for sale in the marketplace. Those willing and able to pay the most are more successful in accomplishing their goals than those with fewer resources.

> Theory may suggest that unregulated markets fail to produce an efficient allocation of resources. This should not lead you to the conclusion that government involvement necessarily leads to efficiency. There are reasons to believe that government attempts to produce the right goods and services in the right quantities efficiently may fail.

GOVERNMENT AND THE MARKET

There is no question that government must be involved in both the provision of public goods and the control of externalities. Although the argument is less clear-cut, a strong case can also be made for government actions to increase the flow of information. No society has ever existed in which citizens did not get together to protect themselves from the abuses of an unrestrained market and to provide for themselves certain goods and services that the market did not provide. The question is not *whether* we need government involvement. The question is *how much* and *what kind* of government involvement we should have.

Critics of government involvement correctly say the existence of an "optimal" level of public-goods production does not guarantee that governments will achieve it. It is easy to show that governments will generally fail to achieve the most efficient level. There is no reason to believe that governments are capable of achieving the "correct" amount of control over externalities or dispersing the proper information to all who need it. Markets may fail to produce an efficient allocation of resources, but governments can fail for a number of reasons.

1. Measurement of social damages and benefits is difficult and imprecise. For example, estimates of the costs of acid rain range from practically nothing to incalculably high amounts.
2. There is no precise mechanism through which citizens' preferences for public goods can be correctly determined. All voting systems lead to inconsistent results. Samuelson's optimal solution works only if individuals in a society pay in accordance with their own preferences. Because this is impossible under our system, we all must be taxed to pay for the mix of public goods that the imperfect voting mechanism provides us.
3. Because government agencies are not subject to the discipline of the market, we have little reason to expect they will be efficient producers. The amount of waste, corruption, and inefficiency in government is a hotly debated issue. Although government is not

subjected to the discipline of the market, it must submit to the discipline of the press, tight budgets, and opinion of the voters.

4. Both elected and appointed officials have needs and preferences of their own, and it is naive to expect them to act selflessly for the good of society (even if they know what would be best for society). Bureaucrats in the Department of Defense, for example, have a clear incentive to increase the size of their budgets, and elected officials rely heavily on those same bureaucrats for information.

Just as critics of government involvement concede that the market fails to achieve full efficiency, defenders of government must acknowledge government's failures. Defenders of government involvement respond that we get closer to an efficient allocation of resources by trying to control externalities and by doing our best to produce the public goods (including information) that people want with the imperfect tools we have than we would by leaving everything to the market.

SUMMARY

EXTERNALITIES AND ENVIRONMENTAL ECONOMICS

1. Often when we engage in transactions or make economic decisions, second or third parties suffer consequences that decision makers have no incentive to consider. These are called *externalities*. A classic example of an external cost is pollution.

2. When external costs are not considered in economic decisions, we may engage in activities or produce products that are not "worth it." When external benefits are not considered, we may fail to do things that are indeed "worth it." The result is an inefficient allocation of resources.

3. A number of alternative mechanisms have been used to control externalities: (1) government-imposed taxes and subsidies, (2) private bargaining and negotiation, (3) legal remedies such as *injunctions* and *liability rules*, (4) sale or auctioning of rights to impose externalities, and (5) direct regulation.

PUBLIC (SOCIAL) GOODS

4. In an unfettered market, certain goods and services that people want will not be produced in adequate amounts. These *public goods* have characteristics that make it difficult or impossible for the private sector to produce them profitably.

5. Public goods are *nonrival in consumption* (their benefits fall collectively on members of society or on groups of members), and/or their benefits are *nonexcludable* (it is generally impossible to exclude people who have not paid from enjoying the benefits of public goods). An example of a public good is national defense.

6. One of the problems of public provision is that it leads to public dissatisfaction. We can choose any quantity of private goods that we want, or we can walk away without buying any. When it comes to public goods such as national defense, the government must choose one and only one kind and quantity of (collective) output to produce.

7. Theoretically, there exists an *optimal level of provision* for each public good. At this level, society's willingness to pay per unit equals the marginal cost of producing the good. To discover such a level, we would need to know the preferences of each individual citizen.

8. According to the *Tiebout hypothesis*, an efficient mix of public goods is produced when local land/housing prices and taxes come to reflect consumer preferences just as they do in the market for private goods.

IMPERFECT INFORMATION

9. Choices made in the presence of imperfect information may not be efficient. In the face of incomplete information, consumers and firms may encounter the problem of *adverse selection*. When buyers or sellers enter into market exchanges with other parties who have more information, low-quality goods are exchanged in greater numbers than high-quality goods. *Moral hazard* arises when one party to a contract passes the cost of its behavior on to the other party to the contract. If a contract absolves one party of the consequences of its actions, and people act in their own self-interest, the result is inefficient.

10. In many cases, the market provides solutions to information problems. Profit-maximizing firms will continue to gather information as long as the marginal benefits from continued search are greater than the marginal costs. Consumers will do the same: More time is afforded to the information search for larger decisions. In other cases, government must be called on to collect and disperse information to the public.

SOCIAL CHOICE

11. Because we cannot know everyone's preferences about public goods, we are forced to rely on imperfect *social choice* mechanisms such as majority rule.

12. The theory that unfettered markets do not achieve an efficient allocation of resources should not lead us to conclude that government involvement necessarily leads to efficiency. Governments also fail.

GOVERNMENT AND THE MARKET

13. Defenders of government involvement in the economy acknowledge its failures but believe we get closer to an efficient allocation of resources with government than without it. By trying to control externalities and by doing our best to provide the public goods that society wants, we do better than we would if we left everything to the market.

REVIEW TERMS AND CONCEPTS

adverse selection, 345

Coase theorem, 335

drop-in-the-bucket problem, 339

externality, 328

free-rider problem, 339

impossibility theorem, 347

injunction, 336

liability rules, 336

logrolling, 348

marginal damage cost (*MDC*), 331

marginal private cost (*MPC*), 331

marginal social cost (*MSC*), 328

market failure, 327

mixed goods, 344

moral hazard, 345

nonexcludable, 339

nonrival in consumption, 338

optimal level of provision for public goods, 343

public goods (social or collective goods), 338

social choice, 347

Tiebout hypothesis, 344

voting paradox, 348

PROBLEM SET

1. "If government imposes on the firms in a polluting industry penalties (taxes) that exceed the actual value of the damages done by the pollution, the result is an inefficient and unfair imposition of costs on those firms and on the consumers of their products." Discuss. Use a diagram to show how consumers are harmed.

2. It has been proposed that toll collection on the Massachusetts Turnpike, a key commuter route into Boston from the west, be discontinued. Proponents argue that tolls have long ago paid for the cost of building the road; now they just provide cash for a fat bureaucracy. A number of economists are opposing the repeal of tolls on the grounds that they serve to internalize externalities. Can you explain their argument briefly?

3. Many people are concerned with the problem of "urban sprawl." As the development of new housing tracts and suburban shopping malls continues over time, metropolitan areas have become more congested and polluted. Open space disappears and the quality of life changes. Think of your own metropolitan area, city, or town. Using the concept of externalities, consider the issue of land use and development. What are the specific decisions made in the development process that lead to externalities? On whom are they imposed? Do you think that they are measurable? In what specific ways can decision makers be given the incentive to consider them? One of the cities that has paid the most attention to urban sprawl is Portland, Oregon. Search the Web to see what you can find out about Portland's approach.

4. The existence of "public goods" is an example of potential market failure. This view suggests a government or public sector working to *improve* the outcome of completely free markets. Write a brief summary of the arguments *for* government provision of public goods. (Be sure to consider the discussion of a prisoners' dilemma in the last chapter.) The following three arguments suggest that government may not improve the outcome as much as we might anticipate.
   a. *Public goods theory:* Because public goods are collective, the government is constrained to pick a single level of output for all of us. National defense is an example. The government must pick one level of defense expenditure, and some of us will think it is too much, some will think it is too little, and no one is happy.

   b. *Problems of social choice:* It is simply impossible to choose collectively in a rational way that satisfies voters/consumers of public goods.
   c. *Public choice and public officials:* Once elected or appointed, public officials tend to act in accordance with their own preferences and not out of concern for the public.
   Which of the three do you find the most persuasive?

5. It has been argued that the following are examples of "mixed goods." They are essentially private but partly public. For each, describe the private and public components and discuss briefly why the government should or should not be involved in their provision.
   a. Elementary and secondary education
   b. Higher education
   c. Medical care
   d. Air-traffic control

6. A paper factory dumps polluting chemicals into the Snake River. Thousands of citizens live along the river, and they bring suit, claiming damages. You are asked by the judge to testify at the trial as an impartial expert. The court is considering four possible solutions, and you are asked to comment on the potential efficiency and equity of each. Your testimony should be brief.
   a. Deny the merits of the case and simply affirm the polluter's right to dump. The parties will achieve the optimal solution without government.
   b. Find in favor of the plaintiff. The polluters will be held liable for damages and must fully compensate citizens for all past and future damages imposed.
   c. Order an immediate end to the dumping, with no damages awarded.
   d. Refer the matter to the Environmental Protection Agency, which will impose a tax on the factory equal to the marginal damage costs. Proceeds will not be paid to the damaged parties.

7. Explain why you agree or disagree with each of the following statements:
   a. The government should be involved in providing housing for the poor because housing is a "public good."
   b. From the standpoint of economic efficiency, an unregulated market economy tends to overproduce public goods.

8. Society is made up of two individuals, A and B, whose demands for public good X are given in Figure 1. Assuming that the pub-

A's Demand

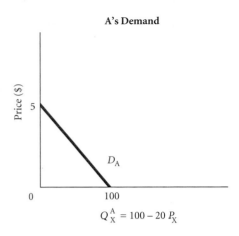

$$Q_X^A = 100 - 20\, P_X$$

B's Demand

$$Q_X^B = 100 - 10\, P_X$$

FIGURE 1

lic good can be produced at a constant marginal cost of $6, what is the optimal level of output? How much would you charge A and B?

9. Government involvement in general scientific research has been justified on the grounds that advances in knowledge are public goods—once produced, information can be shared at virtually no cost. A new production technology in an industry could be made available to all firms, reducing costs of production, driving down price, and benefiting the public. The patent system, however, allows private producers of "new knowledge" to exclude others from enjoying the benefits of that knowledge. Inventors would have little incentive to produce new knowledge if there were no possibility of profiting from their inventions. If one company holds exclusive rights to an advanced production process, it produces at lower cost but can use the exclusion to acquire monopoly power and hold price up.
   a. On balance, is the patent system a good or a bad thing? Explain.
   b. Is government involvement in scientific research a good idea? Discuss.

10. "The Coase theorem implies that we never need to worry about regulating externalities because the private individuals involved will reach the efficient outcome through negotiations." Is this statement true or false? Justify your answer and use examples.

11. Explain how imperfect information problems such as adverse selection and moral hazard might affect the following markets or situations:
   a. Workers applying for disability benefits from a company
   b. The market for used computers
   c. The market for customized telephone systems for college offices and dorms
   d. The market for automobile collision insurance

12. "In recent years, events in Eastern Europe have been dramatic. Those events demonstrate that the best economic system is one in which *all* economic decisions are made by individual households and firms without *any* government involvement." Comment briefly.

Income Distribution and Poverty

16

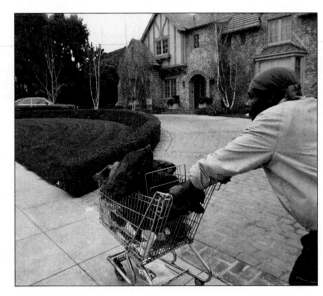

What role should government play in the economy? Thus far, we have focused only on actions the government might be called on to take to improve market efficiency. Even if we achieved markets that are perfectly efficient, would the result be fair? We now turn to the question of **equity**, or fairness.

Somehow, the goods and services produced in every society get distributed among its citizens. Some citizens end up with mansions in Palm Beach, ski trips to Gstaad, and Ferraris; others end up without enough to eat and live in shacks. This chapter focuses on distribution. Why do some people get more than others? What are the sources of inequality? Should the government change the distribution generated by the market?

THE UTILITY POSSIBILITIES FRONTIER

Ideally, in discussing distribution, we should talk not about the distribution of things but about the distribution of well-being. In the nineteenth century, philosophers used the concept of *utility* as a measure of well-being. As they saw it, people make choices among goods and services on the basis of the utility those goods and services yield. People act to maximize utility. If you prefer a night at the symphony to a rock concert, the reason is that you expect to get more utility from the symphony. If we extend this thinking, we might argue that if household A gets more total utility than household B, A is better off than B.

Utility is not directly observable or measurable, but thinking about it as if it were can help us understand some of the ideas that underlie debates about distribution. Suppose society consisted of two people, I and J. Next suppose that the line PP' in Figure 16.1 represents all the combinations of I's utility and J's utility that are possible, given the resources and technology available in their society. (This is an extension of the production possibilities frontier in Chapter 2.)

Any point inside PP', or the **utility possibilities frontier**, is inefficient because both I and J could be better off. A is one such point. B is one of many possible points along PP' that society should prefer to A, because both members are better off at B than they are at A.

While point B is preferable to point A from everyone's point of view, how does point B compare with point C? Both B and C are efficient; I cannot be made better off without making J worse off, and vice versa. All the points along PP' are efficient, but they may not be

equity Fairness.

utility possibilities frontier A graphic representation of a two-person world that shows all points at which A's utility can be increased only if B's utility is decreased.

355

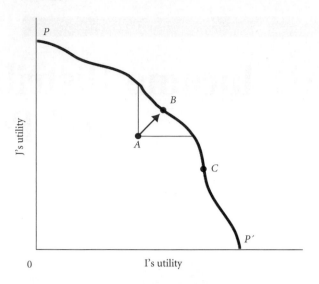

FIGURE 16.1 Utility Possibilities Frontier

If society were made up of two people, I and J, and all the assumptions of perfect competition held, the market system would lead to some point along *PP'*. Every point along *PP'* is efficient; it is impossible to make I better off without making J worse off, and vice versa. Which point is best? Is *B* better than *C*?

equally desirable. If all the assumptions of perfectly competitive market theory held, the market system would lead to one of the points along *PP'*. The actual point reached would depend on I's and J's initial endowments of wealth, skills, and so forth.

In practice, however, the market solution leaves some people out. The rewards of a market system are linked to productivity, and some people in every society are simply not capable of being very productive or have not had the opportunity to become more productive. All societies make some provision for the very poor. Most often, public expenditures on behalf of the poor are financed with taxes collected from the rest of society. Society makes a judgment that those who are better off should give up some of their rewards so that those at the bottom can have more than the market system would allocate to them. In a democratic state, such redistribution is presumably undertaken because a majority of the members of that society think it is fair, or just.

Early economists drew analogies between social choices among alternative outcomes and consumer choices among alternative outcomes. A consumer chooses on the basis of his or her own unique utility function, or measure of his or her own well-being; a society, economists said, chooses on the basis of a social welfare function that embodies the society's ethics.

Such theoretical discussions of fairness and equity focus on the distribution and redistribution of utility. Because utility is neither observable nor measurable, most discussions of social policy center on the *distribution of income* or the *distribution of wealth* as indirect measures of well-being. It is important that you remember throughout this chapter, however, that income and wealth are imperfect measures of well-being. Someone with a profound love of the outdoors may choose to work in a national park for a low wage instead of a consulting firm in a big city for a high wage. The choice reveals that she is better off, even though her measured income is lower. As another example, think about five people with $1 each. Now suppose that one of those people has a magnificent voice, and that the other four give up their dollars to hear her sing. The exchange leads to inequality of measured wealth—the singer has $5 and no one else has any—but all are better off than they were before.

Although income and wealth are imperfect measures of utility, they have no observable substitutes and are therefore the measures we use throughout this chapter. First, we review the factors that determine the distribution of income in a market setting. Second, we look at the data on income distribution, wealth distribution, and poverty in the United States. Third, we talk briefly about some theories of economic justice. Finally, we describe a number of current redistributional programs, including public assistance (or welfare), food stamps, Medicaid, and public housing.

CHAPTER 16 357
Income Distribution and Poverty

THE SOURCES OF HOUSEHOLD INCOME

Why do some people and some families have more income than others? Before we turn to data on the distribution of income, let us review what we already know about the sources of inequality:

> Households derive their incomes from three basic sources: (1) from wages or salaries received in exchange for labor; (2) from property—that is, capital, land, and so forth; and (3) from government.

WAGES AND SALARIES

More than half of personal income in the United States in 2005 was received in the form of wages and salaries. If you add wage supplements, which include contributions for health insurance and pensions, the figure is 64 percent. Hundreds of different wage rates are paid to employees for their labor in thousands of different labor markets. As you saw in Chapter 10, perfectly competitive market theory predicts that all factors of production (including labor) are paid a return equal to their marginal revenue product—the market value of what they produce at the margin. There are reasons why one type of labor might be more productive than another and why some households have higher incomes than others.

Required Skills, Human Capital, and Working Conditions   Some people are born with attributes that translate into valuable skills. Tim Duncan and Shaquille O'Neal are great basketball players, partly because they happen to be 7 feet tall. They did not decide to go out and invest in height; they were born with the right genes. Some people have perfect pitch and beautiful voices; others are tone deaf. Some people have quick mathematical minds; others cannot add 2 and 2.

The rewards of a skill that is in limited supply depend on the demand for that skill. Men's professional basketball is extremely popular, and the top NBA players make millions of dollars per year. There are some great women basketball players, too, but because women's professional basketball has not become popular in the United States, these women's skills go comparatively unrewarded. In tennis, however, people want to see women play, and women therefore earn prize money similar to the money earned by men.

Some people with rare skills can make enormous salaries in an unfettered market economy. Luciano Pavarotti has a voice that millions of people are willing to pay to hear in person and on CDs. Garth Brooks sells a million copies of every album he makes. Before Pablo Picasso died, he could sell small sketches for vast sums of money. Were they worth it? They were worth exactly what the highest bidder was willing to pay.

Not all skills are inborn. Some people have invested in training and schooling to improve their knowledge and skills, and therein lies another source of inequality in wages. When we go to school, we are investing in **human capital** that we expect to yield dividends, partly in the form of higher wages, later on. Human capital is also produced through on-the-job training. People learn their jobs and acquire "firm-specific" skills when they are on the job. Thus, in most occupations there is a reward for experience. Pay scale often reflects numbers of years on the job, and those with more experience earn higher wages than those in similar jobs with less experience.

Some jobs are more desirable than others. Entry-level positions in "glamour" industries such as publishing and television tend to be low-paying. Because talented people are willing to take entry-level jobs in these industries at salaries below what they could earn in other occupations, there must be other, nonwage rewards. It may be that the job itself is more personally rewarding, or that a low-paying apprenticeship is the only way to acquire the human capital necessary to advance. In contrast, less desirable jobs often pay wages that include **compensating differentials**. Of two jobs requiring roughly equal levels of experience and

According to experts, the Alaskan fishing industry faces the most dangerous working conditions in the country. For this reason, Alaskan fishermen are paid compensating differentials that raise their average wage high above the average wage of the U.S. general population.

human capital The stock of knowledge, skills, and talents that people possess; it can be inborn or acquired through education and training.

compensating differentials Differences in wages that result from differences in working conditions. Risky jobs usually pay higher wages; highly desirable jobs usually pay lower wages.

skills that compete for the same workers, the job with the poorer working conditions usually has to pay a slightly higher wage to attract workers away from the job with the better working conditions.

Compensating differentials are also required when a job is very dangerous. Those who take great risks are usually rewarded with high wages. High-beam workers on skyscrapers and bridges command premium wages. Firefighters in cities that have many old, run-down buildings are usually paid more than those in relatively tranquil rural or suburban areas.

Multiple Household Incomes   Another source of wage inequality among households lies in the fact that many households have more than one earner in the labor force. Second, and even third, incomes are becoming more the rule than the exception for U.S. families. In 1960, about 37 percent of women over the age of 16 were in the labor force. By 1978, the figure had increased to over 50 percent, and it continued to climb slowly but steadily to 60 percent in 2005.

The Minimum Wage Controversy   One strategy for reducing wage inequity that has been used for almost 100 years in many countries is the **minimum wage**. (The minimum wage and price floors were discussed in Chapter 4.) A minimum wage is the lowest wage firms are permitted to pay workers. The first minimum wage law was adopted in New Zealand in 1894. The United States adopted a national minimum wage with the passage of the Fair Labor Standards Act of 1938, although many individual states had laws on the books much earlier. Since September 1, 1997, the federal minimum wage has been $5.15 per hour.

In recent years, the minimum wage has come under increasing attack. Opponents argue that minimum wage legislation interferes with the smooth functioning of the labor market and creates unemployment. Proponents argue that it has been successful in raising the wages of the poorest workers and alleviating poverty without creating much unemployment.

These arguments can best be understood with a simple supply and demand diagram. Figure 16.2 shows hypothetical demand and supply curves for unskilled labor. The equilibrium wage rate is $4.00. At that wage, the quantity of unskilled labor supplied and the quantity of unskilled labor demanded are equal. Now suppose that a law is passed setting a minimum wage of $5.15. At that wage rate, the quantity of labor supplied increases from the equilibrium level, L^*, to L_S. At the same time, the higher wage reduces the quantity of labor demanded by firms, from L^* to L_D. As a result, firms lay off $L^* - L_D$ workers.

minimum wage The lowest wage that firms are permitted to pay workers.

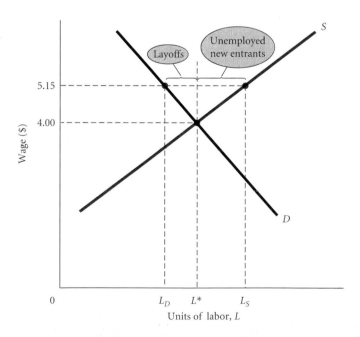

FIGURE 16.2 Effect of Minimum Wage Legislation

If the equilibrium wage in the market for unskilled labor is below the legislated minimum wage, the result is likely to be unemployment. The higher wage will attract new entrants to the labor force (quantity supplied will increase from L^* to L_S), but firms will hire fewer workers (quantity demanded will drop from L^* to L_D).

It is true that those workers who remain on payrolls receive higher wages. With the minimum wage in effect, unskilled workers receive $5.15 per hour instead of $4.00. But is it worth it? Some gain while others (including those who had been employed at the equilibrium wage) suffer unemployment.

In fact, the evidence on the extent to which the minimum wage causes jobs to be lost is changing. Professor Finis Welch at Texas A&M and two colleagues estimated in a recent study that each 10 percent increase in the minimum wage produces job losses of about 1 percent of all minimum wage workers, or about 60,000 workers in total at the time of the study. But other studies find little or no effect on the number of jobs lost when the minimum wage increases. Two studies by David Card of the University of California at Berkeley and one by Lawrence Katz of Harvard and Alan Krueger of Princeton University find that an increase in the minimum wage has virtually no effect at all on unemployment.

Unemployment Before turning to property income, we need to mention another cause of inequality in the United States that is the subject of much discussion in macroeconomics: *unemployment*.

People earn wages only when they have jobs. In recent years, the United States has been through two severe recessions (economic downturns). In 1975, the unemployment rate hit 9 percent, and over 8 million people were unable to find work; in 1982, the unemployment rate was nearly 11 percent, and over 12 million were jobless. More recently, the recovery from the milder recession of 1990 to 1991 was slow at first. By 2000, the number of unemployed dropped below 5.5 million (an unemployment rate of 3.9 percent), but by mid-2005, it was back to 7.5 million, or 5 percent.

Unemployment hurts primarily those who are laid off, and thus its costs are narrowly distributed. For some workers, the costs of unemployment are lowered by unemployment compensation benefits paid out of a fund accumulated with receipts from a tax on payrolls.

INCOME FROM PROPERTY

Another source of income inequality is that some people have **property income**—from the ownership of real property and financial holdings—while many others do not. Some people own a great deal of wealth, and some have no assets at all. Overall, about 22 percent of personal income in the United States in 2005 came from ownership of property.

> The amount of property income that a household earns depends on (1) how much property it owns and (2) what kinds of assets it owns. Such income generally takes the form of profits, interest, dividends, and rents.

Households come to own assets through saving and through inheritance. Many of today's large fortunes were inherited from previous generations. The Rockefellers, the Kennedys, and the Fords, to name a few, still have large holdings of property originally accumulated by previous generations. Thousands of families receive smaller inheritances each year from their parents. (Under 2005 tax laws, $1.5 million can pass from one generation to another free of estate taxes.) Most families receive little through inheritance; most of their wealth or property comes from saving.

Often, fortunes accumulate in a single generation when a business becomes successful. The late Sam Walton built a personal fortune estimated at over $23 billion on a chain of retail stores including Wal-Mart. *Forbes* magazine estimates that Bill Gates, founder and chief executive officer of Microsoft, is worth over $40 billion. Karl and Theo Albrecht made $25 billion, beginning with their mother's corner store in Germany, and expanding to 4,000 stores in Germany and 10 other countries. In the United States, they own the gourmet food-and-beverage chain Trader Joe's.

INCOME FROM THE GOVERNMENT: TRANSFER PAYMENTS

About 14 percent of personal income in 2005 came from governments in the form of **transfer payments**. Transfer payments are payments made by government to people who do not supply goods or services in exchange. Some, but not all, transfer payments are made to

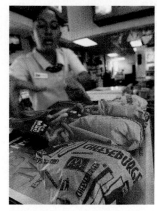

Many fast-food restaurants pay their employees minimum wage. In some locations, however, restaurants find that they must pay above minimum wage to attract and retain staff.

property income Income from the ownership of real property and financial holdings. It takes the form of profits, interest, dividends, and rents.

transfer payments Payments by government to people who do not supply goods or services in exchange.

359

people with low incomes, precisely because they have low incomes. Transfer payments thus reduce the amount of inequality in the distribution of income. Not all transfer income goes to the poor. The biggest single transfer program at the federal level is Social Security.

> Transfer programs are by and large designed to provide income to those in need. They are part of the government's attempts to offset some of the problems of inequality and poverty.

THE DISTRIBUTION OF INCOME

Despite the many problems with using income as a measure of well-being, it is useful to know something about how income is actually distributed. Before we examine these data, we should pin down precisely what the data represent.

economic income The amount of money a household can spend during a given period without increasing or decreasing its net assets. Wages, salaries, dividends, interest income, transfer payments, rents, and so forth are sources of economic income.

Economic income is defined as the amount of money a household can spend during a given period without increasing or decreasing its net assets. Economic income includes anything that enhances your ability to spend—wages, salaries, dividends, interest received, proprietors' income, transfer payments, rents, and so forth. If you own an asset (such as a share of stock) that increases in value, that gain is part of your income, whether you sell the asset to "realize" the gain or not. Normally, we speak of "before-tax" income, with taxes considered a use of income.

INCOME INEQUALITY IN THE UNITED STATES

Table 16.1 presents some estimates of the distribution of several income components and of total income for households in 2000. The measure of income used to calculate these figures is very broad; it includes both taxable and nontaxable items, as well as estimates of realized capital gains. It does not include unrealized capital gains, and so it is not a complete measure of economic income.

The data are presented by "quintiles," that is, the total number of households is first ranked by income and then split into five groups of equal size. In 2000, the top quintile earned 56.7 percent of total income, while the bottom quintile earned just 2.7 percent. The top 1 percent (which is part of the top quintile) earned more than the bottom 40 percent. Labor income was more evenly distributed than total income.

Income from property is more unevenly distributed than wages and salaries. Property income comes from owning things: Land earns rent, stocks earn dividends and appreciate in value, bonds and deposit accounts earn interest, owners of small businesses earn profits, and so forth. The top 20 percent of households earned 73.2 percent of property income, and the top 1 percent earned 31.6 percent.

Transfer payments include Social Security benefits, unemployment compensation, and welfare payments, as well as an estimate of nonmonetary transfers from the government to households—food stamps and Medicaid and Medicare program benefits, for example. Transfers flow to low-income households, but not solely to them. Social Security benefits, for example, which account for about half of all transfer payments, flow to everyone who partic-

TABLE 16.1 Distribution of Total Income and Components in the United States, 2000 (Percentages)

HOUSEHOLDS	TOTAL INCOME	LABOR INCOME	PROPERTY INCOME	TRANSFER INCOME
Bottom fifth	2.7	1.7	0.7	19.2
Second fifth	7.2	6.3	4.2	25.8
Third fifth	12.6	12.7	9.2	23.0
Fourth fifth	21.3	23.6	15.1	17.0
Top fifth	56.7	55.6	73.2	14.8
Top 1 percent	14.8	10.9	31.6	1.2

Source: Julie-Anne Cronin, U.S. Department of the Treasury, OTA paper 85, p. 19.

TABLE 16.2 Distribution of Money Income of U.S. Families by Quintiles, 1947–2002 (Percentages)

	1947	1960	1972	1980	1984	1994	1997	2002
Bottom fifth	5.1	4.8	5.4	5.2	4.7	4.2	4.2	4.2
Second fifth	11.8	12.2	11.9	11.5	11.0	10.0	9.9	9.7
Third fifth	16.7	17.8	17.5	17.5	17.0	15.7	15.7	15.5
Fourth fifth	23.2	24.0	23.9	24.3	24.4	23.3	23.0	23.0
Top fifth	43.3	41.3	41.4	41.5	42.9	46.9	47.2	47.6
Top 5 %	17.5	15.9	15.9	15.3	16.0	20.1	20.7	20.8

Source: *Statistical Abstract of the United States*, various editions; Department of Commerce, HHES Division.

ipated in the system for the requisite number of years and who has reached the required age, regardless of income. Nonetheless, transfers represent a much more important income component at the bottom of the distribution than at the top. Although not shown in Table 16.1, transfers account for more than 80 percent of the income of the bottom 10 percent of households, but only about 3 percent of income among the top 10 percent of households.

Changes in the Distribution of Income
Table 16.2 presents the distribution of money income among U.S. families[1] at a number of points in time. **Money income**, the measure used by the Census Bureau in its surveys and publications, is slightly less complete than the income measure used in the calculations in Table 16.1. It does not include noncash transfer benefits, for example, and does not include capital gains.

As you can see, income distribution in the United States has remained stable over a long time. Between the end of World War II and 1980, there was a slight move toward equality: The share of income going to both the top 5 percent and the top 20 percent declined, while the share going to the bottom 20 percent increased slightly. Between 1980 and 2002, however, the trend reversed, with the top fifth gaining share and the bottom four-fifths losing share.

The Lorenz Curve and the Gini Coefficient
The distribution of income can be graphed in several ways. The most widely used graph is the **Lorenz curve**, shown in Figure 16.3. Plotted along the horizontal axis is the percentage of families, and along the vertical axis is the cumulative percentage of income. The curve shown here represents the year 2002, using data from Table 16.2.

During that year, the bottom 20 percent of families earned only 4.2 percent of total money income. The bottom 40 percent earned 13.9 percent (4.2 percent plus 9.7 percent), and so forth. If income were distributed equally—that is, if the bottom 20 percent earned 20 percent of the income, the bottom 40 percent earned 40 percent of the income, and so forth—the Lorenz curve would be a 45-degree line between 0 and 100 percent. More unequal distributions produce Lorenz curves that are farther from the 45-degree line.

The **Gini coefficient** is a measure of the degree of inequality in a distribution. It is the ratio of the shaded area in Figure 16.3 to the total triangular area below and to the right of the diagonal line 0*A*.

money income The measure of income used by the Census Bureau. Because it excludes noncash transfer payments and capital gains income, it is less inclusive than "economic income."

Lorenz curve A widely used graph of the distribution of income, with cumulative percentage of families plotted along the horizontal axis and cumulative percentage of income plotted along the vertical axis.

Gini coefficient A commonly used measure of inequality of income derived from a Lorenz curve. It can range from 0 to a maximum of 1.

If income is equally distributed, there is no shaded area (because the Lorenz curve and the 45-degree line are the same), and the Gini coefficient is zero. The Lorenz curves for distributions with more inequality are farther down to the right, their shaded areas are larger, and their Gini coefficients are higher. The maximum Gini coefficient is 1. As the Lorenz curve shifts down to the right, the shaded area becomes a larger portion of the total triangular area below 0*A*. If one family earned all the income (with no one else receiving anything), the shaded area and the triangle would be the same, and the ratio would equal 1.

---

[1]The term *family* excludes unmarried individuals living alone and groups of people living together who are not related by blood, marriage, or adoption. In the United States in 2003, there was a total of 111 million households—76 million family households and 35 million nonfamily households.

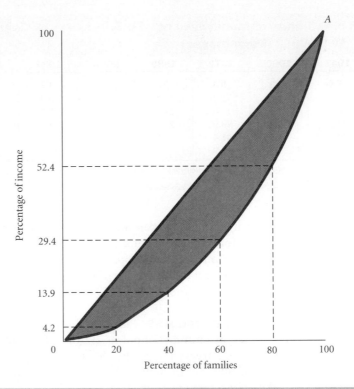

FIGURE 16.3 Lorenz Curve for the United States, 2002

The Lorenz curve is the most common way of presenting income distribution graphically. The larger the shaded area is, the more unequal the distribution. If distribution were equal, the Lorenz curve would be the 45-degree line OA.

Differences Among African-American Households, White Households, and Single-Person Households

So far we have been looking at income distribution among all families. Looking just at families without differentiating them in any way hides some needed distinctions. First, income distribution differs significantly among African-American and Hispanic families and white families. Second, many people do not belong to a family—they may be unmarried and living alone, or they may be part of a group of unrelated people living together.

Table 16.3 presents data on the distribution of money income for different types of households. The differences among the groupings are dramatic. While 27.4 percent of African-American households have annual incomes below $15,000, only 14.5 percent of white households do. At the upper end, 45.5 percent of white households, but only 27 percent of African-American households, have incomes above $50,000.

The category of single-person households includes the elderly living alone, college students, and single people in apartments. While it is hard to generalize about such a mixed bag, the income distribution of this group differs from that of other households in notable ways:

TABLE 16.3 Distribution of Money Income of Households, 2002 (Percentages)

	ALL HOUSEHOLDS	AFRICAN-AMERICAN HOUSEHOLDS	WHITE HOUSEHOLDS	HISPANIC HOUSEHOLDS	ONE-PERSON HOUSEHOLDS
0–15,000	16.1	27.4	14.5	19.1	36.3
15–25,000	13.2	16.4	12.8	17.2	19.8
25–35,000	12.3	14.5	12.0	15.7	13.7
35–50,000	15.1	14.8	15.2	16.4	13.4
50–75,000	18.3	13.9	18.9	16.9	9.7
75–100,000	11.0	6.7	11.6	7.5	3.7
>100,000	14.1	6.4	15.0	7.2	3.5
Total	100.0	100.0	100.0	100.0	100.0

Note: Totals may not add to 100 due to rounding.
Source: Statistical Abstract of the United States, 2004–2005, Tables 665 and 667.

36.3 percent of one-person households have incomes below $15,000, and only 16.9 percent have incomes over $50,000.

The income difference between multiperson households and single-person households is in part due to the fact that many households contain more than one earner. Of the 111.3 million households in the United States in 2003, 47.8 million had at least two earners.[2]

POVERTY

Most of the government's concern with income distribution and redistribution has focused on poverty. *Poverty* is a very complicated word to define. In simplest terms, it means the condition of people who have very low incomes. The dictionary defines the term simply as "lack of money or material possessions," but how low does your income have to be before you are classified as poor?

The Problem of Definition   Philosophers and social policy makers have long debated the meaning of "poverty." One school of thought argues that poverty should be measured by determining how much it costs to buy the "basic necessities of life." For many years, the Bureau of Labor Statistics published "family budget" data designed to track the cost of specific "bundles" of food, clothing, and shelter that were supposed to represent the minimum standard of living.

Critics argue that defining bundles of necessities is a hopeless task. Although it might be possible to define a minimally adequate diet, what is a "minimum" housing unit? Is a car a necessity? What about medical care? In reality, low-income families end up using what income they have in an enormous variety of ways.

Some say poverty is culturally defined and is therefore a relative concept, not an absolute one. Poverty in Bangladesh is very different from poverty in the United States. Even within the United States, urban poverty is very different from rural poverty. If poverty is a relative concept, the definition of it might change significantly as a society accumulates wealth and achieves higher living standards.

Although it is difficult to define precisely, the word *poverty* is one that we all understand intuitively to some degree. It conveys images of run-down, overcrowded, rat-infested housing, homeless people, untreated illness, and so forth. It is also a word that we have been forced to define formally for purposes of keeping statistics and administering public programs.

The Official Poverty Line   In the early 1960s, the U.S. government established an official poverty line. Because poor families tend to spend about one-third of their incomes on food,

> The official **poverty line** has been set at a figure that is simply three times the cost of the Department of Agriculture's minimum food budget.

poverty line The officially established income level that distinguishes the poor from the nonpoor. It is set at three times the cost of the Department of Agriculture's minimum food budget.

Each year the Department of Agriculture sets out a nutritionally sound minimum food bundle. For example, a week's food for a woman between 20 and 34 years old includes 4 eggs; $1\frac{1}{4}$ pounds of meat, fish, or poultry; 3 pounds of potatoes; 12 ounces of dark green or yellow vegetables; 3 pounds of other vegetables; and 8 ounces of fat or oil. In 2005, the department estimated that such a bundle for a family of four would cost about $126.80 per week. Multiply that times 52 weeks for a total of $6,593 per year; triple that, and you have a poverty line for a family of four set at $19,780.

Poverty in the United States Since 1960   In 1962, Michael Harrington published *The Other America: Poverty in the United States*, a book that woke the American people to the problem of poverty and stimulated the government to declare a "war on poverty" in 1964. In 1960, official figures had put the number of the poor in the United States at just under 40 million, or 22 percent of the total population. In his book, Harrington argued that the number had reached over 50 million.

By the late 1960s, the number living below the official poverty line had declined to about 25 million, where it stayed for over a decade. Between 1978 and 1983, the number of poor

---

[2]U.S. Bureau of the Census, **www.census.gov**.

TABLE 16.4 Percentage of Persons in Poverty by Demographic Group, 1964–2002

	OFFICIAL MEASURE 1964	OFFICIAL MEASURE 2004
All	19.0	12.7
White	14.9	10.8
African-American	49.6	24.7
Hispanic	NA	21.9
Female householder— no husband present	45.9	28.4
Elderly (65 +)	28.5	9.8
Children under 18	20.7	17.8

Source: U.S. Census Bureau.

jumped nearly 45 percent, from 24.5 million to 35.3 million, the highest number since 1964. The figure stood at 32.9 million in 2001. As a percentage of the total population, the poor accounted for between 11 percent and 12.6 percent of the population throughout the 1970s. That figure increased sharply to 15.2 percent between 1979 and 1983. From 1983 to 1989, the rate dropped to 12.8 percent, rising back to 14.5 percent in 1995. The rate fell to 12.7 percent in 2004.

While the official 2004 figures put the poverty rate at 12.7 percent of the population, they do not show that some groups in society experience more poverty than others. Table 16.4 shows the official poverty count for 1964 and 2004 by demographic group. One of the problems with the official count is that it considers only money income as defined by the census and is therefore somewhat inflated. Many federal programs designed to help people out of poverty include noncash benefits (sometimes called *in-kind benefits*) such as food stamps, public housing, and so forth. If added to income, these benefits would reduce the number of those officially designated as below the poverty line to about 9 percent of the population.

The poverty rate among African-Americans is more than twice as high as the poverty rate among whites. More than one in five African-Americans live in poverty. In addition, roughly the same proportion of Hispanics as African-Americans had incomes below the poverty line in 2004.

The group with the highest incidence of poverty in 2004 was women living in households with no husband present. In 1964, 45.9 percent of such women lived in poverty. By 2002, the figure was still 26.5 percent. During the 1980s, there was increasing concern about the "feminization of poverty," a concern that continues today.

Poverty rates among the elderly have been reduced considerably over the last few decades, dropping from 28.5 percent in 1964 to 9.8 percent in 2004. Certainly Social Security, supplemental security income, and Medicare have played a role in reducing poverty among the elderly. In 1964, 20.7 percent of all children under 18 lived in poverty, and in 2004 the figure was 17.8 percent.

THE DISTRIBUTION OF WEALTH

Data on the distribution of wealth are not as readily available as data on the distribution of income. Periodically, however, the government conducts a detailed survey of the holdings that make up wealth. Some of the results of this survey for 1998 are presented in Table 16.5. The top 1 percent of households owns 47.7 percent of common stocks. The top 1 percent also owns 34.0 percent of household net worth. In contrast, the bottom 80 percent own just 4.1 percent of common stocks and 18.5 percent of net worth. Housing wealth is more evenly distributed.

The distribution of wealth is much more unequal than the distribution of income. Part of the reason is that wealth is passed from generation to generation and accumulates. Large fortunes also accumulate when small businesses become successful large businesses. Some argue that an unequal distribution of wealth is the natural and inevitable consequence of risk taking in a market economy: It provides the incentive necessary to moti-

Hunger in the United States in 2003

BETWEEN 1991 AND 2001, THE U.S. economy experienced the longest economic expansion in U.S. history. Poverty rates were reduced and unemployment fell to 3.9 percent. While many Americans experienced good times, some were left behind. Between 2001 and 2003, the economy saw unemployment rise to over 9 million and poverty rates increase. The following article from *The Economist* describes the problem of hunger in Oregon in 2003.

A State Going Hungry
—The Economist

Judy Alley, the executive director of a food bank in a suburb east of Portland, Oregon, notices the children in particular. The parents tend to be quiet, embarrassed by their need to claim the boxes of free food which, with luck, will last them three to five days. But the youngsters are eager, darting from item to item. "They reach for anything they can get their hands on," says Mrs Alley.

These days, she says, such scenes are more commonplace. Anywhere from 5–7% of Oregon's 3,500,000 residents live in households where food is inadequate for at least part of most months, compared with figures 3–4% nationwide. Requests for supplies from the food bank Mrs Alley manages, which serves about 3,000 families, are running 40% higher than only a year ago. Across Oregon, bank managers say, requests at food banks are increasing at an annual rate of 10–20%. Oregon, in fact, has for four years claimed the dubious honour of "hungriest" state in the nation: ahead even of Mississippi and Louisiana, which report poverty rates (defined as an income of $18,100 for a family of four) that are half again as high.

How come? Oregon is relatively affluent, with a comfortably middling median income. No more than the average number of households are headed by single parents, usually a strong indicator of poverty. And although its unemployment rate is now the highest in the country, at about 8%, the state also enjoyed rapid economic expansion during the 1990s.

Those figures disguise hard realities, says Michael Leachman, a sociologist who has studied hunger in Oregon. For one thing, he says, Oregon has one of America's fastest-growing gaps between its poorest and wealthiest residents. While prosperous Portland is the centre of a high-tech boom, that boom has bypassed poorer rural communities reeling from downturns in logging and agriculture. Oregon's housing costs have also risen rapidly, and today about one-fifth of the state's renters pay landlords more than half their income. The state government is strapped for cash, forcing cutbacks in medical assistance and other services. And Oregon has a weak social structure, with many recent immigrants who lack the family and community ties to weather hard times.

To an extent, Oregon reflects the realities of a nation where the economy has not performed well for nearly four years. Nationally, June 5th was declared "National Hunger Awareness Day" by Second Harvest, a national network of private food-relief agencies. Growing hunger is reported by nearly all states, and about 10% of all households are classified as "food-insecure," meaning they are apt to have an uncertain food supply at least once a year (a smaller portion face real hunger on a regular basis). In Dayton, Ohio, for instance, the loss of telecoms and government jobs has translated into a 29% jump in food requests at the MidOhio Food Bank, which serves 20 counties. Hungry Americans must often choose between purchasing medicine, paying rent, or eating.

In Oregon, the dubious top hunger ranking has led to a flurry of do-gooding. Ted Kulongoski, the Democratic governor, declared a Hunger Awareness Week in late April. His face adorns posters plastered on the walls of state offices, encouraging employees to donate food. And "food drives" are a regular part of community life. All this is worthy, but also rather odd. In neighbouring Washington state, with demographics nearly identical to Oregon's and a ranking of second on the hungry-states list, hunger is hardly mentioned as a widespread problem. There are food banks and hungry people, but compared with Oregon's they are invisible.

What is also odd is that Oregon's hunger statistics may not be what they seem. In 2000, for instance, a state agency called the Oregon Progress Board did its own survey on hunger. It found that only about 2.9% of state households faced hunger in any year, half the figure culled from United States Department of Agriculture surveys. But the lower figure was discounted. Food-bank managers say the federal surveys were more accurate; but John Charles, a policy analyst at a conservative Oregon think-tank, thinks that political pressure from "hunger-advocacy" groups had an effect.

If hunger is a real problem, it certainly needs defining. Some studies measure it as the inability to buy anything but cheap food, or mere uncertainty about where the next meal is coming from. Food banks, too, may create a need as much as fill one—after all, most did not exist before the 1980s, and their growth may be driven as much by supply as demand. That hunger should be an issue at all in the waddling, all-you-can-eat United States strikes even hunger-watchers as ironic. Hunger certainly exists, but its true prevalence, in Oregon and elsewhere, remains an open question.

Source: From "A State Going Hungry," The Economist, *June 5, 2003. Reprinted by permission.*

TABLE 16.5 Percentage of Different Assets Owned by Households, 1998 Survey of Consumer Finances

PERCENTAGE OF OWNERS	COMMON STOCK EXCLUDING PENSIONS	ALL COMMON STOCK	NONEQUITY FINANCIAL ASSETS	HOUSING EQUITY	NET WORTH
Top .5%	41.4	37.0	24.2	10.2	25.6
Top 1%	53.2	47.7	32.0	14.8	34.0
Top 10%	91.2	86.2	72.2	50.7	68.9
Bottom 80%	1.7	4.1	14.0	29.3	18.5

Source: James Poterba, "Stock Market Wealth and Consumption," *Journal of Economic Perspectives,* 14(2), 99–118, Spring 2000. Courtesy of American Economic Association.

vate entrepreneurs and investors. Others believe that too much inequality can undermine democracy and lead to social conflict. Many of the arguments for and against income redistribution, discussed in the next section, apply equally well to wealth redistribution.

THE REDISTRIBUTION DEBATE

Debates about the role of government in correcting for inequity in the distribution of income revolve around philosophical and practical issues. *Philosophical* issues deal with the "ideal." What should the distribution of income be if we could give it any shape we desired? What is "fair"? What is "just"? *Practical* issues deal with what is, and what is not, possible. Suppose we wanted zero poverty. How much would it cost, and what would we sacrifice? When we take wealth or income away from higher-income people and give it to lower-income people, do we destroy incentives? What are the effects of this kind of redistribution?

Policy makers must deal with both kinds of issues, but it seems logical to confront the philosophical issues first. If you do not know where you want to go, you cannot talk very well about how to get there or how much it costs. You may find that you do not want to go anywhere at all. Many respected economists and philosophers argue quite convincingly that the government should *not* redistribute income.

ARGUMENTS AGAINST REDISTRIBUTION

Those who argue against government redistribution believe that the market, when left to operate on its own, is fair. This argument rests on the proposition that "one is entitled to the fruits of one's efforts."[3] Remember that if market theory is correct, rewards paid in the market are linked to productivity. In other words, labor and capital are paid in accordance with the value of what they produce.

This view also holds that property income—income from land or capital—is no less justified than labor income. All factors of production have marginal products. Capital owners receive profits or interest because the capital they own is productive.

The argument against redistribution also rests on the principles behind "freedom of contract" and the protection of property rights. When I agree either to sell my labor or to commit my capital to use, I do so freely. In return I contract to receive payment, which becomes my "property." When a government taxes me and gives my income to someone else, that action violates these two basic rights.

The more common arguments against redistribution are not philosophical. Instead, they point to more practical problems. First, it is said that taxation and transfer programs interfere with the basic incentives provided by the market. Taxing higher-income people reduces their incentive to work, save, and invest. Taxing the "winners" of the economic game also discourages risk taking. Furthermore, providing transfers to those at the bottom reduces their incentive to work as well. All of this leads to a reduction in total output that is the "cost" of redistribution.

[3]Powerful support for this notion of "entitlement" can be found in the works of the seventeenth-century English philosophers Thomas Hobbes and John Locke.

Another practical argument against redistribution is that it does not work. Some critics see the rise in the poverty rate during the early 1980s, again in the early 1990s, and yet again between 2001 and 2004, as an indication that antipoverty programs simply drain money without really helping the poor out of poverty. Whether or not these programs actually help people out of poverty, the charge of bureaucratic inefficiency in administration always exists. Social programs must be administered by people who must be paid. The Department of Health and Human Services employs over 120,000 people to run the Social Security system, process Medicaid claims, and so forth. Some degree of waste and inefficiency is inevitable in any sizable bureaucracy.

ARGUMENTS IN FAVOR OF REDISTRIBUTION

The argument most often used in favor of redistribution is that a society as wealthy as the United States has a moral obligation to provide all its members with the necessities of life. The Constitution does carry a guarantee of the "right to life." In declaring war on poverty in 1964, President Lyndon Johnson put it this way:

> There will always be some Americans who are better off than others. But it need not follow that the "poor are always with us." . . . It is high time to redouble and to concentrate our efforts to eliminate poverty. . . . We know what must be done and this nation of abundance can surely afford to do it.[4]

Many people, often through no fault of their own, find themselves left out. Some are born with mental or physical problems that severely limit their ability to "produce." Then, there are children. Even if some parents can be held accountable for their low incomes, do we want to punish innocent children for the faults of their parents and thus perpetuate the cycle of poverty? The elderly, without redistribution of income, would have to rely exclusively on savings to survive once they retire, and many conditions can lead to inadequate savings. Should the victims of bad luck be doomed to inevitable poverty? Illness is perhaps the best example. The accumulated savings of very few can withstand the drain of extraordinary hospital and doctors' bills and the exorbitant cost of nursing home care.

Proponents of redistribution refute "practical" arguments against it by pointing to studies that show little negative effect on the incentives of those who benefit from transfer programs. For many—children, the elderly, the mentally ill—incentives are irrelevant, they say, and providing a basic income to most of the unemployed does not discourage them from working when they have the opportunity to do so. We now turn briefly to several more formal arguments.

Utilitarian Justice   First put forth by the English philosophers Jeremy Bentham and John Stuart Mill in the late eighteenth and early nineteenth centuries, the essence of the utilitarian argument in favor of redistribution is that "a dollar in the hand of a rich person is worth less than a dollar in the hand of a poor person." The rich spend their marginal dollars on luxury goods. It is easy to spend over $100 per person for a meal in a good restaurant in New York or Los Angeles. The poor spend their marginal dollars on necessities—food, clothing, and medical care. If the marginal utility of income declines as income rises, the value of a dollar's worth of luxury goods is worth less than a dollar's worth of necessity. Thus, redistributing from the rich to the poor increases total utility. To put this notion of **utilitarian justice** in everyday language: Through income redistribution, the rich sacrifice a little and the poor gain a lot.

The utilitarian position is not without problems. People have very different tastes and preferences. Who is to say that you value a dollar more or less than I do? Because utility is unobservable and unmeasurable, comparisons between individuals cannot be easily made. Nonetheless, many people find the basic logic of the utilitarians persuasive.

utilitarian justice The idea that "a dollar in the hand of a rich person is worth less than a dollar in the hand of a poor person." If the marginal utility of income declines with income, transferring income from the rich to the poor will increase total utility.

---

[4]*Economic Report of the President,* 1964.

Social Contract Theory—Rawlsian Justice

The work of Harvard philosopher John Rawls has generated a great deal of recent discussion, both within the discipline of economics and between economists and philosophers.[5] In the tradition of Hobbes, Locke, and Rousseau, Rawls argues that, as members of society, we have a contract with one another. In the theoretical world that Rawls imagines, an original *social contract* is drawn up, and all parties agree to it without knowledge of who they are or who they will be in society. This condition is called the "original position" or the "state of nature." With no vested interests to protect, members of society are able to make disinterested choices.

As we approach the contract, everyone has a chance to end up very rich or homeless. On the assumption that we are all "risk averse," Rawls believes that people will attach great importance to the position of the least fortunate members of society because anyone could end up there. **Rawlsian justice** is argued from the assumption of risk aversion. Rawls concludes that any contract emerging from the original position would call for an income distribution that would "maximize the well-being of the worst-off member of society."

Any society bound by such a contract would allow for inequality, but only if that inequality had the effect of improving the lot of the very poor. If inequality provides an incentive for people to work hard and innovate, for example, those inequalities should be tolerated as long as some of the benefits go to those at the bottom.

Rawlsian justice A theory of distributional justice that concludes that the social contract emerging from the "original position" would call for an income distribution that would maximize the well-being of the worst-off member of society.

The Works of Karl Marx

For decades, a rivalry existed between the United States and the Soviet Union. At the heart of this rivalry was a fundamental philosophical difference of opinion about how economic systems work and how they should be managed. At the center of the debate were the writings of Karl Marx.

Marx did not write very much about socialism or communism. His major work, *Das Kapital* (published in the nineteenth century), was a three-volume analysis and critique of the capitalist system that he saw at work in the world around him. We know what Marx thought was wrong with capitalism, but he was not very clear about what would replace it. In one essay, late in his life, he wrote, "from each according to his ability, to each according to his needs,"[6] but he was not specific about the applications of this principle.

Marx's view of capital income does have important implications for income distribution. In the preceding chapters, we discussed profit as a return to a productive factor: Capital, like labor, is productive and has a marginal product. However, Marx attributed all value to labor and none to capital. According to Marx's **labor theory of value**, the value of any commodity depends only on the amount of labor needed to produce it. The owners of capital are able to extract profit, or "surplus value," because labor creates more value in a day than it is paid for. Like any other good, labor power is worth only what it takes to "produce" it. In simple words, this means that under capitalism labor is paid a subsistence wage.

labor theory of value Stated most simply, the theory that the value of a commodity depends only on the amount of labor required to produce it.

Marx saw profit as an illegitimate expropriation by capitalists of the fruits of labor's efforts. It follows that Marxians see the property income component of income distribution as the primary source of inequality in the United States today. Without capital income, the distribution of income would be much more equal. (Refer again to Table 16.1.)

Although the Soviet Union no longer exists, Marxism remains a powerful force in the world. China, Vietnam, Cuba, and a number of other countries remain Communist, and many believe that the Marxian critique of capitalism was correct even though one version of an alternative has failed.

Income Distribution as a Public Good

Those who argue that the unfettered market produces a just income distribution do not believe private charity should be forbidden. Voluntary redistribution does not involve any violation of property rights by the state.

In Chapter 15, however, you saw there may be a problem with private charity. Suppose people really do want to end the hunger problem. As they write out their checks to charity, they encounter the classic public-goods problem. First, there are free riders. If hunger and starvation are eliminated, the benefits—even the merely psychological benefits—flow to

---

[5]See John Rawls, *A Theory of Justice* (Cambridge, MA: Harvard University Press, 1972).
[6]Karl Marx, "Critique of the Gotha Program" (May 1875), in *The Marx-Engels Reader*, ed. Robert Tucker (New York: W. W. Norton), p. 388.

everyone, whether they contributed or not. Second, any contribution is a drop in the bucket. One individual contribution is so small that it can have no real effect.

With private charity, as with national defense, nothing depends on whether I pay or not. Thus, private charity may fail for the same reason that the private sector is likely to fail to produce national defense and other public goods. People will find it in their interest not to contribute. Thus, we turn to government to provide things we want that will not be provided adequately if we act separately—in this case, help for the poor and hungry.

REDISTRIBUTION PROGRAMS AND POLICIES

The role of government in changing the *distribution of income* is hotly debated. The debate involves not only what government programs are appropriate to fight poverty but the character of the tax system as well. Unfortunately, the quality of the public debate on the subject is low. Usually it consists of a series of claims and counterclaims about what social programs do to incentives instead of a serious inquiry into what our distributional goal should be.

In this section, we talk about the tools of redistributional policy in the United States. As we do so, you will have a chance to assess for yourself some of the evidence about their effects.

FINANCING REDISTRIBUTION PROGRAMS: TAXES

Redistribution always involves those who end up with less and those who end up with more. Because redistributional programs are financed by tax dollars, it is important to know who the donors and recipients are—who pays the taxes and who receives the benefits of those taxes. The issue of which households bear the burden of the taxes collected by government is actually quite complex and requires some analysis. Oftentimes households, firms, and markets react to the presence of taxes in ways that actually shift burdens off those on whom they were intended to fall and onto others.

A perfect example is the corporation tax. Both at the federal level and at the state level in most states, a special tax is levied on corporations in proportion to their profit or net income. Although this tax is levied on certain firms, the burden ultimately falls on households in one or more of a number of ways. The tax may result in higher prices for corporate products; the tax may result in lower wages for corporate employees; or the tax may result in lower profits for owners/shareholders of corporations. The ultimate impact of a tax, or set of taxes, on the distribution of income depends on which households end up bearing the burden after shifting has taken place.

The term *incidence* refers to the ultimate burden distribution of a tax. Chapter 17 illustrates the way in which economic analysis can be used to estimate the ultimate incidence of taxes.

The mainstay of the U.S. tax system is the individual income tax, authorized in 1913 by the Sixteenth Amendment to the Constitution. The income tax is *progressive*—those with higher incomes pay a higher percentage of their incomes in taxes. Even though the tax is subject to many exemptions, deductions, and so forth that allow some taxpayers to reduce their tax burdens, all studies of the income tax show that its burden as a percentage of income rises as income rises.

With the passage of the Tax Reform Act of 1986, Congress initiated a major change in income tax rates and regulations. The reforms were to simplify the tax and make it easier for people to comply with and harder to avoid. In addition, the act reduced the number of tax brackets and the overall progressivity of the rates. The largest reduction was in the top rate, cut from 50 percent to 28 percent in 1986. It also substantially reduced the tax burdens of those at the very bottom by increasing the amount of income one can earn before paying any tax at all.

In 1993, President Clinton signed into law a tax bill that increased the top rate to 36 percent for families with taxable incomes over $140,000 and individuals with taxable incomes over $115,000. In addition, families with incomes of over $250,000 paid a surtax (a tax rate on a tax rate) of 10 percent, bringing the marginal rate for those families to 39.6 percent. Families with low incomes received grants and credits under the plan. On May 28, 2003, President Bush signed a tax law that reduced the top rate to 35 percent and changed a number of other provisions of the tax code. (See Chapter 17 for details.)

The individual income tax is only one tax among many. More important to the individual is the *overall* burden of taxation, including all federal, state, and local taxes. Most studies

TABLE 16.6 Effective Rates of Federal, State, and Local Taxes, 2000 (Taxes as a Percentage of Total Income)

	FEDERAL	TOTAL
Bottom 20%	5.9	28.1
Second 20	11.7	26.3
Third 20	17.4	29.2
Fourth 20	20.1	32.6
Top 20	24.6	33.9
Top 10	25.7	34.5
Top 5	26.6	34.9
Top 1	29.1	37.0

Source: Julie-Anne Cronin, U.S. Department of the Treasury, OTA paper 85, and authors' estimate.

Social Security system
The federal system of social insurance programs. It includes three separate programs that are financed through separate trust funds: the Old Age and Survivors Insurance (OASI) program, the Disability Insurance (DI) program, and the Health Insurance (HI, or Medicare) program.

public assistance, or welfare Government transfer programs that provide cash benefits to (1) families with dependent children whose incomes and assets fall below a very low level and (2) the very poor regardless of whether or not they have children.

of the effect of taxes on the distribution of income, both before and after the Tax Reform Act, have concluded that the overall burden is roughly proportional. In other words:

All people pay about the same percentage of their income in total taxes.

Table 16.6 presents an estimate of effective tax rates paid in 2000 by families that have been ranked by income. Although some progressivity is visible, it is very slight. The bottom 20 percent of the income earners pay 28 percent of their total incomes in tax. The top 1 percent pay 37.0 percent. We can conclude from these data that the tax side of the equation produces very little change in the distribution of income. (For more on taxes see Chapter 17.)

EXPENDITURE PROGRAMS

Some programs designed to redistribute income or to aid the poor provide cash income to recipients. Others provide benefits in the form of health care, subsidized housing, or food stamps. Still others provide training or help workers find jobs.

Social Security By far the largest income redistribution program in the United States is Social Security. The **Social Security system** is really three programs financed through separate trust funds. The *Old Age and Survivors Insurance (OASI) program*, the largest of the three, pays cash benefits to retired workers, their survivors, and their dependents. The *Disability Insurance (DI) program* pays cash benefits to disabled workers and their dependents. The third, *Health Insurance (HI)*, or Medicare, provides medical benefits to workers covered by OASI and DI and the railroad retirement program. The Social Security system has been credited with substantially reducing poverty among the elderly.

Most workers in the United States must participate in the Social Security system. For many years, federal employees and employees belonging to certain state and municipal retirement systems were not required to participate, but federal employees are now being brought into the system. Today, well over 90 percent of all workers in the United States contribute to Social Security.

Participants and their employers are required to pay a *payroll tax* to the *Federal Insurance Corporation Association (FICA)* to finance the Social Security system. The tax in 2005 was 7.65 percent paid by employers and 7.65 percent paid by employees on wages up to $90,000. Self-employed people assume the entire FICA burden themselves.

You are entitled to Social Security benefits if you participate in the system for 10 years. Benefits are paid monthly to you after you retire or, if you die, to your survivors. A complicated formula based on your average salary while you were paying into the system determines your benefit level. Those who earned more receive a higher level of benefits, but there are maximum and minimum monthly benefits. By and large, low-salaried workers get more out of the system than they paid into it while they were working. High-salaried workers usually get out of the system considerably less than they put in.

The Social Security system is self-financing, but it is different from funded retirement systems. In a *funded system*, deposits (by the employer, the employee, or both) are made to an account in the employee's name. Those funds are invested and earn interest or dividends that accumulate until retirement, when they are withdrawn. Funded retirement plans operate very much like a savings plan that you might set up independently except that you cannot touch the contents until you retire.

In the U.S. Social Security system, the tax receipts from today's workers are used to pay benefits to retired and disabled workers and their dependents today. Currently, the system is collecting more than it is paying out, and the excess is accumulating in the trust funds. This is necessary to keep the system solvent, because after the year 2010 there will be a large increase in the number of retirees and a relative decline in the number of workers. These demographic changes are the result of a high birth rate between 1946 and 1964—the so-called "baby boom." In 2005, 30.4 million retired workers received Social Security benefits and 6.5 million received disability payments.

Public Assistance Next to Social Security, the biggest cash transfer program in the United States is **public assistance**, more commonly called **welfare**. Aimed specifically at the poor, welfare falls into two major categories.

Most welfare is paid in the form of *temporary assistance for needy families.* Benefit levels are set by the states, and they vary widely. In January 2003, the maximum monthly payment to a one-parent family of three was $170 per month in Mississippi, $639 per month in Vermont, and $923 per month in Alaska; the average monthly payment in the United States was $423. To participate, a family must have very low income and virtually no assets. In 2002, there were 5.1 million recipients of Temporary Assistance for Needy Families in the United States. Those who find jobs and enter the labor force lose benefits quickly as their incomes rise. This loss of benefits acts as a tax on beneficiaries, and some argue that it discourages welfare recipients from seeking jobs.

No topics raise passions more than welfare and welfare reform. The issue has been a focal point of "liberal/conservative" name-calling for more than three decades. In 1996, the Congress passed and President Clinton signed a major overhaul of the welfare system in the United States. The name of the program was changed to Temporary Assistance for Needy Families from its former name, Aid to Families with Dependent Children, as of July 1997. The key change mandated that states limit most recipients to no more than 5 years of benefits over a lifetime. Some argue that the result will be a disaster, with some families left with nothing. Others argue that the previous system led to dependency and that there was no incentive to work.

The new legislation provided funds for added services to parents with young children, but leaves a great deal of discretion in states' hands. Only time will tell how it turns out; however, remarkable declines in the Temporary Assistance for Needy Families program (TANF) caseloads occurred between 1994 and 2001. At the end of that year, the average monthly number of TANF recipients was 5.5 million, or 56 percent lower than the Aid to Families with Dependent Children (AFDC) caseload in 1996. From its peak of 14.4 million in March 1994, the number dropped by 64.6 percent to 5.1 million in 2002. Over three-fourths of the reduction in the U.S. average monthly number of recipients since March 1994 occurred following implementation of TANF. These are the largest caseload declines in the history of U.S. public assistance programs.

Supplemental Security Income   The *Supplemental Security Income program (SSI)* is a federal program that was set up under the Social Security Administration in 1974. The program is financed out of general revenues. That is, there is no trust fund, and there are no earmarked taxes from which SSI benefits are paid out.

SSI is designed to take care of the elderly who end up very poor and have no, or very low, Social Security entitlement. In 2005, 7 million people received SSI payments, about half of whom also received some Social Security benefits. The average SSI payment was $437 per month. As with welfare, qualified recipients must have very low incomes and virtually no assets.

Unemployment Compensation   In the first quarter of 2005, governments paid out over $9.5 billion in benefits to 3.3 million recipients. The money to finance this benefit comes from taxes paid by employers into special funds. Companies that hire and fire frequently pay a higher tax rate, while companies with relatively stable employment levels pay a lower tax rate. Tax and benefit levels are determined by the states, within certain federal guidelines.

Workers who qualify for **unemployment compensation** begin to receive benefit checks soon after they are laid off. These checks continue for a period specified by the state. Most unemployment benefits continue for 20 weeks. In times of recession the benefit period is often extended on a state-by-state basis. Average unemployed workers receive only about 36 percent of their normal wages, and not all workers are covered. To qualify for benefits, an unemployed person must have worked recently for a covered employer for a specified time for a given amount of wages. Recipients must also demonstrate willingness and ability to seek and accept suitable employment.

unemployment compensation A state government transfer program that pays cash benefits for a certain period of time to laid-off workers who have worked for a specified period of time for a covered employer.

Unemployment benefits are not aimed at the poor alone, although many of the unemployed are poor. Unemployment benefits are paid regardless of a person's income from other sources and regardless of assets.

Medicaid and Medicare   The largest in-kind transfer programs in the United States are Medicare and Medicaid. The **Medicaid** program provides health and hospitalization benefits to people with low incomes. Although the program is administered by the states, about 57 percent of the cost is borne by the federal government. In 2004, about 44 million people received benefits; total payments exceeded $250 billion.

Medicaid and Medicare In-kind government transfer programs that provide health and hospitalization benefits: Medicare to the aged and their survivors and to certain of the disabled, regardless of income, and Medicaid to people with low incomes.

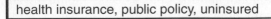

News
ANALYSIS

health insurance, public policy, uninsured   search

○ Further Exploration   ◉ News Analysis

The Drug Wars in 2005

Price-Fixing Cases
in 2005

From a Natural Monopoly
to Near-Perfect
Competition

Footwear Giant Adidas
Buys Reebok in 2005

Externalities Are All
Around Us

Hunger in the United
States in 2003

**The Lack of Health Care
Insurance**

President Bush's
Advisory Panel on
Federal Tax Reform

The Lack of Health Care Insurance

DEBATES ABOUT THE DISTRIBUTION OF income often turn to the fact that some important goods and services, some that we might call necessities, are so expensive that some individuals and families go without them. Perhaps the most obvious one is housing. Homelessness remains a problem in the United States and elsewhere.

One of the biggest problems facing virtually all countries in the world is the high and rapidly growing cost of health care. If you visit the emergency room because of chest pain or have an accident that puts you in the hospital overnight, the bill can easily run over $5,000. If you have a serious injury or disease, the bills can easily run into the hundreds of thousands of dollars.

In the United States if you are very poor, Medicaid covers most of those bills. If you are elderly, Medicare covers most of those bills. If you have employer-sponsored health insurance or can afford to buy your own insurance, you are covered. But millions of working people with no employer-sponsored insurance remain uncovered.

Every year the Census Bureau provides an estimate of the number of households that are uncovered. Here is a summary of their release in 2005.

Income, Poverty, and Health Insurance Coverage in the United States: 2004

■ In 2004, 45.8 million people were without health insurance coverage, up from 45.0 million people in 2003.

■ The historical record is marked by a 12-year period from 1987 to 1998 when the uninsured rate (12.9 percent in 1987) either increased or was unchanged from one year to the next. After peaking at 16.3 percent in 1998, the rate fell for two years in a row to 14.2 percent in 2000, and the rate increased for three years before stabilizing at 15.7 percent in 2004.

■ The percentage of people covered by employment-based health insurance decreased to 59.8 percent in 2004, from 60.4 percent in 2003.

■ The percentage and number of people covered by government health insurance programs increased between 2003 and 2004, from 26.6 percent and 76.8 million to 27.2 percent and 79.1 million, driven by increases in the percentages and number of people covered by Medicaid, from 12.4 percent and 35.6 million to 12.9 percent and 37.5 million.

■ The percentage and number of children (people under 18 years old) without health insurance in 2004 was 11.2 percent and 8.3 million, both unchanged from 2003.

Source: U.S. Department of Commerce, Economics and Statistics Administration, U.S. Census Bureau, Issued August 2005.

Medicare, which is run by the Social Security Administration, is a health insurance program for the aged and certain disabled persons. Most U.S. citizens over age 65 receive Medicare hospital insurance coverage regardless of their income. In addition, they may elect to enroll in a supplementary medical insurance program under Medicare by paying a premium. Medicare pays only a part of total hospital expenses. When their hospital stay is longer than 60 days, for example, patients are responsible for $130 per day.

In 2004, over 41.7 million aged and disabled were covered by Medicare. Benefit payments reached $303 billion in 2004. Medicare has become a political football in Washington in recent years. Projections using conservative assumptions suggest that in 2009 total annual outlays will reach $500 billion and that the Medicare fund will be exhausted by 2020. As the baby boom generation reaches retirement after 2010, the current system is clearly unsustainable. This was an important issue in the most recent presidential election.

Food Stamps   The Food Stamp program is an antipoverty program fully funded out of general federal tax revenues, with states bearing 50 percent of the program's administrative costs. **Food stamps** are vouchers that have a face value greater than their cost and that can be used to purchase food at grocery stores. The amount by which the face value of the stamps exceeds their cost depends on income and family size. Only low-income families and single persons are eligible to receive food stamps.

food stamps Vouchers that have a face value greater than their cost and that can be used to purchase food at grocery stores.

372

It is generally acknowledged that a thriving black market in food stamps exists. Families that want or need cash can sell their food stamps to people who will buy them for less than face value but more than the original recipient paid for them.

In 2004, there were 24 million participants in the Food Stamp program. The total cost of the program in 2004 was $27 billion.

Housing Programs   Over the years, the federal government and state governments have administered many different housing programs designed to improve the quality of housing for low-income people. The biggest is the Public Housing program, financed by the federal government but administered by local public housing authorities. Public housing tenants pay rents equal to no more than 30 percent of their incomes. In many cases, this means they pay zero. The largest housing program, called "Section 8," provides housing assistance payments to tenants and slightly above-market rent guarantees to participating landlords.

In 2003, there were 33.5 million rental housing units in the United States, of which 1.9 million were in public housing projects. Another 2.2 million received a government rent subsidy.

The Earned Income Tax Credit   An important program that is not well understood by most people is the earned income tax credit (EIC). The program is quite complex but essentially allows lower-income families with children a credit equal to a percentage of all wage and salary income against their income taxes. If the credit exceeds the amount of taxes due, the credit is refundable. To see roughly how the EIC works, consider a family made up of two adults and two children with an income of $11,000 per year, all earned as wages. After the standard deduction and exemptions, such a family would owe no taxes, but it would receive (subject to a number of restrictions) a credit of up to $3,800 refundable. That means the family would actually get a check for $3,800.

While not well known, the EIC program is very large. In 2002, the EIC was claimed by over 28 million households and totaled more than $38 billion.

HOW EFFECTIVE ARE ANTIPOVERTY PROGRAMS?

The number of persons officially classified as poor dropped sharply during the 1960s and early 1970s. Between 1978 and 1983, however, the number of poor increased nearly 45 percent. After falling back between 1983 and 1989, the figure hit 39.3 million in 1994, the highest total since 1964. (The figure fell to 34.6 million in 2002.) This increase is at the center of a great debate over the effectiveness of antipoverty programs.

Some say economic growth is the best way to cure poverty. Poverty programs are expensive and must be paid for with tax revenues. The high rates of taxation to support these programs, critics say, have eroded the incentive to work, save, and invest, slowing the rate of economic growth, and the rise in poverty is evidence that antipoverty programs do not work.

The opposite view is that poverty would be much more widespread without antipoverty programs. Poverty has increased not because of *increasing* programs but because the "real" level of transfer payments has actually *fallen* significantly. In other words, transfer payments have not kept up with rising prices.

Despite the anti–big-government rhetoric of recent years, most of what the government did to change the distribution of income 15 years ago it still does today. The volume of redistribution is less, but most major programs have remained largely intact. Many still argue we do too little. The poverty rate was 12.7 percent in 2004, and homelessness was a serious problem in many U.S. cities.

GOVERNMENT OR THE MARKET? A REVIEW

In Part II (Chapters 6 to 12), you were introduced to the behavior of households and firms in input and output markets. You learned that if all the assumptions of perfect competition held in the real world, the outcome would be perfectly efficient.

As we began to relax the assumptions of perfect competition in Part III (Chapters 13 to 17), we began to see a potential role for government in the economy. Some firms acquire market power and tend to underproduce and overprice. Unregulated markets give private decision makers no incentives to weigh the social costs of externalities. Goods that provide collective benefits may not be produced in sufficient quantities without government involvement. As we saw in this chapter, the final distribution of well-being determined by the unfettered market may not be considered equitable by society.

Remember, however, that government is not a cure for all economic woes. There is no guarantee that public-sector involvement will improve matters. Many argue that government involvement may bring about even more inequity and inefficiency because bureaucrats are often driven by self-interest, not public interest.

SUMMARY

THE UTILITY POSSIBILITIES FRONTIER

1. Even if all markets were perfectly efficient, the result might not be fair. Even in relatively unfettered market economies, governments redistribute income and wealth, usually in the name of fairness, or *equity*.

2. Because utility is neither directly observable nor measurable, most policy discussions deal with the distributions of income and wealth as imperfect substitutes for the concept of "the distribution of well-being."

THE SOURCES OF HOUSEHOLD INCOME

3. Households derive their incomes from three basic sources: (1) from wages or salaries received in exchange for labor (about 64 percent); (2) from property such as capital and land (about 22 percent); and (3) from government (about 14 percent).

4. Differences in wage and salary incomes across households result from differences in the characteristics of workers (skills, training, education, experience, and so on) and from differences in jobs (dangerous, exciting, glamorous, difficult, and so on). Household income also varies with the number of household members in the labor force, and it can decline sharply if members become unemployed.

5. The amount of property income that a household earns depends on the amount and kinds of property it owns. Transfer income from governments flows substantially, but not exclusively, to lower-income households. Except for Social Security, transfer payments are by and large designed to provide income to those in need.

THE DISTRIBUTION OF INCOME

6. The 20 percent of families at the top of the income distribution received 47.6 percent of the money income in the United States in 2002, while the bottom 20 percent earned just 4.2 percent. Income distribution in the United States has remained basically stable over a long period of time.

7. The Lorenz curve is a commonly used graphic device for describing the distribution of income. The Gini coefficient is an index of income inequality that ranges from 0 for perfect equality to 1 for total inequality.

8. Poverty is very difficult to define. Nonetheless, the official poverty line in the United States is fixed at three times the cost of the Department of Agriculture's minimum food budget. In 2005, the poverty line for a family of four was $19,780.

9. Between 1960 and 1970, the number of people officially classified as poor fell from 40 million to 25 million. That number did not change much between 1970 and 1978. Between 1978 and 1983, the number of poor people increased by nearly 45 percent to 35.3 million. In 2001, the figure was 32.9 million.

10. Data on the distribution of wealth are not as readily available as data on the distribution of income. The distribution of wealth in the United States is more unequal than the distribution of income. The wealthiest 10 percent of households own 68.9 percent of all household net worth.

THE REDISTRIBUTION DEBATE

11. The basic philosophical argument against government redistribution rests on the proposition that one is entitled to the fruits of one's efforts. It also rests on the principles of freedom of contract and protection of property rights. More common arguments focus on the negative effects of redistribution on incentives to work, save, and invest.

12. The basic philosophical argument in favor of redistribution is that a society as rich as the United States has a moral obligation to provide all its members with the basic necessities of life. More formal arguments can be found in the works of the utilitarians, Rawls, and Marx.

REDISTRIBUTION PROGRAMS AND POLICIES

13. In the United States, redistribution is accomplished through taxation and through a number of government transfer programs. The largest of these are Social Security, public assistance, supplemental security, unemployment compensation, Medicare and Medicaid, food stamps, and various housing subsidy programs, including public housing.

14. The increase in poverty during the 1980s and 1990s is at the center of a great debate over the effectiveness of antipoverty programs. One view holds that the best way to cure poverty is with economic growth. Poverty programs are expensive and must be paid for with tax revenues. The high rates of taxation required to support these programs have eroded the incentive to work, save, and invest, thus slowing the rate of economic growth. In addition, the rise in poverty is cited as evidence that antipoverty programs do not work. The opposite view holds that without antipoverty programs, poverty would be much worse.

REVIEW TERMS AND CONCEPTS

compensating differentials, 357

economic income, 360

equity, 355

food stamps, 372

Gini coefficient, 361

human capital, 357

labor theory of value, 368

Lorenz curve, 361

Medicaid and Medicare, 371

minimum wage, 358

money income, 361

poverty line, 363

property income, 359

public assistance, or welfare, 370

Rawlsian justice, 368

Social Security system, 370

transfer payments, 359

unemployment compensation, 371

utilitarian justice, 367

utility possibilities frontier, 355

PROBLEM SET

1. One of the issues that is debated in virtually every election is whether or not to raise the minimum wage, which stood at $5.15 per hour in 2005. Assume that you are married with a child living on the minimum wage. By assuming that you pay taxes of about 10 percent of your total pay, how much do you "take home" each month? How much does it cost to rent a "reasonable" apartment near where you live? How much would you have left after paying rent? How much would it cost for other items like food? Work out a hypothetical "budget" for this family.

2. In April 2005, the U.S. House of Representatives voted to repeal the federal gift and estate tax. The Senate failed to vote on the bill because of Hurricane Katrina. The gift and estate tax fell heavily on the highest-income families in the United States. What arguments are there for such a change? What are the counterarguments?

3. By using the data in the following table, create two graphs. The first graph should plot the Lorenz curves for African-American families and white families. The second graph should plot the Lorenz curve for the 1980 "all" data and the Lorenz curve for the 1995 "all" data.

   In each graph, which has the higher Gini coefficient? How do you interpret the result?

PERCENT OF INCOME

	African-American	White	1995 All	1980 All
Lowest fifth	3.2	4.6	4.2	5.1
Second fifth	8.5	10.3	10.0	11.6
Third fifth	15.1	15.8	15.7	17.5
Fourth fifth	24.7	23.0	23.3	24.3
Highest fifth	48.7	46.3	46.9	41.6

4. Between 1996 and 2001, the welfare rolls in the United States fell by 56 percent. What explanations can you offer for this rather dramatic drop?

5. Economists call education "an investment in human capital." Define capital. In what sense is education capital? Investments are undertaken to earn a rate of return. Describe the return to an investment in a college education. How would

you go about measuring it? How would you decide if it is good enough to warrant the investment?

6. Below is a list of establishment categories and average weekly earnings for nonsupervisory employees in a recent year. Using the concepts of "human capital" and "compensating differentials," explain why they might be expected to differ in the ways that they do:

Computer programming	$724.85
Heavy construction firms	535.29
Logging firms	447.02
Gas stations	218.13
Car washes	161.19

7. During the mid-1980s and again between 1995 and 2003, house values and rents rose sharply in California and in the northeastern United States. Homeowners, who have higher incomes on average than renters, benefit from house-price increases and are protected from housing-cost increases. Renters experience rising rents and falling standards of living if incomes do not keep up with housing-cost increases. Using the *Statistical Abstract of the United States*, look up residential rent, home prices, and income levels for your area. What has happened in the last 10 years? Do you think the performance of the housing market in recent years has increased or decreased inequality in your area?

8. New Ph.D.'s in economics entering the job market find that academic jobs (jobs teaching at colleges and universities) pay about 30 percent less than nonacademic jobs such as working at a bank or a consulting firm. Those who take academic jobs are clearly worse off than those who take nonacademic jobs. Do you agree? Explain your answer.

9. Should welfare benefits be higher in California and New York than they are in Mississippi? Defend your answer.

10. Poverty among the elderly has been sharply reduced in the last quarter-century. How has this been accomplished?

11. "Income inequality is evidence that our economic system is working well, not poorly." What arguments might one use to support this opinion of income redistribution policies? When racial or gender disparities are pointed out, how might one respond?

Public Finance: The Economics of Taxation

17

The previous chapters in Part III have analyzed the potential role of government in the economy. Together, those chapters discuss much of the field of *public economics*. In this chapter we make the transition to *public finance*. No matter what functions we end up assigning to government, to do anything at all government must first raise revenues. The primary vehicle that the government uses to finance itself is taxation.

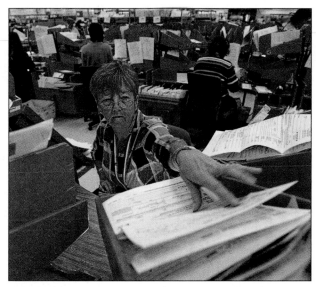

Taxes may be imposed on transactions, institutions, property, meals, and other things, but in the final analysis they are paid by individuals or households.

THE ECONOMICS OF TAXATION

TAXES: BASIC CONCEPTS

To begin our analysis of the U.S. tax system, we need to clarify some terms. There are many kinds of taxes, and tax analysts use a specific language to describe them. Every tax has two parts: a *base* and a *rate structure*. The **tax base** is the measure or value upon which the tax is levied. In the United States, taxes are levied on a variety of bases, including income, sales, property, and corporate profits. The **tax rate structure** determines the portion of the tax base that must be paid in taxes. A tax rate of 25 percent on income, for example, means that I pay a tax equal to 25 percent of my income.

Taxes on Stocks versus Taxes on Flows Tax bases may be either stock measures or flow measures. The local property tax is a tax on the value of residential, commercial, or industrial property. A homeowner, for instance, is taxed on the current assessed value of his or her home. Current value is *stock variable*—that is, it is measured or estimated at a point in time.

Other taxes are levied on *flows*. Income is a flow. Most people are paid on a monthly basis, and they have taxes taken out every month. Retail sales take place continuously, and a retail sales tax takes a portion of that flow. Figure 17.1 diagrams in simple form the important continuous payment flows between households and firms and the points at which the government levies six different taxes.

tax base The measure or value upon which a tax is levied.

tax rate structure The percentage of a tax base that must be paid in taxes—25 percent of income, for example.

377

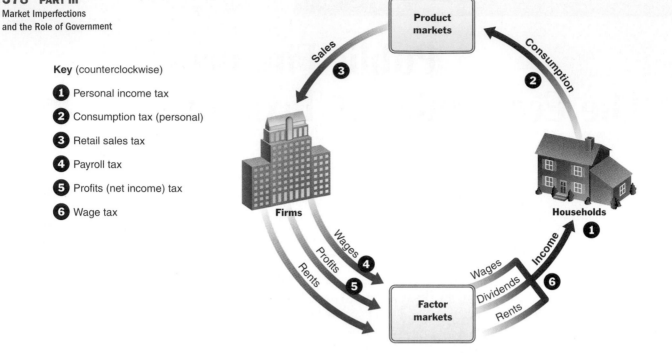

Key (counterclockwise)

1 Personal income tax

2 Consumption tax (personal)

3 Retail sales tax

4 Payroll tax

5 Profits (net income) tax

6 Wage tax

FIGURE 17.1 Taxes on Economic "Flows"

Most taxes are levied on measurable economic flows. For example, a profits, or net income, tax is levied on the annual profits earned by corporations.

Table 17.1 shows the evolution of federal tax receipts since 1960. While the individual income tax has remained around 45 percent of federal receipts since 1960, other taxes have changed share. The corporation income tax, levied on incorporated businesses only, has fallen from 23.2 percent of the total in 1960 to only 11.0 percent of receipts in 2005. The payroll tax, almost all of which is earmarked for the Social Security system and Medicare, has grown from just under 16 percent of the total to nearly 40 percent in 2005.

proportional tax A tax whose burden is the same proportion of income for all households.

progressive tax A tax whose burden, expressed as a percentage of income, increases as income increases.

Proportional, Progressive, and Regressive Taxes   All taxes are ultimately paid out of income. A tax whose burden is a constant proportion of income for all households is a **proportional tax**. A tax of 20 percent on all forms of income, with no deductions or exclusions, is a proportional tax.

A tax that exacts a higher proportion of income from higher-income households than from lower-income households is a **progressive tax**. Because its rate structure increases with income, the U.S. individual income tax is a progressive tax. Under current law, a family with

TABLE 17.1 Federal Government Receipts 1960–2005 (billions of dollars)

	INDIVIDUAL INCOME TAX	CORPORATION INCOME TAX	SOCIAL INSUR. PAYROLL TAXES	EXCISE TAXES	OTHER RECEIPTS	TOTAL
1960	40.7	21.5	14.7	11.7	3.9	92.5
%	**44.0**	**23.2**	**15.9**	**12.6**	**4.2**	**100**
1970	90.4	32.8	44.4	15.7	9.5	192.8
%	**46.9**	**17.0**	**23.0**	**8.1**	**4.9**	**100**
1980	244.1	64.6	157.8	24.3	26.3	517.1
%	**47.2**	**12.5**	**30.1**	**4.7**	**5.1**	**100**
1990	466.9	93.5	380.0	35.3	56.2	1,032.0
%	**45.2**	**9.1**	**36.8**	**3.4**	**5.4**	**100**
2005*	893.7	226.5	773.7	74.0	84.8	2053.0
%	**43.5**	**11.0**	**37.7**	**3.6**	**4.1**	**100**

*OMB estimate
Source: United States, Office of Management and Budget. Percentages may not add to 100 due to rounding.

TABLE 17.2 The Burden of a Hypothetical 5% Sales Tax Imposed on Three Households with Different Incomes

HOUSEHOLD	SAVING INCOME	RATE, %	SAVING	CONSUMPTION	5% TAX ON CONSUMPTION	TAX AS A % OF INCOME
A	$10,000	20	$ 2,000	$ 8,000	$ 400	4.0
B	20,000	40	8,000	12,000	600	3.0
C	50,000	50	25,000	25,000	1,250	2.5

a taxable income of under $14,000 would pay a tax of 10 percent, while a family with an income of $100,000 would pay about 19 percent.

A tax that exacts a lower proportion of income from higher-income families than from lower-income families is a **regressive tax**. *Excise taxes* (taxes on specific commodities such as gasoline and telephone calls) are regressive. The retail sales tax is also a regressive tax. Suppose the retail sales tax in your state is 5 percent. You might assume it is a proportional tax because everyone pays 5 percent. But all people do not spend the same fraction of their income on taxable goods and services. In fact, higher-income households save a larger fraction of their incomes. Even though they spend more on expensive things and may pay more taxes in *dollars* than lower-income families, they end up paying a smaller *proportion* of their incomes in sales tax.

Table 17.2 shows this principle at work in three families. The lowest-income family saves 20 percent of its $10,000 income, leaving $8,000 for consumption. With a hypothetical 5 percent sales tax, the household pays $400, or 4 percent of total income, in tax. The $50,000 family saves 50 percent of its income, or $25,000, leaving $25,000 for consumption. With the 5 percent sales tax, the household pays $1,250, only 2.5 percent of its total income, in tax.

Marginal versus Average Tax Rates

When discussing specific tax or taxes in general, we should distinguish between average tax rate and marginal tax rates. Your **average tax rate** is the total amount of tax you pay divided by your total income. If you earned a total income of $15,000 and paid income taxes of $1,500, your average income tax rate would be 10 percent ($1,500 divided by $15,000). If you paid $3,000 in taxes, your average rate would be 20 percent ($3,000 divided by $15,000). Your **marginal tax rate** is the tax rate you pay on any additional income you earn. If you take a part-time job and pay an additional $280 in tax on the extra $1,000 you've earned, your marginal tax rate is 28 percent ($280 divided by $1,000).

Marginal and average tax rates are usually different. The U.S. individual income tax shows how and why marginal tax rates can differ. Each year, you must file a tax return with the Internal Revenue Service on or before April 15. On that form you first figure out the total tax you are responsible for paying. Next, you determine how much was withheld from your income and sent to the IRS by your employer. If too much was withheld, you get a refund; if not enough, you have to write a check to the government for the difference.

In figuring out the total amount of tax you must pay, you first add up all your income. You are then allowed to subtract certain items from it. Among the things that virtually all taxpayers can subtract are the *personal exemption* and the *standard deduction*.[1] After everything is subtracted, you are left with *taxable income*. Taxable income is then subject to a set of marginal rates that rise with income. Table 17.3 presents the marginal individual income tax rates for 2005.

Suppose you are a single taxpayer who earned $100,000 in 2005. It was a very good year! During 2005 you had tax withheld by your employer. By April 17, 2006, you must file a

regressive tax A tax whose burden, expressed as a percentage of income, falls as income increases.

average tax rate Total amount of tax paid divided by total income.

marginal tax rate The tax rate paid on any additional income earned.

TABLE 17.3 Individual Income Tax Rates, 2005

MARRIED COUPLES FILING JOINTLY

TAXABLE INCOME	TAX RATE
$0–14,600	10%
$14,601–59,400	15%
$59,401–119,950	25%
$119,951–182,800	28%
$182,801–326,450	33%
More than $326,450	35%

SINGLE TAXPAYERS

TAXABLE INCOME	TAX RATE
$0–7,300	10%
$7,301–29,700	15%
$29,701–71,950	25%
$71,951–150,150	28%
$150,151–326,450	33%
More than $326,450	35%

Source: The Internal Revenue Service.

---

[1]Deductions and exemptions have no definition other than that they are amounts that you are allowed to subtract from income before figuring your tax. In 2005, a single taxpayer could subtract a *personal exemption* of $3,200. A married couple could subtract twice that amount plus $3,200 for every dependent child in the family. If your parents claim you as a dependent, you cannot claim an exemption for yourself when you file as an individual. Taxpayers in 2005 were also permitted to subtract either a *standard deduction* of $5,000 ($10,000 for a married couple) or itemized deductions if they exceeded $5,000. Expenditures that can be itemized and deducted include extraordinary medical expenses, state and local income and property taxes, mortgage interest paid, and charitable contributions. The standard deduction is larger for those who are over 65 and/or blind.

return to see if your employer withheld too much or too little. Rushing to meet the deadline, you must do the following calculations, which are summarized in Table 17.4.

First, you take your total income, $100,000, and subtract the personal exemption ($3,200) and the standard deduction ($5,000), leaving "Taxable Income" of $91,800. To figure the tax, in principle, four separate calculations are involved.[2] The first $7,300 is taxed at 10 percent (see Table 17.3). The tax on this amount is simply .10 × $7,300, or $730.

The second "slice" of income, between $7,300 and $29,700, is taxed at 15 percent. The difference between $7,300 and $29,700 is $22,400. The tax on this amount is .15 × $22,400, or $3,360. The third "slice" of income, between $29,700 and $71,950, is taxed at 25 percent. The difference between $29,700 and $71,950 is $42,250. The tax on this amount is .25 × $42,250, or $10,562. Finally, the last "slice" of income, from $71,950 up to $91,800, or $19,850, is taxed at 28 percent. The tax on this amount is .28 × $19,850 or $5,558. Thus, the total tax due is $730 + $3,360 + $10,562 + $5,558 = $20,210. You now check to see if the amount withheld by your employer was too little or too much. If you paid too much, you get a refund; if you did not pay enough, you must send Uncle Sam a check for the shortfall by April 17!

You can now see the difference between average and marginal tax rates. Your average rate in 2005 was $20,210 as a percentage of $100,000, or 20.2 percent. But note that any *additional* income that you might have earned up to $150,150 would be taxed at 28 percent because it is simply more income over $71,950.

How Much Does a Deduction Save You in Taxes? As you saw in the example, you were allowed to subtract $5,000 from your income as a "standard deduction." However, you may be able to do better (that is, pay less tax) if you can come up with "itemized deductions" in excess of $5,000. Taxpayers may deduct income taxes paid to a state, charitable contributions to qualifying organizations, real estate taxes, and interest paid on a mortgage to finance the purchase of a home, as well as other items.

For many taxpayers, itemized deductions are much higher than the standard deduction. Let's say that you paid $7,700 in interest on your condo loan in 2005. Your local property tax on the condo was $2,300, you paid state income taxes of $3,800, and gave $2,000 to your church. Your total deductions are equal to $15,800, which is $10,800 more than the standard deduction of $5,000.

As a result, your taxable income is reduced by $10,800: from $91,800 (see Table 17.4) to $81,000. Now if you figure the tax on $81,000, it is $17,186 instead of $20,210. You can work through the calculations in Table 17.4 to verify this. Your taxes have been reduced by $3,024. If you perform the calculations, you will see that the only thing that has changed is the amount of income taxed at the 28 percent rate. By increasing the amount that I deduct by

---

TABLE 17.4 Tax Calculations for a Single Taxpayer Who Earned $100,000 In 2005

Total income	$100,000
−Personal exemption	3,200
−Standard deduction	5,000
= Taxable income	$ 91,800
Tax Calculation	
0–$7,300 taxed at 10% = 7,300 × .10 =	$730
$7,300–$29,700 taxed at 15% = ($29,700 − $7,300) × .15 = $22,400 × .15 =	$ 3,360
$29,700–$71,950 taxed at 25% = ($71,950 − $29,700) × .25 = $42,250 × .25 =	$ 10,562
Income over $71,950 taxed at 28% = ($91,800 − $71,950) × .28 = $19,850 × .28 =	$5,558
Total tax	$ 20,210
Average tax rate	20.2%
Marginal tax rate	28%

---

[2]Taxpayers do not have to do these calculations. Rather, filers simply look up the tax due for their particular income level in the tax table that accompanies their tax form package. Many use commercial software like Turbo Tax.

$10,800, I reduce my taxes by exactly 28 percent of that amount! That is, my tax savings is $3,024, which is 28 percent of $10,800.

Note that because *marginal* dollars of income are subject to a 28 percent tax rate, any reduction of my taxable income through an additional deduction saves me a tax of 28 percent of that amount. If I were to give an extra $1,000 to the Red Cross, a qualifying charity, I would save $280 (28 percent) in taxes.

Some people complain that high-income households receive a bigger benefit from deductions. For example, if a single person with very high income—let's say over $400,000— gave the same contribution of $1,000, she would save $350 (35 percent in taxes). The highest rate applied to income in the highest bracket is 35 percent. If another person had a taxable income of only $20,000, the same $1,000 charitable contribution would save her only $150, because she would face a marginal rate of only 15 percent.

This example gives you just a taste of the U.S. Individual Income Tax. It is a very complex tax, and most people need help in figuring out how to comply with the law. One of the top priorities of the each of the past five presidents of the United States has been to simplify the tax code, and while the Tax Reform Act of 1986 made some progress, the code seems to get more complex with every passing year.

Marginal tax rates influence behavior. Decisions about how much to work depend on how much of the added income you get to take home. Similarly, a firm's decision about how much to invest depends in part on the additional, or marginal, profits that the investment project would yield after tax.

TAX EQUITY

One of the criteria for evaluating the economy that we defined in Chapter 1 (and returned to in Chapter 16) was fairness, or *equity*. Everyone agrees that tax burdens should be distributed fairly, that all of us should pay our "fair share" of taxes, but there is endless debate about what constitutes a fair tax system.

One theory of fairness is called the **benefits-received principle**. Dating back to the eighteenth-century economist Adam Smith and earlier writers, the benefits-received principle holds that taxpayers should contribute to government according to the benefits they derive from public expenditures. This principle ties the tax side of the fiscal equation to the expenditure side. For example, the owners and users of cars pay gasoline and automotive excise taxes, which are paid into the Federal Highway Trust Fund to build and maintain the federal highway system. The beneficiaries of public highways are thus taxed in rough proportion to their use of those highways.

The difficulty with applying the benefits principle is that the bulk of public expenditures are for public goods—national defense, for example. The benefits of public goods fall collectively on all members of society, and there is no way to determine what value individual taxpayers receive from them.

A different principle, and one that has dominated the formulation of tax policy in the United States for decades, is the **ability-to-pay principle**. This principle holds that taxpayers should bear tax burdens in line with their ability to pay. Here the tax side of the fiscal equation is viewed separately from the expenditure side. Under this system, the problem of attributing the benefits of public expenditures to specific taxpayers or groups of taxpayers is avoided.

benefits-received principle A theory of fairness holding that taxpayers should contribute to government (in the form of taxes) in proportion to the benefits that they receive from public expenditures.

ability-to-pay principle A theory of taxation holding that citizens should bear tax burdens in line with their ability to pay taxes.

Horizontal and Vertical Equity If we accept the idea that ability to pay should be the basis for the distribution of tax burdens, two principles follow. First, the principle of *horizontal equity* holds that those with equal ability to pay should bear equal tax burdens. Second, the principle of *vertical equity* holds that those with greater ability to pay should pay more.

Although these notions seem appealing, we must have answers to two interdependent questions before they can be meaningful. First, how is ability to pay measured? What is the "best" tax base? Second, if A has a greater ability to pay than B, *how much* more should A contribute?

WHAT IS THE "BEST" TAX BASE?

The three leading candidates for best tax base are *income*, *consumption*, and *wealth*. Before we consider each as a basis for taxation, let us see what they mean.

Income—to be precise, *economic income*—is anything that enhances your ability to command resources. The technical definition of economic income is the value of what you consume plus any change in the value of what you own:

> Economic Income = Consumption + Change in Net Worth

This broad definition is essentially consumption + saving but it includes many items not counted by the Internal Revenue Service and some items the Census Bureau does not include in its definition of "money income." Economic income includes all money receipts, whether from employment, interest on savings, dividends, profits, or transfers from the government. It also includes the value of benefits not received in money form, such as medical benefits, employer retirement contributions, paid country club memberships, and so forth. Increases or decreases in the value of stocks or bonds, whether or not they are "realized" through sale, are part of economic income. For income tax purposes, capital gains (increases in the value of assets, like shares of stock) count as income only when they are realized, but for purposes of defining economic income, all increases in asset values count, whether they are realized or not.

A few other items that we do not usually think of as income are included in a comprehensive definition of income. If I own my house outright and live in it rent free, income flows from my house just as interest flows from a bond or profit from a share of stock. By owning the house, I enjoy valuable housing benefits that I would otherwise have to pay rent for. I am my own landlord and I am, in essence, earning my own rent. Other components of economic income include any gifts and bequests received and food grown at home.

> In economic terms, income is income, regardless of source and use.

Consumption is the total value of things that a household consumes in a given period.

Wealth, or *net worth*, is the value of all the things you own after your liabilities are subtracted. If you were to sell off today everything of value you own—stocks, bonds, houses, cars, and so forth—at their current market prices and pay off all your debts—loans, mortgages, and so forth—you would end up with your net worth.

> Net worth = Assets − Liabilities

Remember, income and consumption are *flow* measures. We speak of income per month or per year. Wealth and net worth are *stock* measures at a point in time.

For years, conventional wisdom among economists held that income was the best measure of ability to pay taxes. Many who feel that consumption is a better measure have recently challenged that assumption. The following arguments are not just arguments about fairness and ability to pay; they are also arguments about the best base for taxation.

Remember as you proceed that the issue is which *base* is the best base, not which *tax* is the best tax or whether taxes ought to be progressive or regressive. Sales taxes are regressive, but it is possible to have a personal consumption tax that is progressive. Under such a system, individuals would report their income as they do now, but all documented saving would be deductible. The difference between income and saving is a measure of personal consumption that could be taxed with progressive rates.

Consumption as the Best Tax Base   The view favoring consumption as the best tax base dates back to at least the seventeenth-century English philosopher Thomas Hobbes, who argued that people should pay taxes in accordance with "what they actually take out of the common pot, not what they leave in." The standard of living, the argument goes, depends not on income but on how much income is spent. If we want to redistribute well-being, therefore, the tax base should be consumption, because consumption is the best measure of well-being.

A second argument with a distinguished history dates back to work done by Irving Fisher in the early part of the last century. Fisher and many others have argued that a tax on income discourages saving by taxing savings twice. A story told originally by Fisher illustrates this theory nicely.[3]

Suppose Alex builds a house for Frank. In exchange Frank pays Alex $10,000 and gives him an orchard containing 100 apple trees. Alex spends the $10,000 today, but he saves the orchard, and presumably he will consume or sell the fruit it bears every year in the future. At year's end the state levies a 10 percent tax on Alex's total income, which includes the $10,000 and the orchard. First, the government takes 10 percent of the $10,000, which is 10 percent of Alex's consumption. Second, it takes 10 percent of the orchard—10 trees—which is 10 percent of Alex's saving. If this is all the government did, there would be no double taxation of saving. If, however, the income tax is also levied in the following year, Alex will be taxed on the income generated by the 90 trees that he still owns. If the income tax is levied in the year after that, Alex will again be taxed on the income generated by his orchard, and so on. The income tax is thus taxing Alex's saving more than once. To tax the orchard fairly, the system should take 10 percent of the trees *or* 10 percent of the fruit going forward . . . *but not both!* To avoid the double taxation of savings, either the original savings of 100 trees should not be taxed or the income generated from the after-tax number of trees (90) should not be taxed.

Alex's orchard.

The same logic can be applied to cash savings. Suppose the income tax rate is 25 percent and you earn $20,000. Out of the $20,000 you consume $16,000 and save $4,000. At the end of the year, you owe the government 25 percent of your total income, or $5,000. You can think of this as a tax of 25 percent on consumption ($4,000) and 25 percent on savings ($1,000). Why, then, do we say that the income tax is a double tax on savings? To see why, you have to think about the $4,000 that is saved.

If you save $4,000, you will no doubt put it to some use. Saving possibilities include putting it in an interest-bearing account or buying a bond with it. If you do either, you will earn interest that you can consume in future years. In fact, when we save and earn interest we are spreading some of our present earnings over future years of consumption. Just as the orchard yields future fruit, the bond yields future interest, which is considered income in the year it is earned and is taxed as such. The only way you can earn that future interest income is by leaving your money tied up in the bond or the account. You can consume the $4,000 today *or* you can have the future flow of interest; you can't have both. Yet both are taxed!

Taxing consumption is also more efficient than taxing income. As you will see later, a tax that distorts economic choices creates *excess burdens*. By double-taxing savings, an income tax distorts the choice between consumption and saving, which is really the choice between present consumption and future consumption. Double-taxing also tends to reduce the saving rate and the rate of investment—and ultimately the rate of economic growth.

Income as the Best Tax Base   Your ability to pay is your ability to command resources, and many argue that your income is the best measure of your capacity to command resources today. According to proponents of income as a tax base, you should be taxed not on what you actually draw out of the common pot, but rather on the basis of your *ability* to draw from that pot. In other words, your decision to save or consume is no different from your decision to buy apples, to go out for dinner, or to give money to your mother. It is your *income* that enables you to do all these things, and it is income that should be taxed, regardless of its sources and regardless of how you use it. Saving is just another use of income.

If income is the best measure of ability to pay, the double taxation argument doesn't hold water. An income tax taxes savings twice only if consumption is the measure used to gauge a person's ability to pay. It does not do so if income is the measure used. Acquisition of the orchard enhances your ability to pay today; a bountiful crop of fruit enhances your ability to pay when it is produced. Interest income is no different from any other form of income; it too enhances your ability to pay. Taxing both is thus fair.

---

[3]Irving Fisher and Herbert Fisher, *Constructive Income Taxation: A Proposal for Reform* (New York: Harper, 1942), Ch. 8, p. 56.

Wealth as the Best Tax Base Still others argue that the real power to command resources comes not from any single year's income but from accumulated wealth. Aggregate net worth in the United States is many times larger than aggregate income.

If two people have identical annual incomes of $10,000, but one also has an accumulated net worth of $1 million, is it reasonable to argue that these two people have the same ability to pay, or that they should pay equal taxes? Most people would answer no.

Those who promote a wealth-based system also argue that the only real way to redistribute economic power is to tax the very high concentrations of wealth. Of course, it is important to note that if income is already taxed, a wealth tax in essence taxes the same dollars again.

No Simple Answer Recall that these arguments are about the definition of "horizontal equity": What is the single best measure of ability to pay? In fact, policy debates about the system of taxes in the United States or in any other country involve much more. Virtually every country in the world has a system of taxation that taxes all three bases. In the United States, for example, there are sales and excise taxes (consumption taxes), the Federal Gift and Estate Tax (a wealth tax), the Individual Income Tax, and the local property tax (another wealth tax).

It is important to point out that for many taxpayers, the Individual Income Tax in the United States is probably closer to being a consumption tax than an income tax since much of household savings can be deducted from income before the tax is figured. The tax code (or law) is full of subsidies and incentives. Among the most significant incentives built into the system are provisions designed to encourage people to save. For example, an important exclusion from income for purposes of defining the income tax base is employers' contributions to employee pension accounts. For many workers, retirement is in part financed by payments from pension funds. As long as a person is working, many employers will make deposits or match employee deposits to retirement or pension accounts. Those contributions are part of a household's economic income and part of household savings, but they are not taxed. Recall that income is essentially consumption plus savings (change in net worth). In addition, deposits to specific kinds of accounts (such as Individual Retirement Accounts, or IRAs) can be excluded from income for tax purposes. A good portion of capital gains income (increases in the value of things that a household owns) such as increases in the value of corporate stocks or houses is left out of the base or taxed at lower rates.

There is ongoing debate in the United States about whether it would be better to shift toward a more comprehensive consumption tax. In the fall of 2005, President Bush's Advisory Panel on Federal Tax Reform presented its report on reforming and simplifying the nation's tax code. The commission stopped short of full implementation of a consumption tax such as a national sales tax or a version of a national sales tax called a *value-added tax* (VAT) that is popular in Europe. But the panel did recommend moving to a system that rewards saving and discourages consumption more than the current one. An important goal of the commission was to recommend ways of simplifying the code. (See box on page 394.)

THE GIFT AND ESTATE TAX

estate The property that a person owns at the time of his or her death.

estate tax A tax on the total value of a person's estate.

One of the oldest and most common forms of taxation in the world is the taxation of property held by an individual at the time of his or her death. The property owned at the time of a person's death is called the person's **estate**. An **estate tax** is a tax on the total value of a person's estate regardless of how it is distributed. The United States levies a Gift and Estate Tax on gifts made over a person's lifetime and the value of the person's estate. The Federal Gift and Estate Tax, which raises less than 2 percent of total tax revenues, is scheduled to be phased out in 2010. The law phasing out the Gift and Estate Tax was passed by the Congress in 2001. It gradually raises what is called the unified credit each year until 2010, when the tax is no longer paid. What is strange is that if the Congress and the president do not formally extend the law shutting down the Gift and Estate Tax, it will come back in its pre-2001 form automatically. Most find this outcome to be unlikely. In fact, the House of Representatives voted to repeal the tax in 2005.

Some are strongly opposed to the elimination of the Gift and Estate Tax on the grounds that it is an important progressive element in the tax code. As of 2005, the unified credit effectively exempts estates from the tax that are under two million dollars. Critics say that elimination of the tax will significantly reduce federal revenues precisely when the federal government is having fiscal problems. Those who favor elimination point to the fact that the tax reduces the incentive to save, and thus the nation's saving rate. They also argue that taxing accumulated income that has already been taxed is yet again a form of double taxing.

TAX INCIDENCE: WHO PAYS?

When a government levies a tax, it writes a law assigning responsibility for payment to specific people or specific organizations. To understand a tax, we must look beyond those named in the law as the initial taxpayers.

First, remember the principle of tax analysis: The burden of a tax is ultimately borne by individuals or households; institutions, like business firms or colleges, have no real taxpaying capacity. Taxes paid by a firm ultimately fall on customers, or owners, or workers. Second, the burden of a tax is not always borne by those initially responsible for paying it. Directly or indirectly, tax burdens are often *shifted* to others. When we speak of the **incidence of a tax**, we are referring to the ultimate distribution of its burden.

tax incidence The ultimate distribution of a tax burden.

The simultaneous reactions of many households and/or firms to the presence of a tax may cause relative prices to change, and price changes affect households' well-being. Households may feel the impact of a tax on the sources side or on the uses side of the income equation. (We use the term *income equation* because the amount of income from all *sources* must be exactly equal to the amount of income allocated to all *uses*—including saving—in a given period.) On the **sources side**, a household is hurt if the net wages or profits that it receives fall; on the **uses side**, a household is hurt if the prices of the things that it buys rise. If your wages remain the same but the price of every item that you buy doubles, you are in the same position you would have been in if your wages had been cut by 50 percent and prices hadn't changed. In short:

sources side/uses side The impact of a tax may be felt on one or the other or on both sides of the income equation. A tax may cause net income to fall (damage on the sources side), or it may cause prices of goods and services to rise so that income buys less (damage on the uses side).

> The imposition of a tax or a change in a tax can change behavior. Changes in behavior can affect supply and demand in markets and cause prices to change. When prices change in input or output markets, some households are made better off and some are made worse off. These final changes determine the ultimate burden of the tax.

Tax shifting takes place when households can alter their behavior and do something to avoid paying a tax. Such shifting is easily accomplished when only certain items are singled out for taxation. Suppose a heavy tax were levied on bananas. Initially the tax would make the price of bananas much higher, but there are many potential substitutes for bananas. Consumers can avoid the tax by not buying bananas, and that is what many will do. But as demand drops, the market price of bananas falls and banana growers lose money. The tax shifts from consumers to the growers, at least in the short run.

tax shifting Occurs when households can alter their behavior and do something to avoid paying a tax.

A tax such as the retail sales tax, which is levied at the same rate on *all* consumer goods, is harder to avoid. The only thing consumers can do to avoid such a tax is to consume less of everything. If consumers do, saving will increase, but otherwise there are few opportunities for tax avoidance and therefore for tax shifting.

> Broad-based taxes are less likely to be shifted and more likely to "stick" where they are levied than "partial taxes" are.

THE INCIDENCE OF PAYROLL TAXES

In 2005, 38 percent of federal revenues came from social insurance taxes, also called *payroll taxes*. The revenues from payroll taxes go to support Social Security, unemployment compensation, and other health and disability benefits for workers. (These are discussed in Chapter 16.) Some of these taxes are levied on employers as a percentage of payroll, and some are levied on workers as a percentage of wages or salaries earned.

To analyze the payroll tax, let us take a tax levied on employers and sketch the reactions that are likely to follow. When the tax is first levied, firms find that the price of labor increases. Firms may react in two ways. First, they may substitute capital for the now-more-expensive labor. Second, higher costs and lower profits may lead to a cut in production. Both reactions mean a lower demand for labor. Lower demand for labor reduces wages, and part of the tax is thus passed on (or *shifted to*) the workers, who end up earning less. The extent to which the tax is shifted to workers depends on how workers can react to the lower wages.

We can develop a more formal analysis of this situation with a picture of the market before the tax is levied. Figure 17.2 shows equilibrium in a hypothetical labor market with no payroll tax. Before we proceed, we should review the factors that determine the shapes of the supply and demand curves.

Labor Supply and Labor Demand Curves in Perfect Competition: A Review

Recall that the demand for labor in perfectly competitive markets depends on its productivity. As you saw in Chapter 10, a perfectly competitive, profit-maximizing firm will hire labor up to the point at which the market wage is equal to labor's marginal revenue product. The shape of the demand curve for labor shows how responsive *firms* are to changes in wages.

Recall from Chapter 6 that household behavior and thus the shape of the labor supply curve depend on the relative strengths of income and substitution effects. The labor supply curve represents the reaction of workers to changes in the wage rate. Household behavior depends on the *after-tax* wage that they actually take home per hour of work. In contrast, labor demand is a function of the full amount that firms must pay per unit of labor, an amount that may include a tax if it is levied directly on payroll, as it is in our example. Such a tax, when present, drives a "wedge" between the price of labor that firms face and take-home wages.

Imposing a Payroll Tax: Who Pays?

In Figure 17.2, there were no taxes, and the wage firms paid was the same as the wage workers took home. At a wage of W_0, quantity of labor supplied and quantity of labor demanded were equal, and the labor market was in equilibrium.[4]

But suppose employers must pay a tax of $\$T$ per unit of labor. Figure 17.3 shows a new curve that is parallel to the supply curve but above it by a distance T. The new curve, S_1, shows labor supply as a function of what firms pay. Note that S_1 is not really a new supply curve. Supply is still determined by what workers take home. S_1 simply adds T to the supply

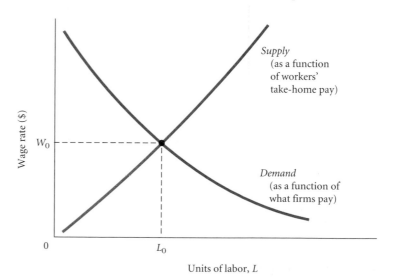

FIGURE 17.2 Equilibrium in a Competitive Labor Market—No Taxes

With no taxes on wages, the wage that firms pay is the same as the wage that workers take home. At a wage of W_0, the quantity of labor supplied and the quantity of labor demanded are equal.

---

[4]Although the supply curve has a positive slope, that slope implies nothing about the actual shape of the labor supply curve in the United States.

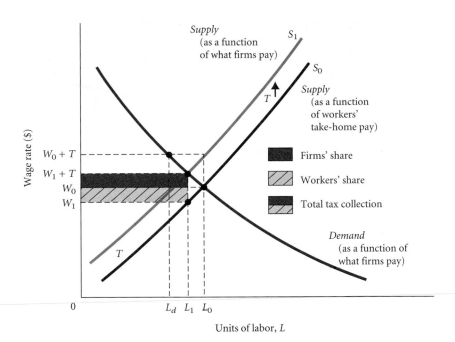

FIGURE 17.3 Incidence of a Per-Unit Payroll Tax in a Perfectly Competitive Labor Market

With a tax on firms of T per unit of labor hired, the market will adjust, shifting the tax partially to workers. When the tax is levied, firms must first pay $W_0 + T$. This reduces the labor demand to L_d. The result is excess supply, which pushes wages down to W_1 and passes some of the burden of the tax on to workers.

curve. Regardless of how the ultimate burden of the tax is shared, there is a difference between what firms pay and what workers take home.

If the initial wage is W_0 per hour, firms will face a price of $W_0 + T$ per unit of labor immediately after the tax is levied. Workers still receive only W_0, however. The higher wage rate—that is, the higher price of labor that firms now face—reduces the quantity of labor demanded from L_0 to L_d, and the firms lay off workers. Workers initially still receive W_0, so that amount of labor supplied does not change, and the result is an excess supply of labor equal to $(L_0 - L_d)$.

The excess supply applies downward pressure to the market wage, and wages fall, shifting some of the tax burden onto workers. The issue is: How far will wages fall? Figure 17.3 shows that a new equilibrium is achieved at W_1, with firms paying $W_1 + T$. When workers take home W_1, they will supply L_1 units of labor; if firms must pay $W_1 + T$, they will demand L_1 units of labor, and the market clears. Quantity supplied again equals quantity demanded.

In this case, then, employers and employees share the burden of the payroll tax. Initially, firms paid W_0; after the tax, they pay $W_1 + T$. Initially, workers received W_0; after the tax, they end up with the lower wage W_1. Total tax collections by the government are equal to $T \times L_1$; geometrically, they are equal to the entire shaded area in Figure 17.3. The workers' share of the tax burden is the lower portion, $(W_0 - W_1) \times L_1$. The firms' share is the upper portion, $[(W_1 + T) - W_0] \times L_1$.

The relative sizes of the firms' share and the workers' share of the total tax burden depend on the shapes of the demand and supply curves. Figure 17.4, parts **a.** and **b.**, shows that the ultimate burden of a payroll tax depends, at least in part, on the *elasticity of labor supply*. If labor supply is very elastic, that is to say, responsive to price, take-home wages do not fall very much, and workers bear only a small portion of the tax. But if labor supply is inelastic, or unresponsive to price, *most* of the burden is borne by workers.

> Workers bear the bulk of the burden of a payroll tax if labor supply is relatively inelastic, and firms bear the bulk of the burden of a payroll tax if labor supply is relatively elastic.

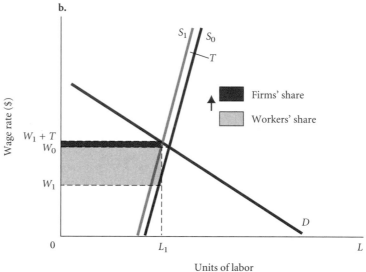

FIGURE 17.4 Payroll Tax with Elastic (a) and Inelastic (b) Labor Supply

The ultimate burden of a payroll tax depends on the elasticities of labor supply and labor demand. For example, if supply is relatively elastic, as in part **a.**, the burden falls largely on employers; if the supply is relatively inelastic, as in part **b.**, the burden falls largely on workers.

Empirical studies of labor supply behavior in the United States suggest that for most of the workforce, the elasticity of labor supply is close to zero. Therefore:

Most of the payroll tax in the United States is probably borne by workers.

The result would be exactly the same if the tax were initially levied on workers rather than on firms. Go back to the equilibrium in Figure 17.3, with wages at W_0. But now assume the tax of $\$T$ per hour is levied on workers rather than firms. The burden will end up being shared by firms and workers in the *exact same proportions*. Initially take-home wages will fall to $W_0 - T$. Workers will supply less labor, creating excess demand and pushing market wages up. That shifts part of the burden back to employers. The "story" is different, but the result is the same.

Table 17.5 presents an estimate of the incidence of payroll taxes (Social Security taxes) in the United States in 2003. This estimate assumes that both the employers' share and employees' share of the payroll taxes are ultimately *borne by employees.*

The payroll tax is regressive for two reasons. First, in 2004 most of the tax (6.2 percent of total wage and salary income levied on both employers and employees) did not apply to wages and salaries above $87,900. The remainder of the total 7.65 percent tax—1.45 per-

TABLE 17.5

Estimated Incidence of Payroll Taxes in the United States in 2003

POPULATION RANKED BY INCOME	TAX AS A % OF TOTAL INCOME
Bottom 20%	7.6
Second 20%	9.8
Third 20%	10.7
Fourth 20%	11.2
Top 20%	8.0
Top 10%	6.7
Top 5%	5.3
Top 1%	3.0

Source: Authors' estimate.

cent—applied to all wage and salary income. Second, wages and salaries fell as a percentage of total income as we move up the income scale. Those with higher incomes earn a larger portion of their incomes from profits, dividends, rents, and so forth, and these kinds of income are not subject to the payroll tax.

Some economists dispute the conclusion that the payroll tax is borne entirely by wage earners. Even if labor supply is inelastic, some wages are set in the process of collective bargaining between unions and large firms. If the payroll tax results in a higher gross wage in the bargaining process, firms may find themselves faced with higher costs. Higher costs either reduce profits to owners or are passed on to consumers in the form of higher product prices.

THE INCIDENCE OF CORPORATE PROFITS TAXES

Another tax that requires careful analysis is the corporate profits tax that is levied by the federal government, as well as by most states. The *corporate profits tax* or *corporation income tax*, is a tax on the profits of firms that are organized as corporations. *Corporations* are firms granted limited liability status by the government. Limited liability means that shareholder/owners can lose only what they have invested. The owners of *partnerships* and *proprietorships* do not enjoy limited liability and do not pay this tax; rather, they report their firms' income directly on their individual income tax returns.

We can think of the corporate tax as a tax on *capital income*, or profits, in one sector of the economy. For simplicity we assume there are only two sectors of the economy, corporate and noncorporate, and only two factors of production, labor and capital. Owners of capital receive profits, and workers (labor) are paid a wage.

Like the payroll tax, the corporate tax may affect households on the sources or the uses side of the income equation. The tax may affect profits earned by owners of capital, wages earned by workers, or prices of corporate and noncorporate products. Once again, the key question is how large these changes are likely to be.

When first imposed, the corporate profits tax initially reduces net (after-tax) profits in the corporate sector. Assuming the economy was in long-run equilibrium before the tax was levied, firms in both the corporate and noncorporate sectors were earning a *normal rate of return*; there was no reason to expect higher profits in one sector than in the other. Suddenly, firms in the corporate sector become significantly less profitable as a result of the tax. (In 2005, for example, the tax rate applicable to most corporations was 35 percent.)

In response to these lower profits, capital investment begins to favor the nontaxed sector because after-tax profits are higher there. Firms in the taxed sector contract in size or (in some cases) go out of business, while firms in the nontaxed sector expand and new firms enter its various industries. As this happens, the flow of capital from the taxed to the nontaxed sector reduces the profit rate in the nontaxed sector: More competition springs up, and product prices are driven down. Some of the tax burden shifts to capital income earners in the noncorporate sector, who end up earning lower profits.

As capital flows out of the corporate sector in response to lower after-tax profits, the profit rate in that sector rises somewhat because fewer firms means less supply, which means higher prices, and so forth. Presumably, capital will continue to favor the nontaxed sector until the after-tax profit rates in the two sectors are equal. Even though the tax is imposed on just one sector, it eventually depresses after-tax profits in all sectors equally.

Under these circumstances, the products of corporations will probably become more expensive and products of proprietorships and partnerships will probably become less expensive. But because almost everyone buys both corporate and noncorporate products, these *excise effects* (that is, effects on the prices of products) are likely to have a minimal impact on the distribution of the tax burden; in essence, the price increases in the corporate sector and the price decreases in the noncorporate sector cancel each other out.

Finally, what effect does the imposition of a corporate income tax have on labor? Wages could actually rise or fall, but the effect is not likely to be large. Taxed firms will have an incentive to substitute labor for capital because capital income is now taxed. This could benefit labor by driving up wages. In addition, the contracting sector will use less labor *and* capital, but if the taxed sector is the capital-intensive corporate sector, the bulk of the effect will be felt by capital; its price will fall more than the price of labor.

The Burden of the Corporate Tax The ultimate burden of the corporate tax appears to depend on several factors: the relative capital/labor intensity of the two sectors, the ease with which capital and labor can be substituted in the two sectors, and elasticities of demand for the products of each sector. In 1962, economist Arnold Harberger, then of the University of Chicago, analyzed this and concluded:

> Owners of corporations, proprietorships, and partnerships all bear the burden of the corporate tax in rough proportion to profits, even though it is directly levied only on corporations.

He also found that wage effects of the corporate tax were small and that excise effects, as we just noted, probably cancel each other out.[5]

Although most economists accept Harberger's view of the corporate tax, there are arguments against it. For example, a profits tax on a monopoly firm earning above-normal profits is *not* shifted to other sectors unless the tax drives profits below the competitive level.

You might be tempted to conclude that because monopolists can control market price, they will simply pass on the profits tax in higher prices to consumers of monopoly products. But theory predicts just the opposite: that the tax burden will remain with the monopolist.

Remember that monopolists are constrained by market demand. That is, they choose the combination of price and output that is consistent with market demand and that maximizes profit. If a proportion of that profit is taxed, the choice of price and quantity will not change. Why not? Quite simply, if you behave so as to maximize profit, and then I come and take half of your profit, you maximize your half by maximizing the whole, which is exactly what you would do in the absence of the tax. Thus, your price and output do not change, the tax is shifted, and you end up paying the tax. In the long run, capital will not leave the taxed monopoly sector, as it did in the competitive case. Even with the tax, the monopolist is earning higher profits than are possible elsewhere.

The great debate about whom the corporate tax hurts illustrates the advantage of broad-based direct taxes over narrow-based indirect taxes. Because it is levied on an institution, the corporate tax is indirect, and therefore it is always shifted. Furthermore, it taxes only one factor (capital) in only one part of the economy (the corporate sector). The income tax, in contrast, taxes all forms of income in all sectors of the economy, and it is virtually impossible to shift. It is difficult to argue that a tax is a good tax if we can't be sure who ultimately ends up paying it.

Table 17.6 presents an estimate of the actual incidence of the U.S. corporate income tax in 2004. The burden of the corporate income tax is clearly progressive, because profits and capital income make up a much bigger part of the incomes of high-income households.

THE OVERALL INCIDENCE OF TAXES IN THE UNITED STATES: EMPIRICAL EVIDENCE

Many researchers have done complete analyses under varying assumptions about tax incidence, and in most cases their results are similar:

> State and local taxes (with sales taxes playing a big role) seem as a group to be mildly regressive. Federal taxes, dominated by the individual income tax but increasingly affected by the regressive payroll tax, are mildly progressive. The overall system is mildly progressive.

TABLE 17.6
Estimated Burden of the U.S. Corporation Income Tax in 2004

POPULATION RANKED BY INCOME	CORPORATE TAX BURDEN AS A % OF TOTAL INCOME
Bottom 20%	0.5
Second 20%	1.0
Third 20%	1.4
Fourth 20%	1.5
Top 20%	4.5
Top 10%	5.7
Top 5%	7.2
Top 1%	9.7

Source: Authors' estimate.

[5]Arnold Harberger, "The Incidence of the Corporate Income Tax," *Journal of Political Economy*, LXX, June 1962.

EXCESS BURDENS AND THE PRINCIPLE OF NEUTRALITY

You have seen that when households and firms make decisions in the presence of a tax that differ from those they would make in its absence, the burden of the tax can be shifted from those for whom it was originally intended. Now we can take the same logic one step further:

> When taxes distort economic conditions, they impose burdens on society that in aggregate exceed the revenue collected by the government.

The amount by which the burden of a tax exceeds the revenue collected by the government is called the **excess burden** of the tax. The *total burden* of a tax is the sum of the revenue collected from the tax and the excess burden created by the tax. Because excess burdens are a form of waste, or lost value, tax policy should be written to minimize them. (Excess burdens are also called *deadweight losses.*)

The size of the excess burden imposed by a tax depends on the extent to which economic decisions are distorted. The general principle that emerges from the analysis of excess burdens is the **principle of neutrality**.

> *Ceteris paribus*, or all else equal,[6] a tax that is neutral with respect to economic decisions is preferred to one that distorts economic decisions.

excess burden The amount by which the burden of a tax exceeds the total revenue collected. Also called deadweight loss.

principle of neutrality All else equal, taxes that are neutral with respect to economic decisions (that is, taxes that do not distort economic decisions) are generally preferable to taxes that distort economic decisions. Taxes that are not neutral impose excess burdens.

In practice, all taxes change behavior and distort economic choices. A product-specific excise tax raises the price of the taxed item, and people can avoid the tax by buying substitutes. An income tax distorts the choice between present and future consumption and between work and leisure. The corporate tax influences investment and production decisions—investment is diverted away from the corporate sector, and firms may be induced to substitute labor for capital.

HOW DO EXCESS BURDENS ARISE?

The idea that a tax can impose an extra cost, or excess burden, by distorting choices can be illustrated by example. Consider a perfectly competitive industry that produces an output, X, using the technology shown in Figure 17.5. Using technology A, firms can produce one unit of output with seven units of capital (K) and three units of labor (L). Using technology B, the production of one unit of output requires four units of capital and seven units of labor. A is thus the more capital-intensive technology.

Technology	Input requirements per unit of output X		Per-unit cost of X $= K(P_K) + L(P_L)$ $P_K = \$2$ $P_L = \$2$	
	K	L		
A	7	3	$20	Least cost
B	4	7	$22	

FIGURE 17.5 Firms Choose the Technology That Minimizes the Cost of Production

If the industry is perfectly competitive, long-run equilibrium price will be $20 per unit of X. If 1,000 units of X are sold, consumers will pay a total of $20,000 for X.

---

[6]The phrase *ceteris paribus* (all else equal) is important. In judging the merits of a tax or a change in tax policy, the degree of neutrality is only one criterion among many, and it often comes into conflict with others. For example, tax A may impose a larger excess burden than tax B, but society may deem A more equitable.

If we assume labor and capital each cost $2 per unit, it costs $20 to produce each unit of output with technology A and $22 with technology B. Firms will choose technology A. Because we assume perfect competition, output price will be driven to cost of production, and the price of output will in the long run be driven to $20 per unit.

Now let us narrow our focus to the distortion of technology choice that is brought about by the imposition of a tax. Assume demand for the good in question is perfectly inelastic at 1,000 units of output. That is, regardless of price, households will buy 1,000 units of product. A price of $20 per unit means consumers pay a total of $20,000 for 1,000 units of X.

Now suppose the government levies a tax of 50 percent on capital. This has the effect of raising the price of capital, P_K, to $3. Figure 17.6 shows what would happen to unit cost of production after the tax is imposed. With capital now more expensive, the firm switches to the more labor-intensive technology B. With the tax in place, X can be produced at a cost of $27 per unit using technology A but for $26 per unit using technology B.

If demand is inelastic, buyers continue to buy 1,000 units of X regardless of its price. (We shall ignore any distortions of consumer choices that might result from the imposition of the tax.) Recall that the tax is 50 percent, or $1 per unit of capital used. Because it takes four units of capital to produce each unit of output, firms—which are now using technology B—will pay a total tax to the government of $4 per unit of output produced. With 1,000 units of output produced and sold, total tax collections amount to $4,000.

But if you look carefully, you will see that the burden of the tax exceeds $4,000. After the tax, consumers will be paying $26 per unit for the good. Twenty-six dollars is now the unit cost of producing the good using the best available technology in the presence of the capital tax. Consumers will pay $26,000 for 1,000 units of the good. This represents an increase of $6,000 over the previous total of $20,000. The revenue raised from the tax is $4,000, but its total burden is $6,000. There is an *excess burden* of $2,000.

How did this excess burden arise? Look back at Figure 17.5. You can see that technology B is less efficient than technology A (unit costs of production are $2 higher per unit using technology B). But the tax on capital has caused firms to switch to this less efficient, labor-intensive mode of production. The result is a waste of $2 per unit of output. The total burden of the tax is equal to the revenue collected plus the loss due to the wasteful choice of technology, and the excess burden is $2 per unit times 1,000 units, or $2,000.

The same principle holds for taxes that distort consumption decisions. Suppose that I prefer to consume bundle X to bundle Y when there is no tax, but choose bundle Y when there is a tax in place. Not only do I pay the tax, I also end up with a bundle of goods that is worth less than the bundle I would have chosen had the tax not been levied. Again, we have the burden of an extra cost.

> The larger the distortion that a tax causes in behavior, the larger the excess burden of the tax. Taxes levied on broad bases tend to distort choices less and impose smaller excess burdens than taxes on more sharply defined bases.

This follows from our discussion earlier in this chapter: The more partial the tax, the easier it is to avoid. An important part of the logic behind the recommendation of the presi-

Technology	Input requirements per unit of output X		Per-unit cost of X $= K(P_K) + L(P_L)$ $P_K = \$2 + \$1$ tax $= \$3$ $P_L = \$2$
	K	L	
A	7	3	$27
B	4	7	$26 → Least cost

FIGURE 17.6 Imposition of a Tax on Capital Distorts the Choice of Technology

If the industry is perfectly competitive, price will be $26 per unit of X when a tax of $1 per unit of capital is imposed. If technology B is used, and if we assume that total sales remain at 1,000 units, total tax collections will be 1,000 × 4 × $1 = $4,000. But consumers will pay a total of $26,000 for the good—$6,000 more than before the tax. Thus, there is an excess burden of $2,000.

dent's tax reform commission in 2005 was that broader bases and lower rates reduce the distorting effects of the tax system and minimize excess burdens.

The only tax that has no excess burden is the lump-sum tax, where the tax you pay does not depend on your behavior or your income or your wealth. Everyone pays the same amount; there is no way to avoid the tax. In 1990, the government of Prime Minister Margaret Thatcher of Great Britain replaced the local property tax with a tax that was very similar to a lump-sum tax. Such a tax is highly regressive, and the perceived unfairness of it led her successor, John Major, to call for its repeal in 1991.

THE PRINCIPLE OF SECOND BEST

Now that we have established the connection between taxes that distort decisions and excess burdens, we can add more complexity to our earlier discussions. Although it may seem that distorting taxes always creates excess burdens, this is not necessarily the case. A distorting tax is sometimes desirable when other distortions already exist in the economy. This is called the **principle of second best**.

> At least two kinds of circumstances favor nonneutral (that is, distorting) taxes: the presence of externalities and the presence of other distorting taxes.

We already examined externalities at some length in Chapter 15. If some activity by a firm or household imposes costs on society that are not considered by decision makers, then firms and households are likely to make economically inefficient choices. Pollution is the classic example of an externality, but there are thousands of others. An efficient allocation of resources can be restored if a tax is imposed on the externality-generating activity that is exactly equal to the value of the damages caused by it. Such a tax forces the decision maker to consider the full economic cost of the decision.

Because taxing for externalities changes decisions that would otherwise be made, it does in a sense "distort" economic decisions. But its purpose is to force decision makers to consider real costs that they would otherwise ignore. In the case of pollution, for example, the distortion caused by a tax is desirable. Instead of causing an excess burden, it results in an efficiency gain. (Review Chapter 15 if this is not clear.)

A distorting tax can also improve economic welfare when there are other taxes present that already distort decisions. Suppose there were only three goods, X, Y, and Z, and a 5 percent excise tax on Y and Z. The taxes on Y and Z distort consumer decisions away from those goods and toward X. Imposing a similar tax on X reduces the distortion of the existing system of taxes. When consumers face equal taxes on all goods, they cannot avoid the tax by changing what they buy. The distortion caused by imposing a tax on X corrects for a preexisting distortion—the taxes on Y and Z.

Let's return to the example described earlier in Figures 17.5 and 17.6. Imposing the tax of 50 percent on the use of capital generated revenues of $4,000 but imposed a burden of $6,000 on consumers. A distortion now exists. But what would happen if the government now imposed an additional tax of 50 percent, or $1 per unit, on labor? Such a tax would push our firm back toward the more efficient technology A. In fact, the labor tax will generate a total revenue of $6,000, but the burden it imposes on consumers would be only $4,000. (It is a good idea for you to work these figures out yourself.)

Optimal Taxation The idea that taxes work together to affect behavior has led tax theorists to search for optimal taxation systems. Knowing how people will respond to taxes would allow us to design a system that would minimize the overall excess burden. For example, if we know the elasticity of demand for all traded goods, we can devise an optimal system of excise taxes that are heaviest on those goods with relatively inelastic demand and lightest on those goods with relatively elastic demands.

Of course, it is impossible to collect all the information required to implement the optimal tax systems that have been suggested. This point brings us full circle, and we end up where we started, with the *principle of neutrality*. All else equal, taxes that are neutral with respect to economic decisions are generally preferable to taxes that distort economic decisions. Taxes that are not neutral impose excess burdens.

principle of second best
The fact that a tax distorts an economic decision does not always imply that such a tax imposes an excess burden. If there are previously existing distortions, such a tax may actually improve efficiency.

President Bush's Advisory Panel on Federal Tax Reform

ON NOVEMBER 1, 2005, PRESIDENT Bush's Advisory Panel on Federal Tax Reform issued its report. The following report in the *New York Times* describes some of the recommendations.

Panel Urges Big Cut in Mortgage Deduction
By DAVID E. ROSENBAUM

President Bush's advisory commission on taxes unanimously recommended a vastly simplified tax system on Tuesday that would limit the deduction of interest payments on large mortgages and erase other tax breaks that many Americans enjoy.

The commission, officially named the President's Advisory Panel on Federal Tax Reform, presented two alternative plans. For individuals, the two plans are similar, but they differ in the way they treat business taxes.

The panel, made up of politicians and tax experts from outside the government, rejected as impractical replacing the income tax with a completely different system like a value-added tax or a national retail sales tax.

In addition to the limits on write-offs for mortgage interest, the main elements of the proposals would abolish the alternative minimum tax, erase deductions for state and local income and property taxes, restrict tax-free employer-paid health insurance, and reduce the deductions that many taxpayers can claim for charitable donations.

Two controversial provisions of the proposed law were (1) elimination of the provision that allows federal taxpayers to deduct state and local taxes from taxable income, and (2) a substantial change in and reduction in the deduction for home mortgage interest paid.

Why eliminate the deduction of state and local taxes? After all, if you pay taxes to a state or a local government, that is income that you do not get. Isn't ability to pay based on "after-tax" income? Clearly people who thought of it that way favored keeping the deduction. But there is a counter-argument. We pay state and local taxes for services that those governments produce for us. Local government, for example, provides police protection, fire protection, and schools. We decide on those budgets, and in a way it is similar to a firm producing a product for us. In the case of a government, deductibility "reduces the price" to taxpayers of services provided by state and local governments. If I and my fellow citizens decide to vote for added school spending, and if I am in the top income tax bracket (which was 35 percent in 2005), each dollar of additional spending costs me only 65 cents! Why? Because for every dollar I am able to deduct, I save 35 cents in tax. This encourages those governments to overspend.

Those who want to disallow the deduction argue the deductibility of home mortgage interest was the largest and most popular of all the provisions of the tax code, and many thought that a proposal to eliminate it would stall the progress of the proposals as they moved through the legislative process. After all, nearly 70 percent of households are home owners and they would, by and large, be hurt. The proposal replaced the deduction with a 15 percent credit. Suppose that I have paid $10,000 in interest this year. That is roughly what I would pay if I had borrowed $160,000 to buy a home. If I were in the 25 percent marginal income tax bracket, I would gain $2,500 from the deduction. But if I got a 15 percent credit, I would only gain $1,500. Recall that a credit is a reduction in taxes, so a $1 credit results in a tax saving of $1. In addition, the proposal called for limits on the deduction by capping the size of the mortgage that would receive full deductibility.

Those in favor of this reduction pointed to inefficient "overinvestment in housing" resulting from the implicit subsidy to home ownership. Those in favor of retaining deductibility pointed to the "external public good" resulting from home ownership. Home owners, it is argued, are better neighbors and citizens because they have a higher stake in the locality.

MEASURING EXCESS BURDENS

It is possible to measure the size of excess burdens if we know something about how people respond to price changes. Look at the demand curve in Figure 17.7. The product originally sold for a price, P_0, equal to marginal cost (which, for simplicity, we assume is constant). Recall that, when input prices are determined in competitive markets, marginal cost reflects the real value of the resources used in producing the product.

To measure the total burden of the tax, we need to recall the notion of consumer surplus from Chapter 4. At any price, some people pay less for a product than it is worth to them. All we reveal when we buy a product is that it is worth *at least* the price being charged. For example, if only one unit of product X were auctioned, someone would pay a price close to D in Figure 17.7. By paying only P_0, that person received a "surplus" equal to $(D - P_0)$. (For a review of consumer surplus and how it is measured, see Chapters 4 and 6.)

Consider what happens when an excise tax raises the price of X from P_0 to $P_1 = P_0 + T$, where T is the tax per unit of X. First, the government collects revenue. The amount of revenue collected is equal to T times the number of units of X purchased (X_1). You can see that $T \times X_1$ is equal to the area of rectangle P_1ABP_0. Second, because consumers must now pay a price of P_1, the consumer surplus generated in the market is reduced from the area of triangle DCP_0 to the area of the smaller triangle DAP_1. The excess burden is equal to the original (pre-tax) consumer surplus *minus* the after-tax surplus *minus* the total taxes collected by the government.

In other words, the original value of consumer surplus (triangle DCP_0) has been broken up into three parts: the area of triangle DAP_1 that is still consumer surplus; the area of rectangle P_1ABP_0 that is tax revenue collected by the government; and the area of triangle ACB that is lost. Thus, the area ACB is an approximate measure of the excess burden of the tax. The total burden of the tax is the sum of the revenue collected and the excess burden: the area of P_1ACP_0.

EXCESS BURDENS AND THE DEGREE OF DISTORTION

The size of the excess burden that results from a decision-distorting tax depends on the degree to which decisions change in response to that tax. In the case of an excise tax, consumer behavior is reflected in elasticity of demand:

> The more elastic the demand curve, the greater is the distortion caused by any given tax rate.

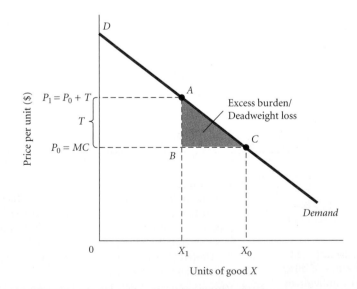

FIGURE 17.7 The Excess Burden of a Distorting Excise Tax

A tax that alters economic decisions imposes a burden that exceeds the amount of taxes collected. An excise tax that raises the price of a good above marginal cost drives some consumers to buy less desirable substitutes, reducing consumer surplus.

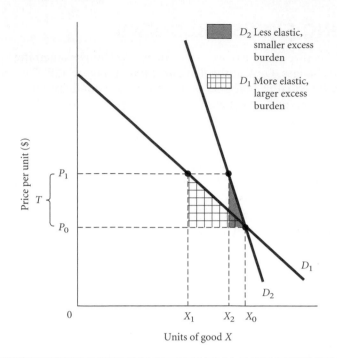

FIGURE 17.8 The Size of the Excess Burden of a Distorting Excise Tax Depends on the Elasticity of Demand

The size of the excess burden from a distorting tax depends on the degree to which decisions or behaviors change in response to it.

Figure 17.8 shows how the size of the consumer response determines the size of the excess burden. At price P_0, the quantity demanded by consumers is X_0. Now suppose that the government imposes a tax of $\$T$ per unit of X. The two demand curves (D_1 and D_2) illustrate two possible responses by consumers. The change in quantity demanded along D_1 (from X_0 to X_1) is greater than the change in quantity demanded along D_2 (from X_0 to X_2). In other words, the response of consumers illustrated by D_1 is more elastic than the response of consumers along D_2.

The excess burdens that would result from the tax under the two assumptions about demand elasticity are approximately equal to the areas of the shaded triangles in Figure 17.8. As you can see, where demand is more responsive (more elastic), the excess burden is larger.

If demand were perfectly inelastic, no distortion would occur, and there would be no excess burden. The tax would simply transfer part of the surplus being earned by consumers to the government. That is why some economists favor uniform land taxes over other taxes. Because land is in perfectly inelastic supply, a uniform tax on all land uses distorts economic decisions less than taxes levied on other factors of production that are in variable supply.

SUMMARY

THE ECONOMICS OF TAXATION

1. Public finance is one of the major subfields of applied economics. A major interest within this subfield is the economics of taxation.

2. Taxes are ultimately paid by people. Taxes may be imposed on transactions, institutions, property, and all kinds of other things, but in the final analysis, taxes are paid by individuals or households.

3. The *base* of a tax is the measure or value upon which the tax is levied. The *rate structure* of a tax determines the portion of the base that must be paid in tax.

4. A tax whose burden is a constant proportion of income for all households is a *proportional tax*. A tax that exacts a higher proportion of income from higher-income households is a *progressive tax*. A tax that enacts a lower proportion of income from higher-income households is a *regressive tax*. In the United States, income taxes are progressive, and sales and excise taxes are regressive.

5. Your average tax rate is the total amount of tax you pay divided by your total income. Your marginal tax rate is the tax rate that you pay on any additional income that you have earned. Marginal tax rates have the most influence on behavior.

6. There is much disagreement over what constitutes a fair tax system. One theory contends that people should bear tax burdens in proportion to the benefits that they receive from government expenditures. This is the *benefits-received principle*. Another contends that people should bear tax burdens in line with their ability to pay. This *ability-to-pay principle* has dominated U.S. tax policy.

7. The three leading candidates for best tax base are income, consumption, and wealth.

TAX INCIDENCE: WHO PAYS?

8. As a result of behavioral changes and market adjustments, tax burdens are often not borne by those initially responsible for paying them. When we speak of the *incidence of a tax*, we are referring to the ultimate distribution of its burden.

9. Taxes change behavior, and changes in behavior can affect supply and demand in markets, causing prices to change. When prices change in input markets or in output markets, some people may be made better off and some worse off. These final changes determine the ultimate burden of a tax.

10. *Tax shifting* occurs when households can alter their behavior and do something to avoid paying a tax. In general, broad-based taxes are less likely to be shifted and more likely to stick where they are levied than partial taxes are.

11. When labor supply is more elastic, firms bear the bulk of a tax imposed on labor. When labor supply is more inelastic, workers bear the bulk of the tax burden. Because the elasticity of labor supply in the United States is close to zero, most economists conclude that most of the payroll tax in the United States is probably borne by workers.

12. The payroll tax is regressive for two reasons. First, in 2004 most of the tax (6.2 percent of total income levied on both employers and employees) did not apply to wages and salaries above $87,900. The remainder of the total 7.65 percent—only 1.45 percent—applied to all wage and salary income. Second, wages and salaries fall as a percentage of total income as we move up the income scale. Those with higher incomes earn a larger portion of their incomes from profits, dividends, rents, and so forth, and these kinds of income are not subject to the payroll tax.

13. The ultimate burden of the corporate tax appears to depend on several factors. One generally accepted study shows that the owners of corporations, proprietorships, and partnerships all bear the burden of the corporate tax in rough proportion to profits, even though it is directly levied only on corporations; that wage effects are small; and that excise effects are roughly neutral. However, there is still much debate about whom the corporate tax "hurts." The burden of the corporate tax is progressive, because profits and capital income make up a much bigger part of the incomes of the high-income households.

14. Under a reasonable set of assumptions about tax shifting, state and local taxes seem as a group to be mildly regressive. Federal taxes, dominated by the individual income tax but increasingly affected by the regressive payroll tax, are mildly progressive. The overall system is mildly progressive.

EXCESS BURDENS AND THE PRINCIPLE OF NEUTRALITY

15. When taxes distort economic decisions, they impose burdens that in aggregate exceed the revenue collected by the government. The amount by which the burden of a tax exceeds the revenue collected by the government is called the *excess burden*. The size of excess burdens depends on the degree to which economic decisions are changed by the tax. The *principle of neutrality* holds that the most efficient taxes are broad-based taxes that do not distort economic decisions.

16. The *principle of second best* holds that a tax that distorts economic decisions does not necessarily impose an excess burden. If previously existing distortions or externalities exist, such a tax may actually improve efficiency.

MEASURING EXCESS BURDENS

17. The excess burden imposed by a tax is equal to the pre-tax consumer surplus minus the after-tax consumer surplus minus the total taxes collected by the government. The more elastic the demand curve, the greater is the distortion caused by any given tax rate.

REVIEW TERMS AND CONCEPTS

ability-to-pay principle, 381

average tax rate, 379

benefits-received principle, 381

excess burden, 391

estate, 384

estate tax, 384

marginal tax rate, 379

principle of neutrality, 391

principle of second best, 393

progressive tax, 378

proportional tax, 378

regressive tax, 379

sources side/uses side, 385

tax base, 377

tax incidence, 385

tax rate structure, 377

tax shifting, 385

PROBLEM SET

1. The president's tax reform commission in 2005 argued for shifting the country's main revenue system closer to being a tax on consumption by expanding opportunities to save tax free. Would you favor such a shift? What are the arguments for and against it?

2. Suppose that in 2006 Congress passed and the president signed a new simple income tax with a flat rate of 25 percent on all income over $25,000 (no tax on the first $25,000). Assume that the tax is imposed on every individual separately. For each of the following total income levels, calculate taxes due and compute the average tax rate. Plot the average tax rate on a graph with income along the horizontal axis. Is the tax proportional, progressive, or regressive? Explain why.
   a. $25,000
   b. $35,000
   c. $45,000
   d. $60,000
   e. $80,000
   f. $100,000

3. Using the tax brackets and rates for 2005 in Table 17.3 and footnote 1, compute the total tax for each of the following. In each case calculate average and marginal tax rates. Assume in each case that the taxpayer chooses the standard deduction.
   a. A single taxpayer earning $35,000
   b. A married couple with two dependent children earning $50,000
   c. A single taxpayer earning $90,000
   d. A married couple with two dependent children earning $110,000

4. A number of specific tax provisions passed the Congress and were enacted into law in 2006. Assume that you were a prospective candidate for Congress in 2006. Write a brief essay describing the changes and explaining why they are good or bad.

5. A citizens' group in the Pacific Northwest has the following statement in its charter:

   "Our goal is to ensure that large, powerful corporations pay their fair share of taxes in this country."

   To implement this goal, the group has recommended and lobbied for an increase in the corporation income tax and a reduction in the individual income tax. Would you support such a petition? Explain your logic.

6. "Taxes imposed on necessities that have low demand elasticities impose large excess burdens because consumers can't avoid buying them." Do you agree or disagree? Explain.

7. For each of the following, do you agree or disagree? Why?
   a. "Economic theory predicts unequivocally that a payroll tax reduction will increase the supply of labor."
   b. "Corporation income taxes levied on a monopolist are likely to be regressive because the monopoly can pass on its burden to consumers."
   c. "All nonneutral taxes are undesirable."

8. In calculating total faculty compensation, the administration of Doughnut University includes payroll taxes (Social Security taxes) paid as a *benefit* to faculty. After all, those tax payments are earning future entitlements for the faculty under Social Security. However, the American Association of University Professors has argued that, far from being a benefit, the employer's contribution is simply a tax and that its burden actually falls on the faculty, even though it is paid by the university. Discuss both sides of this debate.

9. Developing countries rarely have a sophisticated income tax structure like that in the United States. The primary means of raising revenues in many developing countries is through commodity taxes. What problems do you see with taxing particular goods in these countries? (*Hint:* Think about elasticities of demand.)

10. Suppose a special tax were introduced that used the value of one's automobile as the tax base. Each person would pay taxes equal to 10 percent of the value of his or her car. Would the tax be proportional, regressive, or progressive? What assumptions do you make in answering this question? What distortions do you think would appear in the economy if such a tax were introduced?

11. You are given the following information on a proposed "restaurant meals tax" in the Republic of Olympus. Olympus collects no other specific excise taxes, and all other government revenues come from a neutral lump-sum tax. (A lump-sum tax is a tax of a fixed sum paid by all people, regardless of their circumstances.) Assume further that the burden of the tax is fully borne by consumers.

    Now consider the following data:
    - Meals consumed before the tax: 12 million
    - Meals consumed after the tax: 10 million
    - Average price per meal: $15 (not including the tax)
    - Tax rate: 10 percent

    Estimate the size of the excess burden of the tax. What is the excess burden as a percentage of revenues collected from the tax?

Introduction to Macroeconomics

18

Macroeconomics is part of our everyday lives. If the macroeconomy is doing well, few people do not have a job who want one, people's incomes are generally rising, and profits of corporations are generally high. In this type of an economy it is relatively easy for new entrants into the labor force, such as students who have just graduated, to find jobs. On the other hand, if the macroeconomy is in a slump, new jobs are hard to find, incomes are not growing well, and profits are low. Given the large effects that the macroeconomy can have on our lives, it is important that we understand how it works.

We begin by discussing the differences between microeconomics and macroeconomics that we glimpsed in Chapter 1. **Microeconomics** examines the functioning of individual industries and the behavior of individual decision-making units, typically business firms and households. With a few assumptions about how these units behave (firms maximize profits, households maximize utility), we can derive useful conclusions about how markets work, how resources are allocated, and so forth.

Macroeconomics, instead of focusing on the factors that influence the production of particular products and the behavior of individual industries, focuses on the determinants of total national output. Macroeconomics studies not household income but *national* income, not individual prices but the *overall* price level. It does not analyze the demand for labor in the automobile industry but instead total employment in the economy.

Both microeconomics and macroeconomics are concerned with the decisions of households and firms. Microeconomics deals with individual decisions; macroeconomics deals with the sum of these individual decisions. *Aggregate* is used in macroeconomics to refer to sums. When we speak of **aggregate behavior**, we mean the behavior of all households and firms together. We also speak of aggregate consumption and aggregate investment, which refer to total consumption and total investment in the economy.

Because microeconomists and macroeconomists look at the economy from different perspectives, you might expect they would reach somewhat different conclusions about the way the economy behaves. This is true to some extent. Microeconomists generally conclude that markets work well. They see prices as flexible, adjusting to maintain equality between quantity supplied and quantity demanded. Macroeconomists, however, observe that important prices in the economy—for example, the wage rate (or price of labor)—often seem "sticky." **Sticky prices** are prices that do not always adjust rapidly to maintain equality

microeconomics
Examines the functioning of individual industries and the behavior of individual decision-making units—business firms and households.

macroeconomics Deals with the economy as a whole. Macroeconomics focuses on the determinants of total national income, deals with aggregates such as aggregate consumption and investment, and looks at the overall level of prices instead of individual prices.

aggregate behavior The behavior of all households and firms together.

sticky prices Prices that do not always adjust rapidly to maintain equality between quantity supplied and quantity demanded.

microeconomic foundations of macroeconomics The microeconomic principles underlying macroeconomic analysis.

Great Depression The period of severe economic contraction and high unemployment that began in 1929 and continued throughout the 1930s.

between quantity supplied and quantity demanded. Microeconomists do not expect to see the quantity of apples supplied exceeding the quantity of apples demanded, because the price of apples is not sticky. On the other hand, macroeconomists—who analyze aggregate behavior— examine periods of high unemployment, where the quantity of labor supplied appears to exceed the quantity of labor demanded. At such times, it appears that wage rates do not adjust fast enough to equate the quantity of labor supplied and the quantity of labor demanded.

Since about 1970, much work in macroeconomics has been concerned with making macroeconomic analysis consistent with microeconomic postulates—that is, with the idea that firms and households make their decisions along the lines suggested by microeconomic theory. If prices do not appear to equate the quantity supplied and the quantity demanded, for example, macroeconomists now look for solid microeconomic reasons why not. One of the aims of this book is to explain the **microeconomic foundations of macroeconomics**.

THE ROOTS OF MACROECONOMICS

THE GREAT DEPRESSION

Economic events of the 1930s, the decade of the **Great Depression**, spurred a great deal of thinking about macroeconomic issues, especially unemployment. The 1920s had been prosperous years for the U.S. economy. Virtually everyone who wanted a job could get one, incomes rose substantially, and prices were stable. Beginning in late 1929, things took a sudden turn for the worse. In 1929, 1.5 million people were unemployed. By 1933, that had increased to 13 million out of a labor force of 51 million. In 1933, the United States produced about 27 percent fewer goods and services than it had in 1929. In October 1929, when stock prices collapsed on Wall Street, billions of dollars of personal wealth were lost. Unemployment remained above 14 percent of the labor force until 1940.

Classical Models   Before the Great Depression, economists applied microeconomic models, sometimes referred to as "classical" or "market clearing" models, to economy-wide problems. For example, classical supply and demand analysis assumed that an excess supply of labor would drive down wages to a new equilibrium level; as a result, unemployment would not persist.

In other words, classical economists believed that *recessions* (downturns in the economy) were self-correcting. As output falls and the demand for labor shifts to the left, the argument went, the wage rate will decline, thereby raising the quantity of labor demanded by firms, who will want to hire more workers at the new lower wage rate. However, during the Great Depression unemployment levels remained very high for nearly 10 years. In large measure, the failure of simple classical models to explain the prolonged existence of high unemployment provided the impetus for the development of macroeconomics. It is not surprising that what we now call macroeconomics was born in the 1930s.

The Keynesian Revolution   One of the most important works in the history of economics, *The General Theory of Employment, Interest and Money*, by John Maynard Keynes, was published in 1936. Building on what was already understood about markets and their behavior, Keynes set out to construct a theory that would explain the confusing economic events of his time.

Much of macroeconomics has roots in Keynes's work. According to Keynes, it is not prices and wages that determine the level of employment, as classical models had suggested, but instead the level of aggregate demand for goods and services. Keynes believed governments could intervene in the economy and affect the level of output and employment. The government's role during periods when private demand is low, Keynes argued, is to stimulate aggregate demand and, by so doing, to lift the economy out of recession. (See the Further Exploration box, "The Great Depression and John Maynard Keynes.")

RECENT MACROECONOMIC HISTORY

After World War II, and especially in the 1950s, Keynes's views began to gain increasing influence over both professional economists and government policy makers. Governments came to believe they could intervene in their economies to attain specific employment and output goals.

The Great Depression and John Maynard Keynes

Much of the framework of modern macroeconomics comes from the works of John Maynard Keynes, whose *General Theory of Employment, Interest and Money* was published in 1936. The following excerpt by Robert L. Heilbroner provides some insights into Keynes's life and work.

By 1933 the nation was virtually prostrate. On street corners, in homes, in Hoovervilles (communities of makeshift shacks), 14 million unemployed sat, haunting the land. . . .

It was the unemployment that was hardest to bear. The jobless millions were like an embolism in the nation's vital circulation; and while their indisputable existence argued more forcibly than any text that something was wrong with the system, the economists wrung their hands and racked their brains . . . but could offer neither diagnosis nor remedy. Unemployment—this kind of unemployment—was simply not listed among the possible ills of the system: it was absurd, impossible, unreasonable, and paradoxical. But it was there.

It would seem logical that the man who would seek to solve this impossible paradox of not enough production existing side by side with men fruitlessly seeking work would be a Left-winger, an economist with strong sympathies for the proletariat, an angry man. Nothing could be further from the fact. The man who tackled it was almost

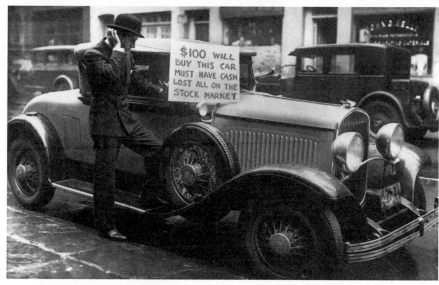

The Great Depression persisted long after the stock market crash in 1929.

John Maynard Keynes.

a dilettante with nothing like a chip on his shoulder. The simple truth was that his talents inclined in every direction. He had, for example, written a most recondite book on mathematical probability, a book that Bertrand Russell had declared "impossible to praise too highly"; then he had gone on to match his skill in abstruse logic with a flair for making money—he accumulated a fortune of £500,000 by way of the most treacherous of all roads to riches: dealing in international currencies and commodities. More impressive yet, he had written his mathematics treatise on the side, as it were, while engaged in Government service, and he piled up his private wealth by applying himself for only half an hour a day while still abed.

But this is only a sample of his many-sidedness. He was an economist, of course—a Cambridge don with all the dignity and erudition that go with such an appointment. . . . He managed to be simultaneously the darling of the Bloomsbury set, the cluster of Britain's most avant-garde intellectual brilliants, and also the chairman of a life insurance company, a niche in life rarely noted for its intellectual abandon. He was a pillar of stability in delicate matters of international diplomacy, but his official correctness did not prevent him from acquiring a knowledge of other European politicians that included their . . . neuroses and financial prejudices. . . . He ran a theater, and he came to be a Director of the Bank

of England. He knew Roosevelt and Churchill and also Bernard Shaw and Pablo Picasso. . . .

His name was John Maynard Keynes, an old British name (pronounced to rhyme with "rains") that could be traced back to one William de Cahagnes and 1066. Keynes was a traditionalist; he liked to think that greatness ran in families, and it is true that his own father was John Neville Keynes, an illustrious enough economist in his own right. But it took more than the ordinary gifts of heritage to account for the son; it was as if the talents that would have sufficed half a dozen men were by happy accident crowded into one person.

By a coincidence he was born in 1883, in the very year that Karl Marx passed away. But the two economists who thus touched each other in time, although each was to exert the profoundest influence on the philosophy of the capitalist system, could hardly have differed from one another more. Marx was bitter, at bay, heavy and disappointed; as we know, he was the draftsman of Capitalism Doomed. Keynes loved life and sailed through it buoyant, at ease, and consummately successful to become the architect of Capitalism Viable.[a]

Source: [a]Reprinted with the permission of Simon & Schuster from *The Worldly Philosophers* by Robert L. Heilbroner. Copyright © 1953, 1961, 1967, 1972, 1980, 1986 by Robert L. Heilbroner. Also reprinted with permission of Penguin Books Limited, U.K.

They began to use their powers to tax and spend, as well as their ability to affect interest rates and the money supply, for the explicit purpose of controlling the economy's ups and downs. This view of government policy became firmly established in the United States with the passage of the Employment Act of 1946. This act established the President's Council of Economic Advisers, a group of economists who advise the president on economic issues. It also committed the federal government to intervening in the economy to prevent large declines in output and employment.

fine-tuning The phrase used by Walter Heller to refer to the government's role in regulating inflation and unemployment.

stagflation Occurs when the overall price level rises rapidly (inflation) during periods of recession or high and persistent unemployment (stagnation).

Fine-Tuning in the 1960s   The notion that the government could, and should, act to stabilize the macroeconomy reached the height of its popularity in the 1960s. During these years, Walter Heller, the chairman of the Council of Economic Advisers under both President Kennedy and President Johnson, alluded to **fine-tuning** as the government's role in regulating inflation and unemployment. During the 1960s, many economists believed the government could use the tools available to manipulate unemployment and inflation levels fairly precisely.

Disillusionment in the 1970s and Early 1980s   In the 1970s and early 1980s, the U.S. economy had wide fluctuations in employment, output, and inflation. In 1974–1975 and again in 1980–1982, the United States experienced a severe recession. Although not as catastrophic as the Great Depression of the 1930s, these two recessions left millions without jobs and resulted in billions of dollars of lost output and income. In 1974–1975 and again in 1979–1981, the United States saw very high rates of inflation.

Moreover, in the 1970s **stagflation** (stagnation + inflation) was born. Stagflation occurs when the overall price level rises rapidly (inflation) during periods of recession or high and persistent unemployment (stagnation). Until the 1970s, rapidly rising prices had been observed only in periods when the economy was prospering and unemployment was low (or at least declining). The problem of stagflation was vexing, both for macroeconomic theorists and for policy makers concerned with the health of the economy.

It was clear by 1975 that the macroeconomy was more difficult to control than either Heller's words or textbook theory had led economists to believe. The events of the 1970s and early 1980s had an important influence on macroeconomic theory. Much of the faith in the simple Keynesian model and the "conventional wisdom" of the 1960s was lost.

Good Times in the 1990s, Pause in 2000–2001, and Recovery in 2002–2005   The economy grew well in the 1980s after the recession of 1980–1982. There was a mild recession in 1990–1991, and then the economy grew for the rest of the 1990s. Growth in 1996–1999 was particularly strong, fueled in part by the stock market boom that began in 1995. Remarkably, inflation was not a problem throughout the entire 1990s. The economy then began slowing down in the middle of 2000, before the terrorist attacks on September 11, 2001. In spite of the attacks, the economy began to pick up at the end of 2001. The growth rate in 2002 and 2003 was moderate, but not large enough to prevent the unemployment rate from rising. During 2000–2001 the unemployment rate rose from about 4 percent to about 5.5 percent. It then rose further to 6.1 percent by the third quarter of 2003. The economy continued to grow fairly well in 2004 and 2005, and by the middle of 2005 the unemployment rate was back down to 5.0 percent. Inflation continued not to be a problem through 2005.

The strong economy in the 1990s and recovery in 2002–2005 did *not* lead to a convergence of views of macroeconomists about how the macroeconomy works. The discipline of macroeconomics is still in flux, and many important issues have yet to be resolved. This makes it hard to teach, but exciting to study.

MACROECONOMIC CONCERNS

Three of the major concerns of macroeconomics are

- Inflation
- Output growth
- Unemployment

Government policy makers would like to have low inflation, high output growth, and low unemployment. They may not be able to achieve these goals, but the goals themselves are clear.

INFLATION AND DEFLATION

inflation An increase in the overall price level.

hyperinflation A period of very rapid increases in the overall price level.

Inflation is an increase in the overall price level. Keeping inflation low has long been a goal of government policy. Especially problematic are **hyperinflations**, or periods of very rapid increases in the overall price level.

Most Americans are unaware of what life is like under very high inflation. In some countries at some times, people were accustomed to prices rising by the day, by the hour, or even by the minute. During the hyperinflation in Bolivia in 1984 and 1985, the price of one egg rose from 3,000 pesos to 10,000 pesos in 1 week. In 1985, three bottles of aspirin sold for the same price as a luxury car had sold for in 1982. At the same time, the problem of handling money became a burden. Banks stopped counting deposits—a $500 deposit was equivalent to about 32 million pesos, and it just did not make sense to count a huge sack full of bills. Bolivia's currency, printed in West Germany and England, was the country's third biggest import in 1984, surpassed only by wheat and mining equipment.

Skyrocketing prices in Bolivia are a small part of the story. When inflation approaches rates of 2,000 percent per year, the economy and the whole organization of a country begin to break down. Workers may go on strike to demand wage increases in line with the high inflation rate, and firms may find it hard to secure credit.

Hyperinflations are rare. Nonetheless, economists have devoted much effort to identifying the costs and consequences of even moderate inflation. Does anyone gain from inflation? Who loses? What costs does inflation impose on society? How severe are they? What causes inflation? What is the best way to stop it? These are some of the main concerns of macroeconomists.

A decrease in the overall price level is called **deflation**. In some periods in U.S. history and recently in Japan, deflation has occurred over an extended period of time. The goal of policy makers is to avoid prolonged periods of deflation as well as inflation in order to pursue the macroeconomic goal of stability.

deflation A decrease in the overall price level.

OUTPUT GROWTH: SHORT RUN AND LONG RUN

Instead of growing at an even rate at all times, economies tend to experience short-term ups and downs in their performance. The technical name for these ups and downs is the **business cycle**. The main measure of how an economy is doing is **aggregate output**, the total quantity of goods and services produced in the economy in a given period. When less is produced (in other words, when aggregate output decreases), there are fewer goods and services to go around, and the average standard of living declines. When firms cut back on production, they also lay off workers, increasing the rate of unemployment.

Recessions are periods during which aggregate output declines. It has become conventional to classify an economic downturn as a "recession" when aggregate output declines for two consecutive quarters. A prolonged and deep recession is called a **depression**, although economists do not agree on when a recession becomes a depression. Since the beginning of the twentieth century, the United States has experienced one depression (during the 1930s), three severe recessions (1946, 1974–1975, and 1980–1982), and a number of less severe, shorter recessions (1954, 1958, 1990–1991, and 2001). Other countries also experienced recessions in the twentieth century, some roughly coinciding with U.S. recessions and some not.

There is more to output than its up-and-down movements during business cycles. The size of the growth rate of output over a long period (longer, say, than the typical length of a business cycle) is also of concern to macroeconomists and policy makers. If the growth rate of output is greater than the growth rate of the population, there is a growing amount of goods and services produced per person. So, on average, people are becoming better off. Policy makers are thus concerned not only with smoothing fluctuations in output during a business cycle but also with policies that might increase the long-run growth rate.

business cycle The cycle of short-term ups and downs in the economy.

aggregate output The total quantity of goods and services produced in an economy in a given period.

recession A period during which aggregate output declines. Conventionally, a period in which aggregate output declines for two consecutive quarters.

depression A prolonged and deep recession.

UNEMPLOYMENT

You cannot listen to the news or read a newspaper without noticing that data on the unemployment rate are released each month. The **unemployment rate**—the percentage of the labor force that is unemployed—is a key indicator of the economy's health. Because the unemployment rate is usually closely related to the economy's aggregate output, announcements of each month's new figure are followed with great interest by economists, politicians, and policy makers.

unemployment rate The percentage of the labor force that is unemployed.

Although macroeconomists are interested in learning why the unemployment rate has risen or fallen in a given period, they also try to answer a more basic question: Why is there any unemployment at all? We do not expect to see zero unemployment. At any time, some firms may go bankrupt due to competition from rivals, bad management, or bad luck. Employees of such firms typically are not able to find new jobs immediately, and while they are looking for work, they will be unemployed. Also, workers entering the labor market for the first time may require a few weeks, or months, to find a job.

If we base our analysis on supply and demand, we would expect conditions to change in response to the existence of unemployed workers. Specifically, when there is unemployment beyond some minimum amount, there is an excess supply of workers—at the going wage rates, there are people who want to work who cannot find work. In microeconomic theory, the response to excess supply is a decrease in the price of the commodity in question and therefore an increase in the quantity demanded, a reduction in the quantity supplied, and the restoration of equilibrium. With the quantity supplied equal to the quantity demanded, the market clears.

The existence of unemployment seems to imply that the aggregate labor market is not in equilibrium—that something prevents the quantity supplied and the quantity demanded from equating. Why do labor markets not clear when other markets do, or is it that labor markets are clearing and the unemployment data are reflecting something different? This is another main concern of macroeconomists.

GOVERNMENT IN THE MACROECONOMY

Much of our discussion of macroeconomics concerns the potential role of government in influencing the economy. There are three kinds of policy that the government has used to influence the macroeconomy:

> **1.** Fiscal policy
> **2.** Monetary policy
> **3.** Growth or supply-side policies

FISCAL POLICY

fiscal policy Government policies concerning taxes and expenditures (spending).

One way the federal government affects the economy is through its tax and expenditure (spending) decisions, or **fiscal policy**. The federal government collects taxes from households and firms and spends these funds on items ranging from missiles to parks to Social Security payments to interstate highways. Both the magnitude and the composition of these taxes and expenditures have a major effect on the economy.

One of Keynes's main ideas in the 1930s was that fiscal policy could and should be used to stabilize the level of output and employment. Specifically, Keynes believed the government should cut taxes and/or raise spending—called *expansionary fiscal policies*—to get the economy out of a slump. Conversely, he held that the government should raise taxes and/or cut spending—called *contractionary fiscal policies*—to bring the economy out of an inflation.

MONETARY POLICY

monetary policy The tools used by the Federal Reserve to control the quantity of money in the economy.

Taxes and spending are not the only variables the government controls. The Federal Reserve, the nation's central bank, determines the quantity of money in the economy. The effects and proper role of **monetary policy** are among the most hotly debated subjects in macroeconomics. Most economists agree that the quantity of money supplied affects the overall price level, interest rates and exchange rates, unemployment rate, and level of output. The main controversies arise concerning how monetary policy manifests itself and exactly how large its effects are.

Macroeconomic Concerns from the Federal Reserve in 2005

As we discuss briefly in this chapter and will discuss in much more detail later, the monetary policy of the United States is determined by the Federal Reserve. As you will see later, the Federal Reserve System is directed by a Board of Governors appointed by the president and approved by Congress. Eight times a year the board's policy-making committee meets to discuss the economy and to decide what, if anything, the nation's central bank should be doing to make things better.

The minutes of each meeting are recorded and released to the public and the press a few weeks after the meeting. The following is excerpted from the minutes of a meeting held on September 20, 2005. It shows precisely what the concerns of macroeconomics are.

Employment

Payroll employment grew at a good pace in August, and the average increase over the most recent three months was largely on par with the advances made since the fourth quarter of last year. Employment gains were widespread across industries, with the exception of the manufacturing sector, which continued to post small job losses. The unemployment rate dipped to 4.9 percent in August, its lowest level since August 2001.

Growth

Industrial production increased only slightly in August; the staff estimated that the curtailment of activity as a result of Hurricane Katrina shaved 0.3 percent from the index. Petroleum refining and crude oil and natural gas extraction were especially hard hit by the storm. The output of utilities declined in August after surging ear-

On February 1, 2006, Ben S. Bernanke became chairman of the Federal Reserve.

lier in the summer in response to unseasonably warm weather. Higher production of motor vehicles and parts boosted manufacturing output. After slowing in the second quarter, the pace of production in the high-tech sector accelerated somewhat in recent months, owing to increased output of communications equipment and semiconductors.

Real personal consumption expenditures, boosted by motor vehicles purchases in response to employee-discount programs, were robust during the summer. Spending on goods outside the automobile sector and on services

was moderate. Strong overall spending along with lackluster real income growth put downward pressure on the saving rate.

Inflation

Core consumer price inflation remained benign in July and August. However, the surge in energy prices considerably boosted overall consumer price inflation over those months. Gasoline prices in particular rose steeply in August, and survey data pointed to a larger increase in early September. Producer price inflation was subdued.

GROWTH POLICIES

Many economists are skeptical about the government's ability to regulate the business cycle with any degree of precision using monetary and fiscal policy. Their view is that the focus of government policy should be to stimulate aggregate supply—to stimulate the potential growth of aggregate output and income. A host of policies have been aimed at increasing the rate of growth. Many of these are targeted at specific markets and are largely discussed in microeconomics. One major worry of macroeconomists is that government borrowing to finance excesses of spending over tax collections (the "deficit") *crowding out* sops up saving that would otherwise flow to businesses to be used for investment in capital. Another focus of progrowth government policies has been the tax system. A major goal of tax reforms in 1981 and 1986 was to increase the incentive to work, save, and invest by lowering tax rates. In addition, the Taxpayer Relief Act of 1997 included a number of progrowth measures. These types of policies are sometimes referred to as **supply-side policies**.

supply-side policies
Government policies that focus on stimulating aggregate supply instead of aggregate demand.

405

THE COMPONENTS OF THE MACROECONOMY

Macroeconomics focuses on four groups: (1) *households* and (2) *firms*, which together compose the private sector, (3) the *government* (the public sector), and (4) the *rest of the world* (the international sector). These four groups interact in a variety of ways, many involving either the receipt or the payment of income.

THE CIRCULAR FLOW DIAGRAM

circular flow A diagram showing the income received and payments made by each sector of the economy.

A useful way of seeing the economic interactions among the four sectors in the economy is a **circular flow** diagram, which shows the income received and payments made by each. A simple circular flow diagram is pictured in Figure 18.1.

Let us walk through the circular flow step-by-step. Households work for firms and the government, and they receive wages for their work. Our diagram shows a flow of wages *into* the household sector as payment for those services. Households also receive interest on corporate and government bonds and dividends from firms. Many households receive other payments from the government, such as Social Security benefits, veterans' benefits, and welfare payments. Economists call these kinds of payments from the government (for which the

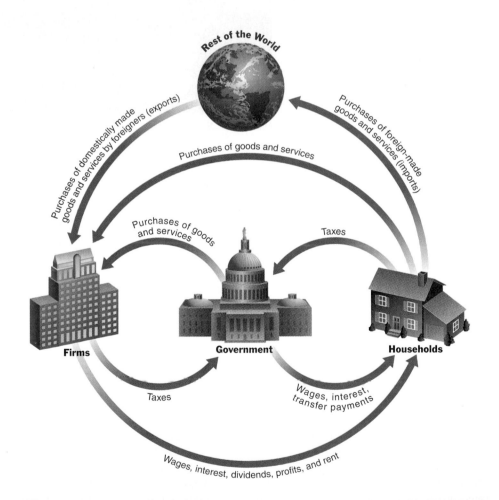

FIGURE 18.1 The Circular Flow of Payments

Households receive income from firms and the government, purchase goods and services from firms, and pay taxes to the government. They also purchase foreign-made goods and services (imports). Firms receive payments from households and the government for goods and services; they pay wages, dividends, interest, and rents to households, and taxes to the government. The government receives taxes from both firms and households, pays both firms and households for goods and services—including wages to government workers—and pays interest and transfers to households. Finally, people in other countries purchase goods and services produced domestically (exports).

Note: Though not shown in this diagram, firms and governments also purchase imports.

recipients do not supply goods, services, or labor) **transfer payments**. Together, all these receipts make up the total income received by the households.

Households spend by buying goods and services from firms and by paying taxes to the government. These items make up the total amount paid out by the households. The difference between the total receipts and the total payments of the households is the amount that the households save or dissave. If households receive more than they spend, they *save* during the period. If they receive less than they spend, they *dissave*. A household can dissave by using up some of its previous savings or by borrowing. In the circular flow diagram, household spending is shown as a flow *out* of the household sector. Saving by households is sometimes termed a "leakage" from the circular flow because it withdraws income, or current purchasing power, from the system.

Firms sell goods and services to households and the government. These sales earn revenue, which shows up in the circular flow diagram as a flow *into* the firm sector. Firms pay wages, interest, and dividends to households, and they pay taxes to the government. These payments are shown flowing *out* of the firm sector.

The government collects taxes from households and firms. The government also makes payments. It buys goods and services from firms, pays wages and interest to households, and makes transfer payments to households. If the government's revenue is less than its payments, the government is dissaving.

Finally, households spend some of their income on *imports*—goods and services produced in the rest of the world. Similarly, people in foreign countries purchase *exports*—goods and services produced by domestic firms and sold to other countries.

One lesson of the circular flow diagram is that everyone's expenditure is someone else's receipt. If you buy a personal computer from Dell, you make a payment to Dell and Dell receives revenue. If Dell pays taxes to the government, it has made a payment and the government has received revenue.

Everyone's expenditures go somewhere. It is impossible to sell something without there being a buyer, and it is impossible to make a payment without there being a recipient. Every transaction must have two sides.

THE THREE MARKET ARENAS

Another way of looking at the ways households, firms, the government, and the rest of the world relate to each other is to consider the markets in which they interact.

The three market arenas are:
1. Goods-and-services market
2. Labor market
3. Money (financial) market

Goods-and-Services Market   Households and the government purchase goods and services from firms in the *goods-and-services market*. In this market, firms also purchase goods and services from each other. For example, Levi Strauss buys denim from other firms to make its blue jeans. In addition, firms buy capital goods from other firms. If General Motors needs new robots on its assembly lines, it may buy them from another firm instead of making them.

Firms *supply* to the goods-and-services market. Households, the government, and firms *demand* from this market. Finally, the rest of the world both buys from and sells to the goods-and-services market. The United States imports hundreds of billions of dollars' worth of automobiles, DVDs, oil, and other goods. At the same time, the United States exports hundreds of billions of dollars' worth of computers, airplanes, and agricultural goods.

Labor Market   Interaction in the *labor market* takes place when firms and the government purchase labor from households. In this market, households *supply* labor, and firms and the government *demand* labor. In the U.S. economy, firms are the largest demanders of labor, although the government is also a substantial employer. The total supply of labor in the economy depends on the sum of decisions made by households. Individuals must decide whether to enter the labor force (whether to look for a job at all) and how many hours to work.

Labor is also supplied to and demanded from the rest of the world. In recent years, the labor market has become an international market. For example, vegetable and fruit farmers in California would find it very difficult to bring their product to market if it were not for the labor of migrant farm workers from Mexico. For years, Turkey has provided Germany with "guest workers" who are willing to take low-paying jobs that more prosperous German workers avoid.

Money Market In the *money market*—sometimes called the *financial market*—households purchase stocks and bonds from firms. Households *supply* funds to this market in the expectation of earning income in the form of dividends on stocks and interest on bonds. Households also *demand* (borrow) funds from this market to finance various purchases. Firms borrow to build new facilities in the hope of earning more in the future. The government borrows by issuing bonds. The rest of the world both borrows from and lends to the money market; every morning there are reports on TV and radio about the Japanese and British stock markets. Much of the borrowing and lending of households, firms, the government, and the international sector are coordinated by financial institutions—commercial banks, savings and loan associations, insurance companies, and the like. These institutions take deposits from one group and lend them to others.

When a firm, a household, or the government borrows to finance a purchase, it has an obligation to pay that loan back, usually at some specified time in the future. Most loans also involve payment of interest as a fee for the use of the borrowed funds. When a loan is made, the borrower nearly always signs a "promise to repay," or *promissory note*, and gives it to the lender. When the federal government borrows, it issues "promises" called **Treasury bonds**, **notes**, or **bills** in exchange for money. Corporations issue **corporate bonds**. A corporate bond might state, for example, "General Electric Corporation agrees to pay $5,000 to the holder of this bond on January 1, 2006, and interest thereon at 5.1 percent annually until that time."

Instead of issuing bonds to raise funds, firms can also issue shares of stock. A **share of stock** is a financial instrument that gives the holder a share in the firm's ownership and therefore the right to share in the firm's profits. If the firm does well, the value of the stock increases, and the stockholder receives a *capital gain*[1] on the initial purchase. In addition, the stock may pay **dividends**—that is, the firm may return some of its profits directly to its stockholders, instead of retaining them to buy capital. If the firm does poorly, so does the stockholder. The capital value of the stock may fall, and dividends may not be paid.

Stocks and bonds are simply contracts, or agreements, between parties. I agree to loan you a certain amount, and you agree to repay me this amount plus something extra at some future date, or I agree to buy part ownership in your firm, and you agree to give me a share of the firm's future profits.

A critical variable in the money market is the *interest rate*. Although we sometimes talk as if there were only one interest rate, there is never just one interest rate at any time. Instead, the interest rate on a given loan reflects the length of the loan and the perceived risk to the lender. A business that is just getting started will have to pay a higher rate than will General Motors. A 30-year mortgage has a different interest rate than a 90-day loan. Nevertheless, interest rates tend to move up and down together, and their movement reflects general conditions in the financial market.

Treasury bonds, notes, and bills Promissory notes issued by the federal government when it borrows money.

corporate bonds Promissory notes issued by corporations when they borrow money.

shares of stock Financial instruments that give to the holder a share in the firm's ownership and therefore the right to share in the firm's profits.

dividends The portion of a corporation's profits that the firm pays out each period to its shareholders.

THE METHODOLOGY OF MACROECONOMICS

Macroeconomists build models based on theories, and they test their models using data. In this sense, the methodology of macroeconomics is similar to the methodology of microeconomics.

---

[1] A *capital gain* occurs whenever the value of an asset increases. If you bought a stock for $1,000 and it is now worth $1,500, you have earned a capital gain of $500. A capital gain is "realized" when you sell the asset. Until you sell, the capital gain is *accrued* but not *realized*.

CONNECTIONS TO MICROECONOMICS

How do macroeconomists try to explain aggregate behavior? One way assumes that the same factors that affect individual behavior also affect aggregate behavior. For example, we know from microeconomics that an individual's wage rate should affect her consumption habits and the amount of labor she is willing to supply. If we were to apply this microeconomic hypothesis to the aggregate data, we would say that the average wage rate in the economy should affect total consumption and total labor supply (which seems to be true).

The reason for looking to microeconomics for help in explaining macroeconomic events is simple:

> Macroeconomic behavior is the sum of all the microeconomic decisions made by individual households and firms. If the movements of macroeconomic aggregates, such as total output or total employment, reflect decisions made by individual firms and households, we cannot understand the former without some knowledge of the factors that influence the latter.

Consider unemployment. The unemployment rate is the number of people unemployed as a fraction of the labor force. To be classified as "in the labor force," a person must either have a job or be seeking one actively. To understand aggregate unemployment, we need to understand individual household behavior in the labor market. Why do people choose to enter the labor force? Under what circumstances will they drop out? Why does unemployment exist even when the economy seems to be doing very well? A knowledge of microeconomic behavior is the logical starting point for macroeconomic analysis.

AGGREGATE DEMAND AND AGGREGATE SUPPLY

A major concern of the next few chapters is the behavior of aggregate demand and aggregate supply. **Aggregate demand** is the total demand for goods and services. **Aggregate supply** is the total supply of goods and services.

Figure 18.2 shows *aggregate demand* and *aggregate supply* curves. Measured on the horizontal axis is aggregate output. Measured on the vertical axis is the *overall price level*, not the price of a particular good or service. The economy is in equilibrium at the point at which these curves intersect.

We will see that aggregate demand and supply curves are much more complicated than the simple demand and supply curves we described in Chapters 3 and 4. The simple logic of

aggregate demand The total demand for goods and services in an economy.

aggregate supply The total supply of goods and services in an economy.

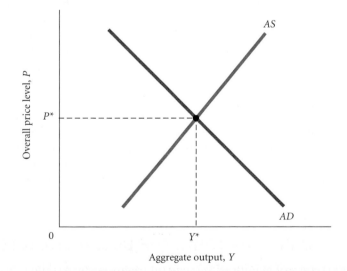

FIGURE 18.2 The Aggregate Demand and Aggregate Supply Curves

A major theme in macroeconomics is the behavior of aggregate demand and aggregate supply. The logic behind the aggregate demand and aggregate supply curves is much more complex than the logic underlying the simple demand and supply curves described in Chapters 3 and 4.

supply, demand, and equilibrium in individual markets does not explain what is depicted in Figure 18.2. It will take the entire next chapter for us to describe what is meant by "aggregate output" and the "overall price level." Furthermore, although we will look to the behavior of households and firms in individual markets for clues about how to analyze aggregate behavior, there are important differences when we move from the individual to the aggregate level.

Consider, for example, *demand*, one of the most important concepts in economics. When the price of a specific good increases, perhaps the most important determinant of consumer response is the availability of other goods that can be substituted for the good whose price has increased. Part of the reason that an increase in the price of airline tickets causes a decline in the quantity of airline tickets demanded is that a higher price relative to other goods means that the opportunity cost of buying a ticket is higher: The sacrifice required in terms of other goods and services has increased. However, when the overall price level changes, there may be no changes in the opportunity cost of goods. For example, a higher-priced airline ticket when compared to higher-priced other goods may involve the same trade-offs as before all prices increased.

Microeconomics teaches us that, *ceteris paribus*, the quantity demanded of a good falls when its price rises and rises when its price falls. (This is the microeconomic law of demand.) In other words, individual demand curves and market demand curves slope downward to the right. The reason the *aggregate* demand curve in Figure 18.2 slopes downward to the right is complex. As we will see later, the downward slope of the aggregate demand curve is related to what goes on in the money (financial) market.

The aggregate supply curve is very different from the supply curve of an individual firm or market. A firm's supply curve is derived under the assumption that all its input prices are fixed. In other words, the firm's input prices are assumed to remain unchanged as the price of the firm's output changes. When we derived Clarence Brown's soybean supply schedule in Chapter 3, we took his input prices as fixed. A change in an input price leads to a shift in Brown's supply curve, not a movement along it. If we are examining changes in the overall price level, however, *all* prices are changing (including input prices), so the aggregate supply curve cannot be based on the assumption of fixed input prices. We will see that the aggregate supply curve is another source of controversy in macroeconomics.

THE U.S. ECONOMY SINCE 1900: TRENDS AND CYCLES

As we said, most macroeconomic variables go through ups and downs over time, and the economy as a whole experiences periods of prosperity and periods of recession. The trend of the U.S. economy, however, has been toward prosperity. One measure of an economy's prosperity is the amount of goods and services that it produces during a year, or its gross domestic product (GDP), which is the subject of the next chapter. An economy is said to grow from one year to another if GDP is larger in the second year than in the first. Between 1900 and 2004, the U.S. economy grew at an average rate of 3.4 percent per year. This means that during those years the economy was on average 3.4 percent richer each year than it had been the year before. This is the economy's "long-run" growth rate.

Remember that we are discussing the average growth rate here. The economy did not actually grow by 3.4 percent every year. In some years, growth was less than 3 percent, and in some years, growth was negative (GDP fell). In other years, the growth rate was greater than 3.4 percent. So, we need to distinguish between *long-term*, or *secular, trends* in economic performance and *short-term*, or *cyclical, variations*.

EXPANSION AND CONTRACTION: THE BUSINESS CYCLE

Macroeconomics is concerned both with long-run trends—why has the U.S. economy done so well over the past 100 years?—and with short-run fluctuations in economic performance—why did the world experience a severe recession in the early 1980s and a mild recession in 2001? The term *business cycle* refers to the short-run fluctuations of an economy. A typical business cycle is illustrated in Figure 18.3.

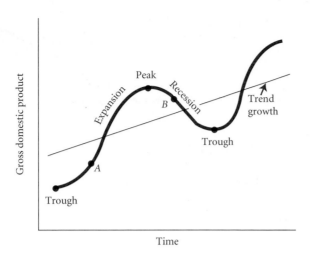

In this business cycle, the economy is expanding as it moves through point *A* from the trough to the peak. When the economy moves from a peak down to a trough, through point *B*, the economy is in recession.

Because the U.S. economy on average grows over time, the business cycle in Figure 18.3 shows a positive trend—the *peak* (the highest point) of a new business cycle is higher than the peak of the previous cycle. The period from a *trough*, or bottom of the cycle, to a peak is called an **expansion** or a **boom**. During an expansion, output and employment grow. The period from a peak to a trough is called a **contraction**, **recession**, or **slump**, when output and employment fall.

In judging whether an economy is expanding or contracting, note the difference between the level of economic activity and its rate of change. If the economy has just left a trough (point *A* in Figure 18.3), it will be growing (rate of change is positive), but its level of output will still be low. If the economy has just started to decline from a peak (point *B*), it will be contracting (rate of change is negative), but its level of output will still be high.

The business cycle in Figure 18.3 is symmetrical, which means the length of an expansion is the same as the length of a contraction. Most business cycles are not symmetrical, however. It is possible, for example, for the expansion phase to be longer than the contraction phase. When contraction comes, it may be fast and sharp, while expansion may be slow and gradual. Moreover, the economy is not nearly as regular as the business cycle in Figure 18.3 indicates. The ups and downs in the economy tend to be erratic.

Figure 18.4 shows the actual business cycles in the United States between 1900 and 2004. Although many business cycles have occurred in the last 100 years, each has been unique. The economy is not so simple that it has regular cycles.

The periods of the Great Depression and the two world wars show the largest fluctuations in Figure 18.4, although other large contractions and expansions have taken place. Note the expansion in the 1960s and the recessions at the beginning of the 1980s and 1990s. Some of the cycles have been long; some have been very short. Note also that GDP actually increased between 1933 and 1937, even though in 1937 it was still quite low. The economy did not really come out of the Depression until the defense buildup prior to the start of World War II. Note also that business cycles were more extreme before World War II than they have been since then.

expansion or **boom** The period in the business cycle from a trough up to a peak, during which output and employment rise.

contraction, recession, or slump The period in the business cycle from a peak down to a trough, during which output and employment fall.

THE U.S. ECONOMY SINCE 1970

Since 1970, the U.S. economy has experienced four recessions and large fluctuations in the rate of inflation. By analyzing how the various parts of the economy behaved during these hectic times, we can learn a lot about macroeconomic behavior.

Figures 18.5, 18.6, and 18.7 show the behavior of three key variables during the period since 1970: GDP, unemployment rate, and rate of inflation. These graphs are based on quarterly data (data compiled for each quarter of the year) instead of annual data. The first quarter of a year consists of January, February, and March; the second quarter consists of April,

FIGURE 18.4 Real GDP, 1900–2004

The periods of the Great Depression and the two world wars show the largest fluctuations in real GDP.

May, and June; and so on. The Roman numerals I, II, III, and IV denote the four quarters. For example, "1972 III" refers to the third quarter, or summer, of 1972.

Figure 18.5 plots GDP for the period 1970 I–2005 II. In the following chapters we will look at four recessionary periods within this period: 1974 I–1975 IV, 1980 II–1983 I, 1990 III–1991 I, and 2001 I–2001 III. These periods make useful reference points when we examine how other variables behaved during the four periods.[2]

One concern of macroeconomists is unemployment. Unemployment generally rises during recessions and falls during expansions. This can be seen in Figure 18.6, which plots

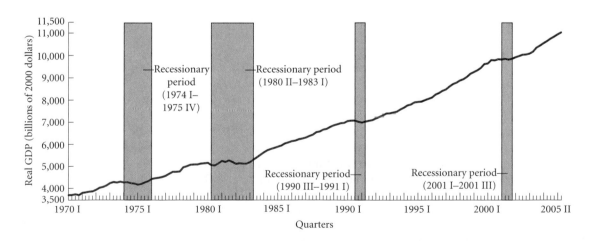

FIGURE 18.5 Real GDP, 1970 I–2005 II

Real GDP in the United States since 1970 has risen overall, but there have been four recessionary periods: 1974 I–1975 IV, 1980 II–1983 I, 1990 III–1991 I, and 2001 I–2001 III.

---

[2]As Figure 18.5 shows, GDP rose in the middle of 1981 before falling again in the last quarter of 1981. Given this fact, one possibility would be to treat the 1980 II–1983 I period as if it included two separate recessionary periods: 1980 II–1981 I and 1981 IV–1983 I. Because the expansion in 1981 was so short-lived, however, we have chosen not to separate the period into two parts.

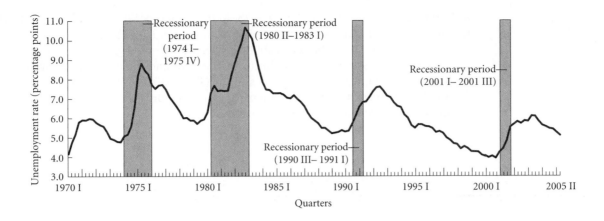

FIGURE 18.6 Unemployment Rate, 1970 I–2005 II

The U.S. unemployment rate since 1970 shows wide variations. The four recessionary reference periods show increases in the unemployment rate.

the unemployment rate for the period 1970 I–2005 II. Note that unemployment rose in all four recessions. In the 1974–1975 recession, the unemployment rate reached a maximum of 8.8 percent in the second quarter of 1975. During the 1980–1982 recession, it reached a maximum of 10.7 percent in the fourth quarter of 1982. The unemployment rate continued to rise after the 1990–1991 recession and reached a peak of 7.6 percent in 1992 III. By the end of 1994, the unemployment rate had fallen to 5.6 percent, and by the second quarter of 2000 it had fallen to 4.0 percent. It then rose to 5.8 percent by the second quarter of 2002. It began falling again in the fourth quarter of 2003.

Macroeconomics is also concerned with the inflation rate. A measure of the overall price level is the GDP deflator. (The construction of the GDP deflator is discussed in the next chapter. It is an index of prices of all domestically produced goods in the economy.) The percentage change in the GDP deflator provides one measure of the overall rate of inflation. Figure 18.7 plots the percentage change in the GDP deflator for the 1970 I–2005 II period.[3] For reference purposes, we have picked two periods within this time as showing particularly high inflation: 1973 IV–1975 IV and 1979 I–1981 IV. In the first period, the inflation rate peaked

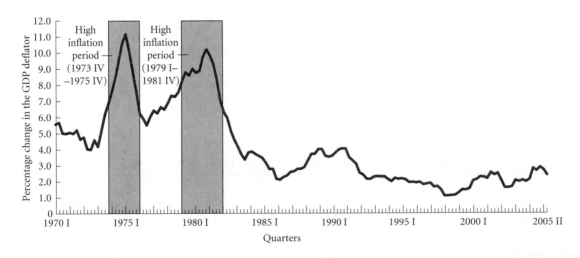

FIGURE 18.7 Percentage Change in the GDP Deflator (Four-Quarter Average), 1970 I–2005 II

The percentage change in the GDP deflator measures the overall rate of inflation. Since 1970, inflation has been high in two periods: 1973 IV–1975 IV and 1979 I–1981 IV. Inflation between 1983 and 1992 was moderate. Since 1992, it has been fairly low.

---

[3]The percentage change in Figure 18.7 is the percentage change over four quarters. For example, the value for 1970 I is the percentage change from 1969 I, the value for 1970 II is the percentage change from 1969 II, and so on.

at 11.0 percent in the first quarter of 1975. In the second period, it peaked at 10.1 percent in the first quarter of 1981. Since 1983, the rate of inflation has been quite low by the standards of the 1970s. Since 1994 it has been about 2.0 percent or less.

Macroeconomics tries to explain the behavior of and the connections among variables such as GDP, the unemployment rate, and the GDP deflator. When you can understand the forces at work in creating the movements shown in Figures 18.5 to 18.7, you will have come a long way in understanding how the economy works.

SUMMARY

1. *Microeconomics* examines the functioning of individual industries and the behavior of individual decision-making units. *Macroeconomics* is concerned with the sum, or aggregate, of these individual decisions—the consumption of *all* households in the economy, the amount of labor supplied and demanded by *all* individuals and firms, and the total amount of *all* goods and services produced.

THE ROOTS OF MACROECONOMICS

2. Macroeconomics was born out of the effort to explain the *Great Depression* of the 1930s. Since that time, the discipline has evolved, concerning itself with new issues as the problems facing the economy have changed. Through the late 1960s, it was believed that the government could "fine-tune" the economy to keep it running on an even keel at all times. The poor economic performance of the 1970s, however, showed that *fine-tuning* does not always work.

MACROECONOMIC CONCERNS

3. The three topics of primary concern to macroeconomists are increases in the overall price level, or *inflation*; the growth rate of aggregate output; and the level of unemployment.

GOVERNMENT IN THE MACROECONOMY

4. Among the tools that governments have available to them for influencing the macroeconomy are *fiscal policy* (decisions on taxes and government spending); *monetary policy* (control of the money supply); and *growth or supply-side policies* (policies that focus on increasing the long-run growth rate).

THE COMPONENTS OF THE MACROECONOMY

5. The *circular flow* diagram shows the flow of income received and payments made by the three sectors of the economy—private, public, and international. Everybody's expenditure is someone else's receipt—every transaction must have two sides.

6. Another way of looking at how households, firms, the government, and the international sector relate is to consider the markets in which they interact: the goods-and-services market, labor market, and money (financial) market.

THE METHODOLOGY OF MACROECONOMICS

7. Because macroeconomic behavior is the sum of all the microeconomic decisions made by individual households and firms, we cannot possibly understand the former without some knowledge of the factors that influence the latter. The movements of macroeconomic aggregates reflect decisions made by individual firms and households.

8. A major theme in macroeconomics is understanding the behavior of *aggregate demand* and *aggregate supply*. The logic underlying the aggregate demand and supply curves is more complex than the logic underlying individual market demand and supply curves.

THE U.S. ECONOMY SINCE 1900: TRENDS AND CYCLES

9. Macroeconomics is concerned with both long-run trends and the short-run fluctuations that are part of the *business cycle*. Since 1970, the U.S. economy has seen four *recessions* and large fluctuations in the rate of *inflation*.

REVIEW TERMS AND CONCEPTS

aggregate behavior, 400
aggregate demand, 409
aggregate output, 403
aggregate supply, 409
business cycle, 403
circular flow, 406
contraction, recession, or slump, 411
corporate bonds, 408
deflation, 403
depression, 403

dividends, 408
expansion or boom, 411
fine-tuning, 402
fiscal policy, 404
Great Depression, 400
hyperinflation, 402
inflation, 402
macroeconomics, 400
microeconomic foundations of macroeconomics, 400

microeconomics, 399
monetary policy, 404
recession, 403
shares of stock, 408
stagflation, 402
sticky prices, 400
supply-side policies, 405
transfer payments, 407
Treasury bonds, notes, and bills, 408
unemployment rate, 403

PROBLEM SET

1. Define inflation. Assume that you live in a simple economy in which only three goods are produced and traded: fish, fruit, and meat. Suppose that on January 1, 2005, fish sold for $2.50 per pound, meat was $3.00 per pound, and fruit was $1.50 per pound. At the end of the year, you discover that the catch was low and that fish prices had increased to $5.00 per pound, but fruit prices stayed at $1.50 and meat prices had actually fallen to $2.00. Can you say what happened to the overall "price level"? How might you construct a measure of the "change in the price level"? What additional information might you need to construct your measure?

2. Define unemployment. Should everyone who does not hold a job be considered "unemployed"? To help with your answer, draw a supply and demand diagram depicting the labor market. What is measured along the demand curve? What factors determine the quantity of labor demanded during a given period? What is measured along the labor supply curve? What factors determine the quantity of labor supplied by households during a given period? What is the opportunity cost of holding a job?

3. During 2000, the chairman of the Board of Governors of the Federal Reserve System, Alan Greenspan, voiced his concern that the unemployment rate, which was below 5 percent, was getting too low. Because employment is certainly a major concern of macroeconomic policy, and because job *creation* is considered a major goal, what was Mr. Greenspan's concern? What other goal(s) of macroeconomic policy might be affected by very low rates of unemployment?

4. A recession occurred in the U.S. economy during the first three quarters of 2001. National output of goods and services fell during this period. But during the fourth quarter of 2001, output began to increase and it increased at a slow rate through the first quarter of 2003. At the same time, between March 2001 and April 2003, employment declined almost continuously with a loss of over 2 million jobs. How is it possible that output can rise while at the same time employment is falling?

5. Describe the economy of your state. What is the most recently reported unemployment rate? How has the number of payroll jobs changed over the last 3 months and over the last year? How does your state's performance compare to the U.S. economy's performance over the last year? What explanations have been offered in the press? How accurate are these?

6. Explain briefly how macroeconomics is different from microeconomics. How can macroeconomists use microeconomic theory to guide them in their work, and why might they wish to do so?

7. During 1993, when the economy was growing very slowly, President Clinton recommended a series of spending cuts and tax increases designed to reduce the deficit. These were passed by Congress in the Omnibus Budget Reconciliation Act of 1993. Some who opposed the bill argue that the United States was pursuing a "contractionary fiscal policy" at precisely the wrong time. Explain their logic.

8. Many of the expansionary periods during the twentieth century occurred during wars. Why do you think this is true?

9. In the 1940s, you could buy a soda for 5 cents, eat dinner at a restaurant for less than $1, and purchase a house for $10,000. From this statement, it follows that consumers today are worse off than consumers in the 1940s. Comment.

10. The box on page 405 presents an excerpt from the minutes of the Federal Reserve System's Federal Open Market Committee (FOMC) in September 2005. Go to **www.federalreserve.gov/ FOMC/** and pull down the minutes from a more recent meeting. How have the views of the FOMC and the Federal Reserve changed since that meeting? Have new concerns arisen? Comparing the two documents, do you think that the committee is more concerned with unemployment relative to growth and inflation or more concerned with inflation relative to growth and unemployment compared to members' concerns at the time of the more recent meeting? Why?

Measuring National Output and National Income

19

Macroeconomics relies on data, much of it collected by the government. To study the economy, we need data on total output, total income, total consumption, and the like. Much of the macroeconomic data are from the **national income and product accounts**, which describe the components of national income in the economy. These accounts are produced by the Bureau of Economic Analysis (BEA) of the U.S. Department of Commerce.

The national income and product accounts do more than convey data about the performance of the economy. They also provide a conceptual framework that macroeconomists use to think about how the pieces of the economy fit together. When economists think about the macroeconomy, the categories and vocabulary they use come from the national income and product accounts.

The national income and product accounts can be compared with the mechanical or wiring diagrams for an automobile engine. The diagrams do not explain how an engine works, but they identify the key parts of an engine and show how they are connected. Trying to understand the macroeconomy without understanding national income accounting is like trying to fix an engine without a mechanical diagram and with no names for the engine parts.

GROSS DOMESTIC PRODUCT

The key concept in the national income and product accounts is **gross domestic product (GDP)**.

> GDP is the total market value of a country's output. It is the market value of all final goods and services produced within a given period of time by factors of production located within a country.

U.S. GDP for 2004—the value of all the output produced by factors of production in the United States in 2004—was $11,734.3 billion.

The centrality of GDP as a working concept cannot be overestimated. Just as an individual firm needs to evaluate the success or failure of its operations each year, so the economy as a whole needs to assess itself. GDP, as a measure of the total production of an economy, provides us with a country's economic report card. Because GDP is such an important concept, we need to take some time to explain exactly what its definition means.

national income and product accounts Data collected and published by the government describing the various components of national income and output in the economy.

gross domestic product (GDP) The total market value of all final goods and services produced within a given period by factors of production located within a country.

FINAL GOODS AND SERVICES

final goods and services
Goods and services produced for final use.

intermediate goods
Goods that are produced by one firm for use in further processing by another firm.

value added The difference between the value of goods as they leave a stage of production and the cost of the goods as they entered that stage.

First note that the definition refers to **final goods and services**. Many goods produced in the economy are not classified as *final* goods, but instead as intermediate goods. **Intermediate goods** are produced by one firm for use in further processing by another firm. For example, tires sold to automobile manufacturers are intermediate goods. The value of intermediate goods is not counted in GDP.

Why are intermediate goods not counted in GDP? Suppose that in producing a car, General Motors (GM) pays $200 to Goodyear for tires. GM uses these tires (among other components) to assemble a car, which it sells for $24,000. The value of the car (including its tires) is $24,000, not $24,000 + $200. The final price of the car already reflects the value of all its components. To count in GDP both the value of the tires sold to the automobile manufacturers and the value of the automobiles sold to the consumers would result in double counting.

Double counting can also be avoided by counting only the value added to a product by each firm in its production process. The **value added** during some stage of production is the difference between the value of goods as they leave that stage of production and the cost of the goods as they entered that stage. Value added is illustrated in Table 19.1. The four stages of the production of a gallon of gasoline are (1) oil drilling, (2) refining, (3) shipping, and (4) retail sale. In the first stage, value added is the value of sales. In the second stage, the refiner purchases the oil from the driller, refines it into gasoline, and sells it to the shipper. The refiner pays the driller $1.00 per gallon and charges the shipper $1.30. The value added by the refiner is thus $0.30 per gallon. The shipper then sells the gasoline to retailers for $1.60. The value added in the third stage of production is $0.30. Finally, the retailer sells the gasoline to consumers for $2.00. The value added at the fourth stage is $0.40, and the total value added in the production process is $2.00, the same as the value of sales at the retail level. Adding the total values of sales at each stage of production ($1.00 + $1.30 + $1.60 + $2.00 = $5.90) would significantly overestimate the value of the gallon of gasoline.

> In calculating GDP, we can either sum up the value added at each stage of production or we can take the value of final sales. We do not use the value of total sales in an economy to measure how much output has been produced.

EXCLUSION OF USED GOODS AND PAPER TRANSACTIONS

GDP is concerned only with new, or current, production. Old output is not counted in current GDP because it was already counted back at the time it was produced. It would be double counting to count sales of used goods in current GDP. If someone sells a used car to you, the transaction is not counted in GDP, because no new production has taken place. Similarly, a house is counted in GDP only at the time it is built, not each time it is resold. In short:

> GDP ignores all transactions in which money or goods change hands but in which no new goods and services are produced.

Sales of stocks and bonds are not counted in GDP. These exchanges are transfers of ownership of assets, either electronically or through paper exchanges, and do not correspond to current production. However, what if I sell the stock or bond for more than I originally paid

TABLE 19.1 Value Added in the Production of a Gallon of Gasoline (Hypothetical Numbers)

STAGE OF PRODUCTION	VALUE OF SALES	VALUE ADDED
(1) Oil drilling	$1.00	$1.00
(2) Refining	1.30	0.30
(3) Shipping	1.60	0.30
(4) Retail sale	2.00	0.40
Total value added		$2.00

Tires taken from that pile and mounted on the wheels of the new car before it is sold are considered intermediate goods to the auto producer. Tires from that pile to replace tires on your old car are considered final goods. If, in calculating GDP, we included the value of the tires (an intermediate good) on new cars and the value of new cars (including the tires), we would be double counting.

for it? Profits from the stock or bond market have nothing to do with current production, so they are not counted in GDP. However, if I pay a fee to a broker for selling a stock of mine to someone else, this fee is counted in GDP, because the broker is performing a service for me. This service is part of current production. Be careful to distinguish between exchanges of stocks and bonds for money (or for other stocks and bonds), which do not involve current production, and fees for performing such exchanges, which do.

EXCLUSION OF OUTPUT PRODUCED ABROAD BY DOMESTICALLY OWNED FACTORS OF PRODUCTION

GDP is the value of output produced by factors of production *located within a country.*

The three basic factors of production are land, labor, and capital. The labor of U.S. citizens counts as a domestically owned factor of production for the United States. The output produced by U.S. citizens abroad—for example, U.S. citizens working for a foreign company—is *not* counted in U.S. GDP because the output is not produced within the United States. Likewise, profits earned abroad by U.S. companies are not counted in U.S. GDP. However, the output produced by foreigners working in the United States is counted in U.S. GDP because the output is produced within the United States. Also, profits earned in the United States by foreign-owned companies are counted in U.S. GDP.

It is sometimes useful to have a measure of the output produced by factors of production owned by a country's citizens regardless of where the output is produced. This measure is called **gross national product (GNP)**. For most countries, including the United States, the difference between GDP and GNP is small. In 2004, GNP for the United States was $11,788.0 billion, which is close to the $11,734.3 billion value for U.S. GDP.

The distinction between GDP and GNP can be tricky. Consider the Honda plant in Marysville, Ohio. The plant is owned by the Honda Corporation, a Japanese firm, but most of the workers employed at the plant are U.S. workers. Although all the output of the plant is included in U.S. GDP, only part of it is included in U.S. GNP. The wages paid to U.S. workers are part of U.S. GNP, while the profits from the plant are not. The profits from the plant are counted in Japanese GNP because this is output produced by Japanese-owned factors of production (Japanese capital in this case). The profits, however, are not counted in Japanese GDP because they were not earned in Japan.

gross national product (GNP) The total market value of all final goods and services produced within a given period by factors of production owned by a country's citizens, regardless of where the output is produced.

CALCULATING GDP

GDP can be computed in two ways. One is to add up the total amount spent on all final goods during a given period. This is the **expenditure approach** to calculating GDP. The other is to add up the income—wages, rents, interest, and profits—received by all factors of

expenditure approach A method of computing GDP that measures the amount spent on all final goods during a given period.

income approach A method of computing GDP that measures the income—wages, rents, interest, and profits—received by all factors of production in producing final goods.

production in producing final goods. This is the **income approach** to calculating GDP. These two methods lead to the same value for GDP for the reason we discussed in the previous chapter: *Every payment (expenditure) by a buyer is at the same time a receipt (income) for the seller.* We can measure either income received or expenditures made, and we will end up with the same total output.

Suppose the economy is made up of just one firm and the firm's total output this year sells for $1 million. Because the total amount spent on output this year is $1 million, this year's GDP is $1 million. (Remember: The expenditure approach calculates GDP on the basis of the total amount spent on final goods and services in the economy.) However, *every one* of the million dollars of GDP is either paid to someone or remains with the owners of the firm as profit. Using the income approach, we add up the wages paid to employees of the firm, the interest paid to those who lent money to the firm, and the rents paid to those who leased land, buildings, or equipment to the firm. What is left over is profit, which is, of course, income to the owners of the firm. If we add up the incomes of all the factors of production, including profits to the owners, we get a GDP of $1 million.

THE EXPENDITURE APPROACH

Recall from the previous chapter the four main groups in the economy: households, firms, the government, and the rest of the world. There are also four main categories of expenditure:

Expenditure Categories:

- Personal consumption expenditures (C): household spending on consumer goods
- Gross private domestic investment (I): spending by firms and households on new capital, i.e., plant, equipment, inventory, and new residential structures
- Government consumption and gross investment (G)
- Net exports ($EX - IM$): net spending by the rest of the world, or exports (EX) minus imports (IM)

The expenditure approach calculates GDP by adding together these four components of spending. In equation form:

$$GDP = C + I + G + (EX - IM)$$

U.S. GDP was $11,734.3 billion in 2004. The four components of the expenditure approach are shown in Table 19.2, along with their various categories.

TABLE 19.2 Components of U.S. GDP, 2004: The Expenditure Approach

	BILLIONS OF DOLLARS		PERCENTAGE OF GDP	
Personal consumption expenditures (C)	8,214.3		70.0	
Durable goods		987.8		8.4
Nondurable goods		2,368.3		20.2
Services		4,858.2		41.4
Gross private domestic investment (I)	1,928.1		16.4	
Nonresidential		1,198.8		10.2
Residential		673.8		5.7
Change in business inventories		55.4		0.5
Government consumption and gross investment (G)	2,215.9		18.9	
Federal		827.6		7.1
State and local		1,388.3		11.8
Net exports (EX − IM)	−624.0		−5.3	
Exports (EX)		1,173.8		10.0
Imports (IM)		1,797.8		15.3
Gross domestic product	11,734.3		100.0	

Note: Numbers may not add exactly because of rounding.
Source: U.S. Department of Commerce, Bureau of Economic Analysis.

Personal Consumption Expenditures (C)   The largest part of GDP consists of **personal consumption expenditures (C)**. Table 19.2 shows that in 2004 the amount of personal consumption expenditures accounted for 70.0 percent of GDP. These are expenditures by consumers on goods and services.

There are three main categories of consumer expenditures: durable goods, nondurable goods, and services. **Durable goods**, such as automobiles, furniture, and household appliances, last a relatively long time. **Nondurable goods**, such as food, clothing, gasoline, and cigarettes, are used up fairly quickly. Payments for **services**—those things that we buy that do not involve the production of physical items—include expenditures for doctors, lawyers, and educational institutions. As Table 19.2 shows, in 2004 durable goods expenditures accounted for 8.4 percent of GDP, nondurables for 20.2 percent, and services for 41.4 percent.

Gross Private Domestic Investment (I)   *Investment*, as we use the term in economics, refers to the purchase of new capital—housing, plants, equipment, and inventory. The economic use of the term is in contrast to its everyday use, where *investment* often refers to purchases of stocks, bonds, or mutual funds.

Total investment in capital by the private sector is called **gross private domestic investment (I)**. Expenditures by firms for machines, tools, plants, and so forth make up **nonresidential investment**.[1] Because these are goods that firms buy for their own final use, they are part of "final sales" and counted in GDP. Expenditures for new houses and apartment buildings constitute **residential investment**. The third component of gross private investment, the **change in business inventories**, is the amount by which firms' inventories change during a period. Business inventories can be looked at as the goods that firms produce now but intend to sell later. In 2004, gross private investment accounted for 16.4 percent of GDP. Of this, 10.2 percent was nonresidential investment, 5.7 percent was residential investment, and 0.5 percent was change in business inventories.

Change in Business Inventories   It is sometimes confusing to students that inventories are counted as capital and that changes in inventory are counted as part of gross private domestic investment, but conceptually it makes sense. The inventory a firm owns has a value, and it serves a purpose, or provides a service, to the firm. That it has value is obvious. Think of the inventory of a new car dealer or of a clothing store, or stocks of newly produced but unsold computers awaiting shipment. All these have value.

However, what *service* does inventory provide? Firms keep stocks of inventory for a number of reasons. One is to meet unforeseen demand. Firms are never sure how much they will sell from period to period. Sales go up and down. To maintain the goodwill of their customers, firms need to be able to respond to unforeseen increases in sales. The only way to do that is with inventory.

Some firms use inventory to provide direct services to customers—the main function of a retail store. A grocery store provides a service—convenience. The store itself does not produce any food at all. It simply assembles a wide variety of items and puts them on display so consumers with varying tastes can come and shop in one place for what they want. The same is true for a clothing or hardware store. To provide their services, such stores need light fixtures, counters, cash registers, buildings, and lots of inventory. Capital stocks are made up of plant, equipment, and inventory; inventory accumulations are part of the change in capital stocks, or investment.

Remember that GDP is not the market value of total final *sales* during a period—it is the market value of total *production*. The relationship between total production and total sales is:

$$\text{GDP} = \text{final sales} + \text{change in business inventories}$$

Total production (GDP) equals final sales of domestic goods plus the change in business inventories. In 2004, production in the United States exceeded sales by $55.4 billion. Inventories at the end of 2004 were $55.4 billion *greater* than they were at the end of 2003.

---

[1]The distinction between what is considered investment and what is considered consumption is sometimes fairly arbitrary. A firm's purchase of a car or a truck is counted as investment, but a household's purchase of a car or a truck is counted as consumption of durable goods. In general, expenditures by firms for items that last longer than a year are counted as investment expenditures. Expenditures for items that last less than a year are seen as purchases of intermediate goods.

personal consumption expenditures (C) A major component of GDP: expenditures by consumers on goods and services.

durable goods Goods that last a relatively long time, such as cars and household appliances.

nondurable goods Goods that are used up fairly quickly, such as food and clothing.

services The things we buy that do not involve the production of physical things, such as legal and medical services and education.

gross private domestic investment (I) Total investment in capital—that is, the purchase of new housing, plants, equipment, and inventory by the private (or nongovernment) sector.

nonresidential investment Expenditures by firms for machines, tools, plants, and so on.

residential investment Expenditures by households and firms on new houses and apartment buildings.

change in business inventories The amount by which firms' inventories change during a period. Inventories are the goods that firms produce now but intend to sell later.

○ Further Exploration ○ News Analysis | gross domestic product | search |

GDP: One of the Great Inventions of the 20th Century—Survey of Current Business

As the 20th century drew to a close, the U.S. Department of Commerce embarked on a review of its achievements. At the conclusion of this review, the Department named the development of the national income and product accounts as "its achievement of the century."

J. Steven Landefeld
Director, Bureau of Economic Analysis

While the GDP and the rest of the national income accounts may seem to be arcane concepts, they are truly among the great inventions of the twentieth century.

Paul A. Samuelson and
William D. Nordhaus

HISTORY OF THE NATIONAL INCOME AND PRODUCT ACCOUNTS (NIPAs)

Prior to the development of the NIPAs, policymakers had to guide the economy using limited and fragmentary information about the state of the economy. The Great Depression underlined the problems of incomplete data and led to the development of the national accounts:

One reads with dismay of Presidents Hoover and then Roosevelt designing policies to combat the Great Depression of the 1930's on the basis of such sketchy data as stock price indices, freight car loadings, and incomplete indices of industrial production. The fact was that comprehensive measures of national income and output did not exist at the time. The Depression, and with it the growing role of government in the economy, emphasized the need for such measures and led to the development of a comprehensive set of national income accounts.

Richard T. Froyen

In response to this need in the 1930's, the Department of Commerce commissioned Nobel laureate Simon Kuznets of the National Bureau of Economic Research to develop a set of national economic accounts. . . . Professor Kuznets coordinated the work of researchers at the National Bureau of Economic Research in New York and his staff at Commerce. The original set of accounts was presented in a report to Congress in 1937 and in a research report, *National Income, 1929–35.* . . .

The national accounts have become the mainstay of modern macroeconomic analysis, allowing policymakers, economists, and the business community to analyze the impact of different tax and spending plans, the impact of oil and other price shocks, and the impact of monetary policy on the economy as a whole and on specific components of final demand, incomes, industries, and regions. . . .

GDP! The right concept of economy-wide output, accurately measured. The U.S. and the world rely on it to tell where we are in the business cycle and to estimate long-run growth. It is the centerpiece of an elaborate and indispensable system of social accounting, the national income and product accounts. This is surely the single most innovative achievement of the Commerce Department in the 20th century. I was fortunate to become an economist in the 1930's when Kuznets, Nathan, Gilbert, and Jaszi were creating this most important set of economic time series. In economic theory, macroeconomics was just beginning at the same time. Complementary, these two innovations deserve much credit for

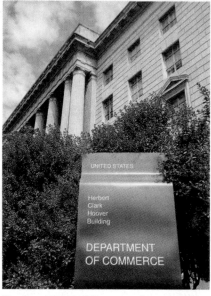

The Department of Commerce is responsible for producing and maintaining the national income and product accounts that keep track of GDP.

the improved performance of the economy in the second half of the century.

James Tobin,
Nobel laureate
Yale University Professor Emeritus of Economics

Source: U.S. Department of Commerce, Bureau of Economics, "GDP: One of the Great Inventions of the 20th Century," Survey of Current Business, *January 2000, pp. 6–9.*

Gross Investment versus Net Investment During the process of production, capital (especially machinery and equipment) produced in previous periods gradually wears out. GDP does not give us a true picture of the real production of an economy. GDP includes newly produced capital goods but does not take account of capital goods "consumed" in the production process.

depreciation The amount by which an asset's value falls in a given period.

gross investment The total value of all newly produced capital goods (plant, equipment, housing, and inventory) produced in a given period.

Capital assets decline in value over time. The amount by which an asset's value falls each period is called its **depreciation.**[2] A personal computer purchased by a business today may be expected to have a useful life of 4 years before becoming worn out or obsolete. Over that period, the computer steadily depreciates.

What is the relationship between gross investment (*I*) and depreciation? **Gross investment** is the total value of all newly produced capital goods (plant, equipment, housing, and

---

[2]This is the formal definition of economic depreciation. Because depreciation is difficult to measure precisely, accounting rules allow firms to use shortcut methods to approximate the amount of depreciation that they incur each period. To complicate matters even more, the U.S. tax laws allow firms to deduct depreciation for tax purposes under a different set of rules.

Investment—the purchase of new capital—includes increases in business inventories: lots full of cars and items at Home Depot.

inventory) produced in a given period. It takes no account of the fact that some capital wears out and must be replaced. **Net investment** is equal to gross investment minus depreciation. Net investment is a measure of how much the stock of capital *changes* during a period. Positive net investment means that the amount of new capital produced exceeds the amount that wears out, and negative net investment means that the amount of new capital produced is less than the amount that wears out. Therefore, if net investment is positive, the capital stock has increased, and if net investment is negative, the capital stock has decreased. Put another way, the capital stock at the end of a period is equal to the capital stock that existed at the beginning of the period plus net investment:

net investment Gross investment minus depreciation.

$$\text{capital}_{\text{end of period}} = \text{capital}_{\text{beginning of period}} + \text{net investment}$$

Government Consumption and Gross Investment (G) Government consumption and gross investment (G) include expenditures by federal, state, and local governments for final goods (bombs, pencils, school buildings) and services (military salaries, congressional salaries, school teachers' salaries). Some of these expenditures are counted as government consumption and some are counted as government gross investment. Government transfer payments (Social Security benefits, veterans' disability stipends, and so on) are not included in G because these transfers are not purchases of anything currently produced. The payments are not made in exchange for any goods or services. Because interest payments on the government debt are also counted as transfers, they are also excluded from GDP on the grounds that they are not payments for current goods or services.

government consumption and gross investment (G) Expenditures by federal, state, and local governments for final goods and services.

As Table 19.2 shows, government consumption and gross investment accounted for $2,215.9 billion, or 18.9 percent of U.S. GDP, in 2004. Federal government consumption and gross investment in 2004 accounted for 7.1 percent of GDP, and state and local government consumption and gross investment accounted for 11.8 percent.

Net Exports (EX − IM) The value of **net exports (EX − IM)** is the difference between *exports* (sales to foreigners of U.S.-produced goods and services) and *imports* (U.S. purchases of goods and services from abroad). This figure can be positive or negative. In 2004, the United States exported less than it imported, so the level of net exports was negative (−$624.0 billion). Before 1976, the United States was generally a net exporter—exports exceeded imports, so the net export figure was positive.

net exports (EX − IM) The difference between exports (sales to foreigners of U.S.-produced goods and services) and imports (U.S. purchases of goods and services from abroad). The figure can be positive or negative.

The reason for including net exports in the definition of GDP is simple. Consumption, investment, and government spending (C, I, and G) include expenditures on goods produced both domestically and by foreigners. Therefore, C + I + G overstates domestic production because it contains expenditures on foreign-produced goods—that is, imports (IM), which have to be subtracted from GDP to obtain the correct figure. At the same time, C + I + G understates domestic production because some of what a nation produces is sold abroad and therefore not included in C, I, or G—exports (EX) have to be added in. If a U.S. firm produces computers and sells them in Germany, the computers are part of U.S. production and should be counted as part of U.S. GDP.

TABLE 19.3 National Income, 2004

	BILLIONS OF DOLLARS	PERCENTAGE OF NATIONAL INCOME
National income	10,275.9	100.0
Compensation of employees	6,687.6	65.1
Proprietors' income	889.6	8.7
Rental income	134.2	1.3
Corporate profits	1,161.5	11.3
Net interest	505.5	4.9
Indirect taxes minus subsidies	809.3	7.9
Net business transfer payments	91.1	0.9
Surplus of government enterprises	−3.0	−0.0

Source: See Table 19.2.

national income The total income earned by the factors of production owned by a country's citizens.

compensation of employees Includes wages, salaries, and various supplements—employer contributions to social insurance and pension funds, for example—paid to households by firms and by the government.

proprietors' income The income of unincorporated businesses.

rental income The income received by property owners in the form of rent.

corporate profits The income of corporate businesses.

net interest The interest paid by business.

indirect taxes minus subsidies Taxes such as sales taxes, customs duties, and license fees, less subsidies that the government pays for which it receives no goods or services in return.

net business transfer payments Net transfer payments by businesses to others.

surplus of government enterprises Income of government enterprises.

THE INCOME APPROACH

We now turn to calculating GDP using the income approach, which looks at GDP in terms of who receives it as income rather than as who purchases it.

We begin with the concept of **national income**, which is defined in Table 19.3. National income is the sum of eight income items. **Compensation of employees**, the largest of the eight items by far, includes wages and salaries paid to households by firms and by the government, as well as various supplements to wages and salaries such as contributions that employers make to social insurance and private pension funds. **Proprietors' income** is the income of unincorporated business. **Rental income**, a minor item, is the income received by property owners in the form of rent. **Corporate profits**, the second-largest item of the eight, is the income of corporations. **Net interest** is the interest paid by business. (Interest paid by households and the government is not counted in GDP because it is not assumed to flow from the production of goods and services.)

The sixth item, **indirect taxes minus subsidies**, includes taxes such as sales taxes, customs duties, and license fees less subsidies that the government pays for which it receives no goods or services in return. (Subsidies are like negative taxes.) The value of indirect taxes minus subsidies is thus net income received by the government. **Net business transfer payments** are net transfer payments by businesses to others and are thus income of others. The final item is the **surplus of government enterprises**, which is the income of government enterprises. Table 19.3 shows that this item was negative in 2004: Government enterprises on net ran at a loss.

National income is the total income of the country, but it is not quite GDP. Table 19.4 shows what is involved in going from national income to GDP. Table 19.4 first shows that in moving from gross domestic product (GDP) to gross national product (GNP), we need to add receipts of factor income from the rest of the world and subtract payments of factor income to the rest of the world. National income is income of the country's citizens, not the

TABLE 19.4 GDP, GNP, NNP, and National Income, 2004

	DOLLARS (BILLIONS)
GDP	11,734.3
Plus: Receipts of factor income from the rest of the world	+415.4
Less: Payments of factor income to the rest of the world	−361.7
Equals: **GNP**	11,788.0
Less: Depreciation	−1,435.3
Equals: **Net national product (NNP)**	10,352.8
Less: Statistical discrepancy	−76.9
Equals: **National income**	10,275.9

Source: See Table 19.2.

TABLE 19.5 National Income, Personal Income, Disposable Personal Income, and Personal Saving, 2004

	DOLLARS (BILLIONS)
National income	10,275.9
Less: Amount of national income not going to households	−562.6
Equals: **Personal income**	9,713.3
Less: Personal income taxes	−1,049.1
Equals: **Disposable personal income**	8,664.2
Less: Personal consumption expenditures	−8,214.3
Personal interest payments	−186.7
Transfer payments made by households	−111.5
Equals: **Personal saving**	151.8
Personal saving as a percentage of disposable personal income:	1.8%

Source: See Table 19.2

income of the residents of the country, and so we need to first move from GDP to GNP. This, as discussed earlier, is a minor adjustment.

We then need to subtract depreciation from GNP, which is a large adjustment. GNP less depreciation is called **net national product (NNP)**. Why is depreciation subtracted? To see why, go back to the example earlier in this chapter in which the economy is made up of just one firm and total output (GDP) for the year is $1 million. Assume that after the firm pays wages, interest, and rent, it has $100,000 left. Assume also that its capital stock depreciated by $40,000 during the year. National income includes corporate profits (see Table 19.3), and in calculating corporate profits the $40,000 depreciation is subtracted from the $100,000, leaving profits of $60,000. When we calculate GDP using the expenditure approach, depreciation is not subtracted. We simply add consumption, investment, government spending, and net exports. In our simple example, this is just $1 million. We thus must subtract depreciation from GDP (actually GNP when there is a rest-of-the-world sector) to get national income.

Table 19.4 shows that net national product and national income are the same except for a **statistical discrepancy**. If the government were completely accurate in its data collection, the statistical discrepancy would be zero. The data collection, however, is not perfect, and the statistical discrepancy is the measurement error in each period. Table 19.4 shows that in 2004 this error was −$76.9 billion, which is small compared to national income of $10,275.9 billion.

We have so far seen from Table 19.3 the various income items that make up total national income, and we have seen from Table 19.4 how GDP and national income are related. A useful way to think about national income is to consider how much of it goes to households. The total income of households is called **personal income**, and it turns out that almost all of national income is personal income. Table 19.5 shows that of the $10,275.9 billion in national income in 2004, $9,713.3 billion was personal income. Although not shown in Table 19.5, one of the differences between national income and personal income is the profits of corporations not paid to households in the form of dividends, called the *retained earnings* of corporations. This is income that goes to corporations rather than to households, and so it is part of national income but not personal income.

Personal income is the income received by households before paying personal income taxes. The amount of income that households have to spend or save is called **disposable personal income**, or **after-tax income**. It is equal to personal income minus personal taxes, as shown in Table 19.5.

Because disposable personal income is the amount of income that households can spend or save, it is an important income concept. Table 19.5 shows there are three categories of spending: (1) personal consumption expenditures, (2) personal interest payments, and (3) transfer payments made by households. The amount of disposable personal income left after total personal spending is **personal saving**. If your monthly disposable income is $500 and you spend $450, you have $50 left at the end of the month. Your personal saving is $50 for the month. Your personal saving level can be negative: If you earn $500 and spend $600 during the month, you have *dissaved* $100. To spend $100 more than you earn, you will

net national product (NNP) Gross national product minus depreciation; a nation's total product minus what is required to maintain the value of its capital stock.

statistical discrepancy Data measurement error.

personal income The total income of households before paying personal income taxes.

disposable personal income or after-tax income Personal income minus personal income taxes. The amount that households have to spend or save.

personal saving The amount of disposable income that is left after total personal spending in a given period.

personal saving rate The percentage of disposable personal income that is saved. If the personal saving rate is low, households are spending a large amount relative to their incomes; if it is high, households are spending cautiously.

either have to borrow the $100 from someone, take the $100 from your savings account, or sell an asset you own.

The **personal saving rate** is the percentage of disposable personal income saved, an important indicator of household behavior. A low saving rate means households are spending a large amount of their income. A high saving rate means households are cautious in their spending. As Table 19.5 shows, the U.S. personal saving rate in 2004 was 1.8 percent. Saving rates tend to rise during recessionary periods, when consumers become anxious about their future, and fall during boom times, as pent-up spending demand gets released.

NOMINAL VERSUS REAL GDP

current dollars The current prices that one pays for goods and services.

nominal GDP Gross domestic product measured in current dollars.

So far, we have looked at GDP measured in **current dollars**, or the current prices we pay for things. When a variable is measured in current dollars, it is described in *nominal terms*. **Nominal GDP** is GDP measured in current dollars—all components of GDP valued at their current prices.

In many applications of macroeconomics, nominal GDP is not a very desirable measure of production. Why? Assume there is only one good—say, pizza. In each year 1 and 2, 100 units (slices) of pizza were produced. Production thus remained the same for year 1 and year 2. Suppose the price of pizza increased from $1.00 per slice in year 1 to $1.10 per slice in year 2. Nominal GDP in year 1 is $100 (100 units × $1.00 per unit), and nominal GDP in year 2 is $110 (100 units × $1.10 per unit). Nominal GDP has increased by $10, even though no more slices of pizza were produced. If we use nominal GDP to measure growth, we can be misled into thinking production has grown when all that has really happened is a rise in the price level (inflation).

If there were only one good in the economy—like pizza—it would be easy to measure production and compare one year's value to another's. We would add up all the pizza slices produced each year. In the example, production is 100 in both years. If the number of slices had increased to 105 in year 2, we would say production increased by 5 slices between year 1 and year 2, which is a 5 percent increase. Alas, however, there is more than one good in the economy.

The following is a discussion of how the BEA adjusts nominal GDP for price changes. As you read the discussion, keep in mind that this adjustment is not easy. Even in an economy of just apples and oranges, it would not be obvious how to add up apples and oranges to get an overall measure of output. The BEA's task is to add up thousands of goods, each of whose price is changing over time.

weight The importance attached to an item within a group of items.

In the following, we will use the concept of a **weight**, either price weights or quantity weights. What is a weight? It is easiest to define the term by an example. Suppose in your economics course there is a final exam and two other tests. If the final exam counts for one-half of the grade and the other two tests for one-fourth each, the "weights" are one-half, one-fourth, and one-fourth. If instead the final exam counts for 80 percent of the grade and the other two tests for 10 percent each, the weights are .8, .1, and .1. The more important an item is in a group, the larger its weight.

CALCULATING REAL GDP

Nominal GDP adjusted for price changes is called *real GDP*. All the main issues involved in computing real GDP can be discussed using a simple three-good economy and 2 years. Table 19.6 presents all the data that we will need. The table presents price and quantity data for 2 years and three goods. The goods are labeled *A*, *B*, and *C*, and the years are labeled 1 and 2. *P* denotes price, and *Q* denotes quantity.

The first thing to note from Table 19.6 is that *nominal output*—in current dollars—in year 1 for good *A* is the price of good *A* in year 1 ($0.50) times the number of units of good *A* produced in year 1 (6), which is $3.00. Similarly, nominal output in year 1 is 7 × $0.30 = $2.10 for good *B* and 10 × $0.70 = $7.00 for good *C*. The sum of these three amounts, $12.10 in column 5, is nominal GDP in year 1 in this simple economy. Nominal GDP in

TABLE 19.6 A Three-Good Economy

	(1)	(2)	(3)	(4)	(5) GDP IN YEAR 1 IN YEAR 1 PRICES $P_1 \times Q_1$	(6) GDP IN YEAR 2 IN YEAR 1 PRICES $P_1 \times Q_2$	(7) GDP IN YEAR 1 IN YEAR 2 PRICES $P_2 \times Q_1$	(8) GDP IN YEAR 2 IN YEAR 2 PRICES $P_2 \times Q_2$
	PRODUCTION YEAR 1 Q_1	YEAR 2 Q_2	PRICE PER UNIT YEAR 1 P_1	YEAR 2 P_2				
Good A	6	11	$0.50	$0.40	$3.00	$5.50	$2.40	$4.40
Good B	7	4	0.30	1.00	2.10	1.20	7.00	4.00
Good C	10	12	0.70	0.90	7.00	8.40	9.00	10.80
Total					$12.10 Nominal GDP in year 1	$15.10	$18.40	$19.20 Nominal GDP in year 2

year 2—calculated by using the year 2 quantities and the year 2 prices—is $19.20 (column 8). Nominal GDP has risen from $12.10 in year 1 to $19.20 in year 2, an increase of 58.7 percent.[3]

You can see that the price of each good changed between year 1 and year 2—the price of good A fell (from $0.50 to $0.40) and the prices of goods B and C rose (B from $0.30 to $1.00; C from $0.70 to $0.90). Some of the change in nominal GDP between years 1 and 2 is due to price changes and not production changes. How much can we attribute to price changes and how much to production changes? Here, things get tricky. The procedure that the BEA used prior to 1996 was to pick a **base year** and to use the prices in that base year as weights to calculate real GDP. This is a **fixed-weight procedure** because the weights used, which are the prices, are the same for all years—namely, the prices that prevailed in the base year.

Let us use the fixed-weight procedure and year 1 as the base year, which means using year 1 prices as the weights. Then in Table 19.6, real GDP in year 1 is $12.10 (column 5), and real GDP in year 2 is $15.10 (column 6). Note that both columns use year 1 prices, and that nominal and real GDP are the same in year 1 because year 1 is the base year. Real GDP has increased from $12.10 to $15.10, an increase of 24.8 percent.

Let us now use the fixed-weight procedure and year 2 as the base year, which means using year 2 prices as the weights. In Table 19.6, real GDP in year 1 is $18.40 (column 7), and real GDP in year 2 is $19.20 (column 8). Note that both columns use year 2 prices, and nominal and real GDP are the same in year 2 because year 2 is the base year. Real GDP has increased from $18.40 to $19.20, an increase of 4.3 percent.

This example shows that growth rates can be sensitive to the choice of the base year—24.8 percent using year 1 prices as weights and 4.3 percent using year 2 prices as weights. The old BEA procedure simply picked one year as the base year and did all the calculations using the prices in that year as weights. The new procedure makes two important changes. The first (using the current example) is to "split the difference" between 24.8 percent and 4.3 percent. What does "splitting the difference" mean? One way would be to take the average of the two numbers, which is 14.55 percent. What the BEA does is to take the *geometric* average, which for the current example is 14.09 percent.[4] These two averages (14.55 percent and 14.09 percent) are quite close, and the use of either would give similar results. The point here is not that the geometric average is used, but that the first change is to split the difference using some average. Note that this new procedure requires two "base" years, because 24.8 percent was computed using year 1 prices as weights and 4.3 percent was computed using year 2 prices as weights.

The second BEA change is to use years 1 and 2 as the base years when computing the percentage change between years 1 and 2, then use years 2 and 3 as the base years when computing the percentage change between years 2 and 3, and so on. The two base years change as the calculations move through time. The series of percentage changes computed in this way is taken to be the series of growth rates of real GDP, and so in this way nominal GDP is

base year The year chosen for the weights in a fixed-weight procedure.

fixed-weight procedure A procedure that uses weights from a given base year.

---

[3]The percentage change is calculated as $[(19.20 - 12.10)/12.10] \times 100 = .587 \times 100 = 58.7$ percent.
[4]The geometric average is computed as the square root of 124.8×104.3, which is 114.09.

adjusted for price changes. To make sure you understand this, review the calculations in Table 19.6, which provides all the data you need to see what is going on.

CALCULATING THE GDP DEFLATOR

We now switch gears from real GDP, a quantity measure, to the GDP deflator, a price measure. One of economic policy makers' goals is to keep changes in the overall price level small. For this reason policy makers need not only good measures of how real output is changing but also good measures of how the overall price level is changing. The GDP deflator is one measure of the overall price level. We can use the data in Table 19.6 to show how the GDP deflator is computed by the BEA.

In Table 19.6, the price of good *A* fell from $0.50 in year 1 to $0.40 in year 2; the price of good *B* rose from $0.30 to $1.00; and the price of good *C* rose from $0.70 to $0.90. If we were interested only in how individual prices change, this is all the information we would need. However, if we are interested in how the overall price *level* changes, we need to weight the individual prices in some way. The obvious weights to use are the quantities produced, but which quantities—those of year 1 or of year 2? The same issues arise here for the quantity weights as for the price weights in computing real GDP.

Let us first use the fixed-weight procedure and year 1 as the base year, which means using year 1 quantities as the weights. Then in Table 19.6, the "bundle" price in year 1 is $12.10 (column 5), and the bundle price in year 2 is $18.40 (column 7). Both columns use year 1 quantities. The bundle price has increased from $12.10 to $18.40, an increase of 52.1 percent.

Next use the fixed-weight procedure and year 2 as the base year, which means using year 2 quantities as the weights. Then the bundle price in year 1 is $15.10 (column 6), and the bundle price in year 2 is $19.20 (column 8). Both columns use year 2 quantities. The bundle price has increased from $15.10 to $19.20, an increase of 27.2 percent.

This example shows that overall price increases can be sensitive to the choice of the base year: 52.1 percent using year 1 quantities as weights and 27.2 percent using year 2 quantities as weights. Again, the old BEA procedure simply picked one year as the base year and did all the calculations using the quantities in the base year as weights. The new procedure first splits the difference between 52.1 percent and 27.2 percent by taking the geometric average, which is 39.1 percent. Second, it uses years 1 and 2 as the base years when computing the percentage change between years 1 and 2, years 2 and 3 as the base years when computing the percentage change between years 2 and 3, and so on. The series of percentage changes computed in this way is taken to be the series of percentage changes in the GDP deflator, that is, a series of inflation rates of the overall price level.

THE PROBLEMS OF FIXED WEIGHTS

To see why the BEA switched to the new procedure, let us consider a number of problems with using fixed-price weights to compute real GDP. First, 1987 price weights, the last price weights the BEA used before it changed procedures, are not likely to be very accurate for, say, the 1950s. Many structural changes have taken place in the U.S. economy in the last 40 to 50 years, and it seems unlikely that 1987 prices are good weights to use for the 1950s.

Another problem is that the use of fixed-price weights does not account for the responses in the economy to supply shifts. Say bad weather leads to a lower production of oranges in year 2. In a simple supply-and-demand diagram for oranges, this corresponds to a shift of the supply curve to the left, which leads to an increase in the price of oranges and a decrease in the quantity demanded. As consumers move up the demand curve, they are substituting away from oranges. If technical advances in year 2 result in cheaper ways of producing computers, the result is a shift of the computer supply curve to the right, which leads to a decrease in the price of computers and an increase in the quantity demanded. Consumers are substituting toward computers. (You should be able to draw supply and demand diagrams for both these cases.) Table 19.6 shows this tendency. The quantity of goodgood A rose between years 1 and 2 and the price decreased (the computer case), whereas the quantity of good B fell and the price increased (the orange case). The computer supply curve has been shifting to the right over time, due primarily to technical advances. The result has been large decreases in the price of computers and large increases in the quantity demanded.

To see why these responses pose a problem for the use of fixed-price weights, consider the data in Table 19.6. Because the price of good A was higher in year 1, the increase in production of good A is weighted more if we use year 1 as the base year than if we used year 2 as the base year. Also, because the price of good B was lower in year 1, the decrease in production of good B is weighted less if we use year 1 as the base year. These effects make the overall change in real GDP larger if we use year 1 price weights than if we use year 2 price weights. Using year 1 price weights ignores the kinds of substitution responses discussed in the previous paragraph and leads to what many feel are too-large estimates of real GDP changes. In the past, the BEA tended to move the base year forward about every 5 years, resulting in the past estimates of real GDP growth being revised downward. It is undesirable to have past growth estimates change simply because of the change to a new base year. The new BEA procedure avoids many of these fixed-weight problems.

Similar problems arise when using fixed-quantity weights to compute price indexes. For example, the fixed-weight procedure ignores the substitution away from goods whose prices are increasing and toward goods whose prices are decreasing or increasing less rapidly. The procedure tends to overestimate the increase in the overall price level. As discussed in the next chapter, there are still a number of price indexes that are computed using fixed weights. The GDP deflator differs because it does not use fixed weights. It is also a price index for all the goods and services produced in the economy. Other price indexes cover fewer domestically produced goods and services but also include some imported (foreign-produced) goods and services.

It should finally be stressed that there is no "right" way of computing real GDP. The economy consists of many goods, each with its own price, and there is no exact way of adding together the production of the different goods. We can say that the BEA's new procedure for computing real GDP avoids the problems associated with the use of fixed weights, and it seems to be an improvement over the old procedure. We will see in the next chapter, however, that the consumer price index (CPI)—a widely used price index—is still computed using fixed weights.

LIMITATIONS OF THE GDP CONCEPT

We generally think of increases in GDP as good. Increasing GDP (or preventing its decrease) is usually considered one of the chief goals of the government's macroeconomic policy. Because some serious problems arise when we try to use GDP as a measure of happiness or well-being, we now point out some of the limitations of the GDP concept as a measure of welfare.

GDP AND SOCIAL WELFARE

If crime levels went down, society would be better off, but a decrease in crime is not an increase in output and is not reflected in GDP. Neither is an increase in leisure time. Yet, to the extent that households desire extra leisure time (instead of having it forced on them by a lack of jobs in the economy), an increase in leisure is also an increase in social welfare. Furthermore, some increases in social welfare are associated with a *decrease* in GDP. An increase in leisure during a time of full employment, for example, leads to a decrease in GDP because less time is spent on producing output.

Most nonmarket and domestic activities, such as housework and child care, are not counted in GDP even though they amount to real production. However, if I decide to send my children to day care or hire someone to clean my house or to drive my car for me, GDP increases. The salaries of day-care staff, cleaning people, and chauffeurs are counted in GDP, but the time I spend doing the same things is not counted. A mere change of institutional arrangements, even though no more output is being produced, can show up as a change in GDP.

Furthermore, GDP seldom reflects losses or social ills. GDP accounting rules do not adjust for production that pollutes the environment. The more production there is, the larger is GDP, regardless of how much pollution results in the process.

GDP also has nothing to say about the distribution of output among individuals in a society. It does not distinguish, for example, between the case in which most output goes to a few people and the case in which output is evenly divided among all people. We cannot use GDP to measure the effects of redistributive policies (which take income from some people and give income to others). Such policies have no direct impact on GDP. GDP is also neutral about the kinds of goods an economy produces. Symphony performances, handguns, cigarettes, professional football games, Bibles, soda pop, milk, economics textbooks, and comic books all get counted similarly without regard to their differing value to society.

Despite these limitations, GDP is a highly useful measure of economic activity and well-being. If you doubt this, answer this simple question: Would you rather live in the United States of 200 years ago, when rivers were less polluted and crime rates were probably lower, or in the United States of today? Most people say they prefer the present. Even with all the "negatives," GDP per person and the average standard of living are much higher today than 200 years ago.

THE UNDERGROUND ECONOMY

Whenever sellers looking for a profit come into contact with buyers willing to pay, markets will arise, often "underground."

underground economy
The part of the economy in which transactions take place and in which income is generated that is unreported and therefore not counted in GDP.

Many transactions are missed in the calculation of GDP, even though in principle they should be counted. Most illegal transactions are missed unless they are "laundered" into legitimate business. Income that is earned but not reported as income for tax purposes is usually missed, although some adjustments are made in the GDP calculations to take misreported income into account. The part of the economy that should be counted in GDP but is not is sometimes called the **underground economy**.

Tax evasion is usually thought to be the major incentive for people to participate in the underground economy. Studies estimate that the size of the U.S. underground economy, ranging from 5 percent to 30 percent of GDP,[5] is comparable to the size of the underground economy in most European countries and probably much smaller than the size of the underground economy in the Eastern European countries. Estimates of Italy's underground economy range from 10 percent to 35 percent of Italian GDP. At the lower end of the scale, estimates for Switzerland range from 3 percent to 5 percent.

Why should we care about the underground economy? To the extent that GDP reflects only a part of economic activity instead of a complete measure of what the economy produces, it is misleading. Unemployment rates, for example, may be lower than officially measured if people work in the underground economy without reporting this fact to the government. Also, if the size of the underground economy varies among countries—as it does—we can be misled when we compare GDP among countries. For example, Italy's GDP would be much higher if we considered its underground sector as part of the economy, while Switzerland's GDP would change very little.

GROSS NATIONAL INCOME PER CAPITA

gross national income (GNI) GNP converted into dollars using an average of currency exchange rates over several years adjusted for rates of inflation.

Making comparisons across countries is difficult because such comparisons need to be made in a single currency, generally U.S. dollars. Converting GNP numbers for Japan into dollars requires converting from yen into dollars. Since exchange rates can change quite dramatically in short periods of time, such conversions are tricky. Recently the World Bank adopted a new measuring system for international comparisons. The concept of **gross national income (GNI)** is GNP converted into dollars using an average of currency exchange rates over several years adjusted for rates of inflation. Table 19.7 lists the gross national income per capita (GNI divided by population) for various countries in 2004. Norway has the highest

---

[5]See, for example, Edgar L. Feige, "Defining and Estimating Underground and Informal Economies: The New Industrial Economic Approach," *World Development* 19(7), 1990; and "The Underground Economy in the United States," Occasional Paper No. 2, U.S. Department of Labor, September 1992.

TABLE 19.7 Per Capita Gross National Income for Selected Countries, 2004

COUNTRY	U.S. DOLLARS	COUNTRY	U.S. DOLLARS
Norway	52,030	Portugal	14,350
Switzerland	48,230	South Korea	13,980
United States	41,400	Czech Republic	9,150
Denmark	40,650	Mexico	6,770
Japan	37,180	Argentina	3,720
Sweden	35,770	Turkey	3,750
Ireland	34,280	South Africa	3,630
United Kingdom	33,940	Brazil	3,090
Finland	32,790	Romania	2,920
Austria	32,300	Jordan	2,140
Netherlands	31,700	Colombia	2,000
Belgium	31,030	China	1,290
Germany	30,120	Philippines	1,170
France	30,090	Indonesia	1,140
Canada	28,390	India	620
Australia	26,900	Pakistan	600
Italy	26,120	Nepal	260
Spain	21,210	Rwanda	220
Greece	16,610	Ethiopia	110

Source: World Bank, July 2005.

per capita GNI followed by Switzerland, the United States, and Demark. Ethiopia was estimated to have per capita GNI of only $110 in 2004.

LOOKING AHEAD

This chapter has introduced many key variables that macroeconomists are interested in, including GDP and its components. There is much more to be learned about the data that macroeconomists use. In the next chapter, we will discuss the data on employment, unemployment, and the labor force, and in Chapters 23 and 24, we will discuss the data on money and interest rates. Finally, in Chapter 33, we will discuss in more detail the data on the relationship between the United States and the rest of the world.

SUMMARY

1. One source of data on the key variables in the macroeconomy is the *national income and product accounts.* These accounts provide a conceptual framework that macroeconomists use to think about how the pieces of the economy fit together.

GROSS DOMESTIC PRODUCT

2. *Gross domestic product* (*GDP*) is the key concept in national income accounting. GDP is the total market value of all final goods and services produced within a given period by factors of production located within a country. GDP excludes *intermediate goods.* To include goods both when they are purchased as inputs and when they are sold as final products would be double counting and an overstatement of the value of production.

3. GDP excludes all transactions in which money or goods change hands but in which no new goods and services are produced. GDP includes the income of foreigners working in the United States and the profits that foreign companies earn in the United States. GDP excludes the income of U.S. citizens working abroad and profits earned by U.S. companies in foreign countries.

4. *Gross national product* (*GNP*) is the market value of all final goods and services produced during a given period by factors of production owned by a country's citizens.

CALCULATING GDP

5. The *expenditure approach* to GDP adds up the amount spent on all final goods and services during a given period. The four main categories of expenditures are *personal consumption expenditures* (*C*), *gross private domestic investment* (*I*), *government consumption and gross investment* (*G*), and *net exports* (*EX − IM*). The sum of these equals GDP.

6. The three main components of *personal consumption expenditures* (*C*) are *durable goods, nondurable goods,* and *services.*

7. *Gross private domestic investment* (*I*) is the total investment made by the private sector in a given period. There are three kinds of investment: *nonresidential investment, residential investment,* and *changes in business inventories*. Gross investment does not take *depreciation*—the decrease in the value of assets—into account. *Net investment* is equal to gross investment minus depreciation.

8. *Government consumption and gross investment* (*G*) include expenditures by state, federal, and local governments for final goods and services. The value of *net exports* (*EX − IM*) equals the differences between exports (sales to foreigners of U.S.-produced goods and services) and imports (U.S. purchases of goods and services from abroad).

9. Because every payment (expenditure) by a buyer is a receipt (income) for the seller, GDP can be computed in terms of who receives it as income—the *income approach* to calculating gross domestic product.

10. GNP minus depreciation is *net national product* (*NNP*). *National income* is the total amount earned by the factors of production in the economy; it is equal to NNP except for a statistical discrepancy. *Personal income* is the total income of households. *Disposable personal income* is what households have to spend or save after paying their taxes. The *personal saving rate* is the percentage of disposable personal income saved instead of spent.

NOMINAL VERSUS REAL GDP

11. GDP measured in current dollars (the current prices that one pays for goods) is *nominal GDP*. If we use nominal GDP to measure growth, we can be misled into thinking that production has grown when all that has happened is a rise in the price level, or inflation. A better measure of production is *real GDP*, which is nominal GDP adjusted for price changes.

12. The GDP deflator is a measure of the overall price level.

LIMITATIONS OF THE GDP CONCEPT

13. We generally think of increases in GDP as good, but some problems arise when we try to use GDP as a measure of happiness or well-being. The peculiarities of GDP accounting mean that institutional changes can change the value of GDP even if real production has not changed. GDP ignores most social ills, such as pollution. Furthermore, GDP tells us nothing about what kinds of goods are being produced or how income is distributed across the population. GDP also ignores many transactions of the *underground economy*.

14. The concept of *gross national income* (*GNI*) is GNP converted into dollars using an average of currency exchange rates over several years adjusted for rates of inflation.

REVIEW TERMS AND CONCEPTS

base year, 427

change in business inventories, 421

compensation of employees, 424

corporate profits, 424

current dollars, 426

depreciation, 422

disposable personal income, or after-tax income, 425

durable goods, 421

expenditure approach, 419

final goods and services, 418

fixed-weight procedure, 427

government consumption and gross investment (*G*), 423

gross domestic product (GDP), 417

gross investment, 422

gross national income (GNI), 430

gross national product (GNP), 419

gross private domestic investment (*I*), 421

income approach, 420

indirect taxes minus subsidies, 424

intermediate goods, 418

national income, 424

national income and product accounts, 417

net business transfer payments, 424

net exports (*EX − IM*), 423

net interest, 424

net investment, 423

net national product (NNP), 425

nominal GDP, 426

nondurable goods, 421

nonresidential investment, 421

personal consumption expenditures (*C*), 421

personal income, 425

personal saving, 425

personal saving rate, 426

proprietors' income, 424

rental income, 424

residential investment, 421

services, 421

statistical discrepancy, 425

surplus of government enterprises, 424

underground economy, 430

value added, 418

weight, 426

Expenditure approach to GDP: GDP = *C* + *I* + *G* + (*EX − IM*)

GDP = final sales − change in business inventories

net investment = capital end of period − capital beginning of period

---

PROBLEM SET

1. In a simple economy suppose that all income is either compensation of employees or profits. Suppose also that there are no indirect taxes. Calculate gross domestic product from the following set of numbers. Show that the expenditure approach and the income approach add up to the same figure.

Consumption	$5,000
Investment	1,000
Depreciation	600
Profits	900
Exports	500
Compensation of employees	5,300
Government purchases	1,000
Direct taxes	800
Saving	1,100
Imports	700

2. How do we know that calculating GDP by the expenditure approach yields the same answer as calculating GDP by the income approach?

3. As the following table indicates, GNP and real GNP were almost the same in 1972, but there was a $300 billion difference by mid-1975. Explain why. Describe what the numbers here suggest about conditions in the economy at the time. How do the conditions compare with conditions today?

DATE	GNP (BILLIONS OF DOLLARS)	REAL GNP (BILLIONS OF DOLLARS)	REAL GNP (% CHANGE)	GNP DEFLATOR (% CHANGE)
72:2	1,172	1,179	7.62	2.93
72:3	1,196	1,193	5.11	3.24
72:4	1,233	1,214	7.41	5.30
73:1	1,284	1,247	10.93	5.71
73:2	1,307	1,248	.49	7.20
73:3	1,338	1,256	2.44	6.92
73:4	1,377	1,266	3.31	8.58
74:1	1,388	1,253	−4.00	7.50
74:2	1,424	1,255	.45	10.32
74:3	1,452	1,247	−2.47	10.78
74:4	1,473	1,230	−5.51	12.03
75:1	1,480	1,204	−8.27	10.86
75:2	1,517	1,219	5.00	5.07

4. What are some of the problems in using fixed weights to compute real GDP and the GDP price index? How does the BEA's approach attempt to solve these problems?

5. Explain what double counting is and discuss why GDP is not equal to total sales.

6. The following table gives some figures from a forecast of real GDP and population done in 2003. According to the forecast, approximately how much real growth will there be between 2005 and 2006? What is per capita GDP projected to be in 2005 and in 2006? Compute the forecast rate of change in real GDP and per capita real GDP between 2005 and 2006.

Real GDP 2005 (billions)	$10,517
Real GDP 2006 (billions)	$10,857
Population 2005 (millions)	295.3
Population 2006 (millions)	297.8

7. Look at a recent edition of *The Economist*. Go to the section on economic indicators. Go down the list of countries and make a list of the ones with the fastest and slowest GDP growth. Look also at the forecast rates of GDP growth. Go back to the table of contents at the beginning of the journal to see if there are articles about any of these countries. Write a paragraph or two describing the events or the economic conditions in one of them. Can you explain why they are growing or are not growing rapidly?

8. During 2002, real GDP in Japan rose about 1.3 percent. During the same period, retail sales in Japan fell 1.8 percent in real terms. What are some possible explanations for retail sales to consumers falling when GDP rises? (*Hint:* Think of the composition of GDP using the expenditure approach.)

9. Which of the following transactions would not be counted in GDP? Explain your answers.
   a. General Motors issues new shares of stock to finance the construction of a plant.
   b. General Motors builds a new plant.
   c. Company A successfully launches a hostile takeover of company B, in which it purchases all the assets of company B.
   d. Your grandmother wins $10 million in the lottery.
   e. You buy a new copy of this textbook.
   f. You buy a used copy of this textbook.
   g. The government pays out Social Security benefits.
   h. A public utility installs new antipollution equipment in its smokestacks.
   i. Luigi's Pizza buys 30 pounds of mozzarella cheese, holds it in inventory for 1 month, and then uses it to make pizza (which it sells).
   j. You spend the weekend cleaning your apartment.
   k. A drug dealer sells $500 worth of illegal drugs.

10. If you buy a new car, the entire purchase is counted as consumption in the year in which you make the transaction. Explain briefly why this is in one sense an "error" in national income accounting. (*Hint:* How is the purchase of a car different from the purchase of a pizza?) How might you correct this error?

11. Explain why imports are subtracted in the expenditure approach to calculating GDP.

12. GDP calculations do not directly include the economic costs of environmental damage—for example, global warming, acid rain. Do you think these costs should be included in GDP? Why or why not? How could GDP be amended to include environmental damage costs?

Long-Run and Short-Run Concerns: Growth, Productivity, Unemployment, and Inflation

20

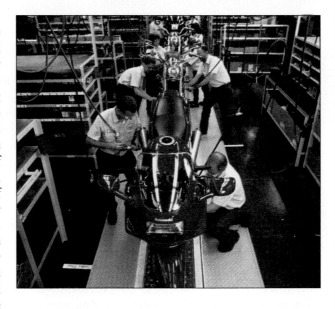

An ideal economy is one in which there is rapid growth of output per worker, low unemployment, and low inflation. In this situation government economic policy makers can sleep well at night. Alas, however, an economy is not always in this ideal state. There can be times of low growth, high unemployment, and high inflation. A key part of macroeconomics is to consider what *determines* output, unemployment, and inflation. Why is the growth of output per worker sometimes high and sometimes low? Why are unemployment and inflation sometimes high? We begin in the next chapter the task of explaining how the macroeconomy works. Before jumping into the analysis, however, in this chapter it will be useful to spend a little more time on description.

We first discuss long-run issues, namely, the rate of growth of output and output per worker over a long period of time. We then move to the short-run issues of unemployment and inflation.

Before discussing output and productivity growth, it will be useful to review a few concepts. **Output growth** is the growth rate of the output of the entire economy. **Per-capita output growth** is the growth rate of output per person in the economy. If the population of a country is growing at the same rate as output, then per-capita output is not growing: Output growth is simply keeping up with population growth. Not everyone in a country works, and so output per worker is not the same as output per person. Output per worker is larger than output per person, and it is called productivity. **Productivity growth** is thus the growth rate of output per worker.

If we take as the measure of economic welfare of a country its per-capita output, then a rapid growth rate of output does not necessarily improve individual welfare. If population is growing as rapidly as output, then per-capita output is not growing, and so the economic welfare of the average person is not growing. If the fraction of the population that is working remains the same and productivity increases, then per-capita output will increase because more output is being produced per person. Per-capita output will also increase if productivity does not change but the fraction of the population that is working increases. In this case, more output is also being produced per person, although this is so because more people are working.

output growth The growth rate of the output of the entire economy.

per-capita output growth The growth rate of output per person in the economy.

productivity growth The growth rate of output per worker.

435

LONG-RUN OUTPUT AND PRODUCTIVITY GROWTH

Figure 18.4 in Chapter 18 shows that the average growth rate of output in the United States economy since 1900 has been about 3.4 percent per year. Some years are better than others, but on average the rate is 3.4 percent. An area of economics called *growth theory* is concerned with the question of what determines this rate. Why 3.4 percent and not 2 percent or 4 percent? We take up this question in Chapter 31, but a few points are useful to make now.

Before we begin our discussion of economic growth, it is important to review what is meant by *capital*. Capital is anything that is produced that is then used as an input to produce other goods and services. Capital can be tangible, such as buildings and equipment, or intangible. The knowledge and skills acquired through education and training can be thought of as intangible *human capital*. Capital can be private or public. The roads and bridges that we drive and walk on are a part of the public capital stock. Capital, thus, can take many forms. To simplify the discussion, however, we will sometimes refer to capital as simply "machines."

In a simplified economy, machines (capital) and workers (labor) are needed to produce output. Suppose that an economy consists of six machines and 60 workers, with 10 workers working on each machine, and also that the length of the workweek is 40 hours, with this workweek resulting in 50 units of output per month per machine. Total output (GDP) for the month is thus 300 units (6 machines times 50 units per machine) in this simple economy.

How can output increase in this economy? There are a number of ways. One way is to add more workers. If, for example, 12 workers are added, 2 extra per machine, then more output can be produced per machine per hour worked because there are more workers helping out on each machine. Another way is to add more machines. For example, if 4 machines are added, then the 60 workers have a total of 10 machines to work with instead of 6, and more output can be produced per worker per hour worked. A third way is to increase the length of the workweek (for example, from 40 hours to 45 hours). With workers and machines working more hours, more output can be produced. Output can thus increase if labor or capital increases or if the amount of time labor and capital are working per week increases.

Education increases skills.

Another way for output to increase in our economy is for the quality of the workers to increase. If, for example, the education of the workers increases, this may add to their skills and thus increase their ability to work on the machines. Output per machine might then rise from 50 units per month to some larger number per month. Also, if workers become more physically fit by exercising more and eating less fat and more whole grains and fresh fruits and vegetables, their greater fitness may increase their output on the machines. People are sometimes said to be adding to their *human capital* when they increase their mental or physical skills.

The quality of the machines may also increase. In particular, new machines that replace old machines may allow more output to be produced per hour with the same number of workers. In our example, it may be that 55 instead of 50 units of output can be produced per month per new machine with 10 workers per machine and a 40-hour work week. An obvious example is the replacement of an old computer with a new, faster one that allows more to be done per minute of work on the computer.

To summarize, output can increase if there are more workers, more skills per worker, more machines, faster machines, or a longer workweek.

Turning now to the actual economy, an interesting variable to look at is the ratio of total output to the total number of worker hours. Output per worker hour is called *labor productivity* or sometimes just *productivity*. Output per worker hour is plotted in Figure 20.1 for the 1952 I–2005 II period. Two features are immediately clear from the figure. First, there is an upward trend, and second, there are fairly sizable short-run fluctuations around the trend. We will see in Chapter 30 why there are short-run fluctuations. This has to do with the possibility that the employed workforce is not always fully utilized. For now, however, the main interest is the long-run trend.

To smooth out the short-run fluctuations in Figure 20.1, we have added straight-line segments to the figure, where the segments roughly go through the high values. The slope of

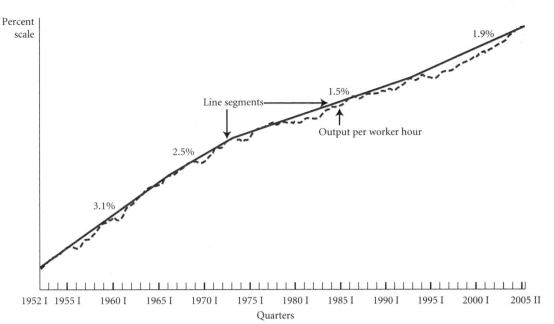

FIGURE 20.1 Output per Worker Hour (Productivity), 1952 I–2005 II

Productivity grew much faster in the 1950s and 1960s than since.

each line segment is the growth rate of productivity along the segment. The growth rates are listed in the figure. The different productivity growth rates in the figure tell an interesting story. From the 1950s through the mid-1960s the growth rate was 3.1 percent. The rate then fell to 2.5 percent in the last half of the 1960s and early 1970s. Between the early 1970s and the early 1990s the growth rate was much lower at 1.5 percent. Since the early 1990s it has been 1.9 percent.

Why are the growth rates positive in Figure 20.1? In other words, why has the amount of output that a worker can produce per hour risen in the last half century? Part of the answer is that the amount of capital per worker has increased. In Figure 20.2 capital per worker is plotted for the same 1952 I–2005 II period. It is clear from the figure that the amount of capital per worker has generally been rising. Therefore, with more capital per worker, more output can be produced per worker. The other part of the answer is that the quality of labor and capital has been increasing. Both the average skill of workers and the average quality of capital have been increasing. This means that more output can be produced per worker for a given quantity of capital, because both workers and capital are getting better.

A harder question to answer concerning Figure 20.1 is why the growth rate of productivity was much higher in the 1950s and 1960s than it has been since the early 1970s. Again, part of the answer is that the amount of capital per worker rose more rapidly in the 1950s and 1960s than it has since then. This can be seen in Figure 20.2. The other part of the answer is, of course, that the quality of labor and capital must have increased more in the 1950s and 1960s than later, although this to some extent begs the question. The key question is, why has the quality of labor and capital grown more slowly since the early 1970s? We take up this question in Chapter 31, where we will see that there seems to be no one obvious answer. An interesting question for the future is whether the continued growth of the Internet will lead to a much larger productivity growth rate, perhaps as large as the growth rate in the 1950s and 1960s. In the present context you can think about the growth of the Internet as an increase in physical capital (wires, servers, switchers, and so on) and an increase in the quality of capital (an increase in what can be done per minute using the Internet). Time will tell whether the Internet will lead to a "new age" of productivity growth.

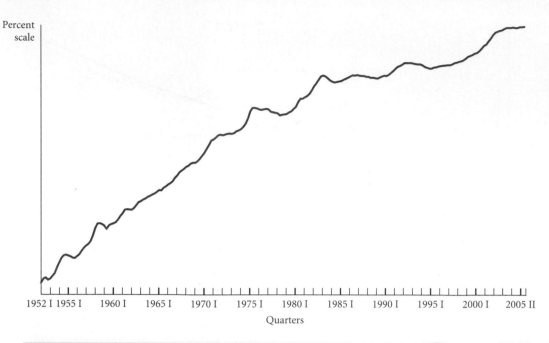

Percent
scale

1952 I 1955 I   1960 I   1965 I   1970 I   1975 I   1980 I   1985 I   1990 I   1995 I   2000 I   2005 II

Quarters

FIGURE 20.2 Capital per Worker, 1952 I–2005 II

Capital per worker grew until about 1980 and then leveled off somewhat.

RECESSIONS, DEPRESSIONS, AND UNEMPLOYMENT

recession Roughly, a period in which real GDP declines for at least two consecutive quarters. Marked by falling output and rising unemployment.

depression A prolonged and deep recession. The precise definitions of prolonged and deep are debatable.

We now move from considering long-run trends to considering deviations of the economy from long-run trends. In other words, we consider business cycles, the periodic ups and downs in the economy.

Recall from Chapter 18 that a **recession** is roughly a period in which real GDP declines for at least two consecutive quarters. Also recall that real GDP is a measure of the actual output of goods and services in the economy during a given period. When real GDP falls, less is being produced. When less output is produced, fewer inputs are used, employment declines, the unemployment rate rises, and a smaller percentage of the capital stock at our disposal is utilized (more plants and equipment are running at less than full capacity). When real output falls, real income declines.

A **depression** is a prolonged and deep recession, although there is disagreement over how severe and how prolonged a recession must be to be called a depression. Nearly everyone agrees the U.S. economy experienced a depression between 1929 and the late 1930s. The most severe recession since the 1930s took place between 1980 and 1982.

In Figure 18.5, we divided the period since 1970 into four "recessionary" periods, 1974–1975, 1980–1982, 1990–1991, and 2001. Table 20.1 summarizes some of the differences between the recession of 1980–1982 and the early part of the Great Depression. Between 1929 and 1933, real GDP declined by 26.6 percent. In other words, in 1933 the United States produced 26.6 percent less than in 1929. Only 3.2 percent of the labor force was unemployed in 1929, but 25.2 percent was unemployed in 1933. By contrast, between 1980 and 1982 real GDP was essentially unchanged rather than declining. The unemployment rate rose from 5.8 percent in 1979 to 9.7 percent in 1982. *Capacity utilization rates*, which show the percentage of factory capacity being used in production, are not available for the 1930s, so we have no point of comparison. However, Table 20.1 shows that capacity utilization fell from 85.2 percent in 1979 to 72.1 percent in 1982. Although the recession in the early 1980s was severe, it did not come close to the severity of the Great Depression.

TABLE 20.1 Real GDP and Unemployment Rates, 1929–1933 and 1980–1982

THE EARLY PART OF THE GREAT DEPRESSION, 1929–1933

	Percentage Change in Real GDP	Unemployment Rate	Number of Unemployed (Millions)
1929		3.2	1.5
1930	−8.6	8.9	4.3
1931	−6.4	16.3	8.0
1932	−13.0	24.1	12.1
1933	−1.3	25.2	12.8

Note: Percentage fall in real GDP between 1929 and 1933 was 26.6 percent.

THE RECESSION OF 1980–1982

	Percentage Change in Real GDP	Unemployment Rate	Number of Unemployed (Millions)	Capacity Utilization (Percentage)
1979		5.8	6.1	85.2
1980	−0.2	7.1	7.6	80.9
1981	2.5	7.6	8.3	79.9
1982	−1.9	9.7	10.7	72.1

Note: Percentage increase in real GDP between 1979 and 1982 was .1 percent.
Sources: Historical Statistics of the United States and U.S. Department of Commerce, Bureau of Economic Analysis.

DEFINING AND MEASURING UNEMPLOYMENT

The most frequently discussed symptom of a recession is unemployment. In September 1982, the United States unemployment rate was over 10 percent for the first time since the 1930s. Although unemployment is widely discussed, most people are unaware of what unemployment statistics mean or how they are derived.

The unemployment statistics released to the press on the first Friday of each month are based on a survey of households conducted by the Bureau of Labor Statistics (BLS), a branch of the Department of Labor. Each month the BLS draws a sample of 65,000 households and completes interviews with all but about 2,500 of them. Each interviewed household answers questions concerning the work activity of household members 16 years of age or older during the calendar week that contains the twelfth of the month. (The survey is conducted in the week that follows the week that contains the twelfth of the month.)

If a household member 16 years of age or older worked 1 hour or more as a paid employee, either for someone else or in his own business or farm, he is classified as **employed**. A household member is also considered employed if he worked 15 hours or more without pay in a family enterprise. Finally, a household member is counted as employed if she held a job from which she was temporarily absent due to illness, bad weather, vacation, labor-management disputes, or personal reasons, regardless of whether she was paid or not.

Those who are not employed fall into one of two categories: (1) unemployed or (2) not in the labor force. To be considered **unemployed**, a person must be available for work and have made specific efforts to find work during the previous 4 weeks. A person not looking for work, because he or she either does not want a job or has given up looking, is classified as **not in the labor force**. People not in the labor force include full-time students, retirees, individuals in institutions, and those staying home to take care of children or elderly parents.

The total **labor force** in the economy is the number of people employed plus the number of unemployed:

$$\text{labor force} = \text{employed} + \text{unemployed}$$

employed Any person 16 years old or older (1) who works for pay, either for someone else or in his or her own business for 1 or more hours per week, (2) who works without pay for 15 or more hours per week in a family enterprise, or (3) who has a job but has been temporarily absent, with or without pay.

unemployed A person 16 years old or older who is not working, is available for work, and has made specific efforts to find work during the previous 4 weeks.

not in the labor force A person who is not looking for work, because he or she either does not want a job or has given up looking.

labor force The number of people employed plus the number of unemployed.

The total population 16 years of age or older is equal to the number of people in the labor force plus the number not in the labor force:

$$\text{population} = \text{labor force} + \text{not in labor force}$$

unemployment rate The ratio of the number of people unemployed to the total number of people in the labor force.

With these numbers, several ratios can be calculated. The **unemployment rate** is the ratio of the number of people unemployed to the total number of people in the labor force:

$$\text{unemployment rate} = \frac{\text{unemployed}}{\text{employed} + \text{unemployed}}$$

In June 2005, the labor force contained 149.123 million people, 141.638 million of whom were employed and 7.485 million of whom were unemployed and looking for work. The unemployment rate was 5.0 percent:

$$\frac{7.485}{141.638 + 7.485} = 5.0\%$$

labor force participation rate The ratio of the labor force to the total population 16 years old or older.

The ratio of the labor force to the population 16 years old or over is called the **labor force participation rate**:

$$\text{labor force participation rate} = \frac{\text{labor force}}{\text{population}}$$

Table 20.2 shows the relationship among these numbers for selected years since 1953. The year 1982 shows the effects of the recession. Although the unemployment rate has gone up and down, the labor force participation rate has grown steadily since 1953. Most of this increase is due to the growth in the participation rate of women between the ages of 25 and 54.

Column 3 in Table 20.2 shows how many new workers the U.S. economy has absorbed in recent years. The number of employed workers increased by about 38 million between 1953 and 1982 and by about 40 million between 1982 and 2004.

COMPONENTS OF THE UNEMPLOYMENT RATE

The unemployment rate by itself conveys a limited amount of information. To understand the level of unemployment better, we must look at unemployment rates across groups of people, regions, and industries.

TABLE 20.2 Employed, Unemployed, and the Labor Force, 1953–2004

	(1) POPULATION 16 YEARS OLD OR OVER (MILLIONS)	(2) LABOR FORCE (MILLIONS)	(3) EMPLOYED (MILLIONS)	(4) UNEMPLOYED (MILLIONS)	(5) LABOR FORCE PARTICIPATION RATE	(6) UNEMPLOYMENT RATE
1953	107.1	63.0	61.2	1.8	58.9	2.9
1960	117.2	69.6	65.8	3.9	59.4	5.5
1970	137.1	82.8	78.7	4.1	60.4	4.9
1980	167.7	106.9	99.3	7.6	63.8	7.1
1982	172.3	110.2	99.5	10.7	64.0	9.7
1990	189.2	125.8	118.8	7.0	66.5	5.6
2000	212.6	142.6	136.9	5.7	67.1	4.0
2004	223.4	147.4	139.3	8.1	66.0	5.5

Note: Figures are civilian only (military excluded).
Source: Economic Report of the President, 2005, Table B-35.

TABLE 20.3 Unemployment Rates by Demographic Group, 1982 and 2005

	YEARS	NOV. 1982	JULY 2005
Total		10.8	5.2
White		9.6	4.4
Men	20+	9.0	3.4
Women	20+	8.1	4.3
Both sexes	16–19	21.8	13.4
African-American		20.2	10.2
Men	20+	19.3	8.3
Women	20+	16.5	8.9
Both sexes	16–19	51.1	36.4

Source: U.S. Department of Labor, Bureau of Labor Statistics. Data are not seasonally adjusted.

Unemployment Rates for Different Demographic Groups There are big differences in rates of unemployment across demographic groups. Table 20.3 shows the unemployment rate for November 1982—the worst month of the recession in 1982—and for July 2005, broken down by race, sex, and age. In November 1982, when the overall unemployment rate hit 10.8 percent, the rate for whites was 9.6 percent while the rate for African-Americans was more than twice that—20.2 percent.

During the recession in 1982, men fared worse than women. In November 1982, 9.0 percent of white men 20 years and over, but only 8.1 percent of white women 20 years and over were unemployed. For African-Americans, 19.3 percent of men 20 years and over and 16.5 percent of women 20 years and over were unemployed. Teenagers between 16 and 19 years of age fared worst. African-Americans between 16 and 19 experienced an unemployment rate of 51.1 percent in November 1982. For whites between 16 and 19 the unemployment rate was 21.8 percent. Although the rates were lower for all groups in July 2005, the pattern was similar. The highest unemployment rates were for African-American teenagers—36.4 percent. The main point of Table 20.3 is that an unemployment rate of, say, 5.2 percent does not mean every group in society has a 5.2 percent unemployment rate.

There are large differences in unemployment rates across demographic groups.

Unemployment Rates in States and Regions Unemployment rates vary by geographic location. For a variety of reasons, not all states and regions have the same level of unemployment. States and regions have different combinations of industries, which do not all grow and decline at the same time and at the same rate. Also, the labor force is not completely mobile—workers often cannot or do not want to pack up and move to take advantage of job opportunities in other parts of the country.

In the last 30 years, remarkable changes have occurred in the relative prosperity of regions, particularly in the Northeast and the oil-rich Southwest. During the early 1970s, the Northeast (New England, in particular) was hit by a serious decline in its industrial base. Textile mills, leather goods plants, and furniture factories closed in the face of foreign competition or moved south to states with lower wages. During the recession of 1975, Massachusetts and Michigan had very high unemployment rates (11.2 percent and 12.5 percent, respectively). Riding the crest of rising oil prices, Texas had one of the lowest unemployment rates at that time (5.6 percent) (Table 20.4).

During the recession of 1982, Texas continued to do well, and Massachusetts took a sharp turn for the better. The unemployment rate in Massachusetts went from nearly three points above the national average during the 1975 recession to nearly two points below during the 1982 recession.

By 1987, things had changed. Although not shown in Table 20.4, Massachusetts had one of the lowest unemployment rates in the country in 1987 (an amazing 2.8 percent) and Texas

TABLE 20.4 Regional Differences in Unemployment, 1975, 1982, 1991, and 2003

	1975	1982	1991	2003
U.S. avg.	8.5	9.7	6.7	6.0
Cal.	9.9	9.9	7.5	6.7
Fla.	10.7	8.2	7.3	5.1
Ill.	7.1	11.3	7.1	6.7
Mass.	11.2	7.9	9.0	5.8
Mich.	12.5	15.5	9.2	7.3
N.J.	10.2	9.0	6.6	5.9
N.Y.	9.5	8.6	7.2	6.3
N.C.	8.6	9.0	5.8	6.5
Ohio	9.1	12.5	6.4	6.1
Tex.	5.6	6.9	6.6	6.8

Sources: Statistical Abstract of the United States, various editions.

(at 8.5 percent) had one of the highest. In Massachusetts, high-tech firms such as Wang Laboratories and Digital Equipment, two firms that employed a total of over 100,000 people, had grown dramatically. In contrast, the fall in crude oil prices from over $30 per barrel to under $15 per barrel in the early 1980s forced the oil-based economy of Texas into a deep and prolonged recession. Then, in 1991, Massachusetts experienced yet another reversal with an unemployment rate of 9 percent.

The economy of Michigan is heavily tied to the fortunes of the automobile industry. During the recession of 1982, Michigan had the highest unemployment rate in the country at 15.5 percent. The automobile industry not only suffered from the decline in the U.S. economy but also faced stiff foreign competition, primarily from Japan. Michigan also suffered in 1991, with an unemployment rate of 9.2 percent.

The recession of 2001 was mild by comparison and the impact was much more uniform around the country. By the second quarter of 2003, the national unemployment rate had risen to 6.1 percent from 3.9 percent in the fourth quarter of 2000. For the states listed in Table 20.4, the unemployment rate in 2003 varied from 5.1 percent for Florida to 7.3 percent for Michigan.

> The national unemployment rate does not tell the whole story. A low national rate of unemployment does not mean that the entire nation is growing and producing at the same rate.

Discouraged-Worker Effects   Remember, people who stop looking for work are classified as having dropped out of the labor force instead of being unemployed. During recessions, people may become discouraged about finding a job and stop looking. This lowers the unemployment rate, because those no longer looking for work are no longer counted as unemployed.

discouraged-worker effect The decline in the measured unemployment rate that results when people who want to work but cannot find jobs grow discouraged and stop looking, thus dropping out of the ranks of the unemployed and the labor force.

To demonstrate how this **discouraged-worker effect** lowers the unemployment rate, suppose there are 10 million unemployed out of a labor force of 100 million. This means an unemployment rate of $10/100 = .10$, or 10 percent. If 1 million of these 10 million unemployed people stop looking for work and drop out of the labor force, there would be 9 million unemployed out of a labor force of 99 million. The unemployment rate would then drop to $9/99 = .091$, or 9.1 percent.

The BLS survey provides some evidence on the size of the discouraged-worker effect. Respondents who indicate that they have stopped searching for work are asked why they stopped. If the respondent cites inability to find employment as the sole reason for not searching, that person might be classified as a discouraged worker.

The number of discouraged workers seems to hover around 1 percent of the size of the labor force in normal times. During the 1980–1982 recession, the number of discouraged workers increased steadily to a peak of 1.5 percent. By the end of the first quarter of 1991, the recession of 1990–1991 had produced 997,000 discouraged workers. Some economists argue

TABLE 20.5 Average Duration of Unemployment, 1979–2004

	WEEKS		WEEKS
1979	10.8	1992	17.7
1980	11.9	1993	18.0
1981	13.7	1994	18.8
1982	15.6	1995	16.6
1983	20.0	1996	16.7
1984	18.2	1997	15.8
1985	15.6	1998	14.5
1986	15.0	1999	13.4
1987	14.5	2000	12.6
1988	13.5	2001	13.1
1989	11.9	2002	16.6
1990	12.0	2003	19.2
1991	13.7	2004	19.6

Sources: U.S. Department of Labor, Bureau of Labor Statistics.

that adding the number of discouraged workers to the number who are now classified as unemployed gives a better picture of the unemployment situation.

The Duration of Unemployment   The unemployment rate measures unemployment at a given point in time. It tells us nothing about how long the average unemployed worker is out of work.

Table 20.5 shows that during recessionary periods the average duration of unemployment rises. Between 1979 and 1983, the average duration of unemployment rose from 10.8 weeks to 20.0 weeks. The slow growth following the 1990–1991 recession resulted in an increase in duration of unemployment to 17.7 weeks in 1992 and to 18.8 weeks in 1994. In 2000, average duration was down to 12.6 weeks, which then rose to 19.6 weeks in 2004.

THE COSTS OF UNEMPLOYMENT

In the Employment Act of 1946, the Congress declared that it was the

> continuing policy and responsibility of the federal government to use all practicable means . . . to promote maximum employment, production, and purchasing power.

In 1978, Congress passed the Full Employment and Balanced Growth Act, commonly referred to as the *Humphrey-Hawkins Act*, which formally established a specific unemployment target of 4 percent. Why should full employment be a policy objective of the federal government? What costs does unemployment impose on society?

Some Unemployment Is Inevitable   Before we discuss the costs of unemployment, we must realize that some unemployment is simply part of the natural workings of the labor market. Remember, to be classified as unemployed, a person must be looking for a job. Every year, thousands of people enter the labor force for the first time. Some have dropped out of high school, some are high school or college graduates, and still others are finishing graduate programs. At the same time, new firms are starting up and others are expanding and creating new jobs, while other firms are contracting or going out of business.

At any moment, there is a set of job seekers and a set of jobs that must be matched with one another. It is important that the right people end up in the right jobs. The right job for a person will depend on that person's skills, preferences concerning work environment (large firm or small, formal or informal), where the individual lives, and willingness to commute. At the same time, firms want workers who can meet the requirements of the job and grow with the company.

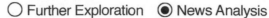

○ Further Exploration ● News Analysis

Jobs and Hurricanes in 2005

EMPLOYMENT DEPENDS ON THE LEVEL of output. Employment expands when there is output growth and contracts when growth slows or when there is a recession. But employment also depends on unforeseen events such as natural disasters and acts of terrorism.

When Hurricane Katrina hit Louisiana and Mississippi in August, 2005, thousands of people, in addition to losing their homes, lost their places of employment as well. New Orleans's mayor C. Ray Nagin was forced to lay off approximately half of 6,000 public employees because there was not enough money to meet the payroll. Yet despite these job losses in Louisiana and Mississippi, unemployment for the rest of the United States remained relatively stable, rising by only .2 percent.

Job Losses Are Below Expectations
By EDUARDO PORTER AND VIKAS BAJAJ
—*New York Times*
October 8, 2005

Employment contracted at an unexpectedly modest pace in September, underscoring the American economy's strength in the first broad snapshot since Hurricane Katrina hit Louisiana and Mississippi in August.

The Department of Labor reported yesterday that the economy lost 35,000 jobs in September, the first contraction since May 2003. The unemployment rate rose for the first time in seven months, inching up to 5.1 percent in September from 4.9 percent in August.

Job losses appeared to be concentrated in the disaster area. They were offset by strong employment growth in the rest of the country, which confirmed the continued strength of the economic expansion.

"The United States economy continues to impress with its resilience," said Scott Anderson, senior economist at Wells Fargo in Milwaukee. "The economic expansion will survive the hurricanes intact."

Philip L. Rones, deputy commissioner of the Labor Department's Bureau of Labor Statistics, told the Joint Economic Committee of Congress that employment growth outside the areas directly affected by the storm continued at a clip of about 194,000 new jobs a month, the same rate as the prior 12 months. This was consistent, he said, with a loss of about 230,000 payroll jobs because of Hurricane Katrina.

"This strikes me as unambiguously good news," said Richard DeKaser, chief economist at the National City Corporation in Cleveland. "This suggests that beyond the most severely affected areas the labor market continues to improve at a healthy clip."

"In a way, it's almost encouraging to see a number that small," said Loren Scott, an economic consultant and professor emeritus at Louisiana State University in Baton Rouge, of the estimated 230,000 jobs lost. He noted that 617,000 people were employed in the New Orleans Metropolitan area alone, and much of it was submerged by Katrina. "The numbers could have been much larger," Mr. Scott added.

To make a good match, workers must acquire information on job availability, wage rates, location, and work environment. Firms must acquire information on worker availability and skills. Information gathering consumes time and resources. The search may involve travel, interviewing, preparation of a résumé, telephone calls, and hours going through the newspaper. To the extent that these efforts lead to a better match of workers and jobs, they are well spent. As long as the gains to firms and workers exceed the costs of search, the result is efficient.

When we consider the various costs of unemployment, it is useful to categorize unemployment into three types:

- Frictional unemployment
- Structural unemployment
- Cyclical unemployment

Frictional and Structural Unemployment   When the BLS does its survey about work activity for the week containing the twelfth of each month, it interviews many people who are involved in the normal search for work. Some are either entering the labor force or switching jobs. This unemployment is both natural and beneficial for the economy.

The portion of unemployment due to the normal working of the labor market is called **frictional unemployment**. The frictional unemployment rate can never be zero. It may, however, change over time. As jobs become more and more differentiated and the number of required skills increases, matching skills and jobs becomes more complex, and the frictional unemployment rate may rise.

The concept of frictional unemployment is somewhat abstract because it is hard to know what "the normal working of the labor market" means. The industrial structure of the U.S. economy is continually changing. Manufacturing, for instance, has yielded part of its share of total employment to services and to finance, insurance, and real estate. Within the manufacturing sector, the steel and textiles industries have contracted sharply, while high-technology sectors, such as electronic components, have expanded.

Although the unemployment that arises from such structural shifts could be classified as frictional, it is usually called **structural unemployment**. The term *frictional unemployment* is used to denote short-run job/skill matching problems, problems that last a few weeks. *Structural unemployment* denotes longer-run adjustment problems—those that tend to last for years. Although structural unemployment is expected in a dynamic economy, it is painful to the workers who experience it. In some ways, those who lose their jobs because their skills are obsolete are the ones who experience the greatest pain. The fact that structural unemployment is natural and inevitable does not mean it costs society nothing.

Economists sometimes use the phrase **natural rate of unemployment** to refer to unemployment that occurs as a normal part of the functioning of the economy. This concept is also somewhat vague, because *natural* is not a precise word. It is probably best to think of the natural rate as the sum of the frictional rate and the structural rate. Estimates of the natural rate range from 4 percent to 6 percent.

Cyclical Unemployment and Lost Output   Although some unemployment is natural, there are times when the unemployment rate seems to be above the natural rate. In 1979, the unemployment rate was 5.8 percent, but it did not fall below 6 percent again until 1987, 8 years later. In the meantime, the United States experienced a major recession, during which the unemployment rate rose substantially. The increase in unemployment that occurs during recessions and depressions is called **cyclical unemployment**.

In one sense, an increase in unemployment during a recession is simply a manifestation of a more fundamental problem. The basic problem is that firms are producing less. Remember that a recession entails a decline in real GDP, or real output. When firms cut back and produce less, they employ fewer workers and less capital. Thus, the first and most direct cost of a recession is the loss of real goods and services that otherwise would have been produced.

Never was the loss of output more dramatic than during the Great Depression. In Table 20.1 you saw that real output fell about 27 percent between 1929 and 1933. It is, of course, the real output of the economy that matters most—the food we eat, the medical care we

frictional unemployment
The portion of unemployment that is due to the normal working of the labor market; used to denote short-run job/skill matching problems.

structural unemployment The portion of unemployment that is due to changes in the structure of the economy that result in a significant loss of jobs in certain industries.

natural rate of unemployment The unemployment that occurs as a normal part of the functioning of the economy. Sometimes taken as the sum of frictional unemployment and structural unemployment.

cyclical unemployment The increase in unemployment that occurs during recessions and depressions.

get, the cars we drive, the movies we watch, the new houses that are built, the pans we cook in, and the education we receive. When output falls by 27 percent, life changes for a lot of people.

During the recession of 1980–1982, the growth rate of real GDP was on average roughly zero. In Table 20.1, had real GDP grown at 3 percent each year from 1979, the total growth in output in the 1980–1982 period would have been about 9 percent instead of the 0.1 percent that actually occurred. This is a substantial loss of output and, consequently, income.

Social Consequences   The costs of recessions and depressions are neither evenly distributed across the population nor easily quantified. The social consequences of the Depression of the 1930s are perhaps the hardest to comprehend. Most people alive today did not live through the Great Depression and can only read about it in books or hear stories told by parents and grandparents. Few emerged from this period unscathed. At the bottom were the poor and the fully unemployed, about 25 percent of the labor force. Even those who kept their jobs found themselves working part-time. Many people lost all or part of their savings as the stock market crashed and thousands of banks failed.

Congressional committees heard story after story. In Cincinnati, where the labor force totaled about 200,000, about 48,000 were wholly unemployed, 40,000 more were on short time, and relief payments to the needy averaged $7 to $8 per week:

> Relief is given to a family one week and then they are pushed off for a week in the hope that somehow or other the breadwinner may find some kind of work. . . . We are paying no rent at all. That, of course, is a very difficult problem because we are continually having evictions, and social workers . . . are hard put to find places for people whose furniture has been put out on the street.[1]

From Birmingham, Alabama, in 1932:

> . . . we have about 108,000 wage and salary workers in my district. Of that number, it is my belief that not exceeding 8000 have their normal incomes. At least 25,000 men are altogether without work. Some of them have not had a stroke of work for more than 12 months. Perhaps 60,000 or 70,000 are working from one to five days a week, and practically all have had serious cuts in wages and many of them do not average over $1.50 per day.[2]

Economic hardship accompanied the 1980–1982 recession as well. Between 1979 and 1983, the number of people officially classified as living in poverty in the United States rose from 26.1 million (11.7 percent of the population) to 35.5 million (15.3 percent). In addition to economic hardship, prolonged unemployment may also bring with it social and personal ills: anxiety, depression, deterioration of physical and psychological health, drug abuse (including alcoholism), and suicide.

THE BENEFITS OF RECESSIONS

Do recessions have any benefits? Yes: Recessions are likely to slow the rate of inflation. We saw in Figure 18.7 two serious inflationary periods since 1970: 1974–1975 and 1979–1981. Each was followed by a recession during which the rate of inflation decreased. As Table 20.6 shows, inflation fell from a 1974 rate of 11.0 percent to 5.8 percent in 1976. In 1983, the inflation rate also fell, to 3.2 percent, from a 1980 rate of 13.5 percent. It appears recessions do help to counteract inflation, but more analysis is needed before we can understand why (see Chapter 26). The point here is:

Recessions may help to reduce inflation.

TABLE 20.6 Inflation Rates, 1974–1976 and 1980–1983

RECESSION BEGINS	INFLATION RATE
→ 1974	11.0
1975	9.1
1976	5.8
→ 1980	13.5
1981	10.3
1982	6.2
1983	3.2

Source: See Table 20.8.

---

[1]U.S. Senate Hearings before a subcommittee of the Committee of Manufacturers, 72nd Congress, first session (1931), p. 239. Cited in Lester Chandler, *America's Greatest Depression, 1929–1941* (New York: Harper & Row, 1970), p. 43.
[2]Senate Hearings, in Lester Chandler, *America's Greatest Depression, 1929–1941* (New York: Harper & Row, 1970), p. 43.

Some argue that recessions may increase efficiency by driving the least efficient firms in the economy out of business and forcing surviving firms to trim waste and manage their resources better. As we will discuss in Chapter 34, a recession leads to a decrease in the demand for imports, which improves a nation's balance of payments—that is, its record of trade with other countries.

INFLATION

Ups in the business cycle often, but not always, seem to encourage inflation. Table 20.7 shows the rate of inflation during the three most recent periods of expansion. The inflation rate rose from 3.2 percent to 11.0 percent from 1972 to 1974. The trend in inflation was also upward from 1976 to 1980. The sustained growth that began in 1983, however, did not seem to bring rapid inflation.

Why is inflation a problem? If you understand that wages and salaries, as well as other forms of income, increase along with prices during periods of inflation, you will see this question is more subtle than you might think. If my income doubles and the prices of the things I buy double, am I any worse off? I can buy exactly the same things that I bought yesterday, so to the extent that my well-being depends on what I am able to buy, the answer is no.

However, incomes and prices do not all increase at the same rate during inflations. For some people, income increases faster than prices; for others, prices increase faster. Some people benefit from inflations, but others are hurt.

The remainder of this chapter focuses on the problem of inflation: its measurement, its costs, and the gains and losses experienced during inflationary periods.

DEFINING INFLATION

What is inflation? Not all price increases constitute inflation. Prices of individual goods and services are determined in many ways. In competitive markets, the interaction of many buyers and many sellers—the operation of supply and demand—determines prices. In imperfectly competitive markets, prices are determined by producers' decisions. (This is the core of microeconomic theory.)

In any economy, prices are continuously changing as markets adjust to changing conditions. Lack of rain may dry up corn and wheat fields, reducing supply and pushing up the price of agricultural products. At the same time, high levels of production by oil producers may be driving down the price of oil and petroleum products. Simultaneously, the United Auto Workers may be negotiating a contract with the Ford Motor Company that raises (or lowers) wage rates.

When the price of one good rises, that price increase may or may not be part of a larger inflation. Remember, **inflation** is an increase in the overall price level. It happens when many prices increase simultaneously. We measure inflation by looking at a large number of goods and services and calculating the average increase in their prices during some period of time. **Deflation** is a decrease in the overall price level. It occurs when many prices decrease simultaneously.

It is useful to distinguish between a *one-time* increase in the overall price level and an increase in the overall price level that continues over time. For example, the overall price level could rise 10 percent in a single month and stop rising, or it could increase steadily over some years. Economists often use *inflation* to refer only to increases in the price level that continue over some significant period. We will refer to such periods as periods of **sustained inflation**.

PRICE INDEXES

Price indexes are used to measure overall price levels. We discussed how these indexes are constructed in the previous chapter. The price index that pertains to all goods and services in the economy is the *GDP deflator*. As we saw in Chapter 19, the Bureau of Economic Analysis (BEA) does not use fixed weights to construct the GDP deflator. Many other price indexes are constructed using fixed weights.

The most popular fixed-weight price index is the **consumer price index (CPI)**. The CPI was first constructed during World War I as a basis for adjusting shipbuilders' wages, which the government controlled during the war. Currently, the CPI is computed by the BLS each

**TABLE 20.7
Inflation During
Three Expansions**

	INFLATION RATE
1972	3.2
1973	6.2
1974	11.0
1976	5.8
1977	6.5
1978	7.6
1979	11.3
1980	13.5
1984	4.3
1985	3.6
1986	1.9
1987	3.6
1988	4.1
1989	4.8

Source: See Table 20.8.

inflation An increase in the overall price level.

deflation A decrease in the overall price level.

sustained inflation An increase in the overall price level that continues over a significant period.

consumer price index (CPI) A price index computed each month by the Bureau of Labor Statistics using a bundle that is meant to represent the "market basket" purchased monthly by the typical urban consumer.

month, using a bundle of goods meant to represent the "market basket" purchased monthly by the typical urban consumer. The quantities of each good in the bundle that are used for the weights are based on extensive surveys of consumers. In fact, the BLS collects prices each month for about 71,000 goods and services from about 22,000 outlets in 44 geographic areas. For example, the cost of housing is included in the data collection by surveying about 5,000 renters and 1,000 homeowners each month. Figure 20.3 shows the CPI market basket at the end of 2002.

Table 20.8 shows values of the CPI since 1950. The percentage changes in the table are calculated using the index. (The base period for this index is 3 years, 1982 to 1984, instead of the more usual 1 year.) For example, from 1970 to 1971 the CPI increased from 38.8 to 40.5. The percentage change is simply $[(40.5 - 38.8)/38.8] \times 100$, which is 4.4 percent.

Remember from the previous chapter that a fixed-weight price index such as the CPI does not account for consumers' substitution away from high-priced goods. For more information, see the Further Exploration box, "World Economy in Transition: Bias in the U.S. Consumer Price Index—Why It Could Be Important."

Changes in the CPI somewhat overstate changes in the cost of living.

In response to the fixed-weight problem, in August 2002 the BLS began publishing a version of the CPI called the Chained Consumer Price Index, which uses changing weights. Although this version is not yet the main version, it may be that within a few years the BLS moves completely away from the fixed-weight version of the CPI. Remember, however, that even if this happens, the CPI will still differ in important ways from the GDP deflator. The CPI covers only consumer goods and services, whereas the GDP deflator covers all goods and services produced in the economy. Also, the CPI includes prices of imported goods, which the GDP deflator does not. Figure 20.3 shows the market basket of goods that was used for the CPI in 2002.

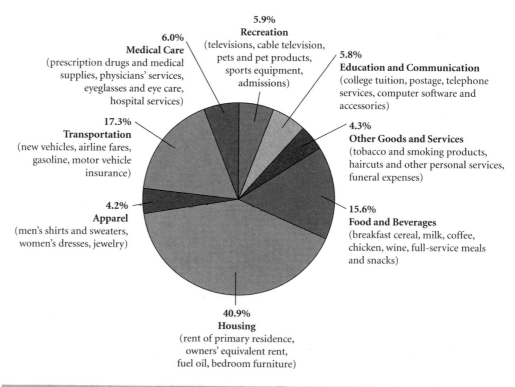

FIGURE 20.3 The CPI Market Basket

The CPI market basket shows how a typical consumer divides his or her money among various goods and services. Most of a consumer's money goes toward housing, transportation, and food and beverages.

Source: The Bureau of Labor Statistics.

TABLE 20.8 The CPI, 1950–2004

	PERCENTAGE CHANGE IN CPI	CPI		PERCENTAGE CHANGE IN CPI	CPI
1950	1.3	24.1	1978	7.6	65.2
1951	7.9	26.0	1979	11.3	72.6
1952	1.9	26.5	1980	13.5	82.4
1953	0.8	26.7	1981	10.3	90.9
1954	0.7	26.9	1982	6.2	96.5
1955	−0.4	26.8	1983	3.2	99.6
1956	1.5	27.2	1984	4.3	103.9
1957	3.3	28.1	1985	3.6	107.6
1958	2.8	28.9	1986	1.9	109.6
1959	0.7	29.1	1987	3.6	113.6
1960	1.7	29.6	1988	4.1	118.3
1961	1.0	29.9	1989	4.8	124.0
1962	1.0	30.2	1990	5.4	130.7
1963	1.3	30.6	1991	4.2	136.2
1964	1.3	31.0	1992	3.0	140.3
1965	1.6	31.5	1993	3.0	144.5
1966	2.9	32.4	1994	2.6	148.2
1967	3.1	33.4	1995	2.8	152.4
1968	4.2	34.8	1996	3.0	156.9
1969	5.5	36.7	1997	2.3	160.5
1970	5.7	38.8	1998	1.6	163.0
1971	4.4	40.5	1999	2.2	166.6
1972	3.2	41.8	2000	3.4	172.2
1973	6.2	44.4	2001	2.8	177.1
1974	11.0	49.3	2002	1.6	179.9
1975	9.1	53.8	2003	2.3	184.0
1976	5.8	56.9	2004	2.7	188.9
1977	6.5	60.6			

Sources: Bureau of Labor Statistics, U.S. Department of Labor.

Other popular price indexes are **producer price indexes (PPIs)**, once called *wholesale price indexes*. These are indexes of prices that producers receive for products at all stages in the production process, not just the final stage. The indexes are calculated separately for various stages in the production process. The three main categories are *finished goods, intermediate materials*, and *crude materials*, although there are subcategories within each of these categories.

One advantage of some of the PPIs is that they detect price increases early in the production process. Because their movements sometimes foreshadow future changes in consumer prices, they are considered to be leading indicators of future consumer prices.

producer price indexes (PPIs) Measures of prices that producers receive for products at all stages in the production process.

THE COSTS OF INFLATION

If you asked most people why inflation is bad, they would tell you that it lowers the overall standard of living by making goods and services more expensive. That is, it cuts into people's purchasing power. People are fond of recalling the days when a bottle of Coca-Cola cost a dime and a hamburger cost a quarter. Just think what we could buy today if prices had not changed. What people usually do not think about is what their incomes were in the "good old days." The fact that the cost of a Coke has increased from 10 cents to a dollar does not mean anything in real terms if people who once earned $5,000 now earn $50,000. Why? The reason is simple:

People's income from wages and salaries, profits, interest, and rent increases during inflations. The wage rate is the price of labor, rent is the price of land, and so on. During inflations, most prices—including input prices—tend to rise together, and input prices determine both the incomes of workers and the incomes of owners of capital and land.

World Economy in Transition: Bias in the U.S. Consumer Price Index—Why It Could Be Important

Changes in the consumer price index (CPI) provide the most commonly used measure of inflation in all countries. . . . In a recent study, the U.S. Advisory Commission to Study the Consumer Price Index (more commonly known as the Boskin Commission, whose chairman was Michael Boskin, former chief of the U.S. Council of Economic Advisers) estimated that the U.S. CPI overstated inflation by 1.1 percentage point in 1996 and by slightly more in each of the previous 20 years. Thus, although the official rate of inflation for 1996 was 2.9 percent, the true rate may have been in the neighborhood of 1.8 percent. This upward bias arises because the CPI methodology does not adequately capture shifts in consumer purchases when relative prices move, the effects of changes in the quality of goods and services, the introduction of new products, or the growing number of discount stores. While some experts have disputed that the upward bias is as large as has been suggested by the Commission, there is a growing consensus that there may indeed be significant bias. . . .

Upward bias in the official inflation rate has important implications. First, real wages—which were widely thought, on the basis of official data, to have stagnated over the last two decades—may, in fact, have increased considerably. Second, in regard to fiscal policy, upward bias has considerable budgetary costs: expenditures indexed to the CPI rise by more than is needed to offset inflation, and inflation adjustments made to tax brackets are overstated, resulting in reduced tax revenues. Recent estimates indicate that if the current inflation bias continues for the next 10

years, the federal government deficit will increase on this account alone by $140 billion, and $650 billion will be added to the national debt by the end of the period. . . .

The Boskin Commission's report identified and quantified three sources of bias, all of which arise because of limitations in the methodology used to calculate the CPI. . . .

■ *Quality change and new product bias*, the largest source of bias, arises because the CPI does not immediately take into account either improvements in the quality of goods and services or the introduction of new products. To the extent that the CPI fails to account for changes in quality, the index will not reflect "true" changes in prices. And new products need to be incorporated into the CPI on a timely basis, so that the early declines in price that are a normal part of the product life cycle are captured.

■ *Substitution bias* occurs because the formula used for CPI calculations assumes that consumers purchase a constant mix of various goods and services despite changes in their relative prices. In actuality, if the price of one good rises relative to that of another good, consumers will tend to substitute cheaper goods for higher-priced ones. Because the weights of goods in the CPI are adjusted infrequently (about once every 10 years), substitution is not taken into account.

■ *Outlet substitution bias* occurs because the CPI does not adequately take into account the extent to which new discount stores have

Not all prices rise at the same rate. When the price of beef rises, the impact on the cost of living is offset by the fact that households can substitute chicken or fish if those prices have risen less.

offered lower prices and enticed consumers away from the traditional outlets that tend to be more fully represented in the CPI market basket. . . .

Source: Adapted from: Paul A. Armknecht and Paula R. De Masi, "United States: Sources and Implications of Bias in the Consumer Price Index," World Economic Outlook, *International Monetary Fund (Washington, D.C., Spring 1997). Available at http://www.worldbank.org.*

Inflation Changes the Distribution of Income Whether you gain or lose during a period of inflation depends on whether your income rises faster or slower than the prices of the things you buy. The group most often mentioned when the impact of inflation is discussed is people living on fixed incomes. If your income is fixed and prices rise, your ability to purchase goods and services falls proportionately. Who are the fixed-income earners?

Most people think of the elderly. Many retired workers living on private pensions receive monthly checks that will never increase. Many pension plans, however, pay benefits that are *indexed* to inflation. The benefits these plans provide automatically increase when the general price level rises. If prices rise 10 percent, benefits also rise 10 percent. The biggest source of income for the elderly is Social Security. These benefits are fully indexed; when prices rise—that is, when the CPI rises—by 5 percent, Social Security benefits also increase by 5 percent.

Effects on Debtors and Creditors   It is also commonly believed that debtors benefit at the expense of creditors during an inflation. Certainly, if I loan you $100 to be paid back in a year, and prices increase 10 percent in the meantime, I get back 10 percent less in real terms than what I loaned you.

Suppose we had both anticipated prices would rise 10 percent. I would have taken this into consideration in the deal that I made with you. I would charge you an interest rate high enough to cover the decrease in value due to the anticipated inflation. If we agree on a 15 percent interest rate, then you must pay me $115 at the end of a year. The difference between the interest rate on a loan and the inflation rate is referred to as the **real interest rate**. In our deal, I will earn a real interest rate of 5 percent. By charging a 15 percent interest rate, I have taken into account the anticipated 10 percent inflation rate. In this sense, I am not hurt by the inflation—I keep pace with inflation and earn a profit on my money, too—despite the fact that I am a creditor.

On the other hand, an unanticipated inflation—an inflation that takes people by surprise—can hurt creditors. If the actual inflation rate during the period of my loan to you turns out to be 20 percent, then I as a creditor will be hurt. I charged you 15 percent interest, expecting to get a 5 percent real rate of return, when I needed to charge you 25 percent to get the same 5 percent real rate of return. Because inflation was higher than expected, I got a negative real return of 5 percent.

> Inflation that is higher than expected benefits debtors; inflation that is lower than expected benefits creditors.

real interest rate The difference between the interest rate on a loan and the inflation rate.

Administrative Costs and Inefficiencies   There are costs associated even with anticipated inflation. One is the administrative cost associated with simply keeping up. During the rapid inflation in Israel in the early 1980s, a telephone hotline was set up to give the hourly price index. Store owners have to recalculate and repost prices frequently, and this takes time that could be used more efficiently.

More frequent banking transactions may be required. For example, interest rates tend to rise with anticipated inflation. When interest rates are high, the opportunity costs of holding cash outside of banks is high. People therefore hold less cash and need to stop at the bank more often. (We discuss this effect in more detail in the next part of this book.) In addition, if people are not fully informed, or if they do not understand what is happening to prices in general, they may make mistakes in their business dealings. These mistakes can lead to a misallocation of resources.

Increased Risk and Slower Economic Growth   When unanticipated inflation occurs regularly, the degree of risk associated with investments in the economy increases. Increases in uncertainty may make investors reluctant to invest in capital and to make long-term commitments. Because the level of investment falls, the prospects for long-term economic growth are lessened.

INFLATION: PUBLIC ENEMY NUMBER ONE?

Economists have debated the seriousness of the costs of inflation for decades. Some, among them Alan Blinder, say, "Inflation, like every teenager, is grossly misunderstood, and this gross misunderstanding blows the political importance of inflation out of all proportion to its economic importance."[3] Others, such as Phillip Cagan and Robert Lipsey, argue, "It was once thought that the economy would in time make all the necessary adjustments [to inflation], but many of them are proving to be very difficult. . . . For financial institutions and markets, the effects of inflation have been extremely unsettling."[4]

No matter what the real economic cost of inflation, people do not like it. It makes us uneasy and unhappy. In 1974, President Ford verbalized some of this discomfort when he said, "Our

---

[3] Alan Blinder, *Hard Heads, Soft Hearts: Tough-Minded Economics for a Just Society* (Reading, MA: Addison-Wesley, 1987).
[4] Phillip Cagan and Robert Lipsey, "The Financial Effects of Inflation," National Bureau of Economic Research (Cambridge, MA: General Series No. 103, 1978), pp. 67–68.

inflation, our public enemy number one, will unless whipped destroy our country, our homes, our liberties, our property, and finally our national pride, as surely as any well-armed wartime enemy."[5] In this belief, our elected leaders have vigorously pursued policies designed to stop inflation. This brings us to where we started. If, as we suggested earlier, the recessions of 1974 to 1975 and 1980 to 1982 were the price we had to pay to stop inflation, stopping inflation is costly.

LOOKING AHEAD

This ends our introduction to the basic concepts and problems of macroeconomics. The first chapter of this part introduced the field, the second discussed the measurement of national product and national income, and this chapter discussed some of the major concerns of macroeconomists. We are now ready to begin the analysis of how the macroeconomy works.

---

[5]U.S. President, Weekly Compilation of Presidential Documents, vol. 10, no. 41, p. 1247. Cited in Blinder, *Hard Heads.*

SUMMARY

LONG-RUN OUTPUT AND PRODUCTIVITY GROWTH

1. Output growth depends on (1) the growth rate of the capital stock, (2) the growth rate of output per unit of the capital stock, (3) the growth rate of labor, and (4) the growth rate of output per unit of labor.

2. Output per worker hour (labor productivity) rose faster in the 1950s and 1960s than it has risen from the 1970s to 2005. An interesting question is whether labor productivity will rise faster in the future because of the Internet.

RECESSIONS, DEPRESSIONS, AND UNEMPLOYMENT

3. A *recession* is a period in which real GDP declines for at least two consecutive quarters. When less output is produced, employment declines, the unemployment rate rises, and a smaller percentage of the capital stock is used. When real output falls, real income declines.

4. A *depression* is a prolonged and deep recession, although there is disagreement over how severe and how prolonged a recession must be to be called a depression.

5. The *unemployment rate* is the ratio of the number of *unemployed* people to the number of people in the *labor force*. To be considered unemployed and in the labor force, a person must be looking for work.

6. Big differences in rates of unemployment exist across demographic groups, regions, and industries. African-Americans, for example, experience much higher unemployment rates than whites.

7. A person who decides to stop looking for work is considered to have dropped out of the labor force and is no longer classified as unemployed. People who stop looking because they are discouraged about finding a job are sometimes called *discouraged workers.*

8. Some unemployment is inevitable. Because new workers are continually entering the labor force, because industries and firms are continuously expanding and contracting, and because people switch jobs, there is a constant process of job

search as workers and firms try to match the best people to the available jobs. This unemployment is both natural and beneficial for the economy.

9. The unemployment that occurs because of short-run job/skill-matching problems is called *frictional unemployment.* The unemployment that occurs because of longer-run structural changes in the economy is called *structural unemployment.* The *natural rate of unemployment* is the sum of the frictional rate and the structural rate. The increase in unemployment that occurs during recessions and depressions is called *cyclical unemployment.*

10. The major costs associated with recessions and unemployment are decreased real output, the damage done to the people who are unemployed, and lost output in the future. Benefits of recessions are that they may help to reduce inflation, increase efficiency, and improve a nation's balance of payments.

INFLATION

11. An *inflation* is an increase in the overall price level. It happens when many prices increase simultaneously. Inflation is measured by calculating the average increase in the prices of a large number of goods during some period of time. A *deflation* is a decrease in the overall price level. A *sustained inflation* is an increase in the overall price level that continues over a significant period of time.

12. A number of different indexes are used to measure the overall price level. Among them are the *GDP deflator, consumer price index (CPI),* and *producer price indexes (PPIs).*

13. Whether people gain or lose during a period of inflation depends on whether their income rises faster or slower than the prices of the things they buy. The elderly are more insulated from inflation than most people think, because Social Security benefits and many pensions are indexed to inflation.

14. Inflation that is higher than expected benefits debtors, and inflation that is lower than expected benefits creditors.

REVIEW TERMS AND CONCEPTS

consumer price index (CPI), 447

cyclical unemployment, 445

deflation, 447

depression, 438

discouraged-worker effect, 442

employed, 439

frictional unemployment, 445

inflation, 447

labor force, 439

labor force participation rate, 440

natural rate of unemployment, 445

not in the labor force, 439

output growth, 435

per-capita output growth, 435

producer price indexes (PPIs), 449

productivity growth, 435

real interest rate, 451

recession, 438

structural unemployment, 445

sustained inflation, 447

unemployed, 439

unemployment rate, 440

1. Labor force = employed + unemployed
2. Population = labor force + not in labor force
3. Unemployment rate $= \dfrac{\text{unemployed}}{\text{employed + unemployed}}$
4. Labor force participation rate $= \dfrac{\text{labor force}}{\text{population}}$

PROBLEM SET

1. Suppose you are hired by the National Bureau of Economic Research to write a formal definition of a depression as distinct from a recession. What are the factors that you consider in making such a distinction formal? Prepare a formal (statistical) definition of a depression and defend it.

2. In September 2005, economists were saying that the U.S. economy was close to full employment even though the unemployment rate was 5.1 percent. How can they make this assertion?

3. The News Analysis box on page 444 notes that while 230,000 jobs were lost as a direct result of Hurricane Katrina in August 2005, job growth in the rest of the economy nearly made up for the entire loss. One example of jobs gained back was a substantial increase in employment in and around the Port of Albany, New York, on the Hudson River. Local officials reported that shipping that was to go up the Mississippi through the severely damaged Port of New Orleans was diverted immediately up the East Coast to the ports on the Hudson. Search the Web and see if you can find evidence of increased employment in and around other port cities. Also, go to **www.bls.gov**, and click on the most recent release of the employment data for the United States. What actually happened in late 2005 and 2006 to employment? To the unemployment rate? Were the job losses of September 2005 quickly erased?

4. "When an inefficient firm or a firm producing a product that people no longer want goes out of business, people are unemployed, but that is part of the normal process of economic growth and development; the unemployment is part of the natural rate and need not concern policy makers." Discuss this statement and its relevance to the economy today.

5. What is the unemployment rate in your state today? What was it in 1970, 1975, and 1982? How has your state done relative to the national average? Do you know, or can you determine, why?

6. Suppose that all wages, salaries, welfare benefits, and other sources of income were indexed to inflation. Would inflation still be considered a problem? Why or why not?

7. What do the CPI and the PPI measure? Why do we need all these price indexes? (Think about what purpose you would use each one for.)

8. The consumer price index (CPI) is a fixed-weight index. It compares the price of a fixed bundle of goods in one year with the price of the same bundle of goods in some base year. Calculate the price of a bundle containing 100 units of good X, 150 units of good Y, and 25 units of good Z in the years 2000, 2001, and 2002. Convert the results into an index by dividing each bundle price figure by the bundle price in year 2000. Calculate the percentage change in your index between 2000 and 2001 and again between 2001 and 2002. Was there inflation between 2001 and 2002?

GOOD	QUANTITY CONSUMED	PRICES 2000	PRICES 2001	PRICES 2002
X	100	$1.00	$1.50	$1.75
Y	150	1.50	2.00	2.00
Z	25	3.00	3.25	3.00

9. Consider the following statements:
   a. "More people are employed in Tappania now than at any time in the past 50 years."
   b. "The unemployment rate in Tappania is higher now than it has been in 50 years."
   Can both of these statements be true at the same time? Explain.

10. Policy makers talk about the "capacity" of the economy to grow. What specifically is meant by the "capacity" of the economy? How might capacity be measured? In what ways is capacity limited by labor constraints, and by capital constraints? What are the consequences if demand in the economy exceeds capacity? What signs would you look for?

11. What was the rate of growth in real GDP during the most recent quarter? You can find the answer in publications such as the *Survey of Current Business, The Economist,* or *Business Week.* Has growth been increasing or decreasing? What policies might you

suggest for increasing the economy's potential long-run rate of growth?

12. Suppose the stock of capital and the workforce are both increasing at 3 percent annually in the country of Wholand. At the same time, real output is growing at 6 percent. How is that possible in the short run, and in the long run?

13. The following table shows that from 1969 to late 1971, real GNP grew by more than $40 billion and employment (the number of jobs) grew by 1.6 million, but the unemployment rate nearly doubled, from 3.4 percent to 5.9 percent. How can that be?

DATE	REAL GNP (BILLIONS OF DOLLARS)	REAL GNP (% CHANGE)	EMPLOYMENT (MILLIONS)	UNEMPLOYMENT (MILLIONS)	U-RATE
69:1	1,084	4.6	81.2	2.7	3.4
69:2	1,088	1.8	81.7	2.8	3.4
69:3	1,091	1.1	82.2	2.9	3.6
69:4	1,086	−2.3	82.6	2.9	3.6
70:1	1,081	−1.6	82.7	3.4	4.2
70:2	1,082	.7	82.4	4.0	4.8
70:3	1,093	3.8	82.3	4.3	5.2
70:4	1,084	−3.0	82.3	4.9	5.8
71:1	1,111	10.3	82.2	5.0	5.9
71:2	1,117	1.9	82.4	5.0	5.9
71:3	1,126	3.2	82.8	5.1	6.0

Aggregate Expenditure and Equilibrium Output

21

W e now begin our discussion of the theory of how the macroeconomy works. We know how to calculate gross domestic product (GDP), but what factors *determine* it? We know how to define and measure inflation and unemployment, but what circumstances *cause* inflation and unemployment? What, if anything, can government do to reduce unemployment and inflation?

Analyzing the various components of the macroeconomy is a complex undertaking. The level of GDP, the overall price level, and the level of employment—three chief concerns of macroeconomists—are influenced by events in three broadly defined "markets":

- Goods-and-services markets
- Financial (money) markets
- Labor markets

We will explore each market, as well as the links between them, in our discussion of macroeconomic theory. Figure 21.1 presents the plan of the next seven chapters, which form the core of macroeconomic theory. In Chapters 21 and 22, we describe the market for goods and services, often called the *goods market*. In Chapter 21, we explain several basic concepts and show how the equilibrium level of national income is determined in a simple economy with no government and no imports or exports. In Chapter 22, we provide a more complete picture of the economy by adding government purchases, taxes, and net exports to the analysis.

In Chapters 23 and 24, we focus on the *money market*. Chapter 23 introduces the money market and the banking system and discusses the way the U.S. central bank (the Federal Reserve) controls the money supply. Chapter 24 analyzes the demand for money and the way interest rates are determined. Chapter 25 then examines the relationship between the goods market and the money market. Chapter 26 explores the aggregate demand and supply curves first mentioned in Chapter 18. Chapter 26 also analyzes how the overall price level is determined, as well as the relationship between output and the price level. Finally, Chapter 27 discusses the supply of and demand for labor and the functioning of the *labor market* in the macroeconomy. This material is essential to an understanding of employment and unemployment.

Before we begin our discussion of aggregate output and aggregate income, we need to stress that production, consumption, and other activities that we will be discussing in the

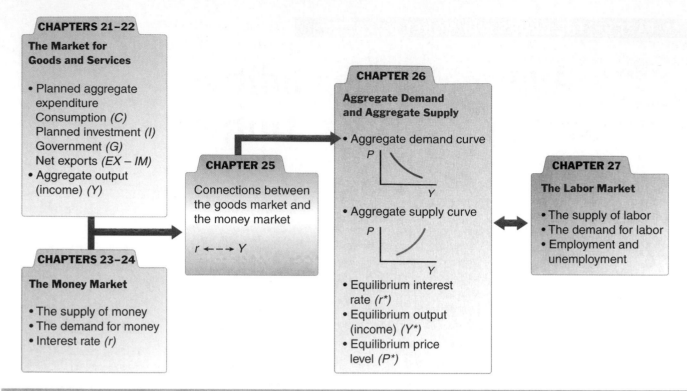

FIGURE 21.1 The Core of Macroeconomic Theory

We build up the macroeconomy slowly. In Chapters 21 and 22 we examine the market for goods and services, and in Chapters 23 and 24 we examine the money market. Then in Chapter 25 we bring the two markets together, in so doing explaining the links between aggregate output (Y) and the interest rate (r). In Chapter 26 we explain how the aggregate demand curve can be derived from Chapters 21 through 25, and we introduce the aggregate supply curve. This sets the stage for an explanation of the price level (P). We then explain in Chapter 27 how the labor market fits into the macroeconomic picture.

following chapters are ongoing activities. Nonetheless, it is helpful to think about these activities as if they took place in a series of *production periods.* A period might be a month long or perhaps 3 months long. During each period, some output is produced, income is generated, and spending takes place. At the end of each period we can examine the results. Was everything that was produced in the economy sold? What percentage of income was spent? What percentage was saved? Is output (income) likely to rise or fall in the next period?

AGGREGATE OUTPUT AND AGGREGATE INCOME (Y)

Each period, firms produce some aggregate quantity of goods and services, which we refer to as *aggregate output* (Y). In Chapter 19, we introduced real gross domestic product as a measure of the quantity of output produced in the economy, Y. Output includes the production of services, consumer goods, and investment goods. It is important to think of these as components of "real" output.

We have already seen that GDP (Y) can be calculated in terms of either income or expenditures. Because every dollar of expenditure is received by someone as income, we can compute total GDP (Y) either by adding up the total spent on all final goods during a period *or* by adding up all the income—wages, rents, interest, and profits—received by all the factors of production.

We will use the variable Y to refer to both **aggregate output** and **aggregate income** because they are the same seen from two different points of view. When output increases, additional income is generated. More workers may be hired and paid; workers may put in, and be paid for, more hours; and owners may earn more profits. When output is cut, income falls, workers may be laid off or work fewer hours (and be paid less), and profits may fall.

aggregate output The total quantity of goods and services produced (or supplied) in an economy in a given period.

aggregate income The total income received by all factors of production in a given period.

aggregate output (income) (Y) A combined term used to remind you of the exact equality between aggregate output and aggregate income.

In any given period, there is an exact equality between aggregate output (production) and aggregate income. You should be reminded of this fact whenever you encounter the combined term **aggregate output (income).**

Aggregate output can also be considered the aggregate quantity supplied, because it is the amount that firms are supplying (producing) during the period. In the discussions that follow, we use the phrase *aggregate output* (*income*), instead of *aggregate quantity supplied*, but keep in mind that the two are equivalent. Also remember that "aggregate output" means "real GDP."

Think in Real Terms   From the outset you must think in "real terms." For example, when we talk about output (*Y*), we mean real output, not nominal output. Although we discussed in Chapter 19 that the calculation of real GDP is complicated, you can ignore these complications in the following analysis. To help make things easier to read, we will frequently use dollar values for *Y*, but do not confuse *Y* with nominal output. The main point is to think of *Y* as being in real terms—the quantities of goods and services produced, not the dollars circulating in the economy.

INCOME, CONSUMPTION, AND SAVING (*Y*, *C*, AND *S*)

Each period (a month or 3 months) households receive some aggregate amount of income (*Y*). We begin our analysis in a simple world with no government and a "closed" economy, that is, no imports and no exports. In such a world, a household can do two, and only two, things with its income: It can buy goods and services—that is, it can *consume*—or it can save. This is shown in Figure 21.2. The part of its income that a household does not consume in a given period is called **saving**. Total household saving in the economy (*S*) is by definition equal to income minus consumption (*C*):

$$\text{saving} \equiv \text{income} - \text{consumption}$$

$$S \equiv Y - C$$

The triple equal sign means this is an **identity**, or something that is always true. You will encounter several identities in this chapter, which you should commit to memory.

Remember that saving does *not* refer to the total savings accumulated over time. Saving (without the final *s*) refers to the portion of a *single period's* income that is not spent in that period. Saving (*S*) is the amount added to *accumulated savings* in any given period. *Saving* is a flow variable; *savings* is a stock variable. (Review Chapter 3 if you are unsure of the difference between stock and flow variables.)

EXPLAINING SPENDING BEHAVIOR

So far, we have said nothing about behavior. We have not described the consumption and saving behavior of households, and we have not speculated about how much aggregate output firms will decide to produce in a given period. Instead, we have only a framework and a set of definitions to work with.

Macroeconomics, you will recall, is the study of behavior. To understand the functioning of the macroeconomy, we must understand the behavior of households and firms. In our

saving (S) The part of its income that a household does not consume in a given period. Distinguished from *savings*, which is the current stock of accumulated saving.

identity Something that is always true.

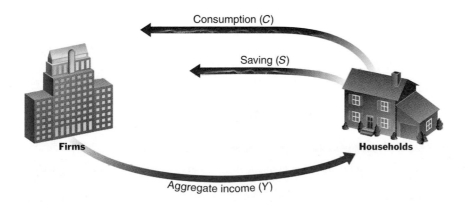

FIGURE 21.2 Saving ≡ Aggregate Income − Consumption

All income is either spent on consumption or saved in an economy in which there are no taxes. Thus, $S \equiv Y - C$.

simple economy in which there is no government, there are two types of spending behavior: spending by households, or *consumption*, and spending by firms, or *investment*.

Household Consumption and Saving How do households decide how much to consume? In any given period, the amount of aggregate consumption in the economy depends on a number of factors.

Some determinants of aggregate consumption include:

1. Household income
2. Household wealth
3. Interest rates
4. Households' expectations about the future

These four factors work together to determine the spending and saving behavior of households, both for individual ones and for the aggregate. This is no surprise. Households with higher income and higher wealth are likely to spend more than households with less income and less wealth. Lower interest rates reduce the cost of borrowing, so lower interest rates are likely to stimulate spending. (Higher interest rates increase the cost of borrowing and are likely to decrease spending.) Finally, positive expectations about the future are likely to increase current spending, whereas uncertainty about the future is likely to decrease current spending.

All these factors are important, but we will concentrate for now on the relationship between income and consumption.[1] In *The General Theory*, Keynes argued that the amount of consumption undertaken by a household is directly related to its income:

> The higher your income is, the higher your consumption is likely to be. People with more income tend to consume more than people with less income.

consumption function
The relationship between consumption and income.

The relationship between consumption and income is called a **consumption function**. Figure 21.3 shows a hypothetical consumption function for an individual household. The

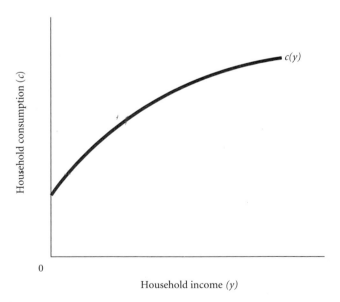

FIGURE 21.3 A Consumption Function for a Household

A consumption function for an individual household shows the level of consumption at each level of household income.

---

[1]The assumption that consumption is dependent solely on income is, of course, overly simplistic. Nonetheless, many important insights about how the economy works can be obtained through this simplification. In Chapter 29, we relax this assumption and consider the behavior of households and firms in the macroeconomy in more detail.

curve is labeled $c(y)$, which is read "c as a function of y," or "consumption as a function of income." There are several things you should notice about the curve. First, it has a positive slope. In other words, as y increases, so does c. Second, the curve intersects the c-axis above zero. This means that even at an income of zero, consumption is positive. Even if a household found itself with a zero income, it still must consume to survive. It would borrow or live off its savings, but its consumption could not be zero.

Keep in mind that Figure 21.3 shows the relationship between consumption and income for an individual household, but also remember that macroeconomics is concerned with aggregate consumption. Specifically, macroeconomists want to know how *aggregate* consumption (the total consumption of all households) is likely to respond to changes in *aggregate* income. If all individual households increase their consumption as income increases, and we assume that they do, it is reasonable to assume that a positive relationship exists between aggregate consumption (C) and aggregate income (Y).

For simplicity, assume that points of aggregate consumption, when plotted against aggregate income, lie along a straight line, as in Figure 21.4. Because the aggregate consumption function is a straight line, we can write the following equation to describe it:

$$C = a + bY$$

Y is aggregate output (income), C is aggregate consumption, and a is the point at which the consumption function intersects the C-axis—a constant. The letter b is the slope of the line, in this case $\Delta C / \Delta Y$ [because consumption (C) is measured on the vertical axis, and income (Y) is measured on the horizontal axis].[2] Every time income increases (say by ΔY), consumption increases by b times ΔY. Thus, $\Delta C = b \times \Delta Y$ and $\Delta C/\Delta Y = b$. Suppose, for example, that the slope of the line in Figure 21.4 is .75 (that is, $b = .75$). An increase in income (ΔY) of $100 would then increase consumption by $b\Delta Y = .75 \times \$100$, or $75.

The **marginal propensity to consume (MPC)** is the fraction of a change in income that is consumed. In the consumption function here, b is the *MPC*. An *MPC* of .75 means consumption changes by .75 of the change in income. The slope of the consumption function is the *MPC*.

marginal propensity to consume (MPC) That fraction of a change in income that is consumed, or spent.

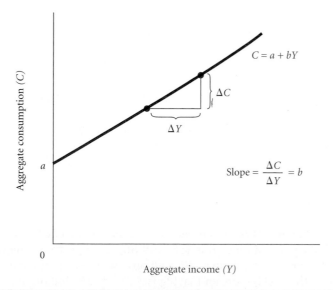

$$C = a + bY$$

$$\text{Slope} = \frac{\Delta C}{\Delta Y} = b$$

FIGURE 21.4 An Aggregate Consumption Function

The consumption function shows the level of consumption at every level of income. The upward slope indicates that higher levels of income lead to higher levels of consumption spending.

---

[2]The Greek letter Δ (delta) means "change in." For example, ΔY (read "delta Y") means the "change in income." If income (Y) in 2004 is $100 and income in 2005 is $110, then ΔY for this period is $110 − $100 = $10. For a review of the concept of slope, see Appendix, Chapter 1.

$$\text{marginal propensity to consume} \equiv \text{slope of consumption function} \equiv \frac{\Delta C}{\Delta Y}$$

marginal propensity to save (MPS) That fraction of a change in income that is saved.

There are only two places income can go: consumption or saving. If $0.75 of a $1.00 increase in income goes to consumption, $0.25 must go to saving. If income decreases by $1.00, consumption will decrease by $0.75 and saving will decrease by $0.25. The **marginal propensity to save (MPS)** is the fraction of a change in income that is saved: $\Delta S/\Delta Y$, where ΔS is the change in saving. Because everything not consumed is saved, the *MPC* and the *MPS* must add up to 1.

$$MPC + MPS \equiv 1$$

Because the *MPC* and the *MPS* are important concepts, it may help to review their definitions.

The marginal propensity to consume (*MPC*) is the fraction of an increase in income that is consumed (or the fraction of a decrease in income that comes out of consumption). The marginal propensity to save (*MPS*) is the fraction of an increase in income that is saved (or the fraction of a decrease in income that comes out of saving).

Because C is aggregate consumption and Y is aggregate income, it follows that the *MPC* is *society's* marginal propensity to consume out of national income and that the *MPS* is *society's* marginal propensity to save out of national income.

Numerical Example The numerical examples used in the rest of this chapter are based on the following consumption function:

$$C = \underbrace{100}_{a} + \underbrace{.75Y}_{b}$$

This equation is simply an extension of the generic $C = a + bY$ consumption function we have been discussing. At a national income of zero, consumption is $100 billion ($a$). As income rises, so does consumption. We will assume that for every $100 billion increase in income (ΔY), consumption rises by $75 billion ($\Delta C$). This means that the slope of the consumption function (b) is equal to $\Delta C/\Delta Y$, or $75 billion/$100 billion = .75. The marginal propensity to consume out of national income is therefore .75; the marginal propensity to save is .25. Some numbers derived from this consumption function are listed and graphed in Figure 21.5.

Now consider saving. We already know $Y \equiv C + S$, income equals consumption plus saving. Once we know how much consumption will result from a given level of income, we know how much saving there will be. Recall that saving is everything that is not consumed.

$$S \equiv Y - C$$

From the numbers in Figure 21.5, we can easily derive the saving schedule that is shown. At an income of $200 billion, consumption is $250 billion; saving is thus a negative $50 billion ($S \equiv Y - C = $200 billion $-$ $250 billion $= -$50 billion). At an aggregate income of $400 billion, consumption is exactly $400 billion, and saving is zero. At $800 billion in income, saving is a positive $100 billion.

The consumption and saving functions we have been discussing are shown in Figure 21.6. To analyze their relationship, we will use the device of the 45° line as a way of comparing C and Y. The 45° line—the solid black line in the top graph—shows all the points at which the value on the horizontal axis equals the value on the vertical axis. Thus, the 45° line in Figure 21.6 represents all the points at which aggregate income equals aggregate consumption.) Where the consumption function is *above* the 45° line, consumption exceeds income, and saving is negative. Where the consumption function

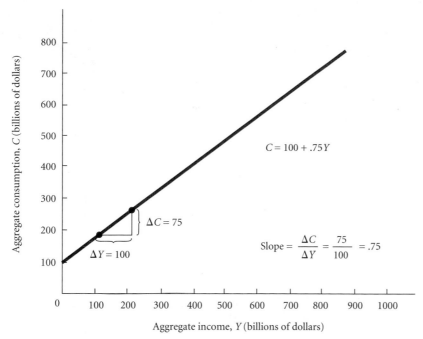

AGGREGATE INCOME, Y (BILLIONS OF DOLLARS)	AGGREGATE CONSUMPTION, C (BILLIONS OF DOLLARS)
0	100
80	160
100	175
200	250
400	400
600	550
800	700
1,000	850

FIGURE 21.5 An Aggregate Consumption Function Derived from the Equation
$C = 100 + .75Y$

In this simple consumption function, consumption is $100 billion at an income of zero. As income rises, so does consumption. For every $100 billion increase in income, consumption rises by $75 billion. The slope of the line is .75.

crosses the 45° line, consumption is equal to income, and saving is zero. Where the consumption function is *below* the 45° line, consumption is less than income, and saving is positive. Note that the slope of the saving function is $\Delta S/\Delta Y$, which is equal to the marginal propensity to save (*MPS*).

> The consumption function and the saving function are mirror images of one another. No information appears in one that does not also appear in the other. These functions tell us how households in the aggregate will divide income between consumption spending and saving at every possible income level. In other words, they embody aggregate household behavior.

PLANNED INVESTMENT (*I*)

Consumption, as we have seen, is the spending by households on goods and services, but what kind of spending do firms engage in? The answer is *investment*.

What Is Investment?   Let us begin with a brief review of terms and concepts. In everyday language, we use *investment* to refer to what we do with our savings: "I invested in a mutual fund and some AOL stock." In the language of economics, however, *investment*

$C = 100 + .75Y$

$S \equiv Y - C$

Y AGGREGATE INCOME (BILLIONS OF DOLLARS)	−	C AGGREGATE CONSUMPTION (BILLIONS OF DOLLARS)	=	S AGGREGATE SAVING (BILLIONS OF DOLLARS)
0		100		−100
80		160		−80
100		175		−75
200		250		−50
400		400		0
600		550		50
800		700		100
1,000		850		150

FIGURE 21.6 Deriving a Saving Function from a Consumption Function

Because $S \equiv Y - C$, it is easy to derive a saving function from a consumption function. A 45° line drawn from the origin can be used as a convenient tool to compare consumption and income graphically. At $Y = 200$, consumption is 250. The 45° line shows us that consumption is larger than income by 50. Thus $S \equiv Y - C = -50$. At $Y = 800$, consumption is less than income by 100. Thus, $S = 100$ when $Y = 800$.

always refers to the creation of capital stock. To an economist, an investment is something produced that is used to create value in the future.

You must not confuse the two uses of the term. When a firm builds a new plant or adds new machinery to its current stock, it is investing. A restaurant owner who buys tables, chairs, cooking equipment, and silverware is investing. When a college builds a new sports center, it is investing. From now on, we use **investment** only to refer to purchases by firms of new buildings and equipment and inventories, all of which add to firms' capital stocks.

Recall that inventories are part of the capital stock. When firms add to their inventories, they are investing—they are buying something that creates value in the future. Most of the

investment Purchases by firms of new buildings and equipment and additions to inventories, all of which add to firms' capital stock.

capital stock of a clothing store consists of its inventories of unsold clothes in its warehouses and on its racks and display shelves. The service provided by a supermarket or department store is the convenience of having a large variety of commodities in inventory available for purchase at a single location.

Manufacturing firms generally have two kinds of inventories: *inputs* and *final products*. General Motors (GM) has stocks of tires, rolled steel, engine blocks, valve covers, and thousands of other things in inventory, all waiting to be used in producing new cars. In addition, GM has an inventory of finished automobiles awaiting shipment.

Investment is a flow variable—it represents additions to capital stock in a specific period. A firm's decision on how much to invest each period is determined by many factors. For now, we will focus simply on the effects that given investment levels have on the rest of the economy.

Actual versus Planned Investment   One of the most important insights of macroeconomics is deceptively simple: A firm may not always end up investing the exact amount that it planned to. The reason is that a firm does not have complete control over its investment decision; some parts of that decision are made by other actors in the economy. (This is not true of consumption, however. Because we assume households have complete control over their consumption, planned consumption is always equal to actual consumption.)

Generally, firms can choose how much new plant and equipment they wish to purchase in any given period. If GM wants to buy a new robot to stamp fenders or McDonald's decides to buy an extra french fry machine, it can usually do so without difficulty. There is, however, another component of investment over which firms have less control—inventory investment.

Suppose GM expects to sell 1 million cars this quarter and has inventories at a level it considers proper. If the company produces and sells 1 million cars, it will keep its inventories just where they are now (at the desired level). Now suppose GM produces 1 million cars, but due to a sudden shift of consumer interest it sells only 900,000 cars. By definition, GM's inventories of cars must go up by 100,000 cars. The firm's **change in inventory** is equal to production minus sales. The point here is:

change in inventory
Production minus sales.

> One component of investment—inventory change—is partly determined by how much households decide to buy, which is not under the complete control of firms. If households do not buy as much as firms expect them to, inventories will be higher than expected, and firms will have made an inventory investment that they did not plan to make.

Because involuntary inventory adjustments are neither desired nor planned, we need to distinguish between actual investment and **desired**, or **planned**, **investment**. We will use I to refer to desired or planned investment only. In other words, I will refer to planned purchases of plant and equipment and planned inventory changes. **Actual investment**, in contrast, is the *actual* amount of investment that takes place. If actual inventory investment turns out to be higher than firms planned, then actual investment is greater than I, planned investment.

desired, or planned, investment Those additions to capital stock and inventory that are planned by firms.

actual investment The actual amount of investment that takes place; it includes items such as unplanned changes in inventories.

For the purposes of this chapter, we will take the amount of investment that firms together plan to make each period (I) as fixed at some given level. We assume this level does not vary with income. In the example that follows, we will assume that $I = \$25$ billion, regardless of income. As Figure 21.7 shows, this means the planned investment function is a horizontal line.

PLANNED AGGREGATE EXPENDITURE (*AE*)

We define total **planned aggregate expenditure (*AE*)** in the economy to be consumption (C) plus planned investment (I).[3]

planned aggregate expenditure (*AE*) The total amount the economy plans to spend in a given period. Equal to consumption plus planned investment: $AE \equiv C + I$.

> planned aggregate expenditure $\equiv$ consumption + planned investment
>
> $$AE \equiv C + I$$

[3]In practice, planned aggregate expenditure also includes government spending (G) and net exports ($EX - IM$): $AE \equiv C + I + G + (EX - IM)$. In this chapter, we are assuming that G and ($EX - IM$) are zero. This assumption is relaxed in the next chapter.

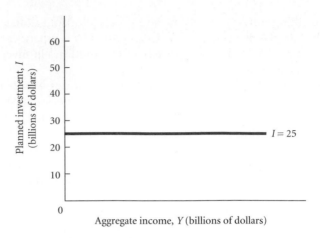

FIGURE 21.7 The Planned Investment Function

For the time being, we will assume that planned investment is fixed. It does not change when income changes, so its graph is a horizontal line.

AE is the total amount that the economy plans to spend in a given period. We will now use the concept of planned aggregate expenditure to discuss the economy's equilibrium level of output.

EQUILIBRIUM AGGREGATE OUTPUT (INCOME)

Thus far, we have described the behavior of firms and households. We now discuss the nature of equilibrium and explain how the economy achieves equilibrium.

A number of definitions of *equilibrium* are used in economics. They all refer to the idea that at equilibrium, there is no tendency for change. In microeconomics, equilibrium is said to exist in a particular market (for example, the market for bananas) at the price for which the quantity demanded is equal to the quantity supplied. At this point, both suppliers and demanders are satisfied. The equilibrium price of a good is the price at which suppliers want to furnish the amount that demanders want to buy.

In macroeconomics, we define **equilibrium** in the goods market as that point at which planned aggregate expenditure is equal to aggregate output.

> aggregate output $\equiv Y$
>
> planned aggregate expenditure $\equiv AE \equiv C + I$
>
> equilibrium: $Y = AE$, or $Y = C + I$

equilibrium Occurs when there is no tendency for change. In the macroeconomic goods market, equilibrium occurs when planned aggregate expenditure is equal to aggregate output.

Note that the equilibrium condition is not an identity.

This definition of equilibrium can hold if, and only if, planned investment and actual investment are equal. (Remember, we are assuming there is no unplanned consumption.) To understand why, consider Y not equal to AE. First, suppose aggregate output is greater than planned aggregate expenditure:

$$Y > C + I$$

aggregate output > planned aggregate expenditure

When output is greater than planned spending, there is unplanned inventory investment. Firms planned to sell more of their goods than they sold, and the difference shows up as an unplanned increase in inventories.

Next, suppose planned aggregate expenditure is greater than aggregate output:

$$C + I > Y$$

planned aggregate expenditure > aggregate output

(1) AGGREGATE OUTPUT (INCOME)(Y)	(2) AGGREGATE CONSUMPTION (C)	(3) PLANNED INVESTMENT (I)	(4) PLANNED AGGREGATE EXPENDITURE (AE) $C + I$	(5) UNPLANNED INVENTORY CHANGE $Y - (C + I)$	(6) EQUILIBRIUM? ($Y = AE$?)
100	175	25	200	−100	No
200	250	25	275	−75	No
400	400	25	425	−25	No
500	475	25	500	0	Yes
600	550	25	575	+25	No
800	700	25	725	+75	No
1,000	850	25	875	+125	No

When planned spending exceeds output, firms have sold more than they planned to. Inventory investment is smaller than planned. Planned and actual investment are not equal. Only when output is exactly matched by planned spending will there be no unplanned inventory investment. If there is unplanned inventory investment, this will be a state of disequilibrium. The mechanism by which the economy returns to equilibrium will be discussed later.

> Equilibrium in the goods market is achieved only when aggregate output (Y) and planned aggregate expenditure ($C + I$) are equal, or when actual and planned investment are equal.

Table 21.1 derives a planned aggregate expenditure schedule and shows the point of equilibrium for our numerical example. (Remember, all our calculations are based on $C = 100 + .75Y$.) To determine planned aggregate expenditure, we add consumption spending (C) to planned investment spending (I) at every level of income. Glancing down columns 1 and 4, we see one, and only one, level at which aggregate output and planned aggregate expenditure are equal: $Y = 500$.

Figure 21.8 illustrates the same equilibrium graphically. Figure 21.8(a) adds planned investment, constant at $25 billion, to consumption at every level of income. Because planned investment is a constant, the planned aggregate expenditure function is simply the consumption function displaced vertically by that constant amount. Figure 21.8(b) plots the planned aggregate expenditure function with the 45° line. The 45° line represents all points on the graph where the variables on the horizontal and vertical axes are equal. Any point on the 45° line is a potential equilibrium point. The planned aggregate expenditure function crosses the 45° line at a single point, where $Y = \$500$ billion. (The point at which the two lines cross is sometimes called the *Keynesian cross*.) At that point, $Y = C + I$.

Now let us look at some other levels of aggregate output (income). First, consider $Y = \$800$ billion. Is this an equilibrium output? Clearly it is not. At $Y = \$800$ billion, planned aggregate expenditure is $725 billion. (See Table 21.1.) This amount is less than aggregate output, which is $800 billion. Because output is greater than planned spending, the difference ends up in inventory as unplanned inventory investment. In this case, unplanned inventory investment is $75 billion.

Next, consider $Y = \$200$ billion. Is this an equilibrium output? No. At $Y = \$200$ billion, planned aggregate expenditure is $275 billion. Planned spending (AE) is greater than output (Y), and there is unplanned inventory disinvestment of $75 billion.

At $Y = \$200$ billion and $Y = \$800$ billion, planned investment and actual investment are unequal. There is unplanned investment, and the system is out of balance. Only at $Y = \$500$ billion, where planned aggregate expenditure and aggregate output are equal, will planned investment equal actual investment.

Finally, let us find the equilibrium level of output (income) algebraically. Recall that we know the following:

(1) $Y = C + I$ (equilbrium)

(2) $C = 100 + .75Y$ (consumption function)

(3) $I = 25$ (planned investment)

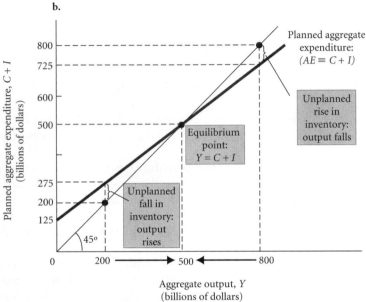

FIGURE 21.8 Equilibrium Aggregate Output

Equilibrium occurs when planned aggregate expenditure and aggregate output are equal. Planned aggregate expenditure is the sum of consumption spending and planned investment spending.

By substituting (2) and (3) into (1), we get:

$$Y = \underbrace{100 + .75Y}_{C} + \underbrace{25,}_{+\ I}$$

There is only one value of Y for which this statement is true, and we can find it by rearranging terms:

$$Y - .75Y = 100 + 25$$

$$Y - .75Y = 125$$

$$.25Y = 125$$

$$Y = \frac{125}{.25} = 500$$

The equilibrium level of output is 500, as seen in Table 21.1 and Figure 21.8.

THE SAVING/INVESTMENT APPROACH TO EQUILIBRIUM

Because aggregate income must either be saved or spent, by definition, $Y \equiv C + S$, which is an identity. The equilibrium condition is $Y = C + I$, but this is not an identity because it does not hold when we are out of equilibrium.[4] By substituting $C + S$ for Y in the equilibrium condition, we can write:

$$C + S = C + I$$

Because we can subtract C from both sides of this equation, we are left with:

$$S = I$$

Thus, only when planned investment equals saving will there be equilibrium.

This saving/investment approach to equilibrium stands to reason intuitively if we recall two things: (1) Output and income are equal, and (2) saving is income that is not spent. Because it is not spent, saving is like a leakage out of the spending stream. Only if that leakage is counterbalanced by some other component of planned spending can the resulting planned aggregate expenditure equal aggregate output. This other component is planned investment (I).

This counterbalancing effect can be seen in Figure 21.9. Aggregate income flows into households, and consumption and saving flow out. The diagram shows saving flowing from households into the financial market. Firms use this saving to finance investment projects. If the planned investment of firms equals the saving of households, then planned aggregate expenditure ($AE \equiv C + I$) equals aggregate output (income) (Y), and there is equilibrium: The *leakage* out of the spending stream—saving—is matched by an equal *injection* of planned investment spending into the spending stream. For this reason, the saving/investment approach to equilibrium is also called the *leakages/injections approach* to equilibrium.

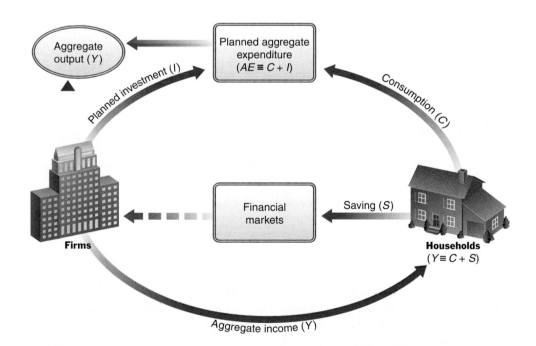

FIGURE 21.9 Planned Aggregate Expenditure and Aggregate Output (Income)

Saving is a leakage out of the spending stream. If planned investment is exactly equal to saving, then planned aggregate expenditure is exactly equal to aggregate output, and there is equilibrium.

---

[4]It would be an identity if I included unplanned inventory accumulations—in other words, if I were actual investment instead of planned investment.

Inventory Changes Signal Slower Growth

Inventory Changes Signal Slower Growth

IN JUNE 2005, THE GOVERNMENT announced that inventories held at U.S. wholesalers increased by 1.1 percent, which was more than analysts and firms had expected. Since inventory increases are part of investment spending, this rise was counted as part of GDP. But what about "planned" investment spending, which measures the total spending on goods and services that firms "plan" to make in a given period?

An unexpected increase in inventories means that actual sales are less than what was expected. This is likely to lead to firms cutting back on production in the future.

Perhaps the unanticipated rise in inventories in 2005 was a signal of things to come?

Bloomberg.com

**U.S. Wholesalers'
Inventories Rose 1.1%
in June (Update 1)**

Aug. 9 (Bloomberg)—Inventories at U.S. wholesalers rose 1.1 percent in June, greater than forecast, as sales failed to increase for the first time in more than a year, a government report showed.

The June increase in inventories, which brought the value of goods at distributors, warehouses and terminals to $309.5 billion, followed a gain of 1.4 percent the month before, the Commerce Department said in Washington. Sales were unchanged after rising for 12 months, including an increase of 0.3 percent in May.

Consumer spending cooled by the most in almost three years during the month.

Inventories at wholesalers of durable goods, which include cars, machinery and appliances, rose 1.4 percent in June after rising 1.9 percent the previous month. Sales rose 0.5 percent after no change the previous month. A 1 percent drop in sales of electrical equipment after a 3.9 percent increase a month earlier limited the gain in all wholesale sales.

Source: Courtesy of Bloomberg LP.

Figure 21.10 reproduces the saving schedule derived in Figure 21.6 and the horizontal investment function from Figure 21.7. Notice that $S = I$ at one, and only one, level of aggregate output, $Y = 500$. At $Y = 500$, $C = 475$ and $I = 25$. In other words, $Y = C + I$, and therefore equilibrium exists.

ADJUSTMENT TO EQUILIBRIUM

We have defined equilibrium and learned how to find it, but we have said nothing about how firms might react to *disequilibrium*. Let us consider the actions firms might take when planned aggregate expenditure exceeds aggregate output (income).

We already know the only way firms can sell more than they produce is by selling some inventory. This means that when planned aggregate expenditure exceeds aggregate output,

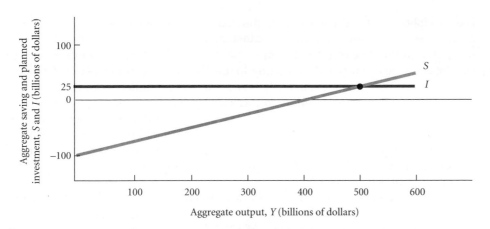

FIGURE 21.10 The S = I Approach to Equilibrium

Aggregate output will be equal to planned aggregate expenditure only when saving equals planned investment (S = I). Saving and planned investment are equal at Y = 500.

unplanned inventory reductions have occurred. It seems reasonable to assume firms will respond to unplanned inventory reductions by increasing output. If firms increase output, income must also increase (output and income are two ways of measuring the same thing). As GM builds more cars, it hires more workers (or pays its existing workforce for working more hours), buys more steel, uses more electricity, and so on. These purchases by GM represent income for the producers of labor, steel, electricity, and so on. If GM (and all other firms) try to keep their inventories intact by increasing production, they will generate more income in the economy as a whole. This will lead to more consumption. Remember, when income rises, consumption also rises.

> The adjustment process will continue as long as output (income) is below planned aggregate expenditure. If firms react to unplanned inventory reductions by increasing output, an economy with planned spending greater than output will adjust to equilibrium, with Y higher than before. If planned spending is less than output, there will be unplanned increases in inventories. In this case, firms will respond by reducing output. As output falls, income falls, consumption falls, and so forth, until equilibrium is restored, with Y lower than before.

As Figure 21.8 shows, at any level of output above $Y = 500$, such as $Y = 800$, output will fall until it reaches equilibrium at $Y = 500$, and at any level of output below $Y = 500$, such as $Y = 200$, output will rise until it reaches equilibrium at $Y = 500$.[5]

THE MULTIPLIER

Now that we know how the equilibrium value of income is determined, we ask: How does the equilibrium level of output change when planned investment changes? If there is a sudden change in planned investment, how will output respond, if it responds at all? As we will see, the change in equilibrium output is *greater* than the initial change in planned investment. Output changes by a multiple of the change in planned investment. So, this multiple is called the multiplier.

---

[5]In discussing simple supply and demand equilibrium in Chapters 3 and 4, we saw that when quantity supplied exceeds quantity demanded, the price falls and the quantity supplied declines. Similarly, when quantity demanded exceeds quantity supplied, the price rises and the quantity supplied increases. In the analysis here we are ignoring potential changes in prices or in the price level and focusing on changes in the level of real output (income). Later, after we have introduced money and the price level into the analysis, prices will be very important. At this stage, however, only aggregate output (income) (Y) adjusts when aggregate expenditure exceeds aggregate output (with inventory falling) or when aggregate output exceeds aggregate expenditure (with inventory rising).

The **multiplier** is defined as the ratio of the change in the equilibrium level of output to a change in some autonomous variable. An **autonomous variable** is a variable that is assumed not to depend on the state of the economy—that is, a variable is autonomous if it does not change in response to changes in the economy. In this chapter, we consider planned investment to be autonomous. This simplifies our analysis and provides a foundation for later discussions.

With planned investment autonomous, we can ask how much the equilibrium level of output changes when planned investment changes. Remember that we are not trying here to explain *why* planned investment changes; we are simply asking how much the equilibrium level of output changes when (for whatever reason) planned investment changes. (Beginning in Chapter 25, we will no longer take planned investment as given and will explain how planned investment is determined.)

Consider a sustained increase in planned investment of $25 billion—that is, suppose I increases from $25 billion to $50 billion and stays at $50 billion. If equilibrium existed at $I = $25 billion, an increase in planned investment of $25 billion will cause a disequilibrium, with planned aggregate expenditure greater than aggregate output by $25 billion. Firms immediately see unplanned reductions in their inventories, and, as a result, they begin to increase output.

Let us say the increase in planned investment comes from an anticipated increase in travel that leads airlines to purchase more airplanes, car rental companies to increase purchases of automobiles, and bus companies to purchase more buses (all capital goods). The firms experiencing unplanned inventory declines will be automobile manufacturers, bus producers, and aircraft producers—GM, Ford, Boeing, and so forth. In response to declining inventories of planes, buses, and cars, these firms will increase output.

Now suppose these firms raise output by the full $25 billion increase in planned investment. Does this restore equilibrium? No, it does not, because when output goes up, people earn more income and a part of that income will be spent. This increases planned aggregate expenditure even further. In other words, an increase in I also leads indirectly to an increase in C. To produce more airplanes, Boeing has to hire more workers or ask its existing employees to work more hours. It also must buy more engines from General Electric, more tires from Goodyear, and so forth. Owners of these firms will earn more profits, produce more, hire more workers, and pay out more in wages and salaries.

> This added income does not vanish into thin air. It is paid to households that spend some of it and save the rest. The added production leads to added income, which leads to added consumption spending.

If planned investment (I) goes up by $25 billion initially *and is sustained at this higher level*, an increase of output of $25 billion will *not* restore equilibrium, because it generates even more consumption spending (C). People buy more consumer goods. There are unplanned reductions of inventories of basic consumption items—washing machines, food, clothing, and so forth—and this prompts other firms to increase output. The cycle starts all over again.[6]

Output and income can rise by significantly more than the initial increase in planned investment, but how much and how large is the multiplier? This is answered graphically in Figure 21.11. Assume the economy is in equilibrium at point A, where equilibrium output is 500. The increase in I of 25 shifts the $AE \equiv C + I$ curve up by 25, because I is higher by 25 at every level of income. The new equilibrium occurs at point B, where the equilibrium level of output is 600. Like

---

[6]Figure 21.9 can help you understand the multiplier effect. Note in the figure how an increase in planned investment makes its way through the circular flow. Initially, aggregate output is at equilibrium with $Y = C + I$. That is, every period, aggregate output is produced by firms, and every period, planned aggregate expenditure is just sufficient to take all those goods and services off the market.

Now note what happens when planned investment spending increases and is sustained at a higher level. Firms experience unplanned declines in inventories and they increase output; more real output is produced in subsequent periods. However, the added output means more income; thus we see added income flowing to households. This means more spending. Households spend some portion of their added income (equal to the added income times the *MPC*) on consumer goods.

The higher consumption spending means that even if firms responded fully to the increase in investment spending in the first round, the economy is still out of equilibrium. Follow the added spending back over to firms in Figure 21.9 and you can see that with higher consumption, planned aggregate expenditure will be greater. Firms again see an unplanned decline in inventories, and they respond by increasing the output of consumer goods. This sets off yet another round of income and expenditure increases: Output rises, and income rises as a result, thus increasing consumption. Higher consumption leads to yet another disequilibrium, inventories fall, and output (income) rises again.

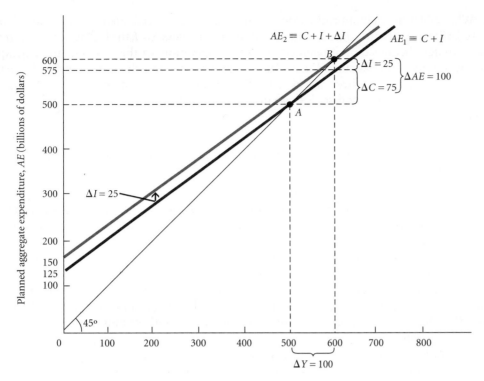

FIGURE 21.11 The Multiplier as Seen in the Planned Aggregate Expenditure Diagram

At point A, the economy is in equilibrium at $Y = 500$. When I increases by 25, planned aggregate expenditure is initially greater than aggregate output. As output rises in response, additional consumption is generated, pushing equilibrium output up by a multiple of the initial increase in I. The new equilibrium is found at point B, where $Y = 600$. Equilibrium output has increased by 100 (600 – 500), or *four times* the amount of the increase in planned investment.

point A, point B is on the 45° line and is an equilibrium value. Output (Y) has increased by 100 (600 − 500), or four times the initial increase in planned investment of 25, between point A and point B. The multiplier in this example is 4. At point B, aggregate spending is also higher by 100. If 25 of this additional 100 is investment (I), as we know it is, the remaining 75 is added consumption (C). From point A to point B then, $\Delta Y = 100$, $\Delta I = 25$, and $\Delta C = 75$.

Why doesn't the multiplier process go on forever? The answer is that only a fraction of the increase in income is consumed in each round. Successive increases in income become smaller and smaller in each round of the multiplier process, due to leakage as saving, until equilibrium is restored.

The size of the multiplier depends on the slope of the planned aggregate expenditure line. The steeper the slope of this line is, the greater the change in output for a given change in investment. When planned investment is fixed, as in our example, the slope of the $AE \equiv C + I$ line is just the marginal propensity to consume ($\Delta C/\Delta Y$). The greater the MPC is, the greater the multiplier. This should not be surprising. A large MPC means that consumption increases a lot when income increases. The more consumption changes, the more output has to change to achieve equilibrium.

THE MULTIPLIER EQUATION

Is there a way to determine the size of the multiplier without using graphic analysis? Yes, there is.

Assume that the market is in equilibrium at an income level of $Y = 500$. Now suppose planned investment (I)—thus planned aggregate expenditure (AE)—increases and remains higher by \$25 billion. Planned aggregate expenditure is greater than output, there is an unplanned inventory reduction, and firms respond by increasing output (income) (Y). This leads to a second round of increases, and so on.

What will restore equilibrium? Look at Figure 21.10 and recall: Planned aggregate expenditure ($AE \equiv C + I$) is not equal to aggregate output (Y) unless $S = I$; the leakage of saving must exactly match the injection of planned investment spending for the economy to be in equilibrium. Recall also we assumed that planned investment jumps to a new, higher level and stays there; it is a *sustained* increase of $25 billion in planned investment spending. As income rises, consumption rises and so does saving. Our $S = I$ approach to equilibrium leads us to conclude:

> Equilibrium will be restored only when saving has increased by exactly the amount of the initial increase in I.

Otherwise, I will continue to be greater than S, and $C + I$ will continue to be greater than Y. (The $S = I$ approach to equilibrium leads to an interesting paradox in the macroeconomy. See the Further Exploration box, "The Paradox of Thrift.")

It is possible to figure how much Y must increase in response to the additional planned investment before equilibrium will be restored. Y will rise, pulling S up with it until the change in saving is exactly equal to the change in planned investment—that is, until S is again equal to I at its new higher level. Because added saving is a *fraction* of added income (the *MPS*), the increase in *income* required to restore equilibrium must be a *multiple* of the increase in planned investment.

Recall that the marginal propensity to save (*MPS*) is the fraction of a change in income that is saved. It is defined as the change in S (ΔS) over the change in income (ΔY):

$$MPS = \frac{\Delta S}{\Delta Y}$$

Because ΔS must be equal to ΔI for equilibrium to be restored, we can substitute ΔI for ΔS and solve:

$$MPS = \frac{\Delta I}{\Delta Y}$$

Therefore,

$$\Delta Y = \Delta I \times \frac{1}{MPS}$$

As you can see, the change in equilibrium income (ΔY) is equal to the initial change in planned investment (ΔI) times $1/MPS$. The multiplier is $1/MPS$:

$$\text{multiplier} \equiv \frac{1}{MPS}$$

Because $MPS + MPC \equiv 1$, $MPS \equiv 1 - MPC$. It follows that the multiplier is equal to

$$\text{multiplier} \equiv \frac{1}{1 - MPC}$$

In our example, the *MPC* is .75, so the *MPS* must equal $1 - .75$, or .25. Thus, the multiplier is 1 divided by .25, or 4. The change in the equilibrium level of Y is $4 \times \$25$ billion, or $100 billion.[7] Also note that the same analysis holds when planned investment falls. If

---

[7]The multiplier can also be derived algebraically, as the appendix to this chapter demonstrates.

The Paradox of Thrift

An interesting paradox can arise when households attempt to increase their saving. What happens if households become concerned about the future and want to save more today to be prepared for hard times tomorrow? If households increase their planned saving, the saving schedule in Figure 1 shifts upward from S_0 to S_1. The plan to save more is a plan to consume less, and the resulting drop in spending leads to a drop in income. Income drops by a multiple of the initial shift in the saving schedule. Before the increase in saving, equilibrium exists at point A, where $S_0 = I$ and $Y = \$500$ billion. Increased saving shifts the equilibrium to point B, the point at which $S_1 = I$. New equilibrium output is $300 billion—a $200 billion decrease ($\Delta Y$) from the initial equilibrium.

By consuming less, households have actually *caused* the hard times about which they were apprehensive. Worse, the new equilibrium finds saving at the same level as it was before consumption dropped ($25 billion). In their attempt to save more, households have caused a contraction in output, and thus in income. They end up consuming less, but they have not saved any more.

It should be clear why saving at the new equilibrium is equal to saving at the old equilibrium. Equilibrium requires that saving equal planned investment, and because planned investment is unchanged, saving must remain unchanged for equilibrium to exist. This paradox shows that the interactions among sectors in the economy can be of crucial importance.

The *paradox of thrift* is "paradoxical" because it contradicts the widely held belief that "a penny saved is a penny earned." This may be true for an individual, but when society as a whole saves

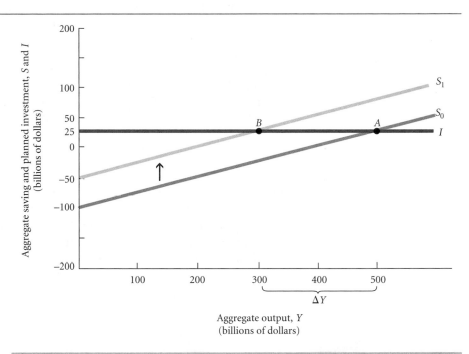

FIGURE 1 The Paradox of Thrift

An increase in planned saving from S_0 to S_1 causes equilibrium output to decrease from $500 billion to $300 billion. The decreased consumption that accompanies increased saving leads to a contraction of the economy and to a reduction of income, but at the new equilibrium, saving is the same as it was at the initial equilibrium. Increased efforts to save have caused a drop in income but no overall change in saving.

more, the result is a drop in income but no increased saving.

Does the paradox of thrift always hold? Recall our assumption that planned investment is fixed. Let us drop this assumption for a moment. If the extra saving that households want to do to ward off hard times is channeled into additional investment

through financial markets, there is a shift up in the I schedule. The paradox could then be averted. If investment increases, a new equilibrium can be achieved at a higher level of saving and income. This result, however, depends critically on the existence of a channel through which additional household saving finances additional investment.

planned investment falls by a certain amount and is sustained at this lower level, output will fall by a multiple of the reduction in I. As the initial shock is felt and firms cut output, they lay people off. The result: Income, and subsequently consumption, falls.

THE SIZE OF THE MULTIPLIER IN THE REAL WORLD

In considering the size of the multiplier, it is important to realize that the multiplier we derived in this chapter is based on a *very* simplified picture of the economy. First, we have assumed that planned investment is autonomous and does not respond to changes in the economy. Second, we have thus far ignored the role of government, financial markets, and the rest of the world in the macroeconomy. For these reasons, it would be a mistake to move on from this chapter thinking that national income can be increased by $100 billion simply by increasing planned investment spending by $25 billion.

As we relax these assumptions in the following chapters, you will see that most of what we add to make our analysis more realistic has the effect of *reducing* the size of the multiplier. For example:

1. The Appendix to Chapter 22 shows that when tax payments depend on income (as they do in the real world), the size of the multiplier is reduced. As the economy expands, tax payments increase and act as a drag on the economy. The multiplier effect is smaller.
2. We will see in Chapter 25 that planned investment (I) is not autonomous; instead, it depends on the interest rate in the economy. This too has the effect of reducing the size of the multiplier.
3. Thus far we have not discussed how the overall price level is determined in the economy. When we do, in Chapter 26, we will see that part of an expansion of the economy is likely to take the form of an increase in the price level instead of an increase in output. When this happens, the size of the multiplier is reduced.
4. The multiplier is also reduced when imports are introduced, in Chapter 34, because some domestic spending leaks into foreign markets.

These juicy tidbits give you something to look forward to as you proceed through the rest of this book. For now, however, it is enough to point out that

> In reality, the size of the multiplier is about 1.4. That is, a sustained increase in autonomous spending of $10 billion into the U.S. economy can be expected to raise real GDP over time by about $14 billion.

This is a far cry from the value of 4.0 that we used in this chapter.

Coffee and food for the unemployed.

THE MULTIPLIER IN ACTION: RECOVERING FROM THE GREAT DEPRESSION

The Great Depression began in 1930 and lasted nearly a decade. Real output in 1938 was lower than real output in 1929, and the unemployment rate never fell below 14 percent of the labor force between 1930 and 1940. How did the economy get "stuck" at such a low level of income and a high level of unemployment? The model that we analyzed in this chapter can help us answer this question.

If firms do not wish to undertake much investment (I is low) or if consumers decide to increase their saving and cut back on consumption, then planned spending will be low. Firms do not want to produce more because, with many workers unemployed, households do not have the income to buy the extra output that firms might produce. Households, who would purchase more if they had more income, cannot find jobs that would enable them to earn additional income. The economy is caught in a vicious circle.

How might such a cycle be broken? One way is for planned aggregate expenditure to increase, increasing aggregate output via the multiplier effect. This increase in *AE* may occur naturally, or it may be caused by a change in government policy.

In the late 1930s, for example, the economy experienced a surge of both residential and nonresidential investment. Between 1935 and 1940, total investment spending (in real terms) increased 64 percent and residential investment more than doubled. There can be no doubt that this increased investment had a multiplier effect. In just 5 years, employment in the construction industry increased by more than 400,000, employment in manufacturing industries jumped by more than 1 million, and total employment grew by more than 5 million. As more workers were employed, more income was generated, and some of this added income was spent on consumption goods. Inventories declined and firms began to expand output. Between 1935 and 1940, real output (income) increased by more than one-third and the unemployment rate dropped from 20.3 percent to 14.6 percent.

However, 14.6 percent is a very high rate of unemployment; the Depression was not yet over. Between 1940 and 1943 the Depression ended, with the unemployment rate dropping to 1.9 percent in 1943. This recovery was triggered by the mobilization for World War II and the significant increase in government purchases of goods and services, which rose from $14 billion in 1940 to $88.6 billion in 1943. In the next chapter, we will explore this *government spending multiplier*, and you will see how the government can help stimulate the economy by increasing its spending.

LOOKING AHEAD

In this chapter, we took the first step in understanding how the economy works. We described the behavior of two sectors (household and firm) and discussed how equilibrium is achieved in the market for goods and services. In the next chapter, we will relax some of the assumptions we have made and take into account the roles of government spending and net exports in the economy. This will give us a more realistic picture of how our economy works.

SUMMARY

AGGREGATE OUTPUT AND AGGREGATE INCOME (Y)

1. Each period, firms produce an aggregate quantity of goods and services called *aggregate output* (Y). Because every dollar of expenditure is received by someone as income, aggregate output and *aggregate income* are the same thing.

2. The total amount of aggregate consumption that takes place in any given period of time depends on factors such as household income, household wealth, interest rates, and households' expectations about the future.

3. If taxes are zero, households do only two things with their income: They can either spend on consumption or save. *C* refers to aggregate consumption by households. *S* refers to aggregate saving by households. By definition, *saving* equals income minus consumption: $S \equiv Y - C$.

4. The higher people's income is, the higher their consumption is likely to be. This is also true for the economy as a whole: There is a positive relationship between aggregate consumption (*C*) and aggregate income (*Y*).

5. The *marginal propensity to consume* (*MPC*) is the fraction of a change in income that is consumed, or spent. The *marginal propensity to save* (*MPS*) is the fraction of a change in income that is saved. Because all income must be either saved or spent, $MPS + MPC \equiv 1$.

6. The primary form of spending that firms engage in is investment. Strictly speaking, *investment* refers to the purchase by firms of new buildings and equipment and additions to inventories, all of which add to firms' capital stock.

7. *Actual investment* can differ from *desired*, or *planned*, *investment* because changes in firms' inventories are part of actual investment and inventory changes are not under the complete control of firms. Inventory changes are partly determined by how much households decide to buy. *I* refers to planned investment only.

EQUILIBRIUM AGGREGATE OUTPUT (INCOME)

8. In an economy in which government spending and net exports are zero, *planned aggregate expenditure* (*AE*) equals consumption plus planned investment: $AE \equiv C + I$. *Equilibrium* in the goods market is achieved when planned aggregate expenditure equals aggregate output: $C + I = Y$. This holds if, and only if, planned investment and actual investment are equal.

9. Because aggregate income must be saved or spent, the equilibrium condition $Y = C + I$ can be rewritten as $C + S = C + I$, or $S = I$. Only when planned investment equals saving will there be equilibrium. This approach to equilibrium is the *saving/investment approach* to equilibrium or the *leakages/injections approach* to equilibrium.

10. When planned aggregate expenditure exceeds aggregate output (*income*), there is an unplanned fall in inventories. Firms will increase output. This increased output leads to increased income and even more consumption. This process will continue as long as output (income) is below planned aggregate expenditure. If firms react to unplanned inventory reductions by increasing output, an economy with planned spending greater than output will adjust to a new equilibrium, with *Y* higher than before.

THE MULTIPLIER

11. Equilibrium output changes by a multiple of the change in planned investment or any other *autonomous variable*. The *multiplier* is 1/*MPS*.

12. When households increase their planned saving, income decreases and saving does not change. Saving does not increase because in equilibrium saving must equal planned investment and planned investment is fixed. If planned investment also increased, this *paradox of thrift* could be averted and a new equilibrium could be achieved at a higher level of saving and income. This result depends on the existence of a channel through which additional household saving finances additional investment.

REVIEW TERMS AND CONCEPTS

identity, 457

investment, 462

marginal propensity to consume (*MPC*), 459

marginal propensity to save (*MPS*), 460

multiplier, 470

planned aggregate expenditure (*AE*), 463

saving (*S*), 457

1. $S \equiv Y - C$
2. $MPC \equiv$ slope of consumption function $\equiv \dfrac{\Delta C}{\Delta Y}$
3. $MPC + MPS \equiv 1$
4. $AE \equiv C + I$
5. Equilibrium condition: $Y = AE$ or $Y = C + I$
6. Saving/investment approach to equilibrium: $S = I$
7. Multiplier $\equiv \dfrac{1}{MPS} \equiv \dfrac{1}{1 - MPC}$

PROBLEM SET

1. The News Analysis box on p. 468 notes that an unanticipated rise in inventories held by U.S. wholesalers was reported by the Department of Commerce in June 2005. The box suggested that this might be the beginning of a slowdown in production, perhaps leading up to a recession. Go to **www.bea.gov**, and click on the most recent release of the GDP data for the United States. What actually happened to real GDP in late 2005 and 2006? Did it fall? Did it continue to grow? At what rate? In light of the actual performance of the economy, what explanation can you offer for the inventory rise in 2005?

2. Briefly define the following terms and explain the relationship between them:

   MPC . . . . Multiplier
   Actual investment . . . . Planned investment
   Aggregate expenditure . . . . Real GDP
   Aggregate output . . . . Aggregate income

3. Expert econometricians in the Republic of Yuck estimate the following:

   Real GNP (Y) . . . . 200 billion Yuck dollars
   Planned investment spending . . . . 75 billion Yuck dollars

   Yuck is a simple economy with no government, no taxes, and no imports or exports. Yuckers (citizens of Yuck) are creatures of habit. They have a rule that everyone saves exactly 25 percent of income. Assume that planned investment is fixed and remains at 75 billion Yuck dollars.

   You are asked by the business editor of the *Weird Herald*, the local newspaper, to predict the economic events of the next few months. By using the data given, can you make a forecast? What is likely to happen to inventories? What is likely to happen to the level of real GDP? Is the economy at an equilibrium? When will things stop changing?

4. Log on to **www.commerce.gov**. Click on Economic Growth, then on Economic Analysis. Click next on National Accounts Data and then on the latest GDP release. Look through the report. Which of the components of aggregate expenditure appear to be growing or falling the fastest? What story can you tell about the current economic events from the data?

5. The following questions refer to this table:

AGGREGATE OUTPUT/INCOME	CONSUMPTION	PLANNED INVESTMENT
2,000	2,100	300
2,500	2,500	300
3,000	2,900	300
3,500	3,300	300
4,000	3,700	300
4,500	4,100	300
5,000	4,500	300
5,500	4,900	300

   a. At each level of output, calculate saving. At each level of output, calculate unplanned investment (inventory change). What is likely to happen to aggregate output if the economy were producing at each of the levels indicated? What is the equilibrium level of output?

   b. Over each range of income (2,000 to 2,500, 2,500 to 3,000, and so on), calculate the marginal propensity to consume. Calculate the marginal propensity to save. What is the multiplier?

   c. By assuming there is no change in the level of the *MPC* and the *MPS*, and planned investment jumps by 200 and is sustained at that higher level, recompute the table. What is the new equilibrium level of *Y*? Is this consistent with what you compute using the multiplier?

6. Explain the multiplier intuitively. Why is it that an increase in planned investment of $100 raises equilibrium output by more than $100? Why is the effect on equilibrium output finite? How do we know that the multiplier is 1/*MPS*?

7. You are given the following data concerning Freedonia, a legendary country:
   (1) Consumption function: $C = 200 + 0.8Y$
   (2) Investment function: $I = 100$
   (3) $AE \equiv C + I$
   (4) $AE = Y$

   a. What is the marginal propensity to consume in Freedonia, and what is the marginal propensity to save?

   b. Graph equations (3) and (4) and solve for equilibrium income.

   c. Suppose equation (2) were changed to (2') $I = 110$. What is the new equilibrium level of income? By how much does the $10 increase in planned investment change equilibrium income? What is the value of the multiplier?

d. Calculate the saving function for Freedonia. Plot this saving function on a graph with equation (2). Explain why the equilibrium income in this graph must be the same as in part b.

8. At the beginning of the section entitled "Household Consumption and Saving," it was argued that saving and spending behavior depended in part on wealth (accumulated savings and inheritance), but our simple model does not incorporate this effect. Consider the following model of a very simple economy:

$$C = 10 + .75Y + .04W$$
$$I = 100$$
$$W = 1,000$$
$$Y = C + I$$
$$S = Y - C$$

If you assume that wealth (W) and investment (I) remain constant (we are ignoring the fact that saving adds to the stock of wealth), what are the equilibrium levels of GDP (Y), consumption (C), and saving (S)? Now suppose that wealth increases by 50 percent to 1,500. Recalculate the equilibrium levels of Y, C, and S. What impact does wealth accumulation have on GDP? Many were concerned with the very large increase in stock values in the late 1990s. Does this present a problem for the economy?

9. You learned earlier that expenditures and income should always be equal. In this chapter, you have learned that AE and aggregate output (income) can be different. Is there an inconsistency here?

APPENDIX

DERIVING THE MULTIPLIER ALGEBRAICALLY

In addition to deriving the multiplier using the simple substitution we used in the chapter, we can also derive the formula for the multiplier by using simple algebra.

Recall that our consumption function is:

$$C = a + bY$$

where b is the marginal propensity to consume. In equilibrium:

$$Y = C + I$$

Now we solve these two equations for Y in terms of I. By substituting the first equation into the second, we get:

$$Y = \underbrace{a + bY}_{C} + I$$

This equation can be rearranged to yield:

$$Y - bY = a + I$$
$$Y(1 - b) = a + I$$

We can then solve for Y in terms of I by dividing through by $(1 - b)$:

$$Y = (a + I)\left(\frac{1}{1 - b}\right)$$

Now look carefully at this expression and think about increasing I by some amount, ΔI, with a held constant. If I increases by ΔI, income will increase by

$$\Delta Y = \Delta I \times \frac{1}{1 - b}$$

Because $b \equiv MPC$, the expression becomes

$$\Delta Y = \Delta I \times \frac{1}{1 - MPC}$$

The multiplier is

$$\frac{1}{1 - MPC}$$

Finally, because $MPS + MPC \equiv 1$, MPS is equal to $1 - MPC$, making the alternative expression for the multiplier $1/MPS$, just as we saw in this chapter.

The Government
and Fiscal Policy

22

N othing in macroeconomics or microeconomics arouses as much controversy as the role of government in the economy.

In microeconomics, the active presence of government in regulating competition, providing roads and education, and redistributing income is applauded by those who believe a free market simply does not work well if left to its own devices. Opponents of government intervention say it is the government, not the market, that performs badly. They say bureaucracy and inefficiency could be eliminated or reduced if the government played a smaller role in the economy.

In macroeconomics, the debate over what the government can and should do has a similar flavor, although the issues are somewhat different. At one end of the spectrum are the Keynesians and their intellectual descendants, who believe that the macroeconomy is likely to fluctuate too much if left on its own and that the government should smooth out fluctuations in the business cycle. These ideas can be traced to Keynes's analysis in *The General Theory*, which suggests that governments can use their taxing and spending powers to increase aggregate expenditure (and thereby stimulate aggregate output) in recessions or depressions. At the other end of the spectrum are those who claim that government spending is incapable of stabilizing the economy, or worse, is destabilizing and harmful.

Perhaps the one thing most people can agree on is that, like it or not, governments are important actors in the economies of virtually all countries. For this reason alone, it is worth our while to analyze the way government influences the functioning of the macroeconomy.

The government has a variety of powers—including regulating firms' entry into and exit from an industry, setting standards for product quality, setting minimum wage levels, and regulating the disclosure of information—but in macroeconomics we study a government with general, but limited, powers. Specifically, government can affect the macroeconomy through two policy channels: fiscal policy and monetary policy. **Fiscal policy**, the focus of this chapter, refers to the government's spending and taxing behavior—in other words, its budget policy. (The word *fiscal* comes from the root *fisc*, which refers to the "treasury" of a government.) Fiscal policy is generally divided into three categories: (1) policies concerning government purchases of goods and services, (2) policies concerning taxes, and (3) policies concerning transfer payments (such as unemployment compensation, Social Security benefits, welfare payments, and veterans' benefits) to households. **Monetary policy**, which we consider in the next two chapters, refers to the behavior of the nation's central bank, the Federal Reserve, concerning the nation's money supply.

fiscal policy The government's spending and taxing policies.

monetary policy The behavior of the Federal Reserve concerning the nation's money supply.

GOVERNMENT IN THE ECONOMY

Given the scope and power of local, state, and federal governments, there are some matters over which they exert great control and some matters beyond their control. We need to distinguish between variables that a government controls directly and variables that are a consequence of government decisions *combined with the state of the economy.*

For example, tax rates are controlled by the government. By law, Congress has the authority to decide who and what should be taxed and at what rate. Tax *revenue,* on the other hand, is not subject to complete control by the government. Revenue from the personal income tax system depends both on personal tax rates (which Congress sets) *and* on the income of the household sector (which depends on many factors not under direct government control, such as how much households decide to work). Revenue from the corporate profits tax depends both on corporate profits tax rates and on the size of corporate profits. The government controls corporate tax rates but not the size of corporate profits.

Government expenditures also depend both on government decisions and on the state of the economy. For example, in the United States the unemployment insurance program pays benefits to unemployed people. When the economy goes into a recession, the number of unemployed workers increases and so does the level of government unemployment insurance payments.

Because taxes and expenditures often go up or down in response to changes in the economy instead of as the result of deliberate decisions by policy makers, we will occasionally use **discretionary fiscal policy** to refer to changes in taxes or spending that are the result of deliberate changes in government policy.

discretionary fiscal policy Changes in taxes or spending that are the result of deliberate changes in government policy.

GOVERNMENT PURCHASES (*G*), NET TAXES (*T*), AND DISPOSABLE INCOME (*Y_d*)

In the previous chapter, we explored the equilibrium level of national output for a simple economy—no taxes, no government spending, and no exports—to provide a general idea of how the macroeconomy operates. To get more realistic, we need to consider an economy in which government is an active participant. We begin by adding the government sector into the simple economy in Chapter 21.

To keep things simple, we will combine two government activities—the collection of taxes and the payment of transfer payments—into a category we call **net taxes (*T*).** Specifically, net taxes are equal to the tax payments made to the government by firms and households minus transfer payments made to households by the government. The other variable we will consider is government purchases of goods and services (*G*).

net taxes (*T*) Taxes paid by firms and households to the government minus transfer payments made to households by the government.

Our earlier discussions of household consumption did not take taxes into account. We assumed that all the income generated in the economy was spent or saved by households. When we take into account the role of government, as Figure 22.1 does, we see that as income (*Y*) flows toward households, the government takes income from households in the form of net taxes (*T*). The income that ultimately gets to households is called **disposable**, or **after-tax, income (*Y_d*):**

disposable, or after-tax, income (*Y_d*) Total income minus net taxes: $Y - T$.

$$\text{disposable income} \equiv \text{total income} - \text{net taxes}$$

$$Y_d \equiv Y - T$$

Y_d excludes taxes paid by households and includes transfer payments made to households by the government. For now we are assuming that T does not depend on Y—that is, net taxes do not depend on income. This assumption is relaxed in Appendix B to this chapter. Taxes that do not depend on income are sometimes called *lump-sum taxes.*

As Figure 22.1 shows, the disposable income (Y_d) of households must end up as either consumption (*C*) or saving (*S*). Thus,

$$Y_d \equiv C + S$$

This equation is an identity—something that is always true.

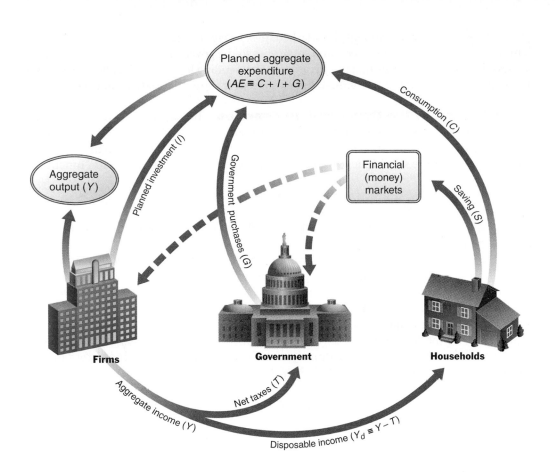

FIGURE 22.1 Adding Net Taxes (*T*) and Government Purchases (*G*) to the Circular Flow of Income

Because disposable income is aggregate income (*Y*) minus net taxes (*T*), we can write another identity:

$$Y - T \equiv C + S$$

By adding *T* to both sides:

$$Y \equiv C + S + T$$

This identity says aggregate income gets cut into three pieces. Government takes a slice (net taxes, *T*), and then households divide the rest between consumption (*C*) and saving (*S*).

Because governments spend money on goods and services, we need to expand our definition of planned aggregate expenditure. Planned aggregate expenditure (*AE*) is the sum of consumption spending by households (*C*), planned investment by business firms (*I*), *and* government purchases of goods and services (*G*).[1]

$$AE \equiv C + I + G$$

A government's **budget deficit** is the difference between what it spends (*G*) and what it collects in taxes (*T*) in a given period:

$$\text{budget deficit} \equiv G - T$$

If *G* exceeds *T*, the government must borrow from the public to finance the deficit. It does so by selling Treasury bonds and bills (more on this later). In this case, a part of household

budget deficit The difference between what a government spends and what it collects in taxes in a given period: *G* − *T*.

---

[1]We are still assuming that net exports (*EX* − *IM*) are zero. In practice, *AE* ≡ *C* + *I* + *G* + (*EX* − *IM*). We bring net exports into the analysis in Chapter 34.

saving (S) goes to the government. The dashed lines in Figure 22.1 mean that some S goes to firms to finance investment projects and some goes to the government to finance its deficit. If G is less than T, which means that the government is spending less than it is collecting in taxes, the government is running a *surplus*. A budget surplus is simply a negative budget deficit.

Adding Taxes to the Consumption Function   In Chapter 21, we examined the consumption behavior of households and noted that aggregate consumption (C) depends on aggregate income (Y): In general, the higher aggregate income is, the higher aggregate consumption. For the sake of illustration, we used a specific linear consumption function:

$$C = a + bY$$

where a is the amount of consumption that would take place if national income were zero and b is the marginal propensity to consume.

We need to modify this consumption function because we have added government to the economy. With taxes a part of the picture, it makes sense to assume that disposable income (Y_d), instead of before-tax income (Y), determines consumption behavior. If you earn a million dollars, but have to pay $950,000 in taxes, you have no more disposable income than someone who earns only $50,000 but pays no taxes. What you have available for spending on current consumption is your disposable income, not your before-tax income.

To modify our aggregate consumption function to incorporate disposable income instead of before-tax income, instead of $C = a + bY$, we write

$$C = a + bY_d$$

or

$$C = a + b(Y - T)$$

Our consumption function now has consumption depending on disposable income instead of before-tax income.

Investment   What about investment? The government can affect investment behavior through its tax treatment of depreciation and other tax policies. Investment may also vary with economic conditions and interest rates, as we will see later. For our present purposes, we continue to assume that planned investment (I) is autonomous.

EQUILIBRIUM OUTPUT: $Y = C + I + G$

We know from Chapter 21 that equilibrium occurs where $Y = AE$—that is, where aggregate output equals planned aggregate expenditure. Remember that planned aggregate expenditure in an economy with a government is $AE \equiv C + I + G$, so the equilibrium condition is

equilibrium condition: $Y = C + I + G$

The equilibrium analysis in Chapter 21 applies here also. If output (Y) exceeds planned aggregate expenditure ($C + I + G$), there will be an unplanned increase in inventories—actual investment will exceed planned investment. Conversely, if $C + I + G$ exceeds Y, there will be an unplanned decrease in inventories.

An example will illustrate the government's effect on the macroeconomy and the equilibrium condition. First, our consumption function, $C = 100 + .75Y$ before we introduced the government sector, now becomes

$$C = 100 + .75Y_d$$

or

$$C = 100 + .75(Y - T)$$

TABLE 22.1 Finding Equilibrium for *I* = 100, *G* = 100, and *T* = 100 (All Figures in Billions of Dollars)

(1) OUTPUT (INCOME) Y	(2) NET TAXES T	(3) DISPOSABLE INCOME $Y_d \equiv Y - T$	(4) CONSUMPTION SPENDING $(C = 100 + .75\,Y_d)$	(5) SAVING S $(Y_d - C)$	(6) PLANNED INVESTMENT SPENDING I	(7) GOVERNMENT PURCHASES G	(8) PLANNED AGGREGATE EXPENDITURE $C + I + G$	(9) UNPLANNED INVENTORY CHANGE $Y - (C + I + G)$	(10) ADJUST- MENT TO DISEQUI- LIBRIUM
300	100	200	250	−50	100	100	450	−150	Output ↑
500	100	400	400	0	100	100	600	−100	Output ↑
700	100	600	550	50	100	100	750	−50	Output ↑
900	100	800	700	100	100	100	900	0	Equilibrium
1,100	100	1,000	850	150	100	100	1,050	+50	Output ↓
1,300	100	1,200	1,000	200	100	100	1,200	+100	Output ↓
1,500	100	1,400	1,150	250	100	100	1,350	+150	Output ↓

Second, we assume that the government is currently purchasing $100 billion of goods and services and collecting net taxes (T) of $100 billion.[2] In other words, the government is running a balanced budget, financing all of its spending with taxes. Third, we assume that planned investment (I) is $100 billion.

Table 22.1 calculates planned aggregate expenditure at several levels of disposable income. For example, at $Y = 500$, disposable income is $Y - T$, or 400.[3] Therefore, $C = 100 + .75(400) = 400$. Assuming that I is fixed at 100, and assuming that G is fixed at 100, planned aggregate expenditure is 600 ($C + I + G = 400 + 100 + 100$). Because output ($Y$) is only 500, planned spending is greater than output by 100. As a result, there is an unplanned inventory decrease of 100, giving firms an incentive to raise output. Thus, output of 500 is below equilibrium.

If $Y = 1,300$, then $Y_d = 1,200$, $C = 1,000$, and planned aggregate expenditure is 1,200. Here, planned spending is *less* than output, there will be an unplanned inventory increase of 100, and firms have an incentive to cut back output. Thus, output of 1,300 is above equilibrium. Only when output is 900 are output and planned aggregate expenditure equal, and only at $Y = 900$ does equilibrium exist.

In Figure 22.2, we derive the same equilibrium level of output graphically. First, the consumption function is drawn, taking into account net taxes of 100. The old function was $C = 100 + .75Y$. The new function is $C = 100 + .75(Y - T)$ or $C = 100 + .75(Y - 100)$, rewritten as $C = 100 + .75Y - 75$, or $C = 25 + .75Y$. For example, consumption at an income of zero is 25 ($C = 25 + .75Y = 25 + .75(0) = 25$). The marginal propensity to consume has not changed—we assume it remains .75. Note that the consumption function in Figure 22.2 plots the points in columns 1 and 4 of Table 22.1.

Planned aggregate expenditure, recall, adds planned investment to consumption. Now, in addition to 100 in investment, we have government purchases of 100. Because I and G are constant at 100 each at all levels of income, we add $I + G = 200$ to consumption at every level of income. The result is the new AE curve. This curve is just a plot of the points in columns 1 and 8 of Table 22.1. The 45° line helps us find the equilibrium level of real output, which, we already know, is 900. If you examine any level of output above or below 900, you will find disequilibrium. Look, for example, at $Y = 500$ on the graph. At this level, planned aggregate expenditure is 600, but output is only 500. Inventories will fall below what was planned, and firms will have an incentive to increase output.

The Leakages/Injections Approach to Equilibrium

As in the last chapter, we can also examine equilibrium using the leakages/injections approach. Look at the circular flow of income in Figure 22.1. The government takes out net taxes (T) from the flow of income—a leakage—and households save (S) some of their income—also a leakage from the

---

[2]As we pointed out earlier, the government does not have complete control over tax revenues and transfer payments. We ignore this problem here, however, and set tax revenues minus transfers at a fixed amount. Things will become more realistic later in this chapter and in Appendix B.
[3]For the rest of this discussion, we will understand but not state that figures are in billions of dollars.

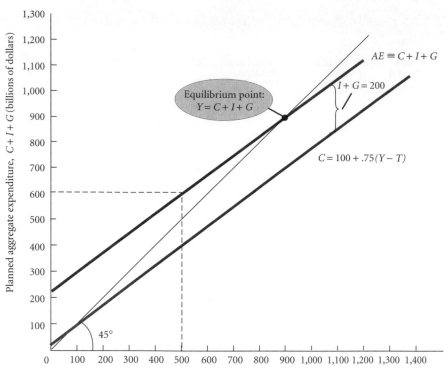

FIGURE 22.2 Finding Equilibrium Output/Income Graphically

Because G and I are both fixed at 100, the aggregate expenditure function is the new consumption function displaced upward by I + G = 200. Equilibrium occurs at Y = C + I + G = 900.

flow of income. The planned spending injections are government purchases (G) and planned investment (I). If leakages ($S + T$) equal planned injections ($I + G$), there is equilibrium:

leakages/injections approach to equilibrium: $S + T = I + G$

To derive this, we know that in equilibrium, aggregate output (income) (Y) equals planned aggregate expenditure (AE). By definition, AE equals $C + I + G$, and by definition Y equals $C + S + T$. Therefore, at equilibrium

$$C + S + T = C + I + G$$

Subtracting C from both sides leaves:

$$S + T = I + G$$

Note that equilibrium does *not* require that $G = T$ (a balanced government budget) or that $S = I$. It is only necessary that the sum of S and T equals the sum of I and G.

Column 5 of Table 22.1 calculates aggregate saving by subtracting consumption from disposal income at every level of disposable income ($S \equiv Y_d - C$). Because I and G are fixed, $I + G$ equals 200 at every level of income. Using the table to add saving and taxes ($S + T$), we see that $S + T$ equals 200 only at $Y = 900$. Thus, the equilibrium level of output (income) is 900, the same answer we arrived at through numerical and graphic analysis.

FISCAL POLICY AT WORK: MULTIPLIER EFFECTS

You can see from Figure 22.2 that if the government were able to change the levels of either G or T, it would be able to change the equilibrium level of output (income). At this point, we are assuming that the government controls G and T. In this section we will review three multipliers:

- Government spending multiplier
- Tax multiplier
- Balanced-budget multiplier

THE GOVERNMENT SPENDING MULTIPLIER

Suppose you are the chief economic adviser to the president and the economy is sitting at the equilibrium output pictured in Figure 22.2. Output and income are being produced at a rate of $900 billion per year, and the government is currently buying $100 billion worth of goods and services each year and is financing them with $100 billion in taxes. The budget is balanced. In addition, the private sector is investing (producing capital goods) at a rate of $100 billion per year.

The president calls you into the Oval Office and says, "Unemployment is too high. We need to lower unemployment by increasing output and income." After some research, you determine that an acceptable unemployment rate could be achieved only if aggregate output increases to $1,100 billion.

You now need to determine: How can the government use taxing and spending policy—fiscal policy—to increase the equilibrium level of national output? Suppose that the president has let it be known that taxes must remain at present levels—the Congress just passed a major tax reform package—so adjusting T is out of the question for several years. That leaves you with G. Your only option is to increase government spending while holding taxes constant.

To increase spending without raising taxes (which provides the government with revenue to spend), the government must borrow. When G is bigger than T, the government runs a deficit, and the difference between G and T must be borrowed. For the moment we will ignore the possible effect of the deficit and focus only on the effect of a higher G with T constant.

Meanwhile, the president is awaiting your answer. How much of an increase in spending would be required to generate a $200 billion increase in the equilibrium level of output, pushing it from $900 billion up to $1,100 billion and reducing unemployment to the president's acceptable level?

You might be tempted to say that because we need to increase income by 200 (1,100 − 900), we should increase government spending by the same amount—but what would happen? The increased government spending will throw the economy out of equilibrium. Because G is a component of aggregate spending, planned aggregate expenditure will increase by 200. Planned spending will be greater than output, inventories will be lower than planned, and firms will have an incentive to increase output. Suppose output rises by the desired 200. You might think, "We increased spending by 200 and output by 200, so equilibrium is restored."

There is more to the story than this. The moment output rises, the economy is generating more income. This was the desired effect: the creation of more employment. The newly employed workers are also consumers and some of their income gets spent. With higher consumption spending, planned spending will be greater than output, inventories will be lower than planned, and firms will raise output, and thus raise income, again. This time firms are responding to the new consumption spending. Already, total income is over 1,100.

This story should sound familiar. It is the multiplier in action. Although this time it is government spending (G) that is changed rather than planned investment (I), the effect is the same as the multiplier effect we described in Chapter 21. An increase in government spending has the same impact on the equilibrium level of output and income as an increase in planned investment. A dollar of extra spending from either G or I is identical with respect to its impact on equilibrium output. The equation for the government spending multiplier is the same as the equation for the multiplier for a change in planned investment.

$$\text{government spending multiplier} \equiv \frac{1}{MPS}$$

We derive the government spending multiplier algebraically in Appendix A to this chapter.

TABLE 22.2 Finding Equilibrium After a $50 Billion Government Spending Increase (All Figures in Billions of Dollars; G Has Increased from 100 in Table 22.1 to 150 Here)

(1) OUTPUT (INCOME) Y	(2) NET TAXES T	(3) DISPOSABLE INCOME $Y_d \equiv Y - T$	(4) CONSUMPTION SPENDING $(C = 100 + .75\, Y_d)$	(5) SAVING S $(Y_d - C)$	(6) PLANNED INVESTMENT SPENDING I	(7) GOVERNMENT PURCHASES G	(8) PLANNED AGGREGATE EXPENDITURE C + I + G	(9) UNPLANNED INVENTORY CHANGE Y − (C + I + G)	(10) ADJUST- MENT TO DISEQUI- LIBRIUM
300	100	200	250	−50	100	150	500	−200	Output ↑
500	100	400	400	0	100	150	650	−150	Output ↑
700	100	600	550	50	100	150	800	−100	Output ↑
900	100	800	700	100	100	150	950	−50	Output ↑
1,100	100	1,000	850	150	100	150	1,100	0	Equilibrium
1,300	100	1,200	1,000	200	100	150	1,250	+50	Output ↓

government spending multiplier The ratio of the change in the equilibrium level of output to a change in government spending.

Formally, the **government spending multiplier** is defined as the ratio of the change in the equilibrium level of output to a change in government spending. This is the same definition we used in the previous chapter, but now the autonomous variable is government spending instead of planned investment.

Remember that we were thinking of increasing government spending (G) by 200. We can use the multiplier analysis to see what the new equilibrium level of Y would be for an increase in G of 200. The multiplier in our example is 4. (Because b—the MPC—is .75, the MPS must be $1 - .75 = .25$, and $1/.25 = 4$). Thus, Y will increase by 800 (4×200). Because the initial level of Y was 900, the new equilibrium level of Y is $900 + 800 = 1,700$ when G is increased by 200.

The level of 1,700 is much larger than the level of 1,100 that we calculated as necessary to lower unemployment to the desired level. Let us back up, then. If we want Y to increase by 200 and if the multiplier is 4, we need G to increase by only $200/4 = 50$. If G changes by 50, the equilibrium level of Y will change by 200, and the new value of Y will be 1,100 ($900 + 200$), as desired.

Looking at Table 22.2, we can check our answer to be sure that it is an equilibrium. Look first at the old equilibrium of 900. When government purchases (G) were 100, aggregate output (income) was equal to planned aggregate expenditure ($AE \equiv C + I + G$) at $Y = 900$. Now G has increased to 150. At $Y = 900$, ($C + I + G$) is greater than Y, there is an unplanned fall in inventories, and output will rise, but by how much? The multiplier told us that equilibrium income would rise by four times the 50 change in G. Y should rise by $4 \times 50 = 200$, from 900 to 1,100, before equilibrium is restored. Let us check. If $Y = 1,100$, then consumption is $C = 100 + .75Y_d = 100 + .75(1,000) = 850$. Because I equals 100 and G now equals 100 (the original level of G) + 50 (the additional G brought about by the fiscal policy change) = 150, then $C + I + G = 850 + 100 + 150 = 1,100$. $Y = AE$, and the economy is in equilibrium.

The graphic solution to the president's problem is presented in Figure 22.3. A 50 increase in G shifts the planned aggregate expenditure function up by 50. The new equilibrium income occurs where the new AE line (AE_2) crosses the 45° line, at $Y = 1,100$.

THE TAX MULTIPLIER

Remember that fiscal policy comprises policies concerning government spending *and* policies concerning taxation. To see what effect a change in tax policy has on the economy, imagine the following. You are still chief economic adviser to the president, but now you are instructed to devise a plan to reduce unemployment to an acceptable level *without* increasing the level of government spending. In your plan, instead of increasing government spending (G), you decide to cut taxes and maintain the current level of spending. A tax cut increases disposable income, which is likely to lead to added consumption spending. (Remember our general rule that increased income leads to increased consumption.) Would the decrease in taxes affect aggregate output (income) the same as an increase in G?

A decrease in taxes would increase income. The government spends no less than it did before the tax cut, and households find they have a larger after-tax, or disposable, income than they had before. This leads to an increase in consumption. Planned aggregate expenditure will increase, which will lead to inventories being lower than planned, which will lead to a rise in output. When output rises, more workers will be employed and more

FIGURE 22.3 The Government Spending Multiplier

Increasing government spending by 50 shifts the *AE* function up by 50. As *Y* rises in response, additional consumption is generated. Overall, the equilibrium level of *Y* increases by 200, from 900 to 1,100.

income will be generated, causing a second-round increase in consumption, and so on. Thus, income will increase by a multiple of the decrease in taxes, but there is a "wrinkle."

The multiplier for a change in taxes is *not the same* as the multiplier for a change in government spending.

Why does the **tax multiplier**—the ratio of change in the equilibrium level of output to a change in taxes—differ from the spending multiplier? To answer this, we need to compare the ways in which a tax cut and a spending increase work their way through the economy.

Look at Figure 22.1. When the government increases spending, there is an immediate and direct impact on the economy's *total* spending. Because *G* is a component of planned aggregate expenditure, an increase in *G* leads to a dollar-for-dollar increase in planned aggregate expenditure. When taxes are cut, there is no direct impact on spending. Taxes enter the picture only because they have an effect on the household's disposable income, which influences household's consumption (which is part of total spending). As Figure 22.1 shows, the tax cut flows through households before affecting aggregate expenditure.

Let us assume the government decides to cut taxes by $1. By how much would spending increase? We already know the answer. The marginal propensity to consume (*MPC*) tells us how much consumption spending changes when disposable income changes. In the example running through this chapter, the marginal propensity to consume out of disposable income is .75. This means that if households' after-tax incomes rise by $1, they will increase their consumption not by the full $1, but by only $0.75.[4]

In summary, when government spending increases by $1, planned aggregate expenditure increases initially by the full amount of the rise in *G*, or $1. When taxes are cut, however, the initial increase in planned aggregate expenditure is only the *MPC* times the change in taxes. Because the initial increase in planned aggregate expenditure is smaller for a tax cut than for a government spending increase, the final effect on the equilibrium level of income will be smaller.

tax multiplier The ratio of change in the equilibrium level of output to a change in taxes.

---

[4]What happens to the other $0.25? Remember that whatever households do not consume is, by definition, saved. The other $0.25 thus gets allocated to saving.

We figure the size of the tax multiplier in the same way we derived the multiplier for an increase in investment and an increase in government purchases. The final change in the equilibrium level of output (income) (Y) is

$$\Delta Y = \text{(initial increase in aggregate expenditure)} \times \left(\frac{1}{MPS}\right)$$

Because the initial change in aggregate expenditure caused by a tax change of ΔT is $(-\Delta T \times MPC)$, we can solve for the tax multiplier by substitution:

$$\Delta Y = (-\Delta T \times MPC) \times \left(\frac{1}{MPS}\right) = -\Delta T \times \left(\frac{MPC}{MPS}\right)$$

Because a tax cut will cause an *increase* in consumption expenditures and output and a tax increase will cause a *reduction* in consumption expenditures and output, the tax multiplier is a negative multiplier:

$$\text{tax multiplier} \equiv -\left(\frac{MPC}{MPS}\right)$$

We derive the tax multiplier algebraically in Appendix A to this chapter.

If the *MPC* is .75, as in our example, the multiplier is $-.75/.25 = -3$. A tax cut of 100 will increase the equilibrium level of output by $-100 \times -3 = 300$. This is very different from the effect of our government spending multiplier of 4. Under these same conditions, a 100 increase in G will increase the equilibrium level of output by 400 or (100×4).

THE BALANCED-BUDGET MULTIPLIER

We have now discussed (1) changing government spending with no change in taxes, and (2) changing taxes with no change in government spending. What if government spending and taxes are increased by the same amount? That is, what if the government decides to pay for its extra spending by increasing taxes by the same amount? The government's budget deficit would not change, because the increase in expenditures would be matched by an increase in tax income.

You might think in this case that equal increases in government spending and taxes have no effect on equilibrium income. After all, the extra government spending equals the extra amount of tax revenues collected by the government. This is not so. Take, for example, a government spending increase of $40 billion. We know from the preceding analysis that an increase in G of 40, with taxes (T) held constant, should increase the equilibrium level of income by 40 × the government spending multiplier. The multiplier is $1/MPS$ or $1/.25 = 4$. The equilibrium level of income should rise by 160 or (40×4).

Now suppose that instead of keeping tax revenues constant, we finance the 40 increase in government spending with an equal increase in taxes, so as to maintain a balanced budget. What happens to aggregate spending as a result of both the rise in G and the rise in T? There are two initial effects. First, government spending rises by 40. This effect is direct, immediate, and positive. Now the government also collects 40 more in taxes. The tax increase has a *negative* impact on overall spending in the economy, but it does not fully offset the increase in government spending.

balanced-budget multiplier The ratio of change in the equilibrium level of output to a change in government spending where the change in government spending is balanced by a change in taxes so as not to create any deficit. The balanced-budget multiplier is equal to 1: The change in Y resulting from the change in G and the equal change in T is exactly the same size as the initial change in G or T itself.

The final impact of a tax increase on aggregate expenditure depends on how households respond to it. The only thing we know about household behavior so far is that households spend 75 percent of their added income and save 25 percent. We know that when disposable income falls, both consumption and saving are reduced. A tax *increase* of 40 reduces disposable income by 40, and that means consumption falls by 40 × MPC. Because $MPC = .75$, consumption falls by 30 or $(40 \times .75)$. The net result in the beginning is that government spending rises by 40 and consumption spending falls by 30. Aggregate expenditure increases by 10 right after the simultaneous balanced-budget increases in G and T.

So, a balanced-budget increase in G and T will raise output, but by how much? How large is this **balanced-budget multiplier**? The answer may surprise you:

$$\text{balanced-budget multiplier} \equiv 1$$

TABLE 22.3 Finding Equilibrium After a $200-Billion Balanced-Budget Increase in *G* and *T* (All Figures in Billions of Dollars; Both *G* and *T* Have Increased from 100 in Table 9.1 to 300 Here)

(1) OUTPUT (INCOME) *Y*	(2) NET TAXES *T*	(3) DISPOSABLE INCOME $Y_d \equiv Y - T$	(4) CONSUMPTION SPENDING $(C = 100 + .75\ Y_d)$	(5) PLANNED INVESTMENT SPENDING *I*	(6) GOVERNMENT PURCHASES *G*	(7) PLANNED AGGREGATE EXPENDITURE *C* + *I* + *G*	(8) UNPLANNED INVENTORY CHANGE *Y* − (*C* + *I* + *G*)	(9) ADJUST- MENT TO DISEQUI- LIBRIUM
500	300	200	250	100	300	650	−150	Output ↑
700	300	400	400	100	300	800	−100	Output ↑
900	300	600	550	100	300	950	−50	Output ↑
1,100	300	800	700	100	300	1,100	0	Equilibrium
1,300	300	1,000	850	100	300	1,250	+50	Output ↓
1,500	300	1,200	1,000	100	300	1,400	+100	Output ↓

Let us combine what we know about the tax multiplier and the government spending multiplier to explain this. To find the final effect of a simultaneous increase in government spending and increase in net taxes, we need to add the multiplier effects of the two. The government spending multiplier is $1/MPS$. The tax multiplier is $-MPC/MPS$. Their sum is $(1/MPS) + (-MPC/MPS) \equiv (1 - MPC)/MPS$. Because $MPC + MPS \equiv 1$, then $1 - MPC \equiv MPS$. This means $(1 - MPC)/MPS \equiv MPS/MPS \equiv 1$. (We also derive the balanced-budget multiplier in Appendix A to this chapter.)

Returning to our example, recall that by using the government spending multiplier, a 40 increase in *G* would *raise* output at equilibrium by 160 (40 × the government spending multiplier of 4). By using the tax multiplier, we know that a 40 tax hike will *reduce* the equilibrium level of output by 120 (40 × the tax multiplier, −3). The net effect is 160 minus 120, or 40. It should be clear, then, that the effect on equilibrium *Y* is equal to the balanced increase in *G* and *T*. In other words, the net increase in the equilibrium level of *Y* resulting from the change in *G* and the change in *T* is exactly the size of the initial change in *G* or *T* itself.

If the president wanted to raise *Y* by 200 without increasing the deficit, a simultaneous increase in *G* and *T* of 200 would do it. To see why, look at the numbers in Table 22.3. In Table 22.1, we saw an equilibrium level of output at 900. With both *G* and *T* up by 200, the new equilibrium is 1,100—higher by 200. At no other level of *Y* do we find $(C + I + G) = Y$.

An increase in government spending has a direct initial effect on planned aggregate expenditure; a tax increase does not. The initial effect of the tax increase is that households cut consumption by the *MPC* times the change in taxes. This change in consumption is less than the change in taxes, because the *MPC* is less than 1. The positive stimulus from the government spending increase is thus greater than the negative stimulus from the tax increase. The net effect is that the balanced-budget multiplier is 1.

Table 22.4 summarizes everything we have said about fiscal policy multipliers. If anything is still unclear, review the relevant discussions in this chapter.

TABLE 22.4 Summary of Fiscal Policy Multipliers

	POLICY STIMULUS	MULTIPLIER	FINAL IMPACT ON EQUILIBRIUM *Y*
Government spending multiplier	Increase or decrease in the level of government purchases: ΔG	$\dfrac{1}{MPS}$	$\Delta G \times \dfrac{1}{MPS}$
Tax multiplier	Increase or decrease in the level of net taxes: ΔT	$\dfrac{-MPC}{MPS}$	$\Delta T \times \dfrac{-MPC}{MPS}$
Balanced-budget multiplier	Simultaneous balanced-budget increase or decrease in the level of government purchases and net taxes: $\Delta G = \Delta T$	1	ΔG

A Warning Although we have added government, the story we have told about the multiplier is still incomplete and oversimplified. For example, we have been treating net taxes (T) as a lump-sum, fixed amount, whereas in practice, taxes depend on income. Appendix B to this chapter shows that the size of the multiplier is reduced when we make the more realistic assumption that taxes depend on income. We continue to add more realism and difficulty to our analysis in the chapters that follow.

THE FEDERAL BUDGET

federal budget The budget of the federal government.

Because fiscal policy is the manipulation of items in the federal budget, we need to consider those aspects of the budget relevant to our study of macroeconomics. The **federal budget** is an enormously complicated document, up to thousands of pages each year. It lists in detail all the things the government plans to spend money on and all the sources of government revenues for the coming year. It is the product of a complex interplay of social, political, and economic forces.

The "budget" is really three different budgets. First, it is a *political document* that dispenses favors to certain groups or regions (the elderly benefit from Social Security, farmers from agricultural price supports, students from federal loan programs, and so on) and places burdens (taxes) on others. Second, it is a *reflection of goals* the government wants to achieve. For example, in addition to assisting farmers, agricultural price supports are meant to preserve the "family farm." Tax breaks for corporations engaging in research and development of new products are meant to encourage research. Finally, the budget may be an *embodiment of some beliefs about how (if at all) the government should manage the macroeconomy*. The macroeconomic aspects of the budget are only a part of a more complicated story, a story that may be of more concern to political scientists than to economists.

THE BUDGET

A highly condensed version of the federal budget is shown in Table 22.5. In 2004, the government had total receipts of $1,974.8 billion, largely from personal income taxes ($801.8 billion) and contributions for social insurance ($802.5 billion). (Contributions for social insurance are employer and employee Social Security taxes.) Receipts from corporate income taxes accounted for $217.4 billion, or only 11.0 percent of total receipts. Not everyone is

TABLE 22.5 Federal Government Receipts and Expenditures, 2004 (Billions of Dollars)

	AMOUNT	PERCENTAGE OF TOTAL
Current receipts		
Personal income taxes	801.8	40.6
Excise taxes and customs duties	94.0	4.8
Corporate income taxes	217.4	11.0
Taxes from the rest of the world	9.2	0.5
Contributions for social insurance	802.5	40.6
Interest receipts and rents and royalties	21.9	1.1
Current transfer receipts from business and persons	28.6	1.4
Current surplus of government enterprises	−0.5	0.0
Total	1,974.8	100.0
Current expenditures		
Consumption expenditures	725.7	30.5
Transfer payments to persons	1,014.0	42.6
Transfer payments to the rest of the world	28.9	1.2
Grants-in-aid to state and local governments	348.3	14.6
Interest payments	221.5	9.3
Subsidies	43.0	1.8
Total	2,381.3	100.0
Net federal government saving—surplus (+) or deficit (−)		
(total current receipts − total current expenditures)	−406.5	

Source: U.S. Department of Commerce, Bureau of Economic Analysis.

fiscal policy, tax policy, government purchases   search

○ Further Exploration   ◉ News Analysis

The Effect of a Natural Disaster on Government Spending and Taxation, 2005

AS THE FOLLOWING ARTICLE FROM THE *New York Times* shows clearly, natural disasters such as Hurricane Katrina in 2005 can cause large increases in the federal budget deficit. Government spending to rebuild and to provide aid to the displaced and injured was large, while tax revenues were lost. The hurricane led to a quite expansionary fiscal policy.

Looking Beyond Floodwaters and Seeing Red Ink

By MARK A. STEIN
—*New York Times*
September 10, 2005

As federal authorities began to deliver significant amounts of aid to the Gulf Coast, government officials in Washington began warning that Hurricane Katrina would also wreak havoc with the economy. Rescue, recovery and reconstruction efforts could cause the federal budget deficit to grow by 15 to 20 percent or more this year and may threaten plans to cut taxes further or to make earlier cuts permanent.

Congress approved another $51.8 billion in federal assistance on Thursday, adding to the $10 billion authorized earlier in the week. More than 400,000 people have already registered for immediate assistance from the govern-

ment and thousands more were calling each day. Federal officials began to distribute $2,000 debit cards to those needing money for food and shelter.

Administration officials said the government was spending almost $700 million a day on the hurricane relief effort and the total cost to the federal government alone could be as much as $100 billion—almost five times the amount sent to New York after the terrorist attacks of Sept. 11, 2001.

The increased spending comes as the storm threatens to slow economic growth, which would reduce tax receipts. Republican leaders in the Senate this week postponed plans to

repeal the estate tax; a repeal would benefit the wealthiest 1 percent of households and reduce tax revenue by at least $70 billion a year.

The Congressional Budget Office, a nonpartisan adviser to Congress, said the disruption caused by the hurricane and flooding could cost 400,000 jobs and slow economic growth by 0.5 to 1 percentage point. The agency had previously predicted that the economy would grow 3.7 percent this year.

aware of the fact that corporate income taxes as a percentage of government receipts are quite small relative to personal income taxes and Social Security taxes.

The federal government also paid $2,381.3 billion in expenditures in 2004. Of this, $1,041.0 billion represented transfer payments to persons (Social Security benefits, military retirement benefits, and unemployment compensation).[5] Consumption ($725.7 billion) was

---

[5]Remember that there is an important difference between transfer payments and government purchases of goods and services (consumption expenditures). Much of the government budget goes for things that an economist would classify as transfers (payments that are grants or gifts) instead of purchases of goods and services. It is only the latter that are included in our variable *G*. Transfers are counted as part of net taxes.

FIGURE 22.4 The Federal Government Surplus (+) or Deficit (−) as a Percentage of GDP, 1970 I–2005 II

The deficits in the 1980s were particularly large by historical standards. The move to surplus in the late 1990s was reversed in 2001.

the next-largest component, followed by grants-in-aid to state and local governments ($348.3 billion), which are grants given to the state and local governments by the federal government, and interest payments on the federal debt ($221.5 billion).

THE SURPLUS OR DEFICIT

federal surplus (+) or deficit (−) Federal government receipts minus expenditures.

The difference between the federal government's receipts and its expenditures is the **federal surplus (+)** or **deficit (−)**, which is net federal government saving. Table 22.5 shows that the federal government spent more than it took in during 2004, resulting in a deficit of $406.5 billion.

The federal deficit was large from the early 1980s until the mid-1990s. You can see this trend in Figure 22.4 where the federal surplus or deficit as a percentage of gross domestic product (GDP) is plotted for 1970 I–2005 II. As the figure shows, the budget was in deficit until 1998 I, when it began to be in surplus. Except for a period in the mid-1970s, the deficit was fairly small until the early 1980s, where it reached 5.4 percent of GDP in 1982 IV. The budget improved rapidly from 1992 until 2000, but it then began falling rapidly. In the third quarter of 2003 the deficit was 4.1 percent of GDP. Since then, the deficit has fallen slowly.

How did such large deficits in the 1980s come about? There are several reasons. First, government purchases as a percentage of GDP rose in the early 1980s and then remained high. This increase primarily reflected the defense buildup of the Reagan years. Second, interest payments as a percentage of GDP rose substantially. Third, personal income tax rates fell as a result of the Economic Recovery Tax Act of 1981. With defense spending and interest payments rising rapidly and personal income tax rates falling, it is not surprising that the deficit rose substantially during the 1980s. The government simply spent a lot more than it collected in taxes.

During the two Clinton administrations (1993–2000) the deficit turned to surplus, and at its peak in the first quarter of 2000 the surplus was 2.3 percent of GDP. Some of this change was due to tax rate increases that were passed at the beginning of the first Clinton administration. The rapid movement from surplus to deficit beginning in 2001 was due in part to a number of large tax rate decreases that were passed during the G. W. Bush administration and increased government spending on Iraq.

THE DEBT

federal debt The total amount owed by the federal government.

When the government runs a deficit, it must borrow to finance it. To borrow, the federal government sells government securities to the public. It issues pieces of paper promising to pay a certain amount, with interest, in the future. In return, it receives funds from the buyers of the paper and uses these funds to pay its bills. This borrowing increases the **federal debt**, the total amount owed by the federal government. The federal debt is the total of all accumulated deficits minus surpluses over time.

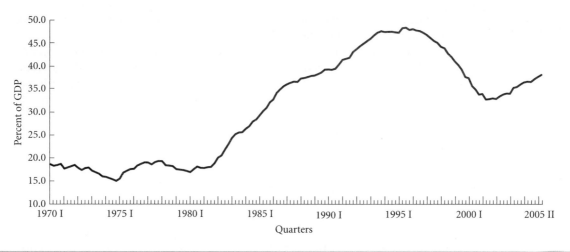

FIGURE 22.5 The Federal Government Debt as a Percentage of GDP, 1970 I–2005 II

The federal government debt increased dramatically in the 1980s as a result of the large deficits. The percentage fell sharply from the mid-1990s to 2000. Since 2000 the percentage has risen slightly.

Some of the securities that the government issues end up being held by the federal government itself at the Federal Reserve or in government trust funds. The term **privately held federal debt** refers only to the *privately held* debt of the U.S. government. At the end of July 2005, the federal debt was $7.9 trillion, of which $4.6 trillion was privately held.

Given the large deficits that the federal government had in the 1980s, it should not be surprising that the federal debt rose sharply in the 1980s. You can see this change in Figure 22.5, where the privately held federal debt as a percentage of GDP is plotted for the 1970 I–2005 II period. The debt rose rapidly between 1982 and 1993—from 19.0 percent of GDP in 1981 IV to 47.5 percent in 1993 IV. From the mid-1990s until 2000 the debt as a percentage of GDP fell sharply. Since 2000 the percent has risen slightly.

privately held federal debt The privately held (non-government-owned) debt of the U.S. government.

THE ECONOMY'S INFLUENCE ON THE GOVERNMENT BUDGET

Some parts of the government's budget depend on the state of the economy, over which the government has no direct control. The following are some of the ways in which the economy affects the budget.

TAX REVENUES DEPEND ON THE STATE OF THE ECONOMY

Consider the revenue side of the budget. The government passes laws that set tax rates and tax brackets, variables the government does control. Tax revenue, on the other hand, depends on taxable income, and income depends on the state of the economy, which the government does *not* control. The government can set a personal income tax rate of 20 percent, but the revenue that the tax brings in will depend on the average income earned by households. The government will collect more revenue when average income is $60,000 than when average income is $40,000.

SOME GOVERNMENT EXPENDITURES DEPEND ON THE STATE OF THE ECONOMY

Some items on the expenditure side of the government budget also depend on the state of the economy. As the economy expands, unemployment falls, and the result is a decrease in unemployment benefits. Welfare payments and food stamp allotments also decrease somewhat. Some of the people who receive these benefits during bad times are able to find jobs when the state of the economy improves, and they begin earning enough income that they no longer qualify. Transfer payments tend to go down automatically during an expansion.

(During a slump, transfer payments tend to increase because there are more people without jobs and more poor people generally.)

Another reason that government spending is not completely controllable is that inflation often picks up when the economy is expanding. This can lead the government to spend more than it had planned to spend. Suppose the government has ordered 20 planes at $2 million each and inflation causes the actual price to be higher than expected. If the government decides to go ahead and buy the planes anyway, it will be forced to increase its spending. Finally, any change in the interest rate changes government interest payments. An increase in interest rates means that the government spends more in interest payments.

AUTOMATIC STABILIZERS

automatic stabilizers
Revenue and expenditure items in the federal budget that automatically change with the state of the economy in such a way as to stabilize GDP.

As the economy expands, the government's tax receipts increase. Also, transfer payments fall as the economy expands, which leads to a decrease in government expenditures. The revenue and expenditure items that change in response to changes in economic activity in such a way as to moderate changes in GDP are known as **automatic stabilizers**. As the economy expands or contracts, "automatic" changes in government revenues and expenditures take place that tend to reduce the change in, or to stabilize, GDP.

The fact that some revenues *automatically* tend to rise and some expenditures *automatically* tend to fall in an expansion means that the government surplus is larger, or the deficit is smaller, in an expansion than it otherwise would be. Suppose we wanted to assess whether a government is practicing a policy designed to increase spending and income. If we looked only at the size of the government budget deficit, we might be fooled into thinking that the government is trying to stimulate the economy when, in fact, the real source of the deficit is a slump in the economy that caused revenues to fall and transfer payments to increase.

FISCAL DRAG

fiscal drag The negative effect on the economy that occurs when average tax rates increase because taxpayers have moved into higher income brackets during an expansion.

If the economy is doing well, income will be high and so will tax revenue. Tax revenue rises with increases in income for two reasons. First, there is more income to be taxed when people are earning more. Second, as people earn more income, they move into higher tax brackets and the average tax rate that they pay increases. This type of increase in tax rates is a **fiscal drag**, because the increase in average tax rates that results when people move into higher brackets acts as a "drag" on the economy. As the economy expands and income increases, the automatic tax increase mechanism built into the system goes to work. Tax rates go up, reducing the after-tax wage, and this slows down the expansion.

Before 1982, people found themselves pushed into higher tax brackets by inflation alone. Suppose my income rose 10 percent in 1981, but the price level also rose by 10 percent in that year. My income did not increase at all in real terms, but because the tax brackets were not legislated in real terms, I ended up paying more taxes. Since 1982, however, tax brackets have been indexed—that is, adjusted for inflation—and this change has substantially reduced the automatic fiscal drag built into the system.

FULL-EMPLOYMENT BUDGET

full-employment budget
What the federal budget would be if the economy were producing at a full-employment level of output.

Because the condition of the economy affects the budget deficit so strongly, we cannot accurately judge either the intent or the success of fiscal policies just by looking at the surplus or deficit. Instead of looking simply at the size of the surplus or deficit, economists have developed an alternative way to measure how effective fiscal policy actually is. By examining what the budget would be like if the economy were producing at the full-employment level of output—the so-called **full-employment budget**—we can establish a benchmark for evaluating fiscal policy.

The distinction between the actual and full-employment budget is important. Suppose the economy is in a slump and the deficit is $250 billion. Also suppose that if there were full employment, the deficit would fall to $75 billion. The $75 billion deficit that would remain even with full employment would be due to the structure of tax and spending programs instead of the state of the economy. This deficit—the deficit that remains at full employment—is sometimes called the **structural deficit**. The $175 billion ($250 billion − $75 billion) part of the deficit caused by the fact the economy is in a slump is known as the **cyclical deficit**. The existence of the cyclical deficit depends on where the economy is in the business cycle, and it ceases to exist when full employment is reached. By definition, the cyclical deficit of the full-employment budget is zero.

structural deficit The deficit that remains at full employment.

cyclical deficit The deficit that occurs because of a downturn in the business cycle.

LOOKING AHEAD

We have now seen how households, firms, and the government interact in the goods market, how equilibrium output (income) is determined, and how the government uses fiscal policy to influence the economy. In the following two chapters we analyze the money market and monetary policy—the government's other major tool for influencing the economy.

SUMMARY

1. The government can affect the macroeconomy through two specific policy channels. *Fiscal policy* refers to the government's taxing and spending behavior. *Discretionary fiscal policy* refers to changes in taxes or spending that are the result of deliberate changes in government policy. *Monetary policy* refers to the behavior of the Federal Reserve concerning the nation's money supply.

GOVERNMENT IN THE ECONOMY

2. The government does not have complete control over tax revenues and certain expenditures, which are partially dictated by the state of the economy.

3. As a participant in the economy, the government makes purchases of goods and services (G), collects taxes, and makes transfer payments to households. *Net taxes* (T) is equal to the tax payments made to the government by firms and households minus transfer payments made to households by the government.

4. *Disposable*, or *after-tax, income* (Y_d) is equal to the amount of income received by households after taxes: $Y_d \equiv Y - T$. After-tax income determines households' consumption behavior.

5. The *budget deficit* is equal to the difference between what the government spends and what it collects in taxes: $G - T$. When G exceeds T, the government must borrow from the public to finance its deficit.

6. In an economy in which government is a participant, planned aggregate expenditure equals consumption spending by households (C) plus planned investment spending by firms (I) plus government spending on goods and services (G): $AE \equiv C + I + G$. Because the condition $Y = AE$ is necessary for the economy to be in equilibrium, it follows that $Y = C + I + G$ is the macroeconomic equilibrium condition. The economy is also in equilibrium when leakages out of the system equal injections into the system. This occurs when saving and net taxes (the leakages) equal planned investment and government purchases (the injections): $S + T = I + G$.

FISCAL POLICY AT WORK: MULTIPLIER EFFECTS

7. Fiscal policy has a multiplier effect on the economy. A change in government spending gives rise to a multiplier equal to $1/MPS$. A change in taxation brings about a multiplier equal to $-MPC/MPS$. A simultaneous equal increase or decrease in government spending and taxes has a multiplier effect of 1.

THE FEDERAL BUDGET

8. The *federal deficit* was quite large in the 1980s. Reasons for the deficit include the defense buildup of the Reagan years, the high amount of interest paid on already-existing debt, and cuts in personal income tax rates. With defense spending and interest payments rising rapidly and personal income tax rates falling, the government has simply been spending more than it has been collecting in taxes.

THE ECONOMY'S INFLUENCE ON THE GOVERNMENT BUDGET

9. *Automatic stabilizers* are revenue and expenditure items in the federal budget that automatically change with the state of the economy and tend to stabilize GDP. For example, during expansions the government automatically takes in more revenue, because people are making more money that is taxed. Higher income and tax brackets also mean fewer transfer payments.

10. *Fiscal drag* is the negative effect on the economy that occurs when average tax rates increase because taxpayers have moved into higher income brackets during an expansion. These higher taxes reduce disposable income and slow down the expansion. Since 1982, tax brackets have been indexed to inflation, and this change has reduced the fiscal drag built into the tax system.

11. The *full-employment budget* is an economist's construction of what the federal budget would be if the economy were producing at a full-employment level of output. The *structural deficit* is the federal deficit that remains even at full employment. A *cyclical deficit* occurs when there is a downturn in the business cycle.

REVIEW TERMS AND CONCEPTS

automatic stabilizers, 494

balanced-budget multiplier, 488

budget deficit, 481

cyclical deficit, 495

discretionary fiscal policy, 480

disposable, or after-tax, income (Y_d), 480

federal budget, 490

federal debt, 492

federal surplus (+) or deficit (−), 492

fiscal drag, 494

fiscal policy, 479

full-employment budget, 494

government spending multiplier, 486

monetary policy, 479

net taxes (T), 480

privately held federal debt, 493

structural deficit, 495

tax multiplier, 487

1. Disposable income $Y_d \equiv Y - T$
2. $AE \equiv C + I + G$
3. Government budget deficit $\equiv G - T$
4. Equilibrium in an economy with a government: $Y = C + I + G$
5. Leakages/injections approach to equilibrium in an economy with a government:
   $S + T = I + G$
6. Government spending multiplier $\equiv \dfrac{1}{MPS}$
7. Tax multiplier $\equiv -\left(\dfrac{MPC}{MPS}\right)$
8. Balanced-budget multiplier $\equiv 1$

PROBLEM SET

1. You are appointed secretary of the treasury of a recently independent country called Rugaria. The currency of Rugaria is the lav. The new nation began fiscal operations this year and the budget situation is that the government will spend 10 million lavs and taxes will be 9 million lavs. The 1-million-lav difference will be borrowed from the public by selling 10-year government bonds paying 5 percent interest. The interest on the outstanding bonds must be added to spending each year, and we assume that additional taxes are raised to cover that interest. Assuming that the budget stays the same except for the interest on the debt for 10 years, what will be the accumulated debt? What will the size of the budget be after 10 years?

2. The News Analysis box on p. 491 describes the impact of Hurricane Katrina on the budget deficit. Go to **www.CBO.gov**, click on "historical budget data," and look at the current federal budget deficit and the deficits of the last 10 years. How does the current deficit compare to those deficits? Have they been consistent with the idea that a slow economy causes deficits to be large? Did the deficit get significantly larger after September 2005?

3. Suppose that the government of Lumpland is enjoying a fat budget surplus with fixed government expenditures of $G = 150$ and fixed taxes of $T = 200$. Assume that consumers of Lumpland behave as described in the following consumption function:

   $$C = 150 + 0.75(Y - T)$$

   Suppose further that investment spending is fixed at 100. Calculate the equilibrium level of GDP in Lumpland. Solve for equilibrium levels of Y, C, and S. Next assume that the Republican Congress in Lumpland succeeds in reducing taxes by 20 to a new fixed level of 180. Recalculate the equilibrium level of GDP using the tax multiplier. Solve for equilibrium levels of Y, C, and S after the tax cut and check to ensure that the multiplier worked. What arguments are likely to be used in support of such a tax cut? What arguments might be used to oppose such a tax cut?

4. For each of the following statements, say whether you agree or disagree and explain your answer:
   a. During periods of budget surplus (when $G < T$), the government debt grows.
   b. A tax cut will increase the equilibrium level of GDP if the budget is in deficit but will decrease the equilibrium level of GDP if the budget is in surplus.
   c. If the $MPS = .90$, the tax multiplier is actually larger than the expenditure multiplier.

5. Define *saving* and *investment*. Data for the simple economy of Newt show that in 2005 saving exceeded investment and the government is running a balanced budget. What is likely to happen? What would happen instead if the government were running a deficit and saving were equal to investment?

6. Expert economists in the economy of Yuk estimate the following:

	BILLION YUKS
Real output/income	1,000
Government purchases	200
Total net taxes	200
Investment spending (planned)	100

   Assume that Yukkers consume 75 percent of their disposable incomes and save 25 percent.
   a. You are asked by the business editor of the *Yuk Gazette* to predict the events of the next few months. By using the data given, can you make a forecast? (Assume that investment is constant.)
   b. If no changes were made, at what level of GDP (Y) would the economy of Yuk settle?
   c. Some local conservatives blame Yuk's problems on the size of the government sector. They suggest cutting government purchases by 25 billion Yuks. What effect would such cuts have on the economy? (Be specific.)

7. "A $1 increase in government spending will raise equilibrium income by more than a $1 tax cut, yet both have the same impact on the budget deficit. So if we care about the budget

deficit, the best way to stimulate the economy is through increases in spending, not cuts in taxes." Comment.

8. Assume that in 2005, the following prevails in the Republic of Nurd:

$Y = \$200$	$G = \$0$
$C = \$160$	$T = \$0$
$S = \$40$	
I (planned) = \$30	

Assume that households consume 80 percent of their income, they save 20 percent of their income, $MPC = .8$, and $MPS = .2$. That is, $C = .8Y_d$ and $S = .2Y_d$.

a. Is the economy of Nurd in equilibrium? What is Nurd's equilibrium level of income? What is likely to happen in the coming months if the government takes no action?

b. If \$200 is the "full-employment" level of Y, what fiscal policy might the government follow if its goal is full employment?

c. If the full-employment level of Y is \$250, what fiscal policy might the government follow?

d. Suppose $Y = \$200$, $C = \$160$, $S = \$40$, and $I = \$40$. Is Nurd's economy in equilibrium?

e. Starting with the situation in part d, suppose the government starts spending \$30 each year with no taxation and continues to spend \$30 every period. If I remains constant, what will happen to the equilibrium level of Nurd's domestic product (Y)? What will the new levels of C and S be?

f. Starting with the situation in part d, suppose the government starts taxing the population \$30 each year without spending anything and continues to tax at that rate every period. If I remains constant, what will happen to the equilibrium level of Nurd's domestic product (Y)? What will be the new levels of C and S? How does your answer to part f differ from your answer to part e? Why?

9. Some economists claim World War II ended the Great Depression of the 1930s. The war effort was financed by borrowing massive sums of money from the public. Explain how a war could end a recession. Look at recent and back issues of the *Economic Report of the President* or the *Statistical Abstract of the United States*. How large was the federal government's debt as a percentage of GDP in 1946? How large is it today?

10. Suppose all tax collections are fixed (instead of dependent on income), and all spending and transfer programs are also fixed (in the sense that they do not depend on the state of the economy, as, for example, unemployment benefits now do). If this were the case, would there be any automatic stabilizers in the government budget? Would there be any distinction between the full-employment deficit and the actual budget deficit? Explain.

11. Answer the following:

a. $MPS = .4$. What is the government spending multiplier?

b. $MPC = .9$. What is the government spending multiplier?

c. $MPS = .5$. What is the government spending multiplier?

d. $MPC = .75$. What is the tax multiplier?

e. $MPS = .1$. What is the tax multiplier?

f. If the government spending multiplier is 6, what is the tax multiplier?

g. If the tax multiplier is -2, what is the government spending multiplier?

h. If government purchases and taxes are both increased by \$100 billion simultaneously, what will the effect be on equilibrium output (income)?

APPENDIX A

DERIVING THE FISCAL POLICY MULTIPLIERS

THE GOVERNMENT SPENDING AND TAX MULTIPLIERS

In the chapter, we noted that the government spending multiplier is $1/MPS$. (This is the same as the investment multiplier.) We can also derive the multiplier algebraically using our hypothetical consumption function:

$$C = a + b(Y - T)$$

where b is the marginal propensity to consume. As you know, the equilibrium condition is

$$Y = C + I + G$$

By substituting for C, we get

$$Y = a + b(Y - T) + I + G$$
$$Y = a + bY - bT + I + G$$

This equation can be rearranged to yield

$$Y - bY = a + I + G - bT$$
$$Y(1 - b) = a + I + G - bT$$

Now solve for Y by dividing through by $(1 - b)$:

$$Y = \frac{1}{(1 - b)}(a + I + G - bT)$$

We see from this last equation that if G increases by 1 with the other determinants of Y (a, I, and T) remaining constant, Y increases by $1/(1 - b)$. The multiplier is, as before, simply $1/(1 - b)$, where b is the marginal propensity to consume. Of course, $1 - b$ equals the marginal propensity to save, so the government spending multiplier is $1/MPS$.

We can also derive the tax multiplier. The last equation says that when T increases by \$1, holding a, I, and G constant, income decreases by $b/(1 - b)$ dollars. The tax multiplier is $-b/(1 - b)$, or $-MPC/(1 - MPC) = -MPC/MPS$. (Remember, the negative sign in the resulting tax multiplier shows that it is a *negative* multiplier.)

THE BALANCED-BUDGET MULTIPLIER

It is easy to show formally that the balanced-budget multiplier = 1. When taxes and government spending are simultaneously increased by the same amount, there are two effects on planned aggregate expenditure: one positive and one negative. The initial impact of a balanced-budget increase in government spending and taxes on aggregate expenditure would be the *increase* in government purchases (ΔG) minus the *decrease* in consumption (ΔC) caused by the tax increase. The decrease in consumption brought about by the tax increase is equal to $\Delta C = \Delta T (MPC)$.

$$
\begin{array}{ll}
\text{increase in spending:} & \Delta G \\
- \text{decrease in spending:} & \Delta C = \Delta T(MPC) \\
\hline
= \text{net increase in spending} & \Delta G - \Delta T(MPC)
\end{array}
$$

In a balanced-budget increase, $\Delta G = \Delta T$, so we can substitute:

net initial increase in spending:
$$\Delta G - \Delta G(MPC) = \Delta G \, (1 - MPC)$$

Because $MPS = (1 - MPC)$, the net initial increase in spending is:

$$\Delta G(MPS)$$

We can now apply the expenditure multiplier $\left(\dfrac{1}{MPS}\right)$ to this net initial increase in spending:

$$\Delta Y = \Delta G(MPS)\left(\frac{1}{MPS}\right) = \Delta G$$

Thus, the final total increase in the equilibrium level of Y is just equal to the initial balanced increase in G and T. That means the balanced-budget multiplier = 1, so the final increase in real output is of the same magnitude as the initial change in spending.

APPENDIX B

THE CASE IN WHICH TAX REVENUES DEPEND ON INCOME

In this chapter, we used the simplifying assumption that the government collects taxes in a lump sum. This made our discussion of the multiplier effects somewhat easier to follow. Now suppose that the government collects taxes not solely as a lump sum that is paid regardless of income, but also partly in the form of a proportional levy against income. This is a more realistic assumption. Typically, tax collections either are based on income (as with the personal income tax) or follow the ups and downs in the economy (as with sales taxes). Instead of setting taxes equal to some fixed amount, let us say that tax revenues depend on income. If we call the amount of net taxes collected T, we can write: $T = T_0 + tY$.

This equation contains two parts. First, we note that net taxes (T) will be equal to an amount T_0 if income (Y) is zero. Second, the tax rate (t) indicates how much net taxes change as income changes. Suppose that T_0 is equal to -200 and t is 1/3. The resulting tax function is $T = -200 + 1/3Y$, which is graphed in Figure 22B.1. Note that when income is zero, the government collects "negative net taxes," which simply means that it makes transfer payments of 200. As income rises, tax collections increase because every extra dollar of income generates $0.33 in extra revenues for the government.

How do we incorporate this new tax function into our discussion? All we do is replace the old value of T (in the example in the chapter, T was set equal to 100) with the new value, $-200 + 1/3Y$. Look first at the consumption equation. Consumption (C) still depends on disposable income, as it did before. Also, disposable income is still $Y - T$, or income minus taxes. Instead of disposable income equaling $Y - 100$, however, the new equation for disposable income is

$$
\begin{aligned}
Y_d &\equiv Y - T \\
Y_d &\equiv Y - (-200 + 1/3Y) \\
Y_d &\equiv Y + 200 - 1/3Y
\end{aligned}
$$

Because consumption still depends on after-tax income, exactly as it did before, we have

$$
\begin{aligned}
C &= 100 + .75Y_d \\
C &= 100 + .75(Y + 200 - 1/3Y)
\end{aligned}
$$

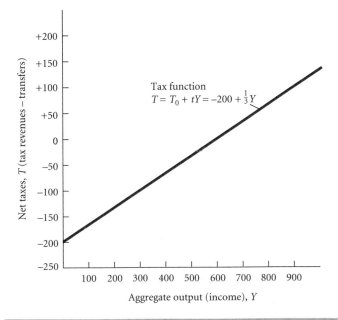

FIGURE 22B.1 The Tax Function

This graph shows net taxes (taxes minus transfer payments) as a function of aggregate income.

Nothing else needs to be changed. We solve for equilibrium income exactly as before, by setting planned aggregate expenditure equal to aggregate output. Recall that planned aggregate expenditure is $C + I + G$, and aggregate output is Y. If we assume, as before, that $I = 100$ and $G = 100$, the equilibrium is

$$Y = C + I + G$$
$$Y = \underbrace{100 + .75(Y + 200 - 1/3Y)}_{C} + \underbrace{100}_{I} + \underbrace{100}_{G}$$

This equation may look difficult to solve, but it is not. It simplifies to

$$Y = 100 + .75Y + 150 - .25Y + 100 + 100$$
$$Y = 450 + .5Y$$
$$.5Y = 450$$

This means that $Y = 450/.5 = 900$, the new equilibrium level of income.

Consider the graphic analysis of this equation as shown in Figure 22B.2, where you should note that when we make taxes a function of income (instead of a lump-sum amount), the AE function becomes *flatter* than it was before. Why? When tax collections do not depend on income, an increase in income of $1 means disposable income also increases by a dollar. Because taxes are a constant amount, adding more income does not raise the amount of taxes paid. Disposable income therefore changes dollar-for-dollar with any change in income.

When taxes depend on income, a $1 increase in income does not increase disposable income by a full dollar, because some of the additional dollar goes to pay extra taxes. Under the

modified tax function of Figure 22B.2, an extra dollar of income will increase disposable income by only $0.67, because $0.33 of the extra dollar goes to the government in the form of taxes.

No matter how taxes are calculated, the marginal propensity to consume out of disposable (or after-tax) income is the same—each extra dollar of disposable income will increase consumption spending by $0.75. However, a $1 change in before-tax income does not have the same effect on disposable income in each case. Suppose we were to increase income by $1. With the lump-sum tax function, disposable income would rise by $1, and consumption would increase by the MPC times the change in Y_d, or $0.75. When taxes depend on income, disposable income would rise by only $0.67 from the $1 increase in income, and consumption would rise by only the MPC times the change in disposable income, or $0.75 \times .67 = $0.50.

If a $1 increase in income raises expenditure by $0.75 in one case, and by only $0.50 in the other, the second aggregate expenditure function must be flatter than the first.

THE GOVERNMENT SPENDING AND TAX MULTIPLIERS ALGEBRAICALLY

All this means that if taxes are a function of income, the three multipliers (investment, government spending, and tax) are less than they would be if taxes were a lump-sum amount. By using the same linear consumption function we used in Chapters 20 and 21, we can derive the multiplier:

$$C = a + b(Y - T)$$
$$C = a + b(Y - T_0 - tY)$$
$$C = a + bY - bT_0 - btY$$

We know that $Y = C + I + G$. Through substitution we get

$$Y = \underbrace{a + bY - bT_0 - btY}_{C} + I + G$$

Solving for Y:

$$Y = \frac{1}{1 - b + bt}(a + I + G - bT_0)$$

This means that a $1 increase in G or I (holding a and T_0 constant) will increase the equilibrium level of Y by

$$\frac{1}{1 - b + bt}$$

If $b = MPC = .75$ and $t = .20$, the spending multiplier is 2.5. (Compare this to 4, which would be the value of the spending multiplier if taxes were a lump sum, that is, if $t = 0$.)

Holding a, I, and G constant, a fixed or lump-sum tax cut (a cut in T_0) will increase the equilibrium level of income by

$$\frac{b}{1 - b + bt}$$

Thus, if $b = MPC = .75$ and $t = .20$, the tax multiplier is −1.875. (Compare this to − 3, which would be the value of the tax multiplier if taxes were a lump sum.)

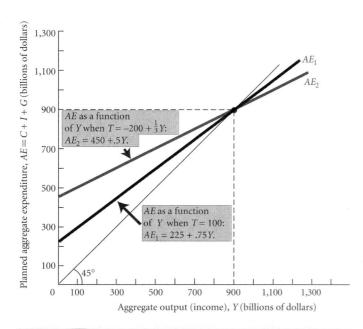

FIGURE 22B.2 Different Tax Systems

When taxes are strictly lump sum ($T = 100$) and do not depend on income, the aggregate expenditure function is steeper than when taxes depend on income.

SUMMARY

1. When taxes depend on income, a $1 increase in income does not increase disposable income by a full dollar, because some of the additional dollar must go to pay extra taxes. This means that if taxes are a function of income, the three multipliers (investment, government spending, and tax) are less than they would be if taxes were a lump-sum amount.

PROBLEM SET

1. Given the following for the economy of a country:
   a. Consumption function: $C = 85 + 0.5Y_d$
   b. Investment function: $I = 85$
   c. Government spending: $G = 60$
   d. Net taxes: $T = -40 + 0.25Y$
   e. Disposable income: $Y_d \equiv Y - T$
   f. Equilibrium: $Y = C + I + G$

Solve for equilibrium income. (*Hint*: Be very careful in doing the calculations. They are not difficult, but it is easy to make careless mistakes that produce very wrong results.) How much does the government collect in net taxes when the economy is in equilibrium? What is the government's budget deficit or surplus?

The Money Supply and the Federal Reserve System

23

In the last two chapters, we explored how consumers, firms, and the government interact in the goods market. In this chapter and the next, we show how money markets work in the macroeconomy. We begin with what money is and the role it plays in the U.S. economy. We then discuss the forces that determine the supply of money and show how banks create money. Finally, we discuss the workings of the nation's central bank, the Federal Reserve (the Fed), and the tools at its disposal to control the money supply.

Microeconomics has little to say about money. Microeconomic theories and models are concerned primarily with *real* quantities (apples, oranges, hours of labor) and *relative* prices (the price of apples relative to the price of oranges, or the price of labor relative to the prices of other goods). Most of the key ideas in microeconomics do not require that we know anything about money. As we shall see, this is not the case in macroeconomics.

AN OVERVIEW OF MONEY

You often hear people say things like, "He makes a lot of money" (in other words, "He has a high income") or "She's worth a lot of money" (meaning "She is very wealthy"). It is true that your employer uses money to pay you your income, and your wealth may be accumulated in the form of money. However, *money is not income, and money is not wealth.*

To see that money and income are not the same, think of a $20 bill. That bill may pass through a thousand hands in a year, yet never be used to pay anyone a salary. Suppose I get a $20 bill from an automatic teller machine, and I spend it on dinner. The restaurant puts that $20 bill in a bank in the next day's deposit. The bank gives it to a woman cashing a check the following day; she spends it at a baseball game that night. The bill has been through many hands but not as part of anyone's income.

WHAT IS MONEY?

We will soon get to a formal definition of money, but let us start out with the basic idea of what money is.

Money is anything that is generally accepted as a medium of exchange.

Most people take the ability to obtain and use money for granted. When the whole monetary system works well, as it generally does in the United States, the basic mechanics of the system are virtually invisible. People take for granted that they can walk into any store, restaurant, boutique, or gas station and buy whatever they want, as long as they have enough green pieces of paper.

The idea that you can buy things with money is so natural and obvious that it seems absurd to mention it, but stop and ask yourself: "How is it that a store owner is willing to part with a steak and a loaf of bread that I can eat in exchange for some pieces of paper that are intrinsically worthless?" Why, on the other hand, are there times and places where it takes a shopping cart full of money to purchase a dozen eggs? The answers to these questions lie in what money is: a means of payment, a store of value, and a unit of account.

A Means of Payment, or Medium of Exchange

Money is vital to the working of a market economy. Imagine what life would be like without it. The alternative to a monetary economy is **barter**, people exchanging goods and services for other goods and services directly instead of exchanging via the medium of money.

How does a barter system work? Suppose you want bacon, eggs, and orange juice for breakfast. Instead of going to the store and buying these things with money, you would have to find someone who has these items and is willing to trade them. You would also have to have something the bacon seller, the orange juice purveyor, and the egg vendor want. Having pencils to trade will do you no good if the bacon, orange juice, and egg sellers do not want pencils.

A barter system requires a *double coincidence of wants* for trade to take place. That is, to effect a trade, I have to find someone who has what I want, and that person must also want what I have. Where the range of goods traded is small, as it is in relatively unsophisticated economies, it is not difficult to find someone to trade with, and barter is often used. In a complex society with many goods, barter exchanges involve an intolerable amount of effort. Imagine trying to find people who offer for sale all the things you buy in a typical trip to the supermarket, and who are willing to accept goods that you have to offer in exchange for their goods.

Some agreed-to **medium of exchange** (or **means of payment**) neatly eliminates the double-coincidence-of-wants problem. Under a monetary system, money is exchanged for goods or services when people buy things; goods or services are exchanged for money when people sell things. No one ever has to trade goods for other goods directly. Money is a lubricant in the functioning of a market economy.

A Store of Value

Economists have identified other roles for money aside from its primary function as a medium of exchange. Money also serves as a **store of value**—an asset that can be used to transport purchasing power from one time period to another. If you raise chickens and at the end of the month sell them for more than you want to spend and consume immediately, you may keep some of your earnings in the form of money until the time you want to spend it.

There are many other stores of value besides money. You could have decided to hold your "surplus" earnings by buying such things as antique paintings, baseball cards, or diamonds, which you could sell later when you want to spend your earnings. Money has several advantages over these other stores of value. First, it comes in convenient denominations and is easily portable. You do not have to worry about making change for a Renoir painting to buy a gallon of gasoline. Second, because money is also a means of payment, it is easily exchanged for goods at all times. (A Renoir is not easily exchanged for other goods.) These two factors compose the **liquidity property of money**. Money is easily spent, flowing out of your hands like liquid. Renoirs and ancient Aztec statues are neither convenient nor portable and are not readily accepted as a means of payment.

The main disadvantage of money as a store of value is that the value of money falls when the prices of goods and services rise. If the price of potato chips rises from $1 per bag to $2 per bag, the value of a dollar bill, in terms of potato chips, falls from one bag to half a bag. When this happens, it may be better to use potato chips (or antiques or real estate) as a store of value.

barter The direct exchange of goods and services for other goods and services.

medium of exchange, or **means of payment** What sellers generally accept and buyers generally use to pay for goods and services.

store of value An asset that can be used to transport purchasing power from one time period to another.

liquidity property of money The property of money that makes it a good medium of exchange as well as a store of value: It is portable and readily accepted and thus easily exchanged for goods.

Real Goods as a Store of Value During Inflation

SOMETIMES GOVERNMENTS IN TROUble resort to printing money in order to pay their bills or to buy foreign currencies with which to buy imported goods. When governments print money excessively, the result is hyperinflation. When the price level rises very rapidly, money stops being a "store of value," and people often resort to real goods rather than money to hold value. The following piece in the *New York Times* describes exactly that situation in Zimbabwe during 2005.

Zimbabwe, Long Destitute, Teeters Toward Ruin
By MICHAEL WINES
New York Times
May 21, 2005

In the weeks before parliamentary elections in March, the leaders of this threadbare nation threw open the national larder, wooing voters with stocks of normally scarce gasoline and corn and a flood of freshly printed money.

Here in the second largest city, lines of cars stretch a quarter mile and more at fuel-parched service stations, and drivers spend the night in their cars' back seats lest they lose their place in line. Milk, cooking oil and, most of all, corn, the national staple, are a distant memory at most stores. At one downtown grocery, tubes of much-prized American toothpaste are kept in a locked case.

Zimbabwe's currency, which traded on the black market at 120 to the dollar in April 2002, went for 6,200 to the dollar last December, 12,000 on April 1, and 17,000 in early May. By mid-May

a single American dollar brought as much as 25,000 Zimbabwean dollars, though the rate has since steadied at about 20,000.

Falling exports made foreign currency more expensive, causing exchange rates to rocket. But the government has generally chosen to print more money instead of readjusting the value of its currency; Zimbabwe's money supply rose 226 percent in 2004.

The result has been hyperinflation and a thriving black market in money and goods. Hyperinflation and the artificial exchange rate, in turn, have crippled gold mining, Zimbabwe's other big export industry. Production fell 18 percent in the first quarter of 2005.

Tony Rowland, the chief executive of Bulawayo-based Zimplow, employs 400 people to make animal-drawn plows from steel rolled at one of Zimbabwe's few domestic mills. To hedge against the

constantly rising price of domestic steel, he reinvests his profits in something that rises with inflation: nuts and bolts.

"I've become a steel dealer," he said. "I've had to expand my business to things beyond my core business to keep going."

So Zimbabweans muddle through. In Harare, the chief of a major consumer products company said recently that he had junked his accounting software until programmers could adapt a Turkish version to his requirements. The problem: The Zimbabwe spreadsheets cannot accommodate the flood of zeros required for transactions that now run into the billions—even the trillions— of Zimbabwean dollars.

"We've run out of noughts," he said.

A Unit of Account   Money also serves as a **unit of account**—a consistent way of quoting prices. All prices are quoted in monetary units. A textbook is quoted as costing $90, not 150 bananas or 5 DVDs, and a banana is quoted as costing 60 cents, not 1.4 apples or 6 pages of a textbook. Obviously, a standard unit of account is extremely useful when quoting prices. This function of money may have escaped your notice—what else would people quote prices in except money?

unit of account A standard unit that provides a consistent way of quoting prices.

COMMODITY AND FIAT MONIES

Some of Yap's stone money wheels are so large that they are never moved.

commodity monies Items used as money that also have intrinsic value in some other use.

fiat, or **token, money** Items designated as money that are intrinsically worthless.

legal tender Money that a government has required to be accepted in settlement of debts.

currency debasement The decrease in the value of money that occurs when its supply is increased rapidly.

Introductory economics textbooks are full of stories about the various items that have been used as money by various cultures—candy bars, cigarettes (in World War II prisoner-of-war camps), huge wheels of carved stone (on the island of Yap in the South Pacific), cowrie shells (in West Africa), beads (among North American Indians), cattle (in southern Africa), and small green scraps of paper (in contemporary North America). The list goes on. These various kinds of money are generally divided into two groups, commodity monies and fiat money.

Commodity monies are those items used as money that also have an intrinsic value in some other use. For example, prisoners of war made purchases with cigarettes, quoted prices in terms of cigarettes, and held their wealth in the form of accumulated cigarettes. Of course, cigarettes could also be smoked—they had an alternative use apart from serving as money. Gold represents another form of commodity money. For hundreds of years gold could be used directly to buy things, but it also had other uses, ranging from jewelry to dental fillings.

By contrast, money in the United States today is mostly fiat money. **Fiat money**, sometimes called **token money**, is money that is intrinsically worthless. The actual value of a 1-, 10-, or 50-dollar bill is basically zero; what other uses are there for a small piece of paper with some green ink on it?

Why would anyone accept worthless scraps of paper as money instead of something that has some value, such as gold, cigarettes, or cattle? If your answer is "because the paper money is backed by gold or silver," you are wrong. There was a time when dollar bills were convertible directly into gold. The government backed each dollar bill in circulation by holding a certain amount of gold in its vaults. If the price of gold were $35 per ounce, for example, the government agreed to sell one ounce of gold for 35 dollar bills. However, dollar bills are no longer backed by any commodity—gold, silver, or anything else. They are exchangeable only for dimes, nickels, pennies, other dollars, and so on.

The public accepts paper money as a means of payment and a store of value because the government has taken steps to ensure that its money is accepted. The government declares its paper money to be **legal tender**. That is, the government declares that its money must be accepted in settlement of debts. It does this by fiat (hence *fiat money*). It passes laws defining certain pieces of paper printed in certain inks on certain plates to be legal tender, and that is that. Printed on every Federal Reserve note in the United States is "This note is legal tender for all debts, public and private." Often, the government can get a start on gaining acceptance for its paper money by requiring that it be used to pay taxes. (Note that you cannot use chickens, baseball cards, or Renoir paintings to pay your taxes.)

Aside from declaring its currency legal tender, the government usually does one other thing to ensure that paper money will be accepted: It promises the public that it will not print paper money so fast that it loses its value. Expanding the supply of currency so rapidly that it loses much of its value has been a problem throughout history and is known as **currency debasement**. Debasement of the currency has been a special problem of governments that lack the strength to take the politically unpopular step of raising taxes. Printing money to be used on government expenditures of goods and services can serve as a substitute for tax increases, and weak governments have often relied on the printing press to finance their expenditures. A recent example is Zimbabwe (see box on p. 503) in 2005. We will discuss money and inflation at great length in later chapters.

MEASURING THE SUPPLY OF MONEY IN THE UNITED STATES

We now turn to the various kinds of money in the United States. Recall that money is used to buy things (a means of payment); to hold wealth (a store of value); and to quote prices (a unit of account). Unfortunately, these characteristics apply to a broad range of assets in the U.S. economy. As we will see, it is not at all clear where we should draw the line and say, "Up to this is money, beyond this is something else."

To solve the problem of multiple monies, economists have given different names to different measures of money. The two most common measures of money are transactions money, also called M1, and broad money, also called M2.

M1: Transactions Money

What should be counted as money? Coins and dollar bills, as well as higher denominations of currency, must be counted as money—they fit all the requirements. What about checking accounts? Checks, too, can be used to buy things and can serve as a store of value. In fact, bankers call checking accounts *demand deposits*, because depositors have the right to go to the bank and cash in (demand) their entire checking account balances at any time. That makes your checking account balance virtually equivalent to bills in your wallet, and it should be included as part of the amount of money you hold.

If we take the value of all currency (including coins) held outside of bank vaults and add to it the value of all demand deposits, traveler's checks, and other checkable deposits, we have defined **M1**, or **transactions money**. As its name suggests, this is the money that can be directly used for transactions—to buy things.

M1, or transactions money Money that can be directly used for transactions.

> M1 ≡ currency held outside banks + demand deposits + traveler's checks + other checkable deposits

A *checkable deposit* is any deposit account with a bank or other financial institution on which a check can be written. Checkable deposits include demand deposits; *negotiable order of withdrawal (NOW) accounts*, which are like checking accounts that pay interest; and *automatic-transfer savings (ATS) accounts*, which automatically transfer funds from savings to checking (or vice versa) when the balance on one of those accounts reaches a predetermined level.

M1 on July 18, 2005, was $1,327.3 billion. M1 is a stock measure—it is measured at a point in time. It is the total amount of coins and currency outside of banks and the total dollar amount in checking accounts *on a specific day*. Until now, we have considered supply as a flow—a variable with a time dimension: the quantity of wheat supplied *per year*, the quantity of automobiles supplied to the market *per year*, and so forth. However, M1 is a stock variable.

M2: Broad Money

Although M1 is the most widely used measure of the money supply, there are others. Should savings accounts be considered money? Many of these accounts cannot be used for transactions directly, but it is easy to convert them into cash or to transfer funds from a savings account into a checking account. What about money market accounts (which allow only a few checks per month but pay market-determined interest rates) and money market mutual funds (which sell shares and use the proceeds to purchase short-term securities)? These can be used to write checks and make purchases, although only over a certain amount.

If we add **near monies**, close substitutes for transactions money, to M1, we get **M2**, called **broad money** because it includes not-quite-money monies such as savings accounts, money market accounts, and other near monies.

near monies Close substitutes for transactions money, such as savings accounts and money market accounts.

M2, or broad money M1 plus savings accounts, money market accounts, and other near monies.

> M2 ≡ M1 + savings accounts + money market accounts + other near monies

On July 18, 2005, M2 was $6,532.2 billion, considerably larger than the total M1 of $1,327.3 billion. The main advantage of looking at M2 instead of M1 is that M2 is sometimes more stable. For instance, when banks introduced new forms of interest-bearing checking accounts in the early 1980s, M1 shot up as people switched their funds from savings accounts to checking accounts. However, M2 remained fairly constant because the fall in savings account deposits and the rise in checking account balances were both part of M2, canceling each other out.

Beyond M2

Because a wide variety of financial instruments bear some resemblance to money, some economists have advocated including almost all of them as part of the money supply. In recent years, for example, credit cards have come to be used extensively in exchange. Everyone who has a credit card has a credit limit—you can charge only a certain amount on your card before you have to pay it off. Usually we pay our credit card bills with a check. One of the very broad definitions of money includes the amount of available credit on credit cards (your charge limit minus what you have charged but not paid) as part of the money supply.

There are no rules for deciding what is money and what is not. This poses problems for economists and those in charge of economic policy. However, *for our purposes here, "money" will always refer to transactions money, or M1*. For simplicity, we will say that M1 is the sum of two *general* categories: currency in circulation and deposits. Keep in mind, however, that M1 has *four* specific components: currency held outside banks, demand deposits, traveler's checks, and other checkable deposits.

THE PRIVATE BANKING SYSTEM

Most of the money in the United States today is "bank money" of one sort or another. M1 is made up largely of checking account balances instead of currency, and currency makes up an even smaller part of M2 and other broader definitions of money. Any understanding of money requires some knowledge of the structure of the private banking system.

Banks and banklike institutions borrow from individuals or firms with excess funds and lend to those who need funds. For example, commercial banks receive funds in various forms, including deposits in checking and savings accounts. They take these funds and loan them out in the form of car loans, mortgages, commercial loans, and so forth. Banks and banklike institutions are called **financial intermediaries** because they "mediate," or act as a link between people who have funds to lend and those who need to borrow.

financial intermediaries
Banks and other institutions that act as a link between those who have money to lend and those who want to borrow money.

The main types of financial intermediaries are commercial banks, followed by savings and loan associations, life insurance companies, and pension funds. Since about 1970, the legal distinctions among the different types of financial intermediaries have narrowed considerably. It used to be, for example, that checking accounts could be held only in commercial banks and that commercial banks could not pay interest on checking accounts. Savings and loan associations were prohibited from offering certain kinds of deposits and were restricted primarily to making loans for mortgages.

The Depository Institutions Deregulation and Monetary Control Act, enacted by Congress in 1980, eliminated many of the previous restrictions on the behavior of financial institutions. Many types of institutions now offer checking accounts, and interest is paid on many types of checking accounts. Savings and loan associations now make loans for many things besides home mortgages.

HOW BANKS CREATE MONEY

So far we have described the general way that money works and the way the supply of money is measured in the United States, but how much money is available at a given time? Who supplies it, and how does it get supplied? We are now ready to analyze these questions in detail. In particular, we want to explore a process that many find mysterious: the way banks *create money*.

A HISTORICAL PERSPECTIVE: GOLDSMITHS

To begin to see how banks create money, consider the origins of the modern banking system. In the fifteenth and sixteenth centuries, citizens of many lands used gold as money, particularly for large transactions. Because gold is both inconvenient to carry around and susceptible to theft, people began to place their gold with goldsmiths for safekeeping. On receiving the gold, a goldsmith would issue a receipt to the depositor, charging him a small fee for looking after his gold. After a time, these receipts themselves, rather than the gold that they represented, began to be traded for goods. The receipts became a form of paper money, making it unnecessary to go to the goldsmith to withdraw gold for a transaction.

At this point, all the receipts issued by goldsmiths were backed 100 percent by gold. If a goldsmith had 100 ounces of gold in his safe, he would issue receipts for 100 ounces of gold, and no more. Goldsmiths functioned as warehouses where people stored gold for safekeeping. The goldsmiths found, however, that people did not come often to withdraw gold. Why should they, when paper receipts that could easily be converted to gold were "as good as gold"? (In fact, receipts were better than gold—more portable, safer from theft, and so on.) As a result, goldsmiths had a large stock of gold continuously on hand.

Because they had what amounted to "extra" gold sitting around, goldsmiths gradually realized that they could lend out some of this gold without any fear of running out of gold. Why would they do this? Because instead of just keeping their gold idly in their vaults, they earned interest on loans. Something subtle, but dramatic, happened at this point. The goldsmiths changed from mere depositories for gold into banklike institutions that had the power to create money. This transformation occurred as soon as goldsmiths began making loans. Without adding any more real gold to the system, the goldsmiths increased the amount of money in circulation by creating additional claims to gold—that is, receipts that entitled the bearer to receive a certain number of ounces of gold on demand.[1] Thus there were more claims than there were ounces of gold.

A detailed example may help to clarify this. Suppose you go to a goldsmith who is functioning only as a depository, or warehouse, and ask for a loan to buy a plot of land that costs 20 ounces of gold. Also suppose that the goldsmith has 100 ounces of gold on deposit in his safe and receipts for exactly 100 ounces of gold out to the various people who deposited the gold. If the goldsmith decides he is tired of being a mere goldsmith and wants to become a real bank, he will loan you some gold. You don't want the gold itself, of course; rather, you want a slip of paper that represents 20 ounces of gold. The goldsmith in essence "creates" money for you by giving you a receipt for 20 ounces of gold (even though his entire supply of gold already belongs to various other people).[2] When he does, there will be receipts for 120 ounces of gold in circulation instead of the 100 ounces worth of receipts before your loan, and the supply of money will have increased.

People think the creation of money is mysterious. Far from it! The creation of money is simply an accounting procedure, among the most mundane of human endeavors. You may suspect the whole process is fundamentally unsound, or somehow dubious. After all, the banking system began when someone issued claims for gold that already belonged to someone else. Here you may be on slightly firmer ground.

Goldsmiths-turned-bankers did face certain problems. Once they started making loans, their receipts outstanding (claims on gold) were greater than the amount of gold they had in their vaults at any given moment. If the owners of the 120 ounces worth of gold receipts all presented their receipts and demanded their gold at the same time, the goldsmith would be in trouble. With only 100 ounces of gold on hand, people could not get their gold at once.

In normal times, people would be happy to hold receipts instead of real gold, and this problem would never arise. If, however, people began to worry about the goldsmith's financial safety, they might begin to have doubts about whether their receipts really were as good as gold. Knowing there were more receipts outstanding than there were ounces of gold in the goldsmith's vault, they might start to demand gold for receipts.

This situation leads to a paradox. It makes perfect sense for people to hold paper receipts (instead of gold) if they know they can always get gold for their paper. In normal times, goldsmiths could feel perfectly safe in loaning out more gold than they actually had in their possession. But once people start to doubt the safety of the goldsmith, then they are foolish not to demand their gold back from the vault.

A **run** on a goldsmith (or in our day, a **run on a bank**) occurs when many people present their claims at the same time. These runs tend to feed on themselves. If I see you going to the goldsmith to withdraw your gold, I may become nervous and decide to withdraw my gold as well. It is the *fear* of a run that usually causes the run. Runs on a bank can be triggered by a variety of causes: rumors that an institution may have made loans to borrowers who cannot repay, wars, failures of other institutions that have borrowed money from the bank, and so on. As you will see later in this chapter, today's bankers differ from goldsmiths—today's banks are subject to a "required reserve ratio." Goldsmiths had no legal reserve requirements, although the amount that they loaned out was subject to the restriction imposed on them by their fear of running out of gold.

run on a bank Occurs when many of those who have claims on a bank (deposits) present them at the same time.

THE MODERN BANKING SYSTEM

To understand how the modern banking system works, you need to be familiar with some basic principles of accounting. Once you are comfortable with the way banks keep their books, the whole process of money creation will seem logical.

---

[1]Remember, these receipts circulated as money, and people used them to make transactions without feeling the need to cash them in—that is, to exchange them for gold itself.

[2]In return for lending you the receipt for 20 ounces of gold, the goldsmith expects to get an IOU promising to repay the amount (in gold itself or with a receipt from another goldsmith) with interest after a certain period of time.

A Brief Review of Accounting   Central to accounting practices is the statement that "the books always balance." In practice, this means that if we take a snapshot of a firm—any firm, including a bank—at a particular moment in time, then by definition:

$$\text{Assets} - \text{Liabilities} \equiv \text{Net Worth,}$$
$$\text{or}$$
$$\text{Assets} \equiv \text{Liabilities} + \text{Net Worth}$$

Assets are things a firm owns that are worth something. For a bank, these assets include the bank building, its furniture, its holdings of government securities, cash in its vaults, bonds, stocks, and so forth. Most important among a bank's assets, for our purposes at least, are its *loans*. A borrower gives the bank an *IOU*, a promise to repay a certain sum of money on or by a certain date. This promise is an asset of the bank because it is worth something. The bank could (and sometimes does) sell the IOU to another bank for cash.

Other bank assets include cash on hand (sometimes called *vault cash*) and deposits with the United States' central bank—the **Federal Reserve Bank (the Fed)**. As we will see later in this chapter, federal banking regulations require that banks keep a certain portion of their deposits on hand as vault cash or on deposit with the Fed.

A firm's *liabilities* are its debts—what it owes. A bank's liabilities are the promises to pay, or IOUs, that it has issued. A bank's most important liabilities are its deposits. *Deposits* are debts owed to the depositors, because when you deposit money in your account, you are in essence making a loan to the bank.

The basic rule of accounting says that if we add up a firm's assets and then subtract the total amount it owes to all those who have lent it funds, the difference is the firm's net worth. *Net worth* represents the value of the firm to its stockholders or owners. How much would you pay for a firm that owns $200,000 worth of diamonds and had borrowed $150,000 from a bank to pay for them? The firm is worth $50,000—the difference between what it owns and what it owes. If the price of diamonds were to fall, bringing their value down to only $150,000, the firm would be worth nothing.

We can keep track of a bank's financial position using a simplified balance sheet called a T-account. By convention, the bank's assets are listed on the left side of the T-account, and its liabilities and net worth are on the right side. By definition, the balance sheet always balances, so that the sum of the items on the left side of the T-account is exactly equal to the sum of the items on the right side.

The T-account in Figure 23.1 shows a bank having $110 million in *assets*, of which $20 million are **reserves**, the deposits that the bank has made at the Fed, and its cash on hand (coins and currency). Reserves are an asset to the bank because it can go to the Fed and get cash for them, just the way you can go to the bank and get cash for the amount in your savings account. Our bank's other asset is its loans, worth $90 million.

Why do banks hold reserves/deposits at the Fed? There are many reasons, but perhaps the most important is the legal requirement that they hold a certain percentage of their deposit liabilities as reserves. The percentage of its deposits that a bank must keep as reserves is known as the **required reserve ratio**. If the reserve ratio is 20 percent, then a bank with

Federal Reserve Bank (the Fed) The central bank of the United States.

reserves The deposits that a bank has at the Federal Reserve bank plus its cash on hand.

required reserve ratio The percentage of its total deposits that a bank must keep as reserves at the Federal Reserve.

	Assets		Liabilities	
Reserves	20		100	Deposits
Loans	90		10	Net worth
Total	110		110	Total

FIGURE 23.1 T-Account for a Typical Bank (millions of dollars)

The balance sheet of a bank must always balance, so that the sum of assets (reserves and loans) equals the sum of liabilities (deposits and net worth).

deposits of $100 million must hold $20 million as reserves, either as cash or as deposits at the Fed. To simplify, we will assume that banks hold all of their reserves in the form of deposits at the Fed.

On the liabilities side of the T-account, the bank has taken deposits of $100 million, so it owes this amount to its depositors. This means that the bank has a net worth of $10 million to its owners ($110 million in assets − $100 million in liabilities = $10 million net worth). The net worth of the bank is what "balances" the balance sheet. Remember:

> When some item on a bank's balance sheet changes, there must be at least one other change somewhere else to maintain balance.

If a bank's reserves increase by $1, then one of the following must also be true: (1) Its other assets (for example, loans) decrease by $1; (2) its liabilities (deposits) increase by $1; or (3) its net worth increases by $1. Various fractional combinations of these are also possible.

THE CREATION OF MONEY

Like the goldsmiths, today's bankers seek to earn income by lending money out at a higher interest rate than they pay depositors for use of their money.

In modern times, the chances of a run on a bank are fairly small; and, even if there is a run, the central bank protects the private banks in various ways. Therefore,

> Banks usually make loans up to the point where they can no longer do so because of the reserve requirement restriction.

A bank's required amount of reserves is equal to the required reserve ratio times the total deposits in the bank. If a bank has deposits of $100 and the required ratio is 20 percent, the required amount of reserves is $20. The difference between a bank's actual reserves and its required reserves is its **excess reserves**:

excess reserves The difference between a bank's actual reserves and its required reserves.

$$\text{excess reserves} \equiv \text{actual reserves} - \text{required reserves}$$

If banks make loans up to the point where they can no longer do so because of the reserve requirement restriction, this means that banks make loans up to the point where their excess reserves are zero.

To see why, note that when a bank has excess reserves, it has credit available, and it can make loans. Actually, a bank can make loans *only* if it has excess reserves. When a bank makes a loan, it creates a demand deposit for the borrower. This creation of a demand deposit causes the bank's excess reserves to fall because the extra deposits created by the loan use up some of the excess reserves the bank has on hand. An example will help demonstrate this.

Assume there is only one private bank in the country, the required reserve ratio is 20 percent, and the bank starts off with nothing, as shown in panel 1 of Figure 23.2. Now suppose dollar bills are in circulation and someone deposits 100 of them in the bank. The bank deposits the $100 with the central bank, so it now has $100 in reserves, as shown in panel 2.

Panel 1		Panel 2		Panel 3	
Assets	Liabilities	Assets	Liabilities	Assets	Liabilities
Reserves 0	0 Deposits	Reserves 100	100 Deposits	Reserves 100 Loans 400	500 Deposits

FIGURE 23.2 Balance Sheets of a Bank in a Single-Bank Economy

In panel 2, there is an initial deposit of $100. In panel 3, the bank has made loans of $400.

The bank now has assets (reserves) of $100 and liabilities (deposits) of $100. If the required reserve ratio is 20 percent, the bank has excess reserves of $80.

How much can the bank lend and still meet the reserve requirement? For the moment, let us suppose anyone who gets a loan keeps the entire proceeds in the bank or pays them to someone else who does. Nothing is withdrawn as cash. In this case, the bank can lend $400 and still meet the reserve requirement. Panel 3 shows the balance sheet of the bank after completing the maximum amount of loans it is allowed with a 20 percent reserve ratio. With $80 of excess reserves, the bank can have up to $400 of additional deposits. The $100 in reserves plus $400 in loans (which are made as deposits) equal $500 in deposits. With $500 in deposits and a required reserve ratio of 20 percent, the bank must have reserves of $100 (20 percent of $500)—and it does. The bank can lend no more than $400 because its reserve requirement must not exceed $100. When a bank has no excess reserves and thus can make no more loans, it is said to be *loaned up*.

Remember, the money supply (M1) equals cash in circulation plus deposits. Before the initial deposit, the money supply was $100 ($100 cash and no deposits). After the deposit and the loans, the money supply is $500 (no cash outside of bank vaults and $500 in deposits). It is clear, then, that when loans are converted into deposits, the supply of money can change.

The bank whose T-accounts are presented in Figure 23.2 is allowed to make loans of $400 based on the assumption that loans that are made *stay in the bank* in the form of deposits. Now suppose I borrow from the bank to buy a personal computer, and I write a check to the computer store. If the store also deposits its money in the bank, my check merely results in a reduction in my account balance and an increase to the store's account balance within the bank. No cash has left the bank. As long as the system is closed in this way—remember that we have so far assumed that there is only one bank—the bank knows that it will never be called on to release any of its $100 in reserves. It can expand its loans up to the point where its total deposits are $500.

Of course, there are many banks in the country, a situation that is depicted in Figure 23.3. As long as the banking system as a whole is closed, it is still possible for an initial deposit of $100 to result in an expansion of the money supply to $500, but more steps are involved when there is more than one bank.

To see why, assume Mary makes an initial deposit of $100 in bank 1, and the bank deposits the entire $100 with the Fed (panel 1 of Figure 23.3). All loans that a bank makes are

FIGURE 23.3 The Creation of Money When There Are Many Banks

In panel 1, there is an initial deposit of $100 in bank 1. In panel 2, bank 1 makes a loan of $80 by creating a deposit of $80. A check for $80 by the borrower is then written on bank 1 (panel 3) and deposited in bank 2 (panel 1). The process continues with bank 2 making loans, and so on. In the end, loans of $400 have been made, and the total level of deposits is $500.

withdrawn from the bank as the individual borrowers write checks to pay for merchandise. After Mary's deposit, bank 1 can make a loan of up to $80 to Bill, because it needs to keep only $20 of its $100 deposit as reserves. (We are assuming a 20 percent required reserve ratio.) In other words, bank 1 has $80 in excess reserves.

Bank 1's balance sheet at the moment of the loan to Bill appears in panel 2 of Figure 23.3. Bank 1 now has loans of $80. It has credited Bill's account with the $80, so its total deposits are $180 ($80 in loans plus $100 in reserves). Bill then writes a check for $80 for a set of shock absorbers for his car. Bill wrote his check to Sam's Car Shop, and Sam deposits Bill's check in bank 2. When the check clears, bank 1 transfers $80 in reserves to bank 2. Bank 1's balance sheet now looks like the top of panel 3. Its assets include reserves of $20 and loans of $80; its liabilities are $100 in deposits. Both sides of the T-account balance: The bank's reserves are 20 percent of its deposits, as required by law, and it is fully loaned up.

Now look at bank 2. Because bank 1 has transferred $80 in reserves to bank 2, it now has $80 in deposits and $80 in reserves (panel 1, bank 2). Its reserve requirement is also 20 percent, so it has excess reserves of $64 on which it can make loans.

Now assume bank 2 loans the $64 to Kate to pay for a textbook and Kate writes a check for $64 payable to the Manhattan College Bookstore. The final position of bank 2, after it honors Kate's $64 check by transferring $64 in reserves to the bookstore's bank, is reserves of $16, loans of $64, and deposits of $80 (panel 3, bank 2).

The Manhattan College Bookstore deposits Kate's check in its account with bank 3. Bank 3 now has excess reserves, because it has added $64 to its reserves. With a reserve ratio of 20 percent, bank 3 can loan out $51.20 (80 percent of $64, leaving 20 percent in required reserves to back the $64 deposit).

As the process is repeated over and over, the total amount of deposits created is $500, the sum of the deposits in each of the banks. Because the banking system can be looked on as one big bank, the outcome here for many banks is the same as the outcome in Figure 23.2 for one bank.[3]

THE MONEY MULTIPLIER

In practice, the banking system is not completely closed—there is some leakage out of the system. Still, the point here is

An increase in bank reserves leads to a greater than one-for-one increase in the money supply. Economists call the relationship between the final change in deposits and the change in reserves that caused this change the **money multiplier**. Stated somewhat differently, the money multiplier is the multiple by which deposits can increase for every dollar increase in reserves.

money multiplier The multiple by which deposits can increase for every dollar increase in reserves; equal to 1 divided by the required reserve ratio.

Do not confuse the money multiplier with the spending multipliers we discussed in the last two chapters. They are not the same thing.

In the example we just examined, reserves increased by $100 when the $100 in cash was deposited in a bank, and the amount of deposits increased by $500 ($100 from the initial deposit, $400 from the loans made by the various banks from their excess reserves). The money multiplier in this case is $500/$100 = 5. Mathematically, the money multiplier can be defined as:

$$\text{money multiplier} \equiv \frac{1}{\text{required reserve ratio}}$$

In the United States, the required reserve ratio varies, depending on the size of the bank and the type of deposit. For large banks and for checking deposits, the ratio is currently 10 percent, which makes the potential money multiplier $1/.10 = 10.0$. This means that an increase in reserves of $1 could cause an increase in deposits of $10 if there were no leakage out of the system.

[3]If banks create money when they make loans, does repaying a loan "destroy" money? The answer is yes.

THE FEDERAL RESERVE SYSTEM

We have seen how the private banking system creates money by making loans. However, private banks are not free to create money at will. Their ability to create money is controlled by the volume of reserves in the system, which is controlled by the Fed. The Fed therefore has the ultimate control over the money supply. We will now examine the structure and function of the Fed.

Founded in 1913 by an act of Congress (to which major reforms were added in the 1930s), the Fed is the central bank of the United States. The Fed is a complicated institution with many responsibilities, including the regulation and supervision of over 8,000 commercial banks. The organization of the Federal Reserve System is presented in Figure 23.4.

The *Board of Governors* is the most important group within the Federal Reserve System. The board consists of seven members, each appointed for 14 years by the president of the United States. The *chair* of the Fed, who is appointed by the president and whose term runs for 4 years, usually dominates the entire Federal Reserve System and is sometimes said to be the second most powerful person in the United States. The Fed is an independent agency in that it does not take orders from the president or from Congress.

Federal Open Market Committee (FOMC) A group composed of the seven members of the Fed's Board of Governors, the president of the New York Federal Reserve Bank, and 4 of the other 11 district bank presidents on a rotating basis; it sets goals concerning the money supply and interest rates and directs the operation of the Open Market Desk in New York.

The United States is divided into 12 Federal Reserve districts, each with its own Federal Reserve bank. These districts are indicated on the map in Figure 23.4. The district banks are like branch offices of the Fed in that they carry out the rules, regulations, and functions of the central system in their districts and report to the Board of Governors on local economic conditions.

U.S. monetary policy—the behavior of the Fed concerning the money supply—is formally set by the **Federal Open Market Committee (FOMC)**. The FOMC consists of the seven members of the Fed's Board of Governors, the president of the New York Federal Reserve

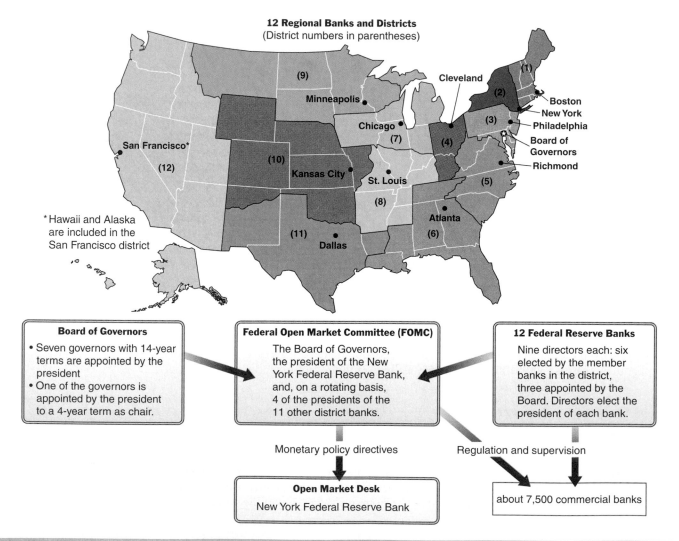

FIGURE 23.4 The Structure of the Federal Reserve System

Bank, and, on a rotating basis, 4 of the presidents of the 11 other district banks. The FOMC sets goals concerning the money supply and interest rates, and it directs the **Open Market Desk** in the New York Federal Reserve Bank to buy and/or sell government securities. (We discuss the specifics of open market operations later in this chapter.)

FUNCTIONS OF THE FEDERAL RESERVE

The Fed is the central bank of the United States. Central banks are sometimes known as "bankers' banks" because only banks (and occasionally foreign governments) can have accounts in them. As a private citizen, you cannot go to the nearest branch of the Fed and open a checking account or apply to borrow money.

Although from a macroeconomic point of view the Fed's crucial role is to control the money supply, the Fed also performs several important functions for banks. These functions include clearing interbank payments, regulating the banking system, and assisting banks in a difficult financial position. The Fed is also responsible for managing exchange rates and the nation's foreign exchange reserves.[4] In addition, it is often involved in intercountry negotiations on international economic issues.

Clearing Interbank Payments   Suppose you write a $100 check, drawn on your bank, the First Bank of Fresno (FBF), to pay for tulip bulbs from Crockett Importers of Miami, Florida. Because Crockett Importers does not bank at FBF, but at Banco de Miami, how does your money get from your bank to the bank in Florida?

The answer: The Fed does it. Both FBF and Banco de Miami have accounts at the Fed. When Crockett Importers receives your check and deposits it at the Banco de Miami, the bank submits the check to the Fed, asking it to collect the funds from FBF. The Fed presents the check to FBF and is instructed to debit FBF's account for the $100 and to credit the account of Banco de Miami. Accounts at the Fed count as reserves, so FBF loses $100 in reserves and Banco de Miami gains $100 in reserves. The two banks effectively have traded ownerships of their deposits at the Fed. The *total* volume of reserves has not changed, nor has the money supply.

This function of clearing interbank payments allows banks to shift money around virtually instantaneously. All they need to do is wire the Fed and request a transfer, and the funds move at the speed of electricity from one computer account to another.

Other Duties of the Fed   Besides facilitating the transfer of funds between banks, the Fed performs several other important duties. It is responsible for many of the regulations governing banking practices and standards. For example, the Fed has the authority to control mergers between banks, and it is responsible for examining banks to ensure they are financially sound and they conform to a host of government accounting regulations. As we saw earlier, the Fed also sets reserve requirements for all financial institutions.

One of the most important responsibilities of the Fed is to act as the **lender of last resort** for the banking system. As our discussion of goldsmiths suggested, banks are subject to the possibility of runs on their deposits. In the United States, most deposits of less than $100,000 are insured by the Federal Deposit Insurance Corporation (FDIC), a U.S. government agency that was established in 1933 during the Great Depression. Deposit insurance makes panics less likely. Because depositors know they can always get their money, even if the bank fails, they are less likely to withdraw their deposits. Not all deposits are insured, so the possibility of bank panics remains. However, the Fed stands ready to provide funds to a troubled bank that cannot find any other sources of funds.

The Fed is the ideal lender of last resort for two reasons. First, providing funds to a bank that is in dire straits is risky and not likely to be very profitable, and it is hard to find private banks or other private institutions willing to do this. The Fed is a nonprofit institution whose function is to serve the overall welfare of the public. Thus, the Fed would certainly be interested in preventing catastrophic banking panics such as those that occurred in the late 1920s and the 1930s.

---

[4]*Foreign exchange reserves* are holdings of the currencies of other countries—for example, Japanese yen—by the U.S. government. We discuss exchange rates and foreign exchange markets at length in Chapter 34.

deflation, Japanese economy, declining prices   search

○ Further Exploration   ◉ News Analysis

Japan's Battle with Deflation

DEFLATION, A DECREASE IN PRICE level, while rare in recent economic history, does occasionally occur, bringing with it a unique set of problems. Some of them are described in the following article from the *New York Times*.

INTERNATIONAL BUSINESS; Japan Consumer Price Drop Is Steepest Since '03
By TODD ZAUN
New York Times
March 26, 2005

Consumer prices in Japan fell 0.4 percent in February from a year earlier, their steepest drop since June 2003 and the latest sign that the country remains mired in a nearly seven-year battle with deflation.

Steep declines in telephone rates and a fall in the price of rice drove overall prices lower in February, according to Japan's statistics bureau. Japanese consumer prices have been flat or have fallen every month but one since April 1998, an unprecedented streak that has sapped some of the country's economic strength.

The long decline in prices has hurt the Japanese economy by dragging down corporate revenue, as well as creating a psychological barrier to consumer spending: Shoppers are likely to put off big purchases if they think prices will be lower in the future.

Friday's new drop in prices made it unlikely that the Bank of Japan would abandon its ultra-easy monetary policy. For nearly four years, the central bank has been trying to kindle growth and a bit of inflation by keeping short-term interest rates near zero and pumping cash into the money markets. The central bank has pledged to maintain this policy until there are convincing signs that prices are headed higher.

The falling prices are a symptom of Japan's larger economic troubles. Japan sank into a mild recession last year amid weak consumer spending and slowing export growth. The economy picked up slightly in the fourth quarter, to an annual pace of 0.5 percent, though the strong export growth that fueled a previous recovery has not returned.

Second, the Fed has an essentially unlimited supply of funds with which to bail out banks facing the possibility of runs. The reason, as we shall see, is that the Fed can create reserves at will. A promise by the Fed that it will support a bank is very convincing. Unlike any other lender, the Fed can never run out of money. Therefore, the explicit or implicit support of the Fed should be enough to assure depositors they are in no danger of losing their funds.

THE FEDERAL RESERVE BALANCE SHEET

Although it is a special bank, the Fed is in some ways similar to an ordinary commercial bank. Like an ordinary bank, the Fed has a balance sheet that records its asset and liability position at any moment in time. The balance sheet for the Fed is presented in Table 23.1.

TABLE 23.1 Assets and Liabilities of the Federal Reserve System, August 3, 2005 (Millions of Dollars)			
ASSETS			**LIABILITIES**
Gold	$ 11,037	$729,601	Federal Reserve notes (outstanding)
Loans to banks	3,330		Deposits:
U.S. Treasury securities	724,700	26,130	Bank Reserves (from depository institutions)
All other assets	81,843	4,813	U.S. Treasury
Total	$820,910	60,366	All other liabilities and net worth
		$820,910	Total

Source: Board of Governors of the Federal Reserve System.

As the asset side of the balance sheet shows, the Fed owns about $11 billion of gold. *Do not think that this gold has anything to do with the supply of money.* Most of the gold was acquired during the 1930s, when it was purchased from the U.S. Treasury Department. Since 1934, the dollar has not been backed by (is not convertible into) gold. You cannot take a dollar bill to the Fed to receive gold for it; all you can get for your old dollar bill is a new dollar bill.[5] Although it is unrelated to the money supply, the Fed's gold counts as an asset on its balance sheet, because it is something of value the Fed owns.

The balance sheet mentions an asset called "loans to banks." These loans are an asset of the Fed in the same way a private commercial bank's loans are among its assets. The Fed sometimes makes loans to commercial banks that are short of reserves.[6] The $3,330 billion in Table 23.1 represents these kinds of loans.

The largest of the Fed's assets by far consists of government (U.S. Treasury) securities: about $724,700 billion worth on August 3, 2005. Government securities are obligations of the federal government, such as Treasury bills and bonds, which the Fed has purchased over the years. The way in which these bonds are acquired has important implications for the Fed's control of the money supply. (We return to this topic after our survey of the Fed's balance sheet.)

The bulk of the Fed's liabilities are Federal Reserve notes. The dollar bill you use to buy a pack of gum is clearly an asset from your point of view—it is something you own that has value. Because every financial asset is by definition a liability of some other agent in the economy, whose liability is that dollar bill? That dollar bill, and bills of all other denominations in the economy, are a liability—an IOU—of the Fed. They are rather strange IOUs, because all they can be redeemed for are other IOUs of exactly the same type. They are, nonetheless, classified as liabilities of the Fed.

The balance sheet shows that, like an ordinary commercial bank, the Fed has accepted deposits. These deposits are liabilities. The bulk of the Fed's deposits come from commercial banks. Remember, commercial banks are required to keep a certain share of their own deposits as deposits at the Fed. A bank's deposits at the Fed (its reserves) are an asset from the bank's point of view, and those same reserves must be a liability from the Fed's point of view.

Table 23.1 shows the Fed has accepted a small volume of deposits from the U.S. Treasury. In effect, the Fed acts as the bank for the U.S. government. When the government needs to pay for something such as a new aircraft carrier, it may write out a check to the supplier of the ship drawn on its "checking account" at the Fed. Similarly, when the government receives revenues from tax collections, fines, or sales of government assets, it may deposit these funds in its account at the Fed.

---

[5]The fact that the Fed is not obliged to provide gold for currency means it can never go bankrupt. When the currency was backed by gold, it would have been possible for the Fed to run out of gold if too many of its depositors came to it at the same time and asked to exchange their deposits for gold. If depositors come to the Fed to withdraw their deposits today, all they can get is dollar bills. The dollar was convertible into gold internationally until August 15, 1971.

[6]Recall that commercial banks are required to keep a set percentage of their deposit liabilities on deposit at the Fed. If a bank suddenly finds itself short of reserves, one of its alternatives is to borrow the reserves it needs from the Fed.

HOW THE FEDERAL RESERVE CONTROLS THE MONEY SUPPLY

To see how the Fed controls the supply of money in the U.S. economy, we need to understand the role of reserves. As we have said, the required reserve ratio establishes a link between the reserves of the commercial banks and the deposits (money) that commercial banks are allowed to create. The reserve requirement effectively determines how much a bank has available to lend. If the required reserve ratio is 20 percent, each $1 of reserves can support $5 in deposits. A bank that has reserves of $100,000 cannot have more than $500,000 in deposits. If it did, it would fail to meet the required reserve ratio.

If you recall that the *money supply* is equal to the sum of deposits inside banks and the currency in circulation outside of banks, you can see that reserves provide the leverage that the Fed needs to control the money supply.

> If the Fed wants to increase the supply of money, it creates more reserves, thereby freeing banks to create additional deposits by making more loans. If it wants to decrease the money supply, it reduces reserves.

Three tools are available to the Fed for changing the money supply: (1) changing the required reserve ratio; (2) changing the discount rate; and (3) engaging in open market operations. Although (3) is almost exclusively used to change the money supply, an understanding of how (1) and (2) work is useful in understanding how (3) works. We thus begin our discussion with the first two tools.

THE REQUIRED RESERVE RATIO

One way for the Fed to alter the supply of money is to change the required reserve ratio. This process is shown in Table 23.2. Let us assume the initial required reserve ratio is 20 percent.

In panel 1, a simplified version of the Fed's balance sheet (in billions of dollars) shows that reserves are $100 billion and currency outstanding is $100 billion. The total value of the Fed's assets is $200 billion, which we assume to be all in government securities. Assuming there are no excess reserves—banks stay fully loaned up—the $100 billion in reserves supports $500 billion in deposits at the commercial banks. [Remember, the money multiplier equals 1/required reserve ratio = $1/.20 = 5$. Thus, $100 billion in reserves can support $500 billion ($100 billion $\times$ 5) in deposits when the required reserve ratio is 20 percent.] The supply of money (M1, or transactions money) is therefore

TABLE 23.2 A Decrease in the Required Reserve Ratio from 20 Percent to 12.5 Percent Increases the Supply of Money (All Figures in Billions of Dollars)

PANEL 1: REQUIRED RESERVE RATIO = 20%

Federal Reserve				Commercial Banks			
Assets		Liabilities		Assets		Liabilities	
Government securities	$200	$100	Reserves	Reserves	$100	$500	Deposits
		$100	Currency	Loans	$400		

Note: Money supply (M1) = currency + deposits = $600.

PANEL 2: REQUIRED RESERVE RATIO = 12.5%

Federal Reserve				Commercial Banks			
Assets		Liabilities		Assets		Liabilities	
Government securities	$200	$100	Reserves	Reserves	$100	$800 (+$300)	Deposits
		$100	Currency	Loans (+$300)	$700		

Note: Money supply (M1) = currency + deposits = $900.

$600 billion: $100 billion in currency and $500 billion in (checking account) deposits at the commercial banks.

Now suppose the Fed wants to increase the supply of money to $900 billion. If it lowers the required reserve ratio from 20 percent to 12.5 percent (as in panel 2 of Table 23.2), then the same $100 billion of reserves could support $800 billion in deposits instead of only $500 billion. In this case, the money multiplier is 1/.125, or 8. At a required reserve ratio of 12.5 percent, $100 billion in reserves can support $800 billion in deposits. The total money supply would be $800 billion in deposits plus the $100 billion in currency, for a total of $900 billion.[7]

Put another way, with the new lower reserve ratio, banks have excess reserves of $37.5 billion. At a required reserve ratio of 20 percent, they needed $100 billion in reserves to back their $500 billion in deposits. At the lower required reserve ratio of 12.5 percent, they need only $62.5 billion of reserves to back their $500 billion of deposits, so the remaining $37.5 billion of the existing $100 billion in reserves is "extra." With that $37.5 billion of excess reserves, banks can lend out more money. If we assume the system loans money and creates deposits to the *maximum* extent possible, the $37.5 billion of reserves will support an additional $300 billion of deposits ($37.5 billion × the money multiplier of 8 = $300 billion). The change in the required reserve ratio has injected an additional $300 billion into the banking system, at which point the banks will be fully loaned up and unable to increase their deposits further.

> Decreases in the required reserve ratio allow banks to have more deposits with the existing volume of reserves. As banks create more deposits by making loans, the supply of money (currency + deposits) increases. The reverse is also true: If the Fed wants to restrict the supply of money, it can raise the required reserve ratio, in which case banks will find that they have insufficient reserves and must therefore reduce their deposits by "calling in" some of their loans.[8] The result is a decrease in the money supply.

For many reasons, the Fed has tended not to use changes in the reserve requirement to control the money supply. In part, this reluctance stems from the era when only some banks were members of the Fed and therefore subject to reserve requirements. The Fed reasoned that if it raised the reserve requirement to contract the money supply, banks might choose to stop being members. (Because reserves pay no interest, the higher the reserve requirement, the more the penalty imposed on those banks holding reserves.) This argument no longer applies. Since the passage of the Depository Institutions Deregulation and Monetary Control Act in 1980, all depository institutions are subject to Fed requirements.

It is also true that changing the reserve requirement ratio is a crude tool. Because of lags in banks' reporting to the Fed on their reserve and deposit positions, a change in the requirement today does not affect banks for about 2 weeks. (However, the fact that changing the reserve requirement expands or reduces credit in every bank in the country makes it a very powerful tool when the Fed does use it.)

THE DISCOUNT RATE

Banks may borrow from the Fed. The interest rate they pay the Fed is the **discount rate**. When banks increase their borrowing, the money supply increases. To see why this is true, assume there is only one bank in the country and the required reserve ratio is 20 percent. The initial position of the bank and the Fed appear in panel 1 of Table 23.3, where the money supply (currency + deposits) is $480. In panel 2, the bank has borrowed $20 from the Fed. By

discount rate Interest rate that banks pay to the Fed to borrow from it.

---

[7]To find the maximum volume of deposits (D) that can be supported by an amount of reserves (R), divide R by the required reserve ratio. If the required reserve ratio is g, because $R = gD$, then $D = R/g$.
[8]Banks never really have to "call in" loans before they are due, to reduce the money supply. First, the Fed is almost always expanding the money supply slowly because the real economy grows steadily and, as we shall see, growth brings with it the need for more circulating money. So when we speak of "contractionary monetary policy," we mean the Fed is slowing down the rate of money growth, not reducing the money supply. Second, even if the Fed were actually to cut reserves (instead of curb their expansion), banks would no doubt be able to comply by reducing the volume of new loans they make while old ones are coming due.

TABLE 23.3 The Effect on the Money Supply of Commercial Bank Borrowing from the Fed (All Figures in Billions of Dollars)

PANEL 1: NO COMMERCIAL BANK BORROWING FROM THE FED

Federal Reserve				Commercial Banks			
Assets		Liabilities		Assets			Liabilities
Securities	$160	$80	Reserves	Reserves	$80	$400	Deposits
		$80	Currency	Loans	$320		

Note: Money supply (M1) = currency + deposits = $480.

PANEL 2: COMMERCIAL BANK BORROWING $20 FROM THE FED

Federal Reserve				Commercial Banks			
Assets		Liabilities		Assets			Liabilities
Securities	$160	$100	Reserves (+$20)	Reserves (+$20)	$100	$500	Deposits (+$300)
Loans	$20	$80	Currency	Loans (+$100)	$420	$20	Amount owed to Fed (+$20)

Note: Money supply (M1) = currency + deposits = $580.

using this $20 as a reserve, the bank can increase its loans by $100, from $320 to $420. (Remember, a required reserve ratio of 20 percent gives a money multiplier of 5; having excess reserves of $20 allows the bank to create an additional $20 × 5, or $100, in deposits.) The money supply has thus increased from $480 to $580. Therefore,

> Bank borrowing from the Fed leads to an increase in the money supply.

The Fed can influence bank borrowing, and thus the money supply, through the discount rate:

> The higher the discount rate, the higher the cost of borrowing, and the less borrowing banks will want to do.

If the Fed wants to curtail the growth of the money supply, for example, it raises the discount rate and discourages banks from borrowing from it, restricting the growth of reserves (and ultimately deposits).

Historically, the Fed has not used the discount rate to control the money supply. Prior to 2003 it usually set the discount rate lower than the rate that banks had to pay to borrow money in the private market. Although this obviously provided an incentive for banks to borrow from the Fed, the Fed discouraged borrowing by putting pressure in various ways on the banks not to borrow. This pressure was sometimes called **moral suasion**. On January 9, 2003, the Fed announced a new procedure. Henceforth the discount rate would be set above the rate that banks pay to borrow money in the private market, and moral suasion would no longer be used. Although banks can now borrow from the Fed if they wish to, they are unlikely to do so except in unusual circumstances because borrowing is cheaper in the private market. It is thus clear that the Fed is not using the discount rate as a tool to try to change the money supply on a regular basis.

moral suasion The pressure that in the past the Fed exerted on member banks to discourage them from borrowing heavily from the Fed.

OPEN MARKET OPERATIONS

open market operations The purchase and sale by the Fed of government securities in the open market; a tool used to expand or contract the amount of reserves in the system and thus the money supply.

By far the most significant of the Fed's tools for controlling the supply of money is **open market operations**. Congress has authorized the Fed to buy and sell U.S. government securities in the open market. When the Fed purchases a security, it pays for it by writing a check that, when cleared, *expands* the quantity of reserves in the system, increasing the money supply. When the Fed sells a bond, private citizens or institutions pay for it with a check that, when cleared, *reduces* the quantity of reserves in the system.

To see how open market transactions and reserve controls work, we need to review several key ideas.

Two Branches of Government Deal in Government Securities The fact that the Fed is able to buy and sell government securities—bills and bonds—may be confusing. In fact, *two* branches of government deal in financial markets for different reasons, and you must keep the two separate in your mind.

First, keep in mind that the Treasury Department is responsible for collecting taxes and paying the federal government's bills. Salary checks paid to government workers, payments to General Dynamics for a new Navy ship, Social Security checks to retirees, and so forth are all written on accounts maintained by the Treasury. Tax receipts collected by the Internal Revenue Service, a Treasury branch, are deposited to these accounts.

If total government spending exceeds tax receipts, the law requires the Treasury to borrow the difference. Recall that the government deficit is $(G - T)$, or government purchases minus net taxes. $(G - T)$ is the amount the Treasury must borrow each year to finance the deficit. This means:

> The Treasury *cannot* print money to finance the deficit.

The Treasury borrows by issuing bills, bonds, and notes that pay interest. These government securities, or IOUs, are sold to individuals and institutions. Often, foreign countries, as well as U.S. citizens, buy them. As discussed in Chapter 22, the total amount of privately held government securities is the *privately held federal debt.*

The Fed is not the Treasury. Instead, it is a quasi-independent agency authorized by Congress to buy and sell *outstanding* (preexisting) U.S. government securities on the open market. The bonds and bills initially sold by the Treasury to finance the deficit are continuously resold and traded among ordinary citizens, firms, banks, pension funds, and so forth. The Fed's participation in that trading affects the quantity of reserves in the system, as we will see.

Because the Fed owns some government securities, some of what the government owes, it owes to itself. Recall that the Federal Reserve System's largest single asset is government securities. These securities are nothing more than bills and bonds initially issued by the Treasury to finance the deficit. They were acquired by the Fed over time through direct open market purchases that the Fed made to expand the money supply as the economy expanded.

The Mechanics of Open Market Operations How do open market operations affect the money supply? Look again at Table 23.1. As you can see, most of the Fed's assets consist of the government securities we have just been talking about.

Suppose the Fed wants to decrease the supply of money. If it can reduce the volume of bank reserves on the liabilities side of its balance sheet, it will force banks in turn to reduce their own deposits (to meet the required reserve ratio). Since these deposits are part of the supply of money, the supply of money will contract.

What will happen if the Fed sells some of its holdings of government securities to the general public? The Fed's holdings of government securities must decrease, because the securities it sold will now be owned by someone else. How do the purchasers of securities pay for what they have bought? By writing checks drawn on their banks and payable to the Fed.

Let us look more carefully at how this works, with the help of Table 23.4. In panel 1, the Fed initially has $100 billion of government securities. Its liabilities consist of $20 billion of deposits (which are the reserves of commercial banks) and $80 billion of currency. With the required reserve ratio at 20 percent, the $20 billion of reserves can support $100 billion of deposits in the commercial banks. The commercial banking system is fully loaned up. Panel 1 also shows the financial position of a private citizen, Jane Q. Public. Jane has assets of $5 billion (a large checking account deposit in the bank) and no debts, so her net worth is $5 billion.

Now imagine that the Fed sells $5 billion in government securities to Jane. Jane pays for the securities by writing a check to the Fed, drawn on her bank. The Fed then reduces the reserve account of her bank by $5 billion. The balance sheets of all the participants after this transaction are shown in panel 2. Note that the supply of money (currency plus deposits) has fallen from $180 billion to $175 billion.

This is not the end of the story. As a result of the Fed's sale of securities, the amount of reserves has fallen from $20 billion to $15 billion, while deposits have fallen from $100 billion to $95 billion. With a required reserve ratio of 20 percent, banks must have .20 × $95 billion, or $19 billion in reserves. Banks are under their required reserve ratio by $4 billion

TABLE 23.4 Open Market Operations (The Numbers in Parentheses in Panels 2 and 3 Show the Differences Between Those Panels and Panel 1. All Figures in Billions of Dollars)

PANEL 1

Federal Reserve				Commercial Banks				Jane Q. Public			
Assets		Liabilities		Assets		Liabilities		Assets		Liabilities	
Securities	$100	$20	Reserves	Reserves	$20	$100	Deposits	Deposits	$5	$0	Debts
		$80	Currency	Loans	$80					$5	Net Worth

Note: Money supply (M1) = currency + deposits = $180.

PANEL 2

Federal Reserve				Commercial Banks				Jane Q. Public			
Assets		Liabilities		Assets		Liabilities		Assets		Liabilities	
Securities (−$5)	$95	$15 (−$5)	Reserves	Reserves (−$5)	$15	$95	Deposits (−$5)	Deposits (−$5)	$0	$0	Debts
		$80	Currency	Loans	$80			Securities (+$5)	$5	$5	Net Worth

Note: Money supply (M1) = currency + deposits = $175.

PANEL 3

Federal Reserve				Commercial Banks				Jane Q. Public			
Assets		Liabilities		Assets		Liabilities		Assets		Liabilities	
Securities (−$5)	$95	$15 (−$5)	Reserves	Reserves (−$5)	$15	$75	Deposits (−$25)	Deposits (−$5)	$0	$0	Debts
		$80	Currency	Loans (−$20)	$60			Securities (+$5)	$5	$5	Net Worth

Note: Money supply (M1) = currency + deposits = $155.

[$19 billion (the amount they should have) minus $15 billion (the amount they do have)]. To comply with the federal regulations, banks must decrease their loans and their deposits.[9]

The final equilibrium position is shown in panel 3, where commercial banks have reduced their loans by $20 billion. Notice that the change in deposits from panel 1 to panel 3 is $25 billion, which is five times the size of the change in reserves that the Fed brought about through its $5 billion open market sale of securities. This corresponds exactly to our earlier analysis of the money multiplier. The change in money (−$25 billion) is equal to the money multiplier (5) times the change in reserves (−$5 billion).

Now consider what happens when the Fed *purchases* a government security. Suppose I hold $100 in Treasury bills, which the Fed buys from me. The Fed writes me a check for $100, and I turn in my Treasury bills. I then take the $100 check and deposit it in my local bank. This increases the reserves of my bank by $100 and begins a new episode in the money expansion story. With a reserve requirement of 20 percent, my bank can now lend out $80. If that $80 is spent and ends up back in a bank, that bank can lend $64, and so forth. (Review Figure 23.3.) The Fed can expand the money supply by buying government securities from people who own them, just the way it reduces the money supply by selling these securities.

Each business day, the Open Market Desk in the New York Federal Reserve Bank buys or sells millions of dollars' worth of securities, usually to large security dealers who act as intermediaries between the Fed and the private markets. We can sum up the effect of these open market operations this way:

- An open market *purchase* of securities by the Fed results in an *increase* in reserves and an *increase* in the supply of money by an amount equal to the money multiplier times the change in reserves.
- An open market *sale* of securities by the Fed results in a *decrease* in reserves and a *decrease* in the supply of money by an amount equal to the money multiplier times the change in reserves.

[9]Once again, banks never really have to call in loans. Loans and deposits would probably be reduced by slowing the rate of new lending as old loans come due and are paid off.

Open market operations are the Fed's preferred means of controlling the money supply for several reasons. First, open market operations can be used with some precision. If the Fed needs to change the money supply by just a small amount, it can buy or sell a small volume of government securities. If it wants a larger change in the money supply, it can buy or sell a larger amount. Second, open market operations are extremely flexible. If the Fed decides to reverse course, it can easily switch from buying securities to selling them. Finally, open market operations have a fairly predictable effect on the supply of money. Because banks are obliged to meet their reserve requirements, an open market sale of $100 in government securities will reduce reserves by $100, which will reduce the supply of money by $100 times the money multiplier.

Where does the Fed get the money to buy government securities when it wants to expand the money supply? The Fed simply creates it! In effect, it tells the bank from which it has bought a $100 security that its reserve account (deposit) at the Fed now contains $100 more than it did previously. This is where the power of the Fed, or any central bank, lies. The Fed has the ability to create money at will. In the United States, the Fed exercises this power when it creates money to buy government securities.

THE SUPPLY CURVE FOR MONEY

Thus far we know how the Fed can control the money supply by controlling the amount of reserves in the economy. If the Fed wants the quantity of money to be $1,350 billion on a given date, it can aim for this target by changing the discount rate, by changing the required reserve ratio, or by engaging in open market operations. (As discussed earlier, the Fed almost always uses open market operations as its tool.) Because the Fed can choose whatever value of the money supply that it wants, it is useful to begin with the case in which the Fed picks a value independent of anything in the economy. In other words, we will assume for now that the Fed's choice of the value of the money supply does not depend on things like the interest rate, inflation, unemployment, and aggregate output. This assumption is relaxed in Chapter 28. We will see in Chapter 28 that in practice the Fed chooses a value of the money supply to hit a particular value of the interest rate, where the Fed's choice for the target interest rate depends on things like inflation and unemployment. But this is jumping ahead of the story.

If the Fed's choice of the value for the money supply does not depend on the interest rate, then in Figure 23.5 we can draw the money supply curve as a vertical line. Therefore, until we get to Chapter 28, we will assume that the money supply curve is vertical.

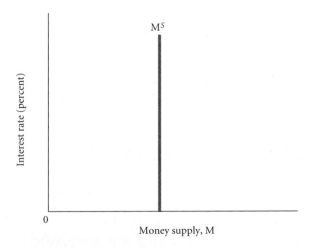

FIGURE 23.5 The Supply of Money

If the Fed's money supply behavior is not influenced by the interest rate, the money supply curve is a vertical line. Through open market operations the Fed can have the money supply be whatever value it wants.

LOOKING AHEAD

This chapter has discussed only the supply side of the money market. We have seen what money is, how banks create money by making loans, and how the Fed controls the money supply. In the next chapter, we turn to the demand side of the money market. We will examine the demand for money and see how the supply of, and demand for, money determine the equilibrium interest rate.

SUMMARY

AN OVERVIEW OF MONEY

1. Money has three distinguishing characteristics: (1) a *means of payment*, or *medium of exchange*; (2) *a store of value*; and (3) *a unit of account*. The alternative to using money is *barter*, in which goods are exchanged directly for other goods. Barter is costly and inefficient in an economy with many different kinds of goods.

2. *Commodity monies* are items that are used as money and also have an intrinsic value in some other use—for example, gold and cigarettes. *Fiat monies* are intrinsically worthless apart from their use as money. To ensure the acceptance of fiat monies, governments use their power to declare money *legal tender* and promise the public they will not debase the currency by expanding its supply rapidly.

3. There are various definitions of money. Currency plus demand deposits plus traveler's checks plus other checkable deposits compose M1, or *transactions money*—money that can be used directly to buy things. The addition of savings accounts and money market accounts (*near monies*) to M1 gives M2, or *broad money*.

HOW BANKS CREATE MONEY

4. The *required reserve ratio* is the percentage of a bank's deposits that must be kept as *reserves* at the nation's central bank, the *Federal Reserve*.

5. Banks create money by making loans. When a bank makes a loan to a customer, it creates a deposit in that customer's account. This deposit becomes part of the money supply. Banks can create money only when they have *excess reserves*—reserves in excess of the amount set by the required reserve ratio.

6. The *money multiplier* is the multiple by which the total supply of money can increase for every dollar increase in reserves. The money multiplier is equal to 1/required reserve ratio.

THE FEDERAL RESERVE SYSTEM

7. The Fed's most important function is controlling the nation's money supply. The Fed also performs several other functions: It clears interbank payments, is responsible for many of the regulations governing banking practices and standards, and acts as a *lender of last resort* for troubled banks that cannot find any other sources of funds. The Fed also acts as the bank for the U.S. government.

HOW THE FEDERAL RESERVE CONTROLS THE MONEY SUPPLY

8. The key to understanding how the Fed controls the money supply is the role of reserves. If the Fed wants to increase the supply of money, it creates more reserves, freeing banks to create additional deposits. If it wants to decrease the money supply, it reduces reserves.

9. The Fed has three tools to control the money supply: (1) changes in the required reserve ratio; (2) changes in the *discount rate* (the interest rate member banks pay when they borrow from the Fed); or (3) engaging in *open market operations* (the buying and selling of already-existing government securities). To increase the money supply, the Fed can create additional reserves by lowering the discount rate or by buying government securities, or the Fed can increase the number of deposits that can be created from a given quantity of reserves by lowering the required reserve ratio. To decrease the money supply, the Fed can reduce reserves by raising the discount rate or by selling government securities, or it can raise the required reserve ratio.

10. If the Fed's money supply behavior is not influenced by the interest rate, the supply curve for money is a vertical line.

REVIEW TERMS AND CONCEPTS

barter, 502

commodity monies, 504

currency debasement, 504

discount rate, 517

excess reserves, 509

Federal Open Market Committee (FOMC), 512

Federal Reserve Bank (the Fed), 508

fiat, or token, money, 504

financial intermediaries, 506

legal tender, 504

lender of last resort, 513

liquidity property of money, 502

M1, or transactions money, 505

M2, or broad money, 505

medium of exchange, or means of payment, 502

money multiplier, 511

moral suasion, 518

near monies, 505

Open Market Desk, 513

open market operations, 518
required reserve ratio, 508
reserves, 508
run on a bank, 507
store of value, 502
unit of account, 503

1. M1 ≡ currency held outside banks + demand deposits + traveler's checks + other checkable deposits
2. M2 ≡ M1 + savings accounts + money market accounts + other near monies
3. Assets ≡ liabilities + net worth
4. Excess reserves ≡ actual reserves − required reserves
5. $\text{Money multiplier} \equiv \dfrac{1}{\text{required reserve ratio}}$

PROBLEM SET

1. In the Republic of Ragu the currency is the rag. During 2004, the Treasury of Ragu sold bonds to finance the Ragu budget deficit. In all, the Treasury sold 50,000 10-year bonds with a face value of 100 rags each. The total deficit was 5 million rags. Further, assume that the Ragu Central Bank reserve requirement was 20 percent, and that in the same year, the bank bought 500,000 rags' worth of outstanding bonds on the open market. Finally, assume that all of the Ragu debt is held by either the private sector (the public) or the central bank.
   a. What is the combined effect of the Treasury sale and the central bank purchase on the total Ragu debt outstanding? On the debt held by the private sector?
   b. What is the effect of the Treasury sale on the money supply in Ragu?
   c. What is the effect of the central bank purchase of bonds on the money supply, assuming no leakage of reserves out of the banking system?

2. In the year 2000, the federal debt was being paid down because the federal budget was in surplus. Recall that surplus means that tax collections (T) exceed government spending (G). The surplus ($T - G$) was used to buy back government bonds from the public, reducing the federal debt. As we discussed in this chapter, the main method by which the Fed increases the money supply is to buy government bonds by using open market operations. What is the impact on the money supply of using the fiscal surplus to buy back bonds? What is the difference between Fed open market purchases of bonds and Treasury purchases of bonds using tax revenues, in terms of their impacts on the money supply?

3. For each of the following, say whether it is an asset or a liability on the accounting books of a bank. Explain why in each case.
   Cash in the vault
   Demand deposits
   Savings deposits
   Reserves
   Loans
   Deposits at the Federal Reserve

4. If the head of the Central Bank of Japan wanted to expand the supply of money in Japan in 2007, which of the following would do it? Explain your answer.
   Increase the required reserve ratio
   Decrease the required reserve ratio
   Increase the discount rate
   Decrease the discount rate
   Buy government securities in the open market
   Sell government securities in the open market

5. Suppose that in the Republic of Madison, the regulation of banking rested with the Madison Congress, including the determination of the reserve ratio. The Central Bank of Madison is charged with regulating the money supply by using open market operations. In April 2006, the money supply was estimated to be 52 million hurls. At the same time, bank reserves were 6.24 million hurls and the reserve requirement was 12 percent. The banking industry, being "loaned up," lobbied the Congress to cut the reserve ratio. The Congress yielded and cut required reserves to 10 percent. What is the potential impact on the money supply? Suppose that the central bank decided that the money supply should not be increased. What countermeasures could it take to prevent the Congress from expanding the money supply?

6. The U.S. money supply (M1) at the beginning of the year 2000 was $1,148 billion, broken down as follows: $523 billion in currency, $8 billion in traveler's checks, and $616 billion in checking deposits. Suppose the Fed decided to reduce the money supply by increasing the reserve requirement from 10 percent to 11 percent. Assuming all banks were initially loaned up (had no excess reserves) and currency held outside of banks did not change, how large a change in the money supply would have resulted from the change in the reserve requirement?

7. As king of Medivalia, you are constantly strapped for funds to pay your army. Your chief economic wizard suggests the following plan: "When you collect your tax payments from your subjects, insist on being paid in gold coins. Take these gold coins, melt them down, and then remint them with an extra 10 percent of brass thrown in. You will then have 10 percent more money than you started with." What do you think of the plan? Will it work?

8. Why is M2 sometimes a more stable measure of money than M1? Explain in your own words, using the definitions of M1 and M2.

9. Do you agree or disagree with each of the following statements? Explain your answers.
   a. When the Treasury of the United States issues bonds and sells them to the public to finance the deficit, the money supply remains unchanged because every dollar of money taken in by the Treasury goes right back into circulation through government spending. This is not true when the Fed sells bonds to the public.
   b. The money multiplier depends on the marginal propensity to save.

*10. When the Fed adds new reserves to the system, some of these new reserves find their way out of the country into foreign banks or foreign investment funds. In addition, some portion of

---

Note: Problems marked with an asterisk are more challenging.

the new reserves ends up in people's pockets and mattresses instead of bank vaults. These "leakages" reduce the money multiplier and sometimes make it very difficult for the Fed to control the money supply precisely. Explain why this is true.

11. You are given this account for a bank:

ASSETS		LIABILITIES	
Reserves	$ 500	$3,500	Deposits
Loans	3,000		

The required reserve ratio is 10 percent.

a. How much is the bank required to hold as reserves, given its deposits of $3,500?

b. How much are its excess reserves?

c. By how much can the bank increase its loans?

d. Suppose a depositor comes to the bank and withdraws $200 in cash. Show the bank's new balance sheet, assuming the bank obtains the cash by drawing down its reserves. Does the bank now hold excess reserves? Is it meeting the required reserve ratio? If not, what can it do?

Money Demand, the Equilibrium Interest Rate, and Monetary Policy

24

Having discussed the supply of money in the last chapter, we now turn to the *demand* for money. One goal of this and the previous chapter is to provide a theory of how the interest rate is determined in the macroeconomy. Once we have seen how the interest rate is determined, we can turn to how the Federal Reserve (Fed) affects the interest rate through **monetary policy**.

It is important that you understand exactly what the interest rate is. **Interest** is the fee borrowers pay to lenders for the use of their funds. Firms and the government borrow funds by issuing bonds, and they pay interest to the firms and households (the lenders) that purchase those bonds. Households and firms that have borrowed from a bank must pay interest on those loans to the bank.

The **interest rate** is the annual interest payment on a loan expressed as a percentage of the loan. A $1,000 bond (representing a $1,000 loan from a household to a firm) that pays $100 in interest per year has an interest rate of 10 percent. The interest rate is expressed as an *annual* rate. It is the amount of interest received *per year* divided by the amount of the loan.

Although there are many different interest rates, we will assume that there is only one. This simplifies our analysis yet provides a valuable tool for us to understand how the parts of the macroeconomy relate to one another. Appendix A to this chapter provides more detail on the various types of interest rates.

THE DEMAND FOR MONEY

What factors and what forces determine the demand for money are central issues in macroeconomics. As we shall see, the interest rate and the level of national income (*Y*) influence how much money households and firms wish to hold.

Before we proceed, we must stress one point that may be troublesome. When we speak of the demand for money, we are not asking these questions: "How much cash do you wish you could have?" "How much income would you like to earn?" "How much wealth would you like?" (The answer to these questions is presumably "as much as possible.") Instead, we are concerned with how much of your financial assets you want to hold *in the form of money*, which does not earn interest, versus how much you want to hold in interest-bearing securities, such as bonds. We take as given the *total* amount of financial assets; our concern here is with how these assets are divided between money and interest-bearing securities.

monetary policy The behavior of the Federal Reserve concerning the money supply.

interest The fee that borrowers pay to lenders for the use of their funds.

interest rate The annual interest payment on a loan expressed as a percentage of the loan. Equal to the amount of interest received per year divided by the amount of the loan.

525

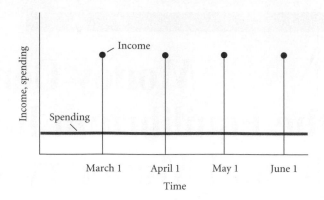

FIGURE 24.1 The Nonsynchronization of Income and Spending
Income arrives only once a month, but spending takes place continuously.

THE TRANSACTION MOTIVE

transaction motive The main reason that people hold money—to buy things.

How much money to hold involves a trade-off between the liquidity of money and the interest income offered by other kinds of assets. The main reason for holding money instead of interest-bearing assets is that money is useful for buying things. Economists call this the **transaction motive**. This rationale for holding money is at the heart of the discussion that follows.[1]

Assumptions To keep our analysis of the demand for money clear, we need a few simplifying assumptions. First, we assume there are only two kinds of assets available to households: bonds and money. By "bonds" we mean interest-bearing securities of all kinds. By "money" we mean currency in circulation and in deposits, neither of which is assumed to pay interest.[2]

Second, we assume that income for the typical household is "bunched up." It arrives once a month, at the beginning of the month. Spending, by contrast, is spread out over time; we assume that spending occurs at a completely uniform rate throughout the month—that is, that the same amount is spent each day (Figure 24.1). The mismatch between the timing of money inflow and the timing of money outflow is sometimes called the **nonsynchronization of income and spending**.

nonsynchronization of income and spending The mismatch between the timing of money inflow to the household and the timing of money outflow for household expenses.

Finally, we assume that spending for the month is exactly equal to income for the month. Because we are focusing on the transactions demand for money and not on its use as a store of value, this assumption is perfectly reasonable.

MONEY MANAGEMENT AND THE OPTIMAL BALANCE

Given these assumptions, how would a rational person (household) decide how much of monthly income to hold as money and how much to hold as interest-bearing bonds? Suppose Jim decides to deposit his entire paycheck in his checking account. Let us say Jim earns $1,200 per month. The pattern of Jim's bank account balance is illustrated in Figure 24.2. At the beginning of the month, Jim's balance is $1,200. As the month rolls by, Jim draws down his balance, writing checks or withdrawing cash to pay for the things he buys. At the end of the month, Jim's bank account balance is down to zero. Just in time, he receives his next month's paycheck, deposits it, and the process begins again.

One useful statistic we will need to calculate is the *average balance* in Jim's account. Jim spends his money at a constant $40 per day ($40 per day times 30 days per month = $1,200).

---

[1]The model that we discuss here is known in the economics profession as the Baumol/Tobin model, after the two economists who independently derived it, William Baumol of Princeton University and the late James Tobin of Yale University.
[2]Remember that the category "deposits" includes checking accounts. Many checking accounts pay interest. This will not matter for the purposes of our discussion, however. Suppose bonds pay 10 percent interest and checking accounts pay 5 percent. (Checking accounts must pay less than bonds. Otherwise, everyone would hold all their wealth in checking accounts and none in bonds, because checking accounts are more convenient.) When it comes to choosing whether to hold bonds or money, the difference in the interest rates on the two matters. People are concerned about how much extra interest they will get from holding bonds instead of money. In the preceding example we could say that bonds pay 5 percent and money pays 0 percent, which makes our discussion simpler.

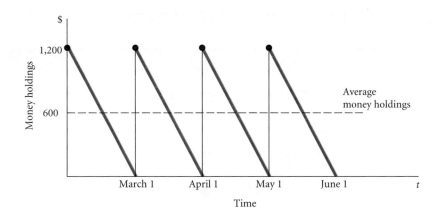

FIGURE 24.2 Jim's Monthly Checking Account Balances: Strategy 1

Jim could decide to deposit his entire paycheck ($1,200) into his checking account at the start of the month and run his balance down to zero by the end of the month. In this case, his average balance would be $600.

His average balance is just his starting balance ($1,200) plus his ending balance (0) divided by 2, or ($1,200 + 0)/2 = $600. For the first half of the month Jim has more than his average of $600 on deposit, and for the second half of the month he has less than his average.

Is anything wrong with Jim's strategy? Yes. If he follows the plan described, Jim is giving up interest on his funds, interest he could be earning if he held some of his funds in interest-bearing bonds instead of in his checking account. How could he manage his funds to give himself more interest?

Instead of depositing his entire paycheck in his checking account at the beginning of the month, Jim could put half his paycheck into his checking account and buy a bond with the other half. By doing this, he would run out of money in his checking account halfway through the month. At a spending rate of $40 per day, his initial deposit of $600 would last only 15 days. Jim would have to sell his bond halfway through the month and deposit the $600 from the sale of the bond in his checking account to pay his bills during the second half of the month.

Jim's money holdings (checking account balances) if he follows this strategy are shown in Figure 24.3. When he follows the buy-a-$600-bond strategy, Jim reduces the average

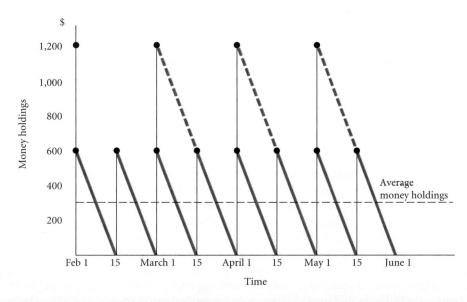

FIGURE 24.3 Jim's Monthly Checking Account Balances: Strategy 2

Jim could also choose to put one-half of his paycheck into his checking account and buy a bond with the other half of his income. At midmonth, Jim would sell the bond and deposit the $600 into his checking account to pay the second half of the month's bills. Following this strategy, Jim's average money holdings would be $300.

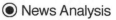

News ANALYSIS

transactions demand for money, wealth holdings   search

○ Further Exploration   ● News Analysis

Money Demand and Interest Rates

THE FOLLOWING TWO SHORT EXCERPTS from the *New York Times* shows just how high and how low interest rates can go. Remember that the *opportunity cost* of holding money (cash and checking accounts) is the interest rate that you can earn by putting your money into bonds or other interest-bearing assets.

1981
Reagan Aide Sees Interest-Rate Drop
AP
New York Times
May 14, 1981

A leading Reagan Administration economist predicted today that surging interest rates would peak within a month or two and then subside significantly in the summer.

"Interest-rate increases are not likely to be durable," said Lawrence Kudlow, an assistant director and chief economist at the Office of Management and Budget. Instead, there should be a "substantial easing of rates in the third quarter" of 1981, which begins in July, Mr. Kudlow said at a news conference.

The prime lending rate that commercial banks charge their best-risk corporate customers is $19\frac{1}{2}$ percent. Other interest rates are at or near record levels. Rates on three-month bills are now 16.4 percent.

2003
Interest Rates Expected to Rise in 2004 and 2005
By JONATHAN FUERBRINGER
New York Times
December 12, 2003

Policy makers [at the Federal Reserve] have pushed their benchmark short-term interest rate to 1 percent, the lowest in 45 years, and have promised to keep it there for "a considerable period." It is that low interest rate that has paved the way for the economic and market recovery.

At its meeting in October, according to minutes released yesterday, policy makers concluded that inflation could remain low until some time in 2005 and that they should wait for concrete signs of inflation before raising interest rates. But with growth picking up, Fed officials at their policy meeting this week gave a first indication that they were laying the groundwork for an eventual increase in interest rates. When rates do rise, the increase could give the stock market a pause.

Here are the results of yesterday's Treasury auction of 10-year notes:

(000 omitted in dollar figures)

Price: 99.076
High Yield: 4.365
Low Yield: 4.260

Sources: Associated Press, "Reagan Aide Sees Interest-Rate Drop," New York Times, May 14, 1981; Jonathan Fuerbringer, "Interest Rates Expected to Rise in 2004 and 2005," New York Times, December 12, 2003. Copyright © 2005 by The New York Times Co. Reprinted with permission.

amount of money in his checking account. Comparing the dashed green lines (old strategy) with the solid green lines (buy-$600-bond strategy), his average bank balance is exactly half of what it was with the first strategy.[3]

The buy-a-$600-bond strategy seems sensible. The object of this strategy was to keep some funds in bonds, where they could earn interest, instead of be "idle" money. Why should he stop there? Another possibility would be for Jim to put only $400 into his checking account on the first of the month and buy two $400 bonds. The $400 in his account will last only 10 days if he spends $40 per day, so after 10 days he must sell one of the bonds and deposit the $400 from the sale in his checking account. This will last through the 20th of the month, at which point he must sell the second bond and deposit the other $400. This strategy lowers Jim's average money holding (checking account balance) even further, reducing his money holdings to an average of only $200 per month, with correspondingly higher average holdings of interest-earning bonds.

You can imagine Jim going even further. Why not hold all wealth in the form of bonds (where it earns interest) and make transfers from bonds to money every time he makes a purchase? If selling bonds, transferring funds to checking accounts, and making trips to the bank were without cost, Jim would never hold money for more than an instant. Each time he needed to pay cash for something or write a check, he would go to the bank or call the bank, transfer the

---

[3]Jim's average balance for the first half of the month is (starting balance + ending balance)/2, or ($600 + 0)/2 = $300. His average for the second half of the month is also $300. His average for the month as a whole is $300.

exact amount of the transaction to his checking account, and either withdraw the cash or write the check to complete the transaction. If he did this constantly, he would squeeze the most interest possible out of his funds because he would never hold assets that did not earn interest.

In practice, money management of this kind is costly. There are brokerage fees and other costs to buy or sell bonds, and time must be spent waiting in line at the bank or at an ATM. At the same time, it is costly to hold assets in non-interest-bearing form, because they lose potential interest revenue.

We have a trade-off problem of the type that pervades economics. Switching more often from bonds to money raises the interest revenue Jim earns (because the more times he switches, the less, on average, he has to hold in his checking account and the more he can keep in bonds), but this increases his money management costs. Less switching means more interest revenue lost (because average money holdings are higher) but lower money management costs (fewer purchases and sales of bonds, less time spent waiting in bank lines, fewer trips to the bank, and so on).

The Optimal Balance   There is a level of average money balances that earns Jim the most profit, taking into account both the interest earned on bonds and the costs paid for switching from bonds to money. This level is his *optimal balance.*

How does the interest rate affect the number of switches that Jim makes and thus the average money balance he chooses to hold? It is easy to see why an increase in the interest rate lowers the optimal money balance. If the interest rate were only 2 percent, it would not be worthwhile to give up much liquidity by holding bonds instead of cash or checking balances. However, if the interest rate were 30 percent, the opportunity cost of holding money instead of bonds would be quite high, and we would expect people to keep most of their funds in bonds and to spend considerable time in managing their money balances. The interest rate represents the opportunity cost of holding money (and therefore not holding bonds, which pay interest). The higher the interest rate is, the higher the opportunity cost of holding money, and the less money people will want to hold. This leads us to conclude:

> When interest rates are high, people want to take advantage of the high return on bonds, so they choose to hold very little money.

Appendix B to this chapter provides a detailed example of this principle.

A demand curve for money, with the interest rate representing the "price" of money, would look like the curve labeled M^d in Figure 24.4. At higher interest rates, bonds are much

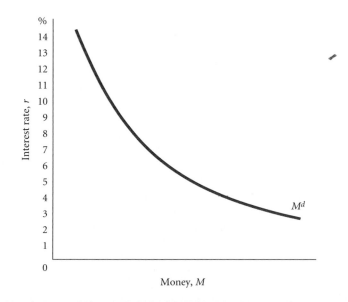

FIGURE 24.4 The Demand Curve for Money Balances

The quantity of money demanded (the amount of money households and firms wish to hold) is a function of the interest rate. Because the interest rate is the opportunity cost of holding money balances, increases in the interest rate will reduce the quantity of money that firms and households want to hold, and decreases in the interest rate will increase the quantity of money that firms and households want to hold.

more attractive than money, so people hold less money because they must make a larger sacrifice in interest for each dollar of money they hold. The curve in Figure 24.4 slopes downward, just like an ordinary demand curve for oranges or shoes. There is an inverse relationship between the interest rate and the quantity of money demanded.[4]

THE SPECULATION MOTIVE

A number of theories have been offered to explain why the quantity of money households desire to hold may rise when interest rates fall, and fall when interest rates rise. One involves household expectations and the relationship of interest rates to bond values.

To understand this theory, you need to realize that the market value of most interest-bearing bonds is inversely related to the interest rate. Suppose I bought an 8 percent bond a year ago for $1,000. Now suppose the market interest rate rises to 10 percent. If I offered to sell my bond for $1,000, no one would buy it because anyone can buy a new bond and earn 10 percent in the market instead of 8 percent of my bond. However, at some lower selling price, my bond becomes attractive to buyers. The reason is that a lower price increases the actual yield to the buyer of my bond. Suppose I sell you my bond for $500. Because the bond is paying 8 percent annually on the original $1,000—that is, $80 per year—it is actually paying you an annual amount that comes to 16 percent of your investment in the bond ($500 × .16 = $80). If you bought that same bond from me for about $800, it would effectively pay you 10 percent interest ($800 × .10 = $80). The point here is simple:

> When market interest rates fall, bond values rise; when market interest rates rise, bond values fall.

Now consider my desire to hold money balances instead of bonds. If market interest rates are higher than normal, I may expect them to come down in the future. If and when interest rates fall, the bonds that I bought when they were high will increase in value. When interest rates are high, the opportunity cost of holding cash balances is high and there is a **speculation motive** for holding bonds in lieu of cash. I am "speculating" that interest rates will fall in the future.

Similarly, when market interest rates are lower than normal, I may expect them to rise in the future. Rising interest rates will bring about a decline in the value of bonds. Thus, when interest rates are low, it is a good time to be holding money and not bonds. When interest rates are low, not only is there the opportunity cost of holding cash balances low, but also there is a speculative motive for holding a larger amount of money. Why should I put money into bonds now when I expect interest rates to rise in the future? (For more on the interaction between the bond market and the money market, see the Further Exploration box "The Bond Market, the Money Market, and the Speculation Motive.")

speculation motive One reason for holding bonds instead of money: Because the market value of interest-bearing bonds is inversely related to the interest rate, investors may wish to hold bonds when interest rates are high with the hope of selling them when interest rates fall.

THE TOTAL DEMAND FOR MONEY

So far we have talked only about household demand for checking account balances. However, the total quantity of money demanded in the economy is the sum of the demand for checking account balances *and cash* by both households *and firms*.

The trade-off for firms is the same as it was for Jim. Like households, firms must manage their money. They have payrolls to meet and purchases to make; they receive cash and checks from sales; and many firms that deal with the public must make change—they need cash in the cash register. Thus, just like Jim, firms need money to engage in ordinary transactions.

However, firms as well as households can hold their assets in interest-earning form. Firms manage their assets just as households do, keeping some in cash, some in their check-

---

[4]The theory of money demand presented here assumes that people know the exact timing of their income and spending. In practice, both have some uncertainty attached to them. For example, some income payments may be unexpectedly delayed a few days or weeks, and some expenditures may arise unexpectedly (such as the cost of repairing a plumbing problem). Because people know that this uncertainty exists, they may choose to hold more money than the strict transactions motive would suggest, as a precaution against unanticipated delays in income receipts or unanticipated expenses. This reason for holding money is sometimes called the *precautionary motive*.

Further exploration

The Bond Market, the Money Market, and the Speculation Motive

People are often confused when business-page headlines read "Bonds Fall, Pushing up Interest Rates" or "Bonds Rise, Driving Yields Down." Nonetheless, it is true that the current market price or value of all fixed-rate bonds, whether U.S. Treasury bonds or German corporate bonds, fall in value when interest rates rise, and rise in value when interest rates fall.

To see why, consider Heidi, a German house painter who bought for $1,000 a 10-year German government bond with a fixed rate of 10 percent. By buying that bond, Heidi has agreed to accept a return on her money of 10 percent for 10 years. This means a check for $100 every year with a promise that her $1,000 will be returned at the end of 10 years.

Though the German government has no obligation to pay the $1,000 back before the bond matures in 10 years, Heidi may need the money before 10 years is up. To get her money back earlier, she can call a broker and sell the bond. In fact, there is a huge market for existing bonds, and existing bond prices are posted in the newspapers every day. To sell the bond, the broker has to find a buyer, and the amount that a buyer would be willing to pay depends on the current rate of interest.

Suppose Heidi wants to sell her bond 2 years after she purchased it. The bond still has 8 years left to maturity. Assume that the Bundesbank (the German central bank) has pushed rates for 8-year bonds to 12 percent. Someone who paid $1,000 for Heidi's bond today would be getting only $100 (10 percent) interest per year. The same person could be getting interest of $120 per year, or 12 percent, by buying a newly issued $1,000 bond. The result: Heidi's broker will not be able to sell her bond for $1,000. Instead, Heidi will have to take a loss because her bond's value has fallen.

Another way to see the same connection between the bond market and the money market is to think of a case in which the demand for bonds increases. Suppose that because of excess demand for bonds in Germany, the value of Heidi's bond goes up to $1,100. Someone who is willing to pay $1,100 for Heidi's bond *must reveal a willingness to accept an annual yield of less than 10 percent*. After all, $100 is only 9.1 percent of $1,100. In addition, the buyer who pays $1,100 will get back only $1,000 when the bond matures. Higher bond prices mean the interest rate bond buyers are willing to accept is lower than before. If buyers are willing to accept 9 percent on old bonds, they will accept 9 percent on new bonds.

Bond prices and interest rates are two sides of the same coin. A rally in the bond market means bond prices have gone up and interest rates, or bond yields, have gone down. Similarly, when the bond market drops, interest rates, or yields, have gone up.

These effects have important implications for money demand. Assume households choose only between holding their assets as money (which does not earn interest) or as bonds (which do earn interest). If households and firms believe interest rates are historically high and they are likely to fall, it is a *good* time to hold bonds. The reason is that a drop in rates means bond values will rise, in a sense earning bondholders a bonus. When interest rates are high and expected to fall, demand for bonds is likely to be high and money demand is likely to be low. Similarly, if people see interest rates as low and expect them to rise, it is *not* a good time to be holding bonds. Why? Because if interest rates rise, bond holders suffer losses. When interest rates are low, money demand is likely to be high and the demand for bonds is likely to be low. Thus, we have another reason for the negative relationship between interest rates and money demand. As we mentioned in the text, this is the *speculation motive* for holding money.

---

ing accounts, and some in bonds. A higher interest rate raises the opportunity cost of money for firms as well as for households and thus reduces the demand for money.

The same trade-off holds for cash. We all walk around with some money in our pockets, but not thousands of dollars, for routine transactions. We carry, on average, about what we think we will need, not more, because there are costs—risks of being robbed and forgone interest.

> At any given moment, there is a demand for money—for cash and checking account balances. Although households and firms need to hold balances for everyday transactions, their demand has a limit. For both households and firms, the quantity of money demanded at any moment depends on the opportunity cost of holding money, a cost determined by the interest rate.

TRANSACTIONS VOLUME AND THE PRICE LEVEL

The money demand curve in Figure 24.4 is a function of the interest rate. There are other factors besides the interest rate that influence total desired money holdings. One is the dollar value of transactions made during a given period of time.

Suppose Jim's income were to increase. Instead of making $1,200 in purchases each month, he will now spend more. He thus needs to hold more money. The reason is simple: To buy more things, he needs more money.

What is true for Jim is true for the economy as a whole. The total demand for money in the economy depends on the total dollar volume of transactions made. The total dollar volume of transactions in the economy, in turn, depends on two things: the total *number* of transactions and the average transaction *amount*. Although there are no data on the actual number of transactions in the economy, a reasonable indicator is likely to be aggregate output (income) (*Y*). A rise in aggregate output—real gross domestic product (GDP)—means there is more economic activity. Firms are producing and selling more output, more people are on payrolls, and household incomes are higher. In short, there are more transactions, and firms and households together will hold more money when they are engaging in more transactions. Thus, an increase in aggregate output (income) will increase the demand for money. Figure 24.5 shows a shift of the money demand curve resulting from an increase in *Y*.

> For a given interest rate, a higher level of output means an increase in the *number* of transactions and more demand for money. The money demand curve shifts to the right when *Y* rises. Similarly, a decrease in *Y* means a decrease in the number of transactions and a lower demand for money. The money demand curve shifts to the left when *Y* falls.

The amount of money needed by firms and households to facilitate their day-to-day transactions also depends on the average *dollar amount* of each transaction. In turn, the average amount of each transaction depends on prices, or instead, on the *price level*. If all prices, including the price of labor (the wage rate) were to double, firms and households would need more money balances to carry out their day-to-day transactions—each transaction would require twice as much money. If the price of your lunch increases from $3.50 to $7.00, you will begin carrying more cash. If your end-of-the-month bills are twice as high as they used to be, you will keep more money in your checking account.

> Increases in the price level shift the money demand curve to the right, and decreases in the price level shift the money demand curve to the left. Even though the number of transactions may not have changed, the quantity of money needed to engage in them has.

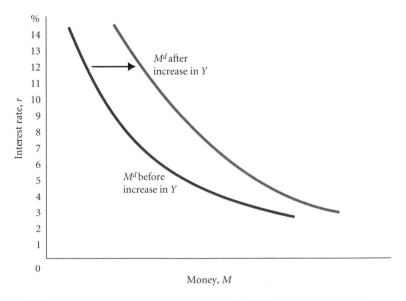

FIGURE 24.5 An Increase in Aggregate Output (Income) (*Y*) Will Shift the Money Demand Curve to the Right

An increase in *Y* means there is more economic activity. Firms are producing and selling more, and households are earning more income and buying more. There are more transactions, for which money is needed. As a result, both firms and households are likely to increase their holdings of money balances at a given interest rate.

TABLE 24.1 Determinants of Money Demand

1. The interest rate: *r* (negative effect causes downward-sloping money demand)
2. The dollar volume of transactions (positive effects shift the money demand curve)
    a. Aggregate output (income): *Y* (positive effect: money demand shifts right when *Y* increases)
    b. The price level: *P* (positive effect: money demand shifts right when *P* increases)

THE DETERMINANTS OF MONEY DEMAND: REVIEW

Table 24.1 summarizes everything we have said about the demand for money. First, because the interest rate (r) is the opportunity cost of holding money balances for both firms and households, increases in the interest rate are likely to decrease the quantity of money demanded; decreases in the interest rate will increase the quantity of money demanded. Thus, the quantity of money demanded is a negative function of the interest rate.

The demand for money also depends on the dollar volume of transactions in a given period. The dollar volume of transactions depends on both aggregate output (income), Y, and the price level, P. The relationship of money demand to Y and the relationship of money demand to P are both positive. Increases in Y or in P will shift the money demand curve to the right; decreases in Y or P will shift the money demand curve to the left.

Some Common Pitfalls We need to consider several pitfalls in thinking about money demand. First, when we spoke in earlier chapters about the demand for goods and services, we were speaking of demand as a *flow variable*—something measured over a period of time. If you say your demand for coffee is three cups, you need to specify whether you are talking about three cups per hour, three cups per day, or three cups per week. In macroeconomics, consumption and saving are flow variables. We consume and save continuously, but we express consumption and saving in time-period terms, such as $600 *per month*.

Money demand is not a flow measure. Instead, it is a *stock variable*, measured at a given point in time. It answers the question: How much money do firms and households desire to hold at a specific point in time, given the current interest rate, volume of economic activity, and price level?

Second, many people think of money demand and saving as roughly the same—they are not. Suppose that in a given year a household had income of $50,000 and expenses of $47,000. It saved $3,000 during the year. At the beginning of the year the household had no debt and $100,000 in assets. Because the household saved $3,000 during the year, it has $103,000 in assets at the end of the year. Some of the $103,000 is held in stocks, some in bonds, some in other forms of securities, and some in money. How much the household chooses to hold in the form of money is its demand for money. Depending on the interest rate and the household's transactions, the amount of the $103,000 that it chooses to hold in the form of money could be anywhere from a few hundred dollars to many thousands. How much of its assets a household retains in the form of money is different from how much of its income it spends during the year.

Finally, recall the difference between a shift in a demand curve and a movement along the curve. The money demand curve in Figure 24.4 shows optimal money balances as a function of the interest rate *ceteris paribus*, all else equal. Changes in the interest rate cause movements *along* the curve—*changes in the quantity of money demanded*. Changes in real GDP (Y) or in the price level (P) cause shifts of the curve as shown in Figure 24.5— *changes in demand*.

THE EQUILIBRIUM INTEREST RATE

We are now in a position to consider one of the key questions in macroeconomics: How is the interest rate determined in the economy?

Financial markets (what we call the money market) work very well in the United States. Almost all financial markets clear—that is, almost all reach an equilibrium where quantity demanded equals quantity supplied. In the money market:

> The point at which the quantity of money demanded equals the quantity of money supplied determines the equilibrium interest rate in the economy.

This explanation sounds simple, but it requires elaboration.

SUPPLY AND DEMAND IN THE MONEY MARKET

We saw in Chapter 23 that the Fed controls the money supply through its manipulation of the amount of reserves in the economy. Because we are assuming that the Fed's money supply behavior does not depend on the interest rate, the money supply curve is a vertical line. (Review Figure 23.5.) In other words, we are assuming that the Fed uses its three tools (the required reserve ratio, the discount rate, and open market operations) to achieve its fixed target for the money supply.

Figure 24.6 superimposes the vertical money supply curve from Figure 23.5 on the downward-sloping money demand curve. Only at interest rate r^* is the quantity of money in circulation (the money supply) equal to the quantity of money demanded. To understand why r^* is an equilibrium, we need to ask what adjustments would take place if the interest rate were not r^*.

To understand the adjustment mechanism, keep in mind that borrowing and lending is a continuous process. The Treasury sells U.S. government securities (bonds) more or less continuously to finance the deficit. When it does, it is borrowing, and must pay interest to attract bond buyers. Buyers of government bonds are, in essence, lending money to the government, just as buyers of corporate bonds are lending money to corporations that wish to finance investment projects.

Consider first r_0 in Figure 24.6. At r_0, the quantity of money demanded is M_0^d, and the quantity of money supplied exceeds the quantity of money demanded. This means there is more money in circulation than households and firms want to hold. At r_0, firms and households will attempt to reduce their money holdings by buying bonds. When there is

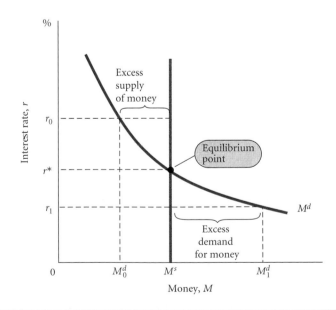

FIGURE 24.6 Adjustments in the Money Market

Equilibrium exists in the money market when the supply of money is equal to the demand for money: $M^d = M^s$. At r_0, the quantity of money supplied exceeds the quantity of money demanded, and the interest rate will fall. At r_1, the quantity demanded exceeds the quantity supplied, and the interest rate will rise. Only at r^* is equilibrium achieved.

money in circulation looking for a way to earn interest—when demand for bonds is high—those looking to borrow money by selling bonds will find that they can do so at a lower interest rate.

> If the interest rate is initially high enough to create an excess supply of money, the interest rate will immediately fall, discouraging people from moving out of money and into bonds.

Now consider r_1, where the quantity of money demanded (M_1^d) exceeds the supply of money currently in circulation—households and firms do not have enough money on hand to facilitate ordinary transactions. They will try to adjust their holdings by shifting assets out of bonds and into their checking accounts. At the same time, the continuous flow of new bonds being issued must also be absorbed. The Treasury and corporations can sell bonds in an environment where people are adjusting their asset holdings to shift *out* of bonds only by offering a higher interest rate to the people who buy them.

> If the interest rate is initially low enough to create an excess demand for money, the interest rate will immediately rise, discouraging people from moving out of bonds and into money.

CHANGING THE MONEY SUPPLY TO AFFECT THE INTEREST RATE

With an understanding of equilibrium in the money market, we can now see how the Fed can affect the interest rate. Suppose the current interest rate is 14 percent and the Fed wants to reduce the interest rate. To do so, it would expand the money supply. Figure 24.7 shows how such an expansion would work. To expand M^s, the Fed can reduce the reserve requirement, cut the discount rate, or buy U.S. government securities on the open market. All these practices expand the quantity of reserves in the system. Banks can make more loans, and the money supply expands. (Review Chapter 23 if you are unsure why.) In Figure 24.7, the initial money supply curve, M_0^s, shifts to the right, to M_1^s.

At the 14 percent interest rate there is an excess supply of money. This immediately puts downward pressure on the interest rate as households and firms try to buy bonds with their money to earn that high interest rate. As this happens, the interest rate falls, and it

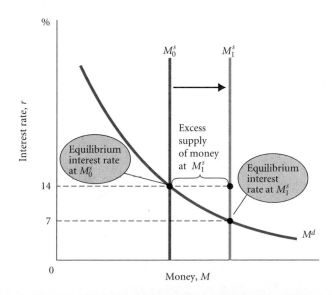

FIGURE 24.7 The Effect of an Increase in the Supply of Money on the Interest Rate

An increase in the supply of money from M_0^s to M_1^s lowers the rate of interest from 14 percent to 7 percent.

will continue to fall until it reaches the new equilibrium interest rate of 7 percent. At this point, $M_1^s = M^d$, and the market is in equilibrium.

If the Fed wanted to drive the interest rate *up*, it would contract the money supply. It could do so by increasing the reserve requirement, by raising the discount rate, or by selling U.S. government securities in the open market. Whichever tool the Fed chooses, the result would be lower reserves and a lower supply of money. M_0^s in Figure 24.7 would shift to the left, and the equilibrium interest rate would rise. (As an exercise, draw a graph of this situation.)

INCREASES IN Y AND SHIFTS IN THE MONEY DEMAND CURVE

Changes in the supply of money are not the only factors that influence the equilibrium interest rate. Shifts in money demand can do the same thing.

Recall that the demand for money depends on both the interest rate and the volume of transactions. As a rough measure of the volume of transactions, we use Y, the level of aggregate output (income). Remember that the relationship between money demand and Y is positive—increases in Y mean a higher level of real economic activity. More is being produced, income is higher, and there are more transactions in the economy. Consequently, the demand for money on the part of firms and households in aggregate is higher.

An increase in Y shifts the money demand curve to the right.

Figure 24.8 illustrates such a shift. Y increases, causing money demand to shift from M_0^d to M_1^d. The result is an increase in the equilibrium level of the interest rate from 7 percent to 14 percent. A decrease in Y would shift M^d to the left, and the equilibrium interest rate would fall.

The money demand curve also shifts when the price level changes. If the price level rises, the money demand curve shifts to the right, because people need more money to engage in their day-to-day transactions. With the quantity of money supplied unchanged, however, the interest rate must rise to reduce the quantity of money demanded to the unchanged quantity of money supplied—a movement *along* the money demand curve.

An increase in the price level is like an increase in Y in that both events increase the demand for money. The result is an increase in the equilibrium interest rate.

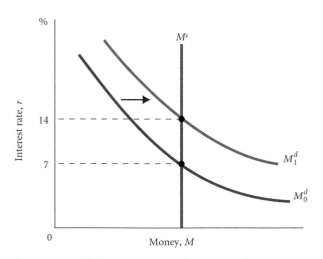

FIGURE 24.8 The Effect of an Increase in Income on the Interest Rate

An increase in aggregate output (income) shifts the money demand curve from M_0^d to M_1^d, which raises the equilibrium interest rate from 7 percent to 14 percent.

If the price level *falls*, the money demand curve shifts to the left, because people need less money for their transactions. However, with the quantity of money supplied unchanged, the interest rate must fall to increase the quantity of money demanded to the unchanged quantity of money supplied.

> A decrease in the price level leads to a decrease in the equilibrium interest rate.

We explore this relationship in more detail in Chapter 26.

LOOKING AHEAD: THE FEDERAL RESERVE AND MONETARY POLICY

We now know that the Fed can change the interest rate by changing the quantity of money supplied. If the Fed increases the quantity of money, the interest rate falls; if it decreases the quantity of money, the interest rate rises.

Nonetheless, we have not yet said *why* the Fed might want to change the interest rate or what happens to the economy when the interest rate changes. We have hinted at why: A low interest rate stimulates spending, particularly investment; a high interest rate reduces spending. By changing the interest rate the Fed can change aggregate output (income). In the next chapter, we will combine our discussions of the goods and money markets and discuss how the interest rate affects the equilibrium level of aggregate output (income) (Y) in the goods market.

The Fed's use of its power to influence events in the goods market, as well as in the money market, is the center of the government's monetary policy. When the Fed moves to contract the money supply in an effort to restrain the economy, economists call it a **tight monetary policy**. Conversely, when the Fed stimulates the economy by expanding the money supply, it has an **easy monetary policy**. The Fed moved aggressively to expand the money supply and lower interest rates in 1975, in 1982, and early in 1991. These easy money policies contributed to economic recovery from the recessions of those years. Tight money policies caused aggregate spending to decline in 1974 and 1981, contributing to the recessions of those years. During the summer of 1981, tight money helped to push some key interest rates above 20 percent.

We will discuss the way in which the economy affects the Fed's behavior in Chapter 28. In that chapter, we will also discuss the Fed's recent policies and examine the effects of these policies on the economy.

tight monetary policy Fed policies that contract the money supply in an effort to restrain the economy.

easy monetary policy Fed policies that expand the money supply in an effort to stimulate the economy.

SUMMARY

1. *Interest* is the fee borrowers pay to lenders for the use of their funds. The *interest rate* is the annual interest payment on a loan expressed as a percentage of the loan; it is equal to the amount of interest received per year divided by the amount of the loan. Although there are many different interest rates in the United States, we assume there is only one interest rate in the economy. This simplifies our analysis but still provides a tool for understanding how the various parts of the macro-economy relate to each other.

THE DEMAND FOR MONEY

2. The demand for money depends negatively on the interest rate. The higher the interest rate, the higher the opportunity cost (more interest forgone) from holding money, and the less money people will want to hold. An increase in the interest rate reduces the quantity demanded for money, and the money demand curve slopes downward.

3. The volume of transactions in the economy affects money demand. The total dollar volume of transactions depends on both the total number of transactions and the average transaction amount.

4. A reasonable measure of the number of transactions in the economy is aggregate output (income) (Y). When Y rises, there is more economic activity, more is being produced and sold, and more people are on payrolls—there are more transactions in the economy. An increase in Y causes the money demand curve to shift to the right. This effect follows because households and firms need more money when they are engaging in more transactions. A decrease in Y causes the money demand curve to shift to the left.

5. Changes in the price level affect the average dollar amount of each transaction. *Increases* in the price level will increase the demand for money (shift the money demand curve to the right) because households and firms will need more money

for their expenditures. *Decreases* in the price level will decrease the demand for money (shift the money demand curve to the left).

THE EQUILIBRIUM INTEREST RATE

6. The point at which the quantity of money supplied equals the quantity of money demanded determines the equilibrium interest rate in the economy. An excess supply of money will cause households and firms to buy more bonds, driving the interest rate down. An excess demand for money will cause households and firms to move out of bonds, driving the interest rate up.

7. The Fed can affect the equilibrium interest rate by changing the supply of money using one of its three tools—the required reserve ratio, the discount rate, or open market operations.

8. An increase in the price level is like an increase in Y in that both events cause an increase in money demand. The result is an increase in the equilibrium interest rate. A decrease in the price level leads to reduced money demand and a decrease in the equilibrium interest rate.

9. *Tight monetary policy* refers to Fed policies that contract the money supply in an effort to restrain the economy. *Easy monetary policy* refers to Fed policies that expand the money supply in an effort to stimulate the economy. The Fed chooses between these two types of policies for different reasons at different times.

REVIEW TERMS AND CONCEPTS

easy monetary policy, 537

interest, 525

interest rate, 525

monetary policy, 525

nonsynchronization of income and spending, 526

speculation motive, 530

tight monetary policy, 537

transaction motive, 526

PROBLEM SET

1. State whether you agree or disagree with the following statements and explain why.
   a. When the real economy expands (Y rises), the demand for money expands. As a result, households hold more cash and the supply of money expands.
   b. Inflation, a rise in the price level, causes the demand for money to decline. Because inflation causes money to be worth less, households desire to hold less of it.
   c. If the Fed buys bonds in the open market and at the same time we experience a recession, interest rates will no doubt rise.

2. During 2003, we began to stop worrying that inflation was a problem. Instead we began to worry about deflation, a decline in the price level. Assume that the Fed decided to hold the money supply constant. What impact would deflation have on interest rates?

3. Look back at the News Analysis box on p. 528. In 1981, interest rates were very high. The opportunity cost of holding money was very high, and thus money demand was low. What did people expect would happen to interest rates in the coming months and years? What would that mean for bond prices? If you shared those expectations, would you hold substantial money balances or would you want to hold more "bonds"? What did people expect to happen to rates in 2005? How would your answers change?

4. What if, at a low level of interest rates, the money demand curve became nearly horizontal, as in the figure below? That is, with interest rates so low, the public would not find it attractive to hold bonds, and thus money demand would be very high. Many argue that this was the position of the U.S. economy in 2003. If the Fed decided to expand the money supply in the diagram, what would be the impact on interest rates?

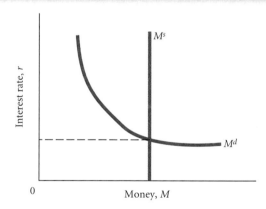

5. During the fourth quarter of 1993, real GDP in the United States grew at an annual rate of over 7 percent. During 1994, the economy continued to expand with modest inflation (Y rose at a rate of 4 percent and P increased about 3 percent). At the beginning of 1994, the prime interest rate (the interest rate that banks offer their best, least risky customers) stood at 6 percent, where it remained for over a year. By the beginning of 1995, the prime rate had increased to over 8.5 percent.
   a. By using money supply and money demand curves, show the effects of the increase in Y and P on interest rates assuming *no change* in the money supply.
   b. On a separate graph, show that the interest rate can rise even if the Federal Reserve expands the money supply as long as it does so more slowly than money demand is increasing.

6. Illustrate the following situations using supply and demand curves for money:
   a. The Fed buys bonds in the open market during a recession.

b. During a period of rapid inflation, the Fed increases the reserve requirement.

c. The Fed acts to hold interest rates constant during a period of high inflation.

d. During a period of no growth in GDP and zero inflation, the Fed lowers the discount rate.

e. During a period of rapid real growth of GDP, the Fed acts to increase the reserve requirement.

7. During a recession, interest rates may fall even if the Fed takes no action to expand the money supply. Why? Use a graph to explain.

8. During the summer of 1997, the Congress and the president agreed on a budget package to balance the federal budget. The "deal," signed into law by President Clinton in August as the Taxpayer Relief Act of 1997, contained substantial tax cuts and expenditure reductions. The tax reductions were scheduled to take effect immediately, however, while the expenditure cuts mostly would come in the years 1999 to 2002. Thus, in 1998, the package was seen by economists to be mildly expansionary. If the result is an increase in the growth of real output/income, what would you expect to happen to interest rates if the Fed holds the money supply (or the rate of growth of the money supply) constant? What would the Fed do if it wanted to raise interest rates? What if it wanted to lower interest rates? Illustrate with graphs.

9. The demand for money in a country is given by

$$M^d = 10,000 - 10,000r + Y$$

where M^d is money demand in dollars, r is the interest rate (a 10 percent interest rate means $r = 0.1$), and Y is national income. Assume Y is initially 5,000.

a. Graph the amount of money demanded (on the horizontal axis) against the interest rate (on the vertical axis).

b. Suppose the money supply (M^s) is set by the central bank at $10,000. On the same graph you drew for part a, add the money supply curve. What is the equilibrium rate of interest? Explain how you arrived at your answer.

c. Suppose income rises from $Y = 5,000$ to $Y = 7,500$. What happens to the money demand curve you drew in part a? Draw the new curve, if there is one. What happens to the equilibrium interest rate if the central bank does not change the supply of money?

d. If the central bank wants to keep the equilibrium interest rate at the same value as it was in part b, by how much should it increase or decrease the supply of money, given the new level of national income?

e. Suppose the shift in part c has occurred, and the money supply remains at $10,000, but there is no observed change in the interest rate. What might have happened that could explain this?

APPENDIX A

THE VARIOUS INTEREST RATES IN THE U.S. ECONOMY

Although there are many different interest rates in the economy, they tend to move up or down with one another. Here, we discuss some of their differences. We first look at the relationship between interest rates on securities with different *maturities*, or terms. We then briefly discuss some of the main interest rates in the U.S. economy.

THE TERM STRUCTURE OF INTEREST RATES

The *term structure of interest rates* is the relationship among the interest rates offered on securities of different maturities. The key here is understanding things like: How are these different rates related? Does a 2-year security (an IOU that promises to repay principal, plus interest, after 2 years) pay a lower annual rate than a 1-year security (an IOU to be repaid, with interest, after 1 year)? What happens to the rate of interest offered on 1-year securities if the rate of interest on 2-year securities increases?

Assume you want to invest some money for 2 years and at the end of the 2 years you want it back. Assume you want to buy government securities. For this analysis, we restrict your choices to two: (1) You can buy a 2-year security today and hold it for 2 years, at which time you cash it in (we will assume that the interest rate on the 2-year security is 9 percent per year), or (2) you can buy a 1-year security today. At the end of 1 year, you must cash this security in; you can then buy another 1-year security. At

the end of the second year, you will cash in the second security. Assume the interest rate on the first 1-year security is 8 percent.

Which would you prefer? Currently, you do not have enough data to answer this question. To consider choice (2) sensibly, you need to know the interest rate on the 1-year security that you intend to buy in the second year. This rate will not be known until the second year. All you know now is the rate on the 2-year security and the rate on the current 1-year security. To decide what to do, you must form an *expectation* of the rate on the 1-year security a year from now. If you expect the 1-year rate (8 percent) to remain the same in the second year, you should buy the 2-year security. You would earn 9 percent per year on the 2-year security but only 8 percent per year on the two 1-year securities. If you expect the 1-year rate to rise to 12 percent a year from now, you should make the second choice. You would earn 8 percent in the first year, and you expect to earn 12 percent in the second year. The expected rate of return over the 2 years is about 10 percent, which is better than the 9 percent you can get on the 2-year security. If you expected the 1-year rate a year from now to be 10 percent, it would not matter very much which of the two choices you made. The rate of return over the 2-year period would be roughly 9 percent for both choices.

We now alter the focus of our discussion to get to the topic we are really interested in—how the 2-year rate is determined. Assume the 1-year rate has been set by the Fed and it is 8 percent. Also assume that people expect the 1-year rate a year from now to be 10 percent. What is the 2-year rate? According to a theory called the *expectations theory of the term structure of interest rates*, the 2-year rate is equal to the average of the current 1-year rate and the 1-year rate expected a year from now. In this example, the 2-year rate would be 9 percent (the average of 8 percent and 10 percent).

If the 2-year rate were lower than the average of the two 1-year rates, people would not be indifferent as to which security they held. They would want to hold only the short-term, 1-year securities. To find a buyer for a 2-year security, the seller would be forced to increase the interest rate it offers on the 2-year security until it is equal to the average of the current 1-year rate and the expected 1-year rate for next year. The interest rate on the 2-year security will continue to rise until people are once again indifferent between one 2-year security and two 1-year securities.[1]

Let us now return to Fed behavior. We know the Fed can affect the short-term interest rate by changing the money supply, but does it also affect long-term interest rates? The answer is "somewhat." Because the 2-year rate is an average of the current 1-year rate and the expected 1-year rate a year from now, the Fed influences the 2-year rate to the extent that it influences the current 1-year rate. The same holds for 3-year rates and beyond. The current short-term rate is a means by which the Fed can influence longer-term rates.

In addition, Fed behavior may directly affect people's expectations of the future short-term rates, which will then affect long-term rates. If the chair of the Fed testifies before Congress that raising short-term interest rates is under consideration, people's expectations of higher future short-term interest rates are likely to increase. These expectations will then be reflected in current long-term interest rates.

TYPES OF INTEREST RATES

The following are some widely followed interest rates in the United States.

THREE-MONTH TREASURY BILL RATE

Government securities that mature in less than a year are called *Treasury bills*, or sometimes *T-bills*. The interest rate on 3-month Treasury bills is probably the most widely followed short-term interest rate.

GOVERNMENT BOND RATE

Government securities with terms of 1 year or more are called *government bonds*. There are 1-year bonds, 2-year bonds, and so on, up to 30-year bonds. Bonds of different terms have different interest rates. The relationship among the interest rates on the various maturities is the term structure of interest rates that we discussed in the first part of this appendix.

FEDERAL FUNDS RATE

Banks borrow not only from the Fed but also from each other. If one bank has excess reserves, it can lend some of those reserves to other banks through the federal funds market. The interest rate in this market is called the *federal funds rate*—the rate banks are charged to borrow reserves from other banks.

The federal funds market is really a desk in New York City. From all over the country, banks with excess reserves to lend and banks in need of reserves call the desk and negotiate a rate of interest. Account balances with the Fed are changed for the period of the loan without any physical movement of money.

This borrowing and lending, which takes place near the close of each working day, is generally for 1 day ("overnight"), so the federal funds rate is a 1-day rate. It is the rate that the Fed has the most effect on through its open market operations.

COMMERCIAL PAPER RATE

Firms have several alternatives for raising funds. They can sell stocks, issue bonds, or borrow from a bank. Large firms can also borrow directly from the public by issuing "commercial paper," which is essentially short-term corporate IOUs that offer a designated rate of interest. The interest rate offered on commercial paper depends on the financial condition of the firm and the maturity date of the IOU.

PRIME RATE

Banks charge different interest rates to different customers depending on how risky the banks perceive the customers to be. You would expect to pay a higher interest rate for a car loan than General Motors would pay for a $1 million loan to finance investment. Also, you would pay more interest for an unsecured loan, a "personal" loan, than for one that was secured by some asset, such as a house or car, to be used as collateral.

The *prime rate* is a benchmark that banks often use in quoting interest rates to their customers. A very low-risk corporation might be able to borrow at (or even below) the prime rate. A less well-known firm might be quoted a rate of "prime plus three-fourths," which means that if the prime rate is, say, 10 percent, the firm would have to pay interest of 10.75 percent. The prime rate depends on the cost of funds to the bank; it moves up and down with changes in the economy.

AAA CORPORATE BOND RATE

Corporations finance much of their investment by selling bonds to the public. Corporate bonds are classified by various bond dealers according to their risk. Bonds issued by General Motors are in less risk of default than bonds issued by a new, risky, biotech research firm. Bonds differ from commercial paper in one important way: Bonds have a longer maturity.

Bonds are graded in much the same way students are. The highest grade is AAA, the next highest AA, and so on. The interest rate on bonds rated AAA is the *triple A corporate bond rate*, the rate that the least risky firms pay on the bonds that they issue.

---

[1]For longer terms, additional future rates must be averaged in. For a 3-year security, for example, the expected 1-year rate a year from now and the expected 1-year rate 2 years from now are added to the current 1-year rate and averaged.

PROBLEM SET

1. The following table gives three key U.S. interest rates in 1980 and again in April 1993:

	1980 (%)	**1993 (%)**
Three-month U.S. government bills	11.39	2.92
Long-term U.S. government bonds	10.81	6.85
Prime rate	15.26	6.00

Can you give an explanation for the extreme differences that you see? Specifically, comment on: (1) the fact that rates in 1980 were much higher than in 1993, and (2) the long-term rate was higher than the short-term rate in 1993 but lower in 1980.

APPENDIX B

THE DEMAND FOR MONEY: A NUMERICAL EXAMPLE

This appendix presents a numerical example showing how optimal money management behavior can be derived.

We have seen that the interest rate represents the opportunity cost of holding funds in non-interest-bearing checking accounts (as opposed to bonds, which yield interest). We have also seen that there are costs involved in switching from bonds to money. Given these costs, our objective is to determine the optimum amount of money for an individual to hold. The optimal average level of money holdings is the amount that maximizes the profits from money management. Interest is earned on average bond holdings, but the cost per switch multiplied by the number of switches must be subtracted from interest revenue to obtain the net profit from money management.

Suppose the interest rate is .05 (5 percent), it costs $2 each time a bond is sold[1] and the proceeds from the sale are

---

[1]In this example we will assume the $2 cost does not apply to the original purchase of bonds.

deposited in one's checking account. Suppose also that the individual's income is $1,200 and that this income is spent evenly throughout the period. This situation is depicted in the top half of Table 24B.1. The optimum value for average money holdings is the value that achieves the largest possible profit in column 6 of the table. When the interest rate is 5 percent, the optimum average money holdings are $150 (which means the individual makes three switches from bonds to money).

In the bottom half of Table 24B.1, the same calculations are performed for an interest rate of 3 percent instead of 5 percent. In this case, the optimum average money holdings is $200 (which means the person/household makes two switches from bonds to money instead of three). The lower interest rate has led to an increase in the optimum average money holdings. Under the assumption that people behave optimally, the demand for money is a negative function of the interest rate: The lower the rate, the more money on average is held, and the higher the rate, the less money on average is held.

TABLE 24B.1 Optimum Money Holdings

1 NUMBER OF SWITCHES[a]	2 AVERAGE MONEY HOLDINGS[b]	3 AVERAGE BOND HOLDINGS[c]	4 INTEREST EARNED[d]	5 COST OF SWITCHING[e]	6 NET PROFIT[f]
		r = 5 percent			
0	$600.00	$ 0.00	$ 0.00	$0.00	$ 0.00
1	300.00	300.00	15.00	2.00	13.00
2	200.00	400.00	20.00	4.00	16.00
3	150.00*	450.00	22.50	6.00	16.50
4	120.00	480.00	24.00	8.00	16.00
Assumptions: Interest rate r = 0.05. Cost of switching from bonds into money equals $2 per transaction.					
		r = 3 percent			
0	$600.00	$ 0.00	$ 0.00	$0.00	$0.00
1	300.00	300.00	9.00	2.00	7.00
2	200.00*	400.00	12.00	4.00	8.00
3	150.00	450.00	13.50	6.00	7.50
4	120.00	480.00	14.40	8.00	6.40
Assumptions: Interest rate r = 0.03. Cost of switching from bonds into money equals $2 per transaction.					

*Optimum money holdings. [a]That is, the number of times you sell a bond. [b]Calculated as 600/(col. 1 + 1). [c]Calculated as 600 − col. 2.
[d]Calculated as r × col. 3, where r is the interest rate. [e]Calculated as t × col. 1, where t is the cost per switch ($2). [f]Calculated as col. 4 − col. 5

PROBLEM SET

1. Sherman Peabody earns a monthly salary of $1,500, which he receives at the beginning of each month. He spends the entire amount each month, at the rate of $50 per day. (Assume 30 days in a month.) The interest rate paid on bonds is 10 percent per month. It costs $4 every time Peabody sells a bond.
   a. Describe briefly how Mr. Peabody should decide how much money to hold.
   b. Calculate Peabody's optimal money holdings. (*Hint:* It may help to formulate a table such as the one in this ap-

   pendix. You can round to the nearest $0.50, and you need to consider only average money holdings of more than $100.)
   c. Suppose the interest rate rises to 15 percent. Find Peabody's optimal money holdings at this new interest rate. What would happen if the interest rate increases to 20 percent?
   d. Graph your answers to **b.** and **c.** with the interest rate on the vertical axis and the amount of money demanded on the horizontal axis. Explain why your graph slopes downward.

Money, the Interest Rate, and Output: Analysis and Policy

25

In Chapters 21 and 22, we discussed the market for goods and services—the **goods market**—without mentioning money, the money market, or the interest rate. We described how the equilibrium level of aggregate output (income) (Y) is determined in the goods market. At given levels of planned investment spending (I), government spending (G), and net taxes (T), we were able to determine the equilibrium level of output in the economy.

In Chapters 23 and 24, we discussed the financial market, or **money market**, barely referring to the goods market, as we explained how the equilibrium level of the interest rate is determined in the money market.

The goods market and the money market do not operate independently, however. Events in the money market affect what goes on in the goods market, and events in the goods market affect what goes on in the money market. Only by analyzing the two markets together can we determine the values of aggregate output (income) (Y) and the interest rate (r) that are consistent with the existence of equilibrium in *both* markets.

Looking at both markets simultaneously also reveals how fiscal policy affects the money market and how monetary policy affects the goods market. This is what we will do in this chapter. By establishing how the two markets affect each other, we will show how open market purchases of government securities (which expand the money supply) affect the equilibrium level of national output and income. Similarly, we will show how fiscal policy measures (such as tax cuts) affect interest rates and investment spending.

goods market The market in which goods and services are exchanged and in which the equilibrium level of aggregate output is determined.

money market The market in which financial instruments are exchanged and in which the equilibrium level of the interest rate is determined.

THE LINKS BETWEEN THE GOODS MARKET AND THE MONEY MARKET

There are two key *links* between the goods market and the money market:

■ **Link 1: Income and the Demand for Money** The first link between the goods market and the money market exists because the demand for money depends on income. As aggregate output (income) (Y) increases, the number of transactions requiring the use of money increases. (You just saw this effect in Chapter 24.) An increase in output, with the interest rate held constant, leads to an increase in money demand.

543

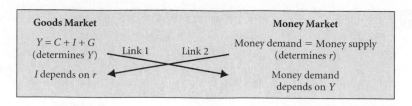

Goods Market		Money Market
$Y = C + I + G$ (determines Y)	Link 1 Link 2	Money demand = Money supply (determines r)
I depends on r		Money demand depends on Y

FIGURE 25.1 Links Between the Goods Market and the Money Market

Planned investment depends on the interest rate, and money demand depends on income.

Income, which is determined in the goods market, has considerable influence on the demand for money in the money market.

- **Link 2: Planned Investment Spending and the Interest Rate** The second link between the goods market and the money market exists because planned investment spending (I) depends on the interest rate (r). In Chapters 21 and 22 we assumed that planned investment spending is fixed at a certain level, but we did so only to simplify that discussion. In practice, investment is not fixed. Instead, it depends on a number of key economic variables. One is the interest rate. The higher the interest rate is, the lower the level of planned investment spending.

The interest rate, which is determined in the money market, has significant effects on planned investment in the goods market.

These two links are summarized in Figure 25.1.

INVESTMENT, THE INTEREST RATE, AND THE GOODS MARKET

It should come as no surprise that there is an inverse relationship between the level of planned investment and the interest rate.

When the interest rate falls, planned investment rises.
When the interest rate rises, planned investment falls.

To see the reason for these effects, recall that *investment* refers to a firm's purchase of new capital—new machines and plants. Whether a firm decides to invest in a project depends on whether the expected profits from the project justify its costs. Usually, a big cost of an investment project is the interest cost.

Consider a firm opening a new plant, or the investment required to open a new ice cream store. When a manufacturing firm builds a new plant, the contractor must be paid at the time the plant is built. When an entrepreneur decides to open a new ice cream parlor, freezers, tables, chairs, light fixtures, and signs are needed. These too must be paid for when they are installed.

The money needed to carry out such projects is generally borrowed and paid back over an extended period. The real cost of an investment project depends in part on the interest rate—the cost of borrowing. When the interest rate rises, it becomes more expensive to borrow, and fewer projects are likely to be undertaken; increasing the interest rate, *ceteris paribus*, is likely to reduce the level of planned investment spending. When the interest rate falls, it becomes less costly to borrow, and more investment projects are likely to be undertaken; reducing the interest rate, *ceteris paribus*, is likely to increase the level of planned investment spending.

The relationship between the interest rate and planned investment is illustrated by the downward-sloping demand curve in Figure 25.2. The higher the interest rate is, the lower the level of planned investment. At an interest rate of 3 percent, planned investment is I_0. When the interest rate rises from 3 percent to 6 percent, planned investment falls from I_0 to I_1. As the interest rate falls, however, more projects become profitable, so more investment is undertaken.

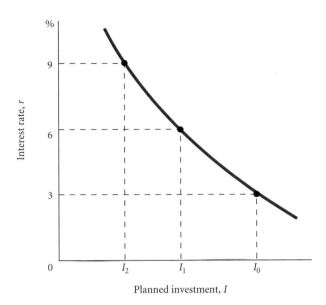

FIGURE 25.2   Planned Investment Schedule

Planned investment spending is a negative function of the interest rate. An increase in the interest rate from 3 percent to 6 percent reduces planned investment from I_0 to I_1.

We can now use the fact that planned investment depends on the interest rate to consider how this relationship affects planned aggregate expenditure (AE). Recall that planned aggregate expenditure is the sum of consumption, planned investment, and government purchases. That is,

$$AE \equiv C + I + G$$

We now know that there are actually many possible levels of I, each corresponding to a different interest rate. When the interest rate changes, planned investment changes. Therefore, a change in the interest rate (r) will lead to a change in total planned spending ($C + I + G$) as well.[1]

Figure 25.3 shows what happens to planned aggregate expenditure when the interest rate rises from 3 percent to 6 percent. At the higher interest rate, planned investment is lower; planned aggregate expenditure thus shifts *downward*. Recall from Chapters 21 and 22: A fall in any component of aggregate spending has an even larger (or "multiplier") effect on equilibrium income (Y). When the interest rate rises, planned investment (and planned aggregate expenditure) falls, and equilibrium output (income) falls by even more than the fall in planned investment. In Figure 25.3, equilibrium Y falls from Y_0 to Y_1 when the interest rate rises from 3 percent to 6 percent.

We can summarize the effects of a change in the interest rate on the equilibrium level of output.

The effects of a change in the interest rate include:

- A high interest rate (r) discourages planned investment (I).
- Planned investment is a part of planned aggregate expenditure (AE).
- Thus, when the interest rate rises, planned aggregate expenditure (AE) at every level of income falls.
- Finally, a decrease in planned aggregate expenditure lowers equilibrium output (income) (Y) by a multiple of the initial decrease in planned investment.

---

[1]When we look at the behavior of households in the macroeconomy in detail in Chapter 30, you will see that consumption spending (C) is also stimulated by lower interest rates and discouraged by higher interest rates.

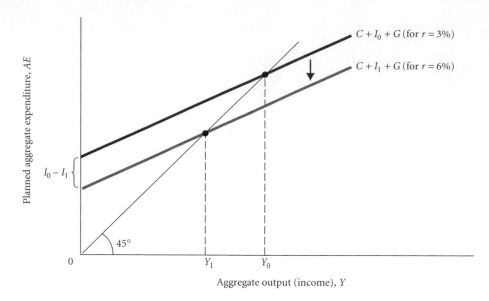

FIGURE 25.3 The Effect of an Interest Rate Increase on Planned Aggregate Expenditure

An increase in the interest rate from 3 percent to 6 percent lowers planned aggregate expenditure and thus reduces equilibrium income from Y_0 to Y_1.

Using a convenient shorthand:

$$r\uparrow \rightarrow I\downarrow \rightarrow AE\downarrow \rightarrow Y\downarrow$$

$$r\downarrow \rightarrow I\uparrow \rightarrow AE\uparrow \rightarrow Y\uparrow$$

As you see, the equilibrium level of output (Y) is not determined solely by events in the goods market, as we assumed in our earlier, simplified discussions. The reason is that the money market affects the level of the interest rate, which then affects planned investment in the goods market. There is a different equilibrium level of Y for every possible level of the interest rate (r). The final level of equilibrium Y depends on what the interest rate turns out to be, which depends on events in the money market.

MONEY DEMAND, AGGREGATE OUTPUT (INCOME), AND THE MONEY MARKET

We have just seen how the interest rate—which is determined in the money market—influences the level of planned investment spending and thus the goods market. Now let us look at the other half of the story: the ways in which the goods market affects the money market.

In Chapter 24, we explored the demand for money by households and firms and explained why the demand for money depends negatively on the interest rate. An increase in the interest rate raises the opportunity cost of holding non-interest-bearing money (as compared with interest-bearing bonds), encouraging people to keep more of their funds in bonds and less in checking account balances. The downward-sloping money demand curve (M^d) is shown in Figure 25.4.

We also saw in Chapter 24 that the demand for money depends on the level of income in the economy. More income means more transactions, and an increased volume of transactions implies a greater demand for money. With more people earning higher incomes and buying more goods and services, more money will be demanded to meet the increased volume of transactions. An increase in income therefore shifts the money demand curve to the right. (Review Figure 24.5.)

If, as we are assuming, the Federal Reserve's (Fed's) choice of the amount of money to supply does not depend on the interest rate, then the money supply curve is simply a vertical

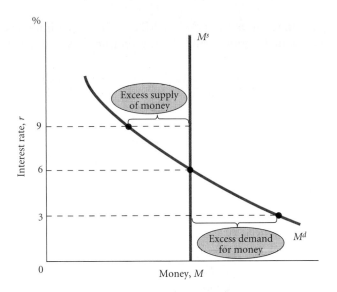

FIGURE 25.4 Equilibrium in the Money Market

If the interest rate were 9 percent, the quantity of money in circulation would exceed the amount households and firms want to hold. The excess money balances would cause the interest rate to drop as people try to shift their funds into interest-bearing bonds. At 3 percent the opposite is true. Excess demand for money balances would push interest rates up. Only at 6 percent would the actual quantity of money in circulation be equal to what the economy wants to hold in money balances.

line. The equilibrium interest rate is the point at which the quantity of money demanded equals the quantity of money supplied. This equilibrium is shown at a 6 percent interest rate in Figure 25.4. If the amount of money demanded by households and firms is less than the amount in circulation as determined by the Fed, as it is at an interest rate of 9 percent in Figure 25.4, the interest rate will fall. If the amount of money demanded is greater than the amount in circulation, as it is at an interest rate of 3 percent in Figure 25.4, the interest rate will rise.

Now consider what will happen to the interest rate when there is an increase in aggregate output (income) (Y). This increase in Y will cause the money demand curve to shift to the right. This is illustrated in Figure 25.5, where an increase in income from Y_0 to Y_1 has

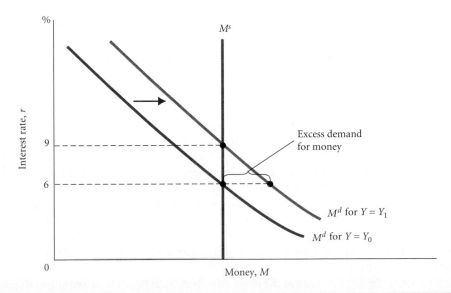

FIGURE 25.5 The Effect of an Increase in Income (Y) on the Interest Rate (r)

An increase in income from Y_0 to Y_1 shifts the M^d curve to the right. With a fixed supply of money, there is now an excess demand for money ($M^d > M^s$) at the initial interest rate of 6 percent. This causes the interest rate to rise. At an interest rate of 9 percent the money market is again in equilibrium with $M^s = M^d$, but at a higher interest rate than before the increase in income.

shifted the money demand curve from M_0^d to M_1^d. At the initial interest rate of 6 percent, there is now excess demand for money, and the interest rate rises from 6 percent to 9 percent.

> The equilibrium level of the interest rate is not determined exclusively in the money market. Changes in aggregate output (income) (Y), which take place in the goods market, shift the money demand curve and cause changes in the interest rate. With a given quantity of money supplied, higher levels of Y will lead to higher equilibrium levels of r. Lower levels of Y will lead to lower equilibrium levels of r, as represented in the following symbols:
>
> $$Y \uparrow \rightarrow M^d \uparrow \rightarrow r \uparrow$$
> $$Y \downarrow \rightarrow M^d \downarrow \rightarrow r \downarrow$$

COMBINING THE GOODS MARKET AND THE MONEY MARKET

Now that we are aware of the links between the goods market and the money market, we can examine the two markets simultaneously. To see how the two markets interact, it will be convenient to consider the effects of changes in fiscal and monetary policy on the economy. We want to examine what happens to the equilibrium levels of aggregate output (income) (Y) and the interest rate (r) when certain key variables—notably government spending (G), net taxes (T), and money supply (M^s)—increase or decrease.

EXPANSIONARY POLICY EFFECTS

expansionary fiscal policy An increase in government spending or a reduction in net taxes aimed at increasing aggregate output (income) (Y).

expansionary monetary policy An increase in the money supply aimed at increasing aggregate output (income) (Y).

Any government policy aimed at stimulating aggregate output (income) (Y) is said to be expansionary. An **expansionary fiscal policy** is an increase in government spending (G) or a reduction in net taxes (T) aimed at increasing aggregate output (income) (Y). An **expansionary monetary policy** is an increase in the money supply aimed at increasing aggregate output (income) (Y).

Expansionary Fiscal Policy: An Increase in Government Purchases (G) or a Decrease in Net Taxes (T)
As you know from Chapter 9, government purchases (G) and net taxes (T) are the two tools of government fiscal policy. The government can stimulate the economy—that is, it can increase aggregate output (income) (Y)—either by *increasing* government purchases or by *reducing* net taxes. Though the impact of a tax cut is somewhat smaller than the impact of an increase in G, both have a multiplier effect on the equilibrium level of Y.

Consider an increase in government purchases (G) of $10 billion. This increase in expenditure causes firms' inventories to be smaller than planned. Unplanned inventory reductions stimulate production, and firms increase output (Y). However, because added output means added income, some of which is subsequently spent, consumption spending (C) also increases. Again, inventories will be smaller than planned and output will rise even further. The final equilibrium level of output is higher by a multiple of the initial increase in government purchases.

This multiplier story is incomplete, however. Until this chapter, we have assumed that planned investment (I) is fixed at a certain level, but we now know that planned investment depends on the interest rate. We can now discuss what happens to the multiplier when investment varies because we now have an understanding of the money market, in which the interest rate is determined.

Return to our multiplier story at the point that firms first begin to raise output in response to an increase in government purchases. As aggregate output (income) (Y) increases, an impact is felt in the money market—the increase in income (Y) increases the demand for money (M^d). (For the moment, assume the Fed holds the quantity of money supplied [M^s] constant.) The resulting disequilibrium, with the quantity of money demanded greater than the quantity of money supplied, causes the interest rate to rise. The increase in G increases both Y and r.

The increase in r has a side effect—a higher interest rate causes planned investment spending (I) to decline. Because planned investment spending is a component of planned aggregate expenditure ($C + I + G$), the decrease in I works against the increase in G. An increase in government spending (G) increases planned aggregate expenditure and increases aggregate output, but a decrease in planned investment reduces planned aggregate expenditure and *decreases* aggregate output.

This tendency for increases in government spending to cause reductions in private investment spending is called the **crowding-out effect**. Without any expansion in the money supply to accommodate the rise in income and increased money demand, planned investment spending is partially crowded out by the higher interest rate. The extra spending created by the rise in government purchases is somewhat offset by the fall in planned investment spending. Income still rises, but the multiplier effect of the rise in G is lessened because of the higher interest rate's negative effect on planned investment.

This crowding-out effect is illustrated graphically in Figure 25.6. An increase in government purchases from G_0 to G_1 shifts the planned aggregate expenditure curve ($C + I_0 + G_0$) upward. The increase in (Y) from Y_0 to Y_1 causes the demand for money to rise, which results in a disequilibrium in the money market. The excess demand for money raises the interest rate, causing I to decrease from I_0 to I_1. The fall in I pulls the planned aggregate expenditure curve back down, which lowers the equilibrium level of income to Y^*. (Remember that equilibrium is achieved when $Y = AE$.)

Note that the size of the crowding-out effect and the ultimate size of the government spending multiplier depend on several things. First, we assumed the Fed did not change the quantity of money supplied. If we were to assume instead that the Fed expanded the quantity of money to accommodate the increase in G, the multiplier would be larger. In this case, the higher demand for money would be satisfied with a higher quantity of money supplied, and the interest rate would not rise. Without a higher interest rate, there would be no crowding out.

Second, the crowding-out effect depends on the **sensitivity** or **insensitivity of planned investment** spending to changes in the interest rate. Crowding out occurs because a higher interest rate reduces planned investment spending. Investment depends on factors other than the interest rate, however, and investment may at times be quite insensitive to changes

crowding-out effect The tendency for increases in government spending to cause reductions in private investment spending.

interest sensitivity or insensitivity of planned investment The responsiveness of planned investment spending to changes in the interest rate. *Interest sensitivity* means that planned investment spending changes a great deal in response to changes in the interest rate; *interest insensitivity* means little or no change in planned investment as a result of changes in the interest rate.

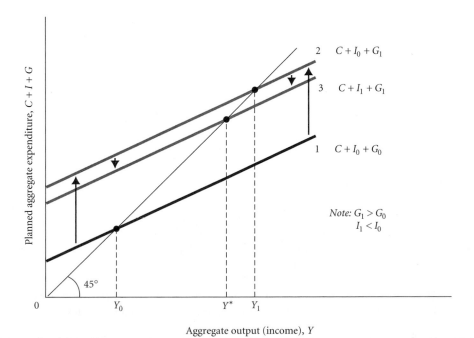

FIGURE 25.6 The Crowding-Out Effect

An increase in government spending G from G_0 to G_1 shifts the planned aggregate expenditure schedule from 1 to 2. The crowding-out effect of the decrease in planned investment (brought about by the increased interest rate) then shifts the planned aggregate expenditure schedule from 2 to 3.

in the interest rate. If planned investment does not fall when the interest rate rises, there is no crowding-out effect. These effects are summarized next.

Effects of an expansionary fiscal policy:

$$G\uparrow \rightarrow Y\uparrow \rightarrow M^d\uparrow \rightarrow r\uparrow \rightarrow I\downarrow$$

Y increases less than if r did not increase

Exactly the same reasoning holds for changes in net taxes. The ultimate effect of a tax cut on the equilibrium level of output depends on how the money market reacts. The expansion of Y that a tax cut brings about will lead to an increase in the interest rate and thus a decrease in planned investment spending. The ultimate increase in Y will therefore be less than it would be if the interest rate did not rise.

Expansionary Monetary Policy: An Increase in the Money Supply   Now let us consider what will happen when the Fed decides to increase the supply of money through open market operations. At first, open market operations inject new reserves into the system and expand the quantity of money supplied (the money supply curve shifts to the right). Because the quantity of money supplied is now greater than the amount households want to hold, the equilibrium rate of interest falls. Planned investment spending (which is a component of planned aggregate expenditure) increases when the interest rate falls.

Increased planned investment spending means planned aggregate expenditure is now greater than aggregate output. Firms experience unplanned decreases in inventories, and they raise output (Y). An increase in the money supply decreases the interest rate and increases Y. However, the higher level of Y increases the demand for money (the demand for money curve shifts to the right), and this keeps the interest rate from falling as far as it otherwise would.

If you review the sequence of events that follows the monetary expansion, you can see the links between the injection of reserves by the Fed into the economy and the increase in output. First, the increase in the quantity of money supplied pushes down the interest rate. Second, the lower interest rate causes planned investment spending to rise. Third, the increased planned investment spending means higher planned aggregate expenditure, which means increased output as firms react to unplanned decreases in inventories. Fourth, the increase in output (income) leads to an increase in the demand for money (the demand for money curve shifts to the right), which means the interest rate decreases less than it would have if the demand for money had not increased.

Effects of an expansionary monetary policy:

$$M^s\uparrow \rightarrow r\downarrow \rightarrow I\uparrow \rightarrow Y\uparrow \rightarrow M^d\uparrow$$

r decreases less than if M^d did not increase

The power of monetary policy to affect the goods market depends on how much of a reaction occurs at each link in this chain. Perhaps the most critical link is the link between r and I. Monetary policy can be effective *only* if I reacts to changes in r. If firms sharply increase the number of investment projects undertaken when the interest rate falls, expansionary monetary policy works well at stimulating the economy. If, however, firms are reluctant to invest even at a low interest rate, expansionary monetary policy will have limited success. In other words, the effectiveness of monetary policy depends on the slope of the investment function. If it is nearly vertical, indicating very little responsiveness of investment to the interest rate, the middle link in this chain is weak, rendering monetary policy ineffective.

Expansionary Policy in Action: The Recessions of 1974–1975, 1980–1982, 1990–1991, and 2001   The United States has experienced four recessions since 1970. In 1974–1975 and 1980–1982 the government engaged in tax cuts that had the effect of stimulating consumer spending (C). Because C is a component of planned aggregate expenditure, these tax cuts had the effect of increasing aggregate output (income) (Y).

Interest Rates and Housing

ONE PART OF INVESTMENT SPENDING (*I*) that is quite sensitive to interest rates is investment in housing. Home purchases are generally financed with a mortgage. A mortgage is a long-term loan. Lower mortgage rates reduce the cost of buying and owning a home.

In 2000, the interest rate on a 30-year fixed-rate mortgage was just

under 8.5 percent. A year later it fell below 7 percent and by March 2003 it was below 6 percent, where it stayed until 2005. Without question, these low rates contributed to the strength of the housing market. Housing starts stayed over 2 million per year through most of the period, sales of existing homes rose to over 7 million, and house prices boomed. Clearly, low interest rates stimulate the housing sector. But when interest rates crept upward in 2005, the demand for housing began to fall. The following *Wall Street Journal* article shows cracks beginning to appear even in New York City's high end market.

Prices Fall in Manhattan as Housing Market Cools
By DANIELLE REED
Dow Jones Newswires
October 4, 2005

NEW YORK—Housing market watchers can exhale. Prices in some of the nation's hottest markets are at least leveling off, and in some cases even coming down.

In New York, a report prepared by appraisal company Miller Samuel Inc. on behalf of real estate firm Prudential Douglas Elliman released Tuesday showed that average Manhattan apartment prices fell nearly 13% in the third quarter 2005 to $1.15 million from $1.32 million in the second quarter.

Housing stock is also staying on the market longer, the report showed, with the number of days it takes to sell an apartment increasing a month to 133 days from 102 days.

The report was confirmed by other research, including reports from two other real estate firms, Brown Harris Stevens and Halstead Property. These showed that average apartment prices in Manhattan were down 11% in the third quarter for co-ops to $1.04 million from $1.17 million in the second quarter, and down 10% for condominiums to $1.28 million from $1.42 million in the previous quarter.

Source: Danielle Reed, "Prices Fall in Manhattan as Housing Market Cools," Dow Jones News-wires, October 4, 2005. Reproduced with permission of DOW JONES & CO INC in the format Textbook via Copyright Clearance Center.

Consider the recession of 1974–1975. The Tax Reduction Act of 1975 resulted in a 1974 tax rebate of $8 billion that was paid to consumers in the second quarter of 1975. This rebate and other tax reductions led to increased consumer spending, which contributed to the economic recovery that began soon after the new tax laws went into effect.

But what about the crowding-out effect? Did the 1975 expansionary fiscal policy drive up interest rates and crowd out private spending? In this case, no. At the same time that Congress was cutting taxes to stimulate spending, the Fed was trying to stimulate the economy by expanding the money supply. Even though the increased output during the expansion caused the *demand* for money to rise, the Fed was simultaneously expanding the *supply* of money, and interest rates did not change very much. This situation is illustrated in Figure 25.7.

A similar sequence of events took place during the recession of 1980–1982. On the recommendation of President Reagan, Congress passed a huge tax cut during the summer of 1981. Like the 1975 tax cut, the 1981 tax cut led to an increase in consumer spending, which helped lift the economy out of the recession.

551

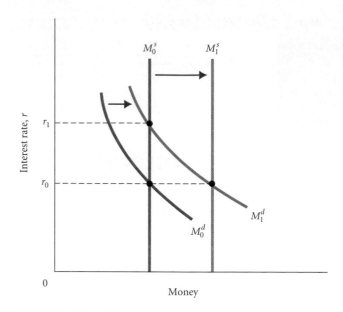

FIGURE 25.7 Fed Accommodation of an Expansionary Fiscal Policy

An expansionary fiscal policy, such as the 1975 tax cut, will increase aggregate output (income) and shift the money demand curve to the right, from M_0^d to M_1^d. If the money supply were unchanged, the interest rate would rise from r_0 to r_1 and planned investment would be negatively affected. If, however, the Fed were to "accommodate" the fiscal expansion by increasing the money supply from M_0^s to M_1^s, the interest rate would not rise.

Recovery from the 1980–1982 recession was also helped along by the Fed, which began to increase the supply of money sharply in the spring of 1982. So, even though output and income were expanding by late 1982, thereby increasing the demand for money, interest rates actually *declined* because the supply of money was expanding at the same time. There was no crowding-out effect.

The recession of 1990–1991 began soon after Iraq's invasion of Kuwait in the late summer of 1990. The recession was short-lived and shallow compared with the two previous recessions. Real GDP began to rise in the second quarter of 1991, but this recovery became known as the "jobless recovery." Because productivity increased and large firms continued to trim payrolls even as output was expanding, the unemployment rate stayed high right into the presidential election of 1992.

The first President Bush debated calling for a tax cut to stimulate the economy, but concern with the already large government deficit and pressure from the Fed convinced him to wait. The Fed did push interest rates lower in an effort to get the economy moving. Even so, little response was evident by election time.

President Clinton called for some modest fiscal stimulus when he took office, but the Congress balked. Then, in the summer of 1993, Congress passed the Clinton deficit reduction package, which *increased* taxes and *reduced* government spending. In the meantime, monetary policy continued to be expansionary. Eventually, interest rates hit 30-year lows. For much of 1993, the 3-month T-bill rate was under 3 percent for the first time since 1962, and the 30-year bond rate fell below 6 percent for the first time since the government began selling 30-year-bonds.

In late 1994, the slow-growth recovery ended and a real expansion began, fueled in large part by the stock market boom that began in 1995. The boom ended in 2000 and the U.S. economy went into a recession in 2001. Monetary policy responded rapidly to the recession. In 2001, the Fed lowered the short-term interest rate by about 4 percentage points. This is perhaps the most expansionary monetary policy action in U.S. history. The recession was fairly mild, and by the fourth quarter of 2001 the economy was expanding again. The recovery was not, however, very strong, and the Fed kept the short-term interest rate low in 2002, 2003, and 2004. In addition, fiscal policy was quite expansive in 2001–2004, as is discussed in Chapter 28.

CONTRACTIONARY POLICY EFFECTS

Any government policy that is aimed at reducing aggregate output (income) (*Y*) is said to be *contractionary*. Where expansionary policy is used to boost the economy, contractionary policy is used to slow the economy.

Considering that one of the four major economic goals is economic growth (Chapter 1), why would the government adopt policies designed to reduce aggregate spending? As we will see in the next two chapters, one way to fight inflation is to reduce aggregate spending. When the inflation rate is high, the government may feel compelled to use its powers to contract the economy. Before we discuss the contractionary policies that the government has undertaken in recent years, we need to discuss how contractionary fiscal and monetary policy work.

Contractionary Fiscal Policy: A Decrease in Government Spending (G) or an Increase in Net Taxes (T)
A **contractionary fiscal policy** is a decrease in government spending (*G*) or an increase in net taxes (*T*) aimed at decreasing aggregate output (income) (*Y*). The effects of this policy are the opposite of the effects of an expansionary fiscal policy.

A decrease in government purchases or an increase in net taxes leads to a decrease in aggregate output (income) (*Y*), a decrease in the demand for money (*M^d*), and a decrease in the interest rate (*r*). The decrease in *Y* that accompanies a contractionary fiscal policy is less than it would be if we did not take the money market into account because the decrease in *r* also causes planned investment (*I*) to *increase*. This increase in *I* offsets some of the decrease in planned aggregate expenditure brought about by the decrease in *G*. (This also means the multiplier effect is smaller than it would be if we did not take the money market into account.) The effects of a decrease in *G*, or an increase in *T*, can be represented as shown.

contractionary fiscal policy A decrease in government spending or an increase in net taxes aimed at decreasing aggregate output (income) (*Y*).

Effects of a contractionary fiscal policy:

$$G\downarrow \text{ or } T\uparrow \rightarrow Y\downarrow \rightarrow M^d\downarrow \rightarrow r\downarrow \rightarrow I\uparrow$$
$$\hookrightarrow Y \text{ decreases less than if } r \text{ did not decrease}$$

Contractionary Monetary Policy: A Decrease in the Money Supply
A **contractionary monetary policy** is a decrease in the money supply aimed at decreasing aggregate output (income) (*Y*). As you recall, the level of planned investment spending is a negative function of the interest rate: The higher the interest rate, the less planned investment there will be. The less planned investment there is, the lower planned aggregate expenditure will be, and the lower the equilibrium level of output (income) (*Y*) will be. The lower equilibrium income results in a decrease in the demand for money, which means that the increase in the interest rate will be less than it would be if we did not take the goods market into account.

contractionary monetary policy A decrease in the money supply aimed at decreasing aggregate output (income) (*Y*).

Effects of a contractionary monetary policy:

$$M^s\downarrow \rightarrow r\uparrow \rightarrow I\downarrow \rightarrow Y\downarrow \rightarrow M^d\downarrow$$
$$\hookrightarrow r \text{ increases less than if } M^d \text{ did not decrease}$$

Contractionary Policy in Action: 1973–1974 and 1979–1981
The Fed pursued strong contractionary policies twice in the 1970s and 1980s: first in 1973–1974 and again in 1979–1981. In 1974, short-term rates exceeded 12 percent, and in 1981, some short-term rates exceeded 20 percent. These high interest rates had a negative effect on planned

aggregate expenditure and contributed to the recessions that followed. The Fed's purpose in following a tight monetary policy was to slow the inflation rate. (We will see in the next chapter why a contractionary policy may bring the inflation rate down.)

THE MACROECONOMIC POLICY MIX

Although we have been treating fiscal and monetary policy separately, it should be clear that fiscal and monetary policy can be used simultaneously. For example, both government purchases (G) and the money supply (M^s) can be increased at the same time. We have seen that an increase in G by itself raises both Y and r, while an increase in M^s by itself raises Y but lowers r. Therefore, if the government wanted to increase Y without changing r, it could do so by increasing both G and M^s by the appropriate amounts.

policy mix The combination of monetary and fiscal policies in use at a given time.

Policy mix refers to the combination of monetary and fiscal policies in use at a given time. A policy mix that consists of a decrease in government spending and an increase in the money supply would favor investment spending over government spending. The reason is that both the increased money supply and the fall in government purchases would cause the interest rate to fall, which would lead to an increase in planned investment. The opposite is true for a mix that consists of an expansionary fiscal policy and a contractionary monetary policy. This mix favors government spending over investment spending. Such a policy will have the effect of increasing government spending and reducing the money supply. Tight money and expanded government spending would drive the interest rate up and planned investment down.

There is no rule about what constitutes the "best" policy mix or the "best" composition of output. On this, as on many other issues, economists (and others) disagree. In part, someone's preference for a certain composition of output—say, one weighted heavily toward private spending with relatively little government spending—depends on how that person stands on such issues as the proper role of government in the economy.

Table 25.1 summarizes the effects of various combinations of policies on several important macroeconomic variables. If you can explain the reasoning underlying each of the effects shown in the table, you can be satisfied that you have a good understanding of the links between the goods market and the money market.

OTHER DETERMINANTS OF PLANNED INVESTMENT

We have assumed in this chapter that planned investment depends only on the interest rate. In reality, planned investment depends on other factors. We will discuss these factors more in Chapter 30, but provide a brief description here.

Expectations and Animal Spirits   Firms' expectations about their future sales play an important role in their investment decisions. When a firm invests, it adds to its capital stock, and capital is used in the production process. If a firm expects that its sales will

TABLE 25.1 The Effects of the Macroeconomic Policy Mix

		FISCAL POLICY	
		Expansionary ($\uparrow G$ or $\downarrow T$)	Contractionary ($\downarrow G$ or $\uparrow T$)
Monetary Policy	Expansionary ($\uparrow M^s$)	$Y\uparrow, r?, I?, C\uparrow$	$Y?, r\downarrow, I\uparrow, C?$
	Contractionary ($\downarrow M^s$)	$Y?, r\uparrow, I\downarrow, C?$	$Y\downarrow, r?, I?, C\downarrow$

Key:
$\uparrow$: Variable increases.
$\downarrow$: Variable decreases.
?: Forces push the variable in different directions. Without additional information, we cannot specify which way the variable moves.

increase in the future, it may begin to build up its capital stock—that is, to invest—now so that it will be able to produce more in the future to meet the increased level of sales. The optimism or pessimism of entrepreneurs about the future course of the economy can have an important effect on current planned investment. Keynes used the phrase *animal spirits* to describe the feelings of entrepreneurs, and he argued that these feelings affect investment decisions.

Capital Utilization Rates   The degree of utilization of a firm's capital stock is also likely to affect planned investment. If the demand for a firm's output has been decreasing and the firm has been lowering output in response to this decline, the firm may have a low rate of capital utilization. It can be costly to get rid of capital quickly once it is in place, and firms sometimes respond to a fall in output by keeping the capital in place but utilizing it less—for example, by running machines fewer hours per day or at slower speeds. Firms tend to invest less in new capital when their capital utilization rates are low than when they are high.

Relative Labor and Capital Costs   The cost of capital (of which the interest rate is the main component) *relative* to the cost of labor can affect planned investment. If labor is expensive relative to capital (high wage rates), firms tend to substitute away from labor toward capital. They aim to hold more capital relative to labor when wage rates are high than when they are low.

The determinants of planned investment are

- The interest rate
- Expectations of future sales
- Capital utilization rates
- Relative capital and labor costs

LOOKING AHEAD: THE PRICE LEVEL

Our discussion of aggregate output (income) and the interest rate in the goods market and the money market is now complete. You should now have a good understanding of how the two markets work together. However, we have not yet discussed the price level in any detail.

   We cannot begin to understand the economic events of the last three decades without an understanding of the aggregate price level. The two periods of rapid increases in the price level, 1974–1975 and 1979–1981, had dramatic effects on the economy. What causes the price level to change? Are there policies that might prevent large changes in the price level or stop them once they have started? Before we can answer such questions, we must understand the factors that affect the overall price level. This is the task of the next chapter. Up to this point we have taken the price level as fixed. Now it is time to relax this assumption.

SUMMARY

1. The *goods market* and the *money market* do not operate independently. Events in the money market have considerable effects on the goods market, and events in the goods market have considerable effects on the money market.

THE LINKS BETWEEN THE GOODS MARKET AND THE MONEY MARKET

2. There are two important links between the goods market and the money market: The level of real output (income) (Y), which is determined in the goods market, determines the volume of transactions each period and thus affects the demand for money in the money market; and the interest

rate (r), which is determined in the money market, affects the level of planned investment spending in the goods market.

3. There is a negative relationship between planned investment and the interest rate because the interest rate determines the cost of investment projects. When the interest rate rises, planned investment will decrease; when the interest rate falls, planned investment will increase.

4. For every value of the interest rate, there is a different level of planned investment spending and a different equilibrium level of output. The final level of equilibrium output depends on what the interest rate turns out to be, which depends on events in the money market.

5. For a given quantity of money supplied, the interest rate depends on the demand for money. Money demand depends on the level of output (income). With a given money supply, increases and decreases in *Y* will affect money demand, which will affect the equilibrium interest rate.

COMBINING THE GOODS MARKET AND THE MONEY MARKET

6. An *expansionary fiscal policy* is an increase in government spending (*G*) or a reduction in net taxes (*T*) aimed at increasing aggregate output (income) (*Y*). An expansionary fiscal policy based on increases in government spending tends to lead to a *crowding-out effect*: Because increased government expenditures mean more transactions in the economy and thus an increased demand for money, the interest rate will rise. The decrease in planned investment spending that accompanies the higher interest rate will then partially offset the increase in aggregate expenditures brought about by the increase in *G*.

7. The size of the crowding-out effect, affecting the size of the government spending multiplier, depends on two things: the assumption that the Fed does not change the quantity of money supplied and the *sensitivity or insensitivity of planned investment* to changes in the interest rate.

8. An *expansionary monetary policy* is an increase in the money supply aimed at increasing aggregate output (income) (*Y*). An increase in the money supply leads to a lower interest rate, increased planned investment, increased planned aggregate expenditure, and ultimately a higher equilibrium level of aggregate output (income) (*Y*). Expansionary policies have been used to lift the economy out of recessions.

9. A *contractionary fiscal policy* is a decrease in government spending or an increase in net taxes aimed at decreasing aggregate output (income) (*Y*). A decrease in government spending or an increase in net taxes leads to a decrease in aggregate output (income) (*Y*), a decrease in the demand for money, and a decrease in the interest rate. However, the decrease in *Y* is somewhat offset by the additional planned investment resulting from the lower interest rate.

10. A *contractionary monetary policy* is a decrease in the money supply aimed at decreasing aggregate output (income) (*Y*). The higher interest rate brought about by the reduced money supply causes a decrease in planned investment spending and a lower level of equilibrium output. However, the lower equilibrium level of output brings about a decrease in the demand for money, which means the increase in the interest rate will be less than it would be if we did not take the goods market into account. Contractionary policies have been used to fight inflation.

11. The *policy mix* is the combination of monetary and fiscal policies in use at a given time. There is no rule about what constitutes the best policy mix or the best composition of output. In part, one's preference for a certain composition of output depends on one's stance concerning such issues as the proper role of government in the economy.

OTHER DETERMINANTS OF PLANNED INVESTMENT

12. In addition to the interest rate, the level of planned investment in the economy also depends on expectations and animal spirits, capital utilization rates, and relative capital and labor costs.

REVIEW TERMS AND CONCEPTS

contractionary fiscal policy, 553

contractionary monetary policy, 553

crowding-out effect, 549

expansionary fiscal policy, 548

expansionary monetary policy, 548

goods market, 543

interest sensitivity or insensitivity of planned investment, 549

money market, 543

policy mix, 554

PROBLEM SET

1. On June 5, 2003, the European Central Bank acted to decrease the short-term interest rate in Europe by half a percentage point, to 2 percent. The bank's president at the time, Willem Duisenberg, suggested that the bank could reduce rates further in the future. The rate cut was made because European countries were growing very slowly or were in recession. What effect did the bank hope the action would have on the economy? Be specific. What was the hoped-for result on *C*, *I*, and *Y*?

2. The News Analysis box on page 551 describes the beginning of a slowdown in the housing sector in October 2005. In part, this sluggishness was in response to the tightening of the Federal Reserve's monetary policy that began in 2004. Go to **www.ofheo.gov** and click on House Price Indexes. Look at the pattern of house prices from 2000 through the present. Was

there a noticeable softening or decline in some cities that began in 2005? Go to **www.bea.gov** and click on National Income and Product Accounts. Can you see a decline or change in the pattern of "residential fixed investment"? What does this seem to say about the impact of interest rates on planned investment spending?

3. During the third quarter of 1997, Japanese GDP was falling at an annual rate of over 11 percent. Many blame the big increase in Japan's taxes in the spring of 1997, which was designed to balance the budget. Explain how an increase in taxes with the economy growing slowly could precipitate a recession; do not skip steps in your answer. If you were head of the Japanese central bank, how would you respond? What impact would your policy have on the level of investment?

4. Some economists argue that the "animal spirits" of investors are so important in determining the level of investment in the economy that interest rates do not matter at all. Suppose that this were true—that investment in no way depends on interest rates.
   a. How would Figure 25.2 be different?
   b. What would happen to the level of planned aggregate expenditures if the interest rate changed?
   c. What would be different about the relative effectiveness of monetary and fiscal policy?

5. For each of the following, tell a story and predict the effects on the equilibrium levels of aggregate output (Y) and the interest rate (r):
   a. During 2005, the Federal Reserve was tightening monetary policy in an attempt to slow the economy. The Congress passed a substantial cut in the individual income tax at the same time.
   b. During the summer of 2003, the Congress passed and President George W. Bush signed the third tax cut in 3 years. Many of the tax cuts took effect in 2005. Assume the Fed holds M^s fixed.
   c. In 1993, the Congress and the president raised taxes. At the same time, the Fed was pursuing an expansionary monetary policy.
   d. In 2005, conditions in Iraq led to a sharp drop in consumer confidence and a drop in consumption. Assume the Fed holds the money supply constant.
   e. The Fed attempts to increase the money supply to stimulate the economy, but plants are operating at 65 percent of their capacities and businesses are pessimistic about the future.

6. Occasionally, the Federal Open Market Committee (FOMC) sets a policy designed to "track" the interest rate. This means that the FOMC is pursuing policies designed to keep the interest rate constant. If, in fact, the Fed were acting to counter any increases or decreases in the interest rate to keep it constant, what specific actions would you expect to see the Fed take if the following were to occur? (In answering, indicate the effects of each set of events on Y, C, S, I, M^s, M^d, and r.)
   a. There is an unexpected increase in investor confidence, leading to a sharp increase in orders for new plants and equipment.
   b. A major New York bank fails, causing a number of worried people (not trusting even the FDIC) to withdraw a substantial amount of cash from other banks and put it in their cookie jars.

7. Paranoia, the largest country in central Antarctica, receives word of an imminent penguin attack. The news causes expectations about the future to be shaken. As a consequence, there is a sharp decline in investment spending plans.
   a. Explain in detail the effects of such an event on the economy of Paranoia, assuming no response on the part of the central bank or the Treasury (M^s, T, and G all remain constant). Be sure to discuss the adjustments in the goods market and the money market.
   b. To counter the fall in investment, the king of Paranoia calls for a proposal to increase government spending. To finance the program, the chancellor of the exchequer has proposed three alternative options:
      (1) Finance the expenditures with an equal increase in taxes
      (2) Keep tax revenues constant and borrow the money from the public by issuing new government bonds
      (3) Keep taxes constant and finance the expenditures by printing new money

   Consider the three financing options and rank them from most expansionary to least expansionary. Explain your ranking.

8. Why might investment not respond positively to low interest rates during a recession? Why might investment not respond negatively to high interest rates during a boom?

APPENDIX

THE *IS-LM* DIAGRAM

There is a useful way of depicting graphically the determination of aggregate output (income) and the interest rate in the goods and money markets. Two curves are involved in this diagram, the *IS* curve and the *LM* curve. In this appendix, we will derive these two curves and use them to see how changes in government purchases (G) and the money supply (M^s) affect the equilibrium values of aggregate output (income) and the interest rate. The effects we describe here are the same as the effects we described in the main text; here we illustrate the effects graphically.

THE *IS* CURVE

We know that in the goods market there is an equilibrium level of aggregate output (income) (Y) for each value of the interest rate (r). For a given value of r, we can determine the equilibrium value of Y. The equilibrium value of Y falls when r rises and rises when r falls. There is thus a *negative* relationship between the equilibrium value of Y and r. The reason for this negative rela-

tionship is the negative relationship between planned investment and the interest rate. When the interest rate rises, planned investment (I) falls, and this decrease in I leads to a decrease in the equilibrium value of Y. The negative relationship between the equilibrium value of Y and r is shown in Figure 25A.1. This curve is called the **IS curve**.[1] Each point on the *IS* curve represents the equilibrium point in the goods market for the given interest rate.

We also know from our earlier analysis of the goods market that when government purchases (G) increase with a constant interest rate, the equilibrium value of Y increases. This means the *IS* curve shifts to the right when G increases. With the same value of r and a higher value of G, the equilibrium value of Y is larger; when G decreases, the *IS* curve shifts to the left.

---

[1]The letter *I* stands for investment, and the letter *S* stands for saving. *IS* refers to the fact that in equilibrium in the goods market, planned investment equals saving.

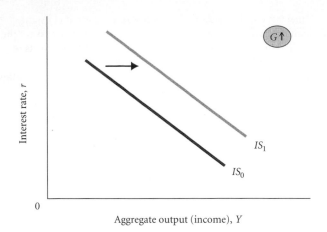

Each point on the *IS* curve corresponds to the equilibrium point in the goods market for the given interest rate. When government spending (G) increases, the *IS* curve shifts to the right, from IS_0 to IS_1.

THE *LM* CURVE

In the money market, there is an equilibrium value of the interest rate (r) for every value of aggregate output (income) (Y). The equilibrium value of r is determined at the point at which the quantity of money demanded equals the quantity of money supplied. For a given value of Y, we can determine the equilibrium value of r in the money market. We also know from Figure 25.5 that the equilibrium value of r rises when Y rises and falls when Y falls—a *positive* relationship between the equilibrium value of r and Y. The reason for this positive relationship is the positive relationship between the demand for money and Y. When Y increases, the demand for money increases because more money is demanded for the increased volume of transactions in the economy. An increase in the demand for money increases the equilibrium value of r —thus the positive relationship between the equilibrium value of r and Y.

The positive relationship between the equilibrium value of r and Y is shown in Figure 25A.2. This curve is called the **LM curve**.[2] Each point on the *LM* curve represents equilibrium in the money market for the given value of aggregate output (income).

We also know from our analysis of the money market that when the money supply (M^s) increases with a constant level of Y, the equilibrium value of r decreases. As Figure 25A.2 shows, this means the *LM* curve shifts to the right when M^s increases. With the same value of Y and a higher value of M^s, the equilibrium value of r is lower. When M^s decreases, the *LM* curve shifts to the left.

---

[2]The letter L stands for liquidity, a characteristic of money, and the letter M stands for money.

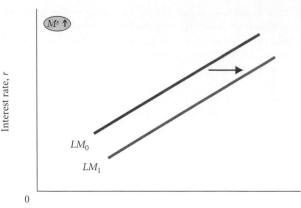

Each point on the *LM* curve corresponds to the equilibrium point in the money market for the given value of aggregate output (income). Money supply (M^s) increases shift the *LM* curve to the right, from LM_0 to LM_1.

THE *IS-LM* DIAGRAM

Figure 25A.3 shows the *IS* and *LM* curves together on one graph. The point at which the two curves intersect is the point at which equilibrium exists in *both* the goods market and the money market. There is equilibrium in the goods market because the point is on the *IS* curve, and there is equilibrium in the money market because the point is on the *LM* curve.

We now have only two tasks left. The first is to see how the equilibrium values of Y and r are affected by changes in G — fiscal policy. This is easy. We have just seen that an increase in G shifts the *IS* curve to the right. Thus, an increase in G leads to

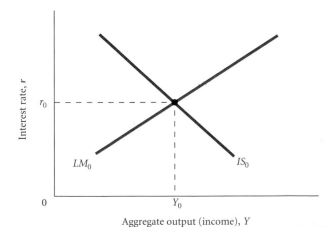

The point at which the *IS* and *LM* curves intersect corresponds to the point at which both the goods market and the money market are in equilibrium. The equilibrium values of aggregate output and the interest rate are Y_0 and r_0.

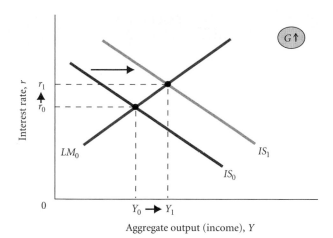

FIGURE 25A.4 An Increase in Government Purchases (G)

When G increases, the IS curve shifts to the right. This increases the equilibrium value of both Y and r.

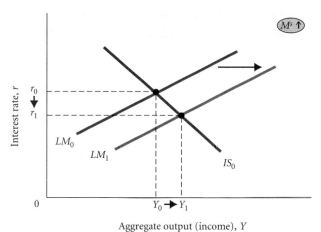

FIGURE 25A.5 An Increase in the Money Supply (M^s)

When M^s increases, the LM curve shifts to the right. This increases the equilibrium value of Y and decreases the equilibrium value of r.

higher equilibrium values of Y and r. This situation is illustrated in Figure 25A.4. Conversely, a decrease in G leads to lower equilibrium values of Y and r because the lower level of G causes the IS curve to shift to the left. (The effects are similar for changes in net taxes, T.)

Our second task is to see how the equilibrium values of Y and r are affected by changes in M^s—monetary policy. This is also easy. We have just seen that an increase in M^s shifts the LM curve to the right. Thus, an increase in M^s leads to a higher equilibrium value of Y and a lower equilibrium value of r. This is illustrated in Figure 25A.5. Conversely, a decrease in M^s leads to a lower equilibrium value of Y and a higher equilibrium value of r because a decreased money supply causes the LM curve to shift to the left.

The IS-LM diagram is a useful way of seeing the effects of changes in monetary and fiscal policies on equilibrium aggregate output (income) and the interest rate through shifts in the two curves. Always keep in mind the economic theory that lies *behind* the two curves. Do not memorize what curve shifts when; be able to understand and explain *why* the curves shift. This means always going back to the behavior of households and firms in the goods and money markets.

It is easy to use the IS-LM diagram to see how there can be a monetary and fiscal policy mix that leads to, say, an increase in aggregate output (income) but no increase in the interest rate. If both G and M^s increase, both curves shift to the right, and the shifts can be controlled in such a way as to bring about no change in the equilibrium value of the interest rate.

SUMMARY

An *IS curve* illustrates the negative relationship between the equilibrium value of aggregate output (income) (Y) and the interest rate in the goods market. An *LM curve* illustrates the positive relationship between the equilibrium value of the interest rate

and aggregate output (income) (Y) in the money market. The point at which the IS and LM curves intersect is the point at which equilibrium exists in both the goods market and the money market.

REVIEW TERMS AND CONCEPTS

IS curve A curve illustrating the negative relationship between the equilibrium value of aggregate output (income) (Y) and the interest rate in the goods market. 557

LM curve A curve illustrating the positive relationship between the equilibrium value of the interest rate and aggregate output (income) (Y) in the money market. 558

PROBLEM SET

1. Illustrate each of the following situations with *IS-LM* curves:
   a. An increase in G with the money supply held constant by the Fed
   b. An increase in G with the Fed changing M^s by enough to keep interest rates constant
   c. A decrease in G and an increase in T while the Fed expands M^s
   d. An increase in G and T while the Fed holds M^s constant during a period of inflation

Aggregate Demand, Aggregate Supply, and Inflation

26

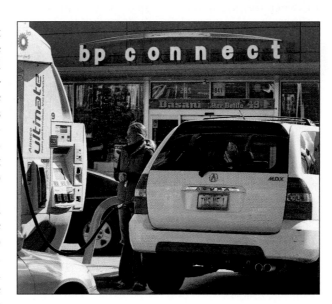

One of the most important issues in macroeconomics is the determination of the overall price level. Recall that inflation—an increase in the overall price level—is one of the key concerns of macroeconomists and government policy makers. Understanding the factors that affect the price level is essential to understanding macroeconomics.

In Chapter 20, we discussed how inflation is measured and the costs of inflation, but made no mention of the *causes* of inflation. For simplicity, our analysis in Chapters 21 through 25 took the price level as fixed. This allowed us to discuss the links between the goods market and the money market without the complication of a changing price level. Having considered how the two markets work, we are ready to take up flexible prices.

We begin by discussing the *aggregate demand curve* and the *aggregate supply curve*, introduced briefly in Chapter 18. We then put the two curves together and discuss how the equilibrium price level is determined in the economy. This analysis allows us to see how the price level affects the economy and how the economy affects the price level. Finally, we consider monetary and fiscal policy effects and the causes of inflation.

THE AGGREGATE DEMAND CURVE

The place to begin our exploration of the price level is the money market. (If you have forgotten the details of how the overall price level is calculated or what it means, review Chapters 19 and 20.) As we saw in Chapter 24, people's demand for money depends on income (Y), the interest rate (r), and the price level (P).

It is not hard to understand why the price level affects the demand for money. Suppose you plan to purchase one pound of chocolate, one bag of potato chips, and a Hostess Twinkie. If these items cost $7.00, $2.00, and $1.00, respectively, you would need $10.00 in cash or in your checking account to make your purchases. Suppose that the price of these goods doubles. To make the same purchases, you will need $20.00.

In general, the amount of money required to make a given number of transactions depends directly and proportionally on the average price of those transactions. As prices and wages rise, households will want to keep more money in their wallets and in their checking accounts, firms will need more in their cash drawers, and so forth. If prices and wages are rising at 6 percent per year, we can expect the demand for money to increase at about 6 percent per year, *ceteris paribus*.

> Money demand is a function of three variables: the interest rate (r), the level of real income (Y), and the price level (P). (Remember, Y is *real* output, or income. It measures the actual volume of output, without regard to changes in the price level.) Money demand will increase if the real level of output (income) increases, the price level increases, or the interest rate declines.

DERIVING THE AGGREGATE DEMAND CURVE

aggregate demand The total demand for goods and services in the economy.

Recall that **aggregate demand** is the total demand for goods and services in the economy. To derive the aggregate demand curve, we examine what happens to aggregate output (income) (Y) when the price level (P) changes. Does it increase, decrease, or remain constant when the price level increases? Our discussions of the goods market and the money market provide the tools to answer this question.

The aggregate demand curve is derived by assuming the fiscal policy variables [government purchases (G) and net taxes (T)] and the monetary policy variable (M^s) remain unchanged. In other words, the assumption is the government does not take any action to affect the economy in response to changes in the price level.

As you know, an increase in the price level increases the demand for money and shifts the money demand curve to the right, as illustrated in Figure 26.1(a). At the initial interest rate of 6 percent, an increase in the price level leads to an excess demand for money. Because of the higher price level, households and firms need to hold larger money balances than before. However, the quantity of money supplied remains the same. [Remember, we are assuming that the Federal Reserve (Fed) takes no action to change the money supply.] The money market is now out of equilibrium. Equilibrium is reestablished at a higher interest rate, 9 percent.

As indicated in Figure 26.1(b) with the interest rate now higher, fewer investment projects are desirable, and planned investment spending (I) falls from I_0 to I_1. Lower I means planned aggregate expenditure (AE) is lower, shown in Figure 26.1(c) as a downward shift of

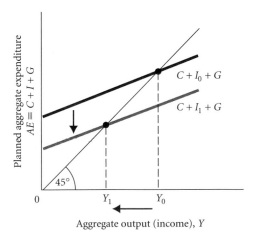

a. An increase in the price level increases the demand for money from M_0^d to M_1^d. With the supply of money unchanged, the interest rate increases from 6 percent to 9 percent.

b. The higher interest rate decreases planned investment from I_0 to I_1.

c. Decreased planned investment reduces planned aggregate expenditure and causes equilibrium output (income) to fall from Y_0 to Y_1.

FIGURE 26.1 The Impact of an Increase in the Price Level on the Economy—Assuming No Changes in *G*, *T*, and *M^s*

the *AE* curve. Lower *AE* means inventories are greater than planned, firms cut back on output, and *Y* falls from Y_0 to Y_1.

> An increase in the price level causes the level of aggregate output (income) to fall.

The situation is reversed when the price level declines. A lower price level causes money demand to fall, which leads to a lower interest rate. A lower interest rate stimulates planned investment spending, increasing planned aggregate expenditure, which leads to an increase in *Y*.

> A decrease in the price level causes the level of aggregate output (income) to rise.

This negative relationship between aggregate output (income) and the price level is called the **aggregate demand (AD) curve**, shown in Figure 26.2. Each point on the aggregate demand curve represents equilibrium in both the goods market *and* the money market. We have derived the *AD* curve by using the analysis we did in Chapter 25, in which the goods market and the money market were linked together. Therefore,

aggregate demand (AD) curve A curve that shows the negative relationship between aggregate output (income) and the price level. Each point on the *AD* curve is a point at which both the goods market and the money market are in equilibrium.

> Each pair of values of *P* and *Y* on the aggregate demand curve corresponds to a point at which both the goods market and the money market are in equilibrium.

THE AGGREGATE DEMAND CURVE: A WARNING

It is very important that you realize what the aggregate demand curve represents. As we pointed out in Chapter 18, the aggregate demand curve is much more complex than a simple individual or market demand curve. The *AD* curve is *not* a market demand curve, and it is *not* the sum of all market demand curves in the economy.

To understand why, recall the logic behind a simple downward-sloping household demand curve. A demand curve shows the quantity of output demanded (by an individual household or in a single market) at every possible price, *ceteris paribus*. In drawing a simple demand curve, we are assuming that *other prices* and *income* are fixed. From these assumptions, it follows that one reason the quantity demanded of a particular good falls when its price rises is that other prices do *not* rise. The good in question therefore becomes more expensive relative to other goods, and households respond by substituting other goods for

FIGURE 26.2 The Aggregate Demand (AD) Curve

At all points along the *AD* curve, both the goods market and the money market are in equilibrium.

the good whose price increased. In addition, if income does not rise when the price of a good does, real income falls. This may also lead to a lower quantity demanded of the good whose price has risen.

Things are different when the *overall price level* rises. When the overall price level rises many prices—including many wage rates (many people's income)—rise together. For this reason, we cannot use the *ceteris paribus* assumption to draw the *AD* curve. The logic that explains why a simple demand curve slopes downward fails to explain why the *AD* curve also has a negative slope.

> Aggregate demand falls when the price level increases because the higher price level causes the demand for money (M^d) to rise. With the money supply constant, the interest rate will rise to reestablish equilibrium in the money market. *It is the higher interest rate that causes aggregate output to fall.*

You do not need to understand anything about the money market to understand a simple individual or market demand curve. However, to understand what the *aggregate* demand curve represents, you must understand the interaction between the goods market and the money market. The *AD* curve in Figure 26.2 embodies everything we have learned about the goods market and the money market up to now.

> The *AD* curve is *not* the sum of all the market demand curves in the economy. It is *not* a market demand curve.

OTHER REASONS FOR A DOWNWARD-SLOPING AGGREGATE DEMAND CURVE

In addition to the effects of money supply and money demand on the interest rate, two other factors lie behind the downward slope of the *AD* curve. These are the consumption link and the real wealth effect.

The Consumption Link   We noted in Chapter 25 (and will discuss in detail in Chapter 30) that consumption (C) and planned investment (I) depend on the interest rate. Other things being equal, consumption expenditures tend to rise when the interest rate falls and to fall when the interest rate rises—just as planned investment does. This tendency is another link between the goods market and the money market. If something happens to change the interest rate in the money market, both consumption and planned investment are affected in the goods market.

The *consumption* link provides another reason for the *AD* curve's downward slope. An increase in the price level increases the demand for money, which leads to an increase in the interest rate, which leads to a decrease in consumption (as well as planned investment), which leads to a decrease in aggregate output (income). The initial decrease in consumption (brought about by the increase in the interest rate) contributes to the overall decrease in output.

> Planned investment does not bear all the burden of providing the link from a higher interest rate to a lower level of aggregate output. Decreased consumption brought about by a higher interest rate also contributes to this effect.

The Real Wealth Effect   We also noted in Chapter 21 (and will discuss in detail in Chapter 30) that consumption depends on wealth. Other things being equal, the more wealth households have, the more they consume. Wealth includes holdings of money, shares of stock, bonds, and housing, among other things. If household wealth decreases, the result will be less consumption now and in the future.

The price level has an effect on some kinds of wealth. Suppose you are holding $1,000 in a checking account or in a money market fund and the price level rises by 10 percent. Your holding is now worth 10 percent less because the prices of the goods that you could buy with your $1,000 have all increased by 10 percent. The purchasing power (or "real value") of your holding has decreased by 10 percent.

An increase in the price level may also lower the real value of stocks and housing, although whether it does depends on what happens to stock prices and housing prices when the overall price level rises. If stock prices and housing prices rise by the same percentage as the overall price level, the real value of stocks and housing will remain unchanged. The point is:

> An increase in the price level lowers the real value of *some* types of wealth.

The fact that the price level lowers the real value of wealth provides another reason for the downward slope of the *AD* curve. An increase in the price level lowers the real value of wealth. This leads to a decrease in consumption, which leads to a decrease in aggregate output (income). So, there is a negative relationship between the price level and output through this **real wealth effect** or **real balance effect**.

real wealth, or real balance, effect The change in consumption brought about by a change in real wealth that results from a change in the price level.

AGGREGATE EXPENDITURE AND AGGREGATE DEMAND

Throughout our discussion of macroeconomics so far, we have referred to the total planned spending by households (C), firms (I), and the government (G) as planned aggregate expenditure. At equilibrium, planned aggregate expenditure ($AE \equiv C + I + G$) and aggregate output (Y) are equal:

$$\text{equilibrium condition: } C + I + G = Y$$

How does planned aggregate expenditure relate to aggregate demand?

> At every point along the aggregate demand curve, the aggregate quantity demanded is exactly equal to planned aggregate expenditure, $C + I + G$.

You can see this in Figures 26.1 and 26.2. When the price level rises, it is planned aggregate expenditure that decreases, moving us up the aggregate demand curve.

However, the aggregate demand curve represents more than just planned aggregate expenditure. Each point on the *AD* curve represents the *particular* level of planned aggregate expenditure that is consistent with equilibrium in the goods market and money market at the given price. Notice that the variable on the horizontal axis of the aggregate demand curve in Figure 26.2 is Y. At every point along the *AD* curve, $Y = C + I + G$.

SHIFTS OF THE AGGREGATE DEMAND CURVE

The aggregate demand curve in Figure 26.2 is based on the assumption that the government policy variables G, T, and M^s are fixed. If any of these variables changes, the aggregate demand curve will shift.

Consider an increase in the quantity of money supplied. If the quantity of money is expanded at any given price level, the interest rate will fall, causing planned investment spending (and planned aggregate expenditure) to rise. The result is an increase in output at the given price level. As Figure 26.3 shows,

> An increase in the quantity of money supplied at a given price level shifts the aggregate demand curve to the right.

An increase in government purchases or a decrease in net taxes also increases aggregate output (income) at each possible price level, even though some of the increase will be crowded out if the money supply is held constant. (If you are unsure of what crowding-out is, review Chapter 25.) An increase in government purchases directly increases planned aggregate expenditure, which leads to an increase in output. A decrease in net taxes results in

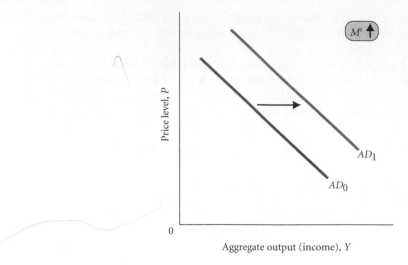

FIGURE 26.3 The Effect of an Increase in Money Supply on the *AD* Curve

An increase in the money supply (M^s) causes the aggregate demand curve to shift to the right, from AD_0 to AD_1. This shift occurs because the increase in M^s lowers the interest rate, which increases planned investment (and thus planned aggregate expenditure). The final result is an increase in output at each possible price level.

a rise in consumption, which increases planned aggregate expenditure, which also leads to an increase in output. As Figure 26.4 shows,

> An increase in government purchases or a decrease in net taxes shifts the aggregate demand curve to the right.

The same kind of reasoning applies to decreases in the quantity of money supplied, decreases in government purchases, and increases in net taxes. All of these shift the aggregate demand curve to the left.

Figure 26.5 summarizes the ways the aggregate demand curve shifts in response to changes in M^s, G, and T. To test your understanding of the AD curve, go through the figure

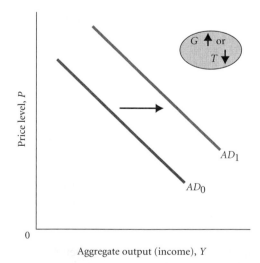

FIGURE 26.4 The Effect of an Increase in Government Purchases or a Decrease in Net Taxes on the *AD* Curve

An increase in government purchases (G) or a decrease in net taxes (T) causes the aggregate demand curve to shift to the right, from AD_0 to AD_1. The increase in G increases planned aggregate expenditure, which leads to an increase in output at each possible price level. A decrease in T causes consumption to rise. The higher consumption then increases planned aggregate expenditure, which leads to an increase in output at each possible price level.

Expansionary monetary policy	Contractionary monetary policy
$M^s \uparrow \rightarrow AD$ curve shifts to the right	$M^s \downarrow \rightarrow AD$ curve shifts to the left
Expansionary fiscal policy	**Contractionary fiscal policy**
$G \uparrow \rightarrow AD$ curve shifts to the right	$G \downarrow \rightarrow AD$ curve shifts to the left
$T \downarrow \rightarrow AD$ curve shifts to the right	$T \uparrow \rightarrow AD$ curve shifts to the left

FIGURE 26.5 Factors That Shift the Aggregate Demand Curve

piece by piece and explain the necessary steps for each of its components to create the shift in aggregate demand.

THE AGGREGATE SUPPLY CURVE

Aggregate supply is the total supply of goods and services in an economy. Although there is little disagreement among economists about the logic behind the aggregate demand curve, there is a great deal of disagreement about the logic behind the aggregate supply curve. There is also disagreement about its shape.

aggregate supply The total supply of all goods and services in an economy.

THE AGGREGATE SUPPLY CURVE: A WARNING

The **aggregate supply (AS) curve** shows the relationship between the aggregate quantity of output supplied by all the firms in an economy and the overall price level. To understand the aggregate supply curve, we need to understand something about the behavior of the individual firms that make up the economy.

aggregate supply (AS) curve A graph that shows the relationship between the aggregate quantity of output supplied by all firms in an economy and the overall price level.

It may seem logical to derive the aggregate supply curve by adding together the supply curves of all the individual firms in the economy. However, the logic behind the relationship between the overall price level in the economy and the level of aggregate output (income)—that is, the *AS* curve—is very different from the logic behind an individual firm's supply curve. The aggregate supply curve is *not* a market supply curve, and it is *not* the simple sum of all the individual supply curves in the economy. (Recall a similar warning for the aggregate demand curve.)

To understand why, recall the logic behind a simple supply curve, first introduced in Chapter 3. A supply curve shows the quantity of output an individual firm would supply at each possible price, *ceteris paribus*. When we draw a firm's supply curve, we assume that input prices, including wage rates, are constant. An individual firm's supply curve shows what would happen to the firm's output if the price of its output changes with *no* corresponding increase in costs. Such an assumption for an individual firm is reasonable because an individual firm is small relative to the economy as a whole. (It is unlikely that one firm raising the price of its output will lead to significant increases in input prices in the economy.) If the price of a profit-maximizing firm's output rises with *no* increase in the costs of any inputs, the firm is likely to increase output.

What would happen, however, if there were an increase in the overall price level? It is unrealistic to believe that costs are constant for individual firms if the overall price level is increasing, for two reasons. First, the outputs of some firms are the inputs of other firms. Therefore, if output prices rise, there will be an increase in at least some input prices. Second, it is unrealistic to assume that wage rates (an important input cost) do not rise at all when the overall price level rises. Because all input prices (including wage rates) are not constant as the overall price level changes, individual firms' supply curves *shift* as the overall price level changes, so we cannot sum them to get an aggregate supply curve.

Another reason the aggregate supply curve cannot be the sum of the supply curves of all the individual firms in the economy is that many firms (some would argue most firms) do not simply respond to prices determined in the market. Instead, they actually *set prices*. Only in perfectly competitive markets do firms simply react to prices determined by market forces. Firms in other kinds of industries (imperfectly competitive industries, to be exact) make both output and price decisions based on their perceptions of demand and costs. Price-setting firms do not have individual supply curves because these firms are choosing both output and price at the same time. To derive an individual supply curve, we need to imagine calling out a price to a firm and having the firm tell us how much output it will supply at that price. We cannot do this if firms are also setting prices. If supply curves do not exist for imperfectly competitive firms, we certainly cannot add them together to get an aggregate supply curve.

What can we say about the relationship between aggregate output and the overall price level? Because input prices change when the overall price level changes and because many firms in the economy set prices as well as output, it is clear that an "aggregate supply curve" in the traditional sense of the word *supply* does not exist. What does exist is what we might call a "price/output response" curve—a curve that traces out the price decisions and output decisions of all the markets and firms in the economy under a given set of circumstances.

What might such a curve look like?

AGGREGATE SUPPLY IN THE SHORT RUN

Many argue that the aggregate supply curve (or the price/output response curve) has a positive slope, at least in the short run. (We will discuss the short-run/long-run distinction in more detail later in this chapter.) In addition, many argue that at very low levels of aggregate output—for example, when the economy is in a recession—the aggregate supply curve is fairly flat, and at high levels of output—for example, when the economy is experiencing a boom—it is vertical or nearly vertical. Such a curve is shown in Figure 26.6.

To understand the shape of the *AS* curve in Figure 26.6, consider the output and price response of markets and firms to a steady increase in aggregate demand brought about by an increasingly expansionary fiscal or monetary policy. The reaction of firms to such an expansion is likely to depend on two factors: (1) how close the economy is to capacity at the time of the expansion, and (2) how rapidly input prices (such as wage rates) respond to increases in the overall price level.

Capacity Constraints   In microeconomics, "short run" describes the time in which firms' decisions are constrained by some *fixed factor of production*. Farmers are constrained in the short run by the number of acres of land on their farm—the amount of land owned is the fixed factor of production. Manufacturing firms' short-run production decisions are

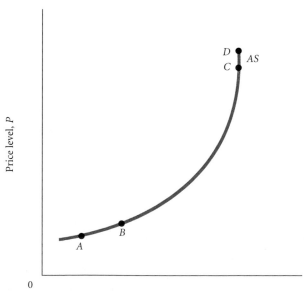

FIGURE 26.6 The Short-Run Aggregate Supply Curve

In the short run, the aggregate supply curve (the price/output response curve) has a positive slope. At low levels of aggregate output, the curve is fairly flat. As the economy approaches capacity, the curve becomes nearly vertical. At capacity, the curve is vertical.

constrained by the size of their physical production facilities. In the longer run, individual firms can overcome these types of constraints by investing in greater capacity—for example, by purchasing more acreage or building a new factory.

The idea of a fixed capacity in the short run also plays a role in macroeconomics. Macroeconomists tend to focus on whether or not *individual firms* are producing at or close to full capacity. A firm is producing at full capacity if it is fully utilizing the capital and labor it has on hand. As we will discuss in detail in Chapter 30, firms may at times have *excess capital* and *excess labor* on hand—amounts of capital and labor not needed to produce the current level of output. If, for example, there are costs of getting rid of capital once it is in place, a firm may choose to hold on to some of this capital, even if the economy is in a downturn and the firm has decreased its output. In this case, the firm will not be fully utilizing its capital stock. Firms may be especially likely to behave this way if they expect that the downturn will be short and that they will need the capital in the future to produce a higher level of output. Firms may have similar reasons for holding excess labor. It may be costly, both in worker morale and administrative costs, to lay off a large number of workers.

The Fed reports on the nation's "capacity utilization rate" monthly. In December 1990, for example, during the recession of 1990–1991, the capacity utilization rate for manufacturing firms was 79.3 percent. This suggests about 20 percent of the nation's factory capacity was idle. During the recessions of 1974–1975 and 1980–1982, capacity utilization fell below 75 percent. During the 2001 recession, capacity utilization also fell below 75 percent. Capacity utilization remained low throughout 2002 and 2003. In July 2003 it was only 72.8 percent.

Macroeconomists also focus on whether or not the *economy as a whole* is operating at full capacity. If there is cyclical unemployment (unemployment above the frictional and structural amounts), the economy is not fully utilizing its labor force. There are people who want to work at the current wage rates who cannot find jobs.

Even if firms are not holding excess labor and capital, the economy may be operating below its capacity if there is cyclical unemployment.

Output Levels and Price/Output Responses   At low levels of output in the economy, there is likely to be excess capacity both in individual firms and in the economy as a whole. Firms are likely to be producing at levels of output below their existing capacity constraints. That is, they are likely to be holding excess capital and labor. It is also likely that there will be cyclical unemployment in the economy as a whole in periods of low output. When this is the case, it is likely that firms will respond to an increase in demand by increasing output much more than they increase prices. Firms are below capacity, so the extra cost of producing more output is likely to be small. In addition, firms can get more labor (from the ranks of the unemployed) without much, if any, increase in wage rates.

An increase in aggregate demand when the economy is operating at low levels of output is likely to result in an increase in output with little or no increase in the overall price level. That is, the aggregate supply (price/output response) curve is likely to be fairly flat at low levels of aggregate output.

Refer to Figure 26.6. Aggregate output is considerably higher at B than at A, but the price level at B is only slightly higher than it is at A.

If aggregate output continues to expand, things will change. As firms and the economy as a whole begin to move closer and closer to capacity, firms' response to an increase in demand is likely to change from mainly increasing output to mainly increasing prices. Why? As firms continue to increase their output, they will begin to bump into their short-run capacity constraints. In addition, unemployment will be falling as firms hire more workers to produce the increased output, so the economy as a whole will be approaching its capacity. As aggregate output rises, the prices of labor and capital (input costs) will begin to rise more rapidly, leading firms to increase their output prices.

At some level of output, it is virtually impossible for firms to expand any further. At this level, all sectors are fully utilizing their existing factories and equipment. Plants are running double shifts, and many workers are on overtime. In addition, there is little or no cyclical unemployment in the economy. At this point, firms will respond to any further increases in demand only by raising prices, since they are unable to expand output any further.

> When the economy is producing at its maximum level of output—that is, at capacity—the aggregate supply curve becomes vertical.

Between C and D in Figure 26.6, the AS curve is vertical. Moving from C to D results in no increase in aggregate output but a large increase in the price level.

The Response of Input Prices to Changes in the Overall Price Level

Whether or not the economy is producing a level of output close to capacity, there must be some time lag between changes in input prices and changes in output prices for the aggregate supply (price/output response) curve to slope upward. If input prices changed at exactly the same rate as output prices, the AS curve would be vertical.

It is easy to see why. It is generally assumed that firms make decisions with the objective of maximizing profits. If all output and input prices increase 10 percent, no firm would find it advantageous to change its level of output. Why? Because the output level that maximized profits before the 10 percent increase will be the same as the level that maximizes profits after the 10 percent increase.[1] So, if input prices adjusted immediately to output prices, the aggregate supply (price/output response) curve would be vertical.

Wage rates may increase at exactly the same rate as the overall price level if the price level increase is *fully anticipated*. If inflation were expected to be 5 percent this year, this expected increase might be built into wage and salary contracts. Most employees, however, do not receive automatic pay raises as the overall price level increases, and sometimes increases in the price level are unanticipated. Input prices—particularly wage rates—tend to lag behind increases in output prices for a variety of reasons. (We discuss these in Chapter 27.) At least in the short run, wage rates tend to be slow to adjust to overall macroeconomic changes. It is precisely this point that has led to an important distinction between the AS curve in the long run and the AS curve in the short run.[2] We will return to this distinction shortly, but for now we will assume that the AS curve is shaped like the one in Figure 26.6.

SHIFTS OF THE SHORT-RUN AGGREGATE SUPPLY CURVE

Just as the aggregate demand curve can shift, so too can the aggregate supply (price/output response) curve. Recall the individual firm behavior we just considered in describing the shape of the short-run AS curve. Firms with the power to set prices choose the price/output combinations that maximize their profits. Firms in perfectly competitive industries choose the quantities of output to supply at given price levels. The AS curve traces out these price/output responses to economic conditions.

Anything that affects these individual firm decisions can shift the AS curve. Some of these factors include cost shocks, economic growth, stagnation, public policy, and natural disasters.

---

[1]All prices going up by the same percentage is analogous to changing the monetary unit of account from, say, green dollars to red dollars, where 1.1 red dollars equals 1 green dollar. A change in the monetary unit of account has no effect on the firms' profit-maximizing decisions. If the nominal value of all output and input prices increases by 10 percent, then nothing *real* happens. When all nominal values go up by 10 percent, firms' decisions concerning *real* output will not change.
[2]Some textbooks derive the short-run aggregate supply curve by assuming *all* input prices are fixed. "Fixed input prices" means input prices do not change as the overall price level changes. This assumption is not realistic because the outputs of some firms (such as intermediate goods and capital goods) are the inputs of other firms. It is also unrealistic to assume that wage rates do not respond at all to changes in the overall price level. It is more realistic to assume that wage rates do not *fully* respond in the short run than it is to assume no response at all.

Cost Shocks Firms' decisions are heavily influenced by costs. Some costs change at the same time the overall price level changes, some costs lag behind changes in the price level, and some may not change at all. Changes in costs that occur at the same time that the price level changes are built into the shape of the short-run *AS* curve. For example, when the price level rises, wage rates might rise by half as much in the short run. (This effect could happen if half of all wage contracts in the economy had cost-of-living increase clauses and half did not.) The shape of the short-run *AS* curve would reflect this response.

Sometimes cost changes occur that are *not* the result of changes in the overall price level—for example, the cost of energy. During the summer of 2005, world crude oil prices doubled from about $35 to $70 a barrel. Once it became clear that the severe hurricanes of that year would not cause a huge disruption of oil supplies, prices fell back below $60. In contrast, in 1973 to 1974 and again in 1979, the price of oil increased substantially and remained at a higher level. Oil is an important input in many firms and industries, and when the price of firms' inputs rises, firms respond by raising prices and lowering output. At the aggregate level, this means an increase in the price of oil (or a similar cost increase) *shifts* the *AS* curve to the left, as in Figure 26.7(a). A leftward shift of the *AS* curve means a higher price level for a given level of output. A decrease in costs shifts the *AS* curve to the right, as in Figure 26.7(b). A rightward shift of the *AS* curve means a lower price level for a given level of output. Shifts in the *AS* curve brought about by a change in costs are referred to as **cost shocks** or **supply shocks**.

Economic Growth Economic growth shifts the *AS* curve to the right. Recall that the vertical part of the short-run *AS* curve represents the economy's maximum (capacity) output. This maximum output is determined by the economy's existing resources and the current state of technology. If the supply of labor increases or the stock of capital grows, the *AS* curve will shift to the right. The labor force is expected to grow naturally with an increase in working-age population, but it can also increase for other reasons. Since the 1960s, for example, the percentage of women in the labor force has grown sharply. This increase in the supply of women workers has shifted the *AS* curve to the right.

Immigration can also shift the *AS* curve. During the 1970s, Germany, faced with a serious labor shortage, opened its borders to large numbers of "guest workers," largely from Turkey. The United States has experienced significant immigration, legal and illegal, from

cost shock, or supply shock A change in costs that shifts the aggregate supply (AS) curve.

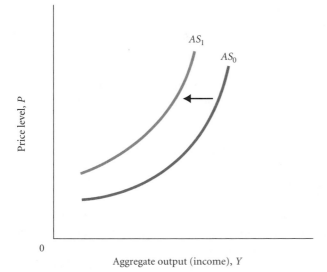

a. A decrease in aggregate supply

A leftward shift of the *AS* curve from AS_0 to AS_1 could be caused by an increase in costs—for example, an increase in wage rates or energy prices—natural disasters, economic stagnation, and the like.

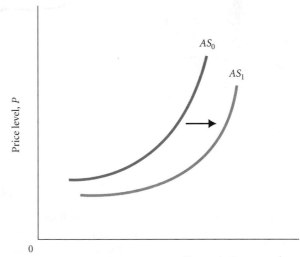

b. An increase in aggregate supply

A rightward shift of the *AS* curve from AS_0 to AS_1 could be caused by a decrease in costs, economic growth, public policy that stimulates supply, and the like.

FIGURE 26.7 Shifts of the Aggregate Supply Curve

Shifts to the Right Increases in Aggregate Supply		Shifts to the Left Decreases in Aggregate Supply	
	Lower costs • lower input prices • lower wage rates	**Higher costs** • higher input prices • higher wage rates	
	Economic growth • more capital • more labor • technological change	**Stagnation** • capital deterioration	
	Public policy • supply-side policies • tax cuts • deregulation	**Public policy** • waste and inefficiency • over-regulation	
	Good weather	**Bad weather, natural disasters, destruction from wars**	

FIGURE 26.8 Factors That Shift the Aggregate Supply Curve

Mexico, from Central and South American countries, and from Asia. Increases in the stock of capital over time and technological advances can also shift the *AS* curve to the right. We will discuss economic growth in more detail in Chapter 33.

Stagnation and Lack of Investment   The opposite of economic growth is stagnation and decline. Over time, capital deteriorates and eventually wears out completely if it is not properly maintained. If an economy fails to invest in both public capital (sometimes called *infrastructure*) and private capital (plant and equipment) at a sufficient rate, the stock of capital will decline. If the stock of capital declines, the *AS* curve will shift to the left.

Public Policy   Public policy can shift the *AS* curve. In the 1980s, for example, the Reagan administration put into effect a form of public policy based on supply-side economics. The idea behind these supply-side policies was to deregulate the economy and reduce taxes to increase the incentives to work, engage in entrepreneurial activity, and invest. The main purpose of these policies was to shift the *AS* curve to the right. (We discuss supply-side economics in Chapter 32.)

Weather, Wars, and Natural Disasters   Changes in weather can shift the *AS* curve. A severe drought will reduce the supply of agricultural goods; the perfect mix of sun and rain will produce a bountiful harvest. If an economy is damaged by war or natural disaster, the *AS* curve will shift to the left. Whenever part of the resource base of an economy is reduced or destroyed, the *AS* curve shifts to the left.

Figure 26.8 shows some factors that might cause the *AS* curve to shift.

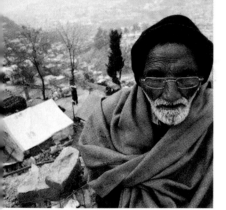

In October 2005, a major earthquake hit Pakistan killing thousands and destroying the homes of over 2 million people. This reduces the capital stock of Pakistan and shifts Pakistan's aggregate supply curve to the left.

equilibrium price level
The price level at which the aggregate demand and aggregate supply curves intersect.

THE EQUILIBRIUM PRICE LEVEL

The **equilibrium price level** in the economy occurs at the point at which the *AD* curve and the *AS* curve intersect, shown in Figure 26.9 where the equilibrium price level is P_0 and the equilibrium level of aggregate output (income) is Y_0.

Figure 26.9 looks simple, but it is a powerful device for analyzing a number of macroeconomic questions. Consider first what is true at the intersection of the *AS* and *AD* curves. Each point on the *AD* curve corresponds to equilibrium in both the goods market and the money market. Each point on the *AS* curve represents the price/output responses of all the firms in the economy. That means:

> The point at which the *AS* and *AD* curves intersect corresponds to equilibrium in the goods and money markets and to a set of price/output decisions on the part of all the firms in the economy.

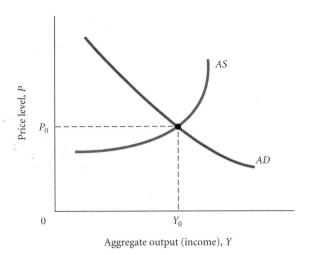

FIGURE 26.9 The Equilibrium Price Level

At each point along the *AD* curve, both the money market and the goods market are in equilibrium. Each point on the *AS* curve represents the price/output decisions of all the firms in the economy. P_0 and Y_0 correspond to equilibrium in the goods market and the money market and to a set of price/output decisions on the part of all the firms in the economy.

We will use this *AS/AD* framework to analyze the effects of monetary and fiscal policy on the economy and to analyze the causes of inflation. First we need to return to the *AS* curve and discuss its shape in the long run.

THE LONG-RUN AGGREGATE SUPPLY CURVE

As we noted earlier, for the *AS* curve not to be vertical, some costs must lag behind increases in the overall price level. If all prices (both input and output prices) change at the same rate, the level of aggregate output does not change. We have assumed that in the short run at least some cost changes lag behind price-level changes, but what happens in the long run?

Many economists believe costs lag behind price-level changes in the short run but ultimately move with the overall price level. For example, wage rates tend to move very closely with the price level *over time*. If the price level increases at a steady rate, inflation may come to be fully anticipated and built into most labor contracts.

If costs and the price level move in tandem over a sufficient time period for these adjustments to be made, in the long run, the *AS* curve is best modeled as vertical. We can see why in Figure 26.10. Initially, the economy is in equilibrium at a price level of P_0 and aggregate output of Y_0 (the point *A* at which AD_0 and AS_0 intersect). Now imagine a shift of the *AD* curve from AD_0 to AD_1. In response to this shift, both the price level and aggregate output rise in the short run, to P_1 and Y_1, respectively (the point *B* at which AD_1 and AS_0 intersect). Recall, however, that the movement along the upward-sloping AS_0 curve as *Y* increases from Y_0 to Y_1 assumes that some costs lag behind the increase in the overall price level.

Assume now that costs fully adjust to prices in the long run, where, for example, labor unions renegotiate wage contracts to catch up with the increase in prices. These kinds of cost increases cause the *AS* curve to shift to the left, from AS_0 to AS_1. If, eventually, costs and prices have risen by exactly the same percentage, aggregate output will be back at Y_0 (the point *C* at which AD_1 and AS_1 intersect).

> If wage rates and other costs fully adjust to changes in prices in the long run, then the long-run *AS* curve is vertical.

POTENTIAL GDP

Recall that even the short-run *AS* curve becomes vertical at some particular level of output. The vertical portion of the short-run *AS* curve exists because there are physical limits to the amount that an economy can produce in any given time period. At the physical limit, all

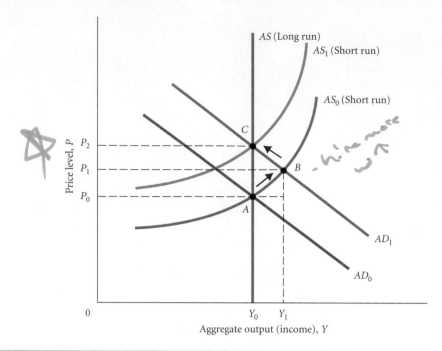

FIGURE 26.10 The Long-Run Aggregate Supply Curve

When the AD curve shifts from AD_0 to AD_1, the equilibrium price level initially rises from P_0 to P_1 and output rises from Y_0 to Y_1. Costs respond in the longer run, shifting the AS curve from AS_0 to AS_1. If costs ultimately increase by the same percentage as the price level, the quantity supplied will end up back at Y_0. Y_0 is sometimes called *potential GDP*.

plants are operating around the clock, many workers are on overtime, and there is no cyclical unemployment.

Note that the vertical portions of the short-run AS curves in Figure 26.10 are to the right of Y_0. If the vertical portions of the short-run AS curves represent "capacity," then what is the nature of Y_0, the level of output corresponding to the long-run AS curve?

Y_0 represents the level of aggregate output that can be *sustained* in the long run without inflation. It is sometimes called **potential output** or **potential GDP**. Output can be pushed above Y_0 under a variety of circumstances, but when it is, there is upward pressure on costs. As the economy approaches short-run capacity, wage rates tend to rise as firms try to attract more people into the labor force and to induce more workers to work overtime. Rising costs shift the short-run AS curve to the left (in Figure 26.10 from AS_0 to AS_1) and drive output back to Y_0.

potential output, or potential GDP The level of aggregate output that can be sustained in the long run without inflation.

Short-Run Equilibrium Below Potential GDP

Thus far we have argued that if the short-run aggregate supply and aggregate demand curves intersect to the right of Y_0 in Figure 26.10, wages and other input prices will rise, causing the short-run AS curve to shift to the left and pushing GDP back down to Y_0. Although different economists have different opinions on how to determine whether an economy is operating at or above potential GDP, there is general agreement that there is a maximum level of output (below the vertical portion of the short-run aggregate supply curve) that can be sustained without inflation.

What about short-run equilibria that occur to the *left* of Y_0? If the short-run aggregate supply and aggregate demand curves intersect at a level of output below potential GDP, what will happen? Here again economists disagree. Those who believe the aggregate supply curve is vertical in the long run believe that when short-run equilibria exist below Y_0, GDP will tend to rise—just as GDP tends to fall when short-run equilibrium exists above Y_0. The argument is that when the economy is operating below full employment with excess capacity and high unemployment, input prices (including wages) are likely to *fall*. A decline in input prices shifts the aggregate supply curve to the *right*, causing the price level to fall and the level of real GDP to rise back to Y_0. This automatic adjustment works only if input prices fall when excess capacity and unemployment exist. We will discuss wage adjustment during periods of unemployment in detail in Chapter 27.

AGGREGATE DEMAND, AGGREGATE SUPPLY, AND MONETARY AND FISCAL POLICY

We are now ready to use the *AS/AD* framework to consider the effects of monetary and fiscal policy. We will first consider the short-run effects.

Recall that the two fiscal policy variables are government purchases (G) and net taxes (T). The monetary policy variable is the quantity of money supplied (M^s). An *expansionary* policy aims at stimulating the economy through an increase in G or M^s or a decrease in T. A *contractionary* policy aims at slowing down the economy through a decrease in G or M^s or an increase in T. We saw earlier in this chapter that an expansionary policy shifts the *AD* curve to the right and that a contractionary policy shifts the *AD* curve to the left. How do these policies affect the equilibrium values of the price level (P) and the level of aggregate output (income)?

When considering the effects of a policy change, we must be careful to note where along the (short-run) *AS* curve the economy is at the time of the change. If the economy is initially on the flat portion of the *AS* curve, as shown by point A in Figure 26.11, then an expansionary policy, which shifts the *AD* curve to the right, results in a small price increase relative to the output increase: The increase in equilibrium Y (from Y_0 to Y_1) is much greater than the increase in equilibrium P (from P_0 to P_1). This is the case in which an expansionary policy works well. There is an increase in output with little increase in the price level.

If the economy is initially on the steep portion of the *AS* curve, as shown by point B in Figure 26.12, then an expansionary policy results in a small increase in equilibrium output (from Y_0 to Y_1) and a large increase in the equilibrium price level (from P_0 to P_1). In this case, an expansionary policy does not work well. It results in a much higher price level with little increase in output. The multiplier is therefore close to zero: Output is initially close to capacity, and attempts to increase it further lead mostly to a higher price level.

Figures 26.11 and 26.12 show that it is important to know where the economy is *before* a policy change is put into effect. The economy is producing on the nearly flat part of the *AS* curve if most firms are producing well below capacity. When this is the case, firms will respond to an increase in demand by increasing output much more than they increase prices. If the economy is producing on the steep part of the *AS* curve, firms are close to capacity and will respond to an increase in demand by increasing prices much more than they increase output.

To see what happens when the economy is on the steep part of the *AS* curve, consider the effects of an increase in G with no change in the money supply. What will happen is that

FIGURE 26.11 A Shift of the Aggregate Demand Curve When the Economy Is on the Nearly Flat Part of the AS Curve

Aggregate demand can shift to the right for a number of reasons, including an increase in the money supply, a tax cut, or an increase in government spending. If the shift occurs when the economy is on the nearly flat portion of the *AS* curve, the result will be an increase in output with little increase in the price level from point *A* to point *A'*.

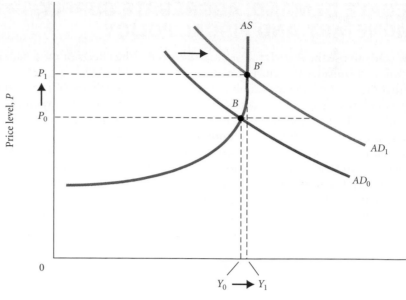

FIGURE 26.12 A Shift of the Aggregate Demand Curve When the Economy Is Operating at or Near Maximum Capacity

If a shift of aggregate demand occurs while the economy is operating near full capacity, the result will be an increase in the price level with little increase in output from point B to point B'.

when G is increased, there will be virtually no increase in Y. In other words, the expansionary fiscal policy will fail to stimulate the economy. To consider this, we need to go back to Chapter 25 and review what is behind the AD curve.

The first thing that happens when G increases is an unanticipated decline in firms' inventories. Because firms are very close to capacity output when the economy is on the steep part of the AS curve, they cannot increase their output very much. The result, as Figure 26.12 shows, is a substantial increase in the price level. The increase in the price level increases the demand for money, which (with a fixed money supply) leads to an increase in the interest rate, decreasing planned investment. *There is nearly complete crowding out of investment.* If firms are producing at capacity, prices and interest rates will continue to rise until the increase in G is completely matched by a decrease in planned investment and there is complete crowding out.

LONG-RUN AGGREGATE SUPPLY AND POLICY EFFECTS

We have so far been considering monetary and fiscal policy effects in the short run. Concerning the long run, it is important to realize:

> If the AS curve is vertical in the long run, neither monetary policy nor fiscal policy has any effect on aggregate output in the long run.

Look back at Figure 26.10. Monetary and fiscal policy shift the AD curve. If the long-run AS curve is vertical, output always comes back to Y_0. In this case, policy affects *only* the price level in the long run, and the multiplier effect of a change in government spending on aggregate output in the long run is zero. Under the same circumstances, the tax multiplier is also zero.

The conclusion that policy has no effect on aggregate output in the long run is perhaps startling. Do most economists agree that the aggregate supply curve is vertical in the long run?

Most economists agree that input prices tend to lag behind output prices in the short run, giving the AS curve some positive slope. Most also agree the AS curve is likely to be steeper in the long run, but how long is the long run? The longer the lag time, the greater the potential impact of monetary and fiscal policy on aggregate output. If the long run is only 3 to 6 months, policy has little chance to affect output; if the long run is 3 or 4 years, policy can

A New Federal Reserve Chairman Nominated in 2005

THE FOLLOWING ARTICLE FROM THE *New York Times* describes the task facing the newly nominated Federal Reserve chairman, Ben Bernanke. The worry was that supply-side increases in oil and other input prices would push up the aggregate supply curve, *AS*, and that price increases would spread to the overall price level. The Fed countered by tightening monetary policy, raising interest rates and shifting the aggregate demand curve to the left. The concern was that real output would not grow as fast or that it would decline.

First on To-Do List: Tame Inflation
By DAVID LEONHARDT
October 25, 2005

President Bush yesterday nominated Ben Bernanke, a senior White House adviser who was a Fed governor from 2002 until this past June, to succeed Mr. Greenspan as chairman early next year.

Mr. Bernanke's first task is likely to be one that temporarily tripped up Mr. Greenspan shortly after he became chairman in 1987: bringing down inflation without causing too much damage to the economy or the stock market along the way.

Over the last year, inflation has reached 4.7 percent, the highest level since 1991, as energy prices have soared. Core inflation, which excludes food and energy and is closely watched at the Fed, has hit 2 percent, the upper limit of what Mr. Bernanke has called his "comfort zone."

Airfares, haircuts, nursery school tuition, new cars, appliances and cigarettes have all become more expensive in recent months. The price of Tide liquid detergent has risen 3.4 percent over the last year, according to the market research firm Information Resources Inc., after years in which inflation on household items was all but nonexistent.

"Bernanke comes in at a difficult juncture," said Laurence H. Meyer, a former Fed governor who is now an economic forecaster.

"So far it's been an easy roll, with interest rates rising at a steady, gradual pace," Mr. Meyer added. But as interest rates reach the point that they could choke off economic growth "there's less of an idea of what the next move should be."

have significant effects. A good deal of research in macroeconomics focuses on the length of time lags between input and output prices. In a sense, the length of the long run is one of the most important open questions in macroeconomics.

Another source of disagreement centers on whether equilibria below potential GDP, Y_0 in Figure 26.10, are self-correcting (that is, without government intervention). Recall that those who believe in a vertical long-run *AS* curve believe that slack in the economy will put downward pressure on input prices (including wages), causing the short-run *AS* curve to shift to the right and pushing GDP back toward Y_0. However, some argue that wages and other input prices do *not* fall during slack periods and that the economy can get "stuck" at an equilibrium below potential GDP. In this case, monetary and fiscal policy would be necessary to restore full employment. We will return to this debate in Chapter 27.

The "new classical" economics, which we discuss in Chapter 32, assumes prices and wages are fully flexible and adjust very quickly to changing conditions. New classical economists

The Simple "Keynesian" Aggregate Supply Curve

There is a great deal of disagreement concerning the shape of the AS curve. One view of the aggregate supply curve, the simple "Keynesian" view, holds that at any given moment, the economy has a clearly defined capacity, or maximum, output. This maximum output, denoted by Y_F, is defined by the existing labor force, the current capital stock, and the existing state of technology. If planned aggregate expenditure increases when the economy is producing *below* this maximum capacity, this view holds, inventories will be lower than planned and firms will increase output, but the price level will not change. Firms are operating with underutilized plants (excess capacity) and there is cyclical unemployment. Expansion does not exert any upward pressure on prices. However, if planned aggregate expenditure increases when the economy is producing near or at its maximum (Y_F), inventories will be lower than planned, but firms cannot increase their output. The result will be an increase in the price level, or inflation.

This view is illustrated in Figure 1. In the top half of the diagram, aggregate output (income) (Y) and planned aggregate expenditure ($C + I + G \equiv AE$) are initially in equilibrium at AE_1, Y_1, and price level P_1. Now suppose a tax cut or an increase in government spending increases planned aggregate expenditure. If such an increase shifts the AE curve from AE_1 to AE_2 and the corresponding aggregate demand curve from AD_1 to AD_2, the equilibrium level of output will rise from Y_1 to Y_F. (Remember, an expansionary policy shifts the AD curve to the right.) Because

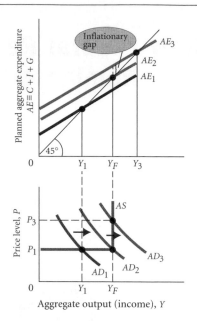

FIGURE 1

With planned aggregate expenditure of AE_1 and aggregate demand of AD_1, equilibrium output is Y_1. A shift of planned aggregate expenditure to AE_2, corresponding to a shift of the AD curve to AD_2, causes output to rise but the price level to remain at P_1. If planned aggregate expenditure and aggregate demand exceed Y_F, however, there is an inflationary gap and the price level rises to P_3.

we were initially producing below capacity output (Y_1 is lower than Y_F), the price level will be unaffected, remaining at P_1.

Now consider what would happen if AE were to increase even further. Suppose planned aggregate expenditure were to shift from AE_2 to AE_3, with a corresponding shift of AD_2 to AD_3. If the economy were producing below capacity output, the equilibrium level of output would rise to Y_3. However, the output of the economy cannot exceed the maximum output of Y_F. As inventories fall below what was planned, firms encounter a fully employed labor market and fully utilized plants. Therefore, they cannot increase their output. The result is that the aggregate supply curve becomes vertical at Y_F, and the price level is driven up to P_3.

The difference between planned aggregate expenditure and aggregate output at full capacity is sometimes referred to as an **inflationary gap**. You can see the inflationary gap in the top half of Figure 1. At Y_F (capacity output), planned aggregate expenditure (shown by AE_3) is greater than Y_F. The price level rises to P_3 until the aggregate quantity supplied and the aggregate quantity demanded are equal.

Despite the fact that the kinked aggregate supply curve provides some insights, most economists find it unrealistic. It does not seem likely that the whole economy suddenly runs into a capacity "wall" at a specific level of output. As output expands, some firms and industries will hit capacity before others.

---

believe, for example, that wage rate changes do not lag behind price changes. The new classical view is consistent with the existence of a vertical *AS* curve, even in the short run. At the other end of the spectrum is what is sometimes called the simple "Keynesian" view of aggregate supply. Those who hold this view believe there is a kink in the *AS* curve at capacity output, as we discuss in the Further Exploration box, "The Simple 'Keynesian' Aggregate Supply Curve."

CAUSES OF INFLATION

We now turn to inflation and use the *AS/AD* framework to consider the causes of inflation.

INFLATION VERSUS SUSTAINED INFLATION: A REMINDER

inflation An increase in the overall price level.

sustained inflation Occurs when the overall price level continues to rise over some fairly long period of time.

Before we discuss the specific causes of inflation, recall the distinction we made in Chapter 20. **Inflation**, as you know, is an increase in the overall price level. Anything that shifts the *AD* curve to the right or the *AS* curve to the left causes inflation, but it is often useful to distinguish between a *one-time increase* in the price level (a one-time inflation) and an inflation that is sustained. A **sustained inflation** occurs when the overall price level continues to rise over some fairly long period of time. When we speak of a sustained inflation rate of 3 percent, for example, we generally mean that the price level has been rising at a rate of 3 percent per year over a number of years.

It is generally accepted that there are many possible causes of a one-time increase in the price level. (We discuss the main causes next.) For the price level to continue to increase period after period, most economists believe it must be "accommodated" by an expanded money supply. This leads to the assertion that a sustained inflation, whatever the initial cause of the increase in the price level, is essentially a monetary phenomenon.

DEMAND-PULL INFLATION

Inflation initiated by an increase in aggregate demand is called **demand-pull inflation**. You can see how demand-pull inflation works by looking at Figures 26.11 and 26.12. In both, the inflation begins with a shift of the aggregate demand schedule from AD_0 to AD_1, which causes the price level to increase from P_0 to P_1. (Output also increases, from Y_0 to Y_1.) If the economy is operating on the steep portion of the AS curve at the time of the increase in aggregate demand, as in Figure 26.12, most of the effect will be an increase in the price level instead of an increase in output. If the economy is operating on the flat portion of the AS curve, as in Figure 26.11, most of the effect will be an increase in output instead of an increase in the price level.

Remember, in the long run the initial increase in the price level will cause the AS curve to shift to the left as input prices (costs) respond to the increase in output prices. If the long-run AS curve is vertical, as depicted in Figure 26.10, the increase in costs will shift the short-run AS curve (AS_0) to the left to AS_1, pushing the price level even higher, to P_2. If the long-run AS curve is vertical, a shift in aggregate demand from AD_0 to AD_1 will result, in the long run, in *no* increase in output and a price-level increase from P_0 to P_2.

demand-pull inflation
Inflation that is initiated by an increase in aggregate demand.

COST-PUSH, OR SUPPLY-SIDE, INFLATION

Inflation can also be caused by an increase in costs, referred to as **cost-push**, or **supply-side, inflation**. Several times in the last two decades oil prices on world markets increased sharply. Because oil is used in virtually every line of business, costs increased.

An increase in costs (a cost shock) shifts the AS curve to the left, as Figure 26.13 shows. If we assume the government does not react to this shift in AS by changing fiscal or monetary

cost-push, or **supply-side, inflation** Inflation caused by an increase in costs.

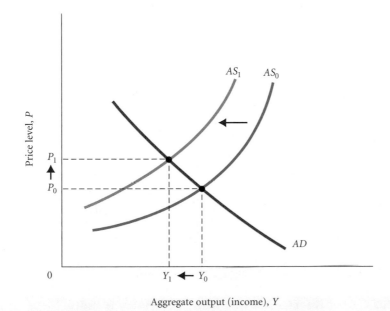

FIGURE 26.13 Cost-Push, or Supply-Side, Inflation

An increase in costs shifts the AS curve to the left. By assuming the government does not react to this shift, the AD curve does not shift, the price level rises, and output falls.

stagflation Occurs when output is falling at the same time that prices are rising.

policy, the AD curve will not shift. The supply shift will cause the equilibrium price level to rise (from P_0 to P_1) and the level of aggregate output to decline (from Y_0 to Y_1). Recall from Chapter 18 that **stagflation** occurs when output is falling at the same time prices are rising—in other words, when the economy is experiencing both a contraction and inflation simultaneously. Figure 26.13 shows that one possible cause of stagflation is an increase in costs.

To return to monetary and fiscal policy for a moment, note from Figure 26.13 that the government could counteract the increase in costs (the cost shock) by engaging in an expansionary policy (an increase in G or M^s or a decrease in T). This would shift the AD curve to the right, and the new AD curve would intersect the new AS curve at a higher level of output. The problem with this policy, however, is that the intersection of the new AS and AD curves would take place at a price even higher than P_1 in Figure 26.13.

> Cost shocks are bad news for policy makers. The only way they can counter the output loss brought about by a cost shock is by having the price level increase even more than it would without the policy action.

This situation is illustrated in Figure 26.14.

EXPECTATIONS AND INFLATION

When firms are making their price/output decisions, their *expectations* of future prices may affect their current decisions. If a firm expects that its competitors will raise their prices, in anticipation it may raise its own price.

Consider a firm that manufactures toasters. The toaster maker must decide what price to charge retail stores for its toaster. If it overestimates price and charges much more than other toaster manufacturers are charging, it will lose many customers. If it underestimates price and charges much less than other toaster makers are charging, it will gain customers but at a considerable loss in revenue per sale. The firm's *optimum price*—the price that maximizes the firm's profits—is presumably not too far from the average of its competitors' prices. If it does not know its competitors' projected prices before it sets its own price, as is often the case, it must base its price on what it expects its competitors' prices to be.

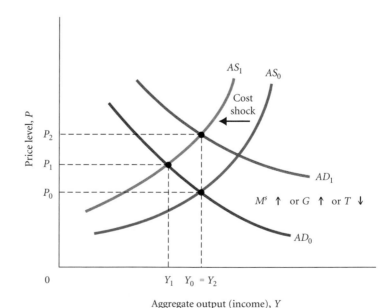

FIGURE 26.14 Cost Shocks Are Bad News for Policy Makers

A cost shock with no change in monetary or fiscal policy would shift the aggregate supply curve from AS_0 to AS_1, lower output from Y_0 to Y_1, and raise the price level from P_0 to P_1. Monetary or fiscal policy could be changed enough to have the AD curve shift from AD_0 to AD_1. This policy would raise aggregate output Y again, but it would raise the price level further, to P_2.

Suppose inflation has been running at about 10 percent per year. Our firm probably expects its competitors will raise their prices about 10 percent this year, so it is likely to raise the price of its own toaster by about 10 percent. This response is how expectations can get "built into the system." If every firm expects every other firm to raise prices by 10 percent, every firm will raise prices by about 10 percent. Every firm ends up with the price increase it expected.

The fact that expectations can affect the price level is vexing. Expectations can lead to an inertia that makes it difficult to stop an inflationary spiral. If prices have been rising, and if people's expectations are *adaptive*—that is, if they form their expectations on the basis of past pricing behavior—then firms may continue raising prices even if demand is slowing or contracting. In terms of the *AS/AD* diagram, an increase in inflationary expectations that causes firms to increase their prices shifts the *AS* curve to the left. Remember that the *AS* curve represents the price/output responses of firms. If firms increase their prices because of a change in inflationary expectations, the result is a leftward shift of the *AS* curve.

Toaster prices.

MONEY AND INFLATION

It is easy to see that an increase in the money supply can lead to an increase in the aggregate price level. As Figures 26.11 and 26.12 show, an increase in the money supply (M^s) shifts the *AD* curve to the right and results in a higher price level. This is simply a demand-pull inflation.

However, the supply of money may also play a role in creating a sustained inflation. Consider an initial increase in government spending (G) with the money supply (M^s) unchanged. Because the money supply is unchanged, this is an increase in G that is not "accommodated" by the Fed. The increase in G shifts the *AD* curve to the right and results in a higher price level. This is shown in Figure 26.15 as a shift from AD_0 to AD_1. (In Figure 26.15, the economy is assumed to be operating on the vertical portion of the *AS* curve.)

Remember what happens when the price level increases. The higher price level causes the demand for money to increase. With an unchanged money supply and an increase in the quantity of money demanded, the interest rate will rise, and the result will be a decrease in planned investment (I) spending. The new equilibrium corresponds to higher G, lower I, a higher interest rate, and a higher price level.

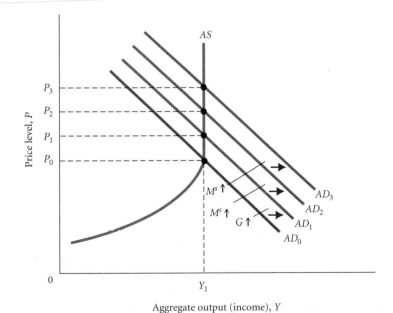

FIGURE 26.15 Sustained Inflation from an Initial Increase in G and Fed Accommodation

An increase in G with the money supply constant shifts the AD curve from AD_0 to AD_1. Although not shown in the figure, this leads to an increase in the interest rate and crowding out of planned investment. If the Fed tries to keep the interest rate unchanged by increasing the money supply, the AD curve will shift farther and farther to the right. The result is a sustained inflation, perhaps even hyperinflation.

hyperinflation A period of very rapid increases in the price level.

Now let us take our example one step further. Suppose that the Fed is sympathetic to the expansionary fiscal policy (the increase in G we just discussed) and decides to expand the supply of money to keep the interest rate constant. As the higher price level pushes up the demand for money, the Fed expands the supply of money with the goal of keeping the interest rate unchanged, eliminating the crowding-out effect of a higher interest rate.

When the supply of money is expanded, the AD curve shifts to the right again, from AD_1 to AD_2. This shift of the AD curve, brought about by the increased money supply, pushes prices up even further. Higher prices in turn increase the demand for money further, which requires a further increase in the money supply, and so on.

What would happen if the Fed tried to keep the interest rate constant when the economy is operating on the steep part of the AS curve? The situation could lead to a **hyperinflation**, a period of very rapid increases in the price level. If no more output can be coaxed out of the economy and if planned investment is not allowed to fall (because the interest rate is kept unchanged), then it is not possible to increase G. As the Fed keeps pumping more and more money into the economy to keep the interest rate unchanged, the price level will keep rising.

SUSTAINED INFLATION AS A PURELY MONETARY PHENOMENON

Virtually all economists agree that an increase in the price level can be caused by anything that causes the AD curve to shift to the right or the AS curve to shift to the left. These include expansionary fiscal policy actions, monetary expansion, cost shocks, changes in expectations, and so forth. It is also generally agreed that for a *sustained* inflation to occur, the Fed must accommodate it. In this sense, a sustained inflation can be thought of as a purely monetary phenomenon.

This argument, first put forth by monetarists (coming in Chapter 32), has gained wide acceptance. It is easy to show, as we just did, how expanding the money supply can continuously shift the AD curve. It is not as easy to come up with other reasons for continued shifts of the AD curve if the money supply is constant. One possibility is for the government to increase spending continuously without increasing taxes, but this process cannot continue forever. To finance spending without taxes, the government must borrow. Without any expansion of the money supply, the interest rate will rise dramatically because of the increase in the supply of government bonds. Now, the public must be willing to buy the government bonds that are being issued to finance the spending increases. At some point, the public may be unwilling to buy any more bonds even though the interest rate is very high.[3] At this point, the government is no longer able to increase non-tax-financed spending without the Fed's cooperation. If this is true, then a sustained inflation cannot exist without the Fed's cooperation.

LOOKING AHEAD

In Chapters 21 and 22, we discussed the concept of an equilibrium level of aggregate output and income, the idea of the multiplier, and the basics of fiscal policy. Those two chapters centered on the workings of the goods market alone.

In Chapters 23 and 24, we analyzed the money market by discussing the supply of money, the demand for money, the equilibrium interest rate, and the basics of monetary policy. In Chapter 25 we brought our analysis of the goods market together with our analysis of the money market.

In this chapter, we used everything learned so far to discuss the aggregate supply and aggregate demand curves, first mentioned in Chapter 18. By using aggregate supply and aggregate demand curves, we can determine the equilibrium price level in the economy and understand some causes of inflation.

We have said little about employment, unemployment, and the functioning of the labor market in the macroeconomy. The next chapter will link everything we have done so far to this third major market arena—the labor market—and to the problem of unemployment.

---

[3]This means that the public's demand for money no longer depends on the interest rate. Even though the interest rate is very high, the public cannot be induced to have its real money balances fall any further. There is a limit concerning how much the public can be induced to have its real money balances fall.

SUMMARY

THE AGGREGATE DEMAND CURVE

1. Money demand is a function of three variables: (1) the interest rate (r); (2) the level of real income (Y); and (3) the price level (P). Money demand will increase if the real level of output (income) increases, the price level increases, or the interest rate declines.

2. At a higher price level, households and firms need to hold larger money balances. If the money supply remains the same, this increased demand for money will cause the interest rate to increase and planned investment spending to fall. As a result, planned aggregate expenditure will be lower, inventories will be greater than planned, firms will cut back on output, and Y will fall. An increase in the price level causes the level of aggregate output (income) to fall. A decrease in the price level causes the level of aggregate output (income) to rise.

3. *Aggregate demand* is the total demand for goods and services in the economy. The *aggregate demand (AD) curve* illustrates the negative relationship between aggregate output (income) and the price level. Each point on the *AD* curve is a point at which both the goods market and the money market are in equilibrium. The *AD* curve is *not* the sum of all the market demand curves in the economy.

4. At every point along the aggregate demand curve, the aggregate quantity demanded in the economy is exactly equal to planned aggregate expenditure.

5. An increase in the quantity of money supplied, an increase in government purchases, or a decrease in net taxes at a given price level shifts the aggregate demand curve to the right. A decrease in the quantity of money supplied, a decrease in government purchases, or an increase in net taxes shifts the aggregate demand curve to the left.

THE AGGREGATE SUPPLY CURVE

6. *Aggregate supply* is the total supply of goods and services in an economy. The *aggregate supply (AS) curve* shows the relationship between the aggregate quantity of output supplied by all the firms in an economy and the overall price level. The *AS* curve is *not* a market supply curve, and it is *not* the simple sum of all the individual supply curves in the economy. For this reason, it is helpful to think of the *AS* curve as a "price/output response" curve—that is, a curve that traces out the price decisions and output decisions of all the markets and firms in the economy under a given set of circumstances.

7. The shape of the short-run *AS* curve is a source of much controversy in macroeconomics. Many economists believe that at very low levels of aggregate output the *AS* curve is fairly flat, and at high levels of aggregate output the *AS* curve is vertical or nearly vertical. Thus, the *AS* curve slopes upward and becomes vertical when the economy reaches its capacity, or maximum, output.

8. Anything that affects an individual firm's decisions can shift the *AS* curve. Some of these factors include *cost shocks*, economic growth, stagnation, public policy, and natural disasters.

THE EQUILIBRIUM PRICE LEVEL

9. The *equilibrium price level* in the economy occurs at the point at which the *AS* and *AD* curves intersect. The intersection of the *AS* and *AD* curves corresponds to equilibrium in the goods and money markets *and* to a set of price/output decisions on the part of all the firms in the economy.

THE LONG-RUN AGGREGATE SUPPLY CURVE

10. For the *AS* curve to slope upward, some input prices must lag behind increases in the overall price level. If wage rates and other costs fully adjust to changes in prices in the long run, then the long-run *AS* curve is vertical.

11. The level of aggregate output that can be sustained in the long run without inflation is called *potential output* or *potential GDP*.

AGGREGATE DEMAND, AGGREGATE SUPPLY, AND MONETARY AND FISCAL POLICY

12. If the economy is initially producing on the flat portion of the *AS* curve, an expansionary policy—which shifts the *AD* curve to the right—will result in a small increase in the equilibrium price level relative to the increase in equilibrium output. If the economy is initially producing on the steep portion of the *AS* curve, an expansionary policy results in a small increase in equilibrium output and a large increase in the equilibrium price level.

13. If the *AS* curve is vertical in the long run, neither monetary nor fiscal policy has any effect on aggregate output in the long run. For this reason, the exact length of the long run is one of the most pressing questions in macroeconomics.

CAUSES OF INFLATION

14. *Inflation* is an increase in the overall price level. A *sustained inflation* occurs when the overall price level continues to rise over some fairly long period of time. Most economists believe that sustained inflations can occur only if the Fed continuously increases the money supply.

15. *Demand-pull inflation* is inflation initiated by an increase in aggregate demand. *Cost-push*, or *supply-side, inflation* is inflation initiated by an increase in costs. An increase in costs may also lead to *stagflation*—the situation in which the economy is experiencing both a contraction and inflation simultaneously.

16. Inflation can become "built into the system" as a result of expectations. If prices have been rising and people form their expectations on the basis of past pricing behavior, firms may continue raising prices even if demand is slowing or contracting.

17. When the price level increases, so too does the demand for money. If the economy is operating on the steep part of the *AS* curve and the Fed tries to keep the interest rate constant by increasing the supply of money, the result could be a *hyperinflation*—a period of very rapid increases in the price level.

REVIEW TERMS AND CONCEPTS

aggregate demand, 562

aggregate demand (*AD*) curve, 563

aggregate supply, 567

aggregate supply (*AS*) curve, 567

cost-push, or supply-side, inflation, 579

cost shock, or supply shock, 571

demand-pull inflation, 579

equilibrium price level, 572

hyperinflation, 582

inflation, 578

inflationary gap, 578

potential output, or potential GDP, 574

real wealth, or real balance, effect, 565

stagflation, 580

sustained inflation, 578

PROBLEM SET

1. In Japan during the first half of 2000, the Bank of Japan kept interest rates at a near zero level in an attempt to stimulate demand. In addition, the government passed a substantial increase in government expenditure and cut taxes. Slowly, Japanese GDP began to grow with absolutely no sign of an increase in the price level. Illustrate the position of the Japanese economy with aggregate supply and demand curves. Where on the short-run *AS* curve was Japan in 2000?

2. In 2005, the prices of lumber and other building materials rose sharply on world markets. What impact would you expect there to be on the aggregate price level and on real GDP? Illustrate your answer with aggregate demand and supply curves. What would you expect to be the effect on interest rates if the Fed held the money supply constant? Tell a complete story.

3. "The aggregate demand curve slopes downward, because when the price level is lower, people can afford to buy more, and aggregate demand rises. When prices rise, people can afford to buy less, and aggregate demand falls." Is this a good explanation of the shape of the *AD* curve? Why or why not?

4. By using aggregate supply and demand curves to illustrate your points, discuss the impacts of the following events on the price level and on equilibrium GDP (*Y*) in the *short run*:
   a. A tax cut holding government purchases constant with the economy operating at near full capacity
   b. An increase in the money supply during a period of high unemployment and excess industrial capacity
   c. An increase in the price of oil caused by a war in the Middle East, assuming that the Fed attempts to keep interest rates constant by accommodating inflation
   d. An increase in taxes and a cut in government spending, supported by a cooperative Fed acting to keep output from falling

5. During 1999 and 2000, a debate raged over whether the United States was at or above potential GDP. Some economists feared the economy was operating at a level of output above potential GDP and inflationary pressures were building. They urged the Fed to tighten monetary policy and increase interest rates to slow the economy. Others argued that a worldwide glut of cheap products was causing input prices to be lower, keeping prices from rising.

   By using aggregate supply and demand curves and other useful graphs, illustrate the following:
   a. Those pushing the Fed to act were right and prices start to rise more rapidly in 2000. The Fed acts belatedly to slow money growth (contract the money supply), driving up interest rates and pushing the economy back to potential GDP.
   b. The worldwide glut gets worse and the result is a *falling* price level (deflation) in the United States despite expanding aggregate demand.

6. Read over the News Analysis box on p. 577. When Ben Bernanke was appointed chairman of the Federal Reserve, he took dead aim at the rate of inflation, which was creeping up in late 2005, for the most part due to a rapid run-up in oil prices. Under Alan Greenspan, the Fed had already tightened the growth of the money supply (in essence contracted the supply of money), pushing the federal funds interest rate from 1 percent to 3.75 percent. How successful was the Fed at preventing inflation in 2006? Go to www.BLS.gov and click on CPI. Look at the rate of inflation (the annual percent change in the CPI) since October 2005. Read over the minutes of a recent Federal Open Market Committee Meeting (go to www.federalreserve.gov and click on Monetary Policy and then on Federal Open Market Committee).

7. By using aggregate supply and aggregate demand curves to illustrate, describe the effects of the following events on the price level and on equilibrium GDP in the *long run*, assuming that input prices fully adjust to output prices after some lag:
   a. An increase occurs in the money supply above potential GDP.
   b. A decrease in government spending and in the money supply with GDP above potential GDP occurs.
   c. Starting with the economy at potential GDP, a war in the Middle East pushes up energy prices temporarily. The Fed expands the money supply to accommodate the inflation.

8. Two separate capacity constraints are discussed in this chapter: (1) the actual physical capacity of existing plants and equipment, shown as the vertical portion of the short-run *AS* curve; and (2) potential GDP, leading to a vertical long-run *AS* curve. Explain the difference between the two. Which is greater, full-capacity GDP or potential GDP? Why?

9. In country A, all wage contracts are indexed to inflation. That is, each month wages are adjusted to reflect increases in the cost of living as reflected in changes in the price level. In country B, there are no cost-of-living adjustments to wages, but the workforce is completely unionized. Unions negotiate 3-year contracts. In which country is an expansionary monetary policy likely to have a larger effect on aggregate output? Explain your answer using aggregate supply and aggregate demand curves.

The Labor Market, Unemployment, and Inflation

27

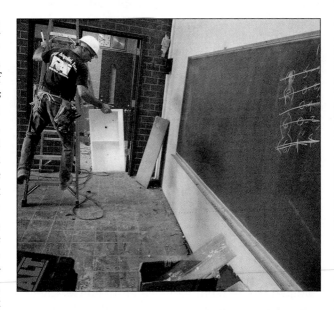

In previous chapters, we stressed the three broadly defined markets in which households, firms, the government, and the rest of the world interact: (1) the *goods market*, discussed in Chapters 21 and 22; (2) the *money market*, discussed in Chapters 23 and 24; and (3) the *labor market*. In Chapter 20 we described some features of the U.S. labor market and explained how the unemployment rate is measured. Then, in Chapter 26, we considered the labor market briefly in our discussion of the aggregate supply curve. Because labor is an input, what goes on in the labor market affects the shape of the aggregate supply (*AS*) curve. If wages and other input costs lag price increases, the *AS* curve will be upward-sloping; if wages and other input costs are completely flexible and rise every time prices rise by the same percentage, the *AS* curve will be vertical.

In this chapter, we look further at the labor market's role in the macroeconomy. First, we consider the classical view, which holds that wages always adjust to clear the labor market, that is, to equate the supply of and demand for labor. We then consider why the labor market may not always clear and why unemployment may exist. Finally, we discuss the relationship between inflation and unemployment. As we go through the analysis, it is important to recall why unemployment is one of the three primary concerns of macroeconomics. Go back and reread the section of Chapter 20 on "The Cost of Unemployment" (see pp. 443–446). It is clear that unemployment imposes heavy costs on the unemployed and on society. In 2005, more than 7 million people in the United States were looking for work and did not have even a part-time job.

THE LABOR MARKET: BASIC CONCEPTS

Let us briefly review what the unemployment rate measures (see Chapter 20). On the first Friday of every month the Labor Department releases the results of a household survey that provides an estimate of the number of people with a job, the employed (E), as well as the number of people who are looking for work but who cannot find a job, the unemployed (U). The labor force (LF) is the number of employed plus unemployed:

$$LF = E + U$$

unemployment rate The
number of people unemployed as
a percentage of the labor force.

The **unemployment rate** is the number of people unemployed as a percentage of the labor force:

$$\text{unemployment rate} = \frac{U}{LF}$$

To repeat, to be unemployed, a person must be out of a job and actively looking for work. When a person stops looking for work, he or she is considered *out of the labor force* and is no longer counted as unemployed.

It is important to realize that even if the economy is running at or near full capacity, the unemployment rate will never be zero. The economy is dynamic. Students graduate from schools and training programs; some businesses make profits and grow, while others suffer losses and go out of business; people move in and out of the labor force and change careers. It takes time for people to find the right job and for employers to match the right worker with the jobs they have. This **frictional** and **structural unemployment** is inevitable and in many ways desirable. (Review Chapter 20 if these terms are hazy to you.)

frictional unemployment
The portion of unemployment
that is due to the normal working
of the labor market; used to
denote short-run job/skill
matching problems.

**structural
unemployment** The portion
of unemployment that is due to
changes in the structure of the
economy that result in a
significant loss of jobs in certain
industries.

In this chapter, we are concerned with **cyclical unemployment**, the increase in unemployment that occurs during recessions and depressions. When the economy contracts, the number of people unemployed and the unemployment rate rise. The United States has experienced several periods of high unemployment. During the Great Depression, the unemployment rate remained over 17 percent for nearly a decade. In December 1982, more than 12 million people were unemployed, putting the unemployment rate at 10.8 percent.

In one sense, the reason employment falls when the economy experiences a downturn is obvious. When firms cut back on production, they need fewer workers, so people get laid off.

cyclical unemployment
The increase in unemployment
that occurs during recessions
and depressions.

> Employment tends to fall when aggregate output falls and to rise when aggregate output rises.

Nevertheless, a decline in the demand for labor does not necessarily mean that unemployment will rise. If markets work as we described in Chapters 3 and 4, a decline in the demand for labor will initially create an excess supply of labor. As a result, the wage rate will fall until the quantity of labor supplied again equals the quantity of labor demanded, restoring equilibrium in the labor market. At the new lower wage rate, everyone who wants a job will have one.

If the quantity of labor demanded and the quantity of labor supplied are brought into equilibrium by rising and falling wage rates, there should be no persistent unemployment above the frictional and structural amount. This was the view held by the classical economists who preceded Keynes, and it is still the view of a number of economists today.

THE CLASSICAL VIEW OF THE LABOR MARKET

The classical view of the labor market is illustrated in Figure 27.1. Classical economists assume the wage rate adjusts to equate the quantity of labor demanded with the quantity of labor supplied, thereby implying that unemployment does not exist. To see how this adjustment takes place, assume there is a decrease in the demand for labor that shifts the demand curve in Figure 27.1 from D_0 to D_1. This decreased demand will cause the wage rate to fall from W_0 to W_1 and the amount of labor demanded to fall from L_0 to L_1. The decrease in the quantity of labor supplied is a movement along the labor supply curve.

labor supply curve A graph
that illustrates the amount of
labor that households want to
supply at each given wage rate.

Each point on the **labor supply curve** in Figure 27.1 represents the amount of labor households want to supply at each given wage rate. Each household's decision concerning how much labor to supply is part of the overall consumer choice problem of a household. Each household member looks at the market wage rate, the prices of outputs, and the value of leisure time (including the value of staying at home and working in the yard or raising children) and chooses the amount of labor to supply (if any). A household mem-

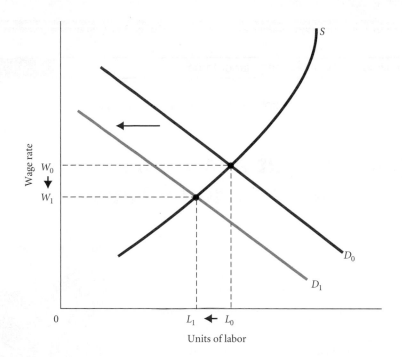

FIGURE 27.1 The Classical Labor Market

Classical economists believe that the labor market always clears. If the demand for labor shifts from D_0 to D_1, the equilibrium wage will fall from W_0 to W_1. Anyone who wants a job at W_1 will have one.

ber not in the labor force has decided his or her time is more valuable in nonmarket activities.

It is easy to see why. If you choose to stay out of the labor force, the reason is that you (a member of society) place a higher value on the use of your time than society is currently placing on the product that you would produce if you were employed. Consider households in less-developed countries. In many such households, the alternative to working for a wage is subsistence farming. If the wage rate in the labor market is very low, many people will choose to farm for themselves. In this case, the value of what these people produce in farming must be greater than the value that society currently places on what they would produce if they worked for a wage. If this were not true, wages would rise and more people would join the labor force.

Each point on the **labor demand curve** in Figure 27.1 represents the amount of labor firms want to employ at each given wage rate. Each firm's decision about how much labor to demand is part of its overall profit-maximizing decision. A firm makes a profit by selling output to households. It will hire workers if the value of its output is sufficient to justify the wage that is being paid. Thus, the amount of labor that a firm hires depends on the value of the output that workers produce.

The classical economists saw the workings of the labor market—the behavior of labor supply and labor demand—as optimal from the standpoint of both individual households and firms and from the standpoint of society. If households want more output than is currently being produced, output demand will increase, output prices will rise, the demand for labor will increase, the wage rate will rise, and more workers will be drawn into the labor force. (Some of those who preferred not to be a part of the labor force at the lower wage rate will be lured into the labor force at the higher wage rate.) At equilibrium, prices and wages reflect a trade-off between the value households place on outputs and the value of time spent in leisure and nonmarket work. At equilibrium, the people who are not working have *chosen* not to work at that market wage. There is always *full employment* in this sense. The classical economists believed the market will achieve the optimal result if left to its own devices, and there is nothing the government can do to make things better.

labor demand curve A graph that illustrates the amount of labor that firms want to employ at each given wage rate.

Employment and Unemployment at the End of 2005

THE EMPLOYMENT REPORT THAT IS released by the U.S. government at the beginning of each month is widely followed by people in both business and politics. The following *New York Times* article describes the report released December 3, 2005. As you can see, this report was dominated by news of the recovery from the two hurricanes. And the White House chimed in.

Jobs Surged Last Month in Rebound from Storm
By LOUIS UCHITELLE
New York Times
December 3, 2005

The nation's employers added 215,000 jobs last month, the government reported yesterday, as the economy rebounded from the devastating impact of Hurricane Katrina.

The strong November number, the biggest monthly increase since July, suggested that employers are scrambling for workers in response to a strongly growing economy. But on the fourth anniversary of the recovery from the 2001 recession, job growth is still below the levels achieved in previous recoveries, and the unemployment rate has been stuck at 5 percent nearly every month since June.

"We're back on track after the ill effects of the hurricanes," said Mark Zandi, chief economist at Economy.com, referring to Wilma, which hit southern

Florida in late October, as well as Katrina in late August. "But it is also fair to conclude that global competition and corporate layoffs are weighing on job growth."

In releasing the employment data for November, the Bureau of Labor Statistics reported that at least 900,000 people age 16 or older—one-third of them black—evacuated in August because of Hurricane Katrina and that half had returned by last month. Most apparently came back to jobs.

The unemployment rate among the returnees was 12.5 percent, while 27.8 percent of those still living elsewhere were unemployed. Hundreds of thousands of other evacuees simply dropped out of the labor force, not even seeking a job, which is necessary to be listed as unemployed.

The November surge in hiring was widespread, covering nearly two-thirds of the nation's industries, the best showing since May of last year. It came after two months in which only 61,000 new jobs were created, because of the hurricanes, and it dispelled concerns that hiring would continue to lag despite robust economic growth.

The White House reacted quickly. "The economy is in good shape," President Bush said in a Rose Garden appearance shortly after the bureau released the November numbers. He declared that the future of the economy is "as bright as it's been in a long time."

The worst news in the November report concerned blacks. Their unemployment rate jumped to 10.6 percent from 9.1 percent in October. That might reverse itself in December. But on top of the national setback, unemployment surged among blacks who evacuated the New Orleans area to escape Hurricane Katrina and have not yet returned.

That rate was 47 percent in November compared with 13 percent for whites who have not gone back.

THE CLASSICAL LABOR MARKET AND THE AGGREGATE SUPPLY CURVE

We can now relate the classical view of the labor market to the theory of the vertical AS curve in Chapter 26. The classical idea that wages adjust to clear the labor market is consistent with the view that wages respond quickly to price changes. Recall that the argument that the AS curve is vertical in the long run involves input-price adjustments. If the short-run AS and aggregate demand (AD) curves intersected above potential GDP (Y_0 in Figure 26.10), then input prices, *including wages*, would rise, shifting the AS curve to the left and pushing Y back down to Y_0. Similarly, if the short-run AS and AD curves intersected to the left of Y_0, unemployment and excess capacity would cause input prices, *including wages*, to fall, shifting the AS curve to the right and pushing Y back up to Y_0. Also remember, if the AS curve is vertical, monetary and fiscal policy cannot affect the level of output and employment in the economy. It therefore follows that those who believe the wage rate adjusts quickly to clear the labor market are likely to believe the *AS* curve is vertical (or almost vertical) and monetary and fiscal policy have little or no effect on output and employment.

THE UNEMPLOYMENT RATE AND THE CLASSICAL VIEW

If, as the classical economists assumed, the labor market works well, how can we account for the fact that the unemployment rate at times seems high? There seem to be times when millions of people who want jobs at prevailing wage rates cannot find them. How can we reconcile this situation with the classical assumption about the labor market?

Some economists answer by arguing that the unemployment rate is not a good measure of whether the labor market is working well. We know the economy is dynamic and at any given time some industries are expanding and some are contracting. Consider, for example, a carpenter who is laid off because of a contraction in the construction industry. He had probably developed specific skills related to the construction industry—skills not necessarily useful for jobs in other industries. If he were earning $40,000 per year as a carpenter, it may be that he could earn only $30,000 per year in another industry. He may eventually work his way back up to a salary of $40,000 in the new industry as he develops new skills, but this process will take time. Will this carpenter take a job at $30,000? There are at least two reasons he may not. First, he may believe the slump in the construction industry is temporary and he will soon get his job back. Second, he may believe he can earn more than $30,000 in another industry and will continue to look for a better job.

If our carpenter decides to continue looking for a job paying more than $30,000 per year, he will be considered unemployed because he is actively looking for work. This does not necessarily mean the labor market is not working properly. The carpenter has *chosen* not to work for a wage of $30,000 per year, but if his value to any firm outside the construction industry is no more than $30,000 per year, we would not expect him to find a job paying more than $30,000. The unemployment rate as measured by the government is not necessarily an accurate indicator of whether the labor market is working properly.

If the degree to which industries are changing in the economy fluctuates over time, there will be more people like our carpenter at some times than at others. This variation will cause the measured unemployment rate to fluctuate. Some economists argue the measured unemployment rate may sometimes *seem* high even though the labor market is working well. The quantity of labor supplied at the current wage is equal to the quantity demanded at the current wage. The fact that there are people willing to work at a wage higher than the current wage does not mean the labor market is not working. Whenever there is an upward-sloping supply curve in a market (as is usually the case in the labor market), the quantity supplied at a price higher than the equilibrium price is always greater than the quantity supplied at the equilibrium price.

Economists who view unemployment in this way do not see it as a major problem. Yet the haunting images of the bread lines in the 1930s are still with us, and many find it difficult to believe everything was optimal when over 12 million people were looking for work at the end of 1982. There are other views of unemployment, as we will now see.

Some economists believe unemployment is not a major problem. However, the images of the 1930s are still with us, and more than 12 million people were looking for work during the recession of 1982.

EXPLAINING THE EXISTENCE OF UNEMPLOYMENT

If unemployment is a major macroeconomic problem—and many economists believe it is—then we need to explore some of the reasons that have been suggested for its existence. Among these are sticky wages, efficiency wage theory, imperfect information, and minimum wage laws.

STICKY WAGES

sticky wages The downward rigidity of wages as an explanation for the existence of unemployment.

One explanation for unemployment (above and beyond normal frictional and structural unemployment) is that wages are **sticky** on the downward side. That is, the equilibrium wage gets stuck at a particular level and does not fall when the demand for labor falls. This situation is illustrated in Figure 27.2, where the equilibrium wage gets stuck at W_0 (the original wage) and does not fall to W^* when demand decreases from D_0 to D_1. The result is unemployment of the amount $L_0 - L_1$, where L_0 is the quantity of labor that households want to supply at wage rate W_0 and L_1 is the amount of labor that firms want to hire at wage rate W_0. $L_0 - L_1$ is the number of workers who would like to work at W_0 but cannot find jobs.

The sticky wage explanation of unemployment begs the question. *Why* are wages sticky, if they are, and why do wages not fall to clear the labor market during periods of high unemployment? Many answers have been proposed, but as yet no one answer has been agreed on. This lack of consensus is one reason macroeconomics has been in a state of flux for so long. The existence of unemployment continues to be a puzzle. Although we will discuss the major theories that economists have proposed to explain why wages may not clear the labor market, we can offer no conclusions. The question is still open.

social, or **implicit, contracts** Unspoken agreements between workers and firms that firms will not cut wages.

Social, or Implicit, Contracts
One explanation for downwardly sticky wages is that firms enter into **social**, or **implicit, contracts** with workers not to cut wages. It seems that extreme events—deep recession, deregulation, or threat of bankruptcy—are necessary for firms to cut wages. Wage cuts did not occur during the Great Depression, in the airline industry following deregulation of the industry in the 1980s, and recently when some U.S. manufacturing firms found themselves in danger of bankruptcy from stiff foreign competition. These are exceptions to the general rule. For reasons that may be more sociological than economic, cutting wages seems close to being a taboo.

relative-wage explanation of unemployment An explanation for sticky wages (and therefore unemployment): If workers are concerned about their wages relative to other workers in other firms and industries, they may be unwilling to accept a wage cut unless they know that all other workers are receiving similar cuts.

A related argument, the **relative-wage explanation of unemployment**, holds that workers are concerned about their wages *relative* to the wages of other workers in other firms and industries and may be unwilling to accept wage cuts unless they know other workers are

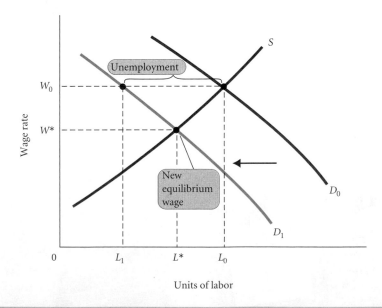

FIGURE 27.2 Sticky Wages

If wages "stick" at W_0 instead of falling to the new equilibrium wage of W^* following a shift of demand from D_0 to D_1, the result will be unemployment equal to $L_0 - L_1$.

receiving similar cuts. Because it is difficult to reassure any one group of workers that all other workers are in the same situation, workers may resist any cut in their wages. There may be an implicit understanding between firms and workers that firms will not do anything that would make their workers worse off relative to workers in other firms.

Explicit Contracts   Many workers—in particular unionized workers—sign 1- to 3-year employment contracts with firms. These contracts stipulate the workers' wages for each year of the contract. Wages set in this way do not fluctuate with economic conditions, either upward or downward. If the economy slows down and firms demand fewer workers, the wage will not fall. Instead, some workers will be laid off.

Although **explicit contracts** can explain why some wages are sticky, a deeper question must also be considered. Workers and firms surely know at the time a contract is signed that unforeseen events may cause the wages set by the contract to be too high or too low. Why do firms and workers bind themselves in this way? One explanation is that negotiating wages is costly. Negotiations between unions and firms can take a considerable amount of time— time that could be spent producing output—and it would be very costly to negotiate wages weekly or monthly. Contracts are a way of bearing these costs at no more than 1-, 2-, or 3-year intervals. There is a trade-off between the costs of locking workers and firms into contracts for long periods of time and the costs of wage negotiations. The length of contracts that minimizes negotiation costs seems to be (from what we observe in practice) between 1 and 3 years.

Some multiyear contracts adjust for unforeseen events by **cost-of-living adjustments (COLAs)** written into the contract. COLAs tie wages to changes in the cost of living: the greater the rate of inflation, the more wages are raised. COLAs thus protect workers from unexpected inflation, although many COLAs adjust wages by a smaller percentage than the percentage increase in prices.

> **explicit contracts**
> Employment contracts that stipulate workers' wages, usually for a period of 1 to 3 years.

> **cost-of-living adjustments (COLAs)**
> Contract provisions that tie wages to changes in the cost of living. The greater the inflation rate, the more wages are raised.

EFFICIENCY WAGE THEORY

Another explanation for unemployment centers on the **efficiency wage theory**, which holds that the productivity of workers increases with the wage rate. If this is true, firms may have an incentive to pay wages *above* the wage at which the quantity of labor supplied is equal to the quantity of labor demanded.

An individual firm has an incentive to hire workers as long as the value of what they produce is equal to or greater than the wage rate. With no efficiency effects, the market in Figure 27.2 would produce an equilibrium wage of W^*. Suppose, however, the firm could increase the productivity of all its workers by raising the wage rate above W^*. The firm's demand for labor would be no lower, but the higher wage rate would cause the quantity of labor supplied to increase. The quantity of labor supplied would exceed the quantity of labor demanded at the new higher wage—the *efficiency wage*—and the result is unemployment.

Empirical studies of labor markets have identified several potential benefits that firms receive from paying workers more than the market-clearing wage. Among them are lower turnover, improved morale, and reduced "shirking" of work. Even though the efficiency wage theory predicts some unemployment, it is unlikely that the behavior it is describing accounts for much of the observed large cyclical fluctuations in unemployment over time.

> **efficiency wage theory**
> An explanation for unemployment that holds that the productivity of workers increases with the wage rate. If this is so, firms may have an incentive to pay wages above the market-clearing rate.

IMPERFECT INFORMATION

Thus far we have been assuming that firms know exactly what wage rates they need to set to clear the labor market. They may not choose to set their wages at this level, but at least they know what the market-clearing wage is. In practice, however, firms may not have enough information at their disposal to know what the market-clearing wage is. In this case, firms are said to have *imperfect information*. If firms have imperfect or incomplete information, they may simply set wages wrong—wages that do not clear the labor market.

If a firm sets its wages too high, more workers will want to work for that firm than the firm wants to employ, and some potential workers will be turned away. The result is, of course, unemployment. One objection to this explanation is that it accounts for the existence of unemployment only in the very short run. As soon as a firm sees that it has made a mistake, why would it not immediately correct its mistake and adjust its wages to the correct, market-clearing level? Why would unemployment *persist*?

If the economy were simple, it should take no more than a few months for firms to correct their mistakes, but the economy is complex. Although firms may be aware of their past mistakes and may try to correct them, new events are happening all the time. Because constant change—including a constantly changing equilibrium wage level—is characteristic of the economy, firms may find it hard to adjust wages to the market-clearing level. The labor market is not like the stock market or the market for wheat, where prices are determined in organized exchanges every day. Instead, thousands of firms are setting wages and millions of workers are responding to these wages. It may take considerable time for the market-clearing wages to be determined after they have been disturbed from an equilibrium position.

MINIMUM WAGE LAWS

minimum wage laws Laws that set a floor for wage rates—that is, a minimum hourly rate for any kind of labor.

Minimum wage laws explain at least a small fraction of unemployment. These laws set a floor for wage rates—a minimum hourly rate for any kind of labor. In 2005, the federal minimum wage was $5.15 per hour. If the market-clearing wage for some groups of workers is below this amount, this group will be unemployed. In Figure 27.2, if the minimum wage is W_0 and the market-clearing wage is W^*, then the number of unemployed will be $L_0 - L_1$.

Teenagers, who have relatively little job experience, are most likely to be hurt by minimum wage laws. If some teenagers can produce only $4.50 worth of output per hour, no firm would be willing to hire them at a wage of $5.15. To do so would incur a loss of $0.65 per hour. In an unregulated market, these teenagers would be able to find work at the market-clearing wage of $4.50 per hour. If the minimum wage laws prevent the wage from falling below $5.15, these workers will not be able to find jobs, and they will be unemployed. Others who may be hurt include people with very low skills and some recent immigrants.

In response to this argument against the minimum wage, Congress established a subminimum wage for teenagers. The new law allows employers to hire teenagers at an "opportunity wage" of $4.25 for up to 90 days.

AN OPEN QUESTION

As we have seen, there are many explanations for why the labor market may not clear. The theories we have just set forth are not necessarily mutually exclusive, and there may be elements of truth in all of them. The aggregate labor market is very complicated, and there are no simple answers to why there is unemployment. Much current work in macroeconomics is concerned directly or indirectly with this question, and it is an exciting area of study. Which argument or arguments will win out in the end is an open question.

THE SHORT-RUN RELATIONSHIP BETWEEN THE UNEMPLOYMENT RATE AND INFLATION

The relationship between the unemployment rate and inflation—two of the most important variables in macroeconomics—has been the subject of much debate. We now have enough knowledge of the macroeconomy to explore this relationship.

We must begin by considering the relationship between aggregate output (income) (Y) and the unemployment rate (U). An increase in Y means firms are producing more output. To produce more output, more labor is needed in the production process. Therefore, an increase in Y leads to an increase in employment. An increase in employment means more people working (fewer people unemployed) and a lower unemployment rate. An increase in Y corresponds to a *decrease* in U. Thus, U and Y are *negatively* related:

> When Y rises, the unemployment rate falls, and when Y falls, the unemployment rate rises.

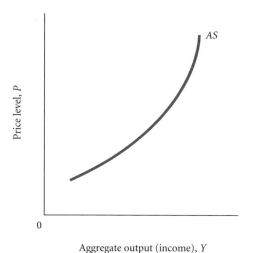

FIGURE 27.3 The Aggregate Supply Curve

The *AS* curve shows a positive relationship between the price level (*P*) and aggregate output (income) (*Y*).

Next consider an upward-sloping *AS* curve, as shown in Figure 27.3. This curve represents the relationship between *Y* and the overall price level (*P*). The relationship is a positive one: When *P* increases, *Y* increases, and when *P* decreases, *Y* decreases.

As you will recall from the last chapter, the shape of the *AS* curve is determined by the behavior of the firms and how they react to an increase in demand. If aggregate demand shifts to the right and the economy is operating on the nearly flat part of the *AS* curve—far from capacity—output will increase but the price level will not change much. However, if the economy is operating on the steep part of the *AS* curve—close to capacity—an increase in demand will drive up the price level, but output will be constrained by capacity and will not increase much.

Think about what will happen following an event that leads to an increase in aggregate demand. First, firms experience an unanticipated decline in inventories. They respond by increasing output (*Y*) and hiring workers—the unemployment rate falls. If the economy is not close to capacity, there will be little increase in the price level. If, however, aggregate demand continues to grow, the ability of the economy to increase output will eventually reach its limit. As aggregate demand shifts farther and farther to the right along the *AS* curve, the price level increases more and more, and output begins to reach its limit. At the point at which the *AS* curve becomes vertical, output cannot rise any further. If output cannot grow, the unemployment rate cannot be pushed any lower.

> There is a negative relationship between the unemployment rate and the price level. As the unemployment rate declines in response to the economy's moving closer and closer to capacity output, the overall price level rises more and more, as shown in Figure 27.4.

The curve in Figure 27.4 has *not* been a major focus of attention in macroeconomics. Instead, the curve that has been extensively studied is shown in Figure 27.5, which plots the inflation rate on the vertical axis and the unemployment rate on the horizontal axis. The **inflation rate** is the percentage change in the price level, not the price level itself.

Figures 27.4 and 27.5 imply different things. Figure 27.4 shows that the *price level* remains the same if the unemployment rate remains unchanged. Figure 27.5 shows that the *inflation rate* remains the same if the unemployment rate remains unchanged. The curve in Figure 27.5 is called the **Phillips Curve**, after the British economist A. W. Phillips, who first examined it using data for the United Kingdom. In simplest terms, the Phillips Curve is a graph showing the relationship between the inflation rate and the unemployment rate.

The rest of this chapter focuses on the Phillips Curve in Figure 27.5 because it is the macroeconomic relationship that has been studied the most. Keep in mind, however, that it

inflation rate The percentage change in the price level.

Phillips Curve A graph showing the relationship between the inflation rate and the unemployment rate.

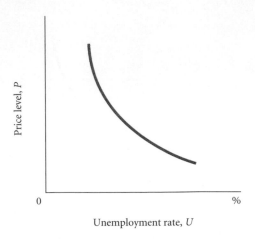

FIGURE 27.4 The Relationship Between the Price Level and the Unemployment Rate

This curve shows a negative relationship between the price level (*P*) and the unemployment rate (*U*). As the unemployment rate declines in response to the economy's moving closer and closer to capacity output, the price level rises more and more.

is not easy to go from the *AS* curve to the Phillips Curve. We have moved from graphs in which the price level is on the vertical axis (Figures 27.3 and 27.4) to a graph in which the *percentage change* in the price level is on the vertical axis (Figure 27.5). Put another way, the theory behind the Phillips Curve is somewhat different from the theory behind the *AS* curve. Fortunately, most of the insights gained from the *AS/AD* analysis concerning the behavior of the price level also apply to the behavior of the inflation rate.

THE PHILLIPS CURVE: A HISTORICAL PERSPECTIVE

In the 1950s and 1960s, there was a remarkably smooth relationship between the unemployment rate and the rate of inflation, as Figure 27.6 shows for the 1960s. As you can see, the data points fit fairly closely around a downward-sloping curve; in general, the higher the unemployment rate is, the lower the rate of inflation. The Phillips Curve in Figure 27.6 shows a trade-off between inflation and unemployment. To lower the inflation rate, we must accept a higher unemployment rate, and to lower the unemployment rate, we must accept a higher rate of inflation.

Textbooks written in the 1960s and early 1970s relied on the Phillips Curve as the main explanation of inflation. Things seemed simple—inflation appeared to respond in a fairly pre-

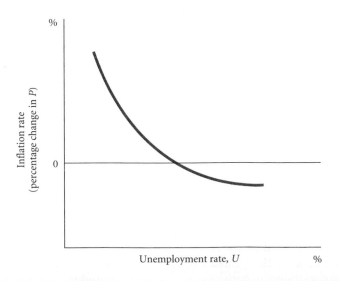

FIGURE 27.5 The Phillips Curve

The Phillips Curve shows the relationship between the inflation rate and the unemployment rate.

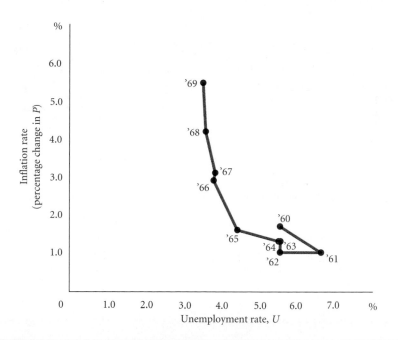

FIGURE 27.6 Unemployment and Inflation, 1960–1969

During the 1960s there seemed to be an obvious trade-off between inflation and unemployment. Policy debates during the period revolved around this apparent trade-off.

Source: See Table 20.8.

dictable way to changes in the unemployment rate. For this reason, policy discussions in the 1960s revolved around the Phillips Curve. The role of the policy maker, it was thought, was to choose a point on the curve. Conservatives usually argued for choosing a point with a low rate of inflation and were willing to accept a higher unemployment rate in exchange for this. Liberals usually argued for accepting more inflation to keep unemployment at a low level.

Life did not turn out to be quite so simple. The Phillips Curve broke down in the 1970s and 1980s. This change can be seen in Figure 27.7, which graphs the unemployment rate and

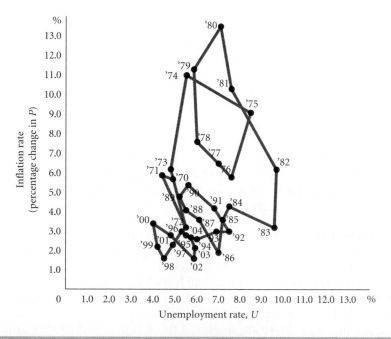

FIGURE 27.7 Unemployment and Inflation, 1970—2004

From the 1970s on, it became clear that the relationship between unemployment and inflation was anything but simple.

Source: See Table 20.8.

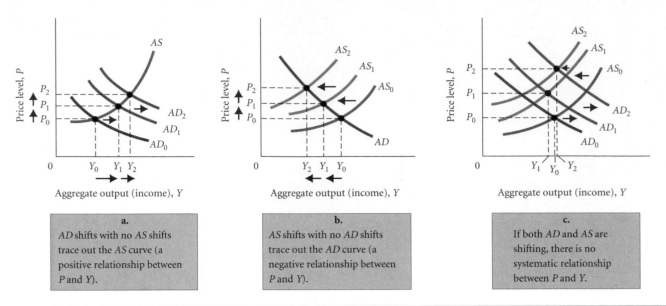

a.	b.	c.
AD shifts with no *AS* shifts trace out the *AS* curve (a positive relationship between *P* and *Y*).	*AS* shifts with no *AD* shifts trace out the *AD* curve (a negative relationship between *P* and *Y*).	If both *AD* and *AS* are shifting, there is no systematic relationship between *P* and *Y*.

FIGURE 27.8 Changes in the Price Level and Aggregate Output Depend on Shifts in Both Aggregate Demand and Aggregate Supply

inflation rate for the period from 1970 to 2004. The points in Figure 27.7 show no particular relationship between inflation and unemployment.

AGGREGATE SUPPLY AND AGGREGATE DEMAND ANALYSIS AND THE PHILLIPS CURVE

How can we explain the stability of the Phillips Curve in the 1950s and 1960s and the lack of stability after that? To answer, we need to return to *AS/AD* analysis.

If the *AD* curve shifts from year to year but the *AS* curve does not, the values of *P* and *Y* each year will lie along the *AS* curve [Figure 27.8(a)]. The plot of the relationship between *P* and *Y* will be upward-sloping. Correspondingly, the plot of the relationship between the unemployment rate (which decreases with increased output) and the rate of inflation will be a curve that slopes downward. In other words, we would expect to see a negative relationship between the unemployment rate and the inflation rate.

However, the relationship between the unemployment rate and the inflation rate will look different if the *AS* curve shifts from year to year but the *AD* curve does not. A leftward shift of the *AS* curve will cause an *increase* in the price level (*P*) and a *decrease* in aggregate output (*Y*) [Figure 27.8(b)]. When the *AS* curve shifts to the left, the economy experiences both inflation *and* an increase in the unemployment rate (because decreased output means increased unemployment). In other words, if the *AS* curve is shifting from year to year, we would expect to see a positive relationship between the unemployment rate and the inflation rate.

If both the *AS* and the *AD* curves are shifting simultaneously, however, there is no systematic relationship between *P* and *Y* [Figure 27.8(c)] and thus no systematic relationship between the unemployment rate and the inflation rate.

The Role of Import Prices One of the main factors that causes the *AS* curve to shift is the price of imports. (Remember, the *AS* curve shifts when input prices change, and input prices are affected by the price of imports, particularly the price of imported oil.) The price of imports is plotted in Figure 27.9 for the 1960 I–2005 II period. As you can see, the price of imports changed very little between 1960 and 1970. There were no large shifts in the *AS* curve in the 1960s due to changes in the price of imports. There were also no other large changes in input prices in the 1960s, so overall the *AS* curve shifted very little during the decade. The main variation in the 1960s was in aggregate demand, so the shifting *AD* curve traced out points along the *AS* curve.

Figure 27.9 also shows that the price of imports increased considerably in the 1970s. This rise led to large shifts in the *AS* curve during the decade, but the *AD* curve was also

596

FIGURE 27.9 The Price of Imports, 1960 I–2005 II

The price of imports changed very little in the 1960s and early 1970s. It increased substantially in 1974 and again in 1979–1980. Since 1981, the price of imports has changed very little.

shifting throughout the 1970s. With both curves shifting, the data point for P and Y were scattered all over the graph, and the observed relationship between P and Y was not at all systematic.

This story about import prices and the AS and AD curves in the 1960s and 1970s carries over to the Phillips Curve. The Phillips Curve was stable in the 1960s because the primary source of variation in the economy was demand, not costs. In the 1970s both demand *and* costs were varying, so no obvious relationship between the unemployment rate and the inflation rate was apparent. To some extent, what is remarkable about the Phillips Curve is not that it was not smooth after the 1960s, but that it ever was smooth.

EXPECTATIONS AND THE PHILLIPS CURVE

Another reason the Phillips Curve is not stable concerns expectations. We saw in Chapter 26 that if a firm expects other firms to raise their prices, the firm may raise the price of its own product. If all firms are behaving this way, then prices will rise because they are expected to rise. In this sense, expectations are self-fulfilling. Similarly, if inflation is expected to be high in the future, negotiated wages are likely to be higher than if inflation is expected to be low. Wage inflation is thus affected by expectations of future price inflation. Because wages are input costs, prices rise as firms respond to the higher wage costs. Price expectations that affect wage contracts eventually affect prices themselves.

If the rate of inflation depends on expectations, then the Phillips Curve will shift as expectations change. For example, if inflationary expectations increase, the result will be an increase in the rate of inflation even though the unemployment rate may not have changed. In this case, the Phillips Curve will shift to the right. If inflationary expectations decrease, the Phillips Curve will shift to the left—there will be less inflation at any given level of the unemployment rate.

It so happened that inflationary expectations were quite stable in the 1950s and 1960s. The inflation rate was moderate during most of this period, and people expected it to remain moderate. With inflationary expectations not changing very much, there were no major shifts of the Phillips Curve, a situation that helps explain its stability during the period.

Near the end of the 1960s, inflationary expectations began to increase, primarily in response to the actual increase in inflation that was occurring because of the tight economy caused by the Vietnam War. Inflationary expectations increased even further in the 1970s as a result of large oil price increases. These changing expectations led to shifts of the Phillips Curve and are another reason the curve was not stable during the 1970s.

IS THERE A SHORT-RUN TRADE-OFF BETWEEN INFLATION AND UNEMPLOYMENT?

Does the fact that the Phillips Curve broke down during the 1970s mean there is no trade-off between inflation and unemployment in the short run? Not at all: It simply means other things affect inflation aside from unemployment. Just as the relationship between price and quantity demanded along a standard demand curve shifts when income or other factors change, so does the relationship between unemployment and inflation change when other factors change.

In 1975, for example, inflation and unemployment were both high. As we explained earlier, this stagflation was caused partly by an increase in oil costs that shifted the aggregate supply curve to the left and partly by expectations of continued inflation that kept prices rising despite high levels of unemployment. In response to this situation, the Federal Reserve (Fed) pursued a contractionary monetary policy, which shifted the *AD* curve to the left and led to even higher unemployment. By 1977, the rate of inflation had dropped from over 11 percent to about 6 percent. So the rise in the unemployment rate did lead to a decrease in inflation, an outcome that reflects the trade-off.

> There *is* a short-run trade off between inflation and unemployment, but other factors besides unemployment affect inflation. Policy involves much more than simply choosing a point along a nice, smooth curve.

Back in Chapter 20, we mentioned that recessions may be the price that the economy pays to eliminate inflation. We can now understand this statement better. When unemployment rises, *other things being equal*, inflation falls.

THE LONG-RUN AGGREGATE SUPPLY CURVE, POTENTIAL GDP, AND THE NATURAL RATE OF UNEMPLOYMENT

Recall from Chapter 26 that many economists believe the *AS* curve is vertical in the long run. In the short run, we know that some input prices (which are costs to firms) lag behind increases in the overall price level. If the price level rises without a full adjustment of costs, firms' profits will be higher and output will increase. In the long run, however, input prices may catch up to output price increases. If input prices rise in subsequent periods, driving up costs, the short-run aggregate supply curve will shift to the left, and aggregate output will fall.

This situation is illustrated in Figure 27.10. Assume the initial equilibrium is at the intersection of AD_0 and the long-run aggregate supply curve. Now consider a shift of the aggregate

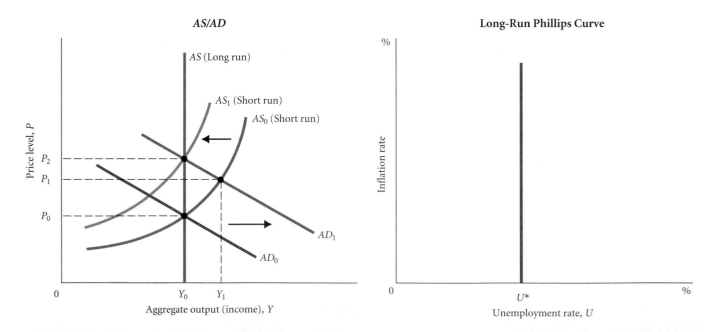

FIGURE 27.10 The Long-Run Phillips Curve: The Natural Rate of Unemployment

If the AS curve is vertical in the long run, so is the Phillips Curve. In the long run, the Phillips Curve corresponds to the natural rate of unemployment—that is, the unemployment rate that is consistent with the notion of a fixed long-run output at potential GDP. U^* is the natural rate of unemployment.

demand curve from AD_0 to AD_1. If input prices lag behind changes in the overall price level, aggregate output will rise from Y_0 to Y_1. (This is a movement along the short-run AS curve AS_0.) In the longer run, input prices may catch up. For example, next year's labor contracts may make up for the fact that wage increases did not keep up with the cost of living this year. If input prices catch up in the longer run, the AS curve will shift from AS_0 to AS_1 and drive aggregate output back to Y_0. If input prices ultimately rise by exactly the same percentage as output prices, firms will produce the same level of output as they did before the increase in aggregate demand.

In Chapter 26 we said Y_0 is sometimes called *potential GDP*. Aggregate output can be pushed above Y_0 in the short run. When aggregate output exceeds Y_0, however, there is upward pressure on input prices and costs. The unemployment rate is already quite low, firms are beginning to encounter the limits of their plant capacities, and so forth. At levels of aggregate output above Y_0, costs will rise, the AS curve will shift to the left, and the price level will rise. Thus, potential GDP is the level of aggregate output that can be sustained in the long run without inflation.

This story is directly related to the Phillips Curve. Those who believe the AS curve is vertical in the long run at potential GDP also believe the Phillips Curve is vertical in the long run at some natural rate of unemployment. Recall from Chapter 20 that the **natural rate of unemployment** refers to unemployment that occurs as a normal part of the functioning of the economy. It is sometimes taken as the sum of frictional unemployment and structural unemployment. The logic behind the vertical Phillips Curve is that whenever the unemployment rate is pushed below the natural rate, wages begin to rise, thus pushing up costs. This leads to a *lower* level of output, which pushes the unemployment rate back up to the natural rate. At the natural rate, the economy can be considered to be at full employment.

natural rate of unemployment The unemployment that occurs as a normal part of the functioning of the economy. Sometimes taken as the sum of frictional unemployment and structural unemployment.

THE NONACCELERATING INFLATION RATE OF UNEMPLOYMENT (NAIRU)

In Figure 27.10 the long-run vertical Phillips Curve is a graph with the inflation rate on the vertical axis and the unemployment rate on the horizontal axis. The natural rate of unemployment is U^*. In the long run, according to advocates of the long-run vertical Phillips Curve, the actual unemployment rate moves to U^* because of the natural workings of the economy.

Another graph of interest is Figure 27.11, which plots the *change in* the inflation rate on the vertical axis and the unemployment rate on the horizontal axis. Many economists believe

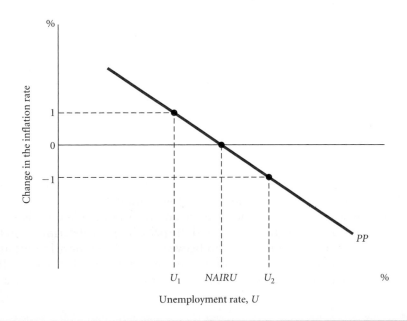

FIGURE 27.11 The NAIRU Diagram

To the left of the NAIRU the price level is accelerating (positive changes in the inflation rate), and to the right of the NAIRU the price level is decelerating (negative changes in the inflation rate). Only when the unemployment rate is equal to the NAIRU is the price level changing at a constant rate (no change in the inflation rate).

NAIRU The nonaccelerating inflation rate of unemployment.

the relationship between the change in the inflation rate and the unemployment rate is as depicted by the *PP* curve in the figure. The value of the unemployment rate where the *PP* curve crosses zero is called the *nonaccelerating inflation rate of unemployment* (**NAIRU**). If the actual unemployment rate is to the left of the NAIRU, the change in the inflation rate will be positive. As depicted in the figure, at U_1 the change in the inflation rate is 1. Conversely, if the actual unemployment rate is to the right of the NAIRU, the change in the inflation rate is negative: At U_2 the change is -1.

Consider what happens if the unemployment rate decreases from the NAIRU to U_1 and stays at U_1 for many periods. Assume also that the inflation rate at the NAIRU was 2 percent. Then in the first period the inflation rate will increase from 2 percent to 3 percent. The inflation rate does not, however, just stay at the higher 3 percent value. In the next period the inflation rate will increase from 3 percent to 4 percent, and so on. The price level will be accelerating—that is, the change in the inflation rate will be positive—when the actual unemployment rate is below the NAIRU. Conversely, the price level will be decelerating—that is, the change in the inflation rate will be negative—when the actual unemployment rate is above the NAIRU.[1]

The *PP* curve in Figure 27.11 is like the *AS* curve in Figure 27.3—the same factors that shift the *AS* curve, such as cost shocks, can also shift the *PP* curve. Figure 26.8 summarizes the various factors that can cause the *AS* curve to shift, and these are also relevant for the *PP* curve. A favorable shift for the *PP* curve is to the left, because the *PP* curve crosses zero at a lower unemployment rate, indicating that the NAIRU is lower. Some have argued that one possible recent source of favorable shifts is increased foreign competition, which may have kept both wage costs and other input costs down.

Before about 1995, proponents of the NAIRU theory argued that the value of the NAIRU in the United States was around 6 percent. By the end of 1995, the unemployment rate declined to 5.6 percent, and by 2000, the unemployment rate was down to 3.9 percent. If the NAIRU were 6 percent, one should have seen a continuing increase in the inflation rate beginning about 1995. In fact, the 1995 to 2000 period saw slightly declining inflation. Not only did inflation not continually increase, it did not even increase once to a new, higher value and then stay there. As the unemployment rate declined during this period, proponents of the NAIRU lowered their estimates of it, more or less in line with the actual fall in the unemployment rate. This recalibration can be justified by arguing that there have been continuing favorable shifts of the *PP* curve, such as possible increased foreign competition. Critics, however, have argued that this procedure is close to making the NAIRU theory vacuous. Can the theory really be tested if the estimate of the NAIRU is changed whenever it is not consistent with the data? How trustworthy is the appeal to favorable shifts?

Macroeconomists are currently debating whether equations estimated under the NAIRU theory are good approximations. More time is needed before any definitive answers can be given.

LOOKING AHEAD

This chapter concludes our basic analysis of how the macroeconomy works. In the preceding seven chapters, we have examined how households and firms behave in the three market arenas—the goods market, the money market, and the labor market. We have seen how aggregate output (income), the interest rate, and the price level are determined in the economy, and we have examined the relationship between two of the most important macroeconomic variables, the inflation rate and the unemployment rate. In Chapter 28, we use everything we have learned up to this point to examine a number of important policy issues.

---

[1]The NAIRU is actually misnamed. It is the *price level* that is accelerating or decelerating, not the inflation rate, when the actual unemployment rate differs from the NAIRU. The inflation rate is not accelerating or decelerating, but simply changing by the same amount each period. The namers of the NAIRU forgot their physics.

SUMMARY

THE LABOR MARKET: BASIC CONCEPTS

1. Because the economy is dynamic, *frictional* and *structural unemployment* are inevitable and in some ways desirable. Times of *cyclical unemployment* are of concern to macroeconomic policy makers.

2. In general, employment tends to fall when aggregate output falls and rise when aggregate output rises.

THE CLASSICAL VIEW OF THE LABOR MARKET

3. Classical economists believe the interaction of supply and demand in the labor market brings about equilibrium and that unemployment (beyond the frictional and structural amounts) does not exist.

4. The classical view of the labor market is consistent with the theory of a vertical aggregate supply curve.

EXPLAINING THE EXISTENCE OF UNEMPLOYMENT

5. Some economists argue that the unemployment rate is not an accurate indicator of whether the labor market is working properly. Unemployed people who are considered part of the labor force may be offered jobs but may be unwilling to take those jobs at the offered salaries. Some of the unemployed may have chosen not to work, but this result does not mean that the labor market has malfunctioned.

6. Those who do not subscribe to the classical view of the labor market suggest several reasons why unemployment exists. Downwardly *sticky wages* may be brought about by *social (implicit)* or *explicit contracts* not to cut wages. If the equilibrium wage rate falls but wages are prevented from falling also, the result will be unemployment.

7. *Efficiency wage theory* holds that the productivity of workers increases with the wage rate. If this is true, firms may have an incentive to pay wages above the wage at which the quantity of labor supplied is equal to the quantity of labor demanded. At all wages above the equilibrium, there will be an excess supply of labor and therefore unemployment.

8. If firms are operating with incomplete or imperfect information, they may not know what the market-clearing wage is. As a result, they may set their wages incorrectly and bring about unemployment. Because the economy is so complex, it may take considerable time for firms to correct these mistakes.

9. *Minimum wage laws*, which set a floor for wage rates, are one factor contributing to unemployment of teenagers and very low-skilled workers. If the market-clearing wage for some groups of workers is below the minimum wage, some members of this group will be unemployed.

THE SHORT-RUN RELATIONSHIP BETWEEN THE UNEMPLOYMENT RATE AND INFLATION

10. There is a negative relationship between the unemployment rate (U) and aggregate output (income) (Y): When Y rises, U falls. When Y falls, U rises.

11. The relationship between the unemployment rate and the price level is negative: As the unemployment rate declines and the economy moves closer to capacity, the price level rises more and more.

12. The *Phillips Curve* represents the relationship between the *inflation rate* and the *unemployment rate*. During the 1950s and 1960s, this relationship was stable, and there seemed to be a predictable trade-off between inflation and unemployment. As a result of import price increases (which led to shifts in aggregate supply) and shifts in aggregate demand brought about partially by inflationary expectations, the relationship between the inflation rate and the unemployment rate was erratic in the 1970s. There *is* a short-term trade-off between inflation and unemployment, but other things besides unemployment affect inflation.

THE LONG-RUN AGGREGATE SUPPLY CURVE, POTENTIAL GDP, AND THE NATURAL RATE OF UNEMPLOYMENT

13. Those who believe the *AS* curve is vertical in the long run also believe the Phillips Curve is vertical in the long run at the *natural rate of unemployment*. The natural rate is generally the sum of the frictional and structural rates. If the Phillips Curve is vertical in the long run, then there is a limit to how low government policy can push the unemployment rate without setting off inflation.

14. The *NAIRU* theory says that the price level will accelerate when the unemployment rate is below the NAIRU and decelerate when the unemployment rate is above the NAIRU.

REVIEW TERMS AND CONCEPTS

cost-of-living adjustments (COLAs), 591
cyclical unemployment, 586
efficiency wage theory, 591
explicit contracts, 591
frictional unemployment, 586
inflation rate, 593

labor demand curve, 587
labor supply curve, 586
minimum wage laws, 592
NAIRU, 600
natural rate of unemployment, 599
Phillips Curve, 593

relative-wage explanation of unemployment, 590
social, or implicit, contracts, 590
sticky wages, 590
structural unemployment, 586
unemployment rate, 586

PROBLEM SET

1. In April 2000, the U.S. unemployment rate dropped below 4 percent for the first time in 30 years. At the same time inflation remained at a very low level by historical standards. Can you offer an explanation for what seems to be an improved trade-off between inflation and unemployment? What factors might improve the trade-off? What factors might make it worse?

2. The box on p. 588 discusses the growth in employment at the end of 2005. At that time, there was much uncertainty about the potential for a slowdown in employment growth. A primary worry was that the housing market, which had been very strong for several years, was beginning to slow significantly. The Fed, however, was beginning to worry about inflation and was raising interest rates. Looking back at the first half of 2005, how successful was the Fed at containing inflation? What happened to the unemployment rate? You can find the answer at **www.bls.gov**.

3. Obtain monthly data on the unemployment rate and the inflation rate for the last 2 years. (These data can be found in a recent issue of the *Survey of Current Business* or in the *Monthly Labor Review* or *Employment and Earnings*, all published by the government and available in many college libraries or at **www.bls.gov**.
   a. What trends do you observe? Can you explain what you see using aggregate supply and aggregate demand curves?
   b. Plot the 24 monthly rates on a graph with the unemployment rate measured on the x-axis and the inflation rate on the y-axis. Is there evidence of a trade-off between these two variables? Can you offer an explanation?

4. In 2006, the country of Ruba was suffering from a period of high unemployment. The new president, Clang, appointed as his chief economist Laurel Tiedye. Ms. Tiedye and her staff estimated these supply and demand curves for labor from data obtained from the secretary of labor, Robert Small:

$$Q_D = 100 - 5W$$
$$Q_S = 10W - 20$$

   where Q is the quantity of labor supplied/demanded in millions of workers and W is the wage rate in slugs, the currency of Ruba.
   a. Currently, the law in Ruba says no worker shall be paid less than nine slugs per hour. Estimate the quantity of labor supplied, the number of unemployed, and the unemployment rate.
   b. President Clang, over the objection of Secretary Small, has recommended to the Congress that the law be changed to allow the wage rate to be determined in the market. If such a law were passed and the market adjusted quickly, what would happen to total employment, the size of the labor force, and the unemployment rate? Show the results graphically.
   c. Will the Rubanese labor market adjust quickly to such a change in the law? Why or why not?

5. The following policies have at times been advocated for coping with unemployment. Briefly explain how each might work, and explain which type or types of unemployment (frictional, structural, or cyclical) each policy is designed to alter.
   a. A computer list of job openings and a service that matches employees with job vacancies (sometimes called an "economic dating service")
   b. Lower minimum wage for teenagers
   c. Retraining programs for workers who need to learn new skills to find employment
   d. Public employment for people without jobs
   e. Improved information about available jobs and current wage rates
   f. The president's going on nationwide TV and attempting to convince firms and workers that the inflation rate next year will be low

6. Your boss offers you a wage increase of 10 percent. Is it possible that you are worse off, even with the wage increase, than you were before? Explain your answer.

7. How will the following affect labor force participation rates, labor supply, and unemployment?
   a. Because the retired elderly are a larger and larger fraction of the U.S. population, Congress and the president decide to raise the Social Security tax on individuals to continue paying benefits to the elderly.
   b. A national child care program is enacted, requiring employers to provide free child care services.
   c. The U.S. government reduces restrictions on immigration into the United States.
   d. The welfare system is eliminated.
   e. The government subsidizes the purchase of new capital by firms (an investment tax credit).

8. Draw a graph to illustrate the following:
   a. A Phillips Curve based on the assumption of a vertical long-run aggregate supply curve
   b. The effect of a change in inflationary expectations on a recently stable Phillips Curve
   c. Unemployment caused by a recently enacted minimum wage law

9. Obtain data on "average hourly earnings of production workers" and the unemployment rate for your state or area over a recent 2-year period. Has unemployment increased or decreased? What has happened to wages? Does the pattern of unemployment help explain the movement of wages? Can you offer an explanation?

10. Suppose the inflation–unemployment relationship depicted by the Phillips Curve was stable. Do you think the U.S. trade-off and the Japanese trade-off would be identical? If not, what kinds of factors might make the trade-offs dissimilar?

Macroeconomic Issues and Policy

28

Newspapers carry articles dealing with macroeconomic problems daily, and macroeconomic issues and policies are an important part of many political campaigns. By using what we have learned about how the macroeconomy works, we can now examine in greater depth various issues and problems.

In this chapter, we look more deeply at monetary and fiscal policy. We first consider a problem that both types of policy makers face, but particularly fiscal policy makers, which is the problem of time lags. We will see that it is not easy to get the timing right when trying to stabilize the economy. We then turn to more detailed looks at monetary and fiscal policy.

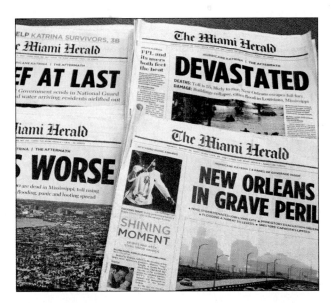

TIME LAGS REGARDING MONETARY AND FISCAL POLICY

One of the objectives of monetary and fiscal policy is stabilization of the economy. Consider the two possible time paths for aggregate output (income) (*Y*) shown in Figure 28.1. In path *B* (the light blue line), the fluctuations in GDP are smaller than those in path *A* (the dark blue line). One aim of **stabilization policy** is to smooth out fluctuations in output, to try to move the economy along a path like *B* instead of *A*. Stabilization policy is also concerned with the stability of prices. Here the goal is not to prevent the overall price level from rising at all but instead to achieve an inflation rate that is as close to zero as possible given the government's other goals of high and stable levels of output and employment.

Stabilization goals are not easy to achieve. The existence of various kinds of **time lags**, or delays in the response of the economy to stabilization policies, can make the economy difficult to control. Economists generally recognize three kinds of time lags: recognition lags, implementation lags, and response lags. We will consider each, but we will begin with an analogy.

STABILIZATION: "THE FOOL IN THE SHOWER"

Milton Friedman, a leading critic of stabilization policy, likened the government's attempts to stabilize the economy to a "fool in the shower." The shower starts out too cold, because the pipes have not yet warmed up. So the fool turns up the hot water. Nothing happens, so he

stabilization policy
Describes both monetary and fiscal policy, the goals of which are to smooth out fluctuations in output and employment and to keep prices as stable as possible.

time lags Delays in the economy's response to stabilization policies.

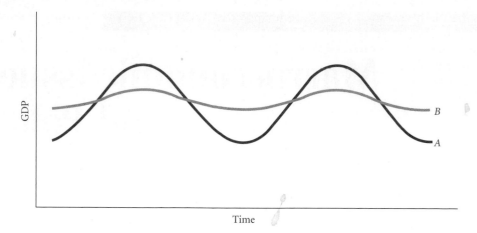

FIGURE 28.1 Two Possible Time Paths for GDP

Path *A* is less stable—it varies more over time—than path *B*. Other things being equal, society prefers path *B* to path *A*.

turns up the hot water further. The hot water comes on and scalds him. He immediately turns up the cold water. Nothing happens right away, so he turns up the cold further. When the cold water finally starts to come up, he finds the shower too cold, and so it goes.

In Friedman's view, the government is constantly behaving like the fool in the shower, stimulating or contracting the economy at the wrong time. How this miscalculation might happen is shown in Figure 28.2. Suppose the economy reaches a peak and begins to slide into recession at point *A* (at time t_0). Policy makers do not observe the decline in GDP until it has sunk to point *B* (at time t_1). By the time they have begun to stimulate the economy (point *C*, time t_2), the recession is well advanced and the economy has almost bottomed out. When the policies finally begin to take effect (point *D*, time t_3), the economy is already on its road to recovery. The policies push the economy to point F'—a much greater fluctuation than point *F*, which is where the economy would have been without the stabilization policy. Sometime after point *D*, policy makers may begin

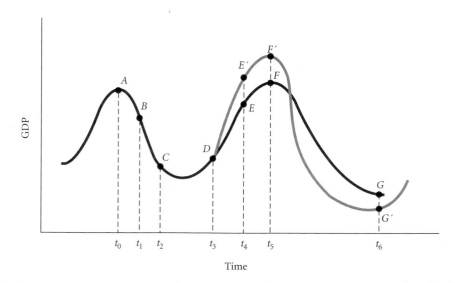

FIGURE 28.2 "The Fool in the Shower"—How Government Policy Can Make Matters Worse

Attempts to stabilize the economy can prove destabilizing because of time lags. An expansionary policy that should have begun to take effect at point *A* does not actually begin to have an impact until point *D*, when the economy is already on an upswing. Hence the policy pushes the economy to points F' and G' (instead of points *F* and *G*). Income varies more widely than it would have if no policy had been implemented.

to realize that the economy is expanding too quickly. By the time they have implemented contractionary policies and the policies have made their effects felt, the economy is starting to weaken. The contractionary policies therefore end up pushing GDP to point G' instead of point G.

Because of the various time lags, the expansionary policies that should have been instituted at time t_0 do not begin to have an effect until time t_3, when they are no longer needed. The light blue line in Figure 28.2 shows how the economy behaves as a result of the "stabilization" policies; the dark blue line shows the time path of GDP if the economy had been allowed to run its course and no stabilization policies had been attempted. In this case, stabilization policy makes income more erratic, not less—the policy results in a peak income of F' as opposed to F and a trough income of G' instead of G.

Critics of stabilization policy argue that the situation in Figure 28.2 is typical of the interaction between the government and the rest of the economy. This claim is not necessarily true. We need to know more about the nature of the various kinds of lags before deciding whether stabilization policy is good or bad.

RECOGNITION LAGS

It takes time for policy makers to recognize a boom or a slump. Many important data—those from the national income and product accounts, for example—are available only quarterly. It usually takes several weeks to compile and prepare even the preliminary estimates for these figures. If the economy goes into a slump on January 1, the recession may not be detected until the data for the first quarter are available at the end of April.

Moreover, the early national income and product accounts data are only preliminary, based on an incomplete compilation of the various data sources. These estimates can, and often do, change as better data become available. This situation makes the interpretation of the initial estimates difficult, and **recognition lags** result.

recognition lag The time it takes for policy makers to recognize the existence of a boom or a slump.

IMPLEMENTATION LAGS

The problems that lags pose for stabilization policy do not end once economists and policy makers recognize that the economy is in a slump or a boom. Even if everyone knows that the economy needs to be stimulated or reined in, it takes time to put the desired policy into effect, especially for actions that involve fiscal policy. **Implementation lags** result.

Each year Congress decides on the federal government's budget for the coming year. The tax laws and spending programs embodied in this budget are not subject to change once they are in place. If it becomes clear that the economy is entering a recession and is in need of a fiscal stimulus during the middle of the year, there is little that can be done. Until Congress authorizes more spending or a cut in taxes, changes in fiscal policy are not possible.[1]

Monetary policy is less subject to the kinds of restrictions that slow down changes in fiscal policy. As we saw in Chapter 23, the Fed's chief tool to control the supply of money or the interest rate is open market operations—buying and selling government securities. Transactions in these securities take place in a highly developed market, and if the Fed wishes, it can buy or sell a large volume of securities in a very short period of time.

implementation lag The time it takes to put the desired policy into effect once economists and policy makers recognize that the economy is in a boom or a slump.

> The implementation lag for monetary policy is generally much shorter than for fiscal policy.

When the Fed wishes to increase the supply of money, it goes into the open market and purchases government securities. This action instantly increases the stock of money (bank reserves held at the Fed), and an expansion of the money supply begins.

---

[1]Do not forget, however, about the existence of automatic stabilizers (see Chapter 22). Many programs contain built-in countercyclical features that expand spending or cut tax collections automatically (without the need for congressional or executive action) during a recession.

response lag The time that it takes for the economy to adjust to the new conditions after a new policy is implemented; the lag that occurs because of the operation of the economy itself.

RESPONSE LAGS

Even after a macroeconomic problem has been recognized and the appropriate policies to correct it have been implemented, there are **response lags**—lags that occur because of the operation of the economy itself. Even after the government has formulated a policy and put it into place, the economy takes time to adjust to the new conditions. Although monetary policy can be adjusted and implemented more quickly than fiscal policy, it takes longer to make its effect felt on the economy because of response lags.

> What is most important is the total lag between the time a problem first occurs and the time the corrective policies are felt.

Response Lags for Fiscal Policy
One way to think about the response lag in fiscal policy is through the government spending multiplier. This multiplier measures the change in GDP caused by a given change in government spending or net taxes. It takes time for the multiplier to reach its full value. The result is a lag between the time a fiscal policy action is initiated and the time the full change in GDP is realized.

The reason for the response lag in fiscal policy—the delay in the multiplier process—is simple. During the first few months after an increase in government spending or a tax cut, there is not enough time for the firms or individuals who benefit directly from the extra government spending or the tax cut to increase their own spending.

> Neither individuals nor firms revise their spending plans instantaneously. Until they can make those revisions, extra government spending does not stimulate extra private spending.

Changes in government purchases are a component of aggregate expenditure. When G rises, aggregate expenditure increases directly; when G falls, aggregate expenditure decreases directly. When personal taxes are changed, however, an additional step intervenes, giving rise to another lag. Suppose a tax cut has lowered personal income taxes across the board. Each household must decide what portion of its tax cut to spend and what portion to save. This decision is the extra step. Before the tax cut gets translated into extra spending, households must take the step of increasing their spending, which usually takes some time.

With a business tax cut, there is a further complication. Firms must decide what to do with their added after-tax profits. If they pay out their added profits to households as dividends, the result is the same as with a personal tax cut. Households must decide whether to spend or to save the extra funds. Firms may also retain their added profits and use them for investment, but investment is a component of aggregate expenditure that requires planning and time.

In practice, it takes about a year for a change in taxes or in government spending to have its full effect on the economy. This response lag means that if we increase spending to counteract a recession today, the full effects will not be felt for 12 months. By that time, the state of the economy might be very different.

Response Lags for Monetary Policy
Monetary policy works by changing interest rates, which then change planned investment. Interest rates can also affect consumption spending, as we discuss further in Chapter 30. For now, it is enough to know that lower interest rates usually stimulate consumption spending and higher interest rates decrease consumption spending.

The response of consumption and investment to interest rate changes takes time. Even if interest rates were to drop by 5 percent overnight, firms would not immediately increase their investment purchases. Firms generally make their investment plans several years in advance. If General Motors wants to respond to a decrease in interest rates by investing more, it will take some time—perhaps up to a year—for the firm to come up with plans for a new factory or assembly line. While drawing up such plans, GM may spend little on new investments. The effect of the decrease in interest rates may not make itself felt for quite some time.

The response lags for monetary policy are even longer than response lags for fiscal policy. When government spending changes, there is a direct change in the sales of firms, which sell more as a result of the increased government purchases. When interest rates change, however, the sales of firms do not change until households change their consumption spending and/or firms change their investment spending. It takes time for households and firms to respond to interest rate changes. In this sense, interest rate changes are like tax-rate changes. The resulting change in firm sales must wait for households and firms to change their purchases of goods.

Summary   Stabilization is not easily achieved. It takes time for policy makers to recognize the existence of a problem, more time for them to implement a solution, and yet more time for firms and households to respond to the stabilization policies taken. Monetary policy can be adjusted more quickly and easily than taxes or government spending, making it a useful instrument in stabilizing the economy. However, because the economy's response to monetary changes is probably slower than its response to changes in fiscal policy, tax and spending changes may also play a useful role in macroeconomic management.

MONETARY POLICY

We have so far in this book talked about monetary policy as consisting of changes in the money supply (M^s). We saw in Chapter 23 that the Fed can change the money supply by (1) changing the required reserve ratio, (2) changing the discount rate, and (3) engaging in open market operations (buying and selling government securities). We also pointed out that the main way in which the Fed changes the money supply is by engaging in open market operations; through these operations the Fed can achieve whatever value of the money supply that it wants.

There are two key points that we must add to the monetary policy story to make the story realistic, as we do in this section. The first point is that *in practice the Fed controls the interest rate rather than the money supply*. The second point is that *the interest rate value that the Fed chooses depends on the state of the economy*. We will first explain these two points and then turn to a discussion of actual Fed policy from 1990 on. Figure 28.3 provides an outline of the way the Fed behaves in practice. It will be useful to keep this figure in mind in the following discussion.

CONTROLLING THE INTEREST RATE

Figure 24.7 on page 535 in Chapter 24 shows that if the Fed increases the money supply the interest rate falls. As the money supply curve shifts to the right, there is a movement of the equilibrium interest rate down the money demand curve. The buying and selling of government securities by the Fed thus has two effects at the same time: It changes the money supply and it changes the interest rate. If the Fed buys securities, this purchase increases the money supply and lowers the interest rate, and if the Fed sells securities, this sale decreases the money supply and raises the interest rate. How much the interest rate changes depends on the shape of the demand for money curve. The steeper the money demand curve, the larger is the change in the interest rate for a given size change in government securities.

What this means is that if the Fed wants to achieve a particular value of the money supply, it must accept whatever interest rate value is implied by this choice. (Again, the interest rate value depends on the shape of the demand for money curve.) Conversely, if the Fed wants to achieve a particular value of the interest rate, it must accept whatever money supply value is implied by this. If, for example, the Fed wants to lower the interest rate by one percentage point, it must keep buying government securities until the interest rate value is reached. As the Fed is buying government securities, the money supply is increasing. In short, the Fed can pick a money supply value and accept the interest rate consequences, or it can pick an interest rate value and accept the money supply consequences.

The first key point is that in practice the Fed chooses the interest rate value and accepts the money supply consequences, rather than vice versa.

FIGURE 28.3 Fed Behavior

The Federal Open Market Committee (FOMC) meets every 6 weeks and sets the value of the interest rate. It then instructs the Open Market Desk at the New York Federal Reserve Bank to keep buying or selling government securities until the desired interest rate value is achieved.

The FOMC announces the interest rate value at 2:15 P.M. eastern time on the day it meets. This is a key time for financial markets around the world. At 2:14 P.M. there are thousands of people staring at their screens waiting for the word from on high. If the announcement is a surprise, it can have very large and immediate effects on bond and stock markets. We will discuss this consequence in the next chapter.

For most of the rest of this text we will talk about monetary policy as being a change in the interest rate. Keep in mind, of course, that monetary policy also changes the money supply. We can talk about an expansionary monetary policy as either one in which the money supply is increased or one in which the interest rate is lowered. We will talk about the interest rate being lowered because the interest rate is what the Fed targets in practice. However we talk about it, an expansionary monetary policy is achieved by the Fed's buying government securities.

THE FED'S RESPONSE TO THE STATE OF THE ECONOMY

When the FOMC meets every 6 weeks to set the value of the interest rate, it does not set the value in a vacuum. An important question in macroeconomics is what influences the interest rate decision. To answer this, we must first consider what the main goals of the Fed are. What ultimately is the Fed trying to achieve?

Two of the Fed's main goals are high levels of output and employment and a low rate of inflation. From the Fed's point of view, the best situation is a fully employed economy with an inflation rate near zero. The worst situation is *stagflation*—high unemployment and high inflation.

If the economy is in a low output/low inflation situation, it will be producing on the relatively flat portion of the aggregate supply (*AS*) curve (Figure 28.4). In this case, the Fed can increase output by lowering the interest rate (and thus increasing the money supply) with little effect on the price level. The expansionary monetary policy will shift the aggregate demand (*AD*) curve to the right, leading to an increase in output with little change in the price level.

The Fed is likely to lower the interest rate (and thus increase the money supply) during times of low output and low inflation.

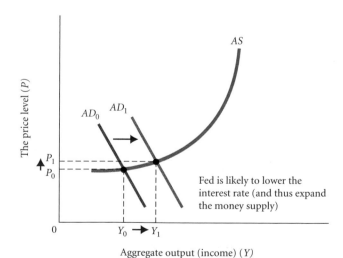

FIGURE 28.4 The Fed's Response to Low Output/Low Inflation

During periods of low output/low inflation, the economy is on the relatively flat portion of the *AS* curve. In this case, the Fed is likely to lower the interest rate (and thus expand the money supply). This will shift the *AD* curve to the right, from AD_0 to AD_1, and lead to an increase in output with very little increase in the price level.

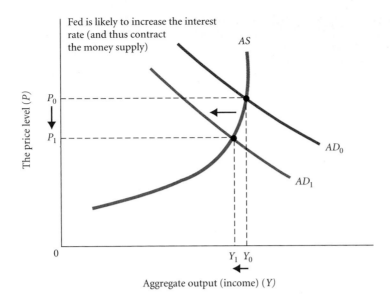

FIGURE 28.5 The Fed's Response to High Output/High Inflation

During periods of high output/high inflation, the economy is on the relatively steep portion of the AS curve. In this case, the Fed is likely to increase the interest rate (and thus contract the money supply). This will shift the AD curve to the left, from AD_0 to AD_1, and lead to a decrease in the price level with very little decrease in output.

The opposite is true in times of high output and high inflation. In this situation, the economy is producing on the relatively steep portion of the AS curve (Figure 28.5), and the Fed can increase the interest rate (and thus decrease the money supply) with little effect on output. The contractionary monetary policy will shift the AD curve to the left, which will lead to a fall in the price level and little effect on output.[2]

> The Fed is likely to increase the interest rate (and thus decrease the money supply) during times of high output and high inflation.

Stagflation is a more difficult problem to solve. If the Fed lowers the interest rate, output will rise, but so will the inflation rate (which is already too high). If the Fed increases the interest rate, the inflation rate will fall, but so will output (which is already too low). (You should be able to draw AS/AD diagrams to see why this is true.) The Fed is faced with a trade-off. In this case, the Fed's decisions depend on how it weights output relative to inflation. If it dislikes high inflation more than low output, it will increase the interest rate; if it dislikes low output more than high inflation, it will lower the interest rate. In practice, the Fed probably dislikes high inflation more than low output, but how the Fed behaves depends in part on the beliefs of the chair of the Fed.

The Fed sometimes "leans against the wind," meaning as the economy expands, the Fed uses open market operations to raise the interest rate gradually to try to prevent the economy from expanding too quickly. Conversely, as the economy contracts, the Fed lowers the interest rate gradually to lessen (and eventually stop) the contraction. This type of stabilization is, of course, not easily achieved, as we saw earlier in this chapter.

MONETARY POLICY SINCE 1990

Table 28.1 presents data on selected variables for the 1989 I–2005 II period. This table may at first look overwhelming, but with a little study you can gain a lot of important information about the U.S. economy since 1990. We will go through it slowly. We will use the table to study

---

[2]In practice, the price level rarely falls. What the Fed actually achieves in this case is a decrease in the *rate of inflation*—that is, in the percentage change in the price level—not a decrease in the price level itself. The discussion here is sliding over the distinction between the price level and the rate of inflation. Recall our discussion of this distinction in Chapter 27.

TABLE 28.1 Data for Selected Variables for the 1989 I–2005 II Period

DATE		REAL GDP GROWTH RATE (%)	UNEMPL. RATE (%)	INFL. RATE (%)	3-MONTH T-BILL RATE	AAA BOND RATE	SURP AS % OF GDP
1989	I	4.1	5.2	4.6	8.5	9.7	−2.1
	II	2.7	5.2	3.9	8.4	9.5	−2.4
	III	2.9	5.3	2.9	7.8	9.0	−2.5
	IV	1.0	5.4	2.8	7.6	8.9	−2.5
1990	I	4.7	5.3	4.9	7.8	9.2	−2.9
	II	1.0	5.3	4.7	7.8	9.4	−3.0
	III	0.0	5.7	3.6	7.5	9.4	−2.8
	IV	−3.0	6.1	3.0	7.0	9.3	−3.1
1991	I	−2.0	6.6	4.8	6.1	8.9	−2.7
	II	2.6	6.8	2.6	5.6	8.9	−3.6
	III	1.9	6.9	2.8	5.4	8.8	−3.9
	IV	1.9	7.1	2.2	4.6	8.4	−4.1
1992	I	4.2	7.4	2.5	3.9	8.3	−4.7
	II	3.9	7.6	2.1	3.7	8.3	−4.6
	III	4.0	7.6	1.8	3.1	8.0	−5.0
	IV	4.5	7.4	2.1	3.1	8.0	−4.5
1993	I	0.5	7.1	3.2	3.0	7.7	−4.6
	II	2.0	7.1	2.2	3.0	7.4	−4.1
	III	2.1	6.8	1.7	3.0	6.9	−4.1
	IV	5.5	6.6	2.1	3.1	6.8	−3.7
1994	I	4.1	6.6	2.4	3.2	7.2	−3.4
	II	5.3	6.2	1.7	4.0	7.9	−2.7
	III	2.3	6.0	2.6	4.5	8.2	−3.0
	IV	4.8	5.6	1.9	5.3	8.6	−3.0
1995	I	1.1	5.5	2.6	5.8	8.3	−2.9
	II	0.7	5.7	1.4	5.6	7.7	−2.7
	III	3.3	5.7	1.9	5.4	7.4	−2.7
	IV	3.0	5.6	1.9	5.3	7.0	−2.4
1996	I	2.9	5.5	2.4	5.0	7.0	−2.4
	II	6.7	5.5	1.6	5.0	7.6	−1.8
	III	3.4	5.3	1.3	5.1	7.6	−1.7
	IV	4.8	5.3	2.1	5.0	7.2	−1.4
1997	I	3.1	5.2	2.6	5.1	7.4	−1.1
	II	6.2	5.0	0.7	5.1	7.6	−0.8
	III	5.1	4.9	1.4	5.1	7.2	−0.4
	IV	3.0	4.7	1.3	5.1	6.9	−0.4
1998	I	4.5	4.6	1.0	5.1	6.7	0.2
	II	2.7	4.4	0.7	5.0	6.6	0.3
	III	4.7	4.5	1.5	4.8	6.5	0.7
	IV	6.2	4.4	1.4	4.3	6.3	0.6
1999	I	3.4	4.3	1.6	4.4	6.4	0.9
	II	3.4	4.2	1.4	4.5	6.9	1.1
	III	4.7	4.2	1.4	4.7	7.3	1.2
	IV	7.3	4.1	1.7	5.0	7.5	1.3
2000	I	1.0	4.1	3.6	5.5	7.7	2.2
	II	6.4	3.9	1.7	5.7	7.8	1.8
	III	−0.5	4.0	2.1	6.0	7.6	1.9
	IV	2.1	3.9	1.6	6.0	7.4	1.7
2001	I	−0.5	4.2	3.3	4.8	7.1	1.6
	II	1.2	4.4	3.3	3.7	7.2	1.2
	III	−1.4	4.8	1.5	3.2	7.1	−0.9
	IV	1.6	5.5	2.0	1.9	6.9	0.0
2002	I	2.7	5.7	1.5	1.8	6.6	−2.0
	II	2.2	5.8	1.4	1.7	6.7	−2.3
	III	2.4	5.7	1.5	1.6	6.3	−2.3
	IV	0.2	5.9	2.2	1.3	6.3	−2.8
2003	I	1.7	5.8	3.1	1.2	6.0	−2.8
	II	3.7	6.1	1.1	1.0	5.3	−3.4
	III	7.2	6.1	1.9	0.9	5.7	−4.1
	IV	3.6	5.9	1.8	0.9	5.7	−3.6
2004	I	4.3	5.6	3.7	0.9	5.5	−3.7
	II	3.5	5.6	3.9	1.1	5.9	−3.5
	III	4.0	5.5	1.3	1.5	5.6	−3.5
	IV	3.3	5.4	2.7	2.0	5.5	−3.1
2005	I	3.8	5.3	3.0	2.5	5.3	−2.4
	II	3.4	5.1	2.6	2.9	5.1	−2.1

Note: The inflation rate is the percentage change in the GDP price deflator. SURP denotes the federal government surplus (+) or deficit (−).

the Fed's interest rate behavior. The short-term interest rate in the table is the 3-month Treasury bill rate, which we will refer to simply as the "bill" rate. It is the interest rate on 3-month U.S. Treasury bills. This is not the interest rate that the FOMC directly controls each day, which is a rate called the *federal funds rate*. The federal funds interest rate is the rate on overnight loans among commercial banks. If, because of reserve requirements, a bank needs to borrow money at the end of the day, it borrows money from banks that have extra reserves, and the rate that it pays is the federal funds rate. The bill rate closely follows the federal funds rate, and we choose here to focus on the bill rate. The other interest rate in the table is the AAA bond rate, which is the interest rate on long-term (about 10 years), high-grade corporate bonds.

1990–1991 Recession   Table 28.1 shows that the real GDP growth rate in 1990 I was 4.7 percent, the unemployment rate was 5.3 percent, the inflation rate was 4.9 percent, and the bill rate was 7.8 percent. You can see that the Fed kept the bill rate fairly high in 1989. The economy was at or close to full employment, and the Fed wanted to keep the inflation rate in check.

In the second half of 1990, the economy went into a recession. Because inflation seemed to be under control at that time, experts expected that the Fed would begin following an expansionary monetary policy to lessen the contraction of the economy. At the end of 1990, the Fed began to follow exactly this policy. Table 28.1 shows that the bill rate fell from 7.0 percent in 1990 IV to 6.1 percent in 1991 I. By 1991 IV, the bill rate was down to 4.6 percent. This lowering of interest rates was designed to stimulate private spending and bring the economy out of the recession.

The Fed's behavior during the 1990–1991 recession is an example of its tendency to lean against the wind. After the Fed became convinced that a recession was at hand, it responded by engaging in open market operations to lower the interest rate. Inflation was not a problem, so the Fed could expand the economy in this way without worrying much about the inflationary consequences of its actions. Some argue that the Fed should have acted sooner, but with the Persian Gulf situation uncertain until February 1991, the Fed did not want to expand too much in the face of a possibly lengthy war that could have led to inflationary pressures. Once the outcome of the Persian Gulf War was known, the Fed responded rapidly.

1993–1994   The economy was slow to recover from the 1990–1991 recession, and the growth rate did not pick up much until the beginning of 1992. Even at the end of 1992, the unemployment rate was still high at 7.4 percent (Table 28.1). The Fed kept the bill rate relatively low in 1992 and 1993 in an attempt to stimulate the economy. This course of action was simply an extension of its expansionary policy in 1991. Again, inflation was not a problem in 1992 and 1993, so the Fed had room to stimulate. By 1993 IV the unemployment rate had fallen to 6.6 percent and the growth rate was 5.5 percent.

At the end of 1993 the Fed decided to begin slowing down the economy. The bill rate rose from 3.1 percent in 1993 IV to 5.8 percent in 1995 I. Why was the Fed pursuing a contractionary policy? You can see from the table that the inflation rate in 1993 and 1994 was quite low, and there were no signs even at the end of 1994 of any inflationary pressures building in the economy. Nevertheless, the Fed was worried that inflation would pick up in the future. The real GDP growth rate in 1994 was relatively high and the unemployment rate was down to 5.6 percent by the fourth quarter, and the Fed felt that these trends might spell inflation problems in the future.

The Fed's behavior in 1994 is an example of leaning against the wind quite far in advance, long before any observed sign of increasing inflation. Some people felt that the Fed was acting too hastily and should have waited for direct signs of inflationary pressures before tightening.

1995–1997   Inflation in fact did not become a problem after 1994. After slow growth in the first half of 1995, the economy picked up the pace, and by the end of 1997, the unemployment rate was down to 4.7 percent. The Fed lowered the bill rate from 5.8 percent in 1995 I to 5.0 percent in 1996 I, and then it kept the bill rate at roughly 5.0 percent throughout 1996 and 1997. You can see from Table 28.1 that the federal government deficit fell to essentially zero by the end of 1997. What better outcome could the Fed want: good growth, low unemployment, low inflation, and a balanced government budget!

1998–2000 By continuing your use of Table 28.1, you can see that the Fed kept the bill rate at about 5 percent in the first three quarters of 1998, but it then suddenly lowered the bill rate to 4.3 percent in 1998 IV. The Fed was concerned about possible negative effects on the U.S. economy from the Asian financial crisis. As it turned out, the U.S. economy was not much affected by the Asia crisis, and the growth rate in 1998–2000 was strong. By the end of 1999, the unemployment rate was down to about 4 percent. Although inflation remained very low in 1998 and 1999, the Fed got nervous in the middle of 1999 about the economy's overheating. It began raising the bill rate, and at the end of 2000 the bill rate was up to 6.0 percent.

2001–2005 We will see in the next chapter that overall stock prices increased dramatically from the beginning of 1995 through the beginning of 2000. We will see that this rise was one of the main reasons for the strong economy in this period. The stock market boom came to an end in the beginning of 2000, and the economy began to slow down in the middle of 2000. Table 28.1 shows that the real GDP growth rate in the last half of 2000 was only about 1 percent and that real growth was negative in two of the first three quarters of 2001. The unemployment rate rose to 5.5 percent by 2001 IV. A recession was declared by the National Bureau of Economic Research in 2001.

The Fed responded to this slowdown by perhaps the most expansionary policy in its history. Table 28.1 shows that the bill rate fell from 6.0 percent in 2000 IV to 1.9 percent in 2001 IV, a fall of over 4 percentage points in a year! The Fed was not worried about inflation because it had not been a problem for years, and so it aggressively lowered the interest rate to try to stimulate the economy. It is interesting to note that even this aggressive policy did not avoid a recession. This outcome shows that the ability of the Fed to stabilize the economy is limited.

Many expected after the attacks on September 11, 2001, that the economy would continue to be in a recession. You can see from Table 28.1, however, that the growth rate was positive from 2001 IV on. The growth rate in 2002 and 2003 was high enough to keep the unemployment rate roughly unchanged. Inflation continued to be low. The Fed kept the interest rate low in 2002 and 2003, as you can see from the table. In 2003 IV the bill rate was only 0.9 percent. Again, the Fed was not worried about inflation and chose to keep the interest rate low to try to stimulate the economy further. At the beginning of 2004, the Fed got nervous again about possible future increases in inflation, and it began gradually to increase the interest rate. By the middle of 2005, the bill rate was up to about 3 percent. The growth rate in 2004 and 2005 remained fairly strong, and by the second quarter of 2005, the unemployment rate was down to 5.1 percent.

Note finally in Table 28.1 the dramatic changes in the federal government budget over time. In the early 1990s, the deficit as a percent of GDP was large; in the late 1990s and early 2000s, there was a fairly large surplus; and from 2002 on, the economy was back to fairly large deficits. We turn to this issue in the last part of this chapter.

INFLATION TARGETING

inflation targeting When a monetary authority chooses its interest rate values with the aim of keeping the inflation rate within some specified band over some specified horizon.

Some monetary authorities in the world engage in what is called **inflation targeting**. If a monetary authority behaves this way, it announces a *target* value of the inflation rate, usually for a horizon of a year or more, and then it chooses its interest rate values with the aim of keeping the actual inflation rate within some specified band around the target value. For example, the target value might be 2 percent with a band of 1 to 3 percent. Then the monetary authority would try to keep the actual inflation rate between 1 and 3 percent. With a horizon of a year or more, the monetary authority would not expect to keep the inflation rate between 1 and 3 percent each month, since there are a number of temporary factors that move the inflation rate around each month (such as weather) that the monetary authority has no control over. But over a year or more, the expectation would be that the inflation rate would be between 1 and 3 percent.

In the discussion at the beginning of this section about the Fed's response to the state of the economy, we assumed that the Fed was concerned about both inflation and output. If output is low, other things being equal, it was argued that the Fed is likely to lower the interest rate to stimulate the economy. If at the same time inflation is high (stagflation), then the Fed is faced with a trade-off, and whether it raises or lowers the interest rate depends on how it weights output relative to inflation. In the case of inflation targeting, all the weight is on inflation. So inflation targeting is a special case of Fed behavior discussed above, namely the case in which all of the Fed's focus is on setting the interest rate to keep the inflation rate within some band over some horizon.

There has been much debate about whether inflation targeting is a good idea. The Fed under Alan Greenspan and previous chairs never engaged in inflation targeting, but the issue arose in the United States with the appointment of Ben Bernanke in 2006 as the new Fed chair. Bernanke has argued in the past in favor of inflation targeting, and it will be interesting to see if the Fed now moves in this direction. (See News Analysis box, "Will the New Fed Chair Change to Inflation Targeting in 2006?" on p. 614.)

FISCAL POLICY: DEFICIT TARGETING

Many fiscal policy discussions revolve around the size of the federal government surplus or deficit. You can see from Table 28.1 that there was a substantial deficit in the first half of the 1990s, which then changed to a surplus by 1998. The surplus then changed back to a deficit in 2002. By 2003 II, the deficit had become fairly large again and a concern to many people.

We begin our discussion of fiscal policy with the reaction of the federal government to the large deficits in the late 1980s and early 1990s. This material is a great macroeconomic learning device. We then turn to a discussion of fiscal policy from 1990 on.

As just noted, the federal government deficit was large in the first half of the 1990s. In fact, the deficit had begun to be a problem in the early 1980s. The government was simply spending much more than it was receiving in taxes. When the deficit reached 4.7 percent of GDP in 1986, the U.S. Congress passed and President Reagan signed the **Gramm-Rudman-Hollings Act** (named for its three congressional sponsors), referred to as GRH.

GRH set a target for reducing the federal deficit by a set amount each year. As Figure 28.6 shows, the deficit was to decline by $36 billion per year between 1987 and 1991, with a deficit of zero slated for fiscal year 1991. What was interesting about the GRH legislation was that the targets were not merely guidelines. If Congress, through its decisions about taxes and spending programs, produced a budget with a deficit larger than the targeted amount, GRH called for automatic spending cuts. The cuts were divided proportionately among most federal spending programs, so that a program that made up 5 percent of total spending was to endure a cut equal to 5 percent of the total spending cut.[3]

In 1986, the U.S. Supreme Court declared part of the GRH bill unconstitutional. In effect, the Court said that Congress would have to approve the "automatic" spending cuts before they could take place. The law was changed in 1986 to meet the Supreme Court ruling and again in 1987, when new targets were established. The new targets had the deficit reaching zero in 1993 instead of 1991. The targets were revised again in 1991, when the year to achieve a zero deficit was changed from 1993 to 1996.

In practice, these targets never came close to being achieved. As time wore on, even the revised targets became completely unrealistic, and by the end of the 1980s the GRH legislation was not taken seriously.

As Table 28.1 shows, the deficit problem continued in the 1990s, and one of President Clinton's goals when he took office in 1993 was to reduce the deficit. The first step was the Omnibus Budget Reconciliation Act of 1993. The act, which barely made it through Congress, was projected to reduce the deficit in the five fiscal years 1994 to 1998 by $504.8 billion—$254.7 billion would come from cuts in federal spending, and $250.1 billion would come from tax increases. Most of the tax increases were levied on high-income taxpayers.

There was also some sentiment in the mid-1990s for the passage of a *balanced-budget amendment*, intended to prevent Congress from doing what it did in the 1980s. The balanced-budget amendment passed the House in early 1995, but it failed by one vote in the Senate. It turned out that the passage of the Omnibus Budget Reconciliation Act of 1993 and

Gramm-Rudman-Hollings Act Passed by the U.S. Congress and signed by President Reagan in 1986, this law set out to reduce the federal deficit by $36 billion per year, with a deficit of zero slated for 1991.

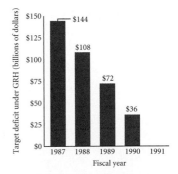

FIGURE 28.6 Deficit Reduction Targets under Gramm-Rudman-Hollings

The GRH legislation, passed in 1986, set out to lower the federal deficit by $36 billion per year. If the plan had worked, a zero deficit would have been achieved by 1991.

---

[3]Programs such as Social Security were exempt from cuts or were treated differently. Interest payments on the federal debt were also immune from cuts.

Will the New Fed Chair Change to Inflation Targeting in 2006?

IN LATE 2005, THE PRESIDENT NOMI-nated Ben Bernanke to chair the Fed. The following article in the *New York Times* points out one controversial issue that was brought up at his confirmation hearings—namely, inflation targeting.

Inflation Issue To Dominate Questioning of Fed Choice

By EDMUND L. ANDREWS

WASHINGTON, Nov. 14—Ben S. Bernanke, President Bush's nominee to lead the Federal Reserve, will have to fend off two contradictory percep-tions at his Senate confirmation hear-ing on Tuesday.

Some Democratic lawmakers worry that Bernanke, who has contended for years that the Fed should set policy according to an explicit inflation target, will be too focused on price stability and not attentive to employment.

Some bond investors, by contrast, fret that Mr. Bernanke will be soft on inflation. As a Fed governor in 2003, he raised alarms about the "jobless recov-ery" and the dangers of deflation. As a top advisor to Mr. Bush since June, he has been more confident than many Fed officials that inflation would remain low.

Mr. Bernanke has argued that the Fed policy would be less personalized, more open and more predictable if it were based on an explicit and public inflation target.

Mr. Bernanke has gone so far as to suggest that inflation should be held to 1 to 2 percent a year, excluding the fluctuations of energy and food.

Critics of inflation-targeting fall into two broad groups. Some, like Mr. Greenspan, contend that the practice would be too rigid and formulaic and would make it harder to deal with unexpected shocks.

Other critics, including some Democrats, worry that inflation-target-ing would conflict with the Fed's dual mandate of pursuing both price stabil-ity and full employment.

Is Mr. Bernanke a hawk or a dove on fighting inflation?

His writings and his record at the Fed suggest that he will be in line with the Fed consensus: the top priority will

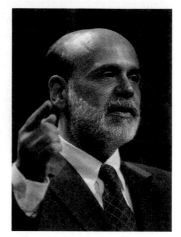

Will Ben Bernanke move toward inflation targeting?

be to maintain price stability, even if it hurts.

Source: Edmund L. Andrews, "Inflation Issue To Dominate Questioning of Fed Choice," NYT, Business Day, November 15, 2005. Copyright © 2005 by The New York Times Co. Reprinted with permission.

a robust economy were enough to lead to a balanced budget by 1998. You can see from Table 28.1 that by 2000 there was a large budget surplus. Between 1998 and 2001 the federal gov-ernment was in the process of paying off its debt, and there was talk that the debt would be completely paid off.

Alas, surplus turned to deficit in 2002. The federal government is again beginning to worry about deficits. It is thus useful to review the approach that the government considered in the late 1980s and early 1990s to cope with the deficit problem, namely the GRH legisla-tion and the balanced-budget amendment. In addition, this material is a great learning tool. If you understand the macroeconomic consequences of the GRH legislation and the balanced-budget amendment, you have come a long way toward being a macroeconomist.

THE EFFECTS OF SPENDING CUTS ON THE DEFICIT

Suppose the terms of the balanced-budget amendment or some other deficit-reduction measure dictate that the deficit must be cut by $20 billion. By how much must government spending be cut to achieve this goal? You might be tempted to think the spending cuts should add up to the amount the deficit is to be cut—$20 billion. (This is what GRH dictated: If the deficit needed to be cut by a certain amount, automatic spending cuts were to be equal to this amount.) This approach seems reasonable. If you decrease your personal spending by $100 over a year, your personal deficit will fall by the full $100 of your spending cut.

However, the government is not an individual household. A cut in government spending shifts the *AD* curve to the left and results in a decrease in aggregate output (income) (*Y*) and a contraction in the economy. When the economy contracts, both the taxable income of households and the profits of firms fall. This effect means in turn that revenue from the personal income tax and the corporate profits tax will fall.

How do these events affect the size of the deficit? To estimate the response of the deficit to changes in government spending, we need to go through two steps. First, we must decide how much a $1 change in government spending will change GDP. That means we need to know the size of the government spending multiplier. [Recall that the government spending multiplier measures the increase (or decrease) in GDP (*Y*) brought about by a $1 increase (or decrease) in government spending.] Based on empirical evidence, a reasonable value for the government spending multiplier seems to be around 1.4 after 1 year, and this is the value we will use. A $1 billion decrease in government spending lowers GDP by about $1.4 billion after 1 year.

Next, we must see what happens to the deficit when GDP changes. We have just noted that when GDP falls—the economy contracts—taxable income and corporate profits fall, so tax revenues fall. In addition, some categories of government expenditures tend to rise when the economy contracts. For example, unemployment insurance benefits (a transfer payment) rise as the economy contracts because more people become unemployed and eligible for benefits. Both the decrease in tax revenues and the rise in government expenditures cause the deficit to increase.

> The deficit tends to rise when GDP falls, and tends to fall when GDP rises.

Assume the **deficit response index (DRI)** is −.22. That is, for every $1 billion decrease in GDP, the deficit rises by $.22 billion. This number seems close to what is true in practice. We can now use the multiplier and the DRI to answer the question that began this section. Suppose government spending is reduced by $20 billion, the exact amount of the necessary deficit reduction. This will lower GDP by 1.4 × $20 billion, or $28 billion, if the value of the multiplier is 1.4. A $28 billion fall in GDP will increase the deficit by .22 × $28 billion, or $6.2 billion, if the value of the DRI is −.22. Because we initially cut government spending (and therefore lowered the deficit from this source) by $20 billion, the net effect of the spending cut is to lower the deficit by $20 billion − $6.2 billion = $13.8 billion.

deficit response index (DRI) The amount by which the deficit changes with a $1 change in GDP.

A $20 billion government spending cut does not lower the deficit by $20 billion. To lower the deficit by $20 billion, we need to cut government spending by about $30 billion. By using 1.4 as the value of the government spending multiplier and −.22 as the value of the DRI, we see that a spending cut of $30 billion lowers GDP by 1.4 × $30 billion, or $42 billion. This raises the deficit by .22 × $42 billion, or $9.2 billion. The net effect on the deficit is −$30 billion (from the government spending cut) + $9.2 billion, which is −$20.8 billion (slightly larger than the necessary $20 billion reduction). This means the spending cut must be nearly 50 percent larger than the deficit reduction we wish to achieve. Congress would have had trouble achieving the deficit targets under the GRH legislation even if it had allowed GRH's automatic spending cuts to take place.

Monetary Policy to the Rescue? Was Congress so poorly informed about macroeconomics that it would pass legislation that could not possibly work? In other words, are there any conditions under which it would be reasonable to assume that a spending cut needs to be only as large as the desired reduction in the deficit? If the government spending multiplier is zero, government spending cuts will not contract the economy, and the cut in the deficit will be equal to the cut in government spending.

Could the government spending multiplier ever be zero? Before the GRH bill was passed, some argued it could. The argument went as follows: If households and firms are worried about the large government deficits and hold back on consumption and investment because of these worries, the passage of GRH might make them more optimistic and induce them to consume and invest more. This increased consumption and investment would offset the effects of the decreased government spending, and the net result would be a multiplier effect of zero.

Another argument in favor of the GRH bill centered on the Fed and monetary policy. We know that an expansionary monetary policy shifts the *AD* curve to the right. Because a cut in government spending shifts the *AD* curve to the left, the Fed could respond to the spending cut enough to shift the *AD* curve back (to the right) to its original position, preventing any change in aggregate output (income). Some argued the Fed would behave in this way after the passage of the GRH bill because it would see that Congress finally "got its house in order."

How large would the interest rate cuts have to be to offset the decrease in *G* completely, thus resulting in a multiplier of zero? Studies at the time of the original GRH bill showed that the decrease in the interest rate that would be necessary for a multiplier of zero—that is, for a government spending cut to have no effect on aggregate output (income)—is quite large. The Fed would have had to engage in extreme behavior with respect to interest rate changes for the multiplier to be zero.

> A zero multiplier can come about through renewed optimism on the part of households and firms or through very aggressive behavior on the part of the Fed, but because neither of these situations is very plausible, the multiplier is likely to be greater than zero. Thus, it is likely that to lower the deficit by a certain amount, the cut in government spending must be larger than that amount.

ECONOMIC STABILITY AND DEFICIT REDUCTION

So, lowering the deficit by a given amount is likely to require a government spending decrease larger than this amount. However, this is not the only point to learn from our analysis of deficit targeting. We will now show how deficit targeting can adversely affect the way the economy responds to a variety of stimuli.

In a world with no GRH, no balanced-budget amendment, and no similar deficit-targeting measure, the Congress and the president make decisions each year about how much to spend and how much to tax. The federal government deficit is a result of these decisions and the state of the economy. However, with GRH or the balanced-budget amendment, the size of the deficit is set in advance. Taxes and government spending must be adjusted to produce the required deficit. In this situation, the deficit is no longer a consequence of the tax and spending decisions. Instead, taxes and spending become a consequence of the deficit decision.

What difference does it make whether Congress chooses a target deficit and adjusts government spending and taxes to achieve this target or decides how much to spend and tax and lets the deficit adjust itself? The difference may be substantial. Consider a leftward shift of the *AD* curve caused by some negative demand shock. A **negative demand shock** is something that causes a negative shift in consumption or investment schedules or that leads to a decrease in U.S. exports.

negative demand shock
Something that causes a negative shift in consumption or investment schedules or that leads to a decrease in U.S. exports.

We know that a leftward shift of the *AD* curve lowers aggregate output (income), which causes the government deficit to increase. In a world without deficit targeting, the increase in the deficit during contractions provides an **automatic stabilizer** for the economy. (Review Chapter 22 if this point is hazy.) The contraction-induced decrease in tax revenues and increase in transfer payments tend to reduce the fall in after-tax income and consumer spending due to the negative demand shock. Thus, the decrease in aggregate output (income) caused by the negative demand shock is lessened somewhat by the growth of the deficit [Figure 28.7(a)].

automatic stabilizers
Revenue and expenditure items in the federal budget that automatically change with the economy in such a way as to stabilize GDP.

In a world with deficit targeting, the deficit is not allowed to rise. Some combination of tax increases and government spending cuts would be needed to offset what would have otherwise been an increase in the deficit. We know that increases in taxes or cuts in spending are contractionary in themselves. The contraction in the economy will therefore be larger than it would have been without deficit targeting, because the initial effect of the negative demand shock is worsened by the rise in taxes or the cut in government

a. Without Deficit Targeting

b. With Deficit Targeting

FIGURE 28.7 Deficit Targeting as an Automatic Destabilizer

Deficit targeting changes the way the economy responds to negative demand shocks because it does not allow the deficit to increase. The result is a smaller deficit but a larger decline in income than would have otherwise occurred.

spending required to keep the deficit from rising. As Figure 28.7(b) shows, deficit targeting acts as an **automatic destabilizer**. It requires taxes to be raised and government spending to be cut during a contraction. This reinforces, rather than counteracts, the shock that started the contraction.

automatic destabilizers
Revenue and expenditure items in the federal budget that automatically change with the economy in such a way as to destabilize GDP.

SUMMARY

It is clear the GRH legislation, the balanced-budget amendment, and similar deficit-targeting measures have some undesirable macroeconomic consequences. Deficit targeting requires cuts in spending or increases in taxes at times when the economy is already experiencing problems. This drawback does not mean that Congress should ignore deficits when they arise. Instead, it means that locking the economy into spending cuts during periods of negative demand shocks, as deficit-targeting measures do, is not a good way to manage the economy.

FISCAL POLICY SINCE 1990

Table 22.5 on page 490 in Chapter 22 shows the main categories of receipts and expenditures of the federal government. The primary ways the government collects money are through the personal income tax and the Social Security tax. Figure 28.8 plots total federal personal income taxes as a percentage of total taxable income for the 1990 I–2005 II period. This is a plot of the average personal income tax rate. As the figure shows, the average tax rate increased substantially in the last half of the 1990s. Much of this increase was due to the Omnibus Budget Reconciliation Act of 1993 mentioned earlier. This act was a major change in fiscal policy.

Figure 28.8 also shows, rather dramatically, the effects of President George W. Bush's tax cuts. The large fall in the average tax rate in 2001 III was due to a tax rebate that was passed after the September 11, 2001, attacks. Although the average tax rate went back up in 2001 IV, it then fell substantially after that as the tax cuts began to be felt.

The tax policy of the federal government from 1990 on is thus rather clear from Figure 28.8. The average tax rate rose sharply under President Clinton and fell sharply under President Bush.

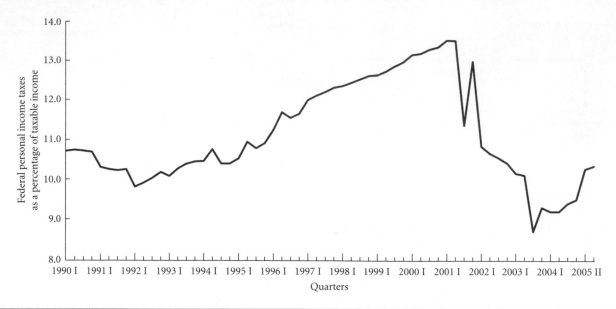

FIGURE 28.8 Federal Personal Income Taxes as a Percentage of Taxable Income, 1990 I–2005 II

Fiscal policy includes spending policies as well as tax policies, and Figures 28.9 and 28.10 plot two spending variables. Figure 28.9 plots the ratio of federal government consumption expenditures to GDP. You can see from Table 22.5 that consumption expenditures make up about one-fourth of total government expenditures. Much of these expenditures are for defense. Figure 28.10 plots the ratio of federal transfer payments and grants-in-aid to GDP. Table 22.5 shows that these two items make up more than half of total government expenditures. Transfer payments include Social Security payments and Medicare/Medicaid payments. Grants-in-aid are grants to state and local government, many of which are used to fund state and local government transfer payments to households.

Figure 28.9 shows that federal consumption expenditures as a percentage of GDP fell until about 1998, remained relatively constant until 2002, and then began to rise. Much of the rise since the beginning of 2002 has been increased expenditures for security and defense. Figure 28.10 shows that federal transfer payments plus grants-in-aid as a percentage of GDP rose rapidly at the beginning of the 1990s, leveled off until about 1996, fell until about 2001, and then rose rapidly. Some of the fall between 1996 and 2000 was

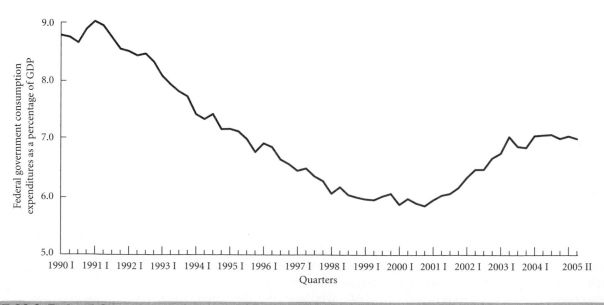

FIGURE 28.9 Federal Government Consumption Expenditures as a Percentage of GDP, 1990 I–2005 II

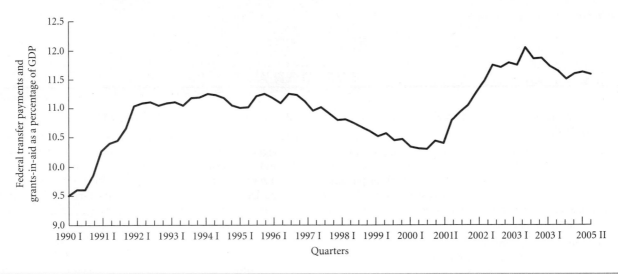

FIGURE 28.10 Federal Transfer Payments and Grants-in-aid as a Percentage of GDP, 1990 I–2005 II

due to the welfare reform legislation passed under President Clinton. Some of the rise from 2001 on is due to increased Medicare payments.

Given Figures 28.8, 28.9, and 28.10, it is not surprising that the federal government budget went from deficit to surplus and then back to deficit. During the last half of the 1990s, the average tax rate rose and government spending as a percentage of GDP fell— both consumption expenditures and transfer payments plus grants-in-aid. The reverse then happened beginning in about 2001. The deficit is again a concern as tax rates are falling and spending is rising.

One final point about the federal government budget is reflected in Figure 28.11, which plots federal government interest payments as a percentage of GDP. You can see that this ratio has fallen dramatically since 1995. Interest payments can fall for two reasons: (1) the size of the federal debt is decreasing, which is true if the government is running a surplus, and (2) interest rates are decreasing. Prior to the large decrease in interest rates in 2001, interest payments were falling because of the decrease in the debt. After 2001 the fall has been due to the decrease in interest rates, because the debt has in fact been increasing because of the deficits.

Regardless of why interest payments are falling, any fall is good for the federal budget. As the government spends less in interest payments, the surplus rises or the deficit falls.

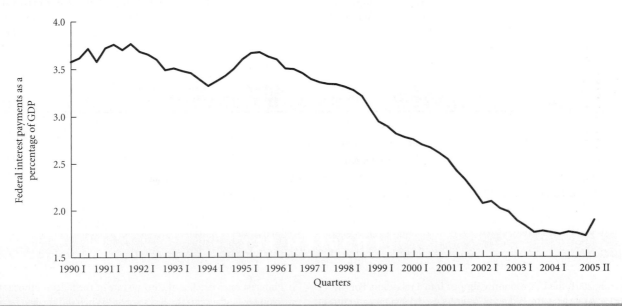

FIGURE 28.11 Federal Interest Payments as a Percentage of GDP, 1990 I–2005 II

SUMMARY

TIME LAGS REGARDING MONETARY AND FISCAL POLICY

1. *Stabilization policy* describes both fiscal and monetary policy, the goals of which are to smooth out fluctuations in output and employment and to keep prices as stable as possible. Stabilization goals are not necessarily easy to achieve because of the existence of certain *time lags*, or delays in the response of the economy to macroeconomic policies.

2. A *recognition lag* is the time it takes for policy makers to recognize the existence of a boom or a slump. An *implementation lag* is the time it takes to put the desired policy into effect once economists and policy makers recognize that the economy is in a boom or a slump. A *response lag* is the time that it takes for the economy to adjust to the new conditions after a new policy is implemented—in other words, a lag that occurs because of the operation of the economy itself. In general, monetary policy can be implemented more rapidly than fiscal policy, but fiscal policy generally has a shorter response lag than monetary policy.

MONETARY POLICY

3. In practice, the Fed controls the interest rate rather than the money supply. The interest rate value that the Fed chooses depends on the state of the economy. The Fed desires high output and low inflation. The Fed is likely to decrease the interest rate during times of low output and low inflation, and it is likely to increase the interest rate during times of high output and high inflation.

4. Monetary policy since 1990 has been one of lowering interest rates to fight the 1990–1991 recession, raising rates during the boom of the last half of the 1990s, and lowering rates dramatically to fight the 2001 recession.

5. Inflation targeting is the case where the monetary authority weights only inflation. It chooses its interest rate values with the aim of keeping the inflation rate within some specified band over some specified horizon.

FISCAL POLICY: DEFICIT TARGETING

6. In fiscal year 1986, Congress passed and President Reagan signed the *Gramm-Rudman-Hollings Act (GRH)*, which set out to reduce the federal deficit by $36 billion per year, with a zero deficit slated for fiscal year 1991. If Congress passed a budget with a deficit larger than the targeted amount, the law called for automatic spending cuts. A Supreme Court ruling later overturned this provision, and the actual figures for each year never came close to the targets. Thanks to the Omnibus Budget Reconciliation Act of 1993, and a robust economy, the federal deficit had been eliminated by 1998.

7. The deficit tends to rise when GDP falls, and to fall when GDP rises. The *deficit response index (DRI)* is the amount by which the deficit changes with a $1 change in GDP.

8. For spending cuts of a certain amount to reduce the deficit by the same amount, the government spending multiplier must be zero. Before GRH was passed, some argued that a government spending multiplier of zero can be achieved through renewed optimism on the part of households or through very aggressive behavior by the Fed to decrease the interest rate. Empirical evidence has shown that both situations are not very plausible, so to lower the deficit by a certain amount, government spending cuts must be larger than that to lower the deficit.

9. Deficit-targeting measures that call for automatic spending cuts to eliminate or reduce the deficit may have the effect of destabilizing the economy because they prevent automatic stabilizers from working.

FISCAL POLICY SINCE 1990

10. The average personal income tax rate rose sharply under President Clinton and fell sharply under President Bush. Federal spending as a percent of GDP began to rise rapidly in 2001. The net effect of falling tax rates and increased spending was a growing federal government deficit beginning in 2001.

REVIEW TERMS AND CONCEPTS

automatic destabilizer, 617

automatic stabilizer, 616

deficit response index (DRI), 615

Gramm-Rudman-Hollings Act, 613

implementation lag, 605

inflation targeting, 612

negative demand shock, 616

recognition lag, 605

response lag, 606

stabilization policy, 603

time lags, 603

PROBLEM SET

1. During 2001, the U.S. economy slipped into a recession. For the next several years, the Fed and Congress used monetary and fiscal policy in an attempt to stimulate the economy. Obtain data on interest rates (such as the prime rate or the federal funds rate). Do you see evidence of the Fed's action? When did the Fed begin its expansionary policy? Obtain data on total federal expenditures,

tax receipts, and the deficit (try **www.commerce.gov**). When did fiscal policy become "expansionary"? Which policy seems to have suffered more from policy lags?

2. Review the box on page 614. Give a grade to Ben Bernanke for his performance in 2006, his first year as Fed chairman. In the fall of 2005 when he was nominated, the Fed had raised the target federal funds rate from 1 percent a year earlier to over 4 percent as worries about inflation crept back into the Fed's discussion. Go to **www.federalreserve.gov** and click on Monetary Policy and Federal Open Market Committee. Read the latest minutes available and write a short essay about current Fed concerns. How successful has the Fed been in containing the inflationary pressures that were building in 2005?

3. Explain carefully why the government deficit rises as the economy contracts.

4. You are given the following information about the economy in 2001 (all in billions of dollars):

Consumption function:	$C = 100 + (.8 \times Y_d)$
Taxes:	$T = -150 + (.25 \times Y)$
Investment function:	$I = 60$
Disposable income:	$Y_d = Y - T$
Government spending:	$G = 80$
Equilibrium:	$Y = C + I + G$

Hint: Deficit is $D = G - T = G - [-150 + (.25 \times Y)]$

a. Find equilibrium income. Show that the government budget deficit (the difference between government spending and tax revenues) is $5 billion.

b. Congress passes the Foghorn-Leghorn (F-L) amendment, which requires that the deficit be zero this year. If the budget adopted by Congress has a deficit that is larger than zero, the deficit target must be met by cutting spending. Suppose spending is cut by $5 billion (to $75 billion). What is the new value for equilibrium GDP? What is the new deficit? Explain carefully why the deficit is not zero.

c. What is the deficit response index and how is it defined? Explain why the DRI must equal .25 in this example. By using this information, by how much must we cut spending to achieve a deficit of zero?

d. Suppose the F-L amendment was not in effect and planned investment falls to $I = 55$. What is the new value of GDP? What is the new government budget deficit? What happens to GDP if the F-L amendment is in effect and spending is cut to reach the deficit target? (*Hint:* Spending must be cut by $21.666 billion to balance the budget.)

5. Some states are required to balance their budgets. Is this measure stabilizing or destabilizing? Suppose all states were committed to a balanced-budget philosophy and the economy moved into a recession. What effects would this philosophy have on the size of the federal deficit?

6. Describe the Fed's tendency to "lean against the wind." Do the Fed's policies tend to stabilize or destabilize the economy?

7. Explain why stabilization policy may be difficult to carry out. How is it possible that stabilization policies can actually be destabilizing?

8. It takes about 1 year for the multiplier to reach its full value. Explain this phenomenon. Does this have any implications for fiscal policy?

The Stock Market and the Economy

29

Introductory macroeconomic texts written a decade ago could more or less ignore the stock market. The effects of the stock market on the macroeconomy were small enough to be put aside in introductory discussions. This changed in the 1990s. We will see that the stock market boom that began in 1995 had a large impact on the economy. The economy grew well in the last half of the 1990s, and many came to believe in the existence of a new economy or a "new age." How much of the growth in the last half of the 1990s was due to the stock market boom? Did the economy in fact enter a new age? We try to answer these questions in this chapter.

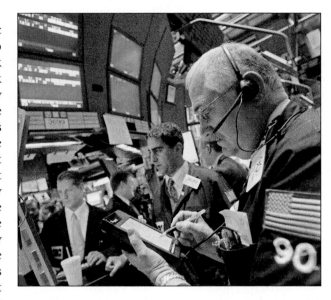

STOCKS AND BONDS

When a firm wishes to make a large purchase—to build a new factory or to buy an expensive piece of machinery—it often cannot pay for the purchase out of its own funds. In that case it must "finance" the investment. One possibility is simply to borrow from a bank. The bank loans the money to the firm; the firm uses the money to buy the factory or machine; and the firm pays back the loan to the bank over time with interest.

BONDS

Another possibility is for the firm to issue a **bond**. If you buy a bond from a firm, you are making a loan to the firm.

    Bonds have several properties. First, they are issued with a *face value*, typically in denominations of $1,000, that represent the amount you (the buyer) agree to lend the bond issuer. They also come with a *maturity date* on which the firm promises to pay back the funds you lent it. (However, you can sell the bond to someone else before the maturity date if you want.) Finally, there is a fixed payment of a specified amount (usually made annually), paid by the bond issuer to the bondholder. This payment, known as the *coupon*, is calculated using the prevailing interest rate at the time the bond is issued. Even if interest rates change over the life of the bond, as they almost always do, the amount you receive as interest on your bond remains fixed. (This is why bonds are sometimes referred to as fixed-income securities.

bond A document that formally promises to pay back a loan under specified terms, usually over a specific time period.

The bondholder receives a set amount, known in advance, no matter what happens to interest rates, stock prices, and so on.)

If you bought a $10,000, 10 percent, 15-year bond from Company XYZ on January 1, 1998, this is what would happen. You would give XYZ, or perhaps your broker, a check for $10,000. Every January for the next 14 years, XYZ would send you a check for $1,000 (10 percent of the $10,000 face value). On January 1, 2013, XYZ would send you a check for the face value of the bond—$10,000—plus the coupon for that year—$1,000—and that would square all accounts.

Does the fact that the coupon on a bond does not change with fluctuations in the interest rate mean that bonds are completely insulated from interest rate movements? Absolutely not! Instead of the coupon's responding to a change in the interest rate, it is the *price of the bond* that changes. To see why, suppose you had a choice of putting $10,000 into the bond described here or into a bank account that pays 10 percent per year interest. In either case, you would earn $1,000 per year in interest payments, so you should be indifferent between the two choices.

But now suppose that the interest rate on the bank account goes up to 20 percent instead of 10 percent. The bond still promises to pay $1,000 per year. If you want to earn $1,000 in interest, you need to put only $5,000 into the bank account (.20 × $5,000 = $1,000). You would obviously prefer to put $5,000 into the bank rather than tie up $10,000 in the bond. The only way anyone would willingly buy the bond is if it cost no more than other investments that yield the same stream of income in the future. The bond would thus be worth much less than $10,000 if the interest rate were 20 percent. It follows, then, that when interest rates rise, bond prices fall, and bondholders suffer a *loss*—that is, a reduction in the value of the securities they own.

See the Further Exploration box for a discussion of how to read bond tables in a newspaper.

STOCKS

stock A certificate that certifies ownership of a certain portion of a firm.

A third way for a firm to finance an investment is for it to issue additional shares of **stock**. When a firm issues new shares of stock, it does not add to its debt. Instead, it brings in additional owners of the firm, owners who agree to supply it with funds. Such owners are treated differently than bondholders, who are owed the amount that they have loaned.

A share of common stock is a certificate that represents the ownership of a share of a business, almost always a corporation. For example, Lincoln Electric is a Cleveland-based company that makes welding and cutting equipment. The company has 41 million shares of common stock that are owned by tens of thousands of shareholders, some of whom are simply private individuals, some of whom are institutions such as Carlton College, and some of whom may be employees of the firm. Shareholders are entitled to a share of the company's profit. When profits are paid directly to shareholders, the payment is called a *dividend*. In a recent year, Lincoln Electric made a profit of $54 million, which was $1.31 per share, of which $0.43 was paid out to shareholders as dividends and the rest was retained for investment.

capital gain An increase in the value of an asset.

Stockholders who own stocks that increase in value earn what are called **capital gains**. **Realized capital gains** (or losses) are increases (or decreases) in the value of assets, including stocks, that households receive when they actually sell those assets. The government considers realized capital gains net of losses to be income, although their treatment under the tax code has been very complex and subject to change every few years. The return that an owner

realized capital gain The gain that occurs when the owner of an asset actually sells it for more than he or she paid for it.

A share of stock represents part ownership of a firm.

Reading a Bond Table

Figure 1 shows a small section of the corporate bond price quotations in the *Wall Street Journal* for July 24, 2003. What do all these signs and symbols mean?

The first column, under "Company," gives the name of the corporation that issued the bond and certain information about the terms under which the bond was originally issued. Let's take the last bond listed in the figure as an example. This bond was issued by the Comcast Cable Communications Holding Company. The "8.375" means the bond pays a coupon of $8.375 per $100 of face value of the bond. The bond matures in 2013. The column titled "Last Yield" shows the annual rate of return on the bond if the bond were purchased at the current price. If the current price were $100, then the annual rate of return would be 8.375 percent. The bond yields only 5.485 percent, however, so the current price of the bond must be higher than its face value of $100. (Remember: A decrease in the interest rate raises the price of a bond.)

The column "Vol" tells how many thousands of dollars in bonds were traded during the day. Here we see $89.953 million (at face value) of the Comcast bond were traded on July 24, 2003.

"Last Price" is the closing price of the bond. This is how much you would have to pay for the bond per $100 of face value. The Comcast bond's closing price was $121.38, which means a $100 bond was worth $121.38 at the end of the trading day.

"Est spread" and "UST" tell us something about the risk associated with the bond. "Est spread" is the difference in yield (stated in "basis points," with 100 basis points being the same as one percentage point) between the last yield on the Comcast bond and the current yield on a 10-year U.S. Treasury bond. Since the current yield on the Comcast bond is 5.485 and the spread is 131 (or 1.31 percent), the 10-year Treasury is paying 4.175 percent. Since the U.S. Treasury is backed by the "full faith and credit of the United States Government," Treasury bonds are the benchmark for a risk-free investment. The Comcast bond pays a higher effective yield because there is a small risk that Comcast will not be able to pay when the bond comes due.

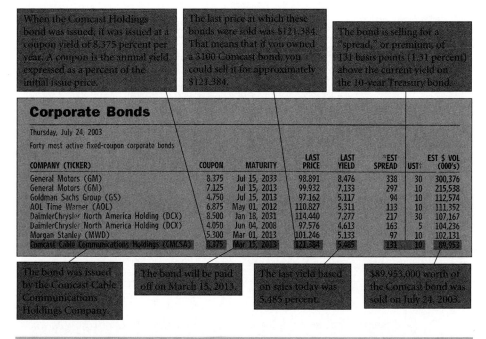

FIGURE 1 New York Stock Exchange Bonds

of common stock earns is the sum of the dividends received and the capital gains. When stock values fall, the returns are sometimes negative. Stocks are generally riskier than bonds.

Shares of common stock are traded openly on private stock exchanges or markets, the biggest of which is the New York Stock Exchange (NYSE). Most of the billions of shares traded every day simply represent one shareholder's selling shares to another, and they have nothing to do with the company. When shares are first issued, the proceeds are used to buy capital or to "buy out" the entrepreneurs who started the firm.

Reading the Stock Pages

Once you buy a stock, you are free to sell it to someone else at any time. Developments in the stock market, where such transactions take place, are constantly followed in the news.

Figure 1 reproduces part of the stock quotations from the *Wall Street Journal* for July 24, 2003. Let's take the stock of Kellogg and see what information the stock pages provide.

The first column, "YTD % Chg," gives the percent change this year to date. Kellogg stock has fallen 2.1 percent since January 1, 2003.

The next two columns, under the heading "52-Week," give the highest and lowest prices over the past year. The price of a share of Kellogg stock reached a high of $36.30 and a low of $27.85 during this period. The column "Div" gives the current annual rate of dividend payment. The current annual rate for Kellogg is $1.01 per share. What sort of return is this? The next column, "Yld %" (yield percent), takes the dividend as a percentage of the day's closing price. (The day's closing price in this case is $33.56, which is given in the column titled "Close.") For Kellogg, the yield is 3.0 percent.

The column "PE" (price-earnings ratio) calculates the ratio of the price of a share of stock to the company's *total earnings per share* (which includes not only dividends paid to shareholders but also retained earnings). The PE ratio is a measure of how highly a stock is valued. Kellogg's PE ratio is 19. The column "Vol 100s" tells how many hundreds of shares changed hands during the day's trading. On July 24, 2003, 689,300 shares of Kellogg's stock were traded.

Source: Wall Street Journal, *July 25, 2003. WALL STREET JOURNAL. EASTERN EDITION [ONLY STAFF-PRODUCED MATERIALS MAY BE USED] by WALL STREET JOURNAL. Copyright 2003 by DOW JONES & CO INC. Reproduced with permission of DOW JONES & CO INC in the format Textbook via Copyright Clearance Center.*

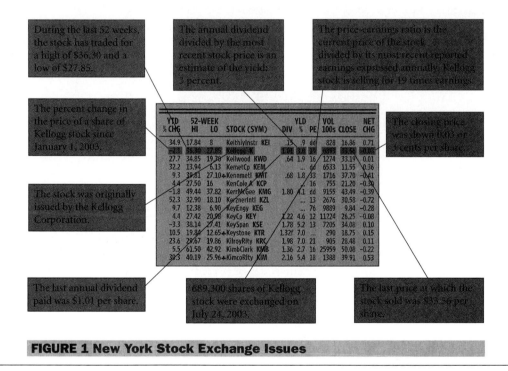

During the last 52 weeks, the stock has traded for a high of $36.30 and a low of $27.85.

The annual dividend divided by the most recent stock price is an estimate of the yield: 3 percent.

The price-earnings ratio is the current price of the stock divided by its most recent reported earnings expressed annually. Kellogg stock is selling for 19 times earnings.

The percent change in the price of a share of Kellogg stock since January 1, 2003.

The closing price was down 0.05 or 5 cents per share.

The stock was originally issued by the Kellogg Corporation.

The last annual dividend paid was $1.01 per share.

689,300 shares of Kellogg stock were exchanged on July 24, 2003.

The last price at which the stock sold was $33.56 per share.

FIGURE 1 New York Stock Exchange Issues

See the Further Exploration box for a discussion of how to read the stock pages in a newspaper.

DETERMINING THE PRICE OF A STOCK

What determines the price of a stock? If a share of stock is selling for $25, why is someone willing to pay that much for it? As we have noted, when you buy a share of stock, you own part of the firm. If a firm is making profits, it may be paying dividends to its shareholders. If it is not paying dividends but is making profits, people may expect that it will pay dividends in the future. Dividends are important in thinking about stocks because dividends are the form in which shareholders receive income from the firm. So one thing that is likely to affect the price of a stock is what people expect its future dividends will be. The larger the expected future dividends, the larger the current stock price, other things being equal.

Another important consideration in thinking about the price of a stock is the time the dividends are expected to be paid. A $2 per share dividend that is expected to be paid four years from now is worth less than a $2 per share dividend that is expected to be paid next year. In other words, the farther into the future the dividend is expected to be paid, the more it will be "discounted." The amount by which expected future dividends are discounted depends on the interest rate. The larger the interest rate, the more expected future dividends will be discounted. If the interest rate is 10 percent, I can invest $100.00 today and receive $110.00 a year from now. I am thus willing to pay $100.00 today to someone who will pay me $110.00 in a year. If instead, the interest rate were only 5 percent, I would be willing to pay $104.76 today to receive $110.00 a year from now because the alternative of $104.76 today at a 5 percent interest rate also yields $110.00 at the end of the year. I am thus willing to pay more for the promise of $110.00 a year from now when the interest rate is lower. In other words, I "discount" the $110.00 less when the interest rate is lower.

There is another discount factor aside from the interest rate that must be taken into account; it is the discount for risk. People prefer certain outcomes to uncertain ones for the same expected values. For example, I prefer a certain $50 over a bet in which there is a 50 percent chance I will get $100 and a 50 percent chance I will get nothing. The expected value of the bet is $50, but I prefer the certain $50 over the bet, where there is a 50 percent chance that I will end up with nothing. The same reasoning holds for future dividends. If, say, I expect dividends for both firms A and B to be $2 per share next year, but firm B has a much wider range of possibilities (is riskier), I will prefer firm A. Put another way, I will "discount" firm B's expected future dividends more than firm A's because the outcome for firm B is more uncertain.

We can thus say that the price of a stock should equal the discounted value of its expected future dividends, where the discount factors depend on the interest rate and risk. If for some reason, say a positive surprise news announcement from the firm, expected future dividends increase, this development should lead to an increase in the price of the stock. If the interest rate falls, this decrease should also lead to a stock price increase. Finally, if the perceived risk of a firm falls, this perception should increase the firm's stock price.

Some stock analysts talk about the possibility of stock market "bubbles." Given the above discussion, what might a bubble be? Say that given your expectations about the future dividends of a firm and given the discount rate, you value the firm's stock at $20 per share. Is there any case in which you would pay more than $20 for a share? You can, of course, buy the stock and sell it later; you don't need to hold the stock forever. If the stock is currently selling for $25, which is above your value of $20, but you think that the stock will rise to $30 in the next few months, you might buy it now in anticipation of selling later for a higher price. If others have similar views, the price of the stock may be driven up.

In this case, what counts is not the discounted value of expected future dividends but rather your view of what others will pay for the stock in the future. If everyone expects that everyone else expects that the price will be driven up, the price may be driven up. One might call this outcome a bubble because the stock price depends on what people expect that other people expect, and so on.

When a firm's stock price has risen rapidly, it is difficult to know whether the reason is that people have increased their expectations of the firm's future dividends or that there is a bubble. Because people's expectations of future dividends are not directly observed, it is hard to test alternative theories.

THE STOCK MARKET SINCE 1948

If you follow the stock market at all, you know that much attention is paid to two stock price indices: the **Dow Jones Industrial Average** and the **NASDAQ Composite**. From a macroeconomic perspective, however, these two indices cover too small a sample of firms. One would like an index that includes firms whose total market value is close to the market value of all firms in the economy. For this purpose a much better measure is the **Standard and Poor's 500** stock price index, called the **S&P 500**. This index includes most of the companies in the economy by market value.

The S&P 500 index is plotted in Figure 29.1 for 1948 I–2005 II. What perhaps stands out most in this plot is the huge increase in the index between 1995 and 2000. Between December 31, 1994, and March 31, 2000, the S&P 500 index rose 226 percent, an annual rate

Dow Jones Industrial Average An index based on the stock prices of 30 actively traded large companies. The oldest and most widely followed index of stock market performance.

NASDAQ Composite An index based on the stock prices of over 5,000 companies traded on the NASDAQ Stock Market. The NASDAQ market takes its name from the National Association of Securities Dealers Automated Quotation System.

Standard and Poor's 500 (S&P 500) An index based on the stock prices of the largest 500 firms traded on the New York Stock Exchange, the NASDAQ Stock Market, and the American Stock Exchange.

Percent scale

FIGURE 29.1 The S&P 500 Stock Price Index, 1948 I–2005 II

of increase of 25 percent. This is by far the largest stock market boom in U.S. history, completely dominating the boom of the 1920s. This boom added roughly $14 trillion to household wealth, about $2.5 trillion per year.

What caused this boom? You can see from Table 28.1 in the previous chapter that interest rates did not change much in the last half of the 1990s, and so the boom cannot be explained by any large fall in interest rates. Perhaps profits rose substantially during this period, and this growth led to a large increase in expected future dividends? We know from the above discussion that if expected future dividends increase, stock prices should increase. Figure 29.2 plots for 1948 I–2005 II the ratio of after-tax profits (as measured in the national income and product accounts). It is clear from the figure that nothing unusual happened in the last half of the 1990s. In fact, the share of profits in GDP fell slightly. Thus there does not appear to be any surge of profits that would have led people to expect much higher future dividends.

It could be that the perceived riskiness of stocks fell in the last half of the 1990s. This change would have led to smaller discount rates for stocks and thus, other things being equal, to higher stock prices. Although this possibility cannot be completely ruled out, there is no strong independent evidence that perceived riskiness fell.

The stock market boom is thus a puzzle, and many people speculate that it was simply a bubble. For some reason stock prices started rising rapidly in 1995, and people expected that other people expected that prices would continue to rise. This led stock prices to rise further, thus fulfilling the expectations, which led to expectations of further increases, and so on.

FIGURE 29.2 Ratio of After-Tax Profits to GDP, 1948 I–2005 II

People of this view note that once stock prices started falling in 2000, they fell a lot. It is not the case that stock prices just leveled out in 2000; they fell rapidly. People of the bubble view argue that this is simply the bubble bursting.

Remember that we are talking about the S&P 500 index, which includes most of the firms in the U.S. economy by market value. We are not just talking about a few dot-com companies. The entire stock market went up by 25 percent per year for 5 years! We will see in the next section the effects of this increase in wealth on the economy.

Before turning to the macroeconomy, it is of interest to reflect on the profound effect that the stock market boom had on countless individuals and families. There are many stories of people putting their life savings in the stock market, many in (with hindsight) questionable dot-com companies, only to lose it all in the end. There are also stories of people who at the peak of the market were worth more than $100 million (and some more than $1 billion) and are now back to essentially nothing. Some people have had to postpone their retirement because of stock market losses. Millions of lives have been affected by the euphoria that existed during the boom and the "correction" that has occurred since.

STOCK MARKET EFFECTS ON THE ECONOMY

We mentioned in Chapter 21 that one of the factors that affects consumption expenditures is wealth. Other things being equal, the more wealth a family has, the more it spends. We discuss this in detail in the next chapter, but all we need for now is to note that an increase in wealth increases consumer spending. An increase in stock prices may also affect investment. If a firm is considering an investment project, one way in which it can finance the project is to issue additional shares of stock. The higher the price of the firm's stock, the more money it can get per additional share. A firm is thus likely to undertake more investment projects the higher its stock price. The cost of an investment project in terms of shares of stock is smaller the larger the price of the stock. This is the way in which a stock market boom may increase investment.

The effect of the stock market on the economy is thus fairly straightforward. If stock prices increase, the wealth of households increases, as in turn does consumer spending. Investment also increases because firms can raise more money per share to finance investment projects. As a rough rule of thumb, a $1.00 change in the value of stocks leads to about a $0.03 to $0.04 change in consumer and investor spending per year. We will use the $0.04 number in the following discussion.

THE CRASH OF OCTOBER 1987

Before considering the boom of the late 1990s, it is useful to review a crash, namely the crash of October 1987. The value of stocks in the United States fell by about a trillion dollars between August 1987 and the end of October 1987. In one day—October 19, 1987—the value of stocks fell nearly $700 billion. If we assume that a $1 decrease in stock prices results in a $0.04 decrease in consumer and investor spending per year, we can see that the $1 trillion decrease in wealth in 1987 implies a $40 billion lower level of spending in 1988. The level of gross domestic product (GDP) was around $4 trillion in 1987, so a $40 billion decrease in spending is around 1.0 percent of GDP. A multiplier effect would also be at work here. A decrease in spending leads to a decrease in aggregate output (income), which leads to a further decrease in spending, and so on. The total decrease in GDP would be somewhat larger than the initial decrease of $40 billion. If the multiplier is 1.4, the total decrease in GDP would be about 1.4 × $40 billion = $56 billion, or about 1.4 percent of GDP.

Although 1.4 percent of GDP is a large amount, it is not large enough to imply that a recession would result from the crash. The life-cycle theory, which we will discuss in Chapter 17, helps explain why. If households are making lifetime decisions and want to have as smooth a consumption path as possible over their lifetimes, they will respond to a decrease in wealth by cutting consumption a little each year. They will *not* decrease their consumption in the current year by the full amount of the decrease in wealth.

Why were people predicting the economy would go into a recession, or worse, a depression, after the crash? The reasons all pertain to expectations. If households and firms

Stock prices are tracked by the stock exchanges on a minute-by-minute basis.

expected the economy would contract sharply after the crash, they probably would have cut back on consumption and investment much more than otherwise. (This reaction would be Keynes's animal spirits at work.) These expectations would have become self-fulfilling in the sense that the economy would have gone into a recession because of the cuts in consumption and investment brought about by lowered expectations.

However, the economy did not go into a recession in 1988. Expectations were not changed drastically following the crash. The Fed helped out by easing monetary policy right after the crash to counteract any large negative reaction. The 3-month Treasury bill rate fell from 6.4 percent to 5.8 percent between October and November 1987. In addition, the value of stocks gradually increased over time to their earlier levels. Because the initial decrease in wealth turned out to be temporary, the negative wealth effect was not nearly as large as it otherwise would have been.

THE BOOM OF 1995–2000

We pointed out earlier that between 1995 and 2000 the value of stocks increased about $2.5 trillion per year. If we assume that a $1 increase in stock prices results in a $0.04 increase in consumption and investment per year and if we use a multiplier of 1.4, the added increase in spending is .04 × $2.5 trillion × 1.4, which is $140 billion per year. In 1998, GDP was around $9 trillion, and so an increase of $140 billion is 1.5 percent of GDP.

The annual growth rate of GDP from the end of 1995 to the middle of 2000 was 4.5 percent. The above numbers thus suggest that about 1.5 of the 4.5 percent was due to the stock market boom. In other words, had there been no boom, the growth rate would likely have been around 3.0 percent instead of 4.5 percent. Households simply spent much more than they would have had there been no huge increase in their wealth, and firms invested much more than they would have had stock prices not risen so much.

A more detailed analysis of the effects of the stock market boom on the economy is presented in Figures 29.3–29.9. This analysis uses a model of the economy[1] to see what

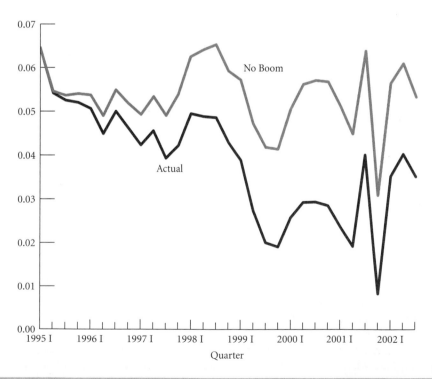

FIGURE 29.3 Personal Saving Rate, 1995 I–2002 III

[1]Ray C. Fair, *Estimating How the Macroeconomy Works* (Cambridge, MA: Harvard University Press, 2004).

the economy would have been like had there been no stock market boom. In each figure, the "actual" line represents the actual values of the variable over the 1995 I–2002 III period. These values reflect the stock market boom (because the boom actually took place!). The "no boom" line represents the values that the model estimates would have taken place had overall stock prices simply grown at a normal rate. In the no boom case, there was neither the huge increase in stock prices between 1995 and 2000 nor the large fall in prices from 2000 on.

The plots in the seven figures are interesting. They show that had there been no stock market boom, the U.S. economy would not have looked unusual in the last half of the 1990s. There would have been no talk of a "new economy" or a "new age." It would have been more or less business as usual. We will now discuss the figures one-by-one. Given what you have learned so far about macroeconomics, you should be able to understand the reasons for the various results.

Figure 29.3 shows that the personal saving rate is considerably higher in the no boom case. No longer are the values below the range of historical experience. This is the wealth effect on consumption at work. With no huge increase in wealth, households consume less.

Figure 29.4 shows that investment is also less in the no boom case. Firms invest less in plant and equipment because the cost to them in terms of extra shares issued is higher (the price per share is lower). Many people feel that investment was excessively high in the late 1990s, a phenomenon that led to the large falls in 2000 and 2001. Figure 29.4 shows that much of this would not have happened had there been no stock market boom.

Figure 29.5 shows that the federal government surplus would not have been as high in the late 1990s and in 2000 were it not for the stock market boom. It should be clear why this is the case. In the no boom case, taxable income and profits are less, and so there is less tax revenue. Also, spending on unemployment benefits is greater because (as we will see below) unemployment is higher.

Figure 29.6 shows that real growth was higher in the last half of the 1990s than would have been the case with no boom. This figure gives a more accurate impression of the growth rate effects than the simple use of the .04 number and the 1.4 multiplier above.

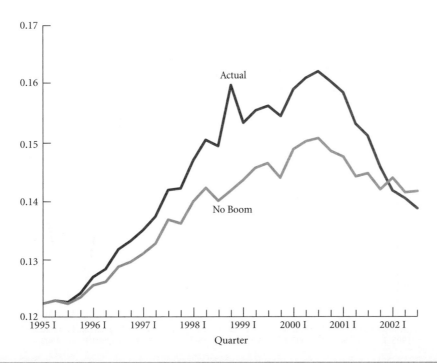

FIGURE 29.4 Investment-Output Ratio, 1995 I–2002 III

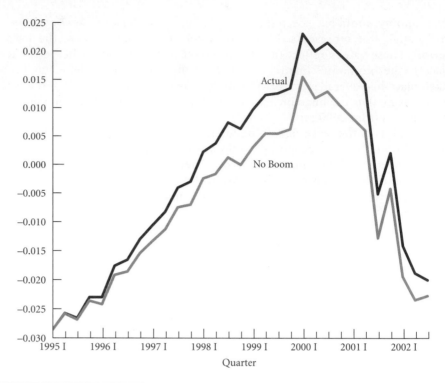

FIGURE 29.5 Ratio of Federal Government Budget Surplus to GDP, 1995 I–2002 III

Note from Figure 29.6 that the growth rate is higher in the no boom case in 2001 and 2002 because in the no boom case there is no large stock market correction in these two years.

Figure 29.7 shows that the fall in the unemployment rate in the last half of the 1990s to 4 percent from 5.5 percent was due to the stock market boom. Had there been no boom, the unemployment rate would have remained at about 5.5 percent.

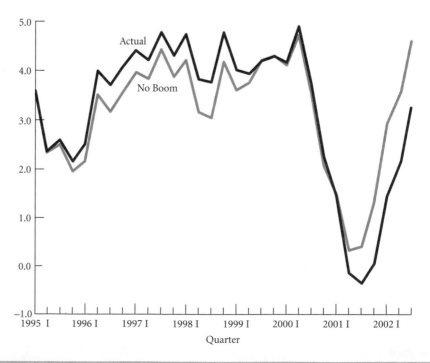

FIGURE 29.6 Growth Rate of Real GDP, 1995 I–2002 III

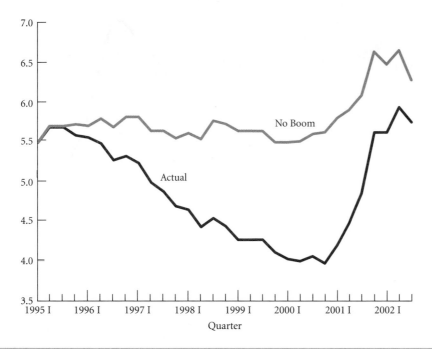

FIGURE 29.7 The Unemployment Rate, 1995 I–2002 III

Figure 29.8 shows that inflation would have been lower in the no boom case. The simple reason is that output would have been lower and thus demand pressure would have been less. In either case, however, the inflation rate is not high by historical standards.

Finally, Figure 29.9 plots the 3-month Treasury bill rate. Remember from the last chapter that this rate reflects the behavior of the Fed. The Fed essentially decides each 6 weeks what it wants the rate to be and uses open market operations to achieve this value. The figure shows that the interest rate would have been lower in the last half of the 1990s had there been no boom. This should make sense from the last chapter. Without the boom, real growth would have been lower and the unemployment rate higher, and the Fed would have responded with lower interest rates.

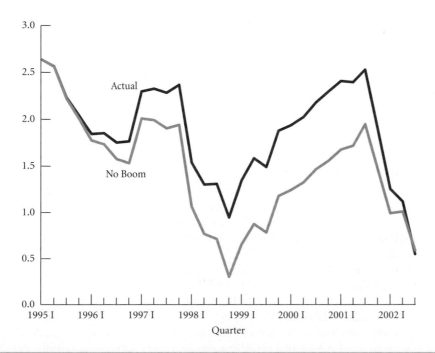

FIGURE 29.8 Inflation Rate, 1995 I–2002 III

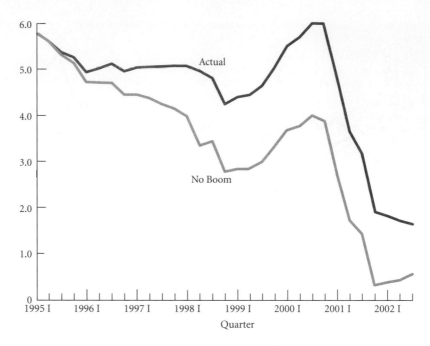

FIGURE 29.9 3-Month Treasury Bill Rate, 1995 I–2002 III

FED POLICY AND THE STOCK MARKET

Figure 29.9 is useful for thinking about how Fed policy is related to the stock market. Policy questions arise from time to time as to whether the Fed should be influenced by the stock market. Should the Fed try to influence stock prices by changing interest rates? Figure 29.9 says that the Fed is in fact influenced by the stock market. The Fed kept the interest rate higher than it would have had there been no stock market boom. It should be clear why this is the case. If ultimately the Fed cares about output, unemployment, and inflation, and if the stock market affects these variables, the Fed will be indirectly affected by the stock market. In other words, the Fed cares about the stock market to the extent that the stock market affects the things that it ultimately cares about, namely, output, unemployment, and inflation.

THE POST-BOOM ECONOMY

Figure 29.1 shows that there was a fairly large fall in stock prices between the fourth quarter of 2000 and the third quarter of 2002. In this period, the fall in household wealth from the stock market was about $7 trillion. We mentioned earlier that the stock market boom in the last half of the 1990s added about $14 trillion to household wealth, and so about half of this increase was reversed in the 2000 IV–2002 III period.

   Given that the stock market boom in the last half of the 1990s led to a more expansionary economy than would otherwise have been the case, it seems likely that the stock market correction in 2000–2002 led to a less expansionary economy. This is in fact the case: The $7 trillion fall in household wealth had a negative effect on the economy. This can be seen from Table 28.1 in the previous chapter. There were two quarters of negative growth in 2001, and the growth rate in 2002 was modest. The economy did not begin growing well again until the middle of 2003.

   What is remarkable about the sluggish economy in 2001 and 2002 is that it came at a time of very expansionary monetary and fiscal policy. Table 28.1 shows that the Fed lowered the bill rate by over 4 percentage points in this period, perhaps the most expansionary policy in its history. Figure 28.7, 28.8, and 28.9 show that fiscal policy was also very expansionary. As discussed in the last chapter, tax rates were lowered substantially in the Bush administration and government spending and transfer payments were increased considerably. Despite these huge expansionary policies, the economy did not do particularly well, and one of the main reasons was the fall in household wealth from the stock market decline. Had there been

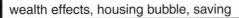
Housing Wealth in 2006

IN 2005, THE BOOM IN HOUSING prices around the globe appeared to be ending, and many observers worried that housing prices would decline in 2006. This drop might then lead to a decline in consumer spending and a period of slow growth or even a recession. The following *Wall Street Journal* article discusses the possibility of negative "wealth effects" in Europe and the United States.

Europe Might Need Some Economic Shelter as Housing Market Cools

By MARCUS WALKER
and KEITH JOHNSON
—*The Wall Street Journal*
November 21, 2005

While observers of the U.S. economy fret about whether the house-price boom will falter and hurt economic growth, Europe is already facing a slowdown in housing markets that could hold back the region's fragile consumer spending, and its economy.

Average home prices in many American cities were rising at a strong pace during the first half of the year. Now there are mounting signs that home sales are cooling, prompting economists to forecast smaller price gains next year. But parts of Europe have already reached that point.

Britain is the most visible example of the trend. The U.K. economy has stumbled badly this year after increases in home prices slowed almost to a halt and heavily indebted consumers closed their wallets. The Bank of England cut short the U.K.'s property boom by raising interest rates steadily from late 2003; its low rates earlier had helped to fuel the house-price increases.

The worst may not be over: Pessimistic observers forecast a 20% fall in house prices over the next three years.

While no crash in home prices or consumption is expected, a slowing property market could be a drag on consumer demand, just when the euro-zone economy was starting to strengthen after four years of painfully slow growth.

The effect on consumer spending is smaller in Europe because unlike Americans, most Europeans can't easily borrow money for consumption against the rising value of their home. But the psychological wealth effect works in Europe, too: People who feel wealthier because their homes are worth more save less of their salaries. That helps explain why the French have cut their savings sharply since 2003, boosting consumer spending even while household incomes have grown only slowly.

A gradual housing-market slowdown won't undermine consumer confidence, and the thinking inside the Bank of Spain is that a cooling could even be healthy. Mathematical models developed at the Organization for Economic Cooperation and Development in Paris say that Spaniards would reduce their spending in shops by only €2 for every €100.

no stock market correction but the same monetary and fiscal policies, the economy would have grown much more rapidly in 2001 and 2002 than it in fact did.

The importance of the stock market in the economy should now be clear. It played a big role in the economic boom of the last half of the 1990s and in the economic slack of 2000–2002. This is why introductory macroeconomic texts can no longer ignore the stock market.

A final point that is interesting to note about the post-boom U.S. economy is the role that housing values played from 2003 through 2005. You can see from Table 28.1 in the previous chapter that the growth rate of output was fairly good in this period and that the unemployment rate fell from 6.1 percent in 2003 III to 5.1 percent in 2005 II. The stock market began to recover in this period, but perhaps more important, the housing market boomed. Many homeowners saw the value of their homes soar. Many responded to this rise by taking out "home equity" loans, which were available at low interest rates, and then increasing their spending on consumer goods and services. Consumption was thus stimulated by this increase in housing wealth, which helped fuel the recovery. *So both stock market wealth and housing wealth have important effects on the economy.*

Some felt by 2005 that there was a housing bubble just waiting to be burst. Would housing prices continue to increase or at least not fall, or was the economy in for a large and rapid fall in prices, as had occurred in the stock market a few years earlier? There was much debate about this issue in late 2005. (See the News Analysis box, "Housing Wealth in 2006," page 635.)

SUMMARY

STOCKS AND BONDS

1. A firm can finance an investment project by borrowing from banks, by issuing *bonds*, or by issuing new shares of its *stock*. People who own shares of stock own a fraction of the firm.

2. The price of a stock should equal the discounted value of its expected future dividends, where the discount factors depend on the interest rate and risk.

3. A bubble exists if the price of a stock exceeds the discounted value of its expected future dividends. In this case, what matters is what people expect that other people expect about how much the stock can be sold for in the future.

THE STOCK MARKET SINCE 1948

4. The largest stock market boom in U.S. history occurred between 1995 and 2000, when the S&P 500 index rose by 25 percent per year. The boom added $14 trillion to household wealth.

5. Why there was a stock market boom in 1995–2000 appears to be a puzzle. There was nothing unusual about earnings that would predict such a boom. Many people believe that the boom was merely a bubble.

6. The boom of 1995–2000 and the large fall in stock prices after that had significant effects on millions of people's lives. Many people overspent during the boom years and were seriously affected when the boom didn't last.

STOCK MARKET EFFECTS ON THE ECONOMY

7. When stock prices increase, household wealth increases, which leads to increased consumer spending. Investment also rises because firms can raise more money per share to finance investment projects. As a rough rule of thumb, a $1.00 change in the value of stocks leads to about a $0.03 to $0.04 change in consumer and investor spending per year.

8. The boom in the economy between 1995 and 2000 was fueled by the stock market boom. Estimates show that had there been no stock market boom, the economy would not have looked historically unusual in the last half of the 1990s.

9. The economy in 2001–2002 was more sluggish than it would have been had there been no stock market "correction" following the boom.

10. The boom in housing prices in 2003–2005 helped sustain the recovery.

REVIEW TERMS AND CONCEPTS

bond, 623

capital gain, 624

Dow Jones Industrial Average, 627

NASDAQ Composite, 627

realized capital gain, 624

Standard and Poor's 500 (S&P 500), 627

stock, 624

PROBLEM SET

1. On July 28, 2003, JPMorgan stock (stock symbol "JPM") traded for $39.50 per share. Suppose that you had bought 100 shares on that date and that you sold them today. Look up the current price of JPMorgan stock in the stock pages of any newspaper.
   a. How much are your shares worth today?
   b. How much did you make or lose in total dollars?

   c. Expressed as a percent of what you initially paid, how big is your gain or loss?
   d. To get a very rough annual percent increase, divide your percent change in c. by the number of years since July 2003, including fractions of a year. For example, if it is November 2004, divide by 1 and 4/12 or 1.33.

e. What is the current dividend yield from the stock table?

f. Now figure your total return by adding the dividend yield in e. to the annualized gain in price from d.

g. How does your total yield compare to interest rates today? Was it a good investment?

2. In July 2003, the S&P 500 index was at 1,000.

a. What is the S&P 500 index?

b. Where is the S&P today?

c. If you had invested $10,000 in July 2003 and your investments had increased in value by the same percentage as the S&P 500 index had increased, how much would you have today?

d. Assume that the total stock market holdings of the household sector were about $12 trillion and that the entire stock market went up/down by the same percentage as the S&P. Evidence suggests that the "wealth effect" of stock market holdings on consumer spending is about 4 percent of wealth annually. How much additional or reduced spending would you expect to see as a result of the stock market moves since July 2003? Assuming a multiplier of 2 and a GDP of $1,100 billion, how much additional/less GDP would you predict for next year if all of this were true?

3. In July 2003, the 10-year Treasury bond was paying 4.25 percent. In the corporate bond table in the box titled "Reading a Bond Table," you can see a bond sold by General Motors due in July 2013 paying a 7.133 percent interest rate. What reasons can you give for the difference between the Treasury's borrowing rate and the rate paid by GM?

4. During 1997, stock markets in Asia collapsed. Hong Kong's was down nearly 30 percent, Thailand's down 62 percent, and Malaysia's down 60 percent. Big drops were also experienced in Japan and Korea. What impacts would these events have on the economies of the countries themselves? Explain your answer. In what ways would you have expected these events to influence the U.S. economy? How might the spending of Asians on American goods be affected? What about Americans who have invested in these countries?

5. The News Analysis box on page 635 discusses the effect of rising home prices on consumer spending. The Federal Reserve Open Market Committee meeting minutes in September 2005 reflects this sentiment: "For the nation as a whole, participants noted that household spending had been fairly robust before the hurricane, supported by strong advances in income and continuing gains in wealth that reflected in part further large increases in home prices." This raises the possibility of a bursting house price bubble that could result in a decline in house prices and spending in 2006 and later years. Go to **www.ofheo.gov** and click on house price index. Look at the most recent press release. What in fact happened to house prices during 2006? What was the likely outcome in terms of the impact on the economy?

Household and Firm Behavior in the Macroeconomy: A Further Look*

I n Chapters 21 through 27, we considered the interactions of households, firms, and the government in the goods, money, and labor markets. The macroeconomy is complicated, and there is a lot to learn about these interactions. To keep our discussions as uncomplicated as possible, we have so far assumed simple behavior of households and firms—the two basic decision-making units in the economy. We assumed household consumption (C) depends only on income, and firms' planned investment (I) depends only on the interest rate. We did not consider that households make consumption and labor supply decisions simultaneously and that firms make investment and employment decisions simultaneously.

Now that we understand the basic interactions in the economy, we must relax these assumptions. In the first part of this chapter, we present a more realistic picture of the influences on households' consumption and labor supply decisions. In the second part, we present a more detailed and realistic picture of the influences on firms' investment and employment decisions. We then use what we have learned to analyze more macroeconomic issues.

HOUSEHOLDS: CONSUMPTION AND LABOR SUPPLY DECISIONS

Before discussing household behavior, let us review what we have learned so far.

THE KEYNESIAN THEORY OF CONSUMPTION: A REVIEW

The assumption that household consumption (C) depends on income, which we have used as the basis of our analysis so far, is one that Keynes stressed in his *General Theory of Employment, Interest, and Money*. While Keynes believed many factors, including interest

---

*This chapter is somewhat more advanced, and it can be skipped, if desired.

rates and wealth, are likely to influence the level of consumption spending, he focused on current income:

> The amount of aggregate consumption depends mainly on the amount of aggregate income. The fundamental psychological law, upon which we are entitled to depend with great confidence both . . . from our knowledge of human nature and from the detailed facts of experience, is that men [and women, too] are disposed, as a rule and on average, to increase their consumption as their incomes increase, but not by as much as the increase in their income.[1]

Keynes is making two points here. First, he suggests that consumption is a positive function of income. The more income you have, the more consuming you are likely to do. Except for a few rich misers who save scraps of soap and bits of string despite million-dollar incomes, this proposition makes sense. Rich people typically consume more than poor people.

average propensity to consume (APC) The proportion of income households spend on consumption. Determined by dividing consumption (C) by income (Y).

Second, Keynes suggests, high-income households consume a smaller proportion of their income than low-income households. (If rich households consume relatively less of their incomes, then by definition they save a higher proportion of their incomes than poor households.) The proportion of income that households spend on consumption is measured by the **average propensity to consume (APC)**.[2] The APC is defined as consumption divided by income:

$$APC = \frac{C}{Y}$$

If a household earns $30,000 per year and spends $25,000 (saving $5,000), it has an *APC* of $25,000/$30,000, or .833. Keynes argues that people who earn, for example, $30,000, are likely to spend a larger portion of their income than those who earn $100,000.

Although the idea that consumption depends on income is a useful starting point, it is far from a complete description of the consumption decision. We need to consider other theories of consumption.

THE LIFE-CYCLE THEORY OF CONSUMPTION

life-cycle theory of consumption A theory of household consumption: Households make lifetime consumption decisions based on their expectations of lifetime income.

The **life-cycle theory of consumption** is an extension of Keynes's theory. The idea of the life-cycle theory is that people make lifetime consumption plans. By realizing that they are likely to earn more in their prime working years than they earn earlier or later, they make consumption decisions based on their expectations of lifetime income. People tend to consume less than they earn during their main working years—they *save* during those years—and they tend to consume more than they earn during their early and later years—they *dissave*, or use up savings, during those years. Students in medical school generally have very low current incomes, but few live in the poverty that those incomes might predict. Instead, they borrow now and plan to pay back later when their incomes improve.

The lifetime income and consumption pattern of a representative individual is shown in Figure 30.1. As you can see, this person has a low income during the first part of her life, high income in the middle, and low income again in retirement. Her income in retirement is not zero because she has income from sources other than her own labor—Social Security payments, interest and dividends, and so forth.

The consumption path as drawn in Figure 30.1 is constant over the person's life. This is an extreme assumption, but it illustrates the point that the path of consumption over a lifetime is likely to be much more stable than the path of income. We consume an amount greater than our incomes during our early working careers. We do so by borrowing against future income, by taking out a car loan, a mortgage to buy a house, or a loan to pay for col-

---

[1]John Maynard Keynes, *The General Theory of Employment, Interest, and Money (1936)*, First Harbinger Ed. (New York: Harcourt Brace Jovanovich, 1964), p. 96.
[2]Whereas the *APC* measures the proportion of total income households spend on consumption, the marginal propensity to consume (*MPC*), which we introduced in Chapter 21, measures the proportion of a *change* in income that households spend on consumption. We could interpret Keynes's theory as implying that the *MPC* falls as income rises. If the *MPC* falls as income rises, it follows that the average propensity to consume (*APC*) falls also.

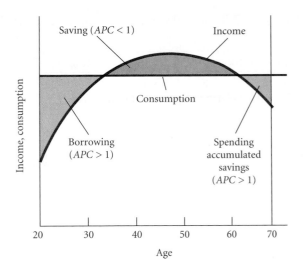

FIGURE 30.1 Life-Cycle Theory of Consumption

In their early working years, people consume more than they earn. This is also true in the retirement years. In between, people save (consume less than they earn) to pay off debts from borrowing and to accumulate savings for retirement.

lege. This debt is repaid when our incomes have risen and we can afford to use some of our income to pay off past borrowing without substantially lowering our consumption. The reverse is true for our retirement years. Here, too, our incomes are low. Because we consume less than we earn during our prime working years, we can save up a "nest egg" that allows us to maintain an acceptable standard of living during retirement.

Fluctuations in wealth are also an important component of the life-cycle story. Many young households borrow in anticipation of higher income in the future. Some households actually have *negative wealth*—the value of their assets is less than the debts they owe. A household in its prime working years saves to pay off debts and to build up assets for its later years, when income typically goes down. Households whose assets are greater than the debts they owe have *positive wealth*. With its wage earners retired, a household consumes its accumulated wealth. Generally speaking, wealth starts out negative, turns positive, and then approaches zero near the end of life. Wealth, therefore, is intimately linked to the cumulative saving and dissaving behavior of households.

The key difference between the Keynesian theory of consumption and the life-cycle theory is that the life-cycle theory suggests consumption and saving decisions are likely to be based not just on current income, but on expectations of future income as well. The consumption behavior of households immediately following World War II clearly supports the life-cycle story. Just after the war ended, income fell as wage earners moved out of war-related work. However, consumption spending did not fall commensurately, as Keynesian theory would predict. People expected to find jobs in other sectors eventually, and they did not adjust their consumption spending to the temporarily lower incomes they were earning in the meantime.

The phrase **permanent income** is sometimes used to refer to the average level of a person's expected future income stream. If you expect your income will be high in the future (even though it may not be high now), your permanent income is said to be high. With this concept, we can sum up the life-cycle theory by saying that current consumption decisions are likely to be based on permanent income instead of current income.[3] This means that policy changes like tax-rate changes are likely to have more of an effect on household behavior if they are expected to be permanent instead of temporary.

Although this insight enriches our understanding of the consumption behavior of households, the analysis is still missing something. What is missing is the other main decision of households: the labor supply decision.

permanent income The average level of one's expected future income stream.

---

[3]The pioneering work on this topic was done by Milton Friedman, *A Theory of the Consumption Function* (Princeton, N.J.: Princeton University Press, 1957). In the mid-1960s, Franco Modigliani did closely related work that included the formulation of the life-cycle theory.

A New Pattern of Consumption and Income, 1946–1947

The following excerpts from an article in the *New York Times* in 1946 and a second article a year later show how economists were beginning to solve the puzzle.

Non-Durable Goods Purchases by Consumers at Record Level

FIRST QUARTER BUYING TOTAL IS AT THE RATE OF $120,000,000,000 A YEAR, DEPARTMENT OF COMMERCE STATISTICS REVEAL

WASHINGTON, April 28—The amount of money spent by consumers on non-durable goods in the first three months of 1946 was high in relation to their incomes, the Department of Commerce said today in announcing that consumer spending in the first quarter had reached the record annual rate of $120,000,000,000.

That Key Man, the Consumer

HOW HE SPENDS HIS MONEY IN TIMES LIKE THESE MAY WELL DETERMINE THE ECONOMIC COURSE OF THE COUNTRY

In the last few years economists have "rediscovered" the crucial importance of consumer behavior in accounting for the ups and downs of business activity. It is becoming clear that if economic policies on a national scale are to have any chance of success, they must be based on a much better understanding than we now have of the complex factors underlying the spending-saving decisions of consumers.

For example, in deciding whether to spend or save a particular dollar of income, the expectations which consumers hold concerning the future undoubtedly carry a lot of weight.

Economists are just beginning to realize the full significance of this phenomenon. Certainly it was the widespread expectation of continued high incomes that helped to set off the explosion of consumer spending at the war's end. And just as certainly the expectation of higher and higher prices in the months that followed was like pouring oil on the flames.

PRIOR TO THE END OF WORLD WAR II, economists basically looked to current income to explain and predict the level of consumer expenditure. At the end of the war, veterans returned home and were discharged, essentially losing their salaries. At the same time, production and employment were cut in the industries that supplied goods and services to the war effort (everything from aircraft and tanks to medical supplies and uniforms for soldiers).

Because of the dramatic loss of income, economic forecasters predicted a major recession. But we now know that consumption spending never dropped after the war. In fact, it rose to record levels during the years immediately following the war's end in 1945.

THE LABOR SUPPLY DECISION

The size of the labor force in an economy is of obvious importance. A growing labor force is one of the ways in which national income/output can be expanded, and the larger the percentage of people who work, the higher the potential output per capita.

So far, we have said little about the things that determine the size of the labor force. Of course, demographics are a key; the number of children born in 2006 will go a long way toward determining the potential number of 20-year-old workers in 2026. In addition, immigration, both legal and illegal, plays a role.

Behavior also plays a role. Households make decisions about whether to work and how much to work. These decisions are closely tied to consumption decisions, because for most households the bulk of their spending is financed out of wages and salaries.

> Households make consumption and labor supply decisions simultaneously. Consumption cannot be considered separately from labor supply, because it is precisely by selling your labor that you earn income to pay for your consumption.

As we discussed in Chapter 3, the alternative to supplying your labor in exchange for a wage or a salary is leisure or other nonmarket activities. Nonmarket activities include raising a child, going to school, keeping a house, or—in a developing economy—working as a subsistence farmer.

What determines the quantity of labor supplied by a household? Among the list of factors are the wage rate, prices, wealth, and nonlabor income.

The Wage Rate   A changing wage rate can affect labor supply, but whether the effect is positive or negative is ambiguous. For example, an increase in the wage rate affects a household in two ways. First, work becomes more attractive relative to leisure and other nonmarket activities. Because every hour spent in leisure now requires giving up a higher wage, the opportunity cost of leisure is higher. As a result, you would expect a higher wage would lead to a larger quantity of labor supplied—a larger workforce. This is called the *substitution effect of a wage rate increase*.

On the other hand, households who work are clearly better off after a wage rate increase. By working the same number of hours as they did before, they will earn more income. If we assume that leisure is a normal good, people with higher income will spend some of it on leisure by working less. This is the *income effect of a wage rate increase*.

When wage rates rise, the substitution effect suggests that people will work more, while the income effect suggests that they will work less. The ultimate effect depends on which separate effect is more powerful. The data suggest that the substitution effect seems to win in most cases. That is, higher wage rates usually lead to a larger labor supply, and lower wage rates usually lead to a lower labor supply.

Prices   Prices also play a major role in the consumption/labor supply decision. In our discussions of the possible effects of an increase in the wage rate, we have been assuming that the prices of goods and services do not rise at the same time. If the wage rate and all other prices rise simultaneously, the story is different. To make things clear we need to distinguish between the nominal wage rate and the real wage rate.

The **nominal wage rate** is the wage rate in current dollars. When we adjust the nominal wage rate for changes in the price level, we obtain the **real wage rate**. The real wage rate measures the amount that wages can buy in terms of goods and services. Workers do not care about their nominal wage—they care about the purchasing power of this wage—the real wage.

nominal wage rate The wage rate in current dollars.

real wage rate The amount that the nominal wage rate can buy in terms of goods and services.

Suppose skilled workers in Indianapolis were paid a wage rate of $20 per hour in 2005. Now suppose that their wage rate rose to $22 in 2006, a 10 percent increase. If the prices of goods and services were exactly the same in 2006 as they were in 2005, the real wage rate would have increased by 10 percent. An hour of work in 2006 ($22) buys 10 percent more than an hour of work in 2005 ($20).

What if the prices of all goods and services also increased by 10 percent between 2005 and 2006? The purchasing power of an hour's wages has not changed. The real wage rate has not increased at all. In 2006, $22 bought the same quantity of goods and services that $20 bought in 2005.

To measure the real wage rate, we adjust the nominal wage rate with a price index. As we saw in Chapter 20, there are several such indexes that we might use, including the consumer price index and the GDP price index.[4]

---

[4]To calculate the real wage rate, we divide the nominal wage rate by the price index. Suppose the wage rate rose from $10.00 per hour in 1994 to $18.00 per hour in 2006 and the price level rose 50 percent during the same period. Using 1994 as the base year, the price index would be 1.00 in 1994 and 1.50 in 2006. The real wage rate is W/P, where W is the nominal wage rate and P is the price level. The real wage rate is $10.00 in 1994 ($10.00/1.00) and $12.00 in 2006 ($18.00/1.50), using 1994 as the base year.

We can now apply what we have learned from the life-cycle theory to our wage/price story. Recall the life-cycle theory says that people look ahead in making their decisions. Translated to real wage rates, this idea says:

> Households look at expected future real wage rates as well as the current real wage rate in making their current consumption and labor supply decisions.

Consider medical students who expect their real wage rate will be higher in the future. This expectation obviously has an effect on current decisions about things like how much to buy and whether or not to take a part-time job.

Wealth and Nonlabor Income   Life-cycle theory says wealth fluctuates over the life cycle. Households accumulate wealth during their working years to pay off debts accumulated when they were young and to support themselves in retirement. This role of wealth is clear, but the existence of wealth poses another question. Consider two households that are at the same stage in their life cycle and have pretty much the same expectations about future wage rates, prices, and so forth. They expect to live the same length of time, and both plan to leave the same amount to their children. They differ only in their wealth. Because of a past inheritance, household 1 has more wealth than household 2. Which household is likely to have a higher consumption path for the rest of its life? Household 1 is, because it has more wealth to spread out over the rest of its life.

> Holding everything else constant (including the stage in the life cycle), the more wealth a household has, the more it will consume, both now and in the future.

nonlabor, or nonwage, income Any income received from sources other than working—inheritances, interest, dividends, transfer payments, and so on.

Now consider a household that has a sudden unexpected increase in wealth, perhaps an inheritance from a distant relative. How will the household's consumption pattern be affected? The household will increase its consumption, both now and in the future, as it spends the inheritance over the course of the rest of its life.

An increase in wealth can also be looked on as an increase in nonlabor income. **Nonlabor, or nonwage, income** is income received from sources other than working—inheritances, interest, dividends, and transfer payments such as welfare payments and Social Security payments. As with wealth:

> An unexpected increase in nonlabor income will have a positive effect on a household's consumption.

What about the effect of an increase in wealth or nonlabor income on labor supply? We already know an increase in income results in an increase in the consumption of normal goods, including leisure. Therefore, an unexpected increase in wealth or nonlabor income results in both an increase in consumption and an increase in leisure. With leisure increasing, labor supply must fall, so:

> An unexpected increase in wealth or nonlabor income leads to a *decrease* in labor supply.

This point should be obvious. If I suddenly win a million dollars in the state lottery or make a killing in the stock market, I will probably work less in the future than I otherwise would have.

INTEREST RATE EFFECTS ON CONSUMPTION

Recall from the last few chapters that the interest rate affects a firm's investment decision. A higher interest rate leads to a lower level of planned investment, and vice versa. This was a key link between the money market and the goods market, and it was the channel through which monetary policy had an impact on planned aggregate expenditure.

We can now expand on this link: The interest rate also affects household behavior. Consider the effect of a fall in the interest rate on consumption. A fall in the interest rate lowers the reward to saving. If the interest rate falls from 10 percent to 5 percent, I earn 5 cents instead of 10 cents per year on every dollar saved. This means that the opportunity cost of spending a dollar today (instead of saving it and consuming it plus the interest income a year from now) has fallen. I will substitute toward current consumption and away from future consumption when the interest rate falls: I consume more today and save less. A rise in the interest rate leads me to consume less today and save more. This effect is called the *substitution effect*.

There is also an *income effect* of an interest rate change on consumption. If a household has positive wealth and is earning interest on that wealth, a fall in the interest rate leads to a fall in interest income. This is a decrease in its nonlabor income, which, as we just saw, will have a negative effect on consumption. For households with positive wealth, the income effect works in the opposite direction from the substitution effect. On the other hand, if a household is a debtor and is paying interest on its debt, a fall in the interest rate leads to a fall in interest payments. The household is better off in this case and will consume more. In this case, the income and substitution effects work in the same direction. The total household sector in the United States has positive wealth, and so in the aggregate the income and substitution effects work in the opposite direction.

On balance, the data suggest that the substitution effect dominates the income effect, so that the interest rate has a negative net effect on consumption. There is also some evidence, however, that the income effect is getting larger over time. U.S. households own most of the U.S. government debt, and the size of this debt has increased dramatically in the last 25 years. This means that the change in government interest payments, and so the change in household interest income, is now larger for a given change in interest rates than before, which leads to a larger income effect than before for a given change in interest rates.

GOVERNMENT EFFECTS ON CONSUMPTION AND LABOR SUPPLY: TAXES AND TRANSFERS

The government influences household behavior mainly through income tax rates and transfer payments. When the government raises income tax rates, after-tax real wages decrease, lowering consumption. When the government lowers income tax rates, after-tax real wages increase, raising consumption. A change in income tax rates also affects labor supply. If the substitution effect dominates, as we are generally assuming, then an increase in income tax rates, which lowers after-tax wages, will lower labor supply. A decrease in income tax rates will increase labor supply.

Transfer payments are payments such as Social Security benefits, veterans' benefits, and welfare benefits. An increase in transfer payments is an increase in nonlabor income, which we have seen has a positive effect on consumption and a negative effect on labor supply. Increases in transfer payments thus increase consumption and decrease labor supply, while decreases in transfer payments decrease consumption and increase labor supply. Table 30.1 summarizes these results.

A POSSIBLE EMPLOYMENT CONSTRAINT ON HOUSEHOLDS

Our discussion of the labor supply decision has so far proceeded as if households were free to choose how much to work each period. If a member of a household decides to work an additional 5 hours a week at the current wage rate, we have assumed the person *can* work 5

TABLE 30.1 The Effects of Government on Household Consumption and Labor Supply

	Income Tax Rates		Transfer Payments	
	INCREASE	**DECREASE**	**INCREASE**	**DECREASE**
Effect on consumption	Negative	Positive	Positive	Negative
Effect on labor supply	Negative*	Positive*	Negative	Positive

*If the substitution effect dominates.
Note: The effects are larger if they are expected to be permanent instead of temporary.

hours more—that work is available. If someone who has not been working decides to work at the current wage rate, we have assumed that the person *can find a job*.

There are times when these assumptions do not hold. The Great Depression, when unemployment rates reached 25 percent of the labor force, led to the birth of macroeconomics in the 1930s. Since the mid-1970s, the United States has experienced four recessions, with millions of unemployed workers unable to find work.

All households face a budget constraint, regardless of the state of the economy. This budget constraint, which separates those bundles of goods that are available to a household from those that are not, is determined by income, wealth, and prices. When there is unemployment, some households feel an additional constraint on their behavior. Some people may want to work 40 hours per week at the current wage rates but may find only part-time work. Others may not find any work at all.

How does a household respond when it is constrained from working as much as it would like? It consumes less. If your current wage rate is $10 per hour and you normally work 40 hours a week, your normal income from wages is $400 per week. If your average tax rate is 20 percent, your after-tax wage income is $320 per week. You are likely to spend much of this income during the week. If you are prevented from working, this income will not be available to you, and you will have less to spend.

You will spend something, of course. You may receive some form of nonlabor income, and you may have assets, such as savings deposits or stocks and bonds, that can be withdrawn or sold. You may also be able to borrow during your period of unemployment. Even though you will spend something during the week, it is almost certain that you will spend less than you would have if you had your usual income of $320 in after-tax wages.

Households consume less if they are constrained from working.

A household constrained from working as much as it would like at the current wage rate faces a different decision from the decision facing a household that can work as much as it wants. The work decision of the former household is, in effect, forced on it. The household works as much as it can—a certain number of hours per week or perhaps none at all—but this amount is less than the household would choose to work at the current wage rate if it could find more work. The amount that a household would like to work at the current wage rate if it could find the work is called its **unconstrained supply of labor**. The amount that the household actually works in a given period at current wage rates is called its **constrained supply of labor**.

unconstrained supply of labor The amount a household would like to work within a given period at the current wage rate if it could find the work.

constrained supply of labor The amount a household actually works in a given period at the current wage rate.

A household's constrained supply of labor is not a variable over which it has any control. The amount of labor the household supplies is imposed on it from the outside by the workings of the economy. However, the household's consumption *is* under its control. We have just seen that the less a household works—that is, the smaller the household's constrained supply of labor is—the lower its consumption. Constraints on the supply of labor are an important determinant of consumption when there is unemployment.

Keynesian Theory Revisited Recall the Keynesian theory that current income determines current consumption. We now know the consumption decision is made jointly with the labor supply decision and the two depend on the real wage rate. It is incorrect to think consumption depends only on income, at least when there is full employment. However, if there is unemployment, Keynes is closer to being correct because income is not determined by households. When there is unemployment, the level of income (at least workers' income) depends exclusively on the employment decisions made by firms. There are unemployed workers who are willing to work at the current wage rate, and their income is in effect determined by firms' hiring decisions. This income affects current consumption, which is consistent with Keynes's theory. This is one of the reasons Keynesian theory is considered to pertain to periods of unemployment. It was, of course, precisely during such a period that the theory was developed.

A SUMMARY OF HOUSEHOLD BEHAVIOR

This completes our discussion of household behavior in the macroeconomy. Household consumption depends on more than current income. Households determine consumption and labor supply simultaneously, and they look ahead in making their decisions.

The following factors affect household consumption and labor supply decisions:

- Current and expected future real wage rates
- Initial value of wealth
- Current and expected future nonlabor income
- Interest rates
- Current and expected future tax rates and transfer payments

If households are constrained in their labor supply decisions, income is directly determined by firms' hiring decisions. In this case, we can say (in the traditional, Keynesian way) that "income" affects consumption.

THE HOUSEHOLD SECTOR SINCE 1970

To better understand household behavior, let us examine how some of the aggregate household variables have changed over time. We will discuss the period 1970 I–2005 II. (Remember, roman numerals refer to quarters, that is, 1970 I means the first quarter of 1970.) Within this span, there have been four recessionary periods, 1974 I–1975 IV, 1980 II–1983 I, 1990 III–1991 I, and 2001 I–2001 III. How did the household variables behave during each period?

Consumption Data on the total consumption of the household sector are in the national income accounts. As we saw in Table 19.2 on page 420, personal consumption expenditures accounted for 70.0 percent of GDP in 2004. The three basic categories of consumption expenditures are services, nondurable goods, and durable goods.

Figure 30.2 plots the data for consumption expenditures on services and nondurable goods combined and for consumption expenditures on durable goods. The variables are in real terms. You can see that expenditures on services and nondurable goods are "smoother" over time than expenditures on durable goods. For example, the decrease in expenditures on services and nondurable goods was much smaller during the three recessionary periods than the decrease in expenditures on durable goods.

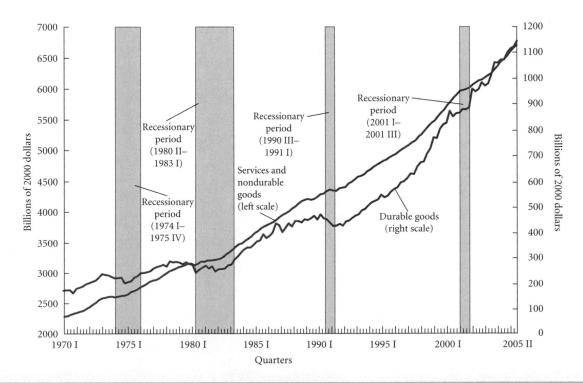

FIGURE 30.2 Consumption Expenditures, 1970 I–2005 II

Over time, expenditures on services and nondurable goods are "smoother" than expenditures on durable goods.

Why do expenditures on durables fluctuate more than expenditures on services and nondurables? When times are bad, people can postpone the purchase of durable goods, and they do. It follows that expenditures on these goods change the most. When times are tough, you do not *have* to have a new car or a new washer-dryer; you can make do with your old Chevy or Maytag until things get better. When your income falls, it is less easy to postpone the service costs of day care or health care. Nondurables fall into an intermediate category, with some items (such as new clothes) easier to postpone than others (such as food).

Housing Investment   Another important expenditure of the household sector is housing investment (purchases of new housing), plotted in Figure 30.3. This variable fluctuates greatly, for at least two reasons. Housing investment is the most easily postponable of all household expenditures. Also, housing investment is sensitive to the general level of interest rates, and interest rates fluctuate considerably over time. When interest rates are low, housing investment is high, and vice versa.

Labor Supply   As we noted in Chapters 20 and 27, a person is considered a part of the labor force when he or she either is working or has been actively looking for work in the past few weeks. The ratio of the labor force to the total working-age population—those 16 and over—is the *labor force participation rate.*

It is informative to divide the labor force into three categories: males 25 to 54, females 25 to 54, and all others 16 and over. Ages 25 to 54 are sometimes called "prime" ages, presuming that a person is in the prime of working life during these ages. The participation rates for these three groups are plotted in Figure 30.4.

As the figure shows, most men of prime age are in the labor force, although the participation rate has fallen slightly since 1970—from .961 in 1970 I to .906 in 2005 II. (A rate of .906 means that 90.6 percent of prime-age men were in the labor force.) The participation rate for prime-age women, on the other hand, rose dramatically between 1970 and 1980—from .501 in 1970 I to .741 in 1990 I. Although economic factors account for some of this increase, a change in social attitudes and preferences probably explains much of the increase. Since 1990 the participation rate for prime-age women has changed very little. In 2005 II it was .751, still considerably below the .906 rate for prime-age men.

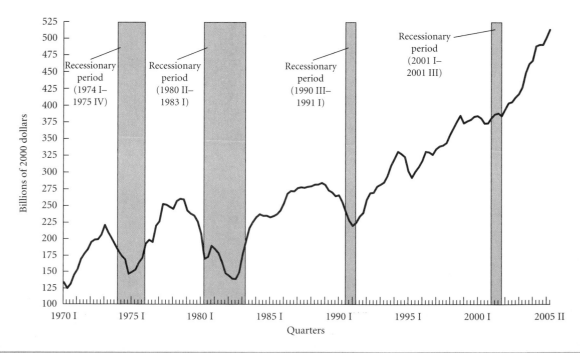

FIGURE 30.3 Housing Investment of the Household Sector, 1970 I–2005 II

Housing investment fell during the four recessionary periods since 1970. Like expenditures for durable goods, expenditures for housing investment are postponable.

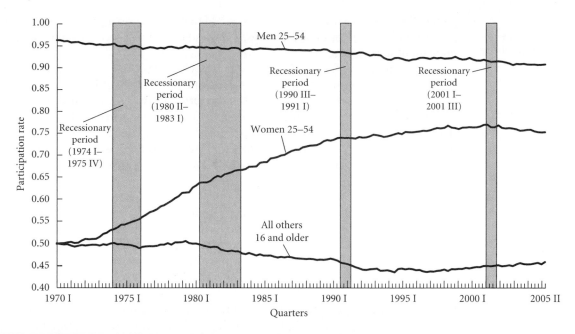

FIGURE 30.4 Labor Force Participation Rates for Men 25 to 54, Women 25 to 54, and All Others 16 and Over, 1970 I–2005 II

Since 1970, the labor force participation rate for prime-age men has been decreasing slightly. The rate for prime-age women has been increasing dramatically. The rate for all others 16 and over has been declining since 1979 and shows a tendency to fall during recessions (the discouraged-worker effect).

Figure 30.4 also shows the participation rate for all individuals 16 and over except prime-age men and women. This rate has some cyclical features—it tends to fall in recessions and to rise or fall less during expansions. These features reveal the operation of the *discouraged-worker effect*, discussed in Chapter 20. During recessions, some people get discouraged about ever finding a job. They stop looking and are then not considered a part of the labor force. During expansions, people become encouraged again. Once they begin looking for jobs, they are again considered a part of the labor force. Because prime-age women and men are likely to be fairly attached to the labor force, the discouraged-worker effect for them is quite small.

FIRMS: INVESTMENT AND EMPLOYMENT DECISIONS

Having taken a closer look at the behavior of households in the macroeconomy, we now look more closely at the behavior of firms—the other major decision-making unit in the economy. In discussing firm behavior earlier, we assumed that planned investment depends only on the interest rate. However, there are several other determinants of planned investment. We now discuss them and the factors that affect firms' employment decisions. Once again, microeconomic theory can help us gain some insights into the working of the macroeconomy.

In a market economy, firms determine which goods and services are available to consumers today and which will be available in the future, how many workers are needed for what kinds of jobs, and how much investment will be undertaken. Stated in macroeconomic terms, the decisions of firms, taken together, determine output, labor demand, and investment.

In this section, we concentrate on the input choices made by firms. By **inputs**, we mean the goods and services that firms purchase and turn into output. Two important inputs that firms use are capital and labor. (Other inputs are energy, raw materials, and semifinished goods.) Each period, firms must decide how much capital and labor to use in producing output. Let us look first at the decision about how much capital to use.

inputs The goods and services that firms purchase and turn into output.

Investment Decisions At any point in time a firm has a certain stock of capital on hand. *Stock of capital* means the factories and buildings (sometimes called "plants") firms own, the equipment they need to do business, and their inventories of partly or wholly finished goods. There are two basic ways a firm can add to its capital stock. One is to buy more machinery or build new factories or buildings. This kind of addition to the capital stock is **plant-and-equipment investment**.

The other way a firm adds to its capital stock is to increase its inventories. When a firm produces more than it sells in a given period, the firm's stock of inventories increases.[5] This type of addition to the capital stock is **inventory investment**. Recall from Chapter 21 that unplanned inventory investment is different from planned inventory investment. When a firm sells less than it expected to, it experiences an unplanned increase in its inventories and is forced to invest more than it planned to. Unplanned increases in inventories result from factors beyond the firm's control. (We take up inventory investment in detail later in this chapter.)

Employment Decisions In addition to investment decisions, firms make *employment* decisions. At the beginning of each period, a firm has a certain number of workers on its payroll. On the basis of its current situation and its upcoming plans, the firm must decide whether to hire additional workers, keep the same number, or reduce its workforce by laying off some employees.

Until this point, our description of firm behavior has been quite simple. In Chapter 21 we argued that firms increase production when they experience unplanned decreases in inventory and reduce production when they experience unplanned increases in inventory. We have also alluded to the fact that the demand for labor increases when output grows. In reality, the set of decisions facing firms is much more complex. A decision to produce additional output is likely to involve additional demand for both labor *and* capital.

The demand for labor is quite important in macroeconomics. If the demand for labor increases at a time of less-than-full employment, the unemployment rate will fall. If the demand for labor increases when there is full employment, wage rates will rise. The demand for capital (which is partly determined by the interest rate) is important as well. Recall, planned investment spending is a component of planned aggregate expenditure. When planned investment spending (*I*, the demand for new capital) increases, the result is additional output (income). We discussed the investment multiplier effect in Chapter 21.

Decision Making and Profit Maximization To understand the complex behavior of firms in input markets, we must assume that firms make decisions to maximize their profits. One of the most important profit-maximizing decisions that a firm must make is how to produce its output. In most cases, a firm must choose among alternative methods of production, or *technologies*. Different technologies generally require different combinations of capital and labor.

Consider a factory that manufactures shirts. Shirts can be made entirely by hand, with workers cutting the pieces of fabric and sewing them together. However, shirts exactly like those can be made on huge complex machines that cut and sew and produce shirts with very little human supervision. Between these two extremes are dozens of alternative technologies. Shirts can be partly hand sewn, with the stitching done on electric sewing machines.

Firms' decisions concerning the amount of capital and labor that they will use in production are closely related. If firms maximize profits, they will choose the technology that minimizes the cost of production. That is, it is logical to assume that firms will choose the technology that is most efficient.

The most efficient technology depends on the relative prices of capital and labor. A shirt factory in the Philippines that decides to increase its production faces a large supply of relatively inexpensive labor. Wage rates in the Philippines are quite low. Capital equipment must be imported and is very expensive. A shirt factory in the Philippines is likely to choose a **labor-intensive technology**—a large amount of labor relative to capital. When labor-intensive technologies are used, expansion is likely to increase the demand for labor substantially while increasing the demand for capital only modestly.

A shirt factory in Germany that decides to expand production is likely to buy a large amount of capital equipment and to hire relatively few new workers. It will probably choose a **capital-intensive technology**—a large amount of capital relative to labor.

---

[5]The change in inventories is exactly equal to the difference between production and sales. If a firm sells 20 units more than it produces in the course of a month, its inventories fall by 20 units; if it produces 20 units more than it sells, its inventories rise by 20 units.

German wage rates are quite high, higher in many occupations than in the United States. Capital, however, is plentiful.

> Firms' decisions about labor demand and investment are likely to depend on the relative costs of labor and capital. The relative impact of an expansion of output on employment and on investment demand depends on the wage rate and the cost of capital.

EXPECTATIONS AND ANIMAL SPIRITS

In addition to the cost of capital and the cost of labor, firms' expectations about the future play a big role in investment and employment decisions.

Time is a key factor in investment decisions. Capital has a life that typically extends over many years. A developer who decides to build an office tower is making an investment that will be around (barring earthquakes, floods, or tornadoes) for several decades. In deciding where to build a plant, a manufacturing firm is committing a large amount of resources to purchase capital that will presumably yield services over a long time. Furthermore, the decision to build a plant or to purchase large equipment must often be made years before the actual project is completed. Whereas the acquisition of a small business computer may take only a few days, the planning process for downtown developments in large U.S. cities has been known to take decades.

For these reasons, investment decisions require looking into the future and forming expectations about it. In forming their expectations, firms consider numerous factors. At a minimum, they gather information about the demand for their specific products, about what their competitors are planning, and about the macroeconomy's overall health. A firm is not likely to increase its production capacity if it does not expect to sell more of its product in the future. Hilton will not put up a new hotel if it does not expect to fill the rooms at a profitable rate. Ford will not build a new plant if it expects the economy to enter a long recession.

Forecasting the future is fraught with dangers. Many events cannot be foreseen. Investments are therefore always made with imperfect knowledge. Keynes pointed this out in 1936:

> The outstanding fact is the extreme precariousness of the basis of knowledge on which our estimates of prospective yield have to be made. Our knowledge of the factors which will govern the yield of an investment some years hence is usually very slight and often negligible. If we speak frankly, we have to admit that our basis of knowledge for estimating the yield ten years hence of a railway, a copper mine, a textile factory, the goodwill of a patent medicine, an Atlantic liner, a building in the City of London amounts to little and sometimes nothing.

Keynes concludes from this line of thought that much investment activity depends on psychology and on what he calls the **animal spirits of entrepreneurs**:

> Our decisions . . . can only be taken as a result of animal spirits. In estimating the prospects of investment, we must have regard, therefore, to nerves and hysteria and even the digestions and reactions to the weather of those upon whose spontaneous activity it largely depends.[6]

animal spirits of entrepreneurs A phrase coined by Keynes to describe investors' feelings.

Because expectations about the future are, as Keynes points out, subject to great uncertainty, they may change often. Thus animal spirits help to make investment a volatile component of GDP.

The Accelerator Effect   Expectations, at least in part, determine the level of planned investment spending. At any interest rate, the level of investment is likely to be higher if businesses are optimistic. If businesses are pessimistic, the level of planned investment will be lower, but what determines expectations?

---

[6]John Maynard Keynes, *The General Theory of Employment, Interest, and Money (1936)*, First Harbinger Ed. (New York: Harcourt Brace Jovanovich, 1964), pp. 149, 152.

One possibility borne out empirically is that expectations are optimistic when aggregate output (Y) is rising and pessimistic when aggregate output is falling.

> At any given level of the interest rate, expectations are likely to be more optimistic and planned investment is likely to be higher when output is growing rapidly than when it is growing slowly or falling.

It is easy to see why. If firms expect future output to grow, they must plan now to add productive capacity. One indicator of future prospects is the current growth rate.

If this is the case in reality, and evidence indicates it is, the ultimate result will be an **accelerator effect**. If aggregate output (income) (Y) is rising, investment will increase even though the level of Y may be low. Higher investment spending leads to an added increase in output, further "accelerating" the growth of aggregate output. If Y is falling, expectations are dampened, and investment spending will be cut even though the level of Y may be high, accelerating the decline.

accelerator effect The tendency for investment to increase when aggregate output increases and to decrease when aggregate output decreases, accelerating the growth or decline of output.

EXCESS LABOR AND EXCESS CAPITAL EFFECTS

We need to make one more point about firms' investment and employment decisions: Firms may sometimes choose to hold **excess labor** and/or **excess capital**. A firm holds excess labor (or capital) if it could reduce the amount of labor it employs (or capital it holds) and still produce the same amount of output.

excess labor, excess capital Labor and capital that are not needed to produce the firm's current level of output.

Why would a firm want to employ more workers or have more capital on hand than it needs? Both labor and capital are costly—a firm has to pay wages to its workers, and it forgoes interest on funds tied up in machinery or buildings. Why would a firm want to incur costs that do not yield revenue?

To see why, suppose a firm suffers a sudden and large decrease in sales, but it expects the lower sales level to last only a few months, after which it believes sales will pick up again. In this case, the firm is likely to lower production in response to the sales change to avoid too large an increase in its stock of inventories. This decrease in production means the firm could get rid of some workers and some machines, because it now needs less labor and less capital to produce the now-lower level of output.

However, things are not this simple. Decreasing its workforce and capital stock quickly can be costly for a firm. Abrupt cuts in the workforce hurt worker morale and may increase personnel administration costs, and abrupt reductions in capital stock may be disadvantageous because of the difficulty of selling used machines. These types of costs are sometimes called **adjustment costs** because they are the costs of adjusting to the new level of output. There are also adjustment costs to increasing output. For example, it is usually costly to recruit and train new workers.

adjustment costs The costs that a firm incurs when it changes its production level—for example, the administration costs of laying off employees or the training costs of hiring new workers.

Adjustment costs may be large enough that a firm chooses not to decrease its workforce and capital stock when production falls. The firm may at times choose to have more labor and capital on hand than it needs to produce its current amount of output, simply because it would be more costly to get rid of them than to keep them. In practice, excess labor takes the form of workers not working at their normal level of activity (more coffee breaks and more idle time, for instance). Some of this excess labor may receive new training so that productivity will be higher when production picks up again.

The existence of excess labor and capital at any given moment is likely to affect future employment and investment decisions. Suppose a firm already has excess labor and capital due to a fall in its sales and production. When production picks up again, the firm will not need to hire as many new workers or acquire as much new capital as it otherwise would need to.

> The more excess capital a firm already has, the less likely it is to invest in new capital in the future. The more excess labor it has, the less likely it is to hire new workers in the future.

INVENTORY INVESTMENT

We now turn to a brief discussion of the inventory investment decision. This decision is quite different from the plant-and-equipment investment decision.

The Role of Inventories   Recall the distinction between a firm's sales and its output. If a firm can hold goods in inventory, which is usually the case unless the good is perishable or unless the firm produces services, then within a given period it can sell a quantity of goods that differs from the quantity of goods it produces during that period. When a firm sells more than it produces, its stock of inventories decreases; when it sells less than it produces, its stock of inventories increases.

> stock of inventories (end of period) = stock of inventories (beginning of period)
> + production − sales

If a firm starts a period with 100 umbrellas in inventory, produces 15 umbrellas during the period, and sells 10 umbrellas in this same interval, it will have 105 umbrellas (100 + 15 − 10) in inventory at the end of the period. A change in the stock of inventories is actually investment because inventories are counted as part of a firm's capital stock. In our example, inventory investment during the period is a positive number, 5 umbrellas (105 − 100). When the number of goods produced is less than the number of goods sold, such as 5 produced and 10 sold, inventory investment is negative.

The Optimal Inventory Policy   We can now consider firms' inventory decisions. Firms are concerned with what they are going to sell and produce in the future, as well as what they are selling and producing currently. At each point in time, a firm has some idea of how much it is going to sell in the current period and in future periods. Given these expectations and its knowledge of how much of its good it already has in stock, a firm must decide how much to produce in the current period.

Inventories are costly to a firm because they take up space and they tie up funds that could be earning interest. However, if a firm's stock of inventories gets too low, the firm may have difficulty meeting the demand for its product, especially if demand increases unexpectedly. The firm may lose sales. The point between too low and too high a stock of inventory is called the **desired**, or **optimal, level of inventories**. This is the level at which the extra cost (in lost sales) from decreasing inventories by a small amount is just equal to the extra gain (in interest revenue and decreased storage costs).

desired, or **optimal, level of inventories** The level of inventory at which the extra cost (in lost sales) from lowering inventories by a small amount is just equal to the extra gain (in interest revenue and decreased storage costs).

A firm that had no costs other than inventory costs would always aim to produce in a period exactly the volume of goods necessary to make its stock of inventories at the end of the period equal to the desired stock. If the stock of inventory fell lower than desired, the firm would produce more than it expected to sell to bring the stock up. If the stock of inventory grew above the desired level, the firm would produce less than it expected to sell to reduce the stock.

There are other costs to running a firm besides inventory costs. In particular, large and abrupt changes in production can be very costly because it is often disruptive to change a production process geared to a certain rate of output. If production is to be increased, there may be adjustment costs for hiring more labor and increasing the capital stock. If production is to be decreased, there may be adjustment costs in laying off workers and decreasing the capital stock.

Because holding inventories and changing production levels are both costly, firms face a trade-off between them. Because of adjustment costs, a firm is likely to smooth its production path relative to its sales path. This means a firm is likely to have its production fluctuate less than its sales, with changes in inventories to absorb the difference each period. However, because there are incentives not to stray too far from the optimal level of inventories, fluctuations in production are not eliminated completely. Production is still likely to fluctuate, just not as much as sales fluctuate.

Two other points need to be made here. First, if a firm's stock of inventories is unusually or unexpectedly high, the firm is likely to produce less in the future than it would have, to decrease its high stock of inventories. In other words, although the stock of inventories fluctuates over time because production is smoothed relative to sales, at any point in time inventories may be unexpectedly high or low because sales have been unexpectedly low or high. An unexpectedly high stock will have a negative effect on production in the future, and an unexpectedly low stock will have a positive effect on production in the future.

> An unexpected increase in inventories has a negative effect on future production, and an unexpected decrease in inventories has a positive effect on future production.

Second, firms do not know their future sales exactly. They have expectations of future sales, and these expectations may not turn out to be exactly right. This has important consequences. If sales turn out to be less than expected, inventories will be higher than expected, and there will be less production in the future. Furthermore, *future* sales expectations are likely to have an important effect on *current* production. If a firm expects its sales to be high in the future, it will adjust its planned production path accordingly. Even though a firm smoothes production relative to sales, over a long time it must produce as much as it sells. If it did not, it would eventually run out of inventories.

> The level of a firm's planned production path depends on the level of its expected future sales path. If a firm's expectations of the level of its future sales path decrease, the firm is likely to decrease the level of its planned production path, including its actual production in the current period. Current production depends on expected future sales.

Because production is likely to depend on expectations of the future, animal spirits may play a role. If firms become more optimistic about the future, they are likely to produce more now. Keynes's view that animal spirits affect investment is also likely to pertain to output.

A SUMMARY OF FIRM BEHAVIOR

> The following factors affect firms' investment and employment decisions:
>
> - Wage rate and cost of capital (the interest rate is an important component of the cost of capital)
> - Firms' expectations of future output
> - Amount of excess labor and excess capital on hand
>
> The most important points to remember about the relationship among production, sales, and inventory investment are:
>
> - Inventory investment—that is, the change in the stock of inventories—equals production minus sales
> - An unexpected increase in the stock of inventories has a negative effect on future production
> - Current production depends on expected future sales

THE FIRM SECTOR SINCE 1970

To close our discussion of firm behavior, we now examine some aggregate investment and employment variables for the period 1970 I–2005 II.

Plant-and-Equipment Investment   Plant-and-equipment investment by the firm sector is plotted in Figure 30.5. Investment fared poorly in the four recessionary periods after 1970. This observation is consistent with the observation that investment depends in part on output. An examination of the plot of real GDP in Figure 18.5 in Chapter 18 and the plot of investment in Figure 30.5 shows investment generally does poorly when GDP does poorly, and investment generally does well when GDP does well.

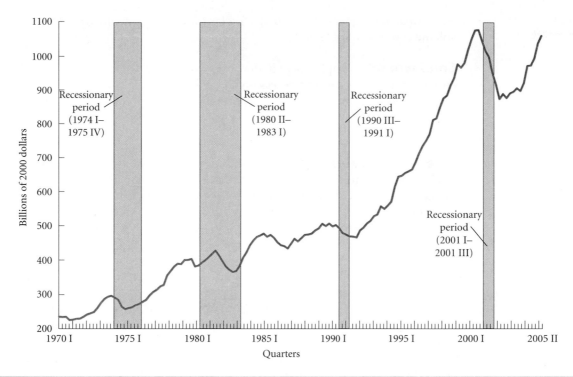

FIGURE 30.5 Plant and Equipment Investment of the Firm Sector, 1970 I–2005 II

Overall, plant and equipment investment declined in the four recessionary periods since 1970.

Figure 30.5 also shows that investment fluctuates greatly. This is not surprising. The animal spirits of entrepreneurs are likely to be volatile, and if animal spirits affect investment, it follows that investment too will be volatile.

Despite the volatility of plant-and-equipment investment, however, it is still true that housing investment fluctuates more than plant-and-equipment investment (as you can see

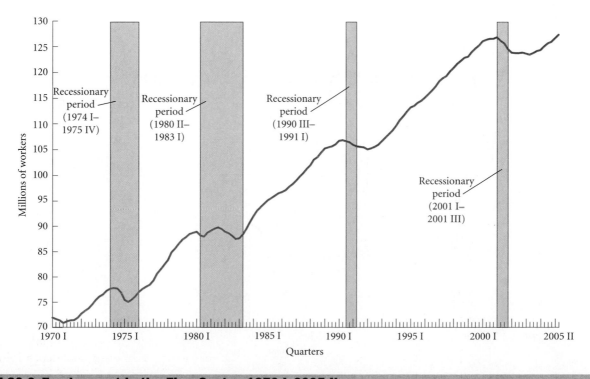

FIGURE 30.6 Employment in the Firm Sector, 1970 I–2005 II

Growth in employment was generally negative in the four recessions the U.S. economy has experienced since 1970.

by comparing Figures 30.3 and 30.5). Plant-and-equipment investment is not the most volatile component of GDP.

Employment Employment in the firm sector is plotted in Figure 30.6, which shows that employment fell in all four recessionary periods. This is consistent with the theory that employment depends in part on output. Otherwise, employment has grown over time in response to the growing economy. Employment in the firm sector rose from 71.2 million in 1970 I to 126.9 million in 2005 II.

Inventory Investment Recall that *inventory investment* is the difference between the level of output and the level of sales. Recall also that some inventory investment is usually unplanned. This occurs when the actual level of sales is different from the expected level of sales.

Inventory investment of the firm sector is plotted in Figure 30.7. Also plotted in this figure is the ratio of the stock of inventories to the level of sales—the *inventory/sales ratio*. The figure shows that inventory investment is very volatile—more volatile than housing investment and plant-and-equipment investment. Some of this volatility is undoubtedly due to the unplanned component of inventory investment, which is likely to fluctuate greatly from one period to the next.

When the inventory/sales ratio is high, the actual stock of inventories is likely to be larger than the desired stock. In such a case, firms have overestimated demand and produced too much relative to sales, and they are likely to want to produce less in the future to draw down their stock. You can find several examples of this trend in Figure 30.7—the clearest occurred during the 1974–1975 period. At the end of 1974, the stock of inventories was very high relative to sales, an indication that firms probably had undesired inventories at the end of 1974. In 1975, firms worked off these undesired inventories by producing less than they sold. Thus inventory investment was very low in 1975. The year 1975 is clearly a year in which output would have been higher had the stock of inventories at the beginning of the year not been so high. There was a huge fall in inventory investment in 2001.

On average the inventory/sales ratio has been declining over time, evidence that firms are becoming more efficient in their management of inventory stocks. They are becoming

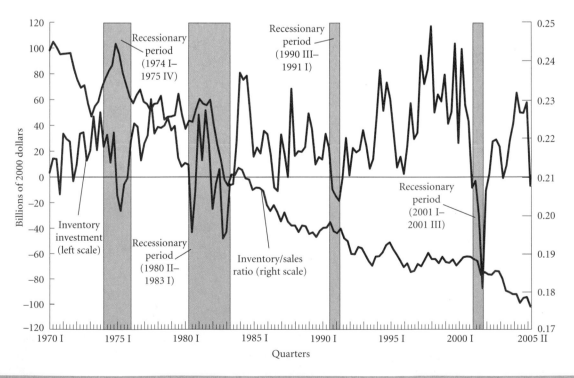

FIGURE 30.7 Inventory Investment of the Firm Sector and the Inventory/Sales Ratio, 1970 I–2005 II

The inventory/sales ratio is the ratio of the firm sector's stock of inventories to the level of sales. Inventory investment is very volatile.

more efficient in the sense of being able (other things equal) to hold smaller and smaller stocks of inventories relative to sales.

PRODUCTIVITY AND THE BUSINESS CYCLE

We can now use what we have just learned about firm behavior to analyze movements in productivity. **Productivity**, sometimes called **labor productivity**, is defined as output per worker hour. If output is Y and the number of hours worked in the economy is H, then productivity is Y/H. Simply stated, productivity measures how much output an average worker produces in 1 hour.

productivity, or labor productivity Output per worker hour; the amount of output produced by an average worker in 1 hour.

Productivity fluctuates over the business cycle, tending to rise during expansions and fall during contractions. The fact that firms at times hold excess labor explains why productivity fluctuates in the same direction as output.

Figure 30.8 shows the pattern of employment and output for a hypothetical economy over time. Employment does not fluctuate as much as output over the business cycle. It is precisely this pattern that leads to higher productivity during periods of high output and lower productivity during periods of low output. During expansions in the economy, output rises by a larger percentage than employment, and the ratio of output to workers rises. During downswings, output falls faster than employment and the ratio of output to workers falls.

The existence of excess labor when the economy is in a slump means productivity as measured by the ratio Y/H tends to fall at such times. Does this trend mean labor is in some sense "less productive" during recessions than before? Not really: It means only that firms choose to employ more labor than they need. For this reason, some workers are in effect idle some of the time, even though they are considered employed. They are not less productive in the sense of having less potential to produce output; they are merely not working part of the time that they are *counted* as working.

Productivity in the Long Run   Theories of long-run economic behavior, which attempt to explain how and why economies grow over time, focus on productivity, usually measured in this case as *output per worker*, or its closely related measure, *GDP per capita*. Productivity defined this way is a key index of an economy's performance over the long run. For example, in comparing how the economies of the United States and Japan have performed over the past 90 years, we would probably begin by noting that although the United States had a substantially higher income per person in 1900, the two countries' incomes per person are now comparable. As we shall see in Chapter 31, the growth of output per worker

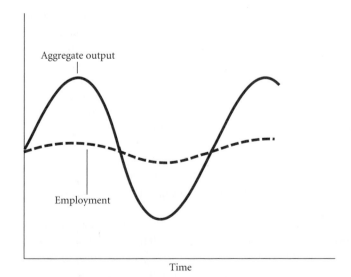

FIGURE 30.8 Employment and Output over the Business Cycle

In general, employment does not fluctuate as much as output over the business cycle. As a result, measured productivity (the output-to-labor ratio) tends to rise during expansionary periods and decline during contractionary periods.

depends on technological progress and on the growth of the capital stock, both of which have been more rapid in Japan than in the United States.

> Productivity figures can be misleading when used to diagnose the health of the economy over the short run, because business cycles can distort the meaning of productivity measurements. Output per worker falls in recessions because firms hold excess labor during slumps. Output per worker rises in expansions because firms put the excess labor back to work. Neither of these conditions has anything to do with the economy's long-run potential to produce output.

THE RELATIONSHIP BETWEEN OUTPUT AND UNEMPLOYMENT

We can also use what we have learned about household and firm behavior to analyze the relationship between output and unemployment. When we discussed the connections between the *AS/AD* diagram and the Phillips Curve in Chapter 27, we mentioned that output (Y) and the unemployment rate (U) are inversely related. When output rises, the unemployment rate falls, and when output falls, the unemployment rate rises. At one time, it was believed that the relationship between the two variables was fairly stable. **Okun's Law** (after U.S. economist Arthur Okun, who first studied the relationship) stated that the unemployment rate decreased about 1 percentage point for every 3 percent increase in real GDP. As with the Phillips Curve, Okun's Law has not turned out to be a "law." The economy is far too complex for there to be such a simple and stable relationship between two macroeconomic variables.

Okun's Law The theory, put forth by Arthur Okun, that the unemployment rate decreases about 1 percentage point for every 3 percent increase in real GDP. Later research and data have shown that the relationship between output and unemployment is not as stable as Okun's "Law" predicts.

Although the relationship between output and the unemployment rate is not the simple relationship Okun believed, it is true that a 1 percent increase in output tends to correspond to a less than 1 percentage point decrease in the unemployment rate. In other words, there are a number of "slippages" between changes in output and changes in the unemployment rate.

The first slippage is between the change in output and the change in the number of jobs in the economy. When output increases by 1 percent, the number of jobs does not tend to rise by 1 percent in the short run. There are two reasons for this. First, a firm is likely to meet some of the increase in output by increasing the number of hours worked per job. Instead of having the labor force work 40 hours per week, the firm may pay overtime and have the labor force work 42 hours per week. Second, if a firm is holding excess labor at the time of the output increase, at least part of the increase in output can come from putting the excess labor back to work. For both reasons, the number of jobs is likely to rise by a smaller percentage than the increase in output.

The second slippage is between the change in the number of *jobs* and the change in the *number of people employed*. If I have two jobs, I am counted twice in the job data but only once in the persons-employed data. Because some people have two jobs, there are more jobs than there are people employed. When the number of jobs increases, some of the new jobs are filled by people who already have one job (instead of by people who are unemployed). This means the increase in the number of people employed is less than the increase in the number of jobs. This is a slippage between output and the unemployment rate because the unemployment rate is calculated from data on the number of people employed, not the number of jobs.

discouraged-worker effect The decline in the measured unemployment rate that results when people who want to work but cannot find work grow discouraged and stop looking for jobs, dropping out of the ranks of the unemployed and the labor force.

The third slippage concerns the response of the labor force to an increase in output. Let E denote the number of people employed, let L denote the number of people in the labor force, and let u denote the unemployment rate. In these terms, the unemployment rate is

$$u = 1 - E/L$$

The unemployment rate is 1 minus the employment rate, E/L.

When we discussed how the unemployment rate is measured in Chapter 20, we introduced the **discouraged-worker effect**. A discouraged worker is one who would like a job but has stopped looking for one because the prospects seem so bleak. When output increases, job prospects begin to look better, and some people who had stopped looking for work begin looking again. When they do, they are once again counted as part of the labor force. The labor force increases when output increases because discouraged workers are moving back into the labor force. This is another reason the unemployment rate does not fall as much as might be expected when output increases.

These three slippages show that the link from changes in output to changes in the unemployment rate is complicated. All three combine to make the change in the unemployment rate less than the percentage change in output in the short run. They also show that the relationship between changes in output and changes in the unemployment rate is not likely to be stable. The size of the first slippage, for example, depends on how much excess labor is being held at the time of the output increase, and the size of the third slippage depends on what else is affecting the labor force (like changes in real wage rates) at the time of the output increase.

> The relationship between output and unemployment depends on the state of the economy at the time of the output change.

THE SIZE OF THE MULTIPLIER

We can finally bring together the material in this chapter and in previous chapters to consider the size of the multiplier. We mentioned in Chapter 21 that much of the analysis we would do after deriving the simple multiplier would have the effect of decreasing the size of the multiplier. We can now summarize why.

- First, there are *automatic stabilizers.* We saw in the Appendix to Chapter 22 that if taxes are not a fixed amount but instead depend on income (which is surely the case in practice), the size of the multiplier is decreased. When the economy expands and income increases, the amount of taxes collected increases. The rise in taxes acts to offset some of the expansion (thus a smaller multiplier). When the economy contracts and income decreases, the amount of taxes collected decreases. This decrease in taxes helps to lessen the contraction. Some transfer payments also respond to the state of the economy and act as automatic stabilizers, lowering the value of the multiplier. Unemployment benefits are the best example of transfer payments that increase during contractions and decrease during expansions.

- Second, there is the *interest rate.* We saw in Chapter 25 that if government spending increases and the money supply remains unchanged, the interest rate increases, which decreases planned investment and aggregate output (income). This *crowding out* of planned investment decreases the value of the multiplier. As we saw earlier in this chapter, increases in the interest rate also have a negative effect on consumption. Consumption is also crowded out in the same way that planned investment is, and this effect lowers the value of the multiplier even further.

- Third, there is the response of the *price level.* We saw in Chapter 26 that some of the effect of an expansionary policy is to increase the price level. The multiplier is smaller because of this price response. The multiplier is particularly small when the economy is on the steep part of the AS curve, where most of the effect of an expansionary policy is to increase prices.

- Fourth, there are *excess capital* and *excess labor.* If firms are holding excess labor and capital, then part of any output increase can come from putting the excess labor and capital back to work instead of increasing employment and investment. This lowers the value of the multiplier because (1) investment increases less than it would have if there were no excess capital, and (2) consumption increases less than it would have if employment (and thus household income) had increased more.

- Fifth, there are *inventories.* Part of any initial increase in sales can come from drawing down inventories instead of increasing output. To the extent that firms draw down their inventories in the short run, the value of the multiplier is lower because output does not respond as quickly to demand changes.

■ Sixth, there are people's *expectations* about the future. People look ahead, and they respond less to temporary changes than to permanent changes. The multiplier effects for policy changes perceived to be temporary are smaller than those for policy changes perceived to be permanent.

The Size of the Multiplier in Practice   In practice, the multiplier probably has a value of around 1.4. Its size also depends on how long ago the spending increase began. For example, in the first quarter of an increase in government spending, the multiplier is only about 1.1. If government spending rises by $1 billion, then GDP increases by only about $1.1 billion during the first quarter. In the second quarter, the multiplier rises to about 1.3. The multiplier then rises to its peak of about 1.4 in the third or fourth quarter.

One of the main points to remember here is that if the government is contemplating a monetary or fiscal policy change, the response of the economy to the change is not likely to be large and quick. It takes time for the full effects to be felt, and in the final analysis the effects are much smaller than the simple multiplier we discussed in Chapter 21 would lead one to believe.

A good way to review much of the material since Chapter 21 is to make sure that you clearly understand how the value of the multiplier is affected by each of the additions to the simple model in Chapter 21. We have come a long way since then, and this review may help you to put all the pieces together.

SUMMARY

HOUSEHOLDS: CONSUMPTION AND LABOR SUPPLY DECISIONS

1. The Keynesian theory of consumption holds that household consumption (C) is positively related to current income: The more income you have, the more you are likely to consume. Keynes also believed high-income households consume a smaller proportion of their income than low-income households. The proportion of income households spend on consumption is measured by the *average propensity to consume* (*APC*), which is equal to consumption divided by income (C/Y).

2. The *life-cycle theory of consumption* says households make lifetime consumption decisions based on their expectations of lifetime income. Generally, households consume an amount less than their incomes during their prime working years and an amount greater than their incomes during their early working years and after they have retired.

3. Households make consumption and labor supply decisions simultaneously. Consumption cannot be considered separately from labor supply, because it is precisely by selling your labor that you earn the income that makes consumption possible.

4. There is a trade-off between the goods and services that wage income will buy and leisure or other nonmarket activities. The wage rate is the key variable that determines how a household responds to this trade-off.

5. Changes in the wage rate have both an income effect and a substitution effect. The evidence suggests the substitution effect seems to dominate for most people, which means the aggregate labor supply responds positively to an increase in the wage rate.

6. Consumption increases when the wage rate increases.

7. The *nominal wage rate* is the wage rate in current dollars. The *real wage rate* is the amount the nominal wage can buy in terms of goods and services. Households look at expected future real wage rates as well as the current real wage rate in making their consumption and labor supply decisions.

8. Holding all else constant (including the stage in the life cycle), the more wealth a household has, the more it will consume, both now and in the future.

9. An unexpected increase in *nonlabor income* (any income received from sources other than working, such as inheritances, interest, and dividends) will have a positive effect on a household's consumption and will lead to a decrease in labor supply.

10. The interest rate also affects consumption, although the direction of the total effect depends on the relative sizes of the income and substitution effects. There is some evidence the income effect is larger now than it used to be, making monetary policy less effective than it used to be.

11. The government influences household behavior mainly through income tax rates and transfer payments. If the substitution effect dominates, an increase in tax rates lowers after-tax income, decreases consumption, and decreases the labor supply; a decrease in tax rates raises after-tax income, increases consumption, and increases labor supply. Increases in transfer payments increase consumption and decrease labor supply; decreases in transfer payments decrease consumption and increase labor supply.

12. During times of unemployment, households' labor supply may be constrained. Households may wish to work a certain number of hours at current wage rates but may not be allowed to do so by firms. In this case, the level of income (at least workers' income) depends exclusively on the employ-

ment decisions made by firms. Households consume less if constrained from working.

FIRMS: INVESTMENT AND EMPLOYMENT DECISIONS

13. Firms purchase *inputs* and turn them into outputs. Each period, firms must decide how much capital and labor (two major inputs) to use in producing output. Firms can invest in plants and equipment or in inventory.

14. Because output can be produced using many different technologies, firms must make capital and labor decisions simultaneously. A *labor-intensive technique* uses a large amount of labor relative to capital. A *capital-intensive technique* uses a large amount of capital relative to labor. Which technology to use depends on the wage rate and the cost of capital.

15. Expectations affect investment and employment decisions. Keynes used the phrase *animal spirits of entrepreneurs* to refer to investors' feelings.

16. At any level of the interest rate, expectations are likely to be more optimistic and planned investment is likely to be higher when output is growing rapidly than when it is growing slowly or falling. The result is an *accelerator effect* that can cause the economy to expand more rapidly during an expansion and contract more quickly during a recession.

17. *Excess labor and capital* are labor and capital not needed to produce a firm's current level of output. Holding excess labor and capital may be more efficient than laying off workers or selling used equipment. The more excess capital a firm has, the less likely it is to invest in new capital in the future. The more excess labor it has, the less likely it is to hire new workers in the future.

18. Holding inventories is costly to a firm because they take up space and they tie up funds that could be earning interest. Not holding inventories can cause a firm to lose sales if demand increases. The *desired*, or *optimal, level of inventories* is the level at which the extra cost (in lost sales) from lowering inventories by a small amount is equal to the extra gain (in interest revenue and decreased storage costs).

19. An unexpected increase in inventories has a negative effect on future production, and an unexpected decrease in inventories has a positive effect on future production.

20. The level of a firm's planned production path depends on the level of its expected future sales path. If a firm's expecta-

tions of its future sales path decrease, the firm is likely to decrease the level of its planned production path, including its actual production in the current period.

PRODUCTIVITY AND THE BUSINESS CYCLE

21. *Productivity*, or *labor productivity*, is output per worker hour—the amount of output produced by an average worker in 1 hour. Productivity fluctuates over the business cycle, tending to rise during expansions and fall during contractions. That workers are less productive during contractions does not mean they have less potential to produce output; it means excess labor exists and workers are not working at their capacity.

THE RELATIONSHIP BETWEEN OUTPUT AND UNEMPLOYMENT

22. There is a negative relationship between output and unemployment: When output (Y) rises, the unemployment rate (U) falls, and when output falls, the unemployment rate rises. *Okun's Law* stated that the unemployment rate decreases about 1 percentage point for every 3 percent increase in GDP. Okun's Law is not a "law"—the economy is too complex for there to be a stable relationship between two macroeconomic variables. In general, the relationship between output and unemployment depends on the state of the economy at the time of the output change.

THE SIZE OF THE MULTIPLIER

23. There are several reasons why the actual value of the multiplier is smaller than the size that would be expected from the simple multiplier model: (1) Automatic stabilizers help to offset contractions or limit expansions. (2) When government spending increases, the increased interest rate crowds out planned investment and consumption spending. (3) Expansionary policies increase the price level. (4) Firms sometimes hold excess capital and excess labor. (5) Firms may meet increased demand by drawing down inventories instead of increasing output. (6) Households and firms change their behavior less when they expect changes to be temporary instead of permanent.

24. In practice, the size of the multiplier at its peak is about 1.4.

REVIEW TERMS AND CONCEPTS

accelerator effect, 652

adjustment costs, 652

animal spirits of entrepreneurs, 651

average propensity to consume (*APC*), 640

capital-intensive technology, 650

constrained supply of labor, 646

desired, or optimal, level of inventories, 653

discouraged-worker effect, 658

excess capital, 652

excess labor, 652

inputs, 649

inventory investment, 650

labor-intensive technology, 650

life-cycle theory of consumption, 640

nominal wage rate, 643

nonlabor, or nonwage, income, 644

Okun's Law, 658

permanent income, 641

plant-and-equipment investment, 650

productivity, or labor productivity, 657

real wage rate, 643

unconstrained supply of labor, 646

$$APC \equiv \frac{C}{Y}$$

PROBLEM SET

1. Between October 2004 and October 2005, real GDP in the United States increased by 3.6 percent while nonfarm payroll jobs increased by only 1.4 percent. How is it possible for output to increase without a proportional increase in the number of workers?

2. The box on page 642 describes a significant increase in consumption that occurred immediately after World War II despite a major drop in household incomes. In 2005, a series of devastating hurricanes all but totally destroyed New Orleans and other areas of the Gulf Coast. In the aftermath of these disasters, over 400,000 households lost their jobs in the region. It is clear that consumer spending did not drop as much as you would predict based on income figures for the states involved. Can you offer an explanation?

3. During 2005, the Federal Reserve Bank raised interest rates in an effort to prevent an increase in the rate of inflation.
   a. What direct effects do higher interest rates have on household and firm behavior?
   b. One of the consequences of higher interest rates was that the value of existing bonds (both corporate bonds and government bonds) fell substantially. Explain why higher interest rates would decrease the value of existing fixed-rate bonds held by the public.
   c. Some economists argue that the wealth effect of higher interest rates on consumption is as important as the direct effect of higher interest rates on investment. Explain what economists mean by "wealth effects on consumption" and illustrate with *AS/AD* curves.

4. In 2005, President Bush's tax reform commission proposed and Congress enacted a decrease in taxes. One of the cuts was in the income tax rate for higher-income wage earners. Republicans claimed that raising the rewards for working (the net after-tax wage rate), would lead to more work effort and a higher labor supply. Critics of the tax cuts replied that this criticism was baseless because it "ignored the income effect of the tax cut (net wage increase)." Explain what these critics meant.

5. Graph the following two consumption functions:

   $C = 300 + .5Y$
   $C = .5Y$

   a. For each function, calculate and graph the average propensity to consume (*APC*) when income is $100, $400, and $800.
   b. For each function, what happens to the *APC* as income rises?
   c. For each function, what is the relationship between the *APC* and the marginal propensity to consume?
   d. Under consumption function (1), a family with income of $50,000 consumes a smaller proportion of its income than a family with income of $20,000; yet if we take a dollar of income away from the rich family and give it to the poor fam-

ily, total consumption by the two families does not change. Explain how this could be.

6. Throughout the late 1990s, the price of houses increased steadily around the country.
   a. What impact would you expect increases and decreases in home value to have on the consumption behavior of home owners? Explain.
   b. In what ways might events in the housing market have influenced the rest of the economy through their effects on consumption spending? Be specific.

*7. Adam Smith is 45 years old. He has assets (wealth) of $20,000 and has no debts or liabilities. He knows he will work for 20 more years and will live 5 years after that when he will earn nothing. His salary each year for the rest of his working career is $14,000. (There are no taxes.) He wants to distribute his consumption over the rest of his life in such a way that he consumes the same amount each year. He cannot consume in total more than his current wealth plus the sum of his income for the next 20 years. Assume the rate of interest is zero and Smith decides not to leave any inheritance to his children.
   a. How much will Adam consume this year, and next year? How did you arrive at your answer?
   b. Plot on a graph Adam's income, consumption, and wealth from the time he is 45 until he is 70 years old. What is the relationship between the annual increase in his wealth and his annual saving (income minus consumption)? In what year does Adam's wealth start to decline? Why? How much wealth does he have when he dies?
   c. Suppose Adam receives a tax rebate of $100 per year, so his income is $14,100 per year for the rest of his working career. By how much does his consumption increase this year and next year?
   d. Now suppose Adam receives a 1-year-only tax refund of $100—his income this year is $14,100, but in all succeeding years his income is $14,000. What happens to his consumption this year? In succeeding years?

8. Explain why a household's consumption and labor supply decisions are interdependent. What impact does this interdependence have on the way in which consumption and income are related?

9. Why do expectations play such an important role in investment demand? How, if at all, does this explain why investment is so volatile?

10. How can a firm maintain a smooth production schedule even when sales are fluctuating? What are the benefits of a smooth production schedule? What are the costs?

---

*Note: Problems marked with an asterisk are more challenging.

Long-Run Growth

31

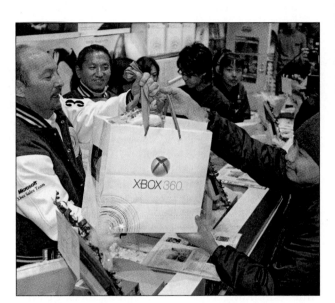

Recall from Chapter 1 that **economic growth** occurs when an economy experiences an increase in total output. The increase in real output that began in the Western World with the Industrial Revolution and continues today has been so sustained and so rapid that economists refer to this as the period of **modern economic growth**. These three simple words describe the complex phenomenon that is the subject of this chapter.

It is through economic growth that living standards improve, but growth brings change. New things are produced, while others become obsolete. Some believe growth is the fundamental objective of a society, because it lifts people out of poverty and enhances the quality of their lives. Others say economic growth erodes traditional values and leads to exploitation, environmental destruction, and corruption.

The first part of this chapter describes economic growth in some detail and identifies sources of economic growth. After a review of the U.S. economy's growth record since the nineteenth century, we examine the role of public policy in the growth process. We conclude with a review of the debate over the benefits and costs of growth.

THE GROWTH PROCESS: FROM AGRICULTURE TO INDUSTRY

The easiest way to understand the growth process and to identify its causes is to think about a simple economy. Recall from Chapter 2, Colleen and Bill washed up on a deserted island. At first they had only a few simple tools and whatever human capital they brought with them to the island. They gathered nuts and berries and built a small cabin. Their "GDP" consisted of basic food and shelter.

Over time, things improved. The first year, they cleared some land and began to cultivate a few vegetables that they found growing on the island. They made some tools and dug a small reservoir to store rainwater. As their agricultural efforts became more efficient, they shifted their resources—their time—into building a larger, more comfortable home.

Colleen and Bill were accumulating capital in two forms. First, they built *physical capital*, material things used in the production of goods and services—a better house, tools, a water system, perhaps a boat to let them fish farther off shore. Second, they acquired more *human*

economic growth An increase in the total output of an economy. Defined by some economists as an increase of real GDP per capita.

modern economic growth The period of rapid and sustained increase in real output per capita that began in the Western World with the Industrial Revolution.

663

capital—knowledge, skills, and talents. Through trial and error, they learned about the island, its soil and its climate, what worked and what did not. Both kinds of capital made them more efficient and increased their productivity. Because it took less time to produce the food they needed to survive, they could devote more energy to producing other things or to leisure.

At any given time, Colleen and Bill faced limits on what they could produce. These limits were imposed by the existing state of their technical knowledge and the resources at their disposal. Over time, they expanded their possibilities, developed new technologies, accumulated capital, and made their labor more productive. In Chapter 2 we defined a society's *production possibility frontier* (*ppf*), which shows all possible combinations of output that can be produced given present technology and if all available resources are fully and efficiently employed. Economic growth expands those limits and shifts society's production possibilities frontier out to the right, as Figure 31.1 shows.

From Agriculture to Industry: The Industrial Revolution
Before the Industrial Revolution in Great Britain, every society in the world was agrarian. Towns and cities existed here and there, but almost everyone lived in rural areas. People spent most of their time producing food and other basic subsistence goods. Then, beginning in England around 1750, technical change and capital accumulation increased productivity significantly in two important industries: agriculture and textiles. New and more efficient methods of farming were developed. New inventions and new machinery in spinning, weaving, and steel production meant that more could be produced with fewer resources. Just as new technology, capital equipment, and resulting higher productivity made it possible for Colleen and Bill to spend time working on other projects and new "products," the British turned from agricultural production to industrial production. In both cases, growth meant new products, more output, and wider choice.

There was one big difference. Colleen and Bill were fully in charge of their own lives. Peasants and workers in eighteenth-century England ended up with a very different set of choices. Those who in the past would have continued in subsistence farming could make a better living as urban workers. A rural agrarian society was very quickly transformed into an urban industrial society.

Growth in Modern Society
Economic growth continues today, and while the underlying process is still the same, the face is different. Just as Colleen and Bill devoted time to building a boat and designing tools, we are still creating capital to make us more

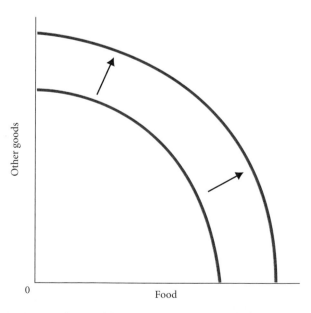

FIGURE 31.1 Economic Growth Shifts Society's Production Possibility Frontier Up and to the Right

The production possibility frontier shows all the combinations of output that can be produced if all society's scarce resources are fully and efficiently employed. Economic growth expands society's production possibilities, shifting the ppf up and to the right.

productive. Just as a shovel makes it possible to dig a bigger hole, new microwave towers bring cell phone service to places that were out of range before. Scientists work on finding a cure for Alzheimer's disease using tools they couldn't have dreamed of a decade ago. Tools available on the Web make it possible for a single law clerk in a busy law office to check hundreds of documents for the opinions of potential expert witnesses in a court case in an hour, a task that took a dozen law clerks weeks to perform just a few years ago. In each case we have become more proficient at producing what we want and need, and we have freed up resources to produce new things that we want and need. For Colleen and Bill it was a better diet; with a boat they could catch more fish in less time. Today it may be better cell phone service; a fast, inexpensive color printer; or a better medical procedure.

The basic building blocks are the same. Growth comes from a bigger workforce and more productive workers. Higher productivity comes from tools (capital), a better-educated and more highly skilled workforce (human capital), and increasingly from innovation and technical change (new techniques of production) and newly developed products and services.

THE SOURCES OF ECONOMIC GROWTH

Economic growth occurs when either (1) society acquires more resources, or (2) society discovers ways of using available resources more efficiently. For economic growth to increase living standards, the rate of growth must exceed the rate of population increase. Economic growth is generally defined as *an increase in real GDP per capita*.

As we discuss the factors that contribute to economic growth, it will be helpful to think of an **aggregate production function**. An individual firm's production function is a mathematical representation of the relationship between the firm's inputs and its output. Output for an aggregate production function is national output, or GDP. Stated simply, GDP (output) (Y), depends on the amount of labor (L) and the amount of capital (K) available in the economy (assuming the amount of land is fixed).[1] If you think of GDP as a function of both labor and capital, you can see that

aggregate production function The mathematical representation of the relationship between inputs and national output, or gross domestic product.

> An increase in GDP can come about through:
>
> **1.** An increase in the labor supply
>
> **2.** An increase in physical or human capital
>
> **3.** An increase in productivity (the amount of product produced by each unit of capital or labor)

AN INCREASE IN LABOR SUPPLY

Consider what would happen if another person joined Colleen and Bill on the island. That individual would join in the work and produce, and so GDP would rise. Suppose that a person who had not been a part of the labor force were to begin to work and use time and energy to produce pottery. Real output would rise in this case also. An increase in labor supply can generate more output.

Whether output *per capita* rises when the labor supply increases is another matter. If the capital stock remains fixed while labor increases, the new labor will likely be less productive than the old labor. This effect is called *diminishing returns*, and it worried Thomas Malthus, David Ricardo, and other early economists.

Malthus and Ricardo, who lived in England during the nineteenth century, were concerned that the fixed supply of land would lead to diminishing returns. With land in strictly limited supply, the ppf could be pushed out only so far as population increased. To increase agricultural output, people would be forced to farm less-productive land or to farm land more intensively. In either case, the returns to successive increases in population would diminish. Both Malthus and Ricardo predicted a gloomy future as population outstripped

---

[1]All the numbers in the tables to follow were derived from the simple production function: $Y = 3 \times K^{1/3} L^{2/3}$.

TABLE 31.1 Economic Growth from an Increase in Labor—More Output but Diminishing Returns and Lower Labor Productivity

PERIOD	QUANTITY OF LABOR L (HOURS)	QUANTITY OF CAPITAL K (UNITS)	TOTAL OUTPUT Y (UNITS)	MEASURED LABOR PRODUCTIVITY Y/L
1	100	100	300	3.0
2	110	100	320	2.9
3	120	100	339	2.8
4	130	100	357	2.7

the land's capacity to produce. What both economists left out of their calculations was technological change and capital accumulation. New and better farming techniques have raised agricultural productivity so much that less than 3 percent of the U.S. population now provides enough food for the country's entire population.

Diminishing returns can also occur if a nation's capital stock grows more slowly than its workforce. Capital enhances workers' productivity. A person with a shovel digs a bigger hole than a person without one, and a person with a steam shovel outdoes them both. If a society's stock of plant and equipment does not grow and the technology of production does not change, additional workers will not be as productive, because they do not have machines to work with.

Table 31.1 illustrates how growth in the labor force, without a corresponding increase in the capital stock or technological change, might lead to growth of output but declining productivity and a lower standard of living. As labor increases, output rises from 300 units in period 1 to 320 in period 2, to 339 in period 3, and so forth, but **labor productivity** (output per worker hour) falls. Output per worker hour, Y/L, is a measure of labor's productivity.

labor productivity Output per worker hour; the amount of output produced by an average worker in 1 hour.

The fear that new workers entering the labor force will displace existing workers and generate unemployment has been with us for a long time. New workers can come from many places. They might be immigrants, young people looking for their first jobs, or older people entering the labor force for the first time. Between 1947 and 2004, the number of women in the labor force quadrupled, jumping from 17 million to 68 million. Table 31.2 shows that in the United States since World War II, the civilian noninstitutional population (those not in jails or mental institutions) over 16 years of age increased by 119.4 percent, while the labor force grew by 148.1 percent. The U.S. economy, however, has shown a remarkable ability to expand right along with the labor force. The number of persons employed jumped by 82.3 million—144.4 percent—during the same period.

As long as the economy and the capital stock are expanding rapidly enough, new entrants into the labor force do not displace other workers.

TABLE 31.2 Employment, Labor Force, and Population Growth, 1947–2004

	CIVILIAN NONINSTITUTIONAL POPULATION OVER 16 YEARS OLD (MILLIONS)	CIVILIAN LABOR FORCE		EMPLOYMENT (MILLIONS)
		Number (Millions)	Percentage of Population	
1947	101.8	59.4	58.3	57.0
1960	117.3	69.6	59.3	65.8
1970	137.1	82.8	60.4	78.7
1980	167.7	106.9	63.7	99.3
1990	189.2	125.8	66.5	118.8
2000	212.6	142.6	67.1	136.9
2004	223.4	147.4	66.0	139.3
Percentage change, 1947–2004	+119.4%	+148.1%		+144.4%
Annual rate	+1.4%	+1.6%		+1.6%

Source: Economic Report of the President, 2005, Table B-35.

TABLE 31.3 Economic Growth from an Increase in Capital—More Output, Diminishing Returns to Added Capital, Higher Measured Labor Productivity

PERIOD	QUANTITY OF LABOR L (HOURS)	QUANTITY OF CAPITAL K (UNITS)	TOTAL OUTPUT Y (UNITS)	MEASURED LABOR PRODUCTIVITY Y/L
1	100	100	300	3.0
2	100	110	310	3.1
3	100	120	319	3.2
4	100	130	327	3.3

INCREASES IN PHYSICAL CAPITAL

An increase in the stock of capital can also increase output, even if it is not accompanied by an increase in the labor force. Physical capital both enhances the productivity of labor and provides valuable services directly.

It is easy to see how capital provides services directly. Consider what happened on Bill and Colleen's island. In the first few years, they built a house, putting many hours of work into it that could have gone into producing other things for immediate consumption. With the house for shelter, Colleen and Bill can spend time on other things. In the same way, capital equipment produced in 1 year can add to the value of a product over many years. For example, we still derive use and value from bridges and tunnels built decades ago.

It is also easy to see how capital used in production enhances the productivity of labor. Computers enable us to do almost instantly tasks that once were impossible or might have taken years to complete. An airplane with a small crew can transport hundreds of people thousands of miles in a few hours. A bridge over a river at a critical location may save thousands of labor hours that would be spent transporting materials and people the long way around. It is precisely this yield in the form of future valuable services that provides both private and public investors with the incentive to devote resources to capital production.

Table 31.3 shows how an increase in capital without a corresponding increase in labor might increase output. Observe several things about these numbers. First, additional capital increases measured productivity; output per worker hour (Y/L) increases from 3.0 to 3.1, to 3.2, and finally to 3.3 as the quantity of capital (K) increases. Second, there are diminishing returns to capital. Increasing capital by 10 units first increases output by 10 units—from 300 in period 1 to 310 in period 2. However, the second increase of 10 units yields only 9 units of output, and the third increase yields only 8 units.

Table 31.4 shows the values of the private nonresidential capital stock in the United States since 1960. The increase in capital stock is the difference between gross investment and depreciation. (Remember, some capital becomes obsolete and some wears out every year.) Between 1960 and 2003, the stock of equipment increased at a rate of 4.6 percent per year and the stock of structures increased at a rate of 2.5 percent per year.

TABLE 31.4 Fixed Private Nonresidential Net Capital Stock, 1960–2003 (Billions of 2000 Dollars)

	EQUIPMENT	STRUCTURES
1960	645.7	2,273.3
1970	1,108.5	3,094.8
1980	1,910.0	4,047.7
1990	2,613.3	5,304.5
2000	4,138.5	6,287.6
2003	4,523.3	6,525.8
Percentage change, 1960–2003	+600.59%	+187.1%
Annual rate	+4.6%	+2.5%

Source: Survey of Current Business, September 2004, Table 15, p. 42 and author's estimates.

By comparing Tables 31.2 and 31.4, you can see that capital has been increasing faster than labor since 1960. In all economies experiencing modern economic growth, capital expands at a more rapid rate than labor. That is, the ratio of capital to labor (K/L) increases, and this too is a source of increasing productivity.

INCREASES IN HUMAN CAPITAL

Investment in human capital is another source of economic growth. People in good health are more productive than people in poor health; people with skills are more productive than people without them.

Human capital can be produced in many ways. Individuals can invest in themselves by going to college or vocational training programs. Firms can invest in human capital through on-the-job training. The government invests in human capital with programs to improve health and to provide schooling and job training.

Table 31.5 shows that the level of educational attainment has risen significantly since 1940. The percentage of the population with at least 4 years of college rose from under 5 percent in 1940 to 27.2 percent in 2003. In 1940, less than 1 person in 4 had completed high school; in 2003, more than 8 in 10 had.

INCREASES IN PRODUCTIVITY

productivity of an input
The amount of output produced per unit of an input.

Growth that cannot be explained by increases in the *quantity* of inputs can be explained only by an increase in the *productivity* of those inputs—each unit of input must be producing more output. The **productivity of an input** can be affected by factors including technological change, other advances in knowledge, and economies of scale.

invention An advance in knowledge.

innovation The use of new knowledge to produce a new product or to produce an existing product more efficiently.

Technological Change   The Industrial Revolution was in part sparked by new technological developments. New techniques of spinning and weaving—the invention of the machines known as the mule and the spinning jenny, for example—were critical. The high-tech boom that swept the United States in the early 1980s was driven by the rapid development and dissemination of semiconductor technology.

Technological change affects productivity in two stages. First, there is an advance in knowledge, or an **invention**. However, knowledge by itself does nothing unless it is used. When new knowledge is used to produce a new product or to produce an existing product more efficiently, there is **innovation**.

Technological change cannot be measured directly. Some studies have presented data on "indicators" of the rate of technical change—the number of new patents, for example—but none are satisfactory. Still, we know technological changes that have improved productivity are all around us. Wireless technology has revolutionized the office, hybrid seeds have

TABLE 31.5 Years of School Completed by People Over 25 Years Old, 1940–2003			
	PERCENTAGE WITH LESS THAN 5 YEARS OF SCHOOL	PERCENTAGE WITH 4 YEARS OF HIGH SCHOOL OR MORE	PERCENTAGE WITH 4 YEARS OF COLLEGE OR MORE
1940	13.7	24.5	4.6
1950	11.1	34.3	6.2
1960	8.3	41.1	7.7
1970	5.5	52.3	10.7
1980	3.6	66.5	16.2
1990	NA	77.6	21.3
2000	NA	84.1	25.6
2003	NA	84.6	27.2

NA = not available.
Source: Statistical Abstract of the United States, 1990, Table 215; and 2005, Table 212.

increased the productivity of land, and more efficient and powerful aircraft have made air travel routine and inexpensive.

Other Advances in Knowledge   Over and above invention and innovation, advances in other kinds of knowledge can also improve productivity. One is what we might call managerial knowledge. For example, because of the very high cost of capital during the early 1980s, firms learned to manage their inventories much better. Many were able to keep production lines and distribution lines flowing with a much lower stock of inventories. Inventories are part of a firm's capital stock, and trimming them reduces costs and raises productivity. This is an example of a *capital-saving* innovation; many of the advances that we are used to thinking about, such as the introduction of robotics, are *labor-saving*.

In addition to managerial knowledge, improved personnel management techniques, accounting procedures, data management, and the like can also make production more efficient, reduce costs, and increase measured productivity.

Economies of Scale   *External economies of scale* are cost savings that result from increases in the size of industries. The economies that accompany growth in size may arise from a variety of causes. For example, as firms in a growing industry build plants at new locations, they may lower transport costs. There may also be some economies of scale associated with research and development (R&D) spending and job-training programs.

Other Influences on Productivity   In addition to technological change, other advances in knowledge, and economies of scale, other forces may affect productivity. During the 1970s and 1980s, the U.S. government required many firms to reduce the air and water pollution they were producing. These requirements diverted capital and labor from the production of measured output, therefore *reducing* measured productivity. Similarly, in recent years requirements imposed by the Occupational Safety and Health Act (OSHA) have required firms to protect workers better from accidental injuries and potential health problems. These laws also divert resources from measured output.

Negative effects such as these are more a problem of *measurement* than of truly declining productivity. The Environmental Protection Agency (EPA) regulates air and water quality because clean air and water presumably have a value to society. The resources diverted to produce that value are not wasted. A perfect measure of output produced that is of value to society would include environmental quality and good health.

Weather can have a big impact on agricultural productivity.

GROWTH AND PRODUCTIVITY IN THE UNITED STATES

Modern economic growth in the United States began in the middle of the nineteenth century. After the Civil War, railroads spread across the country and the economy took off. Table 31.6 shows the growth rate of real output in the United States for selected subperiods since

TABLE 31.6 Growth of Real GDP in the United States, 1871–2000			
PERIOD	AVERAGE GROWTH RATE PER YEAR	PERIOD	AVERAGE GROWTH RATE PER YEAR
1871–1889	5.5	1950–1960	3.5
1889–1909	4.0	1960–1970	4.2
1909–1929	2.8	1970–1980	3.2
1929–1940	1.6	1980–1990	3.2
1940–1950	5.6	1990–2000	3.2

Sources: *Historical Statistics of the United States: Colonial Times to 1970*, Tables F47–70, F98–124; U.S. Department of Commerce, Bureau of Economic Analysis.

COUNTRY	AVERAGE GROWTH RATE PER YEAR
United States	3.1
Japan	2.3
Germany	2.0
France	2.2
Italy	1.8
United Kingdom	2.7
Canada	2.8
Africa	2.8
China	9.1
India	5.8

Source: Economic Report of the President, 2005, computed from Table B-112.

1871. Between 1871 and 1909, the growth rate was very strong—5.5 percent in the 1871–1889 period and 4.0 percent in the 1889–1909 period. The growth rate slowed to 2.8 percent in the 1909–1929 period and even further to 1.6 percent in the period that includes the Great Depression, 1929–1940. The growth rate was a strong 5.6 percent in the period that includes World War II, 1940–1950. It was then 3.5 percent in the 1950s, 4.2 percent in the 1960s, and 3.2 percent in the 1970s, 1980s, and 1990s.

Table 31.7 compares the growth rate in the United States with the growth rates of other countries for the period 1986–2004. This period was a fairly slow time for continental Europe, and the U.S. growth rate exceeded the growth rates of Germany, France, and Italy by about 1 percentage point. The U.S. growth rate was also higher than the growth rates of the United Kingdom, Japan, Canada, and the African countries. The real winners over this period were China and India, where the average growth rate was 9.1 percent for China and 5.8 percent for India.

SOURCES OF GROWTH IN THE U.S. ECONOMY: 1929–1982

For many years, Edward Denison of the Brookings Institution in Washington studied the growth process in the United States and sorted out the relative importance of the various causal factors. Table 31.8 presents some of his results. Denison estimates that about half of U.S. growth in output over the entire period from 1929 to 1982 came from increases in factors of production and the other half from increases in productivity. Growth in the labor force accounted for about 20 percent of overall growth, while growth in capital stock (both human and physical) accounted for 33 percent. Of the capital stock growth figure, human capital (education and training) accounted for 19 percent of the total, and physical capital accounted for 14 percent. Growth of knowledge was the most important factor contributing to increases in the productivity of inputs.

The relative importance of these causes of growth varied considerably over the years. Between 1929 and 1948, for example, physical capital played a much smaller role than it did in other periods. Each period included times that were atypical for one reason or another. The period between 1929 and 1948 included the dislocations and uncertainties of the Great Depression and World War II. From 1948 to 1973, the economy enjoyed a period of unusual stability and expansion.

In looking at the sources of U.S. growth since the 1970s, Professor Dale Jorgenson of Harvard University and a number of colleagues have done a similar accounting that breaks out the contributions of a specific kind of capital: information technology (IT) capital, including computers, software, and communications equipment. The results are presented in Table 31.9. The precise meaning of these numbers is quite complex, but they clearly indicate a number of trends. You can see that the portion of overall growth contributed by productivity is rising and that information technology has played a big role in recent years.

TABLE 31.8 Sources of Growth in the United States, 1929–1982

	Percent of Growth Attributable to Each Source			
	1929–1982	1929–1948	1948–1973	1973–1979
Increases in inputs	**53**	**49**	**45**	**94**
Labor	20	26	14	47
Capital	14	3	16	29
Education (human capital)	19	20	15	18
Increases in productivity	**47**	**51**	**55**	**6**
Advances in knowledge	31	30	39	8
Other factors[a]	16	21	16	−2
Annual growth rate in real national income	2.8	2.4	3.6	2.6

[a]Economies of scale, weather, pollution abatement, worker safety and health, crime, labor disputes, and so forth.
Source: Edward Denison, Trends in American Economic Growth, 1929–1982 (Washington: Brookings Institution, 1985). Reprinted with permission of The Brookings Institution.

TABLE 31.9 Sources of U.S. Growth, 1995–2004	
PERCENT CONTRIBUTION	
Increases in inputs	71.6
Labor	20.6
Capital	50.7
IT capital	22.8
Non-IT capital	27.9
Increases in productivity	28.4

Source: Information Technology and the American Growth Resurgence. Dale W. Jorgenson, Mun S. Ho and Kevin J. Stiroh (Cambridge, MA: MIT Press, 2005). Data update provided by the authors.

LABOR PRODUCTIVITY: 1952 I–2003 II

In Figure 20.1 in Chapter 20 we presented a plot of labor productivity for the 1952 I–2005 II period. It is now time to return to this figure, and it is repeated as Figure 31.2. Productivity in the figure is output per worker hour. Remember that the line segments are drawn to smooth out the short-run fluctuations in productivity. We saw in the last chapter that productivity as it is measured moves with the business cycle because firms tend to hold excess labor in recessions. We are not interested in business cycles in this chapter, and the line segments are a way of ignoring business cycle effects.

There was much talk in the late 1970s and early 1980s about the "productivity problem." Some economics textbooks published in the early 1980s had entire chapters discussing the decline in productivity that seemed to be taking place during the late 1970s. In January 1981, the Congressional Budget Office published a report, "The Productivity Problem: Alternatives for Action."

It is clear from Figure 31.2 that there was a slowdown in productivity growth in the 1970s. The growth rate went from 3.1 percent in the 1950s and first half of the 1960s to 2.5 percent in the last half of the 1960s and early 1970s and then to 1.5 percent from the early 1970s to the 1990s. Many explanations were offered at the time for the productivity slowdown of the late 1970s and early 1980s. Some economists pointed to the low rate of saving in the United States compared with other parts of the world. Others blamed increased environmental and government regulation of U.S. business. Still others argued that the country was not spending as much on R&D as it should be. Finally, some suggested that high energy costs

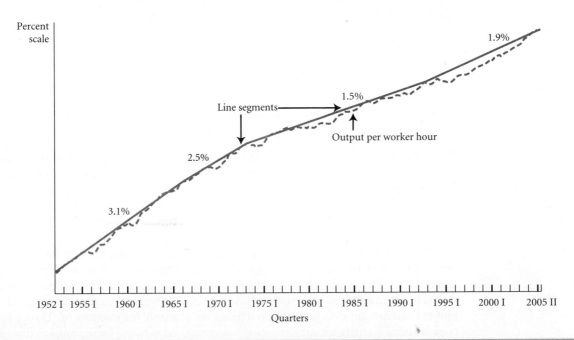

FIGURE 31.2 Output per Worker Hour (Productivity), 1952 I–2005 II

in the 1970s led to investment designed to save energy instead of to enhance productivity. (We discuss how each of these factors influences growth later in this chapter.)

Many of these factors turned around in the 1980s and 1990s and yet, as you can see from Figure 31.2, productivity growth rose to only 1.9 percent in the 1990s. This early discussion is now quite dated. The interesting question as we move into the late 2000s is how large an effect the Internet will have on productivity growth. Are we now in a new age, where long-run productivity growth will return to the rates of the 1950s and 1960s? Notice from Figure 31.2 that the actual growth rate of productivity between 1995 and 2000 was much larger than 1.9 percent (the growth along the 1990s line segment). The actual growth rate between the third quarter of 1995 and the second quarter of 2000 was 2.6 percent (on a per-year basis). Some have argued that this higher productivity growth is the beginning of the new age, the age of e-commerce, and so forth. However, others argue that the higher growth rate is just a cyclical phenomenon and that when actual productivity returns to the line segment (which it did in 2000), the growth rate of productivity will slow down to the rate that has prevailed since the early 1970s. The jury is still out on this one, so stay tuned. We need a few more years of data.

ECONOMIC GROWTH AND PUBLIC POLICY

The decline in productivity in the 1970s that caused so much concern led to a protracted national discussion about the role of government in stimulating economic growth. This debate was spurred in part by increasing concern on the part of many Americans that the United States was not doing as well as the Asian countries.

SUGGESTED PUBLIC POLICIES

Several strategies for increasing the rate of growth in the United States have been suggested, and some have been enacted into law. These strategies include policies aimed toward improving the quality of education, increasing the saving rate, stimulating investment, increasing R&D, reducing regulation, and pursuing an industrial policy.

Policies to Improve the Quality of Education   The Denison study shows that the contribution of education and training (human capital production) to growth in the United States has remained relatively constant at about 20 percent since 1929.

During the 1970s, public education was criticized. Teachers' salaries declined sharply in real terms, while property tax limitations and cuts in federal programs forced the curtailment of school budgets. In the last few years, battles have been waged in Congress over the amount of federal dollars set aside for scholarships and loans to college students. Whatever the policies of the moment, however, all federal, state, and local expenditures on education acknowledge the need to build the nation's stock of human capital.

The Taxpayer Relief Act of 1997 contained provisions that focused on education. First, the HOPE Scholarship credit allows taxpayers to claim a credit up to $1,500 for postsecondary education expenses on behalf of any family member. Other provisions include a new Education Individual Retirement Account that allows savings to earn tax-free returns as long as the balance is used to pay educational expenses.

Policies to Increase the Saving Rate   The amount of capital accumulation in an economy is ultimately constrained by its rate of saving. The more saving in an economy, the more funds are available for investment. Many people have argued that the tax system and the Social Security system in the United States are biased against saving. Some public finance economists favor shifting to a system of consumption taxation instead of income taxation to reduce the tax burden on saving.

Others claim the Social Security system, by providing guaranteed retirement incomes, reduces the incentive for people to save. Private pension plans make deposits to workers' accounts, the balances of which are invested in the stock market and bond market and are made available to firms for capital investment. Social Security benefits, in contrast, are paid out of current tax receipts, and no such accumulations are available for investment. Thus, the argument goes, if Social Security substitutes for private saving, the national saving rate is reduced. Evidence on the extent to which taxes and Social Security reduce the saving rate has not been clear to date.

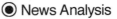
Productivity Gains in Health Care

GROWTH IS DRIVEN BY PRODUCTIVITY. An increase in productivity is measured by an increase in real output per worker. The following news story from the *New York Times* shows how the addition of capital and the application of technology lead to higher productivity on the part of physicians. They not only save time but also produce a higher-quality product.

Doctors Collaborate to Find a Less Costly Way to Add Electronic Medical Records

He is a self-described techie, but that did not help Dr. Eugene P. Heslin harness the wonders of electronic medical records. The technology seemed too complicated and expensive for a small medical group like his six-doctor family practice in rural upstate New York.

"The large groups can afford the software," said Dr. Heslin, a family physician in Saugerties. "For the onesies and twosies, small groups like ours, there is no profit margin."

Now, though, in a collaboration with 500 like-minded doctors, as well as hospitals, insurers and employers in two Hudson Valley counties, Dr. Heslin and his partners are clearing barriers that have made modern information technology inaccessible to the hundreds of thousands of small doctors' offices around the nation.

Electronic records, particularly ones that can be shared online by different doctors and hospitals, can improve the quality and safety of patient care by reducing errors that kill tens of thousands of patients each year.

[Now] Dr. Heslin and his regional colleagues, who call their cooperative effort the Taconic Health Information Network and Community, are pooling their resources and knowledge.

A Web-based, central database approach means that doctors need little more than a few standard PCs, a high-speed Internet connection and the willingness to pay a monthly subscription fee of $500 to $600, eliminating the initial outlay of tens of thousands of dollars.

"My mantra is to ask, How can we make electronic medical records cheaper and more valuable to the doctor?" [said one Federal official].

Under the Taconic system, which is being introduced in phases, doctors can log onto a secure Web site to get prompt laboratory and X-ray and other imaging results for their patients from four local hospitals and two big lab companies. Later this year, the doctors will be able to send prescriptions electronically to participating local drugstores or online pharmacies. The biggest part of the push is to start next year: the introduction of electronic health records accessible online to the patient's doctor.

François de Brantes, a General Electric health care official who is president of the e-Health Initiative Foundation, says early studies show that computerization can yield some savings for physicians, mainly in productivity, by freeing them to see more patients.

A provision of the 1997 Taxpayer Relief Act allowed for new "backloaded" retirement accounts [the so-called Roth individual retirement accounts (IRAs)] to stimulate saving. Individuals can deposit up to $2,000 annually to specified retirement accounts that accumulate earnings without paying income tax. Withdrawals made after age 59 1/2 or for the purchase of a first home can be made tax free.

Policies to Stimulate Investment   For the growth rate to increase, saving must be used to finance new investment. In an effort to revive a slowly growing economy in 1961, President Kennedy proposed and the Congress passed the *investment tax credit*

Can We Really Measure Productivity Changes?

When the government publishes numbers on changes in productivity, most people take them as "true." Even though we don't really know much about how they are constructed, we assume they are the best measurements we can get.

Yet such data are often the source of controversy. Some have argued that the mix of products produced in the United States and the increased pace of technological change in recent years have made it increasingly difficult to measure productivity changes accurately. The observed productivity decline in recent decades may be measurement error.

These arguments make a certain amount of sense at an intuitive level. Even in agriculture, where it is relatively easy to measure productivity growth, the possibility of mismeasurement exists. The output of a soybean farm can be measured in bushels, and labor, capital, and land inputs present no serious measurement problems. So, over time, as farming techniques improved and farmers acquired new and better machinery, output per acre and output per worker rose and have continued to rise. But today we have biotechnology. Genetic engineering now makes it possible to make soybeans higher in protein and more disease resistant. Technology has improved and "output" has increased, but these increases do not show up in the data because of crude measures of output.

A similar problem exists with computers. If you simply counted the number of personal computers produced and measured the cost of the inputs used in their production, you would no doubt see some productivity advances. But computers being produced for under $1,000 in 2005 contained processors capable of performing tasks literally thousands of times faster than computers produced a decade earlier. If we were to measure computer outputs not in terms of units produced but in terms of the actual "services" they provide to users, we would find massive productivity advances. New PCs now contain CD-ROM slots and can be easily connected to the "information superhighway," a source of cheap and plentiful information. In short, the problem is that many of the products we now use are qualitatively different from the comparable products we used only a few years ago, and the standard measures of productivity miss much of these quality changes.

The problems are greater in the service sector, where output is extremely difficult to measure. It is easy to understand the problem if you think of what information technology has done for legal services. As recently as 15 years ago, a lawyer doing research to support a legal case might spend hundreds of hours looking through old cases and public documents. Today's lawyers can log on to a computer and in seconds do a keyword search on a massive legal database. Such time- and labor-saving productivity advances are not counted in the official data.

One of the leading experts on technology and productivity estimates that we have reasonably good measures of output and productivity in only about 31 percent of the U.S. economy. Does this mean that productivity is not a problem? On this topic economists have agreed to disagree.[a]

[a]This argument was described most clearly by Professor Zvi Grilliches of Harvard in his presidential address to the American Economic Association in January 1994. The full text, entitled "Productivity, R&D, and the Data Constraint," is published in the *American Economic Review*, March 1994. The counterargument is best advanced by Professor Dale Jorgenson in *Productivity* (Harvard University Press, 1995).

(ITC). The ITC provided a tax reduction for firms that invest in new capital equipment. For most investments, the reduction took the form of a direct credit equal to 10 percent of the investment. A firm investing in a new computer system costing $100,000 would have its tax liability reduced by $10,000. The ITC was changed periodically over the years, and it was on the books until it was repealed in 1986. Many states have adopted ITCs against their state corporation taxes.

In 1982, the federal Economic Recovery Tax Act contained a number of provisions designed to encourage investment. Among them was the *Accelerated Cost Recovery System (ACRS)*, which gave firms the opportunity to reduce their taxes by using artificially rapid rates of depreciation for purposes of calculating taxable profits. Although these rules were complicated, their effect was similar to the effect of the ITC. The government effectively reduced the cost of capital to firms that undertook investment in plant or equipment.

The Bush tax plan, which became law as the Jobs and Growth Tax Relief Reconciliation Act of 2003, was an attempt to stimulate both labor supply and investment. The centerpiece of the plan was a sharp reduction in the taxation of dividends and capital gains. While long-term capital gains have long been afforded special tax treatment, dividends have essentially always been treated as ordinary income. Under the 2003 act, both are taxed at a reduced rate of 15 percent. In addition, the act generally lowered tax rates for most taxpayers. The top rate, which was 39.6 percent just a few years ago, was reduced to 35 percent, effective in 2003.

In 2005, the president received the report of a federal advisory panel on tax reform. The panel report was entitled *Simple, Fair and Pro-Growth: Proposals to Fix America's Tax System*. The report contained a set of recommendations aimed directly at growth, including allowing businesses to expense all capital purchases immediately rather than depreciating them over time; reducing tax rates on interest; lowering dividends and capital gains to 15 percent; and reducing tax rates in general. Only time will tell which of these provisions will become law.

Policies to Increase Research and Development As Table 31.8 shows, increases in knowledge accounted for 31 percent of total growth in the United States between 1929 and 1982. Although not shown in the table, during the years of high R&D expenditures, 1953 to 1973, the figure reached 40 percent. Research also shows that the rate of return on investment in R&D is quite high. Estimates place the rate of return at around 30 percent.[2]

It can be argued that new knowledge is like a public good. Although the United States has a patent system to protect the gains of R&D for inventors and innovators, many of the benefits flow to imitators and others, including the public. This logic has been used to justify public subsidization of R&D spending.

Reduced Regulations The Reagan and George Bush administrations, and the Republicans' "Contract with America" in 1995, were committed to reducing government regulation, which many believe stands in the way of U.S. industry.

Critics of these policies say many regulations on the books serve legitimate economic purposes. For example, environmental regulations, if properly administered, improve efficiency. Judicious use of antitrust laws, which are designed to promote competition, can also improve the allocation of resources and stimulate investment and production.

Denison estimated that regulation of occupational health and safety, and of the environment, reduced the annual growth rate between 1973 and 1979 by 0.13 percentage points, from 2.74 percent to 2.61 percent per year. Has the value of the improved environment and increased safety been worth it?

Industrial Policy In the last few years, a number of economists have called for increased government involvement in the allocation of capital across manufacturing sectors, a practice known as **Industrial policy**. Those who favor industrial policy believe that because governments of other countries are "targeting" industries for special subsidies and rapid investment, the United States should do likewise to avoid losing out in global competition. The Japanese Ministry of Trade and Industry, for example, picked the automobile industry very early on and decided to expand the automobile industry's role in world markets. The strategy succeeded very well; the Japanese auto industry has been remarkably successful.

Critics of industrial policy argue that having the government too involved in the allocation of capital would be disastrous. Investment always involves risk, they believe, and the best people to judge the extent and appropriateness of that risk are those making the investments and those actually involved in the industry.

industrial policy
Government involvement in the allocation of capital across manufacturing sectors.

GROWTH POLICY: A LONG-RUN PROPOSITION

When President Ford and Congress passed the dramatic tax cuts of 1975 to stimulate the economy and end the deep recession, the results were observable within a few months. Fiscal and monetary policies designed to counteract the cyclical up-and-down swings in the economy can produce measurable results in a short time.

However, the effects of policies designed to increase the rate of growth may not have observable effects for many years—they are by definition designed to mold the economy's long-run growth path. For example, a policy that succeeded in raising the rate of growth by 1 percentage point—for instance, from 2.5 percent to 3.5 percent—would be viewed by all as a tremendous success. Yet it would be almost a decade before such a policy would raise GDP by 10 percent.

The fact that progrowth policies can be costly in the short run and do not produce measurable results for a long time often pushes them far down on politicians' lists of priorities. Some economists who opposed the Tax Reform Act of 1986 argued that the elements of the tax code that had been favorable to capital investment and growth were cut for precisely

---

[2]See M. Nadiri, "Contributions and Determinants of Research and Development Expenditures in the U.S. Manufacturing Industries," in *Capital Efficiency and Growth*, George M. von Furstenberg, ed. (Cambridge, MA: Ballinger Press, 1980).

these reasons. Defenders of the Tax Reform Act claim that it is indeed possible to oversubsidize investment and that the pre-1986 tax code had been doing just that.

Not everyone agrees that the top priority in a developed economy should be continued growth. We will see why as we close the chapter.

THE PROS AND CONS OF GROWTH

There are those who believe growth should be the primary objective of any society and those who believe the costs of growth are too great.

THE PROGROWTH ARGUMENT

Advocates of growth believe growth *is* progress. Resources in a market economy are used to produce what people want; if you produce something people do not want, you are out of business. Even in a centrally planned economy, resources are targeted to fulfill needs and wants. If a society is able to produce those things more efficiently and at less cost, how can that be bad?

By applying new technologies and better production methods, resources are freed to produce new and better products. For Colleen and Bill, accumulating capital—a house, a water system, and so forth—and advancing knowledge were necessary to improve life on a formerly uninhabited island. In a modern industrial society, capital accumulation and new technology improve the quality of life.

One way to think about the benefits of growth is to compare two periods, for instance, 1950 and 1995. In 1995, real GDP per capita was more than twice what it was in 1950. This means incomes have grown twice as fast as prices so that we can buy that much more. (Remember, no one is telling anyone what to buy, and most people can spend much more now than they could then.) Although things available in both periods are not exactly the same, growth has given us *more* choice, not less. Consider transportation. In the 1950s, the interstate highway system (social capital) had not been built. Driving from Chicago to New York took several days. We had automobiles, but the highway system did not compare with what we have today. Greater advances also have been made in air travel. Flying between the two cities was possible, but more costly, less comfortable, and slower in 1950 than it is today.

Do these changes improve the quality of life? Yes, they do, because they give us more freedom. We can travel more frequently. I can see my mother more often. I spend less time getting where I want to go so I can spend more time there. People are able to get to more places for less money.

What about consumer durables—dishwashers, microwave ovens, compact disc players, power lawn mowers, and so forth? Do they enhance the quality of life? If not, why do we buy them? In 1950, about 3 percent of all homes had dishwashers; today close to 50 percent have them. In 1950, fewer than 2 percent of all homes had air conditioners; today over 60 percent do.

What makes a dishwasher worthwhile? It saves the most valuable commodity— *time.* Many consumer durables have no intrinsic value—they do not provide satisfaction directly. They free us from tasks and chores that are not fun (no one likes to wash clothes or dishes). If a product allows us to perform these tasks more easily and quickly, it gives us more time for other things.

Think of the improvement in the *quality* of things that are now available: high-speed Internet connections, music players that weigh a few ounces and hold over 1,000 tunes, plug-in storage devices with 1,000 megabytes, cell phones with video and high-resolution photo capability, almost unbelievable computer games, high-definition flat screen televisions, and, of course, wireless.

Growth also makes it possible to improve conditions for the less fortunate. The logic is simple: When there is more to go around, the sacrifice required to help the needy is smaller. With higher incomes, we can better afford the sacrifices needed to help the poor. Growth also produces jobs. When population growth is not accompanied by growth in output, unemployment and poverty increase.

Those in advanced societies can be complacent about growth, or critical of it, but leaders of developing countries understand its benefits. When 75 percent of a country's population is poor, redistributing existing incomes does not do much. The only hope for improvement in the long run is economic growth.

THE ANTIGROWTH ARGUMENT

Those who argue against economic growth generally make four major points:

1. Any measure of output measures only the value of things exchanged in the market. Many things that affect the quality of life are not traded in the market, and those things generally lose value when growth occurs.
2. For growth to occur, industry must cause consumers to develop new tastes and preferences. Therefore, we have no real need for many of the things we now consume. Wants are created, and consumers have become the servants, instead of the masters, of the economy.
3. The world has a finite quantity of resources, and rapid growth is consuming them at a rate that cannot continue. Because the available resources impose limits to growth, we should begin now to plan for the future, when growth will be impossible.
4. Growth requires that income be distributed unfairly.

Growth Has Negative Effects on the Quality of Life   Perhaps the most significant "unmeasurable" changes that affect the quality of life occur in the early stages of growth when societies become industrialized. More is produced: Agricultural productivity is higher, more manufactured goods are available, and so forth. However, most people are crowded into cities, and their lives change drastically.

Before industrialization, most people in the Western World lived in small towns in the country. Most were poor, and they worked long hours to produce enough food to survive. After industrialization and urbanization in eighteenth-century England, men, women, and children worked long hours at routine jobs in hot, crowded factories. They were paid low wages and had very little control over their lives.

Even today, growth continues to change the quality of life in ways that are observable but not taken into account when we calculate growth rates. U.S. agriculture, for example, is becoming more productive every year. As productivity goes up, food prices drop, and fewer resources are needed in the agricultural sector. States in New England that once had thriving farms have found their climates and soils not good enough to compete anymore. In 1959, 56,000 farms covered 9.3 million acres in the six New England states; in 1998, fewer than 30,000 farms covered fewer than 5 million acres. The agricultural sector had been cut in half.

During the early 1970s, small family farmers all over the United States found that making a living was becoming nearly impossible. The villain was growth and progress. The cost was the decline of a lifestyle that many people want to maintain and that many others think of as an important part of America.

There are other consequences of growth that are not counted in the growth calculation. Perhaps the most significant is environmental damage. As the industrial engine is fed, waste is produced. Often, both the feeding and the waste cause massive environmental damage. A dramatic example is the surface, or strip, mining of coal that has ravaged many parts of the United States. Another is the uncontrolled harvesting of U.S. forests. Modern growth requires paper and wood products, and large areas of timber in many states have been cleared and never replanted.

The disposal of industrial wastes has not begun to keep pace with industrial growth. It is now clear that growing and prosperous chemical companies have for decades been dumping hazardous, often carcinogenic, waste products into the nation's soil and water. It is costing billions to clean them up. Those costs were never taken into account when the market was allocating resources to the growing chemical industry.

Growth-related problems are everywhere. Japan paid little attention to the environment during the early years of its rapid economic growth. Many of the results were disastrous. The best known of these results were the horrifying birth defects following the dumping of industrial mercury into the waters of Minamata Bay. In addition to birth defects, thousands of cases of "Minamata disease" in adults have been documented, and hundreds have died.

Growth Encourages the Creation of Artificial Needs

The nature of preferences has been debated within the economics profession for many years. The orthodox view, which lies at the heart of modern welfare economics, is that preferences exist among consumers and that the economy's purpose is to serve those needs. According to the notion of **consumer sovereignty**, people are free to choose, and things that people do not want will not sell. The consumer rules.

The opposite view is that preferences are formed within the economic system. To continue growing, firms need a continuously expanding set of demands. To ensure that demand develops or grows, firms create it by managing our minds and manipulating our behavior with elaborate advertising, fancy packaging, and other marketing techniques that persuade us to buy things for which we have no intrinsic need.

Growth Means the Rapid Depletion of a Finite Quantity of Resources

In 1972, the Club of Rome, a group of "concerned citizens," contracted with a group at MIT to do a study entitled *The Limits to Growth*.[3] The book-length final report presented the results of computer simulations that assumed present growth rates of population, food, industrial output, and resource exhaustion. According to these data, sometime after the year 2000 the limits will be reached, and the entire world economy will come crashing down:

> Collapse occurs because of nonrenewable resource depletion. The industrial capital stock grows to a level that requires an enormous input of resources. In the very process of that growth, it depletes a large fraction of the resource reserves available. As resource prices rise and mines are depleted, more and more capital must be used for obtaining resources, leaving less to be invested for future growth. Finally, investment cannot keep up with depreciation and the industrial base collapses, taking with it the service and agricultural systems, which have become dependent on industrial inputs (such as fertilizers, pesticides, hospital laboratories, computers, and especially energy for mechanization). . . . Population finally decreases when the death rate is driven upward by the lack of food and health services.[4]

This argument is similar to one offered almost 200 years ago by Thomas Malthus, mentioned earlier in this chapter.

In the early 1970s, many thought that the Club of Rome's predictions had come true. It seemed the world was starting to run up against the limits of world energy supplies; the prices of energy products shot up, and there were serious shortages. In the years since, new reserves have been found, new sources of energy have been discovered and developed, and conservation measures have been tremendously successful (automobile gas mileage has been pushed up to levels that were inconceivable 15 years ago).

In the fall of 2005, it looked as if the world was hitting the wall on oil production yet again. In the aftermath of Hurricane Katrina, which wiped out both production capacity in the Gulf of Mexico and a number of refineries, the price of a barrel of crude climbed to over $70.00, and regular gasoline hit $3.75 per gallon at the pump in some locations. Heating oil headed up sharply. But by early December gasoline was back at $2.00 a gallon and crude was down around $56 a barrel.

The only thing certain about oil is that it will fluctuate with supply and demand. Energy prices have actually fallen to levels that in real terms are about the same as they were before the oil price shocks of the 1970s.

A variation of the depletion-of-resources argument stops short of predicting doomsday. It does point out that unchecked growth in the developed world may have undesirable dis-

---

consumer sovereignty
The notion that people are free to choose, and that things that people do not want will not sell. "The consumer rules."

[3]Dennis L. Meadows et al., *The Limits to Growth* (Washington, DC: Potomac Associates, 1972).
[4]Meadows et al., pp. 131–132.

tributional consequences. To fuel our growth, we are buying vast quantities of minerals and other resources from the developing countries, which have become dependent on the proceeds of those sales to buy food and other commodities on world markets. If this continues, by the time these countries have grown to the point that they need mineral resources, their resources may be gone.

Growth Requires an Unfair Income Distribution and Propagates It

One cause of growth is capital accumulation. Capital investment requires saving, and saving comes mostly from the rich. The rich save more than the poor, and in the developing countries most people are poor and need to use whatever income they have for survival.

Critics also claim that the real beneficiaries of growth are the rich. Choices open to the "haves" in society are greatly enhanced, but the choices open to the "have-nots" remain severely limited. If the benefits of growth trickle down to the poor, why are there more homeless today than there were 20 years ago?

SUMMARY: NO RIGHT ANSWER

We have presented the arguments for and against economic growth in simple terms. In reality, even those who take extreme positions in this debate acknowledge there is no "right answer." To suggest that all economic growth is bad is wrong; to suggest that economic growth should run unchecked is equally wrong. The question is: How can we derive the benefits of growth and at the same time minimize its undesirable consequences?

Society must make some hard choices, and there are many trade-offs. For example, we can grow faster if we pay less attention to environmental concerns, but how much environmental damage should we accept to get how much economic growth? Many argue that we can achieve an acceptable level of economic growth *and* protect the environment at the same time. There is also a trade-off between growth and the distribution of income. More financial inequality would probably lead to more saving and ultimately to more capital and faster growth. Using taxes and income transfers to redistribute some of the benefits of growth to the poor probably does slow the rate of growth. However, it is not a question of all or nothing; society must decide how much inequality is desirable.

As long as these trade-offs exist, people will disagree. The debate in contemporary politics is largely about the costs and benefits of shifting more effort toward the goal of economic growth and away from environmental and social welfare goals.

SUMMARY

1. *Modern economic growth* is the period of rapid and sustained increase in real output per capita that began in the Western World with the Industrial Revolution.

THE GROWTH PROCESS: FROM AGRICULTURE TO INDUSTRY

2. All societies face limits imposed by the resources and technologies available to them. Economic growth expands these limits and shifts society's production possibilities frontier up and to the right.

THE SOURCES OF ECONOMIC GROWTH

3. If growth in output outpaces growth in population, and if the economic system is producing what people want, growth will increase the standard of living. Growth occurs when (1) society acquires more resources, or (2) society discovers ways of using available resources more efficiently.

4. An *aggregate production function* embodies the relationship between inputs—the labor force and the stock of capital—and total national output.

5. A number of factors contribute to *economic growth*: (1) an increase in the labor supply; (2) an increase in physical capital—plant and equipment—and/or human capital—education, training, and health; (3) an increase in productivity brought about by technological change; other advances in knowledge (managerial skills, etc.); and/or economies of scale.

GROWTH AND PRODUCTIVITY IN THE UNITED STATES

6. Modern economic growth in the United States dates to the middle of the nineteenth century. For the last 100 years, the nation's growth in real output has averaged about 3 percent per year. Between 1929 and 1982, about half of U.S. growth in output came from increases in factors of production and half from increases in productivity.

7. There has been much concern that the rate of growth of productivity in the United States is slowing. The growth rate of *labor productivity* decreased from about 3.3 percent in the 1950s and 1960s to about 1.7 percent in the 1990s.

ECONOMIC GROWTH AND PUBLIC POLICY

8. A number of public policies have been pursued with the aim of improving the growth of real output. These policies include efforts to improve the quality of education, to encourage saving, to stimulate investment, to increase research and development, and to reduce regulation. Some economists also argue for increased government involvement in the allocation of capital across manufacturing sectors, a practice known as *industrial policy*.

THE PROS AND CONS OF GROWTH

9. Advocates of growth argue that growth is progress. Growth gives us more freedom—meaning more choices. It saves time, improves the standard of living, and is the only way to improve conditions for the poor. Growth creates jobs and increases income simply because there is more to go around.

10. Those who argue against growth make four points. First, many things that affect the quality of life are not traded in the market, and these things generally lose value when there is growth. Second, to have growth, industry must cause consumers to develop new tastes and preferences for many things that they have no real need for. Third, the world has a finite quantity of resources, and rapid growth is eating them up at a rate that cannot continue. Fourth, growth requires that income be distributed inequitably.

REVIEW TERMS AND CONCEPTS

aggregate production function, 665
consumer sovereignty, 678
economic growth, 663

industrial policy, 675
innovation, 668
invention, 668

labor productivity, 666
modern economic growth, 663
productivity of an input, 668

PROBLEM SET

1. During the 5 years leading up to the recession of 2001, real GDP grew at a very fast pace. The expansion was led by business investment spending on the "new technology." Describe how spending on computer equipment, software, Web sites, and cell phones could have an impact on productivity and the rate of growth. After 2001, however, that sector collapsed, unemployment increased, and we went into a period of decline and very slow growth. Explain how overexpansion and overinvestment can lead to a period of economic decline.

2. Tables 1, 2, and 3 present some data on three hypothetical economies. Complete the tables by figuring the measured productivity of labor and the rate of output growth. What do the data tell you about the causes of economic growth? (*Hint:* How fast are *L* and *K* growing?)

TABLE 1

PERIOD	L	K	Y	Y/L	GROWTH RATE OF OUTPUT
1	1,052	3,065	4,506		
2	1,105	3,095	4,674		
3	1,160	3,126	4,842		
4	1,218	3,157	5,019		

TABLE 2

PERIOD	L	K	Y	Y/L	GROWTH RATE OF OUTPUT
1	1,052	3,065	4,506		
2	1,062	3,371	4,683		
3	1,073	3,709	4,866		
4	1,084	4,079	5,055		

TABLE 3

PERIOD	L	K	Y	Y/L	GROWTH RATE OF OUTPUT
1	1,052	3,065	4,506		
2	1,062	3,095	4,731		
3	1,073	3,126	4,967		
4	1,084	3,157	5,216		

3. Go to a recent issue of *The Economist* magazine. In the back of each issue is a section called "economic indicators." That section lists the most recent growth data for a substantial number of countries. Which countries around the world are growing the most rapidly according to the most recent data? Which countries around the world are growing more slowly? Flip through the stories in *The Economist* to see if there is any explanation for the pattern that you observe. Write a brief essay on current general economic conditions around the world.

4. In the fall of 2005, the president's tax reform commission issued a final report. The commission called for a general cut in marginal tax rates; lower tax rates on dividends, capital gains, and interest income; and, more importantly, the expensing of investment in capital equipment. These provisions were argued to be "pro-growth." In what ways would you expect each of these proposals to be favorable to economic growth?

5. In earlier chapters, you learned that aggregate expenditure $(C + I + G)$ must equal aggregate output for the economy to be in equilibrium. You also saw that when consumption spending rises, $C + I + G$ increases, inventories fall, and aggregate output rises. Thus, policies that simultaneously increase consumer spending and reduce saving would lead to a higher level of GDP. In this chapter, we have argued that a higher saving rate, even

with lower consumption spending, is the key to long-run GDP growth. How can both arguments be correct?

6. Suppose you have just been elected to Congress and you find yourself on the Ways and Means Committee—the committee in the House that decides on tax matters. The committee is debating a bill that would make major changes in tax policy. First, the corporate tax would be lowered substantially in an effort to stimulate investment. The bill contains a 15 percent investment tax credit—firms would be able to reduce their taxes by 15 percent of the value of investment projects that they undertake. To keep revenues constant, the bill would impose a national sales tax that would raise the price of consumer goods and reduce consumption. What trade-offs do you see implied in this bill? What are the pros and cons? How would you vote?

7. If you wanted to measure productivity (output per worker) in the following sectors over time, how would you measure "output"? How easy is it to measure productivity in each of the sectors?

a. Software
b. Vegetable farming
c. Education
d. Airline transportation

8. Economists generally agree high budget deficits today will reduce the growth rate of the economy in the future. Why? Do the reasons for the high budget deficit matter? In other words, does it matter whether the deficit is caused by lower taxes, increased defense spending, more job-training programs, and so on?

9. Why can growth lead to a more unequal distribution of income? By assuming this is true, how is it possible for the poor to benefit from economic growth?

10. The box on p. 673 describes the ways in which investment in information technology raises the quality of rural medical care and increases the productivity of doctors. Pick another profession, such as law or accounting, and describe the ways in which information technology has raised productivity.

Debates in Macroeconomics: Monetarism, New Classical Theory, and Supply-Side Economics

32

Throughout this book, we have noted that there are many disagreements and questions in macroeconomics. For example, economists disagree on whether the aggregate supply curve is vertical, either in the short run or in the long run. Some even doubt that the aggregate supply curve is a useful macroeconomic concept. There are different views on whether cyclical employment exists and, if it does, what causes it. Economists disagree about whether monetary and fiscal policies are effective at stabilizing the economy, and they support different views on the primary determinants of consumption and investment spending.

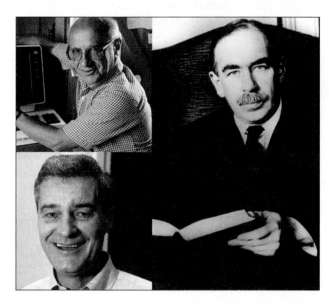

We discussed some of these disagreements in previous chapters, but only briefly. In this chapter, we discuss in more detail a number of alternative views of how the macroeconomy works.

KEYNESIAN ECONOMICS

John Maynard Keynes's *General Theory of Employment, Interest, and Money*, published in 1936, remains one of the most important works in economics. While a great deal of the material in the previous 10 chapters is drawn from modern research that postdates Keynes, much of it is built around a framework constructed by Keynes.

What exactly is *Keynesian economics*? In one sense, it is the foundation of all of macroeconomics. Keynes was the first to stress aggregate demand and links between the money market and the goods market. Keynes also stressed the possible problem of sticky wages. Virtually all the debates in this chapter can be understood in terms of the aggregate output/aggregate expenditure framework suggested by Keynes.

In recent years, the term *Keynesian* has been used narrowly. Keynes believed in an activist federal government. He believed the government had a role to play in fighting inflation and unemployment, and he believed monetary and fiscal policy should be used to manage the macroeconomy. This is why *Keynesian* is sometimes used to refer to economists who advocate active government intervention in the macroeconomy.

During the 1970s and 1980s, it became clear that managing the macroeconomy was more easily accomplished on paper than in practice. The inflation problems of the 1970s and early 1980s and the seriousness of the recessions of 1974 to 1975 and 1980 to 1982 led many

683

economists to challenge the idea of active government intervention in the economy. Some of the challenges were simple attacks on the bureaucracy's ability to act in a timely manner. Others were theoretical assaults that claimed to show that monetary and fiscal policy could have *no effect whatsoever* on the economy, even if it were efficiently managed.

Two major schools decidedly against government intervention developed: monetarism and new classical economics.

MONETARISM

The debate between "monetarist" and "Keynesian" economics is complicated because they mean different things to different people. If we consider the main monetarist message to be that "money matters," then almost all economists would agree. In the aggregate supply/aggregate demand (*AS/AD*) story, for example, an increase in the money supply shifts the *AD* curve to the right, which leads to an increase in both aggregate output (*Y*) and the price level (*P*). Monetary policy thus has an effect on output and the price level. *Monetarism*, however, is usually considered to go beyond the notion that money matters.

THE VELOCITY OF MONEY

velocity of money The number of times a dollar bill changes hands, on average, during a year; the ratio of nominal *GDP* to the stock of money.

To understand monetarist reasoning, you must understand the **velocity of money**. Think of velocity as the number of times a dollar bill changes hands, on average, during a year.

Suppose on January 1 you buy a new ballpoint pen with a $5 bill. The owner of the stationery store does not spend your $5 right away. She may hold it until, say, May 1, when she uses it to buy a dozen doughnuts. The doughnut store owner does not spend the $5 he receives until July 1, when he uses it (along with other cash) to buy 100 gallons of oil. The oil distributor uses the bill to buy an engagement ring for his fiancée on September 1, but the $5 bill is not used again in the remaining 3 months of the year. Because this $5 bill has changed hands four times during the year, its velocity of circulation is 4. A velocity of 4 means the $5 bill stays with each owner for an average of 3 months, or one quarter of a year.

In practice, we use gross domestic product (GDP), instead of the total value of all transactions in the economy, to measure velocity,[1] because GDP data are more available. The income velocity of money (*V*) is the ratio of nominal GDP to the stock of money (*M*):

$$V \equiv \frac{GDP}{M}$$

If $6 trillion worth of final goods and services is produced in a year and if the money stock is $1 trillion, then the velocity of money is $6 trillion ÷ $1 trillion, or 6.0.

We can expand this definition slightly by noting that nominal income (GDP) is equal to real output (income) (*Y*) times the overall price level (*P*):

$$GDP \equiv P \times Y$$

Through substitution:

$$V \equiv \frac{P \times Y}{M}$$

or

$$M \times V \equiv P \times Y$$

---

[1] Recall, GDP does not include transactions in intermediate goods (for example, flour sold to a baker to be made into bread) or in existing assets (for example, the sale of a used car). If these transactions are made using money, however, they do influence the number of times money changes hands during the course of a year. GDP is an imperfect measure of transactions to use in calculating the velocity of money.

At this point, it is worth pausing to ask if our definition has provided us with any insights into the workings of the economy. The answer is no. Because we defined V as the ratio of GDP to the money supply, the statement $M \times V \equiv P \times Y$ is an identity—it is true by definition. It contains no more useful information than the statement "A bachelor is an unmarried man." The definition does not, for example, say anything about what will happen to $P \times Y$ when M changes. The final value of $P \times Y$ depends on what happens to V. If V falls when M increases, the product $M \times V$ could stay the same, in which case the change in M would have had no effect on nominal income. To give monetarism some economic content, we turn to a simple version of monetarism known as the **quantity theory of money**.

THE QUANTITY THEORY OF MONEY

The key assumption of the quantity theory of money is that the velocity of money is constant (or virtually constant) over time. If we let $\overline{V}$ denote the constant value of V, the equation for the quantity theory can be written:

$$M \times \overline{V} = P \times Y$$

quantity theory of money The theory based on the identity $M \times V \equiv P \times Y$ and the assumption that the velocity of money (V) is constant (or virtually constant).

Note the double equal sign has replaced the triple equal sign because the equation is no longer an identity. The equation is true if velocity is constant (and equal to $\overline{V}$), but not otherwise. If the equation is true, it provides an easy way to explain nominal GDP. Given M, which can be considered a policy variable set by the Federal Reserve (Fed), nominal GDP is just $M \times \overline{V}$. In this case, the effects of monetary policy are clear. Changes in M cause equal percentage changes in nominal GDP. For example, if the money supply doubles, nominal GDP also doubles. If the money supply remains unchanged, nominal GDP remains unchanged.

The key is whether the velocity of money is really constant. Early economists believed the velocity of money was determined largely by institutional considerations, such as how often people are paid and how the banking system clears transactions between banks. Because these factors change gradually, early economists believed velocity was essentially constant.

If there is equilibrium in the money market, then the quantity of money supplied is equal to the quantity of money demanded. That could mean that M in the quantity-theory equation equals both the quantity of money supplied and the quantity of money demanded. If the quantity-theory equation is looked on as a demand-for-money equation, it says that the demand for money depends on nominal income (GDP, or $P \times Y$), but *not* on the interest rate.[2] If the interest rate changes and nominal income does not, the equation says that the quantity of money demanded will not change. This is contrary to the theory of the demand for money in Chapter 24, which had the demand for money depending on both income and the interest rate.

Testing the Quantity Theory of Money   One way to test the validity of the quantity theory of money is to look at the demand for money using recent data on the U.S. economy. The key is: Does money demand depend on the interest rate? Most empirical work says yes. When demand-for-money equations are estimated (or "fit to the data"), the interest rate usually turns out to be a factor. The demand for money does not appear to depend only on nominal income.

Another way of testing the quantity theory is to plot velocity over time and see how it behaves. Figure 32.1 plots the velocity of money for the 1960 I–2005 II period. The data show that velocity is far from constant. There is a long-term trend—on average, velocity has been rising during these years—but fluctuations around this trend have also occurred, and some have been quite large. Velocity rose from 6.1 in 1980 III to 6.7 in 1981 III; fell to 6.3 in 1983 I; rose to 6.7 in 1984 III; and fell to 5.7 in 1986 IV. Changes of a few tenths of a point may seem small, but they are actually large. For example, the money supply in 1986 IV was $799 billion. If velocity changes by 0.3 with

---

[2]In terms of the Appendix to Chapter 25, this means the LM curve is vertical.

FIGURE 32.1 The Velocity of Money, 1960 I–2005 II

Velocity has not been constant over the period from 1960 to 2005. There is a long-term trend—velocity has been rising. There are also fluctuations, some of them quite large.

a money supply of this amount, and if the money supply is unchanged, we have a change in nominal GDP ($P \times Y$) of $240 billion ($0.3 \times$ \$799 billion), which is about 5 percent of the level of GDP in 1986.

The debate over monetarist theories is more subtle than our discussion so far indicates. First, there are many definitions of the money supply. M1 is the money supply variable used for the graph in Figure 32.1, but there may be some other measure of the money supply that would lead to a smoother plot. For example, many people shifted their funds from checking account deposits to money market accounts when the latter became available in the late 1970s. Because GDP did not change as a result of this shift while M1 decreased, velocity—the ratio of GDP to M1—must have gone up. Suppose instead we measured the supply of money by M2 (which includes both checking accounts and money market accounts). In this case, the decrease in checking deposits would be exactly offset by the rise in money market account deposits, and M2 would not change. With no change in GDP and no change in M2, the velocity of money would not change. Whether velocity is constant or not may depend partly on how we measure the money supply.

Second, there may be a time lag between a change in the money supply and its effects on nominal GDP. Suppose we experience a 10 percent increase in the money supply today, but it takes 1 year for nominal GDP to increase by 10 percent. If we measured the ratio of today's money supply to today's GDP, it would seem that velocity had fallen by 10 percent. However, if we measured today's money supply against GDP 1 year from now, when the increase in the supply of money had its full effect on income, then velocity would have been constant.

The debate over the usefulness of monetarist theory is primarily empirical. It is a debate that can be resolved by looking at facts about the real world and seeing whether they are in accord with the predictions of theory. Is there a measure of the money supply and a choice of the time lag between a change in the money supply and its effects on nominal GDP such that V is in effect constant? If so, then the monetarist theory is a useful approach to understanding how the macroeconomy works. If not, then some other theory is likely to be more appropriate. (We discuss the testing of alternative theories at the end of this chapter.)

INFLATION AS A PURELY MONETARY PHENOMENON

So far we have talked only about nominal output ($P \times Y$). We have said nothing about how a monetarist would break down a change in nominal output (due to a money-supply change) into a change in P and a change in Y. Here again it is not possible to make a general statement about what all monetarists believe. Some may believe that all of the change occurs in P, and others may believe that at least sometimes some of the change occurs in Y.

If all the change occurs in P, then there is a proportional relationship between changes in the money supply and changes in the price level. For example, a 10 percent change in M will lead to a 10 percent change in P if Y remains unchanged. In this case, inflation (an increase in P) is always a purely monetary phenomenon. The price level will not change if the money supply does not change. We will call this view, that changes in M affect only P and not Y, the "strict monetarist" view.

There is considerable disagreement as to whether the strict monetarist view is a good approximation of reality. For example, the strict view is not compatible with a nonvertical AS curve in the AS/AD model in Chapter 26. In the case of a nonvertical AS curve, an increase in M, which shifts the AD curve to the right, increases both P and Y. (You may want to review why.)

Almost all economists agree, however, that *sustained* inflation—inflation that continues over many periods—is a purely monetary phenomenon. In the context of the AS/AD framework, inflation cannot continue indefinitely unless the Fed "accommodates" it by increasing the money supply. Let us review this.

Consider a continuously increasing level of government spending (G) without any corresponding increase in taxes. The increases in G keep shifting the AD curve to the right, which leads to an increasing price level (P). (You may find it useful to draw a graph now.) With a fixed money supply, the increases in P lead to a higher and higher interest rate, but there is a limit to how far this can go. Because taxes are unchanged, the government must finance the increases in G by issuing bonds, and there is a limit to how many bonds the public is willing to hold regardless of how high the interest rate goes. At the point at which the public cannot be induced to hold any more bonds, the government will be unable to borrow any more to finance its expenditures. Only if the Fed is willing to increase the money supply (buy some of the government bonds) can the government spending (with its inflationary consequences) continue.

Inflation cannot continue indefinitely without increases in the money supply.

THE KEYNESIAN/MONETARIST DEBATE

The leading spokesman for monetarism over the last few decades has been Professor Milton Friedman, formerly of the University of Chicago and currently at the Hoover Institute in California. Most monetarists, including Friedman, blame most of the instability in the economy on the federal government, arguing that the inflation the United States has encountered over the years could have been avoided if only the Fed had not expanded the money supply so rapidly.

Most monetarists do not advocate an activist monetary stabilization policy—expanding the money supply during bad times and slowing the growth of the money supply during good times. Monetarists tend to be skeptical of the government's ability to "manage" the macroeconomy. The most common argument against such management is the one expressed in Chapter 28: Time lags make it likely that conscious attempts to stimulate and contract the economy make the economy more, not less, unstable.

Friedman has for many years advocated a policy of steady and slow money growth—specifically, that the money supply should grow at a rate equal to the average growth of real output (income) (Y). That is, the Fed should pursue a constant policy that accommodates real growth but not inflation.

Keynesianism and monetarism are at odds with each other. Many Keynesians advocate the application of coordinated monetary and fiscal policy tools to reduce instability in the economy—to fight inflation and unemployment. However, not all Keynesians advocate an activist federal government. Some reject the strict monetarist position that changes in money affect only the price level in favor of the view that both monetary and fiscal policies make a difference, and *at the same time* believe the best possible policy for government to pursue is basically noninterventionist.

Most Keynesians agree after the experience of the 1970s that monetary and fiscal tools are not finely calibrated. The notion that monetary and fiscal expansions and contractions can "fine-tune" the economy is gone forever. Still, many believe the experiences of the 1970s also show that stabilization policies can help prevent even bigger economic disasters. Had the government not cut taxes and expanded the money supply in 1975 and in 1982, they argue, the recessions of those years might have been significantly worse. The same people would argue that had the government not resisted the inflations of 1974 to 1975 and 1979 to 1981 with tight monetary policies, they would probably have become much worse.

Thirty years ago, the debate between Keynesians and monetarists was the central controversy in macroeconomics. That controversy, while still alive today, is no longer at the forefront. For the past two decades, the focus of current thinking in macroeconomics has been on the new classical macroeconomics.

NEW CLASSICAL MACROECONOMICS

The challenge to Keynesian and related theories has come from a school sometimes referred to as the *new classical macroeconomics*.[3] Like *monetarism* and *Keynesianism*, this term is vague. No two new classical macroeconomists think exactly alike, and no single model completely represents this school. The following discussion, however, conveys the flavor of the new classical views.

THE DEVELOPMENT OF NEW CLASSICAL MACROECONOMICS

New classical macroeconomics has developed from two different, though related, sources. These sources are the theoretical and the empirical critiques of existing, or traditional, macroeconomics.

On the theoretical level, there has been growing dissatisfaction with the way traditional models treat expectations. Keynes himself recognized that expectations (in the form of "animal spirits") play a big part in economic behavior. The problem is, traditional models have assumed that expectations are formed in naive ways. A common assumption, for example, is that people form their expectations of future inflation by assuming present inflation will continue. If they turn out to be wrong, they adjust their expectations by some fraction of the difference between their original forecast and the actual inflation rate. Suppose I expect 10 percent inflation next year. When next year comes, the inflation rate turns out to be only 5 percent, so I have made an error of 5 percent. I might then predict an inflation rate for the following year of 7.5 percent, halfway between my earlier expectation (10 percent) and actual inflation last year (5 percent).

The problem with this treatment of expectations is that it is not consistent with the assumptions of microeconomics. It implies people systematically overlook information that would allow them to make better forecasts, even though there are costs to being wrong. If, as microeconomic theory assumes, people are out to maximize their satisfaction and firms are out to maximize their profits, they should form their expectations in a smarter way. Instead of naively assuming the future will be like the past or the present, they should actively seek to forecast the future. Any other behavior is not in keeping with the microeconomic view of the forward-looking, rational people who compose households and firms.

On the empirical level, there was stagflation in the U.S. economy during the 1970s. Remember, stagflation is simultaneous high unemployment and rising prices. The Phillips Curve theory of the 1960s predicted that demand pressure pushes up prices, so that when demand is weak—in times of high unemployment, for example—prices should be stable (or perhaps even falling). The new classical theories were an attempt to explain the apparent breakdown in the 1970s of the simple inflation–unemployment trade-off predicted by the Phillips Curve. Just as the Great Depression of the 1930s motivated the development of Keynesian economics, so the stagflation of the 1970s helped motivate the formulation of new classical economics.

---

[3]The term *new classical* is used because many of the assumptions and conclusions of this group of economists resemble those of the classical economists—that is, those who wrote before Keynes.

Inflation and Money Supply in Latin America

THE CONSENSUS VIEW OF THE PROBlem of inflation in Latin America was outlined by the new Fed chair Ben Bernanke nearly a year before his appointment in 2005.

Inflation in Latin America: A New Era?

The Federal Reserve is justly proud of its success in reducing and stabilizing inflation in the United States. When Paul Volcker became Fed chairman twenty-five years ago, Americans were enduring double-digit inflation rates and subpar economic performance. Under the leadership of Volcker and, subsequently, Alan Greenspan, the Federal Open Market Committee took the actions necessary to bring the nation to price stability. In my view, the conquest of inflation has been a major source of the more-rapid economic growth and the greater stability of output and employment that the United States has enjoyed since the mid-1980s (Bernanke, 2004).

Impressive as the Fed's inflation-fighting accomplishments may be, however, inflation developments to our south, in Latin America, may prove to be more impressive yet. For much of the latter half of the twentieth century, Latin America experienced recurrent bouts of high inflation together with erratic growth and periods of economic and financial crisis. Since the mid-

1990s, however, inflation rates in virtually all of Latin America have come down dramatically, to the single digits in most cases.

THE ROOTS OF LATIN AMERICAN INFLATION
For those of us here in the United States, acclimated as we have become to price stability, the severity of inflation in many Latin American countries in recent decades may be difficult to comprehend. A measure of price changes in nine of the most populous Latin American countries shows that inflation in the region averaged nearly 160 percent per year in the 1980s and 235 percent per year in the first half of the 1990s. Indeed, high inflation morphed into hyperinflation—conventionally defined as inflation exceeding 50 percent *per month* (Cagan, 1956)—in a number of Latin countries during the latter part of the 1980s and in the early 1990s. Brazil's inflation rate, for example, exceeded 1,000 percent per year in four of the five years between 1989 and 1993. Other Latin American countries suffering hyperinflations at about that time included Argentina, Bolivia, Nicaragua, and Peru. A particularly striking aspect of this poor inflation performance is that it occurred while most of the rest of the world was reducing inflation to low levels.

Inflation in the region began to moderate in the mid-1990s, however. Inflation in nine major countries—which, as already noted, averaged nearly

235 percent per year in the first half of the 1990s—averaged only 13 percent per year in 1995-99 and less than 8 percent in 2000-04 despite the spike in Argentine inflation that followed that country's crisis in 2002. Why was inflation a perennial problem in Latin America until about 10 years ago, and what explains the recent improvement? Fundamentally, in my view, inflation trends are driven by ideas and politics, which in turn influence economic institutions and economic policies.

In the realm of ideas, the current consensus among economists [is] that money growth generated by fiscal deficits is the driving force behind virtually all episodes of very high inflation.

RATIONAL EXPECTATIONS

In previous chapters, we stressed households' and firms' expectations about the future. A firm's decision to build a new plant depends on its expectations of future sales. The amount of saving a household undertakes today depends on its expectations about future interest rates, wages, and prices.

How are expectations formed? Do people assume things will continue as they are at present (like predicting rain tomorrow because it is raining today)? What information do people use to make their guesses about the future? Questions like these have become central to current macroeconomic thinking and research. One theory, the **rational-expectations hypothesis**, offers a powerful way of thinking about expectations.

rational-expectations hypothesis The hypothesis that people know the "true model" of the economy and that they use this model to form their expectations of the future.

Even though uncertainty exists, if you know the "model" generating the uncertainty, it is possible to have expectations about the future that are "on average" correct. You do not know whether a random coin toss will come up heads or tails. You do know that if you toss a fair coin 100 times, it will come up heads about 50 times.

Suppose we want to forecast inflation. What does it mean to say that my expectations of inflation are "rational"? The rational-expectations hypothesis assumes people know the "true model" that generates inflation—they know how inflation is determined in the economy—and they use this model to forecast future inflation rates. If there were no random, unpredictable events in the economy, and if people knew the true model generating inflation, their forecasts of future inflation rates would be perfect. Because it is true, the model would not permit mistakes, and thus the people using it would not make mistakes.

However, many events that affect the inflation rate are not predictable—they are random. By "true" model, we mean a model that is *on average* correct in forecasting inflation. Sometimes the random events have a positive effect on inflation, which means the model underestimates the inflation rate, and sometimes they have a negative effect, which means the model overestimates the inflation rate. On average, the model is correct. Therefore, rational expectations are correct on average, even though their predictions are not exactly right all the time.

To see why, suppose you have to forecast how many times a fair coin will come up heads out of 100 tosses. The true model in this case is that the coin has a 50–50 chance of coming up heads on any one toss. Because the outcome of the 100 tosses is random, you cannot be sure of guessing correctly. If you know the true model—that the coin is fair—your rational expectation of the outcome of 100 tosses is 50 heads. You are not likely to be exactly right—the actual number of heads is likely to be slightly higher or slightly lower than 50—but *on average* you will be correct.

Sometimes people are said to have rational expectations if they use "all available information" in forming their expectations. This definition is vague, because it is not always clear what "all available information" means. The definition is precise if by "all available information" we mean that people know and use the true model. We cannot have more or better information than the true model.

If information can be obtained at no cost, then people are not behaving rationally if they fail to use all available information. Because there are almost always costs to making a wrong forecast, it is not rational to overlook information that could help improve the accuracy of a forecast as long as the costs of acquiring that information do not outweigh the benefits of improving its accuracy.

Rational Expectations and Market Clearing If firms have rational expectations and if they set prices and wages on this basis, then, on average, prices and wages will be set at levels that ensure equilibrium in the goods and labor markets. When a firm has rational expectations, it knows the demand curve for its output and the supply curve of labor that it faces, except when random shocks disrupt those curves. Therefore, on average the firm will set the market-clearing prices and wages. The firm knows the true model, and it will not set wages different from those it expects will attract the number of workers it wants. If all firms behave this way, then wages will be set in such a way that the total amount of labor supplied will, on average, be equal to the total amount of labor that firms demand. In other words, on average there will be no unemployment.

In Chapter 27, we argued that there might be disequilibrium in the labor market (in the form of either unemployment or excess demand for workers) because firms may make mistakes in their wage-setting behavior due to expectation errors. If, on average, firms do not make errors, then, on average, there is equilibrium. When expectations are rational, disequilibrium exists only temporarily as a result of random, unpredictable shocks—obviously an important conclusion. If true, it means disequilibrium in any market is only temporary, because firms, on average, set market-clearing wages and prices.

The assumption that expectations are rational radically changes the way we can view the economy. We go from a world in which unemployment can exist for substantial periods and the multiplier can operate to a world in which (on average) all markets clear and there is full employment. In this world there is no need for government stabilization policies. Unemployment is not a problem that governments need to worry about; if it exists at all, it is because of unpredictable shocks that, on average, amount to zero. There is no more reason for the government to try to change the outcome in the labor market than there is for it to change the outcome in the banana market. On average, prices and wages are set at market-clearing levels.

The Lucas Supply Function The **Lucas supply function**, after Robert E. Lucas of the University of Chicago, is an important part of a number of new classical macroeconomic theories. It yields, as we shall see, a surprising policy conclusion. The function is deceptively simple. It says real output (Y) depends on (is a function of) the difference between the actual price level (P) and the expected price level (P^e):

Lucas supply function The supply function embodies the idea that output (Y) depends on the difference between the actual price level and the expected price level.

$$Y = f(P - P^e)$$

The actual price level minus the expected price level ($P - P^e$) is the **price surprise**. Before considering the policy implications of this function, we should look at the theory behind it.

price surprise Actual price level minus expected price level.

Lucas begins by assuming people and firms are specialists in production but generalists in consumption. If someone you know is a manual laborer, the chances are she sells only one thing—labor. If she is a lawyer, she sells only legal services. In contrast, people buy a large bundle of goods—ranging from gasoline to ice cream and pretzels—on a regular basis. The same is true for firms. Most companies tend to concentrate on producing a small range of products, but they typically buy a larger range of inputs—raw materials, labor, energy, and capital. According to Lucas, this divergence between buying and selling creates an asymmetry. People know much more about the prices of the things they sell than they do about the prices of the things they buy.[4]

At the beginning of each period, a firm has some expectation of the average price level for that period. If the actual price level turns out to be different, there is a price surprise. Suppose the average price level is higher than expected. Because the firm learns about the actual price level slowly, some time goes by before it realizes all prices have gone up. The firm *does* learn *quickly* that the price of its *output* has gone up. The firm perceives—incorrectly, it turns out—that its price has risen relative to other prices, and this perception leads it to produce more output.

A similar argument holds for workers. When there is a positive price surprise, workers at first believe their "price"—their wage rate—has increased relative to other prices. Workers believe their real wage rate has risen. We know from theory that an increase in the real wage is likely to encourage workers to work more hours.[5] The real wage has not actually risen, but it takes workers a while to figure this out. In the meantime, they supply more hours of work than they would have. This increase means the economy will produce more output when prices are unexpectedly higher than when prices are at their expected level.

This is the rationale for the Lucas supply function. Unexpected increases in the price level can fool workers and firms into thinking relative prices have changed, causing them to alter the amount of labor or goods they choose to supply.

Policy Implications of the Lucas Supply Function The Lucas supply function in combination with the assumption that expectations are rational implies that anticipated policy changes have no effect on real output. Consider a change in monetary policy. In general, the change will have some effect on the average price level. If the policy change is announced to the public, then people know what the effect on the price level will be, because they have rational expectations (and know the way changes in monetary policy affect the price level). This means the change in monetary policy affects both the actual price level and the expected price level in the same way. The new price level minus the new expected price level is zero—no price surprise. In such a case, there will be no change in real output, because the Lucas supply function states that real output can change from its fixed level only if there is a price surprise.

The general conclusion is that *any* announced policy change—in fiscal policy or any other policy—has no effect on real output, because the policy change affects both actual and expected price levels in the same way. If people have rational expectations, known policy changes can produce no price surprises—and no increases in real output. The only way any change in government policy can affect real output is if it is kept in the dark so it is not generally known. Government policy can affect real output only if it surprises people; otherwise,

---

[4]It is not entirely obvious why this should be true, and some critics of the new classical school have argued that this is unrealistic. Some have also criticized the Lucas supply function as too simple, arguing that other things besides price surprises affect aggregate output.

[5]This is true if we assume that the substitution effect dominates the income effect (see Chapter 30).

it cannot. Rational-expectations theory combined with the Lucas supply function proposes a very small role for government policy in the economy.

EVALUATING RATIONAL-EXPECTATIONS THEORY

What are we to make of all this? It should be clear that the key question concerning the new classical macroeconomics is how realistic is the assumption of rational expectations. If it approximates the way expectations are actually formed, then it calls into question any theory that relies at least in part on expectation errors for the existence of disequilibrium. The arguments in favor of the rational-expectations assumption sound persuasive from the perspective of microeconomic theory. If expectations are not rational, there are likely to be unexploited profit opportunities—most economists believe such opportunities are rare and short-lived.

The argument *against* rational expectations is that it requires households and firms to know too much. This argument says it is unrealistic to think these basic decision-making units know as much as they need to know to form rational expectations. People must know the true model (or at least a good approximation of the true model) to form rational expectations, and this knowledge is a lot to expect. Even if firms and households are capable of learning the true model, it may be costly to take the time and gather the relevant information to learn it. The gain from learning the true model (or a good approximation of it) may not be worth the cost. In this sense, there may not be unexploited profit opportunities around. Gathering information and learning economic models may be too costly to bother with, given the expected gain from improving forecasts.

Although the assumption that expectations are rational seems consistent with the satisfaction-maximizing and profit-maximizing postulates of microeconomics, the rational-expectations assumption is more extreme and demanding because it requires more information on the part of households and firms. Consider a firm engaged in maximizing profits. In some way or other, it forms expectations of the relevant future variables, and given these expectations, it figures out the best thing to do from the point of view of maximizing profits. Given a set of expectations, the problem of maximizing profits may not be too hard. What may be hard is forming accurate expectations in the first place. This requires firms to know much more about the overall economy than they are likely to, so the assumption that their expectations are rational is not necessarily realistic. Firms, like the rest of us—so the argument goes—grope around in a world that is difficult to understand, trying to do their best but not always understanding enough to avoid mistakes.

In the final analysis, the issue is empirical. Does the assumption of rational expectations stand up well against empirical tests? This question is difficult to answer. Much work is currently being done to answer it. There are no conclusive results yet, but it is one of the questions that makes macroeconomics an exciting area of research.

REAL BUSINESS CYCLE THEORY

real business cycle theory An attempt to explain business cycle fluctuations under the assumptions of complete price and wage flexibility and rational expectations. It emphasizes shocks to technology and other shocks.

Recent work in new classical macroeconomics has been concerned with whether the existence of business cycles can be explained under the assumptions of complete price and wage flexibility (market clearing) and rational expectations. This work is called **real business cycle theory**. As we discussed in Chapter 26, if prices and wages are completely flexible, then the *AS* curve is vertical, even in the short run. If the *AS* curve is vertical, then events or phenomena that shift the *AD* curve (such as changes in the money supply, changes in government spending, and shocks to consumer and investor behavior) have no effect on real output. Real output does fluctuate over time, so the puzzle is how these fluctuations can be explained if they are not due to policy changes or other shocks that shift the *AD* curve. Solving this puzzle is one of the main missions of real business cycle theory.

It is clear that if shifts of the *AD* curve cannot account for real output fluctuations (because the *AS* curve is vertical), then shifts of the *AS* curve must be responsible. However, the task is to come up with convincing explanations as to what causes these shifts and why they persist over a number of periods. The problem is particularly difficult when it comes to the labor market. If prices and wages are completely flexible, then there is never any unemployment aside from frictional unemployment. For example, because the measured U.S.

unemployment rate was 9.7 percent in 1982 and 4.2 percent in 1999, the puzzle is to explain why so many more people chose not to work in 1982 than in 1999.

Early real business cycle theorists emphasized shocks to the production technology. Suppose there is a negative shock in a given year that causes the marginal product of labor to decline. This leads to a fall in the real wage, which leads to a decrease in the quantity of labor supplied. People have been led to work less because the negative technology shock has led to a lower return from working. The opposite happens when there is a positive shock: The marginal product of labor rises, the real wage rises, and people choose to work more. This early research was not as successful as some had hoped, because it required what seemed to be unrealistically large shocks to explain the observed movements in labor supply over time.

Since this initial work, different types of shocks have been introduced, and work is actively continuing in this area. To date, fluctuations of some variables, but not all, have been explained fairly well. Some argue that this work is doomed to failure because it is based on the unrealistic assumption of complete price and wage flexibility, whereas others hold more hope. Real business cycle theory is another example of the current state of flux in macroeconomics.

SUPPLY-SIDE ECONOMICS

From our discussion of equilibrium in the goods market, beginning with the simple multiplier in Chapter 21 and continuing through Chapter 26, we have focused primarily on *demand*. Supply increases and decreases in response to changes in aggregate expenditure (which is closely linked to aggregate demand). Fiscal policy works by influencing aggregate expenditure through tax policy and government spending. Monetary policy works by influencing investment and consumption spending through increases and decreases in the interest rate. The theories we have been discussing are "demand oriented."

The 1970s were difficult times for the U.S. economy. The United States found itself in 1974 to 1975 with stagflation—high unemployment and inflation. In the late 1970s, inflation returned to the high levels of 1974 to 1975. It seemed as if policy makers were incapable of controlling the business cycle.

As a result of these seeming failures, orthodox economics came under fire. One assault was from a group of economists who expounded *supply-side economics*. The argument of the supply-siders was simple. Basically, they said, all the attention to demand in orthodox macroeconomic theory distracted our attention from the real problem with the U.S. economy. The real problem, said supply-siders, was that high rates of taxation and heavy regulation had reduced the incentive to work, to save, and to invest. What was needed was not a demand stimulus but better incentives to stimulate *supply*.

If we cut taxes so people take home more of their paychecks, the argument continued, they will work harder and save more. If businesses get to keep more of their profits and can get away from government regulations, they will invest more. This added labor supply and investment, or capital supply, will lead to an expansion of the supply of goods and services, which will reduce inflation and unemployment at the same time. The ultimate solution to the economy's woes, the supply-siders concluded, was on the *supply side* of the economy.

At their most extreme, supply-siders argued that the incentive effects of supply-side policies were likely to be so great that a major cut in tax rates would actually *increase* tax revenues. Even though *tax rates* would be lower, more people would be working and earning income and firms would earn more profits, so that the increases in the *tax bases* (profits, sales, and income) would outweigh the decreases in rates, resulting in increased government revenues.

The Laffer Curve Figure 32.2 presents a key diagram of supply-side economics. The tax rate is measured on the vertical axis, and tax revenue is measured on the horizontal axis. The assumption behind this curve is that there is some tax rate beyond which the supply response is large enough to lead to a decrease in tax revenue for further increases in the tax rate. There is obviously some tax rate between zero and 100 percent at which tax revenue is at a maximum. At a tax rate of zero, work effort is high, but there is no tax revenue. At a tax rate of 100, the labor supply is presumably zero, because people are not allowed to keep any of their income. Somewhere in between zero and 100 is the maximum-revenue rate.

The big debate in the 1980s was whether tax rates in the United States put the country on the upper or lower part of the curve in Figure 32.2. The supply-side school claimed the

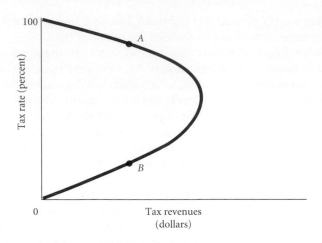

FIGURE 32.2 The Laffer Curve

The Laffer curve shows the amount of revenue the government collects is a function of the tax rate. It shows that when tax rates are very high, an increase in the tax rate could cause tax revenues to fall. Similarly, under the same circumstances, a cut in the tax rate could generate enough additional economic activity to cause revenues to rise.

Laffer Curve With the tax rate measured on the vertical axis and tax revenue measured on the horizontal axis, the Laffer curve shows there is some tax rate beyond which the supply response is large enough to lead to a decrease in tax revenue for further increases in the tax rate.

United States was around *A* and taxes should be cut. Others argued that the United States was nearer *B* and tax cuts would lead to lower tax revenue.

The diagram in Figure 32.2 is the **Laffer Curve**, after economist Arthur Laffer, who, legend has it, first drew it on the back of a napkin at a cocktail party. The Laffer curve had some influence on the passage of the Economic Recovery Tax Act of 1981, the tax package put forward by the Reagan administration that brought with it substantial cuts in both personal and business taxes. The individual income tax was to be cut 25 percent over 3 years. Corporate taxes were cut sharply in a way designed to stimulate capital investment. The new law allowed firms to depreciate their capital at a rapid rate for tax purposes, and the bigger deductions led to taxes that were significantly lower than before.

EVALUATING SUPPLY-SIDE ECONOMICS

Supporters of supply-side economics claim that Reagan's tax policies were successful in stimulating the economy. They point to the fact that almost immediately after the tax cuts of 1981 were put into place, the economy expanded and the recession of 1980 to 1982 came to an end. In addition, inflation rates fell sharply from the high rates of 1980 and 1981. Except for 1 year, federal receipts continued to rise throughout the 1980s despite the cut in tax rates.

Critics of supply-side policies do not dispute these facts but offer an alternative explanation of how the economy recovered. The Reagan tax cuts were enacted just as the U.S. economy was in the middle of its deepest recession since the Great Depression. The unemployment rate stood at 10.8 percent in the fourth quarter of 1982. It was the recession, critics argue, that was responsible for the reduction in inflation—not the supply-side policies. Also among the criticisms of supply-side economics is that it is unlikely a tax cut would substantially increase the supply of labor. In addition, in theory, a tax cut could even lead to a *reduction* in labor supply. Recall our discussion of income and substitution effects in Chapter 30. Although it is true a higher after-tax wage rate provides a higher reward for each hour of work and thus more incentive to work, a tax cut also means households receive a higher income for a given number of hours of work. Because they can earn the same amount of money working fewer hours, households might actually choose to work *less*. They might spend some of their added income on leisure. Research done during the 1980s suggests tax cuts seem to increase the supply of labor somewhat but the increases are very modest.

What about the recovery from the recession? Why did real output begin to grow rapidly in late 1982, precisely when the supply-side tax cuts were taking effect? Two reasons have been suggested. First, the supply-side tax cuts had large *demand*-side effects that stimulated the economy. Second, the Fed pumped up the money supply and drove interest rates down at the same time that the tax cuts were being put into effect. The money supply expanded about 20 percent between 1981 and 1983, and interest rates succumbed. In 1981, the average 3-month U.S. Treasury bill paid 14 percent interest. In 1983, the figure had dropped to 8.6 percent.

Certainly, traditional theory suggests that a huge tax cut will lead to an increase in disposable income and, in turn, an increase in consumption spending (a component of aggregate expenditure). In addition, although an increase in planned investment (brought about by a lower interest rate) leads to added productive capacity and added supply in the long run, it also increases expenditures on capital goods (new plant and equipment investment) in the short run.

Whether the recovery from the 1981–1982 recession was the result of supply-side expansion or supply-side policies that had demand-side effects, one thing is clear: The extreme promises of the supply-siders did not materialize. President Reagan argued that because of the effect depicted in the Laffer curve, the government could maintain expenditures (and even increase defense expenditures sharply), cut tax rates, *and* balance the budget. This was not the case. Government revenues fell sharply from levels that would have been realized without the tax cuts. After 1982, the federal government ran huge deficits, with nearly $2 trillion added to the national debt between 1983 and 1992.

TESTING ALTERNATIVE MACROECONOMIC MODELS

You may wonder why there is so much disagreement in macroeconomics. Why cannot macroeconomists test their models against one another and see which performs best?

One problem is that macroeconomic models differ in ways that are hard to standardize. If one model takes the price level to be given, or not explained within the model, and another one does not, the model with the given price level may do better in, for instance, predicting output—not because it is a better model but simply because the errors in predicting prices have not been allowed to affect the predictions of output. The model that takes prices as given has a head start, so to speak.

Another problem arises in the testing of the rational-expectations assumption. Remember, if people have rational expectations, they are using the true model to form their expectations. Therefore, to test this assumption we need the true model. There is no way to be sure that whatever model is taken to be the true model is in fact the true one. Any test of the rational-expectations hypothesis is therefore a *joint* test (1) that expectations are formed rationally and (2) that the model being used is the true one. If the test rejects the hypothesis, it may be that the model is wrong rather than that the expectations are not rational.

Another problem for macroeconomists is the small amount of data available. Most empirical work uses data beginning in about 1950, which in 2005 was about 56 years' (224 quarters) worth of data. Although this may seem like a lot of data, it is not. Macroeconomic data are fairly "smooth," which means a typical variable does not vary much from quarter to quarter or year to year. For example, the number of business cycles within this 56-year period is small, about eight. Testing various macroeconomic hypotheses on the basis of seven business cycle observations is not easy, and any conclusions must be interpreted with caution.

To give an example of the problem of a small number of observations, consider trying to test the hypothesis that import prices affect domestic prices. Import prices changed very little in the 1950s and 1960s. Therefore, it would have been very difficult at the end of the 1960s to estimate the effect of import prices on domestic prices. The variation in import prices was not great enough to show any effects. We cannot demonstrate that changes in import prices help explain changes in domestic prices if import prices do not change. The situation was different by the end of the 1970s, because by then import prices had varied considerably. By the end of the 1970s, there were good estimates of the import price effect, but not before. This kind of problem is encountered again and again in empirical macroeconomics. In many cases there are not enough observations for much to be said, and hence there is considerable room for disagreement.

We said in Chapter 1 that it is difficult in economics to perform controlled experiments. Economists are for the most part at the mercy of the historical data. If we were able to perform experiments, we could probably learn more about the economy in a shorter time. Alas, we must wait. In time, the current range of disagreements in macroeconomics should be considerably narrowed.

SUMMARY

KEYNESIAN ECONOMICS

1. In a broad sense, Keynesian economics is the foundation of modern macroeconomics. In a narrower sense, *Keynesian* refers to economists who advocate active government intervention in the economy.

MONETARISM

2. The monetarist analysis of the economy places a great deal of emphasis on the *velocity of money*, which is defined as the number of times a dollar bill changes hands, on average, during the course of a year. The velocity of money is the ratio of nominal GDP to the stock of money, or $V \equiv GDP/M \equiv (P \times Y)/M$. Alternately, $M \times V \equiv P \times Y$.

3. The *quantity theory of money* assumes that velocity is constant (or virtually constant). This implies that changes in the supply of money will lead to equal percentage changes in nominal GDP. The quantity theory of money equation is $M \times \overline{V} = P \times Y$. The equation says demand for money does not depend on the interest rate.

4. Most economists believe sustained inflation is a purely monetary phenomenon. Inflation cannot continue indefinitely unless the Fed "accommodates" it by expanding the money supply.

5. Most monetarists blame most of the instability in the economy on the federal government and are skeptical of the government's ability to manage the macroeconomy. They argue that the money supply should grow at a rate equal to the average growth of real output (income) (Y)— the Fed should expand the money supply to accommodate real growth but not inflation.

NEW CLASSICAL MACROECONOMICS

6. The *new classical macroeconomics* has developed from two different but related sources: the theoretical and the empirical critiques of traditional macroeconomics. On the theoretical level, there has been growing dissatisfaction with the way traditional models treat expectations. On the empirical level, the stagflation in the U.S. economy during the 1970s caused

many people to look for alternative theories to explain the breakdown of the Phillips Curve.

7. The *rational-expectations hypothesis* assumes people know the "true model" that generates economic variables. For example, rational expectations assumes that people know how inflation is determined in the economy and use this model to forecast future inflation rates.

8. The *Lucas supply function* assumes that real output (Y) depends on the actual price level minus the expected price level, or the *price surprise*. This function combined with the assumption that expectations are rational implies that anticipated policy changes have no effect on real output.

9. *Real business cycle theory* is an attempt to explain business cycle fluctuations under the assumptions of complete price and wage flexibility and rational expectations. It emphasizes shocks to technology and other shocks.

SUPPLY-SIDE ECONOMICS

10. *Supply-side economics* focuses on incentives to stimulate supply. Supply-side economists believe that if we lower taxes, workers will work harder and save more and firms will invest more and produce more. At their most extreme, supply-siders argue that incentive effects are likely to be so great that a major cut in taxes will actually increase tax revenues.

11. The *Laffer Curve* shows the relationship between tax rates and tax revenues. Supply-side economists use it to argue that it is possible to generate higher revenues by cutting tax rates, but evidence does not appear to support this effect. The lower tax rates of the Reagan administration decreased tax revenues significantly and contributed to the massive increase in the federal debt during the 1980s.

TESTING ALTERNATIVE MACROECONOMIC MODELS

12. Economists disagree about which macroeconomic model is best for several reasons: (1) Macroeconomic models differ in ways that are hard to standardize; (2) when testing the rational-expectations assumption, we are never sure that whatever model is taken to be the true model is the true one; (3) the amount of data available is fairly small.

REVIEW TERMS AND CONCEPTS

Laffer Curve, 694

Lucas supply function, 691

price surprise, 691

quantity theory of money, 685

rational-expectations hypothesis, 689

real business cycle theory, 692

velocity of money (V), 684

$$V \equiv \frac{GDP}{M}$$

$$M \times V \equiv P \times Y$$

$$M \times \overline{V} = P \times Y$$

PROBLEM SET

1. The table gives estimates of the rate of money supply growth and the rate of real GDP growth for five countries in 2000:

	RATE OF GROWTH IN MONEY SUPPLY (M1)	RATE OF GROWTH OF REAL GDP
Australia	+ 9.3	+4.4
Britain	+ 7.6	+4.4
Canada	+18.7	+4.9
Japan	+ 9.0	+0.7
United States	+ 0.2	+5.1

   a. If you were a monetarist, what would you predict about the rate of inflation across the five countries?

   b. If you were a Keynesian, and assuming activist central banks, how might you interpret the same data?

2. The three diagrams in Figure 1 represent in a simplified way the predictions of the three theories presented in this chapter about the likely effects of a major tax cut.

   a. Match each of the following theories with a graph:
   (1) Keynesian economics, (2) supply-side economics, (3) rational expectations/monetarism. Explain the logic behind the three graphs.

   b. Which theory do you find the most convincing? Explain.

3. The remarks by Fed chair Ben Bernanke in early 2005 in the box on page 689 describe the experience of several Latin American countries with rapid inflation. Go online and search for data on current inflation rates for Brazil, Mexico, Peru, Chile, and several other South or Central American countries. Which have maintained relative price stability and which have not? Can you offer or find any explanation for the performance of those countries with low inflation? Those with high inflation?

4. In 2000, a well-known economist was heard to say, "The problem with supply-side economics is that when you cut taxes, they have both supply and demand side effects and you cannot separate them." Explain this comment. Be specific and use either the 1997 tax cuts or the Reagan tax cuts of 1981 as an example.

5. A cornerstone of new classical economics is the notion that expectations are "rational." What do you think will happen to the prices of single-family homes in your community over the next several years? On what do you base your expectations? Is your thinking consistent with the notion of rational expectations? Explain.

6. You are a monetarist given the following information. The money supply is $1,000. The velocity of money is 5. What is nominal income? Real income? What happens to nominal income if the money supply is doubled? What happens to real income?

7. When Bill Clinton took office in January 1993, he faced two major economic problems: a large federal budget deficit and high unemployment resulting from a very slow recovery from the recession of 1990 to 1991. In his first State of the Union message, the president called for spending cuts and substantial tax increases to reduce the deficit. Most of these proposed spending cuts were in the defense budget. The following day, Alan Greenspan, chair of the Federal Reserve Board of Governors, signaled his support for the president's plan. Many elements of the president's original plan were later incorporated into the deficit reduction bill passed in 1993.

   a. Some said at the time that without the Fed's support, the Clinton plan would be a disaster. Explain this argument.

   b. Supply-side economists and monetarists were very worried about the plan and the support it received from the Fed. What specific problems might a monetarist, and a supply-side economist worry about?

   c. Suppose you were hired by the Federal Reserve Bank of St. Louis to report on the events of 1995 and 1996. What specific evidence would you look for to see if the Clinton plan was effective or whether the critics were right to be skeptical?

8. "In an economy with reasonably flexible prices and wages, full employment is almost always maintained." Explain why this is true.

9. During the 1980 presidential campaign, Ronald Reagan promised to cut taxes, increase expenditures on national defense, and balance the budget. During the New Hampshire primary of 1980, George Bush called this policy "voodoo economics." The two men were arguing about the relative merits of supply-side economics. Explain their disagreement.

I.

II.

III.

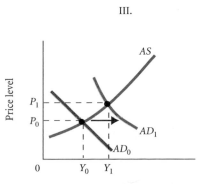

FIGURE 1

*10. In a hypothetical economy there is a simple proportional tax on wages imposed at a rate t. There are plenty of jobs around, so if people enter the labor force they can find work. We define total government receipts from the tax as

$$T = t \times W \times L$$

where t = the tax rate, W = the gross wage rate, and L = the total supply of labor. The net wage rate is

$$W_n = (1 - t)W$$

The elasticity of labor supply is defined as

$$\frac{\text{percentage of change in } L}{\text{percentage of change in } W_n} = \frac{\Delta L / \Delta L}{\Delta W_n / W_n}$$

Suppose t were cut from .25 to .20. For such a cut to *increase* total government receipts from the tax, how elastic must the supply of labor be? (Assume a constant gross wage.) What does your answer imply about the supply-side assertion that a cut in taxes can increase tax revenues?

---

*Note: Problems marked with an asterisk are more challenging.

International Trade, Comparative Advantage, and Protectionism

33

Over the last 35 years, international transactions have become increasingly important to the U.S. economy. In 1970, imports represented only about 7 percent of U.S. gross domestic product (GDP). The share is now around 16 percent. In 2004, the United States imported more than $147 billion worth of goods and services each month.

The "internationalization" or "globalization" of the U.S. economy has occurred in the private and public sectors, in input and output markets, and in business firms and households. Once uncommon, foreign products are now everywhere, from the utensils we eat with to the cars we drive. In 1970, foreign-produced cars made up only a small percentage of all the cars in the United States. At that time, it was difficult to find mechanics who knew how to repair foreign cars, and replacement parts were hard to obtain. Today the roads are full of Toyotas and Nissans from Japan, Volvos from Sweden, and BMWs from Germany, and any service station that cannot repair foreign-produced automobiles probably will not get much business. Half of all the cars and 80 percent of all the consumer electronics (computers, televisions, CD players, and so forth) that U.S. consumers buy are produced abroad.

At the same time, the United States exports billions of dollars' worth of agricultural goods, aircraft, and industrial machinery. In addition, the United States exports and imports large quantities of services. When a Pakistani student enrolls in an American college or university, or a sick woman from Korea seeks medical attention in a U.S. hospital, or a Kenyan hires a lawyer in Miami to help him with a real estate deal, or a tourist from Indonesia eats at a restaurant in New York City, the United States is exporting a service. Similarly, when a student from the United States takes her junior year abroad in Scotland, or a tourist stays in a hotel in Singapore or gets a massage at a spa in Jamaica, the United States is importing a service.

In addition to the fact that goods and services (outputs) flow easily across borders, so too do inputs: capital and labor. Certainly, it is very easy to buy financial assets abroad. Millions of Americans own shares in foreign stocks or have invested in bonds issued by foreign countries. At the same time, millions of foreigners have put money into the U.S. stock and bond markets.

A new phenomenon, outsourcing, is also changing the nature of the global labor market. It is now simple and very common for a customer service call to a software company from a user of its product in Bend, Oregon, to be routed to Bangalore, India, where a young,

TABLE 33.1
U.S. Balance of Trade (Exports Minus Imports), 1929–2004 (Billions of Dollars)

	EXPORTS MINUS IMPORTS
1929	+0.4
1933	+0.1
1945	−0.8
1955	+0.5
1960	+4.2
1965	+5.6
1970	+4.0
1975	+16.0
1976	−1.6
1977	−23.1
1978	−25.4
1979	−22.5
1980	−13.1
1981	−12.5
1982	−20.0
1983	−51.7
1984	−102.7
1985	−115.2
1986	−132.7
1987	−145.2
1988	−110.4
1989	−88.2
1990	−78.0
1991	−27.5
1992	−33.2
1993	−65.0
1994	−93.6
1995	−91.4
1996	−96.2
1997	−101.6
1998	−159.9
1999	−260.5
2000	−379.5
2001	−367.0
2002	−424.4
2003	−500.9
2004	−624.0

Source: U.S. Department of Commerce, Bureau of Economic Analysis.

trade surplus The situation when a country exports more than it imports.

trade deficit The situation when a country imports more than it exports.

Corn Laws The tariffs, subsidies, and restrictions enacted by the British Parliament in the early nineteenth century to discourage imports and encourage exports of grain.

ambitious Indian man provides assistance to a customer over the Internet. The Internet has in essence made it possible for labor to flow smoothly across international borders.

The inextricable connection of the U.S. economy to the economies of the rest of the world has had a profound impact on the discipline of economics and is the basis of one of its most important insights:

> All economies, regardless of their size, depend to some extent on other economies and are affected by events outside their borders.

To get you more acquainted with the international economy, this chapter discusses the economics of international trade. First, we describe the recent tendency of the United States to import more than it exports. Next, we explore the basic logic of trade. Why should the United States or any other country engage in international trade? Finally, we address the controversial issue of protectionism. Should a country provide certain industries with protection in the form of import quotas or tariffs, which are taxes imposed on imports? Should a country help a domestic industry compete in international markets by providing subsidies?

TRADE SURPLUSES AND DEFICITS

Until the 1970s, the United States generally exported more than it imported. When a country exports more than it imports, it runs a **trade surplus**. When a country imports more than it exports, it runs a **trade deficit**. Table 33.1 shows that before 1976 the United States generally ran a trade surplus. This changed in 1976, and since 1976 the United States has run a trade deficit. The deficit reached a local peak of $145.2 billion in 1987, fell to $27.5 billion in 1991, and then rose dramatically to over $600 billion by 2004.

The large trade deficits in the middle and late 1980s touched off political controversy that continues today. Foreign competition hit U.S. markets hard. Less expensive foreign goods—among them steel, textiles, and automobiles—began driving U.S. manufacturers out of business, and thousands of jobs were lost in important industries. Cities such as Pittsburgh, Youngstown, and Detroit had major unemployment problems.

The natural reaction was to call for protection of U.S. industries. Many people wanted the president and Congress to impose taxes and import restrictions that would make foreign goods less available and more expensive, protecting U.S. jobs. This argument was not new. For hundreds of years, industries have petitioned governments for protection, and societies have debated the pros and cons of free and open trade. For the last century and a half, the principal argument against protection has been the theory of comparative advantage, first discussed in Chapter 2.

THE ECONOMIC BASIS FOR TRADE: COMPARATIVE ADVANTAGE

Perhaps the best-known debate on the issue of free trade took place in the British Parliament during the early years of the nineteenth century. At that time, the landed gentry—the landowners—controlled Parliament. For a number of years, imports and exports of grain had been subject to a set of tariffs, subsidies, and restrictions collectively called the **Corn Laws**. Designed to discourage imports of grain and to encourage exports, the Corn Laws' purpose was to keep the price of food high. The landlords' incomes, of course, depended on the prices they got for what their land produced. The Corn Laws clearly worked to the advantage of those in power.

With the Industrial Revolution, a class of wealthy industrial capitalists emerged. The industrial sector had to pay workers at least enough to live on, and a living wage depended greatly on the price of food. Tariffs on grain imports and export subsidies that kept grain and food prices high increased the wages that capitalists had to pay, cutting into their profits. The political battle raged for years. However, as time went by, the power of the landowners in the House of Lords was significantly reduced. When the conflict ended in 1848, the Corn Laws were repealed.

On the side of repeal was David Ricardo, a businessman, economist, member of Parliament, and one of the fathers of modern economics. Ricardo's principal work, *Principles of Political Economy and Taxation*, was published in 1817, 2 years before he entered Parliament. Ricardo's **theory of comparative advantage**, which he used to argue against the Corn Laws, claimed that trade enables countries to specialize in producing the products they produce best. According to the theory:

> Specialization and free trade will benefit all trading partners (real wages will rise), even those that may be absolutely less efficient producers.

theory of comparative advantage Ricardo's theory that specialization and free trade will benefit all trading partners (real wages will rise), even those that may be absolutely less efficient producers.

This basic argument remains at the heart of free-trade debates even today. It was invoked numerous times by presidents Reagan and Bush as they wrestled with Congress over various pieces of protectionist legislation.

Specialization and Trade: The Two-Person Case The easiest way to understand the theory of comparative advantage is to examine a simple two-person society. Suppose Bill and Colleen, stranded on a deserted island in Chapter 2, have only two tasks to accomplish each week: gathering food to eat and cutting logs to construct a house. If Colleen could cut more logs than Bill in a day and Bill could gather more berries and fruits, specialization would clearly benefit both of them.

But suppose Bill is slow and clumsy and Colleen is better at both cutting logs *and* gathering food. Ricardo's point is that it still pays for them to specialize. They can produce more in total by specializing than they can by sharing the work equally. (It may be helpful to review the discussion of comparative advantage in Chapter 2 before proceeding.)

ABSOLUTE ADVANTAGE VERSUS COMPARATIVE ADVANTAGE

A country enjoys an **absolute advantage** over another country in the production of a product if it uses fewer resources to produce that product than the other country does. Suppose country A and country B produce wheat, but A's climate is more suited to wheat and its labor is more productive. Country A will produce more wheat per acre than country B and use less labor in growing it and bringing it to market. Country A enjoys an absolute advantage over country B in the production of wheat.

A country enjoys a **comparative advantage** in the production of a good if that good can be produced at lower cost *in terms of other goods*. Suppose countries C and D both produce wheat and corn and C enjoys an absolute advantage in the production of both—that is, C's climate is better than D's, and fewer of C's resources are needed to produce a given quantity of both wheat and corn. Now C and D must each choose between planting land with either wheat or corn. To produce more wheat, either country must transfer land from corn production; to produce more corn, either country must transfer land from wheat production. The cost of wheat in each country can be measured in bushels of corn, and the cost of corn can be measured in bushels of wheat.

Suppose that in country C, a bushel of wheat has an opportunity cost of 2 bushels of corn. That is, to produce an additional bushel of wheat, C must give up 2 bushels of corn. At the same time, producing a bushel of wheat in country D requires the sacrifice of only 1 bushel of corn. Even though C has an *absolute* advantage in the production of both products, D enjoys a *comparative* advantage in the production of wheat because the *opportunity cost* of producing wheat is lower in D. Under these circumstances, Ricardo claims, D can benefit from trade if it specializes in the production of wheat.

absolute advantage The advantage in the production of a product enjoyed by one country over another when it uses fewer resources to produce that product than the other country does.

comparative advantage The advantage in the production of a product enjoyed by one country over another when that product can be produced at lower cost in terms of other goods than it could be in the other country.

Gains from Mutual Absolute Advantage To illustrate Ricardo's logic in more detail, suppose Australia and New Zealand each have a fixed amount of land and do not trade with the rest of the world. There are only two goods—wheat, to produce bread, and cotton, to produce clothing. This kind of two-country/two-good world does not exist, but its operations can be generalized to many countries and many goods.

To proceed, we have to make some assumptions about the preferences of the people living in New Zealand and the people living in Australia. If the citizens of both countries go

TABLE 33.2 Yield Per Acre of Wheat and Cotton

	NEW ZEALAND	AUSTRALIA
Wheat	6 bushels	2 bushels
Cotton	2 bales	6 bales

around naked, there is no need to produce cotton; all the land can be used to produce wheat. However, assume that people in both countries have similar preferences with respect to food and clothing: The populations of both countries use both cotton and wheat, and preferences for food and clothing are such that both countries consume equal amounts of wheat and cotton.

Finally, we assume that each country has only 100 acres of land for planting, and land yields are as given in Table 33.2. New Zealand can produce three times the wheat that Australia can on 1 acre of land, and Australia can produce three times the cotton that New Zealand can in the same space. New Zealand has an absolute advantage in the production of wheat, and Australia has an absolute advantage in the production of cotton. In cases like this, we say the two countries have *mutual absolute advantage*.

If there is no trade and each country divides its land to obtain equal units of cotton and wheat production, each country produces 150 bushels of wheat and 150 bales of cotton. New Zealand puts 75 acres into cotton but only 25 acres into wheat, while Australia does the reverse (Table 33.3).

We can organize the same information in graphic form as production possibility frontiers for each country. In Figure 33.1, which presents the positions of the two countries before trade, each country is constrained by its own resources and productivity. If Australia put all its land into cotton, it would produce 600 bales of cotton (100 acres × 6 bales/acre) and no wheat; if it put all its land into wheat, it would produce 200 bushels of wheat (100 acres × 2 bushels/acre) and no cotton. The opposite is true for New Zealand. Recall from Chapter 2 that a country's production possibility frontier represents all combinations of goods that can be produced, given the country's resources and state of technology. Each country must pick a point along its own production possibility curve.

Because both countries have an absolute advantage in the production of one product, specialization and trade will benefit both. Australia should produce cotton, New Zealand should produce wheat. Transferring all land to wheat production in New Zealand yields 600 bushels; transferring all land to cotton production in Australia yields 600 bales. An agreement to trade 300 bushels of wheat for 300 bales of cotton would double both wheat and cotton consumption in both countries. (Remember, before trade both countries produced 150 bushels of wheat and 150 bales of cotton. After trade, each country will have 300 bushels of wheat and 300 bales of cotton to consume. Final production and trade figures are in Table 33.4 and Figure 33.2).

Trade enables both countries to move beyond their previous resource and productivity constraints.

The advantages of specialization and trade seem obvious when one country is technologically superior at producing one product and another country is technologically superior

TABLE 33.3 Total Production of Wheat and Cotton Assuming No Trade, Mutual Absolute Advantage, and 100 Available Acres

	NEW ZEALAND	AUSTRALIA
Wheat	25 acres × 6 bushels/acre 150 bushels	75 acres × 2 bushels/acre 150 bushels
Cotton	75 acres × 2 bales/acre 150 bales	25 acres × 6 bales/acre 150 bales

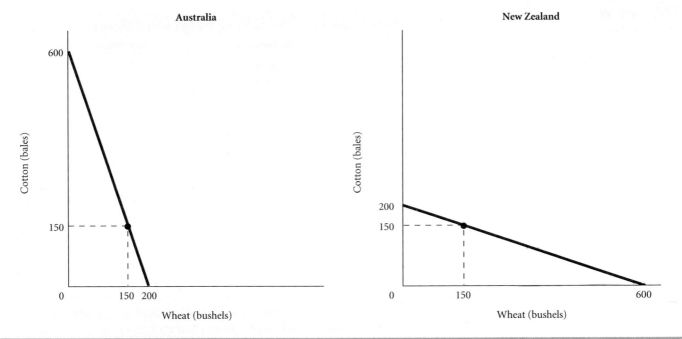

FIGURE 33.1 Production Possibility Frontiers for Australia and New Zealand before Trade

Without trade, countries are constrained by their own resources and productivity.

TABLE 33.4 Production and Consumption of Wheat and Cotton after Specialization

| | PRODUCTION | | | CONSUMPTION | |
	New Zealand	Australia		New Zealand	Australia
Wheat	100 acres × 6 bushels/acre 600 bushels	0 acres 0	Wheat	300 bushels	300 bushels
Cotton	0 acres 0	100 acres × 6 bales/acre 600 bales	Cotton	300 bales	300 bales

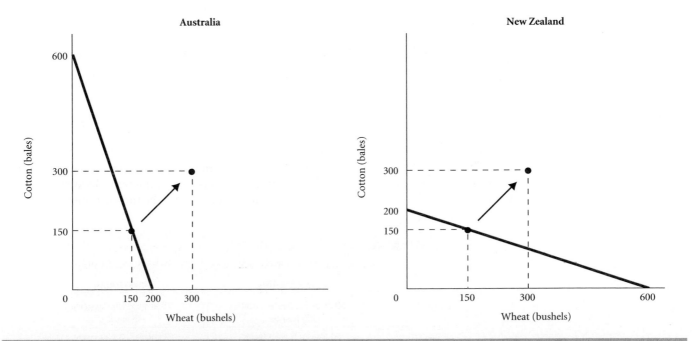

FIGURE 33.2 Expanded Possibilities after Trade

Trade enables both countries to move beyond their own resource constraints—beyond their individual production possibility frontiers.

TABLE 33.5 Yield Per Acre of Wheat and Cotton

	NEW ZEALAND	AUSTRALIA
Wheat	6 bushels	1 bushel
Cotton	6 bales	3 bales

at producing another product. However, let us turn to the case in which one country has an absolute advantage in the production of *both* goods.

Gains from Comparative Advantage
Table 33.5 contains different land yield figures for New Zealand and Australia. Now New Zealand has a considerable absolute advantage in the production of both cotton and wheat, with 1 acre of land yielding six times as much wheat and twice as much cotton as 1 acre in Australia. Ricardo would argue that *specialization and trade are still mutually beneficial.*

Again, preferences imply consumption of equal units of cotton and wheat in both countries. With no trade, New Zealand would divide its 100 available acres evenly, or 50/50, between the two crops. The result would be 300 bales of cotton and 300 bushels of wheat. Australia would divide its land 75/25. Table 33.6 shows that final production in Australia would be 75 bales of cotton and 75 bushels of wheat. (Remember, we are assuming that in each country, people consume equal amounts of cotton and wheat.) Again, before any trade takes place each country is constrained by its own domestic production possibility curve.

Imagine we are at a meeting of trade representatives of both countries. As a special adviser, David Ricardo is asked to demonstrate that trade can benefit both countries. He divides his demonstration into three stages, which you can follow in Table 33.7.

In stage 1, Australia transfers all its land into cotton production. It will have no wheat and 300 bales of cotton. New Zealand cannot completely specialize in wheat because it needs 300 bales of cotton and will not be able to get enough cotton from Australia. The reason is that we are assuming each country wants to consume equal amounts of cotton and wheat.

In stage 2, New Zealand transfers 25 acres out of cotton and into wheat. Now New Zealand has 25 acres in cotton that produce 150 bales and 75 acres in wheat that produce 450 bushels.

Finally, the two countries trade. We assume New Zealand ships 100 bushels of wheat to Australia in exchange for 200 bales of cotton. After the trade, New Zealand has 350 bales of cotton and 350 bushels of wheat; Australia has 100 bales of cotton and 100 bushels of wheat. Both countries are better off than they were before the trade (Table 33.6), and both have moved beyond their own production possibility frontiers.

Why Does Ricardo's Plan Work?
To understand why Ricardo's scheme works, let us return to the definition of comparative advantage.

The real cost of producing cotton is the wheat that must be sacrificed to produce it. *When we think of cost this way, it is less costly to produce cotton in Australia than to produce it in New Zealand, even though an acre of land produces more cotton in New Zealand.* Consider the "cost" of 3 bales of cotton in the two countries. In terms of opportunity cost, 3 bales of cotton in New Zealand cost 3 bushels of wheat; in Australia, 3 bales of cotton cost only 1 bushel of wheat. Because 3 bales are produced by 1 acre of Australian land, to get 3 bales an Australian must transfer 1 acre of land from wheat to cotton production. Because an acre of land produces a bushel of wheat, losing 1 acre to cotton implies the loss of 1 bushel of wheat.

TABLE 33.6 Total Production of Wheat and Cotton Assuming No Trade and 100 Available Acres

	NEW ZEALAND	AUSTRALIA
Wheat	50 acres × 6 bushels/acre 300 bushels	75 acres × 1 bushel/acre 75 bushels
Cotton	50 acres × 6 bales/acre 300 bales	25 acres × 3 bales/acre 75 bales

TABLE 33.7 Realizing a Gain from Trade When One Country Has a Double Absolute Advantage

	STAGE 1			STAGE 2	
	New Zealand	**Australia**		**New Zealand**	**Australia**
Wheat	50 acres × 6 bushels/acre 300 bushels	0 acres 0	Wheat	75 acres × 6 bushels/acre 450 bushels	0 acres 0
Cotton	50 acres × 6 bales/acre 300 bales	100 acres × 3 bales/acre 300 bales	Cotton	25 acres × 6 bales/acre 150 bales	100 acres × 3 bales/acre 300 bales

	STAGE 3	
	New Zealand	**Australia**
	100 bushels (trade)	
	⟶	
Wheat	350 bushels	100 bushels
	(after trade)	
	200 bales (trade)	
	⟵	
Cotton	350 bales	100 bales
	(after trade)	

Australia has a comparative advantage in cotton production because its opportunity cost, in terms of wheat, is lower than New Zealand's. This is illustrated in Figure 33.3.

Conversely, New Zealand has a comparative advantage in wheat production. A unit of wheat in New Zealand costs one unit of cotton; a unit of wheat in Australia costs three units of cotton.

> When countries specialize in producing goods in which they have a comparative advantage, they maximize their combined output and allocate their resources more efficiently.

TERMS OF TRADE

Ricardo might suggest a number of options open to the trading partners. The one we just examined benefited both partners; in percentage terms, Australia made out slightly better. Other deals might have been more advantageous to New Zealand.

The ratio at which a country can trade domestic products for imported products is the **terms of trade**. The terms of trade determine how the gains from trade are distributed

terms of trade The ratio at which a country can trade domestic products for imported products.

FIGURE 33.3 Comparative Advantage Means Lower Opportunity Cost

The real cost of cotton is the wheat sacrificed to obtain it. The cost of 3 bales of cotton in New Zealand is 3 bushels of wheat (a half-acre of land must be transferred from wheat to cotton—refer to Table 33.5). However, the cost of 3 bales of cotton in Australia is only 1 bushel of wheat. Australia has a comparative advantage over New Zealand in cotton production, and New Zealand has a comparative advantage over Australia in wheat production.

among trading partners. In the case just considered, the agreed-to terms of trade were 1 bushel of wheat for 2 bales of cotton. Such terms of trade benefit New Zealand, which can get 2 bales of cotton for each bushel of wheat. If it were to transfer its own land from wheat to cotton, it would get only 1 bale of cotton. The same terms of trade benefit Australia, which can get 1 bushel of wheat for 2 bales of cotton. A direct transfer of its own land would force it to give up 3 bales of cotton for 1 bushel of wheat.

If the terms of trade changed to 3 bales of cotton for every bushel of wheat, only New Zealand would benefit. At those terms of trade *all* the gains from trade would flow to New Zealand. Such terms do not benefit Australia at all because the opportunity cost of producing wheat domestically is *exactly the same* as the trade cost: A bushel of wheat costs 3 bales of cotton. If the terms of trade went the other way—1 bale of cotton for each bushel of wheat—only Australia would benefit. New Zealand gains nothing, because it can already substitute cotton for wheat at that ratio. To get a bushel of wheat domestically, however, Australia must give up 3 bales of cotton, and one-for-one terms of trade would make wheat much less costly for Australia.

Both parties must have something to gain for trade to take place. In this case, you can see that both Australia and New Zealand will gain when the terms of trade are set between 1:1 and 3:1, cotton to wheat.

EXCHANGE RATES

The examples we have used thus far have shown that trade can result in gains to both parties. We have not yet discussed how trade actually comes about.

> When trade is free—unimpeded by government-instituted barriers—patterns of trade and trade flows result from the independent decisions of thousands of importers and exporters and millions of private households and firms.

Private households decide whether to buy Toyotas or Chevrolets, and private firms decide whether to buy machine tools made in the United States or machine tools made in Taiwan, raw steel produced in Germany or raw steel produced in Pittsburgh.

Before a citizen of one country can buy a product made in, or sold by, someone in another country, a currency swap must take place. Consider Shane, who buys a Toyota from a dealer in Boston. He pays in dollars, but the Japanese workers who made the car receive their salaries in yen. Somewhere between the buyer of the car and the producer, a currency exchange must be made. The regional distributor probably takes payment in dollars and converts them into yen before remitting the proceeds to Japan.

To buy a foreign-produced good, I in effect have to buy foreign currency. The price of Shane's Toyota in dollars depends on both the price of the car stated in yen and the dollar price of yen. You probably know the ins and outs of currency exchange very well if you have ever traveled in another country.

In October 2005, the British pound was worth $1.75. Now suppose that you are in London having dinner. On the menu is a nice bottle of wine for 15 pounds. How can you figure out whether you want to buy it? You know what dollars will buy in the United States, so you have to convert the price into dollars. Each pound will cost you $1.75, so 15 pounds will cost you $1.75 × 15 = $26.25.

exchange rate The ratio at which two currencies are traded. The price of one currency in terms of another.

The attractiveness of foreign goods to U.S. buyers and of U.S. goods to foreign buyers depends in part on the **exchange rate**, the ratio at which two currencies are traded. If the price of pounds were to fall to $1.20, that same bottle of wine would cost $18.00.

To understand the patterns of trade that result from the actions of hundreds of thousands of independent buyers and sellers—households and firms—we must know something about the factors that determine exchange rates. Exchange rate determination is very complicated. Here, however, we can demonstrate two things:

> First, for any pair of countries, there is a range of exchange rates that can lead automatically to both countries' realizing the gains from specialization and comparative advantage. Second, within that range, the exchange rate will determine which country gains the most from trade. In short, exchange rates determine the terms of trade.

Trade and Exchange Rates in a Two-Country/Two-Good World Consider first a simple two-country/two-good model. Suppose both the United States and Brazil produce only two goods—raw timber and rolled steel. Table 33.8 gives the current prices of both goods as domestic buyers see them. In Brazil, timber is priced at 3 reals (R) per foot, and steel is priced at 4 R per meter. In the United States, timber costs $1 per foot and steel costs $2 per meter.

**TABLE 33.8
Domestic Prices
of Timber (Per Foot)
and Rolled Steel (Per
Meter) in the United
States and Brazil**

	UNITED STATES	BRAZIL
Timber	$1	3 Reals
Rolled steel	$2	4 Reals

Suppose U.S. and Brazilian buyers have the option of buying at home or importing to meet their needs. The options they choose will depend on the exchange rate. For the time being, we will ignore transportation costs between countries and assume that Brazilian and U.S. products are of equal quality.

Let us start with the assumption that the exchange rate is $1 = 1 R. From the standpoint of U.S. buyers, neither Brazilian steel nor Brazilian timber is competitive at this exchange rate. A dollar buys a foot of timber in the United States, but if converted into a real, it will buy only one-third of a foot. The price of Brazilian timber to an American is $3 because it will take $3 to buy the necessary 3 R. Similarly, $2 buys a meter of rolled steel in the United States, but the same $2 buys only half a meter of Brazilian steel. The price of Brazilian steel to an American is $4, twice the price of domestically produced steel.

At this exchange rate, however, Brazilians find that U.S.-produced steel and timber are both less expensive than steel and timber produced in Brazil. Timber at home—Brazil—costs 3 R, but 3 R buys $3, which buys three times as much timber in the United States. Similarly, steel costs 4 R at home, but 4 R buys $4, which buys twice as much U.S.-made steel. At an exchange rate of $1 = 1 R, Brazil will import steel and timber and the United States will import nothing.

However, now suppose the exchange rate is 1 R = $0.25. This means that 1 dollar buys 4 R. At this exchange rate, the Brazilians buy timber and steel at home and the Americans import both goods. At this exchange rate, Americans must pay a dollar for a foot of U.S. timber, but the same amount of timber can be had in Brazil for the equivalent of $0.75. (Because 1 R costs $0.25, 3 R can be purchased for $0.75.) Similarly, steel that costs $2 per meter in the United States costs an American half as much in Brazil, because $2 buys 8 R, which buys 2 meters of Brazilian steel. At the same time, Brazilians are not interested in importing, because both goods are cheaper when purchased from a Brazilian producer. In this case, the United States imports both goods and Brazil imports nothing.

So far, we can see that at exchange rates of $1 = 1 R and $1 = 4 R we get trade flowing in only one direction. Let us now try an exchange rate of $1 = 2 R, or 1 R = $0.50. First, Brazilians will buy timber in the United States. Brazilian timber costs 3 R per foot, but 3 R buys $1.50, which is enough to buy 1.5 feet of U.S. timber. Buyers in the United States will find Brazilian timber too expensive, but Brazil will import timber from the United States. At this same exchange rate, however, both Brazilian and U.S. buyers will be indifferent between Brazilian and U.S. steel. To U.S. buyers, domestically produced steel costs $2. Because $2 buys 4 R, a meter of imported Brazilian steel also costs $2. Brazilian buyers also find that steel costs 4 R, whether domestically produced or imported. Thus, there is likely to be no trade in steel.

What happens if the exchange rate changes so that $1 buys 2.1 R? While U.S. timber is still cheaper to both Brazilians and Americans, Brazilian steel begins to look good to U.S. buyers. Steel produced in the United States costs $2 per meter, but $2 buys 4.2 R, which buys more than a meter of steel in Brazil. When $1 buys more than 2 R, trade begins to flow in both directions: Brazil will import timber and the United States will import steel.

If you examine Table 33.9 carefully, you will see that trade flows in both directions as long as the exchange rate settles between $1 = 2 R and $1 = 3 R. Stated the other way around, trade will flow in both directions if the price of a real is between $0.33 and $0.50.

Exchange Rates and Comparative Advantage

If the foreign exchange market drives the exchange rate to anywhere between 2 and 3 R per dollar, the countries will automatically adjust and comparative advantage will be realized. At these exchange rates, U.S. buyers begin buying all their steel in Brazil. The U.S. steel industry finds itself in trouble. Plants close, and U.S. workers begin to lobby for tariff protection against Brazilian steel. At the same time, the U.S. timber industry does well, fueled by strong export demand from Brazil. The timber-producing sector expands. Resources, including capital and labor, are attracted into timber production.

The opposite occurs in Brazil. The Brazilian timber industry suffers losses as export demand dries up and Brazilians turn to cheaper U.S. imports. In Brazil, lumber companies

TABLE 33.9 Trade Flows Determined by Exchange Rates		
EXCHANGE RATE	PRICE OF REAL	RESULT
$1 = 1 R	$ 1.00	Brazil imports timber and steel
$1 = 2 R	.50	Brazil imports timber
$1 = 2.1 R	.48	Brazil imports timber; United States imports steel
$1 = 2.9 R	.34	Brazil imports timber; United States imports steel
$1 = 3 R	.33	United States imports steel
$1 = 4 R	.25	United States imports timber and steel

turn to the government and ask for protection from cheap U.S. timber. However, steel producers in Brazil are happy. Not only are they supplying 100 percent of the domestically demanded steel but they are also selling to U.S. buyers. The steel industry expands, and the timber industry contracts. Resources, including labor, flow into steel.

With this expansion-and-contraction scenario in mind, let us look again at our original definition of comparative advantage. If we assume that prices reflect resource use and resources can be transferred from sector to sector, we can calculate the opportunity cost of steel/timber in both countries. In the United States, the production of a meter of rolled steel consumes twice the resources that the production of a foot of timber consumes. Assuming that resources can be transferred, the opportunity cost of a meter of steel is 2 feet of timber (see Table 33.8). In Brazil, a meter of steel uses resources costing 4 R, while a unit of timber costs 3 R. To produce a meter of steel means the sacrifice of only four-thirds (or one and one-third) feet of timber. Because the opportunity cost of a meter of steel (in terms of timber) is lower in Brazil, we say Brazil has a comparative advantage in steel production.

Conversely, consider the opportunity cost of timber in the two countries. Increasing timber production in the United States requires the sacrifice of half a meter of steel for every foot of timber—producing a meter of steel uses $2 worth of resources, while producing a foot of timber requires only $1 worth of resources. Nevertheless, each foot of timber production in Brazil requires the sacrifice of three-fourths of a meter of steel. Because the opportunity cost of timber is lower in the United States, the United States has a comparative advantage in the production of timber.

> If exchange rates end up in the right ranges, the free market will drive each country to shift resources into those sectors in which it enjoys a comparative advantage. Only those products in which a country has a comparative advantage will be competitive in world markets.

THE SOURCES OF COMPARATIVE ADVANTAGE

Specialization and trade can benefit all trading partners, even those that may be inefficient producers in an absolute sense. If markets are competitive, and if foreign exchange markets are linked to goods-and-services exchange, countries will specialize in producing products in which they have a comparative advantage.

So far, we have said nothing about the sources of comparative advantage. What determines whether a country has a comparative advantage in heavy manufacturing or in agriculture? What explains the actual trade flows observed around the world? Various theories and empirical work on international trade have provided some answers. Most economists look to **factor endowments**—the quantity and quality of labor, land, and natural resources—as the principal sources of comparative advantage. Factor endowments seem to explain a significant portion of actual world trade patterns.

factor endowments The quantity and quality of labor, land, and natural resources of a country.

THE HECKSCHER-OHLIN THEOREM

Eli Heckscher and Bertil Ohlin, two Swedish economists who wrote in the first half of the twentieth century, expanded and elaborated on Ricardo's theory of comparative advantage. The **Heckscher-Ohlin theorem** ties the theory of comparative advantage to factor endowments. It assumes that products can be produced using differing proportions of inputs and that inputs are mobile between sectors in each economy, but that factors are not mobile *between* economies. According to this theorem:

> A country has a comparative advantage in the production of a product if that country is relatively well endowed with inputs used intensively in the production of that product.

CHAPTER 33 **709**
International Trade, Comparative
Advantage, and Protectionism

Heckscher-Ohlin theorem A theory that explains the existence of a country's comparative advantage by its factor endowments: A country has a comparative advantage in the production of a product if that country is relatively well endowed with inputs used intensively in the production of that product.

This idea is simple. A country with a lot of good fertile land is likely to have a comparative advantage in agriculture. A country with a large amount of accumulated capital is likely to have a comparative advantage in heavy manufacturing. A country with a lot of human capital is likely to have a comparative advantage in highly technical goods.

OTHER EXPLANATIONS FOR OBSERVED TRADE FLOWS

Comparative advantage is not the only reason countries trade. It does not explain why many countries both import and export the same kinds of goods. The United States, for example, both exports and imports automobiles.

Just as industries within a country differentiate their products to capture a domestic market, so too do they differentiate their products to please the wide variety of tastes that exists worldwide. The Japanese automobile industry, for example, began producing small, fuel-efficient cars long before U.S. automobile makers did. In doing so, they developed expertise in creating products that attracted a devoted following and considerable brand loyalty. BMWs, made only in Germany, and Volvos, made only in Sweden, also have their champions in many countries. Just as product differentiation is a natural response to diverse preferences within an economy, it is also a natural response to diverse preferences across economies.

This idea is not inconsistent with the theory of comparative advantage. If the Japanese have developed skills and knowledge that gave them an edge in the production of fuel-efficient cars, that knowledge can be thought of as a very specific kind of capital not currently available to other producers. The Volvo company invested in a form of intangible capital that we call *goodwill*. That goodwill, which may come from establishing a reputation for safety and quality over the years, is one source of the comparative advantage that keeps Volvos selling on the international market. Some economists distinguish between gains from *acquired comparative advantages* and those from *natural comparative advantages*.

Another explanation for international trade is that some economies of scale may be available when producing for a world market that would not be available when producing for a more limited domestic market. But because the evidence suggests that economies of scale are exhausted at relatively small size in most industries, it seems unlikely that they constitute a valid explanation of world trade patterns.

TRADE BARRIERS: TARIFFS, EXPORT SUBSIDIES, AND QUOTAS

Trade barriers—also called *obstacles to trade*—take many forms; the three most common are tariffs, export subsidies, and quotas. All are forms of **protection** shielding some sector of the economy from foreign competition.

A **tariff** is a tax on imports. The average tariff on imports into the United States is less than 5 percent. Certain protected items have much higher tariffs. For example, in 2005, tariffs on rubber footwear ranged from 20 percent to 48 percent, and on canned tuna it was 35 percent.

protection The practice of shielding a sector of the economy from foreign competition.

tariff A tax on imports.

export subsidies
Government payments made to domestic firms to encourage exports.

dumping A firm or industry's sale of products on the world market at prices below the cost of production.

quota A limit on the quantity of imports.

Smoot-Hawley tariff The U.S. tariff law of the 1930s, which set the highest tariffs in U.S. history (60 percent). It set off an international trade war and caused the decline in trade that is often considered a cause of the worldwide depression of the 1930s.

General Agreement on Tariffs and Trade (GATT) An international agreement signed by the United States and 22 other countries in 1947 to promote the liberalization of foreign trade.

Export subsidies—government payments made to domestic firms to encourage exports—can also act as a barrier to trade. One of the provisions of the Corn Laws that stimulated Ricardo's musings was an export subsidy automatically paid to farmers by the British government when the price of grain fell below a specified level. The subsidy served to keep domestic prices high, but it flooded the world market with cheap subsidized grain. Foreign farmers who were not subsidized were driven out of the international marketplace by the artificially low prices.

Farm subsidies remain a part of the international trade landscape today. Many countries continue to appease their farmers by heavily subsidizing exports of agricultural products. The political power of the farm lobby in many countries has had an important effect on recent international trade negotiations aimed at reducing trade barriers.

Closely related to subsidies is **dumping**. Dumping takes place when a firm or an industry sells products on the world market at prices *below* the cost of production. The charge has been leveled against several specific Japanese industries, including automobiles, consumer electronics, and silicon computer chips. Generally, a company dumps when it wants to dominate a world market. After the lower prices of the dumped goods have succeeded in driving out all the competition, the dumping company can exploit its position by raising the price of its product. A U.S. firm attempting to monopolize a domestic market violates the Sherman Antitrust Act of 1890, prohibiting predatory pricing.

The current U.S. tariff laws contain several provisions aimed at counteracting the effects of dumping. The 1974 Trade Act contains a clause that qualifies an industry for protection if it has been "injured" by foreign competition. Building on that legislation, more recent trade bills, including the Comprehensive Trade Act of 1988, contain clauses that permit the president to impose trade sanctions when investigations reveal dumping by foreign companies or countries.

A **quota** is a limit on the quantity of imports. Quotas can be mandatory or voluntary, and they may be legislated or negotiated with foreign governments. The best-known voluntary quota, or "voluntary restraint," was negotiated with the Japanese government in 1981. Japan agreed to reduce its automobile exports to the United States by 7.7 percent, from the 1980 level of 1.82 million units to 1.68 million units. Many quotas limit trade around the world today. Perhaps the best-known recent case is the textile quota imposed by the European Union on imports of textiles from China in August 2005. Because China had exceeded quotas that had been agreed to earlier in the year, the EU blocked the entry of Chinese-produced textiles into Europe, and more than 100 million garments piled up in European ports.

U.S. Trade Policies and GATT The United States has been a high-tariff nation, with average tariffs of over 50 percent for much of its history. The highest were in effect during the Great Depression following the **Smoot-Hawley tariff**, which pushed the average tariff rate to 60 percent in 1930. The Smoot-Hawley tariff set off an international trade war when U.S. trading partners retaliated with tariffs of their own. Many economists say the decline in trade that followed was one of the causes of the worldwide depression of the 1930s.[1]

In 1947, the United States, with 22 other nations, agreed to reduce barriers to trade. It also established an organization to promote liberalization of foreign trade. This **General Agreement on Tariffs and Trade (GATT)**, at first considered to be an interim arrangement, continues today and has been quite effective. The most recent round of world trade talks sponsored by GATT, the Uruguay Round, began in Uruguay in 1986. It was initialed by 116 countries on December 15, 1993, and was formally approved by the U.S. Congress after much debate following the election in 1994. The Final Act of the Uruguay Round of negotiations is the most comprehensive and complex multilateral trade agreement in history.

Every president who has held office since the first round of this general agreement was signed has argued for free-trade policies, yet each used his powers to protect one economic sector or another. Eisenhower and Kennedy restricted U.S. imports of Japanese textiles;

[1]See especially Charles Kindleberger, *The World in Depression 1929–1939* (London: Allen Lane, 1973).

Johnson restricted meat imports; Nixon restrained imports of steel and tightened restrictions on textiles; Carter protected steel, textiles, and footwear; Reagan restricted imports of sugar and automobiles. In early 2002, President George W. Bush imposed a 30 percent tariff on steel imported into the United States. The U.S. steel industry employed 175,000 workers in 2002, but nearly 20,000 jobs had been lost during the previous 4 years due to cheaper imported steel. The Bush steel tariff was greeted with anger by the other steel-producing countries, many of which threatened a trade war. While the steel tariff has been rolled back for most countries, it remained in place for imports from Japan, Russia, and Brazil at rates as high as 50 percent in 2005.

Nevertheless, the movement in the United States has been away from tariffs and quotas and toward freer trade. The Reciprocal Trade Agreements Act of 1934 authorized the president to negotiate trade agreements on behalf of the United States. As part of trade negotiations, the president can confer *most-favored-nation status* on individual trading partners. Imports from countries with most-favored-nation status are taxed at the lowest negotiated tariff rates. In addition, in recent years several successful rounds of tariff-reduction negotiations have reduced trade barriers to their lowest levels ever.

Economic Integration **Economic integration** occurs when two or more nations join to form a free-trade zone. In 1991, the European Community (EC, or the Common Market) began forming the largest free-trade zone in the world. The economic integration process began that December, when the 12 original members (the United Kingdom, Belgium, France, Germany, Italy, the Netherlands, Luxembourg, Denmark, Greece, Ireland, Spain, and Portugal) signed the Maastricht Treaty. The treaty called for the end of border controls, a common currency, an end to all tariffs, and the coordination of monetary and even political affairs. The **European Union (EU)**, as the EC is now called, has 25 members and 4 applicants (for a list, see the Chapter Summary, p. 718). On January 1, 1993, all tariffs and trade barriers were dropped among the member countries. Border checkpoints were closed in early 1995. Citizens can now travel among member countries without passports.

The United States is not a part of the EU. However, in 1988 the United States (under President Reagan) and Canada (under Prime Minister Mulroney) signed the **U.S.-Canadian Free-Trade Agreement**, which removed all barriers to trade, including tariffs and quotas, between the two countries in 1998.

During the last days of the George H.W. Bush administration, the United States, Mexico, and Canada signed the **North American Free Trade Agreement (NAFTA)**, with the three countries agreeing to establish all North America as a free-trade zone. The North American free-trade area includes 360 million people and a total output of over $7 trillion—larger than the output of the EU. The agreement eliminates all tariffs over a 10- to 15-year period and removes restrictions on most investments.

During the presidential campaign of 1992, NAFTA was hotly debated. Both Bill Clinton and George Bush supported the agreement. Industrial labor unions that might be affected by increased imports from Mexico (like those in the automobile industry) opposed the agreement, while industries whose exports to Mexico might increase as a result of the agreement—for example, the machine tool industry—supported it. Another concern was that Mexican companies were not subject to the same environmental regulations as U.S. firms, so U.S. firms might move to Mexico for this reason.

NAFTA was ratified by the U.S. Congress in late 1993 and went into effect on the first day of 1994. The U.S. Department of Commerce has estimated that as a result of NAFTA, trade between the United States and Mexico increased by nearly $16 billion in 1994. In addition, exports from the United States to Mexico outpaced imports from Mexico during 1994. In 1995, however, the agreement fell under the shadow of a dramatic collapse of the value of the peso. U.S. exports to Mexico dropped sharply, and the United States shifted from a trade surplus to a large trade deficit with Mexico. Aside from a handful of tariffs, however, all of NAFTA's commitments were fully implemented by 2003, and an 8-year report signed by all three countries declared the pact a success. The report concludes, "Eight years of expanded trade, increased employment and investment, and enhanced opportunity for the citizens of all three countries have demonstrated that NAFTA works and will continue to work."

economic integration
Occurs when two or more nations join to form a free-trade zone.

European Union (EU) The European trading bloc composed of 25 countries.

U.S.-Canadian Free Trade Agreement An agreement in which the United States and Canada agreed to eliminate all barriers to trade between the two countries by 1998.

North American Free Trade Agreement (NAFTA) An agreement signed by the United States, Mexico, and Canada in which the three countries agreed to establish all North America as a free-trade zone.

New Trade Agreement with Central America and the Dominican Republic—2005

Outsourcing Is Not Just Customer Service Reps in India

Trade and Development in Africa—2003

Russia's Economy in 2005

New Trade Agreement with Central America and the Dominican Republic—2005

THE FOLLOWING APPEARED ON THE Department of Commerce Web page in September 2005:

> The Central American–Dominican Republic Free Trade Agreement (CAFTA–DR) is currently not in effect. The U.S. Congress approved the CAFTA–DR in July 2005 and the President signed it into law on August 2, 2005. The CAFTA–DR has been approved by the legislatures in El Salvador, Guatemala, and Honduras. Approval is pending in Costa Rica, the Dominican Republic, and Nicaragua. The agreement shall enter into force on a date to be agreed upon among the parties.
>
> The CAFTA–DR is an historic and comprehensive Free Trade Agreement that will strip away barriers to trade, eliminate tariffs, open markets, and promote investment. By promoting economic growth in the Central American countries of Costa Rica, El Salvador, Guatemala, Honduras, and Nicaragua, as well as in the Dominican Republic, this cutting-edge pact will expand U.S. opportunities in important regional markets.

The following piece from the *New York Times* shows just how difficult free-trade pacts can be politically.

U.S. Trade Pact Divides the Central Americans, with Farmers and Others Fearful

By JAMES C. McKINLEY, JR.
August 21, 2005

Bolívar Elizondo barely ekes out a living on his 25-acre farm in the mountains near Bijagua, where he raises chickens, pigs, pineapples and a dozen cows. But his biggest worry these days is a free trade agreement with the United States.

A man who must do everything by hand with a machete or knife, Mr. Elizondo depends on selling about 50 pigs a year to finance the rest of his tiny operation. He says he can never compete with the large mechanized meat producers from the United States that are expected to invade the market over the next 20 years if Costa Rica's legislature approves the accord.

"Without selling the pigs, I don't know how to survive," he said as he fed plantains to his swine. "I can't support myself. I will have to sell this. Who is going to buy it? Not another Costa Rican. It will be a multinational corporation."

If the pact is approved, small farmers like Mr. Elizondo say they will be wiped out. If it is not, Costa Rican manufacturers like Luis Gamboa, whose factory produces stoves and refrigerators, say they may move to another country.

Labor leaders threaten strikes and scream that the treaty will force public-sector layoffs and drive up health care costs. Flower growers say they will go out of business without it.

The accord arouses such passions that the Costa Rican president, Abel Pacheco, dismissed all the negotiators and postponed sending it to the legislature for nearly 18 months. Most political analysts say he plans to let the next president deal with the issue, which is already defining the presidential race this winter.

Rice farmers here see the agreement as an unmitigated disaster. Even though they have 10 years before the

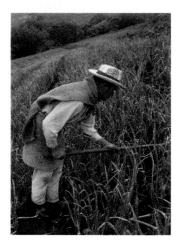

35 percent duty on imported rice begins to disappear, most say they will never be able to compete with rice farmers in the United States.

"If we are in CAFTA, we can survive," said María A. Quirce, the executive director of the Chamber of Textile Exporters. "If we are out of CAFTA, we are out of business."

Defenders of the pact say most of the complaints are baseless and born of fear of change. Freer access to the North American market is the only way, they maintain, for Central American economies to grow.

Source: James C. McKinley, Jr., "U.S. Trade Pact Divides the Central Americans, with Farmers and Others Fearful," The New York Times, August 21, 2005. Reprinted by permission.

One of the great economic debates of all time revolves around the free-trade-versus-protection controversy. We briefly summarize the arguments in favor of each.

THE CASE FOR FREE TRADE

In one sense, the theory of comparative advantage *is* the case for free trade. Trade has potential benefits for all nations. A good is not imported unless its net price to buyers is below the net price of the domestically produced alternative. When the Brazilians in our earlier example found U.S. timber less expensive than their own, they bought it, yet they continued to pay the same price for homemade steel. Americans bought less expensive Brazilian steel, but they continued to buy domestic timber at the same lower price. Under these conditions, *both Americans and Brazilians ended up paying less and consuming more.*

At the same time, resources (including labor) move out of steel production and into timber production in the United States. In Brazil, resources (including labor) move out of timber production and into steel production. The resources in both countries are more efficiently used. Tariffs, export subsidies, and quotas, which interfere with the free movement of goods and services around the world, reduce or eliminate the gains of comparative advantage.

We can use supply and demand curves to illustrate this. Suppose Figure 33.4 shows domestic supply and demand for textiles. In the absence of trade, the market clears at a price of $4.20. At equilibrium, 450 million yards of textiles are produced and consumed.

Assume now that textiles are available at a world price of $2. This is the price in dollars that Americans must pay for textiles from foreign sources. If we assume an unlimited quantity of textiles is available at $2 and there is no difference in quality between domestic and foreign textiles, no domestic producer will be able to charge more than $2. In the absence of trade barriers, the world price sets the price in the United States. As the price in the United States falls from $4.20 to $2.00, the quantity demanded by consumers increases from 450 million yards to

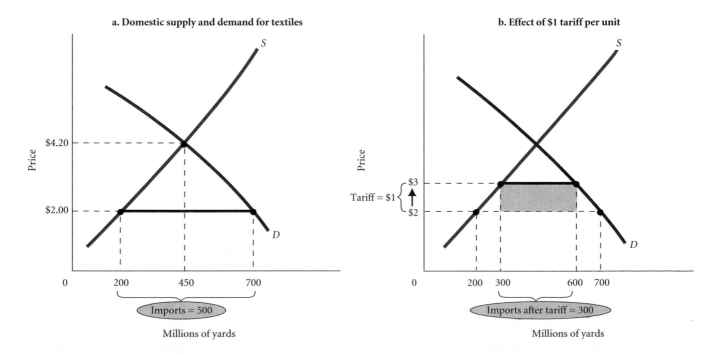

FIGURE 33.4 The Gains from Trade and Losses from the Imposition of a Tariff

A tariff of $1 increases the market price facing consumers from $2 per yard to $3 per yard. The government collects revenues equal to the gray-shaded area. The loss of efficiency has two components. First, consumers must pay a higher price for goods that could be produced at lower cost. Second, marginal producers are drawn into textiles and away from other goods, resulting in inefficient domestic production.

700 million yards, but the quantity supplied by domestic producers drops from 450 million yards to 200 million yards. The difference, 500 million yards, is the quantity of textiles imported.

The argument for free trade is that each country should specialize in producing the goods and services in which it enjoys a comparative advantage. If foreign producers can produce textiles at a much lower price than domestic producers, they have a comparative advantage. As the world price of textiles falls to $2, domestic (U.S.) quantity supplied drops and resources are transferred to other sectors. These other sectors, which may be export industries or domestic industries, are not shown in Figure 33.4a. It is clear that the allocation of resources is more efficient at a price of $2. Why should the United States use domestic resources to produce what foreign producers can produce at a lower cost? U.S. resources should move into the production of the things it produces best.

Now consider what happens to the domestic price of textiles when a trade barrier is imposed. Figure 33.4b shows the effect of a set tariff of $1 per yard imposed on imported textiles. The tariff raises the domestic price of textiles to $2 + $1 = $3. The result is that some of the gains from trade are lost. First, consumers are forced to pay a higher price for the same good; the quantity of textiles demanded drops from 700 million yards under free trade to 600 million yards because some consumers are not willing to pay the higher price.

At the same time, the higher price of textiles draws some marginal domestic producers who could not make a profit at $2 into textile production. (Recall that domestic producers do not pay a tariff.) As the price rises to $3, the quantity supplied by producers rises from 200 million yards to 300 million yards. The result is a decrease in imports from 500 million yards to 300 million yards.

Finally, the imposition of the tariff means that the government collects revenue equal to the shaded area in Figure 33.4b. This shaded area is equal to the tariff rate per unit ($1) times the number of units imported after the tariff is in place (300 million yards). Thus, receipts from the tariff are $300 million.

What is the final result of the tariff? Domestic producers receiving revenues of only $2 per unit before the tariff was imposed now receive a higher price and earn higher profits. However, these higher profits are achieved at a loss of efficiency.

> Trade barriers prevent a nation from reaping the benefits of specialization, push it to adopt relatively inefficient production techniques, and force consumers to pay higher prices for protected products than they would otherwise pay.

THE CASE FOR PROTECTION

A case can also be made in favor of tariffs and quotas. Over the course of U.S. history, protectionist arguments have been made so many times by so many industries before so many congressional committees that it seems all pleas for protection share the same themes. We describe the most frequently heard pleas next.

Protection Saves Jobs   The main argument for protection is that foreign competition costs Americans their jobs. When Americans buy Toyotas, U.S. cars go unsold. Layoffs in the domestic auto industry follow. When Americans buy Japanese or German steel, steelworkers in Pittsburgh lose their jobs. When Americans buy shoes or textiles from Korea or Taiwan, the mill-workers in Maine and Massachusetts, as well as in South Carolina and Georgia, lose their jobs.

It is true that when we buy goods from foreign producers, domestic producers suffer. However, there is no reason to believe that the workers laid off in the contracting sectors will not be ultimately reemployed in other, expanding sectors. Foreign competition in textiles, for example, has meant the loss of U.S. jobs in that industry. Thousands of textile workers in New England lost their jobs as the textile mills there closed over the last 40 years. Nevertheless, with the expansion of high-tech industries, the unemployment rate in Massachusetts fell to one of the lowest in the country in the mid-1980s, and New Hampshire, Vermont, and Maine also boomed. By the 1990s, New England had suffered another severe downturn, due partly to high-technology hardware manufacturing that had moved abroad. But by the late 1990s, its economy was booming again, this time on the back of what was called a "New Industrial Revolution": the rise of Internet-based business.

The adjustment is far from costless. The knowledge that some other industry, perhaps in some other part of the country, may be expanding is of little comfort to the person whose skills become obsolete or whose pension benefits are lost when his or her company abruptly closes a plant or goes bankrupt. The social and personal problems brought about by industry-specific unemployment, obsolete skills, and bankruptcy as a result of foreign competition are significant.

These problems can be addressed in two ways. We can ban imports and give up the gains from free trade, acknowledging that we are willing to pay premium prices to save domestic jobs in industries that can produce more efficiently abroad, or we can aid the victims of free trade in a constructive way, helping to retrain them for jobs with a future. In some instances, programs to relocate people in expanding regions may be in order. Some programs deal directly with the transition without forgoing the gains from trade.

Some Countries Engage in Unfair Trade Practices Attempts by U.S. firms to monopolize an industry are illegal under the Sherman and Clayton acts. If a strong company decides to drive the competition out of the market by setting prices below cost, it would be aggressively prosecuted by the Antitrust Division of the Justice Department. However, the argument goes, if we will not allow a U.S. firm to engage in predatory pricing or monopolize an industry or market, can we stand by and let a German firm or a Japanese firm do so in the name of free trade? This is a legitimate argument and one that has gained significant favor in recent years. How should we respond when a large international company or a country behaves strategically against a domestic firm or industry? Free trade may be the best solution when everybody plays by the rules, but sometimes we have to fight back.

Cheap Foreign Labor Makes Competition Unfair Let us say that a particular country gained its "comparative advantage" in textiles by paying its workers low wages. How can U.S. textile companies compete with companies that pay wages that are less than a quarter of what U.S. companies pay?

First, remember that wages in a competitive economy reflect productivity: a high ratio of output to units of labor. Workers in the United States earn higher wages because they are more productive. The United States has more capital per worker, that is, the average worker works with better machinery and equipment, and its workers are better trained. Second, trade flows not according to *absolute* advantage but according to *comparative* advantage: All countries benefit, even if one country is more efficient at producing everything.

Protection Safeguards National Security Beyond saving jobs, certain sectors of the economy may appeal for protection for other reasons. The steel industry has argued for years with some success that it is vital to national defense. In the event of a war, the United States would not want to depend on foreign countries for a product as vital as steel. Even if we acknowledge another country's comparative advantage, we may want to protect our own resources.

No industry has ever asked for protection without invoking the national defense argument. The testimony on behalf of the scissors and shears industry argued that "in the event of a national emergency and imports cutoff, the United States would be without a source of scissors and shears, basic tools for many industries and trades essential to our national defense." The question lies not in the merit of the argument but in just how seriously it can be taken if *every* industry uses it.

Protection Discourages Dependency Closely related to the national defense argument is the claim that countries, particularly small or developing countries, may come to rely too heavily on one or more trading partners for many items. If a small country comes to rely on a major power for food or energy or some important raw material in which the large nation has a comparative advantage, it may be difficult for the smaller nation to remain politically neutral. Some critics of free trade argue that larger countries, like the United States, Russia, and China, have consciously engaged in trade with smaller countries to create these kinds of dependencies.

A Petition

From the Manufacturers of Candles, Tapers, Lanterns, Sticks, Street Lamps, Snuffers, and Extinguishers, and from Producers of Tallow, Oil, Resin, Alcohol, and Generally of Everything Connected with Lighting.

To the Honourable Members of the Chamber of Deputies.

Gentlemen:

You are on the right track. You reject abstract theories and [have] little regard for abundance and low prices. You concern yourselves mainly with the fate of the producer. You wish to free him from foreign competition, that is, to reserve the domestic market for domestic industry.

We come to offer you a wonderful opportunity for your—what shall we call it? Your theory? No, nothing is more deceptive than theory. Your doctrine? Your system? Your principle? But you dislike doctrines, you have a horror of systems, as for principles, you deny that there are any in political economy; therefore we shall call it your practice—your practice without theory and without principle.

We are suffering from the ruinous competition of a rival who apparently works under conditions so far superior to our own for the production of light that he is flooding the domestic market with it at an incredibly low price; for the moment he appears, our sales cease, all the consumers turn to him, and a branch of French industry whose ramifications are innumerable is all at once reduced to complete stagnation. This rival, which is none other than the sun, is waging war on us so mercilessly we suspect he is being stirred up against us by perfidious Albion (excellent diplomacy nowadays!), particularly because he has for that haughty island a respect that he does not show for us. [A reference to Britain's reputation as a foggy island.]

We ask you to be so good as to pass a law requiring the closing of all windows, dormers, skylights, inside and outside shutters, curtains, casements, bull's-eyes, deadlights, and blinds—in short, all openings, holes, chinks, and fissures through which the light of the sun is wont to enter houses, to the detriment of the fair industries with which, we are proud to say, we have endowed the country, a country that cannot, without betraying ingratitude, abandon us today to so unequal a combat.

Be good enough, honourable deputies, to take our request seriously, and do not reject it without at least hearing the reasons that we have to advance in its support.

First, if you shut off as much as possible all access to natural light, and thereby create a need for artificial light, what industry in France will not ultimately be encouraged? If France consumes more tallow, there will have to be more cattle and sheep, and, consequently, we shall see an increase in cleared fields, meat, wool, leather, and especially manure, the basis of all agricultural wealth.

If France consumes more oil, we shall see an expansion in the cultivation of the poppy, the olive, and rapeseed. These rich yet soil-exhausting plants will come at just the right time to enable us to put to profitable use the increased fertility that the breeding of cattle will impart to the land.

Our moors will be covered with resinous trees. Numerous swarms of bees will gather from our mountains the perfumed treasures that today waste their fragrance, like the flowers from which they emanate. Thus, there is not one branch of agriculture that would not undergo a great expansion.

The same holds true of shipping. Thousands of vessels will engage in whaling, and in a short time we shall have a fleet capable of upholding the honour of France and of gratifying the patriotic aspirations of the undersigned petitioners, chandlers, etc.

Will you tell us that, though we may gain by this protection, France will not gain at all, because the consumer will bear the expense?

We have our answer ready: You no longer have the right to invoke the interests of the consumer. You have sacrificed him whenever you have found his interests opposed to those of the producer. You have done so in order to encourage industry and to increase employment. For the same reason you ought to do so this time too.

Indeed, you yourselves have anticipated this objection. When told that the consumer has a stake in the free entry of iron, coal, sesame, wheat, and textiles, "Yes," you reply, "but the producer has a stake in their exclusion." Very well, surely if consumers have a stake in the admission of natural light, producers have a stake in its interdiction.

"But," you may still say, "the producer and the consumer are one and the same person. If the manufacturer profits by protection, he will make the farmer

Screening out the sun would increase the demand for candles. Should candlemakers be protected from unfair competition?

prosperous. Contrariwise, if agriculture is prosperous, it will open markets for manufactured goods." Very well, if you grant us a monopoly over the production of lighting during the day, first of all we shall buy large amounts of tallow, charcoal, oil, resin, wax, alcohol, silver, iron, bronze, and crystal, to supply our industry; and, moreover, we and our numerous suppliers, having become rich, will consume a great deal and spread prosperity into all areas of domestic industry.

The question, and we pose it formally, is whether what you desire for France is the benefit of consumption free of charge or the alleged advantages of onerous production. Make your choice, but be logical; for as long as you ban, as you do, foreign coal, iron, wheat, and textiles, in proportion as their price approaches zero, how inconsistent it would be to admit the light of the sun, whose price is zero all day long!

Source: Frederic Bastiat (1801 to 1850), New Australian. Reprinted by permission.

Therefore, should small independent countries consciously avoid trading relationships that might lead to political dependence? This objective may involve developing domestic industries in areas where a country has a comparative disadvantage. To do so would mean protecting that industry from international competition.

infant industry A young industry that may need temporary protection from competition from the established industries of other countries to develop an acquired comparative advantage.

Protection Safeguards Infant Industries   Young industries in a given country may have a difficult time competing with established industries in other countries. In a dynamic world, a protected **infant industry** might mature into a strong industry worldwide because of an acquired, but real, comparative advantage. If such an industry is undercut and driven out of world markets at the beginning of its life, that comparative advantage might never develop.

Yet efforts to protect infant industries can backfire. In July 1991, the U.S. government imposed a 62.67 percent tariff on imports of active-matrix liquid crystal display screens (also referred to as "flat-panel displays" and primarily used for laptop computers) from Japan. The Commerce Department and the International Trade Commission agreed that Japanese producers were selling their screens in the U.S. market at a price below cost and that this dumping threatened the survival of domestic laptop screen producers. The tariff was meant to protect the infant U.S. industry until it could compete head-on with the Japanese.

Unfortunately for U.S. producers of laptop computers and for consumers who purchase them, the tariff had an unintended (though predictable) effect on the industry. Because U.S. laptop screens were generally recognized to be of lower quality than their Japanese counterparts, imposition of the tariff left U.S. computer manufacturers with three options: (1) They could use the screens available from U.S. producers and watch sales of their final product decline in the face of *higher-quality* competition from abroad; (2) they could pay the tariff for the higher-quality screens and watch sales of their final product decline in the face of *lower-priced* competition from abroad; or (3) they could do what was the most profitable for them to do—move their production facilities abroad to avoid the tariff completely. The last is exactly what both Apple and IBM did. In the end, not only were the laptop industry and its consumers hurt by the imposition of the tariff (due to higher costs of production and to higher laptop computer prices) but the U.S. screen industry was hurt as well (due to its loss of buyers for its product) by a policy specifically designed to help it.

AN ECONOMIC CONSENSUS

You now know something about how international trade fits into the structure of the economy.

Critical to our study of international economics is the debate between free traders and protectionists. On one side is the theory of comparative advantage, formalized by David Ricardo in the early part of the nineteenth century. According to this view, all countries benefit from specialization and trade. The gains from trade are real, and they can be large; free international trade raises real incomes and improves the standard of living.

On the other side are the protectionists, who point to the loss of jobs and argue for the protection of workers from foreign competition. Although foreign competition can cause job loss in specific sectors, it is unlikely to cause net job loss in an economy, and workers will over time be absorbed into expanding sectors.

> Foreign trade and full employment can be pursued simultaneously. Although economists disagree about many things, the vast majority of them favor free trade.

Chapter 35 picks up this debate on free trade.

SUMMARY

1. All economies, regardless of their size, depend to some extent on other economies and are affected by events outside their borders.

TRADE SURPLUSES AND DEFICITS

2. Until the 1970s, the United States generally exported more than it imported—it ran a *trade surplus.* In the mid-1970s, the United States began to import more merchandise than it exported—a *trade deficit.*

THE ECONOMIC BASIS FOR TRADE: COMPARATIVE ADVANTAGE

3. The *theory of comparative advantage,* dating to David Ricardo in the nineteenth century, holds that specialization

and free trade will benefit all trading partners, even those that may be absolutely less efficient producers.

4. A country enjoys an *absolute advantage* over another country in the production of a product if it uses fewer resources to produce that product than the other country does. A country has a *comparative advantage* in the production of a product if that product can be produced at a lower cost in terms of other goods.

5. Trade enables countries to move beyond their previous resource and productivity constraints. When countries specialize in producing those goods in which they have a comparative advantage, they maximize their combined output and allocate their resources more efficiently.

6. When trade is free, patterns of trade and trade flows result from the independent decisions of thousands of importers and exporters and millions of private households and firms.

7. The relative attractiveness of foreign goods to U.S. buyers and of U.S. goods to foreign buyers depends in part on *exchange rates*, the ratios at which two currencies are traded for each other.

8. For any pair of countries, there is a range of exchange rates that will lead automatically to both countries' realizing the gains from specialization and comparative advantage. Within that range, the exchange rate will determine which country gains the most from trade. This leads us to conclude that exchange rates determine the terms of trade.

9. If exchange rates end up in the right range, that is, in a range that facilitates the flow of goods between nations, the free market will drive each country to shift resources into those sectors in which it enjoys a comparative advantage. Only those products in which a country has a comparative advantage will be competitive in world markets.

THE SOURCES OF COMPARATIVE ADVANTAGE

10. The *Heckscher-Ohlin theorem* looks to relative *factor endowments* to explain comparative advantage and trade flows. According to the theorem, a country has a comparative advantage in the production of a product if that country is relatively well endowed with the inputs that are used intensively in the production of that product.

11. A relatively short list of inputs—natural resources, knowledge capital, physical capital, land, and skilled and unskilled labor—explains a surprisingly large portion of world trade patterns. However, the simple version of the theory of com-

parative advantage cannot explain why many countries import and export the same goods.

12. Some theories argue that comparative advantage can be acquired. Just as industries within a country differentiate their products to capture a domestic market, so too do they differentiate their products to please the wide variety of tastes that exists worldwide. This theory is consistent with the theory of comparative advantage.

TRADE BARRIERS: TARIFFS, EXPORT SUBSIDIES, AND QUOTAS

13. Trade barriers take many forms; the three most common are *tariffs*, *export subsidies*, and *quotas*. All are forms of *protection* through which some sector of the economy is shielded from foreign competition.

14. Although the United States has historically been a high-tariff nation, the general movement is now away from tariffs and quotas. The *General Agreement on Tariffs and Trade (GATT)*, signed by the United States and 22 other countries in 1947, continues in effect today; its purpose is to reduce barriers to world trade and keep them down. Also important are the *U.S.-Canadian Free Trade Agreement*, signed in 1988, and the *North American Free Trade Agreement*, signed by the United States, Mexico, and Canada in the last days of the George H.W. Bush administration, taking effect in 1994.

15. The *European Union (EU)* is a free-trade bloc composed of 25 nations, which are listed below. Four others have applied for membership: Bulgaria, Croatia, Romania, and Turkey. Many economists believe that the advantages of free trade within the bloc, a reunited Germany, and the ability to work well as a bloc will make the EU the most powerful player in the international marketplace in the coming decades.

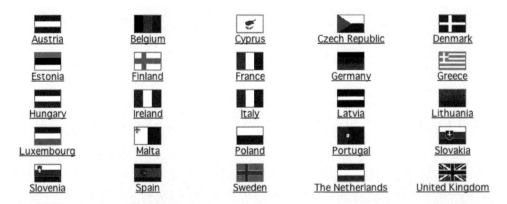

The 25 members of the European Union, 2006

FREE TRADE OR PROTECTION?

16. In one sense, the theory of comparative advantage is the case for free trade. Trade barriers prevent a nation from reaping the benefits of specialization, push it to adopt relatively inefficient production techniques, and force consumers to pay higher prices for protected products than they would otherwise pay.

17. The case for protection rests on a number of propositions, one of which is that foreign competition results in a loss of domestic jobs, but there is no reason to believe that the

workers laid off in the contracting sectors will not be ultimately reemployed in other, expanding sectors. This adjustment process is far from costless, however.

18. Other arguments for protection hold that cheap foreign labor makes competition unfair; that some countries engage in unfair trade practices; and that protection safeguards the national security, discourages dependency, and shields *infant industries*. Despite these arguments, most economists favor free trade.

REVIEW TERMS AND CONCEPTS

absolute advantage, 701

comparative advantage, 701

Corn Laws, 700

dumping, 710

economic integration, 711

European Union (EU), 711

exchange rate, 706

export subsidies, 710

factor endowments, 708

General Agreement on Tariffs and Trade (GATT), 710

Heckscher-Ohlin theorem, 709

infant industry, 716

North American Free Trade Agreement (NAFTA), 711

protection, 709

quota, 710

Smoot-Hawley tariff, 710

tariff, 709

terms of trade, 705

theory of comparative advantage, 701

trade deficit, 700

trade surplus, 700

U.S.-Canadian Free Trade Agreement, 711

PROBLEM SET

1. Suppose Germany and France each produce only two goods, guns and butter. Both are produced using labor alone and the value of a good is equal to the number of labor units required to produce it. Assuming both countries are at full employment, you are given the following information:

   Germany: 10 units of labor required to produce 1 gun
   5 units of labor required to produce 1 pound of butter
   Total labor force: 1,000,000 units

   France: 15 units of labor required to produce 1 gun
   10 units of labor required to produce 1 pound of butter
   Total labor force: 750,000 units

   a. Draw the production possibility frontiers for each country in the absence of trade.
   b. If transportation costs are ignored and trade is allowed, will France and Germany engage in trade? Explain.
   c. If a trade agreement were negotiated, at what rate (number of guns per unit of butter) would they agree to exchange?

2. The box on page 712 describes a new NAFTA-like free-trade zone in Central America including the countries of Costa Rica, El Salvador, Guatemala, Honduras, and Nicaragua as well as the Dominican Republic. Write a short paper on the progress of this treaty to date. Which countries have signed and which have not? What lessons have we been taught by our experience with NAFTA?

3. The United States and Russia each produce only bearskin caps and wheat. Domestic prices are given in the following table:

	RUSSIA	UNITED STATES	
Bearskin caps	10 Ru	$ 7	Per hat
Wheat	15 Ru	$10	Per bushel

   On April 1, the Zurich exchange listed an exchange rate of $1 = 1 Ru.
   a. Which country has an absolute advantage in the production of bearskin caps? Wheat?
   b. Which country has a comparative advantage in the production of bearskin caps? Wheat?
   c. If the United States and Russia were the only two countries engaging in trade, what adjustments would you predict, assuming exchange rates are freely determined by the laws of supply and demand?

4. The following table shows imports and exports of goods during the first half of 2005 for the United States:

	JAN.–JUNE 2005 (BILLIONS OF DOLLARS)	
	Exports	**Imports**
Total	439.0	795.1
Airplanes	15.5	6.1
Clothing	2.1	35.8
Crude oil	.3	81.6
Vehicles	35.4	95.1
Agricultural goods	30.6	29.8

   What, if anything, can you conclude about the comparative advantage that the United States has relative to our trading partners in the production of goods? What stories can you tell about the wide disparities in clothing and airplanes?

5. The following table gives recent figures for yield per acre in Illinois and Kansas:

	WHEAT	SOYBEANS
Illinois	48	39
Kansas	40	24

   Source: U.S. Dept. of Agriculture, *Crop Production.*

   a. If we assume that farmers in Illinois and Kansas use the same amount of labor, capital, and fertilizer, which state has an absolute advantage in wheat production? Soybean production?
   b. If we transfer land out of wheat into soybeans, how many bushels of wheat do we give up in Illinois per additional bushel of soybeans produced? In Kansas?
   c. Which state has a comparative advantage in wheat production? In soybean production?
   d. The following table gives the distribution of land planted for each state in millions of acres in the same year.

	TOTAL ACRES UNDER TILL	WHEAT	SOYBEANS
Illinois	22.9	1.9 (8.3%)	9.1 (39.7%)
Kansas	20.7	11.8 (57.0%)	1.9 (9.2%)

   Are these data consistent with your answer to part c? Explain.

6. You can think of the United States as a set of 50 separate economies with no trade barriers. In such an open environment, each state specializes in the products that it produces best.
   a. What product or products does your state specialize in?
   b. Can you identify the source of the comparative advantage that lies behind the production of one or more of these products (a natural resource, plentiful cheap labor, a skilled labor force, and so on)?
   c. Do you think that the theory of comparative advantage and the Heckscher-Ohlin theorem help to explain why your state specializes in the way that it does? Explain your answer.

7. Australia and the United States produce white and red wines. Current domestic prices for each are given in the following table:

	AUSTRALIA	UNITED STATES
White wine	5 AU$	10 US$
Red wine	10 AU$	15 US$

Suppose that the exchange rate is 1 AU$ = 1 US$.
   a. If the price ratios within each country reflect resource use, which country has a comparative advantage in the production of red wine? White wine?
   b. Assume there are no other trading partners and that the only motive for holding foreign currency is to buy foreign goods. Will the current exchange rate lead to trade flows in both directions between the two countries? Explain.
   c. What adjustments might you expect in the exchange rate? Be specific.
   d. What would you predict about trade flows between Australia and the United States after the exchange rate has adjusted?

Open-Economy Macroeconomics: The Balance of Payments and Exchange Rates

34

The economies of the world have become increasingly interdependent over the last four decades. No economy operates in a vacuum, and economic events in one country can have significant repercussions on the economies of other countries.

International trade is a major part of today's world economy. U.S. imports now account for about 15 percent of U.S. gross domestic product (GDP), and billions of dollars flow through the international capital market each day. In Chapter 33, we explored the main reasons why there is international exchange. Countries trade with

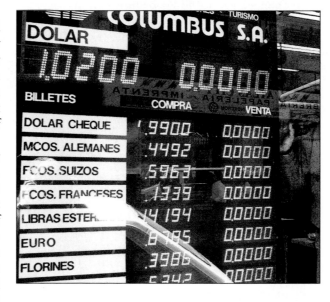

each other to obtain goods and services they cannot produce themselves or because other nations can produce goods and services at a lower cost than they can. You can see the various connections between the domestic economy and the rest of the world in the circular flow diagram in Figure 18.1. Foreign countries supply goods and services to the United States, and the United States supplies goods and services to the rest of the world.

From a macroeconomic point of view, the main difference between an international transaction and a domestic transaction concerns currency exchange:

> When people in different countries buy from and sell to each other, an exchange of currencies must also take place.

Brazilian coffee exporters cannot spend U.S. dollars in Brazil—they need Brazilian reals. A U.S. wheat exporter cannot use Brazilian reals to buy a tractor from a U.S. company or to pay the rent on warehouse facilities. Somehow, international exchange must be managed in a way that allows both partners in the transaction to wind up with their own currency.

As you know from Chapter 33, the direction of trade between two countries depends on **exchange rates**—the price of one country's currency in terms of the other country's currency. If the Japanese yen were very expensive (making the dollar cheap), both Japanese and Americans would buy from U.S. producers. If the yen were very cheap (making the U.S. dollar expensive), both Japanese and Americans would buy from Japanese producers. Within a certain range of exchange rates, trade flows in both directions, each country specializes in producing the goods in which it enjoys a comparative advantage, and trade is mutually beneficial.

exchange rate The price of one country's currency in terms of another country's currency; the ratio at which two currencies are traded for each other.

Representatives of the 44 countries that met in Bretton Woods, New Hampshire, in 1944 to allay the impending chaos in the international monetary system as World War II was ending.

Because exchange rates are a factor in determining the flow of international trade, the way they are determined is very important. Since 1900, the world monetary system has been changed several times by international agreements and events. In the early part of the twentieth century, nearly all currencies were backed by gold. Their values were fixed in terms of a specific number of ounces of gold, which determined their values in international trading—exchange rates.

In 1944, with the international monetary system in chaos as the end of World War II drew near, a large group of experts unofficially representing 44 countries met in Bretton Woods, New Hampshire, and drew up a number of agreements. One of these agreements established a system of essentially fixed exchange rates under which each country agreed to intervene by buying and selling currencies in the foreign exchange market when necessary to maintain the agreed-to value of its currency.

In 1971, most countries, including the United States, gave up trying to fix exchange rates formally and began allowing them to be determined essentially by supply and demand. For example, without government intervention in the marketplace, the price of British pounds in dollars is determined by the interaction of those who want to exchange dollars for pounds (those who "demand" pounds) and those who want to exchange pounds for dollars (those who "supply" pounds). If the quantity of pounds demanded exceeds the quantity of pounds supplied, the price of pounds will rise, just as the price of peanuts or paper clips would rise under similar circumstances. A more detailed discussion of the various monetary systems that have been in place since 1900 is in the Appendix to this chapter.

In this chapter, we explore what has come to be called *open-economy macroeconomics* in more detail. First, we discuss the *balance of payments*—the record of a nation's transactions with the rest of the world. We then go on to consider how the analysis changes when we allow for the international exchange of goods, services, and capital.

THE BALANCE OF PAYMENTS

foreign exchange All currencies other than the domestic currency of a given country.

We sometimes lump all foreign currencies—euros, Swiss francs, Japanese yen, Brazilian reals, and so forth—together as "foreign exchange." **Foreign exchange** is simply all currencies other than the domestic currency of a given country (in the case of the United States, the U.S. dollar). U.S. demand for foreign exchange arises because its citizens want to buy things whose prices are quoted in other currencies, such as Australian jewelry, vacations in Mexico, and bonds or stocks issued by Sony Corporation of Japan. Whenever U.S. citizens make these purchases, Australians, Mexicans, and Japanese gain U.S. dollars, which, from their point of view, are foreign exchange.

Where does the *supply* of foreign exchange come from? The answer is simple: The United States (actually, U.S. citizens or firms) earns foreign exchange when it sells products, services, or assets to another country. Just as Mexico earns foreign exchange when U.S. tourists visit Cancún, the United States earns foreign exchange (in this case, Mexican pesos) when Mexican tourists come to the United States to visit Disney World. Similarly, Saudi Arabian purchases of stock in General Motors or Colombian purchases of real estate in Miami increase the U.S. supply of foreign exchange.

The record of a country's transactions in goods, services, and assets with the rest of the world is its **balance of payments**. The balance of payments is also the record of a country's sources (supply) and uses (demand) of foreign exchange.[1]

THE CURRENT ACCOUNT

The balance of payments is divided up into two major accounts, the *current account* and the *capital account.* These are shown in Table 34.1, which provides data on the U.S. balance of payments for 2004. We begin with the current account.

The first item in the current account is U.S. trade in goods. This category includes exports of computer chips, potato chips, and CDs of U.S. musicians and imports of Scotch whiskey, Japanese calculators, and Mexican oil. U.S. exports *earn* foreign exchange for the United States and are a credit (+) item on the current account. U.S. imports *use up* foreign exchange and are a debit (−) item. In 2004, the United States imported $665.5 billion more in goods than it exported.

Next in the current account is services. Like most other countries, the United States buys services from and sells services to other countries. For example, a U.S. firm shipping wheat to England might purchase insurance from a British insurance company. A Dutch flower grower may fly flowers to the United States aboard an American airliner. In the first case, the United States is importing services and therefore using up foreign exchange; in the second, it is selling services to foreigners and earning foreign exchange. In 2004, the United States exported $48.4 billion more in services than it imported.

The difference between a country's exports of goods and services and its imports of goods and services is its **balance of trade**. If exports of goods and services are less than

balance of payments The record of a country's transactions in goods, services, and assets with the rest of the world; also the record of a country's sources (supply) and uses (demand) of foreign exchange.

balance of trade A country's exports of goods and services minus its imports of goods and services.

TABLE 34.1 United States Balance of Payments, 2004

All transactions that bring foreign exchange into the United States are credited (+) to the current account; all transactions that cause the United States to lose foreign exchange are debited (−) to the current account.

CURRENT ACCOUNT

Goods exports	807.6
Goods imports	−1,473.1
(1) Net export of goods	−665.5
Exports of services	339.6
Imports of services	−291.2
(2) Net export of services	48.4
Income received on investments	369.0
Income payments on investments	−344.9
(3) Net investment income	24.1
(4) Net transfer payments	−72.9
(5) Balance on current account (1 + 2 + 3 + 4)	−665.9

CAPITAL ACCOUNT

(6) Change in private U.S. assets abroad (increase is −)	−821.8
(7) Change in foreign private assets in the United States	1,077.9
(8) Change in U.S. government assets abroad (increase is −)	4.1
(9) Change in foreign government assets in the United States	355.3
(10) Balance on capital account (6 + 7 + 8 + 9)	615.5
(11) Net capital account transactions	−1.5
(12) Statistical discrepancy	51.9
(13) Balance of payments (5 + 10 + 11 + 12)	0

Source: U.S. Department of Commerce, *Survey of Current Business,* April 2005.

[1]Bear in mind the distinction between the balance of payments and a balance sheet. A *balance sheet* for a firm or a country measures that entity's stock of assets and liabilities at a moment in time. The *balance of payments*, by contrast, measures *flows*, usually over a period of a month, a quarter, or a year. Despite its name, the balance of payments is *not* a balance sheet.

trade deficit Occurs when a country's exports of goods and services are less than its imports of goods and services in a given period.

imports of goods and services, a country has a **trade deficit**. The U.S. trade deficit in 2004 was huge: $617.1 billion (that is, $665.5 billion less $48.4 billion).

The third item in the current account concerns investment income. U.S. citizens hold foreign assets (stocks, bonds, and real assets like buildings and factories). Dividends, interest, rent, and profits paid to U.S. asset holders are a source of foreign exchange. Conversely, when foreigners earn dividends, interest, and profits on assets held in the United States, foreign exchange is used up. In 2004, investment income received from foreigners exceeded investment income paid to foreigners by $24.1 billion.

The fourth item in Table 34.1 is net transfer payments. Transfer payments from the United States to foreigners are another use of foreign exchange. Some of these transfer payments are from private U.S. citizens and some are from the U.S. government. You may send a check to a relief agency in Africa. Conversely, some foreigners make transfer payments to the United States. *Net* refers to the difference between payments from the United States to foreigners and payments from foreigners to the United States.

balance on current account Net exports of goods, plus net exports of services, plus net investment income, plus net transfer payments.

If we add net exports of goods, net export of services, net investment income, and net transfer payments, we get the **balance on current account**. The balance on current account shows how much a nation has spent on foreign goods, services, investment income payments, and transfers relative to how much it has earned from other countries. When the balance is negative, which it was for the United States in 2004, a nation has spent more on foreign goods and services (plus investment income and transfers paid) than it has earned through the sales of its goods and services to the rest of the world (plus investment income and transfers received). If a nation has spent more on foreign goods, services, investment income payments, and transfers than it has earned, its net wealth position vis-à-vis the rest of the world must decrease. By *net* we mean a nation's assets abroad minus its liabilities to the rest of the world. The capital account of the balance of payments records the changes in these assets and liabilities. We now turn to the capital account.

THE CAPITAL ACCOUNT

For each transaction recorded in the current account, there is an offsetting transaction recorded in the capital account. Consider the purchase of a Japanese car by a U.S. citizen. Say that the yen/dollar exchange rate is 100 yen to a dollar, and the yen price of the car is 2.0 million yen, which is $20,000. The U.S. citizen (probably an automobile dealer) takes $20,000, buys 2.0 million yen, and then buys the car. In this case, U.S. imports are increased by $20,000 in the current account and foreign assets in the United States (in this case, Japanese holdings of dollars) are increased by $20,000 in the capital account. The net wealth position of the United States vis-à-vis the rest of the world has decreased by $20,000. The key point to realize is that an increase in U.S. imports results in an increase in foreign assets in the United States. The United States must "pay" for the imports, and whatever it pays with (in this example, U.S. dollars) is an increase in foreign assets in the United States. Conversely, an increase in U.S. exports results in an increase in U.S. assets abroad, because foreigners must pay for the U.S. exports.

balance on capital account In the United States, the sum of the following (measured in a given period): the change in private U.S. assets abroad, the change in foreign private assets in the United States, the change in U.S. government assets abroad, and the change in foreign government assets in the United States.

Table 34.1 shows that U.S. assets abroad are divided into private holdings (line 6) and U.S. government holdings (line 8). Similarly, foreign assets in the United States are divided into foreign private (line 7) and foreign government (line 9). The sum of lines 6, 7, 8, and 9 is the **balance on capital account** (line 10). The next item is called net capital account transactions (line 11). It is quite small in value and includes things like U.S. government debt forgiveness. These kinds of transactions affect the capital account but not the current account. Ignoring this item, if there were no errors of measurement in the data collection, the balance on capital account would equal the negative of the balance on current account, because, as mentioned previously, for each transaction in the current account there is an offsetting transaction in the capital account. Another way of looking at the balance on capital account is that it is the change in the net wealth position of the country vis-à-vis the rest of the world. If the balance on capital account is positive, this means that the change in foreign assets in the country is greater than the change in the country's assets abroad, which is a decrease in the net wealth position of the country.

Table 34.1 shows that in 2004 the U.S. balance on current account was −$665.9 billion, which means that the United States spent considerably more than it made vis-à-vis the rest of the world. If the balance on current account is measured correctly, then the net wealth position of the United States vis-à-vis the rest of the world decreased by $665.9 billion in 2004 plus the $1.5 billion in line 11. In this case, the balance on capital account should be $667.4 billion. The balance on capital account (line 10) is in fact $615.5 billion, and so the error of measurement, called the statistical discrepancy, is $51.9 billion (line 12) in 2004. The balance of payments (line 13) is the sum of the balance on current account, the balance on capital account, net capital account transactions, and the statistical discrepancy. By construction, it is always zero.

It is important to note from Table 34.1 that even though the net wealth position of the United States decreased in 2004, the change in U.S. assets abroad increased considerably ($821.8 billion private minus $4.1 billion government). How can this be? Because there was an even larger increase in foreign assets in the United States ($1,077.9 billion private plus $355.3 billion government). It is the *net* change (that is, the change in foreign assets in the United States minus the change in U.S. assets abroad) that is equal to the negative of the balance on current account (aside from the statistical discrepancy), not the change in just U.S. assets abroad. Much of the increase of $355.3 billion in foreign government assets was the accumulation of dollars by Japan and China.

There are many transactions that get recorded in the capital account that do not pertain to the current account. Consider a purchase of a U.K. security by a U.S. resident. This is done by the U.S. resident's selling dollars for pounds and using the pounds to buy the U.K. security. After this transaction, U.S. assets abroad have increased (the United States now holds more U.K. securities) and foreign assets in the United States have increased (foreigners now hold more dollars). The purchase of the U.K. security is recorded as a minus item in line 6 in Table 34.1, and the increase in foreign holdings of dollars is recorded as a plus item in line 7. These two balance out. This happens whenever there is a switch of one kind of asset for another vis-à-vis the rest of the world. When a Japanese company bought Rockefeller Center in New York City in 1990, this was an increase in foreign assets in the United States (the Japanese then owned Rockefeller Center) and an increase in U.S. assets abroad (the United States then had the yen that was used to pay for the center). If the United States subsequently took the yen and bought Japanese securities, this was simply a switch of one kind of U.S. asset abroad (yen) for another (Japanese securities).

THE UNITED STATES AS A DEBTOR NATION

If a country has positive net wealth position vis-à-vis the rest of the world, it can be said to be a creditor nation. Conversely, if it has negative net wealth position, it can be said to be a debtor nation. Remember that a country's net wealth position increases if it has a positive current account balance and decreases if it has a negative current account balance. It is important to realize that the *only* way a country's net wealth position can change is if its current account balance is nonzero. Simply switching one form of asset for another, such as switching Rockefeller Center for Japanese securities in the preceding example, is not a change in a country's net wealth position. Another way of putting this is that a country's net wealth position is the sum of all its past current account balances.

Prior to the mid-1970s, the United States had generally run current account surpluses, and thus its net wealth position was positive. It was a creditor nation. This began to turn around in the mid-1970s, and by the mid-1980s, the United States was running large current account deficits. Sometime during this period the United States changed from having a positive net wealth position vis-à-vis the rest of the world to having a negative position. In other words, the United States changed from a creditor nation to a debtor nation. The current account deficits persisted into the 1990s, and the United States is now the largest debtor nation in the world. In 2003, foreign assets in the United States totaled $10.5 trillion and U.S. assets abroad totaled $7.9 trillion.[2] The U.S. net wealth position was thus −$2.6 trillion. This large negative position reflects the fact that the United States spent much more in the 1980s, 1990s, and 2000s on foreign goods and

---

[2]U.S. Department of Commerce, *Survey of Current Business*, April 2005, Table F.1.

services (plus investment income and transfers paid) than it earned through the sales of its goods and services to the rest of the world (plus investment income and transfers received).

EQUILIBRIUM OUTPUT (INCOME) IN AN OPEN ECONOMY

Everything we have said so far has been descriptive. Now we turn to analysis. How are all these trade and capital flows determined? What impacts do they have on the economies of the countries involved? To simplify our discussion here, we will assume that exchange rates are fixed. We will relax this assumption later.

THE INTERNATIONAL SECTOR AND PLANNED AGGREGATE EXPENDITURE

Our earlier descriptions of the multiplier took into account the consumption behavior of households (C), the planned investment behavior of firms (I), and the spending of the government (G). We defined the sum of these three components as planned aggregate expenditure (AE).

To analyze the international sector, we must include the goods and services a country exports to the rest of the world, as well as what it imports. If we call our exports of goods and services EX, it should be clear that EX is a component of total output and income. A U.S. razor sold to a buyer in Mexico is as much a part of U.S. production as a similar razor sold in Pittsburgh. Exports simply represent demand for domestic products not by domestic households and firms and the government, but by the rest of the world.

What about imports? Remember, imports are *not a part of domestic output* (Y). By definition, imports are not produced by the country that is importing them. Remember also, when we look at households' total consumption spending, firms' total investment spending, and total government spending, imports are included. Therefore, to calculate domestic output correctly, we must subtract the parts of consumption, investment, and government spending that constitute imports. The definition of planned aggregate expenditure becomes:

> Planned aggregate expenditure in an open economy:
>
> $$AE \equiv C + I + G + EX - IM$$

net exports of goods and services (*EX – IM*) The difference between a country's total exports and total imports.

The last two terms ($EX - IM$) together are the country's **net exports of goods and services**.

Determining the Level of Imports What determines the level of imports and exports in a country? For now, we assume that the level of imports is a function of income (Y). The rationale is simple: When U.S. income increases, U.S. citizens buy more of everything, including U.S. cars and peanut butter, Japanese TV sets, and Korean steel and DVD players. When income rises, imports tend to go up. Algebraically,

$$IM = mY$$

marginal propensity to import (*MPM*) The change in imports caused by a $1 change in income.

where Y is income and m is some positive number (m is assumed to be less than 1; otherwise, a $1 increase in income generates an increase in imports of more than $1, which does not make sense). Recall from Chapter 21 that the marginal propensity to consume (MPC) measures the change in consumption that results from a $1 change in income. Similarly, the **marginal propensity to import**, abbreviated as MPM or m, is the change in imports caused by a $1 change in income. If $m = .2$, or 20 percent, and income is $1,000, then imports, IM, are equal to $.2 \times \$1,000 = \$200$. If income rises by $100 to $1,100, then the change in imports will equal $m \times$ (the change in income) $= .2 \times \$100 = \$20$.

For now we will assume that exports (EX) are given (that is, they are not affected, even indirectly, by the state of the economy.) This assumption is relaxed later in this chapter.

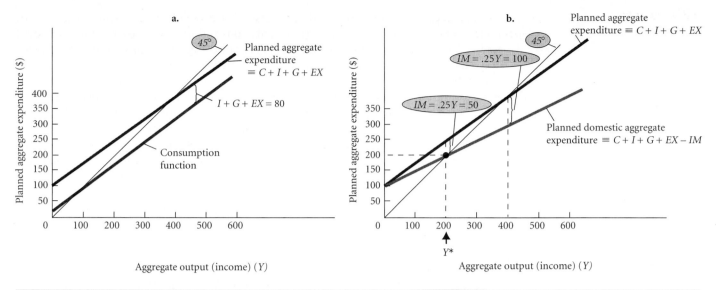

FIGURE 34.1 Determining Equilibrium Output in an Open Economy

In **a**, planned investment spending (*I*), government spending (*G*), and total exports (*EX*) are added to consumption (*C*) to arrive at planned aggregate expenditure. However, *C* + *I* + *G* + *EX* includes spending on imports. In **b**, the amount imported at every level of income is subtracted from planned aggregate expenditure. Equilibrium output occurs at *Y** = 200, the point at which planned domestic aggregate expenditure crosses the 45-degree line.

Solving for Equilibrium   Given the assumption about how imports are determined, we can solve for equilibrium income. This procedure is illustrated in Figure 34.1. Starting from the consumption function (blue line) in Figure 34.1(a), we gradually build up the components of planned aggregate expenditure (red line). Assuming for simplicity that planned investment, government purchases, and exports are all constant and do not depend on income, we move easily from the blue line to the red line by adding the fixed amounts of *I, G*, and *EX* to consumption at every level of income. In this example, we take *I* + *G* + *EX* to equal 80.

$C + I + G + EX$, however, includes spending on imports, which are not part of domestic production. To get spending on domestically produced goods, we must subtract the amount that is imported at each level of income. In Figure 34.1(b), we assume *m* = .25, which is the assumption that 25 percent of total income is spent on goods and services produced in foreign countries. Imports under this assumption are a constant fraction of total income; therefore, at higher levels of income, a larger amount is spent on foreign goods and services. For example, at *Y* = 200, *IM* = .25 *Y*, or 50. Similarly, at *Y* = 400, *IM* = .25 *Y*, or 100. Figure 34.1(b) shows the planned *domestic* aggregate expenditure curve.

Equilibrium is reached when planned domestic aggregate expenditure equals domestic aggregate output (income). This is true at only one level of aggregate output, *Y** = 200, in Figure 34.1(b). If *Y* were below *Y**, planned expenditure would exceed output, inventories would be lower than planned, and output would rise. At levels above *Y**, output would exceed planned expenditure, inventories would be larger than planned, and output would fall.

The Open-Economy Multiplier   All of this has implications for the size of the multiplier. Recall the multiplier, introduced in Chapter 21, and consider a sustained rise in government purchases (*G*). Initially, the increase in *G* will cause planned aggregate expenditure to be greater than aggregate output. Domestic firms will find their inventories to be lower than planned and thus will increase their output, but added output means more income. More workers are hired and profits are higher. Some of the added income is saved, and some is spent. The added consumption spending leads to a second round of inventories being lower than planned and raising output. Equilibrium output rises by a multiple of the initial increase in government purchases. This is the multiplier.

In Chapters 21 and 22, we showed that the simple multiplier equals $1/(1 - MPC)$, or (1/*MPS*). That is, a sustained increase in government purchases equal to ΔG will lead to an increase in aggregate output (income) of $\Delta G \left[1/(1 - MPC) \right]$. If the *MPC* were .75 and government purchases rose by $10 billion, equilibrium income would rise by 4 × $10 billion, or $40 billion. The multiplier is $\left[1/(1 - .75) \right] = \left[1/.25 \right] = 4.0$.

727

In an open economy, some of the increase in income brought about by the increase in G is spent on imports instead of domestically produced goods and services. The part of income spent on imports does not increase domestic income (Y) because imports are produced by foreigners. To compute the multiplier we need to know how much of the increased income is used to increase domestic consumption. (We are assuming all imports are consumption goods. In practice, some imports are investment goods and some are goods purchased by the government.) In other words, we need to know the marginal propensity to consume *domestic* goods. Domestic consumption is $C - IM$. So the marginal propensity to consume domestic goods is the marginal propensity to consume all goods (the MPC) minus the marginal propensity to import (the MPM). The marginal propensity to consume domestic goods is ($MPC - MPM$). Consequently,

$$\text{open-economy multiplier} = \frac{1}{1 - (MPC - MPM)}$$

If the MPC is .75 and the MPM is .25, then the multiplier is 1/.5, or 2.0. This multiplier is smaller than the multiplier in which imports are not taken into account, which is 1/.25, or 4.0. The message of the open-economy multiplier model, put succinctly:

The effect of a sustained increase in government spending (or investment) on income—that is, the multiplier—is smaller in an open economy than in a closed economy. The reason: When government spending (or investment) increases and income and consumption rise, some of the extra consumption spending that results is on foreign products and not on domestically produced goods and services.

IMPORTS AND EXPORTS AND THE TRADE FEEDBACK EFFECT

For simplicity, we have so far assumed that the level of imports depends only on income and that the level of exports is fixed. In reality, the amount of spending on imports depends on factors other than income and exports are not fixed. We will now consider the more realistic picture.

The Determinants of Imports   The same factors that affect households' consumption behavior and firms' investment behavior are likely to affect the demand for imports because some imported goods are consumption goods and some are investment goods. For example, anything that increases consumption spending is likely to increase the demand for imports. We saw in Chapters 21 and 25 that such factors as the after-tax real wage, after-tax nonlabor income, and interest rates affect consumption spending; and thus these should also affect spending on imports. Similarly, anything that increases investment spending is likely to increase the demand for imports. A decrease in interest rates, for example, should encourage spending on both domestically produced goods and foreign-produced goods.

There is one additional consideration in determining spending on imports: the *relative prices* of domestically produced and foreign-produced goods. If the prices of foreign goods fall relative to the prices of domestic goods, people will consume more foreign goods relative to domestic goods. When Japanese cars are cheap relative to U.S. cars, consumption of Japanese cars should be high, and vice versa.

The Determinants of Exports   We now relax our assumption that exports are fixed. The demand for U.S. exports by other countries is identical to their demand for imports from the United States. Germany imports goods, some of which are U.S. produced. France, Spain, and so on do the same. Total expenditure on imports in Germany is a function of the factors we have just discussed, except that the variables are German variables instead of U.S. variables. This is true for all other countries as well. The demand for U.S. exports depends on economic activity in the rest of the world—rest-of-the-world real wages, wealth, nonlabor income, interest rates, and so on—as well as on the prices of U.S. goods relative to the price of rest-of-the-world goods. If foreign output increases, U.S. exports tend to increase. U.S. exports also tend to increase when U.S. prices fall relative to those in the rest of the world.

The Trade Feedback Effect   We can now combine what we know about the demand for imports and the demand for exports to discuss the **trade feedback effect**. Suppose the United States finds its exports increasing, perhaps because the world suddenly decides it prefers U.S. computers to other computers. Rising exports will lead to an increase in U.S. output (income), which leads to an increase in U.S. imports. Here is where the trade feedback begins. Because U.S. imports are somebody else's exports, the extra import demand from the United States raises the exports of the rest of the world. When other countries' exports to the United States go up, their output and incomes also rise, in turn leading to an increase in the demand for imports from the rest of the world. Some of the extra imports demanded by the rest of the world come from the United States, so U.S. exports increase. The increase in U.S. exports stimulates U.S. economic activity even more, triggering a further increase in the U.S. demand for imports, and so on.

> An increase in U.S. imports increases other countries' exports, which stimulates those countries' economies and increases their imports, which increases U.S. exports, which stimulates the U.S. economy and increases its imports, and so on. This is the trade feedback effect. In other words, an increase in U.S. economic activity leads to a worldwide increase in economic activity, which then "feeds back" to the United States.

IMPORT AND EXPORT PRICES AND THE PRICE FEEDBACK EFFECT

We have talked about the price of imports, but we have not yet discussed the factors that influence import prices. The consideration of import prices is complicated because more than one currency is involved. When we talk about "the price of imports," do we mean the price in dollars, in yen, in U.K. pounds, in Mexican pesos, and so on? Because the exports of one country are the imports of another, the same question holds for the price of exports. When Mexico exports auto parts to the United States, Mexican manufacturers are interested in the price of auto parts in terms of pesos, because pesos are what they use for transactions in Mexico. U.S. consumers are interested in the price of auto parts in dollars, because dollars are what they use for transactions in the United States. The link between the two prices is the dollar/peso exchange rate.

Suppose Mexico is experiencing an inflation and the price of radiators in pesos rises from 1,000 pesos to 1,200 pesos per radiator. If the dollar/peso exchange rate remains unchanged at, say, $0.10 per peso, then Mexico's export price for radiators in terms of dollars will also rise, from $100 to $120 per radiator. Because Mexico's exports to the United States are by definition U.S. imports from Mexico, an increase in the dollar prices of Mexican exports to the United States means an increase in the prices of U.S. imports from Mexico. Therefore, when Mexico's export prices rise with no change in the dollar/peso exchange rate, U.S. import prices rise.

> Export prices of other countries affect U.S. import prices.

A country's export prices tend to move fairly closely with the general price level in that country. If Mexico is experiencing a general increase in prices, it is likely this change will be reflected in price increases of all domestically produced goods, both exportable and nonexportable.

> The general rate of inflation abroad is likely to affect U.S. import prices. If the inflation rate abroad is high, U.S. import prices are likely to rise.

The Price Feedback Effect   We have just seen that when a country experiences an increase in domestic prices, the prices of its exports will increase. It is also true that when the prices of a country's *imports* increase, the prices of domestic goods may increase in response. There are at least two ways this effect can occur.

First, an increase in the prices of imported inputs will shift a country's aggregate supply curve to the left. In Chapter 26, we discussed the macroeconomy's response to a cost shock. Recall that a leftward shift in the aggregate supply curve due to a cost increase causes aggregate output to fall and prices to rise (stagflation).

Second, if import prices rise relative to domestic prices, households will tend to substitute domestically produced goods and services for imports. This is equivalent to a rightward shift of the aggregate demand curve. If the domestic economy is operating on the upward-sloping part of the aggregate supply curve, the overall domestic price level will rise in response to an increase in aggregate demand. Perfectly competitive firms will see market-determined prices rise, and imperfectly competitive firms will experience an increase in the demand for their products. Studies have shown, for example, that the price of automobiles produced in the United States moves closely with the price of imported cars.

Still, this is not the end of the story. Suppose a country—say, Mexico—experiences an increase in its domestic price level. This will increase the price of its exports to Canada (and to all other countries). The increase in the price of Canadian imports from Mexico will lead to an increase in domestic prices in Canada. Canada also exports to Mexico. The increase in Canadian prices causes an increase in the price of Canadian exports to Mexico, which then further increases the Mexican price level.

This is called the **price feedback effect**, in the sense that inflation is "exportable." An increase in the price level in one country can drive up prices in other countries, which in turn further increases the price level in the first country. Through export and import prices, a domestic price increase can "feed back" on itself.

It is important to realize that the discussion so far has been based on the assumption of fixed exchange rates. Life is more complicated under flexible exchange rates, to which we now turn.

THE OPEN ECONOMY WITH FLEXIBLE EXCHANGE RATES

To a large extent, the fixed exchange rates set by the Bretton Woods agreements served as international monetary arrangements until 1971. Then, in 1971 the United States and most other countries decided to abandon the fixed exchange rate system in favor of **floating**, or **market-determined, exchange rates**. Although governments still intervene to ensure that exchange rate movements are "orderly," exchange rates today are largely determined by the unregulated forces of supply and demand.

Understanding how an economy interacts with the rest of the world when exchange rates are not fixed is not as simple as when we assume fixed exchange rates. Exchange rates determine the price of imported goods relative to domestic goods and can have significant effects on the level of imports and exports. Consider a 20 percent drop in the value of the dollar against the British pound. Dollars buy fewer pounds and pounds buy more dollars. Both British residents, who now get more dollars for pounds, and U.S. residents, who get fewer pounds for dollars, find that U.S. goods and services are more attractive. Exchange rate movements have important impacts on imports, exports, and the movement of capital between countries.

THE MARKET FOR FOREIGN EXCHANGE

What determines exchange rates under a floating rate system? To explore this question, we assume there are just two countries, the United States and Great Britain. It is easier to understand a world with only two countries, and most of the points we will make can be generalized to a world with many trading partners.

The Supply of, and Demand for, Pounds   Governments, private citizens, banks, and corporations exchange pounds for dollars and dollars for pounds every day. In our two-country case, those who *demand* pounds are holders of dollars seeking to exchange them for pounds. Those who *supply* pounds are holders of pounds seeking to exchange them for dollars. It is important not to confuse the supply of dollars (or pounds) on the foreign exchange market with the U.S. (or British) money supply. The latter is the sum of all the money currently in circulation. The supply of dollars on the foreign exchange market is the number of dollars that holders seek to exchange for pounds in a given time period. The demand for, and supply of, dollars on foreign exchange markets determines *exchange* rates; the demand for money balances and the total domestic money supply determine the *interest* rate.

TABLE 34.2 Some Private Buyers and Sellers in International Exchange Markets: United States and Great Britain

THE DEMAND FOR POUNDS (SUPPLY OF DOLLARS)

1. Firms, households, or governments that import British goods into the United States or wish to buy British-made goods and services
2. U.S. citizens traveling in Great Britain
3. Holders of dollars who want to buy British stocks, bonds, or other financial instruments
4. U.S. companies that want to invest in Great Britain
5. Speculators who anticipate a decline in the value of the dollar relative to the pound

THE SUPPLY OF POUNDS (DEMAND FOR DOLLARS)

1. Firms, households, or governments that import U.S. goods into Great Britain or wish to buy U.S.-made goods and services
2. British citizens traveling in the United States
3. Holders of pounds who want to buy stocks, bonds, or other financial instruments in the United States
4. British companies that want to invest in the United States
5. Speculators who anticipate a rise in the value of the dollar relative to the pound

The common reason for exchanging dollars for pounds is to buy something produced in Great Britain. U.S. importers who purchase Jaguar automobiles or Scotch whiskey must pay with pounds. U.S. citizens traveling in Great Britain who want to ride the train, stay in a hotel, or eat at a restaurant must acquire pounds for dollars to do so. If a U.S. corporation builds a plant in Great Britain, it must pay for that plant in pounds.

At the same time, some people may want to buy British stocks or bonds. Implicitly, when U.S. citizens buy a bond issued by the British government or by a British corporation, they are making a loan, but the transaction requires a currency exchange. The British bond seller must ultimately be paid in pounds.

On the supply side of the market, the situation is reversed. Here we find people—usually British citizens—holding pounds they want to use to buy dollars. Again, the common reason is to buy things produced in the United States. If a British importer decides to import golf carts made in Georgia, the producer must be paid in dollars. British tourists visiting New York may ride in cabs, eat in restaurants, and tour Ellis Island. Doing these things requires dollars. When a British firm builds an office complex in Los Angeles, it must pay the contractor in dollars.

In addition to buyers and sellers who exchange money to engage in transactions, some people and institutions hold currency balances for speculative reasons. If I think the U.S. dollar is going to decline in value relative to the pound, I may want to hold some of my wealth in the form of pounds. Table 34.2 summarizes some of the major categories of private foreign exchange demanders and suppliers in the two-country case of the United States and Great Britain.

Figure 34.2 shows the demand curve for pounds in the foreign exchange market. When the price of pounds (the exchange rate) is lower, it takes fewer dollars to buy British goods and services, to build a plant in Liverpool, to travel to London, and so forth. Lower net prices (in dollars) should increase the demand for British-made products and encourage investment and travel in Great Britain. If prices (in pounds) in Britain do not change, an increase in the quantity of British goods and services demanded by foreigners will increase the quantity of pounds demanded. The demand-for-pounds curve in the foreign exchange market has a negative slope.

Figure 34.3 shows a supply curve for pounds in the foreign exchange market. At a higher exchange rate, each pound buys more dollars, making the price of U.S.-produced goods and services lower to the British. The British are more apt to buy U.S.-made goods when the price of pounds is high (the value of the dollar is low). An increase in British demand for U.S. goods and services is likely to increase the quantity of pounds supplied. The curve representing the supply of pounds in the foreign exchange market has a positive slope.

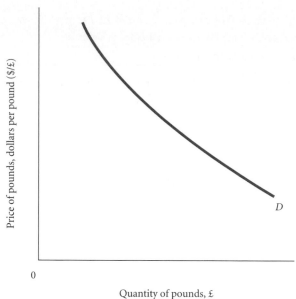

FIGURE 34.2 The Demand for Pounds in the Foreign Exchange Market

When the price of pounds falls, British-made goods and services appear less expensive to U.S. buyers. If British prices are constant, U.S. buyers will buy more British goods and services, and the quantity of pounds demanded will rise.

The Equilibrium Exchange Rate When exchange rates are allowed to float, they are determined the same way other prices are determined:

> The equilibrium exchange rate occurs at the point at which the quantity demanded of a foreign currency equals the quantity of that currency supplied.

This is illustrated in Figure 34.4. An excess demand for pounds (quantity demanded in excess of quantity supplied) will cause the price of pounds to rise—the pound will

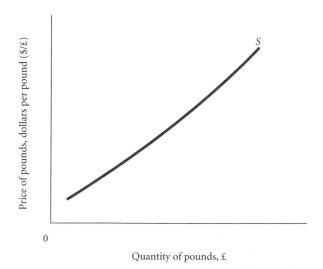

FIGURE 34.3 The Supply of Pounds in the Foreign Exchange Market

When the price of pounds rises, the British can obtain more dollars for each pound. This means that U.S.-made goods and services appear less expensive to British buyers. Thus, the quantity of pounds supplied is likely to rise with the exchange rate.

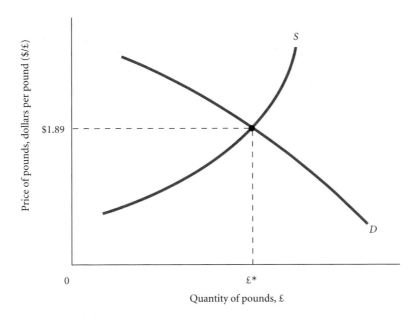

FIGURE 34.4 The Equilibrium Exchange Rate

When exchange rates are allowed to float, they are determined by the forces of supply and demand. An excess demand for pounds will cause the pound to appreciate against the dollar. An excess supply of pounds will lead to a depreciating pound.

appreciate with respect to the dollar. An excess supply of pounds will cause the price of pounds to fall—the pound will **depreciate** with respect to the dollar.[3]

appreciation of a currency The rise in value of one currency relative to another.

depreciation of a currency The fall in value of one currency relative to another.

FACTORS THAT AFFECT EXCHANGE RATES

We now know enough to discuss the factors likely to influence exchange rates. Anything that changes the behavior of the people in Table 34.2 can cause demand and supply curves to shift and the exchange rate to adjust accordingly.

Purchasing Power Parity: The Law of One Price If the costs of transporting goods between two countries are small, we would expect the price of the same good in both countries to be roughly the same. The price of basketballs should be roughly the same in Canada and the United States, for example.

It is not hard to see why. If the price of basketballs is cheaper in Canada, it will pay for someone to buy balls in Canada at a low price and sell them in the United States at a higher price. This decreases the supply and pushes up the price in Canada and increases the supply and pushes down the price in the United States. This process should continue as long as the price differential, and therefore the profit opportunity, persists. For a good with trivial transportation costs, we would expect this **law of one price** to hold. The price of a good should be the same regardless of where we buy it.

law of one price If the costs of transportation are small, the price of the same good in different countries should be roughly the same.

---

[3]Although Figure 34.3 shows the supply-of-pounds curve in the foreign exchange market with a positive slope, under certain circumstances the curve may bend back. Suppose the price of a pound rises from $1.50 to $2.00. Consider a British importer who buys 10 Chevrolets each month at $15,000 each, including transportation costs. When a pound exchanges for $1.50, he will supply 100,000 pounds per month to the foreign exchange market—100,000 pounds brings $150,000, enough to buy 10 cars. Now suppose the cheaper dollar causes him to buy 12 cars. Twelve cars will cost a total of $180,000, but at $2.00 = 1 pound, he will spend only 90,000 pounds per month. The supply of pounds on the market falls when the price of pounds rises. The reason for this seeming paradox is simple. The number of pounds a British importer needs to buy U.S. goods depends on both the quantity of goods he buys and the price of those goods in pounds. If demand for imports is inelastic so that the percentage decrease in price resulting from the depreciated currency is greater than the percentage increase in the quantity of imports demanded, importers will spend fewer pounds and the quantity of pounds supplied in the foreign exchange market will fall. The supply of pounds will slope upward as long as the demand for U.S. imports is elastic.

If the law of one price held for all goods, and if each country consumed the same market basket of goods, the exchange rate between the two currencies would be determined simply by the relative price levels in the two countries. If the price of a basketball were $10 in the United States and $12 in Canada, then the U.S.–Canada exchange rate would have to be $1 U.S. per $1.20 Canadian. If the rate were instead one-to-one, it would pay people to buy the balls in the United States and sell them in Canada. This would increase the demand for U.S. dollars in Canada, thereby driving up their price in terms of Canadian dollars to $1 U.S. per $1.2 Canadian, at which point no one could make a profit shipping basketballs across international lines, and the process would cease.[4]

The theory that exchange rates will adjust so that the price of similar goods in different countries is the same is known as the **purchasing-power-parity theory**. According to this theory, if it takes 10 times as many Mexican pesos to buy a pound of salt in Mexico as it takes U.S. dollars to buy a pound of salt in the United States, then the equilibrium exchange rate should be 10 pesos per dollar.

In practice, transportation costs for many goods are quite large, and the law of one price does not hold for these goods. (Haircuts are often cited as a good example. The transportation costs for a U.S. resident to get a British haircut are indeed large unless that person is an airline pilot.) Also, many products that are potential substitutes for each other are not precisely identical. For instance, a Rolls Royce and a Honda are both cars, but there is no reason to expect the exchange rate between the British pound and the yen to be set so that the prices of the two are equalized. In addition, countries consume different market baskets of goods, so we would not expect the aggregate price levels to follow the law of one price. Nevertheless:

> A high rate of inflation in one country relative to another puts pressure on the exchange rate between the two countries, and there is a general tendency for the currencies of relatively high-inflation countries to depreciate.

Figure 34.5 shows the adjustment likely to occur following an increase in the U.S. price level relative to the price level in Great Britain. This change in relative prices will affect citizens of both countries. Higher prices in the United States make imports relatively less expensive. U.S. citizens are likely to increase their spending on imports from Britain, shifting the demand for pounds to the right, from D_0 to D_1. At the same time, the British see U.S. goods getting more expensive and reduce their demand for exports from the United States. Consequently, the supply of pounds shifts to the left, from S_0 to S_1. The result is an increase in the price of pounds. Before the change in relative prices, 1 pound sold for $1.89; after the change, 1 pound costs $2.25. The pound appreciates and the dollar depreciates.

Relative Interest Rates Another factor that influences a country's exchange rate is the level of its interest rate relative to other countries' interest rates. If the interest rate is 6 percent in the United States and 8 percent in Great Britain, people with money to lend have an incentive to buy British securities instead of U.S. securities. Although it is sometimes difficult for individuals in one country to buy securities in another country, it is easy for international banks and investment companies to do so. If the interest rate is lower in the United States than in Britain, there will be a movement of funds out of U.S. securities into British securities as banks and firms move their funds to the higher-yielding securities.

How does a U.S. bank buy British securities? It takes its dollars, buys British pounds, and uses the pounds to buy the British securities. The bank's purchase of pounds drives up the price of pounds in the foreign exchange market. The increased demand for pounds increases the price of the pound (and decreases the price of the dollar). A high interest rate in Britain relative to the interest rate in the United States tends to depreciate the dollar.

Figure 34.6 shows the effect of rising interest rates in the United States on the pound–dollar exchange rate. Higher interest rates in the United States attract British investors. To buy U.S. securities, the British need dollars. The supply of pounds (the demand for dollars) shifts

purchasing-power-parity theory A theory of international exchange holding that exchange rates are set so that the price of similar goods in different countries is the same.

[4]Of course, if the rate were $1 U.S. to $2 Canadian, then it would pay people to buy basketballs in Canada (at $12 Canadian, which is $6 U.S.) and sell them in the United States. This would weaken demand for the U.S. dollar, and its price would fall from $2 Canadian until it reached $1.20 Canadian.

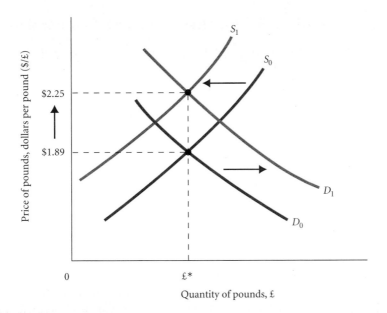

FIGURE 34.5 Exchange Rates Respond to Changes in Relative Prices

The higher price level in the United States makes imports relatively less expensive. U.S. citizens are likely to increase their spending on imports from Britain, shifting the demand for pounds to the right, from D_0 to D_1. At the same time, the British see U.S. goods getting more expensive and reduce their demand for exports from the United States. The supply of pounds shifts to the left, from S_0 to S_1. The result is an increase in the price of pounds. The pound appreciates and the dollar is worth less.

to the right, from S_0 to S_1. The same relative interest rates affect the portfolio choices of U.S. banks, firms, and households. With higher interest rates at home, there is less incentive for U.S. residents to buy British securities. The demand for pounds drops at the same time as the supply increases and the demand curve shifts to the left, from D_0 to D_1. The net result is a depreciating pound and an appreciating dollar. The price of pounds falls from $1.89 to $1.25.

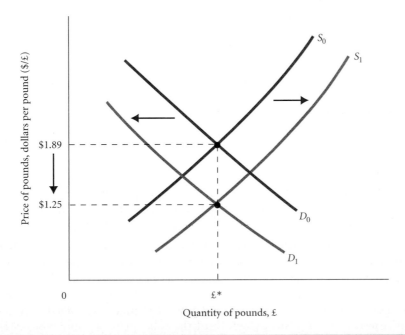

FIGURE 34.6 Exchange Rates Respond to Changes in Relative Interest Rates

If U.S. interest rates rise relative to British interest rates, British citizens holding pounds may be attracted into the U.S. securities market. To buy bonds in the United States, British buyers must exchange pounds for dollars. The supply of pounds shifts to the right, from S_0 to S_1. However, U.S. citizens are less likely to be interested in British securities, because interest rates are higher at home. The demand for pounds shifts to the left, from D_0 to D_1. The result is a depreciated pound and a stronger dollar.

THE EFFECTS OF EXCHANGE RATES ON THE ECONOMY

We are now ready to discuss some of the implications of floating exchange rates. Recall, when exchange rates are fixed, households spend some of their incomes on imports and the multiplier is smaller than it would be otherwise. Imports are a "leakage" from the circular flow, much like taxes and saving. Exports, in contrast, are an "injection" into the circular flow; they represent spending on U.S.-produced goods and services from abroad and can stimulate output.

The world is far more complicated when exchange rates are allowed to float. First, the level of imports and exports depends on exchange rates as well as on income and other factors. When events cause exchange rates to adjust, the levels of imports and exports will change. Changes in exports and imports can in turn affect the level of real GDP and the price level. Further, exchange rates themselves also adjust to changes in the economy. Suppose the government decides to stimulate the economy with an expansionary monetary policy. This will affect interest rates, which may affect exchange rates.

Exchange Rate Effects on Imports, Exports, and Real GDP   As we already know, when a country's currency depreciates (falls in value), its import prices rise and its export prices (in foreign currencies) fall. When the U.S. dollar is cheap, U.S. products are more competitive with products produced in the rest of the world, and foreign-made goods look expensive to U.S. citizens.

A depreciation of a country's currency can serve as a stimulus to the economy. Suppose the U.S. dollar falls in value, as it did sharply between 1985 and 1988. If foreign buyers increase their spending on U.S. goods, and domestic buyers substitute U.S.-made goods for imports, aggregate expenditure on domestic output will rise, inventories will fall, and real GDP (Y) will increase.

A depreciation of a country's currency is likely to increase its GDP.[5]

Exchange Rates and the Balance of Trade: The J Curve   Because a depreciating currency tends to increase exports and decrease imports, you might think it will also reduce a country's trade deficit. In fact, the effect of a depreciation on the balance of trade is ambiguous.

Many economists believe that when a currency starts to depreciate, the balance of trade is likely to worsen for the first few quarters (perhaps three to six). After that, the balance of trade may improve. This effect is graphed in Figure 34.7. The curve in this figure resembles the letter J, and the movement in the balance of trade that it describes is sometimes called the **J-curve effect**. The point of the J shape is that the balance of trade gets worse before it gets better following a currency depreciation.

How does the J curve come about? Recall that the balance of trade is equal to export revenue minus import costs, including exports and imports of services:

$$\text{balance of trade} = \text{dollar price of exports} \times \text{quantity of exports}$$
$$-\text{dollar price of imports} \times \text{quantity of imports}$$

A currency depreciation affects the items on the right side of this equation as follows. First, the quantity of exports increases and the quantity of imports decreases; both have a *positive* effect on the balance of trade (lowering the trade deficit or raising the trade surplus). Second, the dollar price of exports is not likely to change very much, at least not initially. The dollar price of exports changes when the U.S. price level changes, but the initial effect of a depreciation on the domestic price level is not likely to be large. Third, the dollar price of imports increases. Imports

J-curve effect Following a currency depreciation, a country's balance of trade may get worse before it gets better. The graph showing this effect is shaped like the letter *J*, hence the name J-curve effect.

---

[5]For this reason, some countries are tempted at times to intervene in foreign exchange markets, depreciate their currencies, and stimulate their economies. If all countries attempted to lower the value of their currencies simultaneously, there would be no gain in income for any of them. Although the exchange rate system at the time was different, such a situation actually occurred during the early years of the Great Depression. So-called *beggar-thy-neighbor* policies of competitive devaluations were practiced by many countries in a desperate attempt to maintain export sales and employment.

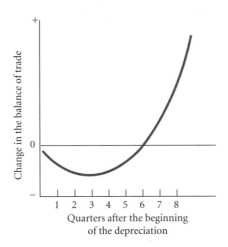

FIGURE 34.7 The Effect of a Depreciation on the Balance of Trade (the J Curve)

Initially, a depreciation of a country's currency may worsen its balance of trade. The negative effect on the price of imports may initially dominate the positive effects of an increase in exports and a decrease in imports.

into the United States are more expensive, because $1 U.S. buys fewer yen, euros, and so on, than before. An increase in the dollar price of imports has a *negative* effect on the balance of trade.

An example to clarify this last point follows: The dollar price of a Japanese car that costs 1,200,000 yen rises from $10,000 to $12,000 when the exchange rate moves from 120 yen per dollar to 100 yen per dollar. After the currency depreciation, the United States ends up spending more (in dollars) for the Japanese car than it did before. Of course, the United States will end up buying fewer Japanese cars than it did before. Does the number of cars drop enough so the quantity effect is bigger than the price effect, or vice versa? Does the value of imports increase or decrease?

The net effect of a depreciation on the balance of trade could go either way. The depreciation stimulates exports and cuts back imports, but it also increases the dollar price of imports. It seems that the negative effect dominates initially. The impact of a depreciation on the price of imports is generally felt quickly, while it takes time for export and import quantities to respond to price changes. In the short run, the value of imports increases more than the value of exports, so the balance of trade worsens. The initial effect is likely to be negative; but after exports and imports have had time to respond, the net effect turns positive. The more elastic the demand for exports and imports, the larger the eventual improvement in the balance of trade.

Exchange Rates and Prices The depreciation of a country's currency tends to increase its price level. There are two reasons for this effect. First, when a country's currency is less expensive, its products are more competitive on world markets, so exports rise. In addition, domestic buyers tend to substitute domestic products for the now-more-expensive imports. This means planned aggregate expenditure on domestically produced goods and services rises, and the aggregate demand curve shifts to the right. The result is a higher price level, higher output, or both. (You may want to draw an *AS/AD* diagram to verify this outcome.) If the economy is close to capacity, the result is likely to be higher prices. Second, a depreciation makes imported inputs more expensive. If costs increase, the aggregate supply curve shifts to the left. If aggregate demand remains unchanged, the result is an increase in the price level.

Monetary Policy with Flexible Exchange Rates Let us now put everything in this chapter together and consider what happens when monetary policy is used first to stimulate the economy and then to contract the economy.

Suppose the economy is below full employment and the Federal Reserve (Fed) decides to expand the money supply. The volume of reserves in the system is expanded, perhaps through open market purchases of U.S. government securities by the Fed. The result is a exchange rates, balance of payments, trade   search

○ Further Exploration ◉ News Analysis

**New Trade Agreement
with Central America
and the Dominican
Republic—2005**

**The Dollar, China,
and Trade in 2006**

The Dollar, China, and Trade in 2006

GOING INTO 2006, A MAJOR SOURCE of concern for the U.S. economy was the exchange rate between the dollar and the Chinese currency, the yuan. The problem was the huge and growing trade deficit between the United States and China, which was blamed on the artificially low value of the yuan. The following article from the *New York Times* describes the dilemma quite well.

China and the U.S. Embark on a Perilous Trip

The dollar may be on a healthier course for now, but that does not silence the prophets of doom who fear a collapse of the currency or some other economic crisis as Americans continue to buy far more abroad than they sell.

The announcement from China on Thursday that it would, at long last, raise the value of the yuan against the dollar and continue to do so gradually quiets the alarmists for the moment. Thanks to the revaluation, no one can claim that the sky is falling—at least this weekend. "The Chicken Littles are really wrong," said James Glassman, chief domestic economist at J. P. Morgan Chase.

Even gradually reducing the value of the dollar by an amount large enough— say 30 percent to 40 percent—so that Americans are finally discouraged from buying increasingly expensive Asian goods, may have unpleasant conse-

quences. Among other dangers there is the risk that China will cut back on its purchases of American government securities, contributing to a sharp rise in long-term interest rates.

The problem stems from America's persistent buying of much more from other countries, particularly China and Japan, than those countries purchase from the United States. The payment for the imports is in dollars, and because the foreigners do not use all of the dollars to make offsetting purchases here, they lend the excess back to Americans, who then use the loans to purchase more from abroad.

That satisfies this country's desire to consume and Asia's desire to step up production and employ-

ment for its vast population. But America's indebtedness to the rest of the world is rising at an annual rate approaching $700 billion. Everyone agrees that this indebtedness cannot continue to go up indefinitely. But while the pessimists see a sharp painful correction in the not-so-distant future, the optimists, a camp that includes the Bush administration and much of Wall Street, argue that the present arrangement is quite sustainable.

decrease in the interest rate. The lower interest rate stimulates planned investment spending and consumption spending.

This added spending causes inventories to be lower than planned and aggregate output (income) (Y) to rise, but there are two additional effects. One, the lower interest rate has an impact in the foreign exchange market. A lower interest rate means a lower demand for U.S. securities by foreigners, so the demand for dollars drops. Two, U.S. investment managers will be more likely to buy foreign securities (which are now paying relatively higher interest rates), so the supply of dollars rises. Both events push down the value of the dollar.

A cheaper dollar is a good thing if the goal of the monetary expansion is to stimulate the domestic economy, because a cheaper dollar means more U.S. exports and fewer imports. If consumers substitute U.S.-made goods for imports, both the added exports and the decrease in imports mean more spending on domestic products, so the multiplier actually increases.

Now suppose inflation is a problem and the Fed wants to slow it down with tight money. Here again, floating exchange rates help. Tight monetary policy works through a higher interest rate. A higher interest rate lowers investment and consumption spending, reducing aggregate expenditure, reducing output, and lowering the price level. The higher interest rate also attracts foreign buyers into U.S. financial markets, driving up the value of the dollar, which reduces the price of imports. The reduction in the price of imports causes a shift of the aggregate supply curve to the right, which helps fight inflation.

Fiscal Policy with Flexible Exchange Rates The openness of the economy and flexible exchange rates do not always work to the advantage of policy makers. Consider a policy of cutting taxes to stimulate the economy. Suppose Congress enacts a major tax cut designed to raise output. Spending by households rises, but not all this added spending is on domestic products—some leaks out of the U.S. economy, reducing the multiplier.

As income rises, so does the demand for money (M^d)—not the demand for dollars in the foreign exchange market, but the amount of money people desire to hold for transactions. Unless the Fed is fully accommodating, the interest rate will rise. A higher interest rate tends to attract foreign demand for U.S. securities. This rise in demand tends to drive the price of the dollar up, which further blunts the effectiveness of the tax cut. If the value of the dollar rises, U.S. exports are less competitive in world markets, and the quantity of exports will decline. Similarly, a strong dollar makes imported goods look cheaper, and U.S. citizens spend more on foreign goods and less on U.S. goods, an affect that again reduces the multiplier.

There is another caveat to the multiplier story of Chapters 21 and 22. Without a fully accommodating Fed, three factors work to reduce the multiplier: (1) A higher interest rate from the increase in money demand may crowd out private investment and consumption; (2) some of the increase in income from the expansion will be spent on imports; and (3) a higher interest rate may cause the dollar to appreciate, discouraging exports and further encouraging imports.

Monetary Policy with Fixed Exchange Rates Although most major countries in the world today have a flexible exchange rate (counting for this purpose the euro zone countries as one country), it is interesting to ask what role monetary policy can play if a country has a fixed exchange rate. The answer is, no role. In order for a country to keep its exchange rate fixed to, say, the U.S. dollar, its interest rate cannot change relative to the U.S. interest rate. If the monetary authority of the country lowered the interest rate because it wanted to stimulate the economy, the country's currency would depreciate (assuming that the U.S. interest rate did not change). People would want to sell the country's currency and buy dollars and invest in U.S. securities, because the country's interest rate would have fallen relative to the U.S. interest rate. In other words, the monetary authority cannot change its interest rate relative to the U.S. interest rate without having its exchange rate change. The monetary authority is at the mercy of the United States, and it has no independent way of changing its interest rate if it wants to keep its exchange rate fixed to the dollar.

This restriction means that when the various European countries moved in 1999 to a common currency, the euro, each of the countries gave up its monetary policy. There is now only one monetary policy for all the euro zone countries, and it is decided by the European Central Bank (ECB).

The one case in which a country can change its interest rate and keep its exchange rate fixed is if it imposes capital controls. Imposing capital controls means that the country limits or prevents people from buying or selling its currency in the foreign exchange markets. A citizen of the country may be prevented, for example, from using the country's currency to buy dollars. The problem with capital controls is that they are hard to enforce, especially for large countries and for long periods of time.

AN INTERDEPENDENT WORLD ECONOMY

The increasing interdependence of countries in the world economy has made the problems facing policy makers more difficult. We used to be able to think of the United States as a relatively self-sufficient region. Forty years ago, economic events outside U.S. borders had relatively little effect on its economy. This situation is no longer true. The events of the past four decades have taught us that the performance of the U.S. economy is heavily dependent on events outside U.S. borders.

This chapter and the previous one have provided only the bare bones of open market macroeconomics. If you continue your study of economics, more will be added to the basic story we have presented.

Also in the international arena, Chapter 35 deals with the problems of developing countries and economies in transition from noncapitalist to capitalist.

SUMMARY

1. The main difference between an international transaction and a domestic transaction concerns currency exchange: When people in different countries buy from, and sell to, each other, an exchange of currencies must also take place.

2. The *exchange rate* is the price of one country's currency in terms of another country's currency.

THE BALANCE OF PAYMENTS

3. *Foreign exchange* is all currencies other than the domestic currency of a given country. The record of a nation's transactions in goods, services, and assets with the rest of the world is its *balance of payments*. The balance of payments is also the record of a country's sources (supply) and uses (demand) of foreign exchange.

EQUILIBRIUM OUTPUT (INCOME) IN AN OPEN ECONOMY

4. In an open economy, some income is spent on foreign-produced goods instead of domestically produced goods. To measure planned domestic aggregate expenditure in an open economy, we add total exports but subtract total imports: $C + I + G + EX - IM$. The open economy is in equilibrium when domestic aggregate output (income) (Y) equals planned domestic aggregate expenditure.

5. In an open economy, the multiplier equals $1/[1 - (MPC - MPM)]$, where MPC is the marginal propensity to consume and MPM is the marginal propensity to import. The *marginal propensity to import* is the change in imports caused by a $1 change in income.

6. In addition to income, other factors that affect the level of imports are the after-tax real wage rate, after-tax nonlabor income, interest rates, and relative prices of domestically produced and foreign-produced goods. The demand for exports is determined by economic activity in the rest of the world and by relative prices.

7. An increase in U.S. economic activity leads to a worldwide increase in economic activity, which then "feeds back" to the United States. An increase in U.S. imports increases other countries' exports, which stimulates economies and increases their imports, which increases U.S. exports, which stimulates the U.S. economy and increases its imports, and so on. This is the *trade feedback effect*.

8. Export prices of other countries affect U.S. import prices. The general rate of inflation abroad is likely to affect U.S. import prices. If the inflation rate abroad is high, U.S. import prices are likely to rise.

9. Because one country's exports are another country's imports, an increase in export prices increases other countries' import prices. An increase in other countries' import prices leads to an increase in their domestic prices—and their export prices. In short, export prices affect import prices, and vice versa. This *price feedback effect* shows that inflation is "exportable"; an increase in the price level in one country can drive up prices in other countries, making inflation in the first country worse.

THE OPEN ECONOMY WITH FLEXIBLE EXCHANGE RATES

10. The equilibrium exchange rate occurs when the quantity demanded of a foreign currency in the foreign exchange market equals the quantity of that currency supplied in the foreign exchange market.

11. *Depreciation of a currency occurs* when a nation's currency falls in value relative to another country's currency. *Appreciation of a currency* occurs when a nation's currency rises in value relative to another country's currency.

12. According to the *law of one price*, if the costs of transportation are small, the price of the same good in different countries should be roughly the same. The theory that exchange rates are set so that the price of similar goods in different countries is the same is known as *purchasing-power-parity* theory. In practice, transportation costs are significant for many goods, and the law of one price does not hold for these goods.

13. A high rate of inflation in one country relative to another puts pressure on the exchange rate between the two countries. There is a general tendency for the currencies of relatively high-inflation countries to depreciate.

14. A depreciation of the dollar tends to increase U.S. GDP by making U.S. exports cheaper (hence more competitive abroad) and by making U.S. imports more expensive

(encouraging consumers to switch to domestically produced goods and services).

15. The effect of a depreciation of a nation's currency on its balance of trade is unclear. In the short run, a currency depreciation may increase the balance-of-trade deficit, because it raises the price of imports. Although this price increase causes a decrease in the quantity of imports demanded, the impact of a depreciation on the price of imports is generally felt quickly; but it takes time for export and import quantities to respond to price changes. The initial effect is likely to be negative; but after exports and imports have had time to respond, the net effect turns positive. The tendency for the balance-of-trade deficit to widen and then to decrease as the result of a currency depreciation is known as the *J-curve effect*.

16. The depreciation of a country's currency tends to raise its price level for two reasons. First, a currency depreciation

increases planned aggregate expenditure, an effect that shifts the aggregate demand curve to the right. If the economy is close to capacity, the result is likely to be higher prices. Second, a depreciation makes imported inputs more expensive. If costs increase, the aggregate supply curve shifts to the left. If aggregate demand remains unchanged, the result is an increase in the price level.

17. When exchange rates are flexible, a U.S. expansionary monetary policy decreases the interest rate and stimulates planned investment and consumption spending. The lower interest rate leads to a lower demand for U.S. securities by foreigners, and a higher demand for foreign securities by U.S. investment-fund managers. As a result, the dollar depreciates. A U.S. contractionary monetary policy appreciates the dollar.

18. Flexible exchange rates do not always work to the advantage of policy makers. An expansionary fiscal policy can appreciate the dollar and work to reduce the multiplier.

REVIEW TERMS AND CONCEPTS

appreciation of a currency, 733

balance of payments, 723

balance of trade, 723

balance on capital account, 724

balance on current account, 724

depreciation of a currency, 733

exchange rate, 721

floating, or market-determined, exchange rates, 730

foreign exchange, 722

J-curve effect, 736

law of one price, 733

marginal propensity to import (*MPM*), 726

net exports of goods and services (*EX − IM*), 726

price feedback effect, 730

purchasing-power-parity theory, 734

trade deficit, 724

trade feedback effect, 729

Planned aggregate expenditure in an open economy:

$$AE \equiv C + I + G + EX - IM$$

Open-economy multiplier:

$$\frac{1}{1 - (MPC - MPM)}$$

PROBLEM SET

1. During 2003, the U.S. dollar fell sharply in value against most currencies, including the Japanese yen and the euro. Most economists point to the actions of the Federal Reserve as an explanation. For each of the following, say whether you agree or disagree, and explain your answer.
   a. This was likely a result of Federal Reserve action to slow the economy with higher interest rates.
   b. This was bad news for U.S. export companies, which now received less for their dollars.
   c. This was actually good news for European exporters, which would receive more dollars for their goods.

2. In December 2005, the euro was trading at $1.18. That is, the exchange rate was $1.18 = 1 euro. Check the Web or any daily newspaper to see what the "price" of a euro is today. What explanations can you give for the change? Be sure to check what has happened to interest rates and economic growth.

3. Suppose the following prevailed on the foreign exchange market in 2006 with floating exchange rates:
   a. Name three phenomena that might shift the demand curve to the right.
   b. Which, if any, of these three might cause a simultaneous shift of the supply curve to the left?

c. What effects might each of the three phenomena have on the balance of trade if the exchange rate floats?

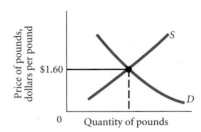

4. Obtain a recent issue of *The Economist*. Turn to the section entitled "Financial Indicators." Look at the table entitled "Trade, exchange rates and budgets." Which country had the largest trade deficit over the last year and during the last month? Which country had the largest trade surplus over the last year and during the last month? How does the current account deficit/surplus compare to the overall trade balance? How can you explain the difference?

5. The box on page 738 describes the U.S. trade deficit with China in 2005. Search the Web to find data on the U.S. trade balance with China. Has it gone up or down since the end of 2005? Has the value of the yuan relative to the dollar gone up or down? What has happened to the interest rate (yield) on the 10-year Treasury bond since 2005? In a few paragraphs, explain the relationship among long-term interest rates, the exchange rate, and the trade deficit.

6. The exchange rate between the U.S. dollar and the Japanese yen is floating freely—both governments do not intervene in the market for each currency. Suppose a large trade deficit with Japan prompts the United States to impose quotas on certain Japanese products imported into the United States and, as a result, the quantity of these imports falls.

   a. The decrease in spending on Japanese products increases spending on U.S.-made goods. Why? What effect will this have on U.S. output and employment, and on Japanese output and employment?

   b. What happens to U.S. imports from Japan when U.S. output (or income) rises? If the quotas initially reduce imports from Japan by $25 billion, why is the final reduction in imports likely to be less than $25 billion?

   c. Suppose the quotas do succeed in reducing imports from Japan by $15 billion. What will happen to the demand for yen? Why?

   d. What will happen to the dollar–yen exchange rate, and why? (*Hint:* There is an excess supply of yen, or an excess demand for dollars.) What effects will the change in the value of each currency have on employment and output in the United States? What about the balance of trade? (Ignore complications such as the J curve.)

   e. Considering the macroeconomic effects of a quota on Japanese imports, could a quota actually reduce employment and output in the United States, or have no effect at all? Explain.

7. What effect will each of the following events have on the current account balance and the exchange rate if the exchange rate is fixed? If it is floating?

   a. The U.S. government cuts taxes, and income rises.

   b. The U.S. inflation rate increases, and prices in the United States rise faster than those in the countries with which the United States trades.

   c. The United States adopts an expansionary monetary policy. Interest rates fall (and are now lower than those in other countries), and income rises.

   d. The textile companies' "Buy American" campaign is successful, and U.S. consumers switch from purchasing imported products to buying those made in the United States.

8. You are given the following model, which describes the economy of Hypothetica.

   (1) Consumption function: $C = 100 + .8Y_d$
   (2) Planned investment: $I = 38$
   (3) Government spending: $G = 75$
   (4) Exports: $EX = 25$
   (5) Imports: $IM = .05\ Y_d$
   (6) Disposable income: $Y_d \equiv Y - T$
   (7) Taxes: $T = 40$
   (8) Planned aggregate expenditure:

   $$AE \equiv C + I + G + EX - IM$$

   (9) Definition of equilibrium income: $Y = AE$

   a. What is equilibrium income in Hypothetica? What is the government deficit? What is the current account balance?

   b. If government spending is increased to $G = 80$, what happens to equilibrium income? Explain, using the government spending multiplier. What happens to imports?

   c. Now suppose the amount of imports is limited to $IM = 40$ by a quota on imports. If government spending is again increased from 75 to 80, what happens to equilibrium income? Explain why the same increase in G has a bigger effect on income in the second case. What is it about the presence of imports that changes the value of the multiplier?

   d. If exports are fixed at $EX = 25$, what must income be to ensure a current account balance of zero? (*Hint:* Imports depend on income, so what must income be for imports to be equal to exports?) By how much must we cut government spending to balance the current account? (*Hint:* Use your answer to the first part of this question to determine how much of a decrease in income is needed. Then use the multiplier to calculate the decrease in G needed to reduce income by that amount.)

APPENDIX

WORLD MONETARY SYSTEMS SINCE 1900

Since the beginning of the twentieth century, the world has operated under a number of different monetary systems. This appendix provides a brief history of each and a description of how they worked.

THE GOLD STANDARD

The gold standard was the major system of exchange rate determination before 1914. All currencies were priced in terms of gold—an ounce of gold was worth so much in each currency. When all currencies exchanged at fixed ratios to gold, exchange rates could be determined easily. For instance, one ounce of gold was worth $20 U.S.; that same ounce of gold exchanged for £4 (British pounds). Because $20 and £4 were each worth one ounce of gold, the exchange rate between dollars and pounds was $20/£4, or $5 to £1.

For the gold standard to be effective it had to be backed up by the country's willingness to buy and sell gold at the determined price. As long as countries maintain their currencies at a fixed value in terms of gold *and* as long as each is willing to buy and sell gold, exchange rates are fixed. If at the given exchange rate the number of U.S. citizens who want to buy things produced in Great Britain is equal to the number of British citizens who want to buy things produced in the United States, the currencies of the two countries will simply be exchanged.

What if U.S. citizens suddenly decide they want to drink imported Scotch instead of domestic bourbon? If the British do not have an increased desire for U.S. goods, they would still accept U.S. dollars because they could be redeemed in gold. This gold could then be immediately turned into pounds.

As long as a country's overall balance of payments remained in balance, no gold would enter or leave the country, and the economy would be in equilibrium. If U.S. citizens bought more from the British than the British bought from the United States, however, the U.S. balance of payments would be in deficit, and the U.S. stock of gold would begin to fall. Conversely, Britain would start to accumulate gold because it would be exporting more than it spent on imports.

Under the gold standard, gold was a big determinant of the money supply.[1] An inflow of gold into a country caused that country's money supply to expand, and an outflow of gold caused that country's money supply to contract. If gold were flowing from the United States to Great Britain, the British money supply would expand and the U.S. money supply would contract.

Now recall from earlier chapters the impacts of a change in the money supply. An expanded money supply in Britain will lower British interest rates and stimulate aggregate demand. As a result, aggregate output (income) and the price level in Britain will increase. Higher British prices will discourage U.S. citizens from buying British goods. At the same time, British citizens will have more income and will face relatively lower import prices, causing them to import more from the States.

On the other side of the Atlantic, U.S. citizens will face a contracting domestic money supply. This will cause higher interest rates, declining aggregate demand, lower prices, and falling output (income). The effect will be lower demand in the United States for British goods. Thus, changes in relative prices and incomes that resulted from the inflow and outflow of gold would automatically bring trade back into balance.

PROBLEMS WITH THE GOLD STANDARD

Two major problems were associated with the gold standard. First, the gold standard implied that a country had little control over its money supply. The reason, as we have just seen, is that the money stock increased when the overall balance of payments was in surplus (gold inflow) and decreased when the overall balance was in deficit (gold outflow). A country that was experiencing a balance-of-payments deficit could correct the problem only by the painful process of allowing its money supply to contract. This contraction brought on a slump in economic activity, a slump that would eventually restore balance-of-payments equilibrium, but only after reductions in income and employment. Countries could (and

often did) act to protect their gold reserves, and this precautionary step prevented the adjustment mechanism from correcting the deficit.

Making the money supply depend on the amount of gold available had another disadvantage. When major new gold fields were discovered (as in California in 1849 and South Africa in 1886), the world's supply of gold (and therefore of money) increased. The price level rose and income increased. When no new gold was discovered, the supply of money remained unchanged and prices and income tended to fall.

When President Reagan took office in 1981, he established a commission to consider returning the nation to the gold standard. The final commission report recommended against such a move. An important part of the reasoning behind this recommendation was that the gold standard puts enormous economic power in the hands of gold-producing nations.

FIXED EXCHANGE RATES AND THE BRETTON WOODS SYSTEM

As World War II drew to a close, a group of economists from the United States and Europe met to formulate a new set of rules for exchange rate determination that they hoped would avoid the difficulties of the gold standard. The rules they designed became known as the **Bretton Woods system**, after the town in New Hampshire where the delegates met. The Bretton Woods system was based on two (not necessarily compatible) premises. First, countries were to maintain fixed exchange rates with each other. Instead of pegging their currencies directly to gold, however, currencies were fixed in terms of the U.S. dollar, which was fixed in value at $35 per ounce of gold. The British pound, for instance, was fixed at roughly $2.40, so that an ounce of gold was worth approximately £14.6. As we shall see, the pure system of fixed exchange rates would work in a manner very similar to the pre-1914 gold standard.

The second aspect of the Bretton Woods system added a new wrinkle to the operation of the international economy. Countries experiencing a "fundamental disequilibrium" in their balance of payments were allowed to change their exchange rates. (The term *fundamental disequilibrium* was necessarily vague, but it came to be interpreted as a large and persistent current account deficit.) Exchange rates were not really fixed under the Bretton Woods system; they were, as someone remarked, only "fixed until further notice."

The point of allowing countries with serious current account problems to alter the value of their currency was to avoid the harsh recessions that the operation of the gold standard would have produced under these circumstances. However, the experience of the European economies in the years between World War I and World War II suggested it might not be a good idea to give countries complete freedom to change their exchange rates whenever they wished.

During the Great Depression, many countries undertook so-called competitive devaluations to protect domestic

---

[1] In the days when currencies were tied to gold, changes in the amount of gold influenced the supply of money in two ways. A change in the quantity of gold coins in circulation had a direct effect on the supply of money; indirectly, gold served as a backing for paper currency. A decrease in the central bank's gold holdings meant a decline in the amount of paper money that could be supported.

output and employment. That is, countries would try to encourage exports—a source of output growth and employment—by attempting to set as low an exchange rate as possible, thereby making their exports competitive with foreign-produced goods. Unfortunately, such policies had a built-in flaw. A devaluation of the pound against the French franc might help encourage British exports to France, but if those additional British exports cut into French output and employment, France would likely respond by devaluing the franc against the pound, a move that, of course, would undo the effects of the pound's initial devaluation.

To solve this exchange rate rivalry, the Bretton Woods agreement created the International Monetary Fund (IMF). Its job was to assist countries experiencing temporary current account problems.[2] It was also supposed to certify that a "fundamental disequilibrium" existed before a country was allowed to change its exchange rate. The IMF is like an international economic traffic cop whose job is to ensure that all countries are playing the game according to the agreed-to rules and to provide emergency assistance where needed.

"PURE" FIXED EXCHANGE RATES

Under a pure fixed exchange rate system, governments set a particular *fixed* rate at which their currencies will exchange for each other and then commit themselves to maintaining that rate. A true fixed exchange rate system is like the gold standard in that exchange rates are supposed to stay the same forever.[3] Because currencies are no longer backed by gold, they have no fixed, or standard, value relative to each other. There is therefore no automatic mechanism to keep exchange rates aligned with each other, as with the gold standard.

The result is that under a pure fixed exchange rate system, governments must at times intervene in the foreign exchange market to keep currencies aligned at their established values. Economists define government intervention in the foreign exchange market as the buying or selling of foreign exchange for the purpose of manipulating the exchange rate. What kind of intervention is likely to occur under a fixed exchange rate system, and how does it work?

We can see how intervention works by looking at Figure 34A.1. Initially, the market for Italian liras is in equilibrium. At the fixed exchange rate of $0.02 per lira, the supply of liras is exactly equal to the demand for liras. No government intervention is necessary to maintain the exchange rate at this level. Now suppose Italian wines are found to be contaminated with antifreeze, and U.S. citizens switch to California wines. This substitution away from the Italian product shifts

---

[2]The idea was that the IMF would make short-term loans to a country with a current account deficit. The loans would enable the country to correct the current account problem gradually, without bringing on a deep recession, running out of foreign exchange reserves, or devaluing the currency.

[3]"Forever" is a very long time. Some countries in Central America have maintained fixed exchange rates with the U.S. dollar for almost 30 years, practically forever in the world of international finance.

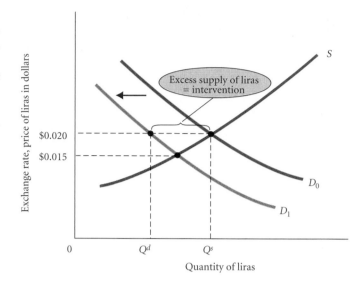

FIGURE 34A.1 Government Intervention in the Foreign Exchange Market

If the price of liras was set by a completely unfettered market, the price of a lira would be $0.020 when demand is D_0 and $0.015 when demand is D_1. If the government has committed itself to keeping the value of a lira at $0.020, it must buy up the excess supply of liras ($Q^s - Q^d$).

the U.S. demand curve for liras to the left: The United States demands fewer liras at every exchange rate (cost of a lira) because it is purchasing less from Italy than it did before.

If the price of liras were set by a completely unfettered market, the shift in the demand curve would lead to a fall in the price of liras, just the way the price of wheat would fall if there was an excess supply of wheat. Remember, the Italian and U.S. governments have committed themselves to maintaining the rate at $0.02 per lira. To do so, either the U.S. government or Italian government (or both) must buy up the excess supply of liras to keep the price of the lira from falling. In essence, the fixed exchange rate policy commits governments to making up any difference between the supply of a currency and the demand so as to keep the price of the currency (exchange rate) at the desired level. The government promises to act as the supplier (or demander) of last resort, who will ensure that the amount of foreign exchange demanded by the private sector will equal the supply at the fixed price.

PROBLEMS WITH THE BRETTON WOODS SYSTEM

As it developed after the end of World War II, the system of more-or-less fixed exchange rates had some flaws that led to its abandonment in 1971.

First, there was a basic asymmetry built into the rules of international finance. Countries experiencing large and persistent current account deficits—what the Bretton Woods agreements termed "fundamental disequilibria"—were obliged to devalue their currencies and/or take measures to cut their deficits by contracting their economies. Both of these alternatives were unpleasant, because devaluation meant rising prices and contraction meant rising unemployment. However, a country with a current account deficit had no choice, because it was losing stock of foreign exchange reserves. When its stock of foreign currencies became exhausted, it had to change its exchange rate, because further intervention (selling off some of its foreign exchange reserves) became impossible.

Countries experiencing current account surpluses were in a different position, because they were gaining foreign exchange reserves. Although these countries were supposed to stimulate their economies and/or revalue their currencies to restore balance to their current account, they were not obliged to do so. They could easily maintain their fixed exchange rate by buying up any excess supply of foreign exchange with their own currency, of which they had plentiful supply.

In practice, this meant some countries—especially Germany and Japan—tended to run large and chronic current account surpluses and were under no compulsion to take steps to correct the problem. The U.S. economy, stimulated by expenditures on the Vietnam War, experienced a large and prolonged current account deficit (capital outflow) in the 1960s, which was the counterpart of these surpluses. The United States was, however, in a unique position under the Bretton Woods system. The value of gold was fixed in terms of the U.S. dollar at $35 per ounce of gold. Other countries fixed their exchange rates in terms of U.S. dollars (and therefore only indirectly in terms of gold). Consequently the United States could never accomplish anything by devaluing its currency in terms of gold. If the dollar was devalued from $35 to $40 per ounce of gold, the yen, pegged at 200 yen per dollar, would move in parallel with the dollar (from 7,000 yen per ounce of gold to 8,000 yen per ounce), with the dollar–yen exchange rate unaffected. To correct its current account deficits vis-à-vis Japan and Germany, it would be necessary for those two countries to adjust their currencies' exchange rates with the dollar. These countries were reluctant to do so for a variety of reasons. As a result, the U.S. current account was chronically in deficit throughout the late 1960s.

A second flaw in the Bretton Woods system was that it permitted devaluations only if a country had a "chronic" current account deficit and was in danger of running out of foreign exchange reserves. This meant devaluations could often be predicted quite far in advance, and they usually had to be rather large if they were to correct any serious current account problem. The situation made it tempting for speculators to "attack" the currencies of countries with current account deficits.

Problems such as these eventually led the United States to abandon the Bretton Woods rules in 1971. The U.S. government refused to continue pegging the value of the dollar in terms of gold. Thus the prices of all currencies were free to find their own levels.

The alternative to fixed exchange rates is a system that allows exchange rates to move freely or flexibly in response to market forces. Two types of flexible exchange rate systems are usually distinguished. In a *freely floating system*, governments do not intervene at all in the foreign exchange market.[4] They do not buy or sell currencies with the aim of manipulating the rates. In a *managed floating system*, governments intervene if markets are becoming "disorderly"—fluctuating more than a government feels is desirable. Governments may also intervene if they think a currency is increasing or decreasing too much in value, even though the day-to-day fluctuations may be small.

Since the demise of the Bretton Woods system in 1971, the world's exchange rate system can be described as "managed floating." One of the important features of this system has been times of large fluctuations in exchange rates. For example, the yen–dollar rate went from 347 in 1971 to 210 in 1978, to 125 in 1988, and to 80 in 1995. These are very large changes, changes that have important effects on the international economy, some of which we have covered in this text.

---

[4]However, governments may from time to time buy or sell foreign exchange for their own needs (instead of influencing the exchange rate). For example, the U.S. government might need British pounds to buy land for a U.S. embassy building in London. For our purposes, we ignore this behavior because it is not "intervention" in the strict sense of the word.

SUMMARY

1. The gold standard was the major system of exchange rate determination before 1914. All currencies were priced in terms of gold. Difficulties with the gold standard led to the *Bretton Woods* agreement following World War II. Under this system, countries maintained fixed exchange rates with each other and fixed the value of their currencies in terms of the U.S. dollar. Countries experiencing a "fundamental disequi-

librium" in their current accounts were permitted to change their exchange rates.

2. The Bretton Woods system was abandoned in 1971. Since then, the world's exchange rate system has been one of managed floating rates. Under this system, governments intervene if foreign exchange markets are fluctuating more than the government thinks desirable.

REVIEW TERMS AND CONCEPTS

Bretton Woods The site in New Hampshire where a group of experts from 44 countries met in 1944 and agreed to an international monetary system of fixed exchange rates. 743

PROBLEM SET

1. The currency of Atlantis is the wimp. In 2005, Atlantis developed a balance-of-payments deficit with the United States as a result of an unanticipated decrease in exports; U.S. citizens cut back on the purchase of Atlantean goods. Assume Atlantis is operating under a system of fixed exchange rates.
   a. How does the drop in exports affect the market for wimps? Identify the deficit graphically.
   b. How must the government of Atlantis act (in the short run) to maintain the value of the wimp?
   c. If originally Atlantis were operating at full employment (potential GDP), what impact would these events have on its economy? Explain your answer.
   d. The chief economist of Atlantis suggests an expansionary monetary policy to restore full employment; the secretary of commerce suggests a tax cut (expansionary fiscal policy). Given the fixed exchange rate system, describe the effects of these two policy options on Atlantis's current account.
   e. How would your answers to **a**, **b**, and **c** change if the two countries operated under a floating rate system?

Globalization

Globalization is an often-used word today. A search reveals that the term was never mentioned in the pages of the *New York Times* during the 1970s, yet it now appears in *Times* stories virtually every day. Using the search engine Google turns up 55 million links using the word. Despite the fact that the word is used so frequently, it is rarely defined clearly. **Globalization** is the process of increasing interdependence among countries and their citizens.

Defined this way, globalization has social, cultural, political, and economic dimensions. It includes increasing international trade, travel, the spread of American movies and music, the incredible worldwide availability of information via the Internet, the problem of disease, global climate change, terrorism, religion, war, and so forth. Any attempt to address all the issues associated with increasing interdependence in a single text chapter, or even a single book, would be hopeless.

An even hotter topic in 2005–2006 is outsourcing, which turns up 83 million links on Google. *Outsourcing* refers generally to the practice of obtaining goods or services from outside sources. In most cases, the word is used to describe U.S. firms' hiring of foreign workers who stay in their own countries but communicate and perform tasks by telephone and over the Internet. Critics argue strongly that this practice amounts to shipping jobs abroad and paying very low wages to foreign workers rather than hiring higher-paid workers in the United States.

The purpose here is to explore the process of **economic globalization**. Economic globalization is the process of increasing *economic* interdependence among countries and their citizens. While the issues that we will discuss all have political and cultural dimensions, we will stick as closely as possible to economics by focusing on the causes and consequences of increased international trade of goods and services, increased cross-border movements of labor, and expanded international financial flows.

globalization The process of increasing interdependence among countries and their citizens.

economic globalization The process of increasing economic interdependence among countries and their citizens.

THE GLOBAL CIRCULAR FLOW

Figure 35.1 inserts the rest of the world on the circular flow diagram introduced in Chapter 3. It has clearly become more complex. The basic diagram of a simple closed economy includes the supply and demand for goods and services, the supply and demand for labor, and the supply and demand for capital (saving and investment). Household income comes

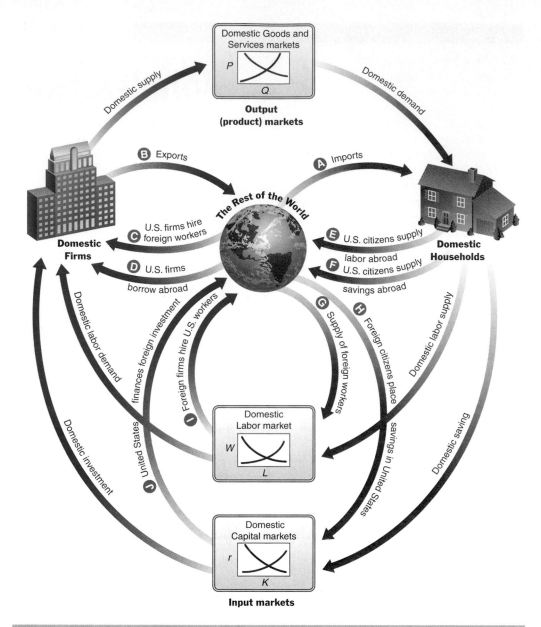

FIGURE 35.1 Economic Globalization: International Flows

A. U.S. citizens buy foreign-produced goods and services (imports)
B. U.S. producers sell their goods and services abroad (exports)
C. U.S. producers hire foreign workers or outsource jobs
D. U.S. producers finance investment with foreign savings—borrowing from a foreign bank
E. U.S. citizens supply labor to foreign companies or in foreign countries
F. U.S. citizens send savings abroad—buy foreign stocks and bonds, put money in foreign banks
G. Foreign citizens supply labor in the U.S. labor market
H. Foreign citizens place savings in the United States—buy U.S. stocks and bonds, put money in U.S. banks
 I. Foreign producers hire workers in the United States
J. Foreign producers finance investment with U.S. savings

from working and from owning assets; firms demand labor and capital and supply products; households demand goods and services and supply labor and capital.

Opening the economy to include the rest of the world adds 10 new flows to the diagram. The 10 new flows are shown in Figure 35.1: (**A.**) Domestic (in this case, U.S.) households can now buy goods and services from abroad—imports. This brings presumably greater choice and potentially lower prices. (**B.**) Domestic firms can now sell in foreign markets—exports. This opens up potential profit opportunities. (**C.**) Firms can hire workers from abroad either by employing immigrants or by outsourcing tasks or jobs to foreign workers, in essence importing labor. (**D.**) U.S. firms can now turn to the rest of the world for capital. A U.S. firm may finance a new factory by borrowing from a German bank or by selling bonds in London. (**E.**) U.S. citizens can now look for a job in foreign labor markets. A laid-off high-tech worker may search for a job in Canada. (**F.**) Domestic households may put their savings into foreign stocks and bonds. During periods of low interest rates in the United States, higher rates in other countries may look attractive.

But that's not all: (**G.**) Foreign workers can work in the United States. Thousands of Mexican immigrants, many legal and many illegal, enter the United States weekly looking for work. (**H.**) Foreign citizens can buy U.S. stocks and bonds or put money into U.S. banks. One of the reasons for the big stock market boom in the late 1990s was that foreigners wanted to buy technology stocks in the United States. (**I.**) Foreign firms can demand labor, making jobs available to U.S. workers. Finally, (**J.**) Foreign firms may look to the United States for funds to use for investment in new capital. An Italian telephone company could finance the acquisition of new switching equipment with a loan from Citibank.

The basic argument for economic globalization can be found in the decisions behind each of these flows. A U.S. consumer buys a good or service from a foreign producer if the good being bought is cheaper than what he would have to pay for it in the United States or if it is of higher quality. Similarly, U.S. citizens put their savings into a foreign bond if it is yielding more than a similar U.S. bond. These choices are made on the basis of self-interest.

Think of the United States as a set of 50 independent states that are totally integrated economically. People, financial capital, and goods and services flow freely across borders in response to people's preferences. If we didn't allow people to move freely across borders, or if we didn't let New Jersey citizens buy shares in California companies, or if we barred the export of fish from the coasts to the interior, the system would clearly be inefficient. Efficiency in any economy, even the world economy, is achieved if capital and labor can move freely to where their productivity is the highest . . . if factors of production are put to work in their "highest and best uses."

But wait a minute. If it were that simple, what is all the fuss about? Why are there such violent demonstrations over the process of globalization? Some contend that trade leads to domestic unemployment and lower wages as foreign workers compete with domestic workers. Others say that U.S. industry cannot compete with goods produced in countries with very low-wage labor. Still others contend that economic openness leads to unfair labor standards and sweatshop conditions in many countries or that openness leads to fierce competition and environmental degradation. Some just dislike the expansion of capitalism that they regard as inherently unjust. We will explore the objections one at a time after looking briefly at the history of globalization.

A BRIEF HISTORY OF ECONOMIC GLOBALIZATION

Economic historian Jeffrey Williamson classifies the period 1820–1914 as the first great period of globalization and the period since World War II as the second. Trade as a percentage of the world's gross domestic product (GDP) rose from 5 percent in the early years of the nineteenth century to 20 percent at the beginning of World War I. The trade barriers that were imposed after 1914, the world wars, and the Great Depression all conspired to cut trade as a percentage of world GDP back to around 5 percent. But the establishment of a new financial order at Bretton Woods, New Hampshire, in 1946 ushered in a new era, and trade grew back to 20 percent of world GDP by 1975.

In 1919, a young John Maynard Keynes said:

> What an extraordinary episode in the economic progress of man that age was which came to an end in August of 1914! . . . The inhabitant of London could order by telephone, sipping his morning tea in bed, the various products of the whole earth, in such quantity as he might see fit, and reasonably expect their early delivery upon his doorstep; he could at the same moment and by the same means adventure his wealth in the natural resources and new enterprises in any quarter of the world, and share, without exertion or even trouble, in their prospective fruits and advantages.[1]

---

[1]Quoted in Stanley Fischer, "Globalization and Its Challenges," *American Economic Review*, May 2003, p. 26.

Although the data are difficult to get, many would argue that with respect to the international mobility of labor, we are less globalized than we were at the beginning of the twentieth century. At that time about 15 percent of the U.S. population was foreign born. The Census Bureau placed that number at 10.4 percent in 2000 up from 7.9 percent in 1990. Clearly, immigration has increased in recent years, but it is unclear whether we are approaching the immigration rates of the 1920s.

International capital flows were blamed for the dramatic events of 1997 in Asia. Volatile exchange rates caused by a rapid withdrawal of loans and credit to Indonesia, Korea, Thailand, and other East Asian countries led to dramatic swings in exchange rates and deep recessions in those countries.

Many dimensions of globalization are new today. Recent years have seen sharp reductions in trade barriers with the signing of the North American Free Trade Agreement (NAFTA) and the General Agreement on Tariffs and Trade (GATT), discussed in earlier chapters. Dramatic increases in the flows of information and commerce over the Internet and the increased speed and lower cost of travel have made the world a much smaller place—far more aware of cultural, political, and religious differences. Another new development is the dramatic increase in outsourcing, or hiring low-wage foreign workers over the Internet. A big issue in the presidential election of 2004 and the subject of a best-selling book by Thomas Friedman in 2005, outsourcing has become a huge political issue.

THE BENEFITS AND COSTS OF GLOBALIZATION

Economic globalization has been criticized on many fronts. To keep the arguments clear, we first review the debate about free trade in goods and services. Next we turn to the debate over the mobility of labor between countries: immigration. Finally we discuss the unique problems of global financial markets.

THE FREE-TRADE DEBATE REVISITED

The potential benefits from trade have been examined several times in this text. The simple story of comparative advantage was first discussed briefly in Chapter 2 and later in more detail in Chapter 33. The argument, first formalized by David Ricardo in the nineteenth century, is simple but powerful, and it has stood the test of time. The argument rests on two pieces of intuition. First, if you have something that I want and I have something that you want, we can exchange and both be better off. Voluntary exchange is efficient. Second, applying the concept to nations, two nations can benefit from free trade by specializing in producing those products in which they enjoy a **comparative advantage**. A country enjoys a comparative advantage in the production of a good if the production of that good has a lower opportunity cost than it would have if produced in another country.

comparative advantage
A country enjoys a comparative advantage in the production of a good if the production of that good has a lower opportunity cost than it would have if produced in another country.

In both Chapter 2 and again in Chapter 33, we showed how trade between two countries allowed both to break out from behind the constraints of their production possibility frontiers. We showed that this is true even if one country is more efficient in the production of all goods. Perhaps even easier to understand, if consumers can buy the same good that they can buy at home at a lower cost in international markets, what is the logic for buying at home or for "protecting" domestically produced goods and services from foreign competition?

As we have seen, those who oppose trade make a number of arguments. First and foremost is that home-produced goods are produced with American workers and that buying imports or outsourcing simply ships jobs abroad. And besides, how can we compete with countries that pay low wages or have workers in sweatshop conditions? Not only do we lose American jobs, but we contribute to substandard working conditions in poor countries.

Proponents of free trade have a number of counterarguments:

1. We can't buy from countries unless they simultaneously buy from us. A number of years ago, presidential candidate Ross Perot opposed NAFTA on the grounds that there would be a "giant sucking sound" as all the good jobs in the United States moved to Mexico, where workers are paid a very low wage. Think about what would happen if this shift occurred.

   If U.S. citizens wanted to buy everything in Mexico, but the Mexicans didn't want to buy anything from us, foreign exchange markets would prevent it from happening.

Mexican workers are paid in pesos. To buy a good produced in Mexico, a buyer has to obtain pesos. But if no Mexicans wanted to buy anything in the United States, there would be no one willing to exchange pesos for dollars. Simply put, there would be no supply of pesos on foreign exchange markets but there would be a big demand for them. As a result, the price of the peso—the exchange rate—would rise.

Now think carefully about what a more expensive peso means. Since U.S. buyers have to buy pesos to buy Mexican goods, Mexican goods just became more expensive. At the same time, the increase in the price of pesos (dollars per peso) makes American goods look cheaper to Mexicans. This will have to go on until the supply and demand for pesos is equal! That means that Mexicans find some goods cheaper in the United States. In fact, exports to Mexico grew from $46 billion in 1995, just after NAFTA went into effect, to $111 billion by 2000. The exchange rate adjusts to make up for the wage differential.

There is one important exception to this story. A country can buy more goods from a second country for an extended period if those purchases are balanced by purchases of stocks and bonds. China, for example, sold more than $10 billion per month more in goods and services to the United States during 2005 than the United States bought from China. To balance that while holding the value of the Chinese currency constant, China accumulated dollars and used them to buy U.S. stocks and bonds. The result is a big trade deficit for the United States. This has been the subject of revived trade talks between the United States and China in recent years. Ultimately, Chinese citizens must be able to buy goods and services to enjoy the benefits of their huge exports.

2. Protecting an industry from foreign competition or attempting to prohibit firms from outsourcing to save jobs will cost jobs in those sectors that would expand with free trade or lower costs. Clearly, when trade opens up, some sectors are hurt by cheaper imports. In fact, that is precisely the point: to get goods at a lower price. If we spend less on vegetables from South America, we can spend more on other goods at home. In addition, demand from our trading partners will spur growth in the production of our export goods. By reducing trade with another country, we also reduce the number of jobs in its export sectors. Similarly, if firms are able to reduce costs through outsourcing, competition will pass those savings on to consumers in the form of lower prices. Consumers will in turn be able to buy goods and services in other sectors, a benefit that will expand and create new jobs to keep the workforce employed.

3. Protecting an industry can lead to inefficiency and a lack of ability to compete in world markets later on. Those industries that are subject to rigorous competition from abroad tend to adopt the newest, most efficient technology and hold costs to a minimum. The U.S. steel industry was heavily protected for many years, and it eventually lost most of the world business in steel to vigorously competitive foreign producers.

4. Keeping the unemployment rate low is a macroeconomic issue. When the economy is expanding, unemployment falls and can be low regardless of the composition of trade. The lowest rate of U.S. unemployment in decades was in the year 2000. In that year, following the expansion of trade from NAFTA and GATT, unemployment averaged just 4 percent, the lowest since 1969. The correct tools for fighting unemployment are fiscal and monetary policies, not antitrade policies.

5. If the objective is to reduce poverty, how can preventing trade help? Opening a country up to trade increases the demand for labor in the export sectors. For many countries, domestic demand is low because income is low. If export demand succeeds in increasing jobs, incomes will rise, not fall.

A second argument against free trade is that it will hurt the environment. The main thrust of this argument is that poor countries are not subject to the same environmental standards as rich countries. Lax environmental standards reduce the cost of doing business for a country's producers. Thus, countries have an incentive to ignore the environment to become more competitive in world markets.

Globalization advocates respond with two points. First, they say, environmental regulation is a problem for all countries regardless of whether they trade. Poor countries, where people are earning subsistence wages, do not have the resources to devote to environmental protection. All you have to do is visit a major city in a poor country to be convinced that the environment is generally a problem. But the real hope for an improved environment is growth and responsible government. Clearly, environmental improvement is a luxury good. Feeding the citizenry comes first, and improving the environment comes later. Second, trade may actually be a lever to increase environmental protection. The World Trade Organization (WTO) and NAFTA have ongoing negotiations designed to pressure countries into improving environmental regulations.

A third argument against free trade is that free-trade rules and the power of organizations like the WTO can undermine national sovereignty by forcing countries to give up various things. This is, of course, true. The classic example is a farm subsidy. The farm lobbies in many countries are strong. With productivity advances, it is increasingly difficult, particularly for small farmers, to make a living farming. Many countries, including the United States, pay significant subsidies to some farmers, enabling them to produce at lower cost. Since farmers can produce at lower cost, they enjoy a significant advantage over farmers producing in countries where there are no subsidies. This has become a huge issue between the developed and developing countries.

genetically modified (GM) foods Strains of food that have been genetically modified. Examples include insect- and herbicide-resistant soybeans, corn, and cotton and rice with increased iron and vitamins.

One final issue is the debate over **genetically modified (GM) foods** or genetically modified organisms. Many companies have been experimenting with strains of food that have been genetically modified for a variety of reasons. Such crops are grown commercially in more than 40 countries. The principal genetically modified crops grown include insect- and herbicide-resistant soybeans, corn, and cotton. Among other GM crops are rice with increased iron and vitamins and a sweet potato resistant to a virus that could decimate much of the African harvest. Microorganisms have been genetically modified to produce enzymes that help make better wine.

The worry is that we don't know everything about the potential dangers of the newly created organisms. They may be harmful. Several European countries have in the past banned the import of GM crops despite their lower cost. As a compromise, in 2003 the European Community opted to drop the ban but to insist on mandatory labeling of any product containing even a trace of a genetically modified ingredient.

U.S. producers have taken up the case with the WTO, claiming that it is just another way to block less costly U.S. products from entering the market and again subsidizing European farmers. The proponents of free trade in GM goods say that while the benefits are clear and certain, the costs are speculative. To date there is no evidence that GM crops have caused any harmful side effects.

TRADE, GROWTH, AND POVERTY

Much of what we have said so far is theory. There is certainly a theoretical case to be made for bringing down trade barriers. But what about evidence? Do those nations that are more open to trade grow faster than countries that are less open? Has poverty declined more rapidly in countries that trade more openly? There are clearly examples of open economies that have grown rapidly and where poverty has been reduced, such as China. There are also examples of countries that trade openly that have seen little growth and increasing poverty rates, such as Haiti. But controlling for other determinants of poverty and growth, is trade a plus or a minus?

The National Bureau of Economic Research and the World Bank sponsored a number of case studies of trade liberalization in the 1970s and 1980s. Most showed that countries that were more integrated into the world economy grew faster than those that were less integrated.[2] An

---

[2]See Jagdish Bhagwati, *Foreign Trade Regimes and Economic Development* (Cambridge, MA: Ballanger Press, 1978).

oft-cited study by Jeffrey Sachs and Andrew Warner concludes that open countries grew 2 percent per year more rapidly than closed economies, controlling for a number of factors.[3] While some studies challenge the strength of the relationship,[4] the bulk of the evidence supports the claim that trade liberalization was an important component of policy reforms that led to more rapid growth. Even one who challenged the strength of the relationship admits, "No country has developed successfully by turning its back on international trade and long-term capital flows."[5]

But does growth necessarily reduce poverty, or do all the benefits of growth find their way into the pockets of the rich? Certainly, as economist Stanley Fischer states in a recent essay on globalization, "Logic dictates that there is no way of lifting the populations of poor countries out of poverty without sustained growth. Globally, the decline in poverty has been the fastest where growth has been the fastest (in developing Asia) and the slowest where growth performance has been the worst (in Africa)."[6] Empirical studies also verify that on average when countries grow, the income of the lowest fifth of the income distribution rises at about the same rate as aggregate income, including when growth is induced by more open trade.[7]

THE GLOBALIZATION OF LABOR MARKETS: THE ECONOMICS OF IMMIGRATION AND OUTSOURCING

Globalization also refers to the increased mobility of labor across international borders. Whenever unemployment rises, the issue of immigration takes center stage in the press. And few topics elicit as much of an emotional response. Back in 1994, voters in California approved by a 3-to-2 margin Proposition 187, a highly controversial referendum that prevents illegal immigrants from receiving state education, welfare, and nonemergency medical benefits. In the same year, Governor Lawton Chiles of Florida declared a statewide emergency and demanded a stop to the tens of thousands of Cuban immigrants flooding into Florida. President Clinton responded by sending the Coast Guard to intercept them and take them to a detention camp at Guantanamo Naval Base in Cuba. Later, some were sent to Panama, and some were allowed to enter the United States. These events provoked memories of the 1980 Mariel boat lift, as a result of which over 125,000 refugees arrived in Florida. Many of these refugees were criminals who still reside in U.S. prisons.

What impact does immigration have on a country's economy? Is it all bad, as many would have us believe? Interestingly, one of the key elements of the agreement among the members of the European Union is the abolition of border controls to encourage the free flow of labor among member countries in response to wage differentials and economic conditions. The relaxation of immigration rules in Europe was done in the name of encouraging economic growth and prosperity.

Many agricultural firms in Texas and California rely on immigration from Mexico, Central America, and South America to supply them with labor during the peak growing season. But does immigration reduce domestic wages and increase unemployment nationally? The evidence is mixed.

A Brief History of Immigration into the United States Immigration into the United States has come in irregular waves. The first "Great Migration" occurred between 1880 and 1924, when 25.8 million immigrants entered the country, a figure that represented more than 40 percent of the period's total population increase. During the 1920s, however, Congress established a national-origins quota system that limited the annual flow from the Eastern Hemisphere countries to 150,000. Under the new laws, visas were issued in proportion to the ethnic composition of the United States in 1920. The result was that 60 percent of the visas went to German and British immigrants.

The flow of immigrants slowed to a trickle during the 1930s but has been expanding ever since. Between 1990 and 2000 immigration averaged just under 1 million annually. Many of today's immigrants are illegal. Studies indicate that during the late 1980s between

[3]Jeffrey Sachs and Andrew Warner, "Economic Reform and the Process of Global Integration," *Brookings Papers on Economic Activity,* 1995 (1).
[4]Francisco Rodriguez and Dani Rodrik, "Trade Policy and Economic Growth: A Skeptic's Guide to the Evidence," in Ben Bernanke and Kenneth Rogoff, *NBER Macroeconomics Annual,* 2000 (Cambridge, MA: MIT Press, 2001).
[5]Dani Rodrik in Rodriguez and Rodrik, p. 23.
[6]Stanley Fischer, "Globalization and Its Challenges," *American Economic Review,* May 2003, p. 13.
[7]For example, David Dollar and Aart Kraay, "Growth Is Good for the Poor," cited in Fischer, p. 13, based on data from 92 countries.

TABLE 35.1 Immigrants into the United States by Country of Origin: 2004

RANK	COUNTRY	IMMIGRANTS (thousands)
1	Mexico	175.4
2	India	70.1
3	Philippines	57.8
4	China	51.2
5	Vietnam	31.5
6	Dominican Republic	30.5
7	El Salvador	29.9
8	Cuba	20.5
9	Korea	19.8
10	Colombia	18.7
11	Guatemala	18.0
12	Canada	15.6
13	United Kingdom	14.9
14	Jamaica	14.4
15	Poland	14.3
16	Haiti	14.0

Source: Statistical Abstract of the United States, 2006, Table 8.

Immigration Reform and Control Act (1986)
Granted amnesty to about 3 million illegal aliens and imposed a strong set of employer sanctions designed to slow the flow of immigrants into the United States.

Immigration Act of 1990
Increased the number of legal immigrants allowed into the United States each year by 150,000.

2 million and 3 million people were illegally residing in the United States and 200,000 to 300,000 new illegals were arriving each year. Though the Border Patrol intercepts and returns about 1.3 million illegals per year, many illegal immigrants enter the country legally. They come in legally through customs and simply remain in the country.

In 1986 Congress enacted the **Immigration Reform and Control Act**, which granted amnesty to about 3 million illegals and imposed a set of strong employer sanctions designed to slow the flow of immigrants into the United States. The **Immigration Act of 1990** increased the number of legal immigrants allowed in each year by 150,000.

Prior to 1960, the largest single group of immigrants into the United States came from Europe. Between 1991 and 2000 the largest group of immigrants came from the Americas, especially Mexico. Beginning in 1970, the number of immigrants from Asia began to grow rapidly. Table 35.1 shows the number of immigrants from the top 14 countries of origin in 2004.

Economic Arguments for Free Immigration   Should a country permit completely free immigration into its borders? The argument for free immigration is that it increases world output. Labor flows across borders in response to wage differentials. Consider the case of Mexico and the United States. Low-wage workers in Mexico migrate to the United States because wages are higher in the United States. If markets are basically competitive, wages reflect the workers' productivity. In other words, because the United States has more capital and uses more advanced technology than Mexico, the productivity of low-wage workers is higher in the United States than in Mexico. Thus, the same labor produces more total output after immigration, and world output rises.

Now consider the case of France and Italy. If a labor shortage develops in France because the demand for French wine increases, French wages will rise and attract workers from other European countries. If at the same time the demand for leather goods produced in Italy drops off, Italian wages will fall, and Italian workers will move to France, where their productivity is higher.

The argument for the free movement of labor among nations is exactly the same as the argument for the free movement of labor among the sectors of the domestic economy. Suppose an economy produces only two goods, X and Y. If demand for good X picks up, the demand for labor used to produce X rises, because the gains to hiring more labor in the production of X are increasing. Labor will move out of the production of good Y if and only if its productivity is higher in X in terms of the value of output. This movement ensures efficiency. Recall the simple definition that an efficient economy is one that produces what people want at least cost.

Those who favor a looser policy toward immigrants believe that immigrants do not displace U.S. workers but rather take jobs that Americans simply do not want. Immigrants serve as domestics and low-wage farm workers, producing things that the United States needs. In addition, the U.S. economy has absorbed wave after wave of immigrants while maintaining virtually full employment. Almost all U.S. citizens except Native Americans have relatively recent ancestors who came to the country as immigrants.

The Argument against Free Immigration   No economist disputes the idea that the distribution of income is likely to change among countries and among groups within each country in response to immigration. Assuming that immigrants are low-wage workers, equilibrium wages in the market for low-skill labor will rise in the country of origin and fall in the country of destination. In addition, the return to capital will rise in the destination country, pushing up profits, while capital income will fall in the country of origin.

The argument in favor of free immigration assumes that all workers get jobs. However, the popular impression is certainly that immigrants (who will usually work for very low wages) take jobs away from low-income Americans and drive up unemployment rates. In addition, many believe that immigrants often end up on welfare rolls and become a burden to taxpayers. Opponents also point to crime in ethnic neighborhoods and rivalries among ethnic groups as evidence of further costs to society.

The Evidence: The Net Costs of Immigration   To determine whether the net benefits of immigration outweigh its net costs, we must ask one important question: To what extent does immigration reduce domestic wages and increase unemployment? A number of recent studies have found that metropolitan areas that have greater numbers of immigrants seem to have only slightly lower wages and only slightly higher unemployment rates.

An influential study by economist David Card of the University of California, Berkeley, looks carefully at wages and employment opportunities in the Miami metropolitan area during and after the Mariel boat lift in 1980. Almost overnight, about 125,000 Cubans arrived in Florida and increased the labor force in Miami by over 7 percent. Card looked at trends in wages and unemployment among Miami workers between 1980 and 1985 and found virtually no effect. In addition, the data he examined mirrored the experience of workers in Los Angeles, Houston, Atlanta, and similar cities that were not hit by the same shock.[8]

However, a more recent study by Borjas, Freeman, and Katz takes issue with much of the work done to date. They argue that immigrants do not stay in the cities at which they arrive, but rather move within the United States in response to job opportunities and wage differentials. Thus, they argue that the effects of immigration on wages and unemployment must be analyzed at the national level, not at the city level. Their study points to the large decline in the wages of high school dropouts relative to workers with more education during the 1980s. Their results suggest that a third of the drop in the relative wages of high school dropouts can be attributed to lower-skilled immigrants.[9]

On the issue of immigration's effects on government costs, mixed evidence also exists. It is clear that earlier generations of immigrants have had a positive effect on both the economy as a whole and on government budgets more specifically. Studies of early immigrants' wage patterns seem to show that their wages on average exceed native workers' wages after 15 years. First-generation immigrants as a group might thus be paying more in taxes than they collect in means-tested benefits such as welfare.

But the data show that over time a very dramatic drop has occurred in the level of education, experience, and skills among immigrants. At the same time, participation in welfare programs among immigrants has jumped sharply. Borjas estimates that in 1990, immigrant households in the United States contributed between $7.6 billion and $10.1 billion in tax revenues while collecting $23.8 billion in benefits from means-tested programs.

---

[8]David Card, "The Impact of the Mariel Boat Lift on the Miami Labor Market," *Industrial and Labor Relations Review*, January 1990, pp. 245–257.

[9]George Borjas, Richard Freeman, and Lawrence Katz, "On the Labor Market Effects of Immigration and Trade," in *Immigration and the Work Force: Economic Consequences for the United States and Source Areas*, eds. George Borjas and Richard Freeman (Chicago: University of Chicago Press, 1992).

Is Immigration Bad or Good? Immigration is another of those economic issues in which no right answer clearly emerges. The evidence on the effects of immigration is mixed, and theory gives us arguments on both sides of the issue. Only time will tell whether the recent wave of immigrants will assimilate as well as past waves. In the meantime, immigration will remain a "hot button" issue politically, and the United States will be called upon to make some important decisions about the treatment of recent immigrants.

In 2001, following the attacks of 9/11, immigration became entangled with issues of international terrorism. With the transfer of the Immigration and Naturalization Service to the newly created Department of Homeland Security, applicants for visas, even student visas, were subject to much more scrutiny. This new policy has led to fears that we will lose some of the benefits that immigration brings with it.

Outsourcing We now turn to outsourcing, one of the biggest issues in the U.S. globalization debate today. Immigration brings workers to jobs in the United States. Outsourcing sends the jobs to low-wage workers in places as disparate as Bulgaria, India, and the Philippines.

At first, the number of outsourcing contracts was small. The word *outsourcing* did not in fact appear in textbooks until a few years ago. In addition, outsourcing was concentrated in relatively low-skill jobs such as customer service. (When you call for assistance with understanding your bank accounts, setting up a wireless port on your computer, or using a new cell phone, you may be talking to a customer service representative in Bangalore, India.) But as the number of outsourcing opportunities grew, the phenomenon spread to areas as unlikely as medicine and the law (see the box on p. 757).

A few years ago forecasters predicted that U.S. firms would outsource several million jobs, and some recent estimates put the number even higher. In fact, hard numbers are hard to come by. Firms are not required to report the number of workers employed by outsource contractors.

Outsourcing has naturally become a very hot political issue. During the first term of George W. Bush, the president's chief economist, Gregory Mankiw, argued that outsourcing brought the benefits of lower production costs and, as a result, lower product prices. He was roundly criticized by the media and politicians on both sides of the aisle.

What made outsourcing possible were technical change and the huge investment in technology that took place in the 1990s. The rise of the Internet and an incredible increase in the quality and speed of information transfer started the ball rolling. Then the world invested hundreds of millions of dollars in broadband connectivity and undersea cable with huge capacity. The cost of computing equipment dropped sharply at the same time as storage capacity increased rapidly.

Where will the outsourcing phenomenon lead, and how will the story end? At this point, no one knows. But the pace of change is dizzying. In fact, the arguments for and against outsourcing are exactly the same as the arguments for and against free trade, and they date to David Ricardo's work in the nineteenth century (see Chapter 33). The fact that Mr. Mankiw was so widely criticized for essentially arguing in favor of free trade suggests that the free trade debate is still far from over.

CAPITAL MOBILITY

Another important aspect of globalization is capital mobility. Look back at the circular flow diagram in Figure 35.1. Six of the 16 flows depicted in the figure refer to the supply of or demand for capital. In the global economy, domestic households can put their wealth to work in foreign or domestic financial markets; domestic firms can finance investment projects by looking to domestic or foreign financial markets. The same applies to foreign households and firms.

Today, virtually all well-diversified portfolios of stocks and bonds owned by households or institutions contain some foreign assets. It is as easy to buy or sell shares in an Italian textile company as it is to buy or sell shares in General Electric. In addition, most of the well-known large corporations in the United States are multinational. That is, they have extensive production, operation, or sales facilities in foreign countries. Purchases and sales of foreign stocks and bonds by U.S. citizens and purchases and sales of U.S. stocks and bonds by foreigners totaled in the trillions of dollars in 2003. One-third of all foreign holdings of U.S. securities are held by the Japanese. Foreign direct investment in the United States, that is, foreign firms' ownership of physical capital in the United

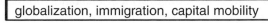
New Trade Agreement
with Central America
and the Dominican
Republic—2005

**Outsourcing Is Not Just
Customer Service Reps
in India**

Trade and Development
in Africa—2003

Russia's Economy
in 2005

Outsourcing Is Not Just Customer Service Reps in India

BY SOME FORECASTS, OUTSOURCING will result in the loss of more than 4 million service-sector jobs in the United States by the year 2015. Firms are finding it less expensive to outsource everything from customer service for cell phone users to legal and medical services. The following *Wall Street Journal* article shows how outsourcing works in the legal profession.

Legal Services Enter Outsourcing Domain

It happened with tech support, financial services and catalog order-taking. Now, a growing number of U.S. and British companies as well as law firms are outsourcing legal work to India.

The practice started a few years ago with simple word processing and filing services performed by nonlawyers. But increasingly, squads of experienced but inexpensive lawyers based in India are doing things ranging from patent applications to divorce papers to legal research for Western clients.

"Short of anything where you have to physically be there or sign on the dotted line, we can do it," says Sanjay Kamlani, co-chief executive officer of Pangea3, a New York–based legal outsourcing firm that opened shop a year ago and already has more than 25 lawyers in India and over 20 U.S. clients.

Not many large American companies will openly admit to sending legal work to India, but a few do. DuPont Co. says it uses Indian lawyers to help draft patent applications. The lawyers conduct searches to ensure that DuPont's proposed patents don't conflict with other companies' existing patents, says

Michelle Reardon, a DuPont spokeswoman.

ANOTHER EXAMPLE OF OUTSOURCING is found in Thomas Friedman's 2005 best seller, *The World is Flat*, which reproduces a letter he received from Bill Brody, president of Johns Hopkins University.

Dear Tom,

I am speaking at a Hopkins continuing education medical meeting for radiologists (I used to be a radiologist). . . . I came upon a very fascinating situation that I thought might interest you. I have just learned that in many small and some medium sized hospitals in the U.S., radiologists are outsourcing reading of CAT scans to doctors in India and Australia!!! Most of this evidently occurs at night (and maybe weekends) when the radiologists do not have sufficient staffing to provide in-hospital coverage. . . . The advantage is that it is daytime in Australia or India when it is night time here—so after-hours coverage becomes more readily done by shipping the images across the globe. Since (CAT and MRI) images are already in digital format and available on a network with a standardized protocol, it is no problem to view them anywhere in the world. . . . I assume that the radiologists on the other end . . . must have trained in [the] U.S. and had appropriate licenses and credentials. . . . The groups abroad that provide these after-hours readings are called "Nighthawks" by the American radiologists that employ them.

States, totaled about $1.2 trillion in 2000, while U.S. firms owned about the same amount of capital in foreign countries.

The argument for free and open financial market mobility is that capital should flow to its highest and best use. Financial markets should allocate capital to those uses that have the highest returns, controlling for risks associated with those investments. If investing in a factory in Nigeria would yield a return of 20 percent annually, while a similar investment of comparable risk in the United States would yield a 14 percent return, financial markets should finance the Nigerian project first regardless of where the financing comes from.

758 PART VII
The World Economy

Rapid and free flows of financial capital have, however, had adverse consequences for some nations. During the mid-1990s, a tremendous volume of financial capital flowed from the United States into the countries of Thailand, Indonesia, and Korea. Mutual funds bought shares of foreign companies, banks and insurance companies financed large real estate deals, and hedge funds speculated by betting on stock markets and exchange rate movements in these countries during the years leading up to 1997.

All of this seemed good for everyone involved. The purchases of physical capital were likely to raise productivity and wages in those countries. The construction of office buildings created jobs directly and provided space for growing businesses, and new factories provided capital (machines) for workers to work with. A side effect was that the currencies of these countries became very strong. For example, the Korean won increased substantially in value. The effect was to make imports very inexpensive. The combination of cheap imports, high demand for investment goods, and prospering financial markets, including booming stock markets, fed on itself and the flows increased.

But what happens quite often in these cases is that capital markets "overshoot." Because no one coordinates the investments being made by individual investors, and because there are often long lags between the decision to invest and the actual creation of new capital, sometimes there is overinvestment. Such was the case in Thailand, Korea, and Indonesia in 1997. When things began to unwind in those countries, creditors all headed for the doors at the same time. That is, mutual funds, banks, and others who were holding assets in those countries tried to liquidate their holdings all at the same time. The result was a dramatic decline in the value of the won (Korea), the baht (Thailand), and the rupiah (Indonesia), which pushed up import prices and hurt consumption spending. Stock markets crashed, business investment dried up, aggregate spending dropped, and all three countries experienced severe recessions. Similar booms and busts in Brazil (1998), Mexico (1994), Russia (1998), Turkey (2000), and Argentina (2001) seem to have roots in similar kinds of rapid financial flows.

Partially as a reaction to these crises, some countries have "capital controls." Such controls place strict limits on the volume of financial flows into and out of a country in a given period of time. In his recent piece on globalization, Stanley Fischer makes the following argument:

> What can be done to reduce the volatility of capital flows to emerging-market countries? The first response would be for countries to shut themselves off from international capital flows. It bears emphasis that despite the crises, and the arguments of many of the critics of globalization, almost no country has taken this route; the revealed preference of the emerging-market countries is to stay involved with the international financial system.[10]

PUBLIC POLICY AND GLOBALIZATION

The increasing interdependence of nations and their citizens brings with it several specific policy debates that go beyond the issues of free trade and labor and capital mobility that we have already discussed. First, there are global public goods and externalities. How should the nations of the world respond to these large-scale problems of coordination, such as global warming? Second, a number of large and powerful institutions, often referred to as nongovernmental organizations (NGOs), play a powerful role in enforcing international monetary agreements and trade rules. The most well known are the World Bank and the International Monetary Fund (IMF). The question is, what role should institutions take in promoting world growth and eliminating poverty?

GLOBAL EXTERNALITIES AND PUBLIC GOODS

Economics by and large deals with the efficient functioning of markets both national and international. But often problems arise that are not efficiently handled by private markets. One such problem involves a class of goods called public goods.

---

[10]Stanley Fischer, "Globalization and Its Challenges," *American Economic Review*, May 2003, p. 16.

Public goods, sometimes called **social goods**, are goods or services that bestow collective benefits on members of society. Generally, no one can be excluded from enjoying their benefits once they are produced. Classic examples are clean air and national defense.

Private goods, such as hamburgers, are produced by the private sector because a firm can exclude those who don't pay. If exclusion is impossible, two problems arise for markets: the "free-rider problem" and the "drop-in-the-bucket problem." Why should I pay for a good if I get the benefits whether I pay or not? Because many people benefit from production, my contribution is so small as to not matter. As a result, the private sector is powerless because it is in peoples' interests to not pay, and it falls to government to arrange for their provision. Governments can appropriate money and collect taxes for such things as national defense, a justice system, and public health, effectively forcing citizens to pay for them. Presumably, governments produce those public goods that its citizens want.

But what about public goods whose benefits are worldwide or at least cross-border? Here, even governments and nations face the "free-rider" and "drop-in-the-bucket" problems. Consider the problem of global warming. Taking action to slow global warming presumably would produce a worldwide public good. Clearly, there is no way to exclude nations from the benefits for not contributing, and the impact of any one nation is small. As a result, nations have an incentive to not contribute. This situation is particularly true for developing countries such as China and India, where cleanup would be costly and the sacrifice great in terms of national income.

Another way to think of global warming is that it is the result of an externality. An **externality** is a cost or a benefit resulting from some activity or transaction that is imposed or bestowed on some party outside the activity or transaction. The classic example is pollution, but there are countless others.

For efficiency, those weighing the costs and benefits of their production or consumption decisions must weigh *all* the costs and benefits. One of the functions of government is to "internalize" externalities. In essence, the idea is to force those who generate externalities to factor those externalities into their decisions. One example of a policy designed to internalize an externality is a charge or tax imposed on a polluting firm in proportion to the damage done. Of course, the situation becomes very complex when one country imposes an external cost on another. If the number of countries involved is small, bargaining and negotiation may simply resolve the issue. But where large numbers of jurisdictions are involved, public goods problems arise.

The United Nations and other international bodies exist to promote those things that have benefits for the world but that require international cooperation and contribution. One interpretation of its purpose is that it exists to ensure the production of international public goods. But its success rate has been spotty. International politics is clearly more complex and problematic than national politics. In addition, international bodies have very little in the way of taxing power.

The concept of public goods also helps to explain the HIV/AIDS pandemic. In 2003, more than 60 million people were infected with the virus. Each day approximately 14,000 infections occurred. More than 20 million have died. HIV/AIDS is the leading cause of death in sub-Saharan Africa, where the disease threatens to reverse the developmental achievements of the last 50 years. The HIV/AIDS problem is more than just a health issue. It decimates the workforce, worsens poverty and inequality, creates huge numbers of orphans, and costs the poorest countries billions of dollars in health expenditures. Basic treatment for an AIDS patient can cost three times the per-capita gross national income. To have an impact on the epidemic, nations must cooperate and be willing to pay. Clearly, this is a problem that will not be solved by the market. It will require a multinational effort if the pandemic is to be brought under control.

public goods, or social goods Goods or services that bestow collective benefits on members of society.

externality A cost or a benefit resulting from some activity or transaction that is imposed or bestowed on some party outside the activity or transaction.

NONGOVERNMENTAL ORGANIZATIONS AND INTERNATIONAL ECONOMICS: THE WASHINGTON CONSENSUS

No single topic in international economics brings up such heated debate as the policy position taken by the IMF a few years back in setting "conditions" that had to be met for countries to qualify for development loans and grants.

Although there is considerable disagreement about exactly who formed it or how strongly it was designed to be enforced, a set of objectives or goals was laid down for countries that the IMF was financing. What came to be referred to as the **Washington Consensus** had 10 elements: (1) fiscal discipline—modest budget deficits or balanced budgets, (2) public expenditure priorities in health and education, (3) tax reform—the tax base should be broad, and marginal tax rates should be low, (4) positive but moderate market-determined interest rates, (5) a competitive—ideally floating—exchange rate as the "first essential element of an outward-oriented economic policy," (6) import liberalization—essentially a free-trade policy for reduced tariffs, (7) openness to foreign investment, (8) privatization—"based on the idea that private industry is managed more efficiently than public enterprises," (9) deregulation, and (10) protection of property rights.

Clearly, considerable room for disagreement existed about the degree to which these elements should or could be enforced. Many believed that the IMF went too far and was too rigid in its dealings with many countries. Taking a country, such as one of the former communist countries of Eastern Europe, and demanding a balanced budget, openness, and privatization in rapid succession was too much too soon.

Out of the bad experiences of the 1990s has emerged a new consensus for gradualism. While the spirit of the Washington Consensus remains intact, the rigor of its application appears to be quite a bit softer.

GLOBALIZATION, CAPITALISM, AND DEMOCRACY

One final topic is important to mention before leaving the discussion of globalization. Very often the issue of openness and globalization intersects with issues concerning political and economic systems. Advocates of globalization often are staunch supporters of laissez-faire capitalism. Certainly, the 10 points of the Washington Consensus would lead one to the conclusion that its advocates are strong believers in the market system.

But does the issue of openness and the desirability of increasing interdependence among national economies depend on the kind of economic or political system that a country chooses to establish? Probably not.

First of all, it is important to separate the debate about political systems from the debate about economic systems. The terms *democracy* and *dictatorship* refer to the institutions of government and to the process of public choice. To what extent are the decisions of the government made through democratic institutions that express the will of the people?

The terms *socialism* and *capitalism* refer, on the other hand, to the economic institutions that determine the allocation of resources. A pure socialist economy is one in which the government owns the land and capital and in which resources are allocated essentially by central government plan. A laissez-faire capitalist economy is one in which the government plays virtually no role in directing the economy. Rather, resource allocation decisions are made by individual households and firms acting in their own self-interest with little or no government involvement. The essential decisions are made through the market.

In fact, most economies are mixed, and the debate is really not about government versus no government. It is instead about the role of government in the economy. Even the most conservative, free enterprise advocates believe that the government must play some role in the economy. In microeconomics we discuss the government's role in providing public goods, regulating monopoly power, internalizing external costs and benefits, and ensuring that all economic agents are well informed. We also discuss the extent to which citizens may want to get the government involved in redistribution of income. In macroeconomics we discuss the potential role of government in stabilizing the economy to hold rates of unemployment and inflation to a minimum.

Even in the strongly free enterprise economic system in the United States, fully 30 percent of total income goes to taxes to support the government, and the government plays a significant role in resource allocation choices.

There are some countries that have had very democratic political systems but that choose to have socialist-leaning economies with very substantial government direction. Examples include Sweden and Denmark. On the other hand, there are countries that have had strong dictatorships but that choose to have very laissez-faire economic systems. Examples include Singapore and Chile under Augusto Pinochet.

While economists as a whole tend to favor globalization, there is a wide range of opinion on the proper role of government in the economy. Although many favor substantial government involvement, most economists believe that the allocation of resources should be left to the market by and large and that profit-maximizing firms and utility-maximizing households should be allowed to respond to market incentives. Those same economists tend by and large to believe that households and firms should be allowed, with as little interference as possible, to engage in trade, invest abroad, or work abroad.

A FINAL WORD

So what is the result of all of this? Is there a consensus about the desirability of globalization? There is not. Probably nothing that we have said here will convince the critics that it is a good thing. But it is important to understand that a powerful logic exists in support of economic openness—the idea that the free flow of resources and goods and services across national borders, driven by efficient economic incentives, including the desire to maximize profit, is likely to make citizens better off than if borders were closed and economies turned inward.

SUMMARY

THE GLOBAL CIRCULAR FLOW

1. *Globalization* is the process of increasing interdependence among countries and their citizens. Globalization has social, cultural, political, and economic dimensions.

2. *Economic globalization* is the process of increasing economic interdependence among countries and their citizens. It involves increased international trade of goods and services, increased cross-border movements of labor, and expanded international financial flows.

3. The global circular flow diagram shows the complexity of the interactions among economies.

4. The basic argument for economic globalization can be found in the decisions behind each of the flows in the circular flow diagram.

5. If we didn't allow people to move freely across borders, or if we didn't let New Jersey citizens invest in California companies, or if we barred the export of fish from the coasts to the interior, the system would clearly be inefficient.

A BRIEF HISTORY OF ECONOMIC GLOBALIZATION

6. Economic historian Jeffrey Williamson classifies the period 1820–1914 as the first great period of globalization and the period since World War II as the second.

THE BENEFITS AND COSTS OF GLOBALIZATION

7. The argument for free trade rests on two pieces of intuition. First, if you have something that I want and I have something that you want, we can exchange and both be better off. Voluntary exchange is efficient. Second, applying the concept to nations, two nations can benefit from free trade by specializing in producing those products in which they enjoy a *comparative advantage*.

8. Those who oppose trade make a number of arguments, and proponents of free trade have a number of counterarguments.

9. There are clearly examples of open economies that have grown rapidly and where poverty has been reduced, such as China. There are also examples of countries that trade openly but that have seen little growth and increasing poverty rates, such as Haiti.

10. The bulk of the evidence supports the claim that trade liberalization was an important component of policy reforms that led to more rapid growth.

11. The argument for free immigration is that it increases world output. Those who favor immigration also point out that the United States has absorbed many waves of immigrants while maintaining virtually full employment. Those who argue against immigration believe that it takes jobs away from low-income U.S. citizens.

12. Another important aspect of globalization is capital mobility. In the global economy, domestic households can put their wealth to work in foreign or domestic financial markets; domestic firms can finance investment projects by looking to domestic or foreign financial markets.

13. The argument for free and open financial market mobility is that capital should flow to its highest and best use. Rapid and free flows of financial capital have, however, had adverse consequences for some nations.

PUBLIC POLICY AND GLOBALIZATION

14. An important world policy issue concerns global public goods or externalities, such as global warming and the HIV/AIDS pandemic.

GLOBALIZATION, CAPITALISM, AND DEMOCRACY

15. Very often, the issue of openness and globalization intersects with issues concerning political and economic systems. Advocates of globalization often are staunch supporters of laissez-faire capitalism.

comparative advantage, 750

economic globalization, 747

externality, 759

genetically modified (GM) foods, 752

globalization, 747

Immigration Act of 1990, 754

Immigration Reform and Control Act (1986), 754

public goods, or social goods, 759

Washington Consensus, 760

PROBLEM SET

1. In 2005, the debate about outsourcing moved onto the political stage. (See the box on outsourcing on p. 757.) Since that time, both Republicans and Democrats have stepped forward with proposals to deal with what the public views as a problem. Search the popular press and write down some of these policy proposals. Do they make any economic sense? Why or why not? What economic arguments can you pull together to counter or to support what you hear out of Washington? Has outsourcing become an even bigger problem in the current year than it was in 2005?

2. In a televised debate in 2004, two Senate candidates were debating the merits of a new trade agreement proposed by the president between the nations of Central America and the United States. Write a brief letter addressed to your own senator explaining the debate as it relates to jobs in your state. What industries in your state tend to export? Which goods does your state import? See if you can find out what products your state exports to the countries of Costa Rica, El Salvador, Guatemala, Honduras, and Nicaragua.

3. From which countries did the largest number of immigrants enter the United States in 2006? You may find the answer by logging on to **www.immigration.gov** and looking for immigration statistics. Do most immigrants come from rich countries or poor countries? See if you can explain the pattern.

4. How is it possible for exports to China to fall short of imports from China by more than $162 billion?

5. A huge problem for the world is the HIV/AIDS pandemic. Advocates of worldwide funding of effective but expensive drugs as well as extensive prevention argue that dealing with the crisis would be the equivalent of producing a worldwide "public good." Define *public good*. In what ways would stopping HIV/AIDS be a public good? What are some of the reasons our efforts have not made significant progress in providing this public good?

Economic Growth in Developing and Transitional Economies

36

Our primary focus in this text has been on countries with modern industrialized economies that rely heavily on markets to allocate resources, but what about the economic problems facing such countries as Somalia or Haiti? Can we apply the same economic principles that we have been studying to these less developed nations?

Yes. All economic analysis deals with the problem of making choices under conditions of scarcity, and the problem of satisfying people's wants and needs is as real for Somalia and Haiti as it is for the United States, Germany, and Japan. The universality of scarcity is what makes economic analysis relevant to all nations, regardless of their level of material well-being or ruling political ideology.

The basic tools of supply and demand, theories about consumers and firms, and theories about the structure of markets all contribute to an understanding of the economic problems confronting the world's developing nations. However, these nations often face economic problems quite different from those faced by richer, more developed countries. In the developing nations, the economist may have to worry about chronic food shortages, explosive population growth, and hyperinflations that reach triple, and even quadruple, digits. The United States and other industrialized economies rarely encounter such difficulties.

The instruments of economic management also vary from nation to nation. The United States has well-developed financial market institutions and a strong central bank (the Federal Reserve) through which the government can control the macroeconomy to some extent. Even limited intervention is impossible in some of the developing countries. In the United States, tax laws can be changed to stimulate saving, to encourage particular kinds of investments, or to redistribute income. In most developing countries, there are neither meaningful personal income taxes nor effective tax policies.

Even though economic problems and the policy instruments available to tackle them vary across nations, economic thinking about these problems can be transferred easily from one setting to another. In this chapter we discuss several of the economic problems specific to developing nations in an attempt to capture some of the insights that economic analysis can offer.

LIFE IN THE DEVELOPING NATIONS: POPULATION AND POVERTY

In the year 2006, the population of the world reached over 6.5 billion people. Most of the world's more than 200 nations belong to the developing world, in which about three-fourths of the world's population lives.

In the early 1960s, the nations of the world could be assigned rather easily to categories: The *developed countries* included most of Europe, North America, Japan, Australia, and New Zealand; the *developing countries* included the rest of the world. The developing nations were often referred to as the *Third World* to distinguish them from the Western industrialized nations (the *First World*) and the former Socialist bloc of Eastern European nations (the *Second World*).

In 2006, the world did not divide easily into three neat parts. Rapid economic progress has brought some developing nations closer to developed economies. Countries such as Argentina and Korea, still considered to be "developing," are often referred to as middle-income, or newly industrialized, countries. Other countries, such as those in much of sub-Saharan Africa and some in South Asia, have stagnated and fallen so far behind the economic advances of the rest of the world that the term *Fourth World* has been used to describe them. It is not clear yet where the republics of the former Soviet Union and other formerly Communist countries of Eastern Europe will end up. Production has fallen sharply in many of them. For example, between 1990 and 1997, real gross domestic product (GDP) fell about 40 percent in the transition economies and over 50 percent in Russia and Central Asia. One estimate puts 2004 per-capita GDP in Russia at around $3,500. Some of the new republics now have more in common with developing countries than with developed countries.

Although the countries of the developing world exhibit considerable diversity, both in their standards of living and in their particular experiences of growth, marked differences continue to separate them from the developed nations. The developed countries have a higher average level of material well-being (the amounts of food, clothing, shelter, and other commodities consumed by the average person). Comparisons of gross national income are often used as a crude index of the level of material well-being across nations. GNI is a new measure of a nation's income, computed using a more accurate way of converting purchasing power into dollars. See Table 36.1, where GNI per capita in the industrial market economies significantly exceeds GNI of both the low- and middle-income developing economies.

Other characteristics of economic development include improvements in basic health and education. The degree of political and economic freedom enjoyed by individual citizens might also be part of what it means to be a developed nation. Some of these criteria are easier to quantify; Table 36.1 presents data for different types of economies according to some of the more easily measured indexes of development. As you see, the industrial market economies enjoy higher standards of living according to whatever indicator of development is chosen.

Behind these statistics lies the reality of the very difficult life facing the people of the developing world. For most, meager incomes provide only the basic necessities. Most meals are the same, consisting of the region's food staple—rice, wheat, or corn. Shelter is primitive. Many people share a small room, usually with an earthen floor and no sanitary facilities. The great majority of the population lives in rural areas where agricultural work

TABLE 36.1 Indicators of Economic Development

COUNTRY GROUP	POPULATION, 2004	GROSS NATIONAL INCOME PER CAPITA, 2004 (DOLLARS)	ANNUAL HEALTH EXPENDITURES PER CAPITA, 2002 (DOLLARS)	INFANT MORTALITY, 2003 (DEATHS BEFORE AGE 5 PER 1,000 BIRTHS)	URBAN POPULATION (PERCENTAGE OF TOTAL), 2003
Low-income	2.3 billion	510	29	122.0	30
Lower middle-income	2.4 billion	1,580	84	42.0	50
Upper middle-income	575.9 million	4,770	310	30.0	75
High-income	1.0 billion	32,040	3,039	7.0[a]	80

[a]For 2002.
Source: World Bank, **www.worldbank.org**.

is hard and extremely time-consuming. Productivity (output produced per worker) is low because household plots are small and only the crudest of farm implements are available. Low productivity means farm output per person is barely sufficient to feed a farmer's own family, with nothing left to sell to others. School-age children may receive some formal education, but illiteracy remains chronic for young and old. Infant mortality runs 10 times higher than in the United States. Although parasitic infections are common and debilitating, there is only one physician per 5,000 people. In addition, many developing nations are engaged in civil and external warfare.

Life in the developing nations is a continual struggle against the circumstances of poverty, and prospects for dramatic improvements in living standards for most people are dim. As with all generalizations, there are exceptions. Some nations are better off than others, and in any given nation an elite group always lives in considerable luxury.

Poverty—not affluence—dominates the developing world. Recent studies suggest that 40 percent of the population of the developing nations has an annual income insufficient to provide for adequate nutrition.

> While the developed nations account for only about one-quarter of the world's population, they are estimated to consume three-quarters of the world's output. This leaves the developing countries with about three-fourths of the world's people, but only one-fourth of the world's income. The simple result is that most of our planet's population is poor.

In the United States, the poorest one-fifth (bottom 20 percent) of the families receives just under 5 percent of total income; the richest one-fifth receives about 46 percent. However, the inequality in the world distribution of income is much greater. When we look at the world population, the poorest one-fifth of the families earns about .5 percent and the richest one-fifth earns 79 percent of total world income.

ECONOMIC DEVELOPMENT: SOURCES AND STRATEGIES

Economists have been trying to understand economic growth and development since Adam Smith and David Ricardo in the eighteenth and nineteenth centuries, but the study of development economics as it applies to the developing nations has a much shorter history. The geopolitical struggles that followed World War II brought increased attention to the developing nations and their economic problems. During this period, the new field of development economics asked simply: Why are some nations poor and others rich? If economists could understand the barriers to economic growth that prevent nations from developing and the prerequisites that would help them to develop, they could prescribe strategies for achieving economic advancement.

THE SOURCES OF ECONOMIC DEVELOPMENT

Although a general theory of economic development applicable to all nations has not emerged and probably never will, some basic factors that limit a poor nation's economic growth have been suggested. These include insufficient capital formation, a shortage of human resources and entrepreneurial ability, a lack of social overhead capital, and the constraints imposed by dependency on the already developed nations.

Capital Formation   One explanation for low levels of output in developing nations is insufficient quantities of necessary inputs. Developing nations have diverse resource endowments—Congo, for instance, is abundant in natural resources, while Bangladesh is resource poor. Almost all developing nations have a scarcity of physical capital relative to other resources, especially labor. The small stock of physical capital (factories, machinery, farm equipment, and other productive capital) constrains labor's productivity and holds back national output.

Nevertheless, citing capital shortages as the cause of low productivity does not explain much. We need to know why capital is in such short supply in developing countries. There

vicious-circle-of-poverty hypothesis Suggests that poverty is self-perpetuating because poor nations are unable to save and invest enough to accumulate the capital stock that would help them grow.

are many explanations. One, the **vicious-circle-of-poverty hypothesis**, suggests that a poor nation must consume most of its income just to maintain its already low standard of living. Consuming most of national income implies limited saving, and this implies low levels of investment. Without investment, the capital stock does not grow, the income remains low, and the vicious circle is complete. Poverty becomes self-perpetuating.

The difficulty with the vicious-circle argument is that if it were true, no nation could ever develop. For example, Japanese GDP per capita in 1900 was well below that of many of today's developing nations. The vicious-circle argument fails to recognize that every nation has some surplus above consumption needs that is available for investment. Often this surplus is most visible in the conspicuous-consumption habits of the nation's richest families.

> Poverty alone cannot explain capital shortages, and poverty is not necessarily self-perpetuating.

In a developing economy, scarcity of capital may have more to do with a lack of incentives for citizens to save and invest productively than with any absolute scarcity of income available for capital accumulation. Many of the rich in developing countries invest their savings in Europe or in the United States instead of in their own country, which may have a riskier political climate. Savings transferred to the United States do not lead to physical capital growth in the developing countries. The term **capital flight** refers to the fact that both human capital and financial capital (domestic savings) leave developing countries in search of higher expected rates of return elsewhere or returns with less risk. In addition, government policies in the developing nations—including price ceilings, import controls, and even outright appropriation of private property—tend to discourage investment.

capital flight The tendency for both human capital and financial capital to leave developing countries in search of higher rates of return elsewhere.

Whatever the causes of capital shortages, it is clear that the absence of productive capital prevents income from rising in any economy. The availability of capital is a necessary, but not a *sufficient*, condition for economic growth. The landscape of the developing countries is littered with idle factories and abandoned machinery. Other ingredients are required to achieve economic progress.

Human Resources and Entrepreneurial Ability   Capital is not the only factor of production required to produce output. Labor is equally important. First of all, in order to be productive the workforce must be healthy. Disease today is the leading threat to development in much of the world. The most devastating health problem in the world today is the HIV/AIDS pandemic. In 2005 alone, 3.1 million people died of AIDS and 4.9 million were newly infected with HIV. At the end of 2005, more than 40 million people were infected with the virus. In total, more than 25 million have died. It is the leading cause of death in sub-Saharan Africa, where the disease threatens to reverse the developmental achievements of the last 50 years. Beyond AIDS, health and nutrition are essential to workforce development. Programs in nutrition and health can be seen as investments in human capital that lead to increased productivity and higher incomes.

But health is not the only issue. To be productive the workforce must be educated and trained. The more familiar forms of human capital investment, including formal education and on-the-job training, are essential. Basic literacy, as well as specialized training in farm management, for example, can yield high returns to both the individual worker and the economy. Education has grown to become the largest category of government expenditure in many developing nations, in part because of the belief that human resources are the ultimate determinant of economic advance.

Just as financial capital seeks the highest and safest return, so does human capital. Thousands of students from developing countries, many of whom were supported by their governments, graduate every year from U.S. colleges and universities as engineers, doctors, scientists, economists, and other professionals. After graduation, these people face a difficult choice: to remain in the United States and earn a high salary or to return home and accept a job at a much lower salary. Many remain in the United States. This **brain drain** siphons off many of the most talented minds from developing countries.

brain drain The tendency for talented people from developing countries to become educated in a developed country and remain there after graduation.

Innovative entrepreneurs who are willing to take risks are an essential human resource in any economy. In a developing nation, new techniques of production rarely need to be invented, because they can usually be adapted from the technology already developed by the technologically advanced nations. However, entrepreneurs who are willing and able to organize and carry out economic activity appear to be in short supply. Family and political ties often seem to be more important than ability when it comes to securing positions of authority. Whatever the explanation:

> Development cannot proceed without human resources capable of initiating and managing economic activity.

Social Overhead Capital   Anyone who has spent time in a developing nation knows how difficult it can be to send a letter, make a local phone call, or travel within the country itself. Add to this problems with water supplies, frequent electrical power outages—in the few areas where electricity is available—and often ineffective mosquito and pest control, and you soon realize how deficient even the simplest, most basic government-provided goods and services can be.

In any economy, developing or otherwise, the government has considerable opportunity and responsibility for involvement where conditions encourage natural monopoly (as in the utilities industries) and where public goods (such as roads and pest control) must be provided. In a developing economy, the government must put emphasis on creating a basic infrastructure—roads, power generation, and irrigation systems. There are often good reasons why such projects, referred to as **social overhead capital**, cannot successfully be undertaken by the private sector. First, many of these projects operate with economies of scale, which means they can be efficient only if they are very large. In that case, they may be too large for any private company or group of companies to carry out.

Second, many socially useful projects cannot be undertaken by the private sector because there is no way for private agents to capture enough of the returns to make such projects profitable. This so-called *free-rider problem* is common in the economics of the developed world. Consider national defense: All persons in a country benefit from national defense, whether they have paid for it or not. Anyone who attempted to go into the private business of providing national defense would go broke. Why should I buy any national defense if your purchase of defense will also protect me? Why should you buy any if my purchase will also protect you?

> The governments of developing countries can do important and useful things to encourage development, but many of their efforts must be concentrated in areas that the private sector would never touch. If government action in these realms is not forthcoming, economic development may be curtailed by a lack of social overhead capital.

social overhead capital
Basic infrastructure projects such as roads, power generation, and irrigation systems.

STRATEGIES FOR ECONOMIC DEVELOPMENT

Just as no single theory appears to explain lack of economic advancement, no one development strategy will likely succeed in all nations. Many alternative development strategies have been proposed over the past years. Although these strategies have been very different, they all recognize that a developing economy faces basic trade-offs. An insufficient amount of both human and physical resources dictates that choices must be made, including those between agriculture and industry, exports and import substitution, and central planning and free markets.

Agriculture or Industry?   Most Third World countries began to gain political independence just after World War II. The tradition of promoting industrialization as the solution to the problems of the developing world dates from this time. The early 5-year development plans of India called for promoting manufacturing; the current government in Ethiopia (an extremely poor country) has similar intentions.

Industry has several apparent attractions over agriculture. First, if it is true that capital shortages constrain economic growth, then the building of factories is an obvious step toward increasing a nation's stock of capital. Second, and perhaps most important, one of the primary characteristics of more developed economies is their structural transition away

TABLE 36.2 The Structure of Production in Selected Developed and Developing Economies, 2003

Country	Per-Capita Gross National Income (GNI)	PERCENTAGE OF GROSS DOMESTIC PRODUCT		
		Agriculture	Industry	Services
Tanzania	$ 300	45	16	39
Bangladesh	400	22	26	52
China	1,100	15	52	33
Colombia	1,810	12	29	58
Thailand	2,190	10	44	46
Brazil	2,720	6	19	75
Korea (Rep.)	12,030	3	35	62
United States	37,870	2	23	75
Japan	34,180	1	30	68

Source: World Bank, World Development Indicators, 2005.

from agriculture and toward manufacturing and modern services. As Table 36.2 shows, agriculture's share in GDP declines substantially as per-capita incomes increase. The share of services increases correspondingly, especially in the early phases of economic development.

Many economies have pursued industry at the expense of agriculture. In many countries, however, industrialization has been either unsuccessful or disappointing—that is, it has not brought the benefits that were expected. Experience suggests that simply trying to replicate the structure of developed economies does not in itself guarantee, or even promote, successful development.

Since the early 1970s, the agricultural sector has received considerably more attention. Agricultural development strategies have had numerous benefits. Although some agricultural projects (such as the building of major dams and irrigation networks) are very capital intensive, many others (such as services to help teach better farming techniques and small-scale fertilizer programs) have low capital and import requirements. Programs like these can affect large numbers of households, and because their benefits are directed at rural areas, they are most likely to help a country's poorest families.

Experience over the last three decades suggests that some balance between these approaches leads to the best outcome—that is, it is important and effective to pay attention to both industry and agriculture. The Chinese have referred to this dual approach to development as "walking on two legs."

Exports or Import Substitution?   As developing nations expand their industrial activities, they must decide what type of trade strategy to pursue, usually one of two alternatives: import substitution or export promotion.

import substitution An industrial trade strategy that favors developing local industries that can manufacture goods to replace imports.

Import substitution is an industrial trade strategy to develop local industries that can manufacture goods to replace imports. For example, if fertilizer is imported, import substitution calls for a domestic fertilizer industry to produce replacements for fertilizer imports. This strategy gained prominence throughout South America in the 1950s. At that time, most developing nations exported agricultural and mineral products, goods that faced uncertain and often unstable international markets. Under these conditions, the call for import-substitution policies was understandable. Special government actions, including tariff and quota protection and subsidized imports of machinery, were set up to encourage new domestic industries. Multinational corporations were also invited into many countries to begin domestic operations.

Most economists believe import-substitution strategies have failed almost everywhere they have been tried. With domestic industries sheltered from international competition by high tariffs (often as high as 200 percent), major economic inefficiencies were created. For example, Peru has a population of 26.7 million, only a tiny fraction of whom can afford to buy an automobile. Yet at one time the country had five or six different automobile manufacturers, each of which produced only a few thousand cars per year. Because there are substantial economies of scale in automobile production, the cost per car was much higher than it needed to be, and valuable resources that could have been devoted to another, more productive, activity were squandered producing cars.

Furthermore, policies designed to promote import substitution often encouraged capital-intensive production methods, which limited the creation of jobs and hurt export activities. A country such as Peru could not export automobiles, because it could produce them only at a cost far greater than their price on the world market. Worse still, import-substitution policies encouraged the use of expensive domestic products, such as tractors and fertilizer, instead of lower-cost imports. These policies taxed the sectors that might have successfully competed in world markets. To the extent that the Peruvian sugar industry had to rely on domestically produced, high-cost fertilizer, for example, its ability to compete in international markets was reduced, because its production costs were artificially raised.

As an alternative to import substitution, some nations have pursued strategies of export promotion. **Export promotion** is simply the policy of encouraging exports. As an industrial market economy, Japan is a striking example to the developing world of the economic success that exports can provide. With an average annual per-capita real GDP growth rate of roughly 6 percent per year since 1960, Japan's achievements are in part based on industrial production oriented toward foreign consumers.

export promotion A trade policy designed to encourage exports.

Several countries in the developing world have attempted to emulate Japan's success. Starting around 1970, Hong Kong, Singapore, Korea, and Taiwan (the "four little dragons" between the two big dragons, China and Japan) all began to pursue export promotion of manufactured goods. Today their growth rates have surpassed Japan's. Other nations, including Brazil, Colombia, and Turkey, have also had some success at pursuing an outward-looking trade policy.

Government support of export promotion has often taken the form of maintaining an exchange rate favorable enough to permit exports to compete with products manufactured in developed economies. For example, many people believe Japan kept the value of the yen artificially low during the 1970s. Because "cheap" yen means inexpensive Japanese goods in the United States, sales of Japanese goods (especially automobiles) increased dramatically. Governments also have provided subsidies to export industries.

A big issue for countries growing or trying to grow by selling exports on world markets is free trade. In 2003, the United States and Europe were accused of protecting their own agricultural producers with large subsidies that allowed domestic farmers a big advantage selling on world markets. The African countries in particular raised the issue during a tour of the continent by President Bush in 2003. (See the News Analysis Box titled "Trade and Development in Africa—2003.")

Central Planning or the Market?
As part of its strategy for achieving economic development, a nation must decide how its economy will be directed. Its basic choices lie between a market-oriented economic system and a centrally planned one.

In the 1950s and into the 1960s, development strategies that called for national planning commanded wide support. The rapid economic growth of the Soviet Union, a centrally planned economy, provided an example of how fast a less developed agrarian nation could be transformed into a modern industrial power. (The often appalling costs of this strategy—severe discipline, gross violation of human rights, and environmental damage—were less widely known.) In addition, the underdevelopment of many commodity and asset markets in the developing world led many experts to believe that market forces could not direct an economy reliably and that major government intervention was therefore necessary. Even the United States, with its commitment to free enterprise in the marketplace, supported early central planning efforts in many developing nations.

Today, planning takes many forms in the developing nations. In some, central planning has replaced market-based outcomes with direct, administratively determined controls over such economic variables as prices, output, and employment. In others, national planning amounts to little more than the formulation of general 5- or 10-year goals as rough blueprints for a nation's economic future.

The economic appeal of planning lies theoretically in its ability to channel savings into productive investment and to coordinate economic activities that private actors in the economy might not otherwise undertake. The reality of central planning, however, is that it is a technically difficult, highly politicized nightmare to administer. Given the scarcity of human resources and the unstable political environment in many developing nations, planning itself—let alone the execution of the plan—becomes a formidable task.

agricultural subsidy, trade barriers, free trade | search

○ Further Exploration ⦿ News Analysis

New Trade Agreement
with Central America
and the Dominican
Republic—2005

Outsourcing Is Not Just
Customer Service Reps
in India

**Trade and Development
in Africa—2003**

Russia's Economy
in 2005

Trade and Development
in Africa—2003

IN JULY 2003, PRESIDENT BUSH toured the African continent, visiting a number of very poor countries. One topic on top of the agenda was the HIV/AIDS crisis. One of the countries on his itinerary was Botswana, where some estimates put the infection rate at 39 percent of adults.

One of the other issues that came up in every country on the tour was agricultural trade. Here the United States was criticized for policies that had a very negative impact on the ability of the continent to grow: agricultural subsidies. In the following piece in the *New York Times*, two African presidents state their case.

Your Farm Subsidies
Are Strangling Us
—New York Times

After too many years of Africa's being pushed to the global background, it's heartening to see the world's attention being focused on our continent. International support—both financial and otherwise—is certainly needed to help combat the severe poverty and disease gripping our nations. But first and foremost, Africa needs to be allowed to take its destiny into its own hands. Only self-reliance and economic growth and development will allow Africa to become a full member of the world community.

With the creation of the New Economic Partnership for African Development in 2001, African leaders have committed themselves to following the principles of good governance and a market economy. Nothing is more central to this goal than participating in world trade. As the presidents of two of Africa's least developed countries—Burkina Faso and Mali—we are eager to participate in the multilateral trading system and to take on its rights and obligations.

Cotton is our ticket into the world market. Its production is crucial to economic development in West and Central Africa, as well as to the livelihoods of millions of people there. Cotton ac-

counts for up to 40 percent of export revenues and 10 percent of gross domestic product in our two countries, as well as in Benin and Chad. More than that, cotton is of paramount importance to the social infrastructure of Africa, as well as to the maintenance of its rural areas.

This vital economic sector in our countries is seriously threatened by agricultural subsidies granted by rich countries to their cotton producers. According to the International Cotton Advisory Committee, cotton subsidies amounted to about $5.8 billion in the production year of 2001 to 2002, nearly equal the amount of cotton trade for this same period. Such subsidies lead to worldwide overproduction and distort cotton prices, depriving poor African countries of their only comparative advantage in international trade.

Not only is cotton crucial to our economies, it is the sole agricultural product for our countries to trade. Although African cotton is of the highest quality, our production costs are about 50 percent lower than in developed countries even though we rely on manual labor. In wealthier countries, by contrast, lower-quality cotton is produced on large mechanized farms, generating little employment and having a questionable impact on the environment. Cotton there could be replaced by other, more valuable crops.

In the period from 2001 to 2002, America's 25,000 cotton farmers received more in subsidies—some $3 billion—than the entire economic output of Burkina Faso, where two million people depend on cotton. Further, United States subsidies are concentrated on just 10 percent of its cotton farmers. Thus, the payments to about 2,500 relatively well-off farmers has the unintended but nevertheless real effect of impoverishing some 10 million rural poor people in West and Central Africa.

Something has to be done. Along with the countries of Benin and Chad, we have submitted a proposal to the

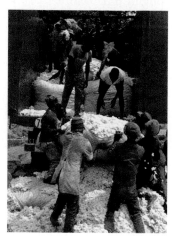

Cotton growers in Africa find that they are unable to compete with heavily subsidized U.S. growers.

World Trade Organization—which is meeting in Cancún, Mexico, in September to discuss agricultural issues—that calls for an end to unfair subsidies granted by developed countries to their cotton producers. As an interim measure, we have also proposed that least-developed countries be granted financial compensation for lost export revenues that are due to those subsidies.

Our demand is simple: apply free trade rules not only to those products that are of interest to the rich and powerful, but also to those products where poor countries have a proven comparative advantage. We know that the world will not ignore our plea for a fair playing field. The World Trade Organization has said it is committed to addressing the problems of developing countries. The United States has convinced us that a free market economy provides the best opportunities for all members of the world community. Let us translate these principles into deeds at Cancún.

Source: Amadou Toumani Touré and Blaise Compaoré, "Your Farm Subsidies Are Strangling Us," New York Times, July 11, 2003. Copyright 2003, The New York Times. Reprinted by permission.

The failure of many central planning efforts has brought increasing calls for less government intervention and more market orientation in developing economies. The elimination of price controls, privatization of state-run enterprises, and reductions in import restraints are examples of market-oriented reforms recommended by such international agencies as the **International Monetary Fund (IMF)**, whose primary goals are to stabilize international exchange rates and to lend money to countries that have problems financing their international transactions, and the **World Bank**, which lends money to a country for projects that promote economic development.

Members' contributions to both organizations are determined by the size of their economies. Only 20 percent of the World Bank's funding comes from contributions; 80 percent comes from retained earnings and investments in capital markets. The developing world is increasingly recognizing the value of market forces in determining the allocation of scarce resources. Nonetheless, government still has a major role to play. In the decades ahead, the governments of developing nations will need to determine those situations where planning is superior to the market and those where the market is superior to planning.

GROWTH VERSUS DEVELOPMENT: THE POLICY CYCLE

Until now, we have used *growth* and *development* as if they meant the same thing, but this may not always be the case. You can easily imagine instances in which a country has achieved higher levels of income (growth) with little or no benefit accruing to most of its citizens (development). Thus, the question is whether economic growth necessarily brings about economic development.

In the past, most development strategies were aimed at increasing the growth rate of income per capita. Many still are, based on the theory that benefits of economic growth will "trickle down" to all members of society. If this theory is correct, then growth should promote development.

By the early 1970s, the relationship between growth and development was being questioned more and more. A study by the World Bank in 1974 concluded

> It is now clear that more than a decade of rapid growth in underdeveloped countries has been of little or no benefit to perhaps a third of their population. . . . Paradoxically, while growth policies have succeeded beyond the expectations of the first development decade, the very idea of aggregate growth as a social objective has increasingly been called into question.

The World Bank study indicated that increases in GDP per capita did not guarantee significant improvements in such development indicators as nutrition, health, and education. Although GDP per capita did rise, its benefits trickled down to a small minority of the population. This very limited success prompted new development strategies that would directly address the problems of poverty. Such new strategies favored agriculture over industry, called for domestic redistribution of income and wealth (especially land), and encouraged programs to satisfy such basic needs as food and shelter.

In the late 1970s and early 1980s, the international macroeconomic crises of high oil prices, worldwide recession, and Third World debt forced attention away from programs designed to eliminate poverty directly. Then, during the 1980s and 1990s, the policy focus turned 180 degrees. The World Bank and the United States began demanding "structural adjustment" in the developing countries as a prerequisite for sending aid to them. **Structural adjustment** programs entail reducing the size of the public sector through privatization and/or expenditure reductions, substantially cutting budget deficits, reining in inflation, and encouraging private saving and investment with tax reforms. These promarket demands were an attempt to stimulate growth; distributional consequences took a back seat.

ISSUES IN ECONOMIC DEVELOPMENT

Every developing nation has a cultural, political, and economic history all its own and therefore confronts a unique set of problems. Still, it is possible to discuss common economic issues that each nation must face in its own particular way. These issues include rapid population growth and growing debt burdens.

International Monetary Fund (IMF) An international agency whose primary goals are to stabilize international exchange rates and to lend money to countries that have problems financing their international transactions.

World Bank An international agency that lends money to individual countries for projects that promote economic development.

structural adjustment A series of programs in developing nations designed to (1) reduce the size of their public sectors through privatization and/or expenditure reductions, (2) decrease their budget deficits, (3) control inflation, and (4) encourage private saving and investment through tax reform.

POPULATION GROWTH

The populations of the developing nations are estimated to be growing at about 1.7 percent per year. (Compare this with a population growth rate of only .5 percent per year in the industrial market economies.) If the Third World's population growth rate remains at 1.7 percent, within 41 years its population will double from the 1990 level of 4.1 billion to over 8 billion by the year 2031. On the other hand, it will take the industrialized nations 139 years to double their populations. What is so immediately alarming about these numbers is that given the developing nations' current economic problems, it is hard to imagine how they can possibly absorb so many more people in such a relatively short period.

Concern over world population growth is not new. The Reverend Thomas Malthus (who became England's first professor of political economy) expressed his fears about the population increases he observed 200 years ago. Malthus believed that populations grow geometrically at a constant growth rate—thus the absolute size of the increase each year gets larger and larger—but that food supplies grow much more slowly because of the diminishing marginal productivity of land.[1] These two phenomena led Malthus to predict the increasing impoverishment of the world's people unless population growth could be slowed.

Malthus's fears for Europe and America proved unfounded. He did not anticipate the technological changes that revolutionized agricultural productivity and the eventual decrease in population growth rates in Europe and North America. Nevertheless, Malthus's prediction may have been right, only premature. Do the circumstances in the developing world now fit his predictions? Although some contemporary observers believe the Malthusian view is correct and the Earth's population will eventually grow to a level that the world's resources cannot support, others say technological change and demographic transitions (to slower population growth rates) will permit further increases in global welfare.

The Consequences of Rapid Population Growth   We know far less about the economic consequences of rapid population growth than you might expect. Conventional wisdom warns of dire economic consequences from the developing nations' "population explosion," but these predictions are difficult to substantiate with the available evidence. The rapid economic growth of the United States, for example, was accompanied by relatively rapid population growth by historical standards. Any slowing of population growth has not been necessary for the economic progress achieved by many of the newly industrialized countries. Nonetheless, population expansion in many of today's poorest nations is of a magnitude unprecedented in world history, as Figure 36.1 clearly shows. From the year 1 A.D. until the mid-1600s, populations grew slowly, at rates of only about .04 percent per year. Since then, and especially since 1950, rates have skyrocketed. Today, populations are growing at rates of 1.5 percent to 4.0 percent per year throughout the developing world.

Because growth rates like these never occurred before the twentieth century, no one knows what impact they will have on future economic development. However, a basic economic concern is that such rapid population growth may limit investment and restrain increases in labor productivity and income. Rapid population growth changes the age composition of a population, generating many dependent children relative to the number of productive working adults. Such a situation may diminish saving rates, and hence investment, as the immediate consumption needs of the young take priority over saving for the future.

Even if low saving rates are not a necessary consequence of rapid population growth, as some authorities contend, other economic problems remain. The ability to improve human capital through a broad range of programs, from infant nutrition to formal secondary education, may be severely limited if the population explosion continues. Such programs are most often the responsibility of the state, and governments that are already weak cannot be expected to improve their services under the burden of population pressures that rapidly increase demands for all kinds of public goods and services.

For example, Mozambique's population growth rate—3.7 percent—is one of the highest in the world. Its 1998 population of over 17 million people grew by about 3.4 million by 2003 and will likely grow by 7 million by 2008. This is a daunting prospect, and it is hard to

---

[1]The law of diminishing marginal productivity says that with a fixed amount of a resource (land), additions of more and more of a variable resource (labor) will produce smaller and smaller gains in output.

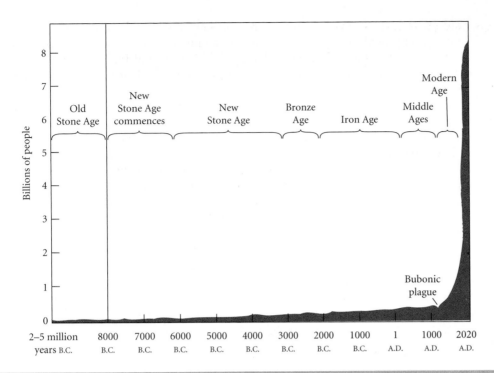

FIGURE 36.1 The Growth of World Population, Projected to 2020 A.D.

For thousands of years, population grew slowly. From 1 A.D. until the mid-1600s, population grew at about .04 percent per year. Since the Industrial Revolution, population growth has occurred at an unprecedented rate.

imagine how in so little time Mozambique, with per-capita GNP under $100, will be able to provide its population with the physical and human capital needed to maintain, let alone improve, already low standards of living.

Causes of Rapid Population Growth   Population growth is determined by the relationship between births and deaths—that is, between **fertility rates** and **mortality rates**. The **natural rate of population increase** is defined as the difference between the birth rate and the death rate. If the birth rate is 4 percent, for example, and the death rate is 3 percent, the population is growing at a rate of 1 percent per year.

Historically, low rates of population growth were maintained because of high mortality rates despite high levels of fertility. That is, families had many children, but average life expectancies were low, and many children (and adults) died young. In Europe and North America, improvements in nutrition, in public health programs (especially those concerned with drinking water and sanitation services), and in medical practices have led to a drop in the mortality rate and hence to more rapid population growth. Eventually, fertility rates also fell, returning population growth to a low and stable rate.

Public health programs and improved nutrition over the past 30 years have brought about precipitous declines in mortality rates in the developing nations also. However, fertility rates have not declined as quickly, and the result has been high natural rates of population growth. Reduced population growth depends to some extent on decreased birth rates, but attempts to lower fertility rates must take account of how different cultures feel and behave with regard to fertility.

Family planning and modern forms of birth control are important mechanisms for decreasing fertility, but by themselves have had rather limited success in most countries where they have been tried. If family-planning strategies are to be successful, they must make sense to the people who are supposed to benefit from them. The planners of such strategies must understand why families in developing nations have so many children.

To a great extent, in developing countries people want large families because they believe they need them. Economists have attempted to understand fertility patterns in the developing countries by focusing on the determinants of the demand for children. In agrarian societies, children are sources of farm labor, and they may make significant contributions to

fertility rate The birth rate. Equal to (the number of births per year divided by the population) × 100.

mortality rate The death rate. Equal to (the number of deaths per year divided by the population) × 100.

natural rate of population increase The difference between the birth rate and the death rate. It does not take migration into account.

household income. In societies without public old-age-support social security programs, children may also provide a source of income for parents who are too old to support themselves. With the high value of children enhanced by high rates of infant mortality, it is no wonder that families try to have many children to ensure that a sufficient number will survive into adulthood.

Cultural and religious values also affect the number of children families want to have, but the economic incentives to have large families are extremely powerful. Only when the relationship between the costs and benefits of having children changes will fertility rates decline. The expansion of employment opportunities for women in an economy increases the opportunity costs of childrearing (by giving women a more highly valued alternative to raising children) and often leads to lower birth rates. Government incentives for smaller families, such as subsidized education for families with fewer than three children, can have a similar effect. In general, rising incomes appear to decrease fertility rates, indicating that economic development itself reduces population growth rates.

Economic theories of population growth suggest that fertility decisions made by poor families should not be viewed as uninformed and uncontrolled. An individual family may find that having many children is a rational strategy for economic survival given the conditions in which it finds itself. This does not mean, however, that having many children is a net benefit to society as a whole. When a family decides to have a large number of children, it imposes costs on the rest of society; the children must be educated, their health provided for, and so forth. In other words, what makes sense for an individual household may create negative effects for the nation as a whole.

> Any nation that wants to slow its rate of population growth will probably find it necessary to have in place economic incentives for fewer children as well as family-planning programs.

DEVELOPING-COUNTRY DEBT BURDENS

In the 1970s, development experts worried about many crises facing the developing world, but not the debt crisis. Within a decade, the picture changed dramatically. The financial plight of nations such as Brazil, Mexico, and the Philippines became front-page news. What alarmed those familiar with the debt situation was not only its potential impact on the developing nations but a belief that it threatened the economic welfare of the developed nations as well.

Between 1970 and 1984, developing nations borrowed so much money from other nations that their combined debt increased by 1,000 percent, to almost $700 billion. Three nations alone—Brazil, Mexico, and Venezuela—had outstanding loans to three major U.S. banks (Citibank, Chase Manhattan, and Manufacturer's Hanover, now part of Chemical) that were more than double the net worth of those financial institutions. As recession took hold in the economically advanced countries during the early 1980s, growth in the exports of the debtor countries slowed, and many found they could no longer pay back the money they owed.

As the situation continued to deteriorate, many feared that debtor nations might repudiate their debts outright and default on their outstanding loans. When *default* (nonpayment) occurs with domestic loans, some collateral is usually available to cover all or part of the remaining debt. For loans to another country, such collateral is virtually impossible to secure. Given their extensive involvement with developing-country borrowers, Western banks did not want to set in motion a pattern of international default and borrowers did not want to default. Leaders of the developing nations recognized that default might result in the denial of access to developed-country banking facilities and to markets in the industrial countries, posing major obstacles to further development efforts.

debt rescheduling An agreement between banks and borrowers through which a new schedule of repayments of the debt is negotiated; often some of the debt is written off and the repayment period is extended.

Various countries rescheduled their debt as an interim solution. Under a **debt rescheduling** agreement, banks and borrowers negotiate a new schedule for the repayment of existing debt, often with some of the debt written off and with repayment periods extended. In return, borrowing countries are expected to sign an agreement with the IMF to revamp their economic policies to provide incentives for higher export earnings and lower imports. This kind of agreement, referred to as a **stabilization program**, usually requires austerity measures such as currency devaluations, reduction in government expenditures, and increase in tax revenues.

By the early 1990s, the debt crisis was not over but it had lessened, mainly as a result of macroeconomic events that led to reduced interest rates. The international economy has revived somewhat, helping some nations to increase their export earnings. Other nations have benefited from new domestic policies. Still others, including Panama and many African nations, however, continue to face debt burdens that are unmanageable in the short run.

During 1998, a number of countries had severe economic problems that required emergency loan guarantees from the IMF. Asian economies such as Indonesia, Thailand, and Korea had sudden currency collapses as short-term loans were called by creditors and as investors headed for the doors. Dramatically falling currency values made it all the more difficult to pay for the interest on dollar-denominated debt and for imports. Similar circumstances occurred in Russia and Brazil in 1998. Russia defaulted on a series of loan agreements in August of that year. In each case emergency credit guarantees were granted by the IMF in exchange for the promise of fiscal discipline and economic austerity. By 2003, these economies were recovering and growing at a fairly rapid pace but each was still saddled with a heavy debt burden.

Between 2000 and 2003, interest rates worldwide dropped considerably, and finally a major step was taken to reduce the problem in September 2005, when the World Bank and the International Monetary Fund agreed to cancel up to $55 billion in debts owed to them by some of the world's poorest countries. A total of 18 countries (14 in Africa and 4 in South and Central America) will be affected. The African Development Fund was expected to do the same thing in early 2006. While debt forgiveness does not solve the problem of development by itself, it loosens a major constraint.

One economic lesson of the last two decades is that proper management of foreign capital in developing countries is essential. Much foreign borrowing was wasted on projects that had little chance of generating the returns necessary to pay back their initial costs. In other cases, domestic policies that used debt as a substitute for adjusting to new economic circumstances proved to be harmful in the long run. Overall, much optimism about the prospects of the developing economies was inappropriate. Whatever else we may have learned from these mistakes, the debt crisis underscored the growing interdependence of all economies—rich and poor, large and small.

stabilization program An agreement between a borrower country and the International Monetary Fund in which the country agrees to revamp its economic policies to provide incentives for higher export earnings and lower imports.

ECONOMIES IN TRANSITION

For 40 years, between the end of World War II and the mid-1980s, a powerful rivalry existed between the Soviet Union and the United States. This "Cold War" pitted the two superpowers against each other in a struggle for influence and fueled the nuclear arms race. At one time the mutual distrust between them was so strong that the concept of "mutual assured destruction" dominated international relations.

However, the world began to change in the mid-1980s as the political and economic structures of the Soviet Union and the Eastern European Communist countries started to crumble. In 1989, relatively peaceful revolutions took place in rapid succession in Poland, Hungary, and Czechoslovakia (now the Czech Republic). A bloody revolution in Romania toppled Nicolae Ceausescu, who had ruled with an iron fist for 24 years. The Berlin Wall, which had separated Berlin since 1961, was knocked down and Germany was reunited. Then, in August 1991, after a failed coup attempt by hard-line Communists, the Soviet Union itself began to come apart. By the end of 1991, the Soviet Union (USSR) had dissolved into 15 independent states, the largest of which is the Russian Republic. Ten of these 15 republics formed the Commonwealth of Independent States (CIS) in December 1991. The Cold War was over.

We reflect on historical political rivalries in an economics text for two reasons. First, the 40-year struggle between the United States and the Soviet Union was fundamentally a struggle between two economic systems: market-based capitalism (the U.S. system) and centrally planned socialism (the Soviet system). Second, the Cold War ended so abruptly in the late 1980s because the Soviet and Eastern European economies virtually collapsed during that period. In a sense, we could say 1991 was the year that the market triumphed.

What now? The independent states of the former Soviet Union and the other former Communist economies of Eastern Europe are struggling to make the transition from centrally planned socialism to some form of market-based capitalism. In some countries, such as Serbia and Bosnia-Herzegovina, economic reforms have taken a back seat to bitter and violent ethnic and political rivalries that have been simmering for decades. In other countries, like Poland and Russia, the biggest issue continues to be economic transformation.

The success or failure of this transition from centrally planned socialism to market-based capitalism will determine the course of history. Although many countries have made the transition from a market-based system to a centrally planned system, the opposite has never occurred. The process has been and will continue to be painful and filled with ups and downs. Between 1989 and 1997, industrial production fell more than 40 percent in countries like the former East Germany, Albania, Poland, and Romania. In Russia, production decreased about 30 percent. In all these nations, fairly prosperous people suddenly found themselves with annual real incomes closer to those of people in developing countries. For many people, the issue became survival: how to get enough food and fuel to get through the winter.

By 1995, things had turned around, and though uncertainty and problems remained, output was rising in much of Eastern and Central Europe. A growing optimism seemed to be spreading. The biggest success story was in East Germany, where real output in 1994 grew by over 9 percent, the fastest growth rate of any region of Europe. A construction boom, rapid development of infrastructure, low inflation, and rising exports all contributed to the region's success. However, East Germany's situation is unique because it was absorbed by a prosperous, fully developed, and modern West Germany that has made development in the East its primary goal.

Central Europe, including Hungary, Poland, the Czech Republic, Bulgaria, and Romania, also achieved basic macroeconomic stability and began to grow in 1993 and 1994. Poland enjoyed the most rapid economic growth in the group (around 4.5 percent). Fueled by foreign investment, privatization, and entrepreneurship, the Polish private sector by 1992 accounted for well over one-third of the nation's total output, although many problems persist. Russia and the former countries of the Soviet Union have achieved less through 2000. Nonetheless, conditions have improved and prospects for success are greater than they were only a few years ago.

POLITICAL SYSTEMS AND ECONOMIC SYSTEMS: SOCIALISM, CAPITALISM, AND COMMUNISM

Every society has both a political system and an economic system. Unfortunately, the political and economic dimensions of a society are often confused.

The terms *democracy* and *dictatorship* refer to *political* systems. A *democracy* is a system of government in which ultimate power rests with the people, who make governmental decisions either directly through voting or indirectly through representatives. A *dictatorship* is a political system in which ultimate power is concentrated in either a small elite group or a single person.

Historically, two major *economic* systems have existed: socialism and capitalism. A **socialist economy** is one in which most capital—factories, equipment, buildings, railroads, and so forth—is owned by the government instead of private citizens. *Social ownership* is another term that is used to describe this kind of system. A **capitalist economy** is one in which most capital is privately owned. Beyond these systems is a purely theoretical economic system called *communism*.

Communism is an economic system in which the people control the means of production (land and capital) directly, without the intervention of a government or state. In the world envisioned by communists, the state would wither away and society would plan the economy in the same way a collective would. Although some countries still consider themselves communist—including China, North Korea, Cuba, and Tanzania—economic planning is done by the government in all of them.

socialist economy An economy in which most capital is owned by the government instead of private citizens. Also called social ownership.

capitalist economy An economy in which most capital is privately owned.

communism An economic system in which the people control the means of production (capital and land) directly, without the intervention of a government or state.

Comparing economies today, the real distinction is between centrally planned socialism and capitalism, not between capitalism and communism.

No pure socialist economies and no pure capitalist economies exist. Even the Soviet Union, which was basically socialist, had a large private sector. Fully one-fourth of agricultural output in what was the USSR was legally produced on private plots and sold. Conversely, the strongly capitalistic United States supports many government enterprises, including the U.S. postal system. Nonetheless, public ownership is the exception in the United States and private ownership was the exception in the Soviet Union.

Whether particular kinds of political systems tend to be associated with particular kinds of economic systems is debated. The United States and Japan are countries with essentially capitalist economic systems and essentially democratic political institutions. China and North Korea have basically socialist economies with political power highly concentrated in a single political party. These observations do not imply that all capitalist countries have democratic political institutions, or that all socialist countries are subject to totalitarian party rule. Some countries—Singapore, for example—have basically capitalist economies without democratic political systems. Other countries that are much closer to the socialist end of the economic spectrum also maintain strong democratic traditions. Sweden is an example of a democratic country that supports strong socialist institutions.

However, do certain kinds of economic systems lead to repressive governments? Austrian economist Friedrich von Hayek argues yes:

> Economic reforms and government coercion are the road to serfdom. . . . Personal and economic freedoms are inseparable. Once you start down the road to government regulation and planning of the economy, the freedom to speak minds and select political leaders will be jeopardized.[2]

The recent events in Eastern Europe and Russia seem to support Hayek's thesis. There, economic and political reforms are proceeding side by side, and the evidence is mounting that the heart of both the market system *and* democracy is individual freedom.

Nonetheless, some counter Hayek's argument by claiming that social reform and active government involvement in the economy are the only ways to prevent the rise of a totalitarian state. They argue that free and unregulated markets lead to inequality and the accumulation of economic power. Accumulated economic power, in turn, leads to political power that is inevitably used in the interests of the wealthy few, not in the interests of all.

CENTRAL PLANNING VERSUS THE MARKET

In addition to ownership of capital, economic systems also differ in the extent to which economic decisions are made through central planning instead of a market system. In some socialist economies, the allocation of resources, the mix of output, and the distribution of output are determined centrally according to a plan. The former Soviet Union, for example, generated 1-year and 5-year plans laying out specific production targets in virtually every sector of the economy. In market economies, decisions are made independently by buyers and sellers responding to market signals. Producers produce only what they expect to sell. Labor is attracted into and out of various occupations by wages that are determined by the forces of supply and demand.

Just as there are no pure capitalist and no pure socialist economies, there are no pure market economies and no pure planned economies. Even in the former Soviet Union markets existed and determined, to a large extent, the allocation of resources. Production targets in the United States are set by many agencies, including the Pentagon.

Generally, socialist economies favor central planning over market allocation, while capitalist economies rely to a much greater extent on the market. Nonetheless, some variety exists. The former Yugoslavia was a socialist country that made extensive use of the market. Ownership of capital and land rested with the government, but individual firms determined their own output levels and prices and made their own investment plans. Yugoslavian firms borrowed from banks to finance investments and paid interest on their loans. This type of system, which combines government ownership with market allocation, is referred to as a **market–socialist economy.**

market–socialist economy An economy that combines government ownership with market allocation.

---

[2]Friedrich Hayek, *The Road to Serfdom* (Chicago: University of Chicago Press, 1944).

THE END OF THE SOVIET UNION

No serious debate about economic matters took place in the Soviet Union until after Josef Stalin's death in 1953. In 1965, official reforms were introduced by the government of Alexei Kosygin. Mikhail Gorbachev announced a series of reforms in 1986 and in 1987, but the structure of the economy was not changed fundamentally.

Although Gorbachev's ideas seemed promising, the situation in the Soviet Union deteriorated sharply after 1987. The attempted transition from central planning to a partly free market system caused major problems. Growth of output slowed to a crawl in 1989 and 1990, and in 1991 the economic system collapsed. Industrial production dropped sharply, food shortages grew worse, inflation became serious, and external debt increased rapidly.

Gorbachev ran out of time in August 1991 as the struggle between the hard-liners and the radical reformers came to a head. The hard-liners took Gorbachev prisoner and assumed control of the government. The coup lasted only 3 days. People took to the streets of Moscow and resisted the tanks, the Soviet army refused to obey orders, and the hard-liners were out.

Nevertheless, the end was near for both Gorbachev and the Soviet Union. In December 1991, the Soviet Union was dissolved, 10 of the former Soviet republics formed the CIS, and Boris Yeltsin became president of the Russian Republic as Gorbachev became part of history. From the beginning, Yeltsin showed himself to be a reformer committed to converting the Russian economy rapidly into a market system while maintaining hard-won political freedoms for the people. His reform plan called for deregulating prices, privatizing public enterprises, and stabilizing the macroeconomy.

Boris Yeltsin was president of the Russian Republic and the champion of reform from 1991 to 1999. Yeltsin deregulated most prices, began the privatization process, and attempted to stabilize the macroeconomy. By 1995 progress had been slow but significant. Privatization had made steady progress, reaching a point in 1994 where the private sector was generating 60 percent of personal income. Inflation was down, and a new "economic constitution" in the form of revised laws to establish property rights and stimulate economic activity went into effect in 1995. Nevertheless, things were not going well across the board.

Most observers estimate that Russian GDP began to grow in the spring of 1997, after falling by about 50 percent from its 1989 level. However, problems remained severe into 1998. The biggest problem was attracting investment, and the biggest barrier was crime and corruption. The Russian government was finding it very difficult to enforce the rule of law. The term *cowboy capitalism* is often used to describe the situation in Russia today.

Vladimir Putin became president in January 2000 and immediately declared his commitment to continue the reforms. The News Analysis box titled "Russia's Economy in 2005" describes recent developments in Russia.

THE TRANSITION TO A MARKET ECONOMY

The reforms under way in the Russian Republic and in the other formerly Communist countries of Eastern Europe have taken shape very slowly and amid debate about how best to proceed. Remember, there is absolutely no historical precedent to provide lessons. Despite this lack of precedent, however, there is substantial agreement among economists about what needs to be done.

SIX BASIC REQUIREMENTS FOR SUCCESSFUL TRANSITION

Economists generally agree on six basic requirements for a successful transition from socialism to a market-based system: (1) macroeconomic stabilization; (2) deregulation of prices and liberalization of trade; (3) privatization of state-owned enterprises and development of new private industry; (4) establishment of market-supporting institutions such as property and contract laws, accounting systems, and so forth; (5) a social safety net to deal with unemployment and poverty; and (6) external assistance.

transitional economics, privatization, market economy	search

○ Further Exploration   ● News Analysis

New Trade Agreement
with Central America
and the Dominican
Republic—2005

Outsourcing Is Not Just
Customer Service Reps
in India

Trade and Development
in Africa—2003

Russia's Economy
in 2005

Russia's Economy in 2005

AFTER A FEW YEARS OF SLOW progress, the Russian economy appeared to be turning a corner at the end of 2005 when the following article appeared in the *Wall Street Journal*.

Russian Economy Begins Revival, as Effects of Yukos Breakup Fade

MOSCOW—Russia's economy is showing signs of picking up steam, evidence the investment climate has begun to recover from the battering it took last year when the Kremlin dismembered oil company OAO Yukos.

Buoyed by surging prices for Russia's main export, oil, growth rates have ticked back up during recent months after a slowdown that began last year. Investment also is rising and outflows of private capital—a key barometer of business confidence—are falling. Meanwhile, rising incomes are fueling a consumer boom.

"Business sentiment has improved significantly compared to a year ago," said John Litwack, lead economist on Russia for the World Bank.

But he warned that a new threat is emerging as oil revenues push up the value of the ruble, hurting the competitiveness of many local industries.

After Russian authorities nationalized Yukos's main production unit late last year in a controversial tax suit, the Kremlin has tried hard to win back shaken investor confidence. President Vladimir Putin has met with Western and Russian business leaders to reassure them on property rights and has proposed measures such as an amnesty on the repatriation of Russian capital from abroad.

Fears that the Kremlin would impose draconian new limits on foreign investment in the energy sector have faded somewhat. The latest version of a new subsoil law, which will set out policy on Russia's natural resources

and comes up for debate in Parliament this week, appears to have taken into account some of the concerns raised by foreign oil companies, according to industry executives.

The Kremlin's confidence-building campaign has had an effect. Inflows of foreign direct investment rose during the first half of this year by 30% from a year earlier to $4.5 billion. Russia's RTS stock index has risen by 55% since mid-May. Russia's credit rating was upgraded by Fitch Ratings in August, and by Moody's Investors Service in October.

In an interview with Dutch journalists this week, Mr. Putin said those developments showed "rumors that confidence in the Russian economy had been undermined [by the Yukos affair] are grossly exaggerated."

Economists also note a slowdown in the amount of capital flowing out of Russia. According to preliminary data, net capital outflows from the private sector came to $2.8 billion in the first nine months of this year, compared with $17.4 billion in the same period of 2004.

Economists attributed the trend to more offshore money flowing into the Russian stock exchange and increased foreign borrowing by Russian banks. "If current trends persist in the fourth quarter, we expect a net inflow of pri-

vate capital this year," Mr. Litwack said.

But the Kremlin's steady tightening of its grip over the energy sector continues to undermine confidence among investors. "The uncertain . . . investment climate and increasing government control are chilling investments," William Ramsay, deputy executive director at the Paris-based International Energy Agency, told an industry conference in Moscow this week.

And the torrent of petrodollars has created new risks, as oil revenues lead to a strengthening of the ruble, making local industry less competitive. That raises questions about the long-term sustainability of Russia's economic recovery.

A World Bank report released Tuesday said eight out of 13 manufacturing industries had reported a "substantial decline" in their growth rates, and said a key cause of the slowdown was "competitive pressures" from the rapid real appreciation of the ruble.

Source: Guy Chazan, "Russian Economy Begins Revival, as Effects of Yukos Breakup Fade," The Wall Street Journal, *November 2, 2005, p. A13. Copyright 2005 by DOW JONES & CO INC. Reproduced by permission of DOW JONES & CO INC. in the format Textbook via Copyright Clearance Center. Reprinted by permission.*

We now discuss each component. Although we focus on the experience of the Russian Republic, these principles apply to all economies in transition.

Macroeconomic Stabilization

Virtually every one of the countries in transition has had a problem with inflation, but nowhere has it been worse than in Russia. As economic conditions worsened, the government found itself with serious budget problems. As revenue flows slowed and expenditure commitments increased, large budget deficits resulted. At the same time, each of the new republics established its own central bank. Each central bank began issuing "ruble credits" to keep important enterprises afloat and to pay the government's bills. The issuance of these credits, which were generally accepted as a means of payment throughout the country, led to a dramatic expansion of the money supply.

Almost from the beginning, the expanded money supply meant too much money was chasing too few goods. This was made worse by government-controlled prices set substantially below market-clearing levels. The combination of monetary expansion and price control was deadly. Government-run shops that sold goods at controlled prices were empty. People waited in line for days and often became violent when their efforts to buy goods at low official prices were thwarted. At the same time, suppliers found that they could charge much higher prices for their products on the black market—which grew bigger by the day, further exacerbating the shortage of goods at government shops. Over time, the ruble became worth less and less as black market prices continued to rise more rapidly. Russia found itself with near hyperinflation in 1992. To achieve a properly functioning market system, prices must be stabilized. To do so, the government must find a way to move toward a balanced budget and to bring the supply of money under control.

Deregulation of Prices and Liberalization of Trade

To move successfully from central planning to a market system, individual prices must be deregulated. A system of freely moving prices forms the backbone of a market system. When people want more of a good than is currently being produced, its price will rise. This higher price increases producers' profits and provides an incentive for existing firms to expand production and for new firms to enter the industry. Conversely, if an industry is producing a good for which there is no market or a good that people no longer want in the same quantity, the result will be excess supply and the price of that good will fall. This outcome reduces profits or creates losses, providing an incentive for some existing firms to cut back on production and for others to go out of business. In short, an unregulated price mechanism ensures an efficient allocation of resources across industries. Until prices are deregulated, this mechanism cannot function.

Trade barriers must also be removed. Reform-minded countries must be able to import capital, technology, and ideas. In addition, it makes no sense to continue to subsidize industries that cannot be competitive on world markets. If it is cheaper to buy steel from an efficient West German steel mill than to produce it in a subsidized antiquated Russian mill, the Russian mill should be modernized or shut down. Ultimately, as the theory of comparative advantage suggests, liberalized trade will push each country to produce the products it produces best.

Deregulating prices and eliminating subsidies can bring serious political problems. Many products in Russia and the rest of the socialist world were priced below market-clearing levels for equity reasons. Housing, food, and clothing were considered by many to be entitlements. Making them more expensive, at least relative to their prices in previous times, is not likely to be popular. In addition, forcing inefficient firms to operate without subsidies will lead many to go out of business, and jobs will be lost. So while price deregulation and trade liberalization are necessary, they are very difficult politically.

tragedy of commons The idea that collective ownership may not provide the proper private incentives for efficiency because Individuals do not bear the full costs of their own decisions but do enjoy the full benefits.

Privatization

One problem with a system of central ownership is a lack of accountability. Under a system of private ownership, owners reap the rewards of their successes and suffer the consequences of their failures. Private ownership provides a strong incentive for efficient operation, innovation, and hard work that is lacking when ownership is centralized and profits are distributed to the people.

The classic story to illustrate this point is called the **tragedy of commons**. Suppose an agricultural community has 10,000 acres of grazing land. If the land were held in common so that all farmers had unlimited rights to graze their animals, each farmer would have an incentive to overgraze. He or she would reap the full benefits from grazing additional calves while the costs of grazing the calves would be borne collectively. The system provides no incentive to manage the land efficiently. Similarly, if the efficiency and benefits of my hard work and managerial skills accrue to others or to the state, what incentive do I have to work hard or to be efficient?

One solution to the tragedy of commons attempted in eighteenth-century Britain was to divide up the land into private holdings. Today, many economists argue, the solution to the incentive problem encountered in state-owned enterprises is to privatize them and let the owners compete.

In addition to increasing accountability, privatization means creating a climate in which new enterprises can flourish. If there is market demand for a product not currently being produced, individual entrepreneurs should be free to set up a business and make a profit. During the last months of the Soviet Union's existence, private enterprises such as taxi services, car repair services, restaurants, and even hotels began to spring up all over the country.

Like deregulation of prices, privatization is difficult politically. Privatization means many protected enterprises will go out of business because they cannot compete at world prices, resulting in a loss of jobs, at least temporarily.

Market-Supporting Institutions Between 1991 and 1997, U.S. firms raced to Eastern Europe in search of markets and investment opportunities and immediately became aware of a major obstacle. The institutions that make the market function relatively smoothly in the United States do not exist in Eastern Europe. For example, the capital market, which channels private saving into productive capital investment in developed capitalist economies, is made up of hundreds of different institutions. The banking system, venture capital funds, the stock market, the bond market, commodity exchanges, brokerage houses, investment banks, and so forth have all developed in the United States over hundreds of years, and they will not simply be replicated overnight in the formerly Communist world.

Many market-supporting institutions are so basic that Americans take them for granted. The institution of private property, for example, is a set of rights that must be protected by laws that the government must be willing to enforce. Suppose that the French hotel chain Novotel decides to build a new hotel in Moscow. Novotel must first acquire land. Then it will construct a building based on the expectation of renting rooms to customers. These investments are made with the expectation that the owner has a right to use them and a right to the profits that they produce. For such investments to be undertaken, these rights must be guaranteed by a set of property laws. This is equally true for large business firms and for Russian entrepreneurs who want to start their own enterprises.

Similarly, the law must provide for the enforcement of contracts. In the United States, a huge body of law determines what happens to you if you break a formal promise made in good faith. Businesses exist on promises to produce and promises to pay. Without recourse to the law when a contract is breached, contracts will not be entered into, goods will not be manufactured, and services will not be provided.

Another seemingly simple matter that turns out to be quite complex is the establishment of a set of accounting principles. In the United States, the rules of the accounting game are embodied in a set of generally accepted accounting principles (GAAP) that carry the force of law. Companies are required to keep track of their receipts, expenditures, and liabilities so their performance can be observed and evaluated by shareholders, taxing authorities, and others who have an interest in the company. If you have taken a course in accounting, you know how detailed these rules have become. Imagine trying to do business in a country operating under hundreds of different sets of rules. That is what has been happening in Russia.

Another institution is insurance. Whenever a venture undertakes a high-risk activity, it buys insurance to protect itself. Several years ago, Amnesty International (a nonprofit organization that works to protect civil liberties around the world) sponsored a worldwide concert tour with a number of well-known rock bands and performers. The most difficult part of organizing the tour was obtaining insurance for the artists and their equipment when they played in the then-Communist countries of Eastern Europe.

Social Safety Net In a centrally planned socialist economy, the labor market does not function freely. Everyone who wants a job is guaranteed one somewhere. The number of jobs is determined by a central plan to match the number of workers. There is essentially no unemployment. This, it has been argued, is one of the great advantages of a planned system. In addition, a central planning system provides basic housing, food, and clothing at very affordable levels for all. With no unemployment and necessities available at very low prices, there is no need for unemployment insurance, welfare, or other social programs.

Transition to a free labor market and liberalization of prices means that some workers will end up unemployed and everyone will pay higher prices for necessities. Indeed, during the early phases of the transition process, unemployment will be high. Inefficient state-owned enterprises will go out of business; some sectors will contract while others expand. As more and more people experience unemployment, popular support for reform is likely to drop unless some sort of social safety net is erected to ease the transition. This social safety net might include unemployment insurance, aid for the poor, and food and housing assistance. The experiences of the developed world have shown that such programs are expensive.

External Assistance Very few believe the transition to a market system can be achieved without outside support and some outside financing. Knowledge of, and experience with, capitalist institutions that exist in the United States, Western Europe, and Japan are of vital interest to the Eastern European nations. The basic skills of accounting, management, and enterprise development can be taught to Eastern Europe; many say it is in everyone's best interest to do so. Many also argue that the world's biggest nightmare is an economically weak or desperate Russia armed with nuclear weapons, giving up on reform or falling to a dictator.

There is little agreement about the extent of *financial* support that should be given, however. The United States has pushed for a worldwide effort to provide billions of dollars in aid. This aid, many argue, will help Russia stabilize its macroeconomy and buy desperately needed goods from abroad. However, critics in the United States and other potential donor countries say pouring money into Russia now is like pouring it into a black hole—no matter how much we donate, it will have little impact on the ultimate success or failure of the reforms.

Shock Therapy or Gradualism? Although economists generally agree on what the former socialist economies need to do, they debate the sequence and timing of specific reforms.

The popular press describes the debate as one between those who believe in "shock therapy" (sometimes called the Big Bang approach) and those who prefer a more gradual approach. Advocates of **shock therapy** believe that the economies in transition should proceed immediately on all fronts. They should stop printing money, deregulate prices and liberalize trade, privatize, develop market institutions, build a social safety net, and acquire external aid—all as quickly as possible. The pain will be severe, the argument goes, but in the end it will be forgotten as the transition raises living standards. Advocates of a *gradualist* approach believe the best course is to build up market institutions first, gradually decontrol prices, and privatize only the most efficient government enterprises first.

Those who favor moving quickly point to the apparent success of Poland, which moved rapidly through the first phases of reform. Russia's experience during the first years of its transition have demonstrated that, at least in that country, change must be to some extent gradual. In theory, stabilization and price liberalization can be achieved instantaneously. To enjoy the benefits of liberalization, a good deal of privatization must have taken place—and that will take more time. One analyst has said privatization means "selling assets with no value to people with no money." Some estimates suggest half of Russian state-owned enterprises are incapable of making a profit at world prices. Simply cutting them loose would create chaos. In a sense, Russia had no choice but to move slowly.

shock therapy The approach to transition from socialism to market capitalism that advocates rapid deregulation of prices, liberalization of trade, and privatization.

SUMMARY

1. The economic problems facing the developing countries are often quite different from those confronting industrialized nations. The policy options available to governments may also differ. Nonetheless, the tools of economic analysis are as useful in understanding the economies of less developed countries as in understanding the U.S. economy.

LIFE IN THE DEVELOPING NATIONS: POPULATION AND POVERTY

2. The central reality of life in the developing countries is poverty. Although there is considerable diversity across the developing nations, most of the people in most developing countries are extremely poor by U.S. standards.

ECONOMIC DEVELOPMENT: SOURCES AND STRATEGIES

3. Almost all developing nations have a scarcity of physical capital relative to other resources, especially labor. The *vicious-circle-of-poverty hypothesis* says poor countries cannot escape from poverty because they cannot afford to postpone consumption—that is, to save—to make investments. In its crude form, the hypothesis is wrong inasmuch as some prosperous countries were at one time poorer than many developing countries are today. However, it is often difficult to mobilize saving efficiently in many developing nations.

4. Human capital—the stock of education and skills embodied in the workforce—plays a vital role in economic development.

5. Developing countries are often burdened by inadequate *social overhead capital,* ranging from poor public health and sanitation facilities to inadequate roads, telephones, and court systems. Such social overhead capital is often expensive to provide, and many governments are simply not in a position to undertake many useful projects because they are too costly.

6. Because developed economies are characterized by a large share of output and employment in the industrial sector, many developing countries seem to believe that development and industrialization are synonymous. In many cases, developing countries have pursued industry at the expense of agriculture, with mixed results. Recent evidence suggests that some balance between industry and agriculture leads to the best outcome.

7. *Import-substitution* policies, a trade strategy that favors developing local industries that can manufacture goods to replace imports, were once very common in the developing nations. In general, such policies have not succeeded as well as those promoting open, export-oriented economies.

8. The failure of many central planning efforts has brought increasing calls for less government intervention and more market orientation in developing economies.

ISSUES IN ECONOMIC DEVELOPMENT

9. Rapid population growth is characteristic of many developing countries. Large families can be economically rational for parents who need support in their old age, or because children offer an important source of labor. However, having many children does not mean a net benefit to society as a whole. Rapid population growth can put a strain on already overburdened public services such as education and health.

10. Between 1970 and 1984, the debts of the developing countries grew 10-fold. As recession took hold in the advanced countries during the early 1980s, growth in the exports of the debtor countries slowed, and many found they could no longer pay back money they owed. The prospect of loan defaults by developing nations threatened the entire international financial system and transformed the debt crisis into a global problem.

ECONOMIES IN TRANSITION

11. In a *socialist economy* most capital is owned by the government instead of private citizens. In a *capitalist economy* most capital is privately owned. *Communism* is a theoretical economic system in which the people directly control the means of production (capital and land) without the intervention of a government or state.

12. Economies differ in the extent to which decisions are made through central planning instead of a market system. Generally, socialist economies favor central planning over market allocation, and capitalist economies rely to a much greater extent on the market. Nonetheless, there are markets in all societies, and planning takes place in all economies.

THE END OF THE SOVIET UNION

13. The Soviet Union grew rapidly through the mid-1970s. During the late 1950s, the Soviet Union's economy was growing much faster than that of the United States. The key to early Soviet success was rapid planned capital accumulation. In the late 1970s, things began to deteriorate. Dramatic reforms were finally introduced by Mikhail Gorbachev after his rise to power in 1985. Nonetheless, the Soviet economy collapsed in 1991. The Soviet Union was dissolved, and the new president of the Russian Republic, Boris Yeltsin, was left to start the difficult task of transition to a market system.

THE TRANSITION TO A MARKET ECONOMY

14. Economists generally agree on six requirements for a successful transition from socialism to a market-based system: (1) macroeconomic stabilization, (2) deregulation of prices and liberalization of trade, (3) privatization, (4) establishment of market-supporting institutions, (5) a social safety net, and (6) external assistance.

15. Much debate exists about the sequence and timing of specific reforms. The idea of *shock therapy* is to proceed immediately on all six fronts, including rapid deregulation of prices and privatization. The *gradualist* approach is to build up market institutions first, gradually decontrol prices, and privatize only the most efficient government enterprises first.

REVIEW TERMS AND CONCEPTS

brain drain, 766
capital flight, 766
capitalist economy, 776
communism, 776
debt rescheduling, 774
export promotion, 769
fertility rate, 773

import substitution, 768
International Monetary Fund (IMF), 771
market–socialist economy, 777
mortality rate, 773
natural rate of population increase, 773
shock therapy, 782
social overhead capital, 767

socialist economy, 776
stabilization program, 775
structural adjustment, 771
tragedy of commons, 780
vicious-circle-of-poverty hypothesis, 766
World Bank, 771

PROBLEM SET

1. The biggest problem facing developing countries across the globe in 2006 was disease. The HIV/AIDS pandemic had infected more than 40 million worldwide and up to 40 percent of the adult populations of some African countries, such as Botswana. Describe the effects of HIV/AIDS on the economies of these countries. Be sure to discuss the sources of economic growth and the use of scarce resources.

2. For a developing country to grow, it needs capital. The major source of capital in most countries is domestic saving, but the goal of stimulating domestic saving usually is in conflict with government policies aimed at reducing inequality in the distribution of income. Comment on this trade-off between equity and growth. How would you go about resolving the issue if you were the president of a small, poor country?

3. The GDP of any country can be divided into two kinds of goods: capital goods and consumption goods. The proportion of national output devoted to capital goods determines, to some extent, the nation's growth rate.
   a. Explain how capital accumulation leads to economic growth.
   b. Briefly describe how a market economy determines how much investment will be undertaken each period.
   c. "Consumption versus investment is a more painful conflict to resolve for developing countries." Comment on this statement.
   d. If you were the benevolent dictator of a developing country, what plans would you implement to increase per capita GDP?

4. The World Bank and the International Monetary Fund were scheduled to formally cancel the debts of 18 very poor countries in 2006, and the African Development Bank was committed to taking the same action during its 2006 annual meeting. Go online and find out whether these debts were indeed canceled. How much debt was forgiven during that year in each of the countries involved? What are the expected benefits to those countries?

5. "Poor countries are trapped in a vicious circle of poverty. For output to grow, they must accumulate capital. To accumulate capital, they must save (consume less than they produce). Because they are poor, they have little or no extra output available for savings—it must all go to feed and clothe the present generation. Thus they are doomed to stay poor forever." Comment on each step in this argument.

6. "Famines are acts of God, resulting from bad weather or other natural disasters. There is nothing we can do about them except to send food relief after they occur." Explain why this position is inaccurate. Concentrate on agricultural pricing policies and distributional issues.

7. The box on p. 779 describes the Russian economy at the end of 2005. Choose one of the transitional economies of Central Europe (Poland, Hungary, Bulgaria, the Czech Republic, Romania, Ukraine, Russia, and so on). Write a brief paper on how the transition to a market economy was proceeding in 2006. Has the economy (prices, employment, and so on) stabilized? Has there been economic growth? How far has privatization progressed? What problems have been encountered? (A good source of information would be the chronological index to a publication like *The Economist* or the *New York Times*.)

8. "The difference between the United States and the Soviet Union is that the United States has a capitalist economic system and the Soviet Union had a totalitarian government." Explain how this comparison confuses the economic and political aspects of the two societies. What words describe the former economic system of the Soviet Union?

9. You are assigned the task of debating the strength of a socialist economy (regardless of your own viewpoint). Outline the points that you would make in the debate. Be sure to define socialism carefully in your presentation.

10. "The U.S. government should institute a policy of subsidizing those firms that are likely to be successful competitors in the international economic wars. Such an 'industrial policy' should have the authority to override the antitrust laws." Do you agree or disagree? Explain your answer.

11. The distribution of income in a capitalist economy is likely to be more unequal than it is in a socialist economy. Why is this so? Is there a tension between the goal of limiting inequality and the goal of motivating risk-taking and hard work? Explain your answer in detail.

Glossary

ability-to-pay principle A theory of taxation holding that citizens should bear tax burdens in line with their ability to pay taxes.

absolute advantage The advantage in the production of a product enjoyed by one country over another when it uses fewer resources to produce that product than the other country does.

accelerator effect The tendency for investment to increase when aggregate output increases and to decrease when aggregate output decreases, accelerating the growth or decline of output.

actual investment The actual amount of investment that takes place; it includes items such as unplanned changes in inventories.

adjustment costs The costs that a firm incurs when it changes its production level—for example, the administration costs of laying off employees or the training costs of hiring new workers.

adverse selection Can occur when a buyer or seller enters into an exchange with another party who has more information.

aggregate behavior The behavior of all households and firms together.

aggregate demand The total demand for goods and services in an economy.

aggregate demand (*AD*) curve A curve that shows the negative relationship between aggregate output (income) and the price level. Each point on the *AD* curve is a point at which both the goods market and the money market are in equilibrium.

aggregate income The total income received by all factors of production in a given period.

aggregate output The total quantity of goods and services produced in an economy in a given period.

aggregate output (income) (*Y*) A combined term used to remind you of the exact equality between aggregate output and aggregate income.

aggregate production function The mathematical representation of the relationship between inputs and national output, or gross domestic product.

aggregate supply The total supply of all goods and services in an economy.

aggregate supply (*AS*) curve A graph that shows the relationship between the aggregate quantity of output supplied by all firms in an economy and the overall price level.

animal spirits of entrepreneurs A phrase coined by Keynes to describe investors' feelings.

Antitrust Division (of the Department of Justice) One of two federal agencies empowered to act against violators of antitrust laws. It initiates action against those who violate antitrust laws and decides which cases to prosecute and against whom to bring criminal charges.

appreciation of a currency The rise in value of one currency relative to another.

automatic destabilizers Revenue and expenditure items in the federal budget that automatically change with the economy in such a way as to destabilize GDP.

automatic stabilizers Revenue and expenditure items in the federal budget that automatically change with the state of the economy in such a way as to stabilize GDP.

autonomous variable A variable that is assumed not to depend on the state of the economy— that is, it does not change when the economy changes.

average fixed cost (AFC) Total fixed cost divided by the number of units of output; a per-unit measure of fixed costs.

average product The average amount produced by each unit of a variable factor of production.

average propensity to consume (*APC*) The proportion of income households spend on consumption. Determined by dividing consumption (*C*) by income (*Y*).

average tax rate Total amount of tax paid divided by total income.

average total cost (ATC) Total cost divided by the number of units of output.

average variable cost (AVC) Total variable cost divided by the number of units of output.

balance of payments The record of a country's transactions in goods, services, and assets with the rest of the world; also the record of a country's sources (supply) and uses (demand) of foreign exchange.

balance of trade A country's exports of goods and services minus its imports of goods and services.

balance on capital account In the United States, the sum of the following (measured in a given period): the change in private U.S. assets abroad, the change in foreign private assets in the United States, the change in U.S. government assets abroad, and the change in foreign government assets in the United States.

balance on current account Net exports of goods, plus net exports of services, plus net investment income, plus net transfer payments.

balanced-budget multiplier The ratio of change in the equilibrium level of output to a change in government spending where the change in government spending is balanced by a change in taxes so as not to create any deficit. The balanced-budget multiplier is equal to 1: The change in *Y* resulting from the change in *G* and the equal change in *T* is exactly the same size as the initial change in *G* or *T* itself.

barrier to entry Something that prevents new firms from entering and competing in imperfectly competitive industries.

barter The direct exchange of goods and services for other goods and services.

base year The year chosen for the weights in a fixed-weight procedure.

benefits-received principle A theory of fairness holding that taxpayers should contribute to government (in the form of taxes) in proportion to the benefits that they receive from public expenditures.

black market A market in which illegal trading takes place at market-determined prices.

bond A contract between a borrower and a lender, in which the borrower agrees to pay the loan at some time in the future, along with interest payments along the way.

brain drain The tendency for talented people from developing countries to become educated in a developed country and remain there after graduation.

breaking even The situation in which a firm is earning exactly a normal rate of return.

budget constraint The limits imposed on household choices by income, wealth, and product prices.

budget deficit The difference between what a government spends and what it collects in taxes in a given period: $G - T$.

business cycle The cycle of short-term ups and downs in the economy.

capital Those goods produced by the economic system that are used as inputs to produce other goods and services in the future.

capital flight The tendency for both human capital and financial capital to leave developing countries in search of higher rates of return elsewhere.

capital gain An increase in the value of an asset.

capital income Income earned on savings that have been put to use through financial capital markets.

capital-intensive technology A production technique that uses a large amount of capital relative to labor.

capital market The input/factor market in which households supply their savings, for interest or for claims to future profits, to firms that demand funds to buy capital goods.

capital stock For a single firm, the current market value of the firm's plant, equipment, inventories, and intangible assets.

capitalist economy An economy in which most capital is privately owned.

cartel A group of firms that gets together and makes joint price and output decisions to maximize joint profits.

Celler-Kefauver Act (1950) Extended the government's authority to ban vertical and conglomerate mergers.

ceteris paribus, **or all else equal** A device used to analyze the relationship between two variables while the values of other variables are held unchanged.

change in business inventories The amount by which firms' inventories change during a period. Inventories are the goods that firms produce now but intend to sell later.

change in inventory Production minus sales.

choice set or **opportunity set** The set of options that is defined and limited by a budget constraint.

circular flow A diagram showing the income received and payments made by each sector of the economy.

Clayton Act Passed by Congress in 1914 to strengthen the Sherman Act and clarify the rule of reason, the act outlawed specific monopolistic behaviors such as tying contracts, price discrimination, and unlimited mergers.

Coase theorem Under certain conditions, when externalities are present, private parties can arrive at the efficient solution without government involvement.

collusion The act of working with other producers in an effort to limit competition and increase joint profits.

command economy An economy in which a central government either directly or indirectly sets output targets, incomes, and prices.

commodity monies Items used as money that also have intrinsic value in some other use.

communism An economic system in which the people control the means of production (capital and land) directly, without the intervention of a government or state.

comparative advantage A country enjoys a comparative advantage in the production of a good if the production of that good has a lower opportunity cost than it would have if produced in another country.

compensating differentials Differences in wages that result from differences in working conditions. Risky jobs usually pay higher wages; highly desirable jobs usually pay lower wages.

compensation of employees Includes wages, salaries, and various supplements—employer contributions to social insurance and pension funds, for example—paid to households by firms and by the government.

complements, complementary goods Goods that "go together"; a decrease in the price of one results in an increase in demand for the other, and vice versa.

consent decrees Formal agreements on remedies between all the parties to an antitrust case that must be approved by the courts. Consent decrees can be signed before, during, or after a trial.

constant returns to scale An increase in a firm's scale of production has no effect on costs per unit produced.

constrained supply of labor The amount a household actually works in a given period at the current wage rate.

consumer goods Goods produced for present consumption.

consumer price index (CPI) A price index computed each month by the Bureau of Labor Statistics using a bundle that is meant to represent the "market basket" purchased monthly by the typical urban consumer.

consumer sovereignty The idea that consumers ultimately dictate what will be produced (or not produced) by choosing what to purchase (and what not to purchase).

consumer surplus The difference between the maximum amount a person is willing to pay for a good and its current market price.

consumption function The relationship between consumption and income.

contraction, recession, or **slump** The period in the business cycle from a peak down to a trough, during which output and employment fall.

contractionary fiscal policy A decrease in government spending or an increase in net taxes aimed at decreasing aggregate output (income) (Y).

contractionary monetary policy A decrease in the money supply aimed at decreasing aggregate output (income) (Y).

Corn Laws The tariffs, subsidies, and restrictions enacted by the British Parliament in the early nineteenth century to discourage imports and encourage exports of grain.

corporate bonds Promissory notes issued by corporations when they borrow money.

corporate profits The income of corporate businesses.

cost-benefit analysis The formal technique by which the benefits of a public project are weighed against its costs.

cost-of-living adjustments (COLAs) Contract provisions that tie wages to changes in the cost of living. The greater the inflation rate, the more wages are raised.

cost-push, or **supply-side, inflation** Inflation caused by an increase in costs.

cost shock, or **supply shock** A change in costs that shifts the aggregate supply (AS) curve.

Cournot model A model of a two-firm industry (duopoly) in which a series of output-adjustment decisions leads to a final level of output between the output that would prevail if the market were organized competitively and the output that would be set by a monopoly.

cross-price elasticity of demand A measure of the response of the quantity of one good demanded to a change in the price of another good.

crowding-out effect The tendency for increases in government spending to cause reductions in private investment spending.

currency debasement The decrease in the value of money that occurs when its supply is increased rapidly.

current dollars The current prices that one pays for goods and services.

cyclical deficit The deficit that occurs because of a downturn in the business cycle.

cyclical unemployment The increase in unemployment that occurs during recessions and depressions.

deadweight loss The net loss of producer and consumer surplus from underproduction or overproduction.

debt rescheduling An agreement between banks and borrowers through which a new schedule of repayments of the debt is negotiated; often

some of the debt is written off and the repayment period is extended.

decreasing returns to scale, or **diseconomies of scale** An increase in a firm's scale of production leads to higher costs per unit produced.

deficit response index (DRI) The amount by which the deficit changes with a $1 change in GDP.

deflation A decrease in the overall price level.

demand curve A graph illustrating how much of a given product a household would be willing to buy at different prices.

demand determined price The price of a good that is in fixed supply; it is determined exclusively by what firms and households are willing to pay for the good.

demand schedule A table showing how much of a given product a household would be willing to buy at different prices.

demand-pull inflation Inflation that is initiated by an increase in aggregate demand.

depreciation The amount by which an asset's value falls in a given period.

depreciation of a currency The fall in value of one currency relative to another.

depression A prolonged and deep recession. The precise definitions of prolonged and deep are debatable.

derived demand The demand for resources (inputs) that is dependent on the demand for the outputs those resources can be used to produce.

descriptive economics The compilation of data that describe phenomena and facts.

desired, or **optimal, level of inventories** The level of inventory at which the extra cost (in lost sales) from lowering inventories by a small amount is just equal to the extra gain (in interest revenue and decreased storage costs).

desired, or **planned, investment** Those additions to capital stock and inventory that are planned by firms.

diamond/water paradox A paradox stating that (1) the things with the greatest value in use frequently have little or no value in exchange, and (2) the things with the greatest value in exchange frequently have little or no value in use.

discount rate Interest rate that banks pay to the Fed to borrow from it.

discouraged-worker effect The decline in the measured unemployment rate that results when people who want to work but cannot find jobs grow discouraged and stop looking, thus dropping out of the ranks of the unemployed and the labor force.

discretionary fiscal policy Changes in taxes or spending that are the result of deliberate changes in government policy.

disposable personal income or **after-tax income** Personal income minus personal income taxes. The amount that households have to spend or save.

disposable, or **after-tax, income** (Y_d) Total income minus net taxes: $Y - T$.

dividends The portion of a corporation's profits that the firm pays out each period to its shareholders.

dominant strategy In game theory, a strategy that is best no matter what the opposition does.

Dow Jones Industrial Average An index based on the stock prices of 30 actively traded large companies. The oldest and most widely followed index of stock market performance.

drop-in-the-bucket problem A problem intrinsic to public goods: The good or service is usually so costly that its provision generally does not depend on whether or not any single person pays.

dumping A firm or industry's sale of products on the world market at prices below the cost of production.

durable goods Goods that last a relatively long time, such as cars and household appliances.

easy monetary policy Fed policies that expand the money supply in an effort to stimulate the economy.

economic globalization The process of increasing economic interdependence among countries and their citizens.

economic growth An increase in the total output of an economy. It occurs when a society acquires new resources or when it learns to produce more using existing resources.

economic income The amount of money a household can spend during a given period without increasing or decreasing its net assets. Wages, salaries, dividends, interest income, transfer payments, rents, and so forth are sources of economic income.

economic integration Occurs when two or more nations join to form a free-trade zone.

economics The study of how individuals and societies choose to use the scarce resources that nature and previous generations have provided.

economic theory A statement or set of related statements about cause and effect, action and reaction.

efficiency In economics, allocative efficiency. An efficient economy is one that produces what people want at the least possible cost.

efficiency wage theory An explanation for unemployment that holds that the productivity of workers increases with the wage rate. If this is so, firms may have an incentive to pay wages above the market-clearing rate.

efficient market A market in which profit opportunities are eliminated almost instantaneously.

elastic demand A demand relationship in which the percentage change in quantity demanded is larger in absolute value than the percentage change in price (a demand elasticity with an absolute value greater than 1).

elasticity A general concept used to quantify the response in one variable when another variable changes.

elasticity of labor supply A measure of the response of labor supplied to a change in the price of labor.

elasticity of supply A measure of the response of quantity of a good supplied to a change in price of that good. Likely to be positive in output markets.

empirical economics The collection and use of data to test economic theories.

employed Any person 16 years old or older (1) who works for pay, either for someone else or in his or her own business for 1 or more hours per week, (2) who works without pay for 15 or more hours per week in a family enterprise, or (3) who has a job but has been temporarily absent, with or without pay.

entrepreneur A person who organizes, manages, and assumes the risks of a firm, taking a new idea or a new product and turning it into a successful business.

equilibrium Occurs when there is no tendency for change. In the macroeconomic goods market, equilibrium occurs when planned aggregate expenditure is equal to aggregate output.

equilibrium price level The price level at which the aggregate demand and aggregate supply curves intersect.

equity Fairness.

estate The property that a person owns at the time of his or her death.

estate tax A tax on the total value of a person's estate.

European Union (EU) The European trading bloc composed of Austria, Belgium, Denmark, Finland, France, Germany, Greece, Ireland, Italy, Luxembourg, the Netherlands, Portugal, Spain, Sweden, and the United Kingdom.

excess burden The amount by which the burden of a tax exceeds the total revenue collected. Also called deadweight loss.

excess demand or shortage The condition that exists when quantity demanded exceeds quantity supplied at the current price.

excess labor, excess capital Labor and capital that are not needed to produce the firm's current level of output.

excess reserves The difference between a bank's actual reserves and its required reserves.

excess supply or **surplus** The condition that exists when quantity supplied exceeds quantity demanded at the current price.

exchange rate The price of one country's currency in terms of another country's currency; the ratio at which two currencies are traded for each other.

expansion or **boom** The period in the business cycle from a trough up to a peak, during which output and employment rise.

expansionary fiscal policy An increase in government spending or a reduction in net taxes aimed at increasing aggregate output (income) (Y).

expansionary monetary policy An increase in the money supply aimed at increasing aggregate output (income) (Y).

expected rate of return The annual rate of return that a firm expects to obtain through a capital investment.

expenditure approach A method of computing GDP that measures the amount spent on all final goods during a given period.

explicit contracts Employment contracts that stipulate workers' wages, usually for a period of 1 to 3 years.

export promotion A trade policy designed to encourage exports.

export subsidies Government payments made to domestic firms to encourage exports.

externality A cost or a benefit resulting from some activity or transaction that is imposed or bestowed on some party outside the activity or transaction.

factor endowments The quantity and quality of labor, land, and natural resources of a country.

factors of production The inputs into the production process. Land, labor, and capital are the three key factors of production.

factor substitution effect The tendency of firms to substitute away from a factor whose price has risen and toward a factor whose price has fallen.

fallacy of composition The erroneous belief that what is true for a part is necessarily true for the whole.

favored customers Those who receive special treatment from dealers during situations of excess demand.

federal budget The budget of the federal government.

federal debt The total amount owed by the federal government.

Federal Open Market Committee (FOMC) A group composed of the seven members of the Fed's Board of Governors, the president of the New York Federal Reserve Bank, and 4 of the other 11 district bank presidents on a rotating basis; it sets goals concerning the money supply and interest rates and directs the operation of the Open Market Desk in New York.

Federal Reserve Bank (the Fed) The central bank of the United States.

federal surplus (+) or **deficit** (−) Federal government receipts minus expenditures.

Federal Trade Commission (FTC) A federal regulatory group created by Congress in 1914 to investigate the structure and behavior of firms engaging in interstate commerce, to determine what constitutes unlawful "unfair" behavior, and to issue cease-and-desist orders to those found in violation of antitrust law.

fertility rate The birth rate. Equal to (the number of births per year divided by the population) × 100.

fiat, or **token, money** Items designated as money that are intrinsically worthless.

final goods and services Goods and services produced for final use.

financial capital market The complex set of institutions in which suppliers of capital (households that save) and the demand for capital (business firms wanting to invest) interact.

financial intermediaries Banks and other institutions that act as a link between those who have money to lend and those who want to borrow money.

fine-tuning The phrase used by Walter Heller to refer to the government's role in regulating inflation and unemployment.

firm An organization that transforms resources (inputs) into products (outputs). Firms are the primary producing units in a market economy.

fiscal drag The negative effect on the economy that occurs when average tax rates increase because taxpayers have moved into higher income brackets during an expansion.

fiscal policy Government policies concerning taxes and expenditures (spending).

fixed cost Any cost that does not depend on the firm's level of output. These costs are incurred even if the firm is producing nothing. There are no fixed costs in the long run.

fixed-weight procedure A procedure that uses weights from a given base year.

floating, or market-determined, exchange rates Exchange rates that are determined by the unregulated forces of supply and demand.

food stamps Vouchers that have a face value greater than their cost and that can be used to purchase food at grocery stores.

foreign exchange All currencies other than the domestic currency of a given country.

free enterprise The freedom of individuals to start and operate private businesses in search of profits.

free-rider problem A problem intrinsic to public goods: Because people can enjoy the benefits of public goods whether they pay for them or not, they are usually unwilling to pay for them.

frictional unemployment The portion of unemployment that is due to the normal working of the labor market; used to denote short-run job/skill matching problems.

full-employment budget What the federal budget would be if the economy were producing at a full-employment level of output.

game theory Analyzes oligopolistic behavior as a complex series of strategic moves and reactive countermoves among rival firms. In game theory, firms are assumed to anticipate rival reactions.

General Agreement on Tariffs and Trade (GATT) An international agreement signed by the United States and 22 other countries in 1947 to promote the liberalization of foreign trade.

genetically modified (GM) foods Strains of food that have been genetically modified. Examples include insect- and herbicide-resistant soybeans, corn, and cotton and rice with increased iron and vitamins.

Gini coefficient A commonly used measure of inequality of income derived from a Lorenz curve. It can range from 0 to a maximum of 1.

globalization The process of increasing interdependence among countries and their citizens.

goods market The market in which goods and services are exchanged and in which the equilibrium level of aggregate output is determined.

government consumption and gross investment (G) Expenditures by federal, state, and local governments for final goods and services.

government failure Occurs when the government becomes the tool of the rent seeker and the allocation of resources is made even less efficient by the intervention of government.

government franchise A monopoly by virtue of government directive.

government spending multiplier The ratio of the change in the equilibrium level of output to a change in government spending.

Gramm-Rudman-Hollings Act Passed by the U.S. Congress and signed by President Reagan in 1986, this law set out to reduce the federal deficit by $36 billion per year, with a deficit of zero slated for 1991.

Great Depression The period of severe economic contraction and high unemployment that began in 1929 and continued throughout the 1930s.

gross domestic product (GDP) The total market value of all final goods and services produced within a given period by factors of production located within a country.

gross investment The total value of all newly produced capital goods (plant, equipment, housing, and inventory) produced in a given period.

gross national income (GNI) GNP converted into dollars using an average of currency exchange rates over several years adjusted for rates of inflation.

gross national product (GNP) The total market value of all final goods and services produced within a given period by factors of production owned by a country's citizens, regardless of where the output is produced.

gross private domestic investment (I) Total investment in capital—that is, the purchase of new housing, plants, equipment, and inventory by the private (or nongovernment) sector.

Heckscher-Ohlin theorem A theory that explains the existence of a country's comparative advantage by its factor endowments: A country has a comparative advantage in the production of a product if that country is relatively well endowed with inputs used intensively in the production of that product.

Herfindahl-Hirschman Index (HHI) A mathematical calculation that uses market share figures to determine whether or not a proposed merger will be challenged by the government.

homogeneous products Undifferentiated outputs; products that are identical to, or indistinguishable from one another.

households The consuming units in an economy.

human capital A form of intangible capital that includes the skills and other knowledge that workers have or acquire through education and training and that yields valuable services to a firm over time.

hyperinflation A period of very rapid increases in the overall price level.

identity Something that is always true.

Immigration Act of 1990 Increased the number of legal immigrants allowed into the United States each year by 150,000.

Immigration Reform and Control Act (1986) Granted amnesty to about 3 million illegal aliens and imposed a strong set of employer sanctions designed to slow the flow of immigrants into the United States.

imperfect competition An industry in which single firms have some control over price and competition. Imperfectly competitive industries give rise to an inefficient allocation of resources.

imperfect information The absence of full knowledge concerning product characteristics, available prices, and so forth.

imperfectly competitive industry An industry in which single firms have some control over the price of their output.

implementation lag The time it takes to put the desired policy into effect once economists and policy makers recognize that the economy is in a boom or a slump.

import substitution An industrial trade strategy that favors developing local industries that can manufacture goods to replace imports.

impossibility theorem A proposition demonstrated by Kenneth Arrow showing that no system of aggregating individual preferences into social decisions will always yield consistent, nonarbitrary results.

income The sum of all a household's wages, salaries, profits, interest payments, rents, and other forms of earnings in a given period of time. It is a flow measure.

income approach A method of computing GDP that measures the income—wages, rents, interest, and profits—received by all factors of production in producing final goods.

income elasticity of demand Measures the responsiveness of demand to changes in income.

increasing returns to scale, or economies of scale An increase in a firm's scale of production leads to lower costs per unit produced.

indirect taxes minus subsidies Taxes such as sales taxes, customs duties, and license fees, less subsidies that the government pays for which it receives no goods or services in return.

industrial policy Government involvement in the allocation of capital across manufacturing sectors.

Industrial Revolution The period in England during the late eighteenth and early nineteenth centuries in which new manufacturing technologies and improved transportation gave rise to the modern factory system and a massive movement of the population from the countryside to the cities.

inelastic demand Demand that responds somewhat, but not a great deal, to changes in price. Inelastic demand always has a numerical value between zero and 21.

infant industry A young industry that may need temporary protection from competition from the established industries of other countries to develop an acquired comparative advantage.

inferior goods Goods for which demand tends to fall when income rises.

inflation An increase in the overall price level.

inflation rate The percentage change in the price level.

inflation targeting When a monetary authority chooses its interest rate values with the aim of keeping the inflation rate within some specified band over some specified horizon.

injunction A court order forbidding the continuation of behavior that leads to damages.

innovation The use of new knowledge to produce a new product or to produce an existing product more efficiently.

input or factor markets The markets in which the resources used to produce products are exchanged.

inputs The goods and services that firms purchase and turn into output.

inputs or **resources** Anything provided by nature or previous generations that can be used directly or indirectly to satisfy human wants.

intangible capital Nonmaterial things that contribute to the output of future goods and services.

interest The fee that borrowers pay to lenders for the use of their funds.

interest rate The annual interest payment on a loan expressed as a percentage of the loan. Equal to the amount of interest received per year divided by the amount of the loan.

interest sensitivity or **insensitivity of planned investment** The responsiveness of planned investment spending to changes in the interest rate. *Interest sensitivity* means that planned investment spending changes a great deal in response to changes in the interest rate; *interest insensitivity* means little or no change in planned investment as a result of changes in the interest rate.

intermediate goods Goods that are produced by one firm for use in further processing by another firm.

International Monetary Fund (IMF) An international agency whose primary goals are to stabilize international exchange rates and to lend money to countries that have problems financing their international transactions.

Interstate Commerce Commission (ICC) A federal regulatory group created by Congress in 1887 to oversee and correct abuses in the railroad industry.

invention An advance in knowledge.

inventory investment Occurs when a firm produces more output than it sells within a given period.

investment New capital additions to a firm's capital stock. Although capital is measured at a given point in time (a stock), investment is measured over a period of time (a flow). The flow of investment increases the capital stock.

J-curve effect Following a currency depreciation, a country's balance of trade may get worse before it gets better. The graph showing this effect is shaped like the letter *J*, hence the name J-curve effect.

kinked demand curve model A model of oligopoly in which the demand curve facing each individual firm has a "kink" in it. The kink results from the assumption that competitor firms will follow if a single firm cuts price but will not follow if a single firm raises price.

labor demand curve A graph that illustrates the amount of labor that firms want to employ at each given wage rate.

labor force participation rate The ratio of the labor force to the total population 16 years old or older.

labor force The number of people employed plus the number of unemployed.

labor market The input/factor market in which households supply work for wages to firms that demand labor.

labor productivity Output per worker hour; the amount of output produced by an average worker in 1 hour.

labor supply curve A diagram that shows the quantity of labor supplied at different wage rates. Its shape depends on how households react to changes in the wage rate.

labor theory of value Stated most simply, the theory that the value of a commodity depends only on the amount of labor required to produce it.

labor-intensive technology A production technique that uses a large amount of labor relative to capital.

laissez-faire economy Literally from the French: "allow [them] to do." An economy in which individual people and firms pursue their own self-interests without any central direction or regulation.

land market The input/factor market in which households supply land or other real property in exchange for rent.

law of demand The negative relationship between price and quantity demanded: As price rises, quantity demanded decreases. As price falls, quantity demanded increases.

law of diminishing marginal utility The more of any one good consumed in a given period, the less satisfaction (utility) generated by consuming each additional (marginal) unit of the same good.

law of diminishing returns When additional units of a variable input are added to fixed inputs after a certain point, the marginal product of the variable input declines.

law of one price If the costs of transportation are small, the price of the same good in different countries should be roughly the same.

law of supply The positive relationship between price and quantity of a good supplied: An increase in market price will lead to an increase in quantity supplied, and a decrease in market price will lead to a decrease in quantity supplied.

legal tender Money that a government has required to be accepted in settlement of debts.

lender of last resort One of the functions of the Fed: It provides funds to troubled banks that cannot find any other sources of funds.

liability rules Laws that require A to compensate B for damages imposed.

life-cycle theory of consumption A theory of household consumption: Households make lifetime consumption decisions based on their expectations of lifetime income.

liquidity property of money The property of money that makes it a good medium of exchange as well as a store of value: It is portable and readily accepted and thus easily exchanged for goods.

logrolling Occurs when congressional representatives trade votes, agreeing to help each other get certain pieces of legislation passed.

long run That period of time for which there are no fixed factors of production: Firms can increase or decrease the scale of operation, and new firms can enter and existing firms can exit the industry.

long-run average cost curve (LRAC) A graph that shows the different scales on which a firm can choose to operate in the long run.

long-run competitive equilibrium When P = SRMC = SRAC = LRAC and profits are zero.

Lorenz curve A widely used graph of the distribution of income, with cumulative percentage of families plotted along the horizontal axis and cumulative percentage of income plotted along the vertical axis.

M1, or **transactions money** Money that can be directly used for transactions.

M2, or **broad money** M1 plus savings accounts, money market accounts, and other near monies.

macroeconomics The branch of economics that examines the economic behavior of aggregates—income, employment, output, and so on—on a national scale.

marginal cost (MC) The increase in total cost that results from producing one more unit of output. Marginal costs reflect changes in variable costs.

marginal damage cost (MDC) The additional harm done by increasing the level of an externality-producing activity by one unit. If producing product × pollutes the water in a river, MDC is the additional cost imposed by the added pollution that results from increasing output by one unit of × per period.

marginal private cost (MPC) The amount that a consumer pays to consume an additional unit of a particular good.

marginal product The additional output that can be produced by adding one more unit of a specific input, ceteris paribus.

marginal product of labor (MPL) The additional output produced by one additional unit of labor.

marginal productivity theory of income distribution At equilibrium, all factors of production end up receiving rewards determined by their productivity as measured by marginal revenue product.

marginal propensity to consume (MPC) That fraction of a change in income that is consumed, or spent.

marginal propensity to import (MPM) The change in imports caused by a $1 change in income.

marginal propensity to save (MPS) That fraction of a change in income that is saved.

marginal rate of transformation (MRT) The slope of the production possibility frontier (ppf).

marginal revenue (MR) The additional revenue that a firm takes in when it increases output by one additional unit. In perfect competition, P = MR.

marginal revenue product (MRP) The additional revenue a firm earns by employing one additional unit of input, ceteris paribus.

marginal social cost (MSC) The total cost to society of producing an additional unit of a good or service. MSC is equal to the sum of the marginal costs of producing the product and the correctly measured damage costs involved in the process of production.

marginal tax rate The tax rate paid on any additional income earned.

marginal utility (MU) The additional satisfaction gained by the consumption or use of one more unit of something.

marginalism The process of analyzing the additional or incremental costs or benefits arising from a choice or decision.

market The institution through which buyers and sellers interact and engage in exchange.

market demand The sum of all the quantities of a good or service demanded per period by all the households buying in the market for that good or service.

market failure Occurs when resources are misallocated, or allocated inefficiently. The result is waste or lost value.

market power An imperfectly competitive firm's ability to raise price without losing all of the quantity demanded for its product.

market supply The sum of all that is supplied each period by all producers of a single product.

market–socialist economy An economy that combines government ownership with market allocation.

maximin strategy In game theory, a strategy chosen to maximize the minimum gain that can be earned.

Medicaid and Medicare In-kind government transfer programs that provide health and hospitalization benefits: Medicare to the aged and their survivors and to certain of the disabled, regardless of income, and Medicaid to people with low incomes.

medium of exchange, or **means of payment** What sellers generally accept and buyers generally use to pay for goods and services.

microeconomic foundations of macroeconomics The microeconomic principles underlying macroeconomic analysis.

microeconomics The branch of economics that examines the functioning of individual industries and the behavior of individual decision-making units—that is, business firms and households.

midpoint formula A more precise way of calculating percentages using the value halfway between P1 and P2 for the base in calculating the percentage change in price, and the value halfway between Q1 and Q2 as the base for calculating the percentage change in quantity demanded.

minimum wage A price floor set under the price of labor.

minimum wage laws Laws that set a floor for wage rates—that is, a minimum hourly rate for any kind of labor.

model A formal statement of a theory, usually a mathematical statement of a presumed relationship between two or more variables.

modern economic growth The period of rapid and sustained increase in real output per capita that began in the Western World with the Industrial Revolution.

monetary policy The behavior of the Federal Reserve concerning the nation's money supply.

money income The measure of income used by the Census Bureau. Because it excludes noncash transfer payments and capital gains income, it is less inclusive than "economic income."

money market The market in which financial instruments are exchanged and in which the equilibrium level of the interest rate is determined.

money multiplier The multiple by which deposits can increase for every dollar increase in reserves; equal to 1 divided by the required reserve ratio.

monopolistic competition A common form of industry (market) structure in the United States, characterized by a large number of firms, none of which can influence market price by virtue of size alone. Some degree of market power is achieved by firms producing differentiated products. New firms can enter and established firms can exit such an industry with ease.

monopoly An industry composed of only one firm that produces a product for which there are no close substitutes and in which significant barriers exist to prevent new firms from entering the industry.

moral hazard Arises when one party to a contract passes the cost of its behavior on to the other party to the contract.

moral suasion The pressure that in the past the Fed exerted on member banks to discourage them from borrowing heavily from the Fed.

mortality rate The death rate. Equal to (the number of deaths per year divided by the population) × 100.

movement along a demand curve The change in quantity demanded brought about by a change in price.

movement along a supply curve The change in quantity supplied brought about by a change in price.

multiplier The ratio of the change in the equilibrium level of output to a change in some autonomous variable.

NAIRU The nonaccelerating inflation rate of unemployment.

NASDAQ Composite An index based on the stock prices of over 5,000 companies traded on the NASDAQ Stock Market. The NASDAQ market takes its name from the National Association of Securities Dealers Automated Quotation System.

Nash equilibrium In game theory, the result of all players' playing their best strategy given what their competitors are doing.

national income The total income earned by the factors of production owned by a country's citizens.

national income and product accounts Data collected and published by the government describing the various components of national income and output in the economy.

natural monopoly An industry that realizes such large economies of scale in producing its product that single-firm production of that good or service is most efficient.

natural rate of population increase The difference between the birth rate and the death rate. It does not take migration into account.

natural rate of unemployment The unemployment that occurs as a normal part of the functioning of the economy. Sometimes taken as the sum of frictional unemployment and structural unemployment.

near monies Close substitutes for transactions money, such as savings accounts and money market accounts.

negative demand shock Something that causes a negative shift in consumption or investment schedules or that leads to a decrease in U.S. exports.

net business transfer payments Net transfer payments by businesses to others.

net exports ($EX - IM$) The difference between exports (sales to foreigners of U.S.-produced goods and services) and imports (U.S. purchases of goods and services from abroad). The figure can be positive or negative.

net exports of goods and services ($EX - IM$) The difference between a country's total exports and total imports.

net interest The interest paid by business.

net investment Gross investment minus depreciation.

net national product (NNP) Gross national product minus depreciation; a nation's total product minus what is required to maintain the value of its capital stock.

net taxes (T) Taxes paid by firms and households to the government minus transfer payments made to households by the government.

nominal GDP Gross domestic product measured in current dollars.

nominal wage rate The wage rate in current dollars.

nondurable goods Goods that are used up fairly quickly, such as food and clothing.

nonexcludable A characteristic of most public goods: Once a good is produced, no one can be excluded from enjoying its benefits.

nonlabor or **nonwage, income** Any income received from sources other than working—inheritances, interest, dividends, transfer payments, and so on.

nonresidential investment Expenditures by firms for machines, tools, plants, and so on.

nonrival in consumption A characteristic of public goods: One person's enjoyment of the benefits of a public good does not interfere with another's consumption of it.

nonsynchronization of income and spending The mismatch between the timing of money inflow to the household and the timing of money outflow for household expenses.

normal goods Goods for which demand goes up when income is higher and for which demand goes down when income is lower.

normal rate of return A rate of return on capital that is just sufficient to keep owners and investors satisfied. For relatively risk-free firms, it should be nearly the same as the interest rate on risk-free government bonds.

normative economics An approach to economics that analyzes outcomes of economic behavior, evaluates them as good or bad, and may prescribe courses of action. Also called *policy economics*.

North American Free Trade Agreement (NAFTA) An agreement signed by the United States, Mexico, and Canada in which the three countries agreed to establish all North America as a free-trade zone.

not in the labor force A person who is not looking for work, because he or she either does not want a job or has given up looking.

Ockham's razor The principle that irrelevant detail should be cut away.

Okun's Law The theory, put forth by Arthur Okun, that the unemployment rate decreases about 1 percentage point for every 3 percent increase in real GDP. Later research and data have shown that the relationship between output and unemployment is not as stable as Okun's "Law" predicts.

oligopoly A form of industry (market) structure characterized by a few dominant firms. Products may be homogenous or differentiated. The behavior of any one firm in an oligopoly depends to a great extent on the behavior of others.

Open Market Desk The office in the New York Federal Reserve Bank from which government securities are bought and sold by the Fed.

open market operations The purchase and sale by the Fed of government securities in the open market; a tool used to expand or contract the amount of reserves in the system and thus the money supply.

operating profit (or **loss**) or **net operating revenue** Total revenue minus total variable cost (TR − TVC).

opportunity cost The best alternative that we forgo, or give up, when we make a choice or a decision.

optimal level of provision for public goods The level at which resources are drawn from the production of other goods and services only to the extent that people want the public good and are willing to pay for it. At this level, society's willingness to pay per unit is equal to the marginal cost of producing the good.

optimal method of production The production method that minimizes cost.

optimal scale of plant The scale of plant that minimizes average cost.

output effect of a factor price increase (decrease) When a firm decreases (increases) its output in response to a factor price increase (decrease), this decreases (increases) its demand for all factors.

output growth The growth rate of the output of the entire economy.

outputs Usable products.

Pareto efficiency or **Pareto optimality** A condition in which no change is possible that will make some members of society better off without making some other members of society worse off.

partial equilibrium analysis The process of examining the equilibrium conditions efficiency. The condition in which the economy is producing what people want at least possible cost.

patent A barrier to entry that grants exclusive use of the patented product or process to the inventor.

per se rule A rule enunciated by the courts declaring a particular action or outcome to be a per se (intrinsic) violation of antitrust law, whether the result is reasonable or not.

per-capita output growth The growth rate of output per person in the economy.

perfect competition An industry structure in which there are many firms, each small relative to the industry and producing virtually identical products, and in which no firm is large enough to have any control over prices.

perfect knowledge The assumption that households possess a knowledge of the qualities and prices of everything available in the market and that firms have all available information concerning wage rates, capital costs, and output prices.

perfectly contestable market A market in which entry and exit are costless.

perfectly inelastic demand Demand in which quantity demanded does not respond at all to a change in price.

perfect price discrimination Occurs when a firm charges the maximum amount that buyers are willing to pay for each unit.

perfect substitutes Identical products.

permanent income The average level of one's expected future income stream.

personal consumption expenditures (*C*) A major component of GDP: expenditures by consumers on goods and services.

personal income The total income of households before paying personal income taxes.

personal saving The amount of disposable income that is left after total personal spending in a given period.

personal saving rate The percentage of disposable personal income that is saved. If the personal saving rate is low, households are spending a large amount relative to their incomes; if it is high, households are spending cautiously.

Phillips Curve A graph showing the relationship between the inflation rate and the unemployment rate.

physical, or **tangible, capital** Material things used as inputs in the production of future goods and services. The major categories of physical capital are nonresidential structures, durable equipment, residential structures, and inventories.

planned aggregate expenditure (*AE*) The total amount the economy plans to spend in a given period. Equal to consumption plus planned investment: $AE = C + I$.

plant-and-equipment investment Purchases by firms of additional machines, factories, or buildings within a given period.

policy mix The combination of monetary and fiscal policies in use at a given time.

positive economics An approach to economics that seeks to understand behavior and the operation of systems without making judgments. It describes what exists and how it works.

post hoc, ergo propter hoc Literally, "after this (in time), therefore because of this." A common error made in thinking about causation: If Event A happens before Event B, it is not necessarily true that A caused B.

potential output, or **potential GDP** The level of aggregate output that can be sustained in the long run without inflation.

poverty line The officially established income level that distinguishes the poor from the nonpoor. It is set at three times the cost of the Department of Agriculture's minimum food budget.

price ceiling A maximum price that sellers may charge for a good, usually set by government.

price discrimination Charging different prices to different buyers.

price elasticity of demand The ratio of the percentage of change in quantity demanded to the percentage of change in price; measures the responsiveness of demand to changes in price.

price feedback effect The process by which a domestic price increase in one country can "feed back" on itself through export and import prices. An increase in the price level in one country can drive up prices in other countries. This in turn further increases the price level in the first country.

price floor A minimum price below which exchange is not permitted.

price leadership A form of oligopoly in which one dominant firm sets prices and all the smaller firms in the industry follow its pricing policy.

price rationing The process by which the market system allocates goods and services to consumers when quantity demanded exceeds quantity supplied.

principle of neutrality All else equal, taxes that are neutral with respect to economic decisions (that is, taxes that do not distort economic decisions) are generally preferable to taxes that distort economic decisions. Taxes that are not neutral impose excess burdens.

principle of second best The fact that a tax distorts an economic decision does not always imply that such a tax imposes an excess burden. If there are previously existing distortions, such a tax may actually improve efficiency.

prisoners' dilemma A game in which the players are prevented from cooperating and in which each has a dominant strategy that leaves them both worse off than if they could cooperate.

private goods Products produced by firms for sale to individual households.

privately held federal debt The privately held (non-government-owned) debt of the U.S. government.

producer price indexes (PPIs) Measures of prices that producers receive for products at all stages in the production process.

producer surplus The difference between the current market price and the full cost of production for the firm.

product differentiation A strategy that firms use to achieve market power. Accomplished by producing products that have distinct positive identities in consumers' minds.

product or **output markets** The markets in which goods and services are exchanged.

production The process that transforms scarce resources into useful goods and services.

production function or **total product function** A numerical or mathematical expression of a relationship between inputs and outputs. It shows units of total product as a function of units of inputs.

production possibility frontier (ppf) A graph that shows all the combinations of goods and services that can be produced if all of society's resources are used efficiently.

production technology The quantitative relationship between inputs and outputs.

productivity growth The growth rate of output per worker.

productivity of an input The amount of output produced per unit of that input.

productivity, or labor productivity Output per worker hour; the amount of output produced by an average worker in 1 hour.

profit The difference between revenues and costs.

progressive tax A tax whose burden, expressed as a percentage of income, increases as income increases.

property income Income from the ownership of real property and financial holdings. It takes the form of profits, interest, dividends, and rents.

proportional tax A tax whose burden is the same proportion of income for all households.

proprietors' income The income of unincorporated businesses.

protection The practice of shielding a sector of the economy from foreign competition.

public assistance, or welfare Government transfer programs that provide cash benefits to (1) families with dependent children whose incomes and assets fall below a very low level and (2) the very poor regardless of whether or not they have children.

public choice theory An economic theory that the public officials who set economic policies and regulate the players act in their own self-interest, just as firms do.

public goods, or social goods Goods or services that bestow collective benefits on members of society. Generally, no one can be excluded from enjoying their benefits. The classic example is national defense.

purchasing-power-parity theory A theory of international exchange holding that exchange rates are set so that the price of similar goods in different countries is the same.

pure monopoly An industry with a single firm that produces a product for which there are no close substitutes and in which significant barriers to entry prevent other firms from entering the industry to compete for profits.

pure rent The return to any factor of production that is in fixed supply.

quantity demanded The amount (number of units) of a product that a household would buy in a given period if it could buy all it wanted at the current market price.

quantity supplied The amount of a particular product that a firm would be willing and able to offer for sale at a particular price during a given time period.

queuing Waiting in line as a means of distributing goods and services: a nonprice rationing mechanism.

quota A limit on the quantity of imports.

ration coupons Tickets or coupons that entitle individuals to purchase a certain amount of a given product per month.

Rawlsian justice A theory of distributional justice that concludes that the social contract emerging from the "original position" would call for an income distribution that would maximize the well-being of the worst-off member of society.

real income Set of opportunities to purchase real goods and services available to a household as determined by prices and money income.

real interest rate The difference between the interest rate on a loan and the inflation rate.

real wage rate The amount that the nominal wage rate can buy in terms of goods and services.

real wealth, or real balance, effect The change in consumption brought about by a change in real wealth that results from a change in the price level.

realized capital gain The gain that occurs when the owner of an asset actually sells it for more than he or she paid for it.

recession Roughly, a period in which real GDP declines for at least two consecutive quarters. Marked by falling output and rising unemployment.

recognition lag The time it takes for policy makers to recognize the existence of a boom or a slump.

regressive tax A tax whose burden, expressed as a percentage of income, falls as income increases.

relative-wage explanation of unemployment An explanation for sticky wages (and therefore unemployment): If workers are concerned about their wages relative to other workers in other firms and industries, they may be unwilling to accept a wage cut unless they know that all other workers are receiving similar cuts.

rental income The income received by property owners in the form of rent.

rent-seeking behavior Actions taken by households or firms to preserve positive profits.

required reserve ratio The percentage of its total deposits that a bank must keep as reserves at the Federal Reserve.

reserves The deposits that a bank has at the Federal Reserve bank plus its cash on hand.

residential investment Expenditures by households and firms on new houses and apartment buildings.

response lag The time that it takes for the economy to adjust to the new conditions after a new policy is implemented; the lag that occurs because of the operation of the economy itself.

rule of reason The criterion introduced by the Supreme Court in 1911 to determine whether a particular action was illegal ("unreasonable") or legal ("reasonable") within the terms of the Sherman Act.

run on a bank Occurs when many of those who have claims on a bank (deposits) present them at the same time.

saving (S) The part of its income that a household does not consume in a given period. Distinguished from *savings*, which is the current stock of accumulated saving.

scarce Limited.

services The things we buy that do not involve the production of physical things, such as legal and medical services and education.

shares of stock Financial instruments that give to the holder a share in the firm's ownership and therefore the right to share in the firm's profits.

Sherman Act Passed by Congress in 1890, the act declared every contract or conspiracy to restrain trade among states or nations illegal and declared any attempt at monopoly, successful or not, a misdemeanor. Interpretation of which specific behaviors were legal fell to the courts.

shift of a demand curve The change that takes place in a demand curve corresponding to a new relationship between quantity demanded of a good and price of that good. The shift is brought about by a change in the original conditions.

shift of a supply curve The change that takes place in a supply curve corresponding to a new relationship between quantity supplied of a good and the price of that good. The shift is brought about by a change in the original conditions.

shock therapy The approach to transition from socialism to market capitalism that advocates rapid deregulation of prices, liberalization of trade, and privatization.

short run The period of time for which two conditions hold: The firm is operating under a fixed scale (fixed factor) of production, and firms can neither enter nor exit an industry.

short-run industry supply curve The sum of the marginal cost curves (above AVC) of all the firms in an industry.

shut-down point The lowest point on the average variable cost curve. When price falls below the minimum point on AVC, total revenue is insufficient to cover variable costs and the firm will shut down and bear losses equal to fixed costs.

Smoot-Hawley tariff The U.S. tariff law of the 1930s, which set the highest tariffs in U.S. history (60 percent). It set off an international trade war and caused the decline in trade that is often considered a cause of the worldwide depression of the 1930s.

social capital, or infrastructure Capital that provides services to the public. Most social capital takes the form of public works (roads and bridges) and public services (police and fire protection).

social choice The problem of deciding what society wants. The process of adding up individual preferences to make a choice for society as a whole.

social overhead capital Basic infrastructure projects such as roads, power generation, and irrigation systems.

Social Security system The federal system of social insurance programs. It includes three separate programs that are financed through separate trust funds: the Old Age and Survivors Insurance (OASI) program, the Disability Insurance (DI) program, and the Health Insurance (HI, or Medicare) program.

social, or implicit, contracts Unspoken agreements between workers and firms that firms will not cut wages.

socialist economy An economy in which most capital is owned by the government instead of private citizens. Also called *social ownership*.

sources side/uses side The impact of a tax may be felt on one or the other or on both sides of the income equation. A tax may cause net income to fall (damage on the sources side), or it may cause prices of goods and services to rise so that income buys less (damage on the uses side).

speculation motive One reason for holding bonds instead of money: Because the market value of interest-bearing bonds is inversely related to the interest rate, investors may wish to hold bonds when interest rates are high with the hope of selling them when interest rates fall.

spreading overhead The process of dividing total fixed costs by more units of output. Average fixed cost declines as quantity rises.

stability A condition in which national output is growing steadily, with low inflation and full employment of resources.

stabilization policy Describes both monetary and fiscal policy, the goals of which are to smooth out fluctuations in output and employment and to keep prices as stable as possible.

stabilization program An agreement between a borrower country and the International Monetary Fund in which the country agrees to revamp its economic policies to provide incentives for higher export earnings and lower imports.

stagflation Occurs when the overall price level rises rapidly (inflation) during periods of recession or high and persistent unemployment (stagnation).

Standard and Poor's 500 (S&P 500) An index based on the stock prices of the largest 500 firms traded on the New York Stock Exchange, the NASDAQ Stock Market, and the American Stock Exchange.

statistical discrepancy Data measurement error.

sticky prices Prices that do not always adjust rapidly to maintain equality between quantity supplied and quantity demanded.

sticky wages The downward rigidity of wages as an explanation for the existence of unemployment.

stock A certificate that certifies ownership of a certain portion of a firm.

store of value An asset that can be used to transport purchasing power from one time period to another.

structural adjustment A series of programs in developing nations designed to (1) reduce the size of their public sectors through privatization and/or expenditure reductions, (2) decrease their budget deficits, (3) control inflation, and (4) encourage private saving and investment through tax reform.

structural deficit The deficit that remains at full employment.

structural unemployment The portion of unemployment that is due to changes in the structure of the economy that result in a significant loss of jobs in certain industries.

substitutes Goods that can serve as replacements for one another; when the price of one increases, demand for the other goes up.

sunk costs Costs that cannot be avoided, regardless of what is done in the future, because they have already been incurred.

supply curve A graph illustrating how much of a product a firm will sell at different prices.

supply schedule A table showing how much of a product firms will sell at different prices.

supply-side policies Government policies that focus on stimulating aggregate supply instead of aggregate demand.

surplus of government enterprises Income of government enterprises.

sustained inflation Occurs when the overall price level continues to rise over some fairly long period of time.

tacit collusion Collusion occurs when price- and quantity-fixing agreements among producers are explicit. Tacit collusion occurs when such agreements are implicit.

tariff A tax on imports.

tax base The measure or value upon which a tax is levied.

tax incidence The ultimate distribution of a tax burden.

tax multiplier The ratio of change in the equilibrium level of output to a change in taxes.

tax rate structure The percentage of a tax base that must be paid in taxes—25 percent of income, for example.

tax shifting Occurs when households can alter their behavior and do something to avoid paying a tax.

technological change The introduction of new methods of production or new products intended to increase the productivity of existing inputs or to raise marginal products.

terms of trade The ratio at which a country can trade domestic products for imported products.

theory of comparative advantage Ricardo's theory that specialization and free trade will benefit all trading partners (real wages will rise), even those that may be absolutely less efficient producers.

Tiebout hypothesis An efficient mix of public goods is produced when local land/housing prices and taxes come to reflect consumer preferences just as they do in the market for private goods.

tight monetary policy Fed policies that contract the money supply in an effort to restrain the economy.

time lags Delays in the economy's response to stabilization policies.

tit-for-tat strategy A company's strategy that lets a competitor know the company will follow the competitor's lead.

total cost (TC) Fixed costs plus variable costs.

total cost (total economic cost) The total of (1) out-of-pocket costs, (2) normal rate of return on capital, and (3) opportunity cost of each factor of production.

total fixed costs (TFC) or **overhead** The total of all costs that do not change with output, even if output is zero.

total revenue (TR) The total amount that a firm takes in from the sale of its product: the price per unit times the quantity of output the firm decides to produce (P × q).

total utility The total amount of satisfaction obtained from consumption of a good or service.

total variable cost (TVC) The total of all costs that vary with output in the short run.

total variable cost curve A graph that shows the relationship between total variable cost and the level of a firm's output.

trade deficit Occurs when a country's exports of goods and services are less than its imports of goods and services in a given period.

trade feedback effect The tendency for an increase in the economic activity of one country to lead to a worldwide increase in economic activity, which then feeds back to that country.

trade surplus The situation when a country exports more than it imports.

tragedy of commons The idea that collective ownership may not provide the proper private incentives for efficiency because individuals do not bear the full costs of their own decisions but do enjoy the full benefits.

transaction motive The main reason that people hold money—to buy things.

transfer payments Cash payments made by the government to people who do not supply goods, services, or labor in exchange for these payments. They include Social Security benefits, veterans' benefits, and welfare payments.

Treasury bonds, notes, and **bills** Promissory notes issued by the federal government when it borrows money.

trust An arrangement in which shareholders of independent firms agree to give up their stock in exchange for trust certificates that entitle them to a share of the trust's common profits. A group of trustees then operates the trust as a monopoly, controlling output and setting price.

U.S.-Canadian Free Trade Agreement An agreement in which the United States and Canada agreed to eliminate all barriers to trade between the two countries by 1998.

unconstrained supply of labor The amount a household would like to work within a given period at the current wage rate if it could find the work.

underground economy The part of the economy in which transactions take place and in which income is generated that is unreported and therefore not counted in GDP.

unemployed A person 16 years old or older who is not working, is available for work, and has made specific efforts to find work during the previous 4 weeks.

unemployment compensation A state government transfer program that pays cash benefits for a certain period of time to laid-off workers who have worked for a specified period of time for a covered employer.

unemployment rate The ratio of the number of people unemployed to the total number of people in the labor force.

unitary elasticity A demand relationship in which the percentage change in quantity of a product demanded is the same as the percentage change in price in absolute value (a demand elasticity of 21).

unit of account A standard unit that provides a consistent way of quoting prices.

utilitarian justice The idea that "a dollar in the hand of a rich person is worth less than a dollar in the hand of a poor person." If the marginal utility of income declines with income, transferring income from the rich to the poor will increase total utility.

utility The satisfaction, or reward, a product yields relative to its alternatives. The basis of choice.

utility possibilities frontier A graphic representation of a two-person world that shows all points at which A's utility can be increased only if B's utility is decreased.

utility-maximizing rule Equating the ratio of the marginal utility of a good to its price for all goods.

value added The difference between the value of goods as they leave a stage of production and the cost of the goods as they entered that stage.

variable A measure that can change from time to time or from observation to observation.

variable cost A cost that depends on the level of production chosen.

vicious-circle-of-poverty hypothesis Suggests that poverty is self-perpetuating because poor nations are unable to save and invest enough to accumulate the capital stock that would help them grow.

voting paradox A simple demonstration of how majority-rule voting can lead to seemingly contradictory and inconsistent results. A commonly cited illustration of the kind of inconsistency described in the impossibility theorem.

Washington Consensus A set of 10 goals prescribed for countries receiving IMF grants and loans.

wealth or **net worth** The total value of what a household owns minus what it owes. It is a stock measure.

weight The importance attached to an item within a group of items.

Wheeler-Lea Act (1938) Extended the language of the Federal Trade Commission Act to include "deceptive" as well as "unfair" methods of competition.

World Bank An international agency that lends money to individual countries for projects that promote economic development.

Solutions to Even-Numbered Problems

CHAPTER 1

2. Answers will vary.

4. Average cost is $1.17(19.95 ÷ 17). Marginal cost is $0.

6. (a) Tuition (which could have been spent on other things), forgone wages, study time, etc.

(b) All the money (gas, depreciation of the car, etc.) could have been spent on other items; time spent en route could have been used for other activities.

(c) A better grade, no headache, perhaps admission to a better grad school, a higher-paying job. He has traded off an investment in human capital (staying in to study) for present consumption (going to the party).

(d) The other things that $200 could buy.

(e) The $1 million could have been invested in other profit-making ventures or projects or it simply could have been put into the bank or loaned out to someone else at interest.

(f) From the standpoint of the store, Alex is free. From Alex's standpoint, he gives up other uses of time and wages that could be earned elsewhere.

CHAPTER 1 APPENDIX

2. Answers will vary.

(a) Negative slope. As price rises, quantity of apples purchased falls.

(b) Positive (and declining) slope. As income rises, taxes rise, but the rise in taxes is less at higher incomes than at lower incomes.

(c) Negative (and declining) slope. As mortgage rates fall, home sales increase, but the increase in home sales is more at lower mortgage rates than at higher mortgage rates.

(d) Negative, then positive slope. As young children get older, they run faster, but as adults get older (beyond a certain age), they run slower.

(e) Positive slope. Greater sunshine leads to greater corn yield.

(f) Positive, then negative slope. Up to a point, more fertilizer increases corn yield, but beyond a certain point, adding more fertilizer actually decreases the yield.

CHAPTER 2

2. Disagree. To be efficient, an economy must produce what people want. This means that in addition to operating on the *ppf* (resources are fully employed, best technology is being used) the economy must be operating at the *right* point on the *ppf*.

4. (a) For Kristen, the "cost" of a potholder is five wristbands; for Anna, the cost of a potholder is six wristbands. Kristen has a comparative advantage in potholders.

(b) Anna has a comparative advantage in the production of wristbands because the opportunity cost (1/6 potholder) is lower for Anna than it is for Kristen (1/5 potholder).

(c)

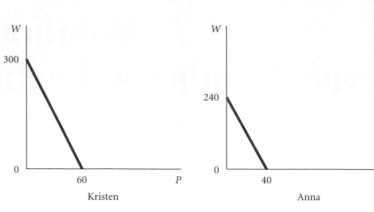

Kristen   Anna

(d) Kristen: 150 wristbands and 30 potholders. Anna: 120 wristbands and 20 potholders. Total wristbands = 270. Total potholders = 50.

(e) 285 wristbands and 51 potholders.

(f) Kristen should completely specialize in potholder production and earn $60 \times \$5.50 = \$330$. Anna should completely specialize in wristband production and earn $240 \times \$1 = \$240$. Maximum combined revenue is $570.

6. (a) Blah.
Blah.

(b) Blah: fruit.
Figistan: timber.

(c)

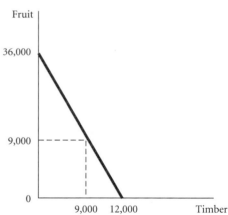

(d) Figistan: 800 workers to timber
                400 workers to fruit
                produces 4,000 of each
    Blah: 900 workers to timber
                300 workers to fruit
                produces 9,000 of each

(e) Figistan moves all labor to timber and produces 6,000 board feet.
Blah moves 150 workers out of timber into fruit.
450 in fruit produces 13,500 baskets; 750 in timber produces 7,500 ft.
Blah trades 4,200 baskets to Figistan for 1,800 board ft.

Blah ends up with 9,300 of each; Figistan ends up with 4,200 of each.
Both move beyond their individual *ppf*s.

8. (a) c; also if you take into account the fact that most members of society like meat not fish you might include d and e.

(b) a, b, d, e, f.

(c) d, e.

(d) e.

(e) b, c, d, e, f.

(f) b.

10. Answers will vary.

CHAPTER 3

2. (a)

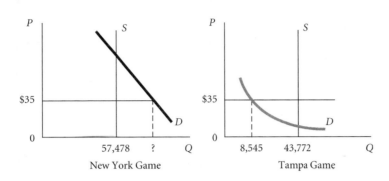

New York Game   Tampa Game

(b) It depends on whether demand responds to the lower price and by how much. The diagram in (a) suggests that if price was lowered by a lot, the stadium would be filled. If demand is "elastic" enough, the quantity demanded will increase by more than the fall in ticket price, and revenues will rise. If demand is not responsive enough, the quantity demanded may not increase enough to offset the fall in ticket prices, and revenues will fall. The easiest example of the latter would occur if demand were "perfectly inelastic," which implies that no one else would come to the game despite the lower price.

(c) The price system was not allowed to work to ration the New York tickets. Some other rationing device must have been used. Perhaps people stood in line or queued. Perhaps there was a lottery. In all likelihood, there would be a secondary market for the tickets ("scalpers"). You could no doubt find them for sale on line at a high price.

4. (a) Disagree. They are complements.

(b) Agree.

(c) Disagree. A rise in income will cause the demand for inferior goods to fall, pushing prices down.

(d) Disagree. Sure they can. Steak and lobster are both normal goods.

(e) Disagree. Price could go down if the shift of supply is larger than the shift of demand.

(f) Agree.

6. (a) A simple demand shift; same diagram for both cities.

(b) Rightward shift of supply with new development; leftward shift of demand with falling incomes; same diagram for both cities. (Assumes the shifts are equal.)

(c) Trade-up buyers shift demand in the higher-income towns and supply in the lower-income towns.

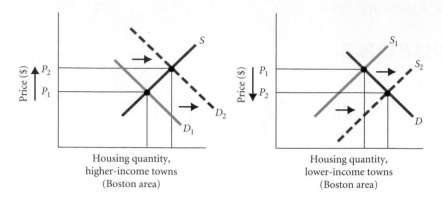

Housing quantity,
higher-income towns
(Boston area)

Housing quantity,
lower-income towns
(Boston area)

8. (a) *P* decreases, *Q* decreases

(b, d) *P* increases, *Q* increases

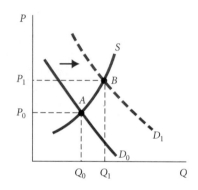

(c) *P* increases, *Q* decreases

(e) *P* decreases, *Q* increases

10. (a)

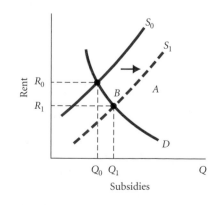

Subsidies

Vouchers

The demand side strategy (vouchers) results in higher rents.

(b) Critics believe that the supply curve for low-income housing looks like this:

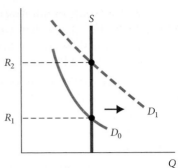

12. The real answer depends on what happened to cause the changes. If the drop in 2004 was due to foreign boycott of U.S. markets, and domestic production was constant, there would have been a big shift of domestic supply to the right pushing down prices in the United States. If, however, it was the case that domestic production had to be cut because the disease was discovered here reducing the availability for export, it would have been a big shift of overall domestic supply to the left. The fact that imports rose substantially, probably means that domestic supply was not plentiful. Since prices rose, this second story is the more likely. We know that the disease was indeed discovered in the United States in 2004 and that demand dropped. If prices rose, supply must have dropped more.

CHAPTER 4

2. Disagree. Every demand curve hits the quantity axis because of diminishing marginal utility . . . at a price of zero, there is a limit to how much one can or wants to consume. The argument that at some price demand goes to zero explains why all demand curves hit the price axis.

4. The subsidy does increase the "cost" of planting—there is now an opportunity cost. (By planting, the farmers will have to give up the subsidy.) The subsidy will clearly lead to fewer acres of production and higher farm prices. In effect, it shifts the supply curve to the left.

6. (a) Wheat market   (b) Hamburger market   (c) Gasoline market

8. (a)

(b) With free trade in oil, Americans would pay $30 per barrel. At this price, the U.S. demand schedule shows that Americans would buy 15 million barrels per day. The U.S. supply schedule shows that U.S. producers would supply 6 million barrels per day, with the remainder—9 million barrels—imported from foreign sources.

(c) With a tax of $4 per barrel, Americans would have to pay $34 for imported oil. Quantity demanded would decrease from 15 million to 13 million barrels. Of this, American producers would supply 10 million barrels, whereas imports would be cut back from 9 million to 3 million barrels. The U.S. government would collect a tax of $4 × 3 million = $12 million per day.

(d) American oil consumers are harmed by the tax; they are paying a higher price for oil. American oil producers are helped by the tax; they receive a higher price for oil, and this induces them to produce more oil. Foreign oil producers are harmed, because Americans buy less imported oil. Finally, the U.S. government (and the U.S. taxpayer generally) benefit from the tax revenue.

10. At $8 and 6 million meals: CS = $18 million; PS = $18 million; total = $36 million
At 3 million meals: CS = $13.5 million; PS = $13.5 million; total = 27 million
Deadweight loss = $9 million

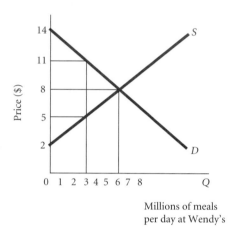

Millions of meals
per day at Wendy's

12. Answers will vary.

CHAPTER 5

2. (a) No. Because demand is elastic, an increase in price will lead to a larger percentage decrease in quantity demanded, so revenue $P \times Q$ will fall if P is increased.

(b) No. Because demand is inelastic. A decrease in prices will lead to a smaller percentage increase in quantity, so revenue $P \times Q$ will fall if P is cut.

4. (a) Between Points A and B: −3.666. Between Points C and D: −1. Between Points E and F: −0.273.

(b) Starting at $50, revenues would fall by $4,000, from $10,000 to $6,000. Starting at $30, revenues would remain constant at $12,000. Starting at $10, revenues would rise by $4,000, from $6,000 to $10,000.

(c) When demand is elastic (e.g., between Points A and B), a price increase will lead to a revenue decline. When elasticity is unitary (e.g., between Points C and D), a price increase will leave revenues unchanged. When demand is inelastic (e.g., between Points E and F), a price will increase revenue.

6. (a) Disagree. The top half of the demand curve is elastic.

(b) Disagree. Price would fall, but firms would earn more revenue because demand is elastic over the range of prices near the equilibrium.

8. (a) $\%\Delta Q \div \%\Delta P = 0.2$

Thus, $\%\Delta P = \%\Delta Q \div 0.2 = 10\% \div 0.2 = 0.10 \div 0.2 = 0.50 = 50\%$. Price would rise to $2.10.

(b) A price ceiling at $1.40 per gallon would create a shortage of gasoline. The result might be long lines at gas stations and perhaps a black market in gasoline.

CHAPTER 6

2.

# OF COOKIES	MARGINAL UTILITY
1	100
2	100
3	75
4	50
5	25
6	10
7	0

The maximum that he would buy would be 6 because the seventh yields no marginal utility.

4. (a)

(b)

(c)

(d)

(e)

(f)

(g)

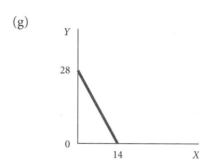

6. This statement is backwards. An increase in the "after tax" wage will have a positive effect on the labor supply only if the substitution effect outweighs the income effect. The substitution effect states that a higher wage makes the opportunity cost of leisure increase. Thus, people tend to substitute working for leisure. The substitution effect alone suggests that a higher after-tax wage leads to *more* labor supply. On the other hand, if the after-tax wage goes up, people are better off. Assuming leisure is a normal good, the higher wage suggests that people will consume more leisure and work *less*.

8. (a) Disagree. If the income effect of a wage change dominates the substitution effect, we know that a wage increase will cause additional consumption of leisure and less work . . . and that lower wages will cause additional work . . . increased labor supply. Thus, if our household works more, it must have been a wage cut.

(b) Disagree. In product markets, a price cut makes households better off . . . higher real income. Thus, for normal goods, the income effect leads to *more* consumption of the good.

10. (a)

# PER MONTH	Movies TU	Movies MU	Movies MU/$	# PER MONTH	Books TU	Books MU	Books MU/$
1	50	50	6.25	1	22	22	1.10
2	80	30	3.75	2	42	20	1.00
3	100	20	2.50	3	52	10	.50
4	110	10	1.25	4	57	5	.25
5	116	6	.75	5	60	3	.15
6	121	5	.63	6	62	2	.10
7	123	2	.25	7	53	1	.05

(b) Yes, these figures are consistent with the law of diminishing marginal utility, which states that as the quantity of a good consumed increases, utility also increases, but by less and less for each additional unit. In the tables, the *TU* figures for both books and movies are increasing, but as more movies or more books are consumed, the *MU* diminishes.

(c) Five movies and two books. To maximize utility, the individual should allocate income toward those goods with the highest marginal utility per dollar. The first four movies have a higher marginal utility per dollar than the first book so the person begins by seeing four movies for $32. The first book has a higher marginal utility than the fifth movie so now the person should buy a book, for total expenditure of $52. Next, the second book, for total spending of $72. And finally, the fifth movie, for total spending of $80.

(d) See graph below.

(e) If the price of books falls to $10, only the *MU/$* column for books needs to be recalculated:

# PER MONTH	Books		
	TU	*MU*	*MU/$*
1	22	22	2.20
2	42	20	2.00
3	52	10	1.00
4	57	5	.50
5	60	3	.30
6	62	2	.20
7	63	1	.10

(f) Now, using the same logic as in (c) above, this individual should purchase six movies and three books, for a total expenditure of $6 \times \$8 = \$48 + 3 \times \$10 = \$30 = \$78$.

(g) See graph below.

(h) The decrease in the price of books increases the purchasing power of the individual's income. This increase in purchasing power—or income effect—will be used to purchase more of one or both goods, depending on the individual's tastes. In this case, the individual chooses to use his or her "increased income" to buy more of both goods.

(*Note:* Another answer to (f) is 5 movies and 4 books. This choice uses up the entire $80, and it results in the same total utility as 6 movies and 3 books.)

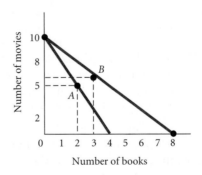

CHAPTER 6 APPENDIX

2. $I/P_{x1} = 100$ and $I = 100$, thus $P_{x1} = \$1.00$
    (Point *A* on demand curve).
$I/P_{x2} = 200$ and $I = 100$, thus $P_{x2} = \$.50$
    (Point *B* on demand curve).
$I/P_{x3} = 300$ and $I = 100$, thus $P_{x3} = \$.33$
    (Point *C* on demand curve).

4. (a) We know that $P_A A + P_N N = 100 \rightarrow 5N + 10A = 100$. We also know that $MU_N/MU_A = A/N = P_N/P_A = 5/10 \rightarrow N = 2A$. Substituting, we find that $5(2A) + 10A = 100 \rightarrow A = 5$; $N = 10$.

(b) If $P_N = 10$, $N = 5$ and if $P_N = 2$, $N = 25$.

(c) Answers will vary, but graph should show an indifference curve tangent to a budget constraint drawn for $P_A = \$10$ and $P_N =$ to one of the prices given in the answer to (b).

CHAPTER 7

2. They are not earning economic profits; they are not considering opportunity costs. The opportunity cost of capital is 10 percent of $50,000 annually, or $5,000. Because simple revenue minus cost yields an accounting profit of only $2,000, adding $5,000 in opportunity cost means the firm is suffering losses of at least $3,000. In addition, they are not considering the opportunity cost of their own labor.

4. (a) The marginal product decreases as a single variable factor increases, holding all other factors constant.

(b) The table does exhibit diminishing returns because the marginal product of labor falls as labor increases:

L	TP	MP
0	0	—
1	5	5
2	9	4
3	12	3
4	14	2
5	15	1

6. Clearly, the labor-intensive way would be to carry the boxes down the hall and up the stairs one at a time. She could get a friend or two to help. If the dorm has an elevator and she can borrow a hand truck, the job would be a piece of cake. She would be using capital to raise her productivity. To go three miles across campus, a car (capital) or a truck (more capital) would be nice, although she could carry the boxes one at a time across campus as well. In the developing world, where capital is scarce, people carry a lot of stuff. To get the boxes to a new campus, she would probably mail them or send them UPS. In this case, they would go in a big truck or in an airplane (a whole lot of capital).

8. The addition of capital (tractors, combines, etc.) and the application of technology (nitrous fertilizers) raise the productivity of labor, just as the new grill discussed in the chapter raised the productivity of workers. Capital is also a substitute input for labor.

10. (a) Tall buildings—skyscrapers.

(b) Product usually has to move along an assembly line and out into a warehouse. An assembly line usually takes a lot of space on a single floor. (Can you imagine a vertical assembly line?)

(c) Offices can be "stacked up." People can move by stairs or elevators easily.

(d) Accessibility!

(e) The area of land increases with the square of distance from the center: When a city grows from a radius of 1 mile to a radius of 5 miles, the new area is 25 times as large as the original: Area $= \pi R^2$.

12. (a) The first step is to calculate the cost for each level of output using each of the three technologies. With capital costing $100 per day, and labor costing $80 per day, the results are as follows:

DAILY OUTPUT	TECHNOLOGY 1	TECHNOLOGY 2	TECHNOLOGY 3
100	860	800	820
150	1,100	960	900
200	1,280	1,140	1,080
250	1,540	1,400	1,340

From the table, we can see that for output of 100, Technology 2 is cheapest. For output levels of 150, 200, and 250, Technology 3 is cheapest.

(b) In a low-wage country, where capital costs $100 per day and labor costs only $40 per day, the cost figures are as follows:

DAILY OUTPUT	TECHNOLOGY 1	TECHNOLOGY 2	TECHNOLOGY 3
100	580	600	660
150	700	680	700
200	840	820	840
250	1,020	1,000	1,020

From the table, we can see that for output of 100, Technology 1 is now cheapest. For output levels of 150, 200, or 250, Technology 2 is now cheapest.

(c) If the firm moves from a high-wage to a low-wage country and continues to produce 200 units per day, it will change from Technology 3 (with six workers) to Technology 2 (with eight workers). Employment increases by two workers.

CHAPTER 7 APPENDIX

2. At A, $MP_L/MP_K > P_L/P_K$ because the slope of the isoquant is greater than the slope of the isocost. That means that $MP_L/P_L > MP_K/P_K$; thus, the firm can cut costs by hiring more labor and less capital.

At B, $MP_L/MP_K < P_L/P_K$ because the slope of the isoquant is less than the slope of the isocost. That means that $MP_K/P_K > MP_L/P_L$; thus, the firm can cut costs by hiring more capital and less labor.

CHAPTER 8

2. At 5 million copies $AFC = \$6$, at 10 million copies $AFC = \$3$ and at 20 million copies $AFC = \$1.50$. If each book costs $1.50, and that is true for every book up to 40 million, then the average variable cost of a volume is $1.50 regardless of how many volumes come off the press, at least up to 40 million. If the producer prints 5 million copies, total fixed cost is $30 million, and total variable cost is 5 million times $1.50 or $7.5 million. Thus, total cost is $37.5 million and average total cost is $37.5 million divided by 5 million or $7.50. You can get this same answer by simply adding average fixed cost of $6 to average variable cost of $1.50. Average total cost of 10 million books is $4.50. The average total cost of producing 20 million copies is $3.00.

4. (a)

Q	TVC	AVC	MC
0	0	–	–
1	45	45.00	45
2	85	42.50	40
3	120	40.00	35
4	155	38.75	35
5	195	39.00	40
6	240	40.00	45
7	290	41.43	50
8	345	43.13	55
9	405	45.00	60
10	470	47.00	65

(b) Yes. Given diminishing returns, *MC* may fall at first but should eventually rise with output.

(c) When *MC* is below *AVC*, *AVC* falls; when *MC* is above *AVC*, *AVC* rises. At 3 units of output, $MC = 35 < AVC = 40$, thus, *AVC* falls. At 6 units, $MC = 45 > AVC = 40$, thus, *AVC* rises.

(d) Marginal cost is the added cost of the resources needed to increase output one unit. The *MC* of the sixth unit of output, for example, is $45; 2 units of *K* at $10 each plus 5 units of *L* at $5 each.

(e) The firm would increase production as long as $P > MC$. The optimal level of output would be 8.

6. (a)

Q	TC $	TFC $	TVC $	AVC $	ATC $	MC $
0	100	100	0	–	–	–
1	130	100	30	30.00	130.00	30
2	150	100	50	25.00	75.00	20
3	160	100	60	20.00	53.33	10
4	172	100	72	18.00	43.00	12
5	185	100	85	17.00	37.00	13
6	210	100	110	18.33	5.00	25
7	240	100	140	20.00	34.29	30
8	280	100	180	22.50	35.00	40
9	330	100	230	25.56	36.66	50
10	390	100	290	29.00	39.00	60

(b)

When *MC* is below *ATC*(*AVC*), *ATC*(*AVC*) is decreasing. When *MC* is above *ATC*(*AVC*), *ATC*(*AVC*) is increasing.

(c) 7 units

$$TR = 7 \times \$30 = \$210$$

$$TR - TC = \$210 - \$240 = -\$30 \text{ loss of } \$30.$$

(d) 9 units

$$TR = 9 \times \$50 - \$450$$

$$TR - TC = \$450 - \$330 = \$120 \text{ profits.}$$

(e) Because a price of \$10 is below the minimum *AVC*, the firm should shut down and incur only fixed costs, for a total loss of \$100.

8.

Units of output

If $P = \$3$, the optimal $q = 200$.
At output below 200 $P > MC$.
At output above 200 $P < MC$.

10. (a) The table gives the marginal product from each day's efforts: 100, 80, 60, and 40 kg.

(b) Marginal cost of a kg of fish is the change in cost divided by the change in *q*. During prime season, each day brings in 100 kg of fish at a cost of 6,000 levs, or $MC = 6{,}000/100 = 60$ levs. During month 7, it's $6{,}000/80 = MC = 75$ levs. During month 8, it's $6{,}000/60 = MC = 100$ levs. During the rest of the year, it's $6{,}000/40 = 150$ levs.

(c) Produce as long as price, which is marginal revenue (80 levs), is greater than *MC*. Thus, the boat should be in the water fishing during prime season and month 7, but should not fish during month 8 or during the rest of the year.

CHAPTER 9

2. The enterprise is suffering a \$20,000 economic loss. $TR = \$100{,}000$, $P \times q = \$5 \times 20{,}000$, $TC = \$120{,}000$. Fixed costs are \$30,000 (10% annually on \$300,000: the opportunity cost of capital). That makes $TVC = \$90{,}000$ ($TC - TFC = 120{,}000 - 30{,}000$). Thus, revenue covers variable cost, profit on operations is $100{,}000 - 90{,}000 = 10{,}000$. The firm should operate in the short run but exit in the long run.

4. One could make a case that some economies probably exist in all five, but the case is much stronger in electric power (needs a big power plant or dam) and aircraft manufacturing (requires a big assembly line and a great deal of cooperation).

Home Building: Home building is usually done by very small independent contractors, although there are some big tract developers (like Ryan Homes) that produce tens of thousands of homes each year. They do quantity buying and use mass-produced parts.

It is hard to find economies of much significance in *software development* and *vegetable farming.* Although some firms in those industries are large, many are quite small and quite competitive.

6. (a) Disagree. A firm will never sell its output for less than the *marginal* cost of producing it, but may indeed sell at less than *average* total cost, as long as it can earn an operating profit.

(b) Disagree. The short-run marginal cost curve assumes at least one input is fixed. The long-run average cost curve allows all inputs to vary. For example, the short-run MC curve for each fixed level of capital could be U-shaped, and yet the $LRAC$ curve could be flat (constant returns to scale).

8. (a) Disagree. Constant returns to scale means that the long-run average cost curve is flat over most of its range.

(b) Disagree. The supply curve of a competitive firm is its marginal cost curve above the average *variable* cost curve. At any point above AVC, total revenue is greater than total variable cost and firms will choose to operate.

(c) Disagree. A firm suffering losses will continue to operate as long as total revenue covers variable cost.

10. Answers will vary.

12. (a, b)

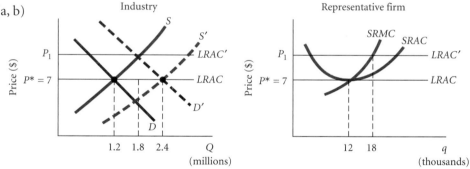

(c) In the short run, demand shifts from D to D', and price rises to P_1. Firms are making profits, and they raise output to 18,000.

In the long run, 100 new firms enter the industry. Supply shifts from S to S', and price falls back to $7.

CHAPTER 9 APPENDIX

2. See the story in the text and Figure 9A.2 for an increasing-cost industry.

CHAPTER 10

2. (a)

Process 1 costs $7 per widget. Process 2 costs $8, and Process 3 costs $10. Process 1 is cheapest.

(b, c) When $q = 10$, $K = 10$ and $L = 40 \rightarrow TVC = \$70$.
When $q = 30$, $K = 30$ and $L = 120 \rightarrow TVC = \$210$.
When $q = 50$, $K = 50$ and $L = 200 \rightarrow TVC = \$350$.

(d) If capital costs \$3 and labor costs \$4 per unit, then process 3 becomes cheapest, with a cost of \$13 per widget.
When $q = 10$, $K = 30$ and $L = 10 \rightarrow TVC = \$130$.
When $q = 30$, $K = 90$ and $L = 30 \rightarrow TVC = \$390$.
When $q = 50$, $K = 150$ and $L = 50 \rightarrow TVC = \$650$.

4.

WORKERS		BUSHELS	MP	MRP
0		0	–	–
1	30	40	40	\$80
2	60	70	30	\$60
3	90	90	20	\$40
4	120	100	10	\$20
5		105	5	\$10
6		102	–3	–\$6

The firm should hire workers as long as $MRP < W$. When $W = \$30$, the firm should hire three workers. If W increases to \$50, the firm should cut back to only two workers because the MRP of the third worker (\$40) is now less than the cost of hiring him/her (\$50).

6. (a) Demand curve for construction workers shifts left; wave decreases; employment decreases.

(b, c) Demand curve for construction workers shifts right; wage increases; employment increases.

Number of workers

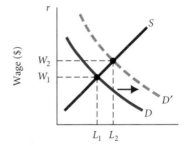

Number of workers

8. Investment tax credits reduce the cost of capital relative to the cost of labor. To the extent that capital is a substitute for labor, these credits can lead to layoffs and slower employment growth.

10. You would weigh the benefits with the costs. The costs are \$40 per week, but the benefits depend on the value of the roommates' time and the displeasure that each gets from mowing. It also depends on their incomes and wealth. There could easily be disagreement. Also, depending on their individual opportunities, one or both of the other two roommates might offer to do the mowing in exchange for money.

12. (a) Even though the ratios MRP_L/P_L and MRP_K/P_K are equal, we still have $MRP_L > P_L$ and $MRP_K > P_K$.

(b) The firm could increase profits by either purchasing more capital or hiring more workers. Either action would add more to revenue than it would add to cost.

CHAPTER 11

2. (a) Disagree strongly. Savings is defined as household income minus consumption spending. It is that portion of income set aside for future consumption. Investment is new purchases of capital, plant, equipment, and inventory. Savings in the simple model is done by households and investment is done by firms. What is often confusing is the fact that saving is the source of resources used to finance investment spending.

(b) Disagree. It is important to remember that when a household buys a share of stock *or* a bond, it is not investing in the economic sense of the word. Only when new capital is produced does investment take place. If a new firm sells shares to households and uses the proceeds to buy new machinery, the purchase of the new machinery is investment.

(c) Disagree. Higher interest rates encourage saving but discourage investment. Interest rates determine in part the cost of investment. If the capital investment is financed with borrowing, higher interest rates increase the cost directly. If capital investment is financed with internal funds by a firm, higher interest rates increase the opportunity cost of the investment.

4.

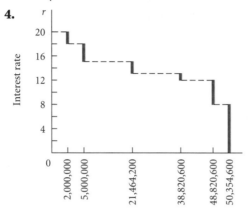

Total investment (Singapore dollars)

Quando Company should invest in all projects that have a rate of return greater than the interest rate. Therefore, it should invest a total of $48,820,600.

6. Savings can be borrowed by business firms, which can purchase new technology, engage in research to develop new technology, expand existing plants, or build new plants. Savings can be borrowed from banks or by a firm issuing bonds. Other channels include the stock market and venture capital funds. Savings can be borrowed by individuals, who can invest in human capital (college education, professional school, technical training) or purchase newly constructed houses.

8. Households supply the funds (saving), which are used by business firms to purchase capital equipment.

10. Physical capital would include the buildings, laboratories, photocopying equipment, chalkboards, desks, and chairs. Intangible capital would include human capital (the education and training possessed by professors, administrators, and staff) and the reputation of the institution.

The value of the physical capital stock could be measured by estimating how much it could sell for on the open market. The value of intangible capital is much more difficult to assess.

Other parts of the answer will vary depending on the school, but some examples might be building new dormitories, athletic centers, or libraries and their impact on the school's reputation and, therefore, admissions and tuition revenue, alumni giving, and the ability to secure grants from private and government sources.

CHAPTER 11 APPENDIX

2. The PDV of the inheritance is $\$10,000/(1.065)^{10} = \$5,327.26$. You should accept your brother's offer. If you invested $6,000 for 10 years at 6.5% you would have $\$6,000 \times (1.065)^{10} = \$11,262$.

4.

	A	B	C	D	E
@8%	$1,000	$1,000	$1,052	$1,092	$1,258
@10%	$924	$903	$1,000	$1,000	$1,208

At 8% interest, flow E is worth a current expense of $1,235 because its *PDV* of $1,258 would exceed the expense. At an interest rate of 10%, the *PDV* of $1,208 is less than the current expense so the investment should not be undertaken.

6. (a) $3,000/(1.10) = $2,727.27.

  (b) $3,000/(1.10)^2 = $2,479.34.

  (c) $1,000/(1.10) + $1,000/(1.10)^2 + $1,000/(1.10)^3 = $909.09 + $826.45 + $751.32 = $2,486.86.

8. Less than 7%. If I can get the same flow of profits by depositing $234,756,000 in a bank paying 7%, and I actually pay $254,000,000 for it, I am earning less than 7% on that investment.

CHAPTER 12

2. Disagree. Even if shareholders are made worse off, the breakup could be a potential Pareto improvement. The term *efficient change* is often used to describe changes in which some are made better off and others worse off but in which those who gain receive benefits that are greater than the costs imposed on those who lose. The theory of the court is that consumers will gain more than shareholders lose, making the breakup efficient.

4. (a) First, calculate *MP* and $P \times MP$:

WORKERS	LOAVES OF BREAD	MP	$P \times MP$
0	0	–	–
1	15	15	210
2	30	15	210
3	42	12	168
4	52	10	140
5	60	8	112
6	66	6	84
7	70	4	56

At a wage of 119 koruna per hour, 4 workers should be hired. The fifth worker would produce less value in an hour (112 koruna) than his/her wage.

  (b) When the price of bread rises to 20 koruna, the last column must be recalculated.

WORKERS	$P \times MP$
0	–
1	300
2	300
3	240
4	200
5	160
6	120
7	80

Now, 6 workers should be hired.

  (c) If the wage rises to 125 koruna per hour, assuming bread still costs 20 koruna, only 5 workers should be hired. (If bread still costs 14 koruna, as in the first example, only 4 workers would be hired.)

  (d) Yes, the allocation of labor would be efficient because each firm would hire labor until the wage was equal to the value of the marginal product of output. If all firms paid the same wage, they would all have the same marginal product of labor, and no reallocation of labor could increase total output.

6. (a) Disagree. The enjoyment of housing can be limited to those who pay for it. Therefore, the private market will supply it. However, housing, if it is attractive, may produce an externality in the nature of a public good.

(b) Disagree. Monopolies produce too little product and charge an artificially high price.

(c) Agree. It is difficult for consumers to evaluate the skills of a doctor or to judge the advice a doctor gives them.

8. The cost of chicken is likely to go up. Substitutes for chicken include fish, turkey, and perhaps pork and beef. In each of these markets, the demand curve will shift right, and both equilibrium price and equilibrium quantity will rise. Complements might include rice and canned and packaged chicken gravy. The demand curves for these goods would shift left, causing both equilibrium price and quantity to decrease. In the market for farmland, we might see more acreage devoted to substitutes when the anchovies disappear because the demand for substitutes will increase, as will their equilibrium prices.

10. Demand for G shifts left (from D_0 to D_1), driving down the price of G from P_0 to P_1 and creating losses in the short run for firms in G. Demand for S shifts to the right, causing the price of S to rise from P_0 to P_1 and creating short-run profits for firms in S. In the long run, firms exit G, shifting the supply curve left (from S_0 to S_1), driving the price of G back up to P_0 and eliminating the losses. At the same time, firms will enter S, shifting the supply curve to the right (from S_0 to S_1) and driving price back down to P_0 eliminating profits. In the long run, employment will expand in S and shrink in G.

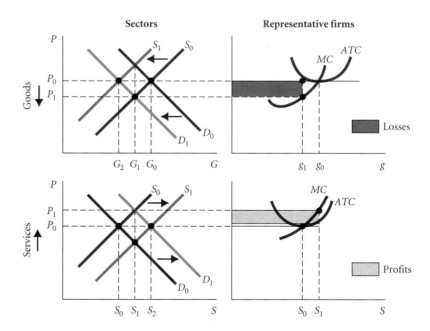

12. (a) Imperfect information—you don't know enough about cars to recognize whether or not you need the repair.

(b) Public good—there is no way to limit enjoyment of the park to those who pay, so the market will not provide it.

(c) Negative externality—there is a byproduct to this activity that affects (harms) parties outside the transaction of buying the album.

(d) Imperfect competition—these firms are not acting like pricetakers. Their decision to raise price above marginal cost will restrict output (ticket sales) below the efficient level.

CHAPTER 13

2. A competitive firm can sell all the output it wants without having any impact on market price. For each additional unit sold, its revenue will rise by the market price. Hence, MR is the same at all levels of output.

Each time a monopolist increases output by one unit, it must lower the price to sell it. The additional revenue the monopolist receives is actually less than the price because consumers who were already buying the output get a price break too. *MR* is, thus, lower than price, and as output increases, both price and *MR* decline.

4.

INTERVAL	MARGINAL REVENUE
0–5	+90
5–10	+70
10–15	+50
15–20	+30
20–25	+10
25–30	−10
30–35	−30
35–40	−50

TR at o is zero; *TR* at 5 is 450; $450 \div 5 = 90$.
Produce as long as $MR > MC$; thus, if $MC = \$20$, optimal output = 20 units.
Profits are $TR = \$1,200(20 \times \$60)$ minus $TC = \$100FC + 400VC(20 \times \$20) = \$500$.
Thus, profit = \$700.
  When $MC = \$40$, optimal output = 15 units, $TR = \$1,050(15 \times \$70)$, $TC = \$100FC + 600VC(15 \times \$40)$. And, finally, profit = \$350(\$1,050 − \$700).

6. (a) $Q^* = 10,000$ (b) $P^* = \$4$

 (c) $TR = \$4 \times 10,000 = \$40,000$ (d) $TC = ATC \times Q = \$5 \times 10,000 = \$50,000$

 (e) profit $= TR - TC = -\$10,000$ (a loss of \$10,000)

8.

Total Profit = $P_T^2 \overline{ABCDEF}$
P_T^1 = Initial price in Taiwan
q_T^1 = Initial quantity in Taiwan
P_T^2 = Price in Taiwan after U.S. Market Opens
q_T^2 = Quantity in Taiwan
$q_{TOTAL}^T - q_T^2$ = Quantity sold in U.S.
Pus = Price in U.S.

CHAPTER 14

2. (a) Disagree. There are no barriers to entry in monopolistic competition, and economic profits are eliminated in the long run.

 (b) Disagree. Oligopoly is an industry in which there are some firms that can control price or influence price because of their size. Dominant firm price leadership is an oligopoly model.

 (c) Disagree. Price does not equal *MC* in the short or long run in monopolistically competitive industries.

4. (a) A good example was AT&T when it held a dominant position in the U.S. telecommunications market. At the same time, it had little competition in the United States, and other countries had big, powerful telecommunications firms producing equipment (telephones, etc.) and services for the world market. World competition was fierce.

(b) The key is the availability of substitutes. A monopoly is a firm producing a product for which there is no close substitute. When they were just another band, clubs could hire a cheap band and consumers didn't know the difference or care. With their success, there became fewer substitutes in the minds of consumers.

6. Both A's and B's potential losses are minimized by cheating. To minimize the maximum loss, A should cheat because it yields higher profit regardless of what B does. The same is true for B. If A cheats, so will B, and if B cheats, so will A. Most likely outcome: Both will cheat.

8. (a) 30 units.

(b) $P = \$14$.

(c) $TR = 30 \times \$14 = \$420$.
$TC = \$9 \times 30 = \$270$.
Profit $= \$420 - \$270 = \$150$.

(d) In the long run, entry will shift the demand and marginal revenue curves left until normal profit is earned at the profit-maximizing output level. This occurs when the demand curve is tangent to the ATC curve.

CHAPTER 15

2. The automobile causes a number of externalities including pollution and congestion. Many advocate tolls as a way to force drivers to weigh these external costs in their decision to drive.

4. Because of the free-rider problem and the drop-in-the-bucket problem, which exist because public goods are non-excludable and non-rival, private producers will find that voluntary contribution to procure public goods will not work. Another argument is that individuals face a prisoner's dilemma in deciding whether to contribute to the production of public goods or not (see last chapter). Thus, we get together and decide what we need to do collectively to procure what we want, we form a government that acts with power to produce what we collectively want, and we make contribution mandatory by collecting a tax.

(a) With private goods, we each get to choose what quantity of each good we want. If I don't like a good, I don't buy it. But with public goods, we all get the same level of output. We all breathe better air if it is cleaned up, and we all get the same amount of national defense. When public goods are produced locally we have more choice (see discussion of the Tiebout hypothesis).

(b) Representative democracy is not guaranteed to produce the socially optimal mix of public goods. Some problems are logrolling, a poorly informed electorate, poor incentives for people to become informed and vote, and the fact that votes are limited to *bundles* of public goods. Also, Arrow's theorem implies that there is no consistent, nonarbitrary way to agree on what the socially optimal mix is. The voting paradox is an example of why majority voting does not provide a consistent social choice mechanism.

(c) An example might be a bureaucrat who is motivated just to increase the power, prestige, and budget of her bureau. This might lead to bloated bureaucracies. Clearly, there has been great pressure in recent years to keep politicians and bureaucrats honest. The press plays an enormous role.

6. (a) This might work in the small numbers case, but here, large numbers of people are involved, and the free-rider problem and the drop-in-the-bucket problem are likely to get in the way of the efficient outcome.

(b) Compensation may be fair, but there are some worries about efficiency. First is Coase's contention that compensation might interfere with the damaged party's incentive to avoid the damage. Compensation for past damages will also overcharge the polluter and potentially put him out of business. For efficiency, the charge must be equal to "marginal damage cost."

(c) This works perfectly in the case where the damages are very high. For example, suppose that the factory was dumping highly radioactive waste! But if the pollution damage was small relative to the benefits of production on the current site, it is inefficient to stop it cold. Also, there may be ways of reducing certain effluents if the tax were set correctly.

(d) This one is efficient assuming that the marginal damages can be measured accurately. You might argue that it is not equitable, but by not compensating the damaged parties, they still have the incentive to avoid the damage if it is the least expensive way of dealing with the problem.

8. Rewrite the demand curves as: $P_X^A = 5 - .05Q_X^A$ and $P_X^B = 10 - .1Q_X^B$. Since X is a public good, $Q_X^A = Q_X^B = Q_X$. Summing vertically, $P_X = P_X^A + P_X^B = 5 - .05Q_X + 10 - .1Q_X = 15 - .15Q_X$. Setting price equal to marginal cost yields $6 = 15 - .15Q_X$ and $Q_X = 60$. Plugging $Q_X = 60$ into each demand equation, we find that A should be charged \$2 per unit and B should be charged \$4 per unit.

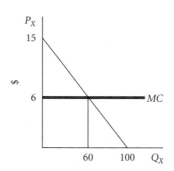

10. False. First, the statement ignores the difficulty of negotiations when large numbers of individuals are involved. Second, externalities involve equity as well as efficiency problems. (Examples used will vary.)

12. Answers will vary, but should mention public goods, externalities, and imperfect market structure at a minimum. Could bring in "public choice" as an issue.

CHAPTER 16

2. Many approaches are possible. Certainly, the change would be to help the very top of the income distribution. There is entitlement theory that says we are entitled to the fruits of our efforts. Wealth is accumulated by saving. Since income has been taxed, this is a double hit on what a household has saved. It also discourages saving and investment and could reduce capital accumulation and slow growth. On the other hand, utilitarian theory argues that taxing high-income households results in a smaller sacrifice since the marginal utility of income is low to a rich family. The social contract theory of Rawls also can be used to support the tax.

4. The biggest reason was that the economy was expanding at a rapid pace during this period. Millions of new jobs had to be filled; employment and labor force participation increased dramatically. In addition, welfare reform was passed and federal law made benefits temporary. In addition, real benefit levels have been falling steadily for years, making the opportunity cost of leisure significantly higher. In other words, the trade-off between work and welfare shifted toward work. The new welfare bill also provided more money for child care and medical insurance. There are many other possible explanations.

6. Computer programming requires a great deal of skill and training. Those who get such jobs have a lot of human capital. Working in a gas station or a car wash does not require great skill. Logging and heavy construction require some skills and are dangerous occupations requiring employers to pay compensation differentials to attract workers.

8. Disagree. The statement ignores different working conditions, differing vacations, and differing time available for other income opportunities (writing books, consulting). Also choices reveal preferences for various jobs. Academic jobs must yield more utility to some or no one would be an academic.

10. Social security, Medicare, private pensions, and the availability of secure vehicles for saving (like FDIC-protected bank accounts) have all contributed to the reduction of poverty among the elderly.

CHAPTER 17

2.

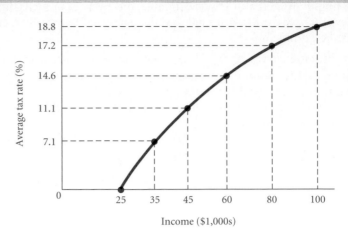

The tax is progressive because the first $25,000 is taxed at a marginal rate of zero. As income rises, the part subject to the 0% rate shrinks as a percentage of total income, and the part subject to the 25% marginal rate rises as a percentage of total income.

4. Answers will vary.

6. Disagree. Excess burdens come about because of distortions in behavior. If a good has a low demand elasticity, the tax will have a relatively small effect on quantity demanded, and the excess burden will be relatively small.

8. If one thinks of the social security tax as payment for future entitlements, it would be correct to list it as part of employee compensation. However, Congress could always change the law so that those "entitlements" aren't received, and faculty may prefer to receive cash rather than future benefits; to this extent, the full value of the payroll tax should not be counted as compensation. Also, it must be pointed out that the imposition of the tax does not raise overall employee compensation. If it really is just another form of compensation, wages will simply fall by the amount of the tax. To the extent that it is a tax because workers prefer to be compensated in a different way, if the supply of labor is inelastic workers, they will bear the burden of the tax and their compensation will be reduced.

10. If the cost of one's car is proportional to one's income, then the tax would be proportional. If high-income people spend a smaller (larger) percentage of their income on cars, then the tax would be regressive (progressive). The tax would distort by discouraging automotive ownership (especially ownership of expensive cars) but might also correct for existing externalities (congestion, air pollution, noise).

CHAPTER 18

2. The unemployed are those who are not working for pay or profit but who have made specific efforts to find a job during the week of the employment survey. In simple terms, it is the excess of labor supplied over labor demanded in the market. The labor demand curve measures the quantity of labor (workers or hours) demanded by firms at each possible wage rate. Firms' demand for labor is derived from the demand for products. Firms will hire workers as long as the product of their labor sells for a price high enough to produce a profit. Thus, the "productivity" of workers is critical. Labor supply reflects the choices made by households to work and how much to work. The alternative to working is leisure or "home production." Home production can include child rearing, subsistence farming, or other unpaid work. The value of leisure and home production is the opportunity cost of working.

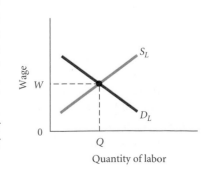

4. The productivity of workers must be increasing. If we are producing more output with fewer workers, output per worker is rising.

6. Macro looks at aggregates in the total economy while micro looks at individual markets and individual economic agents. It is often helpful (and more accurate) to base macroeconomic theories on the behavior of the individuals who make up the macroeconomy.

8. Wars result in high levels of government spending, which helps to increase total spending in the economy.

10. Answers will depend on events.

CHAPTER 19

2. Every payment made by a buyer becomes revenue for the seller, which is paid to someone or held by the seller as profit. Thus, the dollar value of the purchases of new goods and services in a year must be equal to the dollar value of the income generated in that year.

4. With fixed-weight indexes, the percentage change in the index from year to year depends on the weights chosen and, thus, on the base year.

Goods whose output decreases (or increases slowly) because of slowly- or backward-shifting supply curves will have their relative prices increase. If we use the old prices as weights, we will tend to understate the importance of this decrease. Likewise, if we use the new prices as weights, we overstate the importance of the production decline.

Fixed-weight price indexes that use old quantities as weights are generally taken as overestimates of the increase in the price level because these indexes ignore consumers' opportunities to find substitutes for goods whose relative prices rise. Those that use current-year quantities as weights are taken to underestimate changes in the price level because they implicitly assume that the substitutes people chose for the goods whose relative prices rose are considered just as good as the "real thing."

The use of fixed-weight indexes poses special problems when used to make measurements over long periods of time because the use of, for example, 1950 weights for the 1995 economy is not desirable.

The BEA's new approach does two things: First, it takes the (geometric) average of fixed-weight indexes to deal with the overestimation and underestimation issues. Second, it "updates" the base years for the fixed-weight indexes every time it makes a new calculation to ensure that the weights remain appropriate. That is, the indexes whose average it takes are those whose base years are the previous year and the current year.

6. Growth in real GDP: 3.2%.
Per capita GDP for 2005: $35,615.
Per capital GDP for 2006: $36,457.
Growth in real per capita GDP: 2.3%.

8. Consumption as measured by retail sales is just part of GDP. Using the expenditure approach, real GDP is made up of consumption plus investment plus net exports plus government purchases. If the sum of I, G, and $(X - M)$ grows more rapidly than C, real GDP will rise more rapidly than retail sales.

10. The pizza is entirely consumed in the year it was produced while the car will last many years. A car is in reality a capital good. To correct for this, we could count just the value of the services provided by the car *each year*. For example, if the car lasts five years, then 20 percent of its value could be counted in each year's GDP.

12. There is no right or wrong answer here. But counting environmental damage requires a dollar estimate of this damage, about which there will be little consensus.

CHAPTER 20

2. *Full employment* is another term for the natural rate of unemployment. The idea behind this terminology is that if the only unemployment in the economy is the unemployment that comes about as the result of the normal working of the labor market, then there is no "unnecessary" unemployment. Labor is being "fully" utilized because the only unemployment that exists is the natural consequence of an efficiently working market. Unemployment essentially means that people are looking for a job. Every day, people finish school or training, firms in some sectors are expanding and in others contracting, technology is changing, and firms need people with different skills. The normal functioning of the economy means that at any moment some people will be in the process of transition even if the economy is running at full capacity. Thus, the economy can be at full employment with a 4.1 percent unemployment rate, provided that the 4.1 percent unemployment is frictional and structural only.

4. This is structural unemployment, which can sometimes exist for long periods, especially when workers must learn new skills to find jobs. The social costs of this unemployment might be greater than the costs of retraining these workers, providing some justification for government assistance.

6. Yes, inflation would still be a problem. There are other costs of inflation besides the redistribution of income that occurs when incomes are not indexed. One example is the waste of time and resources spent coping with inflation. See the section on "Administrative Costs and Inefficiencies" under the heading "Costs of Inflation."

8.	2000	2001	2002
Bundle price	$400	$531.25	$550
Index	1.00	1.328	1.375
% change		32.8	3.54

Yes. There was a modest increase in the price level between 2001 and 2002.

10. Clearly, in the long run, output can only grow if the quantity of inputs grows or the productivity of those inputs increases. The capacity at any point in time is given by the available capital stock (plant and equipment) and the available labor force. Ultimately, the labor force is limited by the working age population. Since there are always firms going out of business and new firms being born, there are always people looking for work that further limits the number of workers that can actually be working at any given moment of time. Economists often look at the unemployment rate and the "capacity utilization rate" as indicators of how close we are to capacity. When demand exceeds the capacity constraints in an economy, the result is usually an increase in the price level or inflation.

12. In the short run, this can easily happen if more of the labor force becomes employed . . . the unemployment rate falls . . . or more of the existing capital stock is used . . . capacity utilization rises. In the long run, it can happen if technological advance increases factor productivity . . . each unit of labor and capital produces more output over time.

CHAPTER 21

2. *MPC*: Marginal propensity to consume; the fraction of additional income that is spent on consumption. Multiplier: the concept that a sustained increase in one component of aggregate expenditure (like *I*) could lead to an increase in the equilibrium level of income that is a multiple of the initial increase in expenditure. In a simple economy, the multiplier is equal to $1/MPS$ or $1/(1 - MPC)$. Actual investment: The actual amount of investment that takes place; it includes items such as unplanned changes in inventories. Planned investment: Those additions to the capital stock and inventory that are planned by firms. Actual investment and planned investment are equal only in equilibrium; at levels of output below equilibrium actual investment will be less than planned investment, and at levels of output above equilibrium, actual investment will be greater than planned investment. Aggregate expenditure: The total amount the economy spends in a given period. Real GDP: The value of gross domestic product corrected for the effect of higher prices. At equilibrium, planned aggregate expenditure is equal to the level of real GDP. Aggregate output: The total quantity of goods and service produced (or supplied) in an economy in a given period. Aggregate income: The total income received by all factors of production in a given period. Aggregate output and aggregate income are the same (just seen from two different points of view).

4. Answers will depend on future events.

6. Think of the adjustment that occurs when, with the economy at the equilibrium level of output, an increase in planned investment occurs. Inventories are drawn down, and output increases. If firms increase output by the amount of the increase in planned investment, equilibrium will not be reestablished. The increased output (income) will also increase consumption. Thus, there will have been an increase in Y of ΔI, but an increase in aggregate expenditure of more than ΔI. Y must increase further to establish equilibrium. The multiplier is finite because a fraction of income is saved. Thus, as Y grows, S grows; so we will eventually reach a level of Y at which the new planned investment just offsets the leakage into savings. This will be a new equilibrium. At this point, $\Delta S = \Delta 1$. Because $\Delta S = MPS \times \Delta Y$, we can solve for ΔY:

$$\Delta Y = \frac{1}{MPS} \times \Delta I.$$

8. $Y = 600$, $C = 500$, $S = I = 100$; $Y = 680$, $C = 580$, $S = I = 100$. Wealth accumulation increases Y. If the stock market gets overvalued, it inflates GDP on the way up and could deflate it on the way down adding to cyclicality.

CHAPTER 22

2. Answers will depend on events.

4. (a) Disagree. During periods of budget surplus, government debt shrinks. The debt grows only if expenditures exceed taxes.

(b) Disagree. A tax cut will increase the equilibrium level of GDP whether the budget is in surplus or deficit. The only exception might be if the economy were at full employment.

(c) Disagree. The expenditure multiplier is always greater than the tax multiplier if MPC is < 1. If $MPC < MPS$, the tax multiplier is < 1. If $MPS = .90$, the expenditure multiplier is 1.11 and the tax multiplier, MPC/MPS is 0.11.

6. (a) $Y = 1,000$, $Y_d = 800$, $C = 600$, $S = 200$, $I = 100$, $G = 200$.
Because total spending $= C + I + G = 600 + 100 + 200 = 900$ is less than total output of 1,000, one would predict that inventories will pile up, and firms will decide to reduce output.

(b) Y would settle at 600. At this level of output, we would have $C = 300$, $I = 100$, and $G = 200$ so that $Y = C + I + G = 600$.

(c) Cutting government purchases would make the fall in output worse! In particular, a cut of 25 would cause equilibrium Y to decline by $25(1/MPS) = (25)(4) = 100$. This would mean Y would decline to 500.

8. (a) Equilibrium with government requires that output = spending, or that $Y = C + I + G$. Since we know that $Y = C + S + T$ by definition, then equilibrium also requires that $I + G = S + T$. To see if $Y = 200$ is an equilibrium, add $C + I + G$ to obtain $160 + 30 + 0 = 190$. This is not an equilibrium because spending (190) is less than output (200). Alternatively, saving + taxes $= 40 + 0 = 40$, while investment + government spending $= 30 + 0 = 30$. Thus, $S + T$ is not equal to $I + G$. (Notice that there is no autonomous consumption.) In the coming months, we can expect output (Y) to decline and workers to be laid off. Equilibrium $Y = 150$. At $Y = 150$, $C + I + G = 0.8(150) + 30 + 0 = 150$.

10. There would be no automatic stabilizers. (At least none that have been presented in the text thus far. In future chapters, we will see that interest rate changes and price level changes also act as automatic stabilizers.)

There would be no distinction between the actual and full-employment deficit because changes in income would have no impact on the budget deficit.

CHAPTER 23

2. Paying down the debt by buying bonds with tax receipts has no impact on the supply of money. Money that comes to the Treasury in tax payments is immediately returned to the economy as the bonds are paid for by the Treasury. The result is that there is no change in reserves. When the Fed buys bonds in open market operations, it uses what is essentially printed money. The whole point is to expand reserves and, thus, the money supply.

4. Decrease the reserve ratio: that would immediately free up reserves (create excess reserves) system-wide. Banks could lend more, expanding the money supply.

Decrease the discount rate: encouraging banks to borrow reserves and lend more money, expanding the money supply.

Buy government bonds. The Bank of Japan pays with cash or by increasing deposits in banks' accounts. This increases reserves in the system and expands the money supply.

6. If banks are loaned up and the money supply is $1,148 billion, the 10 percent reserve requirement would imply $114.8 billion in reserves. If the reserve requirement were raised to 11 percent, $114.8 billion is 11 percent of $1,044 billion. Raising the reserve requirement to 11 percent would reduce the money supply by $104 billion.

8. $M2$ includes everything in $M1$, plus savings accounts, money market accounts, and some other categories. A shift of funds between, for example, savings accounts and checking accounts, will affect $M1$ but not $M2$, because both savings accounts and checking accounts are part of $M2$.

10. Money injected through open market operations results in a multiple expansion of the money supply only if it leads to loans, and loans can be made only if the new money ends up in banks as reserves. If the Fed buys a bond from James Q. Public, who immediately deposits the proceeds into a dollar-denominated Swiss bank account, the U.S. money supply won't expand at all. If the money ends up in his pockets or in his mattress, the expansion of the money supply will stop right there. If he had deposited the proceeds in a U.S. bank, excess reserves would have been created, stimulating lending and further money creation.

CHAPTER 24

2. A decline in P would shift the money demand curve to the left since transactions would require less money. If the Fed held the money stock constant, interest rates would fall.

4. This is what Keynes called a "liquidity trap." Expanding money supply would not push interest rates lower. The public would essentially hold as much money as we inject into the system. Since, as you will see, monetary policy works through lowering or raising interest rates, it will not work to stimulate the economy if the money demand curve is flat.

6. (a)   (b, e)

(c)   (d)

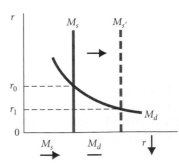

8. Ceteris paribus, an expansionary fiscal policy at a time when the Fed wants to hold the rate of growth of the money supply steady, will drive up interest rates. First, the added expenditure will push up the growth of real GDP. The increased spending and GDP would increase the demand for money, M_d. If the Fed holds the line, $M_d > M_s$ and rates will rise. At the same time these policies hit taxpayers, the Asia crisis of 1998 hit the U.S. economy and slowed down the growth of real GDP as exports to Asia fell. By early 1998, the Fed was even thinking of expanding M_s to push r down to restore GDP growth.

Expansionary fiscal policy; Fed holds

Slowdown from Asia crisis; Fed expands

CHAPTER 25

2. Answers will depend on what happens, and markets are hard to forecast. While in some areas price increases slowed by the end of 2005, there was as yet no evidence of a decline. Residential investment similarly showed no sign of a significant downturn by early 2006. But many believe the market will show more softness as 2006 and 2007 unfold.

4. (a) If investment depended in no way on interest rates, planned investment in Figure 12.2 would be represented as a vertical line.

(b) A change in interest rates would cause no change in planned aggregate expenditure because planned investment would not change. (One could argue that consumption spending might change, but we have not yet discussed the impact of interest rates on consumption spending.)

(c) Fiscal policy would become more effective than monetary policy. Fiscal policy directly influences aggregate output by changing government spending or consumption and would still be effective. (Indeed, it would be more effective since, in this case, there would be no crowding out.) Monetary policy depends on the responsiveness of investment to changes in interest rates to influence aggregate output and would become completely ineffective.

6. (a) Increased investment spending would cause an increase in output (income), which would increase money demand and drive up the interest rate. The Fed could be expected to respond with an increase in the money supply to hold down the interest rate. Output, consumption, saving, and investment spending would increase. The interest rate would remain constant.

(b) The money supply would decrease, causing an increase in the interest rate. The Fed would respond with an increase in the money supply, bringing the interest rate back down to its original level. In the end, there would be no change in output, consumption, saving, investment, or money demand.

8. Investment may not respond positively to low interest rates during a recession because decreased production may have left the firm's existing capital underutilized. In this case, there would be no incentive to buy new plant and equipment. Investment may not respond negatively to high interest rates during a boom because the increased consumer demand arising from increased income may make expansion profitable despite the higher cost of borrowing.

CHAPTER 26

2. An increase in the price of timber and building products increases the cost of production in the housing and real estate sectors. Higher costs will mean that building firms slow down. A cost increase pushes up the aggregate supply curve (the same as a shift to the left).

This has the effect of pushing up the price level and reducing the level of aggregate output in the short run. Assuming the Fed does nothing to the money supply, interest rates could rise or fall. The increase in the price level will cause money demand to shift to the right while falling real output will cause it to shift to the left.

4. (a)

(b)

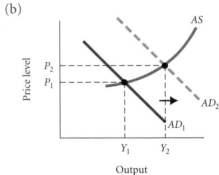

The price level will rise considerably. Equilibrium GDP will rise only a little.

GDP will rise considerably; prices will rise only a little.

(c)

(d)

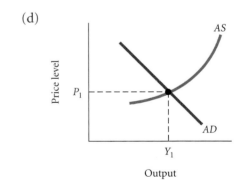

The price level will rise considerably. Equilibrium GDP may fall, but by less than it would if the Fed did not accommodate.

Neither the price level nor output would change. The fiscal and monetary policies have opposing effects on the *AD* curve. If they are of equal strength, there will be no shift in the curve.

6. Answer will depend on events.

8. The actual physical capacity of existing plants represents the maximum output level the economy could produce in the short run. It is where the short-run *AS* curve becomes vertical. Potential GDP is the maximum output the economy could maintain in the long run without exacerbating inflation. It is less than full-capacity output because the bottlenecks and labor shortages that would exist at full-capacity output would cause wages and input prices to rise, leading to worsening inflation.

2. Answers will vary.

4. (a) If the minimum wage is 9 slugs per hour, then:

$$Q_D = 100 - 5(9) = 55 \text{ million workers; } Q_S = 10(9) - 20 = 70 \text{ million workers.}$$

The excess supply of labor (number of unemployed) would be $70 - 55 = 15$ million workers. The unemployment rate would be $15/70 = .214$ or 21.4%.

(b) With no minimum wage, the equilibrium wage is found by setting labor demand equal to labor supply:

$$100 - 5W = 10W - 20 \rightarrow 120 = 15W \rightarrow W = 8 \text{ slugs per hour.}$$

Equilibrium employment is found by substituting $W = 8$ into either the labor-demand or labor-supply equation:

$$Q_D = 100 - 5(8) = 60 \text{ million workers; } Q_S = 10(8) - 20 = 60 \text{ million workers.}$$

The labor force shrinks from 70 million to 60 million workers. Total employment rises from 55 million to 60 million workers. The unemployment rate shrinks from 21.4% to zero. (The model assumes no frictional unemployment.)

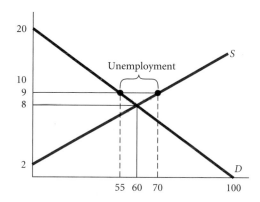

(c) The labor market might not adjust so quickly due to wage rigidity, which has a number of possible causes, including implicit and explicit contracts, worker concerns over their relative wages, and firms' concerns over the decline in productivity that might follow a wage cut.

6. The wage increase may be inefficient to compensate for rising prices. If a wage increase is less than the tax rate of inflation, real wages fall.

8.

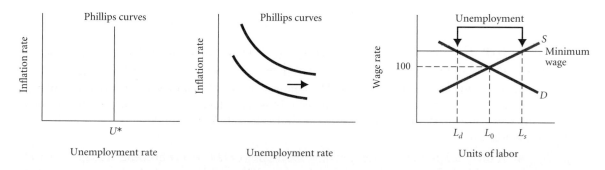

10. The trade-offs would likely not be identical largely because of differences in institutions in the two countries. For example, Japan had a tradition of "lifetime" employment for male workers in the country's largest industries. As a result, there are fewer layoffs in Japan, and it probably has a lower natural rate of unemployment than does the United States.

2. Answers will depend on events.

4. (a) $Y = C + I + G = 100 + .8Y_d + 60 + 80 = 100 + .8[Y - (-150 + .25Y)] + 60 + 80$

$= 100 + .8Y + 120 - .2Y + 60 + 80 = 360 + .6Y$

$Y = 360/.4 = 900$

$D = G - T = 80 - [-150 + .25(900)] = 5$

(b) With $G = 75$

$Y = C + I + G = 100 + .8Y_d + 60 + 75 = 100 + .8[Y - (150 + .25Y)] + 60 + 75$

$= 100 + .8Y + 120 - .2Y + 60 + 75 = 355 + .6Y$

$Y = 355/.4 = 887.5$

$D = G - T = 75 - [-150 + .25(887.5)] = 3.125$

The deficit is not zero because the cut in government spending shifts the *AD* curve to the left, decreasing aggregate output and causing a drop in the net tax revenue. Although the original cut in government spending would seem to eliminate the deficit, the resulting drop in GDP tends to raise the deficit, so the net effect is a deficit that is smaller, but not zero.

(c) The deficit response index (DRI) is the amount by which the deficit changes in response to a one-dollar change in GDP. In this example, the deficit changed for two reasons. The decrease in *G* had a direct effect of decreasing the deficit by $5 billion. The decrease in GDP of 12.5 billion caused the deficit to increase by .25(12.5) = $13.125 billion due to the loss in tax revenue. This latter effect is what is measured by the DRI. $DRI = 3.125/12.5 = .25$.

To find the required change in *G* to eliminate the deficit, note that in this example Δ deficit $= \Delta G - \Delta T = \Delta G - .25(\Delta GDP)$. We also know that $\Delta GDP = 2.5(\Delta G)$. Combining these two equations give us Δ deficit $= \Delta G - .25(2.5\Delta G) = .375\Delta G$. We need Δ deficit to equal -5, so $-5 = .375(\Delta G)$ or $\Delta G = (-5/.375) = -13.33$. Government spending must be cut by $13.33 billion.

(d) With $I = 55$

$Y = C + I + G = 100 + .8Y_d + 55 + 80 = 100 + .8[Y - (-150 + .25Y)] + 55 + 80$

$= 100 + .8Y + 120 - .2Y + 55 + 80 = 355 + .6Y$

$Y = 355/.4 = 887.5$

$D = G - T = 80 - [-150 + .25(887.5)] = 8.125$

Following the methodology of part (c), we need Δ deficit to equal -8.125 so $-8.125 = .375(\Delta G)$ or $\Delta G = (-8.125/.375) = -21.67$.

6. The Fed "leans against the wind" when it increases the money supply to lower interest rates to counteract contraction of the economy, and decreases the money supply to raise interest rates to counteract rapid expansion. These policies are designed to stabilize the economy.

8. It takes a full year for the spending multiplier to take effect because neither individuals nor firms alter their spending plans immediately. It takes time for the additional income derived from increased government spending to be translated into additional purchases, and when taxes are cut, there are also decisions to be made about what portion of the tax cut to spend and what to spend it on. This makes correct timing of fiscal policy more difficult.

2. (a–d) Answers will vary.

4. Certainly such big drops have large effects on the wealth of households in these countries. Consumers in these countries are, therefore, likely to spend less, dropping C and eventually Y. Recessions are likely to result. There are several possible problems for the United States. First, Americans are invested in foreign stock markets so there is a modest wealth effect in the United States. Second, recessions in foreign countries mean that their consumers buy less from the United States and export demand drops. Finally, prices of imports from these countries could fall, competing with U.S. firms.

6. Answers will depend on events.

CHAPTER 30

2. Certainly, there was some relief from government programs such as TANF (Temporary Aid for Needy Families) that replaced some of the lost income. Second, people have to spend a certain amount for things like food, shelter, and health care using savings or temporary employment to pay for them. Third, most people expected to return to their lives eventually and to earn a higher permanent income. In the meantime, they do not fully adjust their lifestyles to their temporary drop in income.

4. When taxes are cut, after-tax wages rise. People keep a larger portion of their wages. The substitution effect refers to the fact that the opportunity cost of leisure is higher after the after-tax wage increase. That would imply that people would work more in response to the Bush tax cuts. On the other hand, when tax rates are cut, people have higher incomes after tax. To the extent that leisure is a normal good—higher income leads to more consumption of normal goods—people would consume more leisure and work fewer hours. The ultimate effect will depend on how strong the two effects are. In reality, some people will work more and others less. Since the two act to offset each other, the aggregate effect is likely to be small.

6. (a) The value of homes is an important component of household wealth. When home prices rise, household wealth rises and consumption tends to increase. When home prices fall, household wealth falls and consumption decreases.

(b) Because changes in consumption are changes in aggregate expenditure, they lead to changes in output and employment in the same direction.

8. A given consumption path requires a given amount of lifetime income to pay for it. But, given initial wealth, lifetime income is determined by working hours. This implies that income is not really an "independent" variable in the consumption function. Rather, the desire to consume and the desire to enjoy leisure together will determine how much income one will earn.

10. Maintaining inventory stocks helps a firm maintain a smooth production level. When sales unexpectedly increase, goods can be sold out of inventory. When sales unexpectedly decrease, goods can be added to inventories. By smoothing production, a firm can save on the adjustment costs associated with frequent changes in capital stock and employment levels. The cost of this policy is the forgone interest from investing funds in inventory stocks instead of lending out the money in financial markets.

CHAPTER 31

2.

Table 1		Table 2		Table 3	
Y/L	GROWTH RATE	Y/L	GROWTH RATE	Y/L	GROWTH RATE
4.28	–	4.28	–	4.28	–
4.23	3.7	4.41	3.9	4.45	5.0
4.17	3.6	4.53	3.9	4.63	5.0
4.12	3.7	4.66	3.9	4.81	5.0

In Table 1, L is growing rapidly while K is growing slowly. It is likely that much of the growth in Y is due to growth in L. Because of diminishing returns to L, it is not surprising that Y/L is declining. In Table 2, L is growing slowly while K is growing rapidly. In this case, it seems that the growth in Y is caused mainly by growth in K. The ratio Y/L is increasing because each worker has more capital with which to work.

Finally, in Table 3, both L and K are growing slowly relative to Y. Technology must be the cause of most of the growth in Y in this case. This technological improvement also has the effect of increasing the amount of output per worker (Y/L).

4. The key focus of the tax law proposals is on capital. When the capital stock grows, output is likely to grow and labor productivity is likely to increase. This can be accomplished by increasing investment directly or by influencing saving. A number of provisions are designed to encourage saving. Lower taxes on capital gains, dividends, and interest income are designed to increase the after-tax returns that people can earn on their saving. That increases the opportunity cost of present consumption. Higher savings increases the pool of available resources to firms and brings down the cost of capital. The investment tax credit is a direct reduction in the cost of capital . . . a 10% ITC reduced taxes by 10% of the amount of investment. This is a direct stimulus to investment.

6. Assuming that the economy stays at full employment, the bill would cause the economy to produce more capital goods and fewer consumption goods. This would lead to a higher growth rate over time. The trade-off is less consumption today. There are also distributional consequences. Capital income earners (who have higher incomes on average) would benefit. Higher-income households (who spend a smaller fraction of their incomes) would bear relatively less of the consumption-tax burden, while low-income households (who spend a higher fraction of their incomes) would bear relatively more of the consumption-tax burden.

8. High budget deficits are financed with private saving. That saving otherwise would have found its way through financial markets into private capital production. If the deficit is used to finance current expenditures such as paying judges and congresspeople, it is not contributing to an expansion of output in the long run. The same is true of a tax cut, which is used to increase current consumption expenditures. But if the government used the money to build capital, such as roads and bridges, or to increase human capital through better education and job training, it would at least offset part of the reduction in private investment spending. Whether the net result for output growth is positive or negative depends on whether private capital or public capital has a higher rate of return. This is a subject of much debate and would depend on the specific capital expenditures undertaken by the government.

10. Answers will vary.

CHAPTER 32

2. (a) Graph I: Supply-side economics: It focuses on the supply-side effects of a tax cut and tends to ignore the demand-side impacts. Tax cuts should increase the incentive to work, save, and invest. If work effort, saving, and investment all increase, the AS curve will shift to the right, increasing output and reducing the price level. The extent to which the supply curve is likely to shift depends on the responsiveness of behavior to the tax cuts. This is the subject of much controversy.

Graph II: Monetarism/New classical economics. Both schools believe that fiscal policy cannot have an impact on the level of real output. Monetarism believes that nominal GDP cannot change as long as the money supply and the velocity of money remain constant. Thus, real GDP will not respond to a tax cut. New classical theories predict that "anticipated" fiscal policies will have no effect on real GDP, which remains at the potential output level determined in the long run in markets such as the labor market.

Graph III: Keynesian economics. As long as the economy is not operating at capacity, and as long as the Fed accommodates somewhat by increasing the money supply, a permanent tax cut can increase the level of real GDP and is likely to be inflationary. The impact on the price level is determined by how close to capacity the economy is operating.

(b) Individual response.

4. The supply-side logic is that cutting taxes increases the incentive to work, save, and invest. Expanding the workforce and the capital stock clearly can have an expansionary effect allowing the economy to grow more rapidly. But a lower T means that disposable income, Y_d, rises. Higher disposable income increases C and, thus, aggregate expenditure. If $AE > Y$, inventories contract and Y rises. Thus, the AD curve shifts; there is an expansionary demand-side effect.

6. Nominal income $= M \times V = (\$1,000)(5) = \$5,000$. If we select the current year as our base year, real income is also $5,000. If you are a strict monetarist you believe V is constant. Therefore, a doubling of the money supply to $2,000 will cause a doubling of nominal GDP to $(\$2,000)(5) = \$10,000$. If, however, velocity is a function of the interest rate as well as institutional factors, then it cannot be assumed a constant. In this case, an increase in the money supply (which reduces interest rates) would lower velocity, so $M \times V$ would not increase by as great a percentage as M itself increased, and nominal GDP would rise by a smaller percentage than the money supply increased. If the money supply doubles (rises by 100 percent), nominal GDP will rise by less than 100 percent. (We cannot know how the rise in nominal GDP is apportioned between a rise in P and a rise in real GDP without knowing more about the current state of the economy).

8. Quite simply, it is because the labor market clears if wages are fully flexible. If there is unemployment, wages will fall, the quantity of labor demanded will rise, and the quantity of labor supplied will fall until there is no more excess supply.

10. A tax cut from .25 to .20 is a 20 percent reduction, and if labor supply did not change, tax revenues would fall 20 percent. Tax revenue $= tWL$. In order for tax revenues not to change, we need to have $.25WL_{OLD} = .2WL_{NEW}$. This implies $L_{NEW} = .25WL_{OLD}/.2W = 1.25 L_{OLD}$. Thus, the new supply of labor must be 25 percent higher than the old supply of labor. What does this tax cut mean to net wages? It means that net wages rise from $.75W$ to $.80W$, an increase of $.05/.75 = .0667$ or 6.67 percent. Thus, in order to keep revenues constant, a 6.67 percent increase in net wages would have to generate a 25 percent increase in labor supply, implying an elasticity of 25/6.67 or 3.75. This is much larger than any empirical estimates of the actual elasticity of labor supply.

CHAPTER 33

2. Answers will vary.

4. Clearly, clothing is produced with cheap labor, and we buy most of our clothing from abroad because of the relatively high cost of labor in the United States. Airplanes are produced on the other hand with highly skilled workers, and the United States does enjoy a comparative advantage there. The United States does not have as large an endowment of oil reserves as the rest of the world, yet we are a big consumer. Both vehicles and agricultural goods are very heterogeneous. Automobiles lend themselves to "acquired comparative advantage." While the United States has a lot of very fertile land for crop production, many things that we consume are not suited for production: coffee, tea, dates, tropical fruits (like bananas), and so forth. The table demonstrates the enormous complexity of the pattern of international trade.

6. Answers will vary.

CHAPTER 34

2. Answers will vary.

4. Answers will vary. The trade balance is simply made up of exports and imports of goods and services. A country with a trade deficit is one that imports more than exports. The current account balance takes into account investment income paid to foreigners as well as foreign investment income paid to a country's citizens. Investment income earned abroad is added to exports, and investment income paid to foreigners is added to imports.

6. (a) The consumption function does not change so instead of spending their money on Japanese goods, U.S. citizens will spend it on domestic goods. All else equal, this will stimulate U.S. output and decrease U.S. unemployment, and decrease output and employment in Japan.

(b) If income rises, consumers are likely to buy more imports as well as more domestic goods. Imports from Japan will increase somewhat after the initial decrease.

(c) If imports decrease, then the demand for yen will also decrease because importers will not need as many yen to purchase Japanese goods.

(d) The yen will depreciate and the dollar will appreciate. This gives U.S. consumers more buying power in the market for foreign goods. Consumers will buy more imports, causing a decrease in aggregate expenditure on domestic output. Output and employment in the United States will fall. The current account deficit will rise, but the total balance of payments will still sum to zero.

(e) The quota would have to increase U.S. output and employment, at least in the short run. The increase in the U.S. trade balance increases U.S. output and employment. This causes the dollar to appreciate, which works to decrease output.

8. (a) $Y = C + I + G + (EX - IM) = 100 + .8(Y - 40) + 38 + 75 + 25 - .05(Y - 40)$

$$= 238 + .8Y - .8(40) - .05Y + .05(40) = 208 + .75Y = 832$$

Government deficit $= G - T = 75 - 40 = 35$.
Current account balance $= EX - IM = 25 - .05(832 - 40) = -14.6$

(b) The multiplier $= 1/[1 - (MPC - MPM)] = 1/[1 - (.8 - .05)] = 4$
When G increases from 75 to 80, Y will increase by $5(4) = 20$. Imports will rise by $.05(20) = 1$.

With the quota, the MPM is zero so the multiplier $= 1/(1 - .8) = 5$. Y will rise by $5(5) = 25$. (This assumes that IM is greater than or equal to 40 without the quota, before the increase in G. Actually, it is 39.6, but assuming $MPM = 0$ is a very close approximation.) Imports that rise with income act as a leakage and reduce the size of the multiplier.

(c) With $EX = 25$, we need $IM = .05(Y - 40) = 25$. This implies $Y = 540$. Income is currently 832 so it must be decreased by $832 - 540 = 292$. With a multiplier of 4, this will require a decrease in government spending of $292/4 = 73$.

CHAPTER 35

2. Answers will vary.

4. If the Chinese economy is running a huge trade surplus, you would think that there would be a big surplus of dollars on the market and that the value of the dollar against the Chinese currency would fall. But the Chinese are using the dollars paid for their goods to buy dollar-denominated assets: Government bonds, U.S. companies, etc. While this maintains a balance of payments equilibrium for a while, there is much debate about how long it can go on.

CHAPTER 36

2. Answers will vary. There is no clear "right answer" to this problem, only trade-offs. Capital accumulation requires saving (reduced consumption), and when most citizens are earning subsistence wages, reducing consumption is not an option for many.

4. Answer will depend on events.

6. Many recent famines have resulted from government policies. In some cases, keeping farm prices artificially low has led to a decrease in production. In other cases, a failure to invest in a distributional infrastructure has led to famine in outlying rural areas.

8. The speaker confuses political systems with economic systems. The Soviet economic system was one of socialism (government ownership of land and capital) and central planning (government direction of resource allocation). Totalitarianism is a political—not an economic—system in which the ruler exercises authoritarian control without the consent of those governed.

10. There are arguments on both sides. Firms that acquire market power tend to overprice and underproduce relative to the efficient price and output levels. Market power, it is argued, stifles both price and quality competition. Microsoft was charged with anticompetitive behavior by packaging its Web browser with its dominant operating system, Windows. After knocking out the competition, they can raise prices without competitive pressure. But what about foreign competition? Isn't it a bigger, tougher game when the competition is a foreign firm receiving government support? The real problem is that the government is likely to be lousy at picking winners. What makes us think that the government can pick winners better than the market? Even recent Japanese attempts to subsidize a winner (fifth-generation computers) have failed.

Index

Notes: Key terms and the page on which they are defined appear in **boldface**. Page numbers followed by *n* refer to information in footnotes.

Currency debasement, **504**
Currency exchange, 721
Current account, in balance of
payments, 723–724
Current dollars, 426
Current market value, 233
Cwiebel, Julia, 27
Cyclical deficit, 495
Cyclical unemployment, 445,
445–446, **586**
Cyclical variations in U.S. economy,
410
Czechoslovakia, 775
Czech Republic, 775, 776

D

Daimler Chrysler Corporation, 263
Das Kapital (Marx), 368
Dave, Nirav, 254
Davis, Yancie, 27
Deadweight losses, 81*n*, **89,** 89–91.
See also Excess burdens
DeBeers Company, 274
Debreu, Gerard, 258
Debtor nation, U.S. as, 725–726
Debtors, 451
Debt rescheduling, 774
Decision making, profit
maximization and, 650–651
Decreasing-cost industry, 208
Decreasing returns to scale, 195,
199–200
Deductions from taxes, savings from,
380–381
Default, 236, 774
Defense, Department of (U.S.), 351
Deficit reduction, economic stability
and, 616–617
Deficit response index (DRI), 615
Deficit targeting, fiscal policy in,
613–617
Deflation, 403, 447
DeKaser, Richard, 444
Dell, Michael, 237
Dell Computers, 237
Demand. *See also* Household
demand; Law of demand
applications, 77–92
for capital, 234
changes in
market adjustment to, 256–258
versus changes in quantity
demanded, 51
cross-price elasticity of, 107
derived, 211–212
determined, 78
diminishing marginal utility and,
125–126
drug wars and, 90
elastic, 98, 105
excess, 64, 65–66
as flows or rates of production, 65*n*
income elasticity of, 107
inelastic, 98, 104
mad cow disease and, 71
market efficiency and, 85–86
in money market, 534–535
in monopolies, 276–282
perfectly elastic, 98
perfectly inelastic, 97
price elasticity of, 96–99
in product/output markets, 50–59
schedule, **51**
shift of, versus movement along
demand curve, 56–57
supply and, in money market,
534–535

Demand curve, 51, 51–54. *See also*
Input demand curves
in monopolistic competition, 307
movement along, 56
versus shift of demand, 56–57,
58
shift of, 56
slope, 51–53
straight-line, elasticity changes
along a, 102–104
Demand deposits, 505
Demand determined, 78
Demand determined price, 221
Demand elasticity
importance of items, 105–106
product differentiation and,
306–307
substitutes, availability of, 105
time dimension, 106–107
Demand-pull inflation, 579
Democracy, 760, 776
Demographic groups, unemployment
rate and, 441
Denison, Edward, 670, 672, 675
Denmark, 431, 711, 760
Depository Institutions Deregulation
and Monetary Control Act,
506, 517
Deposits, 508
Depreciation, 234, 422, 422*n*
of a currency, 733
Depression, 403, 438
Derived demand, 211–212, **212**
Descriptive economics, 10
Descriptive questions, 25
Desired investment, 463
Desired level of inventories, 653
Developing nations
debt burdens, 774–775
economic growth in, 763–783
population and poverty, 764–765
Diamond/water paradox, 129
Dictatorship, 760, 776
Digital Equipment Corporation, 256,
442
Diminishing marginal product, 153
Diminishing marginal productivity,
law of, 772*n*
Diminishing marginal utility,
122–123
downward-sloping demand and,
125–126
law of, 52, 122, 134
Diminishing returns, 152–153, 213,
665
Disability Insurance (DI), 370
Discount rate, 247, 517, 517–518
Discouraged-worker effects, 442,
442–443, 649, **658,** 658–659
Discovery space shuttle, 28
Discretionary fiscal policy, 480
Diseconomies of scale, 195, 199–200
Disequilibrium, 468
fundamental, 743, 744–745
Disposable income (Y_d), 480,
480–482
Disposable personal income, 425
Dissaving, 54, 407, 425
Distribution of output, 41
Dividends, 236, 408, 624
Dominant strategy, 315
Dominican Republic, 712
Dow Jones Industrial Average, 627
Dresdner Kleinwort Wasserstein, 323
Drop-in-the-bucket problem, 336,
339
Drug companies, as monopolies, 275

Drug wars, and supply and demand,
90
Dukakis, Michael, 13
Dumping, 710
Duncan, Tim, 357
Duopoly, 312
DuPont Co., 757
Durable goods, 233*n*, **421**

E

Earned income tax credit (EIC), 373
Earth Summit (1992), 330
Eastern European countries
economic growth, 15
economic systems in, 777
entrepreneurship in, 48
environmental externalities in, 328
market-supporting institutions in,
781
political systems in, 777
privatization in, 6
as Second World countries, 764
as transition economies, 775–776
underground economy in, 430
Washington Consensus and, 760
East Germany, 304, 328, 776
Eastman Kodak, 290
Easy monetary policy, 537
eBay, 40, 66
e-commerce, 241
Econometrics, 9
Economic activity, circular flow of, 49
global, 747–749
Economic costs, 146, 176
Economic development, 9
agriculture and, 767–768
capital formation and, 765–766
centrally planned economy and,
769–771
developing-country debt burdens,
774–775
economic growth versus, 771
entrepreneurial ability and,
766–767
export promotion and, 768–769
human resources and, 766–767
import substitution and, 768–769
industry and, 767–768
issues in, 771–775
market economy and, 769–771
population growth, 772–774
social overhead capital and, 767
sources of, 765–767
strategies for, 767–771
Economic efficiency, in monopolistic
competition, 310
Economic flows, taxes on, 377–378
Economic globalization, 747
history of, 749–750
Economic growth, 15, 35, 663, 665
in developing economies, 763–783
economic development versus,
771
inflation and, 451
inventory changes and, 468
long run, 663–665, 675–676
modern, 663, 664–665
productivity and, in U.S., 669–672
pros and cons, 676–679
public policy and, 672–676
short-run aggregate supply curve
and, 571–572
sources of, 665–669
and dilemma of poor
countries, 35–36
in transitional economies,
763–783

Economic history, 9
Economic income, 360, 383
Economic integration, 711
Economic performance, 320
Economic policy, 14–15
Economic problem, 39
Economic profits. *See* Profit(s)
Economic Recovery Tax Act of 1981,
492, 674, 694
Economics, 2
assumptions, 114–116
fields of, 8–10
method of, 10–15
public choice field, 349
reasons for studying, 2–7
scope of, 7–10
study of, 1–2
theories and models, 11–14
Economic stability, deficit reduction
and, 616–617
Economic systems, 39–42
basic questions of, 26
command economies, 39–40
laissez-faire economies, 40–41
mixed systems, markets, and
governments, 41–42
in transitional economies,
776–777
Economic theory, 10
Economic thought, history of, 9
Economies
exchange rates, effect on, 736–739
federal budget, influence on,
493–495
government in, 480–484
market. *See* Market economy
stock market and, 623–636
Economies of scale, 194, 194–200
in agriculture, 197
in banking, 198
as barrier to entry, 274
graphing, 196–197
in natural markets, 296
productivity and, 669
sources of, 195
The Economist, 334, 365
Economy.com, 588
Edgeworth, F. Y., 50*n*
Education, public policy and
economic growth, 672
Education individual retirement
accounts, 672
Edwards, Wayne, 156
Efficiency, 14, 14–15, **253**
allocative, 14, 259
economic, 310
market, 86–91
Pareto, 259
of perfect competition, 260–263
production, 32
Efficiency wage, 591
Efficiency wage theory, 591
Efficient economy, 259
Efficient market, 3
Efficient mix of output, 33, 261–263
Effluent charges, 332*n*
e-Health Initiative Foundation, 673
Ehrenpreis, Ira, 239
Einstein, Albert, 13
Eisenhower, Dwight, 710
Elastic demand, 98, 105
Elasticity, 95–109, **96**
calculating, 100–105
cross-price, of demand, 107
demand. *See* Demand elasticity
income, of demand, 107
of labor supply, 108, 387–388
midpoint formula, 101–102

Photo Credits

MICROECONOMIC STRUCTURE

Although the authors have chosen to present microeconomics first, they have designed the text so that professors may proceed directly to macroeconomics after teaching the four introductory chapters.

The organization of the microeconomics chapters continues to reflect the authors' belief that the best way to understand how market economies operate—and the best way to understand basic economic theory—is to work through a simple model of a perfectly competitive market system first, including discussions of output markets (goods and services) and input markets (land, labor, and capital), and the connections between them. Only then do the authors turn to noncompetitive market structures such as monopoly and oligopoly. When students have worked through a simple model of a perfectly competitive market system, they begin to understand how the pieces of the economy "fit together." Learning perfect competition first also enables students to see the power of the market system. It is impossible to discuss the efficiency of markets as well as the problems that arise from markets until students have seen how a simple perfectly competitive market produces and distributes goods and services. The accompanying visual gives you an overview of the structure.

- **Chapters 6–8** provide an overview of firm and household decision making in simple perfectly competitive markets.
- **Chapters 9–11** show how firms and households interact in output markets (goods and services) and input markets (labor, land, and capital) to determine prices, wages, and profits.
- **Chapter 12** is a pivotal chapter that links simple perfectly competitive markets with a discussion of market imperfections and the role of government.
- **Chapters 13–17** cover the three noncompetitive market structures (monopoly, monopolistic competition, oligopoly), externalities, public goods, imperfect information, and income distribution as well as taxation and government finance.

FIGURE 6.2 Understanding the Microeconomy and the Role of Government

To understand how the economy works, it helps to build from the ground up. We start in Chapters 6–8 with an overview of **household** and **firm** decision making in simple perfectly competitive markets. In Chapters 9–11 we see how firms and households interact in **output markets** (product markets) and **input markets** (labor/land and capital) to determine prices, wages, and profits. Once we have a picture of how a simple perfectly competitive economy works, we begin to relax assumptions. Chapter 12 is a pivotal chapter that links perfectly competitive markets with a discussion of market imperfections and the role of government. In Chapters 13–17 we cover the three non-competitive market structures (monopoly, monopolistic competition, oligopoly), externalities, public goods, imperfect information, and income distribution as well as taxation and government finance.